# ELEMENTS OF NUMERICAL
# MATHEMATICAL ECONOMICS
# WITH EXCEL

# ELEMENTS OF NUMERICAL MATHEMATICAL ECONOMICS WITH EXCEL

## STATIC AND DYNAMIC OPTIMIZATION

GIOVANNI ROMEO

*Independent Financial Advisor*

ELSEVIER

ACADEMIC PRESS

An imprint of Elsevier

Academic Press is an imprint of Elsevier
125 London Wall, London EC2Y 5AS, United Kingdom
525 B Street, Suite 1650, San Diego, CA 92101, United States
50 Hampshire Street, 5th Floor, Cambridge, MA 02139, United States
The Boulevard, Langford Lane, Kidlington, Oxford OX5 1GB, United Kingdom

**Library of Congress Cataloging-in-Publication Data**
A catalog record for this book is available from the Library of Congress

**British Library Cataloguing-in-Publication Data**
A catalogue record for this book is available from the British Library

ISBN: 978-0-12-817648-1

For information on all Academic Press publications visit our website at
https://www.elsevier.com/books-and-journals

*Publisher:* Brian Romer
*Acquisition Editor:* Brian Romer
*Editorial Project Manager:* Devlin Person
*Production Project Manager:* Paul Prasad Chandramohan
*Cover Designer:* Mark Rogers

Typeset by TNQ Technologies

Working together
to grow libraries in
developing countries

www.elsevier.com • www.bookaid.org

# Contents

# IV
## Special topics

# About the author

Giovanni Romeo is an independent financial advisor in Mergers & Acquisitions and Corporate Finance services. Within his profession, he regularly uses the Excel and VBA programming for finance and business modeling at advanced levels, also connected with the ERP systems for the companies' budgeting, planning, and control. He received his bachelor's and master's degrees in economics and management from the University of Pavia and earned a master in corporate finance from SDA Bocconi Business School. He also passed the three-level examinations required by the CFA Institute.

# Preface

## Mathematics is essentially intuition and so is this book

After using Excel in the financial modeling area, within my finance profession for a long time, I decided to explore how to use this tool for the more scientific and challenging area of math applied to economics.

Driven by my passion for this wonderful subject, all began when I was keeping rereading a page about the calculus of variations in my university textbook of operations research, where there was no proof of the given Euler—Lagrange necessary condition equation. At the end, the functional, seen in a discrete framework, was just a sum and the objective was just to optimize this functional. I tried then to put everything to work in a worksheet using the GRG Solver: after a couple of unsuccessful tests things started working smoothly as I wished and the initial intuition on how to solve the problem was then correct. This was one of the few intuitions that allowed me to begin the long journey to the preparation of this book.

## What this book is about

The book is about the use of numerical techniques applied with Excel and VBA to the discipline of mathematical economics, with some extensions to operations research, data analysis for business and economics, and Monte Carlo analysis.

The book has been then divided in four parts.

**Part I** aims at giving to the reader the fundamental tools of some important advanced worksheet capabilities, including the Excel VBA, as well as the fundamental tools of the mathematical economics applied within a spreadsheet, like standard calculus, linear algebra, differential, and difference equations.

**Part II** is dedicated to the classical static nonlinear and linear programming, with an entire chapter devoted to the mainstream microeconomics, which essentially applies the various optimization techniques. The portfolio optimization is also covered due to its importance.

**Part III** attempts to offer an adequate range of Excel tools to solve at least the standard problems in the following three areas of the dynamic optimization:

- Calculus of Variations
- Theory of Optimal Control
- Discrete Dynamic Optimization

**Part IV** of this book covers some special and important topics that have been chosen not only because of their specific importance, but also because they can be considered perfectly complementary to the mathematical economics, namely the inventory and production optimization, the data analysis for business and economics and the essential elements of Monte Carlo analysis.

Especially regarding the advanced concepts of the dynamic optimization the book can be suggested as ancillary learning material for classical theoretical mathematical economics textbooks, like the one by Alpha C. Chiang (*Elements of Dynamic Optimization*) or the one by Knut Sydsaeter, Peter Hammond, *et al.* (*Further Mathematics for Economic Analysis*).

## Who this book is intended for

The readership is represented by anyone who deals with the mathematical economics discipline, with the desire of seeing the theoretical concepts applied with a common computer language, in a practical and accessible framework.

Target audience can be represented by research economists, students in economic theory, from basic to intermediate and advanced, data analysts, industrial controllers, and research scientists worldwide working in data analytics companies, financial institutions, and other groups that handle economic data.

This book may also be used as a base for developing the same problems with other scientific languages.

## Companion site

This book is accompanied by a companion website (please see the details below) that includes the Excel examples presented in the book, as well as the Excel solutions to the exercises proposed at the end of each chapter. Readers may need to adapt the worksheets for a special use.

Companion site URL: https://www.elsevier.com/books-and-journals/book-companion/9780128176481. Password: 36yfaw4x.

*Giovanni Romeo*

# Excel and fundamental mathematics for economics

Part I of this book aims at giving to the reader the fundamental tools of some important advanced worksheet capabilities, including the Excel VBA, as well as the fundamental tools of the mathematical economics applied within a spreadsheet. These are all tools that will be needed within the course of the whole book and tools that any economist analyst should master within a computer language framework.

Chapter 1 will review some VBA codes, whose prior knowledge would be somehow required from the reader, in order to optimally utilize the worksheets that will be implemented within the book. The Excel macros used within the book are not at a very advanced level, but still, they will require (beside the mathematical knowledge) a certain degree of VBA programming language mastery.

Other advanced features, like the Excel Solver, the *what-if data table analysis* (these two will be used a lot in the book), *contour diagrams*, *scatter charts*, and *trendlines* will be introduced and then developed in detail within the book.

Chapters 2—4 will instead give the essential elements of the mathematical economics applied with Excel.

Three important areas of the mathematical economics are covered here.

Chapter 2 will cover the essential elements of the standard calculus (numerical differentiation and integration) applied within a spreadsheet.

Chapter 3 is dedicated to the essential elements of the linear algebra.

Chapter 4 is instead devoted to the dynamical mathematics (ordinary differential and difference equations, as well as the systems of differential equations). This is a chapter of paramount importance as many of the techniques we will develop in this chapter will be used within the dynamic optimization section and also because the differential and difference equations represent the key constituent area of the economic dynamic modeling.

In all these three chapters, some economic applications are also proposed.

# 1

# Excel VBA, solver, and other advanced worksheet tools

## 1.1 VBA introduction and main statements

### The VBA Editor and the modules

When writing a VBA code, the **VB Editor** needs to be used in Excel. The VB Editor is the working area where we will write a **Macro** and it is accessible from the tab Developer of the Ribbon bar, as shown in Fig. 1.1-1. Then, Fig. 1.1-2 will appear.

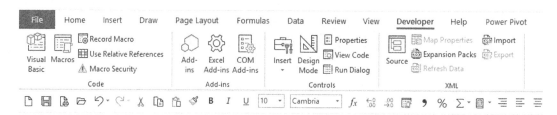

**FIGURE 1.1-1**    The VB Editor in the Excel 2019.

On the left-hand side of Fig. 1.1-2, we have the ***Project Explorer*** (at the top) and a second panel (at the bottom) which contains the ***Properties*** (modifiable by the user when necessary) referred to any ***Excel Object*** we select in the ***VBA Project*** window: a worksheet, a workbook, or a module itself.

Now, what we have to do is to open the actual working area where to write our VBA code, and this is done by inserting a ***Module***, as in Fig. 1.1-3.

A module can be inserted, for example, by clicking on Insert on the ***Menu Bar*** and then selecting Module, and finally the VB Editor will be completed with the Module inserted as in Fig. 1.1-4. If we want, we can rename a Module using the properties window at the bottom of the screen of Fig. 1.1-4. When renaming it, we just need to pay attention to spaces, which are not accepted, and the underscore character should be used in place of a space. Now that we have a module, we can begin writing a code. This is called a ***Macro*** (or procedure, or routine).

Excel VBA also allows to create a ***User Defined Function***, which will enrich the library of the built-in functions.

**FIGURE 1.1-2**    VBA Project Explorer (with Excel Objects) and the Panel Properties at the bottom.

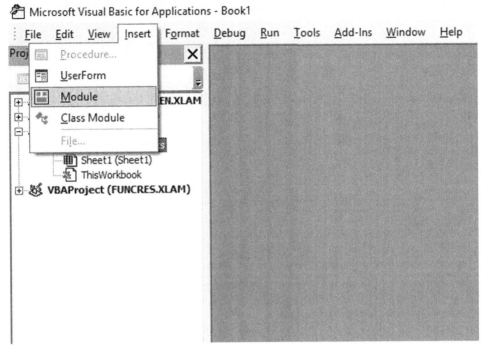

FIGURE 1.1-3    Inserting a Module from the Menu bar.

FIGURE 1.1-4    Module Inserted where to write a VBA program.

I. Excel and fundamental mathematics for economics

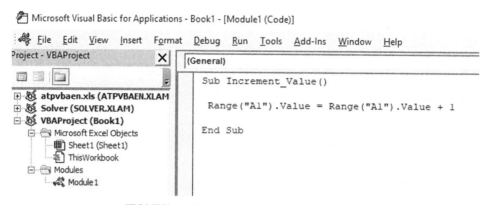

**FIGURE 1.1-5**    Incrementing the value of a Cell.

## 1 Visual Basic Macros

In Excel, the role of a Macro is essentially that of getting an action automated, without manual intervention on the Excel sheet. It is a command we give to Excel, such that it performs something we want to do (e.g., a repeated calculation until a specified cell is equal to zero). The way to do that is to create a *Sub* procedure in the Module.

The procedure is in the following form:

***Sub 'Name' ()***

*VBA Statements*

***End Sub***

Suppose we want to increment the value in *Cell A*1 of a worksheet by 1. The code would be as in Fig. 1.1-5. Now a question arises. How can we get the code activated in the worksheet? In other words, how can we make the macro run? This is normally done inserting a **Button** in the worksheet, which is then associated to the specific code we have created. The button we are referring to is the **Form Control**, as shown in Fig. 1.1-6.

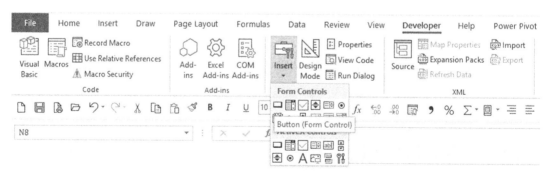

**FIGURE 1.1-6**    Form Control Button to run a Sub.

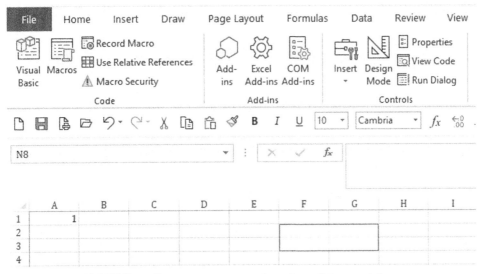

FIGURE 1.1-7    Inserting a Button (form Control) in a worksheet.

Using the Alt-Key to facilitate the Button positioning on the sheet, we decide to position the Button as in Fig. 1.1-7.

Releasing the mouse, Excel will ask us to associate a Macro to this Button, and we choose the only Macro available so far, which is the *Sub Increment_Value* as in Figs. 1.1-8. Then, the

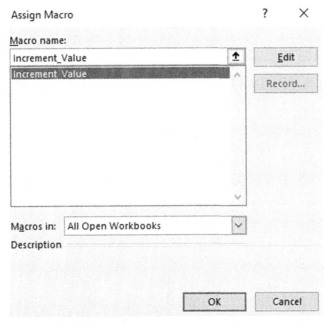

FIGURE 1.1-8    Assigning a macro to a Button.

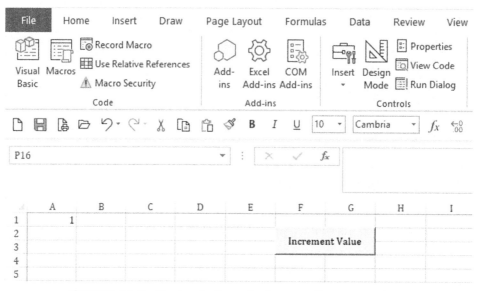

FIGURE 1.1-9   Naming the Button for the macro "Increment_Value".

macro is available to be run through the Button "Increment Value," as in Fig. 1.1-9. We can create a second Macro called "Reduce_Value" as in Fig. 1.1-10, inserting a second Button as in Fig. 1.1-11.

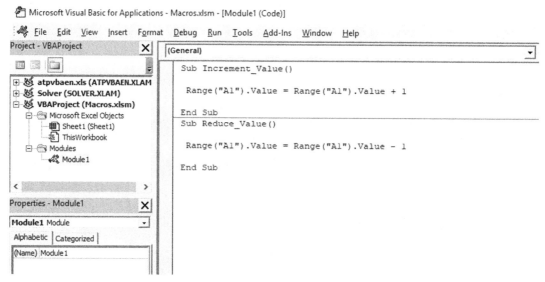

FIGURE 1.1-10   Second macro "Reduce_Value."

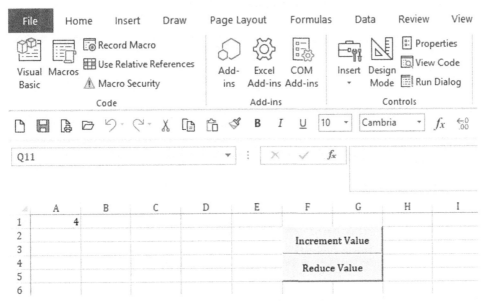

FIGURE 1.1-11    Second Button for the macro "Reduce_Value."

## Using the Macro Recorder

The Macro can be also recorded in Excel using the **Record Macro** option under the **Developer Tab**.

For example, suppose we want to add new sheets to a workbook; we can simply record a macro to do that. What we do is just clicking on the **Record Macro** option adding a new sheet; then, when we finish recording, we click on the little square **Stop Recording** shown in Fig. 1.1-12. The macro will be available in a new module of the Project Explorer.

Recording a macro is useful when we are not sure about the exact code to use and we look for some hints suggested by Excel regarding a specific operation we want to perform. We can record a similar operation, then modify it obtaining the final instruction we were looking for.

The resulting macro (to be found in the VB Editor) would be as follows:

**Sub Add_New_Sheets**()

*Sheets.Add After*:  =  *ActiveSheet*

**End Sub**

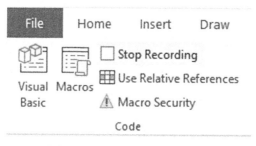

FIGURE 1.1-12   Stop Recording.

If we want to add four sheets in one shot the macro would be modified as follows:

*Sub Add_4_New_Sheets*()

*Sheets.Add After*: = *ActiveSheet, Count*: = 4

***End Sub***

## Main VBA statements used within the book (the looping structures)

Many of the VBA sub procedures need to be entered manually in the VB Editor, and we will show here the main statements used within the book.

These are the *Looping* structures, which are VBA Subs that are finalized at:

1. repeating a set of instructions, until a specific goal is reached, for example, until the Excel sets a specific cell equal to zero, or until a specific target cell is less than a desired $\varepsilon$ (the Steepest Descent VBA code shown in Section 5.4 is an example) or
2. finalized at repeating a set of instructions for a certain number of times.

A *looping* structure belonging to the first category is the **Do Until** statement, sometimes used in conjunction with the **Excel Solver**, to optimize a specific objective function.

Suppose we have a list of 10 numbers like in Fig. 1.1-13, where the last one in effect contains a formula. In this case, it is just a formula that adds the value 1 to the previous cell.

The objective is to add automatically a new row in a new updating sheet round, including the counting formula and removing the formula from the penultimate cell (which was the last cell in the previous updating round).

To do that using the **Do Until** statement can be a perfect solution. The following would be the statement which makes Excel select the *Cell A*1 as a first step and then move forward until the cell is empty:

*Range("A1").Select*

**Do Until** *IsEmpty(ActiveCell)*

*ActiveCell.Offset*(1, 0).*Select*

**Loop**

| | A |
|---|---|
| 1 | 1 |
| 2 | 2 |
| 3 | 3 |
| 4 | 4 |
| 5 | 5 |
| 6 | 6 |
| 7 | 7 |
| 8 | 8 |
| 9 | 9 |
| 10 | =A9+1 |

**FIGURE 1.1-13**    List of numbers from 1 to 10.

Excel moves forward from *Cell A*1 along the same column using the instruction:

*ActiveCell.Offset*(1, 0).*Select*

inserted between **Do Until** and **Loop** (this is always inserted below the instruction we want to repeat).

The complete code of what we want to achieve is shown in Fig. 1.1-14. We can follow step by step the macro by pressing *F8* on the keyboard. This is useful, especially when something does not work as planned and we want to study the macro in detail, investigating at which line of the code the mistake could be located. This can be done also using the **Debug** option from the Menu Bar as shown in Fig. 1.1-15.

There are some other alternatives to test for a blank cell, not only using the **Do Until** Is *Empty(ActiveCell)*; for example, we may also use the following:

**Do Until** *ActiveCell.Value* = " "

Also, a very slightly different code would be the **Loop Until** statement, as described as follows

*Range("A1").Select*

**Do**

```
Sub Add_new_row()

Sheets("Add New Row").Activate

 Range("A1").Select

 Do Until IsEmpty(ActiveCell)

  ActiveCell.Offset(1,0).Select

   Loop

   ActiveCell.Offset(-1,0).Select

   ActiveCell.Offset.Range("A1:AA1").Select

   Selection.Copy

    ActiveCell.Range("A2").Select

    ActiveSheet.Paste

   ActiveCell.Offset(-1,0).Select

  Selection.PasteSpecial Paste := xlValues, Operation := xlNone, SkipBlanks: = _

 False,Transpose: = False

 ActiveCell.Range("A1").Select

 Application.CutCopyMode = False

End Sub
```

FIGURE 1.1-14    Adding a new Row to an Array.

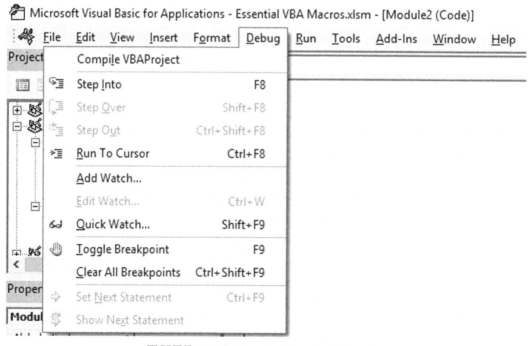

FIGURE 1.1-15    Stepping through a VBA code.

$$ActiveCell.Offset(1, \ 0).Select$$

**Loop Until** *IsEmpty(ActiveCell)*

where we have moved the *Until*, with the condition to be met, after *Loop*.

Another similar statement, the **Do While** statement, would also reach the same solution with the code expressed as follows:

$$Range("A1").Select$$

**Do While** *ActiveCell.Value <> " "*

$$ActiveCell.Offset(1, \ 0).Select$$

**Loop**

In this case, we have replaced the testing condition of the empty cell, to exit the loop, testing whether the cell is different from zero.

Another alternative is to use the *if* statement inside the *Loop* as follows:

**Do**

**If** *ActiveCell.Value* $=$ *" "* **Then Exit** Do

$$ActiveCell.Offset(1, \ 0).Select$$

**Loop**

## EXAMPLE 1 (CONSTRAINED OPTIMIZATION IN $\Re^2$ WITH LAGRANGE MULTIPLIERS USING THE VBA DO UNTIL)

Let us try to set up a VBA code using the **Do Until** Looping statement, for the approximate solution of the following constrained optimization problem (the same example in solved using the Excel Solver in Section 5.5):

$$\min_{\{x_1, x_2\}} x_2^2 + x_2^2 - 4x_1 - 6x_2 + 4$$

$$s.t. \ x_1 + x_2 = 10.$$

The Lagrangian function is:

$$\mathcal{L}(x_1, x_2; \lambda_1) = x_1^2 + x_2^2 - 4x_1 - 6x_2 + 4 + \lambda_1(x_1 + x_2 - 10)$$

I. Excel and fundamental mathematics for economics

| | A | B | C | D | E | F | G | H | I | J |
|---|---|---|---|---|---|---|---|---|---|---|
| 1 | x1 | x2 | | Lagrange Mult | -5 | | | | | |
| 2 | =N14 | =N15 | --> Linked to cells N14 and N15 | | | | | | | |
| 3 | Obj. Funct. | =$A$2^2+B2^2-4*$A$2-6*B2+4 | | | | | | | | |
| 4 | s.t. | =A2+B2 | | | | | | | | |
| 5 | | | | | | | | | | |
| 6 | *If* statement | x1 | Lagrangian | ∂ℒ(x1,x2)/∂x1 | Test on Sign ∂ℒ(x1,x2)/∂x1 | *If* statement | x2 | Lagrangian | ∂ℒ(x1,x2)/∂x2 | Test on Sign ∂ℒ(x1,x2)/∂x2 |
| 7 | =IF(E7=2;1;0) | 0 | =B7^2+$B$2^2-4*B7-6*$B$2+4+$E$1*(B7+$B$2-10) | | | =IF(J7=2;1;0) | 0 | =$A$2^2+G | | |
| 8 | =IF(E8=2;1;0) | 0.1 | =B8^2+$B$2^2-4*B8-6*$B$2+4+$E$1*(B8+$B$2-10) | =(C8-C7)/(B8-B7) | | =IF(J8=2;1;0) | 0.1 | =$A$2^2+G | =(H8-H7)/(G8-G | |
| 9 | =IF(E9=2;1;0) | 0.15 | =B9^2+$B$2^2-4*B9-6*$B$2+4+$E$1*(B9+$B$2-10) | =(C9-C8)/(B9-B8) | =SIGN(D9)-SIGN(D8) | =IF(J9=2;1;0) | 0.15 | =$A$2^2+G | =(H9-H8)/(G9-G | =SIGN(I9)-SIGN(I8) |
| 10 | =IF(E10=2;1;0) | 0.2 | =B10^2+$B$2^2-4*B10-6*$B$2+4+$E$1*(B10+$B$2-10) | =(C10-C9)/(B10-B9) | =SIGN(D10)-SIGN(D9) | =IF(J10=2;1;0) | 0.2 | =$A$2^2+G | =(H10-H9)/(G10 | =SIGN(I10)-SIGN(I9) |
| 11 | =IF(E11=2;1;0) | 0.25 | =B11^2+$B$2^2-4*B11-6*$B$2+4+$E$1*(B11+$B$2-10) | =(C11-C10)/(B11-B10) | =SIGN(D11)-SIGN(D10) | =IF(J11=2;1;0) | 0.25 | =$A$2^2+G | =(H11-H10)/(G1 | =SIGN(I11)-SIGN(I10) |
| 12 | =IF(E12=2;1;0) | 0.3 | =B12^2+$B$2^2-4*B12-6*$B$2+4+$E$1*(B12+$B$2-10) | =(C12-C11)/(B12-B11) | =SIGN(D12)-SIGN(D11) | =IF(J12=2;1;0) | 0.3 | =$A$2^2+G | =(H12-H11)/(G1 | =SIGN(I12)-SIGN(I11) |
| 13 | =IF(E13=2;1;0) | 0.35 | =B13^2+$B$2^2-4*B13-6*$B$2+4+$E$1*(B13+$B$2-10) | =(C13-C12)/(B13-B12) | =SIGN(D13)-SIGN(D12) | =IF(J13=2;1;0) | 0.35 | =$A$2^2+G | =(H13-H12)/(G1 | =SIGN(I13)-SIGN(I12) |
| 14 | =IF(E14=2;1;0) | 0.4 | =B14^2+$B$2^2-4*B14-6*$B$2+4+$E$1*(B14+$B$2-10) | =(C14-C13)/(B14-B13) | =SIGN(D14)-SIGN(D13) | =IF(J14=2;1;0) | 0.4 | =$A$2^2+G | =(H14-H13)/(G1 | =SIGN(I14)-SIGN(I13) |
| 248 | =IF(E248=2;1;0) | 12.1 | =B248^2+$B$2^2-4*B248-6*$B$2+4+$E$1*(B248+$B$2-10) | =(C248-C247)/(B248-B247) | =SIGN(D248)-SIGN(D247) | =IF(J248=2;1;0) | 12.1 | =$A$2^2+G | =(H248-H247)/( | =SIGN(I248)-SIGN(I247) |
| 249 | =IF(E249=2;1;0) | 12.15 | =B249^2+$B$2^2-4*B249-6*$B$2+4+$E$1*(B249+$B$2-10) | =(C249-C248)/(B249-B248) | =SIGN(D249)-SIGN(D248) | =IF(J249=2;1;0) | 12.15 | =$A$2^2+G | =(H249-H248)/( | =SIGN(I249)-SIGN(I248) |
| 250 | =IF(E250=2;1;0) | 12.2 | =B250^2+$B$2^2-4*B250-6*$B$2+4+$E$1*(B250+$B$2-10) | =(C250-C249)/(B250-B249) | =SIGN(D250)-SIGN(D249) | =IF(J250=2;1;0) | 12.2 | =$A$2^2+G | =(H250-H249)/( | =SIGN(I250)-SIGN(I249) |
| 251 | =IF(E251=2;1;0) | 12.25 | =B251^2+$B$2^2-4*B251-6*$B$2+4+$E$1*(B251+$B$2-10) | =(C251-C250)/(B251-B250) | =SIGN(D251)-SIGN(D250) | =IF(J251=2;1;0) | 12.25 | =$A$2^2+G | =(H251-H250)/( | =SIGN(I251)-SIGN(I250) |
| 252 | =IF(E252=2;1;0) | 12.3 | =B252^2+$B$2^2-4*B252-6*$B$2+4+$E$1*(B252+$B$2-10) | =(C252-C251)/(B252-B251) | =SIGN(D252)-SIGN(D251) | =IF(J252=2;1;0) | 12.3 | =$A$2^2+G | =(H252-H251)/( | =SIGN(I252)-SIGN(I251) |

FIGURE 1.1-16 Example 1: constrained optimization excel setup.

from which we obtain the system of (3) **first-order condition** equations:

$$\frac{\partial \mathscr{L}(\boldsymbol{x}, \boldsymbol{\lambda})}{\partial x_1} = 2x_1 - 4 + \lambda_1 = 0 \Rightarrow x_1 = \frac{(4 - \lambda_1)}{2}$$

$$\frac{\partial \mathscr{L}(\boldsymbol{x}, \boldsymbol{\lambda})}{\partial x_2} = 2x_2 - 6 + \lambda_1 = 0 \Rightarrow x_2 = \frac{(6 - \lambda_1)}{2}$$

$$\frac{\partial \mathscr{L}(\boldsymbol{x}, \boldsymbol{\lambda})}{\partial \lambda_1} = x_1 + x_2 - 10 = 0 \Rightarrow \frac{(4 - \lambda_1)}{2} + \frac{(6 - \lambda_1)}{2} = 10.$$

From the third equation, we obtain $\lambda_1 = -5$ and the stationary point $\boldsymbol{x}^*(4.5, 5.5)$.

The way we can solve the problem is first setting up in Excel the equations $\mathscr{L}(x_1, x_2; \lambda_1)$, $\frac{\partial \mathscr{L}(x,\lambda)}{\partial x_1}$, and $\frac{\partial \mathscr{L}(x,\lambda)}{\partial x_2}$ as in Fig. 1.1-16, where:

*Cell A2 Cell B2* $= x_1$ and $x_2$, respectively, linked to the optimization results of Fig. 1.1-17.

$$\textit{Cell B3} = \textit{Objective Function}$$

$$\textit{Cell B4} = \textit{Constraint}$$

$$\textit{Cell E1} = \textit{Lagrange Multiplier } \boldsymbol{\lambda}_1$$

**(It is this value that will be incremented or decremented** via **the VBA code of** Fig. 1.1-18, **until the solution is found)**.

| | M | N |
|---|---|---|
| 12 | **Find Lagrange multiplier such that Cell N18 = 0** | |
| 13 | | |
| 14 | x1 | =VLOOKUP(1;A:B;2;FALSE) |
| 15 | x2 | =VLOOKUP(1;F:G;2;FALSE) |
| 16 | Constraint | =SUM(N14:N15) |
| 17 | | |
| 18 | Must be equal to zero | =IFERROR(ROUND(N16-10;0);"") |
| 19 | | |
| 20 | Sign Test on ∂ℒ | =SUM(E9:E252)+SUM(J9:J252) |

FIGURE 1.1-17 Test Condition for the optimization.

```
Sub Lagrange()

Do Until Range("N18") = 0

  If Range("N18") <> 0 And Range("E1") > 0 Then

    Range("E1").Value = Range("E1").Value − 0.5

  Else

    If Range("N18") <> 0 And Range("E1") < 0 Then

      Range("E1").Value = Range("E1").Value + 0.5

    Else

      If Range("N18") <> 0 And Range("E1")
                = 0 Then MsgBox "Still No Solution Reached: Change Cell E1"

      If Range("N18") <> 0 And Range("E1") = 0 Then Exit Do

  End If

  End If

Loop

End Sub
```

**FIGURE 1.1-18**   VBA Looping structure for the nonlinear constrained optimization (with Lagrange multipliers).

Since before the optimization we do not know which sign the Lagrange multiplier will take on, we will just try a positive value (this must allow a change in the sign of the partial differential under *Column D* and *Column I*).

If the Macro stops without finding the solution, then we try with a negative value in the Lagrange multiplier (again, this must allow a change in the sign of the partial differential under *Column D* and *Column I*).

The worksheet limits the choice up to a maximum value of 3 from a minimum value of −10, using a drop-down list.

The solution will be found when *Cell N18* is equal to zero. See Fig. 1.1-17 and Table 1.1-1.

$$Column\ A = if\ statement\ that\ returns\ x_1^*$$

**TABLE 1.1-1**   Solution of Example 1 with $x_1^* = 4.5$ and $x_2^* = 5.5$.

|  | M | N |
|---|---|---|
| 12 | Find Lagrange multiplier such that Cell N18 = 0 | |
| 13 | | |
| 14 | x1 | 4.5500 |
| 15 | x2 | 5.5500 |
| 16 | Constraint | 10.1000 |
| 17 | | |
| 18 | Must be equal to zero | 0.0000 |
| 19 | | |
| 20 | Sign Test on $\partial\mathcal{L}$ | 4.0000 |

$$Column\ B = x_1$$

$$Column\ C = Lagrangian\ as\ a\ function\ of\ x_1\ holding\ x_2\ constant$$

$$Column\ D = partial\ differential\ \frac{\partial \mathscr{L}(x, \lambda)}{\partial x_1}$$

When the differential changes sign, the value of 2 is returned. At the same row the stationary point will be found.

$$Column\ F = if\ statement\ that\ returns\ x_2^*$$

$$Column\ G = x_2$$

$$Column\ H = Lagrangian\ as\ a\ function\ of\ x_2\ holding\ x_1\ constant$$

$$Column\ I = partial\ differential\ \frac{\partial \mathscr{L}(x, \lambda)}{\partial x_2}$$

$$Column\ J = test\ condition\ on\ the\ sign\ of\ \frac{\partial \mathscr{L}(x, \lambda)}{\partial x_2}.$$

When the differential changes sign the value of 2 is returned. At the same row the stationary point will be found.

Beginning with a positive value in *Cell E1* of Lagrange multiplier the VBA Loop of Fig. 1.1-18 reduces this value repeatedly (this is because of the VBA **Do Until**) by 0.5 until the optimization is reached; i.e., when *Cell N18* = 0 (and constraint $x_1 + x_2 = 10$ is satisfied); when optimization is reached *Cell N20* ≠ 0 must also result, which means that the two partial differentials have changed sign somewhere along the range of the independent variables.

Otherwise, if the *Cell E1* reaches the value of zero without any optimization (namely, *Cell N18* is still different from zero) the VBA exits the Loop and returns a **Message Box**. Therefore, we need to reoptimize inputting in *Cell E1* a negative value, making the macro increase this value until the optimization is reached.

Table 1.1-1 is the final optimization result. In this case, the optimizing Lagrange multiplier turns out to be negative (i.e., $\lambda_1 = -5$) as calculated by the theoretical solution.

## For Next Looping

Another looping structure is the **For Next.** In VBA, this looping structure repeats a set of instructions a certain number of times.

What we need here is a *variable* which allows to count through the loop. This is the **Loop Counter,** and it is normally denoted with a letter.

In VBA, it is defined as an integer as follows:

$$Dim\ i\ As\ Integer$$

The *For Next* statement then begins, recalling the *Loop Counter i* and stating how many times (e.g., 100) we need to repeat a set of instructions:

$$For\ i = 1\ to\ 100$$

which means that the *loop* will count 100 times.

What makes the loop go forward is the word *Next*. Between *For* and *Next* we have therefore to insert the set of instructions to be repeated.

## EXAMPLE 2 (HEAT SHEET HIGHLIGHTING THE BEST PERFORMING FUNDS WITHIN THEIR PEER GROUP)

Let us consider an investment house that has gathered the data of Table 1.1-2 on the funds they manage, where:

$$\%\ Change = performance\ of\ the\ period\ (One\ week,\ One\ Month,\ etc.)$$

$$Rank = Rank\ position\ within\ the\ Peer - Group$$

$$Count = Number\ of\ Funds\ within\ the\ Peer - Group$$

$$Qrtl = In\ which\ Quartile\ (from\ 1\ to\ 4)\ the\ fund\ is\ positioned\ within\ the\ Peer - Group$$

For example, Fund 1 has a performance of $-3.79\%$ over a month, within its peer group (e.g., Euro Equity) made of 55 funds (Count) and it appears to be in the first quartile, as it's been ranked in the eighth position.

Now, using the VBA *For Next* statement, we want to perform a conditional formatting changing the color to the Funds for each performance period (One Week, One Month, Three

**TABLE 1.1-2** Performance and Ranking for each fund within each Peer Group.

| | A | B | C | D | E | F | G | H | I | J | K | L | M | N | O | P | Q | R | S | T | U | V | W | X | Y |
|---|---|---|---|---|---|---|---|---|---|---|---|---|---|---|---|---|---|---|---|---|---|---|---|---|---|
| 1 | Period | One Week | | | | One Month | | | | Three Months | | | | Year to Date | | | | Six Months | | | | One Year | | | |
| 2 | | 14-mag-04 | | | | 23-apr-04 | | | | 20-feb-04 | | | | 31-dic-03 | | | | 21-nov-03 | | | | 23-mag-03 | | | |
| 3 | | 21-mag-04 | | | | 21-mag-04 | | | | 21-mag-04 | | | | 21-mag-04 | | | | 21-mag-04 | | | | 21-mag-04 | | | |
| 4 | Investment Fund | % Change | Rank | Count | Qrtl | % Change | Rank | Count | Qrtl | % Change | Rank | Count | Qrtl | % Change | Rank | Count | Qrtl | % Change | Rank | Count | Qrtl | % Change | Rank | Count | Qrtl |
| 5 | Fund 1 | 1.01 | 4 | 55 | 1 | -3.79 | 8 | 55 | 1 | -3.70 | 6 | 55 | 1 | -1.03 | 6 | 55 | 1 | 6.20 | 6 | 55 | 1 | 17.41 | 8 | 52 | 1 |
| 6 | Fund 2 | 1.61 | 2 | 55 | 1 | -3.41 | 5 | 55 | 1 | -3.90 | 7 | 55 | 1 | -1.31 | 8 | 55 | 1 | 5.95 | 7 | 55 | 1 | 17.82 | 6 | 52 | 1 |
| 7 | Fund 3 | 4.07 | 3 | 8 | 2 | -8.34 | 2 | 8 | 1 | -11.33 | 1 | 8 | 1 | -4.21 | 2 | 8 | 1 | 3.16 | 2 | 8 | 1 | 3.16 | 1 | 8 | 1 |
| 8 | Fund 4 | -0.19 | 24 | 36 | 3 | -5.80 | 5 | 36 | 1 | -2.26 | 2 | 36 | 1 | 3.86 | 1 | 36 | 1 | 9.58 | 1 | 36 | 1 | 36.40 | 2 | 36 | 1 |
| 9 | Fund 5 | 0.06 | 54 | 80 | 3 | -5.00 | 17 | 80 | 1 | -3.54 | 13 | 80 | 1 | 4.55 | 6 | 80 | 1 | 8.72 | 5 | 80 | 1 | 26.49 | 13 | 80 | 1 |
| 10 | Fund 6 | -0.29 | 43 | 58 | 3 | -3.51 | 8 | 58 | 1 | 0.00 | 8 | 58 | 1 | 10.53 | 8 | 58 | 1 | 14.30 | 6 | 58 | 1 | 41.17 | 14 | 57 | 1 |
| 11 | Fund 7 | 0.00 | 60 | 80 | 3 | -4.19 | 10 | 80 | 1 | 0.89 | 1 | 80 | 1 | 9.10 | 1 | 80 | 1 | 13.65 | 1 | 80 | 1 | 39.45 | 2 | 80 | 1 |
| 12 | Fund 8 | 0.00 | 22 | 28 | 4 | -0.10 | 9 | 28 | 2 | 0.00 | 6 | 28 | 1 | 0.29 | 3 | 28 | 1 | 0.48 | 4 | 28 | 1 | 0.67 | 4 | 27 | 1 |
| 13 | Fund 9 | -0.51 | 222 | 237 | 4 | -4.68 | 138 | 237 | 3 | -1.54 | 26 | 236 | 1 | 6.00 | 14 | 235 | 1 | 10.14 | 16 | 234 | 1 | 32.90 | 11 | 225 | 1 |
| 14 | Fund 10 | -0.13 | 22 | 26 | 4 | -3.28 | 12 | 26 | 2 | 0.30 | 7 | 26 | 2 | 4.39 | 3 | 26 | 1 | 6.73 | 4 | 26 | 1 | 24.91 | 1 | 26 | 1 |
| 46 | Fund 42 | 0.77 | 846 | 4400 | 1 | -1.32 | 773 | 4393 | 1 | -1.46 | 2573 | 4322 | 3 | -1.69 | 3864 | 4276 | 4 | 0.14 | 3333 | 4247 | 4 | 1.36 | 3091 | 4027 | 4 |
| 47 | Fund 43 | -2.60 | 47 | 55 | 4 | -4.61 | 24 | 55 | 2 | 1.03 | 47 | 55 | 4 | 3.42 | 50 | 55 | 4 | 2.48 | 53 | 55 | 4 | 5.36 | 53 | 54 | 4 |
| 48 | Fund 44 | 1.14 | 1 | 226 | 1 | 0.42 | 1 | 225 | 1 | 1.19 | 2 | 224 | 1 | 1.43 | 34 | 222 | 1 | N/A | .... | .... | .... | N/A | .... | .... | .... |
| 49 | Fund 45 | 3.87 | 14 | 112 | 1 | -6.69 | 52 | 112 | 2 | N/A | .... | .... | .... | N/A | .... | .... | .... | N/A | .... | .... | .... | N/A | .... | .... | .... |

I. Excel and fundamental mathematics for economics

Months, Year-To-Date, Six Months, One Year), according to their quartile. At the end, we want to color the funds under *Column A* according to the One Year performance.

This will allow us to immediately recognize the best-performing funds and how funds have changed quartile from one period to another.

As follows we have the sub routine that assigns four different colors to each fund for each performance period, according to the quartiles. The color index has been found recording a macro (not shown here) to see which index VBA associates to a specific color. In brackets and in bold the comments (not in the VBA original macro).

*Sub Heat_sheet_colours()*

*Dim i As Integer.*

*Dim n As Integer.*

*For i = 1 To 25* (25 **is the number of coloumns, from column A to Column Y, of** Table 1.1-2)

*If Cells (4,i) = Qrtl Then* (**Excel goes forward for 25 Columns along the** *fourth Row and if it* **meets the word Qrtl then the second For Statement begins**)

*For n = 5 To 49* (**Reference of Rows of** Table 1.1-2)

*If Cells (n,i) = 1 Then* (This is the formatting of Quartile 1)

*Range (Cells (n,i-3), Cells (n,i)). Select* (**Applies the color to the 4 cells**)

*With Selection. Interior*

  *.Color Index = 4*

  *.Pattern = xl Solid*

*End With*

*End If*

*If Cells (n,i) = 2 Then* (**This is the formatting of Quartile 2**)

*Range (Cells (n,i-3), Cells (n,i)). Select*

*With Selection. Interior*

  *.Color Index = 35*

  *.Pattern = xl Solid*

*End with*

*End If*

*If Cells (n,i) = 3 Then* (**This is the formatting of Quartile 3**)

*Range (Cells (n,i-3), Cells (n,i)). Select*

*With Selection. Interior.*

  *.Color Index = 44.*

  *.Pattern = xl Solid.*

*End With.*

*End If.*

*If Cells (n,i) = 4 Then* (**This is the formatting of Quartile 4**)

*Range (Cells (n,i-3), Cells (n,i)). Select*

*With Selection. Interior*

  *.Color Index = 15*

  *.Pattern = xl Solid*

*End With*

*End If*

*Next*

*End If (**ends the beginning if**)*

*Next (**Ends the first For**)*

The result is in Table 1.1-3 where each fund has been colored according to the Sub.

## 2 User Defined Functions (or function procedures)

In their simplest form the function procedures have the following general structure:

**Function** *Function Name (Argument*1, *Argument*2, ⋯)

*Function Name = Result*

*End **Function***

## EXAMPLE 3 (NUMERICAL INTEGRATION)

In Chapter 2, we will introduce the numerical integration.
Suppose we want to integrate the following basic function:

$$y = 5$$

**TABLE 1.1-3**  Heat Sheet Reporting with Colors Assigned to Highlight the Quartile Positioning of each Fund.

| | A | B | C | D | E | F | G | H | I | J | K | L | M | N | O | P | Q | R | S | T | U | V | W | X | Y |
|---|---|---|---|---|---|---|---|---|---|---|---|---|---|---|---|---|---|---|---|---|---|---|---|---|---|
| 1 | Period | One Week | | | | One Month | | | | Three Months | | | | Year to Date | | | | Six Months | | | | One Year | | | |
| 2 | | 14-mag-04 | | | | 23-apr-04 | | | | 20-feb-04 | | | | 31-dic-03 | | | | 21-nov-03 | | | | 23-mag-03 | | | |
| 3 | | 21-mag-04 | | | | 21-mag-04 | | | | 21-mag-04 | | | | 21-mag-04 | | | | 21-mag-04 | | | | 21-mag-04 | | | |
| 4 | Investment Fund | % Change | Rank | Count | Qrtl | % Change | Rank | Count | Qrtl | % Change | Rank | Count | Qrtl | % Change | Rank | Count | Qrtl | % Change | Rank | Count | Qrtl | % Change | Rank | Count | Qrtl |
| 5 | Fund 1 | | | 55 | | | | 25 | | | | 53 | | | | 55 | | | | | | | | 53 | |
| 6 | Fund 2 | | 2 | 58 | | | | 52 | | | | 55 | | | | 23 | | | | 55 | | | | 53 | |
| 7 | Fund 3 | 4.07 | 3 | 8 | 2 | | | | | | | | | | | | | | | | | | | | |
| 10 | Fund 5 | -0.29 | 43 | 58 | 3 | | | | | 0.00 | | 55 | | 10.55 | | | | 14.30 | | 55 | | 4.17 | 54 | 57 | |
| 11 | Fund 7 | 0.00 | 60 | 80 | | | | | | | | 80 | | | | 80 | | 13.65 | | 80 | | | | 85 | |
| 12 | Fund 8 | 0.00 | 22 | 28 | 4 | -0.10 | 9 | 28 | 2 | 0.00 | | | | 0.25 | | 28 | | 0.43 | | 28 | | 0.67 | | 23 | |
| 23 | Fund 19 | 3.91 | 12 | 26 | 2 | -9.61 | 9 | 26 | 2 | | | | | | | 26 | | 0.52 | 15 | 25 | 3 | 47.45 | | | |
| 24 | Fund 20 | -0.21 | 15 | 33 | 2 | -2.77 | 19 | 33 | 3 | -3.48 | 14 | 33 | 2 | 3.29 | 10 | 33 | 3 | 8.35 | 19 | 33 | 3 | 3.44 | | 51 | |
| 25 | Fund 21 | 0.29 | 13 | 13 | 4 | -0.57 | 7 | 13 | 2 | 1.23 | 10 | 13 | 3 | 0.79 | 9 | 13 | 3 | 0.94 | 7 | 12 | 3 | 1.16 | | 12 | |
| 26 | Fund 22 | 0.41 | 92 | 237 | 2 | -4.22 | 95 | 237 | 2 | -3.55 | 120 | 236 | 3 | 3.60 | 71 | 235 | 2 | | | | | 22.46 | 96 | 225 | 2 |
| 27 | Fund 23 | 0.60 | 243 | 357 | | -4.74 | 192 | 357 | 3 | | | | | | | | | 6.49 | 105 | 351 | 2 | 21.99 | 135 | 347 | 2 |
| 34 | Fund 30 | | | | | -3.32 | 7 | 9 | 3 | -4.15 | 7 | 9 | 3 | -1.71 | 8 | 9 | 4 | 0.57 | 7 | 8 | 4 | 7.64 | 4 | 7 | 2 |
| 35 | Fund 31 | 1.22 | 50 | 70 | 3 | -15.14 | 65 | 70 | 4 | -14.55 | 62 | 70 | 4 | -8.61 | 60 | 70 | 4 | 1.01 | 65 | 70 | 4 | 36.34 | 33 | 67 | 2 |
| 36 | Fund 32 | 1.98 | 43 | 48 | 4 | -11.87 | 48 | 48 | 4 | -2.37 | 47 | 48 | 4 | 7.84 | 46 | 48 | 4 | 14.92 | 48 | 48 | 4 | 40.98 | 15 | 48 | 2 |
| 37 | Fund 33 | 0.78 | 36 | 55 | 3 | | | 55 | | | | 55 | | | | 53 | | 0.31 | | | | 1.17 | 28 | 50 | 3 |
| 38 | Fund 34 | 2.88 | 8 | 17 | 2 | | | | | 16.33 | 9 | 17 | 2 | 22.71 | 6 | 17 | 2 | 29.64 | 9 | 17 | 2 | 50.59 | 13 | 17 | 3 |
| 43 | Fund 39 | | | | | 0.00 | 62 | 81 | 4 | 0.08 | 47 | 81 | 3 | 0.16 | 42 | 81 | 3 | 0.18 | 53 | 81 | 3 | 0.34 | 55 | 61 | 3 |
| 44 | Fund 40 | -1.55 | 107 | 117 | 4 | -8.81 | 92 | 117 | 4 | -11.44 | 82 | 117 | 3 | -9.31 | 99 | 117 | 4 | -4.28 | 98 | 116 | 4 | 16.95 | 84 | 114 | 3 |
| 45 | Fund 41 | 2.67 | 71 | 112 | | | | 112 | | | | | | 7.90 | 32 | 107 | 2 | 15.20 | 42 | 107 | 2 | 30.65 | 84 | 103 | 4 |
| 46 | Fund 42 | | | 4440 | | | | 4433 | | -1.46 | 2573 | 4322 | 3 | -1.69 | 3864 | 4276 | 4 | 0.14 | 3333 | 4247 | 4 | 1.36 | 3091 | 4027 | 4 |
| 47 | Fund 43 | -2.60 | 47 | 55 | 4 | -4.61 | 24 | 55 | 2 | 1.03 | 47 | 55 | 4 | 3.42 | 50 | 55 | 4 | 2.48 | 53 | 55 | 4 | 5.36 | 53 | 54 | 4 |
| 48 | Fund 44 | | | | | | | | | | | | | | | | | N/A | ---- | ---- | ---- | N/A | ---- | ---- | ---- |
| 49 | Fund 45 | | | | | -6.69 | 52 | 112 | 2 | N/A | ---- | ---- | ---- | N/A | ---- | ---- | ---- | N/A | ---- | ---- | ---- | N/A | ---- | ---- | ---- |

| | A | B | C | D | E | F | G |
|---|---|---|---|---|---|---|---|
| | x | y'(x) | $x_k$ - $x_{k-1}$ = h | y'(x)*h | $y_k$ = $y_{k-1}$ + y'*h | y Exact | Step |
| 1 | x | y'(x) | $x_k$ - $x_{k-1}$ = h | y'(x)*h | $y_k$ = $y_{k-1}$ + y'*h | y Exact | Step |
| 2 | 0 | | | | 0 | =5*A2 | 0.01 |
| 3 | =A2+$G$2 | 5 | =A3-A2 | =B3*C3 | =INTEGRAL(E2;B3;C3) | =5*A3 | |
| 4 | =A3+$G$2 | 5 | =A4-A3 | =B4*C4 | =INTEGRAL(E3;B4;C4) | =5*A4 | |
| 5 | =A4+$G$2 | 5 | =A5-A4 | =B5*C5 | =INTEGRAL(E4;B5;C5) | =5*A5 | |
| 6 | =A5+$G$2 | 5 | =A6-A5 | =B6*C6 | =INTEGRAL(E5;B6;C6) | =5*A6 | |
| 7 | =A6+$G$2 | 5 | =A7-A6 | =B7*C7 | =INTEGRAL(E6;B7;C7) | =5*A7 | |
| 8 | =A7+$G$2 | 5 | =A8-A7 | =B8*C8 | =INTEGRAL(E7;B8;C8) | =5*A8 | |
| 9 | =A8+$G$2 | 5 | =A9-A8 | =B9*C9 | =INTEGRAL(E8;B9;C9) | =5*A9 | |
| 10 | =A9+$G$2 | 5 | =A10-A9 | =B10*C10 | =INTEGRAL(E9;B10;C10) | =5*A10 | |
| 11 | =A10+$G$2 | 5 | =A11-A10 | =B11*C11 | =INTEGRAL(E10;B11;C11) | =5*A11 | |
| 12 | =A11+$G$2 | 5 | =A12-A11 | =B12*C12 | =INTEGRAL(E11;B12;C12) | =5*A12 | |
| 13 | =A12+$G$2 | 5 | =A13-A12 | =B13*C13 | =INTEGRAL(E12;B13;C13) | =5*A13 | |
| 101 | =A100+$G$: 5 | | =A101-A100 | =B101*C101 | =INTEGRAL(E100;B101;C101) | =5*A101 | |
| 102 | =A101+$G: 5 | | =A102-A101 | =B102*C102 | =INTEGRAL(E101;B102;C102) | =5*A102 | |

FIGURE 1.1-19    Numerical Integration of y = 5 with a user defined Function *INTEGRAL*.

and calculate the area under the curve from 0 to 1 (i.e., 5).

A User Defined Function that can be used is as follows:

Function **INTEGRAL**(*Integral_Step_Before, Integrand, Step_Size*)

**INTEGRAL** = *Integral_Step_Before* + *Integrand* * *Step_Size*

End **Function**

TABLE 1.1-4    Numerical versus Exact Integration of y = 5 (with step-size 0.01).

| x | y'(x) | $x_k$ - $x_{k-1}$ = h | y'(x)*h | $y_k$ = $y_{k-1}$ + y'*h | y Exact | Step |
|---|---|---|---|---|---|---|
| 0.00 | | | | 0.00 | 0.00 | 0.01 |
| 0.01 | 5.00 | 0.01 | 0.05 | 0.05 | 0.05 | |
| 0.02 | 5.00 | 0.01 | 0.05 | 0.10 | 0.10 | |
| 0.03 | 5.00 | 0.01 | 0.05 | 0.15 | 0.15 | |
| 0.04 | 5.00 | 0.01 | 0.05 | 0.20 | 0.20 | |
| 0.05 | 5.00 | 0.01 | 0.05 | 0.25 | 0.25 | |
| 0.06 | 5.00 | 0.01 | 0.05 | 0.30 | 0.30 | |
| 0.07 | 5.00 | 0.01 | 0.05 | 0.35 | 0.35 | |
| 0.08 | 5.00 | 0.01 | 0.05 | 0.40 | 0.40 | |
| 0.09 | 5.00 | 0.01 | 0.05 | 0.45 | 0.45 | |
| 0.10 | 5.00 | 0.01 | 0.05 | 0.50 | 0.50 | |
| 0.11 | 5.00 | 0.01 | 0.05 | 0.55 | 0.55 | |
| 0.99 | 5.00 | 0.01 | 0.05 | 4.95 | 4.95 | |
| 1.00 | 5.00 | 0.01 | 0.05 | 5.00 | 5.00 | |

The name of the new (user defined) function will be added in the library, so that we have, for example, the following excerpts of worksheet (see Fig. 1.1-19 and Table 1.1-4).

The only disadvantage is that one should always check the mathematical operations associated to the User Defined Functions within VBA, as the operations are not displayed in Excel.

Within the book we will always display the custom operations we want to do within the Excel cells, without resorting too much to User Defined Functions.

## 1.2 The Excel Solver: simplex LP, Generalized Reduced Gradient, and evolutionary

The Solver available in Excel is massively used within the optimization problems (both static and dynamic) presented in the book. The Solver is a powerful tool that can be also recalled within a VBA sub routine.

We find the Solver under the Tab Developer as an Add-in, as shown in Figs. 1.2-1. The Solver Add-in should be then always kept flagged as in the following Fig. 1.2-2.

There are three types of Solver available in Excel (see Fig. 1.2-3):

**i.** GRG (Generalized Reduced Gradient) Nonlinear
**ii.** Simplex LP (Linear Programming)
**iii.** Evolutionary

The Solver dialogue box of Fig. 1.2-3 allows to define the **Objective function**, the range of the **Changing Variable Cells** (i.e., the **decision variables** of the problem) to optimize the problem and to define the **constraints** (see Fig. 1.2-4).

The **Reset** option allows instead to eliminate the current Solver parameters to set up new ones. The **Load/Save** options will not be used at all within the spreadsheets of the book, and they allow to save in a range of empty cells the features of the Solver parameters used and stored within the Solver options.

The Solver has some options that apply to all methods, as shown in Fig. 1.2-5. Within the book, Solver resolutions all these options will not be touched, leaving to the reader the choice whether to apply the changes or not, to their own Solver solutions.

### Nonlinear Generalized Reduced Gradient

The **Generalized Reduced Gradient (GRG)** is an extension of the **Frank-Wolfe's Reduced Gradient** algorithm made by **Abadie-Carpenter** to handle nonlinear constraints (see

FIGURE 1.2-1   Excel Add-ins Tab under the Developer Tab.

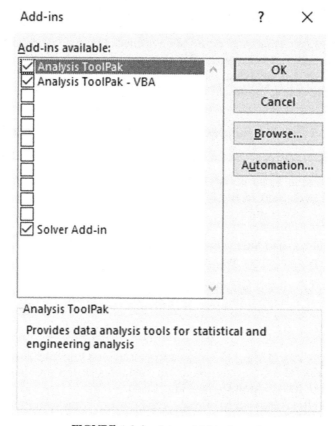

**FIGURE 1.2-2** Solver Add-in flagged.

*Generalization of the Wolfe Reduced Gradient Method to the Case of Nonlinear Constraints.* In R. Fletcher, Ed. Optimization, Academic Press, New York, 1969).

The GRG essentially aims at solving constrained nonlinear problems in the form of:

$$\min_{x \in \Re^n} f(x)$$

subject to

$$h_k(x) = 0 \qquad k = 1,\, 2,\, \cdots,\, q$$

$$g_j(x) \leq 0 \qquad j = 1,\, 2,\, \cdots,\, m$$

$$x_i^l \leq x \leq x_i^u \qquad i = 1,\, 2,\, \cdots,\, n$$

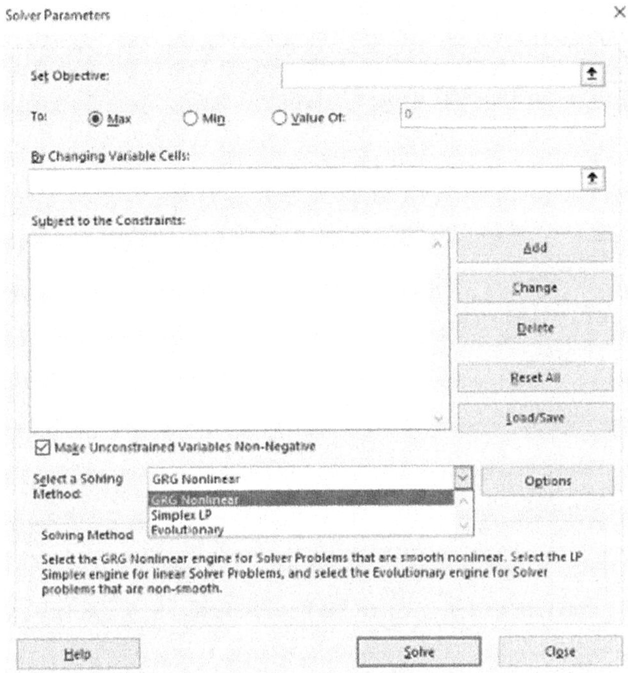

**FIGURE 1.2-3**    Three types of solver.

where $f(x)$, $h(x)$, and $g(x)$ are continuously differentiable real valued functions and $x_i^l$, $x_i^u$ are given *lower* and *upper* bounds.

The idea of the GRG is to use *slack variables* (similarly to what happens in the simplex for the linear programming) to transform the inequality constraints into equality constraints, so that the problem is transformed into the following:

$$\min_{x \in \Re^n} f(x)$$

$$h_k(x) = 0 \qquad k = 1, 2, \cdots, q$$

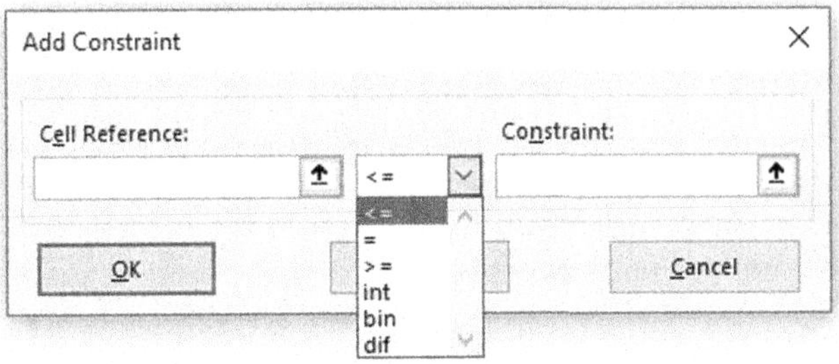

**FIGURE 1.2-4**    Adding a constraint to the Solver.

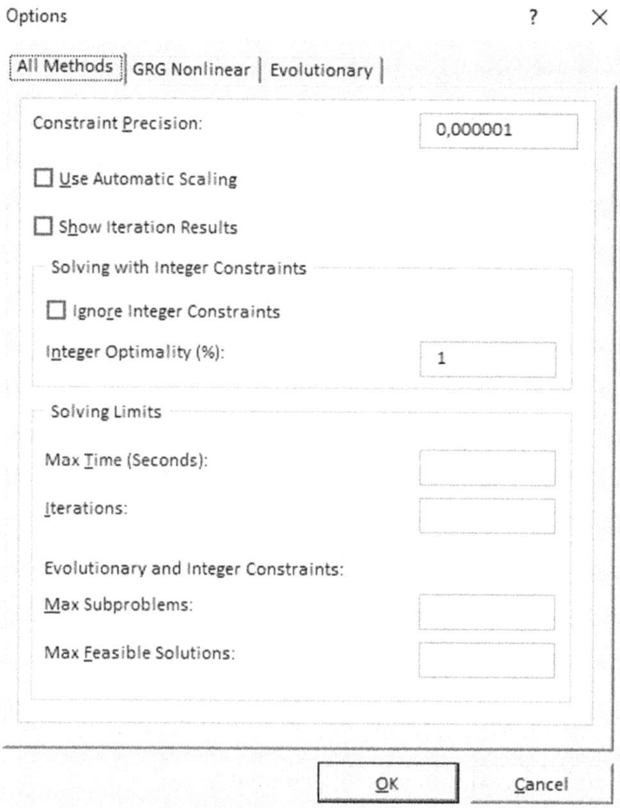

**FIGURE 1.2-5**  Solver options (all methods).

$$g_j(x) + x_{n+j} = 0 \qquad j = 1, 2, \cdots, m$$

$$x_i^l \le x \le x_i^{lu} \qquad i = 1, 2, \cdots, n$$

$$x_{n+j} \ge 0$$

$$x = [x_1, x_2, \cdots, x_n, x_{n+1}, \cdots, x_{n+m}]^T$$

where now $n + m$ is the total number of variables, which are represented by the original $n$ variables and the new $m$ slack variables.

The above problem can be finally expressed as:

$$\min_{x \in \Re^n} f(x)$$

$$H_k(x) = 0 \qquad k = 1, 2, \cdots, s$$

with $s$, new number of constraints.

Then, the algorithm goes through an optimization process via the *gradient vector* search direction, similarly to what happens in the *steepest descent algorithm* (see Section 5.4).

The **GRG Nonlinear** Solver will be utilized within all the static nonlinear problems and all the dynamic optimization problems. The Excel Solver allows for some options in the GRG, as shown in Fig. 1.2-6.

In Fig. 1.2-6, one may decide whether to use a forward or central numerical differentiation, as well as changing the **convergence** tolerance. In the **convergence** box, we can type the amount of relative change that we want to allow in the last five iterations before the Solver stops the optimization procedure.

Then we have the **Multistart** option. This option will automatically run the GRG method from a number of starting points and will display the best of several locally optimal solutions found, as the probable globally optimal solution.

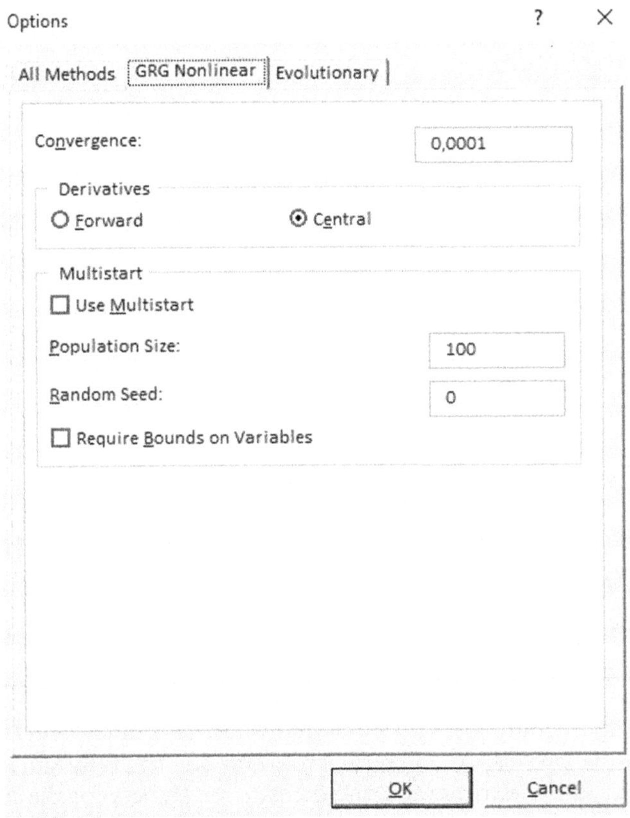

| Options | | ?   ✕ |

All Methods | GRG Nonlinear | Evolutionary

Convergence:     0,0001

Derivatives
   O Forward      ⊙ Central

Multistart
   ☐ Use Multistart

Population Size:     100

Random Seed:     0

   ☐ Require Bounds on Variables

OK      Cancel

FIGURE 1.2-6   Solver options (Generalized Reduced Gradient nonlinear).

In the **Population Size** box, we can type the number of different starting values for the decision variables that we want the multistart method to consider. The minimum population size is 10; if we supply a value less than 10 in this box, or we leave it blank, the multistart method uses a population size of 10 times the number of decision variables, but no more than 200.

The **Random Seed** box uses a positive integer number as a fixed seed for the random number generator used to generate candidate starting points for the GRG nonlinear method. If we enter a number in this box, the multistart method will use the same starting points each time we Solve. If we leave this box blank, the random number generator will use a different seed each time we Solve, which may yield a different (better or worse) final solution. This option will not be used either within the book worksheets.

The **Require Bounds on Variables** check box is to specify that the multistart method should run only if we have defined lower and upper bounds on all decision variables in the Constraints list box. The multistart method is more effective if we define bounds on all variables; the tighter the bounds on the variables that we can specify, the better the multistart method is likely to perform.

All the above option will not be utilized in the book example problems, leaving to the reader to evaluate whether to use them or not.

## Simplex Linear Programming

The **Simplex LP Solver** is to be used within the resolution of the linear programs, namely those optimization problems where both the objective function and the constraints are modeled in a linear form. In Excel it is limited to 200 decision variables.

A general minimizing linear programming problem can be, for example, formulated as:

$$\min_{\{x\}} c \cdot x$$

subject to

$$Ax \lesseqgtr [b]$$

$$x \geq [0]$$

Many of the problems in operations research are modeled via the linear programming, and within the book Chapter 7 will focus on this subject, applying it to some static production optimization models.

One the most used algorithms to solve a multidimensional linear programming problem is the *simplex*.

The *simplex method*, developed by the mathematician George Dantzig, is essentially an iterative algorithm which aims at finding the optimal solution on the corners of the feasible region, and this is possible because in the linear programming the solution, if this ever exists, is always located in one of the *corners* (or *extreme points*, or *vertices*) of the feasible region, this being represented by the linear equation constraints. See Section 7.1 for a more detailed theoretical explanation and geometrical representation.

## Evolutionary

This option of Solver replicates the approach of the **Evolutionary** optimization algorithms, which are different from the classical optimization methods that we will mostly see in the book.

For the sake of a further reader's research, it is just worth mentioning here that the Evolutionary computation is a family of algorithms for global optimization that applies the principles of biological evolution via the *genetic algorithm*. The evolutionary computation is essentially a population-based trial and error problem solver, with a metaheuristic or stochastic optimization underlying approach. You can notice this feature from the Excel Evolutionary Solver options, as shown in Fig. 1.2-7. This kind of approach is studied a lot within the artificial intelligence, and it won't be used at all within the book.

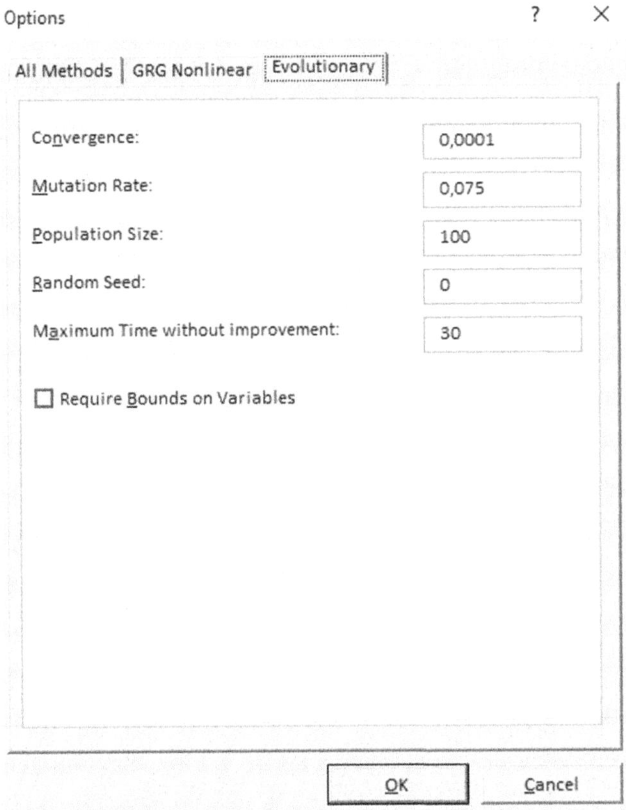

FIGURE 1.2-7    Solver options (evolutionary).

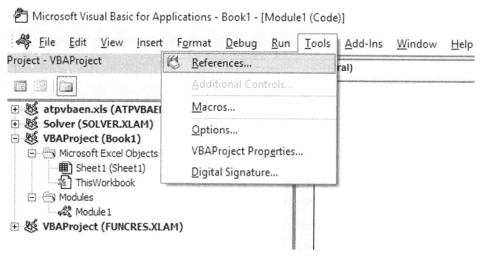

FIGURE 1.2-8    References to recall the solver within VBA.

We have mentioned before that the Solver can be also recalled within the VBA Sub routines, normally because we want to perform a sequential optimization for several times (for example, within the Efficient Frontier construction, see Chapter 8).

In order to do this, when we are under the VB Editor, we need to go to *Tools*, then *References* (see Fig. 1.2-8).

Then, look for the Solver and select it (see Fig. 1.2-9). When we do that, the Solver should be already added from the Excel *Add-ins*.

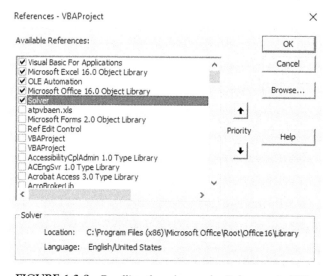

FIGURE 1.2-9    Recalling the solver under References in VBA.

The Solver is now ready to be used within the VBA as an instruction.

When the Solver finds the optimal solution, it returns the following message in Fig. 1.2-10, from which we also have the opportunity to show the Reports (an **Answer Report**, a **Sensitivity Report,** and **Limits Report**).

The Answer Report for the Lagrange constrained optimization problem in Example 1 of Section 1.1 is shown in Figs. 1.2-11.

If the problem is not well specified and the Solver does not find the optimal solution it returns the message of Figs. 1.2-12 of no convergence solution. This may happen, for example, in the unconstrained optimization with more stationary points (local minima or local maxima), where we have to instruct the Solver from which variables to begin searching (e.g., imposing a constraint) otherwise the Solver returns no solutions.

## 1.3 What-if analysis: scenario manager, Goal Seek, Data Table, and contour lines

Under the Ribbon Tab Data, we find another important advanced analysis tool offered by Excel, namely the **What-if Analysis** (see Fig. 1.3-1).

Essentially, this tool answers to the question of **what** will happen to the output function **if** we change the values of the inputs.

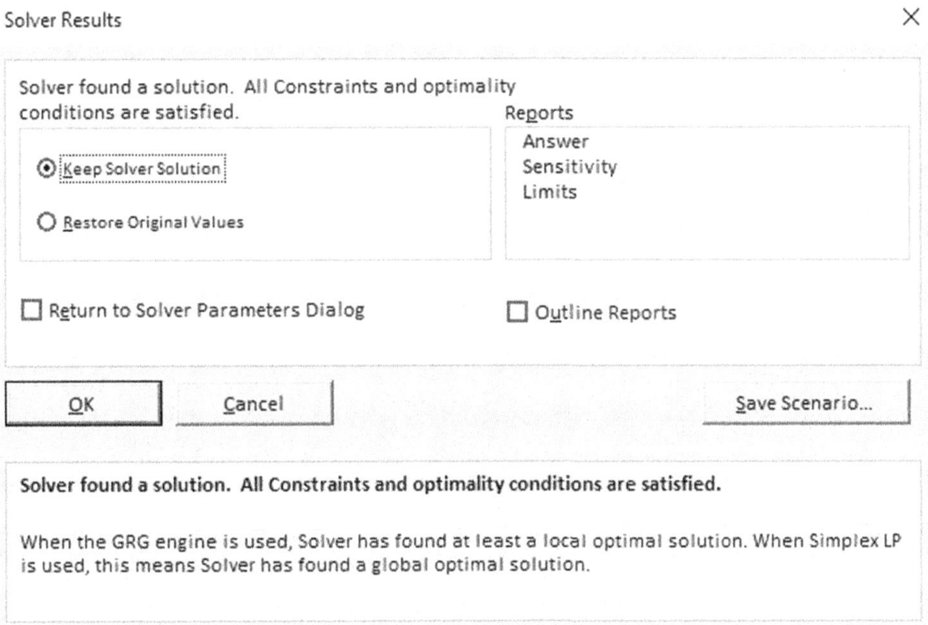

FIGURE 1.2-10   Solver Results (Solver found a Solution).

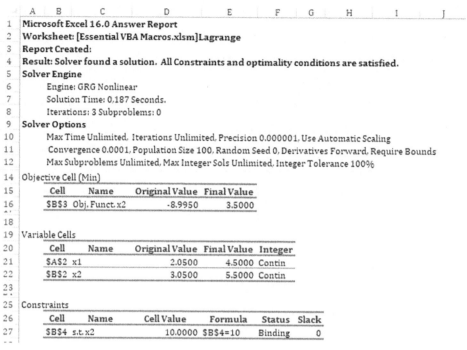

| | A | B | C | D | E | F | G | H | I | J |
|---|---|---|---|---|---|---|---|---|---|---|
| 1 | Microsoft Excel 16.0 Answer Report | | | | | | | | | |
| 2 | Worksheet: [Essential VBA Macros.xlsm]Lagrange | | | | | | | | | |
| 3 | Report Created: | | | | | | | | | |
| 4 | Result: Solver found a solution. All Constraints and optimality conditions are satisfied. | | | | | | | | | |
| 5 | Solver Engine | | | | | | | | | |
| 6 |     Engine: GRG Nonlinear | | | | | | | | | |
| 7 |     Solution Time: 0.187 Seconds. | | | | | | | | | |
| 8 |     Iterations: 3 Subproblems: 0 | | | | | | | | | |
| 9 | Solver Options | | | | | | | | | |
| 10 |     Max Time Unlimited, Iterations Unlimited, Precision 0.000001, Use Automatic Scaling | | | | | | | | | |
| 11 |     Convergence 0.0001, Population Size 100, Random Seed 0, Derivatives Forward, Require Bounds | | | | | | | | | |
| 12 |     Max Subproblems Unlimited, Max Integer Sols Unlimited, Integer Tolerance 100% | | | | | | | | | |
| 14 | Objective Cell (Min) | | | | | | | | | |

**Objective Cell (Min)**

| Cell | Name | Original Value | Final Value |
|---|---|---|---|
| $B$3 | Obj. Funct. x2 | -8.9950 | 3.5000 |

**Variable Cells**

| Cell | Name | Original Value | Final Value | Integer |
|---|---|---|---|---|
| $A$2 | x1 | 2.0500 | 4.5000 | Contin |
| $B$2 | x2 | 3.0500 | 5.5000 | Contin |

**Constraints**

| Cell | Name | Cell Value | Formula | Status | Slack |
|---|---|---|---|---|---|
| $B$4 | s.t. x2 | 10.0000 | $B$4=10 | Binding | 0 |

FIGURE 1.2-11    Solver Answer Report (Example 1 in Section 1.1 and Section 5.5).

Solver Results        ✕

The Objective Cell values do not converge.

Reports

◉ Keep Solver Solution

○ Restore Original Values

☐ Return to Solver Parameters Dialog      ☐ Outline Reports

OK     Cancel        Save Scenario...

**The Objective Cell values do not converge.**

Solver can make the Objective Cell as large (or small when minimizing) as it wants.

FIGURE 1.2-12    Solver message of no convergence in the solution.

FIGURE 1.3-1   What-if analysis.

The What-if Analysis allows to perform three types of activities:

i. Scenarios
ii. Goal Seek
iii. Data Table (of key importance in the standard calculus, involving two independent variables)

The best way to explain the What-if Analysis is through an example. We decide to use a basic Capital Budgeting case of **NPV** (Net Present Value) and **IRR** (Internal Rate of Return) as it fits well with the explanation of the above points **i**, **ii**, and **iii**. Chapter 14 will go deeper into the simulation techniques, using the methods of Monte Carlo.

## EXAMPLE 1 (WHAT-IF ANALYSIS ON NPV AND IRR CALCULATION)

Let us consider the Cash Flows schedule of Table 1.3-1, where the first one is represented by the initial investment:

We assume a required rate of return equal to 9%. The required rate of return is the discount rate that investors should require given the riskiness of the project. This discount rate is also called the **cost of capital** and a weighted average cost of capital (Wacc) is usually calculated, which depends on how the project is financed. This is essentially an **opportunity cost**.

Unless an investment earns more than the cost of capital, the investment should not be undertaken.

The Net Present Value is the present value of the future after-tax cash flows minus the investment outlay as follows:

$$NPV = \sum_{t=1}^{n} \frac{CF_t}{(1+r)^t} - CF_0$$

TABLE 1.3-1   Initial Outlay and Cash Flow Projection of the project.

|   | A | B | C | D | E | F | G | H | I | J | K |
|---|---|---|---|---|---|---|---|---|---|---|---|
| 1 | Year | 0 | 1 | 2 | 3 | 4 | 5 | 6 | 7 | 8 | 9 |
| 2 | Cash Flow | -1.170.00 | -160.00 | 480.00 | 570.00 | 700.00 | 830.00 | 920.00 | 920.00 | 800.00 | 600.00 |
| 3 | | | | | | | | | | | |
| 4 | NPV | 2.292 | | | | | | | | | |
| 5 | Wacc | 9.00% | | | | | | | | | |
| 6 | | | | | | | | | | | |

where

CFt=Cash flow in period t.

$r = $ *required rate of return; the Weighted Average Cost of Capital (Wacc) is considered.*

$CF_0 = $ *Cash Outlay at the beginning of the project.*

Using the following Excel formula:

$$= B2 + NPV(B5; C2: K2)$$

we obtain the NPV equal to £ 2292. The project should be undertaken as the NPV is positive. Here, the cash outlay (this is not discounted as it occurs at $t = 0$) is negatively added separately to the NPV excel formula (which is slightly different from the pure theoretical NPV we defined before).

**i.** Scenario Analysis

Suppose we need to simulate the NPV output changing both the Cash Outlay and the first negative Cash Flow.

The new values would be:

$$CF_0 = -1,500 \text{ and } CF_1 = -300$$

Now, we just go to Scenario Manager on What-if Analysis, following the steps from Figs. 1.3-2—1.3-6.

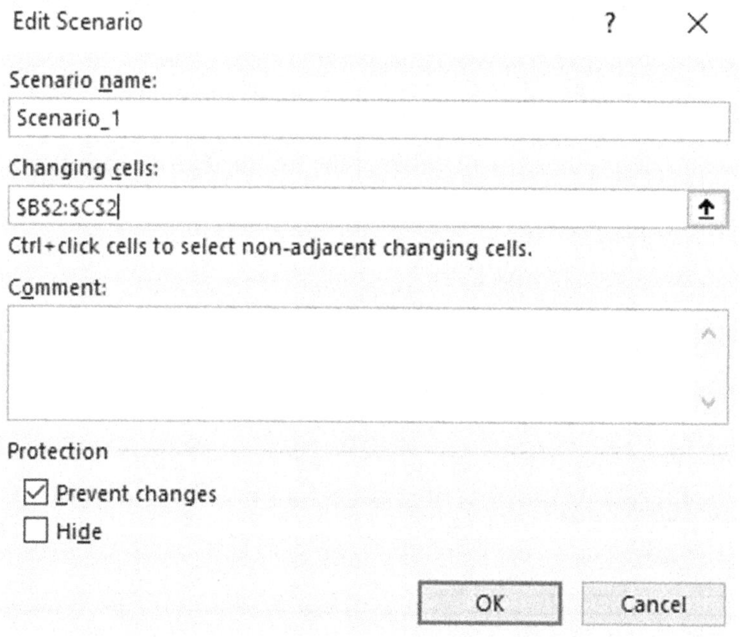

Edit Scenario                                                                    ?     ×

Scenario name:

Scenario_1

Changing cells:

$B$2:$C$2

Ctrl+click cells to select non-adjacent changing cells.

Comment:

Protection

☑ Prevent changes
☐ Hide

OK          Cancel

**FIGURE 1.3-2**   Adding and Editing a Scenario.

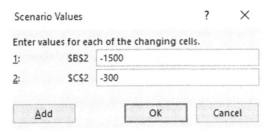

**FIGURE 1.3-3**   Changing $CF_0$ and $CF_1$ to $-1500$ and $-300$.

It is worth noticing that more scenarios can be added simultaneously. Finally, the following report in Fig. 1.3-6 is created.

**ii.** Goal Seek (IRR calculation)

The **internal rate of return** (IRR) is the discount rate that makes the present value of the future after-tax cash flows equal that investment outlay.

The *IRR* is in other words the actual return (ex post, or expected based on the Cash Flows projection), of the project, which is found to satisfy the following equation:

$$\sum_{t=1}^{n} \frac{CF_t}{(1+IRR)^t} - CF_0 = 0.$$

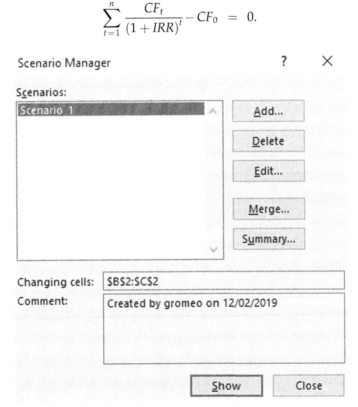

**FIGURE 1.3-4**   Show summary.

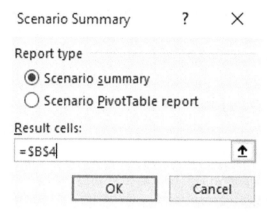

FIGURE 1.3-5    Define the Resulting Cell (NPV): we select Scenario Summary (Scenario in a Pivot Table format is also possible).

A potential supplier of capital will not invest in the project, unless its actual return (i.e., the *IRR*) meets or exceeds what the supplier could earn (the *Wacc*) elsewhere in a comparable risk investment.

We can use the Excel Goal Seek as shown in Figs. 1.3-7 and 1.3-8 to solve the above equation (still considering the data of Table 1.3-1).

The Goal Seek is essentially an optimizer, and sometimes it can be used alternatively to the Solver.

The calculated IRR is equal to 34.51% and corresponds to the one we can calculate using the Excel built-in formula $= IRR(B2:K2)$.

|   | A | B | C | D | E | F | G |
|---|---|---|---|---|---|---|---|
| 1 |   |   |   |   |   |   |   |
| 2 |   | **Scenario Summary** | | | | | |
| 3 |   |   | Current Values: | | Scenario_1 | | |
| 5 |   | **Changing Cells:** | | | | | |
| 6 |   |   | $B$2 | -1,170.00 | -1,500.00 | | |
| 7 |   |   | $C$2 | -160.00 | -300.00 | | |
| 8 |   | **Result Cells:** | | | | | |
| 9 |   |   | $B$4 | 2,292.29 | 1,833.85 | | |

Notes: Current Values column represents values of changing cells at time Scenario Summary Report was created. Changing cells for each scenario are highlighted in gray.

FIGURE 1.3-6    Scenario summary.

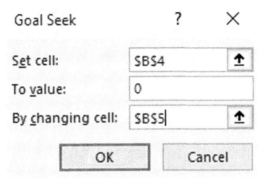

FIGURE 1.3-7    Goal Seek (IRR calculation).

### iii. Data Table Simulation

The third tool offered by Excel to do a simulation on the output variable is the **Data Table**. Throughout the book we will use the Data Table tool within the bivariate optimization analysis.

In the following Fig. 1.3-9, we have set *Cell D9 = Cell B4 = NPV*. This is the simulated output. Now we need the two input variables to be changed, to see how the NPV output will be affected.

This can be easily done as in Fig. 1.3-9, selecting the *Range C9:D20* and inserting a Data Table from the What-if Analysis.

The Data Table will ask two input variables, as a base for the simulation, namely the **Row Input Cell** and the **Column Input Cell**.

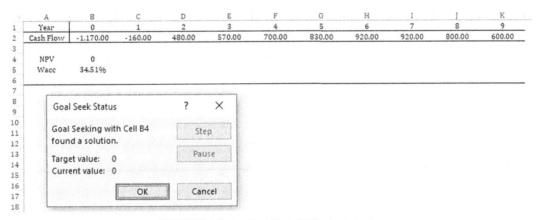

FIGURE 1.3-8    Goal Seek (IRR calculation).

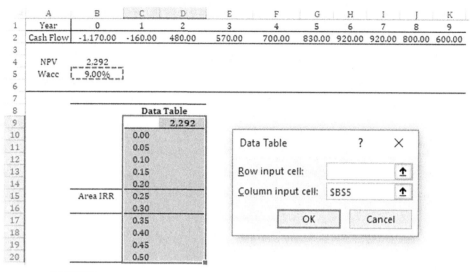

| | A | B | C | D | E | F | G | H | I | J | K |
|---|---|---|---|---|---|---|---|---|---|---|---|
| 1 | Year | 0 | 1 | 2 | 3 | 4 | 5 | 6 | 7 | 8 | 9 |
| 2 | Cash Flow | -1,170.00 | -160.00 | 480.00 | 570.00 | 700.00 | 830.00 | 920.00 | 920.00 | 800.00 | 600.00 |
| 3 | | | | | | | | | | | |
| 4 | NPV | 2,292 | | | | | | | | | |
| 5 | Wacc | 9.00% | | | | | | | | | |
| 6 | | | | | | | | | | | |
| 7 | | | | | | | | | | | |
| 8 | | | | Data Table | | | | | | | |
| 9 | | | | 2,292 | | | | | | | |
| 10 | | | 0.00 | | | | | | | | |
| 11 | | | 0.05 | | | | | | | | |
| 12 | | | 0.10 | | | | | | | | |
| 13 | | | 0.15 | | | | | | | | |
| 14 | | | 0.20 | | | | | | | | |
| 15 | | Area IRR | 0.25 | | | | | | | | |
| 16 | | | 0.30 | | | | | | | | |
| 17 | | | 0.35 | | | | | | | | |
| 18 | | | 0.40 | | | | | | | | |
| 19 | | | 0.45 | | | | | | | | |
| 20 | | | 0.50 | | | | | | | | |

Data Table ? ✕

Row input cell: [ ] ↑

Column input cell: $B$5 ↑

OK    Cancel

FIGURE 1.3-9   Data Table NPV simulation (NPV as a function of the Wacc).

To begin, we decide to change only one variable, the Wacc. This will be our Column Input Cell (i.e., *Cell B5*) because we have arranged the range of possible Wacc under *Column C* (from *Cell C10* to *Cell C20*).

The output is in Fig. 1.3-10, from which we notice that the IRR should be in the range area where the NPV changes sign.

| | A | B | C | D | E | F | G | H | I | J | K |
|---|---|---|---|---|---|---|---|---|---|---|---|
| 1 | Year | 0 | 1 | 2 | 3 | 4 | 5 | 6 | 7 | 8 | 9 |
| 2 | Cash Flow | -1,170.00 | -160.00 | 480.00 | 570.00 | 700.00 | 830.00 | 920.00 | 920.00 | 800.00 | 600.00 |
| 3 | | | | | | | | | | | |
| 4 | NPV | 2,292 | | | | | | | | | |
| 5 | Wacc | 9.00% | | | | | | | | | |
| 6 | | | | | | | | | | | |
| 7 | | | | | | | | | | | |
| 8 | | | | Data Table | | | | | | | |
| 9 | | | | 2,292 | | | | | | | |
| 10 | | | 0.00 | 4,490 | | | | | | | |
| 11 | | | 0.05 | 3,100 | | | | | | | |
| 12 | | | 0.10 | 2,122 | | | | | | | |
| 13 | | | 0.15 | 1,417 | | | | | | | |
| 14 | | | 0.20 | 898 | | | | | | | |
| 15 | | Area IRR | 0.25 | 509 | | | | | | | |
| 16 | | | 0.30 | 211 | | | | | | | |
| 17 | | | 0.35 | -20 | | | | | | | |
| 18 | | | 0.40 | -202 | | | | | | | |
| 19 | | | 0.45 | -348 | | | | | | | |
| 20 | | | 0.50 | -465 | | | | | | | |

FIGURE 1.3-10   Data Table NPV output.

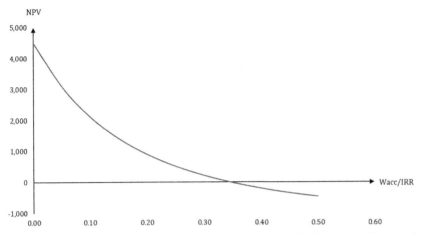

**FIGURE 1.3-11**   NPV profile as a function of various discount rates: if NPV = 0 then Discount Rate = IRR.

The NPV profile is plotted in Fig. 1.3-11 from which we notice that at a discount rate equal to 0% we just have the sum of the undiscounted cash flows equal to £ 4,490. As we have calculated before, at a discount rate of 34.51% we have instead the $NPV = 0$ and therefore 34.51% is the IRR of the project, which compared to the theoretical Wacc (9%) required from the investors for a similar project's class riskiness, make them to decide to undertake the project.

We can also exploit the possibility given by the Data Table changing two variables instead of only one.

For example, we decide to simulate the NPV changing both the Wacc and the initial outlay. In this case the Row Input Cell would be *Cell B2*.

Now we can construct a pure Data Table in two input variables, as in Fig. 1.3-12, where the gray area is because we have selected the entire table before inserting the Data Table formula from the What-if Analysis.

| 2,292 | -2,000 | -1,700 | -1,400 | -1,100 | -800 | -500 |
|-------|--------|--------|--------|--------|------|------|
| 0.00  |        |        |        |        |      |      |
| 0.05  |        |        |        |        |      |      |
| 0.10  |        |        |        |        |      |      |
| 0.15  |        |        |        |        |      |      |
| 0.20  |        |        |        |        |      |      |
| 0.25  |        |        |        |        |      |      |
| 0.30  |        |        |        |        |      |      |
| 0.35  |        |        |        |        |      |      |
| 0.40  |        |        |        |        |      |      |
| 0.45  |        |        |        |        |      |      |
| 0.50  |        |        |        |        |      |      |

**FIGURE 1.3-12**   Arranging the input variable by row (initial outlay) and by Column (Wacc).

| =B4 | -2000 | -1700 | -1400 | -1100 | -800 | -500 |
|---|---|---|---|---|---|---|
| 0 | =TABLE(B2:B5) | =TABLE(B2:B5) | =TABLE(B2:B5) | =TABLE(B2:B5) | =TABLE(B2:B5) | =TABLE(B2:B5) |
| =B27+0.05 | =TABLE(B2:B5) | =TABLE(B2:B5) | =TABLE(B2:B5) | =TABLE(B2:B5) | =TABLE(B2:B5) | =TABLE(B2:B5) |
| =B28+0.05 | =TABLE(B2:B5) | =TABLE(B2:B5) | =TABLE(B2:B5) | =TABLE(B2:B5) | =TABLE(B2:B5) | =TABLE(B2:B5) |
| =B29+0.05 | =TABLE(B2:B5) | =TABLE(B2:B5) | =TABLE(B2:B5) | =TABLE(B2:B5) | =TABLE(B2:B5) | =TABLE(B2:B5) |
| =B30+0.05 | =TABLE(B2:B5) | =TABLE(B2:B5) | =TABLE(B2:B5) | =TABLE(B2:B5) | =TABLE(B2:B5) | =TABLE(B2:B5) |
| =B31+0.05 | =TABLE(B2:B5) | =TABLE(B2:B5) | =TABLE(B2:B5) | =TABLE(B2:B5) | =TABLE(B2:B5) | =TABLE(B2:B5) |
| =B32+0.05 | =TABLE(B2:B5) | =TABLE(B2:B5) | =TABLE(B2:B5) | =TABLE(B2:B5) | =TABLE(B2:B5) | =TABLE(B2:B5) |
| =B33+0.05 | =TABLE(B2:B5) | =TABLE(B2:B5) | =TABLE(B2:B5) | =TABLE(B2:B5) | =TABLE(B2:B5) | =TABLE(B2:B5) |
| =B34+0.05 | =TABLE(B2:B5) | =TABLE(B2:B5) | =TABLE(B2:B5) | =TABLE(B2:B5) | =TABLE(B2:B5) | =TABLE(B2:B5) |
| =B35+0.05 | =TABLE(B2:B5) | =TABLE(B2:B5) | =TABLE(B2:B5) | =TABLE(B2:B5) | =TABLE(B2:B5) | =TABLE(B2:B5) |
| =B36+0.05 | =TABLE(B2:B5) | =TABLE(B2:B5) | =TABLE(B2:B5) | =TABLE(B2:B5) | =TABLE(B2:B5) | =TABLE(B2:B5) |

FIGURE 1.3-13    Data Table construction (changing Wacc by Column and initial outlay by row).

In Fig. 1.3-13, the output returned inside the Table is *Cell B*4 (The NPV) and Table 1.3-2 is the final calculated output table.

We can now also plot the NPV as a function of the two input variables as in Fig. 1.3-14, where essentially the NPV (on the Vertical Axis) is a function : $\Re^2 \rightarrow \Re$, namely $NPV = f(Wacc, CF_0)$.

In the three-dimensional chart of Fig. 1.3-14 the different colors represent the **Contour Map** (or Contour Lines Map).

A **Contour Line** is the locus of points (or a curve) along which the output function (i.e., the NPV) does not change its value, and this will be analyzed in more details in the bivariate constrained optimization analysis.

The **Excel Contour Diagram** (see Fig. 1.3-15 for the NPV example) can be inserted selecting *Contour* from the 3D Surface Excel charts, as shown in Fig. 1.3-16, or alternatively selecting a *Wireframe Contour* (Fig. 1.3-17).

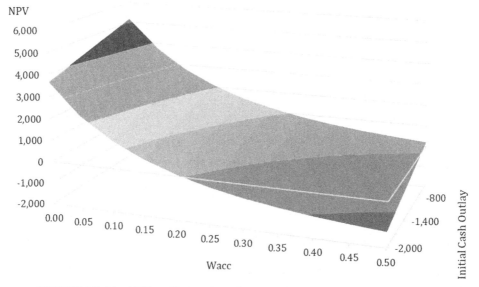

FIGURE 1.3-14    NPV profile in a three-dimensional space, i.e., **NPV** = f(**Wacc**, **CF**$_0$).

**TABLE 1.3-2**  Final Data Table NPV output simulation.

| 2,292 | -2,000 | -1,700 | -1,400 | -1,100 | -800 | -500 |
|-------|--------|--------|--------|--------|------|------|
| 0.00 | 3,660 | 3,960 | 4,260 | 4,560 | 4,860 | 5,160 |
| 0.05 | 2,270 | 2,570 | 2,870 | 3,170 | 3,470 | 3,770 |
| 0.10 | 1,292 | 1,592 | 1,892 | 2,192 | 2,492 | 2,792 |
| 0.15 | 587 | 887 | 1,187 | 1,487 | 1,787 | 2,087 |
| 0.20 | 68 | 368 | 668 | 968 | 1,268 | 1,568 |
| 0.25 | -321 | -21 | 279 | 579 | 879 | 1,179 |
| 0.30 | -619 | -319 | -19 | 281 | 581 | 881 |
| 0.35 | -850 | -550 | -250 | 50 | 350 | 650 |
| 0.40 | -1,032 | -732 | -432 | -132 | 168 | 468 |
| 0.45 | -1,178 | -878 | -578 | -278 | 22 | 322 |
| 0.50 | -1,295 | -995 | -695 | -395 | -95 | 205 |

Notice how in Fig. 1.3-15 (looking at the diagram from the right) on the first line separating the first darkest area from the second less dark area we can read the pair values of Wacc and initial outlay such that NPV is zero (i.e., the IRR of the project is identified for each level of initial outlay). We see that the obvious result is that the less negative the initial outlay read on the vertical axis, the higher the IRR read on the horizontal axis, going upward from the left-hand side to the right-hand side on the first contour line.

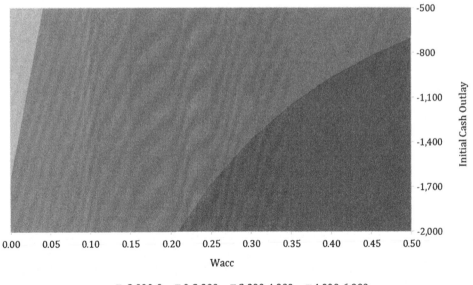

**FIGURE 1.3-15**  Contour Diagram.

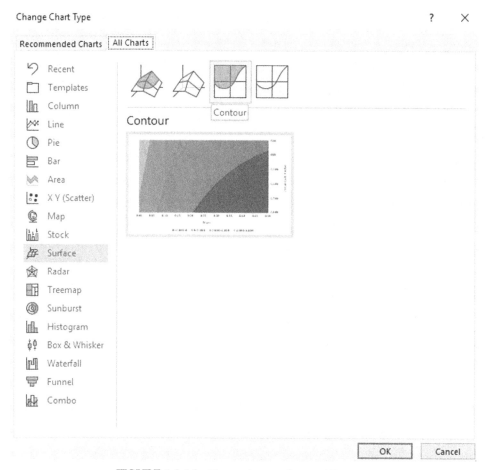

**FIGURE 1.3-16**    How to insert a Contour Diagram.

## 1.4 Scatter charts and trendlines

Another important chart utilized within the book is the **Scatter Chart**.

This chart is essentially used to plot any univariate function $f : \Re \rightarrow \Re$; from a utility function to a cost function, from a profit function to a demand function, as well used to plot the resolution of a differential equation (and system phase diagrams) and optimal trajectories, with time as independent variable, within the dynamic optimizing problems, univariate regressions, and univariate probability density curves.

There are several types of scatter charts as shown in Fig. 1.4-1.

What is important to highlight is that a scatter chart, once run, has an important option, which allows the users to show the equation (not necessarily linear) that best fits the data we are graphing. For example, for a simple univariate linear model this is the same as obtaining the regression equation. This option is activated once the chart is built, just right clicking

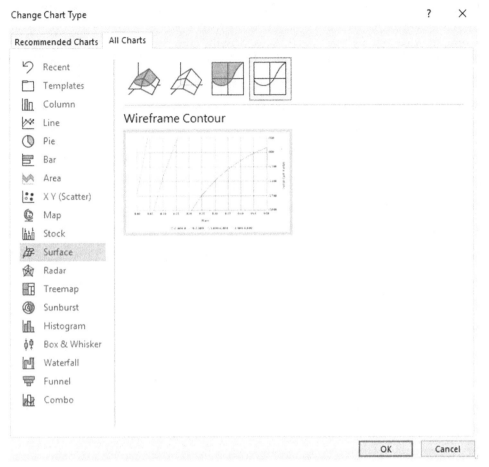

**FIGURE 1.3-17**   How to insert a Wireframe Contour.

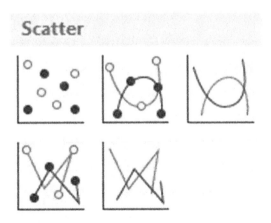

**FIGURE 1.4-1**   Excel Scatter Chart Icons.

I. Excel and fundamental mathematics for economics

on any graphed curve and adding a trendline. Then, the **Format Trendline** window (see Fig. 1.4-2) will appear, in which we set the format trendline. The trendline option also performs some forecast actions that won't be used within the book.

The only limitation is that the equations added are limited to pure exponential, logarithmic, linear, polynomial, and power functions. Therefore, Excel can be right when it shows the exponential equation for an underlying data referring to a function in the form of $y = e^x$ but not in the form of $y = e^{c_1 x} + e^{c_2 x}$. However, we can still select an exponential function or polynomial.

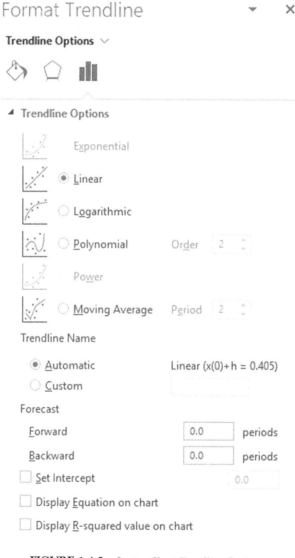

FIGURE 1.4-2    Scatter Chart Trendline Options.

**TABLE 1.4-1**   Two Exponential Functions.

| x | x | y = exp (x) | y = exp (-5x) + exp (0.5x) |
|---|---|---|---|
| 1 | 1 | 3 | 2 |
| 2 | 2 | 7 | 3 |
| 3 | 3 | 20 | 4 |
| 4 | 4 | 55 | 7 |
| 5 | 5 | 148 | 12 |
| 6 | 6 | 403 | 20 |
| 7 | 7 | 1,097 | 33 |
| 8 | 8 | 2,981 | 55 |
| 9 | 9 | 8,103 | 90 |
| 10 | 10 | 22,026 | 148 |
| 11 | 11 | 59,874 | 245 |
| 12 | 12 | 162,755 | 403 |
| 13 | 13 | 442,413 | 665 |
| 14 | 14 | 1,202,604 | 1,097 |
| 15 | 15 | 3,269,017 | 1,808 |
| 16 | 16 | 8,886,111 | 2,981 |

Continuing the example above, let us consider the two basic exponential functions in 2 Table 1.4-1. For the first function, we can show the exact equation in the scatter chart (see Fig. 1.4-3), while for the second function the trendline shown does not represent the exact theoretical equation of the underlying data, but still we can use a good numerical approximation using either the exponential equation (see Fig. 1.4-4) or a polynomial equation of order 5 (see Fig. 1.4-5).

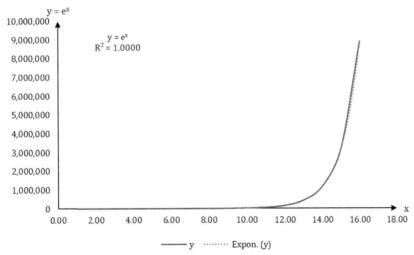

**FIGURE 1.4-3**   Scatter Chart of $y = e^x$ and Exponential Trendline with $R^2$.

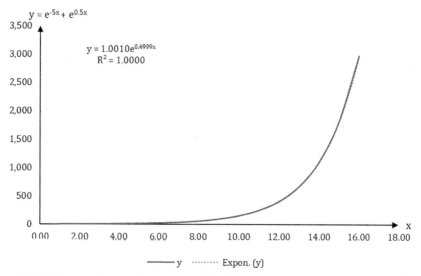

**FIGURE 1.4-4**   Scatter Chart of $y = e^{-5x} + e^{0.5x}$ and Exponential Trendline with $R^2$.

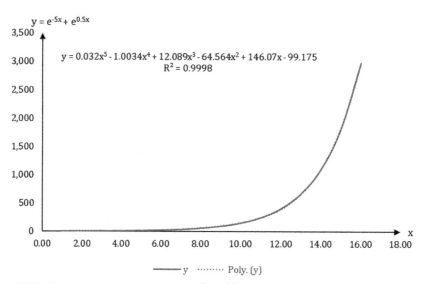

**FIGURE 1.4-5**   Scatter Chart of $y = e^{-5x} + e^{0.5x}$ and a Polynomial Trendline with $R^2$.

We will see throughout the whole book several applications of this chart tool.

# 2

# Univariate and multivariate calculus

## 2.1 Numerical methods for univariate differentiation

Let us begin the basic univariate calculus with the concept of derivative, which is the *rate at which the function $y(x)$ changes with respect to a change of the variable x*. Geometrically, it *represents the slope of the tangent line at each point along the curve of a function*.

The first derivative of a univariate function $f(x)$ in the point $x_n$ is defined as the following limit (if existing):

$$\lim_{h \to 0} \frac{y(x_n + h) - y(x_0)}{h} = \frac{dy}{dx} \tag{2.1-1}$$

Throughout the book we will also use other alternative notations, like $y'(x)$, or $\dot{y}(t)$ in the differential equations and dynamic optimization, where the independent variable is the time.

Within a discrete, worksheet-based framework, Eq. (2.1-1) may simply become the following discrete incremental ratios:

$$\frac{\Delta y}{\Delta x} = y'_n = \frac{y_{n+h} - y_n}{x_{n+h} - x_n} \quad (\textit{forward first order difference})$$

$$\frac{\Delta y}{\Delta x} = y'_n = \frac{y_n - y_{n-h}}{x_n - x_{n-h}} \quad (\textit{backward first order difference})$$

$$\frac{\Delta y}{\Delta x} = y'_n = \frac{y_{n+h} - y_{n-h}}{x_{n+h} - x_{n-h}} \quad (\textit{central first order difference}).$$

We are also interested in the second derivative, which will be represented by the following second-order difference:

$$\frac{\Delta y'}{\Delta x} = y''_n = \frac{y'_{n+h} - y'_n}{x_{n+h} - x_n} \quad (\textit{forward second order difference})$$

$$\frac{\Delta y'}{\Delta x} = y''_n = \frac{y'_n - y'_{n-h}}{x_n - x_{n-h}} \quad (\textit{backward second order difference})$$

$$\frac{\Delta y'}{\Delta x} = y''_n = \frac{y'_{n+h} - y'_{n-h}}{x_{n+h} - x_{n-h}} \quad (\textit{central second order difference}).$$

Let us consider now, for example, the second-order backward difference, this can be reexpressed as follows:

$$y''_n = \frac{\dfrac{y_n - y_{(n-h)}}{h} - \dfrac{y_{(n-h)} - y_{(n-h)-h}}{h}}{h} = \frac{y_n - 2y_{(n-h)} + y_{n-2h}}{h^2}$$

The second-order forward difference is analogously:

$$y''_n = \frac{\dfrac{y_{(n+h)+h} - y_{(n+h)}}{h} - \dfrac{y_{(n+h)} - y_n}{h}}{h} = \frac{y_n - 2y_{(n+h)} + y_{n+2h}}{h^2}$$

Finally, we can also rewrite the numerical central second difference as:

$$y''_n = \frac{\dfrac{y_{(n+h)+h} - y_{(n+h)}}{(x_{n+h} - x_{n-h} = 2h)} - \dfrac{y_{(n-h)+h} - y_{(n-h)}}{(x_{n+h} - x_{n-h} = 2h)}}{h} = \frac{y_{n+2h} - y_{(n+h)} - y_{(n)} + y_{n-h}}{2h^2}.$$

Using the function:

$$y = x^2$$

we want to show the geometrical interpretation of the derivative as a limit of *secants*, passing through the points $P_0 = (x_0, y_0)$, $P_{0+h}(x_0 + h, y_0 + h)$ as $h \to 0$, i.e., as $P_{0+h} \to P_0$. This limit, if existing, will be the *tangent* in $P_0$. The first secant is represented in Fig. 2.1-1, with $x_0 = 0.40$, $h = 0.60$, $x_1 = 1$.

Using the Excel Table (see Fig. 2.1-2), we simulate other secants letting $h \to 0$, i.e., as $x_1 = 1$ $\to x_0 = 0.40$.

The Data Table simulates on the secant formula in *Cell A2*, which includes the linear function between two given points:

$$y = \left( \frac{y_1 - y_0}{x_1 - x_0} \right)(x - x_0) + y_0 = m(x - x_0) + y_0.$$

Along the range *C4:G4*, we have the values that will allow for the simulation of various $x_1$. Essentially, we get $x_1 = 1 \to x_0 = 0.4$. Under the *Column B* we have instead the values of the independent variable $x$.

Table 2.1-1 and Fig. 2.1-3 give the results of the simulation, from which it is apparent that the lowest secant is the approximating tangent in $P_0$, such that $m = y'(x_0) = 0.80$.

We will use now the same Data Table simulation, instead, to plot the tangent in a point for a given function.

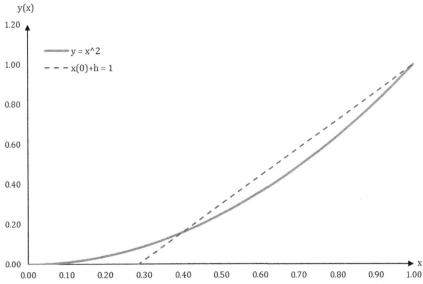

**FIGURE 2.1-1** Secant intersecting $y = x^2$ in $P_0(0.40, 0.16)$ and $P_1(1, 1)$.

| | A | B | C | D | E | F | G |
|---|---|---|---|---|---|---|---|
| 1 | Secant y = m*(x-x₀)+y₀ | m | $x_0$ | 0.4 | $x_1$ | 1 | step |
| 2 | =($F$2-$D$2)/($F$1-$D$1)*(A5-$D$1)+$D$2 | =(F2-D2)/(F1-D1) | $y_0$ | =D1^2 | $y_1$ | =F1^2 | 0.02 |
| 3 | | | | | | | |
| 4 | x | =A2 | 1 | 0.8 | 0.7 | 0.6 | 0.405 |
| 5 | 1 | -1 | =TABLE(F1:A5) | =TABLE(F1:A5) | =TABLE(F1:A5) | =TABLE(F1:A5) | =TABLE(F1:A5) |
| 6 | | -0.98 | =TABLE(F1:A5) | =TABLE(F1:A5) | =TABLE(F1:A5) | =TABLE(F1:A5) | =TABLE(F1:A5) |
| 7 | | -0.96 | =TABLE(F1:A5) | =TABLE(F1:A5) | =TABLE(F1:A5) | =TABLE(F1:A5) | =TABLE(F1:A5) |
| 8 | | -0.94 | =TABLE(F1:A5) | =TABLE(F1:A5) | =TABLE(F1:A5) | =TABLE(F1:A5) | =TABLE(F1:A5) |
| 9 | | -0.92 | =TABLE(F1:A5) | =TABLE(F1:A5) | =TABLE(F1:A5) | =TABLE(F1:A5) | =TABLE(F1:A5) |
| 10 | | -0.9 | =TABLE(F1:A5) | =TABLE(F1:A5) | =TABLE(F1:A5) | =TABLE(F1:A5) | =TABLE(F1:A5) |
| 11 | | -0.88 | =TABLE(F1:A5) | =TABLE(F1:A5) | =TABLE(F1:A5) | =TABLE(F1:A5) | =TABLE(F1:A5) |
| 12 | | -0.86 | =TABLE(F1:A5) | =TABLE(F1:A5) | =TABLE(F1:A5) | =TABLE(F1:A5) | =TABLE(F1:A5) |
| 13 | | -0.84 | =TABLE(F1:A5) | =TABLE(F1:A5) | =TABLE(F1:A5) | =TABLE(F1:A5) | =TABLE(F1:A5) |
| 14 | | -0.82 | =TABLE(F1:A5) | =TABLE(F1:A5) | =TABLE(F1:A5) | =TABLE(F1:A5) | =TABLE(F1:A5) |
| 102 | | 0.94 | =TABLE(F1:A5) | =TABLE(F1:A5) | =TABLE(F1:A5) | =TABLE(F1:A5) | =TABLE(F1:A5) |
| 103 | | 0.96 | =TABLE(F1:A5) | =TABLE(F1:A5) | =TABLE(F1:A5) | =TABLE(F1:A5) | =TABLE(F1:A5) |
| 104 | | 0.98 | =TABLE(F1:A5) | =TABLE(F1:A5) | =TABLE(F1:A5) | =TABLE(F1:A5) | =TABLE(F1:A5) |
| 105 | | 1 | =TABLE(F1:A5) | =TABLE(F1:A5) | =TABLE(F1:A5) | =TABLE(F1:A5) | =TABLE(F1:A5) |

**FIGURE 2.1-2**   Simulating a set of secants as $h \to 0$.

This will be done as described by Fig. 2.1-4 where we make $x_1$ and $x_0$ as close as possible, choosing $\varepsilon = 0.00001$. $x_0$ is the point in which we want to diagram the tangent (Table 2.1-2; Figs. 2.1-5 and 2.1-6).

Let us consider now the following function, which is not defined in zero:

$$y = \frac{1}{x}$$

**TABLE 2.1-1**   Set of secants as $x_1 = 1.00$ approaches $x_0 = 0.40$.

| Secant y = m*(x-x₀)+y₀ | m | $x_0$ | 0.4000 | $x_1$ | 1.0000 | step | |
|---|---|---|---|---|---|---|---|
| **1.0000** | **1.4000** | $y_0$ | 0.1600 | $y_1$ | 1.0000 | 0.0200 | |

| x | 1.0000 | 1.0000 | 0.8000 | 0.7000 | 0.6000 | 0.4050 |
|---|---|---|---|---|---|---|
| **1.0000** | -1.0000 | -1.8000 | -1.5200 | -1.3800 | -1.2400 | -0.9670 |
| | -0.9800 | -1.7720 | -1.4960 | -1.3580 | -1.2200 | -0.9509 |
| | -0.9600 | -1.7440 | -1.4720 | -1.3360 | -1.2000 | -0.9348 |
| | -0.9400 | -1.7160 | -1.4480 | -1.3140 | -1.1800 | -0.9187 |
| | -0.9200 | -1.6880 | -1.4240 | -1.2920 | -1.1600 | -0.9026 |
| | -0.9000 | -1.6600 | -1.4000 | -1.2700 | -1.1400 | -0.8865 |
| | -0.8800 | -1.6320 | -1.3760 | -1.2480 | -1.1200 | -0.8704 |
| | -0.8600 | -1.6040 | -1.3520 | -1.2260 | -1.1000 | -0.8543 |
| | -0.8400 | -1.5760 | -1.3280 | -1.2040 | -1.0800 | -0.8382 |
| | -0.8200 | -1.5480 | -1.3040 | -1.1820 | -1.0600 | -0.8221 |
| | 0.9400 | 0.9160 | 0.8080 | 0.7540 | 0.7000 | 0.5947 |
| | 0.9600 | 0.9440 | 0.8320 | 0.7760 | 0.7200 | 0.6108 |
| | 0.9800 | 0.9720 | 0.8560 | 0.7980 | 0.7400 | 0.6269 |
| | 1.0000 | 1.0000 | 0.8800 | 0.8200 | 0.7600 | 0.6430 |

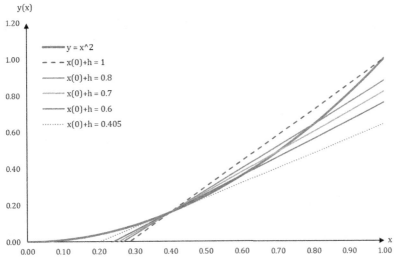

**FIGURE 2.1-3** Clockwise rotation of the secants as $x_1 = 1.000 \rightarrow x_1 = 0.405$.

We want two tangents in $x_0 = \pm 0.50$.

First, we need to remove the Excel Error *Error Type* 2 *#DIV/0!* from the cell where the function is not defined ($x = 0$). See Fig. 2.1-7. This can be done in several ways, from manually to VBA. Fig. 2.1-8 describes one of the several VBA codes that can be implemented to do so. VBA is useful when the function is not defined in more than one point.

Once the database has been cleaned from the points where the function is not defined, we can plot the graph together with the desired tangents. See Fig. 2.1-9.

In Excel, we can also obtain the approximate formula for the general derivative of a function. This can be done using the dialogue box in Fig. 2.1-10, where there are some functions that Excel is able to recognize and approximate. First, we need to calculate the numerical derivative using one of the discrete incremental ratios for Eq. (2.1-1).

| | A | B | C | D | E | F | G |
|---|---|---|---|---|---|---|---|
| 1 | Tangent $y = m^*(x-x_0)+y_0$ | m | $x_0$ | =C4-0.00001 | $x_1$ | 1 | step |
| 2 | =($F$2-$D$2)/($F$1-$D$1)*(A5-$D$1)+$D$2 | =(F2-D2)/(F1-D1) | $y_0$ | =D1^2 | $y_1$ | =F1^2 | 0.02 |
| 3 | | | Simulate tg in C4 changing $x_0$ | | | | |
| 4 | x | | 0.8 | | | y = x^2 | |
| 5 | 1 | -1 | =TABLE(F1;A5) | | | =B5^2 | |
| 6 | | -0.98 | =TABLE(F1;A5) | | | =B6^2 | |
| 7 | | -0.96 | =TABLE(F1;A5) | | | =B7^2 | |
| 8 | | -0.94 | =TABLE(F1;A5) | | | =B8^2 | |
| 9 | | -0.92 | =TABLE(F1;A5) | | | =B9^2 | |
| 10 | | -0.9 | =TABLE(F1;A5) | | | =B10^2 | |
| 11 | | -0.88 | =TABLE(F1;A5) | | | =B11^2 | |
| 12 | | -0.86 | =TABLE(F1;A5) | | | =B12^2 | |

**FIGURE 2.1-4** Data Table for the tangent in a point (e.g., $x_0 = -0.80$).

**TABLE 2.1-2**   Tangent in point $x_0 = -0.80$.

| Tangent y = m*(x-x₀)+y₀ | m | x₀ | -0.8000 | x₁ | 1.0000 | step |
|---|---|---|---|---|---|---|
| 1.0000 | 0.2000 | y₀ | 0.6400 | y₁ | 1.0000 | 0.0200 |

|  |  | Simulate tg in C4 changing x₀ |  |  |
|---|---|---|---|---|

| x | 1.0000 | -0.8000 | y = x^2 |
|---|---|---|---|
| 1.0000 | -1.0000 | 0.9600 | 1.0000 |
|  | -0.9800 | 0.9280 | 0.9604 |
|  | -0.9600 | 0.8960 | 0.9216 |
|  | -0.9400 | 0.8640 | 0.8836 |
|  | -0.9200 | 0.8320 | 0.8464 |
|  | -0.9000 | 0.8000 | 0.8100 |
|  | -0.8800 | 0.7680 | 0.7744 |
|  | -0.8600 | 0.7360 | 0.7396 |
|  | -0.8400 | 0.7040 | 0.7056 |
|  | -0.8200 | 0.6720 | 0.6724 |
|  | -0.8000 | 0.6400 | 0.6400 |
|  | -0.7800 | 0.6080 | 0.6084 |
|  | -0.7600 | 0.5760 | 0.5776 |
|  | -0.7400 | 0.5440 | 0.5476 |
|  | 0.9000 | -2.0800 | 0.8100 |
|  | 0.9200 | -2.1120 | 0.8464 |
|  | 0.9400 | -2.1440 | 0.8836 |
|  | 0.9600 | -2.1760 | 0.9216 |
|  | 0.9800 | -2.2080 | 0.9604 |
|  | 1.0000 | -2.2400 | 1.0000 |

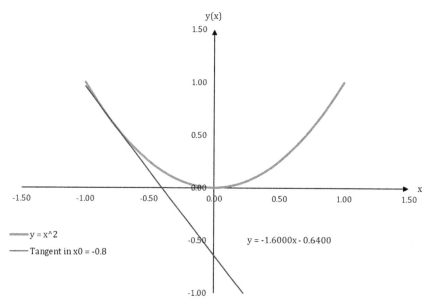

**FIGURE 2.1-5**   Tangent in $x_0 = -0.80$ and its equation.

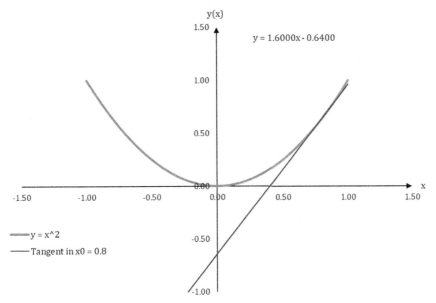

**FIGURE 2.1-6** Tangent in $x_0 = +0.80$ and its equation.

| | A | B | C | D | E | F | G | H |
|---|---|---|---|---|---|---|---|---|
| 4 | **x** | **1.0000** | **0.2000** | | **y = 1/x** | | **-0.2000** | **ErrorType** |
| 5 | 1.0000 | -1.0000 | 35.0015 | | -1.0000 | | 14.9990 | |
| 6 | | -0.9800 | 34.5015 | | -1.0204 | | 14.4990 | |
| 53 | | -0.0400 | 11.0003 | | -25.0000 | | -8.9998 | |
| 54 | | -0.0200 | 10.5003 | | -50.0000 | | -9.4998 | |
| 55 | | 0.0000 | 10.0003 | | #DIV/0! | | -9.9998 | 2.0000 |
| 56 | | 0.0200 | 9.5002 | | 50.0000 | | -10.4997 | |
| 57 | | 0.0400 | 9.0002 | | 25.0000 | | -10.9997 | |
| 58 | | 0.0600 | 8.5002 | | 16.6667 | | -11.4997 | |
| 105 | | 1.0000 | -15.0010 | | 1.0000 | | -34.9985 | |

**FIGURE 2.1-7** $y = 1/x$ is not defined in cell E56.

Let us consider again the function:

$$y = x^2$$

and let us calculate the first derivative, using the first-order backward difference, using a step-size $= 0.02$ as presented in Fig. 2.1-11 and Table 2.1-3.

We plot now together the given function the first derivative: using the trendline option "Linear" in the dialogue box of Fig. 2.1-10, we associate a linear trendline option to the derivative line. For an $n$-polynomial function, we know that its first derivative will be an ($n$-1)-polynomial function (in this case a linear function) (Fig. 2.1-12).

```
Sub clearcontents()

Range("H4").Select

Do Until ActiveCell = 2
  ActiveCell.Offset(1, 0).Select

Loop

    ActiveCell.Offset(0, -3).Select
    Selection.clearcontents
    Range("H4").Select

End Sub
```

**FIGURE 2.1-8**    Removing the cell where $y = 1/x$ is not defined.

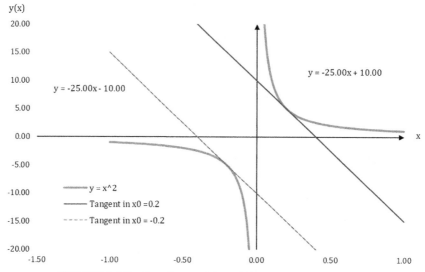

**FIGURE 2.1-9**    Function $y = 1/x$ and the two tangent equations.

Let us have now the following polynomial function:

$$y = x^2 + x^3.$$

Using the trendline polynomial of order $= 2$, we obtain a reasonable approximation of the theoretical derivative equation (Fig. 2.1-13).

In other instances, obtaining the theoretical formula of the derivative via the trendline equations is not possible or, if possible, with a poor approximation.

Consider again the function:

$$y = \frac{1}{x}$$

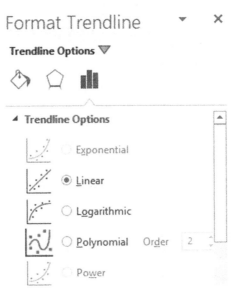

FIGURE 2.1-10   Trendline options.

| | A | B | C | D | E |
|---|---|---|---|---|---|
| | x | y = x^2 | Δy/Δx | $\Delta^2 y/\Delta x^2$ | step |
| 1 | | | | | |
| 2 | -1 | =A2^2 | | | 0.02 |
| 3 | =ROUND(A2+$E$2;2) | =A3^2 | =(B3-B2)/(A3-A2) | | |
| 4 | =ROUND(A3+$E$2;2) | =A4^2 | =(B4-B3)/(A4-A3) | =(C4-C3)/(A4-A3) | |
| 5 | =ROUND(A4+$E$2;2) | =A5^2 | =(B5-B4)/(A5-A4) | =(C5-C4)/(A5-A4) | |
| 6 | =ROUND(A5+$E$2;2) | =A6^2 | =(B6-B5)/(A6-A5) | =(C6-C5)/(A6-A5) | |
| 7 | =ROUND(A6+$E$2;2) | =A7^2 | =(B7-B6)/(A7-A6) | =(C7-C6)/(A7-A6) | |
| 8 | =ROUND(A7+$E$2;2) | =A8^2 | =(B8-B7)/(A8-A7) | =(C8-C7)/(A8-A7) | |
| 9 | =ROUND(A8+$E$2;2) | =A9^2 | =(B9-B8)/(A9-A8) | =(C9-C8)/(A9-A8) | |
| 10 | =ROUND(A9+$E$2;2) | =A10^2 | =(B10-B9)/(A10-A9) | =(C10-C9)/(A10-A9) | |
| 11 | =ROUND(A10+$E$2;2) | =A11^2 | =(B11-B10)/(A11-A10) | =(C11-C10)/(A11-A10) | |
| 12 | =ROUND(A11+$E$2;2) | =A12^2 | =(B12-B11)/(A12-A11) | =(C12-C11)/(A12-A11) | |
| 13 | =ROUND(A12+$E$2;2) | =A13^2 | =(B13-B12)/(A13-A12) | =(C13-C12)/(A13-A12) | |
| 14 | =ROUND(A13+$E$2;2) | =A14^2 | =(B14-B13)/(A14-A13) | =(C14-C13)/(A14-A13) | |
| 15 | =ROUND(A14+$E$2;2) | =A15^2 | =(B15-B14)/(A15-A14) | =(C15-C14)/(A15-A14) | |
| 16 | =ROUND(A15+$E$2;2) | =A16^2 | =(B16-B15)/(A16-A15) | =(C16-C15)/(A16-A15) | |
| 102 | =ROUND(A101+$E$2;2) | =A102^2 | =(B102-B101)/(A102-A101) | =(C102-C101)/(A102-A101) | |

FIGURE 2.1-11   Worksheet setup for the first and second derivatives of $y = x^2$.

and the following diagram in Fig. 2.1-14. Although we are able to plot the numerical derivative function and investigate about its sign (to determine concavity and convexity), we
cannot get any trendline associated to the first derivative).

Now, what we want to do is to approximate as much as possible the exact derivative with
the numerical one. A higher order of approximation can be reached averaging out two points

**TABLE 2.1-3**  Numerical first and second derivatives of $y = x^2$.

| x | y = x^2 | Δy/Δx | Δ²y/Δx² | step |
|---|---|---|---|---|
| -1.0000 | 1.0000 | | | 0.0200 |
| -0.9800 | 0.9604 | -1.9800 | | |
| -0.9600 | 0.9216 | -1.9400 | 2.0000 | |
| -0.9400 | 0.8836 | -1.9000 | 2.0000 | |
| -0.9200 | 0.8464 | -1.8600 | 2.0000 | |
| -0.9000 | 0.8100 | -1.8200 | 2.0000 | |
| -0.8800 | 0.7744 | -1.7800 | 2.0000 | |
| -0.8600 | 0.7396 | -1.7400 | 2.0000 | |
| -0.8400 | 0.7056 | -1.7000 | 2.0000 | |
| -0.8200 | 0.6724 | -1.6600 | 2.0000 | |
| -0.8000 | 0.6400 | -1.6200 | 2.0000 | |
| -0.7800 | 0.6084 | -1.5800 | 2.0000 | |
| -0.7600 | 0.5776 | -1.5400 | 2.0000 | |
| -0.7400 | 0.5476 | -1.5000 | 2.0000 | |
| -0.7200 | 0.5184 | -1.4600 | 2.0000 | |
| 1.0000 | 1.0000 | 1.9800 | 2.0000 | |

in the numerical derivative, as its been done for a specific range of $x$ in Table 2.1-4. This corresponds to the following average:

$$\frac{\left(\dfrac{y_{n+h} - y_n}{h} + \dfrac{y_n - y_{n-h}}{h}\right)}{2} = \frac{y_{n+h} - y_{n-h}}{2h}$$

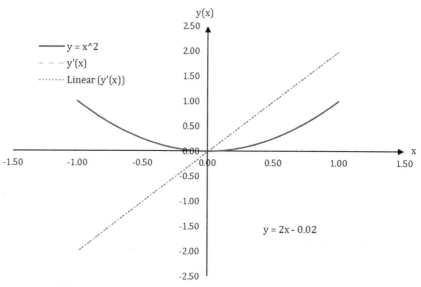

FIGURE 2.1-12  Diagram of $y = x^2$ and its first-derivative linear equation.

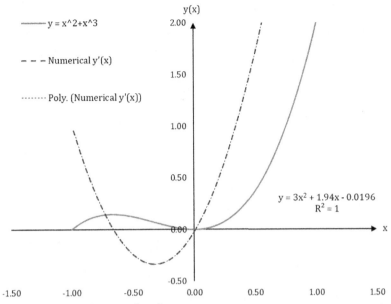

**FIGURE 2.1-13** Diagram of $y = x^2 + x^3$ and its first-derivative approximate polynomial equation.

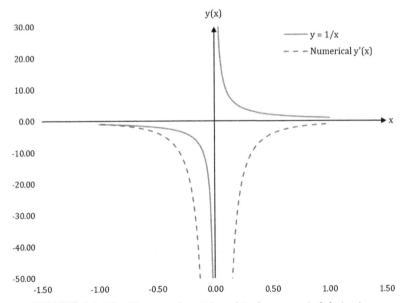

**FIGURE 2.1-14** Diagram of $y = 1/x$ and its first-numerical derivative.

I. Excel and fundamental mathematics for economics

**TABLE 2.1-4**  Numerical first derivative versus exact in the function $y = 1/x$.

| x | $y = 1/x$ | $\Delta y/\Delta x$ | $\Delta y/\Delta x$ Average | $dy/dx$ True |
|---|---|---|---|---|
| 0.1000 | 10.0000 | -125.0000 | -104.1667 | -100.0000 |
| 0.1200 | 8.3333 | -83.3333 | -71.4286 | -69.4444 |
| 0.1400 | 7.1429 | -59.5238 | -52.0833 | -51.0204 |
| 0.1600 | 6.2500 | -44.6429 | -39.6825 | -39.0625 |
| 0.1800 | 5.5556 | -34.7222 | -31.2500 | -30.8642 |
| 0.2000 | 5.0000 | -27.7778 | -25.2525 | -25.0000 |
| 0.2200 | 4.5455 | -22.7273 | -20.8333 | -20.6612 |
| 0.2400 | 4.1667 | -18.9394 | -17.4825 | -17.3611 |

The results are diagrammed in Fig. 2.1-15, from which it is apparent that the small round doted curve approximate better than the dashed numerical derivative curve. Reducing the step-size in the independent variable, i.e., how much increment we give to it along the curve, we can reach an even better approximation. See Fig. 2.1-16 where the small round dotted line is almost overlapping the exact derivative function. This in total accordance with the definition of a derivative as $\lim_{\Delta x \to 0} \frac{\Delta y}{\Delta x} = \frac{dy}{dx}$.

As a last example for numerical differentiation, consider the following fractional function:

$$y = \frac{log^2(x) + 2log(x) - 1}{2x}$$

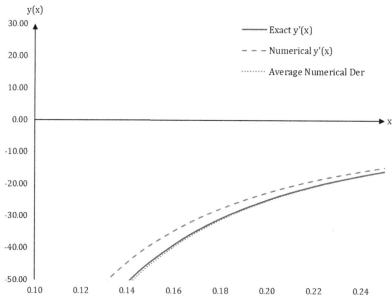

**FIGURE 2.1-15**  Comparing numerical and exact first-order derivative (step 0.02).

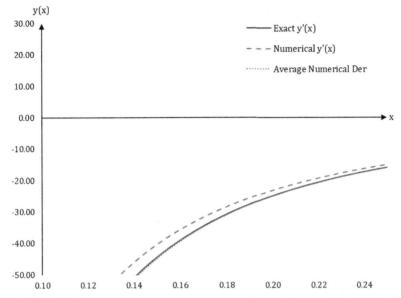

**FIGURE 2.1-16** Comparing numerical and exact first-order derivative (step 0.015).

(log and ln both refer to the natural logarithm, and they may be used interchangeably in the book.)

The exact first derivative of the given function is:

$$y' = \frac{-log^2(x) + 3}{-2x^2}.$$

We calculate the tangent equation together with the numerical derivative in Table 2.1-5. Figs. 2.1-17 and 2.1-18 give the diagram of the given function, of the tangent line equation and the numerical versus exact derivative.

Finally, in Fig. 2.1-19 the function together with its first and second derivatives is diagrammed. From this last figure, the relation between the minimum, inflection point of the function and the sign of the derivatives is apparent.

$$f'(x) > 0 \; Increasing \; function$$

$$f'(x) < 0 \; Decreasing \; function$$

$$f''(x) > 0 \; Strictly \; Convex \; function$$

$$f''(x) < 0 \; Strictly \; Concave \; function$$

**TABLE 2.1-5**   Numerical tangent at $x_0 = 0.15$ and first-order differentiation.

| Tangent y = m*(x-x₀)+y₀ | m | x₀ | 0.1500 | x₁ | 1.0000 | step |
|---|---|---|---|---|---|---|
| **-0.5000** | 4.0985 | y₀ | -3.9838 | y₁ | -0.5000 | 0.0200 |

Simulate tg in C4 changing

| x | -0.5000 | x₀ 0.1500 | y = (log^2(x)+2log(x)-1)/(2x) | Δy/Δx = (yₙ₊ₕ-yₙ₋ₕ)/2h |
|---|---|---|---|---|
| **1.0000** | 0.0400 | -2.5191 | 36.5426 | |
| | 0.0600 | -2.7855 | 10.7372 | -862.3394 |
| | 0.0800 | -3.0518 | 2.0490 | -306.3378 |
| | 0.1000 | -3.3181 | -1.5164 | -128.8314 |
| | 0.1200 | -3.5844 | -3.1042 | -57.3255 |
| | 0.1400 | -3.8508 | -3.8094 | -24.4892 |
| | 0.1600 | -4.1171 | -4.0838 | -8.1727 |
| | 0.1800 | -4.3834 | -4.1363 | 0.3078 |
| | 0.2000 | -4.6497 | -4.0715 | 4.7894 |
| | 0.2200 | -4.9161 | -3.9447 | 7.1214 |
| | 0.2400 | -5.1824 | -3.7866 | 8.2553 |
| | 0.2600 | -5.4487 | -3.6145 | 8.7058 |
| | 0.2800 | -5.7150 | -3.4384 | 8.7627 |
| | 2.0200 | -20.8053 | 0.2229 | 0.3071 |
| | 2.0400 | -29.1516 | 0.2290 | -5.5727 |

To identify the minima and the maxima of a function will be the subject of the static optimization to which Chapter 5 is devoted.

## 2.2  Numerical methods for univariate integration

To solve numerically an integral is of paramount importance because it represents the basis for the numerical dynamic modeling developed within the book, from Chapter 4

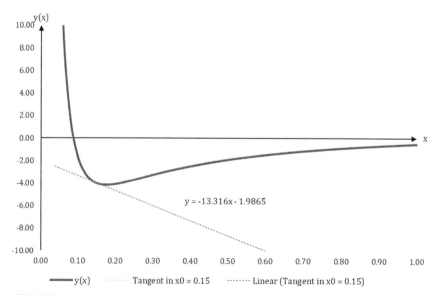

$$y = -13.316x - 1.9865$$

●―― y(x)    ········ Tangent in x0 = 0.15    ------- Linear (Tangent in x0 = 0.15)

**FIGURE 2.1-17**   Diagram of $y = f(x)$ and the equation of the tangent line in $x_0 = 0.15$.

I. Excel and fundamental mathematics for economics

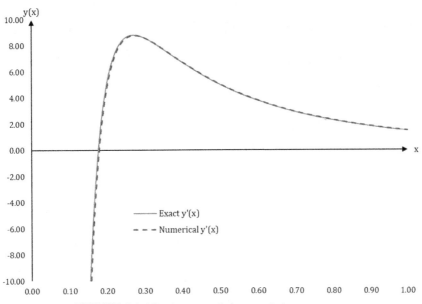

**FIGURE 2.1-18**  Diagram of $y'$: numerical versus exact.

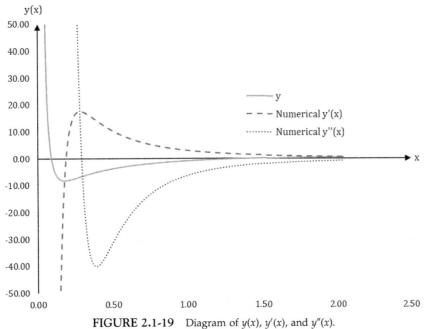

**FIGURE 2.1-19**  Diagram of $y(x)$, $y'(x)$, and $y''(x)$.

(differential equations and systems of differential equations) to Chapter 9 (Calculus of Variations) and Chapter 10 (Theory of Optimal Control).

Consider the following expression, which is also called differential equation:

$$\frac{dy(x)}{dx} = y'(x).$$

In the above equation the unknown variable is $y(x)$, while $y'(x)$ is given. We have therefore to solve the problem to find the appropriate $y(x)$.

The problem is solved as follows, using the Leibniz symbol $\int$ with a long $s$ standing for *sum*:

$$y(x) = \int y'(x)dx + C. \tag{2.2-1}$$

Eq. (2.1-1) is more usually written as:

$$F(x) = \int f(x)dx + C. \tag{2.2-2}$$

$F(x)$ is the sought function that, when derived with respect to $x$, returns the $f(x)$.

The fact that we equated $y(x) = F(x)$ and $y'(x) = f(x)$ directly derives from the *fundamental theorem of Calculus*.

$F(x)$ will be called the *exact antiderivative,* or the *exact integral,* while $f(x)$ is the given *integrand function.*

Now, our problem is to solve Eqs. (2.2-1) and (2.2-2) without the Fundamental Theorem of Calculus and the integration formulas given by theory of integration, but numerically in a discrete framework.

To do this we will resort to another approach, which uses somehow the definition of integral given by Riemann.

Let us go back for a while to Eq. (2.1-1), with backward first-order difference, slightly modified here with the subscripts denoting the step we are in:

$$\frac{\Delta y}{\Delta x} = y'_k = \frac{y_k - y_{k-1}}{x_k - x_{k-1}}$$

setting $x_k = x_{k-1} + h$, at any stage $k$, the following will be true,

$$y_k = y_{k-1} + y'_k \cdot h.$$

Partitioning the $x$ interval, between any two points $a$ and $b$, in $n$ stages as follows:

$$a = x_0 < x_1 < x_2 < \cdots < x_k < \cdots < x_n = b$$

such that:

$$\frac{(b-a)}{n} = h$$

where

$$x_1 = x_0 + h$$

$$x_2 = x_1 + h$$

$$\cdots$$

$$x_k = x_{k-1} + h$$

$$\cdots$$

$$x_n = x_{n-1} + h$$

we obtain the following recursion equation:

$$y_n = \sum_{k=1}^{n} y_k' \cdot h \qquad (2.2\text{-}3)$$

which numerically returns the whole area under the curve of the integrand function $f(x) = y'(x)$, within the specified interval, divided in $n$ partitions.

As $h \to 0$, i.e., as $n \to \infty$ the numerical area between the points $a$ and $b$ will approximate the true area, which is given by the exact integral from the fundamental theorem of calculus:

$$\lim_{h \to 0} y_n = \int_a^b y'(x).$$

The area (integral) is therefore itself a function, and if we plot it against the independent variable, we obtain the diagram of the desired function $F(x) = y(x)$, i.e., $Area(x) = F(x)$.

Let us consider the following differential:

$$\frac{dy(x)}{dx} = 5 \quad x \in [a = 0, \, b = 1]$$

The definite integral, from the fundamental theorem of calculus is:

$$y(x) = \int_0^1 5 \, dx = |5x + C|_0^1 = (5 + C) - (0 + C) = 5$$

| | A | B | C | D | E | F | G |
|---|---|---|---|---|---|---|---|
| 1 | x | y'(x) | $x_k - x_{k-1}$ = h | y'(x)*h | $y_k = y_{k-1} + y'*h$ | y Exact | Step |
| 2 | 0 | | | | 0 | =5*A2 | 0.01 |
| 3 | =A2+$G$2 | 5 | =A3-A2 | =B3*C3 | =E2+D3 | =5*A3 | |
| 4 | =A3+$G$2 | 5 | =A4-A3 | =B4*C4 | =E3+D4 | =5*A4 | |
| 5 | =A4+$G$2 | 5 | =A5-A4 | =B5*C5 | =E4+D5 | =5*A5 | |
| 6 | =A5+$G$2 | 5 | =A6-A5 | =B6*C6 | =E5+D6 | =5*A6 | |
| 23 | =A22+$G$2 | 5 | =A23-A22 | =B23*C23 | =E22+D23 | =5*A23 | |
| 24 | =A23+$G$2 | 5 | =A24-A23 | =B24*C24 | =E23+D24 | =5*A24 | |
| 25 | =A24+$G$2 | 5 | =A25-A24 | =B25*C25 | =E24+D25 | =5*A25 | |
| 26 | =A25+$G$2 | 5 | =A26-A25 | =B26*C26 | =E25+D26 | =5*A26 | |
| 27 | **=A26+$G$2** | **5** | **=A27-A26** | **=B27*C27** | **=E26+D27** | **=5*A27** | |
| 28 | =A27+$G$2 | 5 | =A28-A27 | =B28*C28 | =E27+D28 | =5*A28 | |
| 29 | =A28+$G$2 | 5 | =A29-A28 | =B29*C29 | =E28+D29 | =5*A29 | |
| 101 | =A100+$G$: | 5 | =A101-A100 | =B101*C101 | =E100+D101 | =5*A101 | |
| 102 | **=A101+$G$** | **5** | **=A102-A101** | **=B102*C102** | **=E101+D102** | **=5*A102** | |

FIGURE 2.2-1   Numerical integration worksheet setup.

We want now to apply Eq. (2.2-3) numerically in Excel, partitioning the interval $[a = 0,$ $b = 1]$ in $n = 100$ stages with $h = \frac{b-a}{100} = \frac{1}{100}$.

To do this, we implement the worksheet of Fig. 2.2-1. Under *Column A* we have divided the interval of $x$ from $a = 0$ to $b = 1$, with the step-size $h = 0.01$. *Column B* is the given differential, *Column D* is the quantity $y'_k \cdot h$, at the $k$th stage, while *Column E* returns the numerical integral $y_k$ at the $k$th stage.

If we look at *Column E* of Fig. 2.2-1 (and the correspondent value in Table 2.2-1), we can easily recognize the value of the area under the curve (line), as the independent variable

TABLE 2.2-1   Numerical integration results.

| x | y'(x) | $x_k - x_{k-1}$ = h | y'(x)*h | $y_k = y_{k-1} + y'*h$ | y Exact | Step |
|---|---|---|---|---|---|---|
| 0.00 | | | | 0.00 | 0.00 | 0.01 |
| 0.01 | 5.00 | 0.01 | 0.05 | 0.05 | 0.05 | |
| 0.02 | 5.00 | 0.01 | 0.05 | 0.10 | 0.10 | |
| 0.03 | 5.00 | 0.01 | 0.05 | 0.15 | 0.15 | |
| 0.04 | 5.00 | 0.01 | 0.05 | 0.20 | 0.20 | |
| 0.21 | 5.00 | 0.01 | 0.05 | 1.05 | 1.05 | |
| 0.22 | 5.00 | 0.01 | 0.05 | 1.10 | 1.10 | |
| 0.23 | 5.00 | 0.01 | 0.05 | 1.15 | 1.15 | |
| 0.24 | 5.00 | 0.01 | 0.05 | 1.20 | 1.20 | |
| **0.25** | **5.00** | **0.01** | **0.05** | **1.25** | **1.25** | |
| 0.26 | 5.00 | 0.01 | 0.05 | 1.30 | 1.30 | |
| 0.27 | 5.00 | 0.01 | 0.05 | 1.35 | 1.35 | |
| 0.99 | 5.00 | 0.01 | 0.05 | 4.95 | 4.95 | |
| **1.00** | **5.00** | **0.01** | **0.05** | **5.00** | **5.00** | |

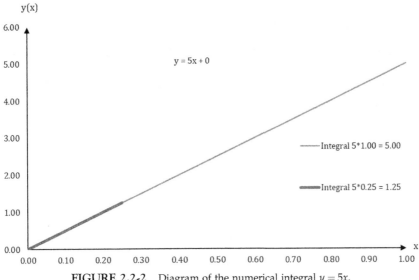

**FIGURE 2.2-2**  Diagram of the numerical integral $y = 5x$.

increases from 0 to 1. The area of the integrand function $y'(x) = 5$ is equal to 5 for $x \in [0, 1]$ or equal to 1.25 for $x \in [0, 0.25]$ (Fig. 2.2-2).

In physics, $y'(x)$ of Fig. 2.2-3 can be interpreted as the constant velocity $v(t)$ measured in km/h, i.e., we have the time measured in hours on the horizontal axis and velocity (km/

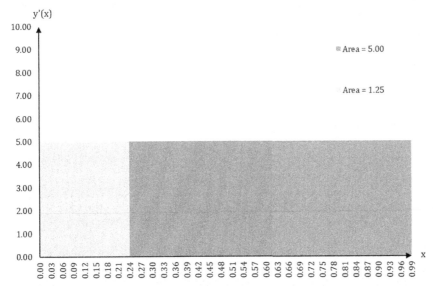

**FIGURE 2.2-3**  Two areas under the integrand function $y'(x) = 5$ at $x = 0.25$ and $x = 1$.

h) on the vertical axis. Then, the two areas represent the distance $S(t) = v(t) \cdot \Delta t$ traveled after 15 min (1.25 km) and after 1 h (5 km).

In the theory of statistics, the integrand function is instead a probability density function of a continuous random variable, with the area underneath representing the cumulative probability of a certain event.

$y'(x)$ equal to a constant, like in Fig. 2.2-3, can be interpreted in economics as a marginal revenue, i.e., the given price for a perfect competitive firm, so that $y(x)$ would be its total revenue function in terms of quantities $x$ (see Section 6.10).

Let us integrate now a standard quadratic function in the range $x \in [0, 1]$:

$$\int_0^1 x^2 dx.$$

The differential can be then formalized as:

$$\frac{dy(x)}{dx} = x^2.$$

The definite integral from the fundamental theorem of calculus is:

$$y(x) = \int_0^1 x^2 dx = \left.\frac{1}{3}x^3 + C\right|_0^1 = \left(\frac{1}{3}+C\right) - (0+C) = \frac{1}{3}.$$

The numerical solution is given by Table 2.2-2.

TABLE 2.2-2   Numerical integral versus exact integral of $y = x^2$.

| x | y'(x) | $x_k - x_{k-1} = h$ | y'(x)*h | $y_k = y_{k-1} + y'*h$ | Average $(y_k ; y_{k-1})$ | y Exact |
|---|---|---|---|---|---|---|
| 0.00000 | 0.00000 | | | 0.00000 | 0.00000 | 0.00000 |
| 0.01000 | 0.00010 | 0.01000 | 0.00000 | 0.00000 | 0.00000 | 0.00000 |
| 0.02000 | 0.00040 | 0.01000 | 0.00000 | 0.00001 | 0.00000 | 0.00000 |
| 0.03000 | 0.00090 | 0.01000 | 0.00001 | 0.00001 | 0.00001 | 0.00001 |
| 0.04000 | 0.00160 | 0.01000 | 0.00002 | 0.00003 | 0.00002 | 0.00002 |
| 0.05000 | 0.00250 | 0.01000 | 0.00003 | 0.00006 | 0.00004 | 0.00004 |
| 0.06000 | 0.00360 | 0.01000 | 0.00004 | 0.00009 | 0.00007 | 0.00007 |
| 0.07000 | 0.00490 | 0.01000 | 0.00005 | 0.00014 | 0.00012 | 0.00011 |
| 0.08000 | 0.00640 | 0.01000 | 0.00006 | 0.00020 | 0.00017 | 0.00017 |
| 0.09000 | 0.00810 | 0.01000 | 0.00008 | 0.00029 | 0.00024 | 0.00024 |
| 0.10000 | 0.01000 | 0.01000 | 0.00010 | 0.00039 | 0.00034 | 0.00033 |
| 0.94000 | 0.88360 | 0.01000 | 0.00884 | 0.28130 | 0.27688 | 0.27686 |
| 0.95000 | 0.90250 | 0.01000 | 0.00903 | 0.29032 | 0.28581 | 0.28579 |
| 0.96000 | 0.92160 | 0.01000 | 0.00922 | 0.29954 | 0.29493 | 0.29491 |
| 0.97000 | 0.94090 | 0.01000 | 0.00941 | 0.30895 | 0.30424 | 0.30422 |
| 0.98000 | 0.96040 | 0.01000 | 0.00960 | 0.31855 | 0.31375 | 0.31373 |
| 0.99000 | 0.98010 | 0.01000 | 0.00980 | 0.32835 | 0.32345 | 0.32343 |
| 1.00000 | 1.00000 | 0.01000 | 0.01000 | 0.33835 | 0.33335 | 0.33333 |

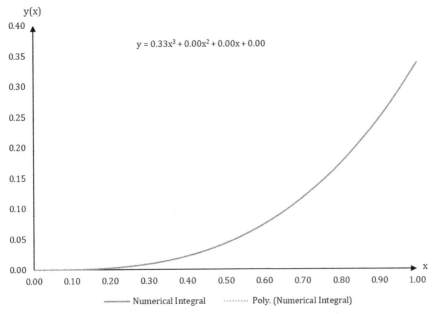

**FIGURE 2.2-4** Numerical integral $y(x) = (1/3)x^3$.

Table 2.2-2 gives the numerical solution compared to the exact integral, while Fig. 2.2-4 plots the diagram of the numerical solution together with the trendline, which returns the equation of the integral. This is only possible if the integral function is expressed in one of the equation forms available in the trendline options. We can approximate further, as we see from Table 2.2-2 that averaging out two points of the numerical solution a better approximation is reached. See also Fig. 2.2-5, where the dotted curve of the exact integral is overlapping with the average.

In other integrand functions like the fractional or the logarithmic and exponential functions, we have to setup the constant of integration such that at $x_0$ the area is always zero.

Let us solve the following integral:

$$\int_0^1 x^2 e^x dx.$$

Integrating by parts the solution would be:

$$y(x) = e^x \left( x^2 - 2x + 2 \right) + C$$

In $x = 0$, we have $y(0) = 0$:

$$2 + C = 0 \Rightarrow C = -2$$

Table 2.2-3 and Fig. 2.2-6 return the numerical solution.

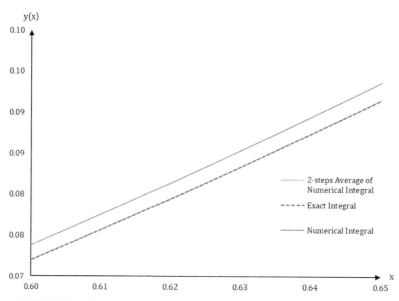

**FIGURE 2.2-5**   Numerical integral averaged out versus exact $y(x) = (1/3)x^3$.

**TABLE 2.2-3**   Integral of $y' = (x^2)(e^x)$ from 0 to 1 equal to $(e - 2) \simeq 0.7182$.

| x | y'(x) | $x_k - x_{k-1} = h$ | y'(x)*h | $y_k = y_{k-1} + y'*h$ | Average $(y_k ; y_{k-1})$ | y Exact | Step | c |
|---|---|---|---|---|---|---|---|---|
| 0.00000 | | | | 0.0000000 | 0.0000000 | 0.0000000 | 0.01 | -2.00 |
| 0.01000 | 0.00010 | 0.01000 | 0.00000 | 0.0000010 | 0.0000005 | 0.0000003 | | |
| 0.02000 | 0.00041 | 0.01000 | 0.00000 | 0.0000051 | 0.0000031 | 0.0000027 | | |
| 0.03000 | 0.00093 | 0.01000 | 0.00001 | 0.0000144 | 0.0000097 | 0.0000092 | | |
| 0.04000 | 0.00167 | 0.01000 | 0.00002 | 0.0000310 | 0.0000227 | 0.0000220 | | |
| 0.05000 | 0.00263 | 0.01000 | 0.00003 | 0.0000573 | 0.0000442 | 0.0000433 | | |
| 0.06000 | 0.00382 | 0.01000 | 0.00004 | 0.0000955 | 0.0000764 | 0.0000753 | | |
| 0.07000 | 0.00526 | 0.01000 | 0.00005 | 0.0001481 | 0.0001218 | 0.0001205 | | |
| 0.08000 | 0.00693 | 0.01000 | 0.00007 | 0.0002174 | 0.0001827 | 0.0001812 | | |
| 0.09000 | 0.00886 | 0.01000 | 0.00009 | 0.0003060 | 0.0002617 | 0.0002600 | | |
| 0.10000 | 0.01105 | 0.01000 | 0.00011 | 0.0004166 | 0.0003613 | 0.0003594 | | |
| 0.99000 | 2.63768 | 0.01000 | 0.02638 | 0.7047584 | 0.6915700 | 0.6915036 | | |
| 1.00000 | 2.71828 | 0.01000 | 0.02718 | 0.7319412 | 0.7183498 | 0.7182818 | | |

## 2.3 Numerical partial differentiation

We will deal now with the numerical differentiation for the following function of $n$ variables:

$$y = f(x) = f(x_1, x_2, \cdots, x_j, \cdots, x_n).$$

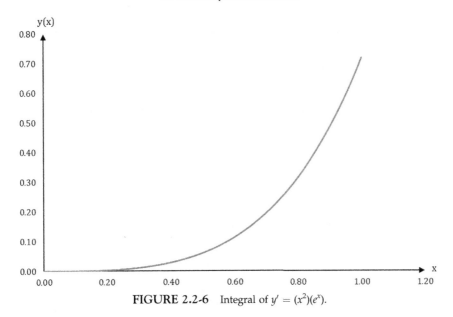

**FIGURE 2.2-6**  Integral of $y' = (x^2)(e^x)$.

In this case, the derivative is generally called *partial derivative*, and the *partial first derivative* of $y = f(x)$ with respect to the variable $x_j$ is calculated considering all the other $(n - 1)$ variables as a constant and it is given by:

$$f_{x_j} = \frac{\partial f}{\partial x_j} \quad (j = 1, \cdots, n) \tag{2.3-1}$$

The notation $f_j$ is also used.

The *gradient* is a vector of dimension equal to $(1 \times n)$ containing all the partial derivatives of the given multivariate function and it is denoted by:

$$grad[f(x)] = \nabla f(x) = \left[\frac{\partial f}{\partial x_1}, \frac{\partial f}{\partial x_2}, \cdots, \frac{\partial f}{\partial x_j}, \cdots, \frac{\partial f}{\partial x_n}\right].$$

A *second partial derivative* is defined as:

$$f_{x_{ij}} = \frac{\partial}{\partial x_i}\left(\frac{\partial f}{\partial x_j}\right)$$

(or more simply as $f_{ij}$) and the *Hessian* matrix is defined instead as the following symmetric matrix containing all the second partial derivatives:

$$H(x) = \begin{bmatrix} f_{11} & f_{12} & \cdots & f_{1n} \\ f_{21} & f_{22} & \cdots & f_{2n} \\ \vdots & \vdots & \vdots & \vdots \\ \vdots & \vdots & \vdots & \vdots \\ f_{n1} & f_{n2} & \cdots & f_{nn} \end{bmatrix} = \begin{bmatrix} \dfrac{\partial}{\partial x_1}\left(\dfrac{\partial f}{\partial x_1}\right) & \dfrac{\partial}{\partial x_1}\left(\dfrac{\partial f}{\partial x_2}\right) & \cdots & \dfrac{\partial}{\partial x_1}\left(\dfrac{\partial f}{\partial x_n}\right) \\ \dfrac{\partial}{\partial x_2}\left(\dfrac{\partial f}{\partial x_1}\right) & \dfrac{\partial}{\partial x_2}\left(\dfrac{\partial f}{\partial x_2}\right) & \cdots & \dfrac{\partial}{\partial x_2}\left(\dfrac{\partial f}{\partial x_n}\right) \\ \vdots & \vdots & \vdots & \vdots \\ \dfrac{\partial}{\partial x_n}\left(\dfrac{\partial f}{\partial x_1}\right) & \dfrac{\partial}{\partial x_n}\left(\dfrac{\partial f}{\partial x_2}\right) & \cdots & \dfrac{\partial}{\partial x_n}\left(\dfrac{\partial f}{\partial x_n}\right) \end{bmatrix}.$$

The gradient and the Hessian matrix will be used in Chapter 5 to identify the minima, the maxima, and *saddle points* of a multivariate function.

Let us consider now the following bivariate linear function:

$$y = 3x_1 - 5x_2 + 1.$$

As we are working with $n = 2$, we are still able to diagram the function, and to do this we will use the Data Table What-if Analysis (Fig. 2.3-1).

*Cell B4* is where the Data Table begins. This cell recalls the formula on which we want to simulate, i.e., *Cell D2* where we have stored the general formula of the given function $y = 3x_1 - 5x_2 + 1$, linked to *Cell B2 Cell B1* for $x_1$ and *Cell C2* for $x_2$, with two arbitrary values for each variable (e.g., $= 1$).

In the range *B5:B16*, we store the simulation on $x_1$, while from *C4* along the same *Row 4* we have the simulation on $x_2$. A step-increment of 1 is given for each variable.

A Data Table What-if analysis is a simulation that is entered going to the ribbon bar, then clicking on Data, What-If analysis, and Data Table as in Fig. 2.3-2.

The dialogue box of Fig. 2.3-3 will appear, where we have to input the *Row Input Cell* and the *Column Input Cell* of the double entry table.

| | A | B | C | D | E | F | G | H | I |
|---|---|---|---|---|---|---|---|---|---|
| 1 | | x1 | x2 | y = 3*x1-5*x2+1 | | | | Step-size | 1 |
| 2 | | 1 | 1 | =3*$B$2-5*$C$2+1 | | | | | |
| 3 | | | | | | | | | x2 |
| 4 | | =D2 | 1 | =C4+$I$1 | =D4+$I$1 | =E4+$I$1 | =F4+$I$1 | =G4+$I$1 | =H4+$I$1 |
| 5 | | 1 | =TABLE(C2;B2) | =TABLE(C2;B2) | =TABLE(C2;B2) | =TABLE(C2;B2) | =TABLE(C2;B2) | =TABLE(C2;B2) | =TABLE(C2;B2) |
| 6 | | =B5+$I$1 | =TABLE(C2;B2) | =TABLE(C2;B2) | =TABLE(C2;B2) | =TABLE(C2;B2) | =TABLE(C2;B2) | =TABLE(C2;B2) | =TABLE(C2;B2) |
| 7 | | =B6+$I$1 | =TABLE(C2;B2) | =TABLE(C2;B2) | =TABLE(C2;B2) | =TABLE(C2;B2) | =TABLE(C2;B2) | =TABLE(C2;B2) | =TABLE(C2;B2) |
| 8 | | =B7+$I$1 | =TABLE(C2;B2) | =TABLE(C2;B2) | =TABLE(C2;B2) | =TABLE(C2;B2) | =TABLE(C2;B2) | =TABLE(C2;B2) | =TABLE(C2;B2) |
| 9 | x1 | =B8+$I$1 | =TABLE(C2;B2) | =TABLE(C2;B2) | =TABLE(C2;B2) | =TABLE(C2;B2) | =TABLE(C2;B2) | =TABLE(C2;B2) | =TABLE(C2;B2) |
| 10 | | =B9+$I$1 | =TABLE(C2;B2) | =TABLE(C2;B2) | =TABLE(C2;B2) | =TABLE(C2;B2) | =TABLE(C2;B2) | =TABLE(C2;B2) | =TABLE(C2;B2) |
| 11 | | =B10+$I$1 | =TABLE(C2;B2) | =TABLE(C2;B2) | =TABLE(C2;B2) | =TABLE(C2;B2) | =TABLE(C2;B2) | =TABLE(C2;B2) | =TABLE(C2;B2) |
| 12 | | =B11+$I$1 | =TABLE(C2;B2) | =TABLE(C2;B2) | =TABLE(C2;B2) | =TABLE(C2;B2) | =TABLE(C2;B2) | =TABLE(C2;B2) | =TABLE(C2;B2) |
| 13 | | =B12+$I$1 | =TABLE(C2;B2) | =TABLE(C2;B2) | =TABLE(C2;B2) | =TABLE(C2;B2) | =TABLE(C2;B2) | =TABLE(C2;B2) | =TABLE(C2;B2) |
| 14 | | =B13+$I$1 | =TABLE(C2;B2) | =TABLE(C2;B2) | =TABLE(C2;B2) | =TABLE(C2;B2) | =TABLE(C2;B2) | =TABLE(C2;B2) | =TABLE(C2;B2) |
| 15 | | =B14+$I$1 | =TABLE(C2;B2) | =TABLE(C2;B2) | =TABLE(C2;B2) | =TABLE(C2;B2) | =TABLE(C2;B2) | =TABLE(C2;B2) | =TABLE(C2;B2) |
| 16 | | =B15+$I$1 | =TABLE(C2;B2) | =TABLE(C2;B2) | =TABLE(C2;B2) | =TABLE(C2;B2) | =TABLE(C2;B2) | =TABLE(C2;B2) | =TABLE(C2;B2) |

**FIGURE 2.3-1** Data Table to diagram a bivariate function $y = f(x_1, x_2)$.

FIGURE 2.3-2   Data Table in Excel.

Data Table                    ?    ✕

Row input cell:        |                    ⬆

Column input cell:                          ⬆

OK                    Cancel

FIGURE 2.3-3   Data Table inputs.

If we look at Fig. 2.3-1, we see that the Row Input Cell is *Cell C2* because we have decided to store $x_2$ along *Row* 4, while the Column Input Cell is *Cell B2* because we have decided to store $x_1$ along *Column B*.

$$y(x_1, \ x_2)y = \ -21(x_1 = 1, \ x_2 = 5)$$

We can see from Table 2.3-1 the results of $y$ as a function of the pair $(x_1, x_2)$ from 1 to 12. Notice the value $y = -21$ inside the table corresponding to the value of the pairs $(x_1 = 1, x_2 = 5)$, $(x_1 = 6, x_2 = 8)$, and $(x_1 = 11, x_2 = 51)$.

The surface chart will allow us to diagram the function as in Fig. 2.3-4.

**TABLE 2.3-1**   Data Table for the given function $y = 3x_1 - 5x_2 + 1$.

| | x1 | x2 | y = 3*x1-5*x2+1 | | | Step-size | 1 | | | | | |
|---|---|---|---|---|---|---|---|---|---|---|---|---|
| | 1.00 | 5.00 | -21.00 | | | | | | | | | |
| | | | | | | | x2 | | | | | |
| | -21.00 | 1.00 | 2.00 | 3.00 | 4.00 | 5.00 | 6.00 | 7.00 | 8.00 | 9.00 | 10.00 | 11.00 | 12.00 |
| | 1.00 | -1.00 | -6.00 | -11.00 | -16.00 | -21.00 | -26.00 | -31.00 | -36.00 | -41.00 | -46.00 | -51.00 | -56.00 |
| | 2.00 | 2.00 | -3.00 | -8.00 | -13.00 | -18.00 | -23.00 | -28.00 | -33.00 | -38.00 | -43.00 | -48.00 | -53.00 |
| | 3.00 | 5.00 | 0.00 | -5.00 | -10.00 | -15.00 | -20.00 | -25.00 | -30.00 | -35.00 | -40.00 | -45.00 | -50.00 |
| | 4.00 | 8.00 | 3.00 | -2.00 | -7.00 | -12.00 | -17.00 | -22.00 | -27.00 | -32.00 | -37.00 | -42.00 | -47.00 |
| x1 | 5.00 | 11.00 | 6.00 | 1.00 | -4.00 | -9.00 | -14.00 | -19.00 | -24.00 | -29.00 | -34.00 | -39.00 | -44.00 |
| | 6.00 | 14.00 | 9.00 | 4.00 | -1.00 | -6.00 | -11.00 | -16.00 | -21.00 | -26.00 | -31.00 | -36.00 | -41.00 |
| | 7.00 | 17.00 | 12.00 | 7.00 | 2.00 | -3.00 | -8.00 | -13.00 | -18.00 | -23.00 | -28.00 | -33.00 | -38.00 |
| | 8.00 | 20.00 | 15.00 | 10.00 | 5.00 | 0.00 | -5.00 | -10.00 | -15.00 | -20.00 | -25.00 | -30.00 | -35.00 |
| | 9.00 | 23.00 | 18.00 | 13.00 | 8.00 | 3.00 | -2.00 | -7.00 | -12.00 | -17.00 | -22.00 | -27.00 | -32.00 |
| | 10.00 | 26.00 | 21.00 | 16.00 | 11.00 | 6.00 | 1.00 | -4.00 | -9.00 | -14.00 | -19.00 | -24.00 | -29.00 |
| | 11.00 | 29.00 | 24.00 | 19.00 | 14.00 | 9.00 | 4.00 | -1.00 | -6.00 | -11.00 | -16.00 | -21.00 | -26.00 |
| | 12.00 | 32.00 | 27.00 | 22.00 | 17.00 | 12.00 | 7.00 | 2.00 | -3.00 | -8.00 | -13.00 | -18.00 | -23.00 |

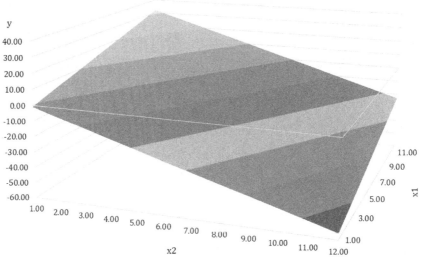

**FIGURE 2.3-4**  Diagram of $y = 3x_1 - 5x_2 + 1$.

Now, the objective is to calculate the gradient of the function:

$$\nabla f(x) = \left[ \frac{\partial f}{\partial x_1}, \frac{\partial f}{\partial x_2} \right].$$

To do this, we will use one of the first-order differences seen in Section 2.1 with respect to one independent variable, keeping constant the other variable, so that for the general case of a multivariate function of $n$ variables, Eq. (2.1-1) with the backward difference can be rewritten as:

$$\frac{\Delta y^j}{\Delta x^j} = y'_n = \frac{y_n^{\ j} - y_{n-h}^{\ j}}{x_n^{\ j} - x_{n-h}^{\ j}}, \quad with\ x^1,\ x^2,\ \cdots, x^{j-1}, x^{j+1}, \cdots, x^n\ constants. \qquad (2.3\text{-}2)$$

The expression (2.3-2) is the numerical partial derivative of the multivariate function $y = f(x) = f(x_1, x_2, \cdots, x_j, \cdots, x_n)$ with respect to $x_j$. The superscript $j$ also in the numerator clearly indicates that $f(x)$ is changing as a function of $x_j$ only. In other words, the numerator of Eq. (2.3-2) is the change of the dependent variable induced by the change of $x_j$ only, for a small increment $h$.

Looking at Fig. 2.3-1, where we have built the bivariate function $y = 3x_1 - 5x_2 + 1$, now we keep on working on the two partial derivatives as described in Fig. 2.3-5. The dollar notation in $C\$2$ and $B\$2$ indicates that we are inducing a change on $y$, changing $x_1$ only and $x_2$ only, respectively, keeping frozen the other variable. See *Column R* and *Column V* of Fig. 2.3-5.

On *Column S* and *Column W* we calculate the usual numerical differentials, with the desired increment.

| Q | R | S | T | U | V | W |
|---|---|---|---|---|---|---|
| x1 | y by changing x1 only | ∂y/∂x1 | | x2 | y by changing x2 only | ∂y/∂x2 |
| =B5 | =3*Q3-5*$C$2+1 | Numerical | | =Q3 | =3*$B$2-5*U3+1 | Numerical |
| =Q3+0.5 | =3*Q4-5*$C$2+1 | =(R4-R3)/(Q4-Q3) | | =Q4 | =3*$B$2-5*U4+1 | =(V4-V3)/(U4-U3) |
| =Q4+0.5 | =3*Q5-5*$C$2+1 | =(R5-R4)/(Q5-Q4) | | =Q5 | =3*$B$2-5*U5+1 | =(V5-V4)/(U5-U4) |
| =Q5+0.5 | =3*Q6-5*$C$2+1 | =(R6-R5)/(Q6-Q5) | | =Q6 | =3*$B$2-5*U6+1 | =(V6-V5)/(U6-U5) |
| =Q6+0.5 | =3*Q7-5*$C$2+1 | =(R7-R6)/(Q7-Q6) | | =Q7 | =3*$B$2-5*U7+1 | =(V7-V6)/(U7-U6) |
| =Q7+0.5 | =3*Q8-5*$C$2+1 | =(R8-R7)/(Q8-Q7) | | =Q8 | =3*$B$2-5*U8+1 | =(V8-V7)/(U8-U7) |
| =Q8+0.5 | =3*Q9-5*$C$2+1 | =(R9-R8)/(Q9-Q8) | | =Q9 | =3*$B$2-5*U9+1 | =(V9-V8)/(U9-U8) |
| =Q9+0.5 | =3*Q10-5*$C$2+1 | =(R10-R9)/(Q10-Q9) | | =Q10 | =3*$B$2-5*U10+1 | =(V10-V9)/(U10-U9) |
| =Q10+0.5 | =3*Q11-5*$C$2+1 | =(R11-R10)/(Q11-Q10) | | =Q11 | =3*$B$2-5*U11+1 | =(V11-V10)/(U11-U10) |
| =Q11+0.5 | =3*Q12-5*$C$2+1 | =(R12-R11)/(Q12-Q11) | | =Q12 | =3*$B$2-5*U12+1 | =(V12-V11)/(U12-U11) |
| =Q12+0.5 | =3*Q13-5*$C$2+1 | =(R13-R12)/(Q13-Q12) | | =Q13 | =3*$B$2-5*U13+1 | =(V13-V12)/(U13-U12) |
| =Q13+0.5 | =3*Q14-5*$C$2+1 | =(R14-R13)/(Q14-Q13) | | =Q14 | =3*$B$2-5*U14+1 | =(V14-V13)/(U14-U13) |
| =Q14+0.5 | =3*Q15-5*$C$2+1 | =(R15-R14)/(Q15-Q14) | | =Q15 | =3*$B$2-5*U15+1 | =(V15-V14)/(U15-U14) |
| =Q15+0.5 | =3*Q16-5*$C$2+1 | =(R16-R15)/(Q16-Q15) | | =Q16 | =3*$B$2-5*U16+1 | =(V16-V15)/(U16-U15) |
| =Q16+0.5 | =3*Q17-5*$C$2+1 | =(R17-R16)/(Q17-Q16) | | =Q17 | =3*$B$2-5*U17+1 | =(V17-V16)/(U17-U16) |
| =Q17+0.5 | =3*Q18-5*$C$2+1 | =(R18-R17)/(Q18-Q17) | | =Q18 | =3*$B$2-5*U18+1 | =(V18-V17)/(U18-U17) |
| =Q18+0.5 | =3*Q19-5*$C$2+1 | =(R19-R18)/(Q19-Q18) | | =Q19 | =3*$B$2-5*U19+1 | =(V19-V18)/(U19-U18) |
| =Q19+0.5 | =3*Q20-5*$C$2+1 | =(R20-R19)/(Q20-Q19) | | =Q20 | =3*$B$2-5*U20+1 | =(V20-V19)/(U20-U19) |
| =Q20+0.5 | =3*Q21-5*$C$2+1 | =(R21-R20)/(Q21-Q20) | | =Q21 | =3*$B$2-5*U21+1 | =(V21-V20)/(U21-U20) |
| =Q21+0.5 | =3*Q22-5*$C$2+1 | =(R22-R21)/(Q22-Q21) | | =Q22 | =3*$B$2-5*U22+1 | =(V22-V21)/(U22-U21) |
| =Q22+0.5 | =3*Q23-5*$C$2+1 | =(R23-R22)/(Q23-Q22) | | =Q23 | =3*$B$2-5*U23+1 | =(V23-V22)/(U23-U22) |
| =Q23+0.5 | =3*Q24-5*$C$2+1 | =(R24-R23)/(Q24-Q23) | | =Q24 | =3*$B$2-5*U24+1 | =(V24-V23)/(U24-U23) |
| =Q24+0.5 | =3*Q25-5*$C$2+1 | =(R25-R24)/(Q25-Q24) | | =Q25 | =3*$B$2-5*U25+1 | =(V25-V24)/(U25-U24) |

FIGURE 2.3-5 Partial derivatives setup for the function $y = 3x_1 - 5x_2 + 1$.

The results are in Table 2.3-2 which returns the schedule of the two partial derivatives for a specific interval in the two independent variables and for a given step-increment. We are going now to diagram these schedules obtaining Fig. 2.3-6, where the trendline associated to each graph will allow us to identify the sought equations of the two partial derivatives. This is possible if and only if the partial derivatives have one of the equation forms of the trendlines available in Excel.

In summary, the gradient of the function $y = 3x_1 - 5x_2 + 1$ is:

$$\nabla f(x) = \left[ \frac{\partial f}{\partial x_1} = 3, \frac{\partial f}{\partial x_2} = -5 \right].$$

We will see that, as these derivatives will never be equal to zero, the function does not have any critical point. The only way to have maxima and minima in linear functions is restricting them with an upper/lower value condition.

Let us consider the nonlinear function:

$$y = x_1^4 + x_1 x_2^3 + x_1^3 x_2^2 + 4$$

The double entry table of the function is represented numerically by Table 2.3-3 and graphically by Fig. 2.3-7.

The two numerical partial derivatives are given in Fig. 2.3-8 and Table 2.3.4.

**TABLE 2.3-2**   Numerical partial derivatives of $y = 3x_1 - 5x_2 + 1$.

| x1 | y by changing x1 only | ∂y/∂x1 | x2 | y by changing x2 only | ∂y/∂x2 |
|---|---|---|---|---|---|
| 1.00 | -1.00 | **Numerical** | 1.00 | -1.00 | **Numerical** |
| 1.50 | 0.50 | 3.00 | 1.50 | -3.50 | -5.00 |
| 2.00 | 2.00 | 3.00 | 2.00 | -6.00 | -5.00 |
| 2.50 | 3.50 | 3.00 | 2.50 | -8.50 | -5.00 |
| 3.00 | 5.00 | 3.00 | 3.00 | -11.00 | -5.00 |
| 3.50 | 6.50 | 3.00 | 3.50 | -13.50 | -5.00 |
| 4.00 | 8.00 | 3.00 | 4.00 | -16.00 | -5.00 |
| 4.50 | 9.50 | 3.00 | 4.50 | -18.50 | -5.00 |
| 5.00 | 11.00 | 3.00 | 5.00 | -21.00 | -5.00 |
| 5.50 | 12.50 | 3.00 | 5.50 | -23.50 | -5.00 |
| 6.00 | 14.00 | 3.00 | 6.00 | -26.00 | -5.00 |
| 6.50 | 15.50 | 3.00 | 6.50 | -28.50 | -5.00 |
| 7.00 | 17.00 | 3.00 | 7.00 | -31.00 | -5.00 |
| 7.50 | 18.50 | 3.00 | 7.50 | -33.50 | -5.00 |
| 8.00 | 20.00 | 3.00 | 8.00 | -36.00 | -5.00 |
| 8.50 | 21.50 | 3.00 | 8.50 | -38.50 | -5.00 |
| 9.00 | 23.00 | 3.00 | 9.00 | -41.00 | -5.00 |
| 9.50 | 24.50 | 3.00 | 9.50 | -43.50 | -5.00 |
| 10.00 | 26.00 | 3.00 | 10.00 | -46.00 | -5.00 |
| 10.50 | 27.50 | 3.00 | 10.50 | -48.50 | -5.00 |
| 11.00 | 29.00 | 3.00 | 11.00 | -51.00 | -5.00 |
| 11.50 | 30.50 | 3.00 | 11.50 | -53.50 | -5.00 |
| 12.00 | 32.00 | 3.00 | 12.00 | -56.00 | -5.00 |
| 12.50 | 33.50 | 3.00 | 12.50 | -58.50 | -5.00 |
| 13.00 | 35.00 | 3.00 | 13.00 | -61.00 | -5.00 |
| 13.50 | 36.50 | 3.00 | 13.50 | -63.50 | -5.00 |
| 14.00 | 38.00 | 3.00 | 14.00 | -66.00 | -5.00 |
| 14.50 | 39.50 | 3.00 | 14.50 | -68.50 | -5.00 |
| 15.00 | 41.00 | 3.00 | 15.00 | -71.00 | -5.00 |
| 15.50 | 42.50 | 3.00 | 15.50 | -73.50 | -5.00 |
| 16.00 | 44.00 | 3.00 | 16.00 | -76.00 | -5.00 |
| 16.50 | 45.50 | 3.00 | 16.50 | -78.50 | -5.00 |

The exact gradient of $y = x_1^4 + x_1 x_2^3 + x_1^3 x_2^2 + 4$ is given by

$$\nabla f(x) = \left[ \frac{\partial f}{\partial x_1} = 4x_1^3 + x_2^3 + 3x_1^2 x_2^2, \frac{\partial f}{\partial x_2} = 3x_1 x_2^2 + 2x_1^3 x_2 \right].$$

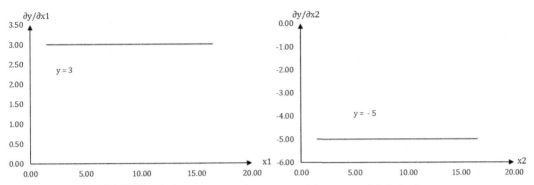

**FIGURE 2.3-6**   Diagram and equations of the two partial derivatives.

**TABLE 2.3-3**   Double entry table for $y = x_1^4 + x_1x_2^3 + x_1^3x_2^2 + 4$.

| x1 | x2 | | y = x1⁴+x1x2³+x1³x2²+4 | | | Step-Size | 1.00 | | | Step dervatives | 0.00200 | 0.02500 |
|---|---|---|---|---|---|---|---|---|---|---|---|---|
| 1.00 | 1.00 | 7.00 | | | | | | | | | | |
| | | | | | | | x2 | | | | | |
| **7.00** | -6.00 | -5.00 | -4.00 | -3.00 | -1.00 | -0.67 | 0.00 | 1.00 | 2.00 | 3.00 | 4.00 | 5.00 |
| -6.00 | -5,180.00 | -3,350.00 | -1,772.00 | -482.00 | 1,090.00 | 1,205.78 | 1,300.00 | 1,078.00 | 388.00 | -806.00 | -2,540.00 | -4,850.00 |
| -5.00 | -2,791.00 | -1,871.00 | -1,051.00 | -361.00 | 509.00 | 574.93 | 629.00 | 499.00 | 89.00 | -631.00 | -1,691.00 | -3,121.00 |
| -4.00 | -1,180.00 | -840.00 | -508.00 | -208.00 | 200.00 | 232.74 | 260.00 | 192.00 | -28.00 | -424.00 | -1,020.00 | -1,840.00 |
| -3.00 | -239.00 | -215.00 | -155.00 | -77.00 | 61.00 | 73.89 | 85.00 | 55.00 | -47.00 | -239.00 | -539.00 | -965.00 |
| **x1** -2.00 | 164.00 | 70.00 | 20.00 | 2.00 | 14.00 | 17.04 | 20.00 | 10.00 | -28.00 | -106.00 | -236.00 | -430.00 |
| -1.00 | 185.00 | 105.00 | 53.00 | 23.00 | 5.00 | 4.85 | 5.00 | 3.00 | -7.00 | -31.00 | -75.00 | -145.00 |
| 0.00 | 4.00 | 4.00 | 4.00 | 4.00 | 4.00 | 4.00 | 4.00 | 4.00 | 4.00 | 4.00 | 4.00 | 4.00 |
| 1.00 | -175.00 | -95.00 | -43.00 | -13.00 | 5.00 | 5.15 | 5.00 | 7.00 | 17.00 | 41.00 | 85.00 | 155.00 |
| 2.00 | -124.00 | -30.00 | 20.00 | 38.00 | 26.00 | 22.96 | 20.00 | 30.00 | 68.00 | 146.00 | 276.00 | 470.00 |
| 3.00 | 409.00 | 385.00 | 325.00 | 247.00 | 109.00 | 96.11 | 85.00 | 115.00 | 217.00 | 409.00 | 709.00 | 1,135.00 |
| 4.00 | 1,700.00 | 1,360.00 | 1,028.00 | 728.00 | 320.00 | 287.26 | 260.00 | 328.00 | 548.00 | 944.00 | 1,540.00 | 2,360.00 |
| 5.00 | 4,049.00 | 3,129.00 | 2,309.00 | 1,619.00 | 749.00 | 683.07 | 629.00 | 759.00 | 1,169.00 | 1,889.00 | 2,949.00 | 4,379.00 |

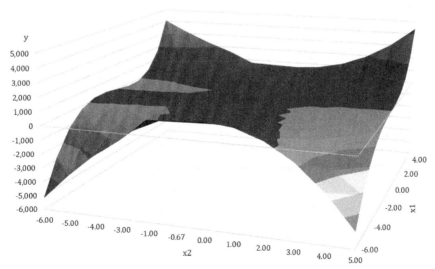

**FIGURE 2.3-7**   Diagram of the function $y = x_1^4 + x_1x_2^3 + x_1^3x_2^2 + 4$.

I. Excel and fundamental mathematics for economics

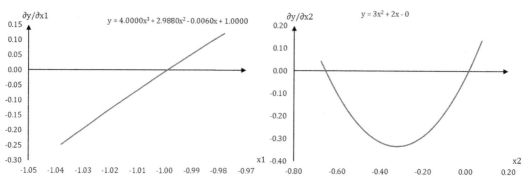

**FIGURE 2.3-8**   Diagram and equations of the two partial derivatives.

**TABLE 2.3-4**   Numerical partial derivatives for $y = x_1^4 + x_1 x_2^3 + x_1^3 x_2^2 + 4$.

| x1 | y by changing x1 only | ∂y/∂x1 | x2 | y by changing x2 only | ∂y/∂x2 |
|---|---|---|---|---|---|
| -1.0400 | 3.0050 | **Numerical** | -0.7000 | 5.1470 | **Numerical** |
| -1.0380 | 3.0045 | -0.2479 | -0.6750 | 5.1481 | 0.0431 |
| -1.0360 | 3.0040 | -0.2345 | -0.6500 | 5.1479 | -0.0081 |
| -1.0340 | 3.0036 | -0.2212 | -0.6250 | 5.1465 | -0.0556 |
| -1.0320 | 3.0032 | -0.2079 | -0.6000 | 5.1440 | -0.0994 |
| -1.0300 | 3.0028 | -0.1948 | -0.5750 | 5.1405 | -0.1394 |
| -1.0280 | 3.0024 | -0.1817 | -0.5500 | 5.1361 | -0.1756 |
| -1.0260 | 3.0021 | -0.1686 | -0.5250 | 5.1309 | -0.2081 |
| -1.0240 | 3.0018 | -0.1557 | -0.5000 | 5.1250 | -0.2369 |
| -1.0220 | 3.0015 | -0.1428 | -0.4750 | 5.1185 | -0.2619 |
| -1.0200 | 3.0012 | -0.1300 | -0.4500 | 5.1114 | -0.2831 |
| -1.0180 | 3.0010 | -0.1173 | -0.4250 | 5.1039 | -0.3006 |
| -1.0160 | 3.0008 | -0.1046 | -0.4000 | 5.0960 | -0.3144 |
| -1.0140 | 3.0006 | -0.0920 | -0.3750 | 5.0879 | -0.3244 |
| -1.0120 | 3.0004 | -0.0795 | -0.3500 | 5.0796 | -0.3306 |
| -1.0100 | 3.0003 | -0.0671 | -0.3250 | 5.0713 | -0.3331 |
| -1.0080 | 3.0002 | -0.0547 | -0.3000 | 5.0630 | -0.3319 |
| -1.0060 | 3.0001 | -0.0424 | -0.2750 | 5.0548 | -0.3269 |
| -1.0040 | 3.0000 | -0.0302 | -0.2500 | 5.0469 | -0.3181 |
| -0.9800 | 3.0012 | 0.1108 | 0.0500 | 5.0026 | 0.0794 |
| -0.9780 | 3.0014 | 0.1221 | 0.0750 | 5.0060 | 0.1369 |

## 2.4 Applications in economics

We will show now some examples of applications of the standard calculus. While three examples are related to mathematical economics, the last example shows the probabilistic application and interpretation of the integral, given a *normal probability density function*.

### EXAMPLE 1 (MARGINAL COST FUNCTION FROM THE TOTAL COST FUNCTION)

Let us assume we have estimated the total cost function of a company with the following statistical relation:

$$TC(Q) = TVC + FC = 10e^{0.2Q} + 80$$

*Fixed Costs* are $FC = 90$ as $TC(0) = 10$, while *Total Variable Costs* are $TVC(Q) = 10e^{0.2Q}$.

The production manager wants to know the marginal cost, that is, the cost of producing one additional unit of a good. This is the derivative of the total cost function with respect to the variable $Q$:

$$MC(Q) = \frac{dTC(Q)}{dQ}.$$

We also refer to the average total costs as:

$$ATC = \frac{TVC + FC}{Q}.$$

Table 2.4-1 returns the numerical values of the cost functions up to $Q = 10$. We see that the $MC = C'(Q)$ is better approximated taking the average of the numerical differential. Figs. 2.4-1 and 2.4-2 give the diagram of the functions. In particular, as the marginal cost is an exponential function, we can obtain from the trendline its equation $MC = 2e^{0.2Q}$.

### EXAMPLE 2 (MARGINAL PROPENSITY TO SAVE FROM THE TOTAL SAVING FUNCTION)

Let us have the following macroeconomic saving function:

$$S(Y) = 0.3Y - 0.2\sqrt{Y}$$

where $Y = Income$.

The marginal propensity to save is defined as the ratio of change in saving to a change in income, that is, the change in saving that has been induced by a change in income:

$$MPS = \frac{\Delta S}{\Delta Y}.$$

I. Excel and fundamental mathematics for economics

**TABLE 2.4-1**  Total cost, marginal cost function, average total cost.

| Q | $TC(Q) = 10e^{0.2Q} + 80$ | $\Delta TC(Q)/\Delta Q$ | $\Delta TC(Q)/\Delta Q$ Average | $dTC(Q)/dQ$ True $C'(Q) = 2e^{0.2Q}$ | Average Total Cost | Step |
|---|---|---|---|---|---|---|
| 0.0000 | 90.0000 | 2.0000 | 2.0000 | 2.0000 | | 0.1000 |
| 0.1000 | 90.2020 | 2.0201 | 2.0405 | 2.0404 | 902.0201 | |
| 0.2000 | 90.4081 | 2.0609 | 2.0818 | 2.0816 | 452.0405 | |
| 0.3000 | 90.6184 | 2.1026 | 2.1238 | 2.1237 | 302.0612 | |
| 0.4000 | 90.8329 | 2.1451 | 2.1667 | 2.1666 | 227.0822 | |
| 0.5000 | 91.0517 | 2.1884 | 2.2105 | 2.2103 | 182.1034 | |
| 0.6000 | 91.2750 | 2.2326 | 2.2551 | 2.2550 | 152.1249 | |
| 0.7000 | 91.5027 | 2.2777 | 2.3007 | 2.3005 | 130.7182 | |
| 0.8000 | 91.7351 | 2.3237 | 2.3472 | 2.3470 | 114.6689 | |
| 0.9000 | 91.9722 | 2.3706 | 2.3946 | 2.3944 | 102.1913 | |
| 1.0000 | 92.2140 | 2.4185 | 2.4430 | 2.4428 | 92.2140 | |
| 1.1000 | 92.4608 | 2.4674 | 2.4923 | 2.4922 | 84.0552 | |
| 9.5000 | 146.8589 | 13.2390 | 13.3727 | 13.3718 | 15.4588 | |
| 9.6000 | 148.2096 | 13.5064 | 13.6428 | 13.6419 | 15.4385 | |
| 9.7000 | 149.5875 | 13.7793 | 13.9184 | 13.9175 | 15.4214 | |
| 9.8000 | 150.9933 | 14.0576 | 14.1996 | 14.1987 | 15.4075 | |
| 9.9000 | 152.4274 | 14.3416 | 14.4865 | 14.4855 | 15.3967 | |
| 10.0000 | 153.8906 | 14.6313 | 14.7791 | 14.7781 | 15.3891 | |

Mathematically, the MPS function is the derivative of the saving function $S(Y)$, with respect to income $Y$:

$$MPS = \frac{dS}{dY}.$$

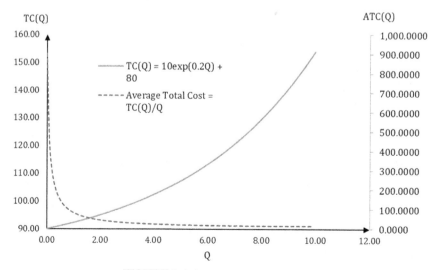

**FIGURE 2.4-1**  TC and ATC diagram.

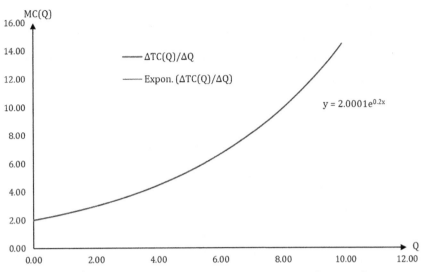

FIGURE 2.4-2 Marginal cost diagram and its equation from trendline.

As usual, we enumerate the problem in Table 2.4-2 where we calculate the numerical derivative versus the exact derivative. We plot the functions in Figs. 2.4-3 and 2.4-4, noticing that the aggregate saving will be positive after $Y = 81$ and the MPS is stabilizing at roughly 30%.

## EXAMPLE 3 (INTEGRATION AND CAPITAL FORMATION FROM A GIVEN INVESTMENT LAW)

Some important applications of differential equations throughout the book attempt to model the capital formation from a given investment policy. The integral is the basis to understand those economic differential equations.

In general, the capital expenditures (capex) within a company are given by:

$$Capex = K_t^g - K_{t-1}^g$$

with $K_t^g = $ *Gross Fixed Capital at a certain time t.*

The capex represents the gross investment made, that is, the money employed by the company to buy new fixed capital and if we leave out for simplicity the depreciations, focusing on the change of the gross fixed capital, we can write the following relation in a continuous time framework:

$$\frac{dK^g(t)}{dt} = I(t).$$

**TABLE 2.4-2**  Saving function and MPS.

| Y | $S(Y) = 0.3Y-0.2Y^{1/2}-22.5$ | $\Delta S(Y)/\Delta Y$ | $\Delta S(Y)/\Delta Y$ Average | dS/dY True $S'(Y)$ $= 0.3-0.1Y^{1/2}$ | Step |
|---|---|---|---|---|---|
| 81.0000 | 0.0000 | | | | 1.0000 |
| 82.0000 | 0.2889 | 0.2889 | 0.2890 | 0.2890 | |
| 83.0000 | 0.5779 | 0.2890 | 0.2890 | 0.2890 | |
| 84.0000 | 0.8670 | 0.2891 | 0.2891 | 0.2891 | |
| 85.0000 | 1.1561 | 0.2891 | 0.2892 | 0.2892 | |
| 86.0000 | 1.4453 | 0.2892 | 0.2892 | 0.2892 | |
| 87.0000 | 1.7345 | 0.2892 | 0.2893 | 0.2893 | |
| 88.0000 | 2.0238 | 0.2893 | 0.2893 | 0.2893 | |
| 89.0000 | 2.3132 | 0.2894 | 0.2894 | 0.2894 | |
| 117.0000 | 10.4367 | 0.2907 | 0.2908 | 0.2908 | |
| 118.0000 | 10.7274 | 0.2908 | 0.2908 | 0.2908 | |
| 119.0000 | 11.0183 | 0.2908 | 0.2908 | 0.2908 | |
| 120.0000 | 11.3091 | 0.2909 | 0.2909 | 0.2909 | |
| 121.0000 | 11.6000 | 0.2909 | 0.2909 | 0.2909 | |
| 174.0000 | 27.0618 | 0.2924 | 0.2924 | 0.2924 | |
| 175.0000 | 27.3542 | 0.2924 | 0.2924 | 0.2924 | |
| 176.0000 | 27.6467 | 0.2925 | 0.2925 | 0.2925 | |
| 177.0000 | 27.9392 | 0.2925 | 0.2925 | 0.2925 | |
| 178.0000 | 28.2317 | 0.2925 | 0.2925 | 0.2925 | |
| 179.0000 | 28.5242 | 0.2925 | 0.2925 | 0.2925 | |
| 180.0000 | 28.8167 | 0.2925 | 0.2925 | 0.2925 | |
| 181.0000 | 29.1093 | 0.2926 | 0.2926 | 0.2926 | |

Therefore, supposing we have $I(t)$, through the integration we can obtain $K^g(t)$. For example, let the following function be the investment law:

$$I(t) = 3t^{1/2}$$

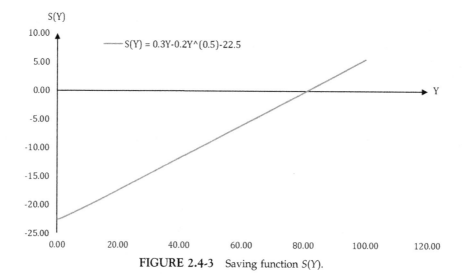

FIGURE 2.4-3  Saving function $S(Y)$.

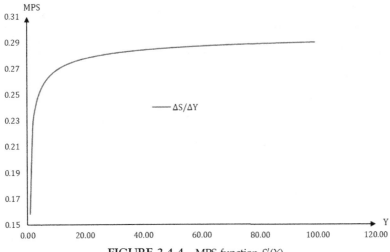

**FIGURE 2.4-4** MPS function $S'(Y)$.

then, through the integral, we obtain:

$$K^8(t) = 2t^{3/2} + C.$$

To calculate the constant of integration we have to know the so-called *initial condition,* which is the beginning value at *time* $= 0$ taken by the integral variable $K(t)$.

Setting for example $K(0) = 5$ the following must result:

$$K(0) = 0 + C = 5 \Rightarrow C = 5.$$

Using the usual tabular format, we obtain Table 2.4-3, where the capital formation over time from $t_0 = 0$ to $t_f = 1$ with step-size $= 0.01$ is enumerated.

The capital available at each instant in time will be therefore given by the initial capital at $t_0 = 0$ plus what has been accumulated until a certain time $t_f$, that is, for $t_f = 1$:

$$K(1) = K(0) + \int_0^1 3t^{1/2} \, dt.$$

The quantity $\int_0^1 I(t)dt = \int_0^1 3t^{\frac{1}{2}}dt$ represents geometrically the area under the curve $I(t) = 3t^{1/2}$ as described by Fig. 2.4-5, i.e., the accumulation of capital (=2) from $t_0 = 0$ to $t_f = 1$, which is then added to $K(0) = 5$ to get $K(1) = 7$ (Fig. 2.4-6).

**TABLE 2.4-3**   Capital path in the time interval $t_0 = 0$, $t_f = 1$.

| t | I(t) = dK/dt = 3t^{1/2} | t_k - t_{k-h} = h | K'(t)*h | K_k = K_{k-h} + K'*h | Average (K_k; K_{k-1}) | K(t) Exact = 2t^{3/2} + K(0) | Step |
|---|---|---|---|---|---|---|---|
| 0.0000 | 0.0000 | | | 5.0000 | 5.0000 | 5.0000 | 0.01 |
| 0.0100 | 0.3000 | 0.0100 | 0.0030 | 5.0030 | 5.0015 | 5.0020 | |
| 0.0200 | 0.4243 | 0.0100 | 0.0042 | 5.0072 | 5.0051 | 5.0057 | |
| 0.0300 | 0.5196 | 0.0100 | 0.0052 | 5.0124 | 5.0098 | 5.0104 | |
| 0.0400 | 0.6000 | 0.0100 | 0.0060 | 5.0184 | 5.0154 | 5.0160 | |
| 0.0500 | 0.6708 | 0.0100 | 0.0067 | 5.0251 | 5.0218 | 5.0224 | |
| 0.0600 | 0.7348 | 0.0100 | 0.0073 | 5.0325 | 5.0288 | 5.0294 | |
| 0.0700 | 0.7937 | 0.0100 | 0.0079 | 5.0404 | 5.0365 | 5.0370 | |
| 0.0800 | 0.8485 | 0.0100 | 0.0085 | 5.0489 | 5.0447 | 5.0453 | |
| 0.0900 | 0.9000 | 0.0100 | 0.0090 | 5.0579 | 5.0534 | 5.0540 | |
| 0.9100 | 2.8618 | 0.0100 | 0.0286 | 6.7499 | 6.7356 | 6.7362 | |
| 0.9200 | 2.8775 | 0.0100 | 0.0288 | 6.7786 | 6.7643 | 6.7649 | |
| 0.9300 | 2.8931 | 0.0100 | 0.0289 | 6.8076 | 6.7931 | 6.7937 | |
| 0.9400 | 2.9086 | 0.0100 | 0.0291 | 6.8367 | 6.8221 | 6.8227 | |
| 0.9500 | 2.9240 | 0.0100 | 0.0292 | 6.8659 | 6.8513 | 6.8519 | |
| 0.9600 | 2.9394 | 0.0100 | 0.0294 | 6.8953 | 6.8806 | 6.8812 | |
| 0.9700 | 2.9547 | 0.0100 | 0.0295 | 6.9248 | 6.9101 | 6.9107 | |
| 0.9800 | 2.9698 | 0.0100 | 0.0297 | 6.9545 | 6.9397 | 6.9403 | |
| 0.9900 | 2.9850 | 0.0100 | 0.0298 | 6.9844 | 6.9695 | 6.9701 | |
| 1.0000 | 3.0000 | 0.0100 | 0.0300 | 7.0144 | 6.9994 | 7.0000 | |

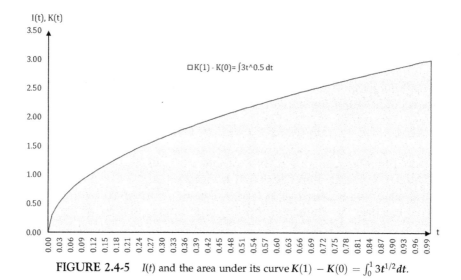

**FIGURE 2.4-5**   $I(t)$ and the area under its curve $K(1) - K(0) = \int_0^1 3t^{1/2}dt$.

## EXAMPLE 4 (INTEGRATION AND THE AREA UNDER A PROBABILITY DENSITY FUNCTION)

An important application of integrals is also related to theory of probability and statistics. As we have pointed out already, given a probability density function $f_X(x)$, the area under its curve represents the cumulative probability $F_X(x)$. The variable $X$ is called random variable.

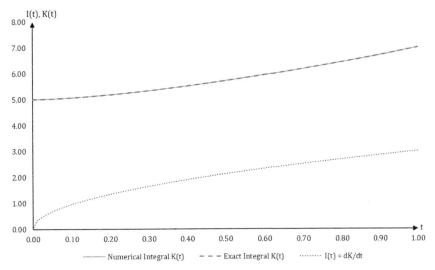

**FIGURE 2.4-6** Diagram of $I(t) = dK(t)/dt$ and time path $K(t)$ from $t_0 = 0$ to $t_f = 1$.

Let us try then to approximate numerically the cumulative probability of the following normal distribution density function, which is used a lot in financial mathematics:

$$f_X(x; \mu, \sigma) = \frac{1}{\sqrt{2\pi}\sigma} e^{-\frac{(x-\mu)^2}{2\sigma^2}}.$$

The cumulative distribution is given by the following integral, which returns the probability $P(X \le x_n)$:

$$F_X(x_n; \mu, \sigma) = \int_{-\infty}^{x_n} \frac{1}{\sqrt{2\pi}\sigma} e^{-\frac{(x-\mu)^2}{2\sigma^2}} dx.$$

The above distribution functions have always the interval [0, 1] as a counter domain.

According to what has been explained so far, Table 2.4-4 has been calculated.

Fig. 2.4-7 represents the probability density function and, under its curve, the integral (area) is given by the cumulative probability $F_X(x_n = 0.55; \mu = 0.50, \sigma = 0.10) \equiv P(X \le 0.55) \cong 0.69$. Fig. 2.4-8 gives the numerical cumulative distribution function versus the exact one represented here instead as curves. To get the exact normal cumulative distribution in Excel the function *NORM.DIST* has been used.

**TABLE 2.4-4** Approximate integration of the normal density function versus exact ($\mu = 0.50$ $\sigma = 0.10$).

| x | p(x) = f(x) | $x_k \cdot x_{k\text{-}h}$ = h | f(x)*h | $F_k = F_{k\text{-}h} + f(x)*h$ | Average ($F_k$ ; $F_{k\text{-}1}$) | F(x) Exact |
|---|---|---|---|---|---|---|
| 0.0000 | 0.0000 | | | 0.00000 | 0.0000 | 0.0000 |
| 0.0100 | 0.0000 | 0.01000 | 0.00000 | 0.00000 | 0.0000 | 0.0000 |
| 0.0200 | 0.0000 | 0.01000 | 0.00000 | 0.00000 | 0.0000 | 0.0000 |
| 0.0300 | 0.0001 | 0.01000 | 0.00000 | 0.00000 | 0.0000 | 0.0000 |
| 0.0400 | 0.0001 | 0.01000 | 0.00000 | 0.00000 | 0.0000 | 0.0000 |
| 0.0500 | 0.0002 | 0.01000 | 0.00000 | 0.00000 | 0.0000 | 0.0000 |
| 0.4700 | 3.8139 | 0.01000 | 0.03814 | 0.40125 | 0.3822 | 0.3821 |
| 0.4800 | 3.9104 | 0.01000 | 0.03910 | 0.44036 | 0.4208 | 0.4207 |
| 0.4900 | 3.9695 | 0.01000 | 0.03970 | 0.48005 | 0.4602 | 0.4602 |
| 0.5000 | 3.9894 | 0.01000 | 0.03989 | 0.51995 | 0.5000 | 0.5000 |
| 0.5100 | 3.9695 | 0.01000 | 0.03970 | 0.55964 | 0.5398 | 0.5398 |
| 0.5200 | 3.9104 | 0.01000 | 0.03910 | 0.59875 | 0.5792 | 0.5793 |
| 0.5300 | 3.8139 | 0.01000 | 0.03814 | 0.63689 | 0.6178 | 0.6179 |
| 0.5400 | 3.6827 | 0.01000 | 0.03683 | 0.67371 | 0.6553 | 0.6554 |
| 0.5500 | 3.5207 | 0.01000 | 0.03521 | 0.70892 | 0.6913 | 0.6915 |
| 0.5600 | 3.3322 | 0.01000 | 0.03332 | 0.74224 | 0.7256 | 0.7257 |
| 0.9600 | 0.0001 | 0.01000 | 0.00000 | 1.00000 | 1.0000 | 1.0000 |
| 0.9700 | 0.0001 | 0.01000 | 0.00000 | 1.00000 | 1.0000 | 1.0000 |
| 0.9800 | 0.0000 | 0.01000 | 0.00000 | 1.00000 | 1.0000 | 1.0000 |
| 0.9900 | 0.0000 | 0.01000 | 0.00000 | 1.00000 | 1.0000 | 1.0000 |
| 1.0000 | 0.0000 | 0.01000 | 0.00000 | 1.00000 | 1.0000 | 1.0000 |

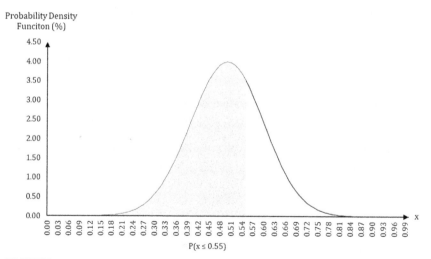

**FIGURE 2.4-7** Normal density function and the area under its curve $F_x (0.55) \cong 0.69$.

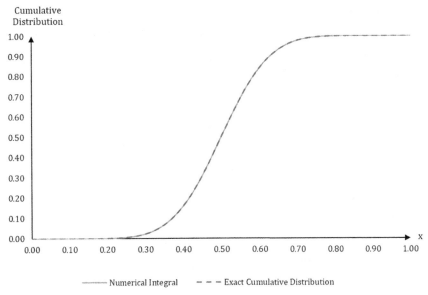

————— Numerical Integral     – – – Exact Cumulative Distribution

**FIGURE 2.4-8**   Numerical and exact cumulative distribution function $f_x(x)$.

## Exercises

1. Using the techniques seen in the chapter, build the Excel Data Table such that you are able to draw the tangent along the points on the curve represented by the following univariate functions:

$$y = x^3$$

$$y = \frac{(x+8)^2}{x^2(x+5)}$$

$$y = \frac{x^2}{x+3}$$

2. Plot the following function:

$$y = -5x^2$$

Then, calculate and plot its numerical first derivative. Using the Excel trendline option find the approximate numerical expression of this derivative.

3. Calculate the following numerical definite integral and compare it versus the exact integral:

$$\int_1^2 \ln x\, dx$$

4. Repeat Exercise 3 for the following expression:

$$\int_1^2 \frac{1}{x}\, dx$$

5. Repeat Exercise 3 for the following expression:

$$\int_0^1 4e^{-4x}\, dx$$

6. Consider the following univariate production function, which relates the level of input labor, $L$, to the output product, $y$:

$$y = L^{0.5}$$

   Plot its graph together with its numerical first derivative, namely the decreasing marginal product of labor. Also, calculate and graph the numerical second derivative and analyze the relation among the various curves.

7. Consider the following Cobb-Douglas production function, which relates the level of inputs $L$ and $K$, to output product, $y$:

$$y = 2L^{0.5}K^{0.5}.$$

   Plot the surface graph and the contour graph of the given production function using the Data Table; then, calculate and plot the numerical partial derivatives, namely the decreasing marginal product of each variable input.

8. Suppose a firm starts at $t = 0$ with a capital stock of $K(0) = £\ 500$ while the investment law detected in the past is equal to $I(t) = 6t^2$ and this will apply over the next 10 years as well. Enumerate the planned level of capital stock. Compare the numerical integral versus the exact integral.

9. The **Consumer Surplus** is defined as the difference between the maximum price the consumers are willing to pay and the price they actually pay. It is the net gain of the buyers. In mathematical terms, we can derive the consumer surplus as follows. Let

$p = D^{-1}(q)$ be the inverse demand function and let $p = p_0$ be the price of the good purchased, i.e., $q_0$ satisfies $p_0 = D^{-1}(q_0)$, then the Consumer Surplus $CS$ is defined as:

$$CS = \int_0^{q_0} D^{-1}(q)dq - p_0 q_0.$$

For a consumer suppose we have $q = 50 - 2p$, namely $D^{-1}(q) = 25 - \frac{1}{2}p$.
Calculate, according to the above definite integral, the Consumer Surplus at $p_0 = 20$ and $q_0 = 10$.

10. Using the following demand function:

$$q = 10 - 2p^{1/2}$$

calculate the Consumer Surplus at $p_0 = 4$ and $q_0 = 6$.

11. You work as a business consultant for a company. Using the econometric techniques, you have estimated the firm's total cost function as $C(q) = q^3 - 5q^2 + 14q + 75$. Enumerate now the marginal cost function $C'(q)$ and obtain the analytical equation form using the Excel trendline.

## 3.1 Built-in Excel matrix functions and basic operations

The Excel spreadsheet is essentially a double-entry table, where we are required to organize the quantitative information in rows and columns. Therefore, it will not be particularly difficult to get used to the matrix calculations in Excel.

To get started with linear algebra in Excel, we will see first the already built-in functions available, to perform calculations on a single matrix (e.g., determinant or inverse). Luckily, under this point of view, the system offers the most important basic operations. Other matrix operations, like the sum of two matrices, can be implemented instead in a standard fashion, or even implemented via VBA, as desired. Having seen these basic operations, in the following paragraphs we will see the more advanced topics.

When working with matrices in Excel, always remember that often we will have to use the so-called *CSE functions,* namely those functions that need, to work, to be entered selecting the appropriate range and pressing the keys combination *Ctrl + Shift + Enter.*

A matrix $A$ of order $(m \cdot n)$ is defined as a set of $(m \cdot n)$ elements, arranged in a rectangular array in *m rows* and *n columns,* as follows:

$$A = \begin{bmatrix} a_{11} & \cdots & a_{1n} \\ \vdots & \ddots & \vdots \\ a_{m1} & \cdots & a_{mn} \end{bmatrix}.$$

More concisely the matrix $A$ can be also denoted by:

$$A = [a_{ij}] \qquad i = 1, \cdots, m \text{ and } j = 1, \cdots, n$$

If $m = n$, we have a square matrix.

If $m = 1$, we have a $(1 \cdot n)$ matrix, namely the *row vector:*

$$A = [a_{11}, \cdots, a_{1j}, \cdots, a_{1n}].$$

If $n = 1$, we have a $(m \cdot 1)$ matrix, namely the *column vector:*

$$A = \begin{bmatrix} a_{11} \\ \vdots \\ a_{i1} \\ \vdots \\ a_{m1} \end{bmatrix}.$$

A matrix can be also seen as the combination of $n$ column vectors as follows:

$$A = [A^1, \cdots, A^j, \cdots, A^n]$$

or the combination of $m$ row vectors as follows:

$$A = \begin{bmatrix} A^1 \\ \vdots \\ A^i \\ \vdots \\ A^m \end{bmatrix}$$

## Built-in Excel functions

Let us consider the following square matrix of order $(3 \cdot 3)$

$$A = \begin{bmatrix} 1 & 4 & 0 \\ -1 & 3 & 7 \\ 2 & 8 & 5 \end{bmatrix}$$

The above matrix is simply translated in the Excel language as in Fig. 3.1-1:
Let us see now a list of major operations in Excel that we can perform on the matrix $A$.

## Determinant of a matrix (=MDETERM)

The determinant of a square matrix, denoted by:

$$det(A) \text{ or } |A|$$

is a scalar associated to a square matrix, which has the important property to investigate about whether the component vectors of the given matrix are *linearly independent* or not. The *necessary and sufficient condition to have the n component vectors of a square matrix linear independent (l.i.) is that det(A) ≠ 0.*

Sometimes, the fact $det(A) \neq 0$ is of paramount importance: for instance, it is a required condition when we want to solve the systems of linear equations. In other instances, instead

| ◢ | A | B | C |
|---|---|---|---|
| 1 | | **A** | |
| 2 | 1.00 | 4.00 | 0.00 |
| 3 | -1.00 | 3.00 | 7.00 |
| 4 | 2.00 | 8.00 | 5.00 |

FIGURE 3.1-1   The A Matrix in Excel.

we require that the determinant be equal to zero, in order to find the so-called *eigenvalues* and the associated *eigenvectors* of the matrix and this is a key step for the resolution of the systems of linear differential equations (see Chapter 4).

The determinant is a scalar, and we do not need to input the *MDETERM* Excel function as CSE function. The way the determinant is calculated on the matrix in Fig. 3.1-1 is shown in Fig. 3.1-2.

From the determinant formula form, we can also obtain the *leading principal minors*, which represent the determinants of the *leading principal submatrices* that we can extract from the given matrix, starting from the upper-leftmost submatrix. **A leading principal submatrix of order $k$ is determined removing the last $(n-k)$ rows and columns.**

This will be important to study whether the Hessian matrix is positive definite, negative definite, or indefinite in the unconstrained multivariate optimization (see Section 3.4 and Section 5.2).

## Inverse of a matrix (=MINVERSE)

In the elementary algebra the inverse of a scalar $\alpha$ is the scalar $\beta$ such that it turns out:

$$\alpha \cdot \beta = 1$$

or equivalently the scalar $\gamma$ such that:

$$\gamma \cdot \beta = 1.$$

A similar concept operates in the context of matrices.

The *inverse matrix* $A^{-1}$ of a square matrix $A$ is defined as:

$$AA^{-1} = A^{-1}A = I$$

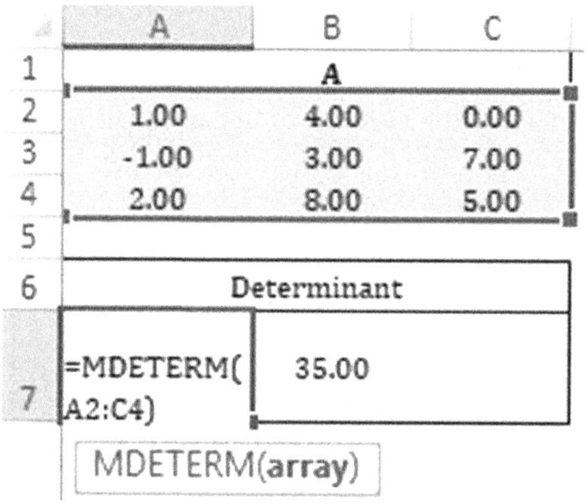

| | A | B | C |
|---|---|---|---|
| 1 | | **A** | |
| 2 | 1.00 | 4.00 | 0.00 |
| 3 | -1.00 | 3.00 | 7.00 |
| 4 | 2.00 | 8.00 | 5.00 |
| 5 | | | |
| 6 | | Determinant | |
| 7 | =MDETERM(A2:C4) | 35.00 | |

MDETERM(**array**)

FIGURE 3.1-2  Determinant of Matrix A det(A) = 35.

where we have denoted with $I$ (or also $I_n$) the *identity matrix*:

$$I = \begin{bmatrix} 1 & \cdots & 0 & 0 \\ \vdots & 1 & 0 & 0 \\ 0 & 0 & 1 & 0 \\ 0 & 0 & 0 & 1 \end{bmatrix}.$$

An identity matrix is essentially a matrix with all elements equal to zero, except for those on the *principal diagonal* which are equal to 1.

The matrix $A$ is said to be **invertible (nonsingular** or **nondegenerate)** if and only if its determinant $\det(A) \neq 0$, otherwise it is said to be **singular**, or **degenerate**, or **nonregular** if $\det(A) = 0$.

Let us calculate in Excel the inverse of the matrix:

$$A = \begin{bmatrix} 1 & 4 & 0 \\ -1 & 3 & 7 \\ 2 & 8 & 5 \end{bmatrix}.$$

We will use the function *MINVERSE*. As the result must be another matrix, this is a CSE function and therefore it needs to be entered as an array formula, pressing $Ctrl + Shift + Enter$.

The way the inverse is calculated is shown in Fig. 3.1-3 (step 1) and Fig. 3.1-4 (step 2). Step 3 is just pressing $Ctrl + Shift + Enter$ obtaining Table 3.1-1.

| | A | B | C |
|---|---|---|---|
| 1 | | **A** | |
| 2 | 1.00 | 4.00 | 0.00 |
| 3 | -1.00 | 3.00 | 7.00 |
| 4 | 2.00 | 8.00 | 5.00 |
| 5 | | | |
| 6 | | Determinant | |
| 7 | | 35.00 | |
| 8 | | | |
| 9 | | Inverse *I* | |
| 10 | | | |
| 11 | | | |
| 12 | | | |

**FIGURE 3.1-3** Step 1: Selection of the array where the Inverse Matrix is needed.

I. Excel and fundamental mathematics for economics

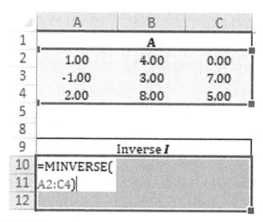

|   | A | B | C |
|---|---|---|---|
| 1 | **A** | | |
| 2 | 1.00 | 4.00 | 0.00 |
| 3 | -1.00 | 3.00 | 7.00 |
| 4 | 2.00 | 8.00 | 5.00 |
| 5 | | | |
| 8 | | | |
| 9 | | Inverse **I** | |
| 10 | =MINVERSE( | | |
| 11 | A2:C4) | | |
| 12 | | | |

**FIGURE 3.1-4**   Step 2: Entering the Inverse Formula.

**TABLE 3.1-1**   Inverse Matrix.

| Inverse **I** | | |
|---|---|---|
| -1.17 | -0.57 | 0.80 |
| 0.54 | 0.14 | -0.20 |
| -0.40 | 0.00 | 0.20 |

## Identity matrix (=MUNIT)

Excel also enables the user to create the identity matrix of any order through the array formula MUNIT.

Let us suppose we want an identity matrix of order $(10 \cdot 10)$, then what we need to do is to select the required range of 10 rows and 10 columns as in Fig. 3.1-5. The array formula MUNIT is inserted in *Cell A1* (Fig. 3.1-6) and finally, pressing *Ctrl + Shift + Enter*, we obtain the identity matrix in Figs 3.1-7.

## Transpose of a matrix (=TRANSPOSE)

From the matrix

$$A = [a_{ij}]$$

we can obtain another matrix $B$ denoted with $A^T$ such that for any element:

$$B = [b_{ij}]$$

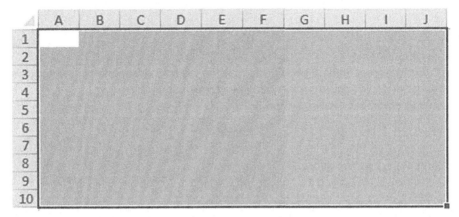

**FIGURE 3.1-5** Selection of the appropriate range (10·10).

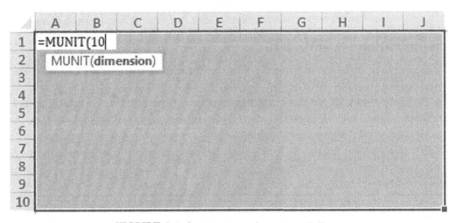

**FIGURE 3.1-6** The Array formula in Cell A1.

| | A | B | C | D | E | F | G | H | I | J |
|---|---|---|---|---|---|---|---|---|---|---|
| 1 | 1 | 0 | 0 | 0 | 0 | 0 | 0 | 0 | 0 | 0 |
| 2 | 0 | 1 | 0 | 0 | 0 | 0 | 0 | 0 | 0 | 0 |
| 3 | 0 | 0 | 1 | 0 | 0 | 0 | 0 | 0 | 0 | 0 |
| 4 | 0 | 0 | 0 | 1 | 0 | 0 | 0 | 0 | 0 | 0 |
| 5 | 0 | 0 | 0 | 0 | 1 | 0 | 0 | 0 | 0 | 0 |
| 6 | 0 | 0 | 0 | 0 | 0 | 1 | 0 | 0 | 0 | 0 |
| 7 | 0 | 0 | 0 | 0 | 0 | 0 | 1 | 0 | 0 | 0 |
| 8 | 0 | 0 | 0 | 0 | 0 | 0 | 0 | 1 | 0 | 0 |
| 9 | 0 | 0 | 0 | 0 | 0 | 0 | 0 | 0 | 1 | 0 |
| 10 | 0 | 0 | 0 | 0 | 0 | 0 | 0 | 0 | 0 | 1 |

**FIGURE 3.1-7** The identity matrix of order (10·10).

I. Excel and fundamental mathematics for economics

it is:

$$b_{ij} = a_{ji}.$$

$A^T$ is called the transpose matrix of $A$, such that the $i$th row of the matrix A becomes the $i$th column of $A^T$ and the $j$th column of A becomes the $j$th row of $A^T$.

If after this operation it turns out that:

$$A = A^T$$

then, $A$ is called a *symmetric matrix*.

Given the matrix $A$ of Table 3.1-2, using the Excel array formula *TRANSPOSE*, $A^T$ is calculated in Table 3.1-3.

The matrix transposition works as well for nonsquare matrices and must be entered as an array formula in a range that has the same number of rows and columns, respectively, as the source range has columns and rows.

## Matrix multiplication ( =MMULT)

Let $A$ be a matrix of order $(m \cdot n)$ and $B$ a matrix of order $(n \cdot q)$, i.e., the number of columns of $A$ is equal to the number of rows of $B$, then the two matrices are *conformable*, and it is possible to multiply them to get the resulting matrix $C$ of order $(m \cdot n)$, such that it is:

$$c_{ij} = A_i B^j$$

TABLE 3.1-2   Matrix A.

| A | | |
|---|---|---|
| 1.00 | 4.00 | 0.00 |
| -1.00 | 3.00 | 7.00 |
| 2.00 | 8.00 | 5.00 |

TABLE 3.1-3   Transpose matrix $A^T$.

| $A^T$ | | |
|---|---|---|
| 1.00 | -1.00 | 2.00 |
| 4.00 | 3.00 | 8.00 |
| 0.00 | 7.00 | 5.00 |

namely, the *scalar product* between the $i$th row of $A$ and the $j$th column of $B$ defined as:

$$A_i B^j = \sum_{k=1}^{n} a_{ik} b_{kj}.$$

When both the products $AB$ and $BA$ are defined, then in general $AB \neq BA$.

Let us multiply in Excel the two matrices $A$ (3·3) and $B$ (3·3) of Fig. 3.1-8. The resulting matrix $C$ will be of order (3·3). First, select the range where to obtain the resulting matrix. Then the array formula *MMULT* has to be input in the activated first *Cell* $c_{11}$ of the matrix $C$. Pressing *Ctrl + Shift + Enter* (see Fig. 3.1-9), we obtain the results in Fig. 3.1-10.

## 3.2 Linear systems and resolution methods in Excel: Cramer, Solver, Inverse

A *nonhomogenous* linear system in $m$ equations, $m$ constant terms, and $n$ unknown $x$ variables is defined as:

$$\begin{cases} a_{11}x_1 + a_{12}x_2 + \cdots + a_{1j}x_j + \cdots + a_{1n}x_n = b_1 \\ a_{21}x_1 + a_{22}x_2 + \cdots + a_{2j}x_j + \cdots + a_{2n}x_n = b_2 \\ \cdots \\ a_{i1}x_1 + a_{i2}x_2 + \cdots + a_{ij}x_j + \cdots + a_{in}x_n = b_i \\ \cdots \\ a_{m1}x_1 + a_{m2}x_2 + \cdots + a_{mj}x_j + \cdots + a_{mn}x_n = b_m \end{cases} \qquad (3.2\text{-}1)$$

The elements $a_{ij}$ are called coefficients of the system and $b_i$ the constant terms. The system 3.2-1 can be also written in the matrix condensed form as:

$$Ax = b$$

with:

$$A = \begin{bmatrix} a_{11} & \cdots & a_{1n} \\ \vdots & \ddots & \vdots \\ a_{m1} & \cdots & a_{mn} \end{bmatrix} ; \quad x = \begin{bmatrix} x_1 \\ \cdots \\ x_j \\ \cdots \\ x_n \end{bmatrix} ; \quad b = \begin{bmatrix} b_1 \\ \cdots \\ b_i \\ \cdots \\ b_m \end{bmatrix}$$

| | A | B | C | D | E | F | G | H | I | J | K |
|---|---|---|---|---|---|---|---|---|---|---|---|
| 1 | | A | | | | B | | | | C | |
| 2 | 1.00 | 4.00 | 0.00 | | 5.00 | 4.00 | 0.00 | | | | |
| 3 | -1.00 | 3.00 | 7.00 | | -1.00 | 6.00 | 7.00 | | | | |
| 4 | 2.00 | 8.00 | 5.00 | | 2.00 | 8.00 | 0.00 | | | | |

FIGURE 3.1-8   Selection of the Range of the resulting Matrix.

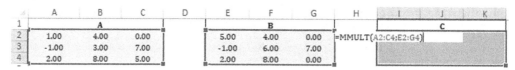

FIGURE 3.1-9    Array formula MMULT.

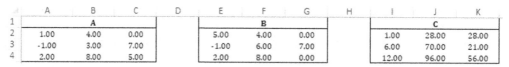

FIGURE 3.1-10    Matrix C = A·B.

The system 3.2-1 is called *homogeneous* if $[b] = 0$ and becomes:

$$Ax = [0].$$

There are also alternative ways to express the system 3.2-1, such as:

$$\sum_{j=1}^{n} a_{ij}x_j = b_i, \quad i = 1, 2, \cdots, m$$

The goal is to find the vector solution $x_1 = \bar{x}_1, x_2 = \bar{x}_2, \cdots, x_j = \bar{x}_j, \cdots x_n = \bar{x}_n$ that satisfies the 3.2-1. To do this in Excel, we will show three techniques:

1. **Cramer's rule.**
2. Resorting to the **inverse matrix** (which is essentially a different formal way of representing the Cramer's rule).
3. **Solver.**

Before advancing, it is highly important, however, that we know the existence of an important theorem, to investigate about the solution of a linear system, which is the following *Rouché–Capelli Theorem.*

## Theorem 1

*Let the system $Ax = b$ have the matrix A of order $(m \cdot n)$ with rank $r(A) = r$. Let $r'$ be the rank of the augmented matrix $[A|b]$. Then, the system $Ax = b$ has a solution if and only if $r = r'$.*

Therefore, when working on a linear system, we should always verify the Rouché–Capelli necessary and sufficient condition, in that if $r \neq r'$ there will not exist any solution.

Some key definitions (theorems) intimately connected are necessary now to be recalled from the theory of linear algebra. The first clarifies the concept of *linear dependence (linear independence)* of a vector, while the second pertains to the *rank of a matrix.*

## Linear dependence (l.d.) versus linear independence (l.i.)

*A set of m vectors $\{x_1, x_2, \cdots, x_m\}$ is said to be l.d. if and only if there exists a set of scalars $\{\lambda_1, \lambda_2, \cdots, \lambda_m\}$, at least one of which is not equal to zero, such that:*

$$\sum_{i=1}^{m} \lambda_i x_i = 0.$$

*If the only set of scalars $\{\lambda_1, \lambda_2, \cdots, \lambda_m\}$ such that $\sum_{i=1}^{m} \lambda_i x_i = 0$ is the set $\{0, 0, \cdots, 0\}$ then the given set of vectors $\{x_1, x_2, \cdots, x_m\}$ is defined to be linearly independent.* The vectors of a matrix A are l.i. if and only if $det(A) \neq 0$.

## Rank of a matrix

The rank of a matrix $A$ corresponds to the maximal number of linearly independent columns (or rows) of $A$. The rank can be found as the maximal order of the nonsingular minors (the determinants of the square submatrices of $A$) that can be extracted from the matrix $A$. The rank can be also seen as a measure of the "nondegenerateness" of the system of linear equations.

From the Rouché–Capelli theorem, for a nonhomogeneous system, it turns out that:

i. if $r(A) = r(A|b) = n$, the solution is unique: we have $\infty^{n-r} = \infty^0 = 1$ solution. **Regular systems.** The $n$ vectors are all l.i.

ii. Otherwise there are infinitely many solutions: if $r(A) = r(A|b) < n$, there exist $\infty^{n-r}$ solutions. If $1 \leq r(A) = r(A|b) < m$, there will be $(m-r)$ redundant equations and there exist $\infty^{n-r}$ solutions. $r$ vectors are l.i., while $(n-r)$ vectors are l.d.

The regular cases where $r(A) = r(A|b) = m = n$ are called **square regular systems** (or **Cramer's systems**), where the coefficient matrix $A$ is square and $det(A) \neq 0$; the solution is unique and to find it we can apply the following **Cramer's rule**.

## Cramer's rule

The solution to the system 3.2-1, with $r(A) = r(A|b) = m = n$, is obtained as follows:

$$x_j = \frac{det(A^j)}{det(A)}, \quad j = 1, 2, \cdots, n$$

*where $det(A^j)$ is the determinant that we can obtain from the matrix A, replacing in A the column $A^j$ with the vector [b].*

## EXAMPLE 1 ($r = m = n$)

Let us have the following system with matrix A of order $(3 \cdot 3)$:

$$\begin{cases} x_1 + x_2 + x_3 = 1 \\ x_1 - x_2 + 4x_3 = 2 \\ 3x_1 + x_3 = 3 \end{cases}$$

The above system can be rewritten as:

$$\begin{bmatrix} 1 & 1 & 1 \\ 1 & -1 & 4 \\ 3 & 0 & 1 \end{bmatrix} \begin{bmatrix} x_1 \\ x_2 \\ x_3 \end{bmatrix} = \begin{bmatrix} 1 \\ 2 \\ 3 \end{bmatrix}.$$

It turns out that $det(A) \neq 0 = 13$ and $A$ is therefore nonsingular. In Excel, we set up the system as in Fig. 3.2-1.

The goal is to find the correct values under *Range D2:D4* such that when this array is premultiplied by the matrix $A$ the result is vector $[b]$. The Cramer's rule in Excel is shown beside the three matrices $A^1$, $A^2$, $A^3$, obtaining the results in Table 3.2-1.

### Inverse matrix resolution

Let us apply now to the system of Example 1 the technique of the inverse matrix. This technique is applicable if and only if $det(A) \neq 0$. In this case, the solution of the system:

$$Ax = b$$

is then

$$x = A^{-1}b.$$

It can be proved that, this is another formal way to look at the Cramer's rule.

| | A | B | C | D | E |
|---|---|---|---|---|---|
| 1 | | A | | x | b |
| 2 | 1 | 1 | 1 | 1 | =MMULT(A2:C4;D2:D4) |
| 3 | 1 | -1 | 4 | 1 | =MMULT(A2:C4;D2:D4) |
| 4 | 3 | 0 | 1 | 1 | =MMULT(A2:C4;D2:D4) |
| 5 | | | | | |
| 6 | | $A^1$ | | | |
| 7 | 1 | 1 | 1 | | |
| 8 | 2 | -1 | 4 | $x_1 = det(A^1)/det(A)$ | =MDETERM(A7:C9)/MDETERM($A$2:$C$4) |
| 9 | 3 | 0 | 1 | | |
| 10 | | | | | |
| 11 | | $A^2$ | | | |
| 12 | 1 | 1 | 1 | | |
| 13 | 1 | 2 | 4 | $x_2 = det(A^2)/det(A)$ | =MDETERM(A12:C14)/MDETERM($A$2:$C$4) |
| 14 | 3 | 3 | 1 | | |
| 15 | | | | | |
| 16 | | $A^3$ | | | |
| 17 | 1 | 1 | 1 | | |
| 18 | 1 | -1 | 2 | $x_3 = det(A^3)/det(A)$ | =MDETERM(A17:C19)/MDETERM($A$2:$C$4) |
| 19 | 3 | 0 | 3 | | |

FIGURE 3.2-1   Cramer's rule Excel set-up of example 1.

**TABLE 3.2-1** Cramer's solution of Example 1.

| A | | | x | b |
|---|---|---|---|---|
| 1.00 | 1.00 | 1.00 | 0.92 | 1.00 |
| 1.00 | -1.00 | 4.00 | -0.15 | 2.00 |
| 3.00 | 0.00 | 1.00 | 0.23 | 3.00 |

| $A^1$ | | | | |
|---|---|---|---|---|
| **1.00** | 1.00 | 1.00 | | |
| **2.00** | -1.00 | 4.00 | $x_1 = det(A^1)/det(A)$ | 0.92 |
| **3.00** | 0.00 | 1.00 | | |

| $A^2$ | | | | |
|---|---|---|---|---|
| 1.00 | **1.00** | 1.00 | | |
| 1.00 | **2.00** | 4.00 | $x_2 = det(A^2)/det(A)$ | -0.15 |
| 3.00 | **3.00** | 1.00 | | |

| $A^3$ | | | | |
|---|---|---|---|---|
| 1.00 | 1.00 | **1.00** | | |
| 1.00 | -1.00 | **2.00** | $x_3 = det(A^3)/det(A)$ | 0.23 |
| 3.00 | 0.00 | **3.00** | | |

With the system of Example 1, we have $det(A) = 13$ and $A$ is nonsingular.

The Excel is organized as in Fig. 3.2-2, where we set the inverse $A^{-1}$ and the vector $[b]$ as inputs, while the vector $[x]$, as output via the *MMULT* formula, is stored in the third column range (Table 3.2-2).

## Solver resolution

Continuing Example 1, via the Excel Solver, we essentially search for the optimal solution $x_1^*, x_2^*, x_3^*$ such that:

$$\begin{bmatrix} 1 & 1 & 1 \\ 1 & -1 & 4 \\ 3 & 0 & 1 \end{bmatrix} \begin{bmatrix} x_1^* \\ x_2^* \\ x_3^* \end{bmatrix} = \begin{bmatrix} 1 \\ 2 \\ 3 \end{bmatrix}.$$

We transform the problem somehow in a sort of optimization problem as in Fig. 3.2-3. As the system is linear, we may want to change the GRG Nonlinear Solver into Linear Simplex (see Fig. 3.2-4).

| A⁻¹ | | | b | x |
|---|---|---|---|---|
| =MINVERSE(A2:C4) | =MINVERSE(A2:C4) | =MINVERSE(A2:C4) | 1 | =MMULT(A24:C26;D24:D26) |
| =MINVERSE(A2:C4) | =MINVERSE(A2:C4) | =MINVERSE(A2:C4) | 2 | =MMULT(A24:C26;D24:D26) |
| =MINVERSE(A2:C4) | =MINVERSE(A2:C4) | =MINVERSE(A2:C4) | 3 | =MMULT(A24:C26;D24:D26) |

FIGURE 3.2-2　Example 1 Calculation of the Inverse to find the vector solution.

TABLE 3.2-2　Solution of Example 1 via the inverse matrix.

| A⁻¹ | | | b | x |
|---|---|---|---|---|
| -0.08 | -0.08 | 0.38 | 1.00 | 0.92 |
| 0.85 | -0.15 | -0.23 | 2.00 | -0.15 |
| 0.23 | 0.23 | -0.15 | 3.00 | 0.23 |

| | A | B | C | D | E |
|---|---|---|---|---|---|
| | | A | | x | b |
| 1 | | | | x | b |
| 2 | 1.00 | 1.00 | 1.00 | 0.92 | 1.00 |
| 3 | 1.00 | -1.00 | 4.00 | -0.15 | 2.00 |
| 4 | 3.00 | 0.00 | 1.00 | 0.23 | 3.00 |
| 5 | | | | | |
| 6 | s.t. | | | | |
| 7 | b1 | 1.00 | | | |
| 8 | b2 | 2.00 | | | |
| 9 | b3 | 3.00 | | | |
| 10 | | | | | |

FIGURE 3.2-3　Solver Solution for the given system [A][x] = [b].

## EXAMPLE 2 (r = m < n)

Let us have the following linear system with matrix A of order $(m \cdot n) = (2 \cdot 3)$:

$$\begin{cases} 3x_1 + 5x_1 - 20x_3 = 1 \\ x_1 - x_2 + 4x_3 = 2 \end{cases}$$

which can be transformed in the following matrix notation:

$$\begin{bmatrix} 3 & 5 & -20 \\ 1 & -1 & 4 \end{bmatrix} \begin{bmatrix} x_1 \\ x_2 \end{bmatrix} = \begin{bmatrix} 1 \\ 2 \end{bmatrix}.$$

The matrix of the system is noninvertible (or singular), and $r(A) = 2 < n = 3$ as we can calculate the following minor of order 2:

$$\begin{vmatrix} 3 & 5 \\ 1 & -1 \end{vmatrix} = -8 \neq 0.$$

**FIGURE 3.2-4**  Solver Setup for the given system [A][x] = [b] in Fig. 3.2-3.

The following augmented matrix $[A|b]$:

$$\begin{bmatrix} 3 & 5 & -20 & 1 \\ 1 & -1 & 4 & 2 \end{bmatrix}$$

as well has the rank $r(A|b) = 2$ and the Rouché–Capelli theorem is satisfied, i.e., $r(A) = r(A|b)$, to guarantee the possibility for at least one solution.

More specifically, the system will have $\infty^{n-r} = \infty^{3-2} = \infty^1$ solutions, and we will see now how to find one solution of these infinite solutions.

The way this is done is solving the following system, where we have moved to the right-hand side of the equations the coefficients not included in the above calculated minor to determine the rank:

$$\begin{cases} 3x_1 + 5x_1 = 1 + 20\bar{x}_3 \\ x_1 - x_2 = 2 - 4\bar{x}_3 \end{cases}$$

and where we also have assigned an arbitrary value to the third unknown, such as $\bar{x}_3 = 1$. Then, the system can be solved via the usual Cramer's rule, inverse, and Solver as shown in Table 3.2-3.

**TABLE 3.2-3**   Solution of a (3•2) system in Example 2.

| A | | | x | b |
|---|---|---|---|---|
| 3.00 | 5.00 | -20.00 | 0.00 | #VALUE! |
| 1.00 | -1.00 | 4.00 | 0.00 | #VALUE! |
| | | | | |
| A (Removing 3rd column) | | | x | b |
| 3.00 | 5.00 | -20.00 | 1.38 | 21.00 |
| 1.00 | -1.00 | 4.00 | 3.38 | -2.00 |

Cramer

| $A^1$ | |
|---|---|
| 21.00 | 5.00 |
| -2.00 | -1.00 |

$x_1 = det(A^1)/det(A)$      1.38

| $A^2$ | |
|---|---|
| 3.00 | 21.00 |
| 1.00 | -2.00 |

$x_2 = det(A^2)/det(A)$      3.38

Solver

| A | | x | b |
|---|---|---|---|
| 3.00 | 5.00 | 1.38 | 21.00 |
| 1.00 | -1.00 | 3.38 | -2.00 |

Inverse

| $A^{-1}$ | | b | x |
|---|---|---|---|
| 0.13 | 0.63 | 21.00 | 1.38 |
| 0.13 | -0.38 | -2.00 | 3.38 |

## EXAMPLE 3 ($1 \le r < m$)

Let us solve the following linear system:

$$\begin{cases} x_1 + x_2 + x_3 = -1 \\ 2x_1 + 2x_2 + 2x_3 = -2 \\ 2x_1 + x_2 + x_3 = 0 \end{cases}$$

The coefficients matrix $A$ is:

$$A = \begin{bmatrix} 1 & 1 & 1 \\ 2 & 2 & 2 \\ 2 & 1 & 1 \end{bmatrix}$$

which is noninvertible (or singular, or degenerate). It is easy to inspect that the nondegenerate submatrix of order 2:

$$A_2 = \begin{bmatrix} 2 & 2 \\ 2 & 1 \end{bmatrix}$$

has the determinant $\det(A_2) \neq 0 = -2$, and therefore the rank of the matrix $A$ is:

$$r(A) = 2 < m = n.$$

It also turns out that the augmented matrix has rank $r(A|b) = 2$, and therefore the Rouché–Capelli theorem is satisfied, making possible the resolution of the system.

More specifically, to find at least one solution we proceed as follows:

i. $(m-r) = (3-2) = 1$ equation is redundant, and it has to be removed from the resolution procedure, and the system will admit $\infty^{n-r} = \infty^{3-2} = \infty^1$ solutions. Which equation do we have to remove? The first one, whose coefficients have not been used to calculate the rank;

ii. $(n-r) = (3-2) = 1$ column coefficients (i.e., the third column coefficients, not used to calculate the rank) must be moved to the right-hand side of the system, having the following new system:

$$\begin{cases} 2x_1 + 2x_2 = -2\bar{x}_3 - 2 \\ 2x_1 + x_2 = -\bar{x}_3 \end{cases}.$$

To obtain one solution among the infinite solutions, we assign the arbitrary value to $\bar{x}_3 = 1$ and we solve the system using the three techniques (Cramer, inverse, Solver) as in Table 3.2-4. The dark area is the information that has been manipulated in order to find the final system of order $(2 \cdot 2)$.

The procedures seen in Examples 1, 2, and 3 can also be applied to the homogeneous system:

$$Ax = [0].$$

with matrix $A$ of order $(m \cdot n)$.

If $r(A) = n$, the system will only admit the trivial solution $[x] = 0$, otherwise if $r(A) < n$, with $m = n$ or $m \neq n$, the system will admit the trivial solution and the nontrivial infinite

**TABLE 3.2-4**   Solution of a $(3 \cdot 3)$ system in Example 3.

| A | | | x | b |
|---|---|---|---|---|
| 1.00 | 1.00 | 1.00 | 1.00 | 3.00 |
| 2.00 | 2.00 | 2.00 | 1.00 | 6.00 |
| 2.00 | 1.00 | 1.00 | 1.00 | 4.00 |

| A (removing 1st row and 3rd column) | | | x | b |
|---|---|---|---|---|
| 1.00 | 1.00 | 1.00 | 1.00 | -1.00 |
| 2.00 | 2.00 | 2.00 | 1.00 | -4.00 |
| 2.00 | 1.00 | 1.00 | -3.00 | -1.00 |

**Cramer**

| $A^1$ | | |
|---|---|---|
| 1.00 | 1.00 | 1.00 |
| -4.00 | 2.00 | 2.00 |
| -1.00 | 1.00 | 1.00 |

$x_1 = det(A^1)/det(A)$     1.00

| $A^2$ | | |
|---|---|---|
| 1.00 | 1.00 | 1.00 |
| 2.00 | -4.00 | 2.00 |
| 2.00 | -1.00 | 1.00 |

$x_2 = det(A^2)/det(A)$     -3.00

**Solver**

| A | | x | b |
|---|---|---|---|
| 2.00 | 2.00 | 1.00 | -4.00 |
| 2.00 | 1.00 | -3.00 | -1.00 |

solutions. It is apparent, therefore, that the system $Ax = [0]$ with square matrix of order $m = n$ will also admit the nontrivial solutions if and only if $det(A)$ 0.

## EXAMPLE 4 (HOMOGENEOUS SYSTEM r < n = m)

Let us solve the following system in three unknowns and three equations:

$$\begin{cases} 3x_1 + 5x_2 + 7x_3 = 0 \\ -x_1 + 7x_2 + 3x_3 = 0 \\ x_1 + 6x_2 + 5x_3 = 0 \end{cases}$$

The system will always admit the trivial solution $[x] = 0$. The objective is now to find at least one nontrivial solution.

The system matrix $A$ of order $(3 \cdot 3)$ is as follows:

$$A = \begin{bmatrix} 3 & 5 & 7 \\ -1 & 7 & 3 \\ 1 & 6 & 5 \end{bmatrix}$$

which is degenerate as $det(A) = 0$. The rank of the matrix is $r(A) = 2$ as the following minor of order 2 can be extracted from the original matrix $A$:

$$\begin{vmatrix} 3 & 5 \\ -1 & 7 \end{vmatrix} = 26 \neq 0.$$

We also have that the augmented matrix $[A|b]$ has rank $r(A|b) = 2$ and the Rouché–Capelli is therefore satisfied, to have at least one nontrivial solution.

Now, what we have to do is to manipulate the system as follows:

i. Removing $(m-r) = (3-2) = 1$ equation from the system. The equation to be removed is the third one, whose coefficients do not enter for the calculation of the rank;

ii. Moving on the right-hand side of the system $(n-r) = (3-2) = 1$ column (i.e., the third one with coefficients not entered in the rank calculation). There will exist $\infty^{n-r} = \infty^{3-2} = \infty^1$ nontrivial solutions.

The original $(3 \cdot 3)$ system is then reformulated into the following $(2 \cdot 2)$:

$$\begin{cases} 3x_1 + 5x_2 = -7\bar{x}_3 \\ -x_1 + 7x_2 = -3\bar{x}_3 \end{cases}$$

which can be solved $\forall \bar{x}_3$ and setting, for example, $\bar{x}_3 = 1$, we have the nontrivial solution in Table 3.2-5.

## Remark 1

The homogeneous system is always solvable, in that it always admits the trivial solution. The system will admit the nontrivial solutions if and only if $det(A) = 0$. This degenerateness condition on the coefficient matrix will be of paramount importance for the eigenvalues and eigenvectors problems.

## Remark 2

The complete system:

$$Ax = [b].$$

**TABLE 3.2-5**  Solution of a (3·3) homogeneous system in Example 4.

| A | | | x | b |
|---|---|---|---|---|
| 3.00 | 5.00 | 7.00 | 1.00 | 15.00 |
| -1.00 | 7.00 | 3.00 | 1.00 | 9.00 |
| 1.00 | 6.00 | 5.00 | 1.00 | 12.00 |

| A (removing 3rd row and 3rd column) | | | x | b |
|---|---|---|---|---|
| 3.00 | 5.00 | 7.00 | 0.00 | -1.00 |
| -1.00 | 7.00 | 3.00 | -1.31 | -3.00 |
| 1.00 | 6.00 | 5.00 | -0.62 | -5.00 |

**Cramer**

| $A^1$ | | | | |
|---|---|---|---|---|
| -7.00 | 5.00 | 7.00 | | |
| -3.00 | 7.00 | 3.00 | $x_1 = \det(A^1)/\det(A)$ | -1.3077 |
| 1.00 | 6.00 | 5.00 | | |

| $A^2$ | | | | |
|---|---|---|---|---|
| 3.00 | -7.00 | 7.00 | | |
| -1.00 | -3.00 | 3.00 | $x_2 = \det(A^2)/\det(A)$ | -0.6154 |
| 1.00 | 6.00 | 5.00 | | |

**Solver**

| A | | x | b |
|---|---|---|---|
| 3.00 | 5.00 | -1.31 | -7.00 |
| -1.00 | 7.00 | -0.62 | -3.00 |

is instead either possible or impossible to solve, depending on the Rouché–Capelli theorem. If this is satisfied, there will exist either one or infinitely many solutions. The case of many finite solutions is therefore excluded. If the Rouché–Capelli is not satisfied the system has no solution.

## Remark 3

The general solution of the complete system can be always obtained as the sum of the general solution of the homogeneous system and the particular solution of the complete system. See the system of linear differential equations Section 4.5.

To show Remark 1, consider the following example, where we have that rank equal to $m$ and equal to $n$ as well.

## EXAMPLE 5 (HOMOGENEOUS SYSTEM $r = n = m$)

$$\begin{cases} x_1 + x_2 + x_3 = 0 \\ x_1 - x_2 + x_3 = 0 \\ x_1 - x_2 - x_3 = 0 \end{cases}$$

The solution is in Table 3.2-6, and since the system has a nondegenerate coefficients matrix, there will only exist the trivial solution.

It is apparent therefore that if we want to search nontrivial solutions, these solutions are linked to the fact that $det(A) = 0$ so that we decrease the rank of the matrix.

Fig. 3.2-5 summarizes within a flowchart framework the steps to follow for the solutions of a linear system.

## 3.3 Eigenvalues and eigenvectors search: analytical and graphical approach

An important section of the theory of linear algebra is dedicated to finding the so-called **eigenvalues** (or **characteristic values**) and **eigenvectors** (or **characteristic vectors**). We will use them to solve the system of linear differential equations using the direct method (see Section 4.5).

Given a square matrix $A$ of order $n$, the problem is to find the values of the parameter $\lambda$ such that the following is satisfied:

$$Ax = \lambda x \tag{3.3-1}$$

Eq. (3.3-1) can be restated as follows:

$$Ax - \lambda x = [0] \Rightarrow Ax - \lambda I x = [0]$$

namely:

$$(A - \lambda I)x = [0] \tag{3.3-2}$$

Eq. (3.3-2) is a homogeneous system, which will always admit the trivial solution if and only if $(A - \lambda I)$ is nondegenerate:

$$\det(A - \lambda I) \neq 0.$$

**TABLE 3.2-6** Trivial solution as $det(A) = 4$.

| A | | | x | b |
|---|---|---|---|---|
| 1.00 | 1.00 | 1.00 | 0.00 | 0.00 |
| 1.00 | -1.00 | 1.00 | 0.00 | 0.00 |
| 1.00 | -1.00 | -1.00 | 0.00 | 0.00 |

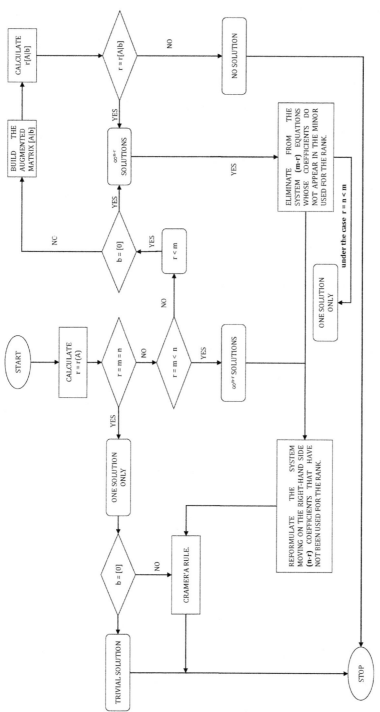

**FIGURE 3.2-5** Flow-chart solution framework for the linear system $Ax = b$.

As our objective is to find the nontrivial solution, we have to set therefore the following "degenerateness" condition:

$$\det(A - \lambda I) = 0 \tag{3.3-3}$$

in order to have $rank(A - \lambda I) < n$.

Eq. (3.3-3) is called the **characteristic equation** of matrix A, and it can also be expressed in the form:

$$\begin{vmatrix} (a_{11} - \lambda) & a_{12} & \cdots & a_{1n} \\ a_{21} & (a_{22} - \lambda) & \cdots & a_{2n} \\ \vdots & \vdots & \vdots & \vdots \\ a_{n1} & \cdots & \cdots & (a_{nn} - \lambda) \end{vmatrix} = 0$$

which is a standard algebraic $n$ *polynomial* in $\lambda$ :

$$(-\lambda)^n + b_{n-1}(-\lambda)^{n-1} + \cdots + b_1(\lambda) + b_0 = 0$$

that will admit the following $n$ real or complex roots:

$$\lambda_1, \lambda_2, \cdots, \lambda_n$$

called **eigenvalues**, or **characteristic values** of the matrix A. Each vector $x \neq [0]$ that satisfies Eq. (3.3-2) for each eigenvalue is called **eigenvector**.

In the case where $n = 2$, we can also notice that the determinant 3.3-3 becomes:

$$\begin{vmatrix} a_{11} - \lambda & a_{12} \\ a_{21} & a_{22} - \lambda \end{vmatrix} = 0$$

which is, after rearranging:

$$\lambda^2 - (a_{11} + a_{22})\lambda + (a_{11}a_{22} - a_{12}a_{21}) = 0.$$

The above characteristic equation can be written also as:

$$\lambda^2 - tr(A)\lambda + |A| = 0 \tag{3.3-4}$$

where $tr(A)$ is the **trace** of the matrix $A$:

$$tr(A) = a_{11} + a_{22}$$

and $|A|$ the determinant of the matrix $A$:

$$a_{11}a_{22} - a_{12}a_{21}.$$

The two roots of the quadratic characteristic Eq. (3.3-4) are then:

$$\lambda_1, \lambda_2 = \frac{tr(A)}{2} \pm \frac{1}{2}\sqrt{tr(A)^2 - 4|A|}. \tag{3.3-5}$$

Once the eigenvalues of matrix $A$ are found, as said before, we need to solve for the eigenvectors the following system:

$$(A - \lambda_k I)x = [0]. \tag{3.3-6}$$

Now, since $\lambda_k$ have been found to make the matrix $(A - \lambda_k I)$ degenerate, i.e., its determinant equal to zero, from the previous paragraph we know that the system 3.3-6 will have rank equal:

$$r(A - \lambda_k I) < m = n$$

and therefore, the system will admit $\infty^{n-r}$ nontrivial solutions (as well as the trivial solution) eliminating $(m-r) = (n-r)$ equations.

To solve the problem of eigenvalues and eigenvectors in Excel, we will resort to these two techniques:

1. Analytical method, following the same steps as the matrix-based calculus, using also the Excel Solver.
2. Graphical approach, for the case $n = 2$, finding the associated characteristic roots of the quadratic equation.

## Example 1

Let us find the eigenvalues and the associated eigenvectors for the following matrix:

$$A = \begin{bmatrix} 4 & -3 \\ 2 & -1 \end{bmatrix}.$$

As $n = 2$, before going to Excel, we will also show the simple procedure. From Eq. (3.3-3), we have the following characteristic equation:

$$\begin{vmatrix} 4 - \lambda & -3 \\ 2 & -1 - \lambda \end{vmatrix} = \lambda^2 - 3\lambda + 2 \Rightarrow \begin{cases} \lambda_1 = 2 \\ \lambda_2 = 1 \end{cases}.$$

Applying directly Eq. (3.3-5), we have:

$$\lambda_1, \lambda_2 = \frac{3}{2} \pm \frac{1}{2}\sqrt{3^2 - 4(-4+6)} = \frac{3}{2} \pm \frac{1}{2}\sqrt{1} \Rightarrow \begin{cases} \lambda_1 = 2 \\ \lambda_2 = 1 \end{cases}.$$

To find the eigenvectors, we proceed as follows:
For $\lambda_1 = 2$, Eq. (3.3-2) becomes:

$$(A - 2I)x^1 = [0]$$

$$\Rightarrow \begin{bmatrix} 2 & -3 \\ 2 & -3 \end{bmatrix} \begin{bmatrix} x_1 \\ x_2 \end{bmatrix} = [0]$$

which is:

$$\begin{cases} 2x_1 - 3x_2 = 0 \\ 2x_1 - 3x_2 = 0 \end{cases} \Rightarrow \begin{cases} x_2 = \dfrac{2}{3}x_1 \\ x_2 = \dfrac{2}{3}x_1 \end{cases}$$

There will be then an infinite number of eigenvectors satisfying the above system. Setting, for example, $x_1 = 3$, we have $x_2 = 2$, the first eigenvector can be:

$$x^1 = \begin{bmatrix} 3 \\ 2 \end{bmatrix}.$$

For $\lambda_2 = 1$, Eq. (3.3-2) becomes

$$(A - 1I)x^1 = [0]$$

$$\Rightarrow \begin{bmatrix} 3 & -3 \\ 2 & -2 \end{bmatrix} \begin{bmatrix} x_1 \\ x_2 \end{bmatrix} = [0]$$

which is:

$$\begin{cases} 3x_1 - 3x_2 = 0 \\ 2x_1 - 2x_2 = 0 \end{cases} \Rightarrow \begin{cases} x_2 = x_1 \\ x_2 = x_1 \end{cases}$$

Setting, for example, $x_1 = 3$, we have $x_2 = 3$ and the second eigenvector can be:

$$x^2 = \begin{bmatrix} 3 \\ 3 \end{bmatrix}.$$

We calculate now the so-called normalized eigenvectors. These can be found satisfying the following Euclidean distance condition, or normalization condition:

$$x_1^2 + x_2^2 = 1.$$

For $\lambda_1 = 2$ and from $x_2 = \frac{2}{3}x_1$ we have:

$$(x_1)^2 + \frac{4}{9}x_1^2 = 1 \Rightarrow \frac{13}{9}x_1^2 = 1 \Rightarrow x_1 = \pm\sqrt{\frac{9}{13}} = \pm\frac{3}{\sqrt{13}}$$

$$x_1 = +\frac{3}{\sqrt{13}} \Rightarrow x_2 = \frac{2}{\sqrt{13}}.$$

For $\lambda_1 = 1$ and from $x_2 = x_1$, we have:

$$x_1^2 + x_1^2 = 1 \Rightarrow 2x_1^2 = 1 \Rightarrow x_1 = \pm\frac{1}{\sqrt{2}}$$

$$x_1 = +\frac{1}{\sqrt{2}} \Rightarrow x_2 = +\frac{1}{\sqrt{2}}$$

Let us go to Excel and let us set up the worksheet represented in Figs. 3.3-1 and 3.3-2. Fig. 3.3-1 is where we set up the homogenous system and where we verify the degenerateness condition $det(A-\lambda I)=0$, while Fig. 3.3-2 is where we store the analytical formula 3.3-4 of the eigenvalues that are recalled in the Cells B2, C3, H2, I3.

To calculate the eigenvectors, we require the assistance of the Excel Solver (see Fig. 3.3-3) where we set the constraints $b1 = b2 = 0$, i.e., the homogeneous system itself. The Solver has to be launched twice for the two eigenvectors, changing the range of the cells: i.e., Fig. 3.3-3 is the optimization for $x^1$ only. It is also advisable to insert two approximate integers into Cells D2 and D3, in order to avoid the trivial solution and to force the Solver to find the nontrivial solutions (see Table 3.3-1).

To find the two eigenvalues, we can also proceed by plotting the characteristic equation for various values of $\lambda$:

$$det(A - \lambda I) = \begin{vmatrix} 4 - \lambda & -3 \\ 2 & -1 - \lambda \end{vmatrix}.$$

This is done in Fig. 3.3-4 (and therefore Fig. 3.3-5), where we have the Excel setup of the determinant as a function of $\lambda$, together with the enumeration of the results.

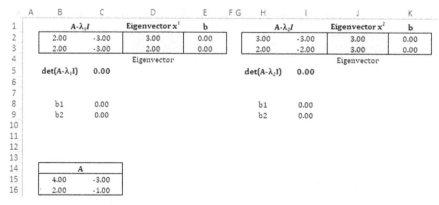

FIGURE 3.3-1   Eigenvalues and eigenvectors Excel setup.

| N | O |
|---|---|
| $\lambda_1$ | $\lambda_2$ |
| =((B15+C16)/2)+1/2*SQRT((B15+C16)^2-4*MDETERM(B15:C16) | =(B15+C16)/2-1/2*SQRT((B15+C16)^2-4*MDETERM(B15:C16)) |

**FIGURE 3.3-2**  Eigenvalue formulas.

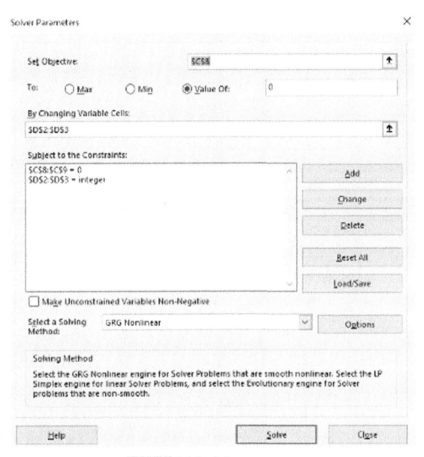

**FIGURE 3.3-3**  Solver parameters.

**TABLE 3.3-1**  Eigenvalues and eigenvectors solutions.

| A-$\lambda_1 I$ | | Eigenvector $x^1$ | b | A-$\lambda_2 I$ | | Eigenvector $x^2$ | b | $\lambda_1$ | $\lambda_2$ |
|---|---|---|---|---|---|---|---|---|---|
| 2.00 | -3.00 | 3.00 | 0.00 | 3.00 | -3.00 | 3.00 | 0.00 | 2.00 | 1.00 |
| 2.00 | -3.00 | 2.00 | 0.00 | 2.00 | -2.00 | 3.00 | 0.00 | | |
| | | Eigenvector | | | | Eigenvector | | | |
| det(A-$\lambda_1 I$) | 0.00 | | | det(A-$\lambda_2 I$) | 0.00 | | | | |
| | | | | | | | | | |
| b1 | 0.00 | | | b1 | 0.00 | | | | |
| b2 | 0.00 | | | b2 | 0.00 | | | | |

| λ | Det = $f(λ)$ | λ | Det = $f(λ)$ |
|------|------------------------------------------------|--------|--------|
| -1 | =($B$15-K16)*($C$16-K16)-($B$16*$C$15) | -1.00 | 6.00 |
| -0.5 | =($B$15-K17)*($C$16-K17)-($B$16*$C$15) | -0.50 | 3.75 |
| 0 | =($B$15-K18)*($C$16-K18)-($B$16*$C$15) | 0.00 | 2.00 |
| 0.5 | =($B$15-K19)*($C$16-K19)-($B$16*$C$15) | 0.50 | 0.75 |
| 1 | =($B$15-K20)*($C$16-K20)-($B$16*$C$15) | 1.00 | 0.00 |
| 1.5 | =($B$15-K21)*($C$16-K21)-($B$16*$C$15) | 1.50 | -0.25 |
| 2 | =($B$15-K22)*($C$16-K22)-($B$16*$C$15) | 2.00 | 0.00 |
| 2.5 | =($B$15-K23)*($C$16-K23)-($B$16*$C$15) | 2.50 | 0.75 |
| 3 | =($B$15-K24)*($C$16-K24)-($B$16*$C$15) | 3.00 | 2.00 |
| 3.5 | =($B$15-K25)*($C$16-K25)-($B$16*$C$15) | 3.50 | 3.75 |
| 4 | =($B$15-K26)*($C$16-K26)-($B$16*$C$15) | 4.00 | 6.00 |
| 4.5 | =($B$15-K27)*($C$16-K27)-($B$16*$C$15) | 4.50 | 8.75 |
| 5 | =($B$15-K28)*($C$16-K28)-($B$16*$C$15) | 5.00 | 12.00 |
| 5.5 | =($B$15-K29)*($C$16-K29)-($B$16*$C$15) | 5.50 | 15.75 |
| 6 | =($B$15-K30)*($C$16-K30)-($B$16*$C$15) | 6.00 | 20.00 |
| 6.5 | =($B$15-K31)*($C$16-K31)-($B$16*$C$15) | 6.50 | 24.75 |
| 7 | =($B$15-K32)*($C$16-K32)-($B$16*$C$15) | 7.00 | 30.00 |
| 7.5 | =($B$15-K33)*($C$16-K33)-($B$16*$C$15) | 7.50 | 35.75 |
| 8 | =($B$15-K34)*($C$16-K34)-($B$16*$C$15) | 8.00 | 42.00 |

FIGURE 3.3-4    Function det = $f(λ)$ and Numerical Solution.

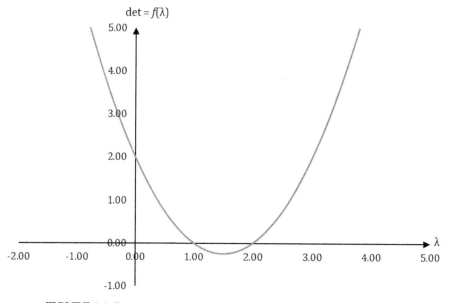

FIGURE 3.3-5    Diagram of the Characteristic Equation and the two Roots.

## 3.4 Quadratic forms and definiteness of a symmetric matrix

Another important problem of linear algebra and economic applications is represented by the **quadratic form**, which is given by the following expression:

$$Q(x) = \sum_{i=1}^{n} \sum_{j=1}^{n} a_{ij} x_i x_j, \tag{3.4-1}$$

or, in a complete extended form, by the following:

$$\begin{cases} a_{11}x_1x_1 + a_{12}x_1x_2 + \cdots + a_{1j}x_1x_j + \cdots + a_{1n}x_1x_n + \\ + a_{21}x_2x_1 + a_{22}x_2x_2 + \cdots + a_{2j}x_2x_j + \cdots + a_{2n}x_2x_n + \\ \cdots \\ + a_{i1}x_ix_1 + a_{i2}x_ix_2 + \cdots + a_{ij}x_ix_j + \cdots + a_{in}x_ix_n + \\ \cdots \\ + a_{n1}x_nx_1 + a_{n2}x_nx_2 + \cdots + a_{nj}x_nx_j + \cdots + a_{nn}x_nx_n, \end{cases}$$

Eq. (3.4-1) can be extremely abbreviated using the matrix notation:

$$Q(x) = x^T A x. \tag{3.4-2}$$

The quadratic form is a **function**, $f : \Re^n \to \Re$, of the vector $x$ and therefore once this vector is assigned, Eq. (3.4-2) reduces to a scalar.

An important quadratic form application is that related to the variance of a portfolio, where the matrix $A$ is the symmetric matrix of variances and covariances (see Chapter 8). Another important application of the quadratic form is also used in the multivariate optimization to investigate whether a stationary point is a maximum, minimum, or a saddle point.

We will always suppose that the matrix $A$ is symmetric. If $A$ is not symmetric, it can always be replaced by the following symmetric matrix:

$$\frac{1}{2}(A + A^T).$$

The fact that $A$ is symmetric helps a lot in shrinking Eq. (3.4-1). In the case $A$ is symmetric the coefficient of $x_i x_j$ is equal to $a_{ij}$ if $i = j$, while it turns out that $a_{ij} = a_{ji}$ if $i \neq j$ and therefore the coefficient of $x_i x_j$ will be equal to $2a_{ij}$.

In case of a symmetric matrix the quadratic form becomes:

$$\begin{aligned} Q(x) ={}& a_{11}(x_1)^2 + a_{22}(x_2)^2 + \cdots + a_{nn}(x_2)^2 + \\ & +2a_{12}x_1x_2 + 2a_{13}x_1x_3 + \cdots + 2a_{n-1,n}x_{n-1}x_n \end{aligned} \tag{3.4-3}$$

## Definiteness of $Q(x)$

The quadratic form can be **definite, semidefinite,** or **indefinite.**

**i.** $Q(x) = x^T Ax$ is definite if it always shows the same sign $\forall x \in \Re^n$, so that:
**1.1.** $Q(x)$ is positive definite if:

$$Q(x) > 0, \qquad \forall\ x \neq [0]$$

**1.2.** $Q(x)$ is negative definite if:

$$Q(x) < 0, \qquad \forall\ x \neq [0].$$

**ii.** $Q(x) = x^T Ax$ is semidefinite if it always shows the same sign but it is equal to zero for some $x \in \Re^n$, being $Q(x) = 0$ at least for one $x$, so that:
**2.1.** $Q(x)$ is positive semidefinite if:

$$Q(x) \geq 0, \qquad \forall\ x \neq [0]$$

**2.2.** $Q(x)$ is negative semidefinite if:

$$Q(x) \leq 0, \qquad \forall\ x \neq [0].$$

**iii.** $Q(x) = x^T Ax$ is indefinite if for a vector $x$, it is positive and for another vector $x$ it is negative.

The structure of the matrix of coefficients will determine to which one of the above definitions the quadratic form will belong. The technique of the principal minors is utilized in the book (see Section 5.2) and the following theorem applies.

## Theorem 2

A symmetric matrix $A$ of order $n$ is:

**i.** **positive definite** iff all the leading principal (upper-leftmost) minors are positive:

$$a_{11} > 0, \quad \begin{vmatrix} a_{11} & a_{12} \\ a_{21} & a_{22} \end{vmatrix} > 0, \quad \begin{vmatrix} a_{11} & a_{12} & a_{13} \\ a_{21} & a_{22} & a_{23} \\ a_{31} & a_{32} & a_{33} \end{vmatrix} > 0, \quad \cdots, \quad \begin{vmatrix} a_{11} & \cdots & a_{1n} \\ \vdots & \vdots & \vdots \\ a_{n1} & \cdots & a_{nn} \end{vmatrix} = |A| > 0;$$

**ii.** **negative definite** iff all the leading principal (upper-leftmost) minors alternate in sign, beginning with a negative minor;

iii. **positive semidefinite** iff all the principal (not necessarily upper-leftmost) minors are $\geq 0$, with the minor of order $n$ equal to zero, i.e., $|A| = 0$;

iv. **negative semidefinite** iff each one of the principal (not necessarily upper-leftmost) minors of **even order is $\geq 0$**, each one of the principal (not necessarily upper-leftmost) minors of **odd order is $\leq 0$**, with the minor of order $n$ equal to zero, i.e., $|A| = 0$;

v. **indefinite** in all the other cases.

Let us see now how we can implement a quadratic form in Excel through the following example.

## EXAMPLE 1

Let us consider the following matrix

$$A = \begin{bmatrix} 1 & 5/2 & 1 \\ 5/2 & 1 & 3/2 \\ 1 & 3/2 & 0 \end{bmatrix}$$

Then, $Q(x)$ will be:

$$x^T A x = \begin{bmatrix} x_1 & x_2 & x_3 \end{bmatrix} \begin{bmatrix} 1 & 5/2 & 1 \\ 5/2 & 1 & 3/2 \\ 1 & 3/2 & 0 \end{bmatrix} \begin{bmatrix} x_1 \\ x_2 \\ x_3 \end{bmatrix}$$

Namely, applying Eq. (3.4-3),

$$Q(x) = (x_1)^2 + (x_2)^2 + 0 + 2 \cdot \left(\frac{5}{2}\right) x_1 x_2 + 2 \cdot (1) x_1 x_3 + 2 \cdot \left(\frac{3}{2}\right) x_2 x_3$$

Setting, for example, $x^1 = \begin{bmatrix} 1 & 1 & 1 \end{bmatrix}$, we have that the quadratic form is equal to $Q(x^1) = 12$.

Using the array formulas *TRANSPOSE* and *MMULT*, we are able to manage and implement the above quadratic form calculation in Excel, as in Fig. 3.4-1:

In Table 3.4-1, we also investigate whether the matrix is positive definite, negative definite, or indefinite, through the analysis of the leading principal minors, via the array formula *MDETERM*.

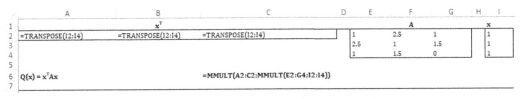

**FIGURE 3.4-1** Quadratic form setup.

**TABLE 3.4-1**   Quadratic form and Theorem 2: A is indefinite.

| $x^T$ | | | | A | | | | x |
|---|---|---|---|---|---|---|---|---|
| 1.00 | 1.00 | 1.00 | | 1.00 | 2.50 | 1.00 | | 1.00 |
| | | | | 2.50 | 1.00 | 1.50 | | 1.00 |
| | | | | 1.00 | 1.50 | 0.00 | | 1.00 |
| $Q(x) = x^T Ax$ | | 12.00 | | | | | | |
| | Minor t = 1 | | | 1.00 | | | | |
| | Minor t = 2 | | | -5.25 | | Indefinite Matrix | | |
| | Minor t = 3 | | | 4.25 | | | | |

We can see that the matrix is indefinite, as it only satisfies the condition **v.** of Theorem 2. It's just worth stressing that we do not have to confuse, with each other, the fact that the given matrix A is positive (all its elements are positive), with the fact that A is positive definite, according to Theorem 2.

## Quadratic form subject to equality constraints

The procedure shown above (via Theorem 2) is a technique that we use to identify minima, maxima, and saddle points, as a second-order condition, in the unconstrained optimization of nonlinear multivariate problems (see Section 5.2). Often in economics the problems are constrained by equality equations leading to linear or nonlinear constrained problems (for nonlinear multivariate constrained problems, see Section 5.5). In this case, Theorem 2 changes.

Suppose we have the following quadratic form with $A$ square matrix of order $(n \cdot n)$:

$$Q(x) = x^T Ax$$

in which the vector components $x_1, x_2, \cdots, x_n$ have to satisfy a system of linear equations defined as:

$$Bx = [0]$$

with matrix B of order $(m \cdot n)$ and $m < n$.

What is the definiteness of the matrix A s.t. to the given linear constraint? In case $Q(x)$ is positive (or negative) definite, being this valid $\forall x \in \Re^n$, as a shortcut we can just stop the analysis to Theorem 2, as $Q(x)$ will be positive (negative) even if we want to use the constrained values $x \in \Re^n$.

Otherwise, in other cases, a more complete and deeper analysis would resort to the following Theorem 3 and to the so-called *bordered* (by the constraints) *matrix*.

# Theorem 3

Let us build the following *bordered matrix* from $A$ and $B$:

$$M = \begin{bmatrix} 0 & B \\ B^T & A \end{bmatrix}$$

Let $\overline{M}_h$ be the leading principal (upper-leftmost) minor of order $h$.

i. **Necessary and sufficient condition to have $Q(x) = x^T A x$ positive definite** for each nontrivial solution of the system $Bx = [0]$ is that:

$$\overline{M}_h(-1)^m > 0, \quad \forall \, h \in \{2m+1, \cdots, m+n\}$$

ii. **Necessary and sufficient condition to have $Q(x) = x^T A x$ negative definite** for each nontrivial solution of the system $Bx = [0]$ is that the sequence:

$$\overline{M}_{2m+1}, \overline{M}_{2m+2}, \cdots, \overline{M}_{m+n}$$

alternate in sign and the last element have the same sign as $(-1)^n$.

## EXAMPLE 2

Let us consider the following quadratic form:

$$Q(x) = (x_1)^2 - 4(x_2)^2 - (x_3)^2 + 2x_1 x_2$$

s.t.

$$2x_1 + x_2 + x_3 = 0.$$

The symmetric matrix associated to the quadratic form is:

$$A = \begin{bmatrix} 1 & 1 & 0 \\ 1 & -4 & 0 \\ 0 & 0 & -1 \end{bmatrix}.$$

Applying Theorem 2, we have the minors of order $t$ calculated in Table 3.4-2:
which leads to no definiteness in the matrix $A$, as the first minor has a positive sign and the second negative. Let us apply Theorem 3 instead and see whether we can draw a more definite conclusion about the quadratic form.

**TABLE 3.4-2**   Minor of order $t$ of the matrix A.

| A | | |
|---|---|---|
| 1.00 | 1.00 | 0.00 |
| 1.00 | -4.00 | 0.00 |
| 0.00 | 0.00 | -1.00 |

| | |
|---|---|
| **Minor t = 1** | 1.00 |
| **Minor t = 2** | -5.00 |
| **Minor t = 3** | 5.00 |

In this case, $B = \begin{bmatrix} 2 & 1 & 1 \end{bmatrix}$ and the bordered matrix is:

$$M = \begin{bmatrix} 0 & b_1 & b_2 & b_3 \\ b_1 & a_{11} & a_{12} & a_{13} \\ b_2 & a_{21} & a_{22} & a_{23} \\ b_3 & a_{31} & a_{32} & a_{33} \end{bmatrix} = \begin{bmatrix} 0 & 2 & 1 & 1 \\ 2 & 1 & 1 & 0 \\ 1 & 1 & -4 & 0 \\ 1 & 0 & 0 & -1 \end{bmatrix}$$

Here $m = 1$, and the minor of order $(2m + 1) = 3$ is:

$$\overline{M}_3 = \begin{vmatrix} 0 & b_1 & b_2 \\ b_1 & a_{11} & a_{12} \\ b_2 & a_{21} & a_{22} \end{vmatrix} = \begin{vmatrix} 0 & 2 & 1 \\ 2 & 1 & 1 \\ 1 & 1 & -4 \end{vmatrix} = 19$$

while the minor (which is also the last one) of order $(2m + 2) = (m + n) = (1 + 3) = 4$ is:

$$\overline{M}_{m+n=4} = |M| = \begin{vmatrix} 0 & 2 & 1 & 1 \\ 2 & 1 & 1 & 0 \\ 1 & 1 & -4 & 0 \\ 1 & 0 & 0 & -1 \end{vmatrix} = -14$$

The condition **ii.** of Theorem 3 is satisfied, requiring that the sign of the last minor be $(-1)^n = (-1)^3 < 0$ and the alternating sign of the two minors; therefore, the matrix A is **negative definite**.

The condition **i.** of Theorem 3 is instead not satisfied, as it turns out, already for $h = (2m + 1) = 3$ that $\overline{M}_{h=3}(-1)^{m=1} = 19 \cdot (-1) < 0$ (while it should be $> 0$).

Using Excel as a calculator, the computations are straightforward and presented in Table 3.4-3.

**TABLE 3.4-3** Bordered matrix negative definite.

| Bordered Matrix M | | | |
|---|---|---|---|
| 0.00 | 2.00 | 1.00 | 1.00 |
| 2.00 | 1.00 | 1.00 | 0.00 |
| 1.00 | 1.00 | -4.00 | 0.00 |
| 1.00 | 0.00 | 0.00 | -1.00 |

| | |
|---|---|
| $\det (M_{2m+1 = 3})$ | 19.00 |
| $\det (M_{m+n = 4})$ | -14.00 |

## 3.5 Leontief open model

Linear algebra has a vast range of applications in micro- and macroeconomics. The first model we are going to show is the one proposed by the Russian economist Wassily Leontief. This model is of paramount importance in the macroeconomic analysis, and it massively resorts to the sectorial double-entry tables. This way to look at macroeconomic aggregates had already been investigated before W. Leontief also by other economists, like—just to mention a few—François Quesnay (i.e., *Tableau Economique*) and Leon Walras (in his works dedicated to the general equilibrium theory).

The model attempts to capture the way an economy, this being based on many interrelated industries, has to work in order to reach the equilibrium, namely a position where the aggregate economic production (i.e., supply) is equal to the aggregate economic consumption (both final and intermediate industrial consumption).

The industries are interrelated, in that the output of one industry is used as input in other industries (e.g., the rubber manufactured is used in the automobile industry as input, to build some car components). Moreover, some of the output needs to be allocated as well to the private consumption.

The following equality in the whole economy must therefore hold:

$$\left\{ \begin{array}{c} \textit{Total quantity produced of the good } j = \textit{quantity } j \textit{ allocated to private consumption} \\ + \textit{quantity } j \textit{ allocted to all industries.} \end{array} \right\}$$

Let us model what has just been said as follows.

First, we denote with the matrix $A$:

$$A = \begin{bmatrix} a_{11} & a_{12} & \cdots & a_{1n} \\ a_{21} & a_{22} & \cdots & a_{2n} \\ \vdots & \vdots & \ddots & \vdots \\ a_{n1} & a_{n2} & \cdots & a_{nn} \end{bmatrix}$$

the money value of the output of industry $i$ needed by the industry $j$ to produce one unit of its output. This is called the *input–output matrix*, or *Leontief matrix*, or *matrix of technological coefficients*.

The element $a_{ij}$ represents the output of the industry $i$ needed for the production of one unit of output in the industry $j$. The element $a_{ii}$ represents the fact that the industry $i$ may use some of its own output within the production process.

We denote instead with the following vector:

$$x = \begin{bmatrix} x_1 \\ x_2 \\ \vdots \\ x_n \end{bmatrix}, \qquad x \geq 0$$

the total amount of goods produced within the economy. There are $n$ goods produced by $n$ industries (or sectors).

The final demand by the consumer of these $n$ goods is represented by the following vector:

$$d = \begin{bmatrix} d_1 \\ d_2 \\ \vdots \\ d_n \end{bmatrix}, \qquad d \geq 0.$$

There are goods such that $d = 0$, as they do not typically enter in by private consumptions. The model is defined *open* because this demand is determined exogenously by the household open sector.

The quantity:

$$a_{ij}x_j \qquad j = 1, 2, \cdots, n$$

represents the money value of input $i$ required by the industry $j$ to produce one unit of the $j$th good.

The total money of value of the output of industry $i$ required by all industries is given by:

$$\sum_{j=1}^{n} a_{ij}x_j$$

We can then set up the following matrix multiplication:

$$Ax = \begin{bmatrix} a_{11} & a_{12} & \cdots & a_{1n} \\ a_{21} & a_{22} & \cdots & a_{2n} \\ \vdots & \vdots & \vdots & \vdots \\ a_{i1} & a_{i2} & a_{ij} & a_{in} \\ \vdots & \vdots & \vdots & \vdots \\ a_{n1} & a_{n2} & \cdots & a_{nn} \end{bmatrix} \begin{bmatrix} x_1 \\ x_2 \\ \vdots \\ x_j \\ \vdots \\ x_n \end{bmatrix} = \begin{bmatrix} \sum_{j=1}^{n} a_{1j}x_j = a_{11}x_1 + a_{12}x_2 + \cdots + a_{1n}x_n \\ \sum_{j=1}^{n} a_{2j}x_j = a_{21}x_1 + a_{22}x_2 + \cdots + a_{2n}x_n \\ \vdots \\ \sum_{j=1}^{n} a_{ij}x_j = a_{i1}x_1 + a_{i2}x_2 + \cdots + a_{in}x_n \\ \vdots \\ \sum_{j=1}^{n} a_{nj}x_j = a_{n1}x_1 + a_{n2}x_2 + \cdots + a_{nn}x_n \end{bmatrix}$$

Each row of the above ($n \cdot 1$) vector is the total amount of good $i$ allocated to all $j = 1, \cdots, n$ sectors within their production processes.

As we have said some of the output also needs to be allocated to private consumption, so that the following equation in the unknown $x$ must be set up:

$$x_i = \sum_{j=1}^{n} a_{ij}x_j + d_i$$

which represents the total demand (industries + private consumption) for the output of sector $i$.

In a matrix notation we have:

$$x = Ax + d$$

The problem is to determine the equilibrium quantities of the unknown $x$ that makes valid the above equation.

The above system can be transformed in the following form:

$$(I - A)x = d \tag{3.5-1}$$

leading to:

$$x = (I - A)^{-1}d. \tag{3.5-2}$$

The system 3.5-1 will admit a solution if and only if the matrix $(I - A)$ is nondegenerate and therefore invertible, i.e.,

$$det(I - A) \neq 0$$

The quantity $(I-A)^{-1}$ in Eq. (3.5-2) is called *Leontief inverse matrix*.

## Numerical example

Let us consider a small economy made of three sectors with the following matrix of technological coefficients:

$$A = \begin{bmatrix} 0.3 & 0.5 & 0.3 \\ 0.2 & 0.2 & 0.3 \\ 0.4 & 0.2 & 0.3 \end{bmatrix}$$

and economy given aggregate demands:

$$d = \begin{bmatrix} 10,000 \\ 7,000 \\ 30,000 \end{bmatrix}$$

The goal is now to solve the following nonhomogeneous system:

$$(I - A)x = d$$

$$\Rightarrow \begin{bmatrix} 1-0.3 & 0.5 & 0.3 \\ 0.2 & 1-0.2 & 0.3 \\ 0.4 & 0.2 & 1-0.3 \end{bmatrix} \begin{bmatrix} x_1 \\ x_2 \\ x_3 \end{bmatrix} = \begin{bmatrix} 10,000 \\ 7,000 \\ 30,000 \end{bmatrix}$$

We will solve the system using the Solver and the inverse. The worksheet for the Solver solution is shown in Fig. 3.5-1 and the Solver parameters, in Fig. 3.5-2, while in Fig. 3.5-3, we have the worksheet setup for the inverse solution. See Table 3.5-1 for both solutions.

Notice how all the leading principal minors of $(I - A)$ are positive, and it is worth mentioning that in these models the **Hawkins–Simon conditions** are normally invoked: if all the principal minors are all positive (i.e., $> 0$), then the required output vector $x$ is nonnegative and the inverse $(I - A)^{-1}$ is nonnegative.

## 3.6 Equilibrium in n markets

The objective of this model is to compute the equilibrium price in $n$-perfect competitive markets via their available schedules of demands and supplies. We will see in Chapter 6, that in the perfect competitive markets the price is determined via the interaction of demand

| | A | B | C | D | E | F | G | H |
|---|---|---|---|---|---|---|---|---|
| 1 | Solver solution | | | | | | | |
| 2 | | A | | x | | d | Ax | x=Ax+d |
| 3 | 0.3 | 0.5 | 0.3 | 174732.14285714 | 10000 | | =MMULT(A3:C5;D3:D5) | =G3+E3 |
| 4 | 0.2 | 0.2 | 0.3 | 118660.71428571 | 7000 | | =MMULT(A3:C5;D3:D5) | =G4+E4 |
| 5 | 0.4 | 0.2 | 0.3 | 176607.14285714 | 30000 | | =MMULT(A3:C5;D3:D5) | =G5+E5 |

FIGURE 3.5-1   Worksheet setup for the Solver solution.

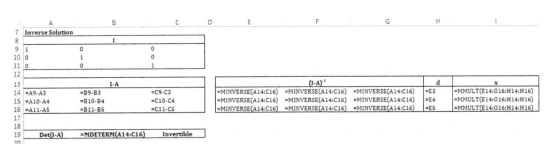

FIGURE 3.5-2   Solver setup for the Leontief model.

and supply, and these prices have to be taken as given by the multitude of firms operating in the market.

In matrix notation, we have the following *n* schedules of supply:

$$q^s = \alpha + \beta p$$

| | A | B | C | D | E | F | G | H | I |
|---|---|---|---|---|---|---|---|---|---|
| 7 | Inverse Solution | | | | | | | | |
| 8 | | I | | | | | | | |
| 9 | 1 | 0 | 0 | | | | | | |
| 10 | 0 | 1 | 0 | | | | | | |
| 11 | 0 | 0 | 1 | | | | | | |
| 12 | | | | | | | | | |
| 13 | | I-A | | | | (I-A)⁻¹ | | d | x |
| 14 | =A9-A3 | =B9-B3 | =C9-C3 | | =MINVERSE(A14:C16) | =MINVERSE(A14:C16) | =MINVERSE(A14:C16) | =E3 | =MMULT(E14:G16;H14:H16) |
| 15 | =A10-A4 | =B10-B4 | =C10-C4 | | =MINVERSE(A14:C16) | =MINVERSE(A14:C16) | =MINVERSE(A14:C16) | =E4 | =MMULT(E14:G16;H14:H16) |
| 16 | =A11-A5 | =B11-B5 | =C11-C5 | | =MINVERSE(A14:C16) | =MINVERSE(A14:C16) | =MINVERSE(A14:C16) | =E5 | =MMULT(E14:G16;H14:H16) |
| 17 | | | | | | | | | |
| 18 | | | | | | | | | |
| 19 | Det(I-A) | =MDETERM(A14:C16) | Invertible | | | | | | |
| 20 | | | | | | | | | |

FIGURE 3.5-3   Worksheet setup for the Leontief inverse solution.

I. Excel and fundamental mathematics for economics

**TABLE 3.5-1**    Solution for the vector $x = [x_1, x_2, x_3]$.

Solver solution

| A | | | x | d | | Ax | x = Ax+d |
|---|---|---|---|---|---|---|---|
| 0.30 | 0.50 | 0.30 | 174,732.14 | 10,000 | | 164,732.14 | 174,732.14 |
| 0.20 | 0.20 | 0.30 | 118,660.71 | 7,000 | | 111,660.71 | 118,660.71 |
| 0.40 | 0.20 | 0.30 | 176,607.14 | 30,000 | | 146,607.14 | 176,607.14 |

Inverse Solution

| I | | |
|---|---|---|
| 1.00 | 0.00 | 0.00 |
| 0.00 | 1.00 | 0.00 |
| 0.00 | 0.00 | 1.00 |

| I-A | | | | $(I-A)^{-1}$ | | | d | x |
|---|---|---|---|---|---|---|---|---|
| 0.70 | -0.50 | -0.30 | | 4.46 | 3.66 | 3.48 | 10,000 | 174,732.14 |
| -0.20 | 0.80 | -0.30 | | 2.32 | 3.30 | 2.41 | 7,000 | 118,660.71 |
| -0.40 | -0.20 | 0.70 | | 3.21 | 3.04 | 4.11 | 30,000 | 176,607.14 |

| Det(I-A) | 0.11 | Invertible |
|---|---|---|

where $q^s$ is the vector of order $(n \cdot 1)$ of the quantities supplied in the $n$ markets, $\alpha$ is the vector of order $(n \cdot 1)$ of the constant terms, $\beta$ is the matrix of order $(n \cdot n)$ of the slopes of the supply curves.

We can then rewrite the above supply schedules as follows:

$$\begin{bmatrix} q_1^s \\ \vdots \\ \vdots \\ q_n^s \end{bmatrix} = \begin{bmatrix} \alpha_1 \\ \vdots \\ \alpha_n \end{bmatrix} + \begin{bmatrix} \beta_{11} & \cdots & \beta_{1n} \\ \vdots & \vdots & \vdots \\ \beta_{n1} & \cdots & \beta_{nn} \end{bmatrix} \begin{bmatrix} p_1 \\ \vdots \\ p_n \end{bmatrix}.$$

We do the same for the $n$ schedules of demand as follows:

$$q^d = a + Bp$$

with:

$$\begin{bmatrix} q_1^d \\ \vdots \\ \vdots \\ q_n^d \end{bmatrix} = \begin{bmatrix} a_1 \\ \vdots \\ a_n \end{bmatrix} + \begin{bmatrix} b_{11} & \cdots & b_{1n} \\ \vdots & \vdots & \vdots \\ b_{n1} & \cdots & b_{nn} \end{bmatrix} \begin{bmatrix} p_1 \\ \vdots \\ p_n \end{bmatrix}.$$

Setting the equilibrium condition, such that the demand is equated to the supply in all markets, we obtain the vector of *market equilibrium prices* (or *market clearing prices*) that must exist under the equilibrium condition.

$$Supply \equiv \alpha + \beta p = a + Bp \equiv Demand$$

which is:

$$\alpha - a = p(B - \beta) \tag{3.6-1}$$

and finally, resorting to the inverse matrix:

$$p = (\alpha - a)(B - \beta)^{-1}. \tag{3.6-2}$$

## Numerical example

Let us consider three competitive markets of tea, sugar, and coffee, whose supply and demand schedules are given in the following systems:

$$q_t^d = 100 - 5p_t + 3p_c - p_s$$

$$q_t^s = -10 + 2p_t$$

$$q_c^d = 120 + 2p_t - 8p_c - 2p_s$$

$$q_c^s = -20 + 5p_c$$

$$q_s^d = 300 - 10p_t - 5p_c - p_s$$

$$q_s^s = 15p_s$$

Sugar, tea, and coffee are often complementary goods. Two goods might be defined complementary when their use is often in pair and using more of one good requires the use of more of the other good. Similarly, if the price of one good falls, people not only will tend to buy more of it, but also they will tend to buy more of the complementary good. Similarly, if the price of one good rises, reducing its demand, the higher might also reduce the demand of the paired good. The coffee and tea are instead often substitute goods. This why the three demand schedules are as described analytically above.

Let us proceed to equate demand and supply as follows:

$$Supply \equiv \alpha + \beta p = a + Bp \equiv Demand$$
$$-10 + 2p_t = 100 - 5p_t + 3p_c - p_s$$
$$-20 + 5p_c = 120 + 2p_t - 8p_c - 2p_s$$
$$15p_s = 300 - 10p_t - 5p_c - p_s$$

From the above system, we derive the vector $[\alpha - a]$ of order $(3 \cdot 1)$

$$[\alpha - a] = \begin{bmatrix} -10 - 100 \\ -20 - 120 \\ 0 - 300 \end{bmatrix} = \begin{bmatrix} -110 \\ -140 \\ -300 \end{bmatrix}.$$

Then, as a second step, we identify $B$ of the demand schedule, of order $(3 \cdot 3)$:

$$B = \begin{bmatrix} -5 & 3 & -1 \\ 2 & -8 & -2 \\ -10 & -5 & 1 \end{bmatrix}$$

and $\beta$ of the supply schedule, of order $(3 \cdot 3)$ as well:

$$\beta = \begin{bmatrix} 2 & 0 & 0 \\ 0 & 5 & 0 \\ 0 & 0 & 15 \end{bmatrix}.$$

Now, we obtain the matrix of coefficients in Eq. (3.6-1):

$$B - \beta = \begin{bmatrix} -7 & 3 & -1 \\ 2 & -13 & -2 \\ -10 & -5 & -16 \end{bmatrix}.$$

and the complete system has the following form:

$$\begin{bmatrix} 7 & -3 & 1 \\ -2 & 13 & 2 \\ 10 & 5 & 16 \end{bmatrix} \begin{bmatrix} p_t \\ p_c \\ p_s \end{bmatrix} = \begin{bmatrix} 110 \\ 140 \\ 300 \end{bmatrix}$$

which will admit a unique solution if and only $[B-\beta]$ is nondegenerate, invertible, therefore with $det(B - \beta) \neq 0$. We know how to solve this system in Excel from the previous sections and the solution using the Solver, as well as the inverse matrix is in Table 3.6-1 with:

$$p^* = \begin{bmatrix} p_t^* = 21.56 \\ p_c^* = 13.94 \\ p_s^* = 0.92 \end{bmatrix}$$

**TABLE 3.6-1** Equilibrium vector prices excel solution in three competitive markets.

Solver Solution

| A | | | Price vector | Constant Terms | | α-a | Constant Terms |
|---|---|---|---|---|---|---|---|
| 7.00 | -3.00 | 1.00 | 21.56 | 110.00 | | α1-a1 | 110.00 |
| -2.00 | 13.00 | 2.00 | 13.94 | 140.00 | | α1-a2 | 140.00 |
| 10.00 | 5.00 | 16.00 | 0.92 | 300.00 | | α1-a3 | 300.00 |

| B-β | | |
|---|---|---|
| 7.00 | -3.00 | 1.00 |
| -2.00 | 13.00 | 2.00 |
| 10.00 | 5.00 | 16.00 |

Inverse Solution

| (B-β)$^{-1}$ | | | α-a | Price vector | p* |
|---|---|---|---|---|---|
| 0.18 | 0.05 | -0.02 | 110.00 | 21.56 | $p_t^*$ |
| 0.05 | 0.09 | -0.01 | 140.00 | 13.94 | $p_c^*$ |
| -0.13 | -0.06 | 0.08 | 300.00 | 0.92 | $p_s^*$ |

| Det(B-β) | 1,090 | Invertible |
|---|---|---|

## 3.7 Economic policy modeling: objectives and instruments

In the theory of economic policy, through the linear algebra and the systems of linear equations, we can model the instruments to be adopted by the decision makers, in order to reach a set of objectives, given some exogenous macroeconomic variables. We will show the basics of these models in a certain and static environment.

Econometrics is massively used in the economic policy and macroeconomic models to estimate the parameters of the models.

Let us introduce **m linear equations, n unknown (endogenous) variables, k instrumental variables,** and **v exogenous variables.** We can formalize the following system of linear equations:

$$
\begin{cases}
(a_{11}y_1 + \cdots + a_{1n}y_n) + (b_{11}x_1 + \cdots + b_{1k}x_k) + (c_{11}z_1 + \cdots c_{1v}z_v) = 0 \\
(a_{21}y_1 + \cdots + a_{2n}y_n) + (b_{21}x_1 + \cdots + b_{2k}x_k) + (c_{21}z_1 + \cdots c_{2v}z_v) = 0 \\
\cdots \\
(a_{i1}y_1 + \cdots + a_{in}y_n) + (b_{i1}x_1 + \cdots + b_{ik}x_k) + (c_{i1}z_1 + \cdots c_{iv}z_v) = 0 \\
\cdots \\
(a_{m1}y_1 + \cdots + a_{mn}y_n) + (b_{m1}x_1 + \cdots + b_{mk}x_k) + (c_{m1}z_1 + \cdots c_{mv}z_v) = 0
\end{cases}
\tag{3.7-1}
$$

Eq. (3.7-1) can be rewritten in a more condensed matrix-based form, where in round brackets the orders of matrices and vectors have been indicated:

$$
\underbrace{A}_{(m \cdot n)} \cdot \underbrace{y}_{(n \cdot 1)} + \underbrace{B}_{(m \cdot k)} \cdot \underbrace{x}_{(k \cdot 1)} + \underbrace{C}_{(m \cdot v)} \cdot \underbrace{z}_{(v \cdot 1)} = 0
\tag{3.7-2}
$$

Eq. (3.7-2) can be solved either in terms of endogenous variables, or in terms of instrumental variables available in the hands of the economic policy maker.

In the first case, we have the followings solution if and only if $\det(A) \neq 0$:

$$y^0 = -A^{-1}Bx - A^{-1}Cz \tag{3.7-3}$$

Eq. (3.7-3) is very useful for comparative statistics, when we want to compare the levels in the endogenous variables when we change the instrumental and exogenous variables.

In the second case, we have the following solution if and only if $y^0 = -A^{-1}Bx - A^{-1}Cz$:

$$x^0 = -B^{-1}Ay^* - B^{-1}Cz \tag{3.7-4}$$

where we have denoted with $x^0 = -B^{-1}Ay^* - B^{-1}Cz$ the economic policy objectives, i.e., the desired level of the endogenous variables involved, at which the economic policy makers are aiming. The vector of instrumental variables implementable to reach these goals is then calculated in Eq. (3.7-4) once the objectives have been established and given the exogeneous variables.

Now, for convenience, let us rewrite Eq. (3.7-4) into the following standard system:

$$\underbrace{B}_{(m\cdot k)} \underbrace{x}_{(k\cdot 1)} = \underbrace{h}_{(m\cdot 1)} \tag{3.7-5}$$

where $h = -\left( \underbrace{Ay^*}_{(m\cdot 1)} + \underbrace{Cz}_{(m\cdot 1)} \right)$.

From the Rouché–Capelli theorem, we know that if the above system is regular, i.e., $r(B) = r(B|h) = m = k$, the solution is unique. We have that the number of objectives is equal to the number of instruments.

In theory, another case where the solution is unique is when $r(B) = r(B|h) = m = k$. Under this circumstance, however, $r(B) = k < m$ instruments (the columns of $k$) are fewer than the number $B$ of objectives (the rows of $m$), and $B$ objectives (equations) have to be removed (see Fig. 3.2-5) to solve the system 3.7-5.

Otherwise, there will be infinite solutions if $(m-k)$ $(r(B) = m < k$ solutions). There is an excess of instruments and we can get around it (A) either setting $(k-m)$ instruments as given exogenous variables or (B) increasing the number $(k-m)$ of objectives.

Let us see an example of this last case of excess of instruments with the following set of equations:

$$Y = C + I + G + NX \tag{3.7.6-1}$$

$$C = (1-s)(Y-T) \tag{3.7.6-2}$$

$$NX = X - M \tag{3.7.6-3}$$

$$M = mY - Z \qquad (3.7.6\text{-}4)$$

where

$Y =$ Income (or Output)
$I =$ Investments
$G =$ Government spending
$NX =$ Net Exports (Balance of Trade)
$X =$ Exports
$M =$ Imports
$T =$ Taxes
$Z =$ Import quotas
$m =$ marginal propensity to import
$s =$ marginal propensity to save

Replacing $s =$ marginal propensity to save in Eq. (1) with Eq. (2) and replacing $C$ in Eq. (3) with Eq. (4) we reduce system 3.7-6 to:

$$sY - I - G - NX + (1-s)T = 0 \qquad (1.a)$$

$$mY + NX - X - Z = 0 \qquad (3.a)$$

Let us separate the variables in endogenous, exogenous, and instrumental.
The variables $mY + NX - X - Z = 0$, $G$ and $T$, are instrumental variables.
The variables $Y$ and $NX$ are endogenous (i.e., explained by other variables in the model).
The variables $Z$ and $I$ are exogenous (i.e., causally independent from other variables in the model).
Let us write, from equations $X$ and (1.a), system 3.7-6 as follows:

$$
\overbrace{\begin{bmatrix} s & -1 \\ m & 1 \end{bmatrix}\begin{bmatrix} Y \\ NX \end{bmatrix}}^{A\cdot y} + \overbrace{\begin{bmatrix} -1 & (1-s) & 0 \\ 0 & 0 & -1 \end{bmatrix}\begin{bmatrix} G \\ T \\ Z \end{bmatrix}}^{B\cdot x} + \overbrace{\begin{bmatrix} -1 & 0 \\ 0 & -1 \end{bmatrix}\begin{bmatrix} I \\ X \end{bmatrix}}^{C\cdot z} = 0
$$

The matrix $B$ is not invertible, and we cannot find a solution for the three instruments $B$ to meet the desired targets of $G$, $T$, $Z$, and $Y^*$.
We can then move $NX^*$ from the set of the instrumental variables to the set of exogenous variables, and we obtain the following new version of the system:

$$
\overbrace{\begin{bmatrix} s & -1 \\ m & 1 \end{bmatrix}\begin{bmatrix} Y \\ NX \end{bmatrix}}^{A\cdot y} + \overbrace{\begin{bmatrix} -1 & 0 \\ 0 & -1 \end{bmatrix}\begin{bmatrix} G \\ Z \end{bmatrix}}^{B\cdot x} + \overbrace{\begin{bmatrix} -1 & (1-s) & 0 \\ 0 & 0 & -1 \end{bmatrix}\begin{bmatrix} I \\ T \\ X \end{bmatrix}}^{C\cdot z} = 0.
$$

Now $B$ is invertible and we can adopt the form 3.7-5 to get the solution of the instruments $B$ and $G$, given the desired level of endogenous variables.

The system 3.7-5 with $Z$ is therefore as follows:

$$\begin{bmatrix} -1 & 0 \\ 0 & -1 \end{bmatrix}\begin{bmatrix} G \\ Z \end{bmatrix} = -\overbrace{\begin{bmatrix} sY - NX \\ mY + NX \end{bmatrix}}^{-A \cdot y} - \overbrace{\begin{bmatrix} -I + (1-s)T \\ -X \end{bmatrix}}^{-C \cdot z}$$

Setting now the desired levels for the objective variables $Y=Y^*$ and $Y = Y^*$, we have the solution:

$$\begin{bmatrix} G^0 \\ Z^0 \end{bmatrix} = -\begin{bmatrix} -1 & 0 \\ 0 & -1 \end{bmatrix}^{-1}\begin{bmatrix} sY^* - NX^* \\ mY^* + NX^* \end{bmatrix} - \begin{bmatrix} -1 & 0 \\ 0 & -1 \end{bmatrix}^{-1}\begin{bmatrix} -I + (1-s)T \\ -X \end{bmatrix}$$

## Numerical example

Let us consider Table 3.7-1 where some data, of the US economy as of the end of year 2017, have been summarized and also estimated. In this case the desired level corresponds to the actual level.

Let us suppose now the economic policy makers want to deviate from the actual levels of the two objective endogenous variables $Y$ and $Y$. Their goal is to increase the economy income to $NX$ and to break-even in the balance of trade, i.e., $Y^* = \mathbf{20,000}$. The instruments to

**TABLE 3.7-1**   US GDP actual data 2017.

| Variable | Desired level (bln) | Actual level (bln) (*) |
|---|---|---|
| Y* | 19,485 | 19,485 |
| NX* | -578 | -578 |
| | | |
| G⁰ | 3,375 | 3,374 |
| Z⁰ | 579 | 579 |
| | Exogenous recalculated | |
| I | 3,368 | 3,368 |
| T | 5,261 | 5,261 |
| X | 2,350 | 2,350 |
| M | 2,929 | 2,929 |
| t | 27% | 27% |
| C | 13,321 | 13,321 |

*(\*) Source: U.S. Bureau of Economic Analysis, except for Z, t, T.*

do so, as we have seen in the model, are represented by the government spending $NX^* = 0$ and the import quotas G.

We assign then the desired level to each of the two endogenous variables in system 3.7-5 to obtain the new levels in the instrumental variables.

We have to set up the system 3.7-5, and the following Table 3.7-2 shows the new levels of the instrumental variables, implied in the economic policy targets.

Table 3.7-3 shows the actual calculations to solve the system, using two of the techniques we have analyzed so far: Solver and the inverse.

The propensity marginal to save and to import have been estimated: the former via the equations of the model, the latter via a linear regression analysis (i.e., Imports vs. Gdp).

The final effect, as expected, is that the economic policy makers should mainly generate more import quotas, while the government spending should be slightly reduced. This is because, before the desired change, the Z component impacted negatively on the income. After this change the consumption:

$$C = (1 - s)(Y - T)$$

increases from

$$13,321 = (1 - 0.06)(19,485 - 5,261)$$

to

$$13,673 = (1 - 0.06)(20,000 - 5,400).$$

From the change, we also expect to have a likely new level in the exogenous variables.

**TABLE 3.7-2** US GDP data actual 2017 and desired levels.

| Variable | Desired level (bln) | Actual level (bln) (*) |
|---|---|---|
| Y* | 20,000 | 19,485 |
| NX* | 0 | -578 |
| $G^0$ | 2,829 | 3,374 |
| $Z^0$ | 1,250 | 579 |
| Exogenous recalculated | | |
| I | 3,498 | 3,368 |
| T | 5,400 | 5,261 |
| X | 2,350 | 2,350 |
| M | 2,350 | 2,929 |
| t | 27% | 27% |
| C | 13,673 | 13,321 |

(*) Source: U.S. Bureau of Economic Analysis, except for Z, t, T.

**TABLE 3.7-3**  System solution for the instruments $G^0$ and $Z^0$.

Solver Solution

| B | | $x^0$ | Constant Terms | -Ay* | -Cz | Ay + Cz |
|---|---|---|---|---|---|---|
| -1.00 | 0.00 | 2,829 | -2,829 | -1,270 | -1,559 | -2,829 |
| 0.00 | -1.00 | 1,250 | -1,250 | -3,600 | 2,350 | -1,250 |

Inverse Solution

| Inverse $B^{-1}$ | | Ay + Cz | $x^0$ | | s | 0.06 |
|---|---|---|---|---|---|---|
| -1.00 | 0.00 | -2,829 | 2,829 | | m | 0.18 |
| 0.00 | -1.00 | -1,250 | 1,250 | | | |

| Government Spending | $G^0$ | 2,829 |
|---|---|---|
| Import Quotas | $Z^0$ | 1,250 |

| A | | y* (bln) | Target Variables | |
|---|---|---|---|---|
| s = 0.06 | -1.00 | 20,000 | Y* | Target Income |
| m = 0.18 | 1.00 | 0 | NX* | Target Trade Balance |

| C | | | z (bln) | Exogenous Variables |
|---|---|---|---|---|
| -1.00 | 0.94 | 0.00 | 3,368 | I |
| 0.00 | 0.00 | -1.00 | 5,261 | T |
| | | | 2,350 | X |

## Exercises

1. Solve the following linear system using the Excel Solver, the inverse, and the Cramer rule:

$$\begin{bmatrix} 1 & 1 & 1 \\ 2 & 3 & -1 \\ 7 & 1 & -2 \end{bmatrix} \begin{bmatrix} x_1 \\ x_2 \\ x_3 \end{bmatrix} = \begin{bmatrix} 9 \\ 16 \\ 57 \end{bmatrix}.$$

Resorting to the Rouché–Capelli theorem, analyze whether the system admits only one solution or not.

2. Solve the following linear system using the Excel Solver, the inverse, and the Cramer rule:

$$\begin{bmatrix} 2 & 1 & 4 \\ 3 & 2 & 1 \\ 1 & 3 & 3 \end{bmatrix} \begin{bmatrix} x_1 \\ x_2 \\ x_3 \end{bmatrix} = \begin{bmatrix} 16 \\ 10 \\ 16 \end{bmatrix}.$$

Resorting to the Rouché–Capelli theorem, analyze whether the system admits only one solution or not.

3. Solve the following linear system using the Excel Solver and the inverse:

$$\begin{bmatrix} 1 & -2 \\ 2 & -3 \end{bmatrix} \begin{bmatrix} x_1 \\ x_2 \end{bmatrix} = \begin{bmatrix} 3 \\ 1 \end{bmatrix}.$$

Resorting to the Rouché–Capelli theorem, analyze whether the system admits only one solution or not.

4. Set up an Excel chart such that the following system of linear inequalities is satisfied:

$$\begin{cases} x_1 + 3x_2 \leq 6 \\ -4x_1 - 2x_2 \leq 4 \\ 2x_1 - x_2 \leq 2 \end{cases}$$

5. Using the model shown in Section 3.7 solve the following problem. Suppose you, as economist, gathered the following macroeconomic annual data for a country:

| Variable | Actual Level (bln) |
|----------|-------------------|
| Y* | 1,700 |
| NX* | 50 |
| $G^0$ | 850 |
| $Z^0$ | 279 |
| I | 200 |
| T | 714 |
| X | 536 |
| M | 486 |
| t | 42% |

The economic policy makers desire to know how they may change the government spending $G^0$ and import quotas $G^0$ in order to achieve the following objectives:

$$Z^0 \text{ and } Y^* = 2,000.$$

6. Resorting to the bordered matrix, determine the sign of the following constrained quadratic form:

$$Q(x) = 3(x_2)^2 + (x_3)^2 + 4x_1x_2 + 2x_2x_3$$

s.t.

$$x_1 - x_3 = 0$$

I. Excel and fundamental mathematics for economics

7. Solve in Excel the Leontief Input–Output problem, determining the equilibrium quantities of the unknown $x_1-x_3=0$, such that:

$$x = Ax + d$$

using the following matrix information:

$$A = \begin{bmatrix} 0.30 & 0.50 & 0.30 \\ 0.20 & 0.20 & 0.30 \\ 0.40 & 0.20 & 0.30 \end{bmatrix}$$

$$d = \begin{bmatrix} 20 \\ 10 \\ 40 \end{bmatrix}$$

The following problems relate to the IS-LM model.

8. The IS-LM model gives the equilibrium conditions in the good and money markets. The goods market (IS) has been econometrically estimated as follows:

$$C = 15 + 0.8(Y - T)$$

$$T = -25 + 0.25Y$$

$$I = 65 - R$$

$$G = 94$$

where $G = 94$ is the private consumption, $C$ the tax revenues, $T$, the private investments, and $I$, the government spending.

The money market (LM) is described instead by the following equations:

$$L = 5Y - 50R$$

$$M = 1,500$$

where $M = 1,500$ is the money demand, $L$ is the money supply. Find in Excel the equilibrium quantities of $M$ and $Y$ using the Solver and the inverse.

(Hint: for this solution, we can express the above equations into the following condensed form:

$$Ax = b$$

where

$$\begin{bmatrix} 1 & 2.5 \\ 1 & -10 \end{bmatrix} \begin{bmatrix} Y \\ R \end{bmatrix} = \begin{bmatrix} 485 \\ 300 \end{bmatrix}.$$

The IS function is found equating aggregate supply and aggregate demand in the goods market, i.e., $Y = C + I + G \Rightarrow Y = 485 - 2.5R$, while the LM is obtained from $L = M \Rightarrow Y = 300 + 10R$).

9. The same set of equations is given below, except for the government spending, that you will use as instrumental variable:

$$C = 15 + 0.8(Y - T)$$

$$T = -25 + 0.25Y$$

$$I = 65 - R$$

$$G = G^0$$

$$L = 5Y - 50R$$

$$M = 1,500.$$

Solve for a target level of government spending, such that the desired level of $M = 1500$.

(Hint: the system can be simply rewritten as:

$$\begin{bmatrix} 0.4 & 1 \\ 1 & -10 \end{bmatrix} \begin{bmatrix} Y \\ R \end{bmatrix} = \begin{bmatrix} G^0 + 100 \\ 300 \end{bmatrix})$$

10. The IS-LM set of equations is given below:

$$C = a + b(1 - t)Y$$

$$I = e - lR$$

$$G = \overline{G}$$

$$L = kY - hR$$

$$M = \overline{M}$$

The economy in equilibrium will satisfy the following:

$$Y = C + I + \overline{G}$$

$$C = a + b(1-t)Y$$

$$I = e - lR$$

$$\overline{M} = kY - hR$$

With four endogenous variables $Y$, $C$, $I$, $R$ and four exogenous variables $\overline{G}$, $a$, $e$, $\overline{M}$, set up the matrix system in Excel in the following form, determining matrix $[A]$:

$$\underbrace{[A]}_{4 \cdot 4} \begin{bmatrix} Y \\ C \\ I \\ R \end{bmatrix} = \begin{bmatrix} \overline{G} \\ a \\ e \\ \overline{M} \end{bmatrix}$$

and determine each one of the endogenous variables using the Solver and the inverse, with the following additional data:

| | | | |
|---|---|---|---|
| $\overline{G}$ | 80 | $l$ | 50 |
| $a$ | 15 | $k$ | 5 |
| $e$ | 65 | $h$ | 1 |
| $M$ | 1,500 | $b$ | 0.8 |
| $t$ | 0.4 | | |

CHAPTER

# 4

# Mathematics for dynamic economic models

OUTLINE

## 4.1 Ordinary differential equations and numerical methods: Euler and Runge-Kutta

Throughout the book we will often encounter differential equations in the form of:

$$\frac{dy(t)}{dt} + a(t)y(t) = b(t)$$

where normally the term $dy(t)/dt$ is denoted with $\dot{y}$.

Eq. (4.1-1) is called *nonautonomous, ordinary, linear first-order differential equation*. It is called nonautonomous because the function $a(t)$ and the function $b(t)$ depend on the independent variable $t$.

On the other hand, Eq. (4.1-1) will be called *autonomous*, if the variable $t$ does not enter the equation explicitly. In this case, Eq. (4.1-1) becomes Eq. (4.1-2) as follows:

$$\frac{dy(t)}{dt} + ay(t) = b$$

where $a$ and $b$ are now two constants.

The general solution of any linear first-order differential equation is given by:

$$y(t) = e^{-A(t)} \left[ \int e^{A(t)} b(t) dt + c \right]$$

where $A(t)$ in the integral of the function $a(t)$.

Throughout the book, to solve numerically in Excel Eqs. (4.1-1) and (4.1-2), we will always use the Euler's method.

We will also show, however, how to implement another important numerical method, namely the Runge-Kutta method.

## Backward Euler's method

The numerical Euler's method has a strong intuitive appeal, and it can be implemented in Excel easily without resorting to any user-defined function or any VBA macro, and therefore it is the preferred method that is used throughout the book.

The minus of the Euler's method is that it requires to fine-tune a sufficiently small step size to reach a reasonable accuracy.

Given Eq. ((4.1-1)):

$$\frac{dy}{dt} + a(t)y(t) = b(t) \qquad \text{4.1-1}$$

we can rearrange the terms as follows:

$$\frac{dy}{dt} = b(t) - a(t)y(t); \qquad \text{(4.1-2)}$$

setting the right part of the equation equal to $f(t, y)$, isolating $dy$ we have:

$$dy = f(t, y)dt$$

so that, to solve for the variable $y(t)$, we can just take the integral on both sides of the equation, as follows:

$$y = \int f(t, y)dt.$$

Setting the step size $dt = h$ as small as desirable, in a discrete numerical environment, the above equation becomes:

$$y = \sum f(t, y)h$$

so that at any stage point $t_n$ the sought function $y(t)$ is:

$$y(t_n) = y(t_{n-1}) + f(t_n, y_n) \cdot h.$$

In case, in Eq. (4.1-2), both the $a(t)$ and $y(t)$ terms are equal to zero, so that we have $\frac{dy}{dt} = b(t)$, then the Euler's method solution simply becomes:

$$y(t_n) = y(t_{n-1}) + b(t_n) \cdot h$$

obtaining the same numerical solution for the integral, where $b(t)$ is the integrand function.

Let us see now how to use this method in Excel.

## EXAMPLE 1 (INITIAL VALUE PROBLEM OR CAUCHY PROBLEM)

The initial value problems (or also Cauchy problems) are those differential equations where the initial value (or initial condition) of the unknown variable $y(t)$ is specified.

Solve the following Cauchy problem:

$$\dot{y}(t) + 2y(t) = 3e^{-2t}$$

$$y(0) = 1$$

The exact general solution is given by Eq. (4.1-3):

$$y(t) = e^{-\int 2dt}\left(\int e^{\int 2dt}3e^{-2t}dt + c\right)$$

$$y(t) = e^{2t}\left(3\int e^{2t}e^{-2t}dt + c\right) \Rightarrow y(t) = e^{-2t}(3t + c) \qquad (4.1\text{-}3)$$

Now, we derive the constant $c$ via the initial value condition:

$$y(0) = 1 \Rightarrow c = 1$$

so that the solution sought is:

$$y(t) = e^{-2t}(3t + 1).$$

Let us go now in Excel and see how to solve this problem via the Euler's method.

First, we need to make sure that under the Excel Options (Formulas) the iterative calculation is always enabled, as in Fig. 4.1-1.

To do the Euler's method, what we need to do is then to set up a spreadsheet as in Fig. 4.1-2.

The formulas have been drug-down for 200 time-steps of size $h = 0.025$ each, to obtain the solution in Table 4.1-1 and Fig. 4.1-3.

## EXAMPLE 2

Solve the following Cauchy problem:

$$\begin{cases} \dot{y}(t) + 2ty(t) = te^{-t^2} \\ y(1) = e^{-1} \end{cases}$$

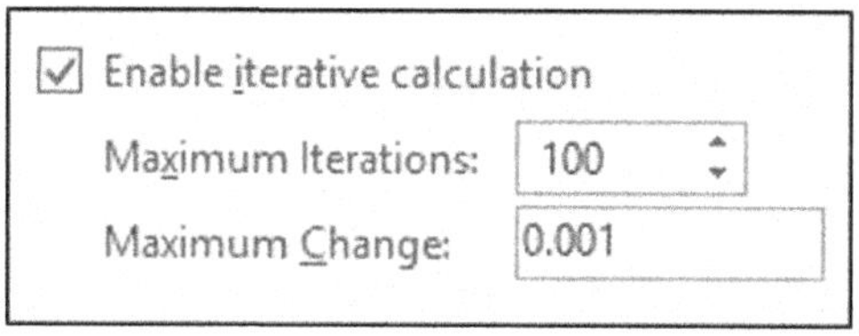

> ☑ Enable iterative calculation
>
> Maximum Iterations: 100
>
> Maximum Change: 0.001

FIGURE 4.1-1   Excel iterative calculation enabled under the Excel Options (Formulas).

| | A | B | C | D | E | F | G | H |
|---|---|---|---|---|---|---|---|---|
| 1 | t | dy/dt = 3exp(-2t) - 2y | dt | dy = [3exp(-2t) - 2y]dt | y = Σ f(t,y)dt | y(t) exact = exp(-2t)*(3t+1) | Error | Step |
| 2 | 0 | =5*A2 | | | =F2 | =EXP(-2*A2)*(3*A2+1) | | 0.025 |
| 3 | =A2+$H$2 | =3*EXP(-2*A3)-2*E3 | =A3-A2 | =B3*C3 | =E2+D3 | =EXP(-2*A3)*(3*A3+1) | =(E3-F3) | |
| 4 | =A3+$H$2 | =3*EXP(-2*A4)-2*E4 | =A4-A3 | =B4*C4 | =E3+D4 | =EXP(-2*A4)*(3*A4+1) | =(E4-F4) | |
| 5 | =A4+$H$2 | =3*EXP(-2*A5)-2*E5 | =A5-A4 | =B5*C5 | =E4+D5 | =EXP(-2*A5)*(3*A5+1) | =(E5-F5) | |
| 6 | =A5+$H$2 | =3*EXP(-2*A6)-2*E6 | =A6-A5 | =B6*C6 | =E5+D6 | =EXP(-2*A6)*(3*A6+1) | =(E6-F6) | |
| 7 | =A6+$H$2 | =3*EXP(-2*A7)-2*E7 | =A7-A6 | =B7*C7 | =E6+D7 | =EXP(-2*A7)*(3*A7+1) | =(E7-F7) | |
| 8 | =A7+$H$2 | =3*EXP(-2*A8)-2*E8 | =A8-A7 | =B8*C8 | =E7+D8 | =EXP(-2*A8)*(3*A8+1) | =(E8-F8) | |
| 9 | =A8+$H$2 | =3*EXP(-2*A9)-2*E9 | =A9-A8 | =B9*C9 | =E8+D9 | =EXP(-2*A9)*(3*A9+1) | =(E9-F9) | |
| 10 | =A9+$H$2 | =3*EXP(-2*A10)-2*E10 | =A10-A9 | =B10*C10 | =E9+D10 | =EXP(-2*A10)*(3*A10+1) | =(E10-F10) | |
| 11 | =A10+$H$2 | =3*EXP(-2*A11)-2*E11 | =A11-A10 | =B11*C11 | =E10+D11 | =EXP(-2*A11)*(3*A11+1) | =(E11-F11) | |
| 12 | =A11+$H$2 | =3*EXP(-2*A12)-2*E12 | =A12-A11 | =B12*C12 | =E11+D12 | =EXP(-2*A12)*(3*A12+1) | =(E12-F12) | |
| 13 | =A12+$H$2 | =3*EXP(-2*A13)-2*E13 | =A13-A12 | =B13*C13 | =E12+D13 | =EXP(-2*A13)*(3*A13+1) | =(E13-F13) | |
| 14 | =A13+$H$2 | =3*EXP(-2*A14)-2*E14 | =A14-A13 | =B14*C14 | =E13+D14 | =EXP(-2*A14)*(3*A14+1) | =(E14-F14) | |
| 15 | =A14+$H$2 | =3*EXP(-2*A15)-2*E15 | =A15-A14 | =B15*C15 | =E14+D15 | =EXP(-2*A15)*(3*A15+1) | =(E15-F15) | |

FIGURE 4.1-2    Euler's method Excel setup.

TABLE 4.1-1    Example 1 Backward Euler's method numerical solution versus exact solution.

| t | dy/dt = 3exp(-2t) - 2y | dt | dy = [3exp(-2t) - 2y]dt | y = Σ f(t,y)dt | y(t) exact = exp(-2t)*(3t+1) | Error |
|---|---|---|---|---|---|---|
| 0.0000 | 0.0000 | | | 1.0000 | 1.0000 | |
| 0.0250 | 0.8130 | 0.0250 | 0.0203 | 1.0203 | 1.0226 | -0.0022 |
| 0.0500 | 0.6418 | 0.0250 | 0.0160 | 1.0364 | 1.0406 | -0.0042 |
| 0.0750 | 0.4851 | 0.0250 | 0.0121 | 1.0485 | 1.0544 | -0.0059 |
| 0.1000 | 0.3421 | 0.0250 | 0.0086 | 1.0571 | 1.0643 | -0.0073 |
| 0.1250 | 0.2117 | 0.0250 | 0.0053 | 1.0623 | 1.0709 | -0.0085 |
| 0.1500 | 0.0931 | 0.0250 | 0.0023 | 1.0647 | 1.0742 | -0.0095 |
| 0.1750 | -0.0146 | 0.0250 | -0.0004 | 1.0643 | 1.0746 | -0.0103 |
| 0.2000 | -0.1121 | 0.0250 | -0.0028 | 1.0615 | 1.0725 | -0.0110 |
| 0.2250 | -0.2001 | 0.0250 | -0.0050 | 1.0565 | 1.0680 | -0.0115 |
| 4.9000 | -0.0017 | 0.0250 | 0.0000 | 0.0009 | 0.0009 | 0.0001 |
| 4.9250 | -0.0017 | 0.0250 | 0.0000 | 0.0009 | 0.0008 | 0.0001 |
| 4.9500 | -0.0016 | 0.0250 | 0.0000 | 0.0009 | 0.0008 | 0.0001 |

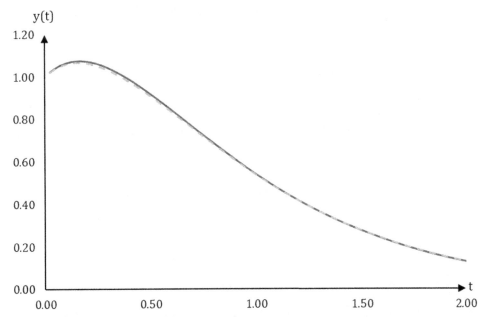

FIGURE 4.1-3    Example 1 backward Euler's method numerical versus exact solution.

Here $a(t) = 2t$ and $b(t) = te^{-t^2}$. The general exact solution is as follows:

$$y(t) = e^{-\int 2t dt} \left( \int e^{\int 2t dt} te^{-t^2} dt + c \right)$$

which becomes:

$$y(t) = e^{-t^2} \left( \int e^{t^2} te^{-t^2} dt + c \right) \Rightarrow y(t) = e^{-t^2} \left( \frac{1}{2}t^2 + c \right).$$

As usual, the constant $c$ is obtained using the initial condition:

$$y(1) = e^{-1} \Rightarrow c = \frac{1}{2}$$

$$y(t) = \frac{1}{2}e^{-t^2} \left( t^2 + 1 \right).$$

For this example, we use a step size $h = 0.005$ in the time interval $[1, 2]$ and the Excel solution is as follows in Table 4.1-2 and Fig. 4.1-4:

## Runge-Kutta of fourth-order method

The Runge-Kutta method attempts to overcome the problem of the Euler's method, as far as the choice of a sufficiently small step size is concerned, to reach a reasonable accuracy in the problem resolution.

On the other hand, the minus of the Runge-Kutta method is that we need to calculate the increments $k_i$ involved in the numerical algorithm, enlarging the utilized space of the Excel

**TABLE 4.1-2**  Example 2 Excel solution of Euler's method.

| t | dy/dt = t*exp(-t^2) - 2ty | dt | dy = f(t,y)Dt | y = Σ f(t,y)dt | y(t) exact = 1/2*exp(-t^2)*(t^2+1) | Error |
|---|---|---|---|---|---|---|
| 1.0000 | 5.0000 | | | 0.3679 | 0.3679 | |
| 1.0050 | -0.3697 | 0.0050 | -0.0018 | 0.3660 | 0.3660 | 0.0000 |
| 1.0100 | -0.3715 | 0.0050 | -0.0019 | 0.3642 | 0.3642 | 0.0000 |
| 1.0150 | -0.3732 | 0.0050 | -0.0019 | 0.3623 | 0.3623 | 0.0000 |
| 1.0200 | -0.3749 | 0.0050 | -0.0019 | 0.3604 | 0.3605 | 0.0000 |
| 1.0250 | -0.3766 | 0.0050 | -0.0019 | 0.3586 | 0.3586 | 0.0000 |
| 1.0300 | -0.3782 | 0.0050 | -0.0019 | 0.3567 | 0.3567 | 0.0000 |
| 1.0350 | -0.3798 | 0.0050 | -0.0019 | 0.3548 | 0.3548 | 0.0000 |
| 1.0400 | -0.3813 | 0.0050 | -0.0019 | 0.3529 | 0.3529 | 0.0000 |
| 1.0450 | -0.3828 | 0.0050 | -0.0019 | 0.3509 | 0.3510 | 0.0000 |
| 1.0500 | -0.3843 | 0.0050 | -0.0019 | 0.3490 | 0.3491 | 0.0000 |
| 1.0550 | -0.3857 | 0.0050 | -0.0019 | 0.3471 | 0.3471 | 0.0000 |
| 1.9750 | -0.1568 | 0.0050 | -0.0008 | 0.0498 | 0.0496 | 0.0002 |
| 1.9800 | -0.1549 | 0.0050 | -0.0008 | 0.0490 | 0.0488 | 0.0002 |
| 1.9850 | -0.1531 | 0.0050 | -0.0008 | 0.0483 | 0.0480 | 0.0002 |
| 1.9900 | -0.1512 | 0.0050 | -0.0008 | 0.0475 | 0.0473 | 0.0002 |
| 1.9950 | -0.1493 | 0.0050 | -0.0007 | 0.0468 | 0.0465 | 0.0002 |
| 2.0000 | -0.1475 | 0.0050 | -0.0007 | 0.0460 | 0.0458 | 0.0002 |

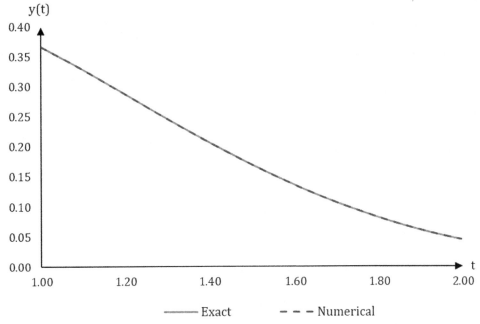

**FIGURE 4.1-4**   Example 2 Euler's method numerical versus exact solution.

worksheet, generating a loss in efficiency, especially when, like in the Optimal Control theory, more variables are involved (i.e., the *state variable*, the *costate variable* and *the control variable*). To have things under a better control, when working with Excel, the goal is always to keep at minimum the worksheet space and the variables utilized, trying to maximize the results we want to achieve.

For the differential equation $\dot{y} = f(t, y)$ where $y(t_0) = y_0$ the Runge-Kutta of fourth-order method (RK4) method is defined using the following recursion formula:

$$y_{n+1} = y_n + \frac{1}{6}(k_1 + 2k_2 + 2k_3 + k_4)h \qquad (4.1\text{-}4)$$

where:

$$\frac{1}{6}(k_1 + 2k_2 + 2k_3 + k_4) = \text{weighted average slope}$$

$$k_1 = f(t_n, y_n)$$

$$k_2 = f\left(t_n + \frac{h}{2}, y_n + \frac{h}{2}k_1\right)$$

$$k_3 = f\left(t_n + \frac{h}{2}, y_n + \frac{h}{2}k_2\right)$$

$$k_4 = hf(t_n + h, y_n + hk_3)$$

$$h = \text{step size}$$

Runge-Kutta methods of any order can be derived, although the derivation of an order higher than four can become extremely complicated. The most popular method used is the RK4, as represented in Eq. (4.1-4).

### EXAMPLE 3 (RK4 vs. EULER's METHOD IN EXCEL)

Let us solve the following simple autonomous differential equation in the form of $\frac{dy}{dt} + ay(t) = b$:

$$\dot{y}(t) + y(t) = 1.$$

$$y(0) = 0.$$

Using Eq. (4.1-3), with $a(t) = 1$ and $b(t) = 1$, the true step-by-step solution would be as follows:

$$y(t) = e^{-A(t)}\left(\int e^{A(t)}b(t)dt + c\right)$$

$$y(t) = e^{-t}\left(\int e^t dt + c\right)$$

namely:

$$y(t) = e^{-t}(e^t + c) = 1 + ce^{-t}.$$

As $y(0) = 0$ we derive the constant $c$ as follows:

$$y(0) = 1 + c \Rightarrow c = -1$$

and the final solution is

$$y(t) = 1 - e^{-t}.$$

In Excel, the setup spreadsheet for the RK4 would be as in Fig. 4.1-5.
The RK4 solution compared with the Euler's method and the exact solution is represented in Table 4.1-3 and Fig. 4.1-6.

| | A | B | C | K | L | M | N |
|---|---|---|---|---|---|---|---|
| 1 | t | dy/dt = - y +1 | y(t) Numerical RK4 | k1 | k2 | k3 | k4 |
| 2 | 0 | =-C2+1 | 0 | =(-C2+1) | =-(C2+$P$1*K2/2)+1 | =-(C2+$P$1*L2/2)+1 | =-(C2+$P$1*M2)+1 |
| 3 | =A2+$P$1 | =-C3+1 | =C2+($P$1*1/6)*(K2+2*L2+2*M2+N2) | =(-C3+1) | =-(C3+$P$1*K3/2)+1 | =-(C3+$P$1*L3/2)+1 | =-(C3+$P$1*M3)+1 |
| 4 | =A3+$P$1 | =-C4+1 | =C3+($P$1*1/6)*(K3+2*L3+2*M3+N3) | =(-C4+1) | =-(C4+$P$1*K4/2)+1 | =-(C4+$P$1*L4/2)+1 | =-(C4+$P$1*M4)+1 |
| 5 | =A4+$P$1 | =-C5+1 | =C4+($P$1*1/6)*(K4+2*L4+2*M4+N4) | =(-C5+1) | =-(C5+$P$1*K5/2)+1 | =-(C5+$P$1*L5/2)+1 | =-(C5+$P$1*M5)+1 |
| 6 | =A5+$P$1 | =-C6+1 | =C5+($P$1*1/6)*(K5+2*L5+2*M5+N5) | =(-C6+1) | =-(C6+$P$1*K6/2)+1 | =-(C6+$P$1*L6/2)+1 | =-(C6+$P$1*M6)+1 |
| 7 | =A6+$P$1 | =-C7+1 | =C6+($P$1*1/6)*(K6+2*L6+2*M6+N6) | =(-C7+1) | =-(C7+$P$1*K7/2)+1 | =-(C7+$P$1*L7/2)+1 | =-(C7+$P$1*M7)+1 |
| 8 | =A7+$P$1 | =-C8+1 | =C7+($P$1*1/6)*(K7+2*L7+2*M7+N7) | =(-C8+1) | =-(C8+$P$1*K8/2)+1 | =-(C8+$P$1*L8/2)+1 | =-(C8+$P$1*M8)+1 |
| 9 | =A8+$P$1 | =-C9+1 | =C8+($P$1*1/6)*(K8+2*L8+2*M8+N8) | =(-C9+1) | =-(C9+$P$1*K9/2)+1 | =-(C9+$P$1*L9/2)+1 | =-(C9+$P$1*M9)+1 |
| 10 | =A9+$P$1 | =-C10+1 | =C9+($P$1*1/6)*(K9+2*L9+2*M9+N9) | =(-C10+1) | =-(C10+$P$1*K10/2)+1 | =-(C10+$P$1*L10/2)+1 | =-(C10+$P$1*M10)+1 |
| 42 | =A41+$P$1 | =-C42+1 | =C41+($P$1*1/6)*(K41+2*L41+2*M41+N41) | =(-C42+1) | =-(C42+$P$1*K42/2)+1 | =-(C42+$P$1*L42/2)+1 | =-(C42+$P$1*M42)+1 |

**FIGURE 4.1-5**   Runge-Kutta of fourth-order implementation.

**TABLE 4.1-3**   Runge-Kutta fourth-order versus Euler's method with step size h = 0.025 and exact solution.

| t | dy/dt = - y +1 | y(t) Numerical RK4 | Euler dy/dt = - y +1 | Numerical Euler | y(t) Exact | k1 | k2 | k3 | k4 |
|---|---|---|---|---|---|---|---|---|---|
| 0.0000 | 1.0000 | 0.0000 | 1.0000 | 0.0000 | 0.0000 | 1.0000 | 0.9875 | 0.9877 | 0.9753 |
| 0.0250 | 0.9753 | 0.0247 | 0.9756 | 0.0244 | 0.0247 | 0.9753 | 0.9631 | 0.9633 | 0.9512 |
| 0.0500 | 0.9512 | 0.0488 | 0.9518 | 0.0482 | 0.0488 | 0.9512 | 0.9393 | 0.9395 | 0.9277 |
| 0.0750 | 0.9277 | 0.0723 | 0.9286 | 0.0714 | 0.0723 | 0.9277 | 0.9161 | 0.9163 | 0.9048 |
| 0.1000 | 0.9048 | 0.0952 | 0.9060 | 0.0940 | 0.0952 | 0.9048 | 0.8935 | 0.8937 | 0.8825 |
| 0.1250 | 0.8825 | 0.1175 | 0.8839 | 0.1161 | 0.1175 | 0.8825 | 0.8715 | 0.8716 | 0.8607 |
| 0.1500 | 0.8607 | 0.1393 | 0.8623 | 0.1377 | 0.1393 | 0.8607 | 0.8499 | 0.8501 | 0.8395 |
| 0.1750 | 0.8395 | 0.1605 | 0.8413 | 0.1587 | 0.1605 | 0.8395 | 0.8290 | 0.8291 | 0.8187 |
| 0.2000 | 0.8187 | 0.1813 | 0.8207 | 0.1793 | 0.1813 | 0.8187 | 0.8085 | 0.8086 | 0.7985 |
| 0.2250 | 0.7985 | 0.2015 | 0.8007 | 0.1993 | 0.2015 | 0.7985 | 0.7885 | 0.7887 | 0.7788 |
| 0.2500 | 0.7788 | 0.2212 | 0.7812 | 0.2188 | 0.2212 | 0.7788 | 0.7691 | 0.7692 | 0.7596 |
| 0.2750 | 0.7596 | 0.2404 | 0.7621 | 0.2379 | 0.2404 | 0.7596 | 0.7501 | 0.7502 | 0.7408 |
| 0.9250 | 0.3965 | 0.6035 | 0.4011 | 0.5989 | 0.6035 | 0.3965 | 0.3916 | 0.3916 | 0.3867 |
| 0.9500 | 0.3867 | 0.6133 | 0.3913 | 0.6087 | 0.6133 | 0.3867 | 0.3819 | 0.3820 | 0.3772 |
| 0.9750 | 0.3772 | 0.6228 | 0.3817 | 0.6183 | 0.6228 | 0.3772 | 0.3725 | 0.3725 | 0.3679 |
| 1.0000 | 0.3679 | 0.6321 | 0.3724 | 0.6276 | 0.6321 | 0.3679 | 0.3633 | 0.3633 | 0.3588 |

Depending on the tolerance accepted by the programmer, one method might be preferred to the other. The Runge-Kutta is quicker in reaching a lower numerical error, even with slight larger step size and a lower number of steps, while the Euler's method is more efficient when there is a larger number of steps with a smaller size.

To analyze better how this phenomenon would work, see Fig. 4.1-7, where the step size has been reduced from 0.025 to 0.005, and the error of the Euler's method is therefore reduced drastically. Fig. 4.1-7 is simply a zoom of the three curves (exact, Euler, and RK4) in the range of $t \in [0.1, 0.11]$.

## 4.2 Force of interest, Walrasian stability, utility functions, and capital formation with ordinary differential equation

Within this section, we will provide some examples of important economic applications of the differential equations of the first order.

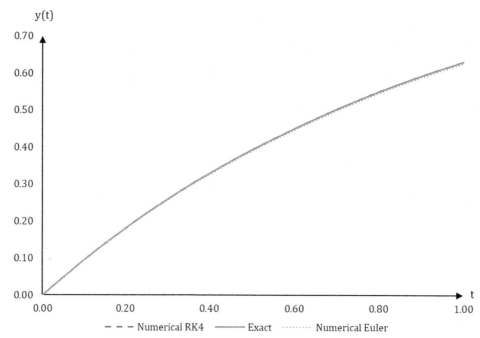

**FIGURE 4.1-6**   Runge-Kutta fourth-order versus Euler's method and exact solution with step size = 0.025.

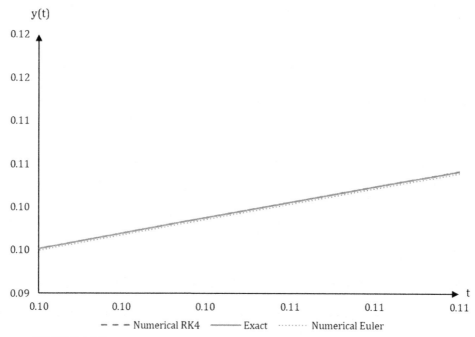

**FIGURE 4.1-7**   Runge-Kutta fourth-order versus Euler's method with step size = 0.005.

## EXAMPLE 1 (FORCE OF INTEREST)

Probably this is one of the most studied applications of the first-order differential equations, within the standard financial calculus.

For the force of interest $\delta(t)$, in the linear first-order differential Eq. (4.1-1):

$$\frac{dy(t)}{dt} + a(t)y(t) = b(t)$$

we set $b(t) = 0$ (homogenous differential equation) and $a(t) = -\delta(t)$ so that we obtain:

$$\frac{dy(t)}{dt} = \delta(t)y(t)$$

namely:

$$\delta(t) = \frac{\dot{y}(t)}{y(t)}.$$

From the force of interest, we can derive directly the form of the accumulation function $y(t)$.

For example, if the following occurs:

$$\delta(t) = \log(1+i)$$

where $i$ = annual interest rate. Then, using the general solution Eq. (4.1-3) setting $b(t) = 0$, we have that the capital accumulation function takes the following standard compounding form:

$$y(t) = e^{t \cdot \log(1+i)} = (1+i)^t.$$

Setting $i = 2\%$ and step size equal to 1, we can set up the following Excel Euler's method worksheet (Fig. 4.2-1), where under *Column E* we store the numerical Euler's method solution for $y(t)$.

| | A | B | C | D | E | F | G | H |
|---|---|---|---|---|---|---|---|---|
| 1 | t | dy/dt = y*ln(1+0.02) | dt | dy = [y*ln(1+0.02)]dt | y = Σf(t,y)dt | y(t) exact = (1+0.02)ᵗ | Error | Step |
| 2 | 0 | =E2*LN(1.02) | | | 1 | =(1+0.02)^A2 | | 1 |
| 3 | =A2+$H$2 | =E3*LN(1.02) | =A3-A2 | =B3*C3 | =E2+D3 | =(1+0.02)^A3 | =E3-F3 | |
| 4 | =A3+$H$2 | =E4*LN(1.02) | =A4-A3 | =B4*C4 | =E3+D4 | =(1+0.02)^A4 | =E4-F4 | |
| 5 | =A4+$H$2 | =E5*LN(1.02) | =A5-A4 | =B5*C5 | =E4+D5 | =(1+0.02)^A5 | =E5-F5 | |
| 6 | =A5+$H$2 | =E6*LN(1.02) | =A6-A5 | =B6*C6 | =E5+D6 | =(1+0.02)^A6 | =E6-F6 | |
| 7 | =A6+$H$2 | =E7*LN(1.02) | =A7-A6 | =B7*C7 | =E6+D7 | =(1+0.02)^A7 | =E7-F7 | |
| 8 | =A7+$H$2 | =E8*LN(1.02) | =A8-A7 | =B8*C8 | =E7+D8 | =(1+0.02)^A8 | =E8-F8 | |
| 9 | =A8+$H$2 | =E9*LN(1.02) | =A9-A8 | =B9*C9 | =E8+D9 | =(1+0.02)^A9 | =E9-F9 | |
| 10 | =A9+$H$2 | =E10*LN(1.02) | =A10-A9 | =B10*C10 | =E9+D10 | =(1+0.02)^A10 | =E10-F10 | |
| 11 | =A10+$H$2 | =E11*LN(1.02) | =A11-A10 | =B11*C11 | =E10+D11 | =(1+0.02)^A11 | =E11-F11 | |
| 12 | =A11+$H$2 | =E12*LN(1.02) | =A12-A11 | =B12*C12 | =E11+D12 | =(1+0.02)^A12 | =E12-F12 | |

**FIGURE 4.2-1**    Excel force of interest and capital accumulation law $y(t)$ via the Euler's method.

**TABLE 4.2-1**  Capital accumulation law y(t) via the Euler's method.

| t | dy/dt = y*ln(1+0.02) | dt | dy = [y*ln(1+0.02)]dt | y = Σ f(t,y)dt | y(t) exact = (1+0.02)$^t$ | Error |
|---|---|---|---|---|---|---|
| 0.0000 | 0.0198 | | | 1.0000 | 1.0000 | |
| 1.0000 | 0.0202 | 1.0000 | 0.0202 | 1.0202 | 1.0200 | 0.0002 |
| 2.0000 | 0.0206 | 1.0000 | 0.0206 | 1.0408 | 1.0404 | 0.0004 |
| 3.0000 | 0.0210 | 1.0000 | 0.0210 | 1.0618 | 1.0612 | 0.0006 |
| 4.0000 | 0.0215 | 1.0000 | 0.0215 | 1.0833 | 1.0824 | 0.0009 |
| 5.0000 | 0.0219 | 1.0000 | 0.0219 | 1.1052 | 1.1041 | 0.0011 |
| 6.0000 | 0.0223 | 1.0000 | 0.0223 | 1.1275 | 1.1262 | 0.0013 |
| 7.0000 | 0.0228 | 1.0000 | 0.0228 | 1.1503 | 1.1487 | 0.0016 |
| 8.0000 | 0.0232 | 1.0000 | 0.0232 | 1.1735 | 1.1717 | 0.0019 |
| 9.0000 | 0.0237 | 1.0000 | 0.0237 | 1.1972 | 1.1951 | 0.0021 |
| 10.0000 | 0.0242 | 1.0000 | 0.0242 | 1.2214 | 1.2190 | 0.0024 |
| 11.0000 | 0.0247 | 1.0000 | 0.0247 | 1.2461 | 1.2434 | 0.0027 |
| 12.0000 | 0.0252 | 1.0000 | 0.0252 | 1.2713 | 1.2682 | 0.0030 |
| 13.0000 | 0.0257 | 1.0000 | 0.0257 | 1.2970 | 1.2936 | 0.0033 |
| 14.0000 | 0.0262 | 1.0000 | 0.0262 | 1.3232 | 1.3195 | 0.0037 |
| 15.0000 | 0.0267 | 1.0000 | 0.0267 | 1.3499 | 1.3459 | 0.0040 |
| 16.0000 | 0.0273 | 1.0000 | 0.0273 | 1.3772 | 1.3728 | 0.0044 |
| 130.0000 | 0.2667 | 1.0000 | 0.2667 | 13.4661 | 13.1227 | 0.3434 |

The output of the numerical accumulation law $y(t)$ is given in Table 4.2-1.

In Fig. 4.2-2 we have graphed the accumulation law $y(t) = (1 + i)^t$. Notice that when we add the exponential trend line, Excel recognizes the typical continuous capital accumulation form $y(t) = e^{it}$.

## EXAMPLE 2 (WALRASIAN EQUILIBRIUM STABILITY IN PERFECT COMPETITIVE MARKETS)

Let the following:

$$z(p) = D(p) - S(p)$$

represent the excess demand in a *flex-price*[1] market, so that

$z(p) = 0$ in case of market equilibrium and $z(p) < 0$ in case of excess supply.

Let $P$ represent instead the deviation of the actual market price $p_m$ from the equilibrium price $p_e$, so that:

$$P \gtreqless 0 \text{ if } \begin{cases} \text{market price} > \text{equilibrium price} \\ \text{market price} = \text{equilibrium price} \\ \text{market price} < \text{equilibrium price} \end{cases}$$

The Walrasian adjustment (also called *groping* process or *tâtonment* in French) postulates that:

**a.** if the economy is *competitive*, in that all the agents (households and firms) take prices as given;

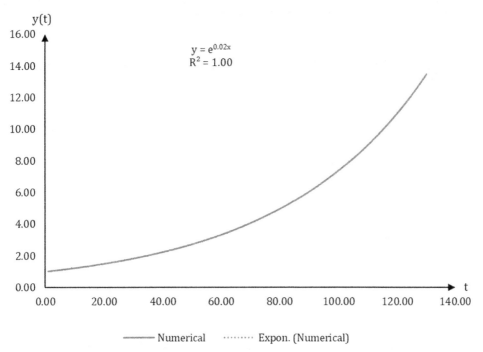

$y(t)$

$$y = e^{0.02x}$$
$$R^2 = 1.00$$

— Numerical    ········ Expon. (Numerical)

**FIGURE 4.2-2**    Capital accumulation law y(t) via the Euler's method.

**b. if** market prices decrease, when there is an excess supply and they decrease proportionally to the excess supply;

**c. if** market prices increase, when there is an excess demand and they increase proportionally to the excess demand;

**d. if** market price > equilibrium price, when there is an excess supply situation and **if** market price < equilibrium price, when there is an excess demand situation (this must imply a negative slope for the demand curve and a positive slope for the supply curve), **then** the equilibrium is stable.

Within the Walrasian adjustment, it is the *auctioneer* that matches supply and demand in a market of perfect competition. Read together with to the point (d), the points (b) and (c) imply that there is a negative feedback in prices. In case of excess supply (demand) and price higher (lower) than equilibrium price, then market prices will move in opposite direction.

The excess demand $z(p)$ can be represented as a linear function of the price deviation $P$ as follows:

$$z(P) = aP$$

and the Walrasian price adjustment can be modeled with a differential equation as follows:

$$\frac{dP}{dt} = k \cdot z(P) = kaP \quad \text{with } k > 0$$

which is a homogenous linear differential equation, such that in Eq. (4.1-1) $b(t) = 0$ and $a(t)$ $y(t) = -kaP(t)$.

Now, applying Eq. (4.1-3) the general solution is:

$$P(t) = c \cdot e^{kat} \quad \text{(where $c$ is the constant of integration).}$$

As $k > 0$, $c \cdot e^{kat}$ decreases over time and $P \to 0$ as $t \to \infty$, and therefore the equilibrium is stable, if and only if $a < 0$. If $P = (p_m - p_e) > 0$ then $z(P) < 0$, namely there is an excess supply, if $P = (p_m - p_e) < 0$ then $z(P) > 0$, namely there is an excess demand.

The graphical quality representation of the Walrasian adjustment would be as in Fig. 4.2-3, where we assume $a = -1$. As $a < 0$ the relation $\frac{dP}{dt} = k \cdot z(P)$ can be represented in a Cartesian coordinate system as a negatively sloped curve. The arrows indicate the direction of the adjustment and this technique to represent qualitatively the stability of the solution of a differential equation is called *phase diagram*. We see that the equilibrium is dynamically stable. The adjustments are explained in the comments within Fig. 4.2-3.

Having $a < 0$, if we start from and excess supply (such that $P' > 0$) the $z(P)$ is then an increasing function moving from the left to the right toward the origin, and the market price $p_m$ must then decrease to the equilibrium price $p_e = 10$, as postulated under (a) On the contrary, if we start from an excess demand (such that $P' < 0$) the $z(P)$ is a decreasing function, moving from the right to the left toward the origin and the market price $p_m$ must then increase to the equilibrium price $p_e = 10$, as postulated under (b).

Now, what we still have to do is to infer numerically in Excel the Euler's approximation of the function $P(t)$.

Setting the usual spreadsheet for the Euler's method, we come out with Table 4.2-2 solution.

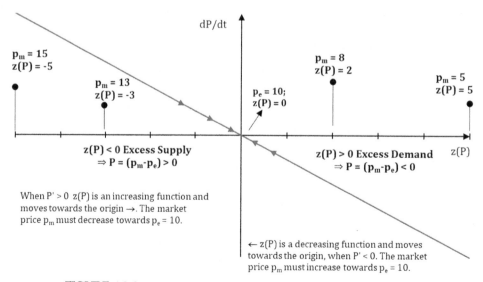

FIGURE 4.2-3   Qualitative analysis of the Walrasian adjustment ($a = -1$).

**TABLE 4.2-2**  Numerical Euler's solution versus exact solution.

| t | dP/dt = kaP | dt | dy = (kaP)*dt | P = Σ f(t,P)dt | P(t) exact = exp(kat) | Error | Step | P = Σ -f(t,P)dt |
|---|---|---|---|---|---|---|---|---|
| 0.0000 | -1.0000 | | | 1.0000 | 1.0000 | | 0.0100 | -1.0000 |
| 0.0100 | -0.9901 | 0.0100 | -0.0099 | 0.9901 | 0.9900 | 0.0000 | | -0.9901 |
| 0.0200 | -0.9803 | 0.0100 | -0.0098 | 0.9803 | 0.9802 | 0.0001 | | -0.9803 |
| 0.0300 | -0.9706 | 0.0100 | -0.0097 | 0.9706 | 0.9704 | 0.0001 | | -0.9706 |
| 0.0400 | -0.9610 | 0.0100 | -0.0096 | 0.9610 | 0.9608 | 0.0002 | | -0.9610 |
| 0.0500 | -0.9515 | 0.0100 | -0.0095 | 0.9515 | 0.9512 | 0.0002 | | -0.9515 |
| 0.0600 | -0.9420 | 0.0100 | -0.0094 | 0.9420 | 0.9418 | 0.0003 | | -0.9420 |
| 0.0700 | -0.9327 | 0.0100 | -0.0093 | 0.9327 | 0.9324 | 0.0003 | | -0.9327 |
| 0.0800 | -0.9235 | 0.0100 | -0.0092 | 0.9235 | 0.9231 | 0.0004 | | -0.9235 |
| 0.0900 | -0.9143 | 0.0100 | -0.0091 | 0.9143 | 0.9139 | 0.0004 | | -0.9143 |
| 0.1000 | -0.9053 | 0.0100 | -0.0091 | 0.9053 | 0.9048 | 0.0004 | | -0.9053 |
| 1.2400 | -0.2912 | 0.0100 | -0.0029 | 0.2912 | 0.2894 | 0.0018 | | -0.2912 |
| 1.2500 | -0.2883 | 0.0100 | -0.0029 | 0.2883 | 0.2865 | 0.0018 | | -0.2883 |
| 1.2600 | -0.2854 | 0.0100 | -0.0029 | 0.2854 | 0.2837 | 0.0018 | | -0.2854 |
| 1.2700 | -0.2826 | 0.0100 | -0.0028 | 0.2826 | 0.2808 | 0.0018 | | -0.2826 |
| 1.2800 | -0.2798 | 0.0100 | -0.0028 | 0.2798 | 0.2780 | 0.0018 | | -0.2798 |
| 1.2900 | -0.2770 | 0.0100 | -0.0028 | 0.2770 | 0.2753 | 0.0018 | | -0.2770 |
| 1.3000 | -0.2743 | 0.0100 | -0.0027 | 0.2743 | 0.2725 | 0.0018 | | -0.2743 |

Fig. 4.2-4 represents the dynamic convergence of $P(t)$ toward the equilibrium point, with two starting points at $t = 0$. We see that wherever the starting point is located, the path converges to zero, where the market price is equal to the equilibrium price and therefore $P(t) = 0$. The negative path represents the Euler's solution in case of constant of integration $c = -1$.

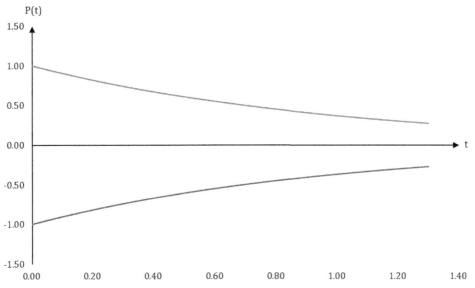

**FIGURE 4.2-4**  Numerical time path $P(t)$ dynamically converging to zero ($p_m = p_e$).

## EXAMPLE 3 (CAPITAL TIME PATH MODEL)

Another important application of differential equations to economics is regarding the capital and investment model.

Let $K(t)$ be the quantity of capital available in a company at time $t$, $\delta$ be the rate of depreciation and $I(t)$ be the gross investment, then the following relation is derived for the change in the company net (of depreciation) capital stock:

$$\dot{K}(t) = \bar{I}(t) - \delta K(t) \qquad \text{with } 0 < \delta \leq 1 \text{ and } K_0 \text{ given.}$$

The net change in the capital stock is given by the gross investment (that here we will suppose constant over time) minus the capital depreciation. The problem consists of finding the capital time path $K(t)$ once we know its differential $\bar{I}(t) - \delta K(t)$, which represents the net capital expenditure (see also Example 3 in Section 2.4, as well as the Sections 10.3 and 10.6 where the investment models have been developed within the Theory of Optimal Control).

What is required to solve in this problem is a linear differential equation of autonomous type (4.1-2):

$$\frac{dy(t)}{dt} + ay(t) = b$$

with $y(t) = K(t)$, $a = \delta$ and $b = \bar{I}(t)$.
Applying Eq. (4.1-3):

$$y(t) = e^{-A(t)} \left( \int e^{A(t)} b(t) dt + c \right)$$

we have:

$$K(t) = e^{-\delta t} \left( \int e^{\delta t} \bar{I}(t) dt + c \right)$$

$$\Rightarrow K(t) = e^{-\delta t} \left( \bar{I}(t) \frac{1}{\delta} e^{\delta t} + c \right) = ce^{-\delta t} + \frac{\bar{I}(t)}{\delta}.$$

Applying the initial value condition $K(0) = K_0$ then the constant of integration is determined as follows:

$$K_0 = c + \frac{\bar{I}(t)}{\delta} \Rightarrow c = K_0 - \frac{\bar{I}(t)}{\delta}$$

so that the general solution for $K(t)$ is:

$$K(t) = \left( K_0 - \frac{\bar{I}(t)}{\delta} \right) e^{-\delta t} + \frac{\bar{I}(t)}{\delta}.$$

| | A | B | C | D | E | F | G |
|---|---|---|---|---|---|---|---|
| 1 | t | dK/dt = Ī-δK | dt | dK = (Ī-δK)dt | K = Σf(t,K,I)dt | K(t) exact = (K₀-Ī/δ)*(exp(-δt)+Ī/δ) | Error |
| 2 | 0 | =$J$2-$I$2*E2 | | | =F2 | =($K$2-$J$2/$I$2)*EXP(-$I$2*A2)+$J$2/$I$2 | |
| 3 | =A2+$H$2 | =$J$2-$I$2*E3 | =A3-A2 | =B3*C3 | =E2+D3 | =($K$2-$J$2/$I$2)*EXP(-$I$2*A3)+$J$2/$I$2 | =E3-F3 |
| 4 | =A3+$H$2 | =$J$2-$I$2*E4 | =A4-A3 | =B4*C4 | =E3+D4 | =($K$2-$J$2/$I$2)*EXP(-$I$2*A4)+$J$2/$I$2 | =E4-F4 |
| 5 | =A4+$H$2 | =$J$2-$I$2*E5 | =A5-A4 | =B5*C5 | =E4+D5 | =($K$2-$J$2/$I$2)*EXP(-$I$2*A5)+$J$2/$I$2 | =E5-F5 |
| 6 | =A5+$H$2 | =$J$2-$I$2*E6 | =A6-A5 | =B6*C6 | =E5+D6 | =($K$2-$J$2/$I$2)*EXP(-$I$2*A6)+$J$2/$I$2 | =E6-F6 |
| 7 | =A6+$H$2 | =$J$2-$I$2*E7 | =A7-A6 | =B7*C7 | =E6+D7 | =($K$2-$J$2/$I$2)*EXP(-$I$2*A7)+$J$2/$I$2 | =E7-F7 |
| 8 | =A7+$H$2 | =$J$2-$I$2*E8 | =A8-A7 | =B8*C8 | =E7+D8 | =($K$2-$J$2/$I$2)*EXP(-$I$2*A8)+$J$2/$I$2 | =E8-F8 |
| 9 | =A8+$H$2 | =$J$2-$I$2*E9 | =A9-A8 | =B9*C9 | =E8+D9 | =($K$2-$J$2/$I$2)*EXP(-$I$2*A9)+$J$2/$I$2 | =E9-F9 |
| 10 | =A9+$H$2 | =$J$2-$I$2*E10 | =A10-A9 | =B10*C10 | =E9+D10 | =($K$2-$J$2/$I$2)*EXP(-$I$2*A10)+$J$2/$I$2 | =E10-F10 |
| 11 | =A10+$H$2 | =$J$2-$I$2*E11 | =A11-A10 | =B11*C11 | =E10+D11 | =($K$2-$J$2/$I$2)*EXP(-$I$2*A11)+$J$2/$I$2 | =E11-F11 |

FIGURE 4.2-5   Capital path Excel setup.

Setting $\delta = 0.15$, $\bar{I}(t) = 0.2$, $K_0 = 5$ and a step size equal to 0.025, we can set up the worksheet of Fig. 4.2-5, using the Euler's method. Table 4.2-3 and Fig. 4.2-6 show the tabular and graphical outputs of the solution, respectively.

## EXAMPLE 4 (LOGARITHMIC CARDINAL UTILITY FUNCTION)

This example deals with deriving one of the most used *Utility* functions in the theory of economics (see Section 6.2), namely the logarithmic (or Bernoulli) Utility function. In this case the independent variable is represented by the usual variable $x$, which measures the quantity of goods demanded.

The assumption behind the logarithmic utility function is that from the quantity demanded $x$ to the quantity $x + h$ the correspondent change of Utility function is proportional to $h$ and inversely proportional to $x$, so that we have:

$$U(x+h) - U(x) = \frac{kh}{x}.$$

As $h \to 0$ we obtain the following first-order differential equation:

$$\frac{dU(x)}{dx} = \frac{k}{x}.$$

TABLE 4.2-3   Capital path model: numerical solution versus exact solution.

| t | dK/dt = Ī-δK | dt | dK = (Ī-δK)dt | K = Σ f(t,K,I)dt | K(t) exact = (K₀-Ī/δ)*(exp(-δt)+Ī/δ) | Error |
|---|---|---|---|---|---|---|
| 0.0000 | -0.5500 | | | 5.0000 | 5.0000 | |
| 0.0250 | -0.5479 | 0.0250 | -0.0137 | 4.9863 | 4.9863 | 0.0000 |
| 0.0500 | -0.5459 | 0.0250 | -0.0136 | 4.9727 | 4.9726 | 0.0001 |
| 0.0750 | -0.5439 | 0.0250 | -0.0136 | 4.9591 | 4.9590 | 0.0001 |
| 0.1000 | -0.5418 | 0.0250 | -0.0135 | 4.9455 | 4.9454 | 0.0001 |
| 0.1250 | -0.5398 | 0.0250 | -0.0135 | 4.9320 | 4.9319 | 0.0001 |
| 0.1500 | -0.5378 | 0.0250 | -0.0134 | 4.9186 | 4.9184 | 0.0002 |
| 0.1750 | -0.5358 | 0.0250 | -0.0134 | 4.9052 | 4.9050 | 0.0002 |
| 0.2000 | -0.5338 | 0.0250 | -0.0133 | 4.8918 | 4.8916 | 0.0002 |
| 0.2250 | -0.5318 | 0.0250 | -0.0133 | 4.8785 | 4.8783 | 0.0002 |
| 0.2500 | -0.5298 | 0.0250 | -0.0132 | 4.8653 | 4.8650 | 0.0002 |
| 3.2500 | -0.3381 | 0.0250 | -0.0085 | 3.5873 | 3.5853 | 0.0021 |

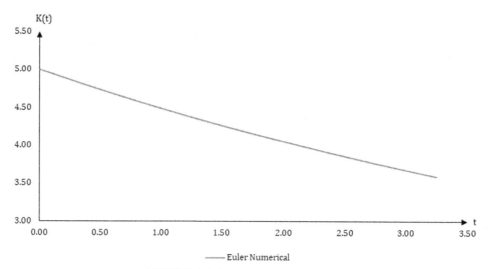

**FIGURE 4.2-6**   Numerical capital path.

Separating the variables, we have:

$$dU(x) = \frac{k}{x}dx$$

and the general solution is simply:

$$U(x) = k \log x + c.$$

One of the fundamental properties of the cardinal utility functions is that if $U(x)$ is a cardinal utility function, then also the increasing linear transformation of $U(x)$ in the form of:

$$\Omega = a \cdot U(x) + b \quad (a > 0)$$

will be a utility function and therefore $U(x) = \log x$ is the sought utility function.

The Excel numerical solution lead to Table 4.2-4 (with step size equal to 0.01) and the graph of Fig. 4.2-7.

## EXAMPLE 5 (HOUSEHOLD STOCKS TIME PATH AND A NONLINEAR FIRST-ORDER DIFFERENTIAL EQUATION)

In this example, we attempt to model the time path of stocks within households, which is similar to the capital path model of Example 3. To do this, we will use here a nonlinear first-order differential equation, solvable separating the variables.

Let $S(t)$ be the household stocks at time $t$, then the change in disposable stocks will be affected by the purchases $P(t)$ and the consumption $C(t)$, given a marginal propensity to consume $c$ $(0 < c < 1)$.

**TABLE 4.2-4**   Logarithmic utility numerical solution.

| x | dU(x)/dx = 1/x | dx | dy = (k/x)dx | Numerical U(x) = Σ f(x)dx | U(x) exact = k*logx | Error | Marginal Utility |
|---|---|---|---|---|---|---|---|
| 1.0000 | 1.0000 | | | 0.0000 | 0.0000 | | |
| 1.0100 | 0.9901 | 0.0100 | 0.0099 | 0.0099 | 0.0100 | 0.0000 | 0.9901 |
| 1.0200 | 0.9804 | 0.0100 | 0.0098 | 0.0197 | 0.0198 | 0.0001 | 0.9804 |
| 1.0300 | 0.9709 | 0.0100 | 0.0097 | 0.0294 | 0.0296 | 0.0001 | 0.9709 |
| 1.0400 | 0.9615 | 0.0100 | 0.0096 | 0.0390 | 0.0392 | 0.0002 | 0.9615 |
| 1.0500 | 0.9524 | 0.0100 | 0.0095 | 0.0486 | 0.0488 | 0.0002 | 0.9524 |
| 1.0600 | 0.9434 | 0.0100 | 0.0094 | 0.0580 | 0.0583 | 0.0003 | 0.9434 |
| 1.0700 | 0.9346 | 0.0100 | 0.0093 | 0.0673 | 0.0677 | 0.0003 | 0.9346 |
| 1.0800 | 0.9259 | 0.0100 | 0.0093 | 0.0766 | 0.0770 | 0.0004 | 0.9259 |
| 1.0900 | 0.9174 | 0.0100 | 0.0092 | 0.0858 | 0.0862 | 0.0004 | 0.9174 |
| 1.1000 | 0.9091 | 0.0100 | 0.0091 | 0.0949 | 0.0953 | 0.0005 | 0.9091 |
| 1.1100 | 0.9009 | 0.0100 | 0.0090 | 0.1039 | 0.1044 | 0.0005 | 0.9009 |
| 1.1200 | 0.8929 | 0.0100 | 0.0089 | 0.1128 | 0.1133 | 0.0005 | 0.8929 |
| 1.1300 | 0.8850 | 0.0100 | 0.0088 | 0.1216 | 0.1222 | 0.0006 | 0.8850 |
| 1.1400 | 0.8772 | 0.0100 | 0.0088 | 0.1304 | 0.1310 | 0.0006 | 0.8772 |
| 2.0000 | 0.5000 | 0.0100 | 0.0050 | 0.6907 | 0.6931 | 0.0025 | 0.5000 |

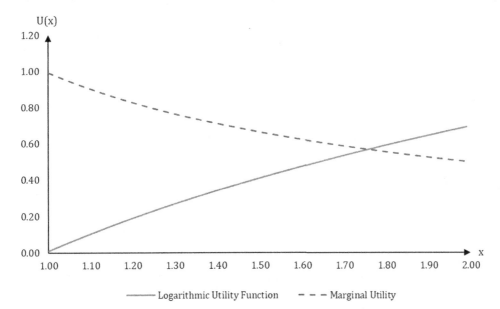

FIGURE 4.2-7   Logarithmic utility function and marginal utility.

In the discrete time interval $t, t+h$ the following will occur:

$$S(t+h) - S(t) = P(t, t+h) - C(t, t+h)$$

where on the right side of the equation we have the purchases and consumption occurred from $t$ to $t+h$.

Dividing both sides of the equation by $h$ and taking $h \rightarrow 0$ we obtain the following first-order differential equation:

$$\frac{dS(t)}{dt} = P(t) - C(t).$$

We will assume then that purchases move as a function of the stocks accumulated, according to the following relation:

$$P(t) = \sqrt{S(t)}.$$

We tend to reduce the purchases as the amount of stocks (or wealth) increases. Similarly, $C(t)$ is also a function of the stocks accumulated:

$$C(t) = f(S(t)).$$

Denoting the marginal propensity to consume with $c$, we can model the following relation between the stocks accumulated and the consumption:

$$C(t) = c\sqrt{S(t)}.$$

The consumption can be also seen therefore as a function of the purchases $P(t)$, and $c$ represents their consumed fraction. In general, we are assuming here that the more disposable stock we have in hands the less we tend to consume, consistently with the diminishing marginal utility.

The nonlinear differential equation model for the household stock is then obtained as:

$$\frac{dS(t)}{dt} = \sqrt{S(t)}(1 - c);$$

separating the variables, we have:

$$\frac{dS}{\sqrt{S}} = (1 - c)dt;$$

integrating both sides of the equation, we obtain:

$$\int \frac{1}{\sqrt{S}} dS = \int (1 - c)dt$$

which leads to the sought time path $S(t)$ (Fig. 4.2-8 and Table 4.2-5):

$$2S^{1/2} = t(1 - c)$$

$$\Rightarrow S = \left[\frac{1}{2}t(1 - c)\right]^2.$$

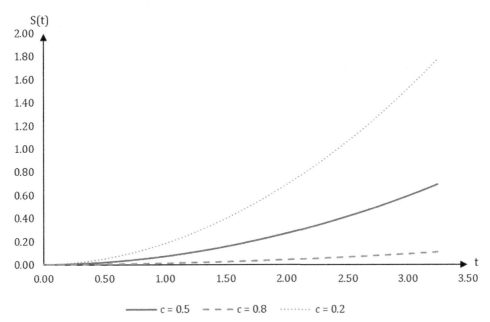

FIGURE 4.2-8 Stock time path with three different levels of marginal propensity to consume.

TABLE 4.2-5 Household stocks model: numerical versus exact solution.

| t | dS/dt = P(t) - C(t) = $S^{1/2}(1-c)$ | dt | dy = [P(t) - C(t)]dt | S(t) = Σ f(t,S)dt | S(t) exact = $[1/2t(1-c)]^2$ | Error | Step | c propensity to consume |
|---|---|---|---|---|---|---|---|---|
| 0.0000 | 0.0000 | | | 0.0000 | 0.0000 | | 0.0250 | 0.5000 |
| 0.0250 | 0.0063 | 0.0250 | 0.0002 | 0.0002 | 0.0000 | 0.0001 | | |
| 0.0500 | 0.0101 | 0.0250 | 0.0003 | 0.0004 | 0.0002 | 0.0003 | | |
| 0.0750 | 0.0137 | 0.0250 | 0.0003 | 0.0008 | 0.0004 | 0.0004 | | |
| 0.1000 | 0.0172 | 0.0250 | 0.0004 | 0.0012 | 0.0006 | 0.0006 | | |
| 0.1250 | 0.0206 | 0.0250 | 0.0005 | 0.0017 | 0.0010 | 0.0007 | | |
| 0.1500 | 0.0240 | 0.0250 | 0.0006 | 0.0023 | 0.0014 | 0.0009 | | |
| 0.1750 | 0.0273 | 0.0250 | 0.0007 | 0.0030 | 0.0019 | 0.0011 | | |
| 0.2000 | 0.0306 | 0.0250 | 0.0008 | 0.0037 | 0.0025 | 0.0012 | | |
| 0.2250 | 0.0339 | 0.0250 | 0.0008 | 0.0046 | 0.0032 | 0.0014 | | |
| 0.2500 | 0.0371 | 0.0250 | 0.0009 | 0.0055 | 0.0039 | 0.0016 | | |
| 0.2750 | 0.0404 | 0.0250 | 0.0010 | 0.0065 | 0.0047 | 0.0018 | | |
| 3.2500 | 0.4159 | 0.0250 | 0.0104 | 0.6919 | 0.6602 | 0.0318 | | |

## 4.3 Difference equations and phase diagrams

A difference equation is any equation that contains a difference of a variable. The classification within the difference equations depends on the following factors.

- **Order of the equation.** The order of the equation is the highest order of difference contained in the equation. A first-order difference equation only contains the first difference of a variable between two consecutive periods, like $y(t+1) - y(t)$. A second-order difference equation also contains the second difference in a variable between every two successive time periods, like $y(t+2) - y(t)$.
- **Autonomous** versus **nonautonomous**: a difference equation is said to be autonomous if it does not depend on time explicitly, and it is this type of equations that will be mainly analyzed here.
- **Linear** versus **nonlinear**.

### Linear first-order autonomous difference equations

Let us start then with the general solution for the following **linear, first-order, autonomous difference equation**:

$$y(t+1) = ay(t) \qquad (4.3\text{-}1)$$

This equation is also homogenous and with constant coefficient $a$.
For its solution it turns out that:

$$\begin{cases} y(1) = ay(0) \\ y(2) = ay(1) = a^2 y(0) \\ y(3) = ay(2) = a^3 y(0) \\ \vdots \\ y(t) = a^t y(0), \end{cases}$$

where $y(0)$ denotes the initial condition.
We can then write the general solution of Eq. (4.3-1) as:

$$y(t) = ca^t \qquad (4.3\text{-}2)$$

where $c$ is the initial condition of the variable $y(t)$.
Let us consider now the following nonhomogeneous equation with constant coefficients:

$$y(t+1) = ay(t) + b \qquad (4.3\text{-}3)$$

which is called nonhomogenous because $b \neq 0$.
We want to find, for Eq. (4.3-3), the conditions under which we have a *stationary solution*, such that $y(t+1) = y(t)$, as $t \to \infty$.
Let us put then Eq. (4.3-3) in the following steady state:

$$y(t+1) = y(t) = \bar{y}$$

then, it must follow:

$$\bar{y} = a\bar{y} + b \Rightarrow \bar{y} = \frac{b}{1-a} \quad a \neq 1 \tag{4.3-4}$$

This is the *steady-state* value for Eq. (4.3-3), while the general complete solution is given by the following (summing the homogenous solution (4.3-2) and the particular solution 4.3-4):

$$y(t) = ca^t + \frac{b}{1-a}. \tag{4.3-5}$$

Now, to find the constant $c$ we use the initial condition $y(t_0) = y_0$:

$$y(t_0) = ca^{t_0} + \frac{b}{1-a} \Rightarrow c = a^{-t_0}\left(y_0 - \frac{b}{1-a}\right)$$

so that Eq. (4.3-5) becomes:

$$y(t) = a^{-t_0}\left(y_0 - \frac{b}{1-a}\right)a^t + \frac{b}{1-a} = a^{t-t_0}\left(y_0 - \frac{b}{1-a}\right) + \frac{b}{1-a}$$

and for $t_0 = 0$ we have the following general solution, satisfying the initial given condition:

$$y(t) = a^t\left(y_0 - \frac{b}{1-a}\right) + \frac{b}{1-a}.$$

We have to analyze how the solution (4.3-6) behaves as $t \to \infty$. It is apparent that the behavior of the solution entirely depends on the factor $a^t$.

$$\lim_{t \to \infty} a^t \left\{ \begin{array}{c} a < -1 \\ a > +1 \\ -1 < a < 1 \end{array} \right\} = \left\{ \begin{array}{c} -\infty \\ +\infty \\ 0 \end{array} \right\} \tag{4.3-6}$$

If $|a| > 1$ the solution (4.3-6) will be divergent, while if $-1 < a < 1$ the solution will converge to $\frac{b}{1-a}$.

The convergence will follow the following paths, depending on the sign that $a$ will take.

**i.** *Monotonic convergence*, when $0 < a < 1$

**ii.** *Oscillatory convergence*, when $-1 < a < 0$

There are also the following cases to analyze.

**iii.** If $a = 0$ then $y(t) = b$.

**iv.** If $a = 1$ then $y(t)$ diverges to infinity if $b > 0$ and to minus infinity if $b < 0$.

**v.** If $a = -1$ then $y(t)$ oscillates between the two values $y(0)$ and $b - y(0)$.

## EXAMPLE 1 (LINEAR FIRST-ORDER AUTONOMOUS DIFFERENCE EQUATION)

Let us develop the following example in Excel:

$$y(t+1) = ay(t) + 10.$$

Setting $y_0 = 10$ as initial condition the general solution is given by the following function:

$$y(t) = a^t \left( 10 - \frac{10}{1-a} \right) + \frac{10}{1-a}.$$

Within the Excel, the difference equation will be simply set up like in Fig. 4.3-1, while the solution path with $a = -0.5$ is in Table 4.3-1.

Notice how in Fig. 4.3-1 and Table 4.3-1 the variable $y(t)$ is always repeated twice, for two consecutive levels of the independent time variable. This is to give to the Excel line scatter chart the typical *step-path* approach of the difference equation solution, as the variable $t$ increases. Let us study now $y(t)$ changing the parameter $a$.

**i.** *Monotonic convergence*, when $0 < a < 1$. The first case is $a = 0.5$ that corresponds to the monotonic convergence as described in Fig. 4.3-2. The convergence steady value is given by $\frac{b}{1-a} = \frac{10}{0.5} = 20$.

| | A | B | C |
|---|---|---|---|
| 1 | t | y(t) = ay(t-1) + 10 | Exact Solution |
| 2 | 0 | 10 | |
| 3 | 1 | =B2 | |
| 4 | =A2+1 | =$E$1*B2+$B$2 | =$E$1^A4*($B$2-10/(1-$E$1))+10/(1-$E$1) |
| 5 | =A3+1 | =B4 | =C4 |
| 6 | =A4+1 | =$E$1*B4+$B$2 | =$E$1^A6*($B$2-10/(1-$E$1))+10/(1-$E$1) |
| 7 | =A5+1 | =B6 | =C6 |
| 8 | =A6+1 | =$E$1*B6+$B$2 | =$E$1^A8*($B$2-10/(1-$E$1))+10/(1-$E$1) |
| 9 | =A7+1 | =B8 | =C8 |
| 10 | =A8+1 | =$E$1*B8+$B$2 | =$E$1^A10*($B$2-10/(1-$E$1))+10/(1-$E$1) |
| 11 | =A9+1 | =B10 | =C10 |
| 12 | =A10+1 | =$E$1*B10+$B$2 | =$E$1^A12*($B$2-10/(1-$E$1))+10/(1-$E$1) |
| 13 | =A11+1 | =B12 | =C12 |
| 14 | =A12+1 | =$E$1*B12+$B$2 | =$E$1^A14*($B$2-10/(1-$E$1))+10/(1-$E$1) |
| 31 | =A29+1 | =B30 | =C30 |
| 32 | =A30+1 | =$E$1*B30+$B$2 | =$E$1^A32*($B$2-10/(1-$E$1))+10/(1-$E$1) |
| 33 | =A31+1 | =B32 | =C32 |
| 34 | =A32+1 | =$E$1*B32+$B$2 | =$E$1^A34*($B$2-10/(1-$E$1))+10/(1-$E$1) |

FIGURE 4.3-1   Example 1 Excel setup.

**TABLE 4.3-1**  Example 1 Excel $y(t)$ solution path $(a = -0.5)$.

| t | y(t) = ay(t-1) + 10 | Exact Solution |
|---|---|---|
| 0.00 | 10.000 | |
| 1.00 | 10.000 | |
| 1.00 | 5.000 | 5.000 |
| 2.00 | 5.000 | 5.000 |
| 2.00 | 7.500 | 7.500 |
| 3.00 | 7.500 | 7.500 |
| 3.00 | 6.250 | 6.250 |
| 4.00 | 6.250 | 6.250 |
| 4.00 | 6.875 | 6.875 |
| 5.00 | 6.875 | 6.875 |
| 5.00 | 6.563 | 6.563 |
| 6.00 | 6.563 | 6.563 |
| 6.00 | 6.719 | 6.719 |
| 15.00 | 6.667 | 6.667 |
| 15.00 | 6.667 | 6.667 |
| 16.00 | 6.667 | 6.667 |
| 16.00 | 6.667 | 6.667 |

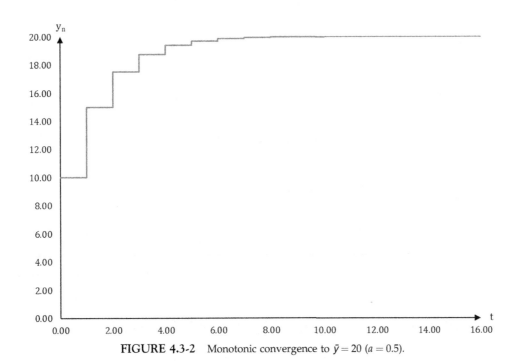

**FIGURE 4.3-2**  Monotonic convergence to $\bar{y} = 20$ ($a = 0.5$).

I. Excel and fundamental mathematics for economics

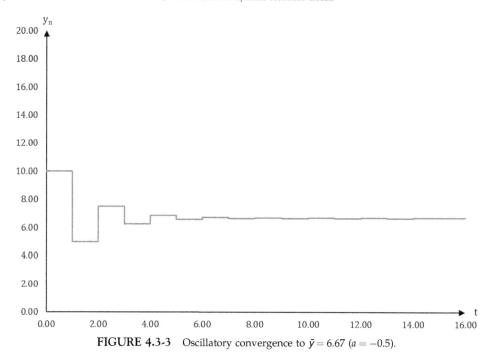

**FIGURE 4.3-3**   Oscillatory convergence to $\bar{y} = 6.67$ ($a = -0.5$).

**ii.** *Oscillatory convergence, when* $-1 < a < 0$. Setting $a = -0.5$ this second case is when $y(t)$ converges to $\frac{b}{1-a} = \frac{10}{1.5} = 6.67$ on an oscillating path, as in Fig. 4.3-3.

**iii.** $a=0$, then $y(t) = B$) See Fig. 4.3-4.

**iv.** If $a = 1$ then $y(t)$ diverges to infinity as $b = 10$. See Fig. 4.3-5.
**v.** If $a = -1$ then $y(t)$ oscillates between the two values $y(0) = 10$ and $b-y(0) = 0$. See Fig. 4.3-6.

**vi.** If $a > 1$ or $a < -1$ then y(t) will be either monotonically divergent or oscillatory divergent.

## Nonlinear first-order difference equations

Let us study now the problem of a *nonlinear difference equation* and how this can be implemented in Excel. The nonlinear difference equations cannot be solved explicitly, and they have to be analyzed resorting to the help of the *phase diagram*.

The phase diagram will help us to understand whether or not $y(t)$ converges to a steady-state equilibrium: if it does converge, no matter what the starting value $y_0$, $y(t)$ will always leads to $\bar{y}$. On the contrary, if $y(t)$ does not converge, we can study qualitatively if $y(t)$ diverges endlessly, if it keeps on oscillating between two particular values, or if it shows a chaotic pattern.

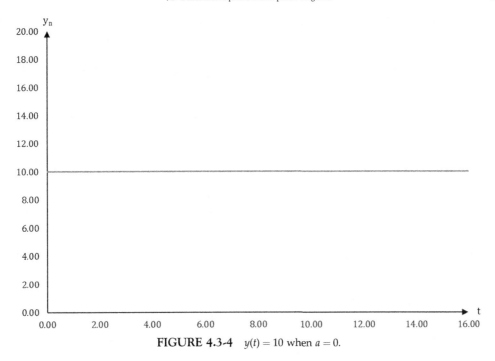

**FIGURE 4.3-4** $y(t) = 10$ when $a = 0$.

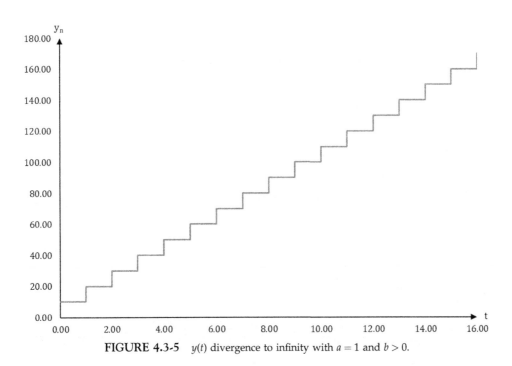

**FIGURE 4.3-5** $y(t)$ divergence to infinity with $a = 1$ and $b > 0$.

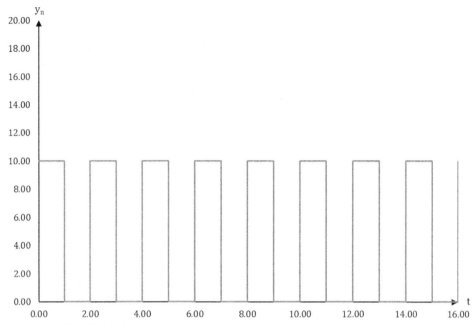

**FIGURE 4.3-6**    $y(t)$ oscillating path between the values 0 and 10 when $a = -1$.

Given the following first-order nonlinear difference equation:

$$y(t+1) = f(y(t))$$

The stationary (or steady-state) points are all the points such that $y(t)$ does not depend on time, namely such that:

$$y(t+1) = y(t).$$

**A phase diagram is a graph where we plot $y(t + 1)$ versus $y(t)$** and as a result the steady-state points will be located on the 45 degrees line as described in Fig. 4.3-7.

EXAMPLE 2 (EXCEL PHASE DIAGRAM FOR A NONLINEAR DIFFERENCE EQUATION)

Let us solve the following nonlinear difference equation:

$$y(t+1) = -y^2(t) + 2y(t).$$

This is a parabola with vertex $V$ in the point $V(1, 1)$ and roots equal to 0 and 2.

The equilibrium points are analytically found solving the following system of two equations:

$$\begin{cases} y(t+1) = 2y(t) - y^2(t) \\ y(t+1) = y(t) \end{cases} \Rightarrow \begin{cases} y_1(t) = 0, y_1(t+1) = 0 \\ y_2(t) = 1, y_2(t+1) = 1 \end{cases}$$

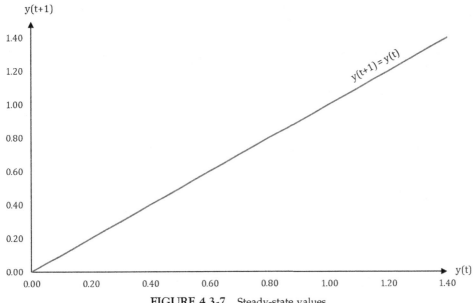

FIGURE 4.3-7    Steady-state values.

If $y(t)$ ever becomes equal to either 0 or 1, then it will stay at that value forever.

As a first point, before analyzing the phase diagram, we can simply examine the behavior of $y(t)$ plotting the data output of Fig. 4.3-8 for some trial values. The resulting values are in Table 4.3-2.

For two starting values $\in (0, 2)$, Figs. 4.3-9 and 4.3-10, in the $(t, y(t))$ Cartesian coordinates system, show the convergence path to the value of 1, beginning from either $y(0) = 0.4$ or $y(0) = 1.5$. If we just choose a slight negative beginning value $y(0) = -0.00005$ $y(t)$ will start diverging to minus infinity, as described in Fig. 4.3-11. The same will happen choosing $y(0) > 2$.

Let us build now the phase diagram, as it is represented in Fig. 4.3-12.

Using the recursion equation:

$$y(t+1) = -y^2(t) + 2y(t)$$

if we begin with $y(0) = 0.40$ then:

$$y(1) = -(0.40^2) + 2 \cdot 0.40 = 0.64$$

$$y(2) = -(0.64^2) + 2 \cdot 0.64 = 0.87$$

$$y(3) = -(0.87^2) + 2 \cdot 0.87 = 0.98 \rightarrow 1$$

| ⊿ | A | B | C | D | E |
|---|---|---|---|---|---|
| 1 | t | y(t) | | t | y(t) |
| 2 | 0 | 0.4 | | 0 | 1.8 |
| 3 | =A2+$G$2 | =B2 | | =D2+$G$2 | =E2 |
| 4 | =A2+$G$2 | =-(B2^2)+2*B | | =D2+$G$2 | =-(E2^2)+2*E2 |
| 5 | =A3+$G$2 | =B4 | | =D3+$G$2 | =E4 |
| 6 | =A4+$G$2 | =-(B4^2)+2*B | | =D4+$G$2 | =-(E4^2)+2*E4 |
| 7 | =A5+$G$2 | =B6 | | =D5+$G$2 | =E6 |
| 8 | =A6+$G$2 | =-(B6^2)+2*B | | =D6+$G$2 | =-(E6^2)+2*E6 |
| 9 | =A7+$G$2 | =B8 | | =D7+$G$2 | =E8 |
| 10 | =A8+$G$2 | =-(B8^2)+2*B | | =D8+$G$2 | =-(E8^2)+2*E8 |
| 11 | =A9+$G$2 | =B10 | | =D9+$G$2 | =E10 |
| 12 | =A10+$G$2 | =-(B10^2)+2* | | =D10+$G$2 | =-(E10^2)+2*E10 |
| 34 | =A32+$G$2 | =-(B32^2)+2* | | =D32+$G$2 | =-(E32^2)+2*E32 |

**FIGURE 4.3-8**    Excel setup of $y(t)$.

**TABLE 4.3-2**    Converging path values.

| t | y(t) | t | y(t) |
|---|---|---|---|
| 0.0000 | 0.4000 | 0.0000 | 1.8000 |
| 0.2000 | 0.4000 | 0.2000 | 1.8000 |
| 0.2000 | 0.6400 | 0.2000 | 0.3600 |
| 0.4000 | 0.6400 | 0.4000 | 0.3600 |
| 0.4000 | 0.8704 | 0.4000 | 0.5904 |
| 0.6000 | 0.8704 | 0.6000 | 0.5904 |
| 0.6000 | 0.9832 | 0.6000 | 0.8322 |
| 0.8000 | 0.9832 | 0.8000 | 0.8322 |
| 0.8000 | 0.9997 | 0.8000 | 0.9719 |
| 1.0000 | 0.9997 | 1.0000 | 0.9719 |
| 1.0000 | 1.0000 | 1.0000 | 0.9992 |
| 3.2000 | 1.0000 | 3.2000 | 1.0000 |

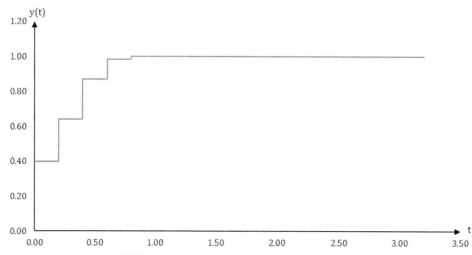

**FIGURE 4.3-9**    Convergence to $\bar{y}=1$ with $y(0)=0.4$.

I. Excel and fundamental mathematics for economics

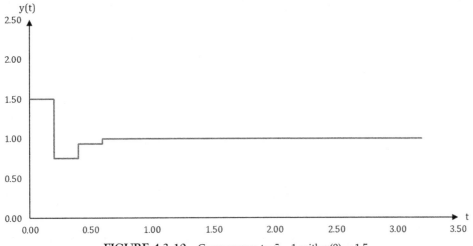

**FIGURE 4.3-10** Convergence to $\bar{y} = 1$ with $y(0) = 1.5$.

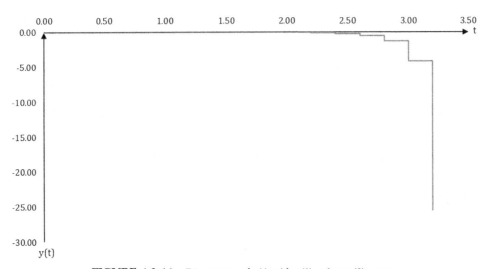

**FIGURE 4.3-11** Divergence of $y(t)$ with $y(0) < 0$ or $y(0) >$ two.

if we begin with $y(0) = 1.80$ then:

$$y(1) = -\left(1.80^2\right) + 2 \cdot 1.80 = 0.36$$

$$y(2) = -\left(0.36^2\right) + 2 \cdot 0.36 = 0.59$$

$$y(3) = -\left(0.87^2\right) + 2 \cdot 0.87 = 0.83 \rightarrow 1$$

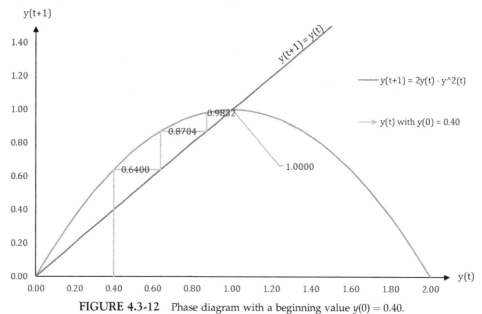

**FIGURE 4.3-12**   Phase diagram with a beginning value $y(0) = 0.40$.

The phase diagrams of $y(t)$ on the Cartesian system $(y(t), y(t+1))$ are found as follows (see Fig. 4.3-12 together with Table 4.3-3):

- consider the value $y(0) = 0.40$;
- the value $y_1 = 0.64$ is read then on the parabola function, following a vertical line;
- transpose $y_1 = 0.64$ onto the horizontal axis. We do this by extending a horizontal line from $y_1$ to the 45 degrees line;
- following a vertical line read now the value 0.64 on the parabola function, obtaining $y_2 = 0.87$;
- transpose this value onto the 45 degrees line; and
- continuing the process, the equilibrium point will be reached at the value equal to 1.

Fig. 4.3-13 shows the phase diagrams for two beginning values $y(0) = 0.40$ and $y(0) = 1.80$, while Fig. 4.3-14 describes the behavior of a diverging path with $y(0) = -0.001$ compared to a converging path.

## 4.4 Cobweb model of price adjustment and other economic models with difference equations

### Cobweb model (price adjustment model in a perfect competitive market)

One of the most studied applications of the phase diagrams and difference equations to economics is the *cobweb model* of price adjustment, typically applied within the *flex-price* perfect competitive markets, namely within those primary sector markets (e.g., commodity

**TABLE 4.3-3** Converging paths with $y(0) = 0.40$ and $y(0) = 1.80$.

| y(t+1) | y(t) | y(t+1) | y(t) |
|--------|--------|--------|--------|
| 0.0000 | 0.4000 | 0.0000 | 1.8000 |
| 0.6400 | 0.4000 | 0.3600 | 1.8000 |
| 0.6400 | 0.6400 | 0.3600 | 0.3600 |
| 0.8704 | 0.6400 | 0.5904 | 0.3600 |
| 0.8704 | 0.8704 | 0.5904 | 0.5904 |
| 0.9832 | 0.8704 | 0.8322 | 0.5904 |
| 0.9832 | 0.9832 | 0.8322 | 0.8322 |
| 0.9997 | 0.9832 | 0.9719 | 0.8322 |
| 0.9997 | 0.9997 | 0.9719 | 0.9719 |
| 1.0000 | 0.9997 | 0.9992 | 0.9719 |
| 1.0000 | 1.0000 | 0.9992 | 0.9992 |
| 1.0000 | 1.0000 | 1.0000 | 0.9992 |
| 1.0000 | 1.0000 | 1.0000 | 1.0000 |
| 1.0000 | 1.0000 | 1.0000 | 1.0000 |
| 1.0000 | 1.0000 | 1.0000 | 1.0000 |
| 1.0000 | 1.0000 | 1.0000 | 1.0000 |
| 1.0000 | 1.0000 | 1.0000 | 1.0000 |
| 1.0000 | 1.0000 | 1.0000 | 1.0000 |
| 1.0000 | 1.0000 | 1.0000 | 1.0000 |
| 1.0000 | 1.0000 | 1.0000 | 1.0000 |
| 1.0000 | 1.0000 | 1.0000 | 1.0000 |
| 1.0000 | 1.0000 | 1.0000 | 1.0000 |
| 1.0000 | 1.0000 | 1.0000 | 1.0000 |

markets) where the price adjustment is typically determined by the interaction of supply and demand. The first articles about this model were written by the British economist Nicholas Kaldor (*A Classificatory Note on the Determination of Equilibrium*, 1934) and by the American agrarian economist Mordecai Ezekiel (*The Cobweb Theorem*, 1938).

The model is based on a time lag between supply and demand decisions and on other key assumptions that we will see throughout the numerical example.

Let us have the following linear demand and supply functions:

$$S_t = a + sp_{t-1} \quad (s > 0)$$

$$D_t = b + dp_t \quad (d < 0).$$

Equating the supply and demand we have:

$$a + sp_{t-1} = b + dp_t$$

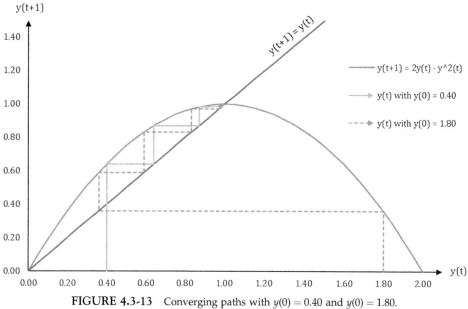

**FIGURE 4.3-13**    Converging paths with $y(0) = 0.40$ and $y(0) = 1.80$.

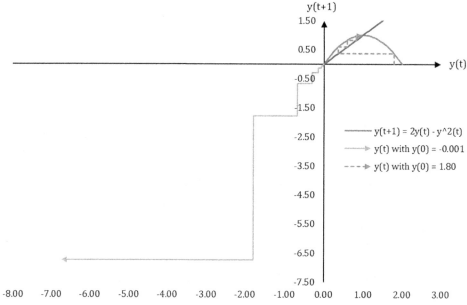

**FIGURE 4.3-14**    Diverging path with $y(0) = -0.001$ versus converging path with $y(0) = 1.80$.

from which we can obtain $p_t$ as a function of $p_{t-1}$ as follows:

$$p_t = \frac{s}{d}p_{t-1} + \frac{a-b}{d}$$

which represents a linear first-order nonhomogeneous difference equation in the form of Eq. (4.3-3):

$$y(t+1) = ay(t) + b$$

with solution:

$$y(t) = a^t\left(y_0 - \frac{b}{1-a}\right) + \frac{b}{1-a}.$$

The general solution of the cobweb price difference equation is therefore:

$$p_t = K\left(\frac{s}{d}\right)^t + \frac{\dfrac{a-b}{d}}{1 - \dfrac{s}{d}} = K\left(\frac{s}{d}\right)^t + \frac{a-b}{d-s}.$$

In $t = 0$ we have:

$$p_0 = K + \frac{a-b}{d-s}$$

so that $K$ becomes:

$$K = p_0 - \frac{a-b}{d-s}$$

and the general solution of the cobweb model is finally obtained as:

$$p_t = \left(p_0 - \frac{a-b}{d-s}\right)\left(\frac{s}{d}\right)^t + \frac{a-b}{d-s}. \tag{4.4-1}$$

The equilibrium price $p_e$ is therefore:

$$p_e = \frac{a-b}{d-s}$$

The equilibrium price can be also found noticing that when the demand equals the supply we have:

$$S_t = a + sp_{t-1} = D_t = b + dp_t$$

$$\Rightarrow S_t - D_t = 0$$

$$a + s p_{t-1} - b - d p_t = 0$$

Setting $p_{t-1} = p_t$ we have:

$$a + s p_t - b - d p_t = 0 \Rightarrow p_t = \frac{(b-a)}{(s-d)}$$

As $d < 0$ the above result corresponds to the equilibrium price found before.

As usual we have to analyze how the solution (4.4-1) behaves as $t \to \infty$. It is apparent that the behavior of the solution entirely depends on the factor $\left(\frac{s}{d}\right)^t$.

$$\lim_{t \to \infty} \left(\frac{s}{d}\right)^t \left\{ \begin{array}{l} \dfrac{s}{d} < -1 \\[2mm] \dfrac{s}{d} = -1 \\[2mm] -1 < \dfrac{s}{d} < 0 \end{array} \right\} \Rightarrow \left\{ \begin{array}{l} Diverging\ Path \\ Oscillatory\ Path \\ Converging\ Path \end{array} \right\}$$

### EXAMPLE 1 (COBWEB MODEL)

Let us have the following supply and demand function parameters:

$$a = 1$$

$$b = 10$$

$$s = 40$$

$$d = -50$$

As usual we set up the solution function (4.4-1) in a worksheet as follows in Fig. 4.4-1 and Table 4.4-1:

With the given parameters we have that:

$$-1 < \frac{s}{d} = -0.80 < 0$$

which corresponds to the converging path case, as described in Table 4.4-1 and Fig. 4.4-2. The convergence is therefore guaranteed by the lower slope of the supply curve compared to that of the demand curve.

| ▲ | A | B |
|---|---|---|
| 1 | t | pt |
| 2 | 0 | 0.2 |
| 3 | 1 | =B2 |
| 4 | =A2+1 | =B2*$N$2/$O$2+($L$2-$M$2)/$O$2 |
| 5 | =A3+1 | =B4 |
| 6 | =A4+1 | =B4*$N$2/$O$2+($L$2-$M$2)/$O$2 |
| 7 | =A5+1 | =B6 |
| 8 | =A6+1 | =B6*$N$2/$O$2+($L$2-$M$2)/$O$2 |
| 9 | =A7+1 | =B8 |
| 10 | =A8+1 | =B8*$N$2/$O$2+($L$2-$M$2)/$O$2 |
| 11 | =A9+1 | =B10 |
| 12 | =A10+1 | =B10*$N$2/$O$2+($L$2-$M$2)/$O$2 |
| 13 | =A11+1 | =B12 |
| 14 | =A12+1 | =B12*$N$2/$O$2+($L$2-$M$2)/$O$2 |
| 15 | =A13+1 | =B14 |
| 16 | =A14+1 | =B14*$N$2/$O$2+($L$2-$M$2)/$O$2 |
| 17 | =A15+1 | =B16 |
| 18 | =A16+1 | =B16*$N$2/$O$2+($L$2-$M$2)/$O$2 |

FIGURE 4.4-1    Excel setup of the solution (4.4-1).

TABLE 4.4-1    Converging path from $p(0) = 0.20$.

| t | pt |
|---|---|
| 0.00 | 0.20 |
| 1.00 | 0.20 |
| 1.00 | 0.02 |
| 2.00 | 0.02 |
| 2.00 | 0.16 |
| 3.00 | 0.16 |
| 3.00 | 0.05 |
| 4.00 | 0.05 |
| 4.00 | 0.14 |
| 5.00 | 0.14 |
| 25.00 | 0.10 |
| 25.00 | 0.10 |
| 26.00 | 0.10 |
| 26.00 | 0.10 |
| 27.00 | 0.10 |
| 27.00 | 0.10 |
| 28.00 | 0.10 |
| 28.00 | 0.10 |

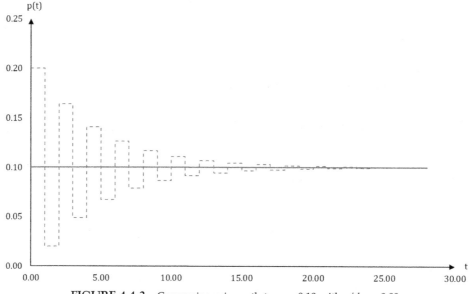

**FIGURE 4.4-2** Converging price path to $p_e = 0.10$ with $s/d = -0.80$.

Fig. 4.4-2 has been created on the basis of the price adjustment described in Table 4.4-2, through which the model will reach a steady-state position such that:

$$S_e = D_e = 5$$

and

$$p_e = 0.10.$$

Fig. 4.4-3 and Table 4.4-2 can be explained by the fundamental assumption of the cobweb model, according to which the producers look at the current price (e.g., $p(0) = 0.2$) to plan the

**TABLE 4.4-2** Demand and supply adjustment and equilibrium price.

| t | p | Dt_quantities/St_quantities | Adjustment |
|---|---|---|---|
| 0.0 | 0.20 | 0.00 | Dt |
| 0.0 | 0.20 | 9.00 | St 9 quantities are offered for the following period at p(0) = 0.2 |
| 1.0 | 0.02 | 9.00 | Dt 9 quantities are purchased at p(1) = 0.02 read on the demand curve |
| 1.0 | 0.02 | 1.80 | St At p(1) = 0.02 only 1.8 quantities are offered |
| 2.0 | 0.16 | 1.80 | Dt 1.8 quantities are purchased at 0.16 |
| 2.0 | 0.16 | 7.56 | St At p(2) = 0.16 only 7.56 quanities are offered |
| 3.0 | 0.05 | 7.56 | Dt etc... |
| 26.0 | 0.10 | 5.01 | |
| 27.0 | 0.10 | 5.01 | |
| 27.0 | 0.10 | 4.99 | |

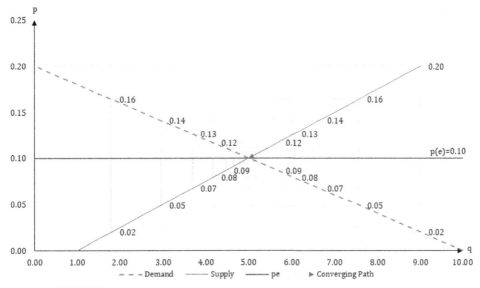

**FIGURE 4.4-3** Cobweb model of price adjustment with a converging path.

production for the next period (e.g., $q(1) = 9.0$). For example, within the agricultural markets, the supply typically depends on the amount previously planned and the amount planned depends on the price at the time of planning.

This implies that the producers have *adaptive expectations* (many economists criticized the adaptive expectations proposing the *rational expectations* of the agents) through which they assume that the current price will also prevail in the next period.

Within this next period, all the production must be sold whatever the price is, as a second assumption of the model is that the goods produced are either perishable from one period to the other or too costly to be stored (i.e., a zero-inventory assumption is made). In the cobweb model, the price is assumed therefore to be set in such a way as to clear the current output of every time period. The model was originally created to explain the corn economic price dynamics.

Figs. 4.4−4−4.4-7 show the other possible paths (diverging and oscillating).

## A basic Keynesian model

Let us set up the following Keynesian system of equations, where consumption decisions for the current period are based on the disposable income in the previous period:

$$\begin{cases} I_t = \bar{I} \\ C_t = \bar{C} + \alpha Y_{t-1} \quad 0 < \alpha < 1 \ (\alpha \text{ is the marginal propensity to consume}) \\ Y_t = C_t + I_t \quad \text{(not considering G and net exports)} \end{cases}$$

from which, we have:

$$Y_t = \bar{C} + \alpha Y_{t-1} + \bar{I},$$

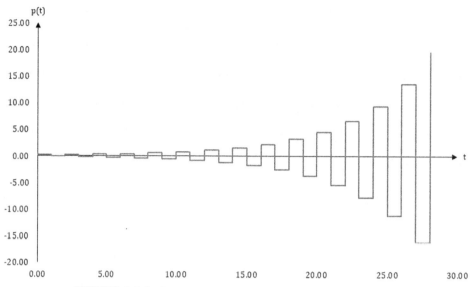

**FIGURE 4.4-4** Diverging path with $s/d = -1.20$ ($s = 60$, $d = -50$).

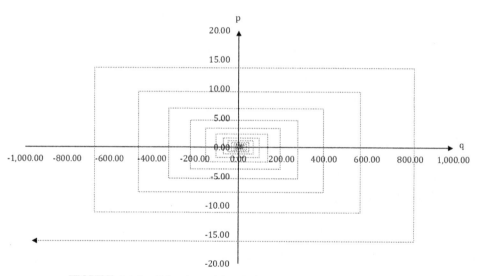

**FIGURE 4.4-5** Cobweb model with diverging path with $s/d = -1.20$.

that we can rearrange into the following linear, nonhomogeneous difference equation:

$$Y_t = \alpha Y_{t-1} + (\overline{C} + \overline{I}).$$

The steady-state value is given by setting:

$$\overline{Y} = \alpha\overline{Y} + (\overline{C} + \overline{I}) \Rightarrow \overline{Y} = \frac{\overline{C} + \overline{I}}{1 - \alpha},$$

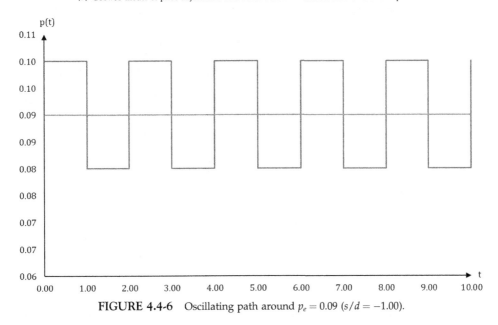

**FIGURE 4.4-6** Oscillating path around $p_e = 0.09$ ($s/d = -1.00$).

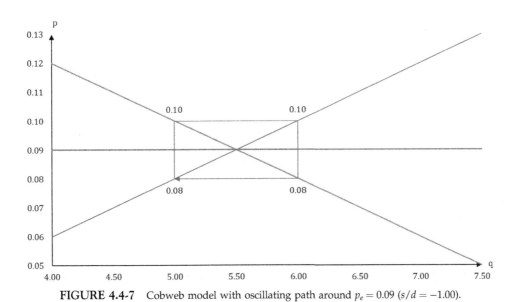

**FIGURE 4.4-7** Cobweb model with oscillating path around $p_e = 0.09$ ($s/d = -1.00$).

while the solution of $Y_t = \alpha Y_{t-1}$ is given by:

$$Y_t = c\alpha^t.$$

The general solution is therefore:

$$Y_t = c\alpha^t + \frac{\overline{C} + \overline{I}}{1 - \alpha}.$$

Now, as usual through the initial condition $Y_0$ at $t = 0$ we calculate the constant $c$ as follows:

$$c = Y_0 - \frac{\overline{C} + \overline{I}}{1 - \alpha}$$

so that the general solution satisfying the initial condition becomes:

$$Y_t = \left(Y_0 - \frac{\overline{C} + \overline{I}}{1 - \alpha}\right)\alpha^t + \frac{\overline{C} + \overline{I}}{1 - \alpha},$$

which is the solution in the form of Eq. (4.3-6).

We have now to analyze how this solution behaves as $t \to \infty$. We do this through the following numerical Excel example.

### EXAMPLE 2 (KEYNESIAN MODEL)

The numerical model is described by Table 4.4-3 (see also Table 4.4-4 and Fig. 4.4-8). The model is simple in its structure, and the convergence is immediately reached after a few steps. The stable level of the national total output $\overline{Y}$ will depend on the assumed marginal propensity to consume.

**TABLE 4.4-3** Keynesian model: converging $Y(t)$ with $Y(0) = 3.00$.

| t | Y(t) | C(t) | Inv. | Exact solution | $\overline{I}$ | C min @ $t_0$ | α |
|------|------|------|------|------|------|------|------|
| 0.00 | 3.00 | 2.00 | 1.00 | 3.00 | 1.00 | 2.00 | 0.20 |
| 1.00 | 3.00 | 2.60 | 1.00 | | | | |
| 1.00 | 3.60 | 2.60 | 1.00 | 3.60 | | Y stable long term | 3.75 |
| 2.00 | 3.60 | 2.72 | 1.00 | | | | |
| 2.00 | 3.72 | 2.72 | 1.00 | 3.72 | | | |
| 3.00 | 3.72 | 2.74 | 1.00 | | | | |
| 3.00 | 3.74 | 2.74 | 1.00 | 3.74 | | | |
| 4.00 | 3.74 | 2.75 | 1.00 | | | | |
| 4.00 | 3.75 | 2.75 | 1.00 | 3.75 | | | |
| 5.00 | 3.75 | 2.75 | 1.00 | | | | |
| 5.00 | 3.75 | 2.75 | 1.00 | 3.75 | | | |
| 6.00 | 3.75 | 2.75 | 1.00 | | | | |
| 6.00 | 3.75 | 2.75 | 1.00 | 3.75 | | | |
| 7.00 | 3.75 | 2.75 | 1.00 | 3.75 | | | |

**TABLE 4.4-4**   Keynesian model: converging $Y(t)$ with $Y(0) = 5.00$.

| t | Yt | Ct | Inv. | Exact solution | İ | C min @ $t_0$ | α |
|------|------|------|------|------|------|------|------|
| 0.00 | 5.00 | 2.00 | 1.00 | 5.00 | 1.00 | 2.00 | 0.20 |
| 1.00 | 5.00 | 3.00 | 1.00 | | | | |
| 1.00 | 4.00 | 3.00 | 1.00 | 4.00 | | Y stable long term | 3.75 |
| 2.00 | 4.00 | 2.80 | 1.00 | | | | |
| 2.00 | 3.80 | 2.80 | 1.00 | 3.80 | | | |
| 3.00 | 3.80 | 2.76 | 1.00 | | | | |
| 3.00 | 3.76 | 2.76 | 1.00 | 3.76 | | | |
| 4.00 | 3.76 | 2.75 | 1.00 | | | | |
| 4.00 | 3.75 | 2.75 | 1.00 | 3.75 | | | |
| 5.00 | 3.75 | 2.75 | 1.00 | | | | |
| 5.00 | 3.75 | 2.75 | 1.00 | 3.75 | | | |
| 6.00 | 3.75 | 2.75 | 1.00 | | | | |
| 6.00 | 3.75 | 2.75 | 1.00 | 3.75 | | | |
| 7.00 | 3.75 | 2.75 | 1.00 | 3.75 | | | |

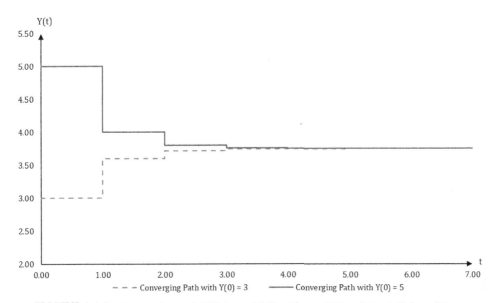

**FIGURE 4.4-8**   Converging path $Y(t)$ toward 3.75 with $\alpha = 0.20$ and two initial conditions.

## 4.5  Systems of linear differential equations

A first-order, nonhomogenous system of autonomous linear differential equations can be expressed formally in the following matrix notation:

$$\begin{bmatrix} \dot{y}_1(t) \\ \vdots \\ \dot{y}_n(t) \end{bmatrix} = A \begin{bmatrix} y_1(t) \\ \vdots \\ y_n(t) \end{bmatrix} + \begin{bmatrix} b_1 \\ \vdots \\ b_n \end{bmatrix} \tag{4.5-1}$$

where $A$ is a $(m, n)$ matrix of constant coefficients.

The system is autonomous because it does not depend explicitly on the variable $t$, namely the coefficients $a_{ij}$ and $b_i$ are constant.

We will only deal with systems of two differential equations represented as follows:

$$\begin{cases} \dot{y}_1(t) = a_{11}y_1(t) + a_{12}y_2(t) + b_1 \\ \dot{y}_2(t) = a_{21}y_1(t) + a_{22}y_2(t) + b_2 \end{cases}$$

The **complete solution**, as usual, will consist of the sum of the **homogeneous solution** and the **particular solution**. As the differential equations are linear, the usual exponential terms will appear. There are two methods to solve Eq. (4.5-1): **by substitution** and the **direct method**. We will utilize the direct method.

## Homogeneous solutions

The homogeneous solution that solves Eq. (4.5-1) can be found as follows. Let us consider the following homogenous system under matrix notation:

$$\dot{y}(t) = Ay(t) \qquad\qquad (4.5\text{-}2)$$

for $n = 1$ it will be:

$$\dot{y}(t) = ay(t)$$

and the solution will be:

$$y(t) = ce^t.$$

Let us consider now a matrix notation of $y(t)$ as:

$$y(t) = ve^{\lambda t} \quad (v \in \Re^n \text{ and } \lambda \in \Re)$$

$$\Rightarrow \dot{y}(t) = \lambda ve^{\lambda t}$$

using this in the system (4.5-2) we have the following:

$$\lambda ve^{\lambda t} = Ave^{\lambda t}$$

$$\lambda v = Av$$

$$(Av - \lambda Iv) = [0]$$

and finally:

$$(A - \lambda I)v = [0] \qquad (4.5\text{-}3)$$

excluding the trivial solution $v = 0$ the above system will admit a nontrivial solution $v \neq 0$ if and only if (see Remark 1 in Section 3.2 and flow chart in Fig. 3.2-5):

$$|A - \lambda I| = 0. \qquad (4.5\text{-}4)$$

Eq. (4.5-4) is called the **characteristic equation** of degree $n$ in the unknown variable $\lambda$. Eq. (4.5-3) has both real and complex roots, and we will limit our attention only to the real case. The roots are called **eigenvalues** of the characteristic equation while $v$ is called the **eigenvector.** For each eigenvalue:

$$\lambda_1, \lambda_2, \cdots, \lambda_n$$

there will be an eigenvector:

$$v^1, v^2, \cdots, v^n$$

and there we will be $n$ solutions for the homogeneous system (4.5-2) in the form:

$$y^1 = v^1 e^{\lambda_1 t}, y^2 = v^2 e^{\lambda_2 t}, \cdots, y^n = v^n e^{\lambda_n t} \quad (y^i, v^i \in \mathcal{R}^n).$$

The objective is to find now a general solution including all the above solutions.

If the eigenvectors $v^1, v^2, \cdots, v^n$ are **linearly independent,** then the following is a solution for Eq. (4.5-2):

$$\begin{cases} y(t) = C_1 v^1 e^{\lambda_1 t} + C_2 v^2 e^{\lambda_2 t} + \cdots + C_n v^n e^{\lambda_n t} \\ y(t) = \displaystyle\sum_{s=1}^{n} C_s v^s e^{\lambda_s t} \quad s.t. \ (v^1, v^2, \cdots, v^n) \text{ are } l.i \end{cases}$$

where $C_s$ are the constants of integration.

*Case* n $= 2$

In this case, the determinant (4.5-4) becomes:

$$\begin{vmatrix} a_{11} - \lambda & a_{12} \\ a_{21} & a_{22} - \lambda \end{vmatrix} = 0$$

which is, after rearranging:

$$\lambda^2 - (a_{11} + a_{22})\lambda + (a_{11}a_{22} - a_{12}a_{21}) = 0.$$

The above characteristic equation can be written also as:

$$\lambda^2 - tr(A)\lambda + |A| = 0 \tag{4.5-5}$$

where $tr(A)$ is the **trace** of the matrix $A$:

$$tr(A) = a_{11} + a_{22}$$

and $|A|$ the determinant of the matrix $A$:

$$a_{11}a_{22} - a_{12}a_{21}.$$

The two roots of the quadratic Eq. (4.5-5) are then:

$$\lambda_1, \lambda_2 = \frac{tr(A)}{2} \pm \frac{1}{2}\sqrt{tr(A)^2 - 4|A|}. \tag{4.5-6}$$

It can be proved via the substitution method that the homogeneous solutions for $y_1(t)$ and $y_2(t)$ have the following forms:

$$y_1(t) = C_1 e^{\lambda_1 t} + C_2 e^{\lambda_2 t}$$

$$y_2(t) = \frac{\lambda_1 - a_{11}}{a_{12}} C_1 e^{\lambda_1 t} + \frac{\lambda_2 - a_{11}}{a_{12}} C_2 e^{\lambda_2 t} \tag{4.5-7}$$

where $C_1$ and $C_2$ are the constants of integrations.

## Particular solutions

Setting $\dot{y}(t) = 0$ in the complete system (4.5-1) we have:

$$A \begin{bmatrix} y_1(t) \\ \vdots \\ y_n(t) \end{bmatrix} + \begin{bmatrix} b_1 \\ \vdots \\ b_n \end{bmatrix} = 0$$

or in a more condensed form:

$$Ay(t) + b = 0,$$

from which we have the particular solution vector:

$$\bar{y} = -A^{-1}b$$

as long as the inverse matrix $A^{-1}$ exists. The inverse matrix will exist if and only if $\det(A) \neq 0$.

## Case n = 2

It can be proved that the complete solutions have the following forms (see Remark 3 in Chapter 3):

$$y_1(t) = C_1 e^{\lambda_1 t} + C_2 e^{\lambda_2 t} + \bar{y}_1$$

$$y_2(t) = \frac{\lambda_1 - a_{11}}{a_{12}} C_1 e^{\lambda_1 t} + \frac{\lambda_2 - a_{11}}{a_{12}} C_2 e^{\lambda_2 t} + \bar{y}_2 \qquad (4.5\text{-}8)$$

## Stability analysis

The eigenvalues play a key role to analyze whether the solutions of the system are stable or not and limiting our attention to the cases of *real* eigenvalues the following three cases may occur:

i. $\lambda_1$, $\lambda_2$ are both *positive* $\Rightarrow$ $y_1(t)$, $y_2(t)$ will both diverge from the steady state, except when the constant of integration are equal to zero. The system has an *unstable node*.

ii. $\lambda_1$, $\lambda_2$ are both negative $\Rightarrow$ $y_1(t)$, $y_2(t)$ will both always converge to the steady state, whatever the values taken by the constants of integration. The system is called to have a *stable node*.

iii. $\lambda_1$, $\lambda_2$ have opposite sign, $\Rightarrow$ the exponential term containing the negative root goes to zero as $t \to \infty$, while the exponential term containing the positive root diverges to infinity as $t \to \infty$, which means that both solutions $y_1(t)$ and $y_2(t)$ will be divergent. The system is called to have a *saddle point* equilibrium. When the constant of integration of the divergent exponential is equal to zero $y_1(t)$, $y_2(t)$ will, however, converge to their steady-state values and $y_1(t)$, $y_2(t)$ will satisfy the following equation (called *saddle path*):

$$y_2 = \frac{\lambda_1 - a_{11}}{a_{12}} (y_1 - \bar{y}_1) + \bar{y}_2. \qquad (4.5\text{-}9)$$

We will show in the next examples how we can deal in Excel with the solution of a two-equations differential system and how a stability qualitative analysis can be performed using the *phase diagrams* technique, that we have already seen in the nonlinear difference equations.

## EXAMPLE 1 (N = 2 HOMOGENEOUS SYSTEM WITH A SADDLE POINT)

Let us solve the following system:

$$\dot{y}(t) = \begin{bmatrix} 1 & 12 \\ 3 & 1 \end{bmatrix} y(t)$$

with initial condition. $y(0) = \begin{bmatrix} 0 \\ 1 \end{bmatrix}$

Using Eq. (4.5-6) we find the two eigenvalues:

$$\lambda_1, \lambda_2 = \frac{2}{2} \pm \frac{1}{2}\sqrt{4 - 4(1 - 3 \cdot 12)} = 1 \pm \frac{1}{2}\sqrt{144} = \begin{cases} \lambda_1 = -5 \\ \lambda_2 = +7 \end{cases}$$

while the eigenvectors associated to these roots can be represented by:

$$v^1 = \begin{bmatrix} 2 \\ -1 \end{bmatrix} \text{ and } v^2 = \begin{bmatrix} 2 \\ 1 \end{bmatrix}$$

found as follows.

For $\lambda_1 = -5$ Eq. (4.5-3) becomes:

$$(A + 5I)v^1 = [0]$$

$$\Rightarrow \begin{bmatrix} 6 & 12 \\ 3 & 6 \end{bmatrix}\begin{bmatrix} v_1 \\ v_2 \end{bmatrix} = [0]$$

which is:

$$\begin{cases} 6v_1 + 12v_2 = 0 \\ 3v_1 + 6v_2 = 0 \end{cases}$$

The second equation is redundant, and we can have infinite solutions from the first:

For $v_2 = -1$ we obtain $v_1 = 2$.

For $\lambda_2 = 7$ Eq. (4.5-3) becomes:

$$(A - 7I)v^2 = [0]$$

$$\Rightarrow \begin{bmatrix} -6 & 12 \\ 3 & -6 \end{bmatrix}\begin{bmatrix} v_1 \\ v_2 \end{bmatrix} = [0]$$

which is:

$$\begin{cases} -6v_1 + 12v_2 = 0 \\ 3v_1 - 6v_2 = 0 \end{cases} \Rightarrow \begin{cases} -v_1 + 2v_2 = 0 \\ v_1 - 2v_2 = 0 \end{cases}.$$

From the first equation we have $v_1 = 2v_2$; then, for $v_2 = 1$ we have $v_1 = 2$.

For the sake of completeness, we also calculate the so-called normalized eigenvectors. These can be found satisfying the Euclidean distance condition or normalization:

$$v_1^2 + v_2^2 = 1.$$

For $\lambda_1 = -5$ and from $v_1 = -2v_2$ we have:

$$(-2v_2)^2 + v_2^2 = 1 \Rightarrow 5v_2^2 = 1 \Rightarrow v_2 = \pm\frac{1}{\sqrt{5}}$$

$$v_2 = +\frac{1}{\sqrt{5}} \Rightarrow v_1 = -\frac{2}{\sqrt{5}}.$$

For $\lambda_1 = 7$ and from $v_1 = 2v_2$ we have:

$$(2v_2)^2 + v_2^2 = 1 \Rightarrow 5v_2^2 = 1 \Rightarrow v_2 = \pm\frac{1}{\sqrt{5}}$$

$$v_2 = +\frac{1}{\sqrt{5}} \Rightarrow v_1 = +\frac{2}{\sqrt{5}}.$$

Avoiding the square roots in the solutions we continue with the nonnormalized vectors $(2 \times 1)$ found before and the two separate solutions are:

$\mathbf{y}^1(t) = \begin{bmatrix} 2 \\ -1 \end{bmatrix} e^{-5t}$ and. $\mathbf{y}^2(t) = \begin{bmatrix} 2 \\ 1 \end{bmatrix} e^{7t}$, while the general solution is represented by the

following linear combination of the above two vectors:

$$\begin{cases} y(t) = C_1 \begin{bmatrix} 2 \\ -1 \end{bmatrix} e^{-5t} + C_2 \begin{bmatrix} 2 \\ 1 \end{bmatrix} e^{7t} \\ \\ s.t.\ y(0) = \begin{bmatrix} 0 \\ 1 \end{bmatrix} \end{cases}$$

with its vector components as follows (according to Eq. 4.5-7):

$$y_1(t) = C_1 2e^{-5t} + C_2 2e^{7t},$$

$$y_2(t) = -C_1 e^{-5t} + C_2 e^{7t}.$$

In $y(2)$ the coefficients are found just multiplying by the scalar 2 the following:

$$\frac{\lambda_1 - a_{11}}{a_{12}} = \frac{-5 - 1}{12} = -\frac{1}{2}$$

$$\frac{\lambda_2 - a_{11}}{a_{12}} = \frac{7 - 1}{12} = \frac{1}{2}.$$

We still have to apply the initial condition $y(0)$:

$$\begin{bmatrix} 0 \\ 1 \end{bmatrix} = C_1 \begin{bmatrix} 2 \\ -1 \end{bmatrix} + C_2 \begin{bmatrix} 2 \\ 1 \end{bmatrix} = \begin{bmatrix} 2C_1 \\ -C_1 \end{bmatrix} + \begin{bmatrix} 2C_2 \\ C_2 \end{bmatrix}$$

obtaining the following system:

$$\begin{cases} 0 = 2C_1 + 2C_2 \\ 1 = -C_1 + C_2 \end{cases} \Rightarrow \begin{cases} 0 = 2C_1 + 2 + 2C_1 \\ 1 + C_1 = C_2 \end{cases} \Rightarrow \begin{cases} C_1 = -1/2 \\ C_2 = +1/2 \end{cases}.$$

The homogenous solution that satisfies the initial condition is therefore:

$$y(t) = -\frac{1}{2} \begin{bmatrix} 2 \\ -1 \end{bmatrix} e^{-5t} + \frac{1}{2} \begin{bmatrix} 2 \\ 1 \end{bmatrix} e^{7t}$$

Let us see now how to develop in Excel the numerical solution. Two techniques are shown to deal with the two-differential equation system.

1. We just follow the steps of the **direct method**, resorting to the Excel to perform the linear algebra calculation to obtain the eigenvalues and the eigenvectors. Once these are obtained it is just a matter of plotting the exact solution trajectories and the phase diagram.
2. **Numerical Euler's method.** We implement the numerical Euler's method the same way as we did for a single differential equation. The matrix-based calculations of the direct method are therefore completely neglected (i.e., as if we did not know the direct method exists). The difference from the Euler's method of a single differential equation will consist now of linking the two following differential equations, to get the numerical solutions for $y_1(t)$ and $y_2(t)$:

$$\begin{cases} \dot{y}_1(t) = a_{11}y_1(t) + a_{12}y_2(t) + b_1 \\ \dot{y}_2(t) = a_{21}y_1(t) + a_{22}y_2(t) + b_2 \end{cases}$$

## 1 Direct method in Excel

As a first step, we need to find the eigenvalues and then the eigenvectors associated to the matrix:

$$A = \begin{bmatrix} 1 & 12 \\ 3 & 1 \end{bmatrix}$$

We already know these steps from linear algebra applied in Excel.

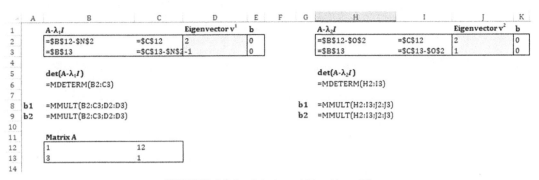

FIGURE 4.5-1   Solution of $(A - \lambda_1)v = [0]$.

Fig. 4.5-1 shows how to implement the system (4.5-3) for each eigenvalue, calculated in Fig. 4.5-2.

The eigenvectors are found using the Solver, such that the vector $b = 0$, in Fig. 4.5-3, which shows the Solver setup for $v^1$ stored in the Excel range $D2:D3$. Similarly, we have found $v^2$ stored in the Excel range $I2:I3$.

Within the Excel cells where the eigenvectors are stored, not to have the trivial solution from the Solver, it is important to start guessing values different from zero, so that the Solver will be able to find the nontrivial solution. The solutions are described in Fig. 4.5-4.

An alternative way to find the eigenvalues is to plot the determinant quadratic function in $\lambda$ and then find the two roots (as in Fig. 4.5-5).

We have now all the necessary elements to build and study the general solution $y(t)$:

$$y_1(t) = C_1 2e^{-5t} + C_2 2e^{7t},$$

$$y_2(t) = -C_1 e^{-5t} + C_2 e^{7t}.$$

First, we will plot the two above functions as explicit functions of time, to see their behavior as time increases. Then, we will plot them together in the Cartesian coordinate system $(y_1(t), y_2(t))$ to study the **phase diagram**.

As described before when $\lambda_1$, $\lambda_2$ have opposite sign, the exponential term containing the negative root goes to zero as $t \to \infty$, while the exponential term containing the positive root diverges to infinity as $t \to \infty$, which means that both solutions $y_1(t)$ and $y_2(t)$ will be divergent. See Fig. 4.5-7.

The system has a *saddle point* equilibrium. However, when the constant of integration of the divergent exponential is equal to zero, $y_1(t)$, $y_2(t)$ will converge to their steady-state values and $y_1(t)$, $y_2(t)$ will satisfy the *saddle path* Eq. (4.5-9). A **phase diagram** for two differential

| N | | O |
|---|---|---|
| $\lambda_1$ | | $\lambda_2$ |
| =(B12+C13)/2-1/2*SQRT((B12+C13)^2-4*MDETERM(B12:C13)) | | =((B12+C13)/2)+1/2*SQRT((B12+C13)^2-4*MDETERM(B12:C13)) |

FIGURE 4.5-2   Eigenvalues $\lambda_1$ and $\lambda_2$ applying the formula (4.5-6).

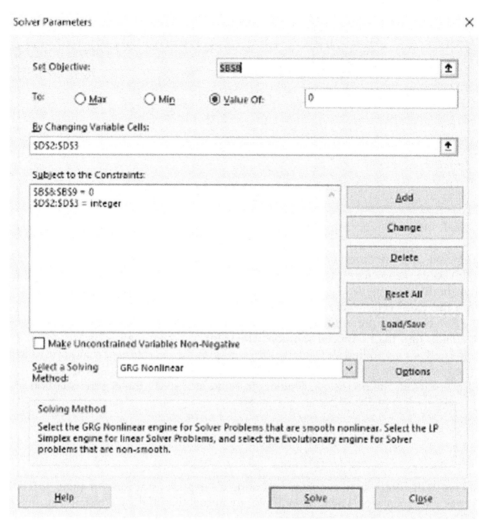

FIGURE 4.5-3    Solver setup for the eigenvector $v^1$

equations is built with $y_1(t)$ on the horizontal axis and $y_2(t)$ on the vertical axis. This Cartesian system is called a **phase plane**, while the behavior followed by the pairs $(y_1(t), y_2(t))$ are called **phase trajectories (or phase paths)**. The saddle path is instead the locus of points where the system is stable (see again Eq. 4.5-9).

[1]J. Hicks distinguishes the markets in two macro categories: *flex-price* markets, where the price adjustment is affected by the interaction of demand and supply (i.e., in the perfect competitive markets) and *fix-price* markets, where the prices are mainly determined via the *full-cost* approach (i.e., in the oligopolistic industries). See comments at the end of Section 6.12.

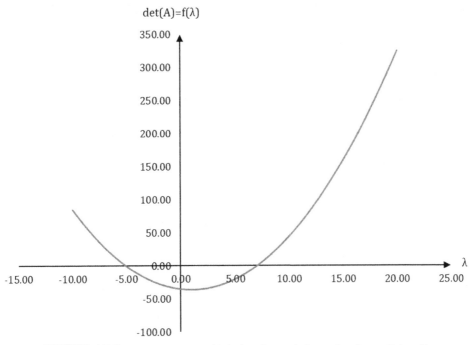

| A-$\lambda_1 I$ | | Eigenvector $v^1$ | b | | A-$\lambda_2 I$ | | Eigenvector $v^2$ | b | | $\lambda_1$ | $\lambda_2$ |
|---|---|---|---|---|---|---|---|---|---|---|---|
| 6.00 | 12.00 | 2.00 | 0.00 | | -6.00 | 12.00 | 2.00 | 0.00 | | -5.00 | 7.00 |
| 3.00 | 6.00 | -1.00 | 0.00 | | 3.00 | -6.00 | 1.00 | 0.00 | | | |
| **det(A-$\lambda_1 I$)** | | | | | **det(A-$\lambda_2 I$)** | | | | | | |
| 0.00 | | | | | 0.00 | | | | | | |
| b1 | 0.00 | | | | b1 | 0.00 | | | | | |
| b2 | 0.00 | | | | b2 | 0.00 | | | | | |

FIGURE 4.5-4    Excel eigenvectors and eigenvalues.

FIGURE 4.5-5    Determinant quadratic function and eigenvalues $\lambda_1 = -5$, $\lambda_2 = 7$.

To build the above charts we organize the Excel worksheet as in Fig. 4.5-6, where under *Column A* we have the time, under *Column B* we have $y_1(t)$, under *Column C* we have $y_2(t)$. Then, all the pairs $(y_1(t), y_2(t))$ are stored in the following columns, with four types of trajectories (with beginning values in each quadrant of the phase plane), changing the constants of integration under *Row* 1. Finally, we have the saddle path equation. Table 4.5-1 shows the calculated data.

From Figs. 4.5-7 and 4.5-8 we see that the trajectories are always divergent, unless we set the constant of integration (of the divergent exponential) $c_2$ equal to zero. In this case, the trajectories are convergent (see Figs. 4.5-9 and 4.5-10).

Changing the set of constants of integration of Table 4.5-1, we are also able to simulate different phase trajectories. For example, with the following pairs $(c_1 = 1, \ c_2 = 0.50)$, $(c_1 = -1, c_2 = 0.50)$, $(c_1 = -1, c_2 = -0.50)$, $(c_1 = 1, c_2 = -0.50)$ we obtain the divergent phase diagram of Fig. 4.5-11.

| | A | B | C | D | E | F |
|---|---|---|---|---|---|---|
| 1 | c1,c2 --> | 10 | 0.5 | | =-B1 | =C1 |
| 2 | t | y1 | y2 | | y1 | y2 |
| 3 | 0 | =B$1*(2)*EXP(-5*$A3)+C$1*2*EXP(7*$A3) | =-B$1*(1)*EXP(-5*$A3)+C$1*EXP(7*$A3) | | =E$1*(2)*EXP( =-E$1*(1)*EXP | |
| 4 | =A3+0.005 | =B$1*(2)*EXP(-5*$A4)+C$1*2*EXP(7*$A4) | =-B$1*(1)*EXP(-5*$A4)+C$1*EXP(7*$A4) | | =E$1*(2)*EXP( =-E$1*(1)*EXP | |
| 5 | =A4+0.005 | =B$1*(2)*EXP(-5*$A5)+C$1*2*EXP(7*$A5) | =-B$1*(1)*EXP(-5*$A5)+C$1*EXP(7*$A5) | | =E$1*(2)*EXP( =-E$1*(1)*EXP | |
| 6 | =A5+0.005 | =B$1*(2)*EXP(-5*$A6)+C$1*2*EXP(7*$A6) | =-B$1*(1)*EXP(-5*$A6)+C$1*EXP(7*$A6) | | =E$1*(2)*EXP( =-E$1*(1)*EXP | |
| 7 | =A6+0.005 | =B$1*(2)*EXP(-5*$A7)+C$1*2*EXP(7*$A7) | =-B$1*(1)*EXP(-5*$A7)+C$1*EXP(7*$A7) | | =E$1*(2)*EXP( =-E$1*(1)*EXP | |
| 8 | =A7+0.005 | =B$1*(2)*EXP(-5*$A8)+C$1*2*EXP(7*$A8) | =-B$1*(1)*EXP(-5*$A8)+C$1*EXP(7*$A8) | | =E$1*(2)*EXP( =-E$1*(1)*EXP | |
| 9 | =A8+0.005 | =B$1*(2)*EXP(-5*$A9)+C$1*2*EXP(7*$A9) | =-B$1*(1)*EXP(-5*$A9)+C$1*EXP(7*$A9) | | =E$1*(2)*EXP( =-E$1*(1)*EXP | |
| 10 | =A9+0.005 | =B$1*(2)*EXP(-5*$A10)+C$1*2*EXP(7*$A10) | =-B$1*(1)*EXP(-5*$A10)+C$1*EXP(7*$A10) | | =E$1*(2)*EXP( =-E$1*(1)*EXP | |
| 11 | =A10+0.005 | =B$1*(2)*EXP(-5*$A11)+C$1*2*EXP(7*$A11) | =-B$1*(1)*EXP(-5*$A11)+C$1*EXP(7*$A11) | | =E$1*(2)*EXP( =-E$1*(1)*EXP | |
| 12 | =A11+0.005 | =B$1*(2)*EXP(-5*$A12)+C$1*2*EXP(7*$A12) | =-B$1*(1)*EXP(-5*$A12)+C$1*EXP(7*$A12) | | =E$1*(2)*EXP( =-E$1*(1)*EXP | |
| 13 | =A12+0.005 | =B$1*(2)*EXP(-5*$A13)+C$1*2*EXP(7*$A13) | =-B$1*(1)*EXP(-5*$A13)+C$1*EXP(7*$A13) | | =E$1*(2)*EXP( =-E$1*(1)*EXP | |
| 14 | =A13+0.005 | =B$1*(2)*EXP(-5*$A14)+C$1*2*EXP(7*$A14) | =-B$1*(1)*EXP(-5*$A14)+C$1*EXP(7*$A14) | | =E$1*(2)*EXP( =-E$1*(1)*EXP | |

| | G | H | I | J | K | L | M | N | O |
|---|---|---|---|---|---|---|---|---|---|
| 1 | =E1 | =-F1 | | =B1 | =-C1 | | | Saddle Path | |
| 2 | y1 | y2 | | y1 | y2 | | | y1 | y2 = -0.5*y1 |
| 3 | =H$1*(2)*EXP| =-H$1*(1)*EXP(-5*$A3)+I$1*EXP(7*$A3) | | =K$1*(2)*EXP( =-K$1*(1)*EXP(-5*$A3)+L$1*EXP(7*$A3) | | | -20 | =-0.5*N3 |
| 4 | =H$1*(2)*EXP| =-H$1*(1)*EXP(-5*$A4)+I$1*EXP(7*$A4) | | =K$1*(2)*EXP( =-K$1*(1)*EXP(-5*$A4)+L$1*EXP(7*$A4) | | | =N3+0.5 | =-0.5*N4 |
| 5 | =H$1*(2)*EXP| =-H$1*(1)*EXP(-5*$A5)+I$1*EXP(7*$A5) | | =K$1*(2)*EXP( =-K$1*(1)*EXP(-5*$A5)+L$1*EXP(7*$A5) | | | =N4+0.5 | =-0.5*N5 |
| 6 | =H$1*(2)*EXP| =-H$1*(1)*EXP(-5*$A6)+I$1*EXP(7*$A6) | | =K$1*(2)*EXP( =-K$1*(1)*EXP(-5*$A6)+L$1*EXP(7*$A6) | | | =N5+0.5 | =-0.5*N6 |
| 7 | =H$1*(2)*EXP| =-H$1*(1)*EXP(-5*$A7)+I$1*EXP(7*$A7) | | =K$1*(2)*EXP( =-K$1*(1)*EXP(-5*$A7)+L$1*EXP(7*$A7) | | | =N6+0.5 | =-0.5*N7 |
| 8 | =H$1*(2)*EXP| =-H$1*(1)*EXP(-5*$A8)+I$1*EXP(7*$A8) | | =K$1*(2)*EXP( =-K$1*(1)*EXP(-5*$A8)+L$1*EXP(7*$A8) | | | =N7+0.5 | =-0.5*N8 |
| 9 | =H$1*(2)*EXP| =-H$1*(1)*EXP(-5*$A9)+I$1*EXP(7*$A9) | | =K$1*(2)*EXP( =-K$1*(1)*EXP(-5*$A9)+L$1*EXP(7*$A9) | | | =N8+0.5 | =-0.5*N9 |
| 10 | =H$1*(2)*EXP| =-H$1*(1)*EXP(-5*$A10)+I$1*EXP(7*$A10) | | =K$1*(2)*EXP( =-K$1*(1)*EXP(-5*$A10)+L$1*EXP(7*$A10) | | | =N9+0.5 | =-0.5*N10 |
| 11 | =H$1*(2)*EXP| =-H$1*(1)*EXP(-5*$A11)+I$1*EXP(7*$A11) | | =K$1*(2)*EXP( =-K$1*(1)*EXP(-5*$A11)+L$1*EXP(7*$A11) | | | =N10+0.5 | =-0.5*N11 |
| 12 | =H$1*(2)*EXP| =-H$1*(1)*EXP(-5*$A12)+I$1*EXP(7*$A12) | | =K$1*(2)*EXP( =-K$1*(1)*EXP(-5*$A12)+L$1*EXP(7*$A12) | | | =N11+0.5 | =-0.5*N12 |
| 13 | =H$1*(2)*EXP| =-H$1*(1)*EXP(-5*$A13)+I$1*EXP(7*$A13) | | =K$1*(2)*EXP( =-K$1*(1)*EXP(-5*$A13)+L$1*EXP(7*$A13) | | | =N12+0.5 | =-0.5*N13 |
| 14 | =H$1*(2)*EXP| =-H$1*(1)*EXP(-5*$A14)+I$1*EXP(7*$A14) | | =K$1*(2)*EXP( =-K$1*(1)*EXP(-5*$A14)+L$1*EXP(7*$A14) | | | =N13+0.5 | =-0.5*N14 |

**FIGURE 4.5-6**    Excel worksheet setup for $y_1(t)$, $y_2(t)$ and phase trajectories.

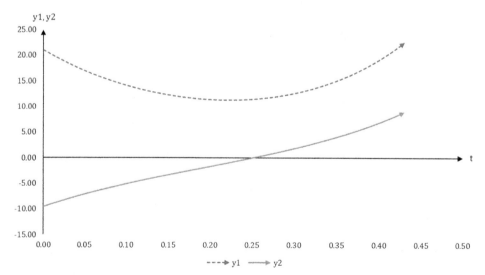

**FIGURE 4.5-7**    $y_1(t)$, $y_2(t)$ both divergent (set of constants of integration of Table 4.5-1).

**TABLE 4.5-1**  Underlying data points for the Pairs $y_1(t)$, $y_2(t)$ and for the phase diagram.

| c1, c2 --> | 10.00 | 0.50 | -10.00 | 0.50 | -10.00 | -0.50 | 10.00 | -0.50 | Saddle Path | |
|---|---|---|---|---|---|---|---|---|---|---|
| t | y1 | y2 | y1 | y2 | y1 | y2 | y1 | y2 | y1 | y2 = -0.5*y1 |
| 0.00 | 21.00 | -9.50 | -19.00 | 10.50 | -21.00 | 9.50 | 19.00 | -10.50 | -20.00 | 10.00 |
| 0.01 | 20.54 | -9.24 | -18.47 | 10.27 | -20.54 | 9.24 | 18.47 | -10.27 | -19.50 | 9.75 |
| 0.01 | 20.10 | -8.98 | -17.95 | 10.05 | -20.10 | 8.98 | 17.95 | -10.05 | -19.00 | 9.50 |
| 0.02 | 19.67 | -8.72 | -17.44 | 9.83 | -19.67 | 8.72 | 17.44 | -9.83 | -18.50 | 9.25 |
| 0.02 | 19.25 | -8.47 | -16.95 | 9.62 | -19.25 | 8.47 | 16.95 | -9.62 | -18.00 | 9.00 |
| 0.03 | 18.84 | -8.23 | -16.46 | 9.42 | -18.84 | 8.23 | 16.46 | -9.42 | -17.50 | 8.75 |
| 0.03 | 18.45 | -7.99 | -15.98 | 9.22 | -18.45 | 7.99 | 15.98 | -9.22 | -17.00 | 8.50 |
| 0.04 | 18.07 | -7.76 | -15.51 | 9.03 | -18.07 | 7.76 | 15.51 | -9.03 | -16.50 | 8.25 |
| 0.04 | 17.70 | -7.53 | -15.05 | 8.85 | -17.70 | 7.53 | 15.05 | -8.85 | -16.00 | 8.00 |
| 0.05 | 17.34 | -7.30 | -14.60 | 8.67 | -17.34 | 7.30 | 14.60 | -8.67 | -15.50 | 7.75 |
| 0.05 | 17.00 | -7.08 | -14.16 | 8.50 | -17.00 | 7.08 | 14.16 | -8.50 | -15.00 | 7.50 |
| 0.06 | 16.66 | -6.86 | -13.72 | 8.33 | -16.66 | 6.86 | 13.72 | -8.33 | -14.50 | 7.25 |
| 0.06 | 16.34 | -6.65 | -13.29 | 8.17 | -16.34 | 6.65 | 13.29 | -8.17 | -14.00 | 7.00 |
| 0.07 | 16.03 | -6.44 | -12.87 | 8.01 | -16.03 | 6.44 | 12.87 | -8.01 | -13.50 | 6.75 |
| 0.07 | 15.73 | -6.23 | -12.46 | 7.86 | -15.73 | 6.23 | 12.46 | -7.86 | -13.00 | 6.50 |
| 0.08 | 15.44 | -6.03 | -12.06 | 7.72 | -15.44 | 6.03 | 12.06 | -7.72 | -12.50 | 6.25 |
| 0.08 | 15.16 | -5.83 | -11.66 | 7.58 | -15.16 | 5.83 | 11.66 | -7.58 | -12.00 | 6.00 |
| 0.09 | 14.89 | -5.63 | -11.26 | 7.44 | -14.89 | 5.63 | 11.26 | -7.44 | -11.50 | 5.75 |
| 0.09 | 14.63 | -5.44 | -10.87 | 7.32 | -14.63 | 5.44 | 10.87 | -7.32 | -11.00 | 5.50 |
| 0.43 | 22.62 | 8.98 | 17.96 | 11.31 | -22.62 | -8.98 | -17.96 | -11.31 | 23.00 | -11.50 |

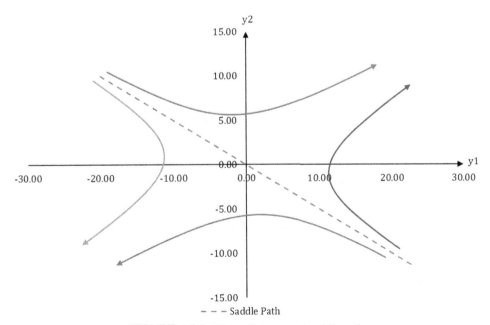

**FIGURE 4.5-8**  Phase diagram and saddle path.

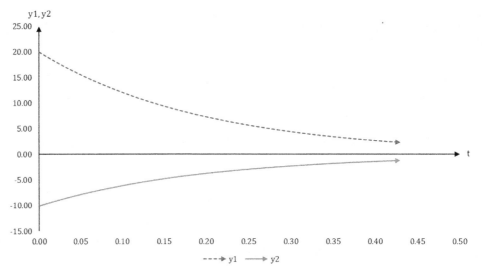

**FIGURE 4.5-9**    $y_1(t)$, $y_2(t)$ both convergent with $c_2 = 0$.

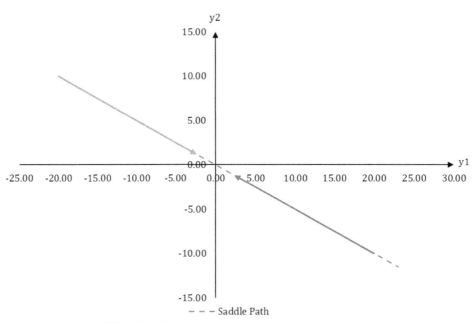

**FIGURE 4.5-10**    Converging phase trajectories setting $c_2 = 0$.

## 2 Euler's method

The Euler's method, neglecting the linear algebra calculations and the Solver optimization, is quicker in building the numerical solutions. As usual, we will need to fine-tune the time step size, to achieve a reasonable approximation of the exact solutions.

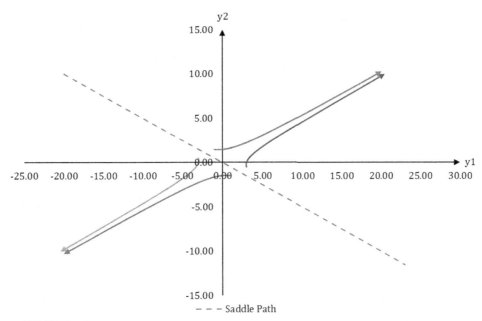

**FIGURE 4.5-11** Diverging phase trajectories with a different set of constants of integration.

Let us build in Excel then the following system (the matrix form associated is in Fig. 4.5-13):

$$\begin{cases} \dot{y}_1(t) = y_1(t) + 12y_2(t) \\ \dot{y}_2(t) = 3y_1(t) + y_2(t) \end{cases}$$

This can be simply done as represented in Fig. 4.5-12, where the two differential equations have been linked together, in the Euler's method framework. Repeating the same columns for other three pairs $(\dot{y}_1(t), \dot{y}_2(t))$ we obtain the numerical results of Table 4.5-2. Figs. 4.5-14 and 4.5-15 plot the Euler's numerical solutions versus the exact solutions.

| | A | B | C | D | E | F | G | H |
|---|---|---|---|---|---|---|---|---|
| 1 | t | dt | dy1/dt = a11y1+a12y2 | dy1 = [a11y1+a12y2]dt | y1 = Σ f(t,y)dt | dy2/dt = a21*y1+a22y2 | dy = [a21*y1+a22y2]dt | y2 = Σ f(t,y)dt |
| 2 | 0 | | | | 21 | | | -9.5 |
| 3 | =A2+$AH$ =A3-A2 | | =$AE$2*E3+$AF$2*H3 | =C3*$B3 | =E2+D3 | =$AE$3*E3+$AF$3*H3 | =F3*$B3 | =H2+G3 |
| 4 | =A3+$AH$ =A4-A3 | | =$AE$2*E4+$AF$2*H4 | =C4*$B4 | =E3+D4 | =$AE$3*E4+$AF$3*H4 | =F4*$B4 | =H3+G4 |
| 5 | =A4+$AH$ =A5-A4 | | =$AE$2*E5+$AF$2*H5 | =C5*$B5 | =E4+D5 | =$AE$3*E5+$AF$3*H5 | =F5*$B5 | =H4+G5 |
| 6 | =A5+$AH$ =A6-A5 | | =$AE$2*E6+$AF$2*H6 | =C6*$B6 | =E5+D6 | =$AE$3*E6+$AF$3*H6 | =F6*$B6 | =H5+G6 |
| 7 | =A6+$AH$ =A7-A6 | | =$AE$2*E7+$AF$2*H7 | =C7*$B7 | =E6+D7 | =$AE$3*E7+$AF$3*H7 | =F7*$B7 | =H6+G7 |
| 8 | =A7+$AH$ =A8-A7 | | =$AE$2*E8+$AF$2*H8 | =C8*$B8 | =E7+D8 | =$AE$3*E8+$AF$3*H8 | =F8*$B8 | =H7+G8 |
| 9 | =A8+$AH$ =A9-A8 | | =$AE$2*E9+$AF$2*H9 | =C9*$B9 | =E8+D9 | =$AE$3*E9+$AF$3*H9 | =F9*$B9 | =H8+G9 |
| 10 | =A9+$AH$ =A10-A9 | | =$AE$2*E10+$AF$2*H10 | =C10*$B10 | =E9+D10 | =$AE$3*E10+$AF$3*H10 | =F10*$B10 | =H9+G10 |
| 11 | =A10+$AH =A11-A10 | | =$AE$2*E11+$AF$2*H11 | =C11*$B11 | =E10+D11 | =$AE$3*E11+$AF$3*H11 | =F11*$B11 | =H10+G11 |
| 12 | =A11+$AH =A12-A11 | | =$AE$2*E12+$AF$2*H12 | =C12*$B12 | =E11+D12 | =$AE$3*E12+$AF$3*H12 | =F12*$B12 | =H11+G12 |
| 13 | =A12+$AH =A13-A12 | | =$AE$2*E13+$AF$2*H13 | =C13*$B13 | =E12+D13 | =$AE$3*E13+$AF$3*H13 | =F13*$B13 | =H12+G13 |
| 14 | =A13+$AH =A14-A13 | | =$AE$2*E14+$AF$2*H14 | =C14*$B14 | =E13+D14 | =$AE$3*E14+$AF$3*H14 | =F14*$B14 | =H13+G14 |
| 15 | =A14+$AH =A15-A14 | | =$AE$2*E15+$AF$2*H15 | =C15*$B15 | =E14+D15 | =$AE$3*E15+$AF$3*H15 | =F15*$B15 | =H14+G15 |

**FIGURE 4.5-12** Euler's method for the system of two linear differential equations of Example 1.

I. Excel and fundamental mathematics for economics

**TABLE 4.5-2**  Euler's method with step size in $t = 0.005$.

| t | dt | dy1/dt = a11y1+a12y2 | dy1 = [a11y1+a12y2]dt | y1 = Σ θ(t,y)dt | dy2/dt = a21*y1+a22y2 | dy = [a21*y1+a22y2] dt | y2 = Σ θ(t,y)dt | dy1/dt | dy1 | y1 | dy2/dt | dy2 | y2 | dy1/dt | dy1 | y1 | dy2/dt | dy2 | y2 | dy1/dt | dy1 | y1 | dy2/dt | dy2 | y2 |
|---|---|---|---|---|---|---|---|---|---|---|---|---|---|---|---|---|---|---|---|---|---|---|---|---|---|
| 0.00 | | | | 21.00 | | | -10.50 | | | -19.00 | | | 10.50 | | | -21.00 | | | 9.50 | | | 19.00 | | | -10.50 |
| 0.01 | 0.01 | -90.31 | -0.45 | 20.55 | 52.41 | 0.26 | -9.24 | 104.81 | 0.52 | -18.48 | -45.19 | -0.23 | 10.27 | 98.31 | 0.45 | -20.55 | -52.41 | -0.26 | 9.24 | -104.81 | -0.52 | 18.48 | 45.15 | 0.23 | -10.27 |
| 0.01 | 0.01 | -87.66 | -0.44 | 20.11 | 51.35 | 0.26 | -8.98 | 102.70 | 0.51 | -17.96 | -43.83 | -0.22 | 10.06 | 87.66 | 0.44 | -20.11 | -51.35 | -0.26 | 8.98 | -102.70 | -0.51 | 17.96 | 43.83 | 0.22 | -10.06 |
| 0.02 | 0.01 | -85.07 | -0.43 | 19.68 | 50.32 | 0.25 | -8.73 | 100.65 | 0.50 | -17.46 | -42.54 | -0.21 | 9.84 | 85.07 | 0.43 | -19.68 | -50.32 | -0.25 | 8.73 | -100.65 | -0.50 | 17.46 | 42.54 | 0.21 | -9.84 |
| 0.02 | 0.01 | -82.52 | -0.41 | 19.27 | 49.33 | 0.25 | -8.48 | 98.67 | 0.49 | -16.97 | -41.26 | -0.21 | 9.64 | 82.52 | 0.41 | -19.27 | -49.33 | -0.25 | 8.48 | -98.67 | -0.49 | 16.97 | 41.26 | 0.21 | -9.64 |
| 0.03 | 0.01 | -80.02 | -0.40 | 18.87 | 48.38 | 0.24 | -8.24 | 96.75 | 0.48 | -16.48 | -40.01 | -0.20 | 9.44 | 80.02 | 0.40 | -18.87 | -48.38 | -0.24 | 8.24 | -96.75 | -0.48 | 16.48 | 40.01 | 0.20 | -9.44 |
| 0.03 | 0.01 | -77.56 | -0.39 | 18.48 | 47.45 | 0.24 | -8.00 | 94.90 | 0.47 | -16.01 | -38.78 | -0.19 | 9.24 | 77.56 | 0.39 | -18.48 | -47.45 | -0.24 | 8.00 | -94.90 | -0.47 | 16.01 | 38.78 | 0.19 | -9.24 |
| 0.04 | 0.01 | -75.14 | -0.38 | 18.11 | 46.55 | 0.23 | -7.77 | 93.11 | 0.47 | -15.54 | -37.57 | -0.19 | 9.05 | 75.14 | 0.38 | -18.11 | -46.55 | -0.23 | 7.77 | -93.11 | -0.47 | 15.54 | 37.57 | 0.19 | -9.05 |
| 0.04 | 0.01 | -72.77 | -0.36 | 17.74 | 45.69 | 0.23 | -7.54 | 91.38 | 0.46 | -15.09 | -36.38 | -0.18 | 8.87 | 72.77 | 0.36 | -17.74 | -45.69 | -0.23 | 7.54 | -91.38 | -0.46 | 15.09 | 36.38 | 0.18 | -8.87 |
| 0.05 | 0.01 | -70.43 | -0.35 | 17.39 | 44.86 | 0.22 | -7.32 | 89.72 | 0.45 | -14.64 | -35.21 | -0.18 | 8.70 | 70.43 | 0.35 | -17.39 | -44.86 | -0.22 | 7.32 | -89.72 | -0.45 | 14.64 | 35.21 | 0.18 | -8.70 |
| 0.05 | 0.01 | -68.12 | -0.34 | 17.05 | 44.04 | 0.22 | -7.10 | 88.12 | 0.44 | -14.20 | -34.06 | -0.17 | 8.53 | 68.12 | 0.34 | -17.05 | -44.04 | -0.22 | 7.10 | -88.12 | -0.44 | 14.20 | 34.06 | 0.17 | -8.53 |
| 0.06 | 0.01 | -65.86 | -0.33 | 16.72 | 43.29 | 0.22 | -6.89 | 86.57 | 0.43 | -13.76 | -32.93 | -0.16 | 8.36 | 65.86 | 0.33 | -16.72 | -43.29 | -0.22 | 6.89 | -86.57 | -0.43 | 13.76 | 32.93 | 0.16 | -8.36 |
| 0.06 | 0.01 | -63.62 | -0.32 | 16.40 | 42.54 | 0.21 | -6.67 | 85.09 | 0.43 | -13.34 | -31.81 | -0.16 | 8.20 | 63.62 | 0.32 | -16.40 | -42.54 | -0.21 | 6.67 | -85.09 | -0.43 | 13.34 | 31.81 | 0.16 | -8.20 |
| 0.07 | 0.01 | -61.42 | -0.31 | 16.10 | 41.83 | 0.21 | -6.46 | 83.67 | 0.42 | -12.92 | -30.71 | -0.15 | 8.05 | 61.42 | 0.31 | -16.10 | -41.83 | -0.21 | 6.46 | -83.67 | -0.42 | 12.92 | 30.71 | 0.15 | -8.05 |
| 0.07 | 0.01 | -59.25 | -0.30 | 15.80 | 41.15 | 0.21 | -6.25 | 82.30 | 0.41 | -12.51 | -29.62 | -0.15 | 7.90 | 59.25 | 0.30 | -15.80 | -41.15 | -0.21 | 6.25 | -82.30 | -0.41 | 12.51 | 29.62 | 0.15 | -7.90 |
| 0.08 | 0.01 | -57.10 | -0.29 | 15.52 | 40.50 | 0.20 | -6.05 | 80.99 | 0.40 | -12.10 | -28.55 | -0.14 | 7.76 | 57.10 | 0.29 | -15.52 | -40.50 | -0.20 | 6.05 | -80.99 | -0.40 | 12.10 | 28.55 | 0.14 | -7.76 |
| 0.08 | 0.01 | -54.99 | -0.27 | 15.24 | 39.87 | 0.20 | -5.85 | 79.74 | 0.40 | -11.70 | -27.49 | -0.14 | 7.62 | 54.99 | 0.27 | -15.24 | -39.87 | -0.20 | 5.85 | -79.74 | -0.39 | 11.70 | 27.49 | 0.14 | -7.62 |
| 0.09 | 0.01 | -52.89 | -0.26 | 14.98 | 39.27 | 0.20 | -5.66 | 78.55 | 0.39 | -11.31 | -26.45 | -0.13 | 7.49 | 52.89 | 0.26 | -14.98 | -39.27 | -0.20 | 5.66 | -78.55 | -0.39 | 11.31 | 26.45 | 0.13 | -7.49 |
| 0.09 | 0.01 | -50.82 | -0.25 | 14.72 | 38.70 | 0.19 | -5.46 | 77.41 | 0.39 | -10.92 | -25.41 | -0.13 | 7.36 | 50.82 | 0.25 | -14.72 | -38.70 | -0.19 | 5.46 | -77.41 | -0.39 | 10.92 | 25.41 | 0.13 | -7.36 |
| 0.10 | 0.01 | -48.76 | -0.24 | 14.48 | 38.16 | 0.19 | -5.27 | 76.33 | 0.38 | -10.54 | -24.39 | -0.12 | 7.24 | 48.76 | 0.24 | -14.48 | -38.16 | -0.19 | 5.27 | -76.33 | -0.38 | 10.54 | 24.39 | 0.12 | -7.24 |
| 0.10 | 0.01 | -46.75 | -0.23 | 14.24 | 37.65 | 0.19 | -5.09 | 75.30 | 0.38 | -10.17 | -23.38 | -0.12 | 7.12 | 46.75 | 0.23 | -14.24 | -37.65 | -0.19 | 5.09 | -75.30 | -0.38 | 10.17 | 23.38 | 0.12 | -7.12 |
| 0.43 | 0.01 | 132.38 | 0.66 | 23.11 | 78.45 | 0.39 | 9.11 | 156.90 | 0.78 | 18.21 | 66.19 | 0.33 | 11.56 | -132.38 | -0.66 | -23.11 | -78.45 | -0.39 | -9.11 | -156.90 | -0.78 | -18.21 | 66.19 | -0.33 | -11.56 |
| 0.43 | 0.01 | 137.92 | 0.69 | 23.80 | 80.92 | 0.40 | 9.51 | 161.94 | 0.81 | 19.02 | 68.96 | 0.34 | 11.90 | -137.92 | -0.69 | -23.80 | -80.92 | -0.40 | -9.51 | -161.94 | -0.81 | -19.02 | 68.96 | -0.34 | -11.90 |

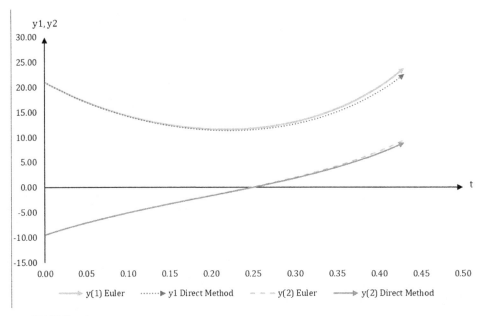

|   | AE | AF |
|---|---|---|
| 1 | **Matrix A** | |
| 2 | 1.00 | 12.00 |
| 3 | 3.00 | 1.00 |

**FIGURE 4.5-13**  Matrix in the worksheet needed for the Euler's method.

**FIGURE 4.5-14**  $y_1(t)$, $y_2(t)$ under the Euler's method and the direct method (exact solution).

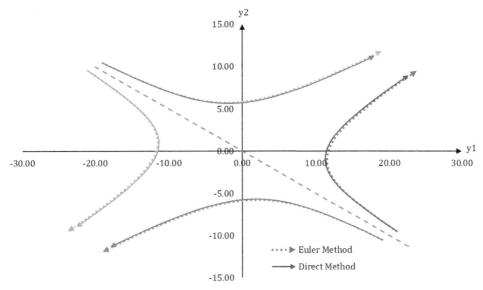

**FIGURE 4.5-15**   Phase trajectories under the Euler's method and the direct method (exact solution).

## EXAMPLE 2 (A CONVERGENT SYSTEM AND A DIVERGENT SYSTEM)

Using the techniques explained within Example 1 let us study the behavior of the two systems below:

**(1)** $\begin{cases} \dot{y}_1(t) = -2y_1(t) + 2 \\ \dot{y}_2(t) = -3y_2(t) + 6 \end{cases}$

**(2)** $\begin{cases} \dot{y}_1(t) = 2y_1(t) - 2 \\ \dot{y}_2(t) = 3y_2(t) - 6 \end{cases}$

The solutions are respectively:

**(1)** $\begin{cases} y_1(t) = C_1 e^{-2t} + 1 \\ y_2(t) = C_2 e^{-3t} + 2 \end{cases}$

**(2)** $\begin{cases} y_1(t) = C_1 e^{2t} + 1 \\ y_2(t) = C_2 e^{3t} + 2 \end{cases}$

The solutions of the first system will be convergent, while the solutions of the second system will be divergent, as described in Figs. 4.5-16 and 4.5-17, respectively.

The phase diagrams for the two systems are in Figs. 4.5-18 and 4.5-19. Let us explain how to read Fig. 4.5-18, then a similar reasoning will be applied to Fig. 4.5-19.

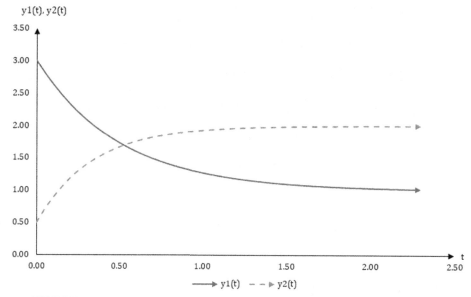

**FIGURE 4.5-16**   Converging solution paths of System (1) as explicit functions of time.

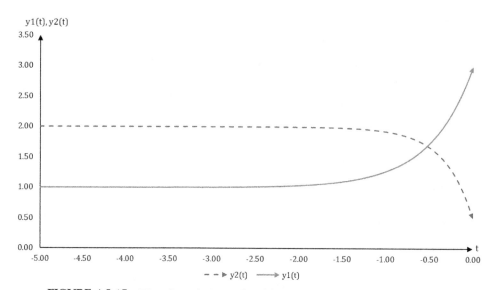

**FIGURE 4.5-17**   Diverging solution paths of System (2) as explicit functions of time.

Let us set in System (1) both differentials equal to zero, so that we have:

**(1)** $\quad \begin{cases} 0 = -2y_1(t) + 2 \\ 0 = -3y_1(t) + 6 \end{cases} \Rightarrow \begin{cases} y_1(t) = 1 \\ y_2(t) = 2 \end{cases}$

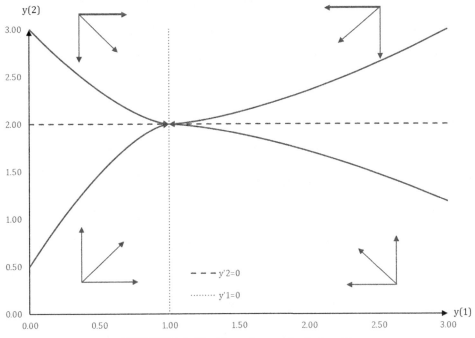

**FIGURE 4.5-18**   Phase diagram for System (1).

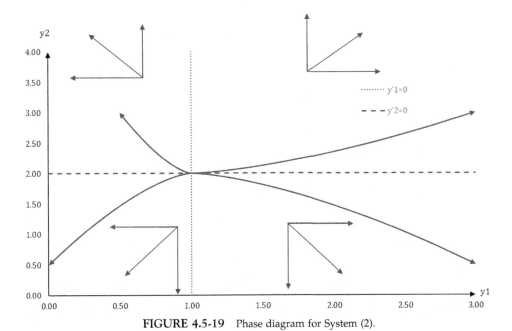

**FIGURE 4.5-19**   Phase diagram for System (2).

The following cases will occur (see the directions of the arrows in Fig. 4.5-18):

- on the right (left) of the vertical **isocline** $y_1(t) = 1$, $\dot{y}_1(t) < 0$ ($>0$) and then $y_1(t)$ decreasing (increasing);
- below (above) the horizontal **isocline** $y_2(t) = 2$, $\dot{y}_2(t) > 0$ ($<0$) and then $y_2(t)$ increasing (decreasing);

### EXAMPLE 3 (THE EULER'S METHOD AND THE CASE OF COMPLEX CHARACTERISTIC ROOTS)

The Euler's method, as it has been exposed in Example 1, will turn to be also useful to the case of complex eigenvalues because it avoids dealing with the analytical cumbersome form of the general solution involving the periodical trigonometric functions. Let us recall that if in the following:

$$\lambda_1, \lambda_2 = \frac{tr(A)}{2} \pm \frac{1}{2}\sqrt{tr(A)^2 - 4|A|}$$

the discriminant $\Delta$ under square root is negative:

$$\Delta = tr(A)^2 - 4|A| < 0$$

then, there are no real roots. Rather, there are two distinct complex roots (complex conjugate). Let us consider the following system:

$$\begin{cases} \dot{y}_1(t) = -y_2(t) + 2 \\ \dot{y}_2(t) = y_1(t) - y_2(t) + 1 \end{cases}$$

which in matrix notation becomes:

$$\begin{bmatrix} \dot{y}_1 \\ \dot{y}_2 \end{bmatrix} = \begin{bmatrix} 0 & -1 \\ 1 & -1 \end{bmatrix} \begin{bmatrix} y_1 \\ y_2 \end{bmatrix}.$$

The characteristic equation is in general:

$$\lambda^2 - (a_{11} + a_{22})\lambda + (a_{11}a_{22} - a_{12}a_{21}) = 0$$

Then we have:

$$\lambda^2 + \lambda + 1 = 0$$

and the complex roots are:

$$\lambda_1, \lambda_2 = -\frac{1}{2} \pm \frac{1}{2}\sqrt{1 - 4} = -\frac{1}{2} \pm i\frac{\sqrt{3}}{2}.$$

**TABLE 4.5-3**   Enumeration of the Euler's method for Pairs of $y_1(t)$ and $y_2(t)$.

| t | dt | dy1/dt = a1·1y1+a1·1d1y1+ 2y2 | dy1 = a12y2/dt | y1 = Σf(t,y)dt | dy2/dt = a21·y1+a21·y1+ 22y2 a22y2)dt | dy = b21·y1+ | y2 = Σf(t,y)dt | dy1/dt | dy1 | y1 | dy2/dt | dy2 | y2 | dy1/dt | dy1 | y1 | dy2/dt | dy2 | y2 | dy1/dt | dy1 | y1 | dy2/dt | dy2 | y2 | dy1/dt | dy1 | y1 | dy2/dt | dy2 | y2 |
|---|---|---|---|---|---|---|---|---|---|---|---|---|---|---|---|---|---|---|---|---|---|---|---|---|---|---|---|---|---|---|
| 0.00 | | | | 0.50 | | | 4.00 | | | 1.50 | | | 4.00 | | | 0.50 | | | 0.00 | | | 1.50 | | | 0.00 |
| 0.05 | 0.05 | -1.88 | -0.09 | 0.41 | -2.47 | -0.12 | 3.88 | 1.92 | -0.10 | 1.40 | -1.52 | -0.08 | 3.92 | 1.92 | -0.10 | 0.60 | 1.52 | 0.08 | 0.08 | 1.88 | 0.09 | 1.59 | 2.47 | 0.12 | 0.12 |
| 0.10 | 0.05 | -1.75 | -0.09 | 0.32 | -2.44 | -0.12 | 3.75 | 1.85 | -0.09 | 1.31 | -1.54 | -0.08 | 3.85 | 1.85 | -0.09 | 0.69 | 1.54 | 0.08 | 0.15 | 1.75 | 0.09 | 1.68 | 2.44 | 0.12 | 0.25 |
| 0.15 | 0.05 | -1.63 | -0.08 | 0.24 | -2.40 | -0.12 | 3.63 | 1.77 | -0.09 | 1.22 | -1.55 | -0.08 | 3.77 | 1.77 | -0.09 | 0.78 | 1.55 | 0.08 | 0.23 | 1.63 | 0.08 | 1.76 | 2.40 | 0.12 | 0.37 |
| 0.20 | 0.05 | -1.52 | -0.08 | 0.16 | -2.36 | -0.12 | 3.52 | 1.69 | -0.08 | 1.14 | -1.55 | -0.08 | 3.69 | 1.69 | -0.08 | 0.86 | 1.55 | 0.08 | 0.31 | 1.52 | 0.08 | 1.84 | 2.36 | 0.12 | 0.48 |
| 0.25 | 0.05 | -1.40 | -0.07 | 0.09 | -2.31 | -0.12 | 3.40 | 1.61 | -0.08 | 1.06 | -1.56 | -0.08 | 3.61 | 1.61 | -0.08 | 0.94 | 1.56 | 0.08 | 0.39 | 1.40 | 0.07 | 1.91 | 2.31 | 0.12 | 0.60 |
| 0.30 | 0.05 | -1.29 | -0.06 | 0.03 | -2.26 | -0.11 | 3.29 | 1.54 | -0.08 | 0.98 | -1.56 | -0.08 | 3.54 | 1.54 | -0.08 | 1.02 | 1.56 | 0.08 | 0.46 | 1.29 | 0.06 | 1.97 | 2.26 | 0.11 | 0.71 |
| 0.35 | 0.05 | -1.18 | -0.06 | -0.03 | -2.21 | -0.11 | 3.18 | 1.46 | -0.07 | 0.91 | -1.55 | -0.08 | 3.46 | 1.46 | -0.07 | 1.09 | 1.55 | 0.08 | 0.54 | 1.18 | 0.06 | 2.03 | 2.21 | 0.11 | 0.82 |
| 0.40 | 0.05 | -1.07 | -0.05 | -0.09 | -2.16 | -0.11 | 3.07 | 1.38 | -0.07 | 0.84 | -1.54 | -0.08 | 3.38 | 1.38 | -0.07 | 1.16 | 1.54 | 0.08 | 0.62 | 1.07 | 0.05 | 2.09 | 2.16 | 0.11 | 0.93 |
| 0.45 | 0.05 | -0.97 | -0.05 | -0.13 | -2.10 | -0.10 | 2.97 | 1.31 | -0.07 | 0.77 | -1.53 | -0.08 | 3.31 | 1.31 | -0.07 | 1.23 | 1.53 | 0.08 | 0.69 | 0.97 | 0.05 | 2.13 | 2.10 | 0.10 | 1.03 |
| 0.50 | 0.05 | -0.86 | -0.04 | -0.18 | -2.04 | -0.10 | 2.86 | 1.23 | -0.06 | 0.71 | -1.52 | -0.08 | 3.23 | 1.23 | -0.06 | 1.29 | 1.52 | 0.08 | 0.77 | 0.86 | 0.04 | 2.18 | 2.04 | 0.10 | 1.14 |
| 0.55 | 0.05 | -0.76 | -0.04 | -0.22 | -1.98 | -0.10 | 2.76 | 1.15 | -0.06 | 0.65 | -1.50 | -0.08 | 3.15 | 1.15 | -0.06 | 1.35 | 1.50 | 0.08 | 0.85 | 0.76 | 0.04 | 2.22 | 1.98 | 0.10 | 1.24 |
| 11.25 | 0.05 | 0.01 | 0.00 | 1.00 | 0.01 | 0.00 | 1.99 | 0.01 | 0.00 | 1.00 | 0.01 | 0.00 | 1.99 | -0.01 | 0.00 | 1.00 | -0.01 | 0.00 | 2.01 | -0.01 | 0.00 | 1.00 | -0.01 | 0.00 | 2.01 |
| 11.30 | 0.05 | 0.01 | 0.00 | 1.00 | 0.01 | 0.00 | 1.99 | 0.01 | 0.00 | 1.00 | 0.01 | 0.00 | 1.99 | -0.01 | 0.00 | 1.00 | -0.01 | 0.00 | 2.01 | -0.01 | 0.00 | 1.00 | -0.01 | 0.00 | 2.01 |

Let us proceed with the Euler's numerical method to study the behavior of the solutions.

First, we enumerate the four pairs of solution as described in Table 4.5-3, according to the given system of two differential equations and the correspondent matrix.

Once the enumeration Table 4.5-3 is ready, we plot the function solutions $y_1(t)$ and $y_2(t)$, together with the isoclines, namely the locus of points where $\dot{y}_1(t) = 0$ and $\dot{y}_2(t) = 0$.

The isoclines are:

$$y_2(t) = 2$$
$$y_2(t) = y_1(t) + 1.$$

The solution paths, as explicit functions of time, are represented in Fig. 4.5-20, while and the phase diagram is represented in Fig. 4.5-21. The step size utilized is 0.05.

As depicted in Fig. 4.5-21 the spiral paths all converge to the point $(1, 2)$, and this is called a **stable focus.** They converge because the real part of the complex root is negative. If this had

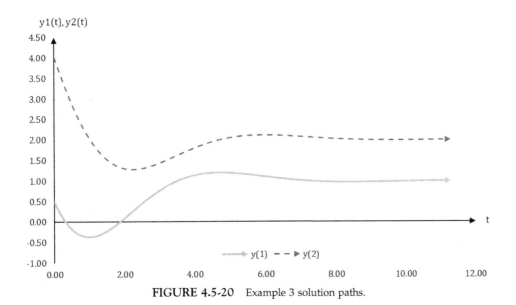

**FIGURE 4.5-20**   Example 3 solution paths.

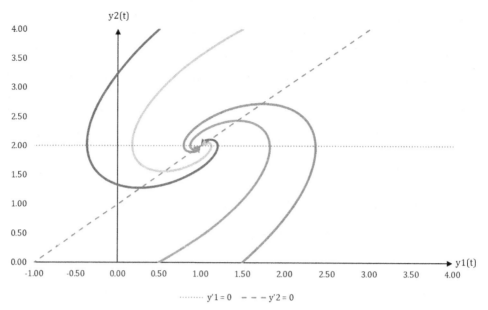

**FIGURE 4.5-21**    Phase diagram and isoclines with stable focus in $(y_1 = 1, y_2 = 2)$.

been positive, we would have had diverging spiral paths, with an **unstable focus**. If the real part were zero, then the spiral would orbit endlessly around the steady state, which would be called **center**.

## 4.6  Tourism fight between two competing regions

As a first economic example, let us model a "fight" between two regions to attract tourists. The system of two differential equations is as follows:

$$\begin{cases} \dot{y}_1(t) = -y_1(t) + 3y_2(t) \\ \dot{y}_2(t) = 5y_1(t) - 3y_2(t) \end{cases}$$

where $y_1(t)$ and $y_2(t)$ represent the deviations from the normal tourism advertising budget for the two competing regions, so that if:

$$\begin{cases} y(t) < 0 \Rightarrow \textit{countries are spending less than the normal budget} \\ y(t) = 0 \Rightarrow \textit{countries are spending in line with the normal budget} \\ y(t) > 0 \Rightarrow \textit{countries are spending more than the normal budget} \end{cases}$$

The matrix of coefficients has the following economic meaning:

- the coefficients $a_{11}$ and $a_{22}$, which appear with a negative sign, make each country's budget move in the opposite direction, that is, if each region is spending too much compared to the normal tourism budget, resulting in $y(t) > 0$, the coefficients pull the advertising back to the normal budget, if each region is spending less than the normal tourism budget, resulting in $y(t) < 0$, the negative coefficient will push the advertising budget to normal levels, resulting in $\dot{y}(t) > 0$ and an increasing $y(t)$. In our example, region 2 is more sensitive to changes in its budget spending than region 1.

- The coefficients $a_{12}$ and $a_{21}$ represent instead the sensitivity (or responsiveness) of each region to the budget policy of the other region, not to lose tourists. They are positive, in that if region 1 sees the region 2 spending more than the normal amount, region 1 will then spend more than normal budget as well. Each differential is then impacted positively by the competing region's budget policy. The coefficients values represent the magnitude of the reaction: the higher the coefficient, the stronger the reaction of the region to the budget policy of the other region. In our example, the reaction of region 2 is stronger than that of region 1.

The general solution of our system is represented by the following linear combination:

$$y(t) = C_1 \begin{bmatrix} 3 \\ -5 \end{bmatrix} e^{-6t} + C_2 \begin{bmatrix} 1 \\ 1 \end{bmatrix} e^{2t}$$

with its vector components (budget policy paths) as follows:

$$y_1(t) = C_1 3 e^{-6t} + C_2 e^{2t},$$

$$y_2(t) = -C_1 5 e^{-6t} + C_2 e^{2t}.$$

Unless the beginning values at $t = 0$ are equal to:

$$y_1(0) = +3 \ (y_1(0) = -3)$$

$$y_2(0) = -5 \ (y_1(0) + 5)$$

the budget policies will both diverge from the equilibrium point (see Fig. 4.6-1). This is a saddle point equilibrium situation and the saddle path equation is:

$$y_2(t) = -\frac{5}{3} y_1(t).$$

The phase diagram is depicted in Fig. 4.6-2. If we set the constant of integration (of the divergent exponential) $C_2 = 0$ the system will be in stable equilibrium, as depicted in Figs. 4.6-3 and 4.6-4.

The economic interpretation is that the two budget spending policies will reach both normal levels (i.e., the departures from the normal budget will be zero) if and only if one region starts with a budget deviation below (above) its normal policy and the other region starts above (below) its normal policy. In all the other cases, both regions will lose, increasing

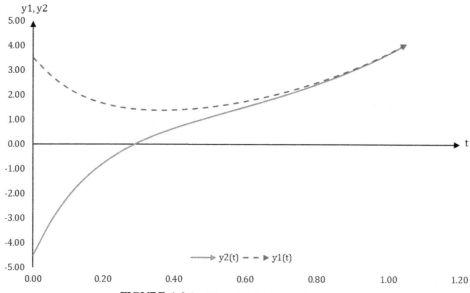

**FIGURE 4.6-1**   Diverging budget policy paths.

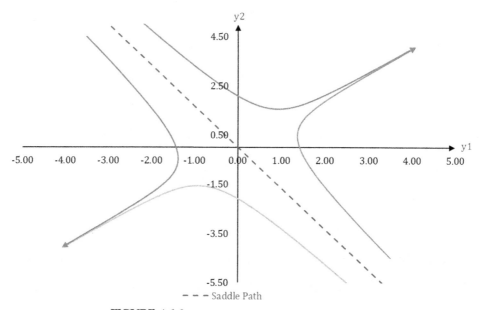

**FIGURE 4.6-2**   Phase diagram of the budget policies.

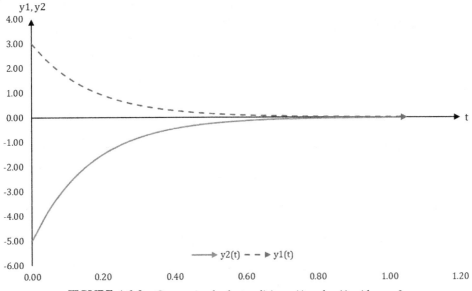

**FIGURE 4.6-3** Converging budget policies $y_1(t)$ and $y_2(t)$ with $c_2 = 0$.

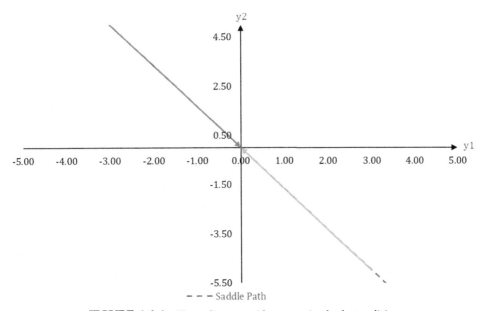

**FIGURE 4.6-4** Phase diagram with converging budget policies.

more and more their budget policies, keeping on fighting each other to attract more tourists, without reaching a stationary value.

## 4.7 Walrasian adjustment with entry

As we have seen in the Example 2 of Section 4.2 the excess demand $z(p) = D(p) - S(p)$ in a competitive market can be represented as a linear function of the price deviation $P$ as follows:

$$z(P) = aP$$

and the Walrasian price adjustment can be modeled with a differential equation as follows:

$$\frac{dP}{dt} = k \cdot z(P) = kaP \quad \text{with } k > 0.$$

where the coefficient $k$ is the speed of the adjustment.

We want to introduce in the model a second variable, the number of firms in the industry. Let the following, respectively, be the demand function and the supply function:

$$D(p) = a - bp$$

$$S(p) = sN$$

where $N$ is the number of firms in the industry.

We can define then the following system in two linear differential equations:

$$\dot{p} = k(a - bp - sN)$$

$$\dot{N} = \gamma(p - \bar{c}), \quad \gamma > 0$$

In matrix notation the system is condensed as follows:

$$\begin{bmatrix} \dot{p} \\ \dot{N} \end{bmatrix} = \begin{bmatrix} -kb & -ks \\ \gamma & 0 \end{bmatrix} \begin{bmatrix} p \\ N \end{bmatrix} + \begin{bmatrix} ka \\ -\gamma\bar{c} \end{bmatrix}.$$

Using the solutions under Eq. (4.5-8) the general solutions are:

$$p(t) = C_1 e^{\lambda_1 t} + C_2 e^{\lambda_2 t} + \bar{p}$$

$$N(t) = \frac{\lambda_1 + kb}{-ks} e^{\lambda_1 t} + \frac{\lambda_2 + kb}{-ks} e^{\lambda_2 t} + \overline{N}$$

The two eigenvalues are:

$$\lambda_1, \lambda_2 = \frac{tr(A)}{2} \pm \frac{1}{2}\sqrt{tr(A)^2 - 4(a_{11}a_{22} - a_{12}a_{21})}$$

namely:

$$\lambda_1, \lambda_2 = \frac{-kb}{2} \pm \frac{1}{2}\sqrt{(-kb)^2 - 4(\gamma ks)}$$

with the discriminant under square root $\Delta$ that may be positive, equal to zero or negative.

Using the following parameters, we represent the phase diagram with the phase trajectories converging to a **stable focus**. N can be expressed in hundreds.

$$k = 5$$

$$a = 2$$

$$b = -0.40$$

$$\gamma = 1$$

$$s = 0.5$$

$$\bar{c} = 2$$

The isoclines are exposed as follows:

$$\dot{p} = 0 \Rightarrow k(a - bp - sN) = 0$$

$$-kbp = ksN - ka \Rightarrow p = \left(\frac{s}{-b}\right)N - \frac{a}{(-b)}$$

so that if N decreases p will increase and vice versa. p will be an increasing function below its isocline.

For N we have the following isocline:
$\dot{N} = 0 \Rightarrow p = \bar{c}$ (N increasing function above $\bar{c}$)

Figs. 4.7-1 and 4.7-2 and Table 4.7-1 show the numerical solutions, using the Euler's method.

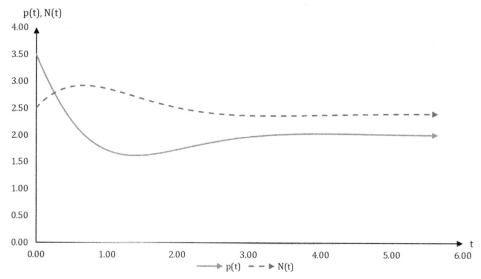

**FIGURE 4.7-1**   Converging paths with beginning values $p(0) = 3.5$ and $N(0) = 2.5$.

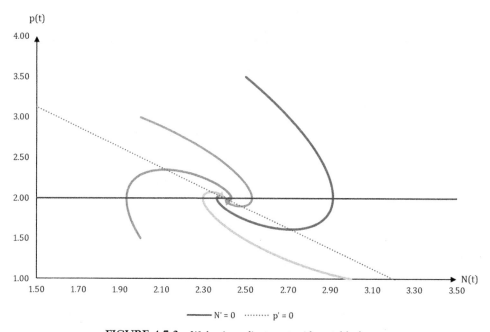

**FIGURE 4.7-2**   Walrasian adjustment with a stable focus.

**TABLE 4.7-1** Euler's method enumeration for a specific pair of $(p, N)$.

| $t$ | $dt$ | $dp/dt = a11^*p+a12^*N+ka$ | $dp = [a11^*p+a12^*N+ka]dt$ | $p = \Sigma f(t,y)dt$ | $dN/dt = a21^*p+a22^*N-\gamma c$ | $dN = [a21^*p+a22^*N-\gamma c]dt$ | $N = \Sigma f(t,y)dt$ |
|---|---|---|---|---|---|---|---|
| 0.00 | | | | 3.50 | | | 2.50 |
| 0.03 | 0.03 | -3.18 | -0.08 | 3.42 | 1.42 | 0.04 | 2.54 |
| 0.05 | 0.03 | -3.11 | -0.08 | 3.34 | 1.34 | 0.03 | 2.57 |
| 0.08 | 0.03 | -3.04 | -0.08 | 3.27 | 1.27 | 0.03 | 2.60 |
| 0.10 | 0.03 | -2.96 | -0.07 | 3.19 | 1.19 | 0.03 | 2.63 |
| 0.13 | 0.03 | -2.89 | -0.07 | 3.12 | 1.12 | 0.03 | 2.66 |
| 0.15 | 0.03 | -2.81 | -0.07 | 3.05 | 1.05 | 0.03 | 2.68 |
| 0.18 | 0.03 | -2.74 | -0.07 | 2.98 | 0.98 | 0.02 | 2.71 |
| 0.20 | 0.03 | -2.66 | -0.07 | 2.92 | 0.92 | 0.02 | 2.73 |
| 0.23 | 0.03 | -2.59 | -0.06 | 2.85 | 0.85 | 0.02 | 2.75 |
| 0.25 | 0.03 | -2.51 | -0.06 | 2.79 | 0.79 | 0.02 | 2.77 |
| 0.28 | 0.03 | -2.43 | -0.06 | 2.73 | 0.73 | 0.02 | 2.79 |
| 0.30 | 0.03 | -2.36 | -0.06 | 2.67 | 0.67 | 0.02 | 2.81 |
| 0.33 | 0.03 | -2.28 | -0.06 | 2.61 | 0.61 | 0.02 | 2.82 |
| 0.35 | 0.03 | -2.21 | -0.06 | 2.56 | 0.56 | 0.01 | 2.84 |
| 0.38 | 0.03 | -2.13 | -0.05 | 2.50 | 0.50 | 0.01 | 2.85 |
| 0.40 | 0.03 | -2.06 | -0.05 | 2.45 | 0.45 | 0.01 | 2.86 |
| 0.43 | 0.03 | -1.98 | -0.05 | 2.40 | 0.40 | 0.01 | 2.87 |
| 0.45 | 0.03 | -1.91 | -0.05 | 2.35 | 0.35 | 0.01 | 2.88 |
| 0.48 | 0.03 | -1.84 | -0.05 | 2.31 | 0.31 | 0.01 | 2.89 |
| 0.50 | 0.03 | -1.76 | -0.04 | 2.26 | 0.26 | 0.01 | 2.89 |
| 5.65 | 0.03 | -0.01 | 0.00 | 2.00 | 0.00 | 0.00 | 2.40 |

# Exercises

**1.** Solve the following first-order difference equations and set up in Excel the step-charts:

$$y(t) = -\frac{1}{3}y(t-1)$$

$$y(t) = \frac{1}{3}y(t-1) + 6$$

$$y(t) = -\frac{1}{4}y(t-1) + 5$$

**2.** Solve the following second-order difference equation and set up in Excel the step-chart:

$$y(t) = -3y(t-1) - 2y(t-2)$$

**3.** The following system of difference equations gives the Samuelson model:

$$Y(t) = C(t) + I(t) + G_0$$

$$C(t) = \gamma Y(t-1)$$

$$I(t) = \alpha[C(t) - C(t-1)]$$

I. Excel and fundamental mathematics for economics

which can be condensed into the following second order difference equation:

$$Y(t) = \gamma(1+\alpha)Y(t-1) - \alpha\gamma Y(t-2) + G_0.$$

Solve in Excel this second-order difference equation and build the step-chart with $\alpha = 1$, $\gamma = 0.80$ and $G_0 = 10$. Simulate various levels of $\alpha$ and $\gamma$, and see what happens to the solution. Set arbitrary initial condition, e.g.,: $y(0) = 1$.

4. Consider the following nonlinear first-order difference equation with initial condition:

$$y(t) = y^\alpha(t-1)$$

construct the step-chart and phase diagram with:

$$\alpha = 0.5$$

$$\alpha = -0.5$$

$$\alpha = -2$$

$$\alpha = 2$$

and analyze the convergence or divergence of the system.

5. Consider the following nonlinear first-order difference equation:

$$y(t) = y^2(t-1) + \frac{3}{16}.$$

Construct the step-chart, phase diagram and examine the global stability.

6. Consider the following economic model:

$$C(t) = C_0 + bY^\alpha(t-1)$$

$$Y(t) = C(t) + \bar{I}$$

which can be condensed in the following nonlinear difference equation:

$$Y(t) = C_0 + bY^\alpha(t-1) + \bar{I}.$$

Construct the step-chart and phase diagram with:

$$\alpha = 0.5$$

$$C_0 = 5$$

$$b = 0.5$$

$$\bar{I} = 5$$

7. Using the Euler method, solve the following first-order differential equation:

$$\dot{y}(t) = y$$

$$y(0) = 1$$

8. Using the Euler method, solve the following nonautonomous first-order differential equation:

$$\dot{y}(t) = t - y$$

$$y(0) = 0.5$$

9. Using the Euler method solve the following nonautonomous first-order differential equation:

$$\dot{y}(t) = 2ty + t$$

$$y(0) = 0$$

10. Using the Euler method solve the following nonautonomous first-order differential equation:

$$\dot{y}(t) = 2ty + 2t$$

$$y(0) = -2$$

11. Given the following expression of force of interest.

$$\delta(t) = 1 + 0.05t$$

calculate the resulting form of the capital accumulation function $y(t)$.
12. Capital growth. Let the following be the function of the aggregate output of economy:

$$Y = (a + \alpha k)t^{1/2}.$$

Then, let the capital accumulation equal to saving (scaled with $s$ marginal propensity to save) as follows:

$$\dot{K}(t) = sY.$$

We can condense the above equations into the following nonautonomous differential equation:

$$\dot{K}(t) = s(a + \alpha k)t^{\frac{1}{2}}.$$

Solve numerically the above differential equation using the Euler method, with;

$$\alpha = 0.15$$

$$a = 0.50$$

$$s = 0.50$$

$$K_0 = 1$$

**13.** The exponential cardinal utility function assumes the following differential equation:

$$\frac{dU(x)}{dx} = -\frac{1}{k}U(x) + 1.$$

Solve the differential equation using the Euler method and plot the total utility function together with the marginal utility. Set the risk aversion factor $k = 1$.

**14.** Solve in Excel using the direct method the following homogenous system of linear ODEs and plot the phase diagram:

$$\dot{y}(t) = \begin{bmatrix} 4 & -1 \\ -4 & 4 \end{bmatrix} y(t)$$

**15.** Solve in Excel using the direct method the following complete system of linear ODEs and plot the phase diagram:

$$\dot{y}(t) = \begin{bmatrix} 0 & 1 \\ 1/4 & 0 \end{bmatrix} y(t) + \begin{bmatrix} -2 \\ -1/2 \end{bmatrix}$$

**16.** Solve the system of two differential equations proposed in Section 4.6 which models the saddle point situation in the tourism battle between two regions using the Euler method shown in Section 4.5 and plot the phase diagram.

$$\dot{y}(t) = \begin{bmatrix} -1 & 3 \\ 5 & -3 \end{bmatrix} y(t)$$

17. The following system presents complex roots. Solve it using the Euler method, and see if the steady state is a focus or a center.

$$\dot{y}(t) = \begin{bmatrix} 0 & 1 \\ -1 & 0 \end{bmatrix} y(t)$$

18. Solve the following Walrasian model using the Euler method:

$$\begin{bmatrix} \dot{p} \\ \dot{N} \end{bmatrix} = \begin{bmatrix} -kb & -ks \\ \gamma & 0 \end{bmatrix} \begin{bmatrix} p \\ N \end{bmatrix} + \begin{bmatrix} ka \\ -\gamma\bar{c} \end{bmatrix}.$$

with

$$k = 5,\ a = 2,\ b = -0.65,\ \gamma = 1,\ s = 0.50,\ \bar{c} = 2$$

Study the discriminant of:

$$\lambda_1, \lambda_2 = \frac{-kb}{2} \pm \frac{1}{2}\sqrt{(-kb)^2 - 4(\gamma ks)}$$

and assess whether the steady state is a stable focus or stable node. Draw the phase diagram and isoclines.

19. The following system presents complex roots. Solve it using the Euler method, and see if the steady state is a focus or a center.

$$\dot{y}(t) = \begin{bmatrix} -1 & 1 \\ -1 & -1 \end{bmatrix} y(t)$$

20. Unemployment versus Inflation and Long-Run Phillips relation: advanced ODEs modeling.

The original formulation of the Phillips curve is as follows:

$$w = f(U) \qquad (f'(U) < 0) \tag{1}$$

where $w$ is the rate of growth of money wage $W$ and $U$ is the rate of unemployment.

Later, economists have used the Phillips curve to relate the rate of unemployment to the rate of inflation $p$, making this rate of inflation $p$, like $w$, a function of $U$ (still with $f'(U) < 0$).

Prices are affected by $w$ itself and a factor of labor productivity, say $T$. The resulting equation of the actual rate of inflation can be modeled as:

$$p = w - T \tag{2}$$

The inflationary pressure of a positive $w$ is offset partially by an increase in labor productivity $T$.

If we assume a linear relation $f(U)$ and combining Eqs. (1) and (2), we can write:

$$p = \alpha - T - \beta U \qquad (\alpha, \ \beta > 0) \tag{3}$$

The expectations-augmented version of the Phillips curve is defined instead as follows:

$$w = f(U) + h\pi \qquad (0 < h \leq 1)$$

where $\pi$ denotes the expected rate of inflation. $h$ is the scale factor for expectations. Therefore, $w$ is an increasing function of $\pi$, in that employees will incorporate their expectations on the rate inflation into their money-wage demand. Also, this will affect the actual rate of inflation, as $w$ will increase or decrease the general level of prices. Eq. (3) becomes then:

$$p = \alpha - T - \beta U + h\pi \qquad (\alpha, \ \beta > 0; \ 0 < h \leq 1) \tag{4}$$

The adaptive expectations hypothesis on the rate of inflation lead to:

$$\frac{d\pi}{dt} = j(p - \pi) \qquad (0 < j \leq 1) \tag{5}$$

whenever $p > \pi$, $\pi$ will be revised upward and vice versa.

The last differential equation we consider is related to the feedback of monetary expansion, hence rate of inflation, on the unemployment. Denoting the nominal money balance $M$ and its rate of growth by $m = \dot{M}/M$ we assume:

$$\frac{dU}{dt} = -k(m - p) \qquad (k > 0) \tag{6}$$

where $(m - p)$ is the rate of growth of real money and therefore $dU/dt$ is negatively related to it.

Now, when Eq. (4) is substituted into Eqs. (5) and (6), we obtain our final system of linear differential equations as follows:

$$\frac{d\pi}{dt} + j(1 - h)\pi + j\beta U = j(\alpha - T)$$

$$\frac{dU}{dt} - kh\pi + k\beta U = k(\alpha - T - m)$$

which is, in matrix notation:

$$\begin{bmatrix} \pi' \\ U' \end{bmatrix} = -\begin{bmatrix} j(1-h) & j\beta \\ -kh & k\beta \end{bmatrix} \begin{bmatrix} \pi \\ U \end{bmatrix} + \begin{bmatrix} j(\alpha - T) \\ k(\alpha - T - m) \end{bmatrix}$$

Assuming $j = 0.75$, $h = 1$ (this case being very important for the shape of the Long-Run Phillips curve) $\beta = 3$, $\alpha = 1$, $T = 0.83$, $m = 2.50\%$ and $k = 0.50$ solve the above system of ODEs using the Euler method, and derive the Long-Run Phillips Curve (vertical isocline) and see how this vertical shape relates to the factor $h = 1$.

# Static optimization

Studying and applying economics means most of the time working on the optimization of a given function subject to some constraints or not.

The goal is always that of finding a critical point (or vector) that optimizes the given univariate (or multivariate) function. In economics, the critical point may typically represent the optimal quantity to be produced, maximizing a certain profit function, while the constraint may be represented by a fixed amount of total costs (equality constraints) or by setting the total costs such that they are equal or below a certain threshold (weak inequality constraints).

In any case, the objective of the *static optimization* is always to find the *optimizing point $x^*$* (*extreme value*) for a given univariate or multivariate function, without any reference to how $x^*$ may evolve in a time framework, while within the *dynamic optimization*, the mathematical problem is that of finding the *optimizing path*, namely the optimal function $y^*(t)$ over time, that minimizes or maximizes a given *functional $J(y(t))$*.

Part II of this book is dedicated to the static optimization, while Part III is dedicated to the dynamic optimization.

Part II is organized in four chapters.

Chapter 5 is devoted to see the classical techniques for the nonlinear optimization (unconstrained and constrained for univariate and multivariate functions).

Chapter 6 will attempt to cover the core concepts of microeconomics applied with Excel and applied with the various techniques of optimization seen in Chapter 5.

Chapter 7 is dedicated to the linear programming case, where both the objective function and constraints are described by linear functions.

Chapter 8 is a special and important case of the nonlinear programming applied to the *portfolio theory*.

# Classical static nonlinear optimization theory

## 5.1  Classical unconstrained optimization of a univariate function

Within this first paragraph, we will show how Excel can be implemented to optimize a univariate function. As said in the abstract this is essentially a continuation of Section 2.1.

Optimizing a function means finding its *minimum* or *maximum*. To do this we always have to identify first the **critical points**, which are also defined **stationary values**, i.e., the points $x^*$ at the slope $f'(x^*) = 0$. This is called the **first-order condition**, and it is a necessary, but not sufficient condition, to optimize the function, in that a critical point can yield either to an **extreme value** (minimum or maximum) or to an **inflection point** (saddle point in a multivariate function). Every extreme value is always a stationary value, but not vice versa.

The study of the sign of the second derivative $f''(x)$ will help instead to identify the inflection points.

The **unconstrained optimization** essentially deals with finding the *global minimum* or *global maximum* of the given function, within the entire real line $\Re$. We can then search for all local extreme values and compare the value of the function at each of them to find the global optimizing point (min or max).

Global minima and global maxima are found when the functions are convex or concave (i.e., they include flat portions for some $x$), while these global extreme values are also *unique* when we are dealing with *strictly concave* or *strictly convex* functions (i.e., they do not show any flat portion). The same is applicable for local extreme points, in the neighborhood of a stationary point, leading to the identification of *strong local minima* and *strong local maxima*, and the same reasoning is valid for multivariate functions (see Section 5.2).

In general, the Excel tools mainly used within the unconstrained optimization will be the following:

- Scatter chart;
- Solver;
- Data Table and 3D Charts (these will be used for a function in two independent variables).

To show all this for the univariate case, we will go through some practical examples.

## EXAMPLE 1 (NUMERICAL STUDY OF A POLYNOMIAL UNIVARIATE FUNCTION)

Let us study the following function:

$$y = 3x^4 - 4x^3.$$

The goal is to find all the critical points (min or max) of the function and the inflection points as well, if ever these exist.

i. As a first step we plot the function in the Cartesian coordinates system $(x, y)$ through the Excel scatter chart. This step is key to choose the most appropriate interval $(a, b)$ in the independent variable domain, so that we can catch all the critical points, to make decisions on how to maximize or to minimize the function.

ii. The second step is to calculate the numerical derivatives as explained in Chapter 2, to see where the derivative is positive, negative, or zero.

iii. The last step is to make Excel highlight the critical points (minima or maxima) and the inflection points, these being identified through the second derivative.

The worksheet we can implement to perform the above steps is like that in Figs. 5.1-1 and 5.1-2.

- Column A stores the independent variable values, within the chosen interval;
- Column B stores the dependent variable values;
- Column C stores the first numerical derivative;
- Column D identifies the critical points (minima and maxima) and whether the function is increasing or decreasing;
- Column E stores the second (numerical) derivative;
- Column F identifies the critical points of the second derivative (for the inflection points in the function) and whether the function is convex or concave.

| | A | B | C | D |
|---|---|---|---|---|
| 1 | x | y=3x^4-4x^3 | dy/dx = 12x^3-12x^2 | Critical points |
| 2 | -1 | =A2^3*(3*A2-4) | | |
| 3 | -0.98 | =A3^3*(3*A3-4) | =(B3-B2)/(A3-A2) | |
| 4 | -0.96 | =A4^3*(3*A4-4) | =(B4-B3)/(A4-A3) | =IF(SIGN(C4)<>SIGN(C3);"CRITICAL POINT";IF(C4>0;"Increasing Function";"Decreasing Function")) |
| 5 | -0.94 | =A5^3*(3*A5-4) | =(B5-B4)/(A5-A4) | =IF(SIGN(C5)<>SIGN(C4);IF(C4<0;"MINIMUM";"MAXIMUM");IF(C5>0;"Increasing Function";"Decreasing Function")) |
| 6 | -0.92 | =A6^3*(3*A6-4) | =(B6-B5)/(A6-A5) | =IF(SIGN(C6)<>SIGN(C5);IF(C5<0;"MINIMUM";"MAXIMUM");IF(C6>0;"Increasing Function";"Decreasing Function")) |
| 7 | -0.9 | =A7^3*(3*A7-4) | =(B7-B6)/(A7-A6) | =IF(SIGN(C7)<>SIGN(C6);IF(C6<0;"MINIMUM";"MAXIMUM");IF(C7>0;"Increasing Function";"Decreasing Function")) |
| 8 | -0.88 | =A8^3*(3*A8-4) | =(B8-B7)/(A8-A7) | =IF(SIGN(C8)<>SIGN(C7);IF(C7<0;"MINIMUM";"MAXIMUM");IF(C8>0;"Increasing Function";"Decreasing Function")) |
| 9 | -0.86 | =A9^3*(3*A9-4) | =(B9-B8)/(A9-A8) | =IF(SIGN(C9)<>SIGN(C8);IF(C8<0;"MINIMUM";"MAXIMUM");IF(C9>0;"Increasing Function";"Decreasing Function")) |
| 10 | -0.84 | =A10^3*(3*A10-4) | =(B10-B9)/(A10-A9) | =IF(SIGN(C10)<>SIGN(C9);IF(C9<0;"MINIMUM";"MAXIMUM");IF(C10>0;"Increasing Function";"Decreasing Function")) |
| 11 | -0.82 | =A11^3*(3*A11-4) | =(B11-B10)/(A11-A10) | =IF(SIGN(C11)<>SIGN(C10);IF(C10<0;"MINIMUM";"MAXIMUM");IF(C11>0;"Increasing Function";"Decreasing Function")) |
| 12 | -0.8 | =A12^3*(3*A12-4) | =(B12-B11)/(A12-A11) | =IF(SIGN(C12)<>SIGN(C11);IF(C11<0;"MINIMUM";"MAXIMUM");IF(C12>0;"Increasing Function";"Decreasing Function")) |
| 13 | -0.78 | =A13^3*(3*A13-4) | =(B13-B12)/(A13-A12) | =IF(SIGN(C13)<>SIGN(C12);IF(C12<0;"MINIMUM";"MAXIMUM");IF(C13>0;"Increasing Function";"Decreasing Function")) |
| 14 | -0.76 | =A14^3*(3*A14-4) | =(B14-B13)/(A14-A13) | =IF(SIGN(C14)<>SIGN(C13);IF(C13<0;"MINIMUM";"MAXIMUM");IF(C14>0;"Increasing Function";"Decreasing Function")) |
| 15 | -0.74 | =A15^3*(3*A15-4) | =(B15-B14)/(A15-A14) | =IF(SIGN(C15)<>SIGN(C14);IF(C14<0;"MINIMUM";"MAXIMUM");IF(C15>0;"Increasing Function";"Decreasing Function")) |
| 16 | -0.72 | =A16^3*(3*A16-4) | =(B16-B15)/(A16-A15) | =IF(SIGN(C16)<>SIGN(C15);IF(C15<0;"MINIMUM";"MAXIMUM");IF(C16>0;"Increasing Function";"Decreasing Function")) |
| 17 | -0.7 | =A17^3*(3*A17-4) | =(B17-B16)/(A17-A16) | =IF(SIGN(C17)<>SIGN(C16);IF(C16<0;"MINIMUM";"MAXIMUM");IF(C17>0;"Increasing Function";"Decreasing Function")) |
| 18 | -0.68 | =A18^3*(3*A18-4) | =(B18-B17)/(A18-A17) | =IF(SIGN(C18)<>SIGN(C17);IF(C17<0;"MINIMUM";"MAXIMUM");IF(C18>0;"Increasing Function";"Decreasing Function")) |
| 19 | -0.66 | =A19^3*(3*A19-4) | =(B19-B18)/(A19-A18) | =IF(SIGN(C19)<>SIGN(C18);IF(C18<0;"MINIMUM";"MAXIMUM");IF(C19>0;"Increasing Function";"Decreasing Function")) |
| 20 | -0.64 | =A20^3*(3*A20-4) | =(B20-B19)/(A20-A19) | =IF(SIGN(C20)<>SIGN(C19);IF(C19<0;"MINIMUM";"MAXIMUM");IF(C20>0;"Increasing Function";"Decreasing Function")) |
| 21 | -0.62 | =A21^3*(3*A21-4) | =(B21-B20)/(A21-A20) | =IF(SIGN(C21)<>SIGN(C20);IF(C20<0;"MINIMUM";"MAXIMUM");IF(C21>0;"Increasing Function";"Decreasing Function")) |
| 22 | -0.6 | =A22^3*(3*A22-4) | =(B22-B21)/(A22-A21) | =IF(SIGN(C22)<>SIGN(C21);IF(C21<0;"MINIMUM";"MAXIMUM");IF(C22>0;"Increasing Function";"Decreasing Function")) |
| 23 | -0.58 | =A23^3*(3*A23-4) | =(B23-B22)/(A23-A22) | =IF(SIGN(C23)<>SIGN(C22);IF(C22<0;"MINIMUM";"MAXIMUM");IF(C23>0;"Increasing Function";"Decreasing Function")) |
| 24 | -0.56 | =A24^3*(3*A24-4) | =(B24-B23)/(A24-A23) | =IF(SIGN(C24)<>SIGN(C23);IF(C23<0;"MINIMUM";"MAXIMUM");IF(C24>0;"Increasing Function";"Decreasing Function")) |
| 25 | -0.54 | =A25^3*(3*A25-4) | =(B25-B24)/(A25-A24) | =IF(SIGN(C25)<>SIGN(C24);IF(C24<0;"MINIMUM";"MAXIMUM");IF(C25>0;"Increasing Function";"Decreasing Function")) |

FIGURE 5.1-1  Excel worksheet for a numerical study of the function (Part I).

| | A | E | F |
|---|---|---|---|
| 1 | x | dy²/d²x = 36x^2-24x | Concavity/Convexity of y |
| 2 | -1 | | |
| 3 | =A2+$H$2 | | |
| 4 | =A3+$H$2 | =(C4-C3)/(A4-A3) | |
| 5 | =A4+$H$2 | =(C5-C4)/(A5-A4) | =IF(SIGN(E5)<>SIGN(E4);"INFLECTION POINT";IF(E5>0;"y Convex";"y Concave")) |
| 6 | =A5+$H$2 | =(C6-C5)/(A6-A5) | =IF(SIGN(E6)<>SIGN(E5);"INFLECTION POINT";IF(E6>0;"y Convex";"y Concave")) |
| 7 | =A6+$H$2 | =(C7-C6)/(A7-A6) | =IF(SIGN(E7)<>SIGN(E6);"INFLECTION POINT";IF(E7>0;"y Convex";"y Concave")) |
| 52 | =A51+$H$2 | =(C52-C51)/(A52-A51) | =IF(SIGN(E52)<>SIGN(E51);"INFLECTION POINT";IF(E52>0;"y Convex";"y Concave")) |
| 53 | =A52+$H$2 | =(C53-C52)/(A53-A52) | =IF(SIGN(E53)<>SIGN(E52);"INFLECTION POINT";IF(E53>0;"y Convex";"y Concave")) |
| 54 | =A53+$H$2 | =(C54-C53)/(A54-A53) | =IF(SIGN(E54)<>SIGN(E53);"INFLECTION POINT";IF(E54>0;"y Convex";"y Concave")) |
| 55 | =A54+$H$2 | =(C55-C54)/(A55-A54) | =IF(SIGN(E55)<>SIGN(E54);"INFLECTION POINT";IF(E55>0;"y Convex";"y Concave")) |
| 56 | =A55+$H$2 | =(C56-C55)/(A56-A55) | =IF(SIGN(E56)<>SIGN(E55);"INFLECTION POINT";IF(E56>0;"y Convex";"y Concave")) |
| 84 | =A83+$H$2 | =(C84-C83)/(A84-A83) | =IF(SIGN(E84)<>SIGN(E83);"INFLECTION POINT";IF(E84>0;"y Convex";"y Concave")) |
| 85 | =A84+$H$2 | =(C85-C84)/(A85-A84) | =IF(SIGN(E85)<>SIGN(E84);"INFLECTION POINT";IF(E85>0;"y Convex";"y Concave")) |
| 86 | =A85+$H$2 | =(C86-C85)/(A86-A85) | =IF(SIGN(E86)<>SIGN(E85);"INFLECTION POINT";IF(E86>0;"y Convex";"y Concave")) |
| 87 | =A86+$H$2 | =(C87-C86)/(A87-A86) | =IF(SIGN(E87)<>SIGN(E86);"INFLECTION POINT";IF(E87>0;"y Convex";"y Concave")) |
| 88 | =A87+$H$2 | =(C88-C87)/(A88-A87) | =IF(SIGN(E88)<>SIGN(E87);"INFLECTION POINT";IF(E88>0;"y Convex";"y Concave")) |
| 89 | =A88+$H$2 | =(C89-C88)/(A89-A88) | =IF(SIGN(E89)<>SIGN(E88);"INFLECTION POINT";IF(E89>0;"y Convex";"y Concave")) |
| 90 | =A89+$H$2 | =(C90-C89)/(A90-A89) | =IF(SIGN(E90)<>SIGN(E89);"INFLECTION POINT";IF(E90>0;"y Convex";"y Concave")) |
| 91 | =A90+$H$2 | =(C91-C90)/(A91-A90) | =IF(SIGN(E91)<>SIGN(E90);"INFLECTION POINT";IF(E91>0;"y Convex";"y Concave")) |
| 92 | =A91+$H$2 | =(C92-C91)/(A92-A91) | =IF(SIGN(E92)<>SIGN(E91);"INFLECTION POINT";IF(E92>0;"y Convex";"y Concave")) |
| 101 | =A100+$H$2 | =(C101-C100)/(A101-A100) | =IF(SIGN(E101)<>SIGN(E100);"INFLECTION POINT";IF(E101>0;"y Convex";"y Concave")) |
| 102 | =A101+$H$2 | =(C102-C101)/(A102-A101) | =IF(SIGN(E102)<>SIGN(E101);"INFLECTION POINT";IF(E102>0;"y Convex";"y Concave")) |
| 103 | =A102+$H$2 | =(C103-C102)/(A103-A102) | =IF(SIGN(E103)<>SIGN(E102);"INFLECTION POINT";IF(E103>0;"y Convex";"y Concave")) |
| 104 | =A103+$H$2 | =(C104-C103)/(A104-A103) | =IF(SIGN(E104)<>SIGN(E103);"INFLECTION POINT";IF(E104>0;"y Convex";"y Concave")) |

**FIGURE 5.1-2**   Excel worksheet for a numerical study of the function (Part II).

The above Excel columns just implement, via the *if function*, the standard rules of calculus, studying the sign of the first and the second derivatives for a univariate function. The numerical values and qualitative description of the given function are in Table 5.1-1, which has been built with a **step-size of 0.02.**

The behavior of the function is as follows:

- Up to the numerical value of $x = 0.04$ the function is decreasing, showing convexity;
- Then, up to the numerical value of $x = 0.70$ the function is decreasing, showing concavity;
- Then, the function is always convex decreasing again until the numerical value of $x = 1$ (strong global minimum), after that point the function is increasing toward infinity as $x$ goes to infinity (there is no global maximum, unless we set an upper bound in the domain of $x$).

We can then plot, choosing the Excel scatter chart, the values of the function alone (Fig. 5.1-3), as well as together with its first derivative and its second derivative (Fig. 5.1-4), to visualize the intimate relations among the three curves and the critical points identified. Notice how through the Excel scatter chart options we can add to the diagram the analytical equations of the function and its derivatives.

**TABLE 5.1-1**   Numerical study of the function $y = 3x^4 - 4x^3$ (minimum point and inflection points).

| x | $y = 3x^4-4x^3$ | $dy/dx = 12x^3-12x^2$ | Critical points | $dy^2/d^2x = 36x^2-24x$ | Concavity/Convexity of y |
|---|---|---|---|---|---|
| -1.0000 | 7.0000 | | | | |
| -0.9800 | 6.5319 | -23.4064 | | | |
| -0.9600 | 6.0870 | -22.2444 | Decreasing Function | 58.0968 | |
| -0.9400 | 5.6646 | -21.1200 | Decreasing Function | 56.2200 | y Convex |
| -0.9200 | 5.2639 | -20.0326 | Decreasing Function | 54.3720 | y Convex |
| -0.9000 | 4.8843 | -18.9815 | Decreasing Function | 52.5528 | y Convex |
| 0.0000 | 0.0000 | -0.0016 | Decreasing Function | 0.4968 | y Convex |
| 0.0200 | 0.0000 | -0.0016 | Decreasing Function | 0.0024 | y Convex |
| 0.0400 | -0.0002 | -0.0108 | Decreasing Function | -0.4632 | **INFLECTION POINT** |
| 0.0600 | -0.0008 | -0.0288 | Decreasing Function | -0.9000 | y Concave |
| 0.0800 | -0.0019 | -0.0550 | Decreasing Function | -1.3080 | y Concave |
| 0.6400 | -0.5453 | -1.7619 | Decreasing Function | -1.0392 | y Concave |
| 0.6600 | -0.5807 | -1.7741 | Decreasing Function | -0.6120 | y Concave |
| 0.6800 | -0.6163 | -1.7772 | Decreasing Function | -0.1560 | y Concave |
| 0.7000 | -0.6517 | -1.7707 | Decreasing Function | 0.3288 | **INFLECTION POINT** |
| 0.7200 | -0.6868 | -1.7538 | Decreasing Function | 0.8424 | y Convex |
| 0.7400 | -0.7213 | -1.7261 | Decreasing Function | 1.3848 | y Convex |
| 0.7600 | -0.7550 | -1.6870 | Decreasing Function | 1.9560 | y Convex |
| 0.7800 | -0.7878 | -1.6359 | Decreasing Function | 2.5560 | y Convex |
| 0.8000 | -0.8192 | -1.5722 | Decreasing Function | 3.1848 | y Convex |
| 0.9800 | -0.9977 | -0.3380 | Decreasing Function | 10.1400 | y Convex |
| 1.0000 | -1.0000 | -0.1168 | Decreasing Function | 11.0568 | y Convex |
| 1.0200 | -0.9975 | 0.1232 | **MINIMUM** | 12.0024 | y Convex |
| 1.0400 | -0.9899 | 0.3828 | Increasing Function | 12.9768 | y Convex |
| 1.0600 | -0.9766 | 0.6624 | Increasing Function | 13.9800 | y Convex |
| 1.4400 | 0.9555 | 10.5530 | Increasing Function | 38.5128 | y Convex |

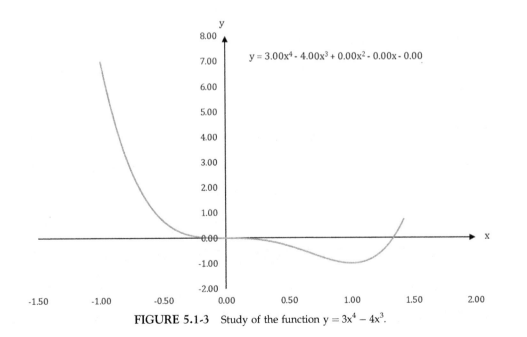

FIGURE 5.1-3   Study of the function $y = 3x^4 - 4x^3$.

II. Static optimization

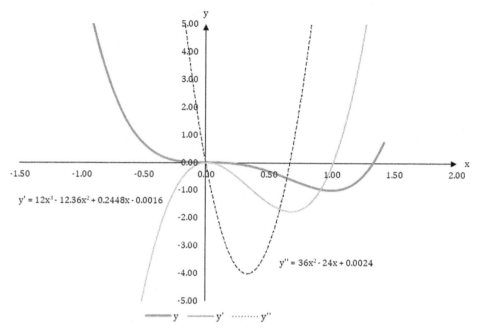

$y' = 12x^3 - 12.36x^2 + 0.2448x - 0.0016$

$y'' = 36x^2 - 24x + 0.0024$

**FIGURE 5.1-4**   Study of the function $y = 3x^4 - 4x^3$ together with its first and second derivatives.

We summarize Fig. 5.1-4 as follows:

- $\frac{d^2y}{dx^2} \gtrless 0$ implies $y$ convex (concave);
- $\frac{dy}{dx} \gtrless 0$ implies $y$ increasing (decreasing) function.

Choosing the best step-size in the above solutions is key. As described in Table 5.5-1 the step-size chosen is 0.02.

Each study function will have its best step-size, reached via trials and errors after an adequate fine-tuning of the interval in the independent variable. The higher the step-size, the larger will be the chosen interval. We essentially proceed by a few iterations.

Iteration 1 (*step-size* = 1). As a first step, we could begin with a step-size of 1 with interval in the independent variable starting from the value $x_0 = -10$. Under this scenario only a minimum has been found, and the calculated values suggest that this would be a unique global minimum. The resulting values are in Table 5.1-2.

Iteration 2 (*step-size* = 0.5). We keep on dividing the step-size, reducing the interval as well. As a second iteration we go for a step-size equal to 0.5 and $x_0 = -5$. The results are in Table 5.1-3. Now, also two inflection points emerge from Table 5.1-3.

Iteration 3 (*step-size* = 0.05). We reduce drastically the step-size. From Table 5.1-3 we notice that beyond point $x = 2$ the function does not have any critical or inflection point and it is just increasing smoothly. We then reduce drastically the interval in the independent variable starting from $x_0 = -1$, focusing only on the range including the minimum point (which is a unique global minimum) and the two inflection points. The third iteration gives Table 5.1-4.

**TABLE 5.1-2**    Iteration N.1 step-size $= 1$ and $x_0 = -10$.

| x | $y = 3x^4-4x^3$ | $dy/dx = 12x^3-12x^2$ | Critical points | $dy^2/d^2x = 36x^2-24x$ | Concavity/Convexity of y |
|---|---|---|---|---|---|
| -10.0000 | 34,000.0000 | | | | |
| -9.0000 | 22,599.0000 | -11,401.0000 | | | |
| -8.0000 | 14,336.0000 | -8,263.0000 | Decreasing Function | 3,138.0000 | |
| -7.0000 | 8,575.0000 | -5,761.0000 | Decreasing Function | 2,502.0000 | y Convex |
| -6.0000 | 4,752.0000 | -3,823.0000 | Decreasing Function | 1,938.0000 | y Convex |
| -5.0000 | 2,375.0000 | -2,377.0000 | Decreasing Function | 1,446.0000 | y Convex |
| -4.0000 | 1,024.0000 | -1,351.0000 | Decreasing Function | 1,026.0000 | y Convex |
| -3.0000 | 351.0000 | -673.0000 | Decreasing Function | 678.0000 | y Convex |
| -2.0000 | 80.0000 | -271.0000 | Decreasing Function | 402.0000 | y Convex |
| -1.0000 | 7.0000 | -73.0000 | Decreasing Function | 198.0000 | y Convex |
| 0.0000 | 0.0000 | -7.0000 | Decreasing Function | 66.0000 | y Convex |
| 1.0000 | -1.0000 | -1.0000 | Decreasing Function | 6.0000 | y Convex |
| 2.0000 | 16.0000 | 17.0000 | MINIMUM | 18.0000 | y Convex |
| 3.0000 | 135.0000 | 119.0000 | Increasing Function | 102.0000 | y Convex |
| 4.0000 | 512.0000 | 377.0000 | Increasing Function | 258.0000 | y Convex |
| 5.0000 | 1,375.0000 | 863.0000 | Increasing Function | 486.0000 | y Convex |
| 6.0000 | 3,024.0000 | 1,649.0000 | Increasing Function | 786.0000 | y Convex |
| 7.0000 | 5,831.0000 | 2,807.0000 | Increasing Function | 1,158.0000 | y Convex |
| 107.0000 | 388,338,631.0000 | 14,359,607.0000 | Increasing Function | 401,958.0000 | y Convex |
| 108.0000 | 403,107,840.0000 | 14,769,209.0000 | Increasing Function | 409,602.0000 | y Convex |
| 109.0000 | 418,294,367.0000 | 15,186,527.0000 | Increasing Function | 417,318.0000 | y Convex |
| 110.0000 | 433,906,000.0000 | 15,611,633.0000 | Increasing Function | 425,106.0000 | y Convex |
| 111.0000 | 449,950,599.0000 | 16,044,599.0000 | Increasing Function | 432,966.0000 | y Convex |
| 112.0000 | 466,436,096.0000 | 16,485,497.0000 | Increasing Function | 440,898.0000 | y Convex |

**TABLE 5.1-3**    Iteration N.2 step-size $= 0.5$ and $x_0 = -5$

| x | $y = 3x^4-4x^3$ | $dy/dx = 12x^3-12x^2$ | Critical points | $dy^2/d^2x = 36x^2-24x$ | Concavity/Convexity of y |
|---|---|---|---|---|---|
| -5.0000 | 2,375.0000 | | | | |
| -4.5000 | 1,594.6875 | -1,560.6250 | | | |
| -4.0000 | 1,024.0000 | -1,141.3750 | Decreasing Function | 838.5000 | |
| -3.5000 | 621.6875 | -804.6250 | Decreasing Function | 673.5000 | y Convex |
| -3.0000 | 351.0000 | -541.3750 | Decreasing Function | 526.5000 | y Convex |
| -2.5000 | 179.6875 | -342.6250 | Decreasing Function | 397.5000 | y Convex |
| -2.0000 | 80.0000 | -199.3750 | Decreasing Function | 286.5000 | y Convex |
| -1.5000 | 28.6875 | -102.6250 | Decreasing Function | 193.5000 | y Convex |
| -1.0000 | 7.0000 | -43.3750 | Decreasing Function | 118.5000 | y Convex |
| -0.5000 | 0.6875 | -12.6250 | Decreasing Function | 61.5000 | y Convex |
| 0.0000 | 0.0000 | -1.3750 | Decreasing Function | 22.5000 | y Convex |
| 0.5000 | -0.3125 | -0.6250 | Decreasing Function | 1.5000 | y Convex |
| 1.0000 | -1.0000 | -1.3750 | Decreasing Function | -1.5000 | INFLECTION POINT |
| 1.5000 | 1.6875 | 5.3750 | MINIMUM | 13.5000 | INFLECTION POINT |
| 2.0000 | 16.0000 | 28.6250 | Increasing Function | 46.5000 | y Convex |
| 2.5000 | 54.6875 | 77.3750 | Increasing Function | 97.5000 | y Convex |
| 3.0000 | 135.0000 | 160.6250 | Increasing Function | 166.5000 | y Convex |
| 3.5000 | 278.6875 | 287.3750 | Increasing Function | 253.5000 | y Convex |
| 53.5000 | 23,964,903.6875 | 1,777,937.3750 | Increasing Function | 99,853.5000 | y Convex |
| 54.0000 | 24,879,312.0000 | 1,828,816.6250 | Increasing Function | 101,758.5000 | y Convex |
| 54.5000 | 25,819,640.6875 | 1,880,657.3750 | Increasing Function | 103,681.5000 | y Convex |
| 55.0000 | 26,786,375.0000 | 1,933,468.6250 | Increasing Function | 105,622.5000 | y Convex |
| 55.5000 | 27,780,004.6875 | 1,987,259.3750 | Increasing Function | 107,581.5000 | y Convex |
| 56.0000 | 28,801,024.0000 | 2,042,038.6250 | Increasing Function | 109,558.5000 | y Convex |

**TABLE 5.1-4**   Iteration N.3 step-size $= 0.05$ and $x_0 = -1$

| x | $y = 3x^4-4x^3$ | $dy/dx = 12x^3-12x^2$ | Critical points | $dy^2/d^2x = 36x^2-24x$ | Concavity/Convexity of y |
|---|---|---|---|---|---|
| -1.0000 | 7.0000 | | | | |
| -0.9500 | 5.8730 | -22.5396 | | | |
| -0.9000 | 4.8843 | -19.7744 | Decreasing Function | 55.3050 | |
| -0.8500 | 4.0225 | -17.2356 | Decreasing Function | 50.7750 | y Convex |
| -0.8000 | 3.2768 | -14.9144 | Decreasing Function | 46.4250 | y Convex |
| -0.7500 | 2.6367 | -12.8016 | Decreasing Function | 42.2550 | y Convex |
| 0.0000 | 0.0000 | -0.0104 | Decreasing Function | 1.3050 | y Convex |
| 0.0500 | -0.0005 | -0.0096 | Decreasing Function | 0.0150 | y Convex |
| 0.1000 | -0.0037 | -0.0644 | Decreasing Function | -1.0950 | INFLECTION POINT |
| 0.1500 | -0.0120 | -0.1656 | Decreasing Function | -2.0250 | y Concave |
| 0.6000 | -0.4752 | -1.6844 | Decreasing Function | -2.2950 | y Concave |
| 0.6500 | -0.5630 | -1.7556 | Decreasing Function | -1.4250 | y Concave |
| 0.7000 | -0.6517 | -1.7744 | Decreasing Function | -0.3750 | y Concave |
| 0.7500 | -0.7383 | -1.7316 | Decreasing Function | 0.8550 | INFLECTION POINT |
| 0.8000 | -0.8192 | -1.6184 | Decreasing Function | 2.2650 | y Convex |
| 0.8500 | -0.8905 | -1.4256 | Decreasing Function | 3.8550 | y Convex |
| 0.9000 | -0.9477 | -1.1444 | Decreasing Function | 5.6250 | y Convex |
| 0.9500 | -0.9860 | -0.7656 | Decreasing Function | 7.5750 | y Convex |
| 1.0000 | -1.0000 | -0.2804 | Decreasing Function | 9.7050 | y Convex |
| 1.0500 | -0.9840 | 0.3204 | MINIMUM | 12.0150 | y Convex |
| 1.1000 | -0.9317 | 1.0456 | Increasing Function | 14.5050 | y Convex |
| 1.1500 | -0.8365 | 1.9044 | Increasing Function | 17.1750 | y Convex |
| 4.9500 | 1,315.9680 | 1,142.4744 | Increasing Function | 746.7750 | y Convex |
| 5.0000 | 1,375.0000 | 1,180.6396 | Increasing Function | 763.3050 | y Convex |
| 5.0500 | 1,435.9820 | 1,219.6404 | Increasing Function | 780.0150 | y Convex |
| 5.1000 | 1,498.9563 | 1,259.4856 | Increasing Function | 796.9050 | y Convex |

Iteration 4 (*step-size* $= 0.02$). This is the iteration which leads to the first Table 5.1-1 that we have shown at the beginning, which allows us to identify, with a reasonable numerical error, the critical points.

## The Solver

At this stage of the numerical analysis we can further fine-tune the unique global minimum value, by simply launching the Solver, suggesting to it that the extreme value is close to 1.

In Fig. 5.1-5, we have input the function $y = 3x^4 - 4x^3$ in *Cell L2*, while in *Cell K2*, the independent variable.

Now, it is just a matter of minimizing *Cell L2*, via the Solver, by changing *Cell K2*, as described in Fig. 5.1-6.

The value we had found before is in fact the exact unique global minimum point $x_{mn}^* = 1$.

The Solver is a powerful tool to solve the optimization problems; however, when the function shows more critical points, we will need to know the properties of these points, to instruct the Solver what and where to search.

| K | L |
|---|---|
| x | y = 3x^4-4x^3 |
| 0.999999 | =K2^3*(3*K2-4) |

| K | L |
|---|---|
| x | y = 3x^4-4x^3 |
| 1.0000 | -1.0000 |

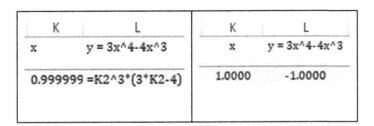

FIGURE 5.1-5 Input of the univariate function.

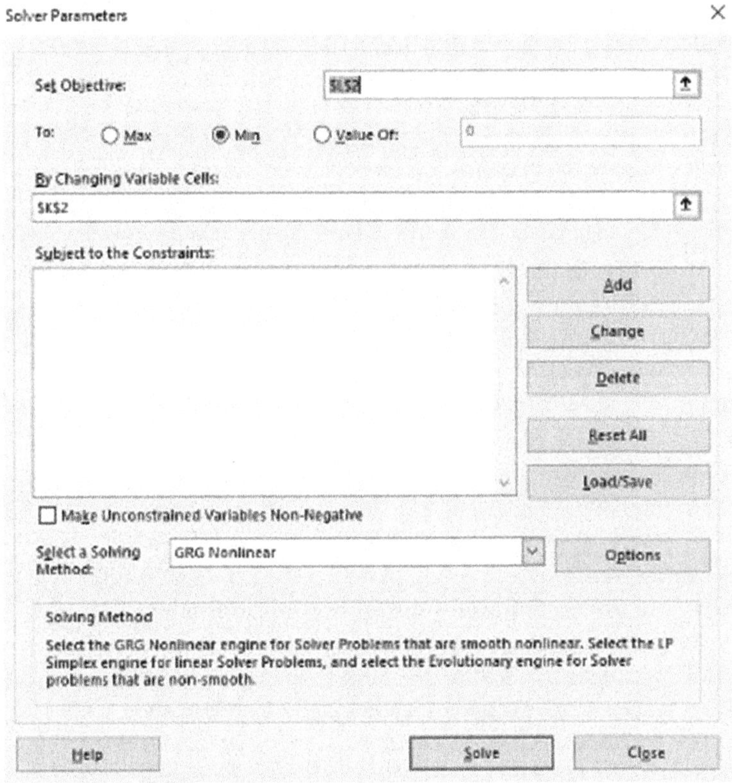

FIGURE 5.1-6 Example 1 Solver setup.

## Example 2 (univariate function with a unique global min and max and two inflection points)

Let us study the behavior of the following function, finding all its extreme values and inflection points.

$$y = xe^{\left(1-x^2\right)}$$

Notice from Table 5.1-5 (and Fig. 5.1-7) how the study of the sign in the second derivative $f''(x)$ is also helpful to identify minima and maxima and not only inflection points. Notice that:

- at the global minimum $x \cong -0.65$ we have $f''(x) > 0$,
- at the global maximum $x \cong 0.75$ we have $f''(x) < 0$.

**TABLE 5.1-5**    Example 2: Enumeration of the function $y = xe^{(1-x^2)}$ Step-Size $= 0.05$

| x | y = x*exp(1-x^2) | dy/dx | Critical points | dy²/d²x | Concavity/Convexity of y |
|---|---|---|---|---|---|
| -4.0000 | 0.0000 | | | | |
| -3.9500 | 0.0000 | 0.0000 | | | |
| -3.9000 | 0.0000 | 0.0000 | Decreasing Function | -0.0001 | |
| -3.8500 | 0.0000 | 0.0000 | Decreasing Function | -0.0001 | y Concave |
| -3.8000 | 0.0000 | 0.0000 | Decreasing Function | -0.0002 | y Concave |
| -1.2500 | -0.7122 | -1.2036 | Decreasing Function | -0.4916 | y Concave |
| -1.2000 | -0.7728 | -1.2123 | Decreasing Function | -0.1742 | y Concave |
| -1.1500 | -0.8330 | -1.2029 | Decreasing Function | 0.1890 | INFLECTION POINT |
| -1.1000 | -0.8916 | -1.1731 | Decreasing Function | 0.5945 | y Convex |
| -1.0500 | -0.9477 | -1.1213 | Decreasing Function | 1.0368 | y Convex |
| -0.7500 | -1.1616 | -0.2992 | Decreasing Function | 3.9409 | y Convex |
| -0.7000 | -1.1657 | -0.0816 | Decreasing Function | 4.3512 | y Convex |
| -0.6500 | -1.1580 | 0.1536 | MINIMUM | 4.7035 | y Convex |
| -0.6000 | -1.1379 | 0.4028 | Increasing Function | 4.9841 | y Convex |
| -0.5500 | -1.1048 | 0.6618 | Increasing Function | 5.1809 | y Convex |
| 0.0000 | 0.0000 | 2.7115 | Increasing Function | 0.8104 | y Convex |
| 0.0500 | 0.1356 | 2.7115 | Increasing Function | 0.0000 | y Convex |
| 0.1000 | 0.2691 | 2.6710 | Increasing Function | -0.8104 | INFLECTION POINT |
| 0.1500 | 0.3987 | 2.5909 | Increasing Function | -1.6007 | y Concave |
| 0.5500 | 1.1048 | 0.9260 | Increasing Function | -5.2835 | y Concave |
| 0.6000 | 1.1379 | 0.6618 | Increasing Function | -5.2834 | y Concave |
| 0.6500 | 1.1580 | 0.4028 | Increasing Function | -5.1809 | y Concave |
| 0.7000 | 1.1657 | 0.1536 | Increasing Function | -4.9841 | y Concave |
| 0.7500 | 1.1616 | -0.0816 | MAXIMUM | -4.7035 | y Concave |
| 0.8000 | 1.1467 | -0.2992 | Decreasing Function | -4.3512 | y Concave |
| 0.8500 | 1.1219 | -0.4962 | Decreasing Function | -3.9409 | y Concave |
| 0.9000 | 1.0883 | -0.6706 | Decreasing Function | -3.4865 | y Concave |
| 0.9500 | 1.0473 | -0.8207 | Decreasing Function | -3.0025 | y Concave |
| 1.2500 | 0.7122 | -1.2123 | Decreasing Function | -0.1890 | y Concave |
| 1.3000 | 0.6520 | -1.2036 | Decreasing Function | 0.1742 | INFLECTION POINT |
| 2.0500 | 0.0834 | -0.3244 | Decreasing Function | 0.9957 | y Convex |
| 2.1000 | 0.0694 | -0.2793 | Decreasing Function | 0.9012 | y Convex |

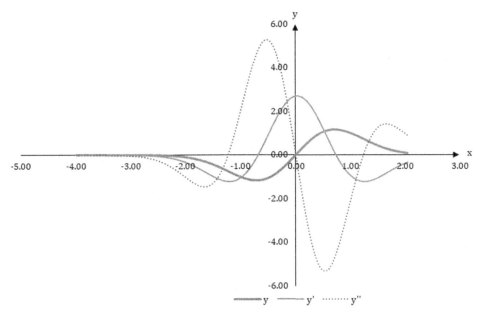

**FIGURE 5.1-7** Example 2: function $y = xe^{(1-x^2)}$ together with its first and second derivatives.

In the range $(-4, 0)$ the function shows concavity and then convexity, reaching within this convex interval a unique global minimum $y^*_{min} \cong -1.16$ at $x^*_{min} \cong -0.65$ and then it shows again concavity, reaching within this concave interval, a global maximum $y^*_{max} \cong 1.16$ at $x^*_{max} \cong 0.75$ showing convexity afterward.

After this numerical analysis, using the Solver, we can easily reach the exact solution with a unique global minimum in $x_{min} = -\frac{\sqrt{2}}{2}$, unique global maximum in $x_{max} = +\frac{\sqrt{2}}{2}$, with $y^*_{min} = -1.1658$, $y^*_{max} = +1.1658$.

An alternative approach to find minima and maxima is given by a geometrical approach, by finding those points where the slope of the tangent is zero. See the following example that continues Example 2.

## EXAMPLE 3 (TANGENT APPROACH FOR MIN AND MAX IDENTIFICATION)

Let us continue with the function:

$$y = xe^{(1-x^2)}.$$

We want to use the tangent geometrical approach to find its extreme values and to do so we resort to the worksheet setup in Fig. 2.1-4, which we modify slightly as in Fig. 5.1-8, where we have added in the second box beneath the study of the sign of the first derivative under *Column G*, together with the difference in the tangent value for each $x$, under *Column H*. The values of the tangent equation are stored within the Data Table.

| | A | B | C | D | E | F |
|---|---|---|---|---|---|---|
| 1 | Tangent y = m*(x-x₀)+y₀ | m | x₀ | =C4-0.00001 | x₁ | 1 |
| 2 | =($F$2-$D$2)/($F$1-$D$1)*(A5-$D$1)+$D$2 | =(F2-D2)/(F1-D1) | y₀ | =D1*EXP(1-D1^2) | y₁ | =F1*EXP(1-F1^2) |
| 3 | | | Simulate tg in C4 changing x₀ | | | |
| | x | | | | y = x*exp(1-x^2) | |
| 4 | | =A2 | -0.5 | | | Δy/Δx |
| 5 | 1 | -3 | =TABLE(F1:A5) | | =B5*EXP(1-B5^2) | |
| 6 | | =B5+$G$2 | =TABLE(F1:A5) | | =B6*EXP(1-B6^2) | =(E6-E5)/(B6-B5) |
| 7 | | =B6+$G$2 | =TABLE(F1:A5) | | =B7*EXP(1-B7^2) | =(E7-E6)/(B7-B6) |
| 8 | | =B7+$G$2 | =TABLE(F1:A5) | | =B8*EXP(1-B8^2) | =(E8-E7)/(B8-B7) |
| 9 | | =B8+$G$2 | =TABLE(F1:A5) | | =B9*EXP(1-B9^2) | =(E9-E8)/(B9-B8) |
| 10 | | =B9+$G$2 | =TABLE(F1:A5) | | =B10*EXP(1-B10^2) | =(E10-E9)/(B10-B9) |
| 11 | | =B10+$G$2 | =TABLE(F1:A5) | | =B11*EXP(1-B11^2) | =(E11-E10)/(B11-B10) |
| 12 | | =B11+$G$2 | =TABLE(F1:A5) | | =B12*EXP(1-B12^2) | =(E12-E11)/(B12-B11) |

| | G | H |
|---|---|---|
| 1 | step | |
| 2 | 0.05 | |
| 3 | | |
| 4 | Incr./Decr. Function | =SUM(H5:H105) |
| 5 | | |
| 6 | | =C6-C5 |
| 7 | =IF(SIGN(F7)<>SIGN(F6);IF(F6<0;"MINIMUM";"MAXIMUM");IF(F7>0;"Increasing Function";"Decreasing Function")) | =C7-C6 |
| 8 | =IF(SIGN(F8)<>SIGN(F7);IF(F7<0;"MINIMUM";"MAXIMUM");IF(F8>0;"Increasing Function";"Decreasing Function")) | =C8-C7 |
| 9 | =IF(SIGN(F9)<>SIGN(F8);IF(F8<0;"MINIMUM";"MAXIMUM");IF(F9>0;"Increasing Function";"Decreasing Function")) | =C9-C8 |
| 10 | =IF(SIGN(F10)<>SIGN(F9);IF(F9<0;"MINIMUM";"MAXIMUM");IF(F10>0;"Increasing Function";"Decreasing Function")) | =C10-C9 |
| 11 | =IF(SIGN(F11)<>SIGN(F10);IF(F10<0;"MINIMUM";"MAXIMUM");IF(F11>0;"Increasing Function";"Decreasing Function")) | =C11-C10 |
| 12 | =IF(SIGN(F12)<>SIGN(F11);IF(F11<0;"MINIMUM";"MAXIMUM");IF(F12>0;"Increasing Function";"Decreasing Function")) | =C12-C11 |

**FIGURE 5.1-8**   Worksheet for the tangent diagram in $x_0$.

If the tangent has slope zero, and this happens when the tangent equation line is built to the curve at its extreme point (either min or max), it will imply that *Column H* of Fig. 5.1-8 will be equal to zero. We will use then *Column G* to identify the numerical approximate extreme values and, as a second step, using the Solver, we will set *Cell H4* equal to zero by changing the value of $x_0$ in *Cell C4*.

Let us consider Fig. 5.1-9 where a tangent has been drawn in the point $x_0 = 0.72$, near to the exact extreme value; it is apparent that, when passing at the maximum point, the tangent, by definition, will have to be horizontal, namely its slope will have to be equal to zero.

What we will do in order to reach this goal is to use the Solver to set *Cell H4* = 0 in Fig. 5.1-8, which means that for any $x$ the tangent equation will always have the same value, by changing the value of $x_0$ in *Cell C4*, as described in Fig. 5.1-10. $x_0$ as found this way from the Solver will be then our final exact value. Before running the Solver, we input in *Cell C4* the approximate numerical value found for the min and the max, according to what indicates *Column G* ($x_0 \cong 0.75$).

Figs. 5.1-11 and 5.1-12 describe the two horizontal tangents drawn at each extreme value, while Tables 5.1-6 and 5.1-7 the numerical values.

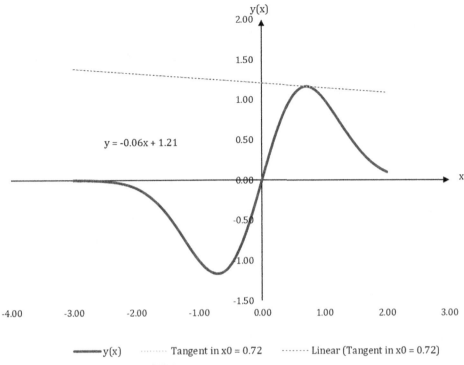

$$y = -0.06x + 1.21$$

──── y(x)    ········ Tangent in x0 = 0.72    ········ Linear (Tangent in x0 = 0.72)

**FIGURE 5.1-9**   Tangent diagram in $x_0 = 0.72$.


## EXAMPLE 4 (UNIVARIATE FUNCTION WITH A SHARP POINT)

Let us study the behavior of the following function:

$$y = x^{\frac{2}{3}}.$$

To study such a function is interesting because it shows the so-called "sharp point," i.e., a point where the first derivative does not exist. In this specific case the sharp point is in zero. Apart from zero the function is, however, differentiable every where.

The enumeration of Table 5.1-8 recognizes the unique global minimum. It recognizes the sharp point as well, however, as inflection point because we are working in a discrete framework. By the same token, in the enumeration table the first derivative in $x = 0$ gives a value different from zero, while in a continuous framework this will not hold.

Figs. 5.1-13 and 5.1-14 represent the function with its derivatives, under two step-size scenarios: 0.5 and 0.015. In this second scenario, the $y(x)$ diagram is getting closer, than the first diagram, to the typical exact sharp-point graph.

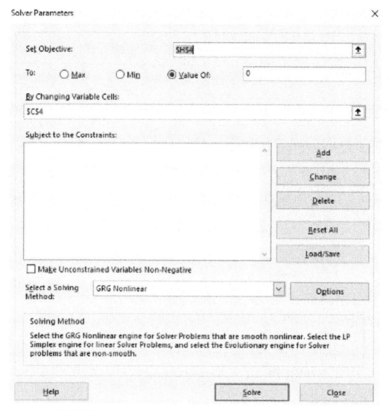

**FIGURE 5.1-10** Horizontal tangent setting via the Solver.

## 5.2 Classical unconstrained optimization of a multivariate function

Let's deal now with the unconstrained optimization of a function of $n$ variables, continuing the concepts introduced in Section 2.3.

For the following $n$-variables function:

$$y = f(x) = f(x_1, x_2, \cdots, x_n)$$

To apply the first-order condition (i.e., first derivative equal to zero), we need to resort to the following quantity, called *gradient* of the $n$-variables function:

$$grad[f(x)] = \nabla f(x) = \left[\frac{\partial f}{\partial x_1}, \frac{\partial f}{\partial x_2}, \cdots, \frac{\partial f}{\partial x_j}, \cdots, \frac{\partial f}{\partial x_n}\right]$$

where

$f_{x_j} = \frac{\partial f}{\partial x_j}$ $(j = 1, \cdots, n)$ is the *partial derivative* of $y = f(x)$ with respect to the variable $x_j$, considering all the other $(n-1)$ variables as a constant. The notation $f_j$ is also used.

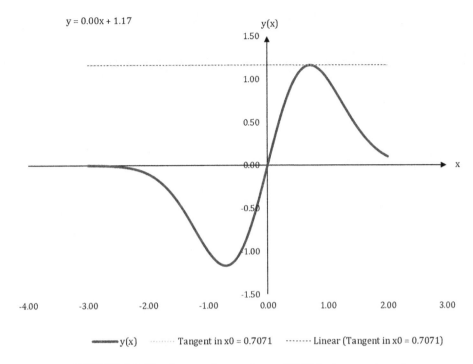

FIGURE 5.1-11    Tangent diagram in $x_0 = 0.7071$ (unique maximum).

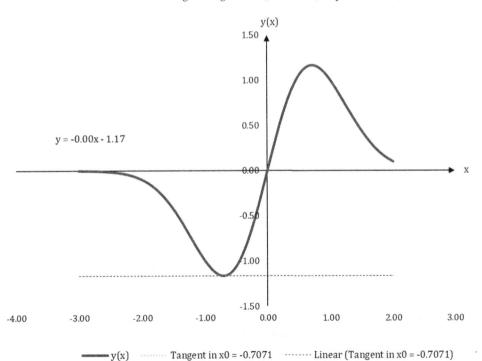

FIGURE 5.1-12    Tangent diagram in $x_0 = -0.7071$ (unique minimum).

II. Static optimization

**TABLE 5.1-6**   Slope equal to zero for $x_0 = 0.7071$ (unique maximum).

| Tangent y = m*(x-x₀)+y₀ | m | x₀ | 0.7071 | x₁ | 1.0000 | step | |
|---|---|---|---|---|---|---|---|
| 1.0000 | -0.5661 | y₀ | 1.1658 | y₁ | 1.0000 | 0.0500 | |

| | | Simulate tg in C4 | | | | | |
| | | changing x₀ | | | | | |

| x | | | | y = | | | |
| | 1.0000 | 0.7071 | | x*exp(1- x^2) | Δy/Δx | Incr./Decr. Function | 0.0000 |
| 1.0000 | -3.0000 | 1.1658 | | -0.001006 | | | |
| | -2.9500 | 1.1658 | | -0.0013 | -0.0065 | | 0.0000 |
| | -2.9000 | 1.1658 | | -0.0018 | -0.0084 | Decreasing Function | 0.0000 |
| | -0.8500 | 1.1658 | | -1.1219 | -0.6706 | Decreasing Function | 0.0000 |
| | -0.8000 | 1.1658 | | -1.1467 | -0.4962 | Decreasing Function | 0.0000 |
| | -0.7500 | 1.1658 | | -1.1616 | -0.2992 | Decreasing Function | 0.0000 |
| | -0.7000 | 1.1658 | | -1.1657 | -0.0816 | Decreasing Function | 0.0000 |
| | **-0.6500** | **1.1658** | | **-1.1580** | **0.1536** | **MINIMUM** | **0.0000** |
| | -0.6000 | 1.1658 | | -1.1379 | 0.4028 | Increasing Function | 0.0000 |
| | 0.6000 | 1.1658 | | 1.1379 | 0.6618 | Increasing Function | 0.0000 |
| | 0.6500 | 1.1658 | | 1.1580 | 0.4028 | Increasing Function | 0.0000 |
| | 0.7000 | 1.1658 | | 1.1657 | 0.1536 | Increasing Function | 0.0000 |
| | **0.7500** | **1.1658** | | **1.1616** | **-0.0816** | **MAXIMUM** | **0.0000** |
| | 0.8000 | 1.1658 | | 1.1467 | -0.2992 | Decreasing Function | 0.0000 |
| | 0.8500 | 1.1658 | | 1.1219 | -0.4962 | Decreasing Function | 0.0000 |
| | 0.9000 | 1.1658 | | 1.0883 | -0.6706 | Decreasing Function | 0.0000 |
| | 0.9500 | 1.1658 | | 1.0473 | -0.8207 | Decreasing Function | 0.0000 |
| | 1.9000 | 1.1658 | | 0.1397 | -0.4876 | Decreasing Function | 0.0000 |
| | 1.9500 | 1.1658 | | 0.1183 | -0.4286 | Decreasing Function | 0.0000 |
| | 2.0000 | 1.1658 | | 0.0996 | -0.3742 | Decreasing Function | 0.0000 |

The gradient is a vector of dimension equal to $(1 \times n)$ containing all the partial derivatives of the given multivariate function.

The point $x^0 = \left[ x_1^0, x_2^0, \cdots, x_j^0, \cdots x_n^0 \right]$ will be called a *critical point* or *stationary point* if the following occurs:

$$\nabla f(x^0) = [0] \tag{5.2-1}$$

namely,

$$\begin{cases} f_{x_1}(x^0) = 0 \\ f_{x_2}(x^0) = 0 \\ \cdots \\ f_{x_j}(x^0) = 0 \\ \cdots \\ f_{x_n}(x^0) = 0 \end{cases}$$

The stationary points are the only points where we can have maxima or minima. Fig. 5.1-1 is however a necessary, not sufficient condition to have maxima or minima and to find them we need to introduce the study of the *Hessian matrix*.

**TABLE 5.1-7**  Slope equal to zero for $x_0 = -0.7071$ (unique minimum).

| Tangent $y = m^*(x-x_0)+y_0$ | m | $x_0$ | -0.7071 | $x_1$ | 1.0000 | step |  |
|---|---|---|---|---|---|---|---|
| **1.0000** | 1.2687 | $y_0$ | -1.1658 | $y_1$ | 1.0000 | 0.0500 |  |

Simulate tg in C4
changing $x_0$

| x |  | 1.0000 | -0.7071 | $y = x^* \exp(1-x^2)$ | $\Delta y/\Delta x$ | Incr./Decr. Function | 0.0000 |
|---|---|---|---|---|---|---|---|
| 1.0000 |  | -3.0000 | -1.1658 | -0.001006 |  |  |  |
|  |  | -2.9500 | -1.1658 | -0.0013 | -0.0065 |  | 0.0000 |
|  |  | -2.9000 | -1.1658 | -0.0018 | -0.0084 | Decreasing Function | 0.0000 |
|  |  | -0.8500 | -1.1658 | -1.1219 | -0.6706 | Decreasing Function | 0.0000 |
|  |  | -0.8000 | -1.1658 | -1.1467 | -0.4962 | Decreasing Function | 0.0000 |
|  |  | -0.7500 | -1.1658 | -1.1616 | -0.2992 | Decreasing Function | 0.0000 |
|  |  | -0.7000 | -1.1658 | -1.1657 | -0.0816 | Decreasing Function | 0.0000 |
|  |  | **-0.6500** | **-1.1658** | **-1.1580** | **0.1536** | **MINIMUM** | **0.0000** |
|  |  | -0.6000 | -1.1658 | -1.1379 | 0.4028 | Increasing Function | 0.0000 |
|  |  | 0.6000 | -1.1658 | 1.1379 | 0.6618 | Increasing Function | 0.0000 |
|  |  | 0.6500 | -1.1658 | 1.1580 | 0.4028 | Increasing Function | 0.0000 |
|  |  | 0.7000 | -1.1658 | 1.1657 | 0.1536 | Increasing Function | 0.0000 |
|  |  | **0.7500** | **-1.1658** | **1.1616** | **-0.0816** | **MAXIMUM** | **0.0000** |
|  |  | 0.8000 | -1.1658 | 1.1467 | -0.2992 | Decreasing Function | 0.0000 |
|  |  | 0.8500 | -1.1658 | 1.1219 | -0.4962 | Decreasing Function | 0.0000 |
|  |  | 0.9000 | -1.1658 | 1.0883 | -0.6706 | Decreasing Function | 0.0000 |
|  |  | 0.9500 | -1.1658 | 1.0473 | -0.8207 | Decreasing Function | 0.0000 |
|  |  | 1.9000 | -1.1658 | 0.1397 | -0.4876 | Decreasing Function | 0.0000 |
|  |  | 1.9500 | -1.1658 | 0.1183 | -0.4286 | Decreasing Function | 0.0000 |
|  |  | 2.0000 | -1.1658 | 0.0996 | -0.3742 | Decreasing Function | 0.0000 |

**TABLE 5.1-8**  Enumeration of the function $y = x^{\frac{2}{3}}$

| x | $y = x^{2/3}$ | dy/dx | Critical points | $dy^2/d^2x$ | Concavity/Convexity of y |
|---|---|---|---|---|---|
| -5.0000 | 2.9240 |  |  |  |  |
| -4.5000 | 2.7257 | -0.3967 |  |  |  |
| -4.0000 | 2.5198 | -0.4117 | Decreasing Function | -0.0300 |  |
| -3.5000 | 2.3052 | -0.4292 | Decreasing Function | -0.0400 | y Concave |
| -3.0000 | 2.0801 | -0.4503 | Decreasing Function | -0.0400 | y Concave |
| -2.5000 | 1.8420 | -0.4761 | Decreasing Function | -0.0517 | y Concave |
| -2.0000 | 1.5874 | -0.5092 | Decreasing Function | -0.0662 | y Concave |
| -1.5000 | 1.3104 | -0.5541 | Decreasing Function | -0.0897 | y Concave |
| -1.0000 | 1.0000 | -0.6207 | Decreasing Function | -0.1334 | y Concave |
| -0.5000 | 0.6300 | -0.7401 | Decreasing Function | -0.2387 | y Concave |
| 0.0000 | 0.0000 | -1.2599 | Decreasing Function | -1.0397 | y Concave |
| 0.5000 | 0.6300 | 1.2599 | MINIMUM | 5.0397 | INFLECTION POINT |
| 1.0000 | 1.0000 | 0.7401 | Increasing Function | -1.0397 | INFLECTION POINT |
| 1.5000 | 1.3104 | 0.6207 | Increasing Function | -0.2387 | y Concave |
| 2.0000 | 1.5874 | 0.5541 | Increasing Function | -0.1334 | y Concave |
| 55.5000 | 14.5500 | 0.1750 | Increasing Function | -0.0011 | y Concave |
| 56.0000 | 14.6372 | 0.1745 | Increasing Function | -0.0010 | y Concave |

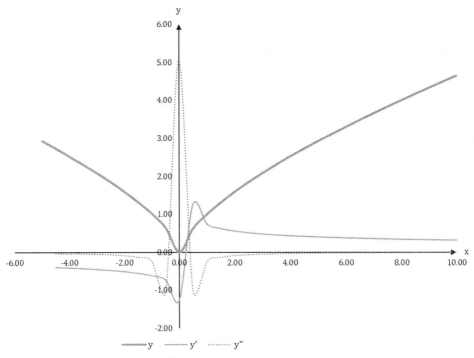

**FIGURE 5.1-13**   Plot of $y = x^{\frac{2}{3}}$ together with its first and second derivatives (step-size 0.50).

The Hessian matrix is a symmetric matrix containing all the second derivatives of the multivariate function.

A second partial derivative is defined as:

$$f_{x_{ij}} = \frac{\partial}{\partial x_i}\left(\frac{\partial f}{\partial x_j}\right)$$

(or more simply as $f_{ij}$).

The Hessian matrix is defined as the following symmetric matrix:

$$H(x) = \begin{bmatrix} f_{11} & f_{12} & \cdots & f_{1n} \\ f_{21} & f_{22} & \cdots & f_{2n} \\ \vdots & \vdots & \vdots & \vdots \\ \vdots & \vdots & \vdots & \vdots \\ f_{n1} & f_{n2} & \cdots & f_{nn} \end{bmatrix} = \begin{bmatrix} \dfrac{\partial}{\partial x_1}\left(\dfrac{\partial f}{\partial x_1}\right) & \dfrac{\partial}{\partial x_1}\left(\dfrac{\partial f}{\partial x_2}\right) & \cdots & \dfrac{\partial}{\partial x_1}\left(\dfrac{\partial f}{\partial x_n}\right) \\ \dfrac{\partial}{\partial x_2}\left(\dfrac{\partial f}{\partial x_1}\right) & \dfrac{\partial}{\partial x_2}\left(\dfrac{\partial f}{\partial x_2}\right) & \cdots & \dfrac{\partial}{\partial x_2}\left(\dfrac{\partial f}{\partial x_n}\right) \\ \vdots & \vdots & \vdots & \vdots \\ \vdots & \vdots & \vdots & \vdots \\ \dfrac{\partial}{\partial x_n}\left(\dfrac{\partial f}{\partial x_1}\right) & \dfrac{\partial}{\partial x_n}\left(\dfrac{\partial f}{\partial x_2}\right) & \cdots & \dfrac{\partial}{\partial x_n}\left(\dfrac{\partial f}{\partial x_n}\right) \end{bmatrix}$$

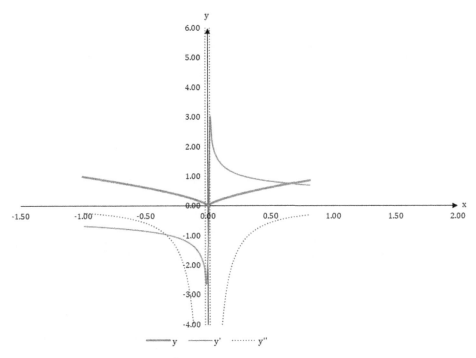

**FIGURE 5.1-14** Plot of $y = x^{\frac{2}{3}}$ together with its first and second derivatives (step-size 0.015).

Now, depending on the sign definiteness of the Hessian matrix, when it is valued at the stationary point ($x^0$), we can have:

- a **minimum point**, which can be a **strong local minimum** ($f$ is strictly convex in the neighborhood of $x^0$), a **global minimum** ($f$ is convex for all $x$) or a **unique global minimum** ($f$ is strictly convex for all $x$, **i.e., it does not contain any line segment**), e.g., Fig. 5.2-1 represents a unique global minimum in a strictly convex function;
- a **maximum point**, which can be a **strong local maximum** ($f$ is strictly concave in the neighborhood of $x^0$), a **global maximum** ($f$ is concave for all $x$) or a **unique global maximum** ($f$ is strictly convex for all $x$, **i.e., it does not contain any line segment**), e.g., Fig. 5.2-2 represents a unique global maximum in a strictly concave function;
- a **saddle point**, like in Fig. 5.2-3.

In more details, as we have seen in Chapter 3, to determine the sign definiteness of a symmetric matrix (or that of its associated quadratic form), we can use the technique of the *leading principal minors*, which represents the determinants of the submatrices that we can extract from the Hessian matrix, starting from the upper-leftmost submatrix. See also Theorem 2 of Section 3.4.

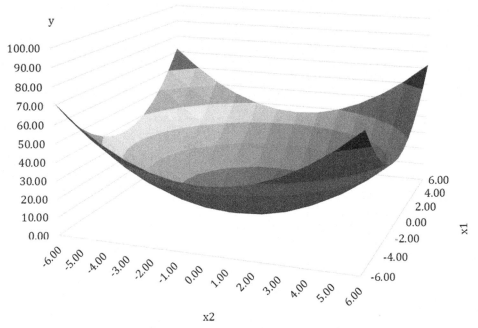

**FIGURE 5.2-1**  Global (and unique) minimum point.

Let $|H_i(x)|$ be the $i$th leading principal of the Hessian matrix. For $n = 2$ the following must be valid:

- a *strong local*, or a *unique global minimum* point when $H$ is *positive definite*, i.e., $|H_1(x)| > 0$ and $|H_2(x)| > 0$;
- a *strong local*, or a *unique global maximum* point when $H$ is *negative definite*, i.e. $|H_1(x)| < 0$ and $|H_2(x)| > 0$;
- a *saddle* point (if the Hessian is *indefinite*) when $|H_1(x)| \gtreqless 0$ and $|H_2(x)| < 0$;
- a *global minimum* when the Hessian is *positive semidefinite*, or a *global maximum* when the Hessian is *negative semidefinite*.

The two leading principal minors $|H_1(x)|$ and $|H_2(x)|$ are defined as:

$$|H_1(x)| = f_{11}; |H_2(x)| = \begin{vmatrix} f_{11} & f_{12} \\ f_{21} & f_{22} \end{vmatrix}$$

Let us see some examples for the case of $n = 2$, developed in Excel.

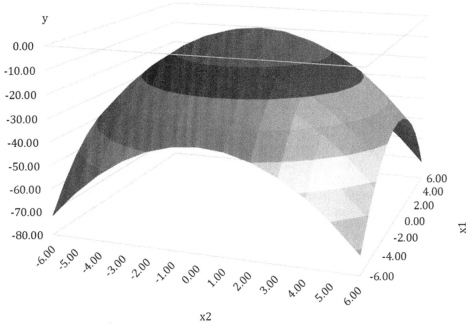

**FIGURE 5.2-2**   Global (and unique) maximum point.

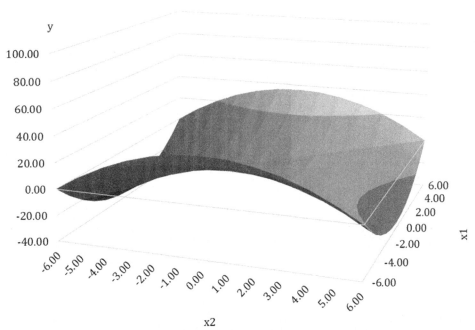

**FIGURE 5.2-3**   Saddle point.

## EXAMPLE 1 (BIVARIATE FUNCTION WITH A UNIQUE GLOBAL MINIMUM)

Let us find the extreme values of the function:

$$f(x_1, x_2) = 2x_1^2 + x_2^2 - 4x_1 + 8x_2.$$

The first method will numerically follow in Excel the test of the first-order and second-order conditions, while as a second method we will use the Excel Solver, to fine-tune our solutions. The following are the main steps.

1. Construction in Excel of the **double entry table**, which will enumerate the values of the given function $f(x_1, x_2)$ for a specific range of $(x_1, x_2)$.

   The Excel Data Table will be used to do this first step. Under *Row* 4 we store the values of $x_2$, while under *Column B* we store the values of $x_1$, and the Data Table function has to be implemented accordingly, as in Fig. 5.2-4. The numerical results of our function are in Table 5.2-1.

FIGURE 5.2-4   Data Table setup for the two-variables function.

TABLE 5.2-1   Numerical values of the given function (step-size = 1).

| x1 | x2 | v = 2*x1²+x2²-4*x1+8*x2 | | Step-Size | 1.00 | | | | | | |
|---|---|---|---|---|---|---|---|---|---|---|---|
| 1.00 | 1.00 | 7.00 | | | | | | | | | |
| | | | | | | x2 | | | | | |
| 7.00 | -6.00 | -5.00 | -4.00 | -3.00 | -2.00 | -1.00 | 0.00 | 1.00 | 2.00 | 3.00 | 4.00 | 5.00 |
| -3.00 | 18.00 | 15.00 | 14.00 | 15.00 | 18.00 | 23.00 | 30.00 | 39.00 | 50.00 | 63.00 | 78.00 | 95.00 |
| -2.00 | 4.00 | 1.00 | 0.00 | 1.00 | 4.00 | 9.00 | 16.00 | 25.00 | 36.00 | 49.00 | 64.00 | 81.00 |
| -1.00 | -6.00 | -9.00 | -10.00 | -9.00 | -6.00 | -1.00 | 6.00 | 15.00 | 26.00 | 39.00 | 54.00 | 71.00 |
| 0.00 | -12.00 | -15.00 | -16.00 | -15.00 | -12.00 | -7.00 | 0.00 | 9.00 | 20.00 | 33.00 | 48.00 | 65.00 |
| x1 1.00 | -14.00 | -17.00 | -18.00 | -17.00 | -14.00 | -9.00 | -2.00 | 7.00 | 18.00 | 31.00 | 46.00 | 63.00 |
| 2.00 | -12.00 | -15.00 | -16.00 | -15.00 | -12.00 | -7.00 | 0.00 | 9.00 | 20.00 | 33.00 | 48.00 | 65.00 |
| 3.00 | -6.00 | -9.00 | -10.00 | -9.00 | -6.00 | -1.00 | 6.00 | 15.00 | 26.00 | 39.00 | 54.00 | 71.00 |
| 4.00 | 4.00 | 1.00 | 0.00 | 1.00 | 4.00 | 9.00 | 16.00 | 25.00 | 36.00 | 49.00 | 64.00 | 81.00 |
| 5.00 | 18.00 | 15.00 | 14.00 | 15.00 | 18.00 | 23.00 | 30.00 | 39.00 | 50.00 | 63.00 | 78.00 | 95.00 |
| 6.00 | 36.00 | 33.00 | 32.00 | 33.00 | 36.00 | 41.00 | 48.00 | 57.00 | 68.00 | 81.00 | 96.00 | 113.00 |
| 7.00 | 58.00 | 55.00 | 54.00 | 55.00 | 58.00 | 63.00 | 70.00 | 79.00 | 90.00 | 103.00 | 118.00 | 135.00 |
| 8.00 | 84.00 | 81.00 | 80.00 | 81.00 | 84.00 | 89.00 | 96.00 | 105.00 | 116.00 | 129.00 | 144.00 | 161.00 |

| Q | R | S | T | U |
|---|---|---|---|---|
| **x1** | **y by changing x1 only** | **∂y/∂x1** | **Critical point** | |
| -5 | =2*Q3^2+$C$2^2-4*Q3+8*$C$2 | Numerical | | |
| =Q3+0.5 | =2*Q4^2+$C$2^2-4*Q4+8*$C$2 | =(R4-R3)/(Q4-Q3) | | |
| =Q4+0.5 | =2*Q5^2+$C$2^2-4*Q5+8*$C$2 | =(R5-R4)/(Q5-Q4) | =IF(SIGN(S5)<>SIGN(S4);"CRITICAL POINT";"") | =IF(T5="CRITICAL POINT";AVERAGE(Q3:Q5);"") |
| =Q5+0.5 | =2*Q6^2+$C$2^2-4*Q6+8*$C$2 | =(R6-R5)/(Q6-Q5) | =IF(SIGN(S6)<>SIGN(S5);"CRITICAL POINT";"") | =IF(T6="CRITICAL POINT";AVERAGE(Q4:Q6);"") |
| =Q6+0.5 | =2*Q7^2+$C$2^2-4*Q7+8*$C$2 | =(R7-R6)/(Q7-Q6) | =IF(SIGN(S7)<>SIGN(S6);"CRITICAL POINT";"") | =IF(T7="CRITICAL POINT";AVERAGE(Q5:Q7);"") |
| =Q7+0.5 | =2*Q8^2+$C$2^2-4*Q8+8*$C$2 | =(R8-R7)/(Q8-Q7) | =IF(SIGN(S8)<>SIGN(S7);"CRITICAL POINT";"") | =IF(T8="CRITICAL POINT";AVERAGE(Q6:Q8);"") |
| =Q8+0.5 | =2*Q9^2+$C$2^2-4*Q9+8*$C$2 | =(R9-R8)/(Q9-Q8) | =IF(SIGN(S9)<>SIGN(S8);"CRITICAL POINT";"") | =IF(T9="CRITICAL POINT";AVERAGE(Q7:Q9);"") |
| =Q9+0.5 | =2*Q10^2+$C$2^2-4*Q10+8*$C$2 | =(R10-R9)/(Q10-Q9) | =IF(SIGN(S10)<>SIGN(S9);"CRITICAL POINT";"") | =IF(T10="CRITICAL POINT";AVERAGE(Q8:Q10);"") |
| =Q10+0.5 | =2*Q11^2+$C$2^2-4*Q11+8*$C$2 | =(R11-R10)/(Q11-Q10) | =IF(SIGN(S11)<>SIGN(S10);"CRITICAL POINT";"") | =IF(T11="CRITICAL POINT";AVERAGE(Q9:Q11);"") |
| =Q11+0.5 | =2*Q12^2+$C$2^2-4*Q12+8*$C$2 | =(R12-R11)/(Q12-Q11) | =IF(SIGN(S12)<>SIGN(S11);"CRITICAL POINT";"") | =IF(T12="CRITICAL POINT";AVERAGE(Q10:Q12);"") |
| =Q12+0.5 | =2*Q13^2+$C$2^2-4*Q13+8*$C$2 | =(R13-R12)/(Q13-Q12) | =IF(SIGN(S13)<>SIGN(S12);"CRITICAL POINT";"") | =IF(T13="CRITICAL POINT";AVERAGE(Q11:Q13);"") |
| =Q13+0.5 | =2*Q14^2+$C$2^2-4*Q14+8*$C$2 | =(R14-R13)/(Q14-Q13) | =IF(SIGN(S14)<>SIGN(S13);"CRITICAL POINT";"") | =IF(T14="CRITICAL POINT";AVERAGE(Q12:Q14);"") |
| =Q14+0.5 | =2*Q15^2+$C$2^2-4*Q15+8*$C$2 | =(R15-R14)/(Q15-Q14) | =IF(SIGN(S15)<>SIGN(S14);"CRITICAL POINT";"") | =IF(T15="CRITICAL POINT";AVERAGE(Q13:Q15);"") |
| =Q15+0.5 | =2*Q16^2+$C$2^2-4*Q16+8*$C$2 | =(R16-R15)/(Q16-Q15) | =IF(SIGN(S16)<>SIGN(S15);"CRITICAL POINT";"") | =IF(T16="CRITICAL POINT";AVERAGE(Q14:Q16);"") |
| =Q16+0.5 | =2*Q17^2+$C$2^2-4*Q17+8*$C$2 | =(R17-R16)/(Q17-Q16) | =IF(SIGN(S17)<>SIGN(S16);"CRITICAL POINT";"") | =IF(T17="CRITICAL POINT";AVERAGE(Q15:Q17);"") |
| =Q17+0.5 | =2*Q18^2+$C$2^2-4*Q18+8*$C$2 | =(R18-R17)/(Q18-Q17) | =IF(SIGN(S18)<>SIGN(S17);"CRITICAL POINT";"") | =IF(T18="CRITICAL POINT";AVERAGE(Q16:Q18);"") |
| =Q18+0.5 | =2*Q19^2+$C$2^2-4*Q19+8*$C$2 | =(R19-R18)/(Q19-Q18) | =IF(SIGN(S19)<>SIGN(S18);"CRITICAL POINT";"") | =IF(T19="CRITICAL POINT";AVERAGE(Q17:Q19);"") |

**FIGURE 5.2-5**  Numerical values of the first derivative with respect to $x_1$ and critical points.

| V | W | X | Y | Z |
|---|---|---|---|---|
| **x2** | **y by changing x2 only** | **∂y/∂x2** | **Critical point** | |
| =Q3 | =2*$B$2^2+V3^2-4*$B$2+8*V | Numerical | | |
| =Q4 | =2*$B$2^2+V4^2-4*$B$2+8*V | =(W4-W3)/(V4-V3) | | |
| =Q5 | =2*$B$2^2+V5^2-4*$B$2+8*V | =(W5-W4)/(V5-V4) | =IF(SIGN(X5)<>SIGN(X4);"CRITICAL POINT";"") | =IF(Y5="CRITICAL POINT";AVERAGE(V3:V5);"") |
| =Q6 | =2*$B$2^2+V6^2-4*$B$2+8*V | =(W6-W5)/(V6-V5) | =IF(SIGN(X6)<>SIGN(X5);"CRITICAL POINT";"") | =IF(Y6="CRITICAL POINT";AVERAGE(V4:V6);"") |
| =Q7 | =2*$B$2^2+V7^2-4*$B$2+8*V | =(W7-W6)/(V7-V6) | =IF(SIGN(X7)<>SIGN(X6);"CRITICAL POINT";"") | =IF(Y7="CRITICAL POINT";AVERAGE(V5:V7);"") |
| =Q8 | =2*$B$2^2+V8^2-4*$B$2+8*V | =(W8-W7)/(V8-V7) | =IF(SIGN(X8)<>SIGN(X7);"CRITICAL POINT";"") | =IF(Y8="CRITICAL POINT";AVERAGE(V6:V8);"") |
| =Q9 | =2*$B$2^2+V9^2-4*$B$2+8*V | =(W9-W8)/(V9-V8) | =IF(SIGN(X9)<>SIGN(X8);"CRITICAL POINT";"") | =IF(Y9="CRITICAL POINT";AVERAGE(V7:V9);"") |
| =Q10 | =2*$B$2^2+V10^2-4*$B$2+8*' | =(W10-W9)/(V10-V9) | =IF(SIGN(X10)<>SIGN(X9);"CRITICAL POINT";"") | =IF(Y10="CRITICAL POINT";AVERAGE(V8:V10);"") |
| =Q11 | =2*$B$2^2+V11^2-4*$B$2+8*' | =(W11-W10)/(V11-V10) | =IF(SIGN(X11)<>SIGN(X10);"CRITICAL POINT";"") | =IF(Y11="CRITICAL POINT";AVERAGE(V9:V11);"") |
| =Q12 | =2*$B$2^2+V12^2-4*$B$2+8*' | =(W12-W11)/(V12-V11) | =IF(SIGN(X12)<>SIGN(X11);"CRITICAL POINT";"") | =IF(Y12="CRITICAL POINT";AVERAGE(V10:V12);"") |
| =Q13 | =2*$B$2^2+V13^2-4*$B$2+8*' | =(W13-W12)/(V13-V12) | =IF(SIGN(X13)<>SIGN(X12);"CRITICAL POINT";"") | =IF(Y13="CRITICAL POINT";AVERAGE(V11:V13);"") |
| =Q14 | =2*$B$2^2+V14^2-4*$B$2+8*' | =(W14-W13)/(V14-V13) | =IF(SIGN(X14)<>SIGN(X13);"CRITICAL POINT";"") | =IF(Y14="CRITICAL POINT";AVERAGE(V12:V14);"") |
| =Q15 | =2*$B$2^2+V15^2-4*$B$2+8*' | =(W15-W14)/(V15-V14) | =IF(SIGN(X15)<>SIGN(X14);"CRITICAL POINT";"") | =IF(Y15="CRITICAL POINT";AVERAGE(V13:V15);"") |
| =Q16 | =2*$B$2^2+V16^2-4*$B$2+8*' | =(W16-W15)/(V16-V15) | =IF(SIGN(X16)<>SIGN(X15);"CRITICAL POINT";"") | =IF(Y16="CRITICAL POINT";AVERAGE(V14:V16);"") |
| =Q17 | =2*$B$2^2+V17^2-4*$B$2+8*' | =(W17-W16)/(V17-V16) | =IF(SIGN(X17)<>SIGN(X16);"CRITICAL POINT";"") | =IF(Y17="CRITICAL POINT";AVERAGE(V15:V17);"") |
| =Q18 | =2*$B$2^2+V18^2-4*$B$2+8*' | =(W18-W17)/(V18-V17) | =IF(SIGN(X18)<>SIGN(X17);"CRITICAL POINT";"") | =IF(Y18="CRITICAL POINT";AVERAGE(V16:V18);"") |

**FIGURE 5.2-6**  Numerical values of the first derivative with respect to $x_2$ and critical points.

2. Setup of the **numerical partial derivatives** with the identification of the **critical values.**
   The two first numerical derivatives have been calculated after building a schedule of values of the function by changing only one variable at a time. In Fig. 5.2-5, we have the computed values for $f_1 = \frac{\partial f}{\partial x_1} = 4x_1 - 4$ while in Fig. 5.2-6, the computed values for $f_2 = \frac{\partial f}{\partial x_2} = 2x_2 + 8$.

   As usual, the critical points are found where the numerical partial derivatives change sign, i.e., where the derivative is zero. Table 5.2-2 returns the values where this happens. Here it is important to give the most appropriate step-size in order to get a reasonable approximation in the numerical derivative and subsequent chart equations.
3. Identification of the minima, maxima, or saddle points, through the **construction** and analysis of the **Hessian matrix** and the **sign of its leading principal minors.** To study the sign of the Hessian we need to build the following matrix:

**TABLE 5.2-2** Critical points identification.

| x1 | y by changing x1 only | ∂y/∂x1 | Critical point | x2 | y by changing x2 only | ∂y/∂x2 | Critical point |
|---|---|---|---|---|---|---|---|
| -1.0000 | -10.0000 | Numerical | | -5.0000 | -17.0000 | Numerical | |
| -0.9000 | -10.7800 | -7.8000 | | -4.5000 | -17.7500 | -1.5000 | |
| -0.8000 | -11.5200 | -7.4000 | | -4.0000 | -18.0000 | -0.5000 | |
| -0.7000 | -12.2200 | -7.0000 | | -3.5000 | -17.7500 | 0.5000 | CRITICAL POINT -4.0000 |
| -0.6000 | -12.8800 | -6.6000 | | -3.0000 | -17.0000 | 1.5000 | |
| 0.4000 | -17.2800 | -2.6000 | | 2.0000 | 18.0000 | 11.5000 | |
| 0.5000 | -17.5000 | -2.2000 | | 2.5000 | 24.2500 | 12.5000 | |
| 0.6000 | -17.6800 | -1.8000 | | 3.0000 | 31.0000 | 13.5000 | |
| 0.7000 | -17.8200 | -1.4000 | | 3.5000 | 38.2500 | 14.5000 | |
| 0.8000 | -17.9200 | -1.0000 | | 4.0000 | 46.0000 | 15.5000 | |
| 0.9000 | -17.9800 | -0.6000 | | 4.5000 | 54.2500 | 16.5000 | |
| 1.0000 | -18.0000 | -0.2000 | | 5.0000 | 63.0000 | 17.5000 | |
| 1.1000 | -17.9800 | 0.2000 | CRITICAL POINT 1.0000 | 5.5000 | 72.2500 | 18.5000 | |
| 1.2000 | -17.9200 | 0.6000 | | 6.0000 | 82.0000 | 19.5000 | |
| 1.3000 | -17.8200 | 1.0000 | | 6.5000 | 92.2500 | 20.5000 | |
| 1.4000 | -17.6800 | 1.4000 | | 7.0000 | 103.0000 | 21.5000 | |
| 2.1000 | -15.5800 | 4.2000 | | 10.5000 | 192.2500 | 28.5000 | |

$$H(x) = \begin{bmatrix} f_{11} & f_{12} \\ f_{21} & f_{22} \end{bmatrix} = \begin{bmatrix} \dfrac{\partial}{\partial x_1}\left(\dfrac{\partial f}{\partial x_1}\right) & \dfrac{\partial}{\partial x_1}\left(\dfrac{\partial f}{\partial x_2}\right) \\[2ex] \dfrac{\partial}{\partial x_2}\left(\dfrac{\partial f}{\partial x_1}\right) & \dfrac{\partial}{\partial x_2}\left(\dfrac{\partial f}{\partial x_2}\right) \end{bmatrix} = \begin{bmatrix} 4 & 0 \\ 0 & 2 \end{bmatrix}$$

The numerical partial derivatives $f_1$ and $f_2$ can be diagrammed and analytically inferred through the scatter charts of Fig. 5.2-7, built on the data of Table 5.2-2. From the diagrams we see that the functions show one critical point in $P(1, -4)$.

Whether this is a maximum, minimum, or saddle point it depends on the sign definiteness of the Hessian matrix.

Using the technique of the leading principal minors we have the results in Table 5.2-3.

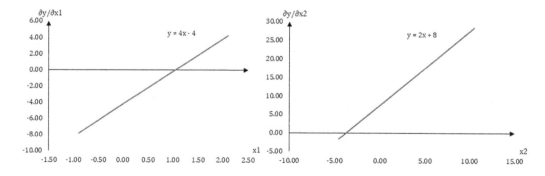

**FIGURE 5.2-7** Diagram of numerical first derivatives.

II. Static optimization

**TABLE 5.2-3** Hessian and leading principal minor.

| Hessian Matrix | |
|---|---|
| 4.0000 | 0.0000 |
| 0.0000 | 2.0000 |
| Leading Principal Minors: | |
| H1 | H2 |
| 4.0000 | 8.0000 |

The principal minor $|H_2|$ has been calculated with the Excel function *MDETERM*, and the conclusion is that the point $P(1, -4)$ is a *unique global minimum*, as the leading principal minors are both positive. The chart of the function in $\Re^3$ is shown in Fig. 5.2-8.

## Solver solution

Using the GRG (Generalized Reduced Gradient) Solver we would have reached the same results. See Fig. 5.2-9 together with Fig. 5.2-4.

As we have a unique global minimum, the Solver has no problem in finding the sought solution. However, when we have more than one local minima, local maxima, and saddle points, we have to instruct the Solver where to search to find the solutions. This is the case of the next example.

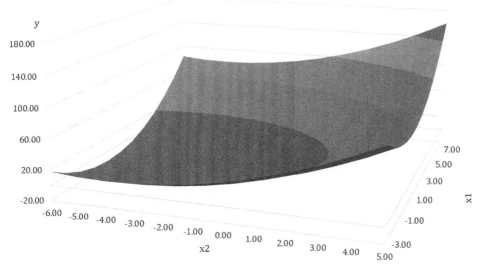

**FIGURE 5.2-8** Diagram of the function $f(x_1, x_2) = 2x_1^2 + x_2^2 - 4x_1 + 8x_2$.

**FIGURE 5.2-9**  Solver setup for the unique
global minimum.

## Example 2 (bivariate function with a local min, a local max, and two saddle points)

Let us consider the following function:

$$y = x_1^3 + x_2^3 - 2x_1^2 + 3x_2^2 - 8$$

1. Construction in Excel of the **double entry table** in Table 5.2-4, which enumerates the values of the given function $f(x_1, x_2)$ for a specific range of $(x_1, x_2)$.
2. Setup of the numerical partial derivatives with the identification of the critical values. See Table 5.2-5 and Fig. 5.2-10. The first partial derivatives are $f_1 = \frac{\partial f}{\partial x_1} = 3x_1^2 - 4x_1$, while in Figs. 5.2-6 the computed values for $f_2 = \frac{\partial f}{\partial x_2} = 3x_2^2 + 6x_2$.
3. Identification of the minima, maxima, or saddle points, through the construction and analysis of the Hessian matrix and the sign of its leading principal minors. See Table 5.2-6. The Hessian is:

$$H(x) = \begin{bmatrix} f_{11} & f_{12} \\ f_{21} & f_{22} \end{bmatrix} = \begin{bmatrix} \frac{\partial}{\partial x_1}\left(\frac{\partial f}{\partial x_1}\right) & \frac{\partial}{\partial x_1}\left(\frac{\partial f}{\partial x_2}\right) \\ \frac{\partial}{\partial x_2}\left(\frac{\partial f}{\partial x_1}\right) & \frac{\partial}{\partial x_2}\left(\frac{\partial f}{\partial x_2}\right) \end{bmatrix} = \begin{bmatrix} 6x_1 - 4 & 0 \\ 0 & 6x_2 + 6 \end{bmatrix}$$

II. Static optimization

**TABLE 5.2-4**  Double entry table.

| x1 | x2 | y = x1^3+x2^3-2x1^2+3x2^2-8 Step-Size 1.00 | | | | | | | | | | |
|---|---|---|---|---|---|---|---|---|---|---|---|---|
| 1.35 | 0.00 | -9.18 | | | | | | | | | | |
| | | | | | | | x2 | | | | | |
| -9.18 | -6.00 | -5.00 | -4.00 | -3.00 | -2.00 | -1.0000 | 0.00 | 1.00 | 2.00 | 3.00 | 4.00 | 5.00 |
| -6.00 | -404.00 | -346.00 | -312.00 | -296.00 | -292.00 | -294.00 | -296.00 | -292.00 | -276.00 | -242.00 | -184.00 | -96.00 |
| -5.00 | -291.00 | -233.00 | -199.00 | -183.00 | -179.00 | -181.00 | -183.00 | -179.00 | -163.00 | -129.00 | -71.00 | 17.00 |
| -4.00 | -212.00 | -154.00 | -120.00 | -104.00 | -100.00 | -102.00 | -104.00 | -100.00 | -84.00 | -50.00 | 8.00 | 96.00 |
| -3.00 | -161.00 | -103.00 | -69.00 | -53.00 | -49.00 | -51.00 | -53.00 | -49.00 | -33.00 | 1.00 | 59.00 | 147.00 |
| x1 -2.00 | -132.00 | -74.00 | -40.00 | -24.00 | -20.00 | -22.00 | -24.00 | -20.00 | -4.00 | 30.00 | 88.00 | 176.00 |
| -1.00 | -119.00 | -61.00 | -27.00 | -11.00 | -7.00 | -9.00 | -11.00 | -7.00 | 9.00 | 43.00 | 101.00 | 189.00 |
| 0.00 | -116.00 | -58.00 | -24.00 | -8.00 | -4.00 | -6.00 | -8.00 | -4.00 | 12.00 | 46.00 | 104.00 | 192.00 |
| 1.35 | -117.18 | -59.18 | -25.18 | -9.18 | -5.18 | -7.18 | -9.18 | -5.18 | 10.82 | 44.82 | 102.82 | 190.82 |
| 2.35 | -114.07 | -56.07 | -22.07 | -6.07 | -2.07 | -4.07 | -6.07 | -2.07 | 13.93 | 47.93 | 105.93 | 193.93 |
| 3.35 | -100.85 | -42.85 | -8.85 | 7.15 | 11.15 | 9.15 | 7.15 | 11.15 | 27.15 | 61.15 | 119.15 | 207.15 |
| 4.35 | -71.53 | -13.53 | 20.47 | 36.47 | 40.47 | 38.47 | 36.47 | 40.47 | 56.47 | 90.47 | 148.47 | 236.47 |
| 5.35 | -20.11 | 37.89 | 71.89 | 87.89 | 91.89 | 89.89 | 87.89 | 91.89 | 107.89 | 141.89 | 199.89 | 287.89 |

**TABLE 5.2-5**  Critical points.

| x1 | y by changing x1 only | ∂y/∂x1 | Critical point | | x2 | y by changing x2 only | ∂y/∂x2 | Critical point | |
|---|---|---|---|---|---|---|---|---|---|
| -0.0500 | 3.9949 | Numerical | | | -3.0000 | -1.0000 | Numerical | | |
| 0.0000 | 4.0000 | 0.1025 | | | -2.8750 | 0.0332 | 8.2656 | | |
| 0.0500 | 3.9951 | -0.0975 | CRITICAL POINT | 0.0000 | -2.7500 | 0.8906 | 6.8594 | | |
| 0.1000 | 3.9810 | -0.2825 | | | -2.6250 | 1.5840 | 5.5469 | | |
| 0.1500 | 3.9584 | -0.4525 | | | -2.5000 | 2.1250 | 4.3281 | | |
| 0.2000 | 3.9280 | -0.6075 | | | -2.3750 | 2.5254 | 3.2031 | | |
| 0.2500 | 3.8906 | -0.7475 | | | -2.2500 | 2.7969 | 2.1719 | | |
| 0.3000 | 3.8470 | -0.8725 | | | -2.1250 | 2.9512 | 1.2344 | | |
| 0.3500 | 3.7979 | -0.9825 | | | -2.0000 | 3.0000 | 0.3906 | | |
| 0.4000 | 3.7440 | -1.0775 | | | -1.8750 | 2.9551 | -0.3594 | CRITICAL POINT | -2.0000 |
| 0.4500 | 3.6861 | -1.1575 | | | -1.7500 | 2.8281 | -1.0156 | | |
| 0.5000 | 3.6250 | -1.2225 | | | -1.6250 | 2.6309 | -1.5781 | | |
| 1.1000 | 2.9110 | -0.8325 | | | -0.1250 | -0.9551 | -1.0156 | | |
| 1.1500 | 2.8759 | -0.7025 | | | 0.0000 | -1.0000 | -0.3594 | | |
| 1.2000 | 2.8480 | -0.5575 | | | 0.1250 | -0.9512 | 0.3906 | CRITICAL POINT | 0.0000 |
| 1.2500 | 2.8281 | -0.3975 | | | 0.2500 | -0.7969 | 1.2344 | | |
| 1.3000 | 2.8170 | -0.2225 | | | 0.3750 | -0.5254 | 2.1719 | | |
| 1.3500 | 2.8154 | -0.0325 | | | 0.5000 | -0.1250 | 3.2031 | | |
| 1.4000 | 2.8240 | 0.1725 | CRITICAL POINT | 1.3500 | 0.6250 | 0.4160 | 4.3281 | | |
| 1.4500 | 2.8436 | 0.3925 | | | 0.7500 | 1.1094 | 5.5469 | | |
| 1.5000 | 2.8750 | 0.6275 | | | 0.8750 | 1.9668 | 6.8594 | | |

The function (represented in Fig. 5.2-11) presents two saddle points in the numerical values (0, 0) and (1.35, −2) a local maximum in (0, −2), and a local minimum in (1.35, 0). The four points have been highlighted in Table 5.2-4.

Tables 5.2-4 makes apparent that the critical point (0, −2) is a local maximum since all four values in its neighborhood point toward $y^* = -4$ increasing their values, while the numerical critical point (1.35, 0) is the numerical local minimum, since all four values in its

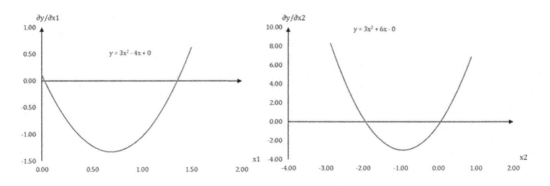

**FIGURE 5.2-10**   Roots of the numerical partial derivatives.

**TABLE 5.2-6**   Hessian and minors evaluation.

| Hessian Valued in P1 (0,-2) | | Hessian Valued in P2 (0, 0) | | Hessian Valued in P3 (1.35, 0) | | Hessian Valued in P4 (1.35, -2) | |
|---|---|---|---|---|---|---|---|
| -4.00 | 0.00 | -4.00 | 0.00 | 4.10 | 0.00 | 4.10 | 0.00 |
| 0.00 | -6.00 | 0.00 | 6.00 | 0.00 | 6.00 | 0.00 | -6.00 |
| Leading Principal Minors: | | Leading Principal Minors: | | Leading Principal Minors: | | Leading Principal Minors: | |
| H1 | H2 | H1 | H2 | H1 | H2 | H1 | H2 |
| -4.00 | 24.00 | -4.00 | -24.00 | 4.10 | 24.60 | 4.10 | -24.60 |

| H1<0,H2>0   Max Point | H1<0,H2<0   Saddle Point | H1>0,H2>0   Min Point | H1<0,H2<0   Saddle Point |
|---|---|---|---|

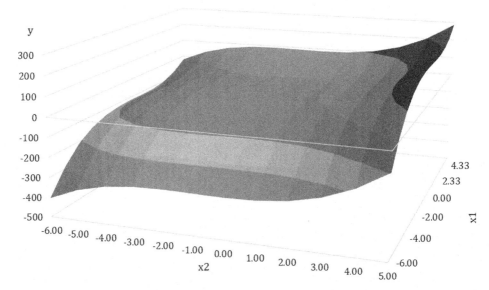

**FIGURE 5.2-11**   Diagram of the function $y = x_1^3 + x_2^2 - 2x_1^2 + 3x_2^2 - 8$.

**TABLE 5.2-7**   Numerical local minimum in (1.35, 0) before running the Solver.

| ⊿ | A | B | C | D | E | F | G |
|---|---|---|---|---|---|---|---|
| | | x1 | x2 | y = x1^3+x2^3-2x1^2+3x2^2-8 | | | |
| 1 | | | | | | | |
| 2 | | 1.35 | 0.00 | -9.18 | | | |

**TABLE 5.2-8**   Exact local minimum in (4/3, 0) after running the Solver.

| ⊿ | A | B | C | D | E | F | G |
|---|---|---|---|---|---|---|---|
| | | x1 | x2 | y = x1^3+x2^3-2x1^2+3x2^2-8 | | | |
| 1 | | | | | | | |
| 2 | | 1.33 | 0.00 | -9.19 | | | |

neighborhood all point toward $y^* = -9.18$ decreasing their values. The other two critical points are not extrema but saddle points, since in their neighborhood there are both figures increasing and decreasing (Tables 5.2-5 and 5.2-6).

## Solver Solution

Now, what we want to do is to use the Solver to fine-tune the extreme local minimum numerical value, which we have left approximated to (1.35, 0), as shown in Table 5.2-7.

What we can do is to instruct the Solver to minimize the function over a specific range of the two independent variables (e.g., from $-2$ to 2), leaving the approximated value $-1.35$ in the *Cell B*2 before running the Solver.

The solution for the exact local minimum is given in Table 5.2-8. The Solver setup is in Fig. 5.2-12.

One of the saddle points found will change slightly as well from $P(1.35, -2)$ to $P(4/3, -2)$.

## 5.3 Some economic applications of the nonlinear unconstrained optimization

There is a vast range of applications of the unconstrained (and constrained optimization) in the economic areas: from the pure consumer and firm optimization problems in microeconomics to the managerial problems of production optimization.

While Chapter 6 is entirely dedicated to the core concepts of microeconomics, whose problems are essentially solved resorting to the constrained optimization, the following two examples will present two typical unconstrained optimization production problems. This class of applied optimization problems to managerial sciences is also studied by the *operations research*.

**FIGURE 5.2-12** Solver setup for local minimum.

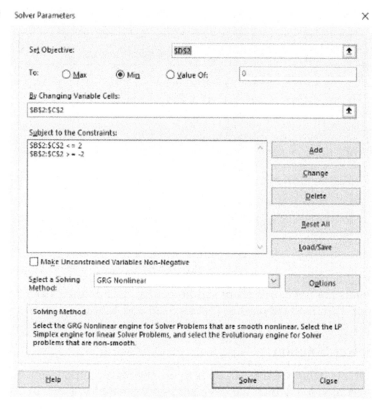

## EXAMPLE 1 (OPTIMIZING PRICES OF TWO COMPLEMENTARY GOODS)

A firm, within its range of products, has a pair of *complementary goods* that have to be bought (and used) together. The problem consists in determining the prices of the two goods in order to maximize the firm's profit function.

A complementary good is a good whose use is related to an associated or paired good and using more of one good requires the use of more of the other good. Similarly, if the price of one good falls, people not only will tend to buy more of it, but also, they will tend to buy more of the complementary good. Similarly, if the price of one good rises, and reduces its demand, it will reduce the demand of the paired good as well.

Whether or not the paired goods are produced by the same business entity, in the real world there are plenty of examples: computer hardware and its software, automobile and fuel (or insurance), printers and ink cartridges, ERP firms' software and the associated consultancy permanent services, etc.

Let us continue the example with the following data.

**a.** *Cost of production = fixed costs + variable direct costs* of the two products (£ 20 for the first good and £ 15 for the second). The fixed costs are £ 2000.

$$Total\ Costs = 2,000 + 20q_1 + 15q_2$$

**b.** Demand functions. The demand of the first good is a linear decreasing function, not only in its price but also in the price of the second good. Similarly, for the second good. We express therefore the two demands as a function of price.

$$q_1 = 900 - 15p_1 - p_2$$

$$q_2 = 600 - 2p_1 - 12p_2$$

Demand schedule. Notice that, within this example the prices are the independent variables to optimize and the demand has the form $q = f(p)$, while in the theory of microeconomics usually its inverse function $p = f(q)$ is used.

*Formation of prices in different types of markets.* It is also important to highlight that the way in which the prices are optimized in this example can be considered compatible with the imperfect oligopolistic markets (see Section 6.12), where the prices are typically determined via the *mark-up* applied to total costs. Also, in the monopolistic markets (see Section 6.11), firms have some flexibility to change the prices, but not as much as in the oligopolistic market. The way in which the prices are optimized in this example is not compatible with the perfect competitive markets (see Section 6.10, e.g., the markets of the natural resources or agricultural products) where the prices are determined by the interaction of demand and supply and where the prices are therefore taken by the firms as given.

With the given data we can define the profit function of the firm as:

$$y = \Pi(p_1, p_2) = TR - TC$$

namely,

$$y = p_1 \cdot q_1 + p_2 \cdot q_2 - (2,000 + 20q_1 + 15q_2).$$

Now, we substitute the quantities $q_1$ and $q_2$ for their analytical forms, obtaining the following total profit as a function of the two independent variables $(p_1, p_2)$:

$$y = p_1 \cdot (900 - 15p_1 - p_2) + p_2 \cdot (600 - 2p_1 - 12p_2)$$
$$- [2,000 + 20 \cdot (900 - 15p_1 - p_2) + 15 \cdot (600 - 2p_1 - 12p_2)].$$

II. Static optimization

After some algebraic arrangements the problem becomes:

$$\max_{\{p_1;p_2\}} \Pi(p_1, p_2) = -15p_1^2 - 3p_1p_2 - 12p_2^2 + 1{,}230p_1 + 800p_2 - 29{,}000.$$

Notice how this function is *not separable*, in that it has a term that incorporates both independent variables. The goal is now to maximize the above function, with respect to $(p_1, p_2)$.

Let us follow the analytical steps of the partial derivatives enumeration and the leading principal minors associated to the Hessian matrix. The Solver will be just used at the end to fine-tune the calculated critical values of the profit function.

1. Construction in Excel of the **double entry table** (see Table 5.3-1).
2. Setup of the numerical partial derivatives with the identification of the critical values. See Table 5.3-2 and Fig. 5.3-1.
3. Identification of the minima, maxima, or saddle points, through the construction and analysis of the Hessian matrix and the sign of its leading principal minors (see Table 5.3-6).

Now, as the function is not separable, the numerical value of $p_1$ will affect $\frac{\partial y}{\partial p_2} = -24p_2 - 3p_1 + 800$, while $p_2$ will affect $\frac{\partial y}{\partial p_1} = -30p_1 - 3p_2 + 1{,}230$, after a first trial in we which we set the values $p_1 = p_2 = 1$ in Table 5.3-1 (first iteration), computing the first iteration numerical partial derivatives in Table 5.3-2, we re-input the computed critical points $p_1 = 40$ and $p_2 = 34$, obtaining Tables 5.3-3 and 5.3-4 and Figs. 5.3-2, with critical values $p_1 = 38$ and $p_2 = 28$.

If we iterate once again (see Table 5.3-5: third iteration), inputting the previous iteration critical values $p_1 = 38$ and $p_2 = 28$, we notice that they remain stable, which means that the optimization process is over.

**TABLE 5.3-1**    Data Table first iteration.

| p1 | p2 | y = -15p1^2-3p1p2-12p2^2+1,230p1+800p2-29,000 | | | | Step-Size | 5.00 | |
|---|---|---|---|---|---|---|---|---|
| 1.00 | 1.00 | -27,000 | | | | | | |
| | | | | | | | p2 | |
| -27,000 | 0.00 | 5.00 | 10.00 | 15.00 | 20.00 | 25.00 | 30.00 | 35.00 |
| 0.00 | -29,000 | -25,300 | -22,200 | -19,700 | -17,800 | -16,500 | -15,800 | -15,700 |
| 5.00 | -23,225 | -19,600 | -16,575 | -14,150 | -12,325 | -11,100 | -10,475 | -10,450 |
| 10.00 | -18,200 | -14,650 | -11,700 | -9,350 | -7,600 | -6,450 | -5,900 | -5,950 |
| 15.00 | -13,925 | -10,450 | -7,575 | -5,300 | -3,625 | -2,550 | -2,075 | -2,200 |
| p1   20.00 | -10,400 | -7,000 | -4,200 | -2,000 | -400 | 600 | 1,000 | 800 |
| 25.00 | -7,625 | -4,300 | -1,575 | 550 | 2,075 | 3,000 | 3,325 | 3,050 |
| 30.00 | -5,600 | -2,350 | 300 | 2,350 | 3,800 | 4,650 | 4,900 | 4,550 |
| 35.00 | -4,325 | -1,150 | 1,425 | 3,400 | 4,775 | 5,550 | 5,725 | 5,300 |
| 40.00 | -3,800 | -700 | 1,800 | 3,700 | 5,000 | 5,700 | 5,800 | 5,300 |
| 45.00 | -4,025 | -1,000 | 1,425 | 3,250 | 4,475 | 5,100 | 5,125 | 4,550 |
| 50.00 | -5,000 | -2,050 | 300 | 2,050 | 3,200 | 3,750 | 3,700 | 3,050 |
| 55.00 | -6,725 | -3,850 | -1,575 | 100 | 1,175 | 1,650 | 1,525 | 800 |

**TABLE 5.3-2** Critical points first iteration.

| p1 | y by changing p1 only | $\partial y/\partial p1$ | Critical point | p2 | y by changing p2 only | $\partial y/\partial p2$ | Critical point |
|---|---|---|---|---|---|---|---|
| 0.0000 | -28,212 | Numerical | | 0.0000 | -27,785 | Numerical | |
| 2.0000 | -25,818 | 1,197 | | 2.0000 | -26,239 | 773.0000 | |
| 4.0000 | -23,544 | 1,137 | | 4.0000 | -24,789 | 725.0000 | |
| 6.0000 | -21,390 | 1,077 | | 6.0000 | -23,435 | 677.0000 | |
| 8.0000 | -19,356 | 1,017 | | 8.0000 | -22,177 | 629.0000 | |
| 10.0000 | -17,442 | 957 | | 10.0000 | -21,015 | 581.0000 | |
| 12.0000 | -15,648 | 897 | | 12.0000 | -19,949 | 533.0000 | |
| 14.0000 | -13,974 | 837 | | 14.0000 | -18,979 | 485.0000 | |
| 16.0000 | -12,420 | 777 | | 16.0000 | -18,105 | 437.0000 | |
| 18.0000 | -10,986 | 717 | | 18.0000 | -17,327 | 389.0000 | |
| 20.0000 | -9,672 | 657 | | 20.0000 | -16,645 | 341.0000 | |
| 22.0000 | -8,478 | 597 | | 22.0000 | -16,059 | 293.0000 | |
| 24.0000 | -7,404 | 537 | | 24.0000 | -15,569 | 245.0000 | |
| 26.0000 | -6,450 | 477 | | 26.0000 | -15,175 | 197.0000 | |
| 28.0000 | -5,616 | 417 | | 28.0000 | -14,877 | 149.0000 | |
| 30.0000 | -4,902 | 357 | | 30.0000 | -14,675 | 101.0000 | |
| 32.0000 | -4,308 | 297 | | 32.0000 | -14,569 | 53.0000 | |
| 34.0000 | -3,834 | 237 | | 34.0000 | -14,559 | 5.0000 | |
| 36.0000 | -3,480 | 177 | | 36.0000 | -14,645 | -43.0000 | CRITICAL POINT 34.0000 |
| 38.0000 | -3,246 | 117 | | 38.0000 | -14,827 | -91.0000 | |
| 40.0000 | -3,132 | 57 | | 40.0000 | -15,105 | -139.0000 | |
| 42.0000 | -3,138 | -3 | CRITICAL POINT 40.0000 | 42.0000 | -15,479 | -187.0000 | |
| 44.0000 | -3,264 | -63 | | 44.0000 | -15,949 | -235.0000 | |
| 46.0000 | -3,510 | -123 | | 46.0000 | -16,515 | -283.0000 | |
| 48.0000 | -3,876 | -183 | | 48.0000 | -17,177 | -331.0000 | |
| 50.0000 | -4,362 | -243 | | 50.0000 | -17,935 | -379.0000 | |
| 52.0000 | -4,968 | -303 | | 52.0000 | -18,789 | -427.0000 | |
| 54.0000 | -5,694 | -363 | | 54.0000 | -19,739 | -475.0000 | |
| 56.0000 | -6,540 | -423 | | 56.0000 | -20,785 | -523.0000 | |
| 58.0000 | -7,506 | -483 | | 58.0000 | -21,927 | -571.0000 | |
| 60.0000 | -8,592 | -543 | | 60.0000 | -23,165 | -619.0000 | |
| 62.0000 | -9,798 | -603 | | 62.0000 | -24,499 | -667.0000 | |

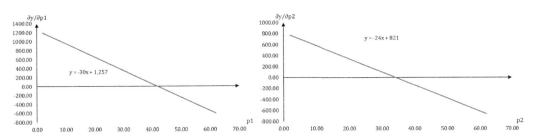

**FIGURE 5.3-1** Numerical partial derivatives first iteration.

## Solver fine-tuning

Now that the two optimal values $p_1 = 38$ and $p_2 = 28$ have been already input in Table 5.3-5 we run the Solver to find the exact solutions obtaining the final two optimal prices as:

$p_1^* = 38.14$ and $p_2^* = 28.57$ with maximum profit $y^* = £\, 5,884$

with the Hessian matrix negative definite (see Table 5.3-6). The diagram of the strictly concave profit function is given in Fig. 5.3-3.

**TABLE 5.3-3**   Data Table second iteration.

| p1 | p2 | y = -15p1^2-3p1p2-12p2^2+1,230p1+800p2-29,000 | Step-Size | 5.00 |
|---|---|---|---|---|
| 40.00 | 34.00 | 5,448 | | |

| 5,448 | 0.00 | 5.00 | 10.00 | 15.00 | 20.00 | 25.00 | p2 30.00 | 35.00 |
|---|---|---|---|---|---|---|---|---|
| 0.00 | -29,000 | -25,300 | -22,200 | -19,700 | -17,800 | -16,500 | -15,800 | -15,700 |
| 5.00 | -23,225 | -19,600 | -16,575 | -14,150 | -12,325 | -11,100 | -10,475 | -10,450 |
| 10.00 | -18,200 | -14,650 | -11,700 | -9,350 | -7,600 | -6,450 | -5,900 | -5,950 |
| 15.00 | -13,925 | -10,450 | -7,575 | -5,300 | -3,625 | -2,550 | -2,075 | -2,200 |
| p1   20.00 | -10,400 | -7,000 | -4,200 | -2,000 | -400 | 600 | 1,000 | 800 |
| 25.00 | -7,625 | -4,300 | -1,575 | 550 | 2,075 | 3,000 | 3,325 | 3,050 |
| 30.00 | -5,600 | -2,350 | 300 | 2,350 | 3,800 | 4,650 | 4,900 | 4,550 |
| 35.00 | -4,325 | -1,150 | 1,425 | 3,400 | 4,775 | 5,550 | 5,725 | 5,300 |
| 40.00 | -3,800 | -700 | 1,800 | 3,700 | 5,000 | 5,700 | 5,800 | 5,300 |
| 45.00 | -4,025 | -1,000 | 1,425 | 3,250 | 4,475 | 5,100 | 5,125 | 4,550 |
| 50.00 | -5,000 | -2,050 | 300 | 2,050 | 3,200 | 3,750 | 3,700 | 3,050 |
| 55.00 | -6,725 | -3,850 | -1,575 | 100 | 1,175 | 1,650 | 1,525 | 800 |

**TABLE 5.3-4**   Critical points found with second Iteration.

| p1 | y by changing p1 only | $\partial y/\partial p1$ | Critical point | p2 | y by changing p2 only | $\partial y/\partial p2$ | Critical point |
|---|---|---|---|---|---|---|---|
| 0.0000 | -15,672 | Numerical | | 0.0000 | -3,800 | Numerical | |
| 2.0000 | -13,476 | 1,098 | | 2.0000 | -2,488 | 656.0000 | |
| 4.0000 | -11,400 | 1,038 | | 4.0000 | -1,272 | 608.0000 | |
| 20.0000 | 888 | 558 | | 20.0000 | 5,000 | 224.0000 | |
| 22.0000 | 1,884 | 498 | | 22.0000 | 5,352 | 176.0000 | |
| 24.0000 | 2,760 | 438 | | 24.0000 | 5,608 | 128.0000 | |
| 26.0000 | 3,516 | 378 | | 26.0000 | 5,768 | 80.0000 | |
| 28.0000 | 4,152 | 318 | | 28.0000 | 5,832 | 32.0000 | |
| 30.0000 | 4,668 | 258 | | 30.0000 | 5,800 | -16.0000 | CRITICAL POINT 28.0000 |
| 32.0000 | 5,064 | 198 | | 32.0000 | 5,672 | -64.0000 | |
| 34.0000 | 5,340 | 138 | | 34.0000 | 5,448 | -112.0000 | |
| 36.0000 | 5,496 | 78 | | 36.0000 | 5,128 | -160.0000 | |
| 38.0000 | 5,532 | 18 | | 38.0000 | 4,712 | -208.0000 | |
| 40.0000 | 5,448 | -42 | CRITICAL POINT 38.0000 | 40.0000 | 4,200 | -256.0000 | |
| 42.0000 | 5,244 | -102 | | 42.0000 | 3,592 | -304.0000 | |
| 44.0000 | 4,920 | -162 | | 44.0000 | 2,888 | -352.0000 | |
| 46.0000 | 4,476 | -222 | | 46.0000 | 2,088 | -400.0000 | |
| 48.0000 | 3,912 | -282 | | 48.0000 | 1,192 | -448.0000 | |
| 60.0000 | -1,992 | -642 | | 60.0000 | -6,200 | -736.0000 | |
| 62.0000 | -3,396 | -702 | | 62.0000 | -7,768 | -784.0000 | |

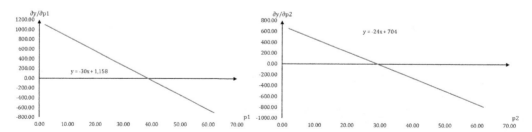

**FIGURE 5.3-2**   Numerical partial derivatives with second iteration.

**TABLE 5.3-5** Double entry table with third Iteration before Solver (optimal prices $p_1 = 38$ and $p_2 = 28$).

| | p1 | p2 | y = -15p1^2-3p1p2-12p2^2+1,230p1+800p2-29,000 | | | Step-Size | 5.00 | |
|---|---|---|---|---|---|---|---|---|
| | 38.00 | 28.00 | 5,880 | | | | | |
| | | | | | | | p2 | |
| | 5,880 | 0.00 | 5.00 | 10.00 | 15.00 | 20.00 | 25.00 | 30.00 | 35.00 |
| | 0.00 | -29,000 | -25,300 | -22,200 | -19,700 | -17,800 | -16,500 | -15,800 | -15,700 |
| | 5.00 | -23,225 | -19,600 | -16,575 | -14,150 | -12,325 | -11,100 | -10,475 | -10,450 |
| | 10.00 | -18,200 | -14,650 | -11,700 | -9,350 | -7,600 | -6,450 | -5,900 | -5,950 |
| | 15.00 | -13,925 | -10,450 | -7,575 | -5,300 | -3,625 | -2,550 | -2,075 | -2,200 |
| p1 | 20.00 | -10,400 | -7,000 | -4,200 | -2,000 | -400 | 600 | 1,000 | 800 |
| | 25.00 | -7,625 | -4,300 | -1,575 | 550 | 2,075 | 3,000 | 3,325 | 3,050 |
| | 30.00 | -5,600 | -2,350 | 300 | 2,350 | 3,800 | 4,650 | 4,900 | 4,550 |
| | 35.00 | -4,325 | -1,150 | 1,425 | 3,400 | 4,775 | 5,550 | 5,725 | 5,300 |
| | 40.00 | -3,800 | -700 | 1,800 | 3,700 | 5,000 | 5,700 | 5,800 | 5,300 |
| | 45.00 | -4,025 | -1,000 | 1,425 | 3,250 | 4,475 | 5,100 | 5,125 | 4,550 |
| | 50.00 | -5,000 | -2,050 | 300 | 2,050 | 3,200 | 3,750 | 3,700 | 3,050 |
| | 55.00 | -6,725 | -3,850 | -1,575 | 100 | 1,175 | 1,650 | 1,525 | 800 |

**TABLE 5.3-6** Hessian matrix negative definite with H1 < 0 and H2 > 0 (unique maximum point).

| Hessian Matrix | |
|---|---|
| -30 | -3 |
| -3 | -24 |
| **Leading Principal Minors** | |
| H1 | H2 |
| -30 | 711 |

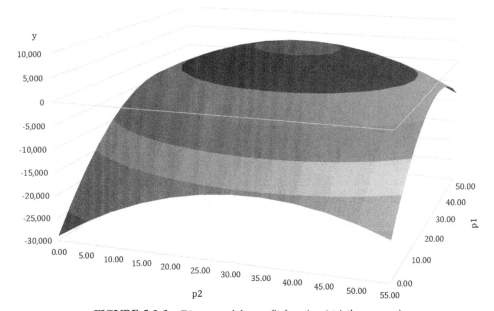

**FIGURE 5.3-3** Diagram of the profit function (strictly concave).

II. Static optimization

5. Classical static nonlinear optimization theory

## EXAMPLE 2 (OPTIMIZING THE QUANTITIES OF TWO PRODUCTS FOR TWO SEPARATE COUNTRY MARKETS)

In the previous example the problem was that of searching the optimal prices that maximizes the given function; in this example, we will see instead an optimization problem based on quantities.

Let us have a firm selling the same good into two different country markets. For each country market the firm experiences a different demand schedule as follows:

$$p_1 = 60 - 2q_1$$

$$p_2 = 80 - 4q_2$$

being the demand function therefore expressed in the form $p = f(q)$.

The total costs function is:

$$TC = 50 + 40(q_1 + q_2).$$

The profit function to maximize is then:

$$y = \Pi(q_1, q_2) = (60 - 2q_1) \cdot q_1 + (80 - 4q_2) \cdot q_2 - [50 + 40(q_1 + q_2)]$$

and the problem finally becomes:

$$\max_{\{q_1; q_2\}} \Pi(q_1, q_2) = 20q_1 - 2q_1^2 + 40q_2 - 4q_2^2 - 50.$$

In this case, the terms of the functions are associated only to one variable and we do not need to iterate further on the numerical partial derivatives and the critical values, as we did in the previous example. After proceeding as explained so far, we have obtained Table 5.3-7 and the numerical partial derivatives in Table 5.3-8 (Fig. 5.3-4).

TABLE 5.3-7   Enumeration of the profit function.

| q1 | q2 | y = 20q1-2q1^2+40q2-4q2^2-50 | | | | Step-Size | 1.00 | | | | | |
|---|---|---|---|---|---|---|---|---|---|---|---|---|
| 5.00 | 5.00 | 100.00 | | | | | | | | | | |
| | | | | | | | **p2** | | | | | |
| **100.00** | 0.00 | 1.00 | 2.00 | 3.00 | 4.00 | 5.00 | 6.00 | 7.00 | 8.00 | 9.00 | 10.00 | 11.00 |
| 0.00 | -50.00 | -14.00 | 14.00 | 34.00 | 46.00 | 50.00 | 46.00 | 34.00 | 14.00 | -14.00 | -50.00 | -94.00 |
| 1.00 | -32.00 | 4.00 | 32.00 | 52.00 | 64.00 | 68.00 | 64.00 | 52.00 | 32.00 | 4.00 | -32.00 | -76.00 |
| 2.00 | -18.00 | 18.00 | 46.00 | 66.00 | 78.00 | 82.00 | 78.00 | 66.00 | 46.00 | 18.00 | -18.00 | -62.00 |
| 3.00 | -8.00 | 28.00 | 56.00 | 76.00 | 88.00 | 92.00 | 88.00 | 76.00 | 56.00 | 28.00 | -8.00 | -52.00 |
| **p1** 4.00 | -2.00 | 34.00 | 62.00 | 82.00 | 94.00 | 98.00 | 94.00 | 82.00 | 62.00 | 34.00 | -2.00 | -46.00 |
| 5.00 | 0.00 | 36.00 | 64.00 | 84.00 | 96.00 | 100.00 | 96.00 | 84.00 | 64.00 | 36.00 | 0.00 | -44.00 |
| 6.00 | -2.00 | 34.00 | 62.00 | 82.00 | 94.00 | 98.00 | 94.00 | 82.00 | 62.00 | 34.00 | -2.00 | -46.00 |
| 7.00 | -8.00 | 28.00 | 56.00 | 76.00 | 88.00 | 92.00 | 88.00 | 76.00 | 56.00 | 28.00 | -8.00 | -52.00 |
| 8.00 | -18.00 | 18.00 | 46.00 | 66.00 | 78.00 | 82.00 | 78.00 | 66.00 | 46.00 | 18.00 | -18.00 | -62.00 |
| 9.00 | -32.00 | 4.00 | 32.00 | 52.00 | 64.00 | 68.00 | 64.00 | 52.00 | 32.00 | 4.00 | -32.00 | -76.00 |
| 10.00 | -50.00 | -14.00 | 14.00 | 34.00 | 46.00 | 50.00 | 46.00 | 34.00 | 14.00 | -14.00 | -50.00 | -94.00 |
| 11.00 | -72.00 | -36.00 | -8.00 | 12.00 | 24.00 | 28.00 | 24.00 | 12.00 | -8.00 | -36.00 | -72.00 | -116.00 |

**TABLE 5.3-8**  Partial derivatives and critical points.

| p1 | y by changing p1 only | $\partial y/\partial p1$ | Critical point | p2 | y by changing p2 only | $\partial y/\partial p2$ | Critical point |
|---|---|---|---|---|---|---|---|
| 3.00 | 92 | Numerical | | 3.00 | 84 | Numerical | |
| 3.10 | 93 | 8 | | 3.10 | 86 | 15.60 | |
| 3.20 | 94 | 7 | | 3.20 | 87 | 14.80 | |
| 3.30 | 94 | 7 | | 3.30 | 88 | 14.00 | |
| 4.60 | 100 | 2 | | 4.60 | 99 | 3.60 | |
| 4.70 | 100 | 1 | | 4.70 | 100 | 2.80 | |
| 4.80 | 100 | 1 | | 4.80 | 100 | 2.00 | |
| 4.90 | 100 | 1 | | 4.90 | 100 | 1.20 | |
| 5.00 | 100 | 0 | | 5.00 | 100 | 0.40 | |
| 5.10 | 100 | 0 | CRITICAL POINT 5.0000 | 5.10 | 100 | -0.40 | CRITICAL POINT 5.00 |
| 5.20 | 100 | -1 | | 5.20 | 100 | -1.20 | |
| 5.30 | 100 | -1 | | 5.30 | 100 | -2.00 | |
| 5.40 | 100 | -1 | | 5.40 | 99 | -2.80 | |
| 5.50 | 100 | -2 | | 5.50 | 99 | -3.60 | |
| 5.60 | 99 | -2 | | 5.60 | 99 | -4.40 | |
| 5.70 | 99 | -3 | | 5.70 | 98 | -5.20 | |
| 5.80 | 99 | -3 | | 5.80 | 97 | -6.00 | |
| 5.90 | 98 | -3 | | 5.90 | 97 | -6.80 | |
| 6.00 | 98 | -4 | | 6.00 | 96 | -7.60 | |
| 6.10 | 98 | -4 | | 6.10 | 95 | -8.40 | |

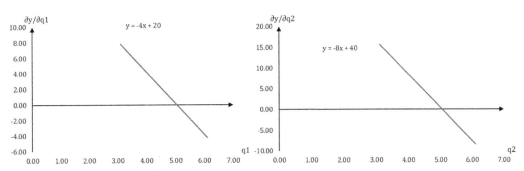

**FIGURE 5.3-4**  Diagrams of the numerical partial derivatives.

**TABLE 5.3-9**  Hessian matrix with H1 < 0 and H2 > 0 (maximum point).

| Hessian Matrix | |
|---|---|
| -4 | 0 |
| 0 | -8 |
| **Leading Principal Minors** | |
| H1 | H2 |
| -4 | 32 |

II. Static optimization

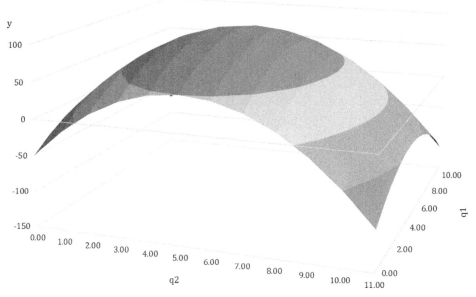

**FIGURE 5.3-5**    Diagram of the profit function.

The Hessian matrix is represented in Table 5.3-9.
The critical vector point:

$$q_1^* = 5 \text{ and } q_2^* = 5$$

is a global maximum, leading to the maximum profit $y^* = £\ 100$.

The prices corresponding to the optimal quantities are as follows, while the diagram of the profit function is in Fig. 5.3-5.

$$p_1 = 60 - 2 \cdot 5 = £\ 50$$

$$p_2 = 80 - 4 \cdot 5 = £\ 60.$$

## 5.4 Numerical steepest descent method applied to the unconstrained optimization with VBA

The *steepest descent* is a numerical method applied to the unconstrained optimization that can be both applied to the case of multivariate and univariate functions.

The algorithm works by iterations through the following steps (e.g., for a minimum):

- **Step 1.** Start with a first approximation $x_0$ to the minimum $x^*$.
- **Step 2.** Evaluate in $x_0$ the following function:

$$g(t) = F(x - t\nabla F(x))$$

such that it turns out:

$$g(t_0) = F(x_0 - t_0\nabla F(x_0))$$

- **Step 3.** Find $t_0^*$ so that $g(t_0)$ is minimized.
- **Step 4.** Find the second approximation of the minimum $x^*$ as

$$x_1 = \left[x_0 - t_0^*\nabla F(x_0)\right]$$

In general, for the $k$th step, we will have the following:

$$g(t_k) = F(x_k - t_k\nabla F(x_k))$$

to be minimized for $t_k^*$ and

$$x_{k+1} = \left[x_k - t_k^*\nabla F(x_k)\right].$$

As a stopping criterion the following is usually considered:

$$\frac{|F(x_{k+1}) - F(x_k)|}{1 + |F(x_k)|} < \varepsilon.$$

## EXAMPLE 1 (STEEPEST DESCENT FOR A MAXIMUM POINT)

Consider again the function of Example 2 in the previous Section 5.3 expressed as:

$$F = 20x_1 - 2x_1^2 + 40x_2 - 4x_2^2 - 50.$$

### Iteration 1

Let us begin the procedure with the point $x_0 = (0, 0)$.
The gradient of the given function is:

$$\nabla F(x) = \left[\frac{\partial F}{\partial x_1} = 20 - 4x_1; \frac{\partial f}{\partial x_2} = 40 - 8x_2\right]$$

which, evaluated in $x_0=(0, 0)$, becomes:

$$\nabla F(x_0) = [20; 40].$$

As a second step let us build the following function:

$$g(t_0) = F(x_0 - t_0 \nabla F(x_0))$$

that must be evaluated in $x_0=(0, 0)$, so that we have:

$$g(t_0) = F(x_0 - t_0 \nabla F(x_0)) = F(0 - t_0 20; 0 - t_0 40)$$

which becomes:

$$g(t_0) = 20(0 - t_0 20) - 2(0 - t_0 20)^2 + 40(0 - t_0 40) - 4(0 - t_0 40)^2 - 50$$

that we need to maximize with respect to $t_0$.

Taking the first derivative of $g(t_0)$ and setting it to zero we obtain $t_0^*$:

$$g\prime(t_0) = -400 - 4 \cdot 20^2 \cdot t_0 - 1,600 - 8 \cdot 40^2 \cdot t_0 = 0$$

$$g\prime(t_0) = -2,000 - 14,400 \cdot t_0 = 0 \Rightarrow t_0^* = -0.1389$$

Now we determine the numerical value of $x_{0+1} = \left[x_0 - t_0^* \nabla F(x_k)\right]$ as:

$$x_{0+1} = [0 + 0.1389 \cdot 20; 0 + 0.1389 \cdot 40] = [2.7780; 5.5560]$$

**Iteration 2**

$$\nabla F(x_{0+1}) = [20 - 4 \cdot 2.7780; 40 - 8 \cdot 5.5560] = [8.8880; -4.4480]$$

$$g(t_{0+1}) = F(x_{0+1} - t_{0+1} \nabla F(x_{0+1}))$$

$$g(t_{0+1}) = 20(2.7780 - t_{0+1} 8.888) - 2(2.7780 - t_{0+1} 8.888)^2 + 40(5.5560 + t_0 4.448)$$
$$- 4(5.5560 + t_{0+1} 4.448)^2 - 50$$

Taking the first derivative of $g(t_{0+1})$ and setting it to zero we obtain $t_{0+1}^* = -0.2082$, and then continue the iterations until the stopping criterion is satisfied.

The whole process can be performed via a VBA instruction in Excel. In Fig. 5.4-1, we have the worksheet setup for each iteration, while Fig. 5.4-3 is the VBA code implemented. The convergence process is diagrammed in Fig. 5.4-2 with numerical values in Table 5.4-1.

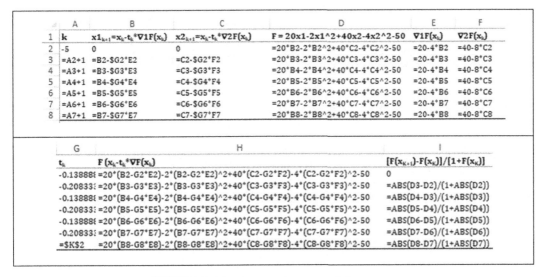

**FIGURE 5.4-1**    Steepest descent worksheet setup.

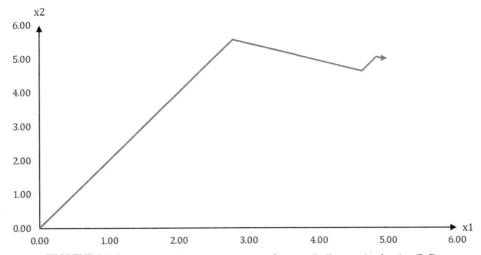

**FIGURE 5.4-2**    Steepest descent convergence from $x_0$ (0, 0) to optimal point (5, 5).

**TABLE 5.4-1**    Steepest descent: values at each Iteration.

| k | $x1_{k+1}=x_k-t_k*\nabla1F(x_k)$ | $x2_{k+1}=x_k-t_k*\nabla2F(x_k)$ | $F = 20x1-2x1^2+40x2-4x2^2-50$ | $\nabla1F(x_k)$ | $\nabla2F(x_k)$ | $t_k$ | $F(x_k-t_k*\nabla F(x_k))$ | $[F(x_{k+1})-F(x_k)]/[1+F(x_k)]$ |
|---|---|---|---|---|---|---|---|---|
| -5.0000 | 0.0000 | 0.0000 | -50.0000 | 20.0000 | 40.0000 | -0.1389 | 88.8889 | 0.0000 |
| -4.0000 | 2.7778 | 5.5556 | 88.8889 | 8.8889 | -4.4444 | -0.2083 | 99.1770 | 2.7233 |
| -3.0000 | 4.6296 | 4.6296 | 99.1770 | 1.4815 | 2.9630 | -0.1389 | 99.9390 | 0.1145 |
| -2.0000 | 4.8354 | 5.0412 | 99.9390 | 0.6584 | -0.3292 | -0.2083 | 99.9955 | 0.0076 |
| -1.0000 | 4.9726 | 4.9726 | 99.9955 | 0.1097 | 0.2195 | -0.1389 | 99.9997 | 0.0006 |
| 0.0000 | 4.9878 | 5.0030 | 99.9997 | 0.0488 | -0.0244 | -0.2083 | 100.0000 | 0.0000 |
| 1.0000 | 4.9980 | 4.9980 | 100.0000 | 0.0081 | 0.0163 | -0.2083 | 100.0000 | 0.0000 |

## Remark

Notice in the VBA code where it says *MaxMinVal* $= 1$, which means that we are maximizing, otherwise the VBA code would be *MaxMinVal* $= 2$ in case of minimization (Fig. 5.4-3).

As the VBA code needs the Solver, before running the macro the Solver has to be recalled within the Excel VBA *References*.

In order to do this, when we are under the VBA working area, we need to go to *Tools*, then *References*, look for the Solver and select it (see Fig. 5.4-4). The Solver should be already added from the Excel *Add-ins*.

Let us change now the starting point from $x_0 = (0, 0)$ to $x_0 = (50, 50)$ and to $x_0 = (-50, -50)$. As the function presents a global unique maximum the algorithm will converge, even if we begin from a value located far from the optimal point, and the algorithm will make the iterations converge to that unique maximum point. See Figs. 5.4-5 and 5.4-6.

This will not be the case for more than one maxima or minima. In this case, ideally, we should have some preliminary info about the function, to know what and where to search. See Example 2 for a function of one variable with a min and max.

```
Sub Steepest_Descent_Max()
 ' Run first time solver
   SolverOk SetCell:="$H$2", MaxMinVal:=1, ValueOf:=0, ByChange:="$G$2", Engine:=1 _
        , EngineDesc:="GRG Nonlinear"
     SolverSolve UserFinish:=True

   ' Run Solver until column I equals to 0
     Range("I3").Select

Do Until Range("J2") < 0.00001

     SolverOk SetCell:="L2", MaxMinVal:=1, ValueOf:=0, ByChange:="K2", Engine _
     :=1, EngineDesc:="GRG Nonlinear"
     SolverSolve UserFinish:=True

'Copies last row down
   Range("A1").Select

Do Until ActiveCell = ""
   ActiveCell.Offset(1, 0).Select

Loop
   ActiveCell.Offset(-1, 0).Select
   ActiveCell.Offset.Range("al:I1").Select
   Selection.Copy
   ActiveCell.Range("a2").Select
   ActiveSheet.Paste
   Application.CutCopyMode = False
   ActiveCell.Offset.Range("gl:gl").Select
   ActiveCell.Offset(-1, 0).Select
'Copy penultimate cell value
   Selection.Copy
   Selection.PasteSpecial xlPasteValues
   Application.CutCopyMode = False

Loop

End Sub
```

**FIGURE 5.4-3**    Steepest descent code in VBA

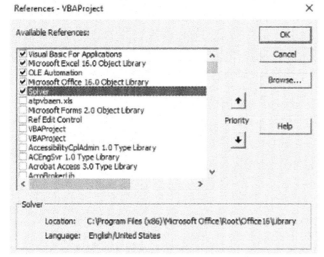

**FIGURE 5.4-4** Recalling the Solver under references in VBA.

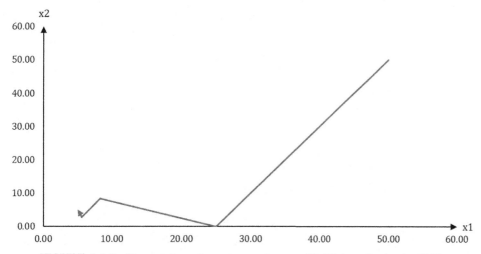

**FIGURE 5.4-5** Steepest descent convergence from $x_0$ (50, 50) to optimal point (5, 5).

## Example 2

The steepest descent can be also be implemented for a function of one variable. We just set $x_2 = 0$. Let us consider the following univariate function:

$$y = x_1^3 + 3x_1^2 - 9x_1 + 5$$

Let us apply the steepest descent to verify the convergence to the minimum and to the maximum.

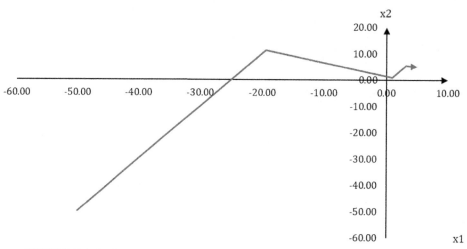

**FIGURE 5.4-6** Steepest descent convergence from $x_0$ $(-50, -50)$ to optimal point $(5, 5)$.

After diagramming the function in Fig. 5.4-7, we set $x_0$ accordingly, to find the maximum point and the minimum point, either running the macro in Fig. 5.4-3 with *MaxMinVal* $= 1$ or *MaxMinVal* $= 2$.

The results are from Figs. 5.4-8 to 5.4-11.

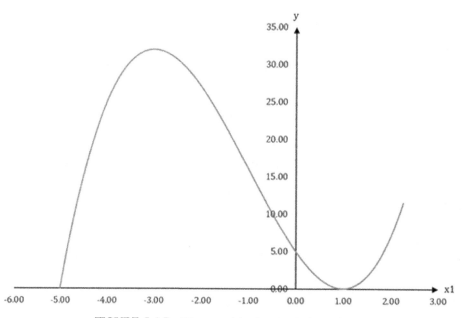

**FIGURE 5.4-7** Diagram of the function in Example 2.

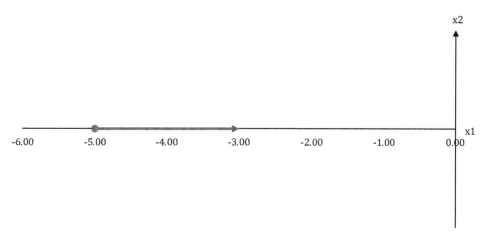

**FIGURE 5.4-8**    Steepest descent convergence from $x_0$ $(-5, 0)$ to maximum point $(-3, 0)$.

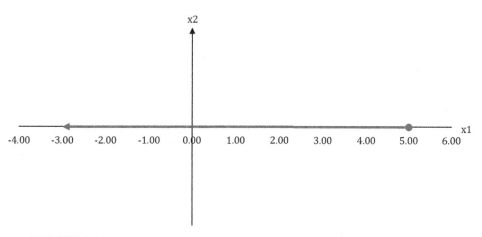

**FIGURE 5.4-9**    Steepest descent convergence from $x_0$ $(5, 0)$ to maximum point $(-3, 0)$.

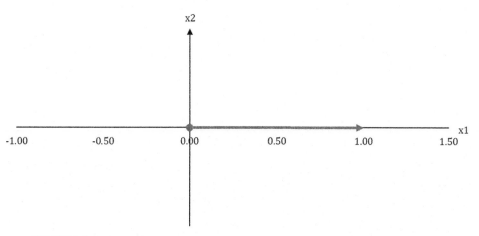

**FIGURE 5.4-10**    Steepest descent convergence from $x_0$ $(0, 0)$ to minimum point $(1, 0)$.

II. Static optimization

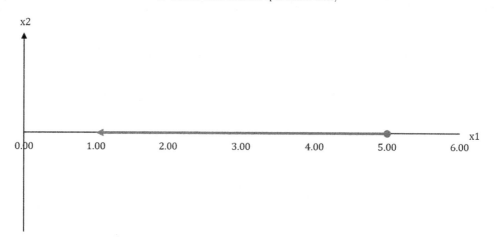

FIGURE 5.4-11    Steepest descent convergence from $x_0$ (5, 0) to minimum point (1, 0).

FIGURE 5.4-12    Button (form control).

In this example, as we either minimize or maximize, we can insert in our worksheet two Excel *Buttons (Form Control)* in order to launch the two macros (min and max) separately. Fig. 5.4-12 is where we have to go to insert the two buttons (form control).

Then, when we insert the Excel button in the worksheet (and the usual cross will appear to guide us where to insert the button), the dialogue box of Fig. 5.4-13 will appear and each macro will need to be assigned to each button. We can change the name of the two macros and the two buttons as we wish, as in Figs. 5.4-13 and 5.4-14.

## 5.5 Nonlinear problems in $\mathbf{R}^n$ with equality constraints: Lagrange multipliers and Solver

A nonlinear optimization problem in $\Re^n$, namely with $f : \Re^n \to \Re$, with $m$-equality constraints, is a problem where we have to minimize (or maximize) a multivariate function of

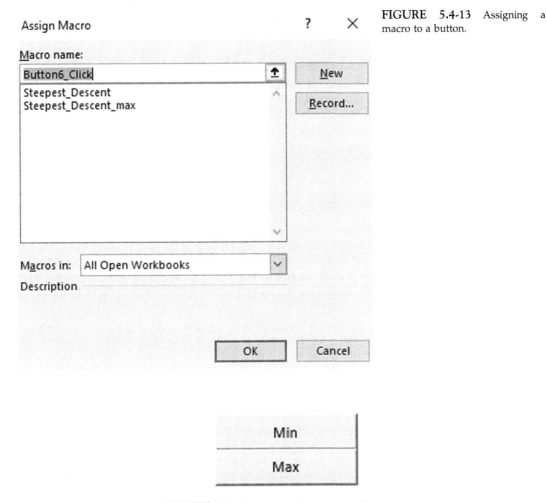

FIGURE 5.4-13 Assigning a macro to a button.

FIGURE 5.4-14  Naming the two Excel buttons.

$n$ variables, subject to the given $m$-equality constraints, that can be expressed as follows, with $m < n$:

$$\min_{\{x_1, x_2, \cdots, x_n\}} (or\ max)\, f(x_1, x_2, \cdots, x_n)$$

s.t.

$$g_1(x_1, x_2, \cdots, x_n) = c_1$$

$$g_2(x_1, x_2, \cdots, x_n) = c_2$$

...

$$g_m(x_1, x_2, \cdots, x_n) = c_m \tag{5.5-1}$$

The problem 5.5-1 is one of the most important forms used in economics (e.g., within the consumer and the firm's theory) and can be solved resorting to the technique of the *Lagrange multipliers*.

To solve 5.5-1, we need to introduce the *Lagrangian* function:

$$\boxed{\mathscr{L}(x_1, x_2, \cdots, x_n; \lambda_1, \lambda_2, \cdots, \lambda_n) = f(x_1, x_2, \cdots, x_n) + \sum_{i=1}^{m} \lambda_i[g_i(x_1, x_2, \cdots, x_n) - c_i]} \tag{5.5-2}$$

which is essentially the new objective function of $(n + m)$ variables, where the $\lambda_i$s introduced are called *Lagrange multipliers*.

The 5.5-2 can be then optimized with the usual technique of the unconstrained optimization of multivariate function. The following equations represent the conditions of first order for an optimum to exist:

$$\frac{\partial \mathscr{L}(x, \lambda)}{\partial x_j} = \frac{\partial f(x)}{\partial x_j} + \sum_{i=1}^{m} \lambda_i \frac{\partial g_i(x)}{\partial x_j} = 0 \quad j = 1, \cdots, n \tag{5.5-3}$$

$$\frac{\partial \mathscr{L}(x, \lambda)}{\partial \lambda_i} = g_i(x_1, x_2, \cdots, x_n) - c_i \quad i = 1, \cdots, m$$

The solution of the 5.5-3 yields to a stationary point $(x^*, \lambda^*)$. A set of various second-order condition methods apply in this case to establish which kind of extreme value has been found (e.g., maximum or minimum).

These approaches use similar techniques used in Section 5.2, that investigate the so-called *bordered Hessian matrix according to Theorem 3 of Section 3.4.*

Let us turn our attention to the numerical approach to the problem 5.5-1.

Without a doubt, the Excel GRG Solver is able to solve this class of problems with a great efficiency, in the light of the constraints given by the problem, which forces the algorithm to search the optimal solutions within a specific range of values.

As a second approach, that we will apply to the case of a function of two variables with one constraint, is using the Data Table as well. This is essentially a simulation made on the various solutions to find the one that optimizes and satisfies the given constraint.

Let us see then some general examples, beginning with the simplest case of a function of two variables, where it is easier to check also the second-order conditions of the bordered Hessian matrix.

Chapter 6 includes the most important applications of the nonlinear constrained dynamic programming to the theory of economics (e.g., consumer optimization), while another important application of the nonlinear constrained programming is represented by the *portfolio theory* and to this is dedicated Chapter 8.

# EXAMPLE 1 ($N = 2$, $M = 1$)

Let us solve the following problem:

$$\min_{\{x_1, x_2\}} x_2^2 + x_2^2 - 4x_1 - 6x_2 + 4$$

s.t. $x_1 + x_2 = 10$.

The Lagrangian function is:

$$\mathscr{L}(x_1, x_2; \lambda_1) = x_1^2 + x_2^2 - 4x_1 - 6x_2 + 4 + \lambda_1(x_1 + x_2 - 10)$$

from which we obtain the system of $(2 + 1)$ **first-order condition** equations (as in 5.5-3):

$$\frac{\partial \mathscr{L}(x, \lambda)}{\partial x_1} = 2x_1 - 4 + \lambda_1 = 0 \Rightarrow x_1 = \frac{(4 - \lambda_1)}{2}$$

$$\frac{\partial \mathscr{L}(x, \lambda)}{\partial x_2} = 2x_2 - 6 + \lambda_1 = 0 \Rightarrow x_2 = \frac{(6 - \lambda_1)}{2}$$

$$\frac{\partial \mathscr{L}(x, \lambda)}{\partial \lambda_1} = x_1 + x_2 - 10 = 0 \Rightarrow \frac{(4 - \lambda_1)}{2} + \frac{(6 - \lambda_1)}{2} = 10.$$

From the third equation, we obtain $\lambda_1 = -5$ and the stationary point $x^*(4.5, 5.5)$.

**Second-order conditions. Bordered Hessian.** Is this stationary point a minimum or a maximum? The answer lies in studying the following *bordered* (by the constraint) Hessian matrix:

$$H(x) = \begin{bmatrix} 0 & g_1 & g_2 \\ g_1 & \mathscr{L}_{11} & \mathscr{L}_{12} \\ g_2 & \mathscr{L}_{21} & \mathscr{L}_{22} \end{bmatrix}$$

where $g_1$ and $g_2$ are the first-order partials of the constraint function. The bordered Hessian is therefore:

$$H(x) = \begin{bmatrix} 0 & 1 & 1 \\ 1 & 2 & 0 \\ 1 & 0 & 2 \end{bmatrix}.$$

We apply Theorem 3 in Section 3.4.

According to this theorem, we have $m = 1$ constraint and $n = 2$ variables. Therefore, it is

$$\overline{M}_{2m+1=3}(-1)^1 = \begin{vmatrix} 0 & 1 & 1 \\ 1 & 2 & 0 \\ 1 & 0 & 2 \end{vmatrix} = -4 \cdot (-1) = 4$$

FIGURE 5.5-1 Example 1: constrained
problem worksheet.

| | A | B |
|---|---|---|
| 1 | **x1** | **x2** |
| 2 | 4.50000000000004 | 5.50000000000004 |
| 3 | Obj. Funct. | =$A$2^2+B2^2-4*$A$2-6*B2+4 |
| 4 | s.t.---> | =A2+B2 |

and the point **i.** of Theorem 3 in Section 3.4 is satisfied, being the bordered Hessian **positive definite**; therefore, the stationary value $x^*(4.5, 5.5)$ does minimize the objective function.

Another important application of the bordered Hessian, that has to be mentioned, is when we want to identify the **quasiconcavity** or **quasiconvexity** of a multivariate function.

## Solver solution

When we use the Excel Solver we immediately instruct the Solver either to minimize or to maximize the objective function.

In Excel, this problem does not present any particular issue to be solved. We just need to store our problem in the worksheet as represented in Fig. 5.5-1.

As a second step we open the Solver (from the Excel Ribbon, go to Data) and we set it up as in Fig. 5.5-2.

In this case, as we are dealing with a nonlinear problem, we must use the option *GRG Nonlinear*.

The solution is given in Table 5.5-1.

Selecting, in Fig. 5.5-3, the option Sensitivity we obtain the information about the Lagrange multiplier together with the other data of the problem (see Fig. 5.5-4).

## Problem defined in stages and the use of Data Table (relation with the discrete dynamic programming)

The same problem can be also approached in stages, i.e., two stages as $n = 2$, via the dynamic programming (see Chapter 11). We can study the problem using the Data Table, which is quite often a little used tool within Excel.

The problem setup is in Fig. 5.5-5, and the results are in Table 5.5-2. Essentially, we input the value of the function in *Cell J*3, building a Data Table simulation from *Cell B*7 to *Cell H*13. Data Table is an Excel *CSE* function and needs to be entered therefore pressing *Ctrl + Shift + Enter*, as it is an array function. Beneath the Data Table, we construct the table of the constraint, where we focus the attention only to values equal to 10, minimizing the values in the Data Table. The result is a minimum in x*(4.5, 5.5). See Table 5.5-2.

This approach is somehow similar to what has been done in Section 11.2 with discrete dynamic systems. The Data Table construction, however, is to be prepared with some trials and errors, to define and narrow the optimization range.

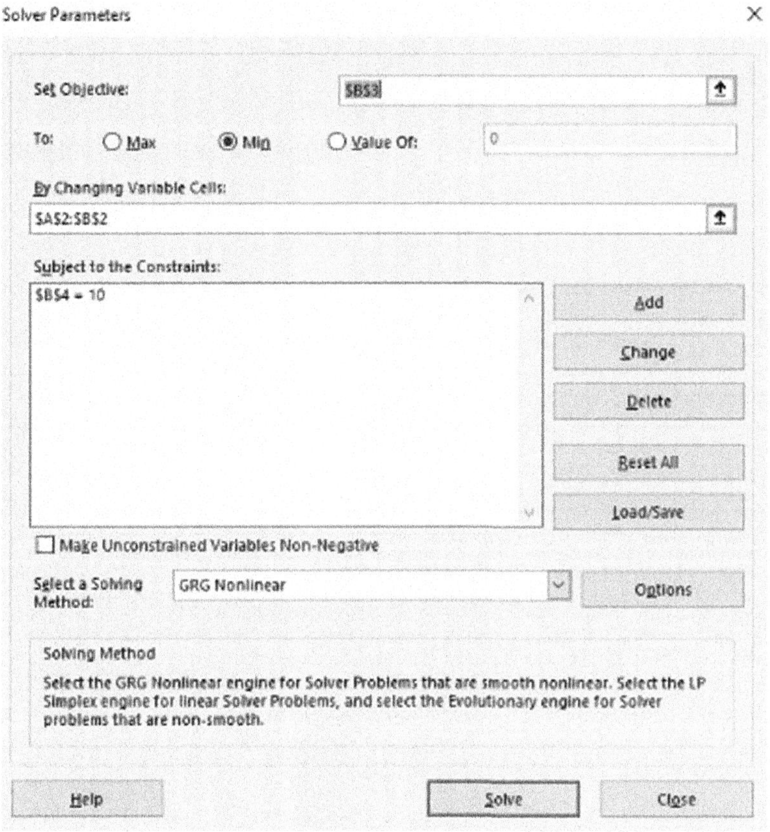

**FIGURE 5.5-2**  Solver setup.

**TABLE 5.5-1**  Solver solution x*(4.5, 5.5).

| x1 | x2 |
|:---:|:---:|
| 4.5000 | 5.5000 |
| Obj. Funct. | 3.5000 |
| s.t. | 10.0000 |

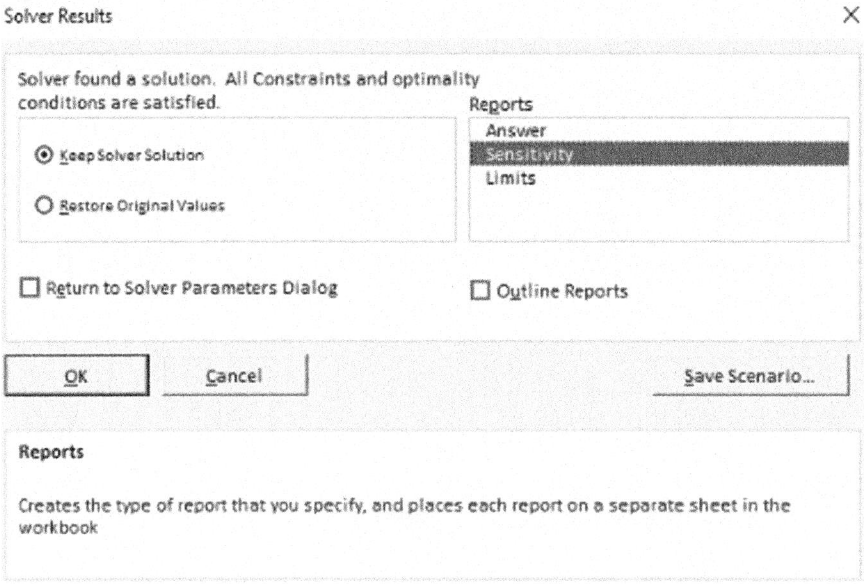

FIGURE 5.5-3   Solver reports.

| 6 | Variable Cells | | | |
|---|---|---|---|---|
| 7 | | | **Final** | **Reduced** |
| 8 | **Cell** | **Name** | **Value** | **Gradient** |
| 9 | $A$2 | x1 | 4.5 | 0 |
| 10 | $B$2 | x2 | 5.5 | 0 |
| 11 | | | | |
| 12 | Constraints | | | |
| 13 | | | **Final** | **Lagrange** |
| 14 | **Cell** | **Name** | **Value** | **Multiplier** |
| 15 | $B$4 | s.t. x2 | 10 | 5.000010859 |

FIGURE 5.5-4   Solver sensitivity report.

| | A | B | C | D | E | F | G | H |
|---|---|---|---|---|---|---|---|---|
| 1 | | t | x | S | J | | | |
| 2 | | 1 | 4.5 | =C2 | | | | |
| 3 | | 2 | 5.5 | =C2+C3 | =C2^2+C3^2-4*C2-6*C3+4 | | | |
| 4 | | | | | | | | |
| 5 | s.t.---> | =SUM(C2:C4) | | | | | | |
| 6 | | | | | x1 | | | |
| 7 | | =E3 | 3 | 3.5 | 4 | 4.5 | 5 | 5.5 |
| 8 | | 3 | =TABLE(C3;B4) | =TABLE(C3;B4) | =TABLE(C3;B4) | =TABLE(C3;B4) | =TABLE(C3;B4) | =TABLE(C3;B4) |
| 9 | | 3.5 | =TABLE(C3;B4) | =TABLE(C3;B4) | =TABLE(C3;B4) | =TABLE(C3;B4) | =TABLE(C3;B4) | =TABLE(C3;B4) |
| 10 | x2 | 4 | =TABLE(C3;B4) | =TABLE(C3;B4) | =TABLE(C3;B4) | =TABLE(C3;B4) | =TABLE(C3;B4) | =TABLE(C3;B4) |
| 11 | | 4.5 | =TABLE(C3;B4) | =TABLE(C3;B4) | =TABLE(C3;B4) | =TABLE(C3;B4) | =TABLE(C3;B4) | =TABLE(C3;B4) |
| 12 | | 5 | =TABLE(C3;B4) | =TABLE(C3;B4) | =TABLE(C3;B4) | =TABLE(C3;B4) | =TABLE(C3;B4) | =TABLE(C3;B4) |
| 13 | | 5.5 | =TABLE(C3;B4) | =TABLE(C3;B4) | =TABLE(C3;B4) | =TABLE(C3;B4) | =TABLE(C3;B4) | =TABLE(C3;B4) |
| 14 | | | | | | | | |
| 15 | | s.t. x1+x2=10 | | | | | | |
| 16 | | | =$B8+C$7 | =$B8+D$7 | =$B8+E$7 | =$B8+F$7 | =$B8+G$7 | =$B8+H$7 |
| 17 | | | =$B9+C$7 | =$B9+D$7 | =$B9+E$7 | =$B9+F$7 | =$B9+G$7 | =$B9+H$7 |
| 18 | | | =$B10+C$7 | =$B10+D$7 | =$B10+E$7 | =$B10+F$7 | =$B10+G$7 | =$B10+H$7 |
| 19 | | | =$B11+C$7 | =$B11+D$7 | =$B11+E$7 | =$B11+F$7 | =$B11+G$7 | =$B11+H$7 |
| 20 | | | =$B12+C$7 | =$B12+D$7 | =$B12+E$7 | =$B12+F$7 | =$B12+G$7 | =$B12+H$7 |
| 21 | | | =$B13+C$7 | =$B13+D$7 | =$B13+E$7 | =$B13+F$7 | =$B13+G$7 | =$B13+H$7 |

FIGURE 5.5-5　Data Table setup.

TABLE 5.5-2　Optimization via Data Table.

| | t | x | S | J | | | |
|---|---|---|---|---|---|---|---|
| | 1.00 | 4.50 | 4.50 | | | | |
| | 2.00 | 5.50 | 10.00 | 3.50 | | | |
| | | | | | | | |
| s.t ---> | 10.00 | | | | | | |
| | | | | x1 | | | |
| | 3.50 | 3.00 | 3.50 | 4.00 | 4.50 | 5.00 | 5.50 |
| | 3.00 | -2.75 | -2.50 | -1.75 | -0.50 | 1.25 | 3.50 |
| | 3.50 | -2.75 | -2.50 | -1.75 | -0.50 | 1.25 | 3.50 |
| x2 | 4.00 | -2.75 | -2.50 | -1.75 | -0.50 | 1.25 | 3.50 |
| | 4.50 | -2.75 | -2.50 | -1.75 | -0.50 | 1.25 | 3.50 |
| | 5.00 | -2.75 | -2.50 | -1.75 | -0.50 | 1.25 | 3.50 |
| | 5.50 | -2.75 | -2.50 | -1.75 | -0.50 | 1.25 | 3.50 |
| | | | | | | | |
| | s.t. x1+x2=10 | | | | | | |
| | | 6.00 | 6.50 | 7.00 | 7.50 | 8.00 | 8.50 |
| | | 6.50 | 7.00 | 7.50 | 8.00 | 8.50 | 9.00 |
| | | 7.00 | 7.50 | 8.00 | 8.50 | 9.00 | 9.50 |
| | | 7.50 | 8.00 | 8.50 | 9.00 | 9.50 | 10.00 |
| | | 8.00 | 8.50 | 9.00 | 9.50 | 10.00 | 10.50 |
| | | 8.50 | 9.00 | 9.50 | 10.00 | 10.50 | 11.00 |

|   | A | B | C |
|---|---|---|---|
| 1 | **x1** | **x2** | **x3** |
| 2 | 1 | 1 | 1 |
| 3 | Obj. Funct. | =5*A2+2*B2-C2 | |
| 4 | | | |
| 5 | s.t. | =A2*B2 | 3 |
| 6 | | =A2*C2 | 1 |

**FIGURE 5.5-6**   Example 2 problem in Excel.

## EXAMPLE 2 (N = 3, M = 2)

$$\min_{\{x_1,x_2\}} 5x_1 + 2x_2 - x_3$$

s.t.

$$x_1 x_2 = 3.$$

$$x_1 x_3 = 1.$$

The problem is translated into an Excel form as in Fig. 5.5-6:

Two constraints are added in the Solver dialogue box as in Fig. 5.5-7 and the solution found is in Table 5.5-3.

## 5.6 Nonlinear problems in $R^2$ with equality constraints: contour lines

In the case where $f : \Re^2 \to \Re$, the objective function can be represented graphically in a three-dimensional space and we can solve the constrained optimization problem using the *contour lines* technique. A contour line of a function is the locus of points where the function does not change its value.

The contour lines may be of any type (e.g., hyperbolas, circumferences, straight lines, etc.) depending on the objective function.

For a function representing the consumer's utility, they are called *indifference curves* (see Section 6.3), while for a function representing the firm's production, they are called *isoquants* (see Section 6.7). Let us see how to make them in Excel with some practical examples. Applications to economics of the contour lines will be also shown in Chapter 6.

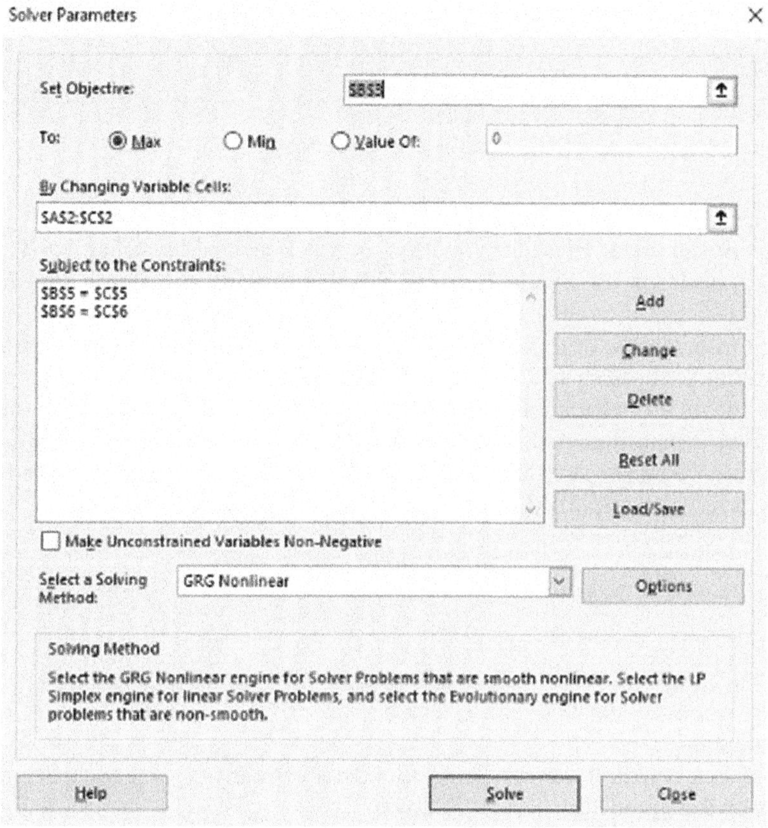

FIGURE 5.5-7   Example 2 Solver setup.

TABLE 5.5-3   Solver solution.

| x1 | x2 | x3 |
|---|---|---|
| 1.000 | 3.000 | 1.000 |
| Obj. Funct. | 10.0000 | |
| | | |
| s.t. | 3.00 | 3.00 |
| | 1.00 | 1.00 |

## Example 1 (Contour Map with Excel, for Linear and Quadratic Bivariate Functions)

**a.** Let us have the following linear bivariate function:

$$y = 3x_1 + 4x_2 + 10$$

which can be represented in a Data Table format as in Table 5.6-1:

The chart of the linear bivariate function, in a 3D surface, is in Fig. 5.6-1, while its contour map, built via the available Excel 3D **contour** and **wireframe contour** is in Fig. 5.6-2.

Although informative, the problem of the Excel contour map is that it cannot be treated together with other charts: for instance, if we want to visualize the point of tangency between a contour line associated to the objective function and a line representing a given constraint, this is not possible. What we need to do is then to build step by step our own contour map in Excel, using the scatter plot, to which we can add then any other curve we want. To do this, transform the given function:

$$y = 3x_1 + 4x_2 + 10$$

into

$$k = 3x_1 + 4x_2 + 10$$

where $k$ is a constant.

Now, as $k$ is a constant we can build the locus of point $(x_1, x_2)$ such that we have the same value of the given function as follows:

$$x_2 = -\frac{3}{4}x_1 + \frac{(k - 10)}{4}.$$

**TABLE 5.6-1**   Data table for $y = 3x_1 + 4x_2 + 10$.

|  |  | -6.00 | -5.00 | -4.00 | -3.00 | -2.00 | -1.00 | 0.00 | 1.00 | 2.00 | 3.00 | 4.00 | 5.00 | 6.00 |
|---|---|---|---|---|---|---|---|---|---|---|---|---|---|---|
|  | -6.00 | -32.00 | -28.00 | -24.00 | -20.00 | -16.00 | -12.00 | -8.00 | -4.00 | 0.00 | 4.00 | 8.00 | 12.00 | 16.00 |
|  | -5.00 | -29.00 | -25.00 | -21.00 | -17.00 | -13.00 | -9.00 | -5.00 | -1.00 | 3.00 | 7.00 | 11.00 | 15.00 | 19.00 |
|  | -4.00 | -26.00 | -22.00 | -18.00 | -14.00 | -10.00 | -6.00 | -2.00 | 2.00 | 6.00 | 10.00 | 14.00 | 18.00 | 22.00 |
|  | -3.00 | -23.00 | -19.00 | -15.00 | -11.00 | -7.00 | -3.00 | 1.00 | 5.00 | 9.00 | 13.00 | 17.00 | 21.00 | 25.00 |
|  | -2.00 | -20.00 | -16.00 | -12.00 | -8.00 | -4.00 | 0.00 | 4.00 | 8.00 | 12.00 | 16.00 | 20.00 | 24.00 | 28.00 |
| **x1** | -1.00 | -17.00 | -13.00 | -9.00 | -5.00 | -1.00 | 3.00 | 7.00 | 11.00 | 15.00 | 19.00 | 23.00 | 27.00 | 31.00 |
|  | 0.00 | -14.00 | -10.00 | -6.00 | -2.00 | 2.00 | 6.00 | 10.00 | 14.00 | 18.00 | 22.00 | 26.00 | 30.00 | 34.00 |
|  | 1.00 | -11.00 | -7.00 | -3.00 | 1.00 | 5.00 | 9.00 | 13.00 | 17.00 | 21.00 | 25.00 | 29.00 | 33.00 | 37.00 |
|  | 2.00 | -8.00 | -4.00 | 0.00 | 4.00 | 8.00 | 12.00 | 16.00 | 20.00 | 24.00 | 28.00 | 32.00 | 36.00 | 40.00 |
|  | 3.00 | -5.00 | -1.00 | 3.00 | 7.00 | 11.00 | 15.00 | 19.00 | 23.00 | 27.00 | 31.00 | 35.00 | 39.00 | 43.00 |
|  | 4.00 | -2.00 | 2.00 | 6.00 | 10.00 | 14.00 | 18.00 | 22.00 | 26.00 | 30.00 | 34.00 | 38.00 | 42.00 | 46.00 |
|  | 5.00 | 1.00 | 5.00 | 9.00 | 13.00 | 17.00 | 21.00 | 25.00 | 29.00 | 33.00 | 37.00 | 41.00 | 45.00 | 49.00 |
|  | 6.00 | 4.00 | 8.00 | 12.00 | 16.00 | 20.00 | 24.00 | 28.00 | 32.00 | 36.00 | 40.00 | 44.00 | 48.00 | 52.00 |

*x2*

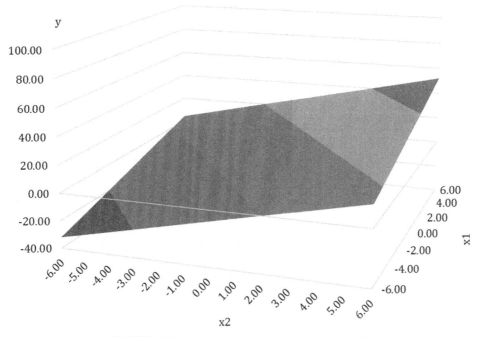

**FIGURE 5.6-1**    Bivariate function $y = 3x_1 + 4x_2 + 10$.

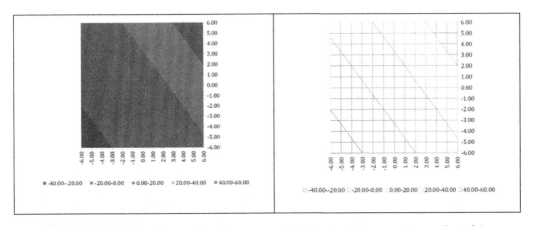

**FIGURE 5.6-2**    Excel contour lines (contour on the left and wireframe contour on the right).

We input the above formula in Excel as in Fig. 5.6-3, where under *Cell T2* we have the dependent variable $x_2$ while in *Cell R1* the value of $k$ and in *Cell R2* the independent variable.

Fig. 5.6-3 represents the Data Table formulas, where we simulate the values of $x_2$, changing the values in the constant $k$ from 10 to 60 and for values $x_1$ from $-10$ to 20.

| | Q | R | | T | |
|---|---|---|---|---|---|
| 1 | k | 1 | | x2 = -(3/4)x1+(k-10)/4 | |
| 2 | x1 | =1 | | =-3/4*R2+(R1-10)/4 | |

**FIGURE 5.6-3** Locus of points $(x_1, x_2)$ for a given value of $y = k$.

**TABLE 5.6-2**  Data Table results.

| | k (constant levels of y) | | | | | |
|---|---|---|---|---|---|---|
| -3.00 | 10.00 | 20.00 | 30.00 | 40.00 | 50.00 | 60.00 |
| -10.00 | 7.50 | 10.00 | 12.50 | 15.00 | 17.50 | 20.00 |
| -5.00 | 3.75 | 6.25 | 8.75 | 11.25 | 13.75 | 16.25 |
| 0.00 | 0.00 | 2.50 | 5.00 | 7.50 | 10.00 | 12.50 |
| 2.00 | -1.50 | 1.00 | 3.50 | 6.00 | 8.50 | 11.00 |
| 4.00 | -3.00 | -0.50 | 2.00 | 4.50 | 7.00 | 9.50 |
| 6.00 | -4.50 | -2.00 | 0.50 | 3.00 | 5.50 | 8.00 |
| 8.00 | -6.00 | -3.50 | -1.00 | 1.50 | 4.00 | 6.50 |
| 10.00 | -7.50 | -5.00 | -2.50 | 0.00 | 2.50 | 5.00 |
| 12.00 | -9.00 | -6.50 | -4.00 | -1.50 | 1.00 | 3.50 |
| 16.00 | -12.00 | -9.50 | -7.00 | -4.50 | -2.00 | 0.50 |
| 20.00 | -15.00 | -12.50 | -10.00 | -7.50 | -5.00 | -2.50 |

The results are in Table 5.6-2 and the contour map is in Figs. 5.6-5, which can now be treated together with other functions.

**b.** Let us study now the following quadratic function:

$$y = ax_1^2 + bx_2^2$$

| | k (constant levels of y) | | | | | |
|---|---|---|---|---|---|---|
| =T2 | 10 | 20 | 30 | 40 | 50 | 60 |
| -10 | =TABLE(R1;R2) | =TABLE(R1;R2) | =TABLE(R1;R2) | =TABLE(R1;R2) | =TABLE(R1;R2) | =TABLE(R1;R2) |
| -5 | =TABLE(R1;R2) | =TABLE(R1;R2) | =TABLE(R1;R2) | =TABLE(R1;R2) | =TABLE(R1;R2) | =TABLE(R1;R2) |
| 0 | =TABLE(R1;R2) | =TABLE(R1;R2) | =TABLE(R1;R2) | =TABLE(R1;R2) | =TABLE(R1;R2) | =TABLE(R1;R2) |
| 2 | =TABLE(R1;R2) | =TABLE(R1;R2) | =TABLE(R1;R2) | =TABLE(R1;R2) | =TABLE(R1;R2) | =TABLE(R1;R2) |
| 4 | =TABLE(R1;R2) | =TABLE(R1;R2) | =TABLE(R1;R2) | =TABLE(R1;R2) | =TABLE(R1;R2) | =TABLE(R1;R2) |
| 6 | =TABLE(R1;R2) | =TABLE(R1;R2) | =TABLE(R1;R2) | =TABLE(R1;R2) | =TABLE(R1;R2) | =TABLE(R1;R2) |
| 8 | =TABLE(R1;R2) | =TABLE(R1;R2) | =TABLE(R1;R2) | =TABLE(R1;R2) | =TABLE(R1;R2) | =TABLE(R1;R2) |
| 10 | =TABLE(R1;R2) | =TABLE(R1;R2) | =TABLE(R1;R2) | =TABLE(R1;R2) | =TABLE(R1;R2) | =TABLE(R1;R2) |
| 12 | =TABLE(R1;R2) | =TABLE(R1;R2) | =TABLE(R1;R2) | =TABLE(R1;R2) | =TABLE(R1;R2) | =TABLE(R1;R2) |
| 16 | =TABLE(R1;R2) | =TABLE(R1;R2) | =TABLE(R1;R2) | =TABLE(R1;R2) | =TABLE(R1;R2) | =TABLE(R1;R2) |
| 20 | =TABLE(R1;R2) | =TABLE(R1;R2) | =TABLE(R1;R2) | =TABLE(R1;R2) | =TABLE(R1;R2) | =TABLE(R1;R2) |

**FIGURE 5.6-4**  Locus of points $(x_1, x_2)$ by changing the value in k from 20 to 60.

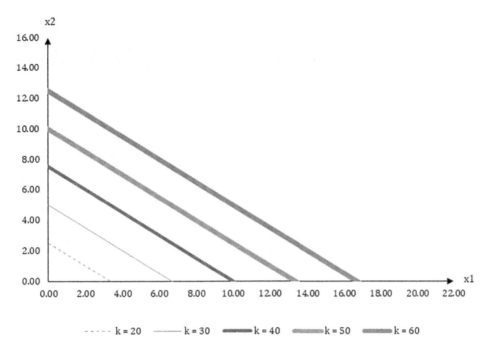

**FIGURE 5.6-5**   Contour map: locus of points $(x_1, x_2)$ where $y = k$ has the same value, from 10 to 60.

From Table 5.6-3 and from Fig. 5.6-6, we notice that the function is a paraboloid with global minimum in zero and with a contour map represented by circumferences. Setting $y = k^2$ and $a = b = 1$, Fig. 5.6-7 depicts the contour lines from the following equations:

$$x_2 = \pm \sqrt{k^2 - x_1^2}$$

**TABLE 5.6-3**   Data Table of the quadratic function with $a = 1$ and $b = 1$ highlight values giving $y = 25$.

| | | x2 | | | | | | | | | | | | |
|---|---|---|---|---|---|---|---|---|---|---|---|---|---|---|
| | | -6.00 | -5.00 | -4.00 | -3.00 | -2.00 | -1.00 | 0.00 | 1.00 | 2.00 | 3.00 | 4.00 | 5.00 | 6.00 |
| | -6.00 | 72.00 | 61.00 | 52.00 | 45.00 | 40.00 | 37.00 | 36.00 | 37.00 | 40.00 | 45.00 | 52.00 | 61.00 | 72.00 |
| | -5.00 | 61.00 | 50.00 | 41.00 | 34.00 | 29.00 | 26.00 | **25.00** | 26.00 | 29.00 | 34.00 | 41.00 | 50.00 | 61.00 |
| | -4.00 | 52.00 | 41.00 | 32.00 | **25.00** | 20.00 | 17.00 | 16.00 | 17.00 | 20.00 | **25.00** | 32.00 | 41.00 | 52.00 |
| | -3.00 | 45.00 | 34.00 | **25.00** | 18.00 | 13.00 | 10.00 | 9.00 | 10.00 | 13.00 | 18.00 | **25.00** | 34.00 | 45.00 |
| | -2.00 | 40.00 | 29.00 | 20.00 | 13.00 | 8.00 | 5.00 | 4.00 | 5.00 | 8.00 | 13.00 | 20.00 | 29.00 | 40.00 |
| x1 | -1.00 | 37.00 | 26.00 | 17.00 | 10.00 | 5.00 | 2.00 | 1.00 | 2.00 | 5.00 | 10.00 | 17.00 | 26.00 | 37.00 |
| | 0.00 | 36.00 | **25.00** | 16.00 | 9.00 | 4.00 | 1.00 | 0.00 | 1.00 | 4.00 | 9.00 | 16.00 | 25.00 | 36.00 |
| | 1.00 | 37.00 | 26.00 | 17.00 | 10.00 | 5.00 | 2.00 | 1.00 | 2.00 | 5.00 | 10.00 | 17.00 | 26.00 | 37.00 |
| | 2.00 | 40.00 | 29.00 | 20.00 | 13.00 | 8.00 | 5.00 | 4.00 | 5.00 | 8.00 | 13.00 | 20.00 | 29.00 | 40.00 |
| | 3.00 | 45.00 | 34.00 | **25.00** | 18.00 | 13.00 | 10.00 | 9.00 | 10.00 | 13.00 | 18.00 | **25.00** | 34.00 | 45.00 |
| | 4.00 | 52.00 | 41.00 | 32.00 | **25.00** | 20.00 | 17.00 | 16.00 | 17.00 | 20.00 | **25.00** | 32.00 | 41.00 | 52.00 |
| | 5.00 | 61.00 | 50.00 | 41.00 | 34.00 | 29.00 | 26.00 | **25.00** | 26.00 | 29.00 | 34.00 | 41.00 | 50.00 | 61.00 |
| | 6.00 | 72.00 | 61.00 | 52.00 | 45.00 | 40.00 | 37.00 | 36.00 | 37.00 | 40.00 | 45.00 | 52.00 | 61.00 | 72.00 |

II. Static optimization

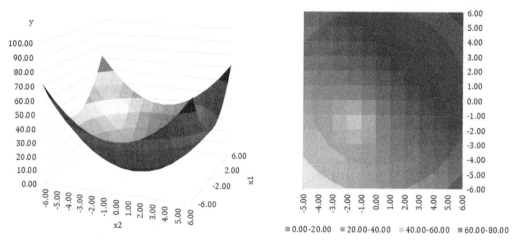

**FIGURE 5.6-6**   Quadratic function and contour map (a = 1 and b = 1).

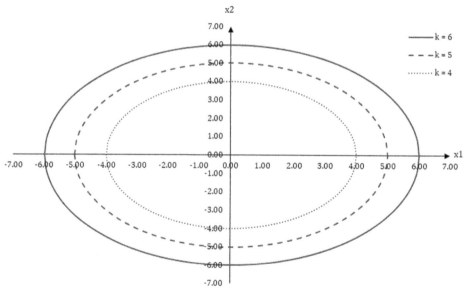

**FIGURE 5.6-7**   Circle contour lines equations $x_2 = \pm\sqrt{k^2 - x_1^2}$.

c. Setting in the quadratic equation $a = 1$, $b = -1$, we have instead following function (Table 5.6-4) (Fig. 5.6-8):

$$y = x_1^2 - x_2^2$$

which leads to a saddle point in zero.

**TABLE 5.6-4** Data Table of the quadratic function with a = 1 and b = −1 highlighting y = (−k, k).

| | | x2 | | | | | | | | | | | | |
|---|---|---|---|---|---|---|---|---|---|---|---|---|---|---|
| | | -6.86 | -5.00 | -4.00 | -3.00 | -2.00 | -1.00 | 0.00 | 1.00 | 2.00 | 3.00 | 4.00 | 5.00 | 6.86 |
| | -6.00 | **-11.00** | **11.00** | 20.00 | 27.00 | 32.00 | 35.00 | 36.00 | 35.00 | 32.00 | 27.00 | 20.00 | **11.00** | **-11.00** |
| | -5.00 | -22.00 | 0.00 | **9.00** | 16.00 | 21.00 | 24.00 | 25.00 | 24.00 | 21.00 | 16.00 | **9.00** | 0.00 | -22.00 |
| | -4.00 | -31.00 | **-9.00** | 0.00 | **7.00** | 12.00 | 15.00 | 16.00 | 15.00 | 12.00 | **7.00** | 0.00 | **-9.00** | -31.00 |
| | -3.00 | -38.00 | -16.00 | **-7.00** | 0.00 | **5.00** | 8.00 | 9.00 | 8.00 | **5.00** | 0.00 | **-7.00** | -16.00 | -38.00 |
| | -2.00 | -43.00 | -21.00 | -12.00 | **-5.00** | 0.00 | **3.00** | 4.00 | **3.00** | 0.00 | **-5.00** | -12.00 | -21.00 | -43.00 |
| x1 | -1.00 | -46.00 | -24.00 | -15.00 | -8.00 | **-3.00** | 0.00 | **1.00** | 0.00 | **-3.00** | -8.00 | -15.00 | -24.00 | -46.00 |
| | 0.00 | -47.00 | -25.00 | -16.00 | -9.00 | -4.00 | **-1.00** | 0.00 | **-1.00** | -4.00 | -9.00 | -16.00 | -25.00 | -47.00 |
| | 1.00 | -46.00 | -24.00 | -15.00 | -8.00 | **-3.00** | 0.00 | **1.00** | 0.00 | **-3.00** | -8.00 | -15.00 | -24.00 | -46.00 |
| | 2.00 | -43.00 | -21.00 | -12.00 | **-5.00** | 0.00 | **3.00** | 4.00 | **3.00** | 0.00 | **-5.00** | -12.00 | -21.00 | -43.00 |
| | 3.00 | -38.00 | -16.00 | **-7.00** | 0.00 | **5.00** | 8.00 | 9.00 | 8.00 | **5.00** | 0.00 | **-7.00** | -16.00 | -38.00 |
| | 4.00 | -31.00 | **-9.00** | 0.00 | **7.00** | 12.00 | 15.00 | 16.00 | 15.00 | 12.00 | **7.00** | 0.00 | **-9.00** | -31.00 |
| | 5.00 | -22.00 | 0.00 | **9.00** | 16.00 | 21.00 | 24.00 | 25.00 | 24.00 | 21.00 | 16.00 | **9.00** | 0.00 | -22.00 |
| | 6.00 | **-11.00** | **11.00** | 20.00 | 27.00 | 32.00 | 35.00 | 36.00 | 35.00 | 32.00 | 27.00 | 20.00 | **11.00** | **-11.00** |

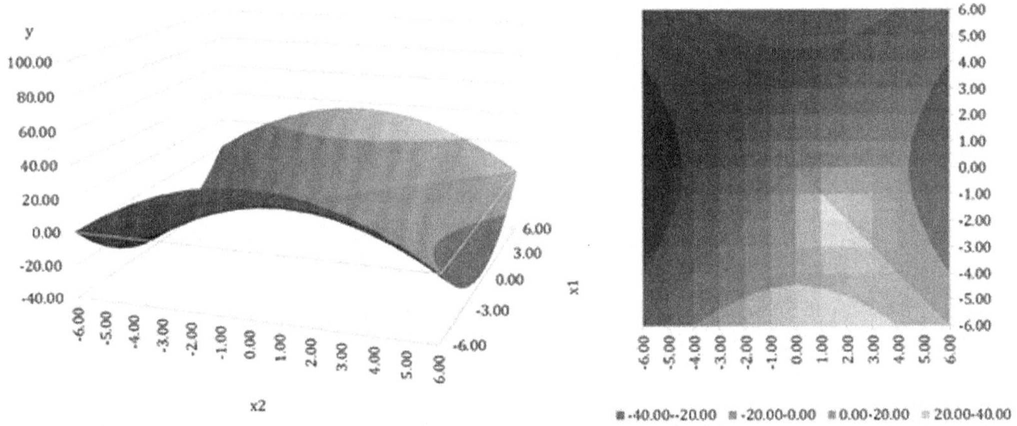


FIGURE 5.6-8 Quadratic function with saddle point and contour map (a = 1 and b = −1).

The contour lines are obtained via the following equations:

$$x_2 = \pm\sqrt{x_1^2 - k}.$$

Using the Data Table functionality, we can build our own hyperbolas, and this is shown in Table 5.6-5 and Fig. 5.6-9. Notice how the contour map plot here is found inverting the horizontal axis with the vertical axis from the Data Table. This is due to the quadratic form of the contour lines equation.

To show this look, in Table 5.6-5, at the first column, beginning with $x_1 = -10.00$ and the second column under the value $k = -11.00$, beginning with $x_2 = 10.54$. The same column values, inverted, appear in the last two columns of the table with the positive value $k = 11$.

**TABLE 5.6-5**   Data Table of the quadratic function with $a = 1$ and $b = -1$ highlighting $y = (-11, 11)$.

| x1 | 4.47 | -11.00 | -9.00 | -7.00 | -5.00 | -3.00 | -1.00 | 4.47 | k (constant levels of y) 11.00 |
|---|---|---|---|---|---|---|---|---|---|
| -10.00 | 10.54 | 10.44 | 10.34 | 10.25 | 10.15 | 10.05 | 10.54 | 10.00 |
| -8.00 | 8.66 | 8.54 | 8.43 | 8.31 | 8.19 | 8.06 | 8.66 | 8.00 |
| -6.00 | 6.86 | 6.71 | 6.56 | 6.40 | 6.24 | 6.08 | 6.86 | 6.00 |
| -4.00 | 5.20 | 5.00 | 4.80 | 4.58 | 4.36 | 4.12 | 5.20 | 4.00 |
| -2.00 | 3.87 | 3.61 | 3.32 | 3.00 | 2.65 | 2.24 | 3.87 | 2.00 |
| 0.00 | 3.32 | 3.00 | 2.65 | 2.24 | 1.73 | 1.00 | 3.32 | 0.00 |
| 2.00 | 3.87 | 3.61 | 3.32 | 3.00 | 2.65 | 2.24 | 3.87 | -2.00 |
| 4.00 | 5.20 | 5.00 | 4.80 | 4.58 | 4.36 | 4.12 | 5.20 | -4.00 |
| 6.00 | 6.86 | 6.71 | 6.56 | 6.40 | 6.24 | 6.08 | 6.86 | -6.00 |
| 8.00 | 8.66 | 8.54 | 8.43 | 8.31 | 8.19 | 8.06 | 8.66 | -8.00 |
| 10.00 | 10.54 | 10.44 | 10.34 | 10.25 | 10.15 | 10.05 | 10.54 | -10.00 |
| 10.00 | -10.54 | -10.44 | -10.34 | -10.25 | -10.15 | -10.05 | -10.54 | -10.00 |
| 8.00 | -8.66 | -8.54 | -8.43 | -8.31 | -8.19 | -8.06 | -8.66 | -8.00 |
| 6.00 | -6.86 | -6.71 | -6.56 | -6.40 | -6.24 | -6.08 | -6.86 | -6.00 |
| 4.00 | -5.20 | -5.00 | -4.80 | -4.58 | -4.36 | -4.12 | -5.20 | -4.00 |
| 2.00 | -3.87 | -3.61 | -3.32 | -3.00 | -2.65 | -2.24 | -3.87 | -2.00 |
| 0.00 | -3.32 | -3.00 | -2.65 | -2.24 | -1.73 | -1.00 | -3.32 | 0.00 |
| -2.00 | -3.87 | -3.61 | -3.32 | -3.00 | -2.65 | -2.24 | -3.87 | 2.00 |
| -4.00 | -5.20 | -5.00 | -4.80 | -4.58 | -4.36 | -4.12 | -5.20 | 4.00 |
| -6.00 | -6.86 | -6.71 | -6.56 | -6.40 | -6.24 | -6.08 | -6.86 | 6.00 |
| -8.00 | -8.66 | -8.54 | -8.43 | -8.31 | -8.19 | -8.06 | -8.66 | 8.00 |
| -10.00 | -10.54 | -10.44 | -10.34 | -10.25 | -10.15 | -10.05 | -10.54 | 10.00 |

The last two columns of Table 5.6-5 give then the hyperbolas in Fig. 5.6-9 of the *quadrants I–IV* and *quadrants II–III* with the solid lines ($k = 11$), while the first two columns give the hyperbolas of the *quadrants I–II* and *quadrants III–IV*, with squared dots ($k = -11$). Repeating this for all possible values we can obtain Fig. 5.6-10.

## EXAMPLE 2 (NONLINEAR PROGRAMMING WITH INEQUALITY CONSTRAINTS)

Let us solve geometrically the following problem:

$$\max_{\{x_1; x_2\}} x_1 + x_2$$

s.t.

$$x_1 + 2x_2 \geq 2$$

$$x_1^2 + x_2^2 \leq 4$$

$$x_1 \geq 0, \; x_2 \geq 0$$

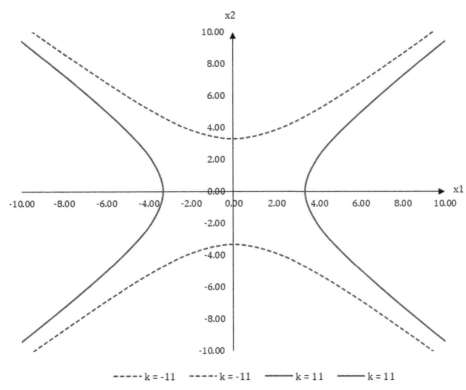

x2

FIGURE 5.6-9 Hyperbolas contour map $k = (-11, 11)$.

The numerical solution is given in Fig. 5.6-11 at the point $\left(x_1^* \cong 1.40; \ x_2^* \cong 1.43\right)$ of tangency between the circumference and the contour line associated to the objective function, such that it is:

$$x_1 + x_2 = 2.83.$$

Essentially, using the Data Table technique, we make the objective function contour straight line increase, for various values of $k$, moving it on the upper right side of the graph till (1) it goes past the first linear constraint and (2) it meets the second circumference constraint. After some trials and errors, we identify the numerical value in $k^* = 2.83$.

Solving analytically the three equations of the problem, for the three variables $x_1, x_2, k$, the exact solution would be instead:

$$x^* = \left(x_1^* = \sqrt{2}; \ x_2^* = \sqrt{2}\right) \text{ and } k^* = 2\sqrt{2}.$$

## EXAMPLE 3 (ECONOMIC POLICY MODEL)

The constrained optimization is also used within the theory of *economic policy*, where different policy instruments have to be implemented in order to reach the economic policy

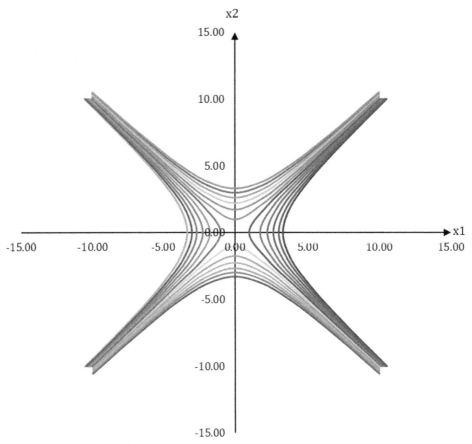

**FIGURE 5.6-10**   Hyperbolas contour map for various values of k.

goals. A typical instrument is the government spending, normally denoted by $G$, while a typical goal is reaching a specific national aggregate income $Y$. A simple economic policy model can be then represented as follows:

$$\min_{\{Y, G\}} V = (Y - Y^*)^2 + g(G - G^*)^2, \qquad g \geq 0$$

s.t.

$$Y = C + I + G$$

$$C = (1 - s)Y$$

where $V$ is the *macroeconomic cost function* that incorporates the deviations from the desired levels of government spending and national income. It quantifies the level of government nonsatisfaction when $Y$, $G$ deviate from their desired levels. $I$ represents the given national

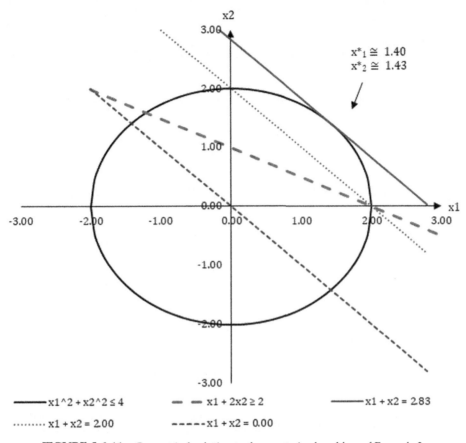

$x*_1 \cong 1.40$
$x*_2 \cong 1.43$

——— x1^2 + x2^2 ≤ 4          — — x1 + 2x2 ≥ 2          ——— x1 + x2 = 2.83

········· x1 + x2 = 2.00          - - - - - x1 + x2 = 0.00

**FIGURE 5.6-11**   Geometrical solution to the constrained problem of Example 2

investments, and it is an exogeneous variable, while $s$ is the marginal propensity to save of the economy. $g$ is the relative cost associated to the deviations in $G$, assuming equal to 1, the one associated to the deviations in $Y$.

From the two constraint equations the cost function becomes:

$$V = \left(\frac{I+G}{s} - Y^*\right)^2 + g(G - G^*)^2.$$

From the first-order condition:

$$\frac{dV}{dG} = 0$$

**TABLE 5.6-6**  Economic policy model data.

| I | G* | Y* | s | g |
|------|------|------|------|------|
| 2.00 | 5.00 | 5.00 | 0.50 | 1.00 |

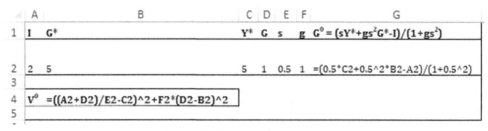

**FIGURE 5.6-12**   Excel model.

we obtain the minimizing value we have to assign to the instrument $G$, as a function of the desired levels of $(Y^*, G^*)$ as:

$$G^0 = \frac{sY^* + gs^2G^* - I}{1 + gs^2}.$$

As an example, let us use the data in Table 5.6-6: we will use then the Solver to find the optimal solution to this quadratic programming problem.

The data and the objective function are organized as described in Fig. 5.6-12.

After launching the Solver, minimizing *Cell B*4 by changing *Cell D*2 we obtain the solution in Table 5.6-7.

Fig. 5.6-13 represents the geometrical solution where three circumferences have been drawn, of which just the one corresponding to the value of $V^0 = 16.20$ minimizes the cost function, as well as satisfying the given constraint.

**TABLE 5.6-7**  Economic policy model solution $G^0 = 1.40$ and $V^0 = 16.20$

| I | G* | Y* | G | s | g | $G^0 = (sY^* + gs^2 G^* - I)/(1 + gs^2)$ |
|------|------|------|------|------|------|------|
| 2.00 | 5.00 | 5.00 | 1.40 | 0.50 | 1.00 | 1.40 |

| $V^0$ | 16.20 |
|------|------|

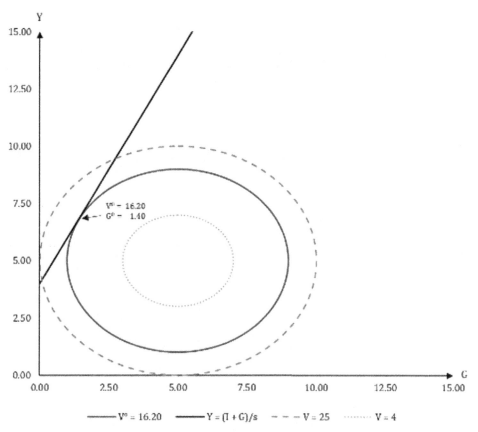

FIGURE 5.6-13    Geometrical solution of the economic policy model.

## 5.7 Nonlinear problems with inequality constraints

A more general form of problem 5.5-1 is given by the following, where the equality constraints have been replaced by the weak inequality constraints.

$$\min_{\{x_1, x_2, \cdots, x_n\}} (or \ \max) f(x_1, x_2, \cdots, x_n) \qquad (5.7\text{-}1)$$

$$s.t.$$

$$g_1(x_1, x_2, \cdots, x_n) \le c_1$$

$$g_2(x_1, x_2, \cdots, x_n) \le c_2$$

$$\cdots$$

$$g_m(x_1, x_2, \cdots, x_n) \le c_m$$

The first-order conditions that apply to the 5.7-1 are of paramount importance in the nonlinear programming theory, and they are called **Kuhn–Tucker** (or **Karush–Kuhn–Tucker**) **necessary conditions**, which, for an optimal point $(x^*, \lambda^*)$, in case of a maximum, are formally stated as:

$$\frac{\partial \mathscr{L}(x^*, \lambda^*)}{\partial x_j} \le 0 \quad \forall\, j$$

$$x_j^* \frac{\partial \mathscr{L}(x^*, \lambda^*)}{\partial x_j} = 0 \quad \forall\, j \quad \text{and} \quad x_j^* \ge 0$$

$$\frac{\partial \mathscr{L}(x^*, \lambda^*)}{\partial \lambda_i} \ge 0 \quad \forall\, i \tag{5.7-2}$$

$$\lambda_i^* \frac{\partial \mathscr{L}(x^*, \lambda^*)}{\partial \lambda_i} = 0 \quad \forall\, i \quad \text{and} \quad \lambda_i^* \ge 0$$

while for a minimum they become:

$$\frac{\partial \mathscr{L}(x^*, \lambda^*)}{\partial x_j} \ge 0 \quad \forall\, j$$

$$x_j^* \frac{\partial \mathscr{L}(x^*, \lambda^*)}{\partial x_j} = 0 \quad \forall\, j \quad \text{and} \quad x_j^* \ge 0$$

$$\frac{\partial \mathscr{L}(x^*, \lambda^*)}{\partial \lambda_i} \le 0 \quad \forall\, i \tag{5.7-3}$$

$$\lambda_i^* \frac{\partial \mathscr{L}(x^*, \lambda^*)}{\partial \lambda_i} = 0 \quad \forall\, i \quad \text{and} \quad \lambda_i^* \ge 0$$

The **sufficiency conditions** instead aim, in this case, at verifying the concavity (convexity) in the objective function $f(x)$, as well as convexity (concavity) in the constraint functions $g_i$, for an optimal point to be a maximum (or a minimum).

Our aim is not to solve problem 5.7-1 going through all the steps of the Kuhn–Tucker necessary and sufficient conditions, but rather to show that the Excel Solver can also deal with this type of situation.

Let us see the following example of a sales-maximizing firm (vs. profit-maximizing), such that the profit $\pi$ does not fall below a certain minimum threshold $\pi_0$.

## EXAMPLE 1 (SALES-MAXIMIZING FIRM VS. PROFIT-MAXIMIZING FIRM)

For a sales-maximizing firm the problem is formalized as:

$$\max_{\{Q\}} R(Q)$$

s.t.

$$R(Q) - C(Q) \geq \pi_0 \quad Q \geq 0 \text{ and } \pi_0 > 0$$

Let the following be the revenue function $R(Q)$ and the cost function $C(Q)$:

$$R = 32Q - Q^2$$

$$C = Q^2 + 8Q + 4.$$

Let the minimum profit be $\pi_0 = 18$, so that the problem is:

$$\max_{\{Q\}} 32Q - Q^2$$

s.t.

$$\left[32Q - Q^2\right] - \left[Q^2 + 8Q + 4\right] \geq 18 \quad Q \geq 0 \text{ and } \pi_0 > 0$$

The solution of the problem via the GRG Solver is enumerated in Table 5.7-1, where the optimal solution is $Q^* = 11$.

For the profit-maximizing firm, instead, the solution (implying the marginalist rule $R' = C'$) would be $Q^* = 6$ (Table 5.7-2).

**TABLE 5.7-1** Sales-maximizing firm.

| R(Q) | C(Q) | $\pi_0$ | Q* |
|------|------|---------|-----|
| 231 | 213 | 18 | 11 |
| | | | |
| Max R(Q) | 231 | | |
| | | | |
| s.t. | | | |
| R - Q ≥ 18 | 18 | | |

**TABLE 5.7-2**   Profit-maximizing firm.

| R(Q) | C(Q) | $\pi_0$ | Q* |
|------|------|---------|-----|
| 156  | 88   | 18      | 6  |
| | | | |
| Max R(Q) - C(Q) | 68 | | |
| | | | |
| s.t. | | | |
| R - Q ≥ 18 | 68 | | |

## Exercises

1. Enumerate in Excel the following univariate functions and study the concavity, convexity. Find the critical points and assess whether they are maxima or minima. Find then the exact minima or maxima of the function using the Solver. Using the numerical second derivative also find the inflexion points. Plot each function together with its first and second derivatives.

$$y = \frac{(x^2 - 5x + 6)}{(x - 1)^2}$$

$$y = x^3 + 0.13x^2 - 0.0005x - 0.0009$$

$$y = x^3$$

2. Using the technique of the graphical tangent, via the Excel Data Table shown in the Example 3 find, using the Solver, the exact minima or maxima of the following univariate functions and visualize the tangent equation on the chart at the critical points:

$$y = x^2 + x^3$$

$$y = \left(4x^2 + 15x\right)e^{-x}$$

$$y = \frac{(x - 1)(x - 6)^2}{x}$$

3. Bivariate functions nonlinear optimization. Find the critical points of the following functions ad assess whether they are minima, maxima, or saddle points, studying the sign definiteness of the Hessian matrix. Plot the surface charts using the Excel Data

Table. Enumerate also the partial derivatives in Excel and visualize them in a chart, together with their equations obtained using the chart trendline.

$$f(x_1, x_2) = x_1^2 + x_2^2$$

$$f(x_1, x_2) = -x_1^2 - x_2^2$$

$$f(x_1, x_2) = x_1^2 - x_2^2$$

$$f(x_1, x_2) = 3x_1^2 + 4x_2^2 - x_1x_2 - 5x_1 - 8x_2$$

$$f(x_1, x_2) = 32 - 8x_1 - 16x_2 + x_1^2 + 4x_2^2$$

$$f(x_1, x_2) = x_1^2 + 2x_2$$

4. Construct in Excel the circle contour lines for various levels of $f$ for the following function:

$$f(x_1, x_2) = x_1^2 + x_2^2$$

5. Using the Solver find the solution to the following nonlinear constrained optimization problem:

$$\min_{\{x_1, x_2, x_3\}} x_1^2 - 2x_1x_2 + x_2^2 + 5x_3^2$$

s.t.

$$x_1 + x_2 + 2x_3 = 10.$$

6. Using the Solver find the solution to the following nonlinear constrained optimization problem:

$$\max_{\{x_1, x_2, x_3\}} x_1^2 + x_2^2 + x_3^2$$

s.t.

$$x_1^2 - x_1x_2 + x_2^2 - x_3^2 = 1$$

$$x_1^2 + x_2^2 = 1$$

7. Using the Solver find the solution to the following nonlinear constrained optimization problem:

$$\min_{\{x_1,x_2,x_3\}} 5x_1 + 2x_2 - x_3$$

s.t.

$$x_1 x_2 = 3$$

$$x_1 x_3 = 1$$

8. Using the Solver find the solution to the following nonlinear constrained optimization problem:

$$\min_{\{x_1,x_2,x_3\}} x_1^2 + x_2^2 + x_3^2$$

s.t.

$$x_1 + x_2 + 2x_3 = 10$$

9. Using the Solver find the solution to the following nonlinear constrained optimization problem:

$$\min_{\{x_1,x_2\}} x_1^2 + 4x_2^2 - 8x_1 - 16x_2 + 32$$

s.t.

$$x_1 + x_2 \leq 5$$

$$x_1, x_2 \geq 0$$

10. Using the graphical approach in Excel solve the following nonlinear optimization constrained problem:

$$\min_{\{x_1,x_2\}} (x_1 - 4)^2 + (x_2 - 4)^2$$

s.t.

$$2x_1 + 3x_2 \geq 6$$

$$-3x_1 - 2x_2 \geq -12$$

$$x_1, x_2 \geq 0$$

11. Using the graphical approach in Excel solve the following nonlinear optimization constrained problem:

$$\min_{\{x_1, x_2\}} x_1^2 + x_2^2$$

s.t.

$$x_1 x_2 \geq 25$$

$$x_1, x_2 \geq 0$$

12. Steepest descent. Using the numerical steepest descent technique and the VBA macro shown in the chapter, find the critical points of the following functions:

$$f(x_1, x_2) = 32 - 8x_1 - 16x_2 + x_1^2 + 4x_2^2$$

$$f(x_1) = 3x_1^4 - 4x_1^3$$

The following set of problems shows the typical applications of the nonlinear optimization to some production problems.

13. Output cost minimization problem. A company has the following total cost function for the production of two items:

$$C(q_1, q_2) = q_1^2 + q_2^2 - 10q_1 - 12q_2 + 151.$$

Find the optimal quantities to produce to minimize the total cost function.

14. Output Profit Maximization problem. A company shows the following total cost function:

$$C(q) = 12,000 + 500q - q^2$$

The sale price depends on the quantities sold according to the following equation:

$$p = 700 - 1.5q$$

Identify the objective function profit

$$\Pi = Pq - C(q)$$

and find the optimal quantity to produce in order to maximize the profit.

15. Output Profit Maximization problem. A company wishes to find the optimal program for a production of a product in order to maximize its profit (i.e., the objective function). The total cost function has been estimated as follows:

$$C(q) = 30,000 + 600q - 0.5q^2$$

while the demand faced by the company for this product is as follows:

$$p = 900 - 0.6q$$

(the company estimated this demand law using econometric techniques).
Find the optimal quantity to produce in order to maximize the profit:

$$\pi = pq - C(q) = (900 - 0.6q)q - (30,000 + 600q - 0.5q^2)$$

Assume $q \leq 1000$ (we cannot produce more than 1000 quantities).
Use the tangent technique built with the Excel Data Table and the Solver. Plot the profit function and visualize the tangent at the maximum point.

16. Output Profit Maximization problem. A company produces monthly a certain number of products of one type, which are sold at a unit price of £ 800. The monthly fixed cost is £ 180,000 and the unit production variable cost is £ 50. The company also faces selling costs equal to half products sold (e.g., for 10 products, selling costs equal to £ 5). Find the optimal quantity to produce in a month in order to maximize the objective function:

$$\pi = 800q - \left(180,000 + 50q + \frac{q}{2}q\right)$$

Use the tangent technique built with the Excel Data Table and the Solver. Plot the profit function and visualize the tangent at the maximum point.

17. Output Profit Maximization Problem. A printing company faces the following total cost function:

$$C(q) = 900 + 400q - q^2$$

where $q^2$ denotes the volume savings.
The income due to the advertisement is instead as follows:

$$I(q) = 600q - 6q^2.$$

Sales is £ 600 per advertisement to which we subtract $6q^2$ for diminishing returns. The profit function is therefore:

$$\pi = (600q - 6q^2) - (900 + 400q - q^2)$$

Find the optimal quantity that maximizes the profit. Use the tangent technique built with the Excel Data Table and the Solver. Plot the profit function and visualize the tangent at the maximum point.

**18.** Inventory and optimal procurement policy (deterministic single item inventory model). A company employs a certain raw material whose consumption in the production cycle is constant over time and it wishes to find the optimal policy of procurement. We have the following information:

- Consumption rate of raw material: 150 tons/day (54,000 tons/year).
- Fixed cost for each order: £ 60,000.
- Inventory carrying cost: £ 2/day.

Now, the number of orders in a year is then found as:

$$\frac{54,000}{Q}.$$

Assuming on every day we have stock, the average quantity is:

$$\frac{Q}{2}$$

The total cost of orders in a year is equal to:

$$60,000 \cdot \frac{54,000}{Q}$$

while total inventory carrying cost is equal to (days in a year 360):

$$2 \cdot \frac{q}{2} \cdot 360.$$

The objective function you are required to minimize with respect to $q$ in Excel is therefore:

$$C(Q) = 360 \cdot \left( \frac{9Mln}{Q} + Q \right)$$

Use the tangent technique built with the Excel Data Table and the Solver. Plot the cost function and visualize the tangent at the minimum point.

## 6.1  The consumer problem: cardinal versus ordinal utility approach

The consumer problem is a particular case of the general scope of the theory of economics.

Given a commodity bundle $(x) = (x_1, x_2,..., x_n)$, where $x_i \geq 0$ is the quantity of the $i$th commodity, and a commodity price vector $(p) = (p_1, p_2,..., p_n)$, the consumer problem consists of formalizing the conditions under which to find the optimal combination of quantities $x_i$ the consumer will have to purchase, to have the maximum utility $U(x)$, considering the money income available (*budget constraint*). The standard consumer problem theory departed from two main approaches of the *neoclassical* (or *marginalism*) theory of microeconomics.

### Cardinal utility

The *cardinal utility approach*, developed by the *subjectivist school* in the late 19th century and beginning of 20th century, is due to the works of economists like Gossen, Jevons, Menger, Wieser, Marshall, and Walras; the main concept is that the consumer utility can be measured in monetary units. According to this approach, we can postulate a mathematical function $U = U(x_i)$ which associates to each quantity $x_i$ of a good *utility measure* $U(x_i)$, which represents the cardinal degree of satisfaction that the consumer derives from consuming $x_i$ quantities of good $i$. Going back in history, this problem was also investigated in some works by Daniel Bernoulli, from which the standard logarithmic utility function $U(x) = \log(x)$ has been derived. Besides the concept of total utility, the cardinal approach also postulates the existence of its derivative $U'(x) = \frac{dU}{dx}$ called *marginal utility*, which represents the additional utility received from the consumption of an additional unit of good. Another important assumption of this school is that, in the context of consumption of many goods, the total utility is separable, which means that it is just the sum of the separate utilities of the goods $x_i$ comprising the *commodity bundle* $x$:

$$U(x) = U(x_1) + U(x_2) + \cdots + U(x_n).$$

## Ordinal utility

Economists like Pareto, Slutsky, Hicks, and Allen disagreed with the cardinal utility approach and developed a different theory, the *ordinal utility approach*, according to which the utility is not measured in quantitative cardinal terms, but it can only be expressed on an *ordinal scale* basis. This implies that a consumer is only able to express *preferences* or *indifferences* among the various goods. The key concept around which this theory is developed is the *indifference map*: *the locus of points showing different combinations of two goods providing equal utility to the consumer*. The *ordinal utility* will work instead as an ordinal mapping that must preserve the order of the preferences expressed by the consumer, rather than dealing with the quantitative differences of utilities derived from different goods. Then, if we decide to use $u$ as an index of ordinal utility, it must follow that:

$$u(x) > u(y) \text{ if and only if } xPy$$

$$u(x) = u(y) \text{ if and only if } xIy$$

where $P$ means *preferred to* and $I$ means *indifferent to*. There will be infinite utility functions satisfying the relations $P$ and $I$ and each utility function will be a monotonic transformation of another, that is to say, if $u$ satisfies the relations $P$ and $I$, then also $\bar{u} = \phi(u)$ can be taken as ordinal utility, as long as the function $\phi$ is a strictly increasing monotonic function.

## 6.2 Consumer optimization and derivation of the demand curve in the cardinal approach

The cardinal utility approach, to set the theory of the consumer equilibrium, postulates the so-called **law of diminishing marginal utility** which states that *as the rate of consumption increases, the marginal utility derived from consuming additional units of a good will decline as well.* This principle is directly derived from the *Gossen's first law*, which always implies $U''(x) = \frac{d^2U}{dx^2} < 0$. Using the Alfred Marshall's *Principles of Economics* words, it is stated as "the additional benefit which a person derives from a given increase of his stock of a thing, diminishes with every increase in the stock that he already has" *(see Principles, p. 79)*.

A list of Excel-based charts of the most used utility functions, together with their decreasing marginal utilities is given below.

- Exponential: $U(x) = k\left\{1 - e^{-\frac{k}{x}}\right\}$ with $x \geq 0$, $k > 0$ (see Fig. 6.2-1)

In a context of consumption of many goods, in the cardinal utility approach the *consumer equilibrium* is found according to a second principle, which is the **principle of equi-marginal utility** which is expressed as follows:

$$\frac{U'(x_1)}{p_1} = \frac{U'(x_2)}{p_2} = \cdots = \frac{U'(x_i)}{p_i} = \cdots = \frac{U'(x_n)}{p_n} = U'(M)$$

- Logarithmic (Bernoulli): $U(x) = \log(x) \ \forall \ x > 0$ (see Fig. 6.2-2 and Section 4.2)
- Quadratic: $U(x) = x - kx^2$ $\qquad\qquad \forall \ x \leq \frac{1}{2k}$ (see Fig. 6.2-3)
- Squared Root (Cramer): $U(x) = \sqrt{x}$ $\qquad \forall \ x \geq 0$ (see Fig. 6.2-4)
- Constant Relative Risk Aversion (CRRA): $\frac{x^{1-\gamma}-1}{1-\gamma}$, $\forall \ x \geq 0$, $\gamma > 0$, $\gamma \neq 1$; $\lim\limits_{\gamma \to 1}[\text{CRRA}] = (\log(x)$ see Fig. 6.2-5).

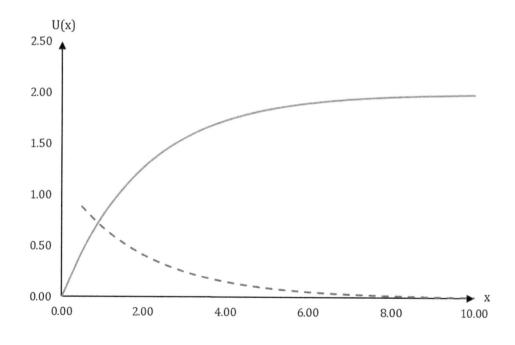

$$-\,-\,-\ U'(x) \qquad \longrightarrow U(x)$$

**FIGURE 6.2-1**   Exponential utility function with $k = 2$.

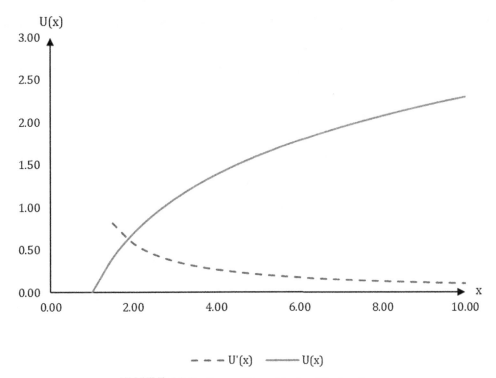

FIGURE 6.2-2    Bernoulli logarithmic utility function.

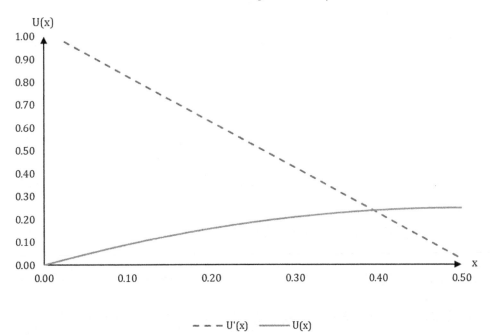

FIGURE 6.2-3    Quadratic utility with $k = 1$.

II. Static optimization

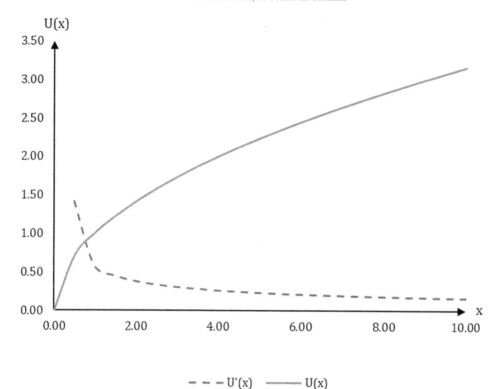

$$-\,-\,-\;U'(x) \quad\quad \text{——} \;U(x)$$

**FIGURE 6.2-4**   Cramer's squared root utility function.

where $U'(M)$ = marginal utility of money and $p_i$ = price of good $i$ and from which we derive the following $(n-1)$ equations:

$$\frac{p_2}{p_1}=\frac{U'(x_2)}{U'(x_1)}; \cdots ; \frac{p_i}{p_{i-1}}=\frac{U'(x_i)}{U'(x_{i-1})}; \cdots ; \frac{p_n}{p_{n-1}}=\frac{U'(x_n)}{U'(x_{n-1})}.$$

The principle of equi-marginal utility states that the consumer, to be in equilibrium, must choose the various goods such that the utility obtained from spending a unit more of money in an additional unit of good is the same for all the goods.

The marginal utility of money represents a subtle economic concept and it measures the quantity of money that a consumer will be able to forgo to obtain the utility for the additional unit of good purchased. It serves, according to Marshall, as a constant index to measure the increment of utility derived from the consumption of goods.

The ratio $\frac{U'(x_i)}{p_i}$ represents the utility of the good compared to its price (the weighted consumer benefit). Put it differently, this ratio can be seen as the ratio between the *use value* and *exchange value* of a good. Essentially, when purchasing a good the consumer is always confronted with four variables. (1) How much money one wants to allocate to a good; (2) Utility exploitable from that good; (3) Price of the good ("is it worth for its use value?"); (4) Money available.

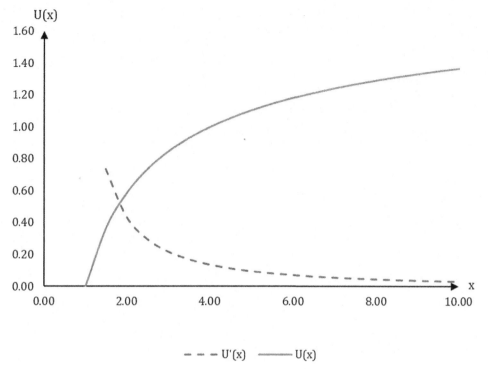

FIGURE 6.2-5   Constant relative risk aversion utility function with $\gamma = 1.50$.

The consumer optimization problem, under the cardinal approach, assuming the additive property of utility function, can be then formalized in the following problem 6.2-1:

$$
\begin{cases}
\displaystyle \max_{\{x\}} U(x) = \max_{\{x_i\}} \sum_{i=1}^{n} U(x_i) \\[2ex]
\displaystyle s.t. \ \frac{p_i}{p_{i-1}} = \frac{U'(x_i)}{U'(x_{i-1})} \qquad \text{for } i = 2, \cdots, n \\[2ex]
\displaystyle \text{and } s.t. \sum_{i=1}^{n} p_i x_i = m \qquad \text{with } x_i \geq 0
\end{cases}
\qquad (6.2\text{-}1)
$$

where, together with the $(n-1)$ equations constraints of equi-marginal utility, we also have the $n$th equation $\sum p_i x_i = m$ representing the budget constraint, expenditures = money available. Let us see now how this problem can be modeled end solved in Excel with a simple example.

## EXAMPLE 1 (CONSUMER OPTIMIZATION IN THE CARDINAL UTILITY APPROACH)

Let us suppose we have $n = 5$, with the vector of prices specified as $p_1 = 5$, $p_2 = 3$, $p_3 = 2$, $p_4 = 4$, $p_5 = 10$.

The maximization problem can be solved resorting to the Lagrange multipliers technique, and therefore the Excel Solver can be used. The following worksheet can be set up in Excel (Fig. 6.2-6 and Table 6.2-1).

The Solver Parameters have to be set up in such a way that we maximize the sum of total utilities for each good, subject to the fourth equation $\frac{p_i}{p_{i-1}} = \frac{U'(x_i)}{U'(x_{i-1})}$ and the fifth equation of budget constraint. The solution of optimal quantities to demand is found by changing the range A2:E2, where the quantities $x_i$ are stored.

We also flag the nonnegative option of the unconstrained variables. Also, as this is a nonlinear programming problem we use the Generalized Reduced Gradient (GRG) method to optimize (Fig. 6.2-7).

## Demand curve derivation under the cardinal utility approach (using VBA)

To derive the demand curve under the Cardinal Utility framework we need to resort again to the principle of equi-marginal utility equilibrium condition. Let us suppose we have now $n = 2$, so that we have:

$$\frac{U'(x_1)}{p_1} = \frac{U'(x_2)}{p_2} = U'(M) \Rightarrow \frac{p_2}{p_1} = \frac{U'(x_2)}{U'(x_1)},$$

which represents the initial equilibrium situation.

Let us suppose now we have a decrease in $p_1$ so that:

|    | A | B | C | D | E |
|----|---|---|---|---|---|
| 1 | x1 | x2 | x3 | x4 | x5 |
| 2 | 40.0000002988954 | 66.6666672337588 | 100.000000953668 | 50.0000005277934 | 20.0000002285737 |
| 3 | | | | | |
| 4 | p1 | p2 | p3 | p4 | p5 |
| 5 | 5 | 3 | 2 | 4 | 10 |
| 6 | | | | | |
| 7 | | U'(x₁)/p₁ for p₁ = 1, 2, ..., 5 | | | |
| 8 | =1/A2/A5 | =1/B2/B5 | =1/C2/C5 | =1/D2/D5 | =1/E2/E5 |
| 9 | | | | | |
| 10 | | | | Utility Function | U(x) = ln(x) |
| 11 | | | | Marginal Utility | U'(x) = 1/x |
| 12 | | | | | |
| 13 | | pᵢ/Pᵢ₋₁ | | U'(xᵢ)/U'(xᵢ₋₁) | U(xᵢ) = ln(xᵢ) |
| 14 | | =B5/A5 | = | =(1/B2)/(1/A2) | =LN(A2) |
| 15 | n-1 equations: | =C5/B5 | = | =(1/C2)/(1/B2) | =LN(B2) |
| 16 | | =D5/C5 | = | =(1/D2)/(1/C2) | =LN(C2) |
| 17 | | =E5/D5 | = | =(1/E2)/(1/D2) | =LN(D2) |
| 18 | | | | | =LN(E2) |
| 19 | | | | | |
| 20 | | | | Σ U(xᵢ) = | =SUM(E14:E18) |
| 21 | | | | | |
| 22 | nᵗʰ equation: | | | | |
| 23 | Total Expenditure | = | Money available | | |
| 24 | =SUMPRODUCT(A2:E2;A5:E5) | = | 1000 | | |

FIGURE 6.2-6   Example 1: cardinal utility consumer optimization Excel setup.

**TABLE 6.2-1** Example 1: cardinal utility approach consumer optimal solution.

| x1 | x2 | x3 | x4 | x5 |
|---|---|---|---|---|
| 40.0000 | 66.6667 | 100.0000 | 50.0000 | 20.0000 |

| p1 | p2 | p3 | p4 | p5 |
|---|---|---|---|---|
| 5.0000 | 3.0000 | 2.0000 | 4.0000 | 10.0000 |

|  |  | $U'(x_i)/p_i$ for $p_i = 1, 2, ..., 5$ |  |  |
|---|---|---|---|---|
| 0.0050 | 0.0050 | 0.0050 | 0.0050 | 0.0050 |

|  |  |  |  |
|---|---|---|---|
|  |  | Utility Function | $U(x) = \ln(x)$ |
|  |  | Marginal Utility | $U'(x) = 1/x$ |

|  | $p_i/p_{i-1}$ |  | $U'(x_i)/U'(x_{i+1})$ | $U(x_i) = \ln(x_i)$ |
|---|---|---|---|---|
|  | 0.6000 | = | 0.6000 | 3.6889 |
| **n-1 equations:** | 0.6667 | = | 0.6667 | 4.1997 |
|  | 2.0000 | = | 2.0000 | 4.6052 |
|  | 2.5000 | = | 2.5000 | 3.9120 |
|  |  |  |  | 2.9957 |

|  |  |  | $\Sigma U(x_i) =$ | 19.4015 |
|---|---|---|---|---|

| $n^{th}$ **equation:** |  |  |
|---|---|---|
| Total Expenditure | = | Money available |
| **1,000** | = | **1,000** |

$$\frac{U'(x_1)}{p_1} > \frac{U'(x_2)}{p_2} = U'(M).$$

The only way to reach the new equilibrium is that $U'(x_1)$ should decrease as well, to restore the equality $\frac{U'(x_1)}{p_1} = \frac{U'(x_2)}{p_2}$. As $U'(x_1)$ is a decreasing function, when it decreases in value, the quantity $x_1$ will have to increase, therefore proving the *law of demand*, according to which there is an inverse relationship between the price and the quantity demanded of a good. Marshall writes:

> There is then one general law of demand: The greater the amount to be sold, the smaller must be the price at which it is offered in order that it may find purchasers; or, in other words, the amount demanded increases with a fall in price, and diminishes with a rise in price (*see Principles, chapter III, p. 84*).

It is worth to notice that this inverse relation (negative slope of demand curve) is always true for the *normal goods*, while it is not valid for the *inferior goods*, like the *Giffen goods*, where

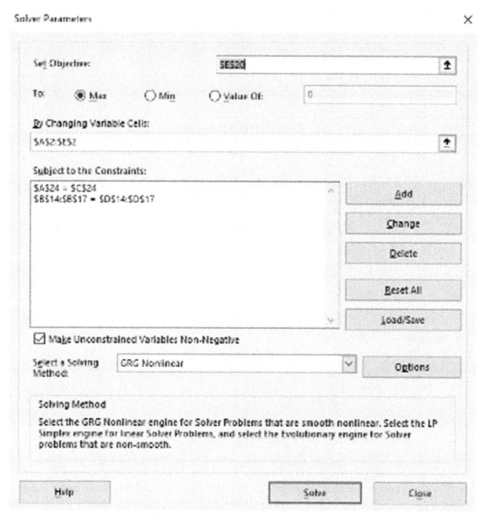

**FIGURE 6.2-7**   Example 1: solver parameters.

there is a positive relation between price and quantity purchased. This is called the *Giffen paradox*.

According to Marshall, however, these cases are rare:

> There are however some exceptions. For instance, as Sir R. Giffen has pointed out, a rise in the price of bread makes so large a drain on the resources of the poorer laboring families and raises so much the marginal utility of money to them, that they are forced to curtail their consumption of meat and the more expensive farinaceous foods: and, bread being still the cheapest food which they can get and will take, they consume more, and not less of it. But such cases are rare. (*see Principles, chapter VI, p. 110*).

Let us go back now to the problem of the computational derivation of the demand curve. In essence, what we need to do is to rerun the Solver optimizer several times, for each simulated price in one good, in order to find the associated schedule of quantities demanded that satisfies the optimization problem 6.2-1. We will perform this using a VBA macro as described in the following example.

## EXAMPLE 2 (DEMAND DERIVATION IN THE CARDINAL APPROACH USING VBA)

Let us consider again $n = 2$ for simplicity and $p_2 = 3$. $p_1$ will be changed from 10 to 0.5 to plot the entire demand schedule, optimizing problem 6.2-1 several times. Therefore, the equality $\frac{p_2}{p_1} = \frac{U'(x_2)}{U'(x_1)}$ must be always satisfied, together with the budget constraint $p_1 x_1 + p_2 x_2 = m$. Furthermore, we set $m = 600$, and we assume a logarithmic utility function. The problem is set up in Excel as in Fig. 6.2-8:

We have arranged the information about the quantities $x_1$ and $x_2$ by row in the *Range A2:B2*, while the information about the prices by column in *Range D1:D2. MMULT* is instead the Excel matrix multiplication function.

We start then changing *Cell D2* with the highest price that $p_1$ can take and therefore the macro will run the solver maximizing *Cell E8* s.t. the two equations constraints (with nonnegative quantities), until *Cell D2* reaches the minimum price that $p_1$ can take (e.g., 0.50). This is done via the VBA code of Fig. 6.2-9/10/11.

The macro just keeps running the Solver, keeping memory of the optimal solution $x_1^*$, together with each correspondent simulated price, under *Columns G and H*, until the price in *Cell D1 = 0.50*. This is done with the part of the macro following the *Do until Range* ("D1") = 0.5.

Before running the macro in the VBA, one should always make sure that the Solver is activated, not only as a standard *Add-in* in Excel from the *Ribbon* menu, but also under *References*, within the VBA application tool (Fig. 6.2-12). This is because the Solver is to be run within the VBA. The steps are described as follows:

**1** Go to your VBA from the Ribbon menu (Fig. 6.2-13)
**2** Go to tools and references (Fig 6.2-14)
**3** Search Solver in the References dialog box and flag it (Fig. 6.2-15).

| | A | B | C | D | E |
|---|---|---|---|---|---|
| 1 | x1 | x2 | Start changing p1 (e.g. 10) and then run solver | 10 | |
| 2 | 599.999977898214 | 100.0000031 | p2 | 3 | |
| 3 | | | | | |
| 4 | | | | | |
| 5 | p2/p1 | | U'(x2)/U'(x1) | | U(x̦) = ln(x̦) |
| 6 | =D2/D1 | = | =(1/B2)/(1/A2) | | =LN(A2) |
| 7 | Total Expenditure | = | Money Available | | =LN(B2) |
| 8 | =MMULT(A2:B2;D1:D2) | = | 600 | | =SUM(E6:E7) |

FIGURE 6.2-8   Example 1: Excel setup for curve derivation.

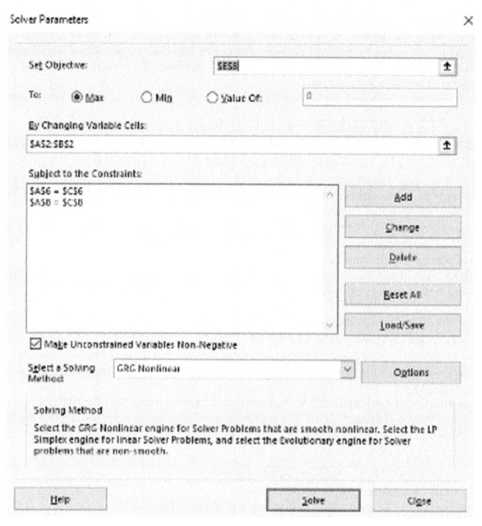

**FIGURE 6.2-9**  Example 2: Solver set-up.

Table 6.2-2 gives the Demand Schedule for $x_1^*$ for each price from 10 to 0.5, and the demand elasticity is also derived at each point simply as (see the demand schedule in Fig. 6.2-16):

$$\varepsilon = \frac{\%\ variation\ in\ quantity}{\%\ variation\ in\ price} = \frac{\Delta x_1 / x_1}{\Delta p_1 / p_1}.$$

```
Sub demand_derivation_cardinal()

' Clear content old results

Range("G2:H2").Select
Range(Selection, Selection.End(xlDown)).Select
Selection.ClearContents

Range("A2") = 10
Range("B2") = 10

' Run 1st iteration Solver with constraints

SolverOk SetCell:="$E$8", MaxMinVal:=1, ValueOf:=0, ByChange:="$A$2:$B$2", _
Engine:=1, EngineDesc:="GRG Nonlinear"
SolverSolve UserFinish:=True

    ' Copying price

    Range("D1").Copy
    Range("G1").Select

    Do Until ActiveCell = ""

  ActiveCell.Offset(1, 0).Select

 Loop

    ActiveCell.Offset(0, 0).PasteSpecial xlPasteValues
    Application.CutCopyMode = False
```

FIGURE 6.2-10   Example 2: Solver run within a VBA macro (part I).

## 6.3 Consumer optimization and derivation of the demand curve in the ordinal approach

Let us turn now the attention to the second fundamental approach to the consumer theory, namely the *ordinal utility* approach.

The main concept to which the ordinal approach resorts, to solve the consumer problem, is the indifference curve (see Vilfredo Pareto, *Manual of Political Economy*, Appendix) which is defined as the locus of points showing different combinations of two goods providing equal utility to the consumer.

The indifference curves have some basic properties that serve to find the consumer equilibrium:

- they have downward (negative) slope to the right;
- convexity to the origin;
- they cannot intersect each other.
- higher curves represent greater level of total utility;
- the curves are everywhere dense (we can draw an indifference curve through any point on the diagram).

```
' Copying quantity

Range("A2").Copy
Range("H1").Select

  Do Until ActiveCell = ""
  ActiveCell.Offset(1, 0).Select
  Loop

    ActiveCell.Offset(0, 0).PasteSpecial xlPasteValues
    Application.CutCopyMode = False


' Run the other iterative solver adding the constraint until quantity = 0.5

Do Until Range("D1") = 0.5

  Range("D1").Value = Range("D1").Value - 0.5

  SolverOk SetCell:="$F$8", MaxMinVal:=1, ValueOf:=0, ByChange:="$A$2:$B$2", _
  Engine:=1, EngineDesc:="GRG Nonlinear"

    SolverAdd CellRef:="$A$6", Relation:=2, FormulaText:="$C$6"
    SolverAdd CellRef:="$A$8", Relation:=2, FormulaText:="$C$8"

    ' Delete constraint from solver to reinitialize macro

    SolverDelete CellRef:="$A$6", Relation:=2, FormulaText:="$C$6"
    SolverDelete CellRef:="$A$8", Relation:=2, FormulaText:="$C$8"

SolverSolve UserFinish:=True
```

FIGURE 6.2-11    Example 2: Solver run within a VBA macro (part II).


How can we derive mathematically an indifference curve? These are simply represented by the contour lines map of a multidimensional surface of the ordinal utility function $U(x) = U(x_1, x_2,..., x_n)$.

An ordinal utility function, concept introduced by Pareto, is a function representing the preferences of the consumer on an ordinal basis, rather than on a cardinal-quantitative basis. According to this school, the study of the rational consumer behavior essentially implies that we know how the consumer orders the various commodities in terms of preferences.

A set of *preferences axioms,* from which the properties of the indifference curve derive, will then guarantee the existence of an ordinal utility function on a commodity-bundle space:

- monotonicity (or nonsatiety)
- continuity
- convexity

Then, in the ordinal utility approach the consumer problem can be formalized as the following constrained maximization problem:

$$\begin{cases} \max_{\{x_i\}} U(x_1, x_2, \cdots, x_n) \\ s.t. \ \sum_{i=1}^{n} p_i x_i = m \quad \text{with } x_i \geq 0. \end{cases} \qquad (6.3\text{-}1)$$

```
' Copying price

Range("D1").Copy
Range("G1").Select

  Do Until ActiveCell = ""
  ActiveCell.Offset(1, 0).Select
   Loop

     ActiveCell.Offset(0, 0).PasteSpecial xlPasteValues
     Application.CutCopyMode = False

 'Copying quantity

Range("A2").Copy
Range("H1").Select

  Do Until ActiveCell = ""
  ActiveCell.Offset(1, 0).Select
  Loop

     ActiveCell.Offset(0, 0).PasteSpecial xlPasteValues
     Application.CutCopyMode = False

  Loop


End Sub
```

FIGURE 6.2-12    Example 2: solver run within a VBA macro (part III).

The assumption behind the budget constraint is that the whole wealth available is to be utilized. It comes from the *nonsatiety* postulate according to which the consumer can always increase the level of utility, purchasing more of a commodity until the budget constraint is satisfied.

The maximization problem 6.3-1 is a typical nonlinear constraint problem that can be solved either via the Lagrange multipliers or geometrically via the iso-curves method. Both methods lead to the same solution.

Let us suppose now we have two commodities. The budget constraint becomes:

$$p_1 x_1 + p_2 x_2 = m.$$

Setting $x_2$ as dependent variable and $x_1$ as independent variable, we can then plot on a Cartesian system the budget constraint as the following locus of points, as a straight line with negative slope:

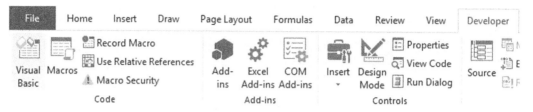

FIGURE 6.2-13   The recall of the solver in VBA (Step 1).

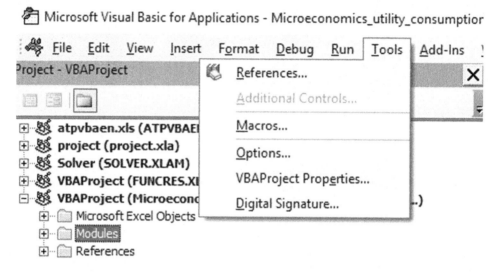

FIGURE 6.2-14   The recall of the solver in VBA (Step 2).

$$x_2 = \frac{m}{p_2} - \frac{p_1}{p_2}x_1.$$

Equivalently, let us suppose we know the form of the three-dimensional ordinal utility function $U(x) = U(x_1, x_2)$, representing the consumer preferences over the commodity bundle $x=(x_1, x_2)$.

The consumer problem 6.3-1 is solved geometrically at the point where the slope of budget line is equal to the slope of the maximum attainable indifference curve. In mathematical terms, the following equality must result:

$$\left|\frac{dx_2}{dx_1}\right| = \frac{p_1}{p_2}.$$

The absolute quantity on the left is called *Marginal Rate of Substitution (MRS)* which is the rate at which the commodity 2 is substituted for an additional quantity of the commodity 1 maintaining the same level of utility. In formal terms, it is the derivative (slope) of the function expressed by the indifference curve.

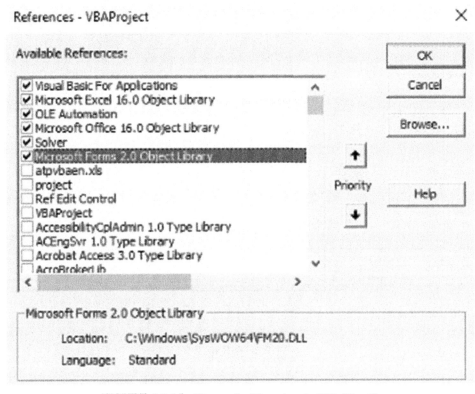

FIGURE 6.2-15    The recall of the solver in VBA (Step 3).

**TABLE 6.2-2**    Demand Schedule for ×1 by changing p1 from 10 to 0.50; $m = 600$ and log utility function.

| x1 | x2 | Start changing p1 (e.g. 10) and then run solver | 0.50 | | Demand curve p1 = f(x1) for x1 --> | x1* with solver | Demand Elasticity = % Var q/ % Var p |
|---|---|---|---|---|---|---|---|
| 600.00 | 100.00 | p2 | 3.00 | | 10.00 | 30.00 | |
| | | | | | 9.50 | 31.58 | 1.05 |
| | | | | | 9.00 | 33.33 | 1.06 |
| p2/p1 | | U'(x2)/U'(x1) | | U(x₁) = ln(x₁) | 8.50 | 35.29 | 1.06 |
| 6.00 | = | 6.00 | | 6.3969 | 8.00 | 37.50 | 1.06 |
| Total Expenditure | = | Money Available | | 4.6052 | 7.50 | 40.00 | 1.07 |
| 600.00 | = | 600.00 | | 11.0021 | 7.00 | 42.86 | 1.07 |
| | | | | | 6.50 | 46.15 | 1.08 |
| | | | | | 6.00 | 50.00 | 1.08 |
| | | The macro runs the Solver s.t constraints above | | | 5.50 | 54.55 | 1.09 |
| | | for each level of price p1 to determine the quantity x1 | | | 5.00 | 60.00 | 1.10 |
| | | and then the individual consumer demand curve is found. | | | 4.50 | 66.67 | 1.11 |
| | | | | | 4.00 | 75.00 | 1.13 |
| | | In the cardinal approach equi-marginal utility situation | | | 3.50 | 85.71 | 1.14 |
| | | must be reached by the consumer. | | | 3.00 | 100.00 | 1.17 |
| | | | | | 2.50 | 120.00 | 1.20 |
| | | The consumer is in equilibrium position when marginal utility of | | | 2.00 | 150.00 | 1.25 |
| | | money expenditure on each good is the same. | | | 1.50 | 200.00 | 1.33 |
| | | | | | 1.00 | 300.00 | 1.50 |
| | | The marginal utility of money expenditure on a good is equal to | | | 0.50 | 600.00 | 2.00 |
| | | the ratio of marginal utility of a good and the price of that good, namely the ratio U'(x₁)/p₁ | | | | | |
| | | | | | | | |
| | | In equilibrium must be (together with income equation) | | | | | |
| | | U'(x1)/p1        = U'(x2)/p2        = ... U'(xi)/pi | | | | | |

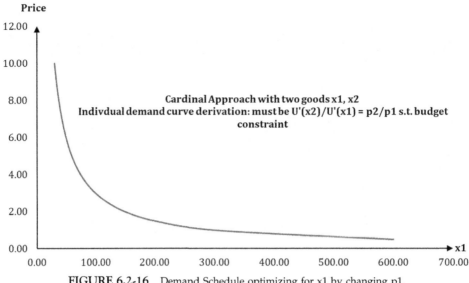

**FIGURE 6.2-16**   Demand Schedule optimizing for x1 by changing p1.

We can define it as:

$$\left|\frac{dx_2}{dx_1}\right| = MRS_{1,2.}$$

In the ordinal utility approach, the consumer should demand the two goods in quantities such that the *MRS* is equal to the ratio of the two prices.

## EXAMPLE 1 (CONSUMER OPTIMIZATION IN THE ORDINAL UTILITY APPROACH)

Let us work with two goods, so that the geometrical approach of the solution can be graphically represented.

Suppose we have a Cobb–Douglas ordinal utility function described as follows:

$$U(x_1, x_2) = (x_1 x_2)^{0.5}.$$

Then, the commodity prices are given as $p_1 = 2$, $p_2 = 3$, together with the budget constraint:

$$2x_1 + 3x_2 = 600.$$

The consumer problem can be then formalized as:

$$\max_{\{x_1, x_2\}} (x_1 x_2)^{0.5}$$

$$s.t.\ 2x_1 + 3x_2 = 600 \quad \text{with } x_1, x_2 \geq 0$$

II. Static optimization

## Solver solution

The problem is set up in Excel as in Fig. 6.3-1:

As this is a nonlinear constrained problem, we use the GRG Solver, as depicted in Fig. 6.3-2.

The solution is easily reached by the Solver, and it is represented in Table 6.3-1.

## Indifference curves method

What we need to do is first working on the utility function to derive the indifference curves map.

From the function:

$$U(x_1, x_2) = (x_1 x_2)^{0.5},$$

setting $U$ equal to a constant $k$ we obtain:

$$k = (x_1 x_2)^{0.5} \Rightarrow k^2 = (x_1 x_2),$$

from which all the combinations $(x_1, x_2)$ returning the same level of utility $U = k$ can be represented as the rectangular hyperbolas:

$$x_2 = \frac{k^2}{x_1} \quad \text{(indifference curve equations obtained by changing } k\text{)}.$$

Secondly, we have to plot the locus of points belonging to the budget line as follows:

$$x_2 = \frac{m}{p_2} - \frac{p_1}{p_2} x_1.$$

The optimal commodity bundle solution $x^* = (x_1^*, x_2^*)$ is found setting the slope of the indifference curve equal to the slope of the budget line as follows:

$$\frac{k^2}{x_1^2} = \frac{p_1}{p_2},$$

| | A | B | C | D | E |
|---|---|---|---|---|---|
| 1 | x1 | x2 | p1 | 2 | |
| 2 | 150.000004135675 | 100.000007469327 | p2 | 3 | |
| 3 | | | | | |
| 4 | | | | | |
| 5 | Max Utility | =(A2*B2)^(0.5) | | Cobb-Douglas Utility $U(x1,x2) = (x1 \cdot x2)^{0.5}$ | |
| 6 | | | | | |
| 7 | s.t. | | Money available | | |
| 8 | =MMULT(A2:B2;D1:D2) = | | 600 | | |

FIGURE 6.3-1  Example 1: ordinal utility approach consumer problem Excel setup.

**FIGURE 6.3-2**    Example 1: ordinal utility approach consumer problem Excel setup.

**TABLE 6.3-1**    Example 1: solver solution.

| x1 | x2 | p1 | 2.00 |
|---|---|---|---|
| 150.00 | 100.00 | p2 | 3.00 |

**Max Utility 122.47**         **Cobb-Douglas Utility**   U(x1,x2) = (x1·x2)$^{0.5}$

| s.t. | | Money available |
|---|---|---|
| 600.00 | = | 600.00 |

from which we can obtain the optimal value $x_1^*$:

$$x_1^2 = \frac{p_2}{p_1}k^2 \Rightarrow x_1^* = k\sqrt{\frac{p_2}{p_1}}.$$

As the relation $k^2 = (x_1 \cdot x_2)$ must be satisfied, it follows that:

$$k^2 = \left(k\sqrt{\frac{p_2}{p_1}}x_2\right) \Rightarrow x_2^* = \frac{k}{\sqrt{\frac{p_2}{p_1}}}$$

so that also $x_2^*$ has been obtained.

With $m = 600$, $p_1 = 2$, $p_2 = 3$, and setting $k = 122.47$, namely the value of maximum utility we have found before using the Lagrange method, we find again the same optimal values as before:

$$x_1^* = 122.47\sqrt{\frac{3}{2}} = 150; \ x_2^* = \frac{122.47}{\sqrt{\frac{3}{2}}} = 100,$$

which plugged in the budget constraint give the following:

$$2 \cdot 150 + 3 \cdot 100 = 600.$$

This implies that among the infinite indifference curves that one can obtain by changing the constant $k$, only that corresponding to the level of utility $k = 122.47$ can be attained by the consumer.

In particular, the optimal solution is found at the point where the budget line is tangent to the indifference curve with $k = 122.47$.

Let us assume instead $k = 200$ and see what happens at the point where the indifference curve slope is equal to that of the budget line:

$$x_1^* = 200\sqrt{\frac{3}{2}} = 245;$$

As the relation $k^2 = (x_1 x_2)$ must be also satisfied, it follows that:

$$200^2 = (245x_2) \Rightarrow x_2^* = 163.$$

If we plug these values in the budget constraint we obtain:

$$2 \cdot 245 + 3 \cdot 163 = 979 > 600$$

which implies that all the commodity bundles lying on the indifference curve returning a level of utility equal to $k = 200$ is not attainable.

We use now the What–if Analysis Data Table tool to build and plot the indifference curves map within the Excel, together with the consumer equilibrium point.

The objective here is to plot the equations of the indifference curves:

$$x_2 = \frac{k^2}{x_1}$$

by changing the constant $k$.

The excerpt of spreadsheet of Fig. 6.3-3 helps us to understand the way the contour lines are developed.

In the *Cell Z2*, we have inserted the equation $x_2 = \frac{k^2}{x_1}$, while in *Cell AA2* $= x_1 = 5$ and *Cell AB2* $= k = 60$. To build the data table, we recall *Cell Z2* in *Cell AE2* and from *Cell AF2* to *Cell AI2* we assume some hypothetical values of $k$, including the optimal value $k = 122.47$ to plot the equilibrium point. The quantity $x_1$ is simulated under *Column AE* from 5 to 400. The Data Table formulas inside the table will return then the values of $x_2 = \frac{k^2}{x_1}$.

As described in Fig. 6.3-4, the What—if Analysis is carried out selecting first the Table Excel *Range AE2:AI43* and assigning in the Excel input box the inputs by row (the values of $k$) and by column (the values of $x_1$). The table simulation is finalized pressing Ok. The Data Table has to be selected from the Ribbon menu as described in Figs. 6.3-5.

Let's look at Fig. 6.3-6. The optimal commodity bundle solution $x^* = (x_1^* = 150, x_2^* = 100)$ is given for $p_1 = 2$, $p_2 = 3$ on the tangent point between the indifference curve *I3* and the Budget Constraint (equilibrium point *E1*).

The New Budget Line of Fig. 6.3-6, instead, is given assuming a higher price $p_1 = 3$ so that the equilibrium point *E2* is found at the tangent point with a lower indifference curve *I1*, implying a lower level of quantity demanded for $x_1$ and a lower level of utility $U = 100$.

| | Z | AA | AB | AD | AE | AF | AG | AH | AI |
|---|---|---|---|---|---|---|---|---|---|
| 1 | Contour line for utility at 60 | x1 | k | | | | Indifference curves with different level of U(x1,x2) | | |
| 2 | =($AB$2^2)/AA2 | 5 | 60 | x1 | =Z2 | 100 | 145 | =B5 | 173.2051 |
| 3 | | | | x1 | 5 | =TABLE(AB2:AA2) | =TABLE(AB2:AA2) | =TABLE(AB2:AA2) | =TABLE(AB2:AA2) |
| 4 | | | | x1 | 10 | =TABLE(AB2:AA2) | =TABLE(AB2:AA2) | =TABLE(AB2:AA2) | =TABLE(AB2:AA2) |
| 5 | | | | x1 | 20 | =TABLE(AB2:AA2) | =TABLE(AB2:AA2) | =TABLE(AB2:AA2) | =TABLE(AB2:AA2) |
| 6 | | | | x1 | 30 | =TABLE(AB2:AA2) | =TABLE(AB2:AA2) | =TABLE(AB2:AA2) | =TABLE(AB2:AA2) |
| 7 | | | | x1 | 40 | =TABLE(AB2:AA2) | =TABLE(AB2:AA2) | =TABLE(AB2:AA2) | =TABLE(AB2:AA2) |
| 8 | | | | x1 | 50 | =TABLE(AB2:AA2) | =TABLE(AB2:AA2) | =TABLE(AB2:AA2) | =TABLE(AB2:AA2) |
| 9 | | | | x1 | 60 | =TABLE(AB2:AA2) | =TABLE(AB2:AA2) | =TABLE(AB2:AA2) | =TABLE(AB2:AA2) |
| 41 | | | | x1 | 380 | =TABLE(AB2:AA2) | =TABLE(AB2:AA2) | =TABLE(AB2:AA2) | =TABLE(AB2:AA2) |
| 42 | | | | x1 | 390 | =TABLE(AB2:AA2) | =TABLE(AB2:AA2) | =TABLE(AB2:AA2) | =TABLE(AB2:AA2) |
| 43 | | | | x1 | 400 | =TABLE(AB2:AA2) | =TABLE(AB2:AA2) | =TABLE(AB2:AA2) | =TABLE(AB2:AA2) |

FIGURE 6.3-3    Example 1: indifference curves with Data Table.

| | AA | AB | AD | AE | AF | AG | AH | AI |
|---|---|---|---|---|---|---|---|---|
| 1 | x1 | k | | | | Indifference curves with different level of U(x1,x2) | | |
| 2 | 5.00 | 60.00 | x1 | 720.00 | 100.00 | 145.00 | 122.47 | 173.21 |
| 3 | | | x1 | 5.00 | 2,000.00 | 4,205.00 | 3,000.00 | 6,000.00 |
| 4 | | | x1 | 10.00 | 1,000.00 | 2,102.50 | 1,500.00 | 3,000.00 |
| 5 | | | x1 | 20.00 | 500.00 | 1,051.25 | 750.00 | 1,500.00 |
| 6 | | | | 30.00 | 333.33 | 700.83 | 500.00 | 1,000.00 |
| 7 | Data Table | ? | X | 40.00 | 250.00 | 525.63 | 375.00 | 750.00 |
| 40 | | | | 370.00 | 27.03 | 56.82 | 40.54 | 81.08 |
| 41 | Row input cell: | $AB$2 | ↑ | 380.00 | 26.32 | 55.33 | 39.47 | 78.95 |
| 42 | | | | 390.00 | 25.64 | 53.91 | 38.46 | 76.92 |
| 43 | Column input cell: | $AA$2 | ↑ | 400.00 | 25.00 | 52.56 | 37.50 | 75.00 |
| 44 | | | | | | | | |
| 45 | OK | Cancel | | | | | | |
| 46 | | | | | | | | |

FIGURE 6.3-4    Example 1: indifference curves with Data Table (the input cells).

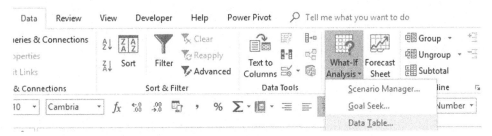

FIGURE 6.3-5   Example 1: the Data Table under what-if analysis.

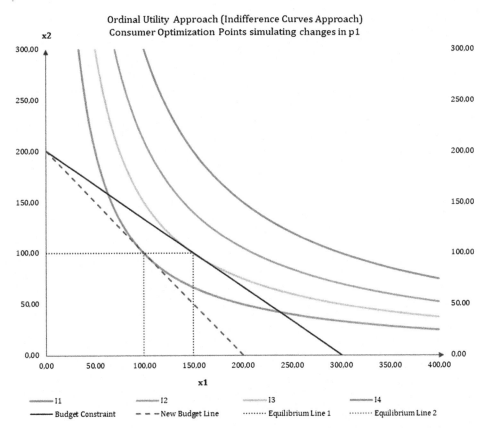

FIGURE 6.3-6   Example 1: indifference curves and equilibrium points (normal goods).

This effect of lower quantity demanded for a higher price is called *Price Effect*, which is decomposed by the ordinal utility approach economists into two imaginary effects:

- *Income Effect*: the part of the increase (decrease) in real wealth, as a result of a decrease (increase) in the price of a good, with the same nominal income.

- *Substitution Effect*: the part of the increase (decrease) of the consumption of a good, as a result of decrease (increase) in the price of a good.

For *normal goods* the two abovementioned effects have always each one negative sign, and this will ensure the typical downward slope in the demand curve, causing consumers to purchase more as the price falls and less as the price rise; for the *Giffen goods*, however, the income effect works in the reverse positive direction, dominating the substitution effect, leading to an upward slope in the demand curve.

As a conclusion, differently from the cardinal approach, in the ordinal utility approach the standard shape of the demand curve (with negative slope) is always guaranteed, as long as the negative sign of the substitution effect goes together with a negative sign in the income effect.

In our example, the set of preferences behind the Cobb–Douglas utility function is assumed to be expressed by the consumer for normal goods.

## EXAMPLE 2 (DEMAND DERIVATION IN THE ORDINAL APPROACH USING VBA)

As we have done in the cardinal utility approach ordinal, the demand curve derivation can be done optimizing problem 6.3-1 several times, to find the complete schedule of the demand curve, by changing the price of a good from a maximum to a minimum value.

As the geometrical and Lagrange methods lead to the same results for problem 6.3-1, it is much more efficient to rerun the optimization sequence using the Excel Solver, than finding the equilibrium points geometrically in sequence.

With a similar VBA macro to the one we have seen in Figs. 6.2-9 to 6.2-11, we obtain the demand schedule of Table 6.3-2 and is graphed in Fig. 6.3-7.

**TABLE 6.3-2**    Demand curve schedule derivation under the ordinal approach.

| x1 | x2 | Change starting p1 (e.g. 10) and then run solver | 0.50 | Demand curve for x1 --> | p1 = f(x1) x1* with solver | Demand Elasticity = % Var q/ % Var p |
|---|---|---|---|---|---|---|
| 600.00 | 100.00 | p2 | 3.00 | | 10.00 | 30.00 | |
| | | | | | 9.50 | 31.58 | 1.05 |
| | | | | | 9.00 | 33.33 | 1.06 |
| Max Utility | 244.95 | U(x1,x2) = (x1·x2)^{0.5} | | | 8.50 | 35.29 | 1.06 |
| | | | | | 8.00 | 37.50 | 1.06 |
| Total Expenditure = | | Income Available | | | 7.50 | 40.00 | 1.07 |
| 600.00 | = | 600.00 | | | 7.00 | 42.86 | 1.07 |
| | | | | | 6.50 | 46.15 | 1.08 |
| | | | | | 6.00 | 50.00 | 1.08 |
| | | | | | 5.50 | 54.55 | 1.09 |
| | | | | | 5.00 | 60.00 | 1.10 |
| | | The macro runs the Solver to maximize utility | | | 4.50 | 66.67 | 1.11 |
| | | for each level of price p1 to determine the quantity x1 | | | 4.00 | 75.00 | 1.13 |
| | | and then the individual consumer demand curve is found. | | | 3.50 | 85.71 | 1.14 |
| | | | | | 3.00 | 100.00 | 1.17 |
| | | We can find the market demand with the sum | | | 2.50 | 120.00 | 1.20 |
| | | of all these individual demands. | | | 2.00 | 150.00 | 1.25 |
| | | | | | 1.50 | 200.00 | 1.33 |
| | | In the ordinal approach the demand curve is derived | | | 1.00 | 300.00 | 1.50 |
| | | via the indifference map analysis: | | | 0.50 | 600.00 | 2.00 |
| | | the consumer must reach the highest indifference | | | | | |
| | | curve s.t. budget constraint | | | | | |

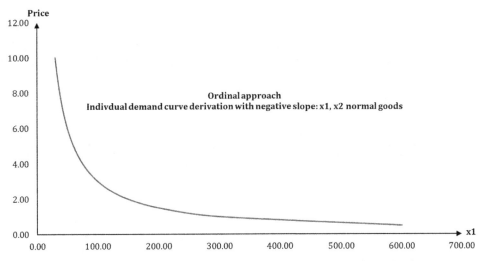

**FIGURE 6.3-7** Demand schedule in the ordinal approach optimizing for ×1 by changing $p_1$.

The Solver will maximize the Cobb–Douglas utility function subject to the budget constraint.

## 6.4 The firm problem

Let us turn now the attention to the second basic institution of the economic system, which is the firm.

The firm faces the economic problem of deciding how much to produce and how much of the various inputs to use within the production process, considering the costs the firm must sustain, the prices and demand of the output and considering the important technological relations between output and inputs.

Similarly to what we have seen with the consumer problem, the *firm problem* is that of finding the optimal combination of inputs that maximizes the total output production with a given total cost constraint (or minimizing the total costs for a given output production, which is the mathematical *dual problem*).

In general, a production function can be represented as follows:

$$y = f(x_1, x_2, \cdots, x_n; K)$$

which means that the output $y$ depends on the vector of inputs $x = (x_1, x_2,..., x_n)$, where $x_i \geq 0$, and also on the available capital (plants and equipment) employed within the production process.

As we have seen the firm problem is that of maximizing the production obtainable, subject to the budget constraint for total costs to incur, finding the optimal combination of the various inputs.

Leaving out for simplicity $K$, it can be formalized then as a standard nonlinear maximization constrained problem, to be solved with the Lagrange multipliers:

$$\begin{cases} \max\limits_{\{x_i\}} y(x_1, x_1, \cdots, x_n) \\ s.t. \sum\limits_{i=1}^{n} p_i x_i = C \quad \text{with } x_i \geq 0, \end{cases} \quad (6.4\text{-}1)$$

where $c = $ total costs and $p_i = $ price of input $i$.

It can be also stated as a dual problem, finding the optimal combination among the various inputs minimizing the total costs for a given level of production.

$$\begin{cases} \min\limits_{\{x_i\}} C(x_i) = \sum\limits_{i=1}^{n} p_i x_i \\ s.t. \ y(x_1, x_1, \cdots, x_n) - \bar{y} \quad \text{with } x_i \geq 0 \end{cases} \quad (6.4\text{-}2)$$

## 6.5 One-input classical production function

The one-input production function is represented as a function of one input only (e.g.,:$x_1$) keeping constant all the other inputs:

$$y = f(x_1, \bar{x}_2, \cdots, \bar{x}_n).$$

Such a production function must satisfy the axiom of the *law of diminishing returns*, which states that the *marginal (incremental) output of a production process decreases, as the amount of a single input of production is incrementally increased, while the amounts of all other inputs of production remain constant.*

A typical production function can be then represented by the following function:

$$y = ax_1^3 + bx_1^2 + cx_1 \qquad \text{where } x_i \geq 0, a < 0, b > 0 \text{ and } c > 0.$$

### Example 1

Let us assume the following data: $C = 600$, $p_1 = 5$, $a = -0.0025$, $b = 1$, and $c = 10$.

The production function has the form presented in Fig. 6.5-1. The exact marginal product of Fig. 6.5-2 has been drawn from:

$$\frac{dy}{dx_1} = -3(0.0025)x_1^2 + 2x_1 + 10$$

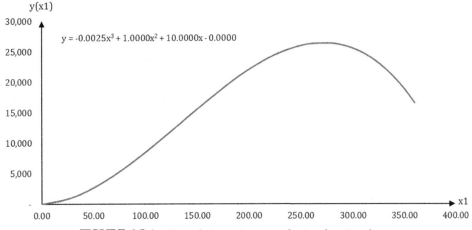

y(x1)

$y = -0.0025x^3 + 1.0000x^2 + 10.0000x - 0.0000$

FIGURE 6.5-1   Example 1: one-input production function shape.

The law of diminishing returns is shown in Fig. 6.5-2, where both the average product and marginal product are represented. The second derivative $\frac{d^2y}{dx_1^2}$ gives the shape of the marginal product, which is an increasing function until $x_1 \cong 133$, then a decreasing function:

$$\frac{d^2y}{dx_1^2} = -0.015x_1 + 2 > 0 \text{ for } x_1 > 133.35.$$

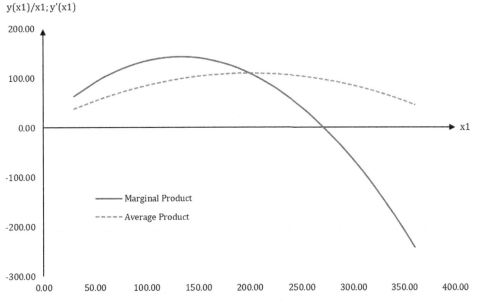

y(x1)/x1; y'(x1)

——— Marginal Product

----- Average Product

FIGURE 6.5-2   Example 1: average product and marginal product of $x_1$.

II. Static optimization

**TABLE 6.5-1**   Example 1: one-input production function solution for $x_1 = 120$.

| x1 Quantity of Input 1 | Quantity Production Function $y = -ax1^3+bx1^2+cx1$ | Average Product | Exact Marginal Product | Costs Constraint |
|---|---|---|---|---|
| 0.00 | 0.00 | | | |
| 30.00 | 1,132.50 | 37.75 | 63.25 | 150.00 |
| 60.00 | 3,660.00 | 61.00 | 103.00 | 300.00 |
| 90.00 | 7,177.50 | 79.75 | 129.25 | 450.00 |
| 120.00 | 11,280.00 | 94.00 | 142.00 | 600.00 |
| 150.00 | 15,562.50 | 103.75 | 141.25 | 750.00 |
| 180.00 | 19,620.00 | 109.00 | 127.00 | 900.00 |
| 200.00 | 22,000.00 | 110.00 | 110.00 | 1,000.00 |
| 220.00 | 23,980.00 | 109.00 | 87.00 | 1,100.00 |
| 230.00 | 24,782.50 | 107.75 | 73.25 | 1,150.00 |
| 240.00 | 25,440.00 | 106.00 | 58.00 | 1,200.00 |
| 250.00 | 25,937.50 | 103.75 | 41.25 | 1,250.00 |
| 260.00 | 26,260.00 | 101.00 | 23.00 | 1,300.00 |
| 280.00 | 26,320.00 | 94.00 | -18.00 | 1,400.00 |
| 290.00 | 26,027.50 | 89.75 | -40.75 | 1,450.00 |
| 300.00 | 25,500.00 | 85.00 | -65.00 | 1,500.00 |
| 310.00 | 24,722.50 | 79.75 | -90.75 | 1,550.00 |
| 320.00 | 23,680.00 | 74.00 | -118.00 | 1,600.00 |
| 330.00 | 22,357.50 | 67.75 | -146.75 | 1,650.00 |
| 340.00 | 20,740.00 | 61.00 | -177.00 | 1,700.00 |
| 350.00 | 18,812.50 | 53.75 | -208.75 | 1,750.00 |
| 360.00 | 16,560.00 | 46.00 | -242.00 | 1,800.00 |

The marginal product of the factor $x_1$ is diminishing everywhere to the right of point $x_1 \cong 133$.

The problem of the firm is solved finding the optimal quantity of the factor $x_1$ to be used to maximize the production output function, considering the total costs constraint $C = 5x_1 = 600$. The problem is simply solved for $x_1 = 120$. See Table 6.5-1 with the whole schedule of production.

## 6.6 Two-inputs production functions

### 1. Cobb–Douglas production function

Probably the most used in the economic production theory, the Cobb–Douglas is a production function that implements labor $L$ and capital $K$ as inputs and it is expressed as:

$$y = A\left(L^\alpha K^\beta\right)$$

where:

- $y$ = total production.
- $L$ = labor input (e.g., man-hours of the workforce).
- $K$ = capital input (e.g., machine-hours referred to the fixed capital employed or real value of equipment).
- $A$ = factor productivity.
- $\alpha$ and $\beta$ are the output elasticities of capital and labor, respectively. Output elasticity measures the responsiveness of output to a change in levels of either labor or capital used in production. For example, if $\alpha = 0.8$, it means that a 1% increase in labor will determine a 0.80% increase in production, other things remaining equal.

## The Returns to scale

$\alpha$ and $\beta$ also determine the *returns to scale*, which describe what happens in the long run to the output production $y$ when both inputs production $L$ and $K$ change equi-proportionally.

We can have the following three cases:

i. $\alpha + \beta = 1$ (Constant Returns to Scale).
ii. $\alpha + \beta < 1$ (Decreasing Returns to Scale).
iii. $\alpha + \beta > 1$ (Increasing Returns to Scale).

It is important to recall that the returns to scale concept is different from the *economies of scale*, which refer instead to the cost advantages that the firms obtain due to the scale of operations (these being measured by the amount of output produced), with cost per unit of output decreasing with increasing scale.

The ratio $\frac{\alpha}{\beta}$ also determines the "intensity" of the input factors; the higher the ratio the higher the labor intensity, compared to the capital factor.

In this book, we will always refer to a Cobb–Douglas function with constant returns to scale, so that once we know the parameter $\alpha$ we have $\beta = 1 - \alpha$ and the Cobb–Douglas becomes:

$$y_{CD} = A\left(L^{\alpha} K^{1-\alpha}\right).$$

It is worth to notice that the Cobb–Douglas is a special case of another important class of production functions, called *Constant Elasticity of Substitution (CES)* defined as:

$$y_{CES} = A[\alpha K^{\gamma} + (1 - \alpha)L^{\gamma}]^{\frac{1}{\gamma}} \qquad \text{with } \lim_{\gamma \to 0} y_{CES} = y_{CD}.$$

Similarly to what we have done within the consumer theory, we can derive the *MRS* between the two inputs, which measures the rate at which one input is substituted for an additional quantity of the other input, so that the total output is constant. The $MRS_{L,K}$ is defined as:

$$MRS_{L,K} = \frac{\partial y}{\partial L} \Big/ \frac{\partial y}{\partial K} = \frac{MP_L}{MP_K} = \frac{\alpha}{1 - \alpha} \cdot \frac{K}{L},$$

where $MP_L = \frac{\partial y}{\partial L} = \alpha \frac{y}{L}$ and $MP_K = \frac{\partial y}{\partial K} = (1-\alpha)\frac{y}{K}$ are the marginal product of labor and marginal product of capital, respectively.

Moreover, the theory of the firm often resorts to the concept of *elasticity of substitution* between inputs, and this is denoted as follows by $|\sigma_{K,L}|$:

$$|\sigma_{K,L}| = \frac{d\log\frac{K}{L}}{d\log(MRS_{L,K})}.$$

For the Cobb–Douglas $y = A(L^\alpha K^\beta)$ this ratio is equal to 1.
We have:

$$d\log\left(\frac{K}{L}\right) = \frac{d\left(\frac{K}{L}\right)}{K/L} = d\left(\frac{K}{L}\right) \cdot \frac{L}{K}$$

$$d\log(MRS_{L,K}) = \frac{dMRS_{L,K}}{MRS_{L,K}} = \frac{d\left(\frac{\alpha}{\beta}\cdot\frac{K}{L}\right)}{\frac{\alpha}{\beta}\cdot\frac{K}{L}}.$$

Therefore:

$$|\sigma_{K,L}| = \frac{d\left(\frac{K}{L}\right)\cdot\frac{L}{K}}{d\left(\frac{\alpha}{\beta}\cdot\frac{K}{L}\right)/\frac{\alpha}{\beta}\cdot\frac{K}{L}} = \frac{d\left(\frac{K}{L}\right)\cdot\frac{L}{K}\cdot\frac{K}{L}}{\frac{\alpha}{\beta}d\left(\frac{K}{L}\right)\cdot\frac{\beta}{\alpha}} = 1.$$

The elasticity of substitution measures the substitutability between inputs, i.e., how easy it is to substitute one input (or good) for the other.

After having examined the main features of the Cobb–Douglas production, let us see how it can be implemented in an Excel spreadsheet. As we are dealing with a two-independent-variables function, we will use the Excel What–if Data Table and the surface charts. See Example 1.

## EXAMPLE 1 (COBB–DOUGLAS PRODUCTION FUNCTION IMPLEMENTED IN EXCEL)

Let us assume we have a constant return of scale Cobb–Douglas function with the following data parameters: $A = 0.5$ $\alpha = 0.80$ and $1 - \alpha = 0.20$.

Referring to Fig. 6.6-1, in *Cell D2* we input the Cobb–Douglas function as a function of *Cell B2* and *Cell C2* (the input factors of production). Then, it is just a matter of recalling the *Cell D2* in *Cell B4* where the two variables double entry table begins. Along the *Row 4* we store the capital input, while along the *Column B* we store the labor input. Step of increment for both inputs is 1. We will make the inputs change from 0 to 11. The result is given in Table 6.6-1.

|  | A | B | C | D | E | F | G | H | I | J |
|---|---|---|---|---|---|---|---|---|---|---|
| 1 |  | L | K | y = A(L^a K^(1-a)) | α = | 0.8 | A = | 0.5 | Step | 1 |
| 2 |  | 1 | 1 | =$H$1*(B2^F1)+(C2)^(1-$F$1) |  |  |  |  |  |  |
| 3 |  |  |  |  |  |  |  |  | Capital K |  |
| 4 |  | =D2 | 0 | 1 | =D4+$J$1 | =E4+$J$1 | =F4+$J$1 | =G4+$J$1 | =H4+$J$1 | =I4+$J$1 |
| 5 |  | 0 | =TABLE(C2:B2) | =TABLE(C2:B2) | =TABLE(C2:B2) | =TABLE(C2:B2) | =TABLE(C2:B2) | =TABLE(C2:B2) | =TABLE(C2:B2) | =TABLE(C2:B2) |
| 6 |  | 1 | =TABLE(C2:B2) | =TABLE(C2:B2) | =TABLE(C2:B2) | =TABLE(C2:B2) | =TABLE(C2:B2) | =TABLE(C2:B2) | =TABLE(C2:B2) | =TABLE(C2:B2) |
| 7 |  | =B6+$J$1 | =TABLE(C2:B2) | =TABLE(C2:B2) | =**TABLE(C2:B2)** | =TABLE(C2:B2) | =TABLE(C2:B2) | =TABLE(C2:B2) | =TABLE(C2:B2) | =TABLE(C2:B2) |
| 8 |  | =B7+$J$1 | =TABLE(C2:B2) | =TABLE(C2:B2) | =TABLE(C2:B2) | =TABLE(C2:B2) | =TABLE(C2:B2) | =TABLE(C2:B2) | =TABLE(C2:B2) | =TABLE(C2:B2) |
| 9 | Labour L | =B8+$J$1 | =TABLE(C2:B2) | =TABLE(C2:B2) | =TABLE(C2:B2) | =TABLE(C2:B2) | =TABLE(C2:B2) | =**TABLE(C2:B2)** | =TABLE(C2:B2) | =TABLE(C2:B2) |
| 10 |  | =B9+$J$1 | =TABLE(C2:B2) | =TABLE(C2:B2) | =TABLE(C2:B2) | =TABLE(C2:B2) | =TABLE(C2:B2) | =TABLE(C2:B2) | =TABLE(C2:B2) | =TABLE(C2:B2) |
| 11 |  | =B10+$J$1 | =TABLE(C2:B2) | =TABLE(C2:B2) | =TABLE(C2:B2) | =TABLE(C2:B2) | =TABLE(C2:B2) | =TABLE(C2:B2) | =TABLE(C2:B2) | =TABLE(C2:B2) |
| 12 |  | =B11+$J$1 | =TABLE(C2:B2) | =TABLE(C2:B2) | =TABLE(C2:B2) | =TABLE(C2:B2) | =TABLE(C2:B2) | =TABLE(C2:B2) | =TABLE(C2:B2) | =TABLE(C2:B2) |
| 13 |  | =B12+$J$1 | =TABLE(C2:B2) | =TABLE(C2:B2) | =TABLE(C2:B2) | =TABLE(C2:B2) | =TABLE(C2:B2) | =TABLE(C2:B2) | =TABLE(C2:B2) | =TABLE(C2:B2) |
| 14 |  | =B13+$J$1 | =TABLE(C2:B2) | =TABLE(C2:B2) | =TABLE(C2:B2) | =TABLE(C2:B2) | =TABLE(C2:B2) | =TABLE(C2:B2) | =TABLE(C2:B2) | =TABLE(C2:B2) |
| 15 |  | =B14+$J$1 | =TABLE(C2:B2) | =TABLE(C2:B2) | =TABLE(C2:B2) | =TABLE(C2:B2) | =TABLE(C2:B2) | =TABLE(C2:B2) | =TABLE(C2:B2) | =TABLE(C2:B2) |
| 16 |  | =B15+$J$1 | =TABLE(C2:B2) | =TABLE(C2:B2) | =TABLE(C2:B2) | =TABLE(C2:B2) | =TABLE(C2:B2) | =TABLE(C2:B2) | =TABLE(C2:B2) | =TABLE(C2:B2) |

**FIGURE 6.6-1**    Example 1 Cobb–Douglas Excel implementation.

**TABLE 6.6-1**    Example 1: Cobb–Douglas double entry table.

| | L | K | y = A(L^a K^(1-a)) | α = | 0.8000 | A = | 0.5000 | Step | 1.0000 | | | |
|---|---|---|---|---|---|---|---|---|---|---|---|---|
| | 1.0000 | 1.0000 | 0.5000 | | | | | | | | | |
| | | | | | | | | **Capital K** | | | | |
| | 0.5000 | 0.0000 | 1.0000 | 2.0000 | 3.0000 | 4.0000 | 5.0000 | 6.0000 | 7.0000 | **8.0000** | 9.0000 | 10.0000 | 11.0000 |
| | 0.0000 | 0.0000 | 0.0000 | 0.0000 | 0.0000 | 0.0000 | 0.0000 | 0.0000 | 0.0000 | 0.0000 | 0.0000 | 0.0000 | 0.0000 |
| | 1.0000 | 0.0000 | 0.5000 | 0.5743 | 0.6229 | 0.6598 | 0.6899 | 0.7155 | 0.7379 | 0.7579 | 0.7759 | 0.7924 | 0.8077 |
| | 2.0000 | 0.0000 | 0.8706 | **1.0000** | 1.0845 | 1.1487 | 1.2011 | 1.2457 | 1.2847 | 1.3195 | 1.3510 | 1.3797 | 1.4063 |
| | 3.0000 | 0.0000 | 1.2041 | 1.3832 | 1.5000 | 1.5888 | 1.6613 | 1.7230 | 1.7770 | 1.8251 | 1.8686 | 1.9084 | 1.9451 |
| Labour L | 4.0000 | 0.0000 | 1.5157 | 1.7411 | 1.8882 | **2.0000** | 2.0913 | 2.1689 | 2.2369 | 2.2974 | 2.3522 | 2.4022 | 2.4485 |
| | 5.0000 | 0.0000 | 1.8119 | 2.0814 | 2.2572 | 2.3909 | 2.5000 | 2.5928 | 2.6740 | 2.7464 | 2.8119 | 2.8717 | 2.9270 |
| | 6.0000 | 0.0000 | 2.0965 | 2.4082 | 2.6117 | 2.7663 | 2.8926 | 3.0000 | 3.0939 | 3.1777 | 3.2534 | 3.3227 | 3.3866 |
| | 7.0000 | 0.0000 | 2.3716 | 2.7243 | 2.9544 | 3.1294 | 3.2722 | 3.3937 | 3.5000 | 3.5947 | 3.6804 | 3.7588 | 3.8311 |
| | **8.0000** | 0.0000 | 2.6390 | 3.0314 | 3.2875 | 3.4822 | 3.6411 | 3.7764 | 3.8946 | **4.0000** | 4.0953 | 4.1826 | 4.2631 |
| | 9.0000 | 0.0000 | 2.8998 | 3.3310 | 3.6123 | 3.8263 | 4.0009 | 4.1495 | 4.2794 | 4.3952 | 4.5000 | 4.5958 | 4.6843 |
| | 10.0000 | 0.0000 | 3.1548 | 3.6239 | 3.9300 | 4.1628 | 4.3528 | 4.5144 | 4.6557 | 4.7818 | 4.8957 | 5.0000 | 5.0962 |
| | 11.0000 | 0.0000 | 3.4047 | 3.9110 | 4.2414 | 4.4926 | 4.6976 | 4.8721 | 5.0246 | 5.1606 | 5.2836 | 5.3962 | 5.5000 |

The highlighted cells of Table 6.6-1 show how the constant returns to scale work: when the inputs increase by a factor of 2 we have twice as much as the previous output, or also, an increase of 100% in the inputs have led to an equal increase of 100% in the output.

Now, what we want to do is to take the partial derivatives (i.e., marginal products) of $y = A(L^\alpha K^{1-\alpha})$ with respect to both $L$ and $K$. This is done first by enumerating the production function as a function of one input only, keeping constant the other, and then taking the numerical derivative in Excel. This is done in Fig. 6.6-2 where also the exact marginal products are calculated (Fig. 6.6-3).

We can then plot the marginal product functions with the data of Table 6.6-2.

From Table 6.6-2, we can also easily see that if we apply an increment of 1% to $L$ the output will increment by 0.80% (which is the elasticity of output with respect to labor) and if we apply a 1% increment to $K$ we will have an increment of 0.20% in the output (which is the elasticity of output with respect to capital).

It is interesting to notice, from Fig. 6.6-4, how the marginal product of labor is always plotted higher than the marginal product of capital and this is due to the higher intensity of labor given via the parameter $\alpha = 0.80$.

| Q | R | S | T | U | V | W | X | Y |
|---|---|---|---|---|---|---|---|---|
| | y = A(L^a K^{1-a}) by changing L only | ∂y/∂L = αy/L | | | | y = A(L^a K^{1-a}) by changing K only | ∂y/∂K = (1-α)y/K | |
| L | only | Numerical | Exact | | K | only | Numerical | Exact |
| =B5 | =$H$1*(Q3*$C$2)^$F$1 | | | | =Q3 | =$H$1*(V3*$B$2)^(1-$F$1) | | |
| =Q3+0.5 | =$H$1*(Q4*$C$2)^$F$1 | =(R4-R3)/(Q4-Q3) | =$F$1*R4/Q4 | | =Q4 | =$H$1*(V4*$B$2)^(1-$F$1) | =(W4-W3)/(V4-V3) | =(1-$F$1)*W4/V4 |
| =Q4+0.5 | =$H$1*(Q5*$C$2)^$F$1 | =(R5-R4)/(Q5-Q4) | =$F$1*R5/Q5 | | =Q5 | =$H$1*(V5*$B$2)^(1-$F$1) | =(W5-W4)/(V5-V4) | =(1-$F$1)*W5/V5 |
| =Q5+0.5 | =$H$1*(Q6*$C$2)^$F$1 | =(R6-R5)/(Q6-Q5) | =$F$1*R6/Q6 | | =Q6 | =$H$1*(V6*$B$2)^(1-$F$1) | =(W6-W5)/(V6-V5) | =(1-$F$1)*W6/V6 |
| =Q6+0.5 | =$H$1*(Q7*$C$2)^$F$1 | =(R7-R6)/(Q7-Q6) | =$F$1*R7/Q7 | | =Q7 | =$H$1*(V7*$B$2)^(1-$F$1) | =(W7-W6)/(V7-V6) | =(1-$F$1)*W7/V7 |
| =Q7+0.5 | =$H$1*(Q8*$C$2)^$F$1 | =(R8-R7)/(Q8-Q7) | =$F$1*R8/Q8 | | =Q8 | =$H$1*(V8*$B$2)^(1-$F$1) | =(W8-W7)/(V8-V7) | =(1-$F$1)*W8/V8 |
| =Q8+0.5 | =$H$1*(Q9*$C$2)^$F$1 | =(R9-R8)/(Q9-Q8) | =$F$1*R9/Q9 | | =Q9 | =$H$1*(V9*$B$2)^(1-$F$1) | =(W9-W8)/(V9-V8) | =(1-$F$1)*W9/V9 |
| =Q9+0.5 | =$H$1*(Q10*$C$2)^$F$1 | =(R10-R9)/(Q10-Q9) | =$F$1*R10/Q10 | | =Q10 | =$H$1*(V10*$B$2)^(1-$F$1) | =(W10-W9)/(V10-V9) | =(1-$F$1)*W10/V10 |
| =Q10+0.5 | =$H$1*(Q11*$C$2)^$F$1 | =(R11-R10)/(Q11-Q10) | =$F$1*R11/Q11 | | =Q11 | =$H$1*(V11*$B$2)^(1-$F$1) | =(W11-W10)/(V11-V10) | =(1-$F$1)*W11/V11 |
| =Q11+0.5 | =$H$1*(Q12*$C$2)^$F$1 | =(R12-R11)/(Q12-Q11) | =$F$1*R12/Q12 | | =Q12 | =$H$1*(V12*$B$2)^(1-$F$1) | =(W12-W11)/(V12-V11) | =(1-$F$1)*W12/V12 |
| =Q12+0.5 | =$H$1*(Q13*$C$2)^$F$1 | =(R13-R12)/(Q13-Q12) | =$F$1*R13/Q13 | | =Q13 | =$H$1*(V13*$B$2)^(1-$F$1) | =(W13-W12)/(V13-V12) | =(1-$F$1)*W13/V13 |
| =Q13+0.5 | =$H$1*(Q14*$C$2)^$F$1 | =(R14-R13)/(Q14-Q13) | =$F$1*R14/Q14 | | =Q14 | =$H$1*(V14*$B$2)^(1-$F$1) | =(W14-W13)/(V14-V13) | =(1-$F$1)*W14/V14 |
| =Q14+0.5 | =$H$1*(Q15*$C$2)^$F$1 | =(R15-R14)/(Q15-Q14) | =$F$1*R15/Q15 | | =Q15 | =$H$1*(V15*$B$2)^(1-$F$1) | =(W15-W14)/(V15-V14) | =(1-$F$1)*W15/V15 |

**FIGURE 6.6-2**  Taking the partial derivatives $\nabla y(K, L) = [\partial y(K, L)/\partial K, \partial y(K, L)/\partial L]$ of the Cobb–Douglas.

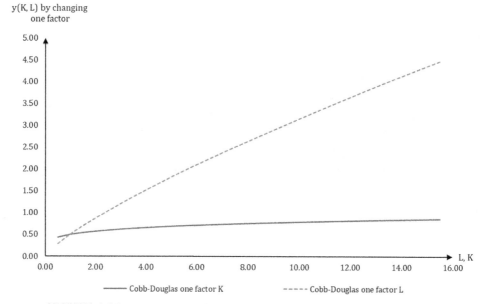

y(K, L) by changing one factor

——— Cobb-Douglas one factor K   - - - - Cobb-Douglas one factor L

**FIGURE 6.6-3**  Example 1: Cobb–Douglas as a function of one input factor only.

Finally, the surface chart of the Cobb–Douglas is represented in Fig. 6.6-5.

## 2. Input–Output (or Leontief) production function

The Input–Output production function assumes that the two input factors are used in fixed predetermined proportions, as there is no substitutability between the factors. This implies that the elasticity of substitution between inputs is $\sigma = 0$.

The Input–Output production function is formalized as follows:

$$y(x_1, x_2) = \min\left(\frac{x_1}{a_1}; \frac{x_2}{a_2}\right)$$

where $a_1$ and $a_2$ are the technology constant parameters.

**TABLE 6.6-2**  Marginal products of the Cobb–Douglas.

| L | $y = A(L^\alpha K^{1\text{-}\alpha})$ by changing L only | $\partial y/\partial L = \alpha y/L$ | | K | $y = A(L^\alpha K^{1\text{-}\alpha})$ by changing K only | $\partial y/\partial K = (1\text{-}\alpha)y/K$ | |
|---|---|---|---|---|---|---|---|
| | | Numerical | Exact | | | Numerical | Exact |
| 0.0000 | 0.0000 | | | 0.0000 | 0.0000 | | |
| 0.5000 | 0.2872 | 0.5743 | 0.4595 | 0.5000 | 0.4353 | 0.8706 | 0.1741 |
| 1.0000 | 0.5000 | 0.4257 | 0.4000 | 1.0000 | 0.5000 | 0.1294 | 0.1000 |
| 1.5000 | 0.6916 | 0.3832 | 0.3688 | 1.5000 | 0.5422 | 0.0845 | 0.0723 |
| 2.0000 | 0.8706 | 0.3579 | 0.3482 | 2.0000 | 0.5743 | 0.0642 | 0.0574 |
| 2.5000 | 1.0407 | 0.3403 | 0.3330 | 2.5000 | 0.6006 | 0.0524 | 0.0480 |
| 3.0000 | 1.2041 | 0.3268 | 0.3211 | 3.0000 | 0.6229 | 0.0446 | 0.0415 |
| 3.5000 | 1.3621 | 0.3161 | 0.3113 | 3.5000 | 0.6424 | 0.0390 | 0.0367 |
| 4.0000 | 1.5157 | 0.3071 | 0.3031 | 4.0000 | 0.6598 | 0.0348 | 0.0330 |
| 4.5000 | 1.6655 | 0.2995 | 0.2961 | 4.5000 | 0.6755 | 0.0315 | 0.0300 |
| 5.0000 | 1.8119 | 0.2929 | 0.2899 | 5.0000 | 0.6899 | 0.0288 | 0.0276 |
| 5.5000 | 1.9555 | 0.2871 | 0.2844 | 5.5000 | 0.7031 | 0.0266 | 0.0256 |
| 6.0000 | 2.0965 | 0.2819 | 0.2795 | 6.0000 | 0.7155 | 0.0247 | 0.0238 |
| 6.5000 | 2.2351 | 0.2773 | 0.2751 | 6.5000 | 0.7270 | 0.0231 | 0.0224 |
| 7.0000 | 2.3716 | 0.2730 | 0.2710 | 7.0000 | 0.7379 | 0.0217 | 0.0211 |
| 7.5000 | 2.5062 | 0.2692 | 0.2673 | 7.5000 | 0.7481 | 0.0205 | 0.0200 |
| 8.0000 | 2.6390 | 0.2656 | 0.2639 | 8.0000 | 0.7579 | 0.0194 | 0.0189 |
| 8.5000 | 2.7702 | 0.2623 | 0.2607 | 8.5000 | 0.7671 | 0.0185 | 0.0180 |
| 9.0000 | 2.8998 | 0.2592 | 0.2578 | 9.0000 | 0.7759 | 0.0176 | 0.0172 |
| 9.5000 | 3.0280 | 0.2564 | 0.2550 | 9.5000 | 0.7844 | 0.0169 | 0.0165 |
| 10.0000 | 3.1548 | 0.2537 | 0.2524 | 10.0000 | 0.7924 | 0.0162 | 0.0158 |
| 10.5000 | 3.2804 | 0.2511 | 0.2499 | 10.5000 | 0.8002 | 0.0155 | 0.0152 |
| 11.0000 | 3.4047 | 0.2488 | 0.2476 | 11.0000 | 0.8077 | 0.0150 | 0.0147 |
| 11.5000 | 3.5280 | 0.2465 | 0.2454 | 11.5000 | 0.8149 | 0.0144 | 0.0142 |
| 12.0000 | 3.6502 | 0.2444 | 0.2433 | 12.0000 | 0.8219 | 0.0139 | 0.0137 |
| 12.5000 | 3.7714 | 0.2423 | 0.2414 | 12.5000 | 0.8286 | 0.0135 | 0.0133 |
| 13.0000 | 3.8916 | 0.2404 | 0.2395 | 13.0000 | 0.8351 | 0.0131 | 0.0128 |
| 13.5000 | 4.0109 | 0.2386 | 0.2377 | 13.5000 | 0.8415 | 0.0127 | 0.0125 |
| 14.0000 | 4.1293 | 0.2368 | 0.2360 | 14.0000 | 0.8476 | 0.0123 | 0.0121 |
| 14.5000 | 4.2468 | 0.2351 | 0.2343 | 14.5000 | 0.8536 | 0.0119 | 0.0118 |
| 15.0000 | 4.3636 | 0.2335 | 0.2327 | 15.0000 | 0.8594 | 0.0116 | 0.0115 |
| 15.5000 | 4.4796 | 0.2320 | 0.2312 | 15.5000 | 0.8650 | 0.0113 | 0.0112 |

Using the Data Table function, similarly to what we have done with the Cobb–Douglas, we are able to plot the two-variables function. Setting, for example, $a_1 = a_2 = 5$ we obtain the surface production represented in Fig. 6.6-6.

## 3. Linear Production Function

The production function is formalized as:

$$y(x_1, x_2) = a_1 x_1 + a_2 x_2.$$

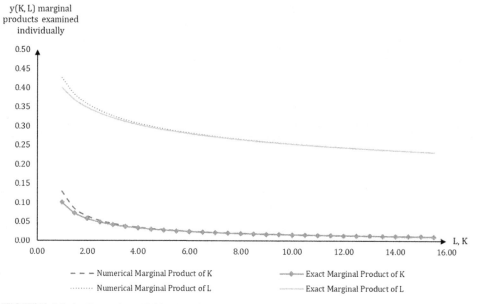

**FIGURE 6.6-4**    Example 1: Cobb–Douglas decreasing marginal products: numerical versus Exact.

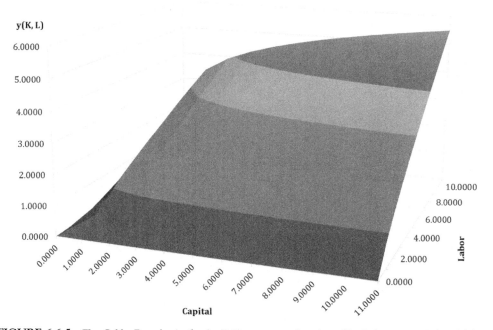

**FIGURE 6.6-5**    The Cobb–Douglas in the $(y, K, L)$ space as a function of both factors: capital and labor.

$y = \min(x_1/5; x_2/5)$

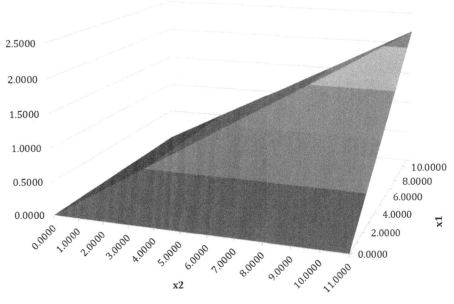

FIGURE 6.6-6    Input–output production function.

The elasticity of substitution between the two inputs is equal to $\sigma = \infty$, implying the two inputs are perfect substitutes.

The surface chart is given in Fig. 6.6-7.

## 4. Constant Elasticity substitution production function

The CES production function generalizes the three production functions described so far and it is defined as follows (Fig. 6.6-8):

$$y_{CES} = A[\alpha x_1^\gamma + (1 - \alpha)x_2^\gamma]^{\frac{1}{\gamma}}$$

where $-\infty \leq \gamma \leq 1, A = $ factor productivity and $\sigma = 1/(1 - \gamma)$.

- If $\gamma \to 0$ then $y_{CES} \to$ Cobb–Douglas Production Function.
- If $\gamma \to -\infty$ then $y_{CES} \to$ Leontief Production Function (inputs are perfect complements).
- If $\gamma \to 1$ then $y_{CES} \to$ Linear Production (inputs are perfect substitutes).

$y = a_1x_1 + a_2x_2$

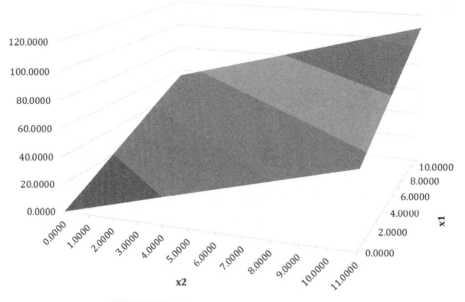

**FIGURE 6.6-7** Linear production function.

$y = A[\alpha x_1^\gamma + (1-\alpha)x_2^\gamma]^{1/\gamma}$

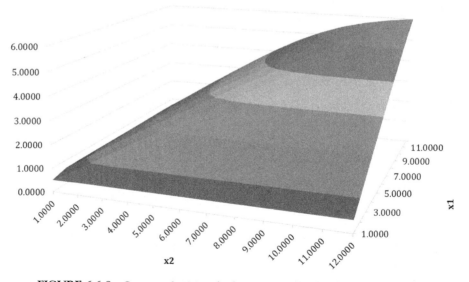

**FIGURE 6.6-8** Constant elasticity of substitution production function, $\gamma = 5$

## 6.7 Isoquants and the constrained production optimization with two inputs

Let us go back now to the original firm, consisting of finding the optimal inputs combination to maximize the obtainable output, subject to the total costs the firm must sustain.

The problem is described as follows (see Section 6.4: Problem 6.4-1 with its Dual 6.4-2):

$$
\begin{cases}
\max_{\{x_i\}} y\,(x_1, x_1, \cdots, x_n) \\[2mm]
s.t. \displaystyle\sum_{i=1}^{n} p_i x_i = C \quad \text{with } x_i \geq 0 \text{ (isocost line)}
\end{cases}
$$

and it is a standard constrained problem that can be solved either analytically via the Lagrange multipliers or geometrically using the *isoquant* curves and *isocosts* line.

The isoquants are contour lines derived from the production function, showing all combinations of inputs giving the same amount of production, while the isocost line gives the combinations of inputs with the same total costs and it represents the budget constraint faced by the firm.

For each one of the four production functions we have a specific behavior of isoquants, depending on the index $\sigma$, the elasticity of substitution.

- Cobb–Douglas $\sigma = 1$
- Input–Output $\sigma = 0$
- Linear $\sigma = \infty$
- CES $\sigma = 1/(1 - \gamma)$    with $-\infty \leq \gamma \leq 1$

In Fig. 6.7-1, we have graphed the four types of isoquants directly from Excel, selecting from the Surface charts the Contour.

The alternative way to graph the isoquants is via the Excel Data Table, as we have done in Figs. 6.3-3 and 6.3-4 for the indifference curve case and as we will do in the following numerical Example 1, which will apply the production optimization using the Cobb–Douglas function.

Given a production function $y = h(x_1, x_2)$, as along the isoquant the production level is constant, the following fundamental property must be satisfied:

$$
dy = \frac{\partial h}{\partial x_1} dx_1 + \frac{\partial h}{\partial x_2} dx_2 = 0,
$$

which becomes:

$$
\frac{\partial h}{\partial x_1} \bigg/ \frac{\partial h}{\partial x_2} = MP_{x_1}/MP_{x_2} = |dx_2 / dx_1|
$$

### EXAMPLE 1 (OPTIMIZATION OF PRODUCTION WITH A COBB–DOUGLAS)

With the help of statistical modeling, we can assume that the total output of a firm can be numerically approximated by a Cobb–Douglas two-inputs function. Let us assume therefore we have the following data: total direct costs constraint $C = 1\ Mln$, price of inputs $p_L = 2, p_K = 3$.

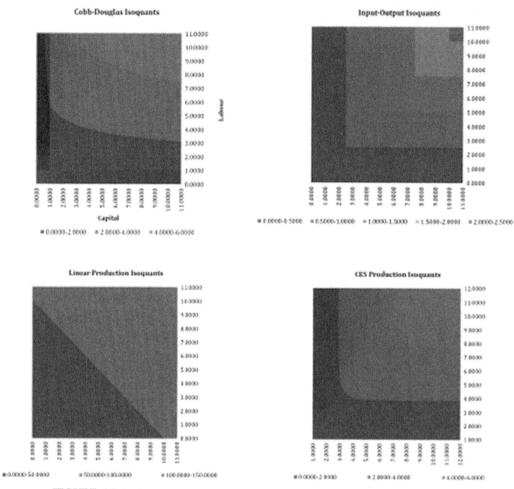

**FIGURE 6.7-1**    Isoquants representation for different degrees of input substitutability.

These input costs may be interpreted as the average estimated direct costs per hour of labor and machines, so that $L$ and $K$ may measure the two direct factors, man-hours and machine-hours (these calculated for the total amount of workforce and machineries employed by the firm on a yearly basis, i.e., 365 days).

The Cobb–Douglas estimated parameters are $A = 0.5$ and $\alpha = 0.5$. We assume therefore a Cobb–Douglas with constant returns to scale in the form of:

$$y = 0.5\left(L^{0.5}\,K^{0.5}\right).$$

Setting $y = k$, we derive the isoquant equation as:

$$k = 0.5\left(L^{0.5}\,K^{0.5}\right)$$

$$K^{0.5} = \frac{k}{0.5(L^{0.5})} \Rightarrow K = \frac{4k^2}{L}.$$

The isocost line will be derived instead from the following equality:

$$C = p_L \cdot L + p_k \cdot K = 2 \cdot L + 3 \cdot K.$$

Setting $x_2 = K$ as a dependent variable and $x_1 = L$ as independent variable we have the following isocost line:

$$K = \frac{C}{p_K} - \frac{p_L}{p_K}L = \frac{1\,Mln}{3} - \frac{2}{3}L,$$

which is the equation that satisfies the total cost constraint.

The production optimization is found at the point where the isocost line is tangent to the maximum isoquant attainable by the firm.

The slope of the isocost is equal to $-\frac{2}{3} = -0.67$ and at the optimal point the following relation must be satisfied (slope of the isoquant = slope of the isocost line):

$$MRS_{L,K} = \frac{p_L}{p_K}.$$

As:

$$MRS_{L,K} = \left|\frac{dK}{dL}\right| = \frac{MP_L}{MP_K},$$

the equilibrium condition becomes:

$$\frac{MP_L}{MP_K} = \frac{p_L}{p_K} \Rightarrow \frac{MP_L}{p_L} = \frac{MP_K}{p_K}$$

which is a familiar condition that we have seen in the cardinal utility approach, the ratio between marginal utility and price must be the same for all goods, which becomes here: the ratio between marginal product and price of input must be the same for all inputs.

As described in Fig. 6.7-2 the attainable isoquant is $I3$, which returns a level of output equal to $y = 102, 062$.

At the tangent point we have:

$$MRS_{L,K} = \frac{\alpha}{1-\alpha} \cdot \frac{K}{L} = \frac{166, 667}{250, 000} = 0.67 = \frac{p_L}{p_K} = \frac{2}{3}.$$

The budget constraint is also satisfied by easily inspecting that:

$$1\,Mln = 2 \cdot 250, 000 + 3 \cdot 166, 667.$$

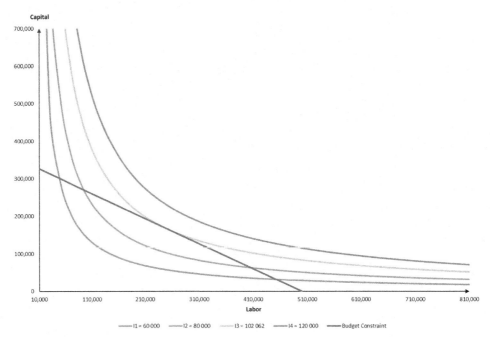

**FIGURE 6.7-2**   Example 1: firm optimal point at $L = 250{,}000$ and $K = 166{,}667$ with $y = 102{,}062$.

The analytical solution via the Lagrange multipliers (i.e., Excel GRG Solver) is given in Table 6.7-1, together with the marginal products information:

## Estimating the Cobb–Douglas function

At the beginning of Example 1, we have mentioned that we can estimate the Cobb–Douglas function from a statistical model.

This can be easily performed through the transformation of the nonlinear Cobb–Douglas:

$$y = A\left(L^{\alpha}K^{\beta}\right)$$

into the following linear logarithmic form, which is a linear multiple regression in two independent variables:

$$\log(y) = \log(A) + \alpha \cdot \log(L) + \beta \cdot \log(K).$$

Using available data, we have to take the *natural* log *level* of each data series. At this point having gathered the log level data on output, employment, and capital stock (or machine hours), we are ready to regress $y$ on $L$ and $K$.

**TABLE 6.7-1**   Example 1: analytical solution.

| x1 | x2 | p1 | 2 |
|---|---|---|---|
| 250,000 | 166,667 | p2 | 3 |
| L | K | | |
| | | | |
| **Max Poduction** | 102,062 | $y = A(L^{\alpha}K^{1-\alpha})$ | |
| | | | |
| s.t. | | | |
| 1,000,000 | = | 1,000,000 | |
| | | | |
| A | 0.50 | | |
| $\alpha$ | 0.50 | | |

| $MP_L = \partial y/\partial L = \alpha y/L$ | $MP_K = \partial y/\partial K = (1-\alpha)y/K$ |
|---|---|
| 0.2041 | 0.3062 |

| $MP_L/P_L$ | $MP_K/P_K$ |
|---|---|
| 0.1021 | 0.1021 |

## 6.8 Production Edgeworth box, contract curve, and the possibility frontier construction

Another problem the firm faces is to search for optimal combinations between outputs, derived from different production processes.

To solve this problem, we resort to the *Edgeworth box* and the *contract curve*.

A production Edgeworth box is a way to represent together two production processes (or two different firms), to which two production functions are associated, generating, respectively, output $y_1$ and $y_2$ as:

$$y_1 = f_1(x_1, x_2)$$

$$y_2 = f_2(x_1, x_2).$$

All the isoquants are reachable by the firm in each production process; the issue is to select the efficient combination of output, subject to a given *endowment* of factors.

If we assume for both processes a common Cobb–Douglas function as the following:

$$y = 0.5(L^{0.5}K^{0.5}),$$

the isoquant equation will all have the common form, by changing the parameter $k$:

$$x_2 = 4k^2/x_2.$$

Now, it is just a matter of plotting the isoquants on the Excel graph, where the primary axis will be used for the isoquants of $y_1$ and the secondary axis, in a reverse order scale, will be used for the isoquants of $y_2$.

The result will be a set of isoquants, all convex to the origins, as in Fig. 6.8-1.

Each point of the box identifies an allocation of inputs to the two different production processes.

The underlying data chart has been built via the usual Excel Data Table (see Table 6.8-1).

Each axis sum values represent the total *endowment* for the two inputs, that have to be allocated to both production processes: the endowment for labor is the sum between values read on the two horizontal axes on the same imaginary vertical line (see Fig. 6.8-1 the major grid vertical lines), while the endowment for capital is the sum between values read on the two horizontal axes on the same imaginary horizontal line (see Fig. 6.8-1 the major grid horizontal lines). Therefore, on each point where the two curves touch it must be numerically, approximately true that:

$$L_1 + L_2 \cong 820,000$$

$$K_1 + K_2 \cong 1,600,000.$$

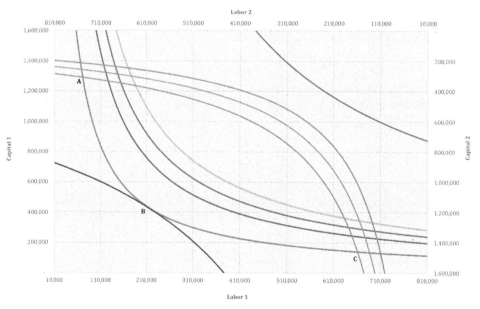

**FIGURE 6.8-1**   Production Edgeworth box.

**TABLE 6.8-1** Production Edgeworth box isoquants data.

| | Firm 1 (Or Production Process 1) Isoquants Map Output y1 = k --> | | | | step isoquants 20,000 | Firm 2 (Or Production Process 2) Isoquants Map Output y2 = k --> | | | |
|---|---|---|---|---|---|---|---|---|---|
| **440,076** | 200,000 | 220,000 | 240,000 | 152,000 | 1,201,634 | 200,000 | 220,000 | 240,000 | 421,000 |
| x1 = Labor | | | | | x2 = Capital K (within the table) | | | | |
| 10,000 | 16,000,000 | 19,360,000 | 23,040,000 | 9,241,600 | 10,000 | 16,000,000 | 19,360,000 | 23,040,000 | 70,896,400 |
| 30,000 | 5,333,333 | 6,453,333 | 7,680,000 | 3,080,533 | 30,000 | 5,333,333 | 6,453,333 | 7,680,000 | 23,632,133 |
| 50,000 | 3,200,000 | 3,872,000 | 4,608,000 | 1,848,320 | 50,000 | 3,200,000 | 3,872,000 | 4,608,000 | 14,179,280 |
| 70,000 | 2,285,714 | 2,765,714 | 3,291,429 | 1,320,229 | 70,000 | 2,285,714 | 2,765,714 | 3,291,429 | 10,128,057 |
| 90,000 | 1,777,778 | 2,151,111 | 2,560,000 | 1,026,844 | 90,000 | 1,777,778 | 2,151,111 | 2,560,000 | 7,877,378 |
| 110,000 | 1,454,545 | 1,760,000 | 2,094,545 | 840,145 | 110,000 | 1,454,545 | 1,760,000 | 2,094,545 | 6,445,127 |
| 130,000 | 1,230,769 | 1,489,231 | 1,772,308 | 710,892 | 130,000 | 1,230,769 | 1,489,231 | 1,772,308 | 5,453,569 |
| 150,000 | 1,066,667 | 1,290,667 | 1,536,000 | 616,107 | 150,000 | 1,066,667 | 1,290,667 | 1,536,000 | 4,726,427 |
| 170,000 | 941,176 | 1,138,824 | 1,355,294 | 543,624 | 170,000 | 941,176 | 1,138,824 | 1,355,294 | 4,170,376 |
| 190,000 | 842,105 | 1,018,947 | 1,212,632 | 486,400 | 190,000 | 842,105 | 1,018,947 | 1,212,632 | 3,731,389 |
| **210,000** | 761,905 | 921,905 | 1,097,143 | **440,076** | 210,000 | 761,905 | 921,905 | 1,097,143 | 3,376,019 |
| 230,000 | 695,652 | 841,739 | 1,001,739 | 401,809 | 230,000 | 695,652 | 841,739 | 1,001,739 | 3,082,452 |
| 250,000 | 640,000 | 774,400 | 921,600 | 369,664 | 250,000 | 640,000 | 774,400 | 921,600 | 2,835,856 |
| 270,000 | 592,593 | 717,037 | 853,333 | 342,281 | 270,000 | 592,593 | 717,037 | 853,333 | 2,625,793 |
| 570,000 | 280,702 | 339,649 | 404,211 | 162,133 | 570,000 | 280,702 | 339,649 | 404,211 | 1,243,796 |
| 590,000 | 271,186 | 328,136 | 390,508 | 156,637 | **590,000** | 271,186 | 328,136 | 390,508 | **1,201,634** |
| 610,000 | 262,295 | 317,377 | 377,705 | 151,502 | 610,000 | 262,295 | 317,377 | 377,705 | 1,162,236 |
| 730,000 | 219,178 | 265,205 | 315,616 | 126,597 | 730,000 | 219,178 | 265,205 | 315,616 | 971,184 |
| 750,000 | 213,333 | 258,133 | 307,200 | 123,221 | 750,000 | 213,333 | 258,133 | 307,200 | 945,285 |
| 770,000 | 207,792 | 251,429 | 299,221 | 120,021 | 770,000 | 207,792 | 251,429 | 299,221 | 920,732 |
| 790,000 | 202,532 | 245,063 | 291,646 | 116,982 | 790,000 | 202,532 | 245,063 | 291,646 | 897,423 |
| 810,000 | 197,531 | 239,012 | 284,444 | 114,094 | 810,000 | 197,531 | 239,012 | 284,444 | 875,264 |

The box has the property that the points A and C in Fig. 6.8-1 are less efficient than point B, as in B we can reach a higher isoquant for $y_2$. At point A, we have that the isoquant, such that the production is $y_1 = 152,000$, crosses the isoquant such that the production is $y_2 = 240,000$, and the following inputs are needed (see Table 6.8-1):

$$L_1 = 70,000; K_1 = 1,320,229 \Rightarrow MRS1 = \frac{\alpha}{1 - \alpha} \cdot K_1/L_1 \cong 18.86$$

$$L_2 = 750,000; K_2 = 307,000 \Rightarrow MRS2 = \frac{\alpha}{1 - \alpha} \cdot K_2/L_2 \cong 0.41.$$

In B, we have instead:

$$L_1 = 210,000; K_1 = 440,076 \Rightarrow MRS1 \cong 2$$

$$L_2 = 590,000; K_2 = 1,201,634 \Rightarrow MRS2 \cong 2,$$

so that $L_2$ and $K_2$ lie on a higher isoquant, corresponding to the production level $y_2 = 421,000$. It is also apparent how in B the two isoquants are tangent and have the same slope and this identifies an optimal allocation (defined also *Pareto allocation*). The point B is defined *contract point*.

The contract curve represents therefore the locus of the various contract points where the isoquants of each production process are tangent each other and where they have the same slope. In other words, the contract curve is the locus of efficient output points obtainable from the given input factors of the two production processes.

How can we graph the contract curve? We will use two methods: the first one derives from the geometrical inspection of the slopes of the various isoquants, the other is analytically derived via a standard constrained maximization problem.

## EXAMPLE 1 (CONTRACT CURVE DERIVATION AND PRODUCTION POSSIBILITY FRONTIER)

Let us continue with a constant return to scale Cobb–Douglas with $A = 0.5$ and $\alpha = 0.50$ described as follows:

$$y_{1,2} = 0.5\left(L^{0.5}\, K^{0.5}\right)$$

with

$$L_1 + L_2 \cong 820,000$$

$$K_1 + K_2 \cong 1,600,000.$$

To have the maximum efficiency the firm should move along the isoquants of Table 6.8-2, which are different from Table 6.8-1, where only one efficient allocation point could be identified.

Differently from Fig. 6.8-1, in Fig. 6.8-2 we do not have only a tangent point but as many tangent points as the number of isoquants, and the ideal line connecting them is the contract curve.

In each contract point, we have the same $MRS$ ($\cong 2$) between inputs for both production processes and what we need to do then is to find the co-ordinates of the two inputs in

**TABLE 6.8-2**  Example 1: isoquants data tangent each other.

| x1=Labour Hor.Axis | Firm 1 (Or Production Process 1) Isoquants Map Output Y1 = k -> | | | | | Firm 2 (Or Production Process 2) Isoquants Map Output Y2 = k -> | | | | |
|---|---|---|---|---|---|---|---|---|---|---|
| | 1,440,000 | 152,000 | 213,000 | 350,000 | 421,000 | 1,440,000 | 152,000 | 223,000 | 340,000 | 421,000 |
| | 10,000 | 9,241,600 | 21,715,600 | 49,000,000 | 70,896,400 x2=Capital | 10,000 | 9,241,600 | 19,891,600 | 46,240,000 | 70,896,400 |
| | 30,000 | 3,080,533 | 7,238,533 | 16,333,333 | 23,632,133 Vert.Axis | 30,000 | 3,080,533 | 6,630,533 | 15,413,333 | 23,632,133 |
| | 50,000 | 1,848,320 | 4,343,120 | 9,800,000 | 14,179,280 | 50,000 | 1,848,320 | 3,978,320 | 9,248,000 | 14,179,280 |
| | 70,000 | 1,320,229 | 3,102,229 | 7,000,000 | 10,128,057 | 70,000 | 1,320,229 | 2,841,657 | 6,605,714 | 10,128,057 |
| | 90,000 | 1,026,844 | 2,412,844 | 5,444,444 | 7,877,378 | 90,000 | 1,026,844 | 2,210,178 | 5,137,778 | 7,877,378 |
| | 110,000 | 840,145 | 1,974,145 | 4,454,545 | 6,445,127 | 110,000 | 840,145 | 1,808,327 | 4,203,636 | 6,445,127 |
| | 130,000 | 710,892 | 1,670,431 | 3,769,231 | 5,453,569 | 130,000 | 710,892 | 1,530,123 | 3,556,923 | 5,453,569 |
| | 150,000 | 616,107 | 1,447,707 | 3,266,667 | 4,726,427 | 150,000 | 616,107 | 1,326,107 | 3,082,667 | 4,726,427 |
| | 170,000 | 543,624 | 1,277,388 | 2,882,353 | 4,170,376 | 170,000 | 543,624 | 1,170,094 | 2,720,000 | 4,170,376 |
| | 190,000 | 486,400 | 1,142,926 | 2,578,947 | 3,731,389 | 190,000 | 486,400 | 1,046,926 | 2,433,684 | 3,731,389 |
| | 590,000 | 156,637 | 368,061 | 830,508 | 1,201,634 | 590,000 | 156,637 | 337,146 | 783,729 | 1,201,634 |
| | 610,000 | 151,502 | 355,993 | 803,279 | 1,162,236 | 610,000 | 151,502 | 326,092 | 758,033 | 1,162,236 |
| | 630,000 | 146,692 | 344,692 | 777,778 | 1,125,340 | 630,000 | 146,692 | 315,740 | 733,968 | 1,125,340 |
| | 650,000 | 142,178 | 334,086 | 753,846 | 1,090,714 | 650,000 | 142,178 | 306,025 | 711,385 | 1,090,714 |
| | 670,000 | 137,934 | 324,113 | 731,343 | 1,058,155 | 670,000 | 137,934 | 296,890 | 690,149 | 1,058,155 |
| | 690,000 | 133,936 | 314,719 | 710,145 | 1,027,484 | 690,000 | 133,936 | 288,284 | 670,145 | 1,027,484 |
| | 710,000 | 130,163 | 305,854 | 690,141 | 998,541 | 710,000 | 130,163 | 280,163 | 651,268 | 998,541 |
| | 730,000 | 126,597 | 297,474 | 671,233 | 971,184 | 730,000 | 126,597 | 272,488 | 633,425 | 971,184 |
| | 750,000 | 123,221 | 289,541 | 653,333 | 945,285 | 750,000 | 123,221 | 265,221 | 616,533 | 945,285 |
| | 770,000 | 120,021 | 282,021 | 636,364 | 920,732 | 770,000 | 120,021 | 258,332 | 600,519 | 920,732 |
| | 790,000 | 116,982 | 274,881 | 620,253 | 897,423 | 790,000 | 116,982 | 251,792 | 585,316 | 897,423 |
| | 810,000 | 114,094 | 268,094 | 604,938 | 875,264 | 810,000 | 114,094 | 245,575 | 570,864 | 875,264 |

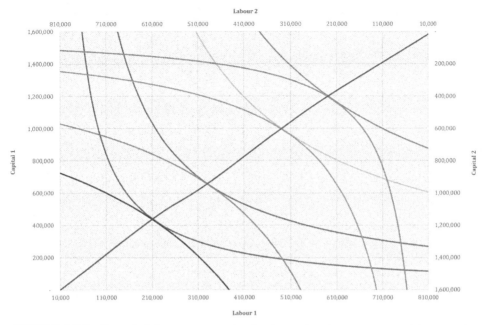

**FIGURE 6.8-2** Example 1: isoquants tangent each other and contract curve geometric approach.

each of those contract points, connecting these co-ordinates and then plotting the resulting line as our contract curve. The result is in Fig. 6.8-2.

The analytical method resorts instead to the following optimization problem (see Fig. 6.8-3 and Table 6.8-3):

$$\max_{\{L_1,K_1,L_2,K_2\}} b \cdot y_1(L_1, K_1) + (1-b) \cdot y_2(L_2, K_2) \qquad 0 < b < 1$$

subject to the following endowment constraint:

$$L_1 + L_2 = L^{tot}$$

$$K_1 + K_2 = K^{tot}$$

and subject to the following production processes constraint (we move along the tangent iso-quants, such that we have the same slope):

$$y_1(L_1, K_1) = \bar{y}_1 \big| MRS1 = MRS2$$

$$y_2(L_2, K_2) = \bar{y}_2 \big| MRS2 = MRS1$$

For each of the output identified by the isoquants we can plot in the co-ordinates space $(y_1, y_2)$ what is called the *production possibility frontier* (see Fig. 6.8-4), which shows the efficient

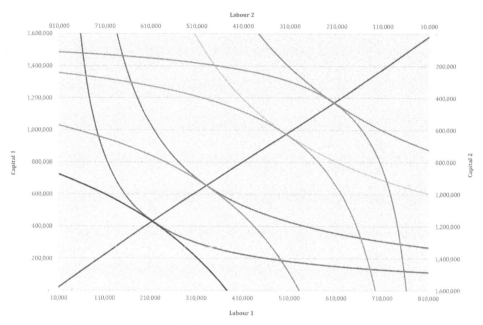

**FIGURE 6.8-3**    Example 1: contract curve from analytical approach.

infinite combinations of the two outputs obtainable from the most efficient employment combinations of the two inputs.

## 6.9 Short-run, long-run costs and the envelope average total costs derivation

In the previous sections we have analyzed the output produced as a function of the inputs.

In the current section, we will analyze, within the traditional costs theory, the costs as a function of the obtainable output.

The costs the firm faces fall in the following four macrocategories.

**i.** Short-run and long-run costs.
**ii.** Fixed and variable costs.

Normally, in the short-run the firm is constrained by a maximum production capacity, given by the equipment, plants, labor, and investment capacity available (i.e., equity capital available for a particular investment choice), while in the long-run the firm can better adapt the higher/lower levels of output demanded through the most adequate investment/divestment policies. For example, after a 5-years expansion period the company can have access to more debt-capital and undertake the best capital investments it desires, to maintain the new larger scale of the business than it had 5 years before.

**TABLE 6.8-3**  Contract curve solver numerical solution.

|  | | **Max** |  |
|---|---|---|---|
| b Factor | | 286,500 | |
| **0.50** | | | |
| | | | |
| s.t. Endowments | | 1,601,722 = | 1,601,722 |
| | | 820,000 = | 820,000 |

| | **Contract Curve Data Chart** | |
|---|---|---|
| | **x2 Capital** | **x1 Labour** |
| | 0 | 0 |
| **Firm1** | 430,932 | 214,457 |
| **Firm2** | 1,170,790 | 605,543 |
| | 1,601,722 | 820,000 |
| | | |
| **Endowment** | **1,601,722** | **820,000** |

**Constraints on y1 and y2**

| | | |
|---|---|---|
| y1 | 152,000 | 152,000 |
| y2 | 421,000 | 421,000 |

In the short run, the firm faces both variable and fixed/semi-fixed costs: the variable costs are typically represented by the direct costs incurred to produce the output (i.e., direct labor, row materials used in the production process, transportation costs, sales costs, direct energy costs, etc.), while there are other costs that are quite independent from the output produced (at least in the short-run), and these are, for example, the administrative costs, the portion of energy costs not related to the production area, IT maintenance costs, insurance expenses, bank charges, advertising costs, rents, and depreciation (which depends on the long-run investment policy).

In the long run we have that, if the company increases the business, all the costs will be usually automatically higher, due to the larger dimension of the business that is being run by the firm: for example, a higher number of employees will lead to higher total labor and administrative costs, compared to the previous period and, as a consequence of that, the distinction between fixed and variable costs in the long run practically vanishes.

In other words, in the long run the firm can alter the plant size and can vary all production factors, while in the short-run the plant size cannot be altered, and the firm is unable to change all the factors of production together.

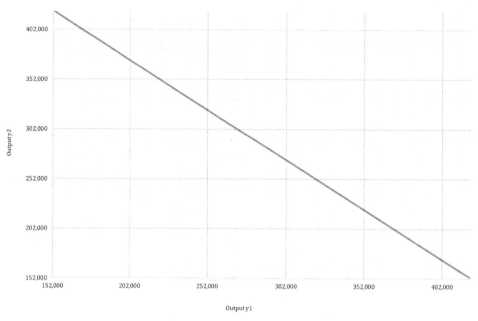

**FIGURE 6.8-4**   Example 1: linear production possibility frontier.

What are then the main costs functions analyzed in the short-run, within the traditional costs theory of microeconomics? The answer is the following set of functions, which determine the typical U-shaped cost curves.

- Variable-Costs function defined for the U-shaped costs as a polynomial function:

$$VC = ay^3 + by^2 + cy \qquad \text{with } a > 0,\ b < 0 \text{ and } c > 0.$$

- Fixed-Costs function, which is simply a horizontal line returning the constant C:

$$FC = Constant.$$

- Total-Costs function, $TC = VC + FC$:

$$TC = ay^3 + by^2 + cy + FC.$$

- Average-Total-Costs function, $ATC = \frac{TC}{y} = \frac{(VC + FC)}{y}$:

$$ATC = \frac{(ay^3 + by^2 + cy + FC)}{y} = ay^2 + by + c + \frac{FC}{y}.$$

- Average-Variable-Total-Costs function, $AVC = \frac{VC}{y}$ :

$$AVC = \frac{(ay^3 + by^2 + cy)}{y} = ay^2 + by + c .$$

- Marginal-Total-Costs function (cost of producing one additional unit of output):

$$MTC = \frac{dTC}{dy} = 3ay^2 + 2by + c.$$

- Marginal-Variable-Costs function:

$$MVC = \frac{dVC}{dy} = 3ay^2 + 2by + c.$$

As usual, some basic econometric regression modeling will help us to estimate the parameters $a$, $b$, $c$ from the actual data series that we want to investigate. Moreover, in reality, firms may have different costs paths from the ones described before, not necessarily U-shaped, and this depends on the type of business they are in and on other specific conditions under which they operate, that it is possible to investigate only case-by-case.

In the long run, the functions change slightly, as we do not have the Fixed-Costs, so that the long-run Average-Total-Cost function, for example, becomes:

$$LR\,ATC = \frac{(ay^3 + by^2 + cy)}{y} = ay^2 + by + c$$

## EXAMPLE 1 (U-SHAPED COST CURVES FOR A THREE-PLANTS FIRM CASE AND APPROXIMATE LONG-RUN ENVELOPE)

Let us suppose we have three plants for three different levels of output capacity, up to 100, up to 120, and up to 140 units, respectively. Each plant is used in the short-run while the three periods $T_1$, $T_2$, and $T_3$, taken as a whole, is the long-run period, in the sense that it takes some years to reach an increase of +40% in the production capacity and to undertake the adequate plants size investment policy.

In each period we estimate the following total costs function:

$$TC_1 = 0.01y_1^3 - 0.80y_1^2 + 50y_1 + 100;$$

$$TC_2 = 0.01y_1^3 - 1.00y_1^2 + 50y_1 + 400;$$

$$TC_3 = 0.01y_1^3 - 1.20y_1^2 + 50y_1 + 1.500.$$

We can then simply plot the total cost functions for each period, like in Fig. 6.9-1.

Notice that the Fixed-Costs, considered in the 3 years period as a whole, are variable (they jump from 100 to 1.500), and this is due to the larger dimension of the firm.

The Long-Run Total Cost curve is the envelope of all the Short-Run Total Cost curves; the Long-Run Total Cost curve starts from the origin, as in the long-run all costs are variable. It has been numerically derived as:

$$Long\ Run\ TC = Quantity \times Envelope\ Long\ Run\ ATC.$$

A polynomial order-3 (without intercept) equation has been added to the Excel graph of Fig. 6.9-1 to estimate the equation of the long-run costs.

The ATC for each period will be the one related to each plant used in each period. In the first period, we will use the small plant, in the second period the average plant, while in the third period we will use the large plant. The Long-Run Average Total Costs will be represented by the minimum costs incurred among the three plants (i.e., the most efficient plant is selected for each level of production). The line connecting all these minimum costs is called *discrete envelope curve* as represented in Fig. 6.9-2.

The LR ATC shows the minimum average cost of producing each output level when the firm is free to choose among all possible plant sizes. We can notice that:

- up to almost 40 units of output the small plant is most suitable; beyond that level of production the unit costs will start increasing and the average second plant would be ideally chosen for the production;

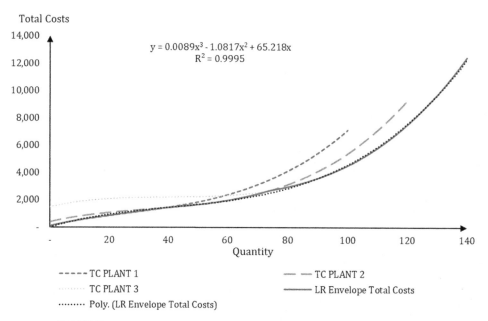

FIGURE 6.9-1　Total cost curves in the short- and long-run (envelope curve).

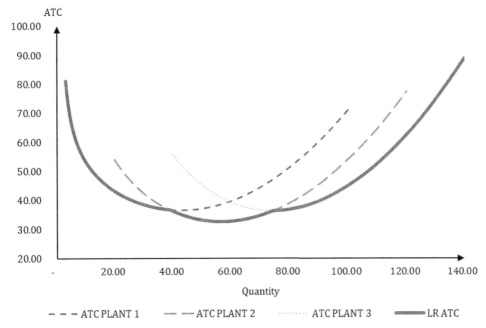

**FIGURE 6.9-2**  Average total cost curves in the short- and long-run (discrete envelope curve).

- up to almost 75 units of output, the average second plant is most suitable;
- up to maximum capacity of 140 units of output, the large third plant is most suitable.

The shape of the short-run costs reflects the diminishing marginal returns law.

The MC in Fig. 6.9-3 declines as long as the marginal product of the variable input is rising (see Fig. 6.5-2), and this result is because in this range smaller additions of the variable inputs are needed to produce each extra unit of output.

Once diminishing returns set in, more and more units of the variable inputs are needed to produce an extra unit of output and MC will rise because the marginal product of the variable input is declining. Eventually, MC will exceed both AVC and ATC causing these costs rise as well.

From the given functions of the Short-Run Total Costs, we can easily derive them to obtain the Short-Run Marginal Cost curves as depicted in Fig. 6.9-3.

The Long-Run Marginal Cost curve of Fig. 6.9-4 is instead obtained by deriving the polynomial function we have in Fig. 6.9-1, which approximates the envelope Long-Run Total Cost curve.

We can now use the Excel Solver GRG to estimate the *Long-Run Continuous Envelope*, as represented in Fig. 6.9-5.

The Envelope is a curve constructed from the underlying ATC curves, which has the mathematical property that it touches these curves in only one point (having therefore the same values), having at this point also the same slope, as the underlying curve (it is tangent).

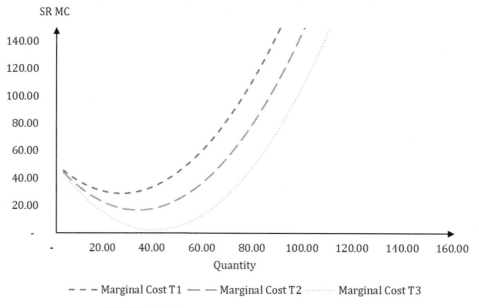

**FIGURE 6.9-3** Marginal cost curves in the short-run.

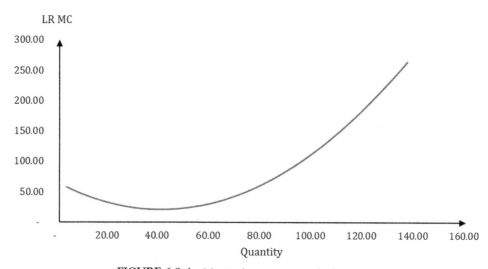

**FIGURE 6.9-4** Marginal cost curves in the long-run.

The way we have proceeded to solve this problem is first setting up the worksheet as in Fig. 6.9-6, where we have (condensed by row) the following information:

- *Column A* represents the quantity produced.
- under *Columns B, C, D* we have stored the data of SR ATC.

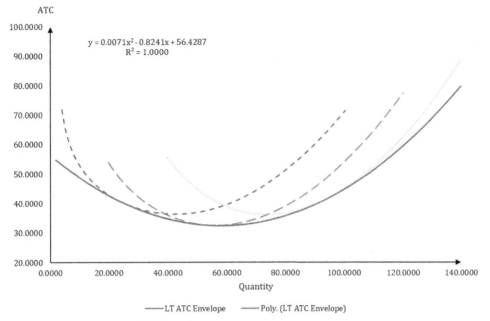

**FIGURE 6.9-5** Long-run ATC continuous envelope.

| | A | B | C | D | E | F | G | H | I | J | L | M | N | O |
|---|---|---|---|---|---|---|---|---|---|---|---|---|---|---|
| 1 | y | ATC1 | ATC2 | ATC3 | ENVELOPE | dATC1 | dATC2 | dATC3 | dATC Envelope | dATC LR-dATC SR | a | b | c | FC |
| 2 | ='ST a | | | | | | | | | | 0.0070 | -0.824 | 56.428 | No FC in long-run |
| 3 | ='ST a | ='ST a | | | =$L$2*'LT AT | | | | | | | | | |
| 4 | ='ST a | ='ST a | | | =$L$2*'LT AT | =(B4-B3)/( | =(C4-C3)/(A4 | =(D4-D3)/(A4-A3) | =(E4-E3)/(A4-A3) | =I4-F4 | | | | |
| 50 | ='ST a | ='ST a | ='ST an | | =$L$2*'LT AT | =(B50-B49), | =(C50-C49)/( | =(D50-D49)/(A50-A49) | =(E50-E49)/(A50-A49) | =I50-F50 | | | | |
| 51 | ='ST a | ='ST a | ='ST an | | =$L$2*'LT AT | =(B51-B50), | =(C51-C50)/( | =(D51-D50)/(A51-A50) | =(E51-E50)/(A51-A50) | =I51-F51 | | | | |
| 52 | ='ST a | ='ST a | ='ST an | | =$L$2*'LT AT | =(B52-B51), | =(C52-C51)/( | =(D52-D51)/(A52-A51) | =(E52-E51)/(A52-A51) | =I52-F52 | Here the only point where they touch and also have same slope | | | |
| 53 | ='ST a | ='ST a | ='ST an | | =$L$2*'LT AT | =(B53-B52), | =(C53-C52)/( | =(D53-D52)/(A53-A52) | =(E53-E52)/(A53-A52) | =I53-F53 | | | | |
| 108 | ='ST a | ='ST a | ='ST an | ='ST a | =$L$2*'LT AT | =(B108-B10 | =(C108-C107 | =(D108-D107)/(A108-A107) | =(E108-E107)/(A108-A107) | =I108-G108 | | | | |
| 109 | ='ST a | ='ST a | ='ST an | ='ST a | =$L$2*'LT AT | =(B109-B10 | =(C109-C108 | =(D109-D108)/(A109-A108) | =(E109-E108)/(A109-A108) | =I109-G109 | | | | |
| 110 | ='ST a | ='ST a | ='ST an | ='ST a | =$L$2*'LT AT | =(B110-B10 | =(C110-C109 | =(D110-D109)/(A110-A109) | =(E110-E109)/(A110-A109) | =I110-G110 | | | | |
| 111 | ='ST a | ='ST a | ='ST an | ='ST a | =$L$2*'LT AT | =(B111-B11 | =(C111-C110 | =(D111-D110)/(A111-A110) | =(E111-E110)/(A111-A110) | =I111-G111 | Here the only point where they touch and also have same slope | | | |
| 112 | ='ST a | ='ST a | ='ST an | ='ST a | =$L$2*'LT AT | =(B112-B11 | =(C112-C111 | =(D112-D111)/(A112-A111) | =(E112-E111)/(A112-A111) | =I112-G112 | | | | |
| 188 | ='ST a | ='ST a | ='ST an | ='ST a | =$L$2*'LT AT | =(B188-B18 | =(C188-C187 | =(D188-D187)/(A188-A187) | =(E188-E187)/(A188-A187) | =I188-H188 | | | | |
| 189 | ='ST a | ='ST a | ='ST an | ='ST a | =$L$2*'LT AT | =(B189-B18 | =(C189-C188 | =(D189-D188)/(A189-A188) | =(E189-E188)/(A189-A188) | =I189-H189 | | | | |
| 190 | ='ST a | ='ST a | ='ST an | ='ST a | =$L$2*'LT AT | =(B190-B18 | =(C190-C189 | =(D190-D189)/(A190-A189) | =(E190-E189)/(A190-A189) | =I190-H190 | Here the only point where they touch and also have same slope | | | |
| 191 | ='ST a | ='ST a | ='ST an | ='ST a | =$L$2*'LT AT | =(B191-B19 | =(C191-C190 | =(D191-D190)/(A191-A190) | =(E191-E190)/(A191-A190) | =I191-H191 | | | | |
| 207 | ='ST a | | ='ST an | ='ST a | =$L$2*'LT AT | =(B207-B20 | =(C207-C206 | =(D207-D206)/(A207-A206) | =(E207-E206)/(A207-A206) | =I207-H207 | | | | |
| 282 | ='ST a | | ='ST an | ='ST a | =$L$2*'LT AT | =(B282-B28 | =(C282-C281 | =(D282-D281)/(A282-A281) | =(E282-E281)/(A282-A281) | =I282-H282 | | | | |

**FIGURE 6.9-6** Excel setup for the LR ATC envelope curve.

- *Column E* is the Envelope ATC cost function linked to the cost parameters stored in *Cells L2, M2, N2*.
- *Columns F, G, H, I* store the numerical derivatives of the ATC costs.
- Column J is just the difference between the numerical derivative of the Envelope and corresponding SR curve for each period. For example, after producing quantity 40 the second plant is activated.

Using the Excel Solver (see Fig. 6.9-7), we can minimize any value under *Column J* (we have selected *Cell J* 111), by changing the costs parameters under *Cells L2, M2, N2*, subject to the constraints that in just one point each SR cost function and the LR cost function have to touch (have the same values) and have the same slope.

After a geometric inspection (and trials and errors), these three points can be visualized and selected in correspondence of the *Row* 52, *Row* 111 and *Row* 190.

The second tangent point can be, for example, found in the range including the minimum value of the ATC2. The solution is given in Table 6.9-1, where at each point the slope and values of Envelope and each underlying SR curve is the same. Once the numerical data have been found the polynomial approximate equation of the LR Envelope can be found as represented in Fig. 6.9-5 just adding the order-2 trend line to the data points.

The U-shaped LR ATC curve, as represented in Fig. 6.9-5, reflects the long-run economies and diseconomies of scale depending on the production undertaken. The unit cost declines once the output increases, until a minimum point. Then, as organizational inefficiencies may result from producing larger and larger levels of outputs the effect of higher marginal costs operates and diseconomies of scale set in, increasing the average total costs.

Also, economists relate the U-shape of the long-run ATC to the concept of returns to scale as follows:

| | | |
|---|---|---|
| *LR ATC decreasing* | *iff* | *increasing returns to scale* |
| *LR ATC constant* | *iff* | *constant returns to scale* |
| *LR ATC increasing* | *iff* | *decreasing returns to scale* |

## Importance of costs for the supply curve

The costs analysis is of paramount importance because economists through the costs are interested in analyzing the supply behavior.

**TABLE 6.9-1**  Envelope Solver Solution at points y = 25, y = 54.50, and y = 94.

| y | ATC1 | ATC2 | ATC3 | ENVELOPE | dATC1 | dATC2 | dATC3 | dATC Envelope | dATC LR-dATC SR |
|---|---|---|---|---|---|---|---|---|---|
| 0.0000 | | | | | | | | | |
| 0.5000 | 249.6025 | | | 56.0184 | | | | | |
| 1.0000 | 149.2100 | | | 55.6116 | -200.7850 | 0.0000 | 0.0000 | -0.8135 | 199.9715 |
| 1.5000 | 115.4892 | | | 55.2084 | -67.4417 | 0.0000 | 0.0000 | -0.8064 | 66.6352 |
| 24.5000 | 40.4841 | 47.8290 | | 40.4868 | -0.4851 | -1.1953 | 0.0000 | -0.4808 | 0.0043 |
| **25.0000** | **40.2500** | 47.2500 | | **40.2500** | **-0.4683** | -1.1581 | 0.0000 | **-0.4737** | **-0.0054** |
| 25.5000 | 40.0241 | 46.6888 | | 40.0167 | -0.4519 | -1.1225 | 0.0000 | -0.4666 | -0.0147 |
| 53.0000 | 37.5768 | 32.6372 | 42.7919 | 32.6365 | 0.2191 | -0.0888 | -0.6841 | -0.0772 | 0.0115 |
| 53.5000 | 37.6917 | 32.5991 | 42.4599 | 32.6015 | 0.2297 | -0.0761 | -0.6640 | -0.0701 | 0.0059 |
| 54.0000 | 37.8119 | 32.5674 | 42.1378 | 32.5699 | 0.2404 | -0.0635 | -0.6442 | -0.0631 | 0.0004 |
| **54.5000** | 37.9374 | **32.5419** | 41.8254 | **32.5419** | 0.2510 | **-0.0509** | -0.6247 | **-0.0560** | **-0.0051** |
| 55.0000 | 38.0682 | 32.5227 | 41.5227 | 32.5175 | 0.2616 | -0.0384 | -0.6054 | -0.0489 | -0.0104 |
| 55.5000 | 38.2043 | 32.5097 | 41.2295 | 32.4966 | 0.2722 | -0.0260 | -0.5864 | -0.0418 | -0.0158 |
| 93.0000 | 63.1653 | 47.7911 | 41.0190 | 41.0176 | 1.0434 | 0.8085 | 0.4806 | 0.4892 | 0.0086 |
| 93.5000 | 63.6920 | 48.2006 | 41.2653 | 41.2658 | 1.0535 | 0.8190 | 0.4925 | 0.4963 | 0.0038 |
| **94.0000** | 64.2238 | 48.6153 | **41.5174** | **41.5174** | 1.0636 | 0.8295 | **0.5043** | **0.5033** | **-0.0010** |
| 94.5000 | 64.7607 | 49.0353 | 41.7755 | 41.7727 | 1.0737 | 0.8400 | 0.5161 | 0.5104 | -0.0057 |
| 95.0000 | 65.3026 | 49.4605 | 42.0395 | 42.0314 | 1.0839 | 0.8504 | 0.5279 | 0.5175 | -0.0104 |
| 140.0000 | | 0.0000 | 88.7143 | 79.8154 | 0.0000 | 0.0000 | 1.5182 | 1.1547 | -0.3635 |

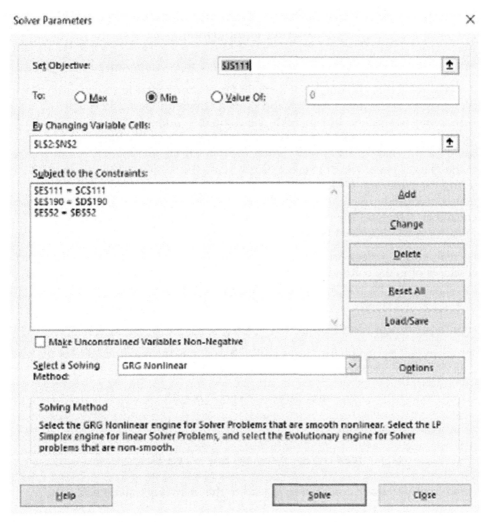

FIGURE 6.9-7   Solver set up for envelope resolution.

In the short-run, when making supply decisions the marginal cost of producing additional units is the relevant cost consideration: the production will be expanded by the profit maximizing firm until the marginal cost will be equal to marginal revenue.

In the long run, the ATC is of key importance for the long-run supply of the perfect-competitive firm. In the long run, the new entrants, before entering the industry, will compare the price versus LR ATC and the firms will supply the product as long as the price at least covers the LR ATC.

These analyses will be developed in the next section dedicated to the perfect (or pure) competitive markets.

## 6.10 Perfect competitive markets: short-run, long-run supply curves and market equilibrium

The main features of the *perfect competition markets* can be summarized as follows:

- the demand related to the output of a single firm is horizontal in the co-ordinates space $(p, y)$ and equal to the price; the demand curve is therefore perfectly elastic;
- there are many sellers and buyers each one completely independent from the other;
- the firms are called *price-takers* because the consumers are not willing to pay more for the same good, which is also produced by the other firms; the sellers are not able to affect the market price, which is taken as given (see in Section 4.2 the Example 2 regarding the Walrasian *tâtonment*);
- the goods produced are identical for all firms and they are perfectly homogeneous to the consumer; therefore, the price applied will be the same for all firms;
- the industry is characterized by low *barriers to entry*.

In the real world, perfect competitive markets can be typically found in the agriculture product sectors or in the commodity sectors. Also, the minority stocks traded at the stock exchange every day can be seen as a peculiar form of perfect competitive market.

### Short-run equilibrium conditions

The problem that the single firm faces in the short-run is the maximization of the profit $\Pi$, defined as the difference between Total-Revenues and Total-Costs:

$$\max \Pi(y) = TR(y) - TC(y),$$

which is in more details defined as:

$$\max \Pi(y) = \overline{p}y - \left(ay^3 + by^2 + cy + FC\right).$$

The first-order necessary condition will lead to the following equation:

$$\frac{d\Pi(y)}{dy} = \overline{p} - MTC = 0 \Rightarrow \overline{p} = MTC$$

where $MTC = 3ay^2 + 2by + c$, with $a > 0$ and $b < 0$.

It turns out that the sufficient condition is:

$$\frac{d^2\Pi(y)}{dy^2} = \frac{d^2TC(y)}{dy^2} = -(6ay + 2b) < 0 (6ay + 2b) > 0$$

which implies that in correspondence of the quantity $y^*$, such that $\overline{p} = MTC$, the marginal cost is an increasing function.

Let us see now a perfect-competition case applied in Excel in Example 1.

## EXAMPLE 1 (PERFECT COMPETITIVE FIRM SHORT-RUN EQUILIBRIUM)

Let us consider the same short-run Total Cost function in T1 as the one considered in the previous section, defined as:

$$TC(y) = 0.01y^3 - 0.80y^2 + 50y + 100;$$

where $0 \leq y \leq 100$ is the output produced in period T1.

The Total Revenue function is simply the price times the output, for period T1:

$$TR(y) = \bar{p}y$$

setting $\bar{p} = 50$.

It is easy to see that the Marginal Revenue is $MR = \frac{dTR(y)}{dy}$ equal to $\bar{p} = 50$ while, also the Average Revenue $AR = \frac{\bar{p}y}{y} = \bar{p}$ is equal to $\bar{p} = 50$ so that we have, for the perfect-competitive firm, the following relationship:

$$\bar{p} = 50 = MR = AR = D.$$

Letting $y$ move from zero to 100, we can simply plot the Total Cost and Total Revenue functions as in Fig. 6.10-1.

The excerpt of the Excel setup worksheet is in Fig. 6.10-2, where we have built the relevant cost-curves (TC, ATC, MC and AVC) together with TR, $\bar{p}$ and profit $= \Pi$:

Now, the issue is to find the optimal point $y^*$ that maximizes *Cell T5* (the profit function) by changing *Cell T7* (the optimal quantity to seek), and this is done simply via the Excel GRG Solver, as in Fig. 6.10-3.

The solution returned by the Solver is given by the optimal quantity (see Fig. 6.10-3):

$$y^* = 53.33$$

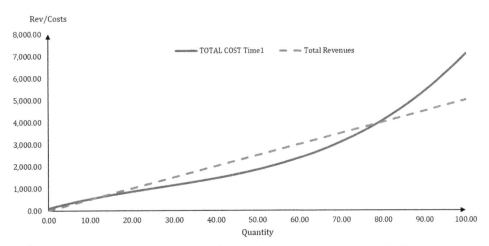

**FIGURE 6.10-1**  Total costs and total revenue for the perfect-competitive firm.

II. Static optimization

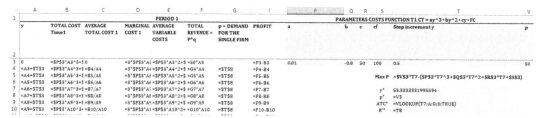

**FIGURE 6.10-2**    Excel setup for the perfect-competitive, maximizing profit firm.

**Solver Parameters**    ✕

Se_t Objective:    $T$5    ⬆

To:    ⦿ _M_ax    ○ Mi_n_    ○ _V_alue Of:    0

_B_y Changing Variable Cells:

$T$7    ⬆

S_u_bject to the Constraints:

|  |
|--|

_A_dd

_C_hange

_D_elete

_R_eset All

Load/Save

☑ Ma_k_e Unconstrained Variables Non-Negative

S_e_lect a Solving Method:    GRG Nonlinear    ⌄    O_p_tions

**Solving Method**

Select the GRG Nonlinear engine for Solver Problems that are smooth nonlinear. Select the LP Simplex engine for linear Solver Problems, and select the Evolutionary engine for Solver problems that are non-smooth.

Help    _S_olve    Close

**FIGURE 6.10-3**    Excel Solver perfect-competitive firm maximizing profit.

at which point the ATC is:

$$ATC^* = 37.65$$

and also the Marginal Cost is equal to the price.

Looking at Fig. 6.10-4, we can see that the Profit $\Pi$ can be measured in geometrical terms by the following rectangular area:

$$Profit\ \Pi = y^*(\bar{p} - ATC^*) \cong 658$$

When $\bar{p} > MR$, geometrically speaking, looking at Fig. 6.10-4, we can expand the production until the MC is equal to the given price (at the point where MC is an increasing function, recalling the sufficient conditions) and then we can draw from that point a vertical line that will determine the optimal quantity. The ATC* is also determined for that optimal quantity produced.

Let us suppose now that the price is $P = 36$, namely lower than the ATC but higher than AVC.

The graph of the maximizing profit firm would be as in Fig. 6.10-5. We have canceled any (extra) profit, but it is still convenient for the firm to keep producing because the price is higher than the AVC. The point where the price is equal to the minimum AVC (i.e., $p_c = 34$) is called *shut-down point*; at this point for the firm will not be anymore possible to continue the production and it will be forced to shut down.

In a perfect competition market, as the price is a variable determined exogenously, the firm can only work on the costs side of the business and the better the firm manages its cost the higher the profit, otherwise it will be pushed out of the industry.

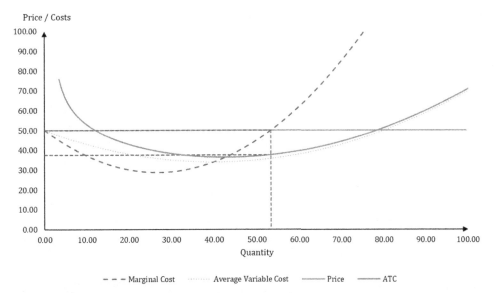

**FIGURE 6.10-4** Maximum profit area for a perfect-competitive firm $P = 50$.

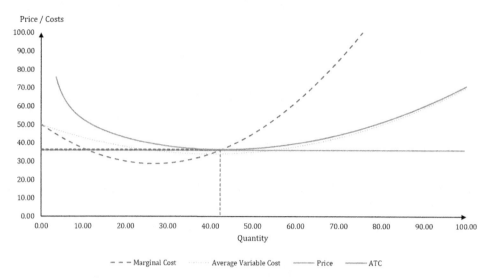

**FIGURE 6.10-5**  Zero profit area for a perfect-competitive firm when $P = 36$.

Now, we are able to build the SR Supply curve for the perfect competitive firm: this will be represented by each point read on the MC curve, above the shutting-down point as depicted in Fig. 6.10-6.

Summing horizontally all the supply curves we obtain the aggregate supply of the sector that in the short-run will have the typical upward shape. In the perfect competition industry, the horizontal sum of the supply curves is possible because each firm operates independently from the others.

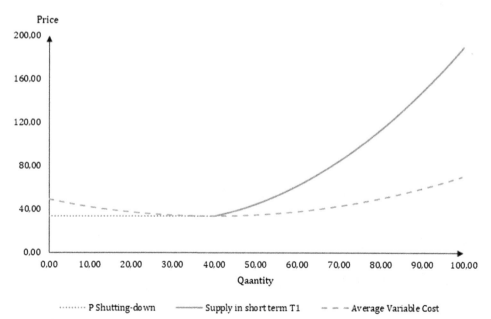

**FIGURE 6.10-6**  Short-run supply curve (part of the MC curve above the shutting-down point).

Assuming then a linear demand function for all the consumers, as:

$$p = a - by$$

and setting $a = 100$ and $b = 1$, we can sum the demand curves horizontally to derive the aggregate demand of the industry and draw the short-run equilibrium of the market, as described in Fig. 6.10-7.

With a market equilibrium such that the price is $P = 48$ the industry will attract new entrants because (extra) profit will exist and push down the price.

Assuming instead the following aggregate demand function, keeping the same aggregate supply function:

$$p = 60 - y$$

the market equilibrium will be obtained as in Fig. 6.10-8. In this situation the price is at the shutting-down level, and this will create no profit generation, preventing the new players from entering the market.

## The long-run

In the long-run the supply curve will be derived considering the long-run marginal and average costs (see Fig. 6.10-9).

The long-run supply curve will correspond to the portion of the MC curve of Fig. 6.9-4 above the minimum point of the LR ATC of Fig. 6.9-2.

This is described by Fig. 6.10-8.

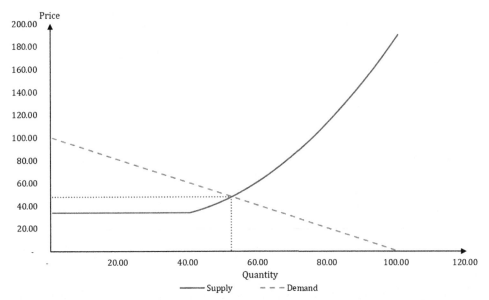

**FIGURE 6.10-7**  Supply and Demand with clearing price $P = 48$ and quantity $= 52$.

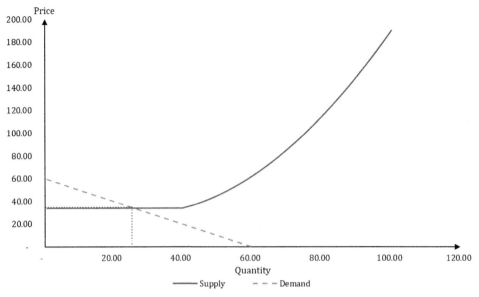

**FIGURE 6.10-8**    Supply and Demand with clearing price $P = 34$ and quantity $= 26$.

The aggregate LR supply curve of the industry will be instead different from the shape of each firm LR supply curve, depending on the three following cases.

1. Constant costs industry (the shape of the long-run supply will be horizontal).
2. Increasing costs industry (upward long-run supply curve).
3. Decreasing costs industry (downward long-run supply curve).

## 6.11 Monopolistic market equilibrium: the Chamberlin model

The second type of market described here is the monopolistic competition (see E. Chamberlin, *The Theory of Monopolistic Competition*, 1933).

The main features of this form of competition can be summarized as follows:

- large number of players (households and sellers);
- low barriers to entry;
- differentiated products; however, the differences are not so great as to eliminate other goods as substitutes;
- players operate independently in the market, from each other;
- the firms face a downward-sloping demand curve. The sellers can slightly leverage on prices, which are not completely taken as given. This, together with the fact that the products are slightly differentiated, represents the main difference from a perfect competitive market.

Within this form of competitive market, the firm is called *price-searcher*.

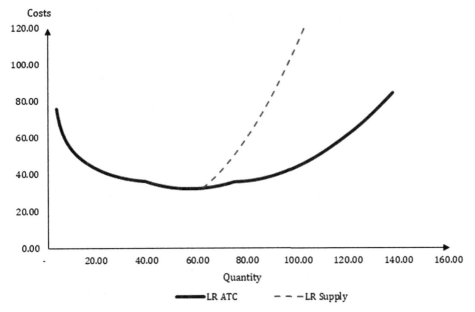

Costs

FIGURE 6.10-9   Long-run supply for the perfect-competitive firm.

We can find hundreds of examples of this type of competition (e.g., ice creams, toothpaste, soap, hand creams, etc.). Also, the restaurants in downtown are good examples of a monopolistic competition: prices of meals are different from one restaurant to the other, as the "product" is clearly different, and decisions of the agents are independent from each other. However, the pricing power is limited, as each seller must consider the fact that goods are somehow homogenous and replaceable.

## EXAMPLE 1 (SHORT-RUN AND LONG-RUN EQUILIBRIUM)

As usual, the problem that the single firm faces in the short-run is the maximization of the profit $\Pi$, defined as the difference between Total-Revenues and Total-Costs:

$$\max \Pi(y) = TR(y) - TC(y),$$

which is in more details defined as:

$$\max \Pi(y) = py - \left(ay^3 + by^2 + cy + FC\right).$$

Now, the difference from the price-takers competition is the downward-sloping demand curve faced by the firm, which, if assumed to be linear, can be defined as:

$$p = a - by,$$

so that the total revenues become:

$$\Pi(y) = (ay - by^2) - (ay^3 + by^2 + cy + FC).$$

Let us assume now we have the following short-run total costs function:

$$TC(y) = 0.01y^3 - 0.80y^2 + 50y + 100$$

and the following short-run demand function:

$$p = 100 - y.$$

The maximization problem leads to the following nonlinear objective function:

$$\max \Pi(y) = (100y - y^2) - (0.01y^3 + 0.80y^2 + 50y + 100)$$

$$\frac{d\Pi(y)}{dy} = 100 - 2y - MC \Rightarrow MR = MC,$$

namely, marginal revenue must be equal to marginal cost.

In Excel, the short-run equilibrium is simply found with the GRG Solver at the point $y^* = 34.70$, such that $MR = MC \cong 31$. The price will be read on the demand line, in correspondence of the optimal point $y^*$.

Figs. 6.11-1 to 6.11-3 represent the way the firm in the monopolistic market reaches the short-run and long-run equilibrium points.

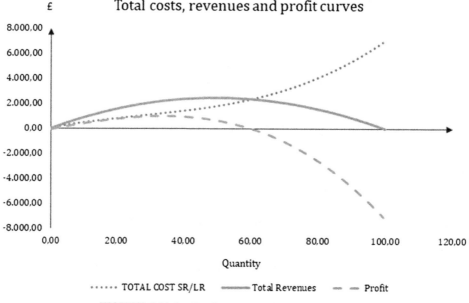

FIGURE 6.11-1   Total costs, total revenues, and profit.

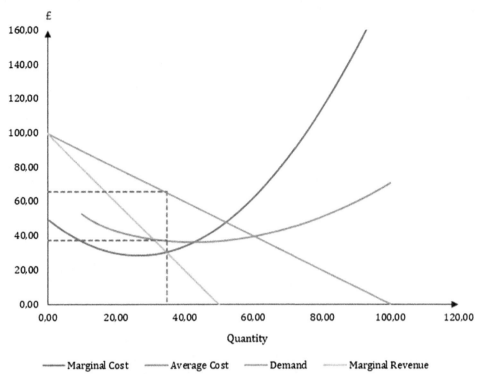

FIGURE 6.11-2 Monopolistic competition: short-run equilibrium point.

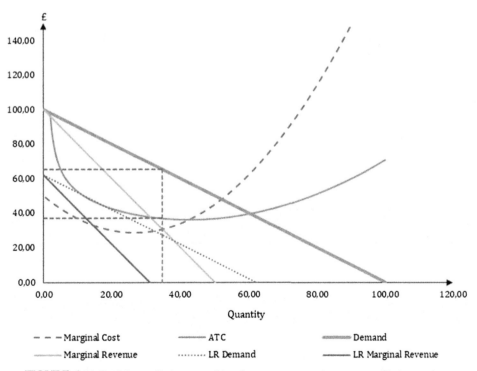

FIGURE 6.11-3 Monopolistic competition: long-run versus short-run equilibrium points.

```
Sub Find_LR_Monopolistic_Equilibrium()

'Starting point resets for parameter (a) of long run demand p=a-by moving the curve on the left

 Range("AE3") = 40

'Increments parameter (a) of the long run demand p=a-by until tangent point with ATC is met.
'Columns N and O will tests if demand is equal to average total cost in only one point

Do Until Range("O205") = 1

    Range("AE3").Value = Range("AE3").Value + 0.05

'This increment function will move to the right the long run demand (parallel to short term demand)
'until tangent point is met then copies the equilibrium quantity from column A

Loop
Range("O3").Select

 Do Until ActiveCell = 1

   ActiveCell.Offset(1, 0).Select

Loop

ActiveCell.Offset(0, -14).Copy

Range("AJ7").PasteSpecial xlPasteValues


Application.CutCopyMode = False

End Sub
```

**FIGURE 6.11-4**    VBA code for LR equilibrium point.

While in the short-run the usual rule $MR = MC$ applies, in the long-run the optimal point is found where the long-term demand is tangent to the LR ATC (here we have assumed for simplicity the same ATC from the SR total costs function).

According to the Chamberlin model, what is happening, essentially, is that at the short-run equilibrium price = 65.50 extra profits will be generated by the firm and new firms will enter the industry, causing a parallel shift on the left for each firm's demand curve (this is because the same number of buyers has to be divided among a larger number of firms) until it is tangent to LR ATC and this will cancel any extra profit (LR Equilibrium price = 47.40).

We can also simulate on various long-run demand curves and find the optimal LR equilibrium tangent point to ATC, using a VBA code as represented in Fig. 6.11-4.

## 6.12 Markets with high-entry barriers: monopoly and the Cournot duopoly model

In the previous Sections 6.10 and 6.11, we have analyzed how the firms behave in competitive markets with low-entry barriers.

We now turn the attention to the following two competitive markets with high-entry barriers.

- Monopoly.
- Oligopoly (as analyzed in the classical Cournot Duopoly Model).

## Monopoly

The monopoly is characterized by the following points:

- single seller;
- no goods substitutes;
- high barriers to entry (e.g., legal, economic, capital requirement barriers, etc.).
- downward sloping demand, as in the monopolistic market.

In the monopoly we have the same objective function to maximize, as in the monopolistic market:

$$\max \Pi(y) = TR(y) - TC(y) = (ay - by^2) - (ay^3 + by^2 + cy + FC).$$

$$\frac{d\Pi(y)}{dy} = 0 \Rightarrow MR = MC.$$

In Excel, we can implement the various functions as described in Table 6.12-2. Fig. 6.12-1 represents the way the monopolist acts to reach the optimum: once the optimal quantity is analytically found, such that $MC = MR$, the correspondent price will be read on the demand curve. The optimal quantity $y^*$ is found via the Excel GRG Solver (see Table 6.12-1).

Notice that in monopoly there is no such thing as the supply curve of the pure competitive markets. There is just a supply point. Once the marginal cost and the demand curve are known the monopolist will find the optimal price and the optimal quantity. It does not make any sense wondering the quantity offered for each level of price: given the marginal cost curve the same quantity may be offered at different price levels, depending on the demand curve.

In broad terms the same reasoning is valid in the long-run, as there will not be any new entry in the industry. The existence of high barriers to entry will allow the monopolist to generate extra profits in the long run as well.

This does not imply that the monopolist will charge higher prices (monopolists are often accused of price gouging) because this conduct might have a negative impact on the quantity sold, as the demand is downward sloping. Therefore, a higher price is not always good for monopolists.

**TABLE 6.12-1** Excel solver solution.

| Max P | 976.36 |
| --- | --- |
| $y^*$ | 34.70 |
| $p^*$ | 65.50 |
| ATC* | 37.20 |
| R'* | 31.00 |
| C'* | 30.51 |

**TABLE 6.12-2**   monopoly functions underlying data and the optimal solution.

| | MONOPOLIST COST AND REVENUE FUNCTIONS | | | | | | | |
|---|---|---|---|---|---|---|---|---|
| y | TOTAL COST SR/LR | AVERAGE TOTAL COST | MARGINAL COST | AVERAGE VARIABLE COSTS | TOTAL REVENUE = $p^*y = (a-by)y$ $= ay-by^2$ | DEMAND FOR THE MONOPOLIST (PRICE) $p = a-by$ | PROFIT | $R'=a-2by$ |
| 0.00 | 100.00 | 0.00 | | | 0.00 | 100.00 | | 100.00 |
| 0.50 | 124.80 | 249.60 | 49.21 | 49.60 | 49.75 | 99.50 | -75.05 | 99.00 |
| 1.00 | 149.21 | 149.21 | 48.43 | 49.21 | 99.00 | 99.00 | -50.21 | 98.00 |
| 1.50 | 173.23 | 115.49 | 47.67 | 48.82 | 147.75 | 98.50 | -25.48 | 97.00 |
| 34.00 | 1,268.24 | 37.30 | 30.28 | 34.36 | 2,244.00 | 66.00 | 975.76 | 32.00 |
| **34.50** | **1,283.44** | **37.20** | **30.51** | **34.30** | **2,259.75** | **65.50** | **976.31** | **31.00** |
| 35.00 | 1,298.75 | 37.11 | 30.75 | 34.25 | 2,275.00 | 65.00 | 976.25 | 30.00 |
| 35.50 | 1,314.19 | 37.02 | 31.01 | 34.20 | 2,289.75 | 64.50 | 975.56 | 29.00 |
| 36.00 | 1,329.76 | 36.94 | 31.28 | 34.16 | 2,304.00 | 64.00 | 974.24 | 28.00 |
| 36.50 | 1,345.47 | 36.86 | 31.57 | 34.12 | 2,317.75 | 63.50 | 972.28 | 27.00 |
| 37.00 | 1,361.33 | 36.79 | 31.87 | 34.09 | 2,331.00 | 63.00 | 969.67 | 26.00 |
| 37.50 | 1,377.34 | 36.73 | 32.19 | 34.06 | 2,343.75 | 62.50 | 966.41 | 25.00 |
| 38.00 | 1,393.52 | 36.67 | 32.52 | 34.04 | 2,356.00 | 62.00 | 962.48 | 24.00 |
| 98.50 | 6,819.92 | 69.24 | 183.47 | 68.22 | 147.75 | 1.50 | -6,672.17 | -97.00 |
| 99.00 | 6,912.19 | 69.82 | 185.63 | 68.81 | 99.00 | 1.00 | -6,813.19 | -98.00 |
| 99.50 | 7,005.55 | 70.41 | 187.81 | 69.40 | 49.75 | 0.50 | -6,955.80 | -99.00 |
| 100.00 | 7,100.00 | 71.00 | 190.00 | 70.00 | 0.00 | 0.00 | -7,100.00 | -100.00 |

## Oligopoly (the Cournot Duopoly Model)

The oligopoly is a market competition where only a small number of sellers compose the market. It is essentially a competition market among the few. What is the key difference between the oligopoly and the perfect or monopolistic competitive markets? The answer lies in the *interdependence* among the few firms that constitute the oligopoly.

While in the perfect and monopolistic markets each firm is independent from each other, in the oligopoly the firms are strategically connected each other. While the perfect competitive firm and the monopolistic firm know their demand curve this is not possible in the oligopoly, where each firm does not exactly know which portion of the total demand will compete for. The action of each firm influences the demand faced by rival sellers.

The first mathematical economic model of oligopoly (in the form of a *duopoly*) was developed by the French mathematician and economist Augustin Cournot in 1838 (*Researches into the Mathematical Principles of Wealth,* Chapter 7). The Cournot model is often compared with the Bertrand and the Stackelberg models, developed later in the 20th century, which kept the original theoretical structure of Cournot, modifying it with different assumptions. All these models represent somehow the *classical approach* to the oligopoly.

In the 20th century a new way to analyze several problems in economics was developed by economists and mathematician-economists, like John von Neumann, Oskar Morgestern, and John Nash. This is the *Game Theory* (see Section 6.13), which provided, compared to the classical approach, a set of different theoretical tools to approach the behavior of firms in the oligopolistic market. This represents the *strategic approach* to the oligopoly.

The Cournot model is summarized as follows:

- goods are homogenous;
- demand curve is linear $p(Y) = a - bY$ (from now on we will set $b = 1$);
- no costs of production;
- only two sellers $A$ and $B$ exist (we are in a duopoly), so that $Y = Y_A + Y_B$;
- each *duopolist*, independently from the other, wants to maximize its profit. In the real economy, there are many examples of duopoly like Visa versus Mastercard or Coca-Cola versus Pepsi.

Firm A maximizes the following equation (no costs exist):

$$\Pi_A(Y_A, Y_B) = p(Y)Y_A = (a - Y_A - Y_B)Y_A = aY_A - Y_A^2 - Y_A Y_B.$$

As this is a function of two independent variables we can derive the *isoprofit curve* for $A$, for each level of $(Y_A, Y_B)$.

The isoprofit curve has the following properties:

**i.** it is strictly concave;
**ii.** the level of profit lowers as the curve moves away from the origin.

The isoprofit for $A$ is derived from the profit function, keeping constant different levels of $\Pi_A$, that we will denote with $\overline{\Pi}_A$.

The equation of the isoprofit for $A$ is then:

$$Y_B = \left(aY_A - Y_A^2 - \overline{\Pi}_A\right)/Y_A$$

The isoprofit for B will be instead (specular):

$$Y_A = \left(aY_B - Y_B^2 - \overline{\Pi}_B\right)/Y_B$$

Setting the parameter $a = 100$ and using the Excel Data Table we can build and graph each isoprofit function in the $(Y_A, Y_B)$ space (Fig. 6.12-2).

Graphs of Fig. 6.12-3 and Fig. 6.12-4 are both plotted in the $(Y_A, Y_B)$ space, with $Y_A$ always graphed on the horizontal axis and $Y_B$ always on the vertical axis (IP stands for isoprofit).

In his model, Cournot makes the following assumptions.

**a.** The duopolist chose the quantity to produce to maximize the profit.
**b.** The strategic variable that determines the decision of each duopolist is the quantity (while in the Bertrand model is the price).

Let us consider the point P of Fig. 6.12-5. If the duopolist B decides for a quantity $Y_B = 36.70$, the duopolist A, to maximize the profit, will have to choose to stay on the isoprofit curve such that the slope is zero (i.e., the isoprofit IP A 1000) producing therefore the quantity $Y_A = 30.50$.

II. Static optimization

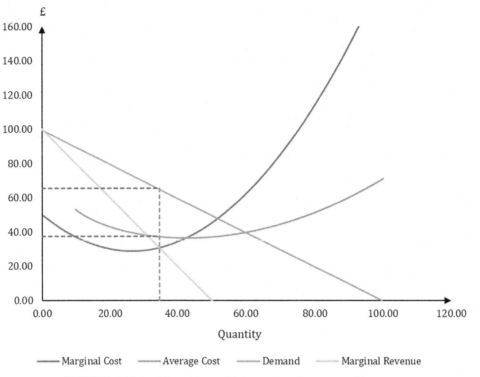

FIGURE 6.12-1 Monopoly equilibrium point: short-run and long-run.

| | A | B | C | D | F | G | H | I | J | M | N | O | P | Q | R | U | V | W | X |
|---|---|---|---|---|---|---|---|---|---|---|---|---|---|---|---|---|---|---|---|
| 1 | $Y_A$ (Horizontal Axis) | $Y_B$ (Vertical Axis) | Πa | a | $Y_B$ (Vertical Axis) | $Y_A$ (Horizontal Axis) | Πb | a | | | $Y_A$↓ | Πa→ | | | | $Y_B$↓ | Πb→ | | |
| 2 | 0.5 | =($D$2*A2-A2^2-$C$2)/A2 | 100 | 100 | 0.5 | =($I$2*F2-F2^2-$H$2)/F2 | 100 | =D2 | | | =B2 | 100 | 500 | 1000 | | =G2 | 100 | 500 | 1000 |
| 3 | | | | | | | | | | | 0.5 | =TABLE(C2;A2) | =TABLE(C2;A2) | =TABLE(C2;A2) | | 0.5 | =TABLE(H | =TABLE(H | =TABLE(H |
| 4 | | | | | | | | | | | 1 | =TABLE(C2;A2) | =TABLE(C2;A2) | =TABLE(C2;A2) | | 1 | =TABLE(H | =TABLE(H | =TABLE(H |
| 5 | | | | | | | | | | | 1.5 | =TABLE(C2;A2) | =TABLE(C2;A2) | =TABLE(C2;A2) | | 1.5 | =TABLE(H | =TABLE(H | =TABLE(H |
| 6 | | | | | | | | | | | 2 | =TABLE(C2;A2) | =TABLE(C2;A2) | =TABLE(C2;A2) | | 2 | =TABLE(H | =TABLE(H | =TABLE(H |
| 7 | | | | | | | | | | | 2.5 | =TABLE(C2;A2) | =TABLE(C2;A2) | =TABLE(C2;A2) | | 2.5 | =TABLE(H | =TABLE(H | =TABLE(H |
| 8 | | | | | | | | | | | 3 | =TABLE(C2;A2) | =TABLE(C2;A2) | =TABLE(C2;A2) | | 3 | =TABLE(H | =TABLE(H | =TABLE(H |
| 9 | | | | | | | | | | | 3.5 | =TABLE(C2;A2) | =TABLE(C2;A2) | =TABLE(C2;A2) | | 3.5 | =TABLE(H | =TABLE(H | =TABLE(H |
| 10 | | | | | | | | | | | 4 | =TABLE(C2;A2) | =TABLE(C2;A2) | =TABLE(C2;A2) | | 4 | =TABLE(H | =TABLE(H | =TABLE(H |
| 11 | | | | | | | | | | | 4.5 | =TABLE(C2;A2) | =TABLE(C2;A2) | =TABLE(C2;A2) | | 4.5 | =TABLE(H | =TABLE(H | =TABLE(H |

FIGURE 6.12-2 Excel Data Table setup for the isoprofit curves.

The locus of points connecting each isoprofit curve where the slope is zero (maximum point) is called *reaction curve.*

The reaction curve is essentially the locus of points where, given the demand curve in the market and given the quantity of the competitor, each duopolist finds the optimal quantity to produce.

The curve of reaction for A (Fig. 6.12-6) will be denoted by $r_A$, and it is analytically determined taking the derivative of $\Pi_A(Y_A, Y_B)$ with respect to $Y_A$ and setting it equal to zero, as follows:

$$\frac{\partial \Pi_A(Y_A, Y_B)}{\partial Y_A} = a - Y_B - 2Y_A = 0 \Rightarrow Y_A = \frac{(a - Y_B)}{2}.$$

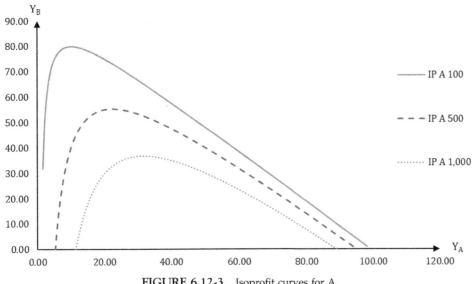

**FIGURE 6.12-3** Isoprofit curves for A.

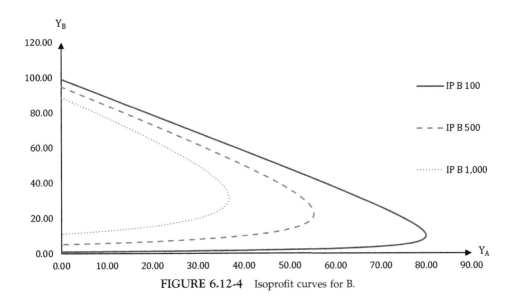

**FIGURE 6.12-4** Isoprofit curves for B.

We do the same for the duopolist B (Fig. 6.12-7) and we obtain $r_B$ as:

$$Y_B = \frac{(a - Y_A)}{2}.$$

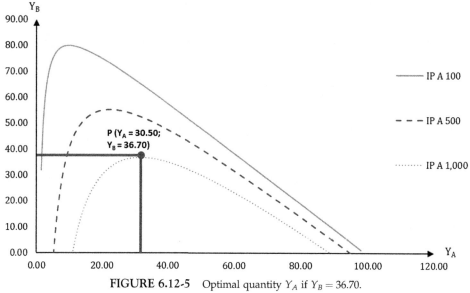

**FIGURE 6.12-5**    Optimal quantity $Y_A$ if $Y_B = 36.70$.

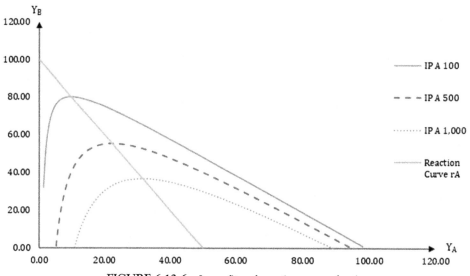

**FIGURE 6.12-6**    Isoprofit and reaction curves for $A$.

We have then the following system of two equations:

$$Y_A = \frac{(a - Y_B)}{2}$$

$$Y_B = \frac{(a - Y_A)}{2}.$$

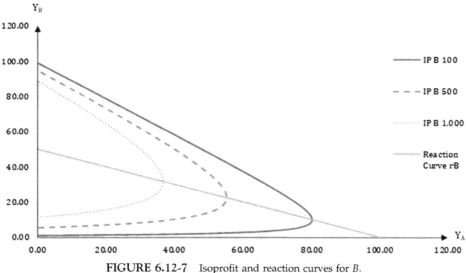

FIGURE 6.12-7   Isoprofit and reaction curves for $B$.

The solution of this system $(Y_A^*, Y_B^*)$ is the *Cournot Equilibrium* and it is represented by the following quantities:

$$Y_A^* = Y_B^* = \frac{a}{3}.$$

The Cournot Equilibrium is found at the intersection point between the two reaction curves as represented in Fig. 6.12-8.

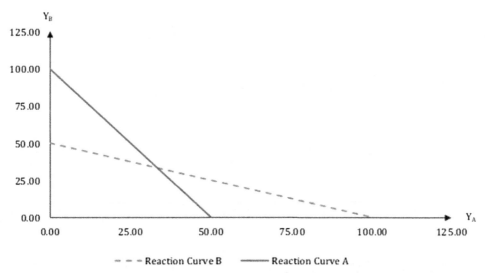

FIGURE 6.12-8   Reaction curves for $A$ and $B$ and Cournot equilibrium at $Y_A^* = Y_B^* = 100/3$ with $a = 100$.

On the reaction curve $r_A$, it turns out:

$$Y_A = 0 \Rightarrow Y_B = a$$

and:

$$Y_B = 0 \Rightarrow Y_A = \frac{a}{2}.$$

On the reaction curve $r_B$, we have vice versa the following:

$$Y_A = 0 \Rightarrow Y_B = \frac{a}{2}$$

and:

$$Y_B = 0 \rightarrow Y_A = a.$$

The optimal total output in the market will be therefore:

$$Y^* = Y_A^* + Y_B^* = \frac{2a}{3} = \frac{200}{3},$$

and the price at which the consumers will buy this quantity is determined via the market demand $p(Y) = a - Y$ as:

$$p^*(Y) = a - Y^* = 100 - \frac{200}{3} \cong 33.34.$$

In the model, we can also simulate various equilibrium points by changing the parameter $a$ in the market demand (see Fig. 6.12-8 and 6.12-9).

A different way the reaction curve is considered by the duopolist in the Cournot model lead to the Stackelberg model and the Stackelberg Equilibrium.

Assuming no costs and looking at the profit for A (normally referred as the leader company), this is done simply plugging the reaction curve of B (normally referred as the follower company), $Y_B = \frac{(a-Y_A)}{2}$, in the profit function for A:

$$\Pi_A(Y_A, Y_B) = p(Y)Y_A = (a - Y_A - Y_B)Y_A$$

namely,

$$\Pi_A(Y_A) = p(Y)Y_A = \left( a - Y_A - \frac{(a - Y_A)}{2} \right)Y_A,$$

which becomes:

$$\Pi_A(Y_A) = \left( aY_A - Y_A^2 - \frac{a}{2}Y_A + \frac{Y_A^2}{2} \right) = \frac{a}{2}Y_A - \frac{1}{2}Y_A^2.$$

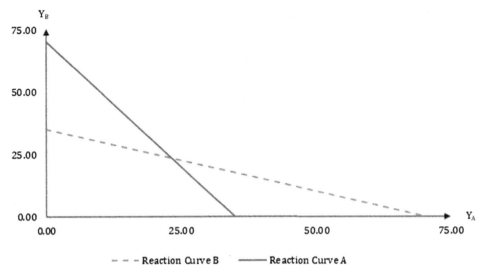

**FIGURE 6.12-9** Reaction curves for $A$ and $B$ and Cournot equilibrium at $Y_A^* = Y_B^* = 70/3$ with $a = 70$.

The necessary maximum condition leads to the optimal quantity for $Y_A$ as follows:

$$\frac{d\Pi_A(Y_A)}{dY_A} = \frac{a}{2} - Y_A = 0 \Rightarrow Y_A = \frac{a}{2}$$

while the equilibrium quantity $Y_B$ is determined, from the reaction curve $r_B$, as:

$$Y_B = \frac{\left(a - \dfrac{a}{2}\right)}{2} = \frac{a}{4}.$$

## Oligopoly, post-Keynesian theory of the firm and full-cost pricing

The oligopoly has drawn the attention of many post-Keynesian economists in the 20th century, as far as the formation of prices is concerned, leading to the *post-Keynesian theory of the firm*.

An important research by R. Hall and C. Hitch published in 1939 on the "Oxford Economic Papers," called *Price Theory and Business Behavior*, aimed at investigating the pricing decision processes within the firms, discovered that the pricing of the firms did not follow the marginalist maximizing rules, but rather a *full-cost pricing* rule.

The pricing rule within the oligopolistic markets emphasized the difference between the neoclassical approach and post-Keynesian economists. The oligopoly is a *fix-price* market (as defined by John Hicks), in that the pricing rule normally followed is the *full-cost pricing*:

$$p = (ULC + UMC)(1 + m)$$

where *ULC* is the unit cost of direct labor, *UMC* is the unit cost of raw materials, and *m* is the mark-up applied to the direct costs, to cover the general costs and to guarantee the required remuneration of the invested capital (i.e., WACC).

It is apparent how this rule is completely different from the following neoclassical maximizing rule:

$$Marginal\ Revenue\ =\ Marginal\ Cost$$

which proved to be inconsistent therefore with the empirical evidence detected within the oligopolistic firm's managerial practice.

In such an industrial manufacturing market, as the price is not taken as given, differently from what happens in the primary sectors of the natural resources, there is no room neither for the Walrasian price adjustment (i.e., the Walrasian auctioneer, see Section 4.2), nor for the mathematical neoclassical framework of the perfect competitive maximizing firms.

The post-Keynesian economists that contributed most to this view of the oligopolistic firm's behavior were J. Hicks, M. Kalecki, P. Sylos Labini, J.S. Bain, and F. Modigliani. They essentially brought back the theory of the oligopolistic firm closer to the daily firm's accounting and financial managerial practice.

## 6.13 Game theory. Zero-sum games and minimax criterion: matrix and graphical resolutions

The modern *Game Theory* was officially born when an article was written by John von Neumann in 1928, called *On the Theory of Games of Strategy*, and a following book, by John von Neumann and Oskar Morgestern, *Theory of Games and Economics Behavior* was published in 1944.

The *Game Theory* is adopted in economics when there are more decision-makers and the objective function of one decision-maker also depends on the choices (or strategies) of the other decision maker.

As the situation represented is essentially similar to what happens in a game (e.g., chess or cards), the terminology is often taken from the games (i.e., *player, payoff, loss, move, strategy*).

There are many types of games, and within this section we will show how to implement in Excel the *two-person zero-sums* games, resolving them using both the matrix and the graphical approach. The *minimax* criterion of resolution is adopted (the Theorem of minimax is due to John von Neumann).

A zero-sum game is a game where the payoffs to the players sum to zero. In the two-person zero-sum game what one player gains the other loses. The matrix representation is normally used in the game theory. Let us see the following example with two players, where we will also introduce some other important and necessary concepts of the game theory.

6.13 Game theory. Zero-sum games and minimax criterion: matrix and graphical resolutions

371

## EXAMPLE 1 (ZERO-SUM GAME WITH SADDLE POINT AND MINIMAX CRITERION)

The first step in a two-person game problem is to formalize the *payoff matrix* for the two players.

The payoff matrix is simply a double entry table, with all the payments made by one player to the other, for each strategy adopted, like in Table 6.13-1. As the payment of one player is equal to the gain of the other player, the game is called zero-sum (which is a type of constant-sum game):

$$\Pi_{i,j}^{A} + \Pi_{i,j}^{B} = 0 \Rightarrow \Pi_{i,j}^{A} = -\Pi_{i,j}^{B}$$

In Table 6.13-1, we have labeled the strategies of A with $A_i$ for $i = 1, 2, 3$ and the strategies of B, with $B_j$ for $j = 1, 2, 3, 4$. The positive numbers are the payments made by B to A, while the negative numbers are the payments that B receives from A. It is implicitly meant that in each cell of the payoff matrix the sum of the two players' profit is zero.

Once the matrix is defined, we need to operate on it to find the solution of the game, according to some criteria.

We will follow the Von Neuman *minimax criterion*, which suggests *maximizing the minimum profit* and *minimizing the maximum loss*. This is seen as a risk-averse criterion.

In formal terms the following will happen for Player A (maximizing the minimum profit):

$$\max_{i} \min_{j} \Pi_{i,j}$$

and for Player B (minimizing the maximum loss):

$$\min_{i} \max_{j} \Pi_{i,j}.$$

The solution of the game is easily reachable using the Excel functions Min and Max, and it is described in Fig. 6.13-1 and Table 6.13-2.

The solution of the game is found at the Excel *Cell C3*, with value equal to zero and strategies B2 and A1. Notice, also that the maximin value is equal to the minimax:

$$\max_{i} \min_{j} \Pi_{i,j} = \min_{i} \max_{j} \Pi_{i,j} = \Pi_{i,j}^{*} \Rightarrow v.$$

TABLE 6.13-1 Payoff matrix.

| ↓ Strategies → | Payments made from B to A | | | |
|---|---|---|---|---|
| | B1 | B2 | B3 | B4 |
| A1 | 8 | 0 | 6 | 8 |
| A2 | 16 | -2 | -8 | -8 |
| A3 | -6 | -4 | 8 | 8 |

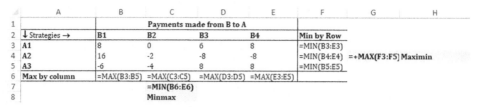

|  | A | B | C | D | E | F | G | H |
|---|---|---|---|---|---|---|---|---|
| 1 |  | Payments made from B to A | | | | | | |
| 2 | ↓ Strategies → | B1 | B2 | B3 | B4 | Min by Row | | |
| 3 | A1 | 8 | 0 | 6 | 8 | =MIN(B3:E3) | | |
| 4 | A2 | 16 | -2 | -8 | -8 | =MIN(B4:E4) | =+MAX(F3:F5) Maximin | |
| 5 | A3 | -6 | -4 | 8 | 8 | =MIN(B5:E5) | | |
| 6 | Max by column | =MAX(B3:B5) | =MAX(C3:C5) | =MAX(D3:D5) | =MAX(E3:E5) | | | |
| 7 |  |  | =MIN(B6:E6) | | | | | |
| 8 |  |  | Minmax | | | | | |

FIGURE 6.13-1   Example 1 Excel setup of minimax criterion.

TABLE 6.13-2   Example 1 solution of the game.

|  | Payments made from B to A | | | | |  |
|---|---|---|---|---|---|---|
| ↓ Strategies → | B1 | B2 | B3 | B4 | Min by Row |  |
| A1 | 8 | 0 | 6 | 8 | 0 |  |
| A2 | 16 | -2 | -8 | -8 | -8 | 0 Maximin |
| A3 | -6 | -4 | 8 | 8 | -6 |  |
| Max by column | 16 | 0 | 8 | 8 |  |  |
|  |  | 0 | | | |  |
|  |  | Minmax | | | |  |

When this happens, the game is said to have a *saddle point* at $\Pi^*_{i,j}$, namely the $i, j$ element of the matrix being both the minimum in its row and the maximum in its column. In Example 1, we have $\Pi^*_{i,j} = \Pi^*_{1,2} = 0$, which is the *value of the game v* and the strategies A1 and B1 are called *pure strategies*, in the sense that only one strategy is utilized by each player. On the contrary, a strategy is called *mixed strategy* if the player adopts a portion of more strategies. In the games with saddle point the strategies are always pure.

## EXAMPLE 2 (NO SADDLE POINT AND MIXED STRATEGIES)

Let us see now an example of game where mixed strategies are implemented with the Excel Solver.

Let us have the following payoff matrix (Table 6.13-3):

According to the minimax criterion we would have the following table and optimal strategies S(A) and S(B) (Table 6.13-4).

What happens here is that we do not have any saddle point, as the following turns out:

$$\max_i \min_j \Pi_{i,j} > \min_i \max_j \Pi_{i,j}.$$

TABLE 6.13-3   Example 2 payoff matrix.

|  | B1 | B2 |
|---|---|---|
| A1 | 2.00 | 5.00 |
| A2 | 3.00 | 0.00 |

**TABLE 6.13-4**   Minimax solutions.

|  |  | B1 | B2 | Min Profit For A | S(A): MaxMin Profit |
|---|---|---|---|---|---|
|  | A1 | 2.00 | 5.00 | 2.00 | 2.00 |
|  | A2 | 3.00 | 0.00 | 0.00 |  |
| Max Loss For B |  | 3.00 | 5.00 |  |  |
| S(B): MinMax Loss |  | 3.00 |  |  |  |

Von Neuman and Morgestern proved that in such a game, without a saddle point, if mixed strategies are allowed, the game will always have a saddle point, and this will correspond to the value of the game $v$.

Mixed strategies are probability combinations of pure strategies, and they can be found as follows.

The pure strategies have to be combined such that the expected value (probability weighted) of the game is equal to the exact value of the game. We can set up then a system in the following three equations (and three variables) $p_1$, $p_2$, and $v$, where $p_1$, $p_2$ are the probability weights that sum to one. As follows the first system to find the mixed strategy for Player A, $S^*(A)$.

$$p_1 a_{11} + p_2 a_{21} = v$$
$$p_1 a_{12} + p_2 a_{22} = v \qquad (6.13\text{-}1)$$
$$p_1 + p_2 = 1$$

For Player B and mixed strategy $S^*(B)$, we set up the following three equations:

$$p_1 a_{11} + p_2 a_{12} = v$$
$$p_1 a_{21} + p_2 a_{22} = v \qquad (6.13\text{-}2)$$
$$p_1 + p_2 = 1$$

Let us go then to Excel and solve Systems 6.13-1 and 6.13-2 as set up in Fig. 6.13-2.

To solve the two systems, we use sequentially the Solver as described in Fig. 6.13-3.

The optimal mixed strategies are formalized as follows (i.e., mixed strategies are like a discrete random variable):

$$S^*(A) = \begin{bmatrix} A_1 & A_2 \\ 5/6 & 1/6 \end{bmatrix} = \begin{bmatrix} 2 & 5 \\ 5/6 & 1/6 \end{bmatrix} or \begin{bmatrix} 3 & 0 \\ 5/6 & 1/6 \end{bmatrix} \Rightarrow v = 2.50$$

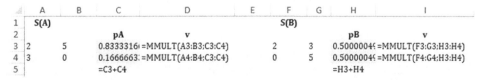

| ◢ | A | B | C | D | E | F | G | H | I |
|---|---|---|---|---|---|---|---|---|---|
| 1 | S(A) |  |  |  |  | S(B) |  |  |  |
| 2 |  |  | pA | v |  |  |  | pB | v |
| 3 | 2 | 5 | 0.8333316 | =MMULT(A3:B3;C3:C4) | 2 | 3 | 0.5000004 | =MMULT(F3:G3;H3:H4) |
| 4 | 3 | 0 | 0.1666663 | =MMULT(A4:B4;C3:C4) | 0 | 5 | 0.5000004 | =MMULT(F4:G4;H3:H4) |
| 5 |  |  | =C3+C4 |  |  |  |  | =H3+H4 |  |

**FIGURE 6.13-2**   Excel setup for mixed strategy $S^*(A)$ and mixed strategy $S^*(B)$.

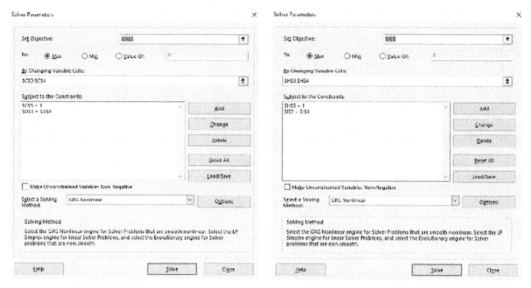

**FIGURE 6.13-3** Solver parameters for $S^*(A)$ on the left and $S^*(B)$ on the right.

$$S^*(B) = \begin{bmatrix} B_1 & B_2 \\ 1/2 & 1/2 \end{bmatrix} = \begin{bmatrix} 2 & 3 \\ 1/2 & 1/2 \end{bmatrix} or \begin{bmatrix} 5 & 0 \\ 1/2 & 1/2 \end{bmatrix} \Rightarrow v = 2.50$$

See Table 6.13-5.

## Graphical resolution method

Let us consider again the payoff matrix of Example 2 (Table 6.13-6): and let us represent in a Cartesian co-ordinate system $(x, y)$ the payoffs as follows, to solve the game from Player A's perspective:

From the data points, we derive the linear equations, adding the linear trend line in the Excel chart, and the results are like in Fig. 6.13-4.

**TABLE 6.13-5** Example 2 Solution: probabilities $p_A$, $p_B$, and value of the game $v = 2.50$.

| S(A) | | | | S(B) | | | |
|---|---|---|---|---|---|---|---|
| | | pA | v | | | pB | v |
| 2.00 | 5.00 | 0.83 | 2.50 | 2.00 | 3.00 | 0.50 | 2.50 |
| 3.00 | 0.00 | 0.17 | 2.50 | 0.00 | 5.00 | 0.50 | 2.50 |
| | | 1.00 | | | | 1.00 | |
| Solution pA | | 5/6 | | Solution pB | | 1/2 | |
| | | 1/6 | | | | 1/2 | |

6.13 Game theory. Zero-sum games and minimax criterion: matrix and graphical resolutions

375

**TABLE 6.13-6**   Example 2 payoff matrix for graphical resolution.

|     | B1   | B2   |
| --- | ---- | ---- |
| A1  | 2.00 | 5.00 |
| A2  | 3.00 | 0.00 |

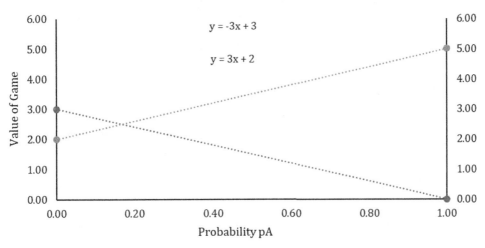

**FIGURE 6.13-4**   Payoffs in a Cartesian co-ordinate system (for Player A).

From the coefficients of the two equations, we can derive the following linear system for the Player A, to find the value of the game and the optimal portion of strategies:

$$\begin{bmatrix} 1 & -3 \\ 1 & 3 \end{bmatrix}\begin{bmatrix} y \\ x \end{bmatrix} = \begin{bmatrix} 2 \\ 3 \end{bmatrix}.$$

Using the Solver as described in Fig. 6.13-6, we find the solution for the value of the game $y = 2.5$ and the probability of portion of strategies $x = p_1 = 0.17$ and $(1 - p_1) = 0.83$. (Fig. 6.13-5).

The same solution can be read at the point where the two lines in Fig. 6.13-4 intersect. This is the maximum point lying on the lower line, that results connecting the lower boundary points on the graph, as represented by the thick segment in Fig. 6.13-7.

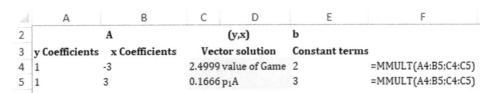

| ◢ | A | B | C | D | E | F |
| --- | --- | --- | --- | --- | --- | --- |
| 2 | | A | | (y,x) | b | |
| 3 | y Coefficients | x Coefficients | | Vector solution | Constant terms | |
| 4 | 1 | -3 | | 2.4999 value of Game | 2 | =MMULT(A4:B5;C4:C5) |
| 5 | 1 | 3 | | 0.1666 $p_1$A | 3 | =MMULT(A4:B5;C4:C5) |

**FIGURE 6.13-5**   Linear system from payoff matrix.

II. Static optimization

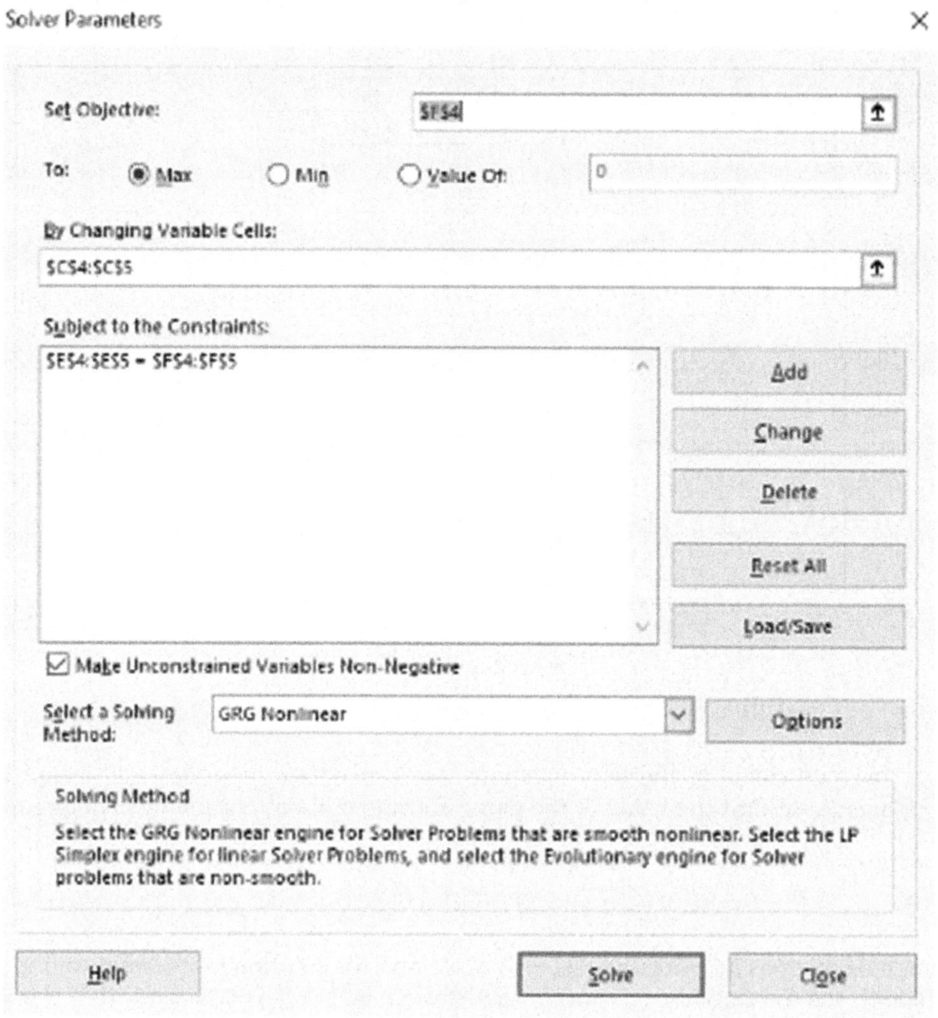

FIGURE 6.13-6   Solver set-up for the linear system in Fig. 6.13-5.

## Exercises

1. Given a commodity bundle $(x) = (x_1, x_2,..., x_5)$ and the vector of prices $(p) = (£\ 20, £\ 5, £\ 2, £\ 4, £\ 10)$ under the cardinal approach, assuming the additive property of total utility function, solve the following consumer problem:

$$\max_{\{x\}} U(x) = \max_{\{x_i\}} \sum_{i=1}^{5} U(x_i)$$

where $U(x_i) = \sqrt{x_i}$ and given a budget constraint of £ 1000.

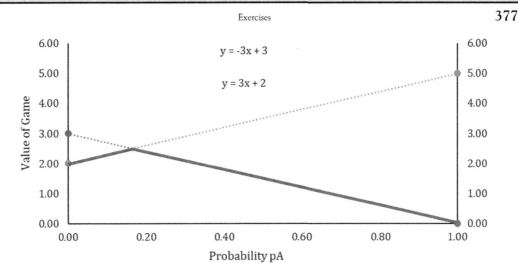

**FIGURE 6.13-7**  Graphical solution for player A: max point on the lower boundary segment.

2. Suppose we have Cobb–Douglas utility function described as follows:

$$U(x_1, x_2) = x_1^{0.6} x_2^{0.4}$$

Then, the commodity prices are given as $p_1 = £\ 3$, $p_2 = £\ 1$, together with the budget constraint:

$$3x_1 + 1x_2 = £\ 10.$$

The neoclassical consumer problem can be then formalized as:

$$\max_{\{x_1, x_2\}} x_1^{0.6} x_2^{0.4}$$

$$s.t.$$

$$3x_1 + 1x_2 = 10 \quad \text{with } x_1, x_2 \geq 0$$

a. Find with Solver the optimal quantities the consumer has to choose to maximize the utility, subject to the given constraint.
b. Plot a set of indifference curves.
c. Plot the budget constraint and visualize the tangency point, between the constraint and the attainable indifference curve.
d. Find a new equilibrium point for the case the budget constraint changes to:

$$3x_1 + 1x_2 = £\ 20$$

**3.** Suppose we have a nonlinear utility function described as follows:

$$U(x_1, x_2) = x_1 x_2$$

Then, the commodity prices are given as $p_1 = £\ 24$, $p_2 = £\ 8$, together with the budget constraint:

$$3x_1 + 1x_2 = £\ 80.$$

    **a.** Find with Solver the optimal quantities the consumer has to choose to maximize the utility, subject to the given constraint.
    **b.** Plot a set of indifference curves.
    **c.** Plot the budget constraint and visualize the tangency point, between the constraint and the attainable indifference curve.

**4.** Consider two consumers. The first consumer has the following Leontief utility function:

$$U(x_1, x_2) = \min\left(\frac{x_1}{5}; \frac{x_2}{5}\right)$$

(i.e., the two goods are perfect complements).
While the second consumer has the following Linear utility function:

$$U(x_1, x_2) = 2x_1 + x_2$$

(i.e., the two goods are somehow substitutable)
    **a.** Plot for each case a set of indifference curves.
    **b.** Build the Edgeworth Box and identify the optimal bargaining area, within which both consumers can increase their expected utility.
    **c.** Show that the contract curve is represented by the diagonal running between the southwest to northeast corners of the box.

**5.** A firm has estimated the following Cobb–Douglas production function:

$$y = 2\left(L^{1/3} K^{1/2}\right)$$

while total direct costs budget constraint is $C = £\ 90$, and unit prices of inputs are $p_L = 4$, $p_K = 9$.

    **a.** Find with Solver the optimal combination of inputs, subject to the given cost constraint.
    **b.** Plot a set of production isoquants.
    **c.** Plot the budget constraint and visualize the tangency point, between the constraint and the attainable production isoquants.
    **d.** Calculate the MRS at the tangent point.

**6.** Consider the following Leontief Input–Output production function:

$$y(x_1, x_2) = \min\left(\frac{x_1}{5}; \frac{x_2}{5}\right)$$

    **a.** Plot the surface chart using the Excel Data Table.
    **b.** Construct the chart for a set of isoquants.

**7.** Consider the following Leontief Input–Output production function, with inputs represented by labor, $L$, and capital, $K$:

$$y(L, K) = \min\left(\frac{L}{0.5}; \frac{K}{0.2}\right).$$

    The unit prices of the two inputs are $p_L = 6$, $p_K = 3$ while budget constraint of the firm for the total expenditure in inputs is $C = £\ 600$,
    **a.** Find with Solver the optimal combination of inputs, subject to the given cost constraint.
    **b.** Plot the surface chart of the production function using the data table.
    **c.** Plot a set of production isoquants.
    **d.** Plot the budget constraint and visualize the tangency point, between the constraint and the attainable production isoquants.

**8.** Input profit optimization problem. A firm sells a product at a unit price of £ 8, while the production function to produce this type of item is represented by the following Cobb–Douglas function:

$$q = \left(L^{1/8}K^{3/8}\right)$$

    The unit prices of inputs are $p_L = 4$, $p_K = 12$.
    The profit function is therefore given as usual by:

$$\pi = pq - TC = 8 \cdot \left(L^{1/8}K^{3/8}\right) - 4L - 12K$$

    Find the optimal demand of inputs that maximizes the profit $\pi$.

**9.** Input profit optimization problem. A firm sells a product at a unit price of £ 100, while the production function to produce this type of item is represented by the following Cobb–Douglas function, where, as we are operating in the short-run, the availability of capital quantity is given at 81 and it can not be changed:

$$q = \left(L^{1/2}81^{1/2}\right).$$

The unit prices of inputs are $p_L = 18$, $p_K = 8$. The profit function is therefore given by:

$$\pi = pq - TC = 100 \cdot \left( L^{1/2}81^{1/2} \right) - 18L - 8 \cdot (81)$$

Find the optimal demand of Labor that maximizes the profit $\pi$.

10. **Perfect Competition.** On a natural resource perfect competition market, we have 100 firms that face the following short-run total cost function (see the constant term representing the fixed costs):

$$TC = 2y^2 + 50.$$

where the variable $y$ measures the quantity produced.
The demand function of the market is given instead by the following:

$$y = 2,600 - p$$

  a. Find each firm's short-run supply curve and plot the relevant revenue/cost curves for the PC firm operating in this market.
  b. After summing horizontally all the supply curves, find the *market clearing equilibrium price* $p^*$.
  c. Using the Excel Solver, find then the optimal quantity at which each firm produces with this equilibrium price and measure the extra profit area (or economic profit[1]).
  d. Plot the chart of demand versus supply and equilibrium lines.

11. There are 30 firms in a perfect competitive market that faces total costs according to the following total cost function:

$$TC = 5y^2$$

while the demand function of the market is as follows:

$$y = 300 - 72p.$$

Repeat Exercise 10 in this new scenario. Then answer to the following point.
  a. Once you have assessed the extra profit of each firm also say whether there is still room for new market entrants at the market equilibrium price found.

---

[1]"Remember, economic profits are defined using the market prices of all factors of production. The market prices measure the opportunity cost of those factors - what they could earn elsewhere. Any amount of money earned in excess of the payments to the factors of production is a pure economic profit. It is this attempt to capture economic profits that eventually drives them to zero in a competitive industry with free entry." From Hal Varian, Intermediate Microeconomics: A Modern Approach, Ch. 23, eighth Ed.

**12.** A perfect competitive firm has the following short-run total cost function:

$$TC = 2y^2 + 98$$

while the market clearing price is $p* = 40$.
   **a.** Calculate the optimal quantity to produce for the firm, together with its profit area.
   **b.** Plot the relevant revenue and cost functions and identify in the chart the trend line associated to the marginal cost function.

**13.** A monopolist has the following total cost function:

$$TC = 6 + y^2$$

while its downward sloping demand is as follows:

$$p = 40 - y$$

   **a.** Set up the profit function, and using the Solver calculate the optimal quantity $y*$ to produce and the equilibrium price $p*$ for a maximum profit.
   **b.** Plot the relevant revenue and cost functions and visualize the equilibrium point.

**14.** Chamberlin monopolistic firm. Consider a firm in a monopolistic market that has the following total cost function:

$$TC = 0.03y^3 - 0.1y^2 + 50y + 100$$

while the short-run demand of the firm is:

$$p = 100 - \frac{1}{2}y$$

   **a.** Set up the profit function and using the Solver find the optimal quantity $y*$ to produce and the short-run equilibrium price $p*$ for a maximum profit.
   **b.** Visualize the profit area in a chart together with the relevant revenue, cost curves, and demand function.
      Extra profit will be now generated, causing new players enter the market and causing a new demand curve for each monopolistic firm.
   **c.** Using the VBA macro provided, find the new optimal quantity and equilibrium price for the long-run period, as well as the new firm long-run demand that generates zero extra profit, tangent to the ATC curve. Assume the ATC curve is the same both for short-run and the long-run. Assume the slope changes to $b = 1$ in the long-run demand.

**15.** Cournot Duopoly Model with no costs. Suppose the following linear demand curve in the market:

$$p(Y) = 20 - Y$$

   **a.** Build a set of isoprofit curves for each duopolist and visualize them in a chart.
   **b.** Visualize the reaction curves and calculate the market equilibrium quantity $Y^* = Y_A^* + Y_B^*$ and the equilibrium price $p^*$.

**16.** Cournot Duopoly Model with costs. Suppose the following linear demand curve in the market:

$$Y = 100 - 2p$$

and equal linear total cost function for each duopolist as follows:

$$TC(A) = \frac{1}{2}Y_A + 10Y_A$$

and

$$TC(B) = \frac{1}{2}Y_B + 10Y_A$$

   **a.** Setting up the maximum profit conditions, build a set of isoprofit curves for each duopolist, visualizing them in a chart.
   **b.** Visualize then the reaction curves and calculate the market equilibrium quantity $Y^* = Y_A^* + Y_B^*$ and the equilibrium price $p^*$.

**17.** Solve the zero-sum games with respect to Player A with the graphical method, considering the following $(2 \cdot 2)$ pay-off matrices.

|        | B1  | B2  |
|--------|-----|-----|
| **a.** A1 | 1   | 0   |
| A2     | 0   | 0.5 |

|        | B1  | B2  |
|--------|-----|-----|
| **b.** A1 | 3   | 6   |
| A2     | 4   | 5   |

|        | B1  | B2  |
|--------|-----|-----|
| **c.** A1 | 1   | 2   |
| A2     | 6   | 4   |

|        | B1  | B2  |
|--------|-----|-----|
| **d.** A1 | -2  | 5   |
| A2     | 7   | 2   |

|        | B1  | B2  |
|--------|-----|-----|
| **e.** A1 | 9   | -3  |
| A2     | -2  | 14  |

|        | B1  | B2  |
|--------|-----|-----|
| **f.** A1 | 2   | 1   |
| A2     | -1  | 3   |

## 7.1 Standard formulation of a linear program and resolution methods

The standard form of a linear program in $n$ decision variables and subject to $m$ constraints is represented as follows:

$$\max_{\{x_j\}} c_1 x_1 + c_2 x_2 + \cdots + c_j x_j + \cdots + c_n x_n$$
$$x_j \geq 0 \qquad j = 1, 2 \cdots, n$$

$$
\begin{cases}
s.t. \\
a_{11} x_1 + a_{12} x_2 + \cdots + a_{1j} x_j + \cdots + a_{1n} x_n \lesseqgtr b_1 \\
a_{21} x_1 + a_{22} x_2 + \cdots + a_{2j} x_j + \cdots + a_{2n} x_n \lesseqgtr b_2 \\
\cdots \\
a_{i1} x_1 + a_{i2} x_2 + \cdots + a_{ij} x_j + \cdots + a_{in} x_n \lesseqgtr b_i \\
\cdots \\
a_{m1} x_1 + a_{m2} x_2 + \cdots + a_{m_j} x_j + \cdots + a_{mn} x_n \lesseqgtr b_m
\end{cases}
\tag{7.1-1}
$$

Eq. (7.1-1) can be shortened as follows:

$$\max_{\{x\}} f(x) \quad x_j \geq 0 \, (j = 1, 2, \cdots, m) \quad \begin{cases} s.t. \\ \sum_{j=1}^{n} a_{ij} x_j \lessgtr b_i \quad (i = 1, 2, \cdots, m) \end{cases} \tag{7.1-2}$$

For Eqs. (7.1-1) and (7.1-2), we can also adopt the matrix notation and write the problem in the following new and more condensed form:

$$\max_{\{x\}} c \cdot x \begin{cases} s.t. \\ Ax \lessgtr [b] \\ x \geq [0] \end{cases} \tag{7.1-3}$$

where $A$ is the matrix of coefficients of order $(m \cdot n)$, $c$ is the row vector of order $(1 \cdot n)$ of the coefficients of the decision variables, and $x$ is the *programming vector* of order $(n \cdot 1)$ of the decision variables.

Eqs. (7.1-1) and (7.1-3) can be transformed into a minimization problem leading to the following problem in matrix notation:

$$\min_{\{x\}} c \cdot x \begin{cases} s.t. \\ Ax \lessgtr [b] \\ x \geq [0] \end{cases} \tag{7.1-4}$$

Among the various linear programming theorems there is one of key importance, which leads to identify the symmetric problem from the original problem. The symmetric problem is called the *dual problem*, while the original problem is called the *primal problem*. Given, for example, problem (7.1-3) we can build its *dual problem*, as follows:

$$\min_{\{y\}} b \cdot y \begin{cases} s.t. \\ A^T y \lessgtr [c] \\ y \geq [0] \end{cases} \tag{7.1-5}$$

**Upper bounds on decision variables**: Together with the nonnegativity restriction $x_j \geq 0$ sometimes we can also require that the decision variable is bounded from above as follows:

$$x_j \leq u_j \quad j = 1, 2, \cdots, n$$

## Resolution methods in Excel

The way a linear program can be solved in Excel can be both geometrical and analytical with the Simplex Linear Programming Excel Solver.

The geometrical approach is possible only if we are dealing up three decision variables, and it resorts for $n = 2$ to the technique of the contour lines we have explained in **Section 5.6**.

The *simplex method*, developed by the mathematician George Dantzig, is one of the most important finding in the theory of linear programming, and it is essentially an iterative algorithm which aims at finding the optimal solution on the corners of the feasible region, and this is possible because in the linear programming the solution, if this ever exists, is always located in one of the *corners* (or *extreme points*, or *vertices*) of the feasible region, this being represented by the linear equation constraints.

The *simplex* is the name of the $n$-dimensional convex polyhedron (or $n$-dimensional convex polytope) obtained from the intersection of the hyperplanes (i.e., the constraints), with corners representing the extreme points of the convex polyhedron (see Fig. 7.1-4/7.1-5) and the simplex method provides the iterative procedure such that we move from one corner of the feasible region to another, until the optimal solution is reached.

Numerically, the simplex method is a cumbersome process, and luckily the Excel has got the simplex option embedded within the Solver (see Figs. 7.1-1) and this will be used in the applied problems that we will show next.

## Global, local solutions and corner solutions

It is important to recall that as we are dealing with linear functions, these are concave and convex at the same time and a local optimal solution can be also a global optimal solution. This is represented in Fig. 7.1-2 where we have a closed convex set $K$ of feasible solutions on which we can have an infinite number of solutions located on the segment $\overline{cd}$, whose values maximize the linear objective function. In Fig. 7.1-2, we have $m = 3$ constraints, to which we have to add the nonnegativity constraints.

In Fig. 7.1-3, we represent instead a unique maximum point (i.e., a *corner solution*), which is located on the corner $c$ of the region $K$.

In Fig. 7.1-4, we have the representation of an infinite number of solutions in case of a convex three-dimensional polyhedron while Fig. 7.1-5 represents a unique optimal corner solution. The hyperplanes touching the feasible region $K$ represent the various levels of the objective functions. We have here $n = 3$ decision variables and $m = 5$ constraints, these leading to the origination of $K$.

Therefore, in the linear programming problems, when the admissible region $K$ is closed, we may either have an **infinite number of optimal solutions** or just one **unique (corner) solution**. We exclude the case of more than one finite solutions, similarly to what happens in the linear systems (see Remark 2 of **Section 3.2**).

In general, the following will be true when the admissible region $K$ is closed.

**i.** If we have a unique optimal point, this is located on the corner of the feasible region $K$.

**ii.** If there are more than one optimum, then at least one optimal point is located on the corner of $K$.

FIGURE 7.1-1   The simplex in the Solver.

**iii.** If there are more optima, each of these can be a linear combination of at least two extreme points of $K$.

**iv.** Each linear combination of two optimal points is itself an optimal solution.

Some linear programming problems lead to **no solution** when the region of feasible solutions is empty or not bounded (e.g., for a maximum problem with the region unbounded from above or for a minimum with the region unbounded from below).

There may be also cases where the admissible region degenerates in a segment, and this happens when we have inequality constraints together with an **equational constraint**.

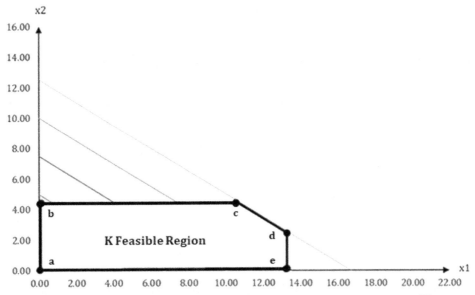

**FIGURE 7.1-2**   Closed set $K$ and Local solutions that are also Global on the segment $\overline{cd}$ ($n = 2$).

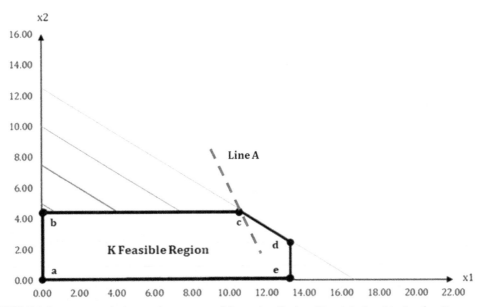

**FIGURE 7.1-3**   Unique solution on the corner c of the region $K$ when Line A is the objective function ($n = 2$).

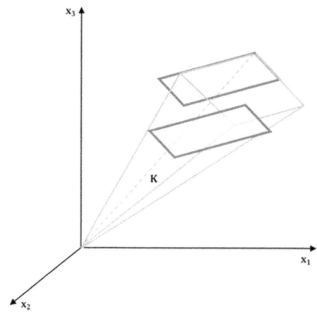

**FIGURE 7.1-4**   Infinite solutions on the highest plane touching $K$ on the border ($n = 3$ decision variables).

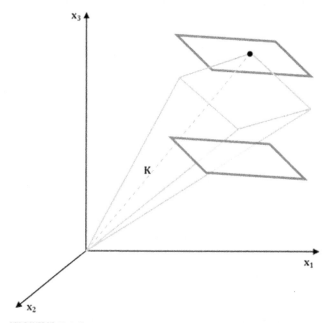

**FIGURE 7.1-5**   Unique corner solution ($n = 3$ decision variables).

## 7.2 Applications to the static production planning and capital budgeting

We will show here some Excel examples on how the linear programming technique can be applied to the static production planning.

There are several classes of problems in production planning that can be tackled using the linear programming, and the following deterministic production problems (stochastic models are also possible) will be shown:

- Product mix decisions
- Process selection problems
- Blending problem

Then, we will show how the linear programming can be also applied to a standard capital budgeting problem, which is usually referred to as the classical Lorie-Savage capital rationing problem.

### Product mix decisions

As already seen in the production Edgeworth box theory, one of the most important problems of the firms is to find the optimal mix of outputs in order to optimize a certain performance measure, subject to the given constraints.

We want to model now a problem that finds a production mix program that maximizes the performance measure of total contribution margin to overhead costs. We illustrate this using the following linear program information.

$$x_j = quantity\ of\ product \quad i = 1,\ 2,\ \cdots,\ n$$

$$b_i = amount\ of\ resources \quad i = 1,\ 2,\ \cdots,\ m\ avaialble\ in\ the\ period$$

$$a_{ij} = number\ of\ units\ of\ resource\ i\ required\ to\ produce\ one\ unit\ of\ product\ j$$

$$U_j = maximum\ sales\ potential\ of\ product\ i\ in\ the\ period$$

$$L_j = maximum\ quanitity\ of\ product\ i\ in\ the\ period$$

$$r_j = net\ revenue\ from\ selling\ one\ unit\ of\ product\ i$$

$$c_j = unit\ variable\ cost\ of\ producing\ one\ unit\ of\ product\ i.$$

The performance measure we want to maximize is the contribution margin of each product:

$$Contribution\ Margin\ of\ Product\ j = (r_j - c_j)$$

The linear program is then written as follows:

$$
\begin{cases}
\max_{\{x_j\}} Z = \sum_{j=1}^{n}(r_j - c_j)x_j & \qquad x_j \le U_j \ \ j = 1, 2, \cdots, n \\
s.t. & \\
\sum_{i=1}^{n} a_{ij}x_j \le b_i \quad i = 1, 2, \cdots, m & \qquad x_j \ge L_j \ \ j = 1, 2, \cdots, n
\end{cases}
$$

The cases from Example 1 to Example 4 are taken from Lynwood A. Johnson, Douglas C. Montgomery, *Operations Research in Production planning, Scheduling, and Inventory Control,* Chapter 3, Copyright © 1974 by John Wiley and Sons, Inc.


## EXAMPLE 1 (PRODUCT MIX)

We have a manufacturer that produces four lines of household products from sheet metal. The production chain consists of five departments: stamping, drilling, assembly, finishing, and packaging. For a given month the manufacturer has to decide how much to produce, considering that only 2000 square feet of the type of metal used for products 2 and 4 will be available during the month. Product 2 requires 2.0 square feet per unit and Product 4 uses 1.2 square feet per unit. Furthermore, all the other essential information of the problem is gathered in Tables 7.2-1 and 7.2-2.

We are ready now to set up the linear program. The problem is to find the optimal quantities of nonnegative $x_j$ that maximize the contribution margin, given the constraints of production.

$$
\max_{\{x_j\}} Z = 4x_1 + 10x_2 + 5x_3 + 6x_4
$$

**TABLE 7.2-1** Production data.

| DEPARTMENT | PRODUCTION RATES IN HOURS PER UNIT | | | | PRODUCTION HOURS AVAILABLE |
|---|---|---|---|---|---|
| | PRODUCT 1 | PRODUCT 2 | PRODUCT 3 | PRODUCT 4 | |
| Stamping | 0.03 | 0.15 | 0.05 | 0.10 | 400 |
| Drilling | 0.06 | 0.12 | 0.00 | 0.10 | 400 |
| Assembly | 0.05 | 0.10 | 0.05 | 0.12 | 500 |
| Finishing | 0.04 | 0.20 | 0.03 | 0.12 | 450 |
| Packaging | 0.02 | 0.06 | 0.02 | 0.05 | 400 |

Source: Lynwood A. Johnson, Douglas C. Montgomery, *Operations Research in Production Planning, Scheduling and Inventory Control,* Table 3.1, p.109, Copyright © 1974 by John Wiley and Sons, Inc.

**TABLE 7.2-2** Product data.

| PRODUCT | NET SELLING PRICE (Rj) | VARIABLE COST (Cj) | SALES POTENTIAL | |
|---------|------------------------|--------------------|-----------------|-----|
| | | | MIN | MAX |
| 1 | 10 | 6 | 1,000 | 6,000 |
| 2 | 25 | 15 | 0 | 500 |
| 3 | 16 | 11 | 500 | 3,000 |
| 4 | 20 | 14 | 100 | 1,000 |

**Source:** Lynwood A. Johnson, Douglas C. Montgomery, *Operations Research in Production Planning, Scheduling and Inventory Control*, Table 3.2, p.110, Copyright © 1974 by John Wiley and Sons, Inc.

*s.t.*

**(1)** Constraints on production time (production hours available):

$$0.03x_1 + 0.15x_2 + 0.05x_3 + 0.10x_4 \leq 400 \quad (Stamping)$$

$$0.06x_1 + 0.12x_2 + 0.10x_4 \leq 400 \quad (Drilling)$$

$$0.05x_1 + 0.10x_2 + 0.05x_3 + 0.12x_4 \leq 500 \quad (Assembly)$$

$$0.04x_1 + 0.20x_2 + 0.03x_3 + 0.12x_4 \leq 450 \quad (Finishing)$$

$$0.02x_1 + 0.06x_2 + 0.02x_3 + 0.05x_4 \leq 400 \quad (Packaging)$$

**(2)** Constraint on sheet metal availability:

$$2.0x_2 + 1.2x_4 \leq 2,000$$

**(3)** Constraints on minimum production and maximum sales:

$$1,000 \leq x_1 \leq 6,000$$

$$0 \leq x_2 \leq 500$$

II. Static Optimization

$$500 \leq x_3 \leq 3,000$$

$$100 \leq x_4 \leq 1,000$$

The problem is implemented in Excel as in Fig. 7.2-2. In the objective function we can either use the *SUMPRODUCT* function or the *MMULT* function. In this case the latter has been used and the two multiplying vectors need to be arranged accordingly.

The Solver is set up as in Fig. 7.2-2 where we have selected the option Simplex LP and where all the constraints have added as stated in the problem. The changing variable cells represent the program vector of decision variables $x_i$ ($i = 1, 2, 3, 4, 5$) (Fig. 7.2-2).

The optimal solution is reached for:

$$x_1^* = 5,500 \; ; x_2^* = 500 \; ; \; x_3^* = 3,000 \; ; \; x_4^* = 100$$

with maximum contribution margin to overheads is equal to:

$$Z_{max} = \pounds \, 42,600.$$

Notice from the linear program that the optimal solution generates some unused resources (Table 7.2-3).

## Process selection problems

Similarly to what happens in the production Edgeworth box with two production processes, the objective here is to determine how much to produce of an output, within each production process, in order to minimize the production costs, subject to the constraints of resource limitations and production requirement.

|    | A | B | C | D | E | F | G | H | I |
|----|---|---|---|---|---|---|---|---|---|
| 1 | MAX Z | =MMULT(F1:I1;C5:C8) | | Gross profit (rj-cj) --> | | =L12-M12 | =L13-M13 | =L14-M14 | =L15-M15 |
| 2 | (Total contribution margin) | | | | | | | | |
| 3 | | | | | | | | | |
| 4 | | Program Vector $x_i$ | | | | | | | |
| 5 | Units of products --> | x1 | 5500 | | | | | | |
| 6 | Units of products --> | x2 | 500 | | | | | | |
| 7 | Units of products --> | x3 | 3000 | | | | | | |
| 8 | Units of products --> | x4 | 100 | | | | | | |
| 9 | | | | | | | | | |
| 10 | s.t. | | | | | | | | |
| 11 | (1) | duction time machine ho | | | | Unused | | | |
| 12 | =0.03*C5+0.15*C6+0.05*C7+0.1*C8 | ≤ | 400 | Stamping | | =C12-A12 | | | |
| 13 | =0.06*C5+0.12*C6+0.1*C8 | ≤ | 400 | Drilling | | =C13-A13 | | | |
| 14 | =0.05*C5+0.1*C6+0.05*C7+0.12*C8 | ≤ | 500 | Assembly | | =C14-A14 | | | |
| 15 | =0.04*C5+0.2*C6+0.03*C7+0.12*C8 | ≤ | 450 | Finishing | | =C15-A15 | | | |
| 16 | =0.02*C5+0.06*C6+0.02*C7+0.05*C8 | ≤ | 400 | Packaging | | =C16-A16 | | | |
| 17 | | | | | | | | | |
| 18 | (2) | Sheet metal availability | | | | | | | |
| 19 | =2*C6+1.2*C8 | ≤ | 2000 | | | =C19-A19 | | | |
| 20 | | | | | | | | | |
| 21 | (3) | Min prod max sales | | | | | | | |
| 22 | 1000 | ≤1≤ | 6000 | | | Product 1 | | | |
| 23 | 0 | ≤2≤ | 500 | | | Product 2 | | | |
| 24 | 500 | ≤3≤ | 3000 | | | Product 3 | | | |
| 25 | 100 | ≤4≤ | 1000 | | | Product 4 | | | |

FIGURE 7.2-1    Excel setup of the product mix linear program.

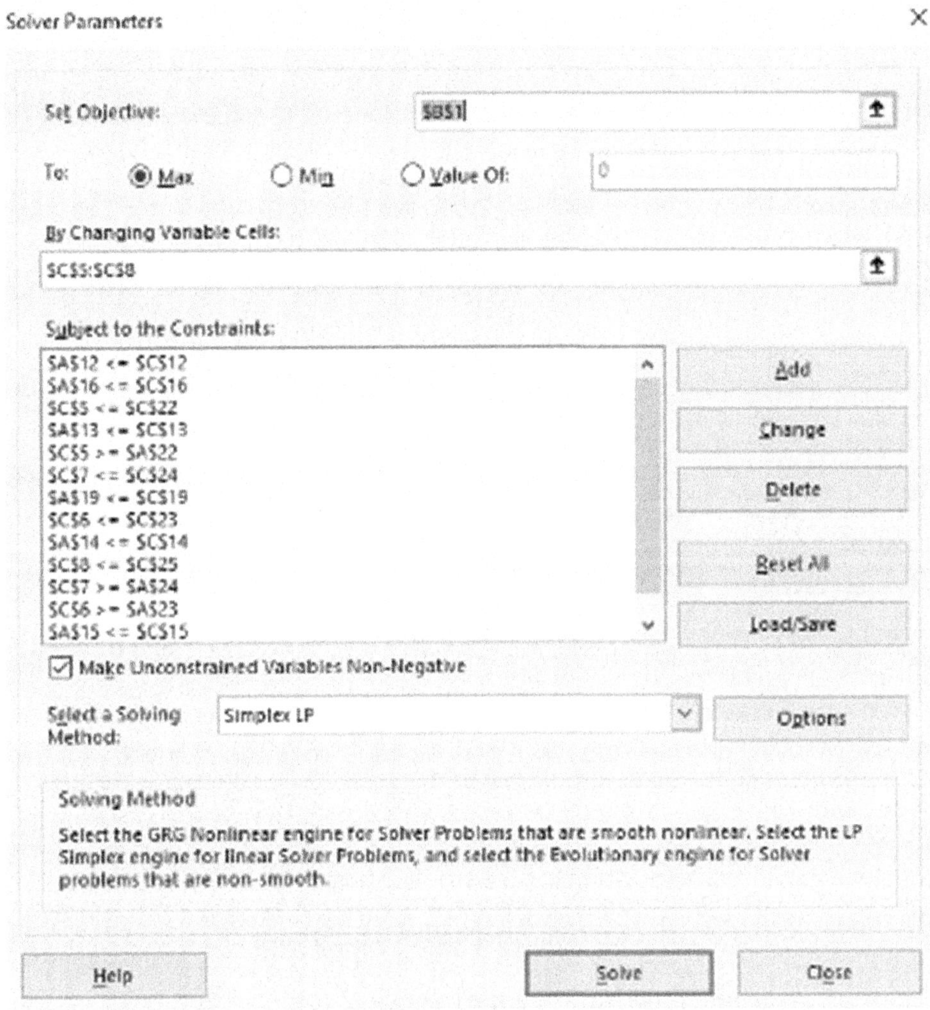

FIGURE 7.2-2   Solver parameters of the product mix linear program.

We have the following linear program formulation, which slightly modifies the product mix linear program.

$$x_{jk} = quantity\ of\ product\ j\ = \ 1,\ 2,\ \cdots,\ n\ produced\ by\ the\ process\ k\ = \ 1,\ 2,\ \cdots,\ K_j\ in\ the\ period$$

$$D_j = required\ production\ of\ product\ j\ in\ the\ period$$

$$b_i = amount\ of\ resources\ i\ = \ 1,\ 2,\ \cdots,\ m\ avaialble\ in\ the\ period$$

$$a_{jki} = number\ of\ units\ of resource\ i\ rquired\ to\ produce\ one\ unit\ of\ product\ j\ within\ the\ process\ k$$

**TABLE 7.2-3**  Linear program solution.

| MAX Z | | 42,600 | Gross profit (rj-cj) --> | | 4 | 10 | 5 | 6 |
|---|---|---|---|---|---|---|---|---|
| (Total contribution margin) | | | | | | | | |

**Program Vector xᵢ**

| Units of products --> | x1 | 5,500 |
|---|---|---|
| Units of products --> | x2 | 500 |
| Units of products --> | x3 | 3,000 |
| Units of products --> | x4 | 100 |

s.t.

(1)

| | Production time machine hours | | | | Unused |
|---|---|---|---|---|---|
| 400 | ≤ | 400 | Stamping | 0 |
| 400 | ≤ | 400 | Drilling | 0 |
| 487 | ≤ | 500 | Assembly | 13 |
| 422 | ≤ | 450 | Finishing | 28 |
| 205 | ≤ | 400 | Packaging | 195 |

(2)

| | Sheet metal availability | | |
|---|---|---|---|
| 1,120 | ≤ | 2,000 | 880 |

(3)

| | Min prod max sales | | |
|---|---|---|---|
| 1,000 | ≤ 1 ≤ | 6,000 | Product 1 |
| 0 | ≤ 2 ≤ | 500 | Product 2 |
| 500 | ≤ 3 ≤ | 3,000 | Product 3 |
| 100 | ≤ 4 ≤ | 1,000 | Product 4 |

$$c_{jk} = \text{unit variable cost of producing one unit of product } j \text{ by process } k$$

$$Z = \text{total production cost in the period}$$

The linear programming problem is specified as follows:

$$\min_{\{x_j\}} Z = \sum_{j=1}^{n} \sum_{k=1}^{K_j} c_{jk} x_{jk}$$

s.t.

$$\sum_{k=1}^{K_j} x_{jk} = D_j \quad \text{(required production for all } j\text{)}$$

$$\sum_{j=1}^{n} \sum_{k=1}^{K_j} a_{jki} x_{jk} \leq b_i \quad \text{(amount of resources for all } i\text{)}$$

$$x_{jk} \geq 0 \quad (nonnegativity\ constraint)$$

## EXAMPLE 2 (EXAMPLE 1 EXPANDED)

Example 1 is modified as follows.

i. The manufacturer may decide to resort to the subcontracting for both the stamping and the drilling activities, and this will imply an increase in direct variable costs of 20%, while the assembly, finishing, and packaging are all retained by the manufacturer.
ii. Furthermore, if necessary, the manufacturer will operate his finishing department on overtime up to 100 machine hours and this will increase the costs of Table 7.2-2 for product 1 by 20 cents, product 2 by 40 cents, product 3 by 20 cents, and product 4 by 30 cents.

iii. Also, the subcontractor may operate overtime with the same increases in the variable costs as in (ii) applied on the overtime manufacturer cost. The variable costs are then summarized in Table 7.2-4.

**TABLE 7.2-4** Unit variable costs.

| $x_{jk}$ | Process k = 1, 2, 3, 4 | Product | £ | Delta |
|------|-------------------------------|-----------|-------|-------|
| x11 | Internal stamping regular time | Product 1 | 6.00 | 0.00 |
| x12 | Internal stamping over time time | Product 1 | 6.20 | 0.20 |
| x13 | Subcontracting regular time | Product 1 | 7.20 | 20% |
| x14 | Subcontracting over time | Product 1 | 7.40 | 0.20 |
| x21 | Internal stamping regular time | Product 2 | 15.00 | 0.00 |
| x22 | Internal stamping over time time | Product 2 | 15.40 | 0.40 |
| x23 | Subcontracting regular time | Product 2 | 18.00 | 20% |
| x24 | Subcontracting over time | Product 2 | 18.40 | 0.40 |
| x31 | Internal stamping regular time | Product 3 | 11.00 | 0.00 |
| x32 | Internal stamping over time time | Product 3 | 11.20 | 0.20 |
| x33 | Subcontracting regular time | Product 3 | 13.20 | 20% |
| x34 | Subcontracting over time | Product 3 | 13.40 | 0.20 |
| x41 | Internal stamping regular time | Product 4 | 14.00 | 0.00 |
| x42 | Internal stamping over time time | Product 4 | 14.30 | 0.30 |
| x43 | Subcontracting regular time | Product 4 | 16.80 | 20% |
| x44 | Subcontracting over time | Product 4 | 17.10 | 0.30 |

iv. The sheet metal availability for products 2 and 4 applies only to internally stamped and drilled production.

v. The regular hours constraints are taken from Table 7.2-1 and repeated in the following Table 7.2-5, together with the overtime constraint.

vi. The quantities required for each product are in Table 7.2-6.

We identify four processes:

1. Internal stamping, regular time finishing.
2. Internal stamping, overtime finishing.
3. Subcontracting, regular time finishing.
4. Subcontracting, overtime finishing.

We are ready to completely write out the linear programming problem as follows:

$$\min_{\{x_j\}} Z = 6.0x_{11} + 6.2x_{12} + 7.2x_{13} + 7.4x_{14} + 15.0x_{21} + 15.4x_{22} + 18.0x_{23} + 18.4x_{24} + 11.0x_{31}$$

$$+ 11.2x_{32} + 13.2x_{33} + 13.4x_{34} + 14.0x_{41} + 14.3x_{42} + 16.8x_{43} + 17.1x_{44}$$

**TABLE 7.2-5**  Hours required.

|  | HOURS CONSTRAINTS | |
| --- | --- | --- |
|  | REGULAR TIME HOURS | OVERTIME HOURS |
| STAMPING | 400 | |
| DRILLING | 400 | |
| ASSEMBLY | 500 | |
| FINISHING | 450 | 100 |
| PACKAGING | 400 | |

**TABLE 7.2-6**  Quantities.

| PRODUCT | QUANTITY REQUIRED |
| --- | --- |
| 1 | 3,000 |
| 2 | 500 |
| 3 | 1,000 |
| 4 | 2,000 |

*s.t.*

**(1)** Constraints on regular time capacity:

$$\sum_{k=1}^{2} 0.03x_{1k} + 0.15x_{2k} + 0.05x_{3k} + 0.10x_{4k} \leq 400 \quad (Stamping)$$

$$\sum_{k=1}^{2} 0.06x_{1k} + 0.12x_{2k} + 0.10x_{4k} \leq 400 \quad (Drilling)$$

$$\sum_{k=1}^{4} 0.05x_{1k} + 0.10x_{2k} + 0.05x_{3k} + 0.12x_{4k} \leq 500 \quad (Assembly)$$

$$0.04(x_{11} + x_{13}) + 0.20(x_{21} + x_{23}) + 0.03(x_{31} + x_{33}) + 0.12(x_{41} + x_{43}) \leq 450 \quad (Finishing)$$

$$\sum_{k=1}^{4} 0.02x_{1k} + 0.06x_{2k} + 0.02x_{3k} + 0.05x_{4k} \leq 400 \quad (Packaging)$$

**(2)** Constraints on overtime finishing:

$$0.04(x_{12} + x_{14}) + 0.20(x_{22} + x_{24}) + 0.03(x_{32} + x_{34}) + 0.12(x_{42} + x_{44}) \leq 100 \quad (Overtime\ Finishing)$$

**(3)** Constraint on sheet metal availability:

$$2.0(x_{21} + x_{22}) + 1.2(x_{41} + x_{42}) \leq 2,000$$

**(4)** Constraint on quantity required:

$$x_{11} + x_{12} + x_{13} + x_{14} = 3,000$$

$$x_{21} + x_{22} + x_{23} + x_{24} = 500$$

$$x_{31} + x_{32} + x_{33} + x_{34} = 1,000$$

$$x_{41} + x_{42} + x_{43} + x_{44} = 2,000$$

Using the Solver (Simplex LP), by changing the range of *Cells H3:H18* of Fig. 7.2-3, the optimal linear program vector is:

$$x_{11}^* = 3,000 \; ; x_{23}^* = 300 \; ; \; x_{24}^* = 200 \; ; \; x_{31}^* = 1,000 \; ; x_{41}^* = 1,667 \; ; \; x_{43}^* = 333$$

with minimum value in the objective function equal to:

$$Z_{min} = \pounds \, 67,013.$$

See Figs. 7.2-3 and 7.2-4 (Excel Setup) and Table 7.2-7.

## EXAMPLE 3 (EXAMPLE 1 COMBINED WITH EXAMPLE 2)

In this example, we change the objective function of Example 2 to maximize the total contribution margin to overhead costs, still considering the four production processes.

We replace then the constraint (4) of quantities required in Table 7.2-7 with the constraint (3) of min-max sales in Table 7.2-3.

The objective function becomes:

$$\max_{\{x_j\}} Z = 4.0x_{11} + 3.8x_{12} + 2.8x_{13} + 2.6x_{14} + 10.0x_{21} + 9.6x_{22} + 7.0x_{23} + 6.6x_{24} + 5.0x_{31} + 4.8x_{32}$$

$$+ 2.8x_{33} + 2.6x_{34} + 6.0x_{41} + 5.7x_{42} + 3.2x_{43} + 2.9x_{44}.$$

The coefficients of the above objective functions are the contribution margin for the product $j = 1, 2, 3, 4$ produced within the process $k = 1, 2, 3, 4$ combining the unit variable costs of Table 7.2-4 with the unit selling prices of Table 7.2-2. The problem formulated in Excel is in Fig. 7.2-5 (with optimal solution) while the Solver setup is in Fig. 7.2-6.

| | G | H | I | J | K | L |
|---|---|---|---|---|---|---|
| 1 | | | UNIT OF PRODUCT (j) PRODUCED BY PROCESS (k) | | UNIT VARIABLE COSTS | |
| 2 | $x_{jk}$ | $x_{jk}$ Optimal | Process k = 1, 2, 3, 4 | Product | £ | Delta |
| 3 | x11 | 3,000 | Internal stamping regular time | Product 1 | 6.00 | 0.00 |
| 4 | x12 | 0 | Internal stamping over time time | Product 1 | 6.20 | 0.20 |
| 5 | x13 | 0 | Subcontracting regular time | Product 1 | 7.20 | 20% |
| 6 | x14 | 0 | Subcontracting over time | Product 1 | 7.40 | 0.20 |
| 7 | x21 | 0 | Internal stamping regular time | Product 2 | 15.00 | 0.00 |
| 8 | x22 | 0 | Internal stamping over time time | Product 2 | 15.40 | 0.40 |
| 9 | x23 | 300 | Subcontracting regular time | Product 2 | 18.00 | 20% |
| 10 | x24 | 200 | Subcontracting over time | Product 2 | 18.40 | 0.40 |
| 11 | x31 | 1,000 | Internal stamping regular time | Product 3 | 11.00 | 0.00 |
| 12 | x32 | 0 | Internal stamping over time time | Product 3 | 11.20 | 0.20 |
| 13 | x33 | 0 | Subcontracting regular time | Product 3 | 13.20 | 20% |
| 14 | x34 | 0 | Subcontracting over time | Product 3 | 13.40 | 0.20 |
| 15 | x41 | 1,667 | Internal stamping regular time | Product 4 | 14.00 | 0.00 |
| 16 | x42 | 0 | Internal stamping over time time | Product 4 | 14.30 | 0.30 |
| 17 | x43 | 333 | Subcontracting regular time | Product 4 | 16.80 | 20% |
| 18 | x44 | 0 | Subcontracting over time | Product 4 | 17.10 | 0.30 |

FIGURE 7.2-3   Example 2 optimal solution.

| | A | B | C | D | E |
|---|---|---|---|---|---|
| 1 | MIN Z | =SUMPRODUCT(H3:H18;K3:K18) | | | |
| 2 | (Total variable costs) | | | | |
| 3 | | | | | |
| 4 | | | | | |
| 5 | s.t. | | | | |
| 6 | (1) | Regular time capacity | | | |
| 7 | Scheduled | | Available (Table 7.2-5) | | |
| 8 | | | | | |
| 9 | =0.03*SUM(H3:H4)+0.15*SUM(H7:H8)+0.05*SUM(H11:H12)+0.1*SUM(H15:H16) | ≤ | 400 | Stamping | Applies to internal prod only |
| 10 | =0.06*SUM(H3:H4)+0.12+SUM(H7:H8)+0.1*SUM(H15:H16) | ≤ | 400 | Drilling | Applies to internal prod only |
| 11 | =0.05*SUM(H3:H6)+0.1*SUM(H7:H10)+0.05*SUM(H11:H14)+0.12*SUM(H15:H18) | ≤ | 500 | Assembly | All quantities considered for assembly |
| 12 | =0.04*(H3+H5)+0.2*(H7+H9)+0.03*(H11+H13)+0.12*(H15+H17) | ≤ | 450 | Finishing | Applies to internal an subcontractor production |
| 13 | =0.02*SUM(H3:H6)+0.06*SUM(H7:H10)+0.02*SUM(H11:H14)+0.05*SUM(H15:H18) | ≤ | 400 | Packaging | All quantities considered for packaging |
| 14 | | | | | |
| 15 | (2) | Over time finishing capacity | | | |
| 16 | Scheduled | | Available (Table 7.2-5) | | |
| 17 | | | | | |
| 18 | =0.04*(H4+H6)+0.2*(H8+H10)+0.03*(H12+H14)+0.12*(H16+H18) | ≤ | 100 | | |
| 19 | | | | | |
| 20 | (3) | Sheet metal availability | | | |
| 21 | | | | | |
| 22 | =2*(H7+H8)+1.2*(H15+H16) | ≤ | 2000 | | |
| 23 | | | | | |
| 24 | (3) | Quantities required | (Table 7.2-6) | | |
| 25 | | | | | |
| 26 | =SUM(H3:H6) | = | 3000 | | |
| 27 | =SUM(H7:H10) | = | 500 | | |
| 28 | =SUM(H11:H14) | = | 1000 | | |
| 29 | =SUM(H15:H18) | = | 2000 | | |

FIGURE 7.2-4    Example 2 excel set-up.

TABLE 7.2-7    Example 2 linear program solution.

| MIN Z | | 67,013 | | | |
|---|---|---|---|---|---|
| (Total variable costs) | | | | | |
| | | | | | |
| s.t | | | | | |
| (1) | | Regular time capacity | | | |
| | Scheduled | | Available (Table 7.2-5) | | |
| | 306.67 | ≤ | 400 | Stamping | Applies to internal prod only |
| | 346.79 | ≤ | 400 | Drilling | Applies to internal prod only |
| | 490.00 | ≤ | 500 | Assembly | All quantities considered for assembly |
| | 450.00 | ≤ | 450 | Finishing | Applies to internal an subcontractor production |
| | 210.00 | ≤ | 400 | Packaging | All quantities considered for packaging |
| | | | | | |
| (2) | | Over time finishing capacity | | | |
| | Scheduled | | Available (Table 7.2-5) | | |
| | 40.00 | ≤ | 100 | | |
| | | | | | |
| (3) | | Sheet metal availability | | | |
| | Scheduled | | Available | | |
| | 2,000 | ≤ | 2,000 | | |
| | | | | | |
| (4) | | Quantities required | (Table 7.2-6) | | |
| | Scheduled | | | | |
| | 3,000 | = | 3,000 | | |
| | 500 | = | 500 | | |
| | 1,000 | = | 1,000 | | |
| | 2,000 | = | 2,000 | | |

The optimal solution is

$$x_{11}^* = 5,500 \; ; x_{13}^* = 260 \; ; \; x_{21}^* = 500 \; ; \; x_{31}^* = 3,000 \; ; x_{41}^* = 100 \; ; \; x_{43}^* = 333$$

with maximum value in the objective function equal to:

$$Z_{max} = £\,43,328.$$

II. Static Optimization

COMBIN    ×   ✓   *fx*   =SUMPRODUCT(H3:H18:K3:K18)

SUMPRODUCT(array1; [array2]; [array3]; [array4]; ...)

| | A | B | C | | | UNIT OF PRODUCT (j) PRODUCED BY PROCESS (k) | | | CONTRIBUTION MARGIN | |
|---|---|---|---|---|---|---|---|---|---|---|
| 1 | Max Z | K18 | | | | $x_{jk}$ | $x_{jk}$ Optimal | Process k = 1, 2, 3, 4 | Product | £ |
| 2 | (gross profit by product/process) | | | | | $x_{11}$ | 5,800 | Internal stamping regular time | Product 1 | 4.00 |
| 3 | | | | | | $x_{12}$ | 0 | Internal stamping over time time | Product 1 | 3.80 |
| 4 | | | | | | $x_{13}$ | 260 | Subcontracting regular time | Product 1 | 2.80 |
| 5 | | z.L | | | | $x_{14}$ | 0 | Subcontracting over time | Product 1 | 2.60 |
| 6 | (1) | | Regular time capacity | | | $x_{21}$ | 900 | Internal stamping regular time | Product 2 | 10.00 |
| 7 | | Scheduled | | Available (Table 7.2-5) | | $x_{22}$ | 0 | Internal stamping over time time | Product 2 | 9.60 |
| 8 | | | | | | $x_{23}$ | 0 | Subcontracting regular time | Product 2 | 7.00 |
| 9 | | 400 | ≤ | 400 | | $x_{24}$ | 0 | Subcontracting over time | Product 2 | 6.60 |
| 10 | | 400 | ≤ | 400 | | $x_{31}$ | 3,000 | Internal stamping regular time | Product 3 | 5.00 |
| 11 | | 500 | ≤ | 500 | | $x_{32}$ | 0 | Internal stamping over time time | Product 3 | 4.80 |
| 12 | | 432 | ≤ | 450 | | $x_{33}$ | 0 | Subcontracting regular time | Product 3 | 2.80 |
| 13 | | 210 | ≤ | 400 | | $x_{34}$ | 0 | Subcontracting over time | Product 3 | 2.60 |
| 14 | | | | | | $x_{41}$ | 100 | Internal stamping regular time | Product 4 | 6.00 |
| 15 | (2) | | Over time finishing capacity | | | $x_{42}$ | 0 | Internal stamping over time time | Product 4 | 5.70 |
| 16 | | Scheduled | | Available (Table 7.2-5) | | $x_{43}$ | 0 | Subcontracting regular time | Product 4 | 3.20 |
| 17 | | | | | | $x_{44}$ | 0 | Subcontracting over time | Product 4 | 2.90 |
| 18 | | 0 | ≤ | 100 | | | | | | |
| 19 | | | | | | | | | | |
| 20 | (3) | | Sheet metal availability | | | | | | | |
| 21 | | Scheduled | | | | | | | | |
| 22 | | 1,120 | ≤ | 2,000 | | | | | | |
| 23 | | | | | | | | | | |
| 24 | (4 new) | | Max sales min production from Example 1 added | (Table 7.2-1) | | | | | | |
| 25 | | Scheduled | | | | | | | | |
| 26 | | 1,000 | ≤ | 5,760 | ≤ | 6,000 | | | | |
| 27 | | 0 | ≤ | 500 | ≤ | 500 | | | | |
| 28 | | 900 | ≤ | 3,000 | ≤ | 3,000 | | | | |
| 29 | | 100 | ≤ | 100 | ≤ | 1,000 | | | | |

FIGURE 7.2-5    Example 3 linear program formulation.

## Blending production problems

These problems arise when a production process must involve the blending of several raw materials to make a product, according to a specific requirement and there are several combinations (blends) of these raw materials that will lead to an acceptable product. Examples are the blending of ingredients in the food and beverage industry, crude oils in the petroleum industry, mineral bearing ores in the production of metals and alloy, cotton, or wool fibers in the textile industry, or, in the cement concrete the blending of the aggregates (sand, crushed stones, gravels, etc.) with the fluid cement paste.

The problem consists of finding the least-cost blend of raw materials that is also meeting the required specifications. The available quantities, as well as the product specifications generate the constraints to obtain the optimal blend. The optimal solution returns the quantity of each material to be mixed to produce one unit of product.

Assuming we have a linear relationship within the underlying variables the mathematical problem can be formalized as follows.

We have *n* different raw materials with *m* specifications. Let:

$$x_j = \text{quantity of raw material } j \text{ used per unit of product}$$

$$c_j = \text{unit cost of material } j$$

$$a_{ij} = \text{contribution of a unit of material } j \text{ to the value of property } i \text{ of the product}$$

$$b_i = \text{specification on property } i \text{ of the product}$$

$$Z = \text{objective function total material cost}$$

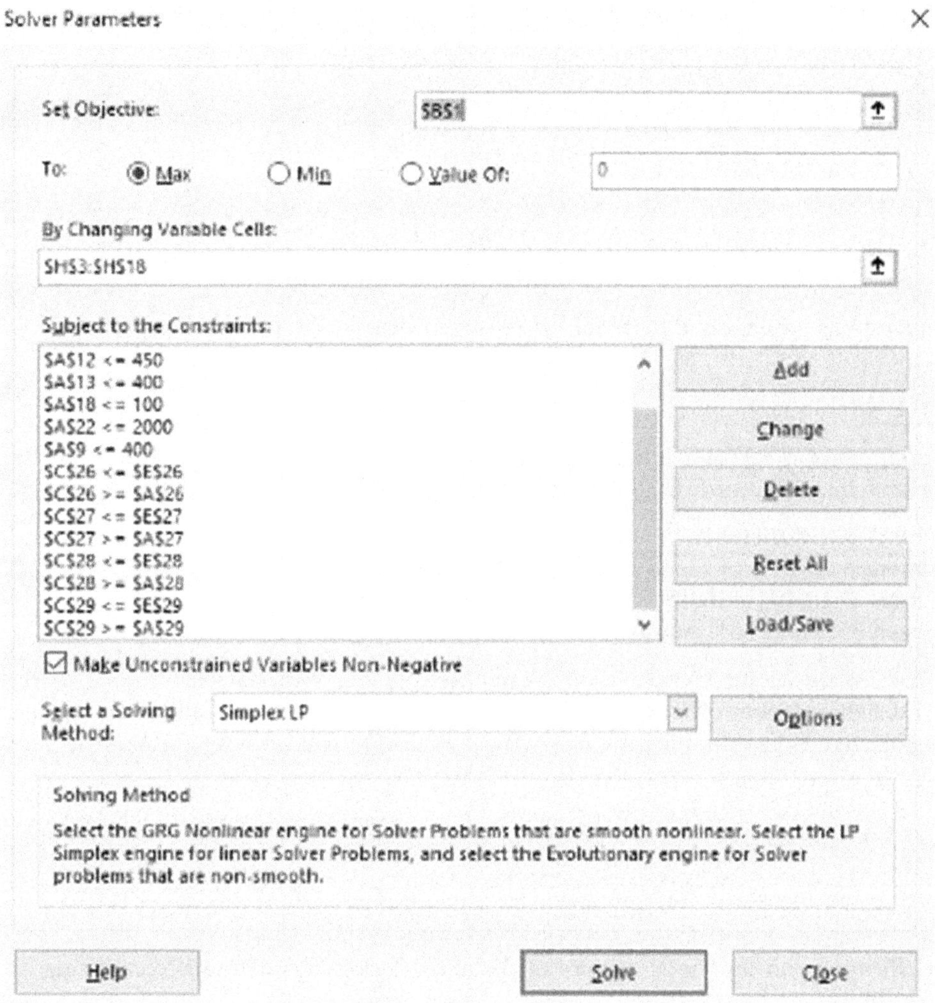

Solver Parameters                                                                                        ✕

Se*t* Objective:                              $B$1                                                          ⬆

To:        ⦿ Ma*x*        ○ Mi*n*        ○ *V*alue Of:        0

By Changing Varsable Cells:

$H$3:$H$18                                                                                                 ⬆

S*u*bject to the Constraints:

| $A$12 <= 450 | ^ | Add |
| $A$13 <= 400 | | |
| $A$18 <= 100 | | Change |
| $A$22 <= 2000 | | |
| $A$9 <= 400 | | |
| $C$26 <= $E$26 | | Delete |
| $C$26 >= $A$26 | | |
| $C$27 <= $E$27 | | |
| $C$27 >= $A$27 | | Reset All |
| $C$28 <= $E$28 | | |
| $C$28 >= $A$28 | | |
| $C$29 <= $E$29 | | Load/Save |
| $C$29 >= $A$29 | ⌄ | |

☑ Ma*k*e Unconstrained Variables Non-Negati*v*e

S*e*lect a Solving      Simplex LP                                    ⌄        Options
Method:

Solving Method

Select the GRG Nonlinear engine for Solver Problems that are smooth nonlinear. Select the LP
Simplex engine for linear Solver Problems, and select the Evolutionary engine for Solver
problems that are non-smooth.

Help                              Solve                              Close

**FIGURE 7.2-6**   Solver setup for Example 3

The problem is to find the nonnegative quantities $x_j$ ($j = 1, 2, \cdots, n$) to minimize:

$$Z = \sum_{j=1}^{n} c_j x_j$$

s.t.

$$\sum_{j=1}^{n} a_{ij} x_j \left\{ \begin{array}{c} \leq \\ = \\ \geq \end{array} \right\} b_i \quad (i = 1, 2, \cdots, m)$$

II. Static Optimization

$$\sum_{j=1}^{n} x_j = 1 \quad (material\ balance\ constraint)$$

Also, if we let $d_j$ the fraction of the unit of input of material $j$ contained in a unit of finished product the material balance constraint becomes:

$$\sum_{j=1}^{n} d_j x_j = 1$$

This happens when some material $j$ is removed during the production process.

## EXAMPLE 4

A producer of metal alloys has a special order from a customer to produce an alloy containing four metals according to the following specifications.

1. At least 23% of metal A.
2. No more than 15% of metal B.
3. No more than 4% of metal C.
4. Between 35% and 65% of metal D.

Table 7.2-8 shows the composition of each ore together with its cost.
Let $x_j$ be the number of tons of ore $j = 1, 2, \cdots, 6$ used per ton of alloy.
The objective is to minimize the following function of total raw materials cost per ton of alloy:

$$\min_{\{x_j\}} Z = 23x_1 + 20x_2 + 18x_3 + 10x_4 + 27x_5 + 12x_6$$

s.t.

(1) Specifications on the metal content of the alloy (last two constraints concerning metal D):

TABLE 7.2-8  Ore Composition and its cost per ton (to be read by row).

| ORE (j =1,..., 6) | METAL A | METAL B | METAL C | METAL D | IMPURITIES | TOTAL | COST/TON £ |
|---|---|---|---|---|---|---|---|
| 1 | 25% | 10% | 10% | 25% | 30% | 100% | 23 |
| 2 | 40% | 0% | 0% | 30% | 30% | 100% | 20 |
| 3 | 20% | 10% | 0% | 30% | 40% | 100% | 18 |
| 4 | 0% | 15% | 5% | 20% | 60% | 100% | 10 |
| 5 | 20% | 20% | 0% | 40% | 20% | 100% | 27 |
| 6 | 8% | 5% | 10% | 17% | 60% | 100% | 12 |

Source: Lynwood A. Johnson, Douglas C. Montgomery, *Operations Research in Production Planning, Scheduling and Inventory Control*, Table 3.7, p.121, Copyright © 1974 by John Wiley and Sons, Inc.

$$0.25x_1 + 0.40x_2 + 0.20x_3 + 0.20x_5 + 0.08x_6 \geq 0.23$$

$$0.10x_1 + 0.10x_3 + 0.15x_4 + 0.20x_5 + 0.05x_6 \leq 0.23$$

$$0.10x_1 + 0.05x_4 + 0.10x_6 \leq 0.23$$

$$0.25x_1 + 0.30x_2 + 0.30x_3 + 0.20x_4 + 0.40x_5 + 0.17x_6 \geq 0.35$$

$$0.25x_1 + 0.30x_2 + 0.30x_3 + 0.20x_4 + 0.40x_5 + 0.17x_6 \leq 0.65$$

**(2)** Material balance constraint:

$$0.70x_1 + 0.70x_2 + 0.60x_3 + 0.40x_4 + 0.80x_5 + 0.40x_6 = 1$$

The Excel linear problem is fully described in Fig. 7.2-7 and the Solver setup is in Fig. 7.2-8. The optimal solution is:

$$x_2^* = 0.9714 \; ; \; x_4^* = 0.80 \; ; \; x_1^* = x_3^* = x_5^* = x_6^* = 0$$

With the minimum value of the objective function equal to:

$$Z_{min} = £\ 27.43$$

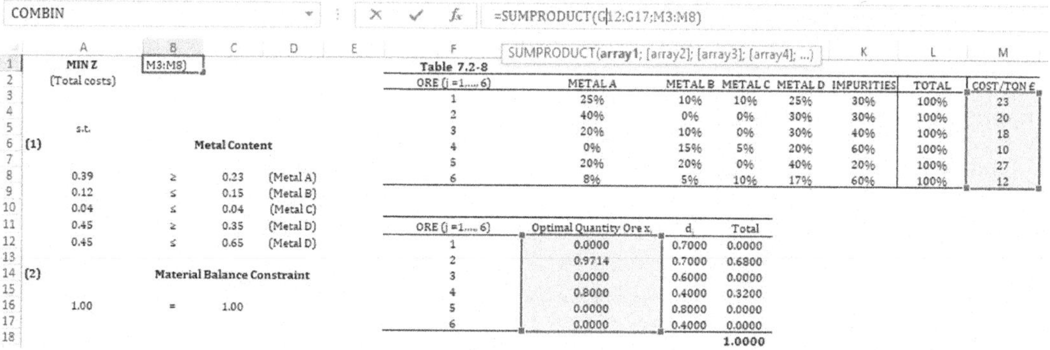

FIGURE 7.2-7  Example 4 Excel linear program (blending).

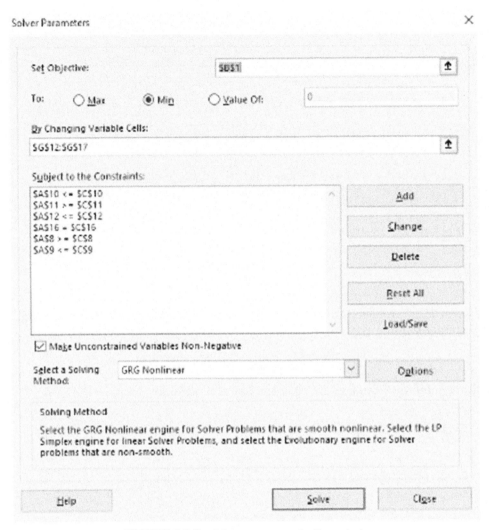

FIGURE 7.2-8    Solver parameters for Example 4.

## Lorie-Savage capital rationing

Capital budgeting is the process that companies use for decision-making on capital projects. Decisions are based on the cash flows generated by the project, using some investment criteria, e.g., Net Present Value (NPV) or Internal Rate of Return (IRR).

The capital rationing occurs instead when the company's capital budget has a size constraint. In its multiperiod general form, the Lorie–Savage capital rationing problem can be formalized as follows.

Let $n$ be the number of investment projects available and $c_j$ the NPV of each investment project. Also, let $x_j$ be the binary decision variable, which will either take the value 1 if the project is undertaken or the value 0 if it is not undertaken and $a_{ij}$ be the outlay of the investment $j$ in the period $i$.

The problem is then subject to the constraint of maximum resources available, $b_i$ to be employed for the $i$th period.

The linear program is specified as follows:

$$\max_{\{x_j\}} Z = \sum_{j=1}^{n} c_j x_j$$

s.t.

$$\sum_{j=1}^{n} a_{ij} x_j \leq b_i \quad (i = 1, 2, \cdots, m)$$

$x_j$ binary variable otherwise fractional investments undertaken

## EXAMPLE 5 (CAPITAL RATIONING)

Let us consider Table 7.2-9 which includes the same data as the ones appearing in the original article, by Lorie–Savage, *Three Problems in Rationing Capital*, Journal of Business, Oct. 1954.

The problem will be set up as in Fig. 7.2-9, and the Solver will be set up instead as in Fig. 7.2-10 which optimizes the objective function stored in *Cell B1* by changing the binary decision variables in *Range I4:I12*. The optimal solution of the binary program vector $x$ is in Table 7.2-10.

**TABLE 7.2-9** Investment projects data.

| Investment Project | PV of Outlay | | NPV |
|:---:|:---:|:---:|:---:|
| | Period1 | Period 2 | |
| 1 | 12.0 | 3.0 | 14.0 |
| 2 | 54.0 | 7.0 | 17.0 |
| 3 | 6.0 | 6.0 | 17.0 |
| 4 | 6.0 | 2.0 | 15.0 |
| 5 | 30.0 | 35.0 | 40.0 |
| 6 | 6.0 | 6.0 | 12.0 |
| 7 | 48.0 | 4.0 | 14.0 |
| 8 | 36.0 | 3.0 | 10.0 |
| 9 | 18.0 | 3.0 | 12.0 |

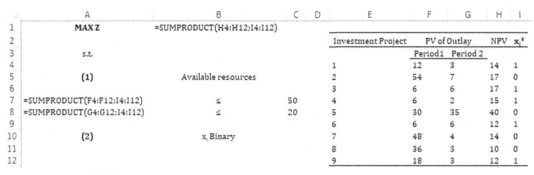

| | A | B | C | D | E | F | G | H | I |
|---|---|---|---|---|---|---|---|---|---|
| 1 | MAX Z | =SUMPRODUCT(H4:H12;I4:I12) | | | | | | | |
| 2 | | | | | Investment Project | PV of Outlay | | NPV | $x_i^*$ |
| 3 | s.t. | | | | | Period1 | Period 2 | | |
| 4 | | | | | 1 | 12 | 3 | 14 | 1 |
| 5 | (1) | Available resources | | | 2 | 54 | 7 | 17 | 0 |
| 6 | | | | | 3 | 6 | 6 | 17 | 1 |
| 7 | =SUMPRODUCT(F4:F12;I4:I12) | ≤ | 50 | | 4 | 6 | 2 | 15 | 1 |
| 8 | =SUMPRODUCT(G4:G12;I4:I12) | ≤ | 20 | | 5 | 30 | 35 | 40 | 0 |
| 9 | | | | | 6 | 6 | 6 | 12 | 1 |
| 10 | (2) | $x_i$ Binary | | | 7 | 48 | 4 | 14 | 0 |
| 11 | | | | | 8 | 36 | 3 | 10 | 0 |
| 12 | | | | | 9 | 18 | 3 | 12 | 1 |

FIGURE 7.2-9    Excel set up of the Lorie–Savage capital budgeting problem.

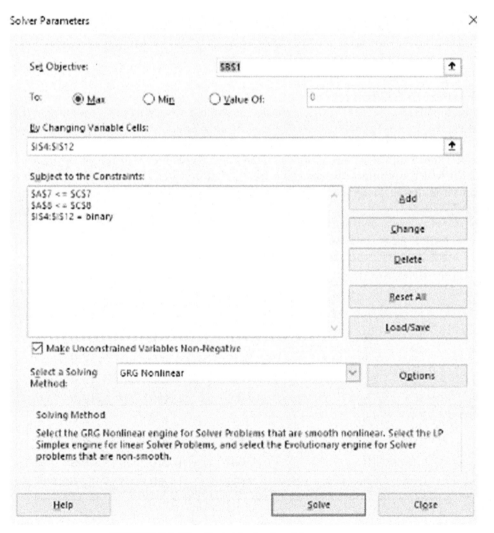

FIGURE 7.2-10    Capital budgeting Solver parameters.

**TABLE 7.2-10**  Optimal solution $x_j^*$.

| | | | Investment Project | PV of Outlay | | NPV | $x_j^*$ |
|---|---|---|---|---|---|---|---|
| MAX Z | 70.0 | | | Period1 | Period 2 | | |
| s.t. | | | 1 | 12.0 | 3.0 | 14.0 | 1 |
| **(1)** | Available resources | | 2 | 54.0 | 7.0 | 17.0 | 0 |
| | | | 3 | 6.0 | 6.0 | 17.0 | 1 |
| 48.0 | ≤ | 50.0 | 4 | 6.0 | 2.0 | 15.0 | 1 |
| 20.0 | ≤ | 20.0 | 5 | 30.0 | 35.0 | 40.0 | 0 |
| | | | 6 | 6.0 | 6.0 | 12.0 | 1 |
| **(2)** | $x_j$ Binary | | 7 | 48.0 | 4.0 | 14.0 | 0 |
| | | | 8 | 36.0 | 3.0 | 10.0 | 0 |
| | | | 9 | 18.0 | 3.0 | 12.0 | 1 |

**TABLE 7.2-11**  Optimal solution removing the binary constraint.

| | | | Investment Project | PV of Outlay | | NPV | $x_j^*$ |
|---|---|---|---|---|---|---|---|
| MAX Z | 70.3 | | | Period1 | Period 2 | | |
| s.t. | | | 1 | 12.0 | 3.0 | 14.0 | 1.000 |
| **(1)** | Available resources | | 2 | 54.0 | 7.0 | 17.0 | 0.000 |
| | | | 3 | 6.0 | 6.0 | 17.0 | 1.000 |
| 50.0 | ≤ | 50.0 | 4 | 6.0 | 2.0 | 15.0 | 1.000 |
| 20.0 | ≤ | 20.0 | 5 | 30.0 | 35.0 | 40.0 | 0.000 |
| | | | 6 | 6.0 | 6.0 | 12.0 | 0.970 |
| **(2)** | $x_j$ Not Necessarily Binary | | 7 | 48.0 | 4.0 | 14.0 | 0.045 |
| | | | 8 | 36.0 | 3.0 | 10.0 | 0.000 |
| | | | 9 | 18.0 | 3.0 | 12.0 | 1.000 |

The Solver is set up as in Fig. 7.2-10 where the binary constraint has been added to the constraint of resources available. Although the problem is linear, in this case we have used the GRG as this works better in finding the optimal solution, with the binary constraint and other constraints. We also notice from Table 7.2-10 that some resources have been not employed fully. In this case, we can relax the assumption of undertaking/not undertaking the project, removing the binary constraint in the Solver, so that the company can also invest in fractional projects. In this case, the solution changes as in Table 7.2-11, from which we see that the resources have been now fully exploited at their maximum level. The new Solver parameters are instead as in Fig. 7.2-11.

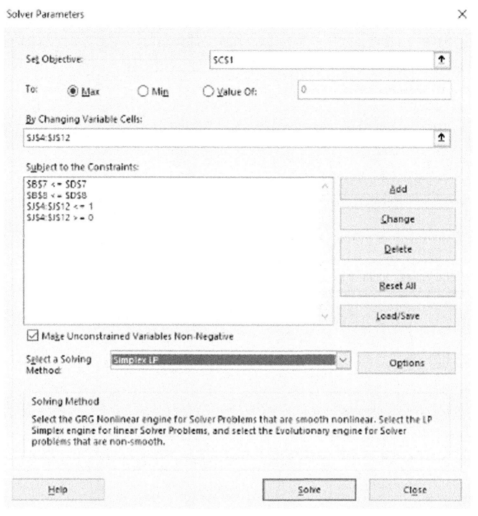

FIGURE 7.2-11    solver parameters without binary constraint.

# Exercises

1. Three products A, B, and C are produced in a plant, and for a given period there is the problem of deciding how much of each product to produce. Table 1 below contains information on the production process, profitability, and sales potential of each item.
   Identify the objective function, formalize the various constraints, and formulate the linear programming model.

**TABLE 1**

| PRODUCT | PROCESSING TIME IN HOURS PER UNIT | | | | | UNIT PROFIT £ | SALES CAPACITY | |
| | DEPT I | DEPT II | DEPT III | INSPECTION | SHIPPING | | MIN | MAX |
|---|---|---|---|---|---|---|---|---|
| A | 0.14 | 0.60 | 0.20 | 0.04 | 0.10 | 42 | 150 | 250 |
| B | 0.10 | 0.40 | 0.20 | 0.04 | 0.10 | 40 | 200 | 400 |
| C | | 0.20 | 0.10 | 0.04 | 0.12 | 36 | 360 | 500 |
| Hours of Capacity | 160 | 320 | 160 | 80 | 80 | | | |

**Source**: Lynwood A. Johnson, Douglas C. Montgomery, *Operations Research in Production Planning, Scheduling and Inventory Control*, Exercise 3.1, p.167, Copyright © 1974 by John Wiley and Sons, Inc.

2. A plant can manufacture three products A, B, and C. The plant has four departments, I, II, III, and IV. Product A must be processed in departments I and II; product B in departments I, II, III, and IV; and product C in departments I, III, and IV.

   Departments I and II must each be scheduled for at least 100 h, while at least 1000 pieces of product A must be manufactured. Then, a purchase part used in the assembly of products A and C is scarce and only 3500 parts are available for the month. Two parts are used in each piece of product A and three parts are used in each piece of product C.

   Table 2 below contains the relevant information.

**TABLE 2**

| PRODUCT | OUTPUT RATE IN PIECES PER HOUR | | | | UNIT PROFIT £ | PRODUCTION MIN CONSTR. | |
| | DEPT I | DEPT II | DEPT III | DEPT IV | | MIN | MAX |
|---|---|---|---|---|---|---|---|
| A | 20.00 | 40.00 | 0.00 | 0.00 | 3.10 | 1000 | |
| B | 30.00 | 25.00 | 10.00 | 22.00 | 2.05 | | |
| C | 60.00 | 0.00 | 20.00 | 5.00 | 6.17 | | |
| Available Hours | 150 | 160 | 130 | 100 | | | |
| MIN | 100 | 100 | | | | | |

**Source**: Lynwood A. Johnson, Douglas C. Montgomery, *Operations Research in Production Planning, Scheduling and Inventory Control*, Exercise 3.3, p.168, Copyright © 1974 by John Wiley and Sons, Inc.

Identify the objective function, formalize the various constraints, and determine the most profitable product mix for the month.

3. Consider again the blending production problem of Example 4 shown in the chapter and suppose that the customer order is for 4000 tons of alloy and that the producer has only the following amounts of the six ores available (in tons); 2500; 2200; 800; 3000; 1000, and 1600.

Write a general linear programming formulation for the resource constrained blending problem, where the raw materials are in limited supply.

4. Three products A, B, and C are produced in a plant with three departments I, II, and III. The three departments have a limited number of available hours. Product A must be processed according to the following department order:

$$I \Rightarrow III \Rightarrow II \Rightarrow III.$$

Product B according to the following:

$$I \Rightarrow II \Rightarrow III.$$

Product C according to the following:

$$II \Rightarrow III.$$

The output rate in pieces per hour, unit profits, and constraints are shown in Table 3.

TABLE 3

| PRODUCT | OUTPUT RATE IN PIECES PER HOUR | | | | UNIT PROFIT £ | PRODUCT CAPACITY |
| | DEPT I | DEPT II | DEPT III | DEPT III | | |
|---|---|---|---|---|---|---|
| A | 0.35 | 12.00 | 30.00 | 15.00 | 350 | 250 |
| B | 0.28 | 12.00 | 15.00 | 0.00 | 250 | 1,250 |
| C | 0.00 | 9.60 | 12.00 | 0.00 | 400 | 1,500 |
| Available Hours | 2,700 | 624 | 416 | | | |

Identify the objective function, formalize the various constraints, and determine the most profitable product vector mix.

5. Using the Solver find the solution of the following linear problem and represent it geometrically in a chart:

$$\min_{\{x_1; x_2\}} 9x_1 + 12x_2$$

s.t.

$$3x_1 + x_2 \geq 12$$

$$x_1 + x_2 \geq 9$$

$$x_1 + 2x_2 \geq 8$$

$$x_1 \geq 0, \ x_2 \ \textit{Free}$$

II. Static Optimization

**6.** Using the Solver find the solution of the following linear problem and represent it geometrically in a chart:

$$\max_{\{x_1;x_2\}} 4x_1 + 2x_2$$

s.t.

$$3x_1 + 4x_2 \leq 24$$

$$700x_1 + 225x_2 \leq 3,150$$

$$1.8x_1 + 2x_2 \leq 18$$

$$7x_1 + 6x_2 \leq 42$$

$$x_1 \geq 0, \; x_2 \geq 0$$

**7.** Using the Solver find the solution of the following linear problem and represent it geometrically in a chart:

$$\max_{\{x_1;x_2\}} 4x_1 + 7x_2$$

s.t.

$$2x_1 + 5x_2 \leq 10$$

$$6x_1 + 3x_2 \leq 18$$

$$x_1 \geq 0, \; x_2 \geq 0$$

**8.** Using the Solver find the solution of the following linear problem and represent it geometrically in a chart:

$$\max_{\{x_1;x_2\}} 8x_1 + 2x_2$$

s.t.

$$4x_1 + x_2 \geq 16$$

II. Static Optimization

$$2x_1 + 3x_2 \geq 12$$

$$x_1 \geq 0, \; x_2 \geq 0$$

(*This problem allows infinite optimal solutions.*)

**9.** Using the Solver find the solution of the following linear problem and represent it geometrically in a chart:

$$\max_{\{x_1;x_2\}} 4x_1 + 6x_2$$

s.t.

$$3x_1 + 2x_2 \geq 6$$

$$x_1 + 5x_2 \geq 10$$

$$x_1 \geq 0, \; x_2 \geq 0$$

(*This maximum problem is not determined as the admissible region is unbounded from above.*)

**10.** A firm produces an item of two types: for the high-end market and for the mass market. Both products require the same type of raw materials but in different proportions. For each ton of output produced, the required resources expressed in hours are as follows in Table 4:

**TABLE 4**

|                  | Mass market | High-end market |
|------------------|:-----------:|:---------------:|
| Person-hours     | 1.0         | 1.8             |
| Machine-hours A  | 0.5         | 0.6             |
| Machine-hours B  | 0.3         | 0.2             |

The firm employs eight people in the workshop, three machines of Type A and two machines of Type B. The working hours are 8 h per day for 25 days in a month. The hours available are therefore 1600 person hours, 600 machine hours A and 400 machine hours B. The contribution margin for each ton produced is £600 for the mass-market product, while £ 1050 for the high-end product:

**a.** Identify the objective function, formalize the various constraints, and determine the most profitable product vector mix.

**b.** Represent the linear problem geometrically in a chart.

11. Implement a linear binary program for the investment opportunities shown in Table 5, with investment budget constraint equal to £ 1000.

TABLE 5

| Investment Project | PV of Outlay Period1 | NPV |
|---|---|---|
| 1 | 600.0 | 300.0 |
| 2 | 600.0 | 270.0 |
| 3 | 200.0 | 80.0 |
| 4 | 400.0 | 100.0 |

Transportation problems modeling.

The linear programming has vast applications in the management and industrial engineering area. An important topic is solving the transportation problems. Essentially, given a matrix of costs $c_{ij}$ for shipping the goods from the *source i* (i.e., the production center) to the *destination j* (i.e., depository center) the problem consists of finding the optimal flow of units $x_{ij}$ in order to minimize the total transportation cost, subject to the production capacity of each source center (supply capacity), demands required in each destination center, and nonnegativity constraints. The linear problem is formalized therefore as follows:

$$\min_{\{x_{ij}\}} \sum_{i=1}^{m} \sum_{j=1}^{n} c_{ij} x_{ij}$$

$$s.t.$$

$$\sum_{i=1}^{m} x_{ij} = d_j \quad (j = 1, \cdots, n)$$

$$\sum_{j=1}^{n} x_{ij} = s_i \quad (i = 1, \cdots, m)$$

$$x_{ij} \geq 0$$

Solve the following problems in Excel using the Simplex LP Solver.

12. A company owns three production centers P1, P2, and P3, whose production capacity is of units 50, 80, and 110, respectively. These products have to be shipped in three depositary centers D1, D2, and D3 which have demanded units 100, 80, and 60,

respectively. The matrix of transportation costs is as given in Table 6, where in each cell we have the transportation cost from the production center $i$ to the depositary center $j$.

TABLE 6

|    | D1 | D2 | D3 |
|----|----|----|----|
| P1 | 5  | 7  | 3  |
| P2 | 4  | 8  | 2  |
| P3 | 6  | 9  | 1  |

Determine the best transportation policy that minimizes the total cost using a linear program in Excel.

13. A company owns three production centers P1, P2, and P3, whose production capacity is of units 61, 49, and 90, respectively. These products have to be shipped in three depositary centers D1, D2, and D3 which have demanded units 52, 68, and 80, respectively. The matrix of transportation costs is given in (Table 7), where in each cell we have the transportation cost from the production center $i$ to the depositary center $j$.

Determine the best transportation policy that minimizes the total cost using a linear program in Excel.

TABLE 7

|    | D1 | D2 | D3 |
|----|----|----|----|
| P1 | 26 | 23 | 10 |
| P2 | 14 | 13 | 21 |
| P3 | 16 | 17 | 29 |

14. A company owns three production centers P1, P2, and P3, whose production capacity is of units 5, 7, and 3, respectively. These products have to be shipped in three depositary centers D1, D2, and D3 which have demanded units 7, 3, and 5, respectively. The matrix of transportation costs is as given in (Table 8), where in each cell we have the transportation cost from the production center $i$ to the depositary center $j$.

TABLE 8

|    | D1    | D2 | D3    |
|----|-------|----|-------|
| P1 | 3     | 1  | 1,000 |
| P2 | 4     | 2  | 4     |
| P3 | 1,000 | 3  | 3     |

The figurative amounts of 1000 indicate that the shipping is not possible. Determine the best transportation policy that minimizes the total cost using a linear program in Excel.

15. A company owns three production centers P1, P2, and P3, whose production capacity is of units 10, 15, and 8, respectively. These products have to be shipped in four depositary centers D1, D2, D3, and D4 which have demanded units 5, 3, 8, and 17, respectively. The matrix of transportation costs is as given in Table 9, where in each cell we have the transportation cost from the production center $i$ to the depositary center $j$.

### TABLE 9

|    | D1 | D2 | D3 | D4 |
|----|----|----|----|----|
| P1 | 10 | 10 | 6  | 15 |
| P2 | 5  | 15 | 10 | 12 |
| P3 | 11 | 8  | 7  | 21 |

# Nonlinear optimization applied to the portfolio theory

## 8.1 Portfolio modeling and the efficient frontier construction

As usually done in the finance textbooks to introduce the portfolio concepts, let us consider initially the simplest case where we have a portfolio made of only two assets; then, we will expand the problem to a portfolio of n-assets.

### The case of two assets

We will denote the **portfolio return** with $r_p$ as follows (sometimes it is also referred to as the expected return of the portfolio):

$$r_p = w_1 r_1 + w_2 r_2.$$

The return is always associated to the risk of a portfolio, and finance takes from statistics its measure of risk, which is a measure of dispersion around a central tendency of the given random variable. The standard deviation or equivalently its square, the variance, is taken therefore as one of the principal risk indicators of a portfolio. See also Section 13.3.

Theory of finance introduced as well some other "combined" measures, like the portfolio returns adjusted by the risk, and within this class of risk-adjusted performance indicators, the Sharpe Ratio plays a key role.

The **variance of a portfolio** of two assets is calculated as follows (from the property of the variance of two variables in statistics and probability theory):

$$\sigma_p^2 = w_1^2 \sigma_1^2 + w_2^2 \sigma_2^2 + 2 w_1 w_2 \rho_{12} \sigma_1 \sigma_2$$

where

$$\sigma_1 = \textit{standard deviation of asset 1}$$

$$\sigma_1 = \textit{standard deviation of asset 2}$$

$$\rho_{12} = \frac{Cov(r_1,\ r_2)}{\sigma_1 \sigma_2} \textit{ correlation coefficient between the two financial assets.}$$

The index of **covariance** $Cov(r_1, r_2)$ is an index to study the relationship between two assets returns (normally the fund's returns and the benchmark's returns) which represent the statistical (or random) variables we are studying. The covariance ranges from negative values to positive values. A positive covariance indicates that the two variables tend to move together and with the same sign, a negative covariance indicates that the two variables tend to move in the opposite direction. A covariance close to zero indicates that the relation between the fund's returns and the benchmark's returns is neutral and therefore there is little relationship between the two variables.

The formula of the covariance considers the two variables $(r_1, r_2)$ at the same time, and it is as follows:

$$Cov(r_1,\ r_2) = \frac{1}{N} \sum_{i=1}^{N} (r_{1i} - \mu_1) \cdot (r_{2i} - \mu_2)$$

with $\mu_1$ and $\mu_2$ the expected (average) returns of the first and the second assets, respectively.

To measure the correlation between two variables, we calculate the **correlation coefficient** $\rho_{12}$ with:

$$-1 \le \rho_{12} \le +1.$$

Since via the covariance we can only recognize the magnitude of the relationship in absolute terms, this index helps us to investigate more about the magnitude of the relationship in relative terms. This means that $\rho_{12}$ ranges from $-1$ to $+1$, and therefore we can recognize immediately the strength and the quality of the relationship between the two variables that we are studying.

When we find values of $\rho_{12} = 1$ we have got perfect positive correlation, when we find values of $\rho_{12} = -1$ we have got perfect negative correlation. Values close to zero indicate neutral correlation between the two variables, in other words they indicate independence between the two variables.

Let us represent the variances and covariances of the portfolio in the following symmetric matrix, called the **matrix of variances and covariances** associated to the portfolio $p$:

$$\Sigma = \begin{bmatrix} Cov(r_1, \ r_1) & Cov(r_1, \ r_2) \\ Cov(r_2, \ r_1) & Cov(r_2, \ r_2) \end{bmatrix}$$

then $\sigma_p^2$ can be represented as a quadratic form notation (see Eq. 3.4-2):

$$\sigma_p^2 = w^T \Sigma \ w$$

which is, recalling that $Cov(r_i, \ r_i) \ = \ \sigma_i^2$:

$$\sigma_p^2 = [w_1 \quad w_2] \begin{bmatrix} \sigma_1^2 & Cov(r_1, \ r_2) \\ Cov(r_2, \ r_1) & \sigma_2^2 \end{bmatrix} \begin{bmatrix} w_1 \\ w_2 \end{bmatrix}$$

$$\sigma_p^2 = [w_1\sigma_1^2 + w_2Cov(r_2, \ r_1) \quad w_1Cov(r_1, \ r_2) + w_2\sigma_2^2] \begin{bmatrix} w_1 \\ w_2 \end{bmatrix}$$

which corresponds to a scalar, namely the sought portfolio variance:

$$\sigma_p^2 = w_1^2\sigma_1^2 + w_1w_2Cov(r_2, \ r_1) + w_1w_2Cov(r_1, \ r_2) + w_2^2\sigma_2^2$$

$$= w_1^2\sigma_1^2 + w_2^2\sigma_2^2 + 2w_1w_2Cov(r_1, \ r_2)$$

$$= w_1^2\sigma_1^2 + w_2^2\sigma_2^2 + 2w_1w_2\rho_{12}\sigma_1\sigma_2.$$

### The case of three assets

Let us introduce a third asset, and in this case the portfolio return is as follows:

$$r_p = w_1r_1 + w_2r_2 + w_3r_3 \ = \ \sum_{j=1}^{3} w_jr_j.$$

The portfolio volatility measure, using the matrix notation, is:

$$\sigma_p^2 = \begin{bmatrix} w_1 & w_2 & w_3 \end{bmatrix} \begin{bmatrix} \sigma_1^2 & Cov(r_1,\, r_2) & Cov(r_1,\, r_3) \\ Cov(r_2,\, r_1) & \sigma_2^2 & Cov(r_2,\, r_3) \\ Cov(r_3,\, r_1) & Cov(r_3,\, r_2) & \sigma_3^2 \end{bmatrix} \begin{bmatrix} w_1 \\ w_2 \\ w_3 \end{bmatrix}.$$

The expanded form of the portfolio variance with three assets becomes therefore:

$$\sigma_p^2 = w_1^2\sigma_1^2 + w_2^2\sigma_2^2 + w_3^2\sigma_3^2 + 2w_1w_2Cov(r_1, r_2) + 2w_1w_3Cov(r_1, r_3) + 2w_2w_3Cov(r_2, r_3).$$

Using $Cov(r_i,\, r_j) = \rho_{ij}\sigma_i\sigma_j$, we have:

$$\sigma_p^2 = w_1^2\sigma_1^2 + w_2^2\sigma_2^2 + w_3^2\sigma_3^2 + 2w_1w_2\rho_{12}\sigma_1\sigma_2 + 2w_1w_3\rho_{13}\sigma_1\sigma_3 + 2w_2w_3\rho_{23}\sigma_2\sigma_3$$

## The case of n-assets

For the n-assets portfolio, the returns and variance can be formalized as follows:

$$r_p = \sum_{j=1}^{n} w_j r_j$$

$$\sigma_p^2 = w_1^2\sigma_1^2 + \cdots + w_n^2\sigma_n^2 + 2\sum_{i\neq j}^{n} w_i w_j Cov(r_i, r_j)$$

or equivalently:

$$\sigma_p^2 = \sum_{i=1}^{n}\sum_{j=1}^{n} w_i w_j Cov(r_i, r_j)$$

We want to determine now the best combination of assets in order to have the minimum portfolio standard deviation for a given return. This is called the **minimum variance frontier** (MVF).

Once the MVF is obtained, we will determine the **efficient frontier**, which represents the set of efficient portfolios and which is part of the MVF. The **global minimum variance** (GMV) portfolio can be then also deducted.

In mathematical terms, the optimization problem is to find the optimal weights $w_j$ that minimize the volatility of the portfolio, for a given return, that is:

$$\min_{w} \sum_{i=1}^{n}\sum_{j=1}^{n} w_i w_j Cov(r_i, r_j) \tag{1}$$

s.t.

$$\sum_{j=1}^{n} w_j r_j = z \tag{2}$$

$$\sum_{j=1}^{n} w_j = 1 \tag{3}$$

$$w_j \geq 0 \tag{4}$$

**(1)** The nonlinear objective function that we need to minimize (i.e., the portfolio variance).
**(2)** The minimization program needs to be run sequentially for every level of expected return, $z$, between $r_{min}$ and $r_{max}$. In practice, we will run the optimization starting with $z = r_{min}$ then, we will increase $z$ by a few basis points and solving for the optimal weights until we reach $z = r_{max}$ at which level the optimization program stops.
**(3)** This is the constraint such that the sum of weights will give 1.
**(4)** Read together with **(3)**, it characterizes the problem as having **no short selling, no riskless lending, and no borrowing** opportunities.

We show now in the following examples how we can approach this problem in Excel.

## EXAMPLE 1 (TWO ASSETS EFFICIENT FRONTIER)

Three years of data observations for two standard indices are provided in Table 8.1-1.

Now, supposing we have access to some tracking investment of the two indices the problem is to find the efficient frontier from the two indices, i.e., the best combinations of investment weights leading to the MVF.

The inputs of the problem are the average returns (using arithmetic average), standard deviation, and the correlation between the two assets, as in Table 8.1-2. In Fig. 8.1-1, we have the computations that we need to graph the efficient frontier. We build an Excel Data Table over the mean and standard deviation of the portfolio, and we let the weight in *Cell J9* move from 0% to 100%. The MVF and GMV portfolio are enumerated in Table 8.1-3, while the curve of minimum variance frontier, together with its two component assets is in Fig. 8.1-2.

**Efficient frontier**: The portion of the minimum variance frontier beginning with the GMV portfolio (see Figs. 8.1-2) and continuing above is called efficient frontier. Portfolios lying on the efficient frontier offer the maximum expected return for their level of standard deviation of returns.

Would the curvature of the efficient frontier change, if we had a different correlation index? The answer is yes of course. The following cases may happen as far as the correlation index is concerned:

**i.** Positive correlation, up to perfect positive correlation, i.e., $\rho = +1$.
**ii.** No correlation, i.e., $\rho = 0$.

**TABLE 8.1-1**  Three-years historical data for JP Morgan Euro bond index and MSCI Euro equity index.

| Euro Bond Index Date | Euro Bond Index Px Last | % Variation | Euro Equity Index Date | Euro Equity Index Px Last | % Variation |
|---|---|---|---|---|---|
| 28/02/2003 | 362.893 |  | 28/02/2003 | 62.56 |  |
| 31/03/2003 | 361.108 | -0.49% | 31/03/2003 | 59.78 | -4.44% |
| 30/04/2003 | 360.957 | -0.04% | 30/04/2003 | 67.6 | 13.08% |
| 30/05/2003 | 367.848 | 1.91% | 30/05/2003 | 68.14 | 0.80% |
| 30/06/2003 | 368.609 | 0.21% | 30/06/2003 | 70.44 | 3.38% |
| 31/07/2003 | 362.414 | -1.68% | 31/07/2003 | 73.53 | 4.39% |
| 29/08/2003 | 363.544 | 0.31% | 29/08/2003 | 75.31 | 2.42% |
| 30/09/2003 | 368.742 | 1.43% | 30/09/2003 | 71.19 | -5.47% |
| 31/10/2003 | 364.25 | -1.22% | 31/10/2003 | 76.56 | 7.54% |
| 28/11/2003 | 362.418 | -0.50% | 28/11/2003 | 78.09 | 2.00% |
| 31/12/2003 | 367.333 | 1.36% | 31/12/2003 | 80.79 | 3.46% |
| 30/01/2004 | 370.394 | 0.83% | 30/01/2004 | 83.37 | 3.19% |
| 27/02/2004 | 376.143 | 1.55% | 27/02/2004 | 84.93 | 1.87% |
| 31/03/2004 | 379.785 | 0.97% | 31/03/2004 | 82.38 | -3.00% |
| 30/04/2004 | 375.355 | -1.17% | 30/04/2004 | 82.93 | 0.67% |
| 31/05/2004 | 374.879 | -0.13% | 31/05/2004 | 81.85 | -1.30% |
| 30/06/2004 | 376.073 | 0.32% | 30/06/2004 | 83.85 | 2.44% |
| 30/07/2004 | 379.726 | 0.97% | 30/07/2004 | 81.36 | -2.97% |
| 31/08/2004 | 384.197 | 1.18% | 31/08/2004 | 80.3 | -1.30% |
| 30/09/2004 | 385.532 | 0.35% | 30/09/2004 | 82.1 | 2.24% |
| 29/10/2004 | 388.711 | 0.82% | 29/10/2004 | 84.28 | 2.66% |
| 30/11/2004 | 393.244 | 1.17% | 30/11/2004 | 86.56 | 2.71% |
| 31/12/2004 | 395.145 | 0.48% | 31/12/2004 | 88.97 | 2.78% |
| 31/01/2005 | 400.807 | 1.43% | 31/01/2005 | 90.66 | 1.90% |
| 28/02/2005 | 398.776 | -0.51% | 28/02/2005 | 93.14 | 2.74% |
| 31/03/2005 | 401.089 | 0.58% | 31/03/2005 | 92.77 | -0.40% |
| 29/04/2005 | 407.957 | 1.71% | 29/04/2005 | 89.09 | -3.97% |
| 31/05/2005 | 412.741 | 1.17% | 31/05/2005 | 93.44 | 4.88% |
| 30/06/2005 | 417.655 | 1.19% | 30/06/2005 | 96.62 | 3.40% |
| 29/07/2005 | 414.281 | -0.81% | 29/07/2005 | 100.81 | 4.34% |
| 31/08/2005 | 419.335 | 1.22% | 31/08/2005 | 99.76 | -1.04% |
| 30/09/2005 | 419.069 | -0.06% | 30/09/2005 | 104.48 | 4.73% |
| 31/10/2005 | 415.235 | -0.91% | 31/10/2005 | 100.98 | -3.35% |
| 30/11/2005 | 415.431 | 0.05% | 30/11/2005 | 104.8 | 3.78% |
| 30/12/2005 | 418.829 | 0.82% | 30/12/2005 | 108.9 | 3.91% |
| 31/01/2006 | 417.589 | -0.30% | 31/01/2006 | 113.25 | 3.99% |
| 28/02/2006 | 418.292 | 0.17% | 28/02/2006 | 116.42 | 2.80% |

**TABLE 8.1-2** Average return and standard deviation.

| | Bond Euro | Equity Euro |
|---|---|---|
| Mean | 0.40% | 1.80% |
| SD | 0.91% | 3.59% |

iii. Negative correlation (up to perfect negative correlation, i.e., $\rho = -1$. We have here the maximum effect of diversification.

iv. Imperfect positive/negative correlation.

The cases are summarized and graphed in Fig. 8.1-3.

## EXAMPLE 2 (MVF WITH SIX ASSETS OPTIMIZING SEQUENTIALLY WITH VBA)

Let us consider now the case of six assets. In this case, the Excel data table is not sufficient for the various combinations of assets and we need to resort to the Solver (GRG). We will

| | I | J | K | L |
|---|---|---|---|---|
| 1 | | | | |
| 2 | | | | |
| 3 | | Bond Euro | | Equity Euro |
| 4 | Mean | =+AVERAGE(C4:C39) | | =+AVERAGE(F4:F39) |
| 5 | SD | =STDEV(C4:C39) | | =STDEV(F4:F39) |
| 6 | | | | |
| 7 | Correlation | =CORREL(F4:F39;C4:C39) | | |
| 8 | | | | |
| 9 | Weight | 0.111261133056975 | | |
| 10 | SD | =SQRT(J9^2*L5^2+(1-J9)^2*J5^2+2*J7*J9*(1-J9)*J5*L5) | | |
| 11 | Mean | =+J9*L4+(1-J9)*J4 | | |
| 12 | | | | |
| 13 | | | Mean | St. Dev. |
| 14 | | Weight | =+J11 | =+J10 |
| 15 | | 0 | =TABLE(;J9) | =TABLE(;J9) |
| 16 | | 0.05 | =TABLE(;J9) | =TABLE(;J9) |
| 17 | | 0.111261133056975 | =TABLE(;J9) | =TABLE(;J9) |
| 18 | | 0.15 | =TABLE(;J9) | =TABLE(;J9) |
| 19 | | 0.2 | =TABLE(;J9) | =TABLE(;J9) |
| 20 | | 0.25 | =TABLE(;J9) | =TABLE(;J9) |
| 21 | | 0.3 | =TABLE(;J9) | =TABLE(;J9) |
| 22 | | 0.35 | =TABLE(;J9) | =TABLE(;J9) |
| 23 | | 0.4 | =TABLE(;J9) | =TABLE(;J9) |
| 24 | | 0.45 | =TABLE(;J9) | =TABLE(;J9) |
| 25 | | 0.5 | =TABLE(;J9) | =TABLE(;J9) |
| 35 | | 1 | =TABLE(;J9) | =TABLE(;J9) |

**FIGURE 8.1-1** Excel Data Table computations for the efficient frontier.

**TABLE 8.1-3**  Minimum variance frontier enumeration and the global minimum variance portfolio (highlighted).

| Weight | Mean 0.56% | St. Dev. 0.80% |
|---|---|---|
| 0.0000% | 0.3995% | 0.9120% |
| 5.0000% | 0.4696% | 0.8354% |
| **11.1261%** | **0.5555%** | **0.7997%** |
| 15.0000% | 0.6098% | 0.8141% |
| 20.0000% | 0.6799% | 0.8728% |
| 25.0000% | 0.7500% | 0.9688% |
| 30.0000% | 0.8201% | 1.0921% |
| 35.0000% | 0.8902% | 1.2348% |
| 40.0000% | 0.9603% | 1.3908% |
| 45.0000% | 1.0304% | 1.5562% |
| 50.0000% | 1.1005% | 1.7282% |
| 55.0000% | 1.1706% | 1.9050% |
| 60.0000% | 1.2407% | 2.0855% |
| 65.0000% | 1.3108% | 2.2688% |
| 70.0000% | 1.3809% | 2.4541% |
| 75.0000% | 1.4510% | 2.6412% |
| 80.0000% | 1.5211% | 2.8296% |
| 85.0000% | 1.5912% | 3.0192% |
| 90.0000% | 1.6613% | 3.2096% |
| 95.0000% | 1.7314% | 3.4008% |
| 100.0000% | 1.8015% | 3.5926% |

essentially minimize the portfolio variance (1) subject to (2)–(4) in sequence, letting $z$ move from $r_{min}$ to $r_{max}$.

Consider the data in Table 8.1-4 which show the arithmetic mean and the standard deviation of four indices calculated on historical return observations, from January 1999 to September 2004.

The variance–covariance matrix is given in Table 8.1-5, while in Fig. 8.1-4, we describe how the Excel should be set up for the optimization. See Section 13.3 to analyze how the descriptive statistics and the matrix of variances and covariances can be obtained.

The VBA macro, that sequentially optimizes, is in Figs. 8.1-5. The Solver has to be recalled in VBA under Tools (References) from the menu bar of the VBA working area (see also Section 5.4).

We let $z$ in *Cell K*14 move from a minimum return of 0.033% to a maximum return of 1.333% increasing it by two basis points (0.02%), and then we minimize *Cell B*28 by changing *Cells C*15:*C*20 for each return level. The constraints are better to be left into the Solver dialogue box as in Fig. 8.1-6, rather than including them into the macro.

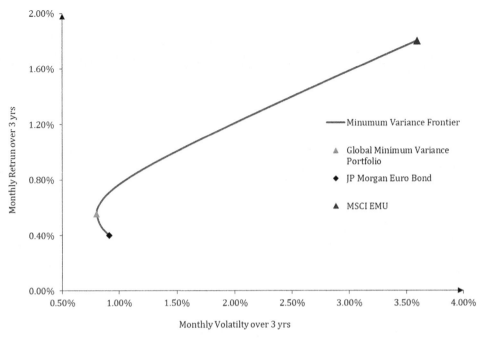

**FIGURE 8.1-2**　Minimum variance frontier and global minimum variance portfolio.

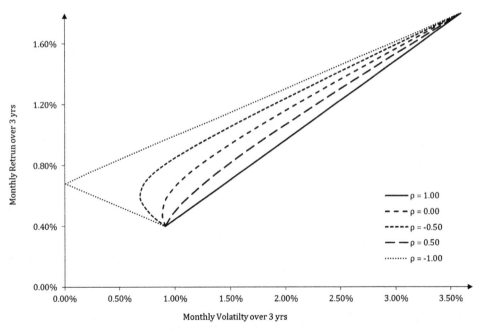

**FIGURE 8.1-3**　Minimum variance frontier from two assets for varied correlations.

II. Static optimization

**TABLE 8.1-4** Means and standard deviation for six indices (TR standing for total return).

| Index | Means | Sigma |
|---|---|---|
| MSCI Europe Net | 0.0489% | 4.9880% |
| EONIA Capit. 90j Micropal (TR) | 0.2697% | 0.0803% |
| S&P 500 (Composite) | 0.0323% | 5.5759% |
| Japan TSE 1st Section(Topix) (TR) | 0.2668% | 6.6022% |
| S&P/IFCI EMEA (TR) | 1.3336% | 6.4879% |
| Lehman Euro-Aggregate (TR) | 0.4208% | 0.9081% |

**TABLE 8.1-5** Variance–covariance matrix for the six asset indices.

| | 1 | 2 | 3 | 4 | 5 | 6 |
|---|---|---|---|---|---|---|
| 1 | 0.2488% | -0.0008% | 0.2373% | 0.1462% | 0.2334% | -0.0184% |
| 2 | -0.0008% | 0.0001% | -0.0005% | -0.0015% | -0.0012% | 0.0001% |
| 3 | 0.2373% | -0.0005% | 0.3109% | 0.2086% | 0.2510% | -0.0195% |
| 4 | 0.1462% | -0.0015% | 0.2086% | 0.4359% | 0.2435% | -0.0146% |
| 5 | 0.2334% | -0.0012% | 0.2510% | 0.2435% | 0.4209% | -0.0146% |
| 6 | -0.0184% | 0.0001% | -0.0195% | -0.0146% | -0.0146% | 0.0082% |

| | A | B | C | D | E | F | G | H | I | J | K |
|---|---|---|---|---|---|---|---|---|---|---|---|
| 1 | | | | | | | | | | | |
| 2 | | | | | | | | | | | |
| 3 | | 1 | 2 | 3 | 4 | 5 | 6 | | Index | Means | Sigma |
| 4 | 1 | 0.2488% | -0.0008% | 0.2373% | 0.1462% | 0.2334% | -0.0184% | | MSCI Europe Net | 0.0489% | 4.9880% |
| 5 | 2 | -0.0008% | 0.0001% | -0.0005% | -0.0015% | -0.0012% | 0.0001% | | EONIA Capit. 90j Micropal (TR) | 0.2697% | 0.0803% |
| 6 | 3 | 0.2373% | -0.0005% | 0.3109% | 0.2086% | 0.2510% | -0.0195% | | S&P 500 (Composite) | 0.0323% | 5.5759% |
| 7 | 4 | 0.1462% | -0.0015% | 0.2086% | 0.4359% | 0.2435% | -0.0146% | | Japan TSE 1st Section(Topix) (TR) | 0.2668% | 6.6022% |
| 8 | 5 | 0.2334% | -0.0012% | 0.2510% | 0.2435% | 0.4209% | -0.0146% | | S&P/IFCI EMEA (TR) | 1.3336% | 6.4879% |
| 9 | 6 | -0.0184% | 0.0001% | -0.0195% | -0.0146% | -0.0146% | 0.0082% | | Lehman Euro-Aggregate (TR) | 0.4208% | 0.9081% |
| 10 | | | | | | | | | | | |
| 11 | | | | | | | | | | | |
| 12 | | | | | | | | | | | |
| 13 | | | | | | | | | | | |
| 14 | | **Optimal portfolio proportions** | | | | | | | | z | 0.0330% |
| 15 | | $x_1$ | 0.0000 | | | | | | | | |
| 16 | | $x_2$ | 0.0000 | | | | | | | | |
| 17 | | $x_3$ | 0.0000 | | | | | | | | |
| 18 | | $x_4$ | 0.0000 | | | | | | | | |
| 19 | | $x_5$ | 0.9994 | | | | | | | | |
| 20 | | $x_6$ | 0.0006 | | | | | | | | |
| 21 | | | | | | | | | | | |
| 22 | | | | | | | | | | | |
| 23 | | Total | 1.0000 | | | | | | | | |
| 24 | | | | | | | | | | | |
| 27 | **Portfolio mean** | 1.33% | <-- {=MMULT(TRANSPOSE(C15:C20);J4:J9)} | | | | | | | | |
| 28 | **Portfolio sigma** | 6.48% | <-- {=SQRT(MMULT(TRANSPOSE(C15:C20);MMULT(B4:G9;C15:C20)))} | | | | | | | | |

FIGURE 8.1-4 Worksheet setup for the MVF with six asset indices.

```
Sub eff_frontier()

Range("m2").Select

   Do Until Range("Zero") = 0

   Solverok SetCell:="$B$28", MaxMinVal:=2, ValueOf:="0", ByChange:="$C$15:$C$20"
   SolverSolve UserFinish:=True

   Range("m2").Select

   Do Until ActiveCell = ""

   ActiveCell.Offset(1, 0).Select

   Loop

     ActiveCell.Offset(-1, 0).Select
     ActiveCell.Offset.Range("a1:aa1").Select
     Selection.Copy
     ActiveCell.Range("a2").Select
     ActiveSheet.Paste

     ActiveCell.Offset(-1, 0).Select
     Selection.PasteSpecial Paste:=xlValues, Operation:=xlNone, SkipBlanks:= _
         False, Transpose:=False

     ActiveCell.Offset(1, 0).FormulaR1C1 = "=R[-1]C+0.0002"


   Loop

   Solverok SetCell:="$B$28", MaxMinVal:=2, ValueOf:="0", ByChange:="$C$15:$C$20"
   SolverSolve UserFinish:=True

End Sub
```

**FIGURE 8.1-5**   VBA optimization for the minimum variance frontier.

The graph of the MVF is in Fig. 8.1-7, while its enumeration is in Table 8.1-6. From the graph, we notice that the GMV asset is the Eonia risk-free rate index, and from this point continuing above, the efficient frontier curve begins, offering higher returns for a given standard deviation.

## 8.2 Investor's utility and the optimal portfolio choice

In Section 8.1, we have seen how to graph, from a feasible set of investments, the minimum variance frontier and consequently the efficient frontier, which is a portion of the MVF.

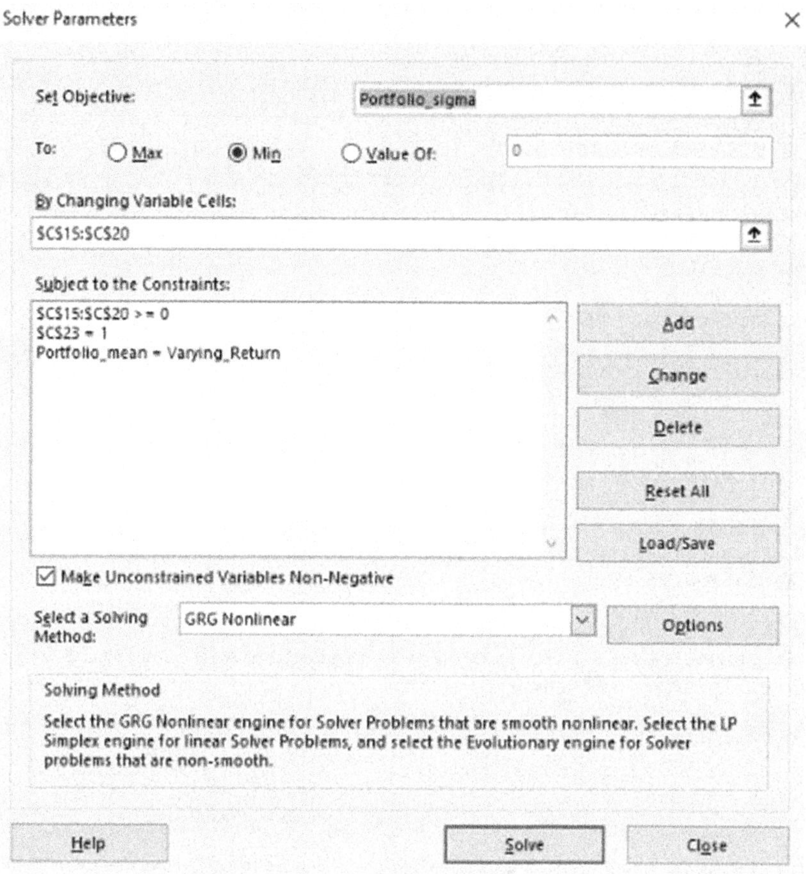

FIGURE 8.1-6  Solver parameters for the MVF.

A question now arises: once we have identified the efficient frontier what is that unique portfolio that the investor should choose? In other words, what is the optimal portfolio among the various portfolios on the efficient frontier?

The answer lies on the so-called *investor's preferences*, or *investor's utility*. The optimal portfolio to choose on the efficient frontier is that portfolio offering the highest utility to the investor. *It lies at the point of tangency between the efficient frontier and the indifference utility curve with the highest possible utility.*

The investor's utility function usually considered has the following analytical form:

$$U_p = r_p - \frac{1}{T}\sigma_p^2$$

where

$U_p$ = *utility associated to an efficient portfolio.*

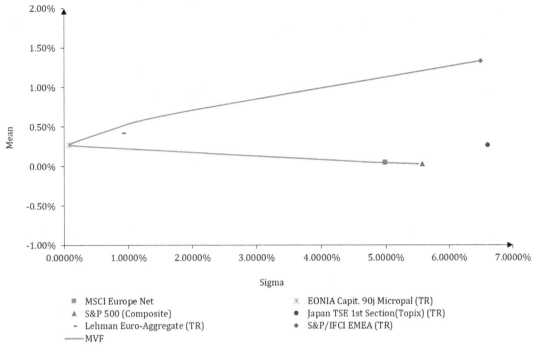

**FIGURE 8.1-7**    MVF in the case of six assets (portion of the curve above being the efficient frontier).

**TABLE 8.1-6**    Enumeration of the MVF of Example 2.

| M | N | O | P | Q | R | S | T | U |
|---|---|---|---|---|---|---|---|---|
| z | Sigma | Mean | $x_1$ | $x_2$ | $x_3$ | $x_4$ | $x_5$ | $x_6$ |
| 0.0330% | 5.52% | 0.03% | 4.38% | 0.00% | 95.62% | 0.00% | 0.00% | 0.00% |
| 0.0530% | 4.79% | 0.05% | 61.98% | 4.40% | 33.62% | 0.00% | 0.00% | 0.00% |
| 0.0730% | 4.35% | 0.07% | 56.30% | 13.22% | 30.48% | 0.00% | 0.00% | 0.00% |
| 0.0930% | 3.90% | 0.09% | 50.62% | 22.04% | 27.33% | 0.00% | 0.00% | 0.00% |
| 0.1130% | 3.46% | 0.11% | 44.94% | 30.87% | 24.19% | 0.00% | 0.00% | 0.00% |
| 0.1330% | 3.02% | 0.13% | 39.26% | 39.69% | 21.05% | 0.00% | 0.00% | 0.00% |
| 0.1530% | 2.57% | 0.15% | 33.59% | 48.51% | 17.90% | 0.00% | 0.00% | 0.00% |
| 0.1730% | 2.13% | 0.17% | 27.91% | 57.33% | 14.76% | 0.00% | 0.00% | 0.00% |
| 0.1930% | 1.69% | 0.19% | 22.23% | 66.15% | 11.62% | 0.00% | 0.00% | 0.00% |
| 0.2130% | 1.24% | 0.21% | 16.55% | 74.98% | 8.47% | 0.00% | 0.00% | 0.00% |
| 0.2330% | 0.80% | 0.23% | 10.87% | 83.80% | 5.33% | 0.00% | 0.00% | 0.00% |
| 0.2530% | 0.36% | 0.25% | 5.19% | 92.62% | 2.19% | 0.00% | 0.00% | 0.00% |
| 0.2730% | 0.08% | 0.27% | 0.00% | 99.17% | 0.00% | 0.21% | 0.27% | 0.35% |
| 0.2930% | 0.11% | 0.29% | 0.00% | 92.13% | 0.00% | 0.00% | 1.25% | 6.62% |
| 0.3130% | 0.17% | 0.31% | 0.00% | 84.39% | 0.00% | 0.00% | 2.17% | 13.44% |
| 0.3330% | 0.24% | 0.33% | 0.00% | 76.72% | 0.00% | 0.00% | 3.09% | 20.19% |
| 0.3530% | 0.31% | 0.35% | 0.00% | 69.02% | 0.00% | 0.00% | 4.00% | 26.98% |
| 1.2530% | 5.90% | 1.25% | 0.00% | 0.00% | 0.00% | 0.00% | 91.18% | 8.82% |
| 1.2730% | 6.04% | 1.27% | 0.00% | 0.00% | 0.00% | 0.00% | 93.37% | 6.63% |
| 1.2930% | 6.19% | 1.29% | 0.00% | 0.00% | 0.00% | 0.00% | 95.56% | 4.44% |
| 1.3130% | 6.34% | 1.31% | 0.00% | 0.00% | 0.00% | 0.00% | 97.75% | 2.25% |
| 1.3330% | 6.48% | 1.33% | 0.00% | 0.00% | 0.00% | 0.00% | 99.94% | 0.06% |

$$r_p = \text{expected return of the efficient portfolio.}$$

$$\sigma_p^2 = \text{expected variance of the efficient portfolio.}$$

$T = \text{risk tolerance of the investor; higher values will denote that a higher degree of risk is tolerated.}$

## EXAMPLE 1

Fig. 8.2-1 describes the situation of an efficient frontier, which has been derived using the techniques shown in Section 8.1 from four assets, together with three separate indifference curves associated, respectively, to a lower risk tolerance ($T = 10$), average-high risk tolerance ($T = 40$), and a high-risk tolerance (low risk aversion) with $T = 100$. Each of the three investors will choose his own optimal portfolio on the efficient frontier.

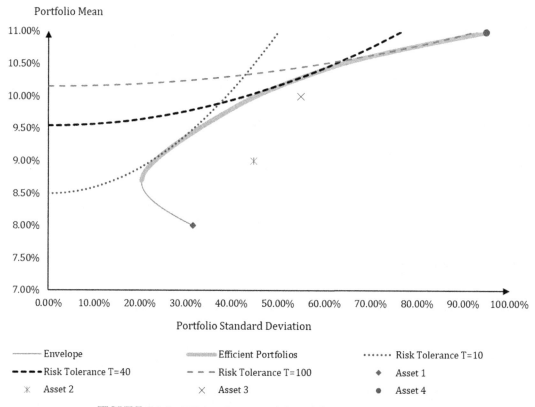

FIGURE 8.2-1   Efficient frontier and three different optimal portfolios.

Essentially, to identify the optimal investment we calculate for each portfolio lying on the efficient frontier the index of utility $U_p$, and the investor will choose the portfolio offering the highest utility. The indifference curves graphed in Fig. 8.2-1 are plotted in the $\sigma_p, r_p$ space using the following relation:

$$r_p = \overline{U}_p + \frac{1}{T}\sigma_p^2$$

which, for each pair $\sigma_p, r_p$ returns the same level of utility along the curve.

In particular, for the indifference curves graphed in Figs. 8.2-1, we take into account the maximum utility level as constant level of utility, and the above equation should be more precisely written as:

$$r_p = \overline{U}_p^{max} + \frac{1}{T}\sigma_p^2$$

Figs. 8.2-2 and 8.2-3 show instead a set of indifference curves and tangency portfolios for $T = 10$ (risk averse investor) and $T = 40$ average-high risk tolerant investor.

In this example, we have four assets, and the data for building the efficient frontier are enumerated from Tables 8.2-1 to 8.2-3. The efficient portfolio returning the highest expected utility for $T = 10$ has been highlighted in Table 8.2-3.

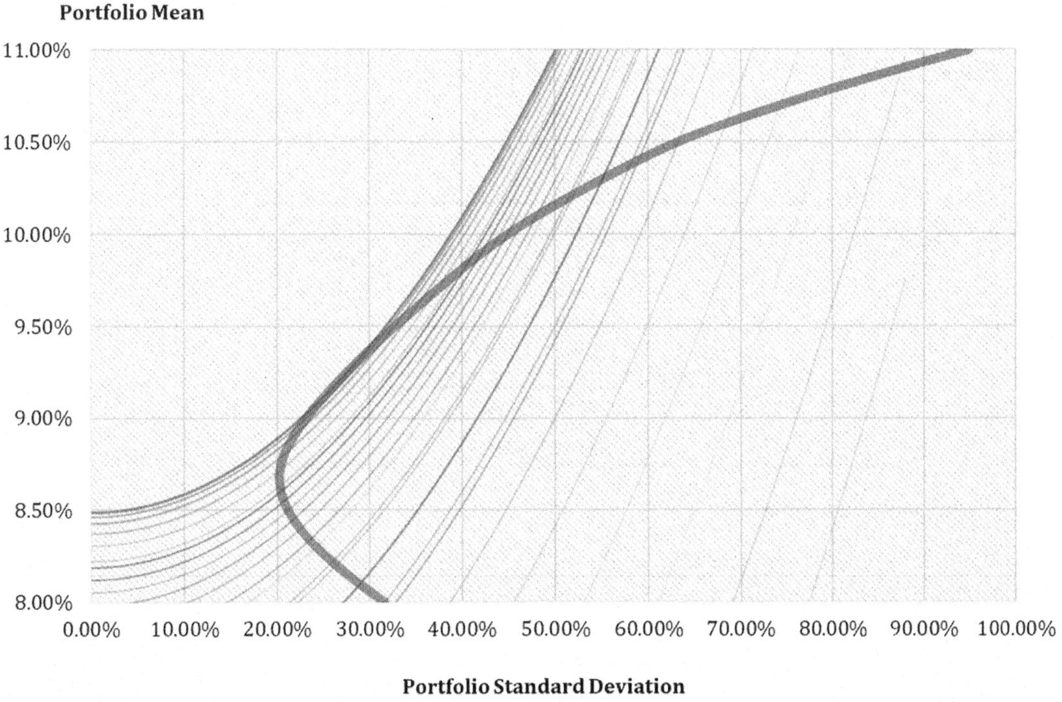

FIGURE 8.2-2 Efficient frontier, tangency portfolio, and a set of indifference curves for a risk averse investor ($T = 10$).

**Portfolio Mean**

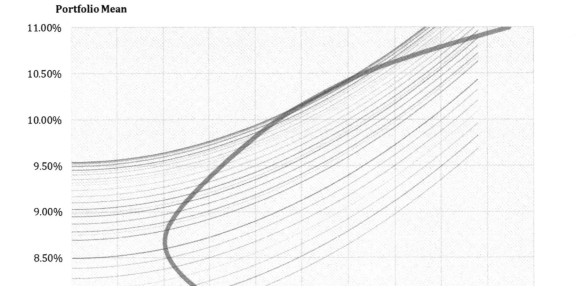

**Portfolio Standard Deviation**

**FIGURE 8.2-3**   Efficient frontier, tangency portfolio, and a set of indifference curves for an investor with higher risk tolerance ($T = 40$).

**TABLE 8.2-1**   Example 1: matrix of variances and covariances.

|   | 1 | 2 | 3 | 4 |
|---|---|---|---|---|
| 1 | 10.00% | 3.00% | -8.00% | 5.00% |
| 2 | 3.00% | 20.00% | 2.00% | 3.00% |
| 3 | -8.00% | 2.00% | 30.00% | 20.00% |
| 4 | 5.00% | 3.00% | 20.00% | 90.00% |

# Exercises

## Asset management case

You work as a senior investment analyst in a wealth management house, whose business is to manage the assets of the customers (individuals, insurances, foundations, etc.) through the activity of *fund of funds* management.

The board of your company has recently signed a mandate from an insurance company to manage for them a new fund of funds, in which the insurance company would like to direct some of their excess liquidity, according to the insurance guidelines.

TABLE 8.2-2 Example 1: returns and standard deviation for the four assets.

| Means | Sigma |
|-------|-------|
| 8.00% | 31.62% |
| 9.00% | 44.72% |
| 10.00% | 54.77% |
| 11.00% | 94.87% |

The fund of funds management mandate with the insurance company has a series of restrictions, and the most important one is that they restrict the investable funds only to those that are labeled as *ethical funds* in the financial databases and within the funds investment prospectuses.

After conducting a research in the mutual funds database that you use within the company, according to some investment criteria (e.g., absolute historical performances, risk-adjusted performance measures vs. benchmark, management fees, track record of the fund manager) you have decided to select 16 ethical funds.

TABLE 8.2-3 Example 1: enumeration of the minimum variance frontier and optimal portfolio for $T = 10$.

| z | Sigma | Mean | $x_1$ | $x_2$ | $x_3$ | $x_4$ | Portfolio Utility T =10 |
|---|-------|------|-------|-------|-------|-------|-------------------------|
| 8.000% | 31.62% | 8.00% | 100.00% | 0.00% | 0.00% | 0.00% | 7.0000% |
| 8.10% | 28.88% | 8.10% | 95.00% | 0.00% | 5.00% | 0.00% | 7.2660% |
| 8.20% | 26.38% | 8.20% | 90.00% | 0.00% | 10.00% | 0.00% | 7.5042% |
| 8.30% | 24.21% | 8.30% | 85.00% | 0.00% | 15.00% | 0.00% | 7.7142% |
| 8.40% | 22.45% | 8.40% | 79.52% | 0.95% | 19.52% | 0.00% | 7.8962% |
| 8.50% | 21.15% | 8.50% | 73.21% | 3.57% | 23.21% | 0.00% | 8.0527% |
| 8.60% | 20.39% | 8.60% | 66.90% | 6.19% | 26.90% | 0.00% | 8.1840% |
| 8.70% | 20.24% | 8.70% | 60.60% | 8.81% | 30.60% | 0.00% | 8.2903% |
| 8.80% | 20.70% | 8.80% | 54.28% | 11.43% | 34.29% | 0.00% | 8.3715% |
| 8.90% | 21.74% | 8.90% | 48.11% | 14.00% | 37.68% | 0.21% | 8.4275% |
| 9.00% | 23.14% | 9.00% | 43.09% | 16.12% | 38.49% | 2.30% | 8.4645% |
| 9.10% | 24.77% | 9.10% | 38.08% | 18.24% | 39.29% | 4.39% | 8.4864% |
| 9.20% | 26.58% | 9.20% | 33.05% | 20.36% | 40.10% | 6.48% | 8.4934% |
| 9.30% | 28.54% | 9.30% | 28.04% | 22.49% | 40.91% | 8.57% | 8.4853% |
| 9.40% | 30.62% | 9.40% | 23.02% | 24.61% | 41.71% | 10.66% | 8.4622% |
| 9.50% | 32.80% | 9.50% | 18.00% | 26.73% | 42.52% | 12.75% | 8.4241% |
| 9.60% | 35.06% | 9.60% | 12.99% | 28.85% | 43.32% | 14.84% | 8.3711% |
| 10.60% | 68.41% | 10.60% | 0.00% | 0.00% | 40.00% | 60.00% | 5.9200% |
| 10.70% | 74.30% | 10.70% | 0.00% | 0.00% | 30.00% | 70.00% | 5.1800% |
| 10.80% | 80.75% | 10.80% | 0.00% | 0.00% | 20.00% | 80.00% | 4.2800% |
| 10.90% | 87.64% | 10.90% | 0.00% | 0.00% | 10.00% | 90.00% | 3.2200% |
| 11.00% | 94.87% | 11.00% | 0.00% | 0.00% | 0.00% | 100.00% | 2.0000% |

You have now collected all the historical monthly performance data over 3 years, for these 16 funds, together with a benchmark, and the objective now is to calculate the following.

1. Matrix of correlation for all these 16 funds.
2. Funds monthly relative returns and relative Tracking Error Volatility (TEV) for each fund versus the benchmark given by the insurance company in the 3 years period. The TEV is the volatility of the relative returns of the fund versus those of the benchmark.
3. The *alpha* of each of the 16 funds. The *alpha* of a fund is a financial indicator of over/ under performance of the mutual fund versus the benchmark, and it is measured via the following linear regression:

$$Fund\ Retruns_t = \alpha + \beta(Benchmark\ Returns_t) + \varepsilon_t$$

4. On the basis of the Tracking Error Volatility and Alpha of the funds, run the optimization program and build a Minimum Variance Frontier (MVF).
5. The insurance company restricts then to invest in a portfolio of funds which could possibly show no more than 1.50% Tracking Error Volatility versus the benchmark. Identify on the MVF the optimal portfolio of funds that could meet this requirement.
6. Another restriction is that the resulting asset allocation should have no more than 30% invested in the Emerging Markets area. Is the allocation you have chosen satisfying this constraint?

# Dynamic optimization

In Part II of this book, dedicated to the Static Optimization, the fundamental mathematical problem was essentially that of finding an *optimal point $x^*$* of a given function $y(x)$. For example, the problems of microeconomics in a static environment are all focused on finding an optimal point, usually subject to some types of constraints.

Part III of this book, beginning with a chapter dedicated to the Calculus of Variations, will cover a challenging area of the mathematical economics called Dynamic Optimization, where the independent variable of the functions considered is normally represented by the variable $t$ (*time*), while the dependent variable $y(t)$ is normally referred as the *state variable*. In the discrete version of the problem, the time is usually divided in *stages*, while the state variable can only take values belonging to a finite set.

In contrast to the Static Optimization within the Dynamic Optimization, the mathematical problem is that of finding the *optimal path*, namely the optimal function $y^*(t)$ over time, to minimize or maximize a given *functional* $J(y(t))$.

Like the static problems, the dynamic problems may be subject to some types of constraints.

The Dynamic Optimization, in its continuous forms of the Calculus of Variations and the Theory of Optimal Control, is similar to a differential equation problem because we are asked to find a function, but differently from the differential equations in the Dynamic Optimization, we also have to investigate whether the function found minimizes or maximizes an *objective functional*.

Part III of the book attempts to offer an adequate range of Excel tools to solve at least the standard problems in the following three areas of the Dynamic Optimization:
- Calculus of Variations (Chapter 9)
- Theory of Optimal Control (Chapter 10)
- Discrete Dynamic Optimization (Chapter 11)

Especially with regards to Chapters 9 and 10, this book will show how a continuous optimal time path problem can be transformed into a discrete time problem in Excel and solved numerically without passing directly from the resolution steps of complex differential equations derived from the Euler–Lagrange equation. The exact continuous solutions and the numerical solution are then compared to show to the reader the often unexploited, hidden power, and efficiency of a worksheet discrete analysis.

Some general cases will be developed step by step to understand the underlying logic of the numerical approach proposed and then also developed in Excel; as usual some important models in economics will be also developed.

## 9.1 The fundamental problem of the Calculus of Variations

The *fundamental problem* of the Calculus of Variations (CoV) is simply that of minimizing or maximizing a *functional*, and Fig. 9.1-1 helps us to understand how a *functional* works in very general terms.

Let us assume that our problem is to find the optimal continuous path, namely the optimal function $y(t)$, that connects point $P_0(t_0, y(t_0))$ with point $P_1(t_1, y(t_1))$ of Fig. 9.1-1, with the shortest distance. As you can imagine there are infinite ways to connect the two points, and Fig. 9.1-1 only depicts three paths, from which just one is to be selected.

The *functional* is nothing more than a *mapping* between paths (or trajectories) and real numbers. The real number (or scalar) resulting from this *mapping* will be denoted by $J(y(t))$, or just by $J(y)$, which is also called *performance measure*. The notation $J(y)$ clearly indicates that it is the *variation* in the path $y(t)$ that results in a change of the *functional*.

Essentially, the objective of the CoV is to find the extreme value (minimum or maximum) of the *functional* $J(y)$, namely to find the optimal path $y^*(t)$ that yields an extremum of $J(y)$. This optimal path is called *extremal*.

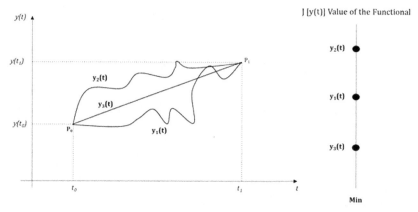

FIGURE 9.1-1  Admissible time paths.

In the *objective functional*, associated to the path $y(t)$, also the slope of $y(t)$, $y\prime(t) = \frac{dy(t)}{dt}$, usually appears.

Going back to Fig. 9.1-1, the optimal path that minimizes the value of $J(y)$ is $y_3(t)$, which is a linear equation path, with the associated shortest distance from point $P_0$ to point $P_1$.

Now, to give a more formal representation of the CoV and the related *functional*, let us continue with our *shortest path* problem.

From the Pythagorean theorem, the Euclidean distance between the two points $P_0$ and $P_1$ can be obtained by the following:

$$distance\ (P_0 - P_1) = \sqrt{(\Delta t)^2 + (\Delta y)^2}$$

which is, after algebraic rearrangement:

$$distance\ (P_0 - P_1) = \sqrt{(\Delta t)^2 \left[1 + \frac{(\Delta y)^2}{(\Delta t)^2}\right]}$$

which finally becomes:

$$distance\ (P_0 - P_1) = \sqrt{1 + \frac{(\Delta y)^2}{(\Delta t)^2}} \Delta t$$

where,

$$\Delta y = y(t_1) - y(t_0)$$

$$\Delta t = t_1 - t_0$$

To obtain the total distance, we can also divide the time between $t_0$ and $t_1$ into $n$ subintervals as desired, with the correspondent subintervals in the state variable $y(t_i)$ for $i = 1, 2, \cdots, n$ so that we can obtain Fig. 9.1-2, where the total distance between $P_0$ and $P_1$ (which is our functional) is calculated as follows:

$$J = \sum_{i=1}^{n} \sqrt{1 + \frac{(\Delta_i y)^2}{(\Delta_i t)^2}} \Delta_i t$$

The continuous transposition of this discrete sum leads to the following:

$$J = \int_{t_0}^{t_1} \sqrt{1 + \frac{(dy)^2}{(dt)^2}} dt \tag{9.1-1}$$

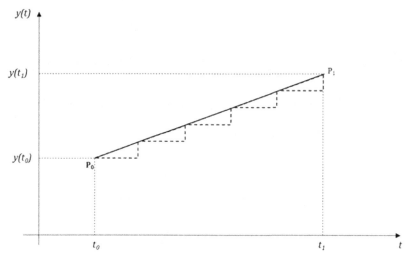

**FIGURE 9.1-2**    Summation of various interval distances from $P_0$ and $p_1$.

In mathematical terms, the CoV problem is finally expressed as the following general form:

$$\text{maximize or minimize } J(y) = \int_{t_0}^{T} (F(t, y(t), y'(t)))dt$$

$$\text{subject to (s.t.) } y(t_0) = A \ (A \ given)$$

$$y(T) = Z \ (T, \ Z \ given), \tag{9.1-2}$$

where $y(t)$ is our unknown path of the problem and $y'(t)$ is its given derivative.

Such a problem, with an integrand function $F(t, y(t), y'(t))$ in a single state variable $y(t)$ and its slope $y'(t)$, with completely specified initial and terminal points, and with no constraints, is known as the *fundamental problem* (or *simplest problem*) of CoV.

In Section 9.8 we will also deal with CoV with functional with integrand functions involving two state variables, while for a discrete version of the shortest path problem proposed in Fig. 9.1-1 (see Chapter 11).

The general solution of Problem 9.1-2 is given by finding and solving a differential equation associated to the following Euler–Lagrange equation (*first-order necessary condition of CoV*):

$$\frac{\partial F}{\partial y}(t, y(t), y'(t)) - \frac{d}{dt}\left[\frac{\partial F}{\partial y}(t, y(t), y'(t))\right] = 0$$

which we will not use much, except for verifying the numerical solutions and for solving the CoV problems involving two functions and the constrained CoV problems.

## Transversality conditions

In Eq. (9.1-2), while the initial condition is always specified by the problem, the different assumptions that you can make on the terminal state position $y(T)$, and $T$ itself as well, lead to a set of assumptions called *transversality conditions*.

Within the CoV, we will mostly see cases with specified initial and terminal point like in *simplest problem*, but we will also see some examples where the terminal value of $y(T)$ is free with a specified $T$ and also where $T$ is free with a specified value of $y(T)$.

In CoV we can have the following three basic *transversality conditions*:

1. *Fixed time problem*, when terminal $T$ is specified while $y(T)$ is free. It is also called *vertical-terminal-line* problem;
2. *Fixed endpoint problem*, when terminal $y(T)$ is specified but not $T$. It is also called *horizontal-terminal-line* problem;
3. *Terminal curve problem*, when neither $y(T)$ nor $T$ are specified.

Further on we will see some examples on the *vertical-terminal-line*, as well as on the *horizontal-terminal-line*, and we will see some more about *transversality conditions* in Chapter 10, dedicated to the Theory of Optimal Control.

## EXAMPLE 1 (DISTANCE BETWEEN TWO POINTS AND CALCULUS OF VARIATIONS)

Let us assume we have $P_0(1,7)$ and $P_1(3,17)$ and let us divide both the total interval of $t$ and the total interval of $y(t)$ in four subintervals as follows (Table 9.1-1):

Applying Eq. (9.1-1), the distance between the two given points $P_0$ and $P_1$ is simply given by the following:

$$10.20 = \sum_{i=1}^{4} \sqrt{\left[1 + \frac{(2.5)^2}{(0.5)^2}\right] 0.5}$$

The linear equation passing through the two given points $P_0$ and $P_1$ is:

$$y^*(t) = 5t + 2$$

**TABLE 9.1-1**  Example 1 data points.

| $t$ | $y(t)$ |
|------|--------|
| 1.00 | 7.00 |
| 1.50 | 9.50 |
| 2.00 | 12.00 |
| 2.50 | 14.50 |
| 3.00 | 17.00 |

whose derivative $y'(t)$ is 5, which allows us to check Eq. (9.1-2) of the CoV in the following continuous definite integral:

$$J = \int_1^3 \sqrt{1+5^2}dt = \int_1^3 \sqrt{26}dt = \sqrt{26}\cdot 3 - \sqrt{26}\cdot 1 = 10.20$$

## 9.2 Discrete approximate Calculus of Variations: Lagrange multipliers and contour lines solutions

We have now all the essential necessary elements to solve our CoV problem in a discrete numerical manner without passing through the Euler–Lagrange equation.

### First approach to solve the Calculus of Variations in a numerical framework: Lagrange multipliers

Let us propose the following general discretization of the *simplest problem* 9.1-2:

$$\text{maximize or minimize } J_{discrete} = \sum_{i=1}^{n} F_i\left[\left(y_0 + \sum_{k=1}^{i}\Delta_k y\right), \frac{(\Delta_i y)}{(\Delta_i t)}, t_i\right]\Delta_i t \qquad (9.2\text{-}1)$$

$$s.t. \sum_{i=1}^{n}\Delta_i y = y(T) - y(0)$$

and let us apply to it the standard Lagrange multipliers method of equality constrained optimization, to find the optimal value of the discrete *functional*.

Some simple examples resolved manually are provided next to show how this approach works and then the same cases will be solved on a larger scale and computer Excel basis, in the following paragraphs..

### EXAMPLE 1 (SHORTEST DISTANCE PROBLEM)

Find the shortest distance between the two points $P_0(1,7)$ and $P_\downarrow 1(3, 17)$, being the CoV problem in its standard continuous form as follows:

$$\text{minimize } J = \int_1^3 \left[1 + \frac{(dy)^2}{(dt)^2}\right]^{1/2} dt$$

$$\text{with continuous } F = \left[1 + \frac{(dy)^2}{(dt)^2}\right]^{1/2}$$

$$\text{s.t. } y(1) = 7 \text{ and } y(3) = 17$$

To discretize the problem and to make it simpler, let us divide both the total interval of time and $y(t)$ into two subintervals and transform, according to Eq. (9.2-1), the above continuous problem into a discrete problem to solve it with the Lagrange multipliers technique.

In this example, pay attention to the fact that $y(t)$ does not appear in the integrand function, while only $y'(t) = dy/dt$ appears, so that the discrete form of the problem becomes as follows:

$$J = \sum_{i=1}^{2}\left[1 + \frac{(\Delta_i y)^2}{(\Delta_i t)^2}\right]^{1/2}\Delta_i t = \left[1 + \frac{(\Delta_1 y)^2}{(\Delta_1 t)^2}\right]^{1/2}\Delta_1 t + \left[1 + \frac{(\Delta_2 y)^2}{(\Delta_2 t)^2}\right]^{1/2}\Delta_2 t$$

$$\text{s.t. } \Delta_1 y + \Delta_2 y = y(3) - y(1) = 17 - 7 = 10$$

The discrete modified Lagrange objective *functional J* in two variables, plus the Lagrange multiplier variable is as follows:

$$J(\Delta_1 y, \Delta_2 y, \lambda) = \left[1 + \frac{(\Delta_1 y)^2}{(\Delta_1 t)^2}\right]^{\frac{1}{2}}\Delta_1 t + \left[1 + \frac{(\Delta_2 y)^2}{(\Delta_2 t)^2}\right]^{\frac{1}{2}}\Delta_2 t + \lambda(\Delta_1 y + \Delta_2 y - 10)$$

Now we can apply the Lagrange multipliers method: the goal is just to find the optimal solutions for $\Delta_1 y$ and $\Delta_2 y$ to obtain the numerical complete path of $y(t)$ over the interval given by the problem. Essentially, what we are doing is transforming a classical CoV continuous dynamic problem into a numerical, two-variable, constrained optimization problem.

The three partial derivatives of $J(\Delta_1 y; \Delta_2 y; \lambda)$ are:

$$\frac{\partial J(\cdot)}{\partial \Delta_1 y} = \frac{2\Delta_1 y/(\Delta_1 t)^2}{2\left[1 + \frac{(\Delta_1 y)^2}{(\Delta_1 t)^2}\right]^{1/2}}\Delta_1 t + \lambda = 0$$

$$\frac{\partial J(\cdot)}{\partial \Delta_2 y} = \frac{2\Delta_2 y/(\Delta_2 t)^2}{2\left[1 + \frac{(\Delta_2 y)^2}{(\Delta_2 t)^2}\right]^{1/2}}\Delta_2 t + \lambda = 0$$

$$\frac{\partial J(\cdot)}{\partial \lambda} = \Delta_1 y + \Delta_2 y - 10 = 0$$

**TABLE 9.2-1**   Example 1: optimal path.

| t | y(t) |
|---|------|
| 1 | 7 |
| 2 | = 7+$\Delta_1 y$=12 |
| 3 | =12+$\Delta_2 y$=17 |

So, it must follow that:

$$\frac{2\Delta_1 y/(\Delta_1 t)^2}{2\left[1+\dfrac{(\Delta_1 y)^2}{(\Delta_1 t)^2}\right]^{1/2}}\Delta_1 t = \frac{2\Delta_2 y/(\Delta_2 t)^2}{2\left[1+\dfrac{(\Delta_2 y)^2}{(\Delta_2 t)^2}\right]^{1/2}}\Delta_2 t$$

namely,

$$\Delta_1 y = \Delta_2 y$$

Setting $\Delta_1 t = \Delta_2 t = 1$, according to the constraint $\Delta_1 y + \Delta_2 y = 10$ it turns out $2\Delta_1 y = 10$, namely $\Delta_1 y = 5$ and $\Delta_2 y = 5$, while the Lagrange multiplier is $\lambda = 0.9806$.

Now we are ready to solve numerically our original CoV problem just plugging the information we have found on $\Delta_1 y$ and $\Delta_2 y$, together with the initial condition on $y(t)$, in the following table (Table 9.2-1):

The result is finally given by the linear equation passing through these points, which is the same solution as the one we have calculated before $y^*(t) = 5t + 2$, being the scalar solution for the *functional* $J(y) = 10.20$, which is the shortest distance sought.

We can plug the data into Excel, build a scatter chart, and then associate a trendline to the data points. The result is in the following Fig. 9.2-1:

Notice that, by default settings in the trendline labels, Excel always identifies the independent variable with $x$.

Within the next sections, it is this approach of Lagrange multipliers that will be followed in the Excel framework GRG Solver optimization, and it will be our main method to use for CoV.

Let us solve two more complicated examples taken from Alpha Chiang[1] and then we will see the same problems, together with some economic cases, fully developed in Excel.

## EXAMPLE 2

Find the extremal of the *functional* in the following problem:

$$\min J = \int_0^2 \left(12ty + y'^2\right)dt$$

---

[1]For the continuous complete solutions via the Euler–Lagrange equation, see Alpha Chiang, *Elements of Dynamic Optimization*, Mc-Graw-Hill, 1992, chapter 2.

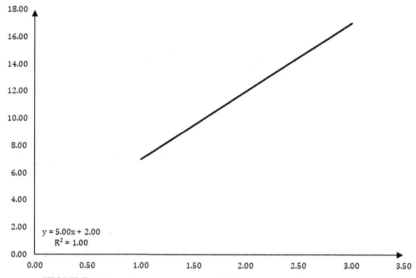

FIGURE 9.2-1    Example 1: shortest distance optimal numerical path.

$$s.t.\ y(0) = 0 \text{ and } y(2) = 8$$

Applying Eq. (9.2-1) and beginning with $n = 2$ to make the calculations simpler, we have:

$$J = \left[12t_1(0 + \Delta_1 y) + \frac{(\Delta_1 y)^2}{(\Delta_1 t)^2}\right]\Delta_1 t + \left[12t_2(0 + \Delta_1 y + \Delta_2 y) + \frac{(\Delta_2 y)^2}{(\Delta_2 t)^2}\right]\Delta_2 t$$

$$s.t.\ \Delta_1 y + \Delta_2 y = 8$$

The modified Lagrange multipliers objective functional is instead:

$$J = \left[12t_1(0 + \Delta_1 y) + \frac{(\Delta_1 y)^2}{(\Delta_1 t)^2}\right]\Delta_1 t + \left[12t_2(0 + \Delta_1 y + \Delta_2 y) + \frac{(\Delta_2 y)^2}{(\Delta_2 t)^2}\right]\Delta_2 t + \lambda(\Delta_1 y + \Delta_2 y - 8)$$

Taking the partial derivatives, we have the following three equations:

$$\frac{\partial J(\cdot)}{\partial \Delta_1 y} = 12t_1\Delta_1 t + 2\frac{(\Delta_1 y)}{(\Delta_1 t)} + 12t_2\Delta_2 t + \lambda = 0$$

$$\frac{\partial J(\cdot)}{\partial \Delta_2 y} = 12t_2\Delta_2 t + 2\frac{(\Delta_2 y)}{(\Delta_2 t)} + \lambda = 0$$

$$\frac{\partial J(\cdot)}{\partial \lambda} = \Delta_1 y + \Delta_2 y - 8 = 0$$

III. Dynamic optimization

Setting $\Delta_1 t = \Delta_2 t = 1$ with $t_1 = 1$ and $t_2 = 2$ we simplify in:

$$\frac{\partial J(\cdot)}{\partial \Delta_1 y} = 36 + 2\Delta_1 y + \lambda = 0$$

$$\frac{\partial J(\cdot)}{\partial \Delta_2 y} = 24 + 2\Delta_2 y + \lambda = 0$$

$$\frac{\partial J(\cdot)}{\partial \lambda} = \Delta_1 y + \Delta_2 y - 8 = 0$$

We have then:

$$\Delta_1 y = \frac{-\lambda - 36}{2}$$

$$\Delta_2 y = \frac{-\lambda - 24}{2}$$

$$\frac{-\lambda - 36}{2} + \frac{-\lambda - 24}{2} = 8.$$

After obtaining the multiplier $\lambda = -38$, we can plug it into the equations of $\Delta_1 y$ and $\Delta_2 y$ as follows:

1. $\Delta_1 y = \frac{38-36}{2} = 1$
2. $\Delta_2 y = \frac{38-24}{2} = 7$

Now we have our numerical CoV solution in the following Table 9.2-2: which satisfies the boundary conditions. In Example 2, not linear in the exact path like Example 1, with just two subintervals numerical solution, we are still in doubt whether to pick $y = t^3$ or a second path $y = 3t^2 - 2t$ as the exact path. In fact, the exact solution that solves our example is the cubic function $y = t^3$.

TABLE 9.2-2  Example 2:
optimal path.

| $t$ | $y(t)$ |
|---|---|
| 0 | 0 |
| 1 | $= 0 + \Delta_1 y = 1$ |
| 2 | $= 1 + \Delta_2 y = 1 + 7 = 8$ |

We will see in the next Excel applications that just with one subinterval more we will reach immediately the exact equation solution. We will see that the more we divide the total interval of $t$ and $y(t)$ into subintervals, the more the numerical solution will approximate the exact solution, and it will be also easy for the Excel trendline to show the exact optimal path.

The scalar for the *functional* $J(y)$ associated to these two intervals numerical approximate solution can be found plugging the above numerical solution in the discrete *functional*:

$$J(y) = \left[12t_1(0 + \Delta_1 y) + \frac{(\Delta_1 y)^2}{(\Delta_1 t)^2}\right]\Delta_1 t + \left[12t_2(0 + \Delta_1 y + \Delta_2 y) + \frac{(\Delta_2 y)^2}{(\Delta_2 t)^2}\right]\Delta_2 t$$

$$J(y) = [12 \cdot 1 \cdot (1) + 1] \cdot 1 + [12 \cdot 2 \cdot (8) + 7^2] \cdot 1 = 254.00$$

while the sought exact minimum scalar of the *functional* is $J(y) = 134.40$, with the definite integral of the problem simply plugged in with the path $y^*(t) = t^3$, is as follows:

$$J(y^*(t)) = \int_0^2 (12t^4 + 9t^4)dt = \int_0^2 (21t^4)dt = 134.40$$

To verify that this path is the optimal one (minimizing) compared to $y = 3t^2 - 2t$ we evaluate the definite integral with this second path as well, obtaining a higher number for the *functional*, which is not evidently the path solution we are seeking:

$$J(y(3t^2 - 2t)) = 166.67$$

## EXAMPLE 3.A (LAGRANGE MULTIPLIERS)

Find the extremal of the *functional* in the following problem:

$$\min J = \int_0^1 (ty + 2y'^2)dt$$

$$s.t.\ y(0) = 1 \quad \text{and} \quad y(1) = 2$$

Using the Euler–Lagrange equation, we obtain the exact path $y^*(t) = \frac{1}{24}t^3 + \frac{23}{24}t + 1$.

For our numerical solution as usual we discretize the *functional* as follows, with two subintervals of length 0.5:

$$J = \left[t_1(1 + \Delta_1 y) + 2\frac{(\Delta_1 y)^2}{(\Delta_1 t)^2}\right]\Delta_1 t + \left[t_2(1 + \Delta_1 y + \Delta_2 y) + 2\frac{(\Delta_2 y)^2}{(\Delta_2 t)^2}\right]\Delta_2 t$$

$$s.t.\ \Delta_1 y + \Delta_2 y = 1$$

The modified Lagrange multipliers objective functional is instead:

III. Dynamic optimization

$$J = \left[ t_1(1+\Delta_1 y) + 2\frac{(\Delta_1 y)^2}{(\Delta_1 t)^2} \right] \Delta_1 t + \left[ t_2(1+\Delta_1 y + \Delta_2 y) + 2\frac{(\Delta_2 y)^2}{(\Delta_2 t)^2} \right] \Delta_2 t + \lambda(\Delta_1 y + \Delta_2 y - 1)$$

Taking the partial derivatives, we have the following three equations:

1. $\frac{\partial J(\cdot)}{\partial \Delta_1 y} = t_1 \Delta_1 t + 4\frac{(\Delta_1 y)}{(\Delta_1 t)} + t_2 \Delta_2 t + \lambda = 0$

2. $\frac{\partial J(\cdot)}{\partial \Delta_2 y} = t_2 \Delta_2 t + 4\frac{(\Delta_2 y)}{(\Delta_2 t)} + \lambda = 0$

3. $\frac{\partial J(\cdot)}{\partial \lambda} = \Delta_1 y + \Delta_2 y - 1 = 0$

Setting $\Delta_1 t = \Delta_2 t = 0.5$ with $t_1 = 0.5$ and $t_2 = 1$ we simplify in:

1. $\frac{\partial J(\cdot)}{\partial \Delta_1 y} = 0.25 + 4\frac{(\Delta_1 y)}{(0.5)} + 0.5 + \lambda = 0$

2. $\frac{\partial J(\cdot)}{\partial \Delta_2 y} = 0.5 + 4\frac{(\Delta_2 y)}{(0.5)} + \lambda = 0$

3. $\frac{\partial J(\cdot)}{\partial \lambda} = \Delta_1 y + \Delta_2 y - 1 = 0$

We have then:

1. $\Delta_1 y = \frac{-\lambda - 0.75}{8}$
2. $\Delta_2 y = \frac{-\lambda - 0.50}{8}$
3. $\frac{-\lambda - 0.75}{8} + \frac{-\lambda - 0.50}{8} = 1$

After obtaining the multiplier $\lambda = -4.625$ we can plug it into the equations of $\Delta_1 y$ and $\Delta_2 y$ as follows:

1. $\Delta_1 y = \frac{4.625 - 0.75}{8} = 0.4844$
2. $\Delta_2 y = \frac{4.625 - 0.50}{8} = 0.5156$

We have our usual numerical CoV solution in the following table (Table 9.2-3):

Table 9.2-3 is numerically exact as it returns the same values as $y^*(t) = \frac{1}{24}t^3 + \frac{23}{24}t + 1$, while in Fig. 9.2-2 we have plotted the numerical path, with the correspondent equation, which is slightly different from $y^*(t)$ because of the just two data intervals we are working on.

The scalar for the *functional* $J(y)$ associated to the two intervals numerical approximate solution can be found plugging the above numerical solution into the discrete *functional*:

$$J(y) = \left[ t_1(1+\Delta_1 y) + 2\frac{(\Delta_1 y)^2}{(\Delta_1 t)^2} \right] \Delta_1 t + \left[ t_2(1+\Delta_1 y + \Delta_2 y) + 2\frac{(\Delta_2 y)^2}{(\Delta_2 t)^2} \right] \Delta_2 t$$

$$J(y) = \left[ 0.5 \cdot 1.4844 + 2 \cdot \frac{(0.4844)^2}{(0.5)^2} \right] \cdot 0.5 + \left[ 1 \cdot 2 + 2 \cdot \frac{(0.5156)^2}{(0.5)^2} \right] \cdot 0.5 = 1.3097 + 2.0634$$

$$= 3.3731$$

while the sought exact minimum scalar of the *functional* is $J(y) = 2.8305$, with the definite integral of the problem simply plugged in with the exact path $y^*(t) = \frac{1}{24}t^3 + \frac{23}{24}t + 1$ as follows:

TABLE 9.2-3   Example 3.a. optimal path.

| $t$ | $y(t)$ |
| --- | --- |
| 0.00 | 1.0000 |
| 0.50 | $= 1 + \Delta_1 y = 1.4844$ |
| 1.00 | $= 1.4844 + \Delta_2 y = 1.4844 + 0.5156 = 2.0000$ |

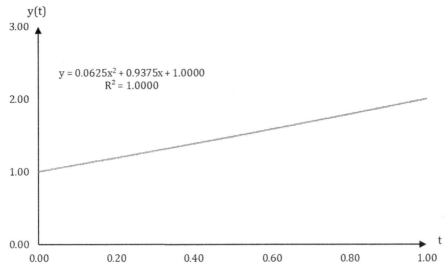

FIGURE 9.2-2   Example 3.a: optimal numerical path optimizing in two steps.

$$J(y^*(t)) = \int_0^1 \left[ t\left( \frac{1}{24}t^3 + \frac{23}{24}t + 1 \right) + 2\left( \frac{1}{8}t^2 + \frac{23}{24} \right)^2 \right] dt = 2.8305$$

## Second approach to solve the Calculus of Variations in a numerical framework: contour lines

The Lagrange multipliers technique presented above is nothing more than an equality-constrained optimization problem in two independent variables, when we decide to approximate the problem with two subintervals. Then, in that case we can easily also apply the geometrical approach of the *contour lines*, which are curves along which our *functional* $J(y(t))$ assumes a constant level, say $c$, till the optimal solution is found and the constraint is satisfied.

### EXAMPLE 3.B (CONTOUR LINES)

Let us continue Example 3 where the discrete problem was:

$$\min J = \left[ t_1(1 + \Delta_1 y) + 2\frac{(\Delta_1 y)^2}{(\Delta_1 t)^2} \right] \Delta_1 t + \left[ t_2(1 + \Delta_1 y + \Delta_2 y) + 2\frac{(\Delta_2 y)^2}{(\Delta_2 t)^2} \right] \Delta_2 t$$

III. Dynamic optimization

$$s.t. \; \Delta_1 y + \Delta_2 y = 1$$

With $t_1 = 0.5$ and $t_2 = 1$, we have:

$$J = \left[ 0.5(1 + \Delta_1 y) + 2 \frac{(\Delta_1 y)^2}{(\Delta_1 t)^2} \right] \Delta_1 t + \left[ 1(2) + 2 \frac{(\Delta_2 y)^2}{(\Delta_2 t)^2} \right] \Delta_2 t$$

where $J$ is a function of two independent variables $\Delta_1 y$ and $\Delta_2 y$, problem that we can transform into a one-independent variable problem just setting $J = c$ and taking $\Delta_1 y$ as the only independent variable and $\Delta_2 y$ as the dependent variable. We can then map all the curves as a function of $c$ to see when the given constraint $\Delta_1 y + \Delta_2 y = 1$ is met, and at the same time, $J = c$ is chosen at its optimal level.

Carrying on with our example we have:

$$c = \left[ 0.5(1 + \Delta_1 y) + 2 \frac{(\Delta_1 y)^2}{(0.5)^2} \right] 0.5 + \left[ 1(2) + 2 \frac{(\Delta_2 y)^2}{(0.5)^2} \right] 0.5$$

which is:

$$c = \left[ 0.25 + 0.25 \Delta_1 y + 4(\Delta_1 y)^2 \right] + \left[ 1 + 4(\Delta_2 y)^2 \right]$$

isolating $(\Delta_2 y)$ we have:

$$4(\Delta_2 y)^2 = c - 0.25 - 0.25 \Delta_1 y - 4(\Delta_1 y)^2 - 1$$

and finally our *contour map* is found:

$$\Delta_2 y = \left[ \frac{c - 1.25 - \Delta_1 y(0.25 + 4\Delta_1 y)}{4} \right]^{\frac{1}{2}}$$

This function returns all the *contour lines* positions as a function of the constant *cc*.

We can also check the numerical solution $\Delta_1 y = 0.4844$ and $\Delta_2 y = 0.5156$ which simultaneously returns $c = 3.3731$.

Geometrically speaking, as usual, the optimal point is found where the constraint equation $\Delta_1 y + \Delta_2 y = 1$ is tangent to one of the contour lines, as represented in Fig. 9.2-3, where only the first quadrant is of our interest; $\Delta_1 y$, $\Delta_2 y$ are then univocally determined together with the scalar $c$ associated to the functional $J(y(t))$.

The method of contour lines is somehow limited by the fact that we approximate the optimal path by just two intervals and so it works best when the optimal path is linear.

In the following section dedicated to Excel, we will see how to implement this method with a simple VBA macro code.

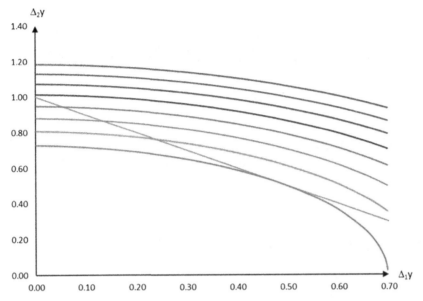

**FIGURE 9.2-3**  Example 3.b: contour map and the point of tangency to find $\Delta_1 y$, and $\Delta_2 y$.

## 9.3 Set up of the Excel worksheet for Calculus of Variations problems: the Solver solution

Now that the numerical approaches proposed have been investigated we are ready to go into our Excel worksheet to see how the problems can be implemented and solved on a much larger-scale basis.

Let us start with our CoV *simplest problem* of finding the shortest distance between the two points $P_0(1, 7)$ and $P_1(3, 17)$, being the CoV problem in its standard continuous form as follows:

$$\text{minimize } J = \int_{1}^{3} \left[ 1 + \frac{(dy)^2}{(dt)^2} \right]^{1/2} dt$$

$$s.t. \ y(1) = 7 \quad \text{and} \quad y(3) = 17$$

which discretized in $n$ steps becomes:

$$J = \sum_{i=1}^{n} \left[ 1 + \frac{(\Delta_i y)^2}{(\Delta_i t)^2} \right]^{1/2} \Delta_i t$$

$$s.t. \ \Delta_1 y + \Delta_2 y + \cdots \Delta_n y = y(3) - y(1) = 17 - 7 = 10$$

III. Dynamic optimization

Let us open Excel and let us set up the format of Excel worksheet of Fig. 9.3-1, where we have proposed the *simplest problem* in its discrete form, with 20 steps $\Delta_i t$ of length 0.1, from $t_0 = 1$ and terminal $T = 3$.

Now, what we have to do, Excel computer based, is exactly the same as we did in Section 9.2 within the Lagrange multipliers technique, on a much larger scale than the manual procedure implemented in Examples 1, 2, and 3 of the previous Section 9.2.

Our objective is to minimize the cell F24, where the *functional* scalar result is stored, changing the values in *Column C*, where all the optimal $\Delta_i y$ will be stored, subject to the constraint of the boundary conditions under cells C24, C27. In *Column E* we have stored instead our integrand function.

So, once Fig. 9.3-1 is ready in a worksheet let us go to Data in the Quick Access Toolbar, open the Solver and launch it as follows in Fig. 9.3-2.

We leave unflagged the option of *Make Unconstrained Variables Non-Negative*, and the Solver will find the desired solution and it will store it under *Column C*. Finally click OK when the message of Fig. 9.3-3 appears. You can also investigate about the Lagrange multiplier value if you choose Sensitivity.

| | A | B | C | D | E | F |
|---|---|---|---|---|---|---|
| 1 | t | y | dy | dt | $F = [1+(dy/dt)^2]^{0.5}$ | Functional $= \Sigma[1+(dy/dt)^2]^{0.5}dt$ |
| 2 | 1 | 7 | | | | |
| 3 | =A2+0.1 | =B2+C3 | 0.50000005 | =A3-A2 | =SQRT(1+(C3/D3)^2) | =E3*D3 |
| 4 | =A3+0.1 | =B3+C4 | 0.50000005 | =A4-A3 | =SQRT(1+(C4/D4)^2) | =E4*D4 |
| 5 | =A4+0.1 | =B4+C5 | 0.50000005 | =A5-A4 | =SQRT(1+(C5/D5)^2) | =E5*D5 |
| 6 | =A5+0.1 | =B5+C6 | 0.50000005 | =A6-A5 | =SQRT(1+(C6/D6)^2) | =E6*D6 |
| 7 | =A6+0.1 | =B6+C7 | 0.50000005 | =A7-A6 | =SQRT(1+(C7/D7)^2) | =E7*D7 |
| 8 | =A7+0.1 | =B7+C8 | 0.50000005 | =A8-A7 | =SQRT(1+(C8/D8)^2) | =E8*D8 |
| 9 | =A8+0.1 | =B8+C9 | 0.50000005 | =A9-A8 | =SQRT(1+(C9/D9)^2) | =E9*D9 |
| 10 | =A9+0.1 | =B9+C10 | 0.50000005 | =A10-A9 | =SQRT(1+(C10/D10)^2) | =E10*D10 |
| 11 | =A10+0.1 | =B10+C11 | 0.50000005 | =A11-A10 | =SQRT(1+(C11/D11)^2) | =E11*D11 |
| 12 | =A11+0.1 | =B11+C12 | 0.50000005 | =A12-A11 | =SQRT(1+(C12/D12)^2) | =E12*D12 |
| 13 | =A12+0.1 | =B12+C13 | 0.50000005 | =A13-A12 | =SQRT(1+(C13/D13)^2) | =E13*D13 |
| 14 | =A13+0.1 | =B13+C14 | 0.50000005 | =A14-A13 | =SQRT(1+(C14/D14)^2) | =E14*D14 |
| 15 | =A14+0.1 | =B14+C15 | 0.50000005 | =A15-A14 | =SQRT(1+(C15/D15)^2) | =E15*D15 |
| 16 | =A15+0.1 | =B15+C16 | 0.50000005 | =A16-A15 | =SQRT(1+(C16/D16)^2) | =E16*D16 |
| 17 | =A16+0.1 | =B16+C17 | 0.50000005 | =A17-A16 | =SQRT(1+(C17/D17)^2) | =E17*D17 |
| 18 | =A17+0.1 | =B17+C18 | 0.50000005 | =A18-A17 | =SQRT(1+(C18/D18)^2) | =E18*D18 |
| 19 | =A18+0.1 | =B18+C19 | 0.50000005 | =A19-A18 | =SQRT(1+(C19/D19)^2) | =E19*D19 |
| 20 | =A19+0.1 | =B19+C20 | 0.50000005 | =A20-A19 | =SQRT(1+(C20/D20)^2) | =E20*D20 |
| 21 | =A20+0.1 | =B20+C21 | 0.50000005 | =A21-A20 | =SQRT(1+(C21/D21)^2) | =E21*D21 |
| 22 | =A21+0.1 | =B21+C22 | 0.50000005 | =A22-A21 | =SQRT(1+(C22/D22)^2) | =E22*D22 |
| 23 | | | | | | |
| 24 | | | =B22-B2 | | | =SUM(F3:F22) |
| 25 | | | set equal to: | | | |
| 26 | y(1) | =B2 | | | | |
| 27 | y(3) | 17 | =B27-B26 | | | |

FIGURE 9.3-1    Excel set-up of the shortest distance problem in CoV.

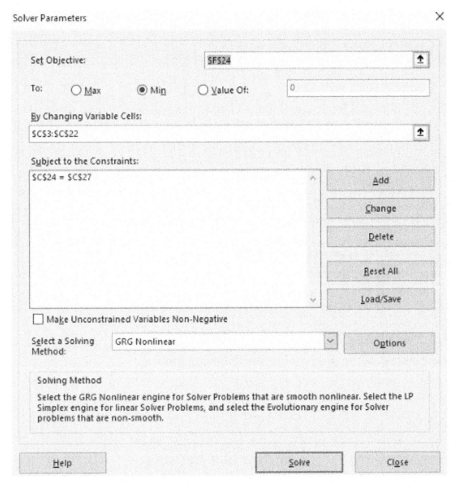

**FIGURE 9.3-2**    Solver parameters.

The output solution with 20 steps of $\Delta_i t = 0.10$ from $t_0 = 1$ and final $T = 3$ is included in Table 9.3-1, while the sought optimal linear equation path $y = 5t + 2$ is in Fig. 9.3-4, where the chart selected is the Scatter from the ones proposed by Excel.

The trendline equation is added to the chart easily by first right-clicking on the data series of the scatter chart, selecting the option Add Trendline, then going into Format Trendline and flagging the options Linear, Display Equation on chart, as well as Display R-squared value on chart, if you want this information as well (Fig. 9.3.5).

## 9.4 General cases developed in Excel with fixed and variable terminal points

Now we are ready to develop and analyze fully some general cases, as well as some CoV economic models applied with Excel in the following sections.

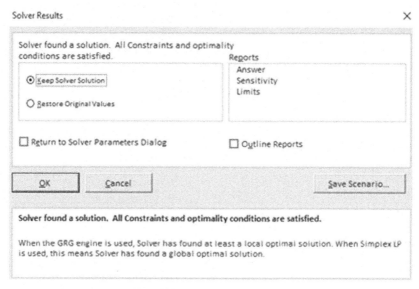

**FIGURE 9.3-3**    Solver results.

## EXAMPLE 1 (EXAMPLE 2 OF SECTION 9.2 CONTINUED)

Find the extremal of the *functional* in the following problem:

$$\min J = \int_0^2 \left(12ty + y'^2\right)dt$$

$$s.t.\ y(0) = 0 \ \text{ and } \ y(2) = 8$$

If you apply the Euler–Lagrange equation, you obtain the continuous exact solution $y = t^3$, while the numerical worksheet solution with 20 steps of $\Delta_i t = 0.10$ from $t_0 = 1$ and final $T = 2$ is represented in Table 9.4-1, together with the path equation, that we can derive from, in the chart of Fig. 9.4-1.

We can see from Fig. 9.4-1 that the numerical path is $y = t_3 + negligible factor(t)$, which corresponds to the exact solution sought and that we can use it as well to find the exact scalar of $J(y(t))$.

The exact minimum scalar of the *functional* is $J(y) = 134.40$, with the definite integral of the problem simply plugged in with the path $y^*(t) = t^3$ as follows:

$$J(y^*(t)) = \int_0^2 \left(12t^4 + 9t^4\right)dt = \int_0^2 \left(21t^4\right)dt = 134.40$$

TABLE 9.3-1    The shortest distance problem numerical solution.

| t | y | dy | dt | $[1+(dy/dt)^2]^{0.}$ | $\Sigma[1+(dy/dt)^2]$ |
|---|---|---|---|---|---|
| **1.00** | **7.00** | | | | |
| 1.10 | 7.50 | 0.50 | 0.10 | 5.10 | 0.51 |
| 1.20 | 8.00 | 0.50 | 0.10 | 5.10 | 0.51 |
| 1.30 | 8.50 | 0.50 | 0.10 | 5.10 | 0.51 |
| 1.40 | 9.00 | 0.50 | 0.10 | 5.10 | 0.51 |
| 1.50 | 9.50 | 0.50 | 0.10 | 5.10 | 0.51 |
| 1.60 | 10.00 | 0.50 | 0.10 | 5.10 | 0.51 |
| 1.70 | 10.50 | 0.50 | 0.10 | 5.10 | 0.51 |
| 1.80 | 11.00 | 0.50 | 0.10 | 5.10 | 0.51 |
| 1.90 | 11.50 | 0.50 | 0.10 | 5.10 | 0.51 |
| 2.00 | 12.00 | 0.50 | 0.10 | 5.10 | 0.51 |
| 2.10 | 12.50 | 0.50 | 0.10 | 5.10 | 0.51 |
| 2.20 | 13.00 | 0.50 | 0.10 | 5.10 | 0.51 |
| 2.30 | 13.50 | 0.50 | 0.10 | 5.10 | 0.51 |
| 2.40 | 14.00 | 0.50 | 0.10 | 5.10 | 0.51 |
| 2.50 | 14.50 | 0.50 | 0.10 | 5.10 | 0.51 |
| 2.60 | 15.00 | 0.50 | 0.10 | 5.10 | 0.51 |
| 2.70 | 15.50 | 0.50 | 0.10 | 5.10 | 0.51 |
| 2.80 | 16.00 | 0.50 | 0.10 | 5.10 | 0.51 |
| 2.90 | 16.50 | 0.50 | 0.10 | 5.10 | 0.51 |
| **3.00** | **17.00** | 0.50 | 0.10 | 5.10 | 0.51 |
| | | **10.00** | | | **10.20** |
| | | **set equal to:** | | | |
| **y(1)** | **7.00** | | | | |
| **y(3)** | **17.00** | **10.00** | | | |

We can also insist on our Excel worksheet to find a closer value in the functional, increasing the number of steps in $\Delta_i t$. The more we divide the total interval into subintervals, the more the value of $J(y(t))$ will go closer to the solution.

So let us just try for this example in Excel to divide the total interval into 200 steps and launch the Solver. The numerical solution found in Table 9.4-2 has an error of less than 1%, compared to the exact solution.

The reasons why we want to stop at a lesser number of steps are listed below:

1. Time. When Excel is required to optimize over 200 steps, it takes longer before having the Solver solution, while we desire the most efficient solution also in terms of time that we want to spend to have that solution.
2. Amount of space in terms of the worksheet organization that will be definitely higher with a higher level of attentions required by us.

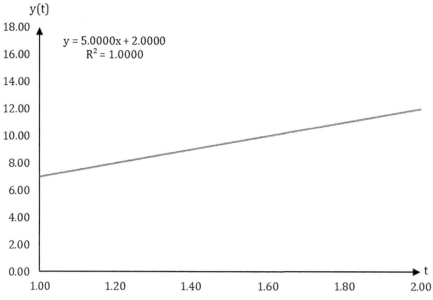

**FIGURE 9.3-4** The shortest distance problem optimal path.

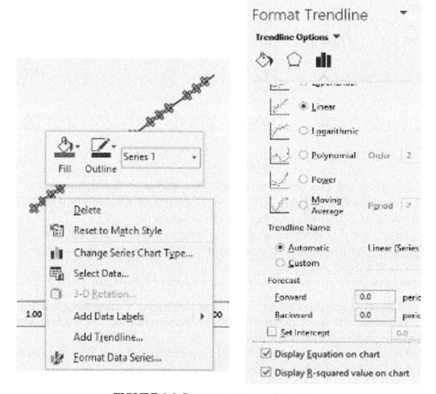

**FIGURE 9.3-5** Setting the trendline chart.

**TABLE 9.4-1**   Example 1: Numerical solution.

| t | y | dy | dt | $F = 12ty+(dy/dt)^2$ | Functional $= \Sigma[12ty+(dy/dt)^2]dt$ |
|---|---|---|---|---|---|
| 0.0000 | 0.0000 | | | | |
| 0.1000 | 0.0011 | 0.0011 | 0.1000 | 0.0015 | 0.0001 |
| 0.2000 | 0.0138 | 0.0127 | 0.1000 | 0.0492 | 0.0049 |
| 0.3000 | 0.0324 | 0.0186 | 0.1000 | 0.1512 | 0.0151 |
| 0.4000 | 0.0695 | 0.0371 | 0.1000 | 0.4711 | 0.0471 |
| 0.5000 | 0.1297 | 0.0602 | 0.1000 | 1.1401 | 0.1140 |
| 0.6000 | 0.2202 | 0.0905 | 0.1000 | 2.4049 | 0.2405 |
| 0.7000 | 0.3470 | 0.1268 | 0.1000 | 4.5218 | 0.4522 |
| 0.8000 | 0.5156 | 0.1687 | 0.1000 | 7.7954 | 0.7795 |
| 0.9000 | 0.7324 | 0.2167 | 0.1000 | 12.6054 | 1.2605 |
| 1.0000 | 1.0030 | 0.2707 | 0.1000 | 19.3641 | 1.9364 |
| 1.1000 | 1.3337 | 0.3307 | 0.1000 | 28.5414 | 2.8541 |
| 1.2000 | 1.7304 | 0.3967 | 0.1000 | 40.6551 | 4.0655 |
| 1.3000 | 2.1991 | 0.4687 | 0.1000 | 56.2744 | 5.6274 |
| 1.4000 | 2.7458 | 0.5467 | 0.1000 | 76.0178 | 7.6018 |
| 1.5000 | 3.3765 | 0.6307 | 0.1000 | 100.5555 | 10.0555 |
| 1.6000 | 4.0972 | 0.7207 | 0.1000 | 130.6067 | 13.0607 |
| 1.7000 | 4.9139 | 0.8167 | 0.1000 | 166.9420 | 16.6942 |
| 1.8000 | 5.8326 | 0.9187 | 0.1000 | 210.3849 | 21.0385 |
| 1.9000 | 6.8593 | 1.0267 | 0.1000 | 261.8027 | 26.1803 |
| 2.0000 | 8.0000 | 1.1407 | 0.1000 | 322.1195 | 32.2120 |

|  |  |  |
|---|---|---|
| | **8.00** | **144.2405** |
| | **Set equal to:** | |
| y(0) | 0.00 | |
| y(2) | 8.00 | 8.00 |

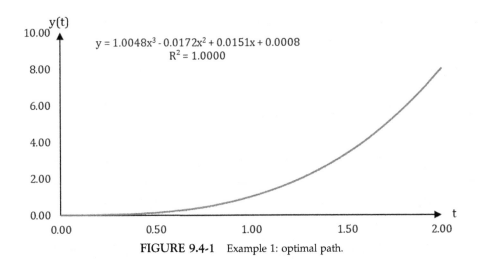

$y = 1.0048x^3 - 0.0172x^2 + 0.0151x + 0.0008$
$R^2 = 1.0000$

**FIGURE 9.4-1**   Example 1: optimal path.

III. Dynamic optimization

**TABLE 9.4-2** Example 1: Optimization over 200 steps.

| t | y | dy | dt | F = 12ty+(dy/dt)² | Functional = Σ[12ty+(dy/dt)²]dt |
|---|---|----|----|-------------------|-------------------------------|
| **0.0000** | **0.0000** | | | | |
| 0.0100 | 0.0001 | 0.0001 | 0.0100 | 0.0001 | 0.0000 |
| 0.0200 | 0.0009 | 0.0008 | 0.0100 | 0.0065 | 0.0001 |
| 0.0300 | 0.0029 | 0.0020 | 0.0100 | 0.0408 | 0.0004 |
| 0.0400 | 0.0062 | 0.0033 | 0.0100 | 0.1094 | 0.0011 |
| 0.0500 | 0.0102 | 0.0040 | 0.0100 | 0.1695 | 0.0017 |
| 0.0900 | 0.0248 | 0.0039 | 0.0100 | 0.1792 | 0.0018 |
| 0.1000 | 0.0296 | 0.0048 | 0.0100 | 0.2706 | 0.0027 |
| 0.1100 | 0.0345 | 0.0049 | 0.0100 | 0.2827 | 0.0028 |
| 0.1200 | 0.0393 | 0.0048 | 0.0100 | 0.2873 | 0.0029 |
| 0.1300 | 0.0437 | 0.0044 | 0.0100 | 0.2585 | 0.0026 |
| 1.9100 | 6.9835 | 0.1077 | 0.0100 | 276.0349 | 2.7603 |
| 1.9200 | 7.0923 | 0.1088 | 0.0100 | 281.7879 | 2.8179 |
| 1.9300 | 7.2023 | 0.1099 | 0.0100 | 287.6284 | 2.8763 |
| 1.9400 | 7.3133 | 0.1110 | 0.0100 | 293.5567 | 2.9356 |
| 1.9500 | 7.4255 | 0.1122 | 0.0100 | 299.5810 | 2.9958 |
| 1.9600 | 7.5388 | 0.1133 | 0.0100 | 305.6925 | 3.0569 |
| 1.9700 | 7.6532 | 0.1144 | 0.0100 | 311.8973 | 3.1190 |
| 1.9800 | 7.7688 | 0.1156 | 0.0100 | 318.1897 | 3.1819 |
| 1.9900 | 7.8844 | 0.1156 | 0.0100 | 321.8822 | 3.2188 |
| 2.0000 | 8.0000 | 0.1156 | 0.0100 | 325.6024 | 3.2560 |
| | | 8.00 | | | 135.41 |
| | | **Set equal to:** | | | |
| y(0) | 0.00 | | | | |
| y(2) | 8.00 | 8.00 | | | |

3. When we work with 20 steps, we already got our numerical optimal path $y^*(t)$ and we can use this one in the definite integral to get the scalar $J(y^*(t))$.
4. As we will see, in Economics, we are mostly interested in the behavior of the optimal path, rather than in the exact scalar solution of the *functional*.

On ad hoc basis, one can decide the steps that consider the best to reach the desired numerical solution of the specific problem.

## EXAMPLE 2 (EXAMPLE 3 OF SECTION 9.2 CONTINUED)

Find the extremal of the *functional* in the following problem:

$$\min J = \int_0^1 (ty + 2y'^2)\,dt$$

$$s.t.\ y(0) = 1 \text{ and } y(1) = 2$$

**TABLE 9.4-3** Example 2: numerical solution.

| t | y | dy | dt | $F = [ty+2(dy/dt)^2]$ | Functional $= \Sigma[ty+2(dy/dt)^2]dt$ |
|---|---|---|---|---|---|
| 0.0000 | 1.0000 | | | | |
| 0.0500 | 1.0479 | 0.0479 | 0.0500 | 1.8894 | 0.0945 |
| 0.1000 | 1.0959 | 0.0480 | 0.0500 | 1.9490 | 0.0975 |
| 0.1500 | 1.1439 | 0.0480 | 0.0500 | 2.0159 | 0.1008 |
| 0.2000 | 1.1920 | 0.0481 | 0.0500 | 2.0900 | 0.1045 |
| 0.2500 | 1.2402 | 0.0482 | 0.0500 | 2.1714 | 0.1086 |
| 0.3000 | 1.2886 | 0.0484 | 0.0500 | 2.2601 | 0.1130 |
| 0.3500 | 1.3372 | 0.0486 | 0.0500 | 2.3561 | 0.1178 |
| 0.4000 | 1.3860 | 0.0488 | 0.0500 | 2.4596 | 0.1230 |
| 0.4500 | 1.4351 | 0.0490 | 0.0500 | 2.5705 | 0.1285 |
| 0.5000 | 1.4844 | 0.0493 | 0.0500 | 2.6890 | 0.1344 |
| 0.5500 | 1.5340 | 0.0496 | 0.0500 | 2.8151 | 0.1408 |
| 0.6000 | 1.5840 | 0.0500 | 0.0500 | 2.9491 | 0.1475 |
| 0.6500 | 1.6344 | 0.0504 | 0.0500 | 3.0910 | 0.1546 |
| 0.7000 | 1.6851 | 0.0508 | 0.0500 | 3.2411 | 0.1621 |
| 0.7500 | 1.7363 | 0.0512 | 0.0500 | 3.3996 | 0.1700 |
| 0.8000 | 1.7880 | 0.0517 | 0.0500 | 3.5665 | 0.1783 |
| 0.8500 | 1.8402 | 0.0522 | 0.0500 | 3.7419 | 0.1871 |
| 0.9000 | 1.8929 | 0.0527 | 0.0500 | 3.9260 | 0.1963 |
| 0.9500 | 1.9462 | 0.0533 | 0.0500 | 4.1185 | 0.2059 |
| 1.0000 | 2.0000 | 0.0538 | 0.0500 | 4.3197 | 0.2160 |
| | | 1.0000 | | | 2.8810 |

Set equal to:

| | | |
|---|---|---|
| y(0) | 1.00 | |
| y(1) | 2.00 | 1.00 |

If you apply the Euler–Lagrange equation, you obtain the continuous exact $y^*(t) = \frac{1}{24}t^3 + \frac{23}{24}t + 1$ and the numerical solution found with the Excel Solver is represented in Table 9.4-3 as follows.

The associated chart with the numerical path solution equation found is represented in Fig. 9.4-2. Neglecting the $t^2 \cong 0$ factor, the equation corresponds to the exact path.

Even if we select an order 4 Polynomial trendline format, Excel will recognize that the coefficient associated to $t^4$ must be set to zero. On the contrary, if you select Linear, the statistic $R^2$ will be lower and you can reach $R^2 \cong 1$ just selecting a Polynomial trendline.

## EXAMPLE 3

So far, we have covered cases in which the CoV problem is presented with fixed initial and ending points boundary conditions (like in the *simplest problem*), but we have seen that a CoV problem may also be presented with the so called *transversality conditions* and one of this common condition is when the terminal point y(T) is free.

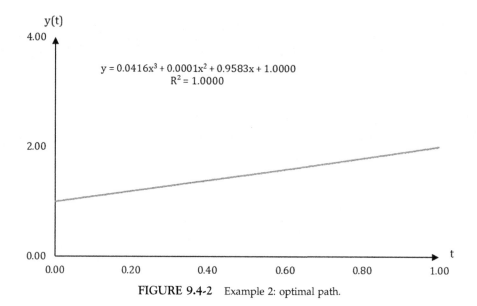

**FIGURE 9.4-2**  Example 2: optimal path.

Let us solve then the following problem:

$$\min J = \int_0^2 (y'^2 + 2yy' + 4y^2)\,dt$$

$$s.t.\ y(0)\ =\ 1 \text{ and } y(2)\ =\ \textit{free}$$

Now, the resolution of this case does not change a lot compared to the ones we have seen before, except for the inclusion of the *vertical-terminal-line transversality* condition. The Excel Solver can deal with these types of problems just simply omitting the constraint on $y(T)$ within the Solver menu.

However, the theory of CoV requires that we also define the following constraint, which is the mathematical form of the *vertical-terminal-line transversality* condition, which is sometimes referred as *natural boundary condition*:

$$\left[\frac{\partial F(T, y(T), y'(T))}{\partial y'}\right] = y'(2) + y(2) = 0 \tag{9.4-1}$$

So, what we have to do in our worksheet is just storing somewhere this condition and add it as a constraint in the Solver, setting it to zero. The output of the Solver numerical solution is in the following Table 9.4-4.

From the Euler–Lagrange equation the exact solution path is given by the equation:

$$y^*(t) = c_1 e^{-2t} + c_2 e^{2t}$$

with $c_1 + c_2 = 1$

**TABLE 9.4-4**   Example 3: Numerical solution.

| t | y | dy | dt | $F=[(y')^2+2yy'+4(y)^2]$ | Functional $= \Sigma\,[(y')^2+2yy'+4(y)^2]dt$ | $\partial F(T)/\partial y'=0$ |
|---|---|---|---|---|---|---|
| 0.0000 | 1.0000 | | | | | |
| 0.1000 | 0.8267 | -0.1733 | 0.1000 | 2.8720 | 0.2872 | -0.9066 |
| 0.2000 | 0.6834 | -0.1433 | 0.1000 | 1.9625 | 0.1962 | -0.7492 |
| 0.3000 | 0.5650 | -0.1184 | 0.1000 | 1.3410 | 0.1341 | -0.6191 |
| 0.4000 | 0.4671 | -0.0979 | 0.1000 | 0.9163 | 0.0916 | -0.5115 |
| 0.5000 | 0.3863 | -0.0809 | 0.1000 | 0.6261 | 0.0626 | -0.4225 |
| 0.6000 | 0.3194 | -0.0668 | 0.1000 | 0.4278 | 0.0428 | -0.3489 |
| 0.7000 | 0.2642 | -0.0552 | 0.1000 | 0.2923 | 0.0292 | -0.2880 |
| 0.8000 | 0.2186 | -0.0456 | 0.1000 | 0.1998 | 0.0200 | -0.2375 |
| 0.9000 | 0.1809 | -0.0377 | 0.1000 | 0.1365 | 0.0137 | -0.1957 |
| 1.0000 | 0.1498 | -0.0311 | 0.1000 | 0.0933 | 0.0093 | -0.1610 |
| 1.1000 | 0.1242 | -0.0256 | 0.1000 | 0.0637 | 0.0064 | -0.1321 |
| 1.2000 | 0.1031 | -0.0211 | 0.1000 | 0.0436 | 0.0044 | -0.1081 |
| 1.3000 | 0.0857 | -0.0174 | 0.1000 | 0.0298 | 0.0030 | -0.0880 |
| 1.4000 | 0.0715 | -0.0143 | 0.1000 | 0.0204 | 0.0020 | -0.0711 |
| 1.5000 | 0.0598 | -0.0117 | 0.1000 | 0.0140 | 0.0014 | -0.0567 |
| 1.6000 | 0.0503 | -0.0095 | 0.1000 | 0.0096 | 0.0010 | -0.0445 |
| 1.7000 | 0.0427 | -0.0076 | 0.1000 | 0.0066 | 0.0007 | -0.0338 |
| 1.8000 | 0.0366 | -0.0061 | 0.1000 | 0.0046 | 0.0005 | -0.0244 |
| 1.9000 | 0.0318 | -0.0048 | 0.1000 | 0.0033 | 0.0003 | -0.0159 |
| 2.0000 | 0.0289 | -0.0029 | 0.1000 | 0.0025 | 0.0003 | 0.0000 |

0.9066

| $y(0)$ | 0.00 |
|---|---|
| $y(2)$ | Free |

$$c_1 = \frac{3e^4}{e^{-4}+3e^4} \text{ and } c_2 = \frac{e^{-4}}{e^{-4}+3e^4}$$

The exact path is represented numerically in Table 9.4-5, with the error compared to the numerical solution.

In Figs. 9.4-3 and 9.4-4, we compare the exact solution with the numerical solution, associating to each of them the best fitting polynomial curve; we can easily inspect that the absolute error is close to zero.

From Fig. 9.4-5, we see how the Solver has been set up to reach the numerical solution. The *natural boundary condition (Cell G22 = 0)* has been added to the Solver Parameters.

## EXAMPLE 4

Find the extremal of the *functional* in the following problem:

$$\min J = \int_0^T (ty' + y'^2)dt$$

with boundary conditions specified as follows:

**a.** $y(0) = 1$, $T = 1$, $y(1) = 2.75$ (*fixed endpoint problem*)

III. Dynamic optimization

**TABLE 9.4-5** Exact optimal path and error vs. numerical path.

| t | y Exact | Error |
|---|---|---|
| 0.0000 | 1.0000 | |
| 0.1339 | 1.2633 | 0.00 |
| 0.2680 | 1.5180 | -0.01 |
| 0.4085 | 1.7754 | -0.01 |
| 0.5520 | 2.0278 | -0.02 |
| 0.6985 | 2.2750 | -0.02 |
| 0.8483 | 2.5167 | -0.03 |
| 1.0018 | 2.7527 | -0.03 |
| 1.1592 | 2.9825 | -0.04 |
| 1.3212 | 3.2060 | -0.04 |
| 1.4882 | 3.4228 | -0.05 |
| 1.6609 | 3.6321 | -0.05 |
| 1.8402 | 3.8338 | -0.05 |
| 2.0272 | 4.0270 | -0.06 |
| 2.2233 | 4.2108 | -0.06 |
| 2.4307 | 4.3844 | -0.06 |
| 2.6527 | 4.5462 | -0.07 |
| 2.8941 | 4.6943 | -0.07 |
| 3.1647 | 4.8256 | -0.07 |
| 3.4871 | 4.9342 | -0.07 |
| 4.0289 | 4.9998 | 0.00 |

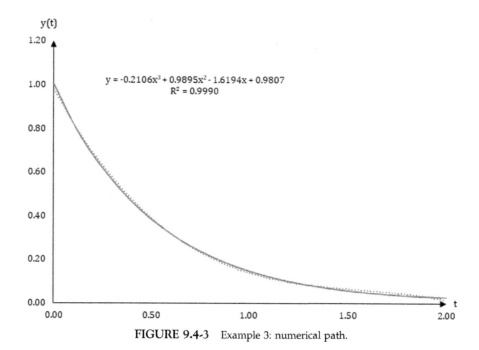

**FIGURE 9.4-3** Example 3: numerical path.

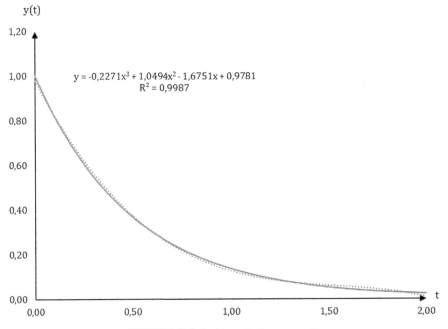

y(t)

y = -0,2271x³ + 1,0494x² - 1,6751x + 0,9781
R² = 0,9987

**FIGURE 9.4-4**    Example 3: exact path.

**b.** $y(0) = 1$, $T = 1$, $y(1) =$ free (*vertical terminal—line problem*)
**c.** $y(0) = 1$, $T =$ free, $y(T) = 5$ (*horizontal terminal—line problem*)

So, let us solve the problem with each one of the three specified boundary conditions, two of which are *transversality conditions*.

**a.** The exact solution path for this problem, via the Euler—Lagrange equation, is:

$$y^*(t) = -\frac{1}{4}t^2 + 2t + 1$$

while the Excel numerical solution is given below in Table 9.4-6 and Fig. 9.4-6, with the numerical equation path exactly corresponding to the exact Euler—Lagrange solution.

**b.** The exact solution path for this problem is:

$$y^*(t) = -\frac{1}{4}t^2 + 1$$

Here, to solve the problem we also need to set the *transversality condition* 9.4-1:

$$\left[\frac{\partial F(T, y(T), y'(T))}{\partial y'}\right] = T + 2y'(T) = 1 + 2y'(2) = 0$$

III. Dynamic optimization

**FIGURE 9.4-5**   Natural boundary condition constraint.

The numerical path equation is a good approximation of the exact one, neglecting the factor $t \cong 0$ (Fig. 9.4-7) (Table 9.4-7).

**c.** The exact solution path for this problem is again:

$$y^*(t) = -\frac{1}{4}t^2 + 2t + 1$$

In the *horizontal-terminal-line problem*, the theory of CoV requires that the following new *transversality condition* is introduced, that must be satisfied at terminal time $T$:

$$F((T, y(T), y'(T)) - \left[\frac{\partial F(T, y(T), y'(T))}{\partial y'}\right] y'(T) = \left[Ty'(T) + y'^2(T)\right] - [T + 2y'(T)]y'(T) = 0$$

$$(9.4\text{-}2)$$

**TABLE 9.4.6** Example 4.a. Numerical solution.

| t | y | dy | dt | $F = [t(dy/dt)+(dy/dt)^2]$ | Functional $= \Sigma[t(dy/dt)+(dy/dt)^2]\,dt$ |
|---|---|---|---|---|---|
| 0.0000 | 1.0000 | | | | |
| 0.0500 | 1.0994 | 0.0994 | 0.0500 | 4.0492 | 0.2025 |
| 0.1000 | 1.1975 | 0.0981 | 0.0500 | 4.0477 | 0.2024 |
| 0.1500 | 1.2944 | 0.0969 | 0.0500 | 4.0447 | 0.2022 |
| 0.2000 | 1.3900 | 0.0956 | 0.0500 | 4.0404 | 0.2020 |
| 0.2500 | 1.4844 | 0.0944 | 0.0500 | 4.0347 | 0.2017 |
| 0.3000 | 1.5775 | 0.0931 | 0.0500 | 4.0277 | 0.2014 |
| 0.3500 | 1.6694 | 0.0919 | 0.0500 | 4.0195 | 0.2010 |
| 0.4000 | 1.7600 | 0.0906 | 0.0500 | 4.0101 | 0.2005 |
| 0.4500 | 1.8494 | 0.0894 | 0.0500 | 3.9994 | 0.2000 |
| 0.5000 | 1.9375 | 0.0881 | 0.0500 | 3.9875 | 0.1994 |
| 0.5500 | 2.0244 | 0.0869 | 0.0500 | 3.9744 | 0.1987 |
| 0.6000 | 2.1100 | 0.0856 | 0.0500 | 3.9600 | 0.1980 |
| 0.6500 | 2.1944 | 0.0844 | 0.0500 | 3.9445 | 0.1972 |
| 0.7000 | 2.2775 | 0.0831 | 0.0500 | 3.9277 | 0.1964 |
| 0.7500 | 2.3594 | 0.0819 | 0.0500 | 3.9096 | 0.1955 |
| 0.8000 | 2.4400 | 0.0806 | 0.0500 | 3.8903 | 0.1945 |
| 0.8500 | 2.5194 | 0.0794 | 0.0500 | 3.8697 | 0.1935 |
| 0.9000 | 2.5975 | 0.0781 | 0.0500 | 3.8477 | 0.1924 |
| 0.9500 | 2.6744 | 0.0769 | 0.0500 | 3.8242 | 0.1912 |
| 1.0000 | 2.7500 | 0.0756 | 0.0500 | 3.8004 | 0.1900 |
| | | | | | **3.9605** |

| | | |
|---|---|---|
| | 1.75 | |
| | **Set equal to:** | |
| y(0) | 1.00 | 1.75 |
| y(1) | 2.75 | 1.75 |

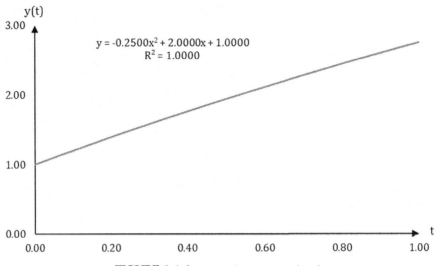

**FIGURE 9.4-6**  Example 4.a: optimal path.

**TABLE 9.4-7**  Example 4.b. Numerical solution.

| t | y | dy | dt | $F = [t(dy/dt)+(dy/dt)^2]$ | Functional $= \Sigma[t(dy/dt)+(dy/dt)^2]\,dt$ | Natural Boundary condition |
|---|---|---|---|---|---|---|
| 0.0000 | 1.0000 | | | | | |
| 0.0500 | 0.9987 | -0.0013 | 0.0500 | -0.0006 | 0.0000 | 0.0000 |
| 0.1000 | 0.9962 | -0.0025 | 0.0500 | -0.0025 | -0.0001 | 0.0000 |
| 0.1500 | 0.9925 | -0.0038 | 0.0500 | -0.0056 | -0.0003 | 0.0000 |
| 0.2000 | 0.9875 | -0.0050 | 0.0500 | -0.0100 | -0.0005 | 0.0000 |
| 0.2500 | 0.9812 | -0.0063 | 0.0500 | -0.0156 | -0.0008 | 0.0000 |
| 0.3000 | 0.9737 | -0.0075 | 0.0500 | -0.0225 | -0.0011 | 0.0000 |
| 0.3500 | 0.9650 | -0.0088 | 0.0500 | -0.0306 | -0.0015 | 0.0000 |
| 0.4000 | 0.9550 | -0.0100 | 0.0500 | -0.0400 | -0.0020 | 0.0000 |
| 0.4500 | 0.9437 | -0.0113 | 0.0500 | -0.0506 | -0.0025 | 0.0000 |
| 0.5000 | 0.9312 | -0.0125 | 0.0500 | -0.0625 | -0.0031 | 0.0000 |
| 0.5500 | 0.9175 | -0.0138 | 0.0500 | -0.0756 | -0.0038 | 0.0000 |
| 0.6000 | 0.9025 | -0.0150 | 0.0500 | -0.0900 | -0.0045 | 0.0000 |
| 0.6500 | 0.8862 | -0.0163 | 0.0500 | -0.1056 | -0.0053 | 0.0000 |
| 0.7000 | 0.8687 | -0.0175 | 0.0500 | -0.1225 | -0.0061 | 0.0000 |
| 0.7500 | 0.8500 | -0.0188 | 0.0500 | -0.1406 | -0.0070 | 0.0000 |
| 0.8000 | 0.8300 | -0.0200 | 0.0500 | -0.1600 | -0.0080 | 0.0000 |
| 0.8500 | 0.8087 | -0.0212 | 0.0500 | -0.1806 | -0.0090 | 0.0000 |
| 0.9000 | 0.7862 | -0.0225 | 0.0500 | -0.2025 | -0.0101 | 0.0000 |
| 0.9500 | 0.7625 | -0.0237 | 0.0500 | -0.2256 | -0.0113 | 0.0000 |
| 1.0000 | 0.7375 | -0.0250 | 0.0500 | -0.2500 | -0.0125 | 0.0000 |
| | | | | | **-0.0897** | |

| | | |
|---|---|---|
| y(0) | 1.00 | |
| y(1) | Free | |

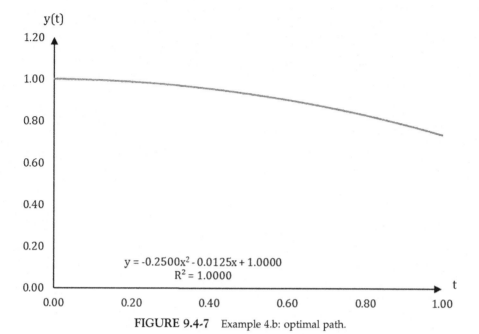

**FIGURE 9.4-7** Example 4.b: optimal path.

which becomes:

$$[T + y'(T) - T - + 2y'(T)]y'(T) = 0$$

which requires that $y'(T) = 0$:

$$-\frac{1}{2}T + c_1 = 0$$

Having also

$$5 = -\frac{1}{4}T^2 + c_1 T + 1$$

it implies that $T = 4$ *and* $c_1 = 2$.

Now we try to find the same result numerically in Excel and we present in Table 9.4-8 and Fig. 9.4-8 the output obtained from the Solver solution. See how a new *Column* has been inserted to store the *transversality* condition.

In this example, the Solver is set up as follows, where the *horizontal-terminal-line transversality condition* 9.4-1 at $T$ has been inserted through the Change Constraint module of the Solver in *Cell G22* (Fig. 9.4-9):

Differently from all the previous cases, here we ask the Solver to optimize not only over *Column C*, where the optimal $\Delta y_i$ are stored, but also over the *Column D*, where the optimal $\Delta t_i$ need to be stored as well, as we have to find the optimal terminal point $T$. So, in *Column A* of the worksheet we have changed the formula as $t_{i+1} = t_i + \Delta t_{i,i+1}$.

III. Dynamic optimization

**TABLE 9.4-8**  Example 4.c. Numerical solution.

| t | y | dy | dt | $F = [t(dy/dt)+(dy/dt)^2]$ | Functional $= \Sigma[t(dy/dt)+(dy/dt)^2]dt$ | Transversality Condition |
|---|---|---|---|---|---|---|
| 0.0000 | 1.0000 | | | | | |
| 0.1339 | 1.2679 | 0.2679 | 0.1339 | 4.2728 | 0.5720 | -4.0049 |
| 0.2680 | 1.5272 | 0.2592 | 0.1341 | 4.2559 | 0.5706 | -3.7378 |
| 0.4085 | 1.7891 | 0.2620 | 0.1406 | 4.2344 | 0.5953 | -3.4730 |
| 0.5520 | 2.0461 | 0.2570 | 0.1434 | 4.1998 | 0.6024 | -3.2107 |
| 0.6985 | 2.2979 | 0.2517 | 0.1465 | 4.1538 | 0.6085 | -2.9535 |
| 0.8483 | 2.5442 | 0.2463 | 0.1498 | 4.0978 | 0.6139 | -2.7031 |
| 1.0018 | 2.7847 | 0.2405 | 0.1535 | 4.0235 | 0.6176 | -2.4541 |
| 1.1592 | 3.0191 | 0.2345 | 0.1575 | 3.9432 | 0.6209 | -2.2171 |
| 1.3212 | 3.2470 | 0.2279 | 0.1620 | 3.8386 | 0.6218 | -1.9796 |
| 1.4882 | 3.4681 | 0.2210 | 0.1670 | 3.7203 | 0.6214 | -1.7510 |
| 1.6609 | 3.6819 | 0.2138 | 0.1726 | 3.5905 | 0.6199 | -1.5337 |
| 1.8402 | 3.8876 | 0.2058 | 0.1793 | 3.4283 | 0.6147 | -1.3167 |
| 2.0272 | 4.0847 | 0.1971 | 0.1870 | 3.2472 | 0.6073 | -1.1107 |
| 2.2233 | 4.2724 | 0.1877 | 0.1960 | 3.0456 | 0.5971 | -0.9168 |
| 2.4307 | 4.4493 | 0.1769 | 0.2075 | 2.7990 | 0.5808 | -0.7268 |
| 2.6527 | 4.6140 | 0.1646 | 0.2220 | 2.5181 | 0.5589 | -0.5503 |
| 2.8941 | 4.7640 | 0.1501 | 0.2414 | 2.1852 | 0.5276 | -0.3863 |
| 3.1647 | 4.8953 | 0.1313 | 0.2706 | 1.7714 | 0.4793 | -0.2355 |
| 3.4871 | 4.9999 | 0.1046 | 0.3224 | 1.2365 | 0.3987 | -0.1052 |
| 4.0289 | 5.0000 | 0.0001 | 0.5418 | 0.0006 | 0.0003 | 0.0000 |

|   |   | 4.00 | | | 11.0288 | |
|   |   | Set equal to: | | | | |
| y(0) | 1.00 | | | | | |
| y(T) | 5.00 | 4.00 | | | | |

As you can see from Fig. 9.4-8, the numerical solution is slightly different (still very acceptable error) from the exact solution $y^*(t) = -\frac{1}{4}t^2 + 2t + 1$ because in this specific case we have forced Excel to do something more difficult compared to the previous cases, optimizing over the two *Columns* with a second constraint, returning a very good approximate solution.

In such an example with terminal $T$ free, we may need to iterate numerically in Excel many times before finding the solution, and it may happen that the Solver does not return always the same optimal $T$.

Finally, the error of the numerical solution is as follows (Table 9.4-9):

Now that we have covered the general examples in CoV, together with the most important *transversality conditions*, it is time to see some applications.

From Section 9.5 until Section 9.7, we will be covering some interesting applications of CoV to Economics proposed in the literature. Section 9.8 is a classical application to the dynamic Inventory modeling, while the case 9.9 is a basic application of the numerical Excel CoV framework to the theory of Corporate Finance, in particular, to the dynamic optimization of the firm capital structure, together with the cost of capital.

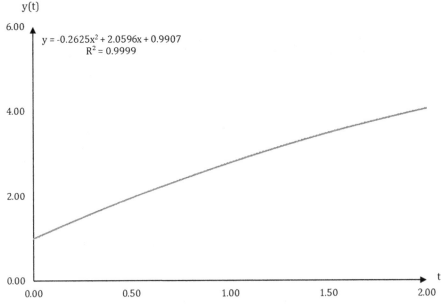

y(t)

$y = -0.2625x^2 + 2.0596x + 0.9907$
$R^2 = 0.9999$

FIGURE 9.4-8   Example 4.c: optimal path.

**(A)**                    **(B)**

| | A | B | C | D | E | F | G |
|---|---|---|---|---|---|---|---|
| | $t$ | $y$ | $dy$ | $dt$ | $F = [t(dy/dt) \cdot (dy/dt)^2]$ | Functional $= \Sigma[t(dy/dt) \cdot (dy/dt)^2]dt$ | Transversality Condition |
| 1 | | | | | | | |
| 5 | 0.4085 | 1.7891 | 0.2620 | 0.1406 | 4.2344 | 0.5953 | -3.4730 |
| 6 | 0.5520 | 2.0461 | 0.257 | | | | -3.2107 |
| 7 | 0.6985 | 2.2979 | 0.251 | | | | -2.9535 |
| 8 | 0.8483 | 2.5442 | 0.246 | | | | -2.7031 |
| 9 | 1.0018 | 2.7847 | 0.240 | | | | -2.4541 |
| 10 | 1.1592 | 3.0191 | 0.234 | | | | -2.2171 |
| 11 | 1.3212 | 3.2470 | 0.227 | | | | -1.9796 |
| 12 | 1.4882 | 3.4681 | 0.221 | | | | -1.7510 |
| 13 | 1.6609 | 3.6819 | 0.213 | | | | -1.5337 |
| 14 | 1.8402 | 3.8876 | 0.205 | | | | -1.3167 |
| 15 | 2.0272 | 4.0847 | 0.1971 | 0.1870 | 3.2472 | 0.6073 | -1.1107 |
| 16 | 2.2233 | 4.2724 | 0.1877 | 0.1960 | 3.0456 | 0.5971 | -0.9168 |
| 17 | 2.4307 | 4.4493 | 0.1769 | 0.2075 | 2.7990 | 0.5808 | -0.7268 |
| 18 | 2.6527 | 4.6140 | 0.1646 | 0.2220 | 2.5181 | 0.5589 | -0.5503 |
| 19 | 2.8941 | 4.7640 | 0.1501 | 0.2414 | 2.1852 | 0.5276 | -0.3863 |
| 20 | 3.1647 | 4.8953 | 0.1313 | 0.2706 | 1.7714 | 0.4793 | -0.2355 |
| 21 | 3.4871 | 4.9999 | 0.1046 | 0.3224 | 1.2365 | 0.3987 | -0.1052 |
| 22 | 4.0289 | 5.0000 | 0.0001 | 0.5418 | 0.0006 | 0.0003 | 0.0000 |

FIGURE 9.4-9   Setting the transversality condition constraint in the Solver (A) and (B).

## 9.5 Dynamic optimization for a monopolist

The first economic application of the CoV is a classical model taken from the literature[2] regarding the monopoly.

As we have seen in the section of Microeconomics in this imperfect competitive market, there is no such thing as the supply curve, like in the perfect competitive markets, but

[2]For the models proposed in this section and next Sections 9.6 and 9.7, see Alpha Chiang, Elements of Dynamic Optimization, Mc-Graw-Hill, 1992.

**TABLE 9.4-9** Example 4.c
exact optimal
path and error
vs. numerical
path.

| t | y Exact | Error |
|---|---|---|
| 0.0000 | 1.0000 | |
| 0.1339 | 1.2633 | 0.00 |
| 0.2680 | 1.5180 | -0.01 |
| 0.4085 | 1.7754 | -0.01 |
| 0.5520 | 2.0278 | -0.02 |
| 0.6985 | 2.2750 | -0.02 |
| 0.8483 | 2.5167 | -0.03 |
| 1.0018 | 2.7527 | -0.03 |
| 1.1592 | 2.9825 | -0.04 |
| 1.3212 | 3.2060 | -0.04 |
| 1.4882 | 3.4228 | -0.05 |
| 1.6609 | 3.6321 | -0.05 |
| 1.8402 | 3.8338 | -0.05 |
| 2.0272 | 4.0270 | -0.06 |
| 2.2233 | 4.2108 | -0.06 |
| 2.4307 | 4.3844 | -0.06 |
| 2.6527 | 4.5462 | -0.07 |
| 2.8941 | 4.6943 | -0.07 |
| 3.1647 | 4.8256 | -0.07 |
| 3.4871 | 4.9342 | -0.07 |
| 4.0289 | 4.9998 | 0.00 |

only a supply point exists. In the static environment, the optimal output depends on the specific shape of the demand curve. Through the demand curve, we read the price level at which the monopolist maximizes its profit, which is equal to total revenues minus total costs, namely $\pi = pq - (aq^3 + bq^2 + c)$, where $p = a - bq$ is the demand shape at a certain time. The solution in the static environment is then the optimal quantity to offer at a certain price, this being implied by the demand curve.

The objective in the dynamic model is instead to find the optimal price path $P^*(t)$ that maximizes the profit over a finite time period $[0, T]$.

The assumptions of the dynamic optimization model for a monopolist are as follows:

1. The cost production function is:
   $c(Q) = \alpha Q^2 + \beta Q + \gamma$ with $\alpha, \beta, \gamma > 0$.
2. The quantity demanded depends on $P(t)$ and also on $P'(t)$:
   $Q(t, P(t), P'(t)) = a - bP(t) + hP'(t)$ where $a, b > 0; h \neq 0$.
3. The profit function $\pi$ is:

$$\pi(t, P(t), P'(t)) = PQ - C = P(a - bP + hP') - \alpha(a - bP + hP')^2 - \beta(a - bP - bP') - \gamma$$

which will be our integrand function in the following CoV problem:

$$\max \Pi(P) = \int_0^T \pi(t, P, P')dt = \min \Pi(P) = \int_0^T -\pi(t, P, P')dt \qquad (9.5\text{-}1)$$

III. Dynamic optimization

s.t. $P(0) = P_0$ and $P(T) = P_T$ (T given)

where a maximization problem is transformed in minimization problem for more numerical convenience.

From the Euler–Lagrange equation, the following second-order differential equation is obtained:

$$P'' - \frac{b(1 + \alpha b)}{\alpha h^2} P = -\frac{a + 2\alpha ab + \beta b}{2\alpha h^2}$$

to solve it for the function $P(t)$, as:

$$P^*(t) = A_1 e^{rt} + A_2 e^{-rt} + \overline{P}$$

with $A_1 = \frac{P_0 - \overline{P} - (P_T - \overline{P})e^{rT}}{1 - e^{2rT}}$, $A_2 = \frac{P_0 - \overline{P} - (P_T - \overline{P})e^{-rT}}{1 - e^{-2rT}}$, $\overline{P} = \frac{a + 2\alpha ab + \beta b}{2b(1 + \alpha b)}$ (particular solution).

$r_1, r_2 = \pm\sqrt{\frac{b(1+\alpha b)}{\alpha h^2}}$ (characteristic roots, or eigenvalues).

To solve the problem numerically we assume the following parameters:

$$a = b = 1; \quad \alpha = \beta = 1; \quad h = 0.5; \quad \gamma = 0.5; \quad P_0 = 1; \quad P_1 = 2; \quad T = 1$$

So, now we just have to set up our usual Excel worksheet and find the optimal solution price path $P^*(t)$ that maximizes the *functional* $\Pi(P)$.

The Excel output is as follows dividing $T = 1$ in the usual 20 steps of length 0.05 Table 9.5-1.

The chart solution is in the following Figs. 9.5-1 and 9.5-2, where the exact solution and the approximate numerical solution are compared, and where an order 4 polynomial equation has been used as a chart trendline for both curves. This polynomial trendline equation in the chart helps us to associate also to the exact solution an equation that we can compare to the numerical path. The exact path curve is built from the exact exponential function $P^*(t) = A_1 e^{rt} + A_2 e^{-rt} + \overline{P}$.

## 9.6 Unemployment and inflation

The second model is concerning an important issue of Macroeconomics, which is the trade-off between the unemployment rate and inflation, studied thoroughly by the economist William Phillips.

The CoV can help to understand what the best combination of inflation and unemployment over time would be.

The model proposed here is the same as proposed in Alpha Chiang, op.cit., Chapter 2, which is itself an adapted model of the original one proposed by Taylor,[3] where the planning horizon has been changed from $\infty$ to a finite $T$.

---

[3]Dean Taylor, "Stopping Inflation in the Dornbush Model: Optimal Monetary Policies with Alternate Price-Adjustments Equations", *Journal of Macroeconomics*, Spring 1989, pp. 199–216.

**TABLE 9.5-1**   Monopoly numerical optimal price path.

| t | y = Optimal Price Path P | dy | dt | F = [y(1-1y+0.5y')-1(1-1y+0.5y')²-1(1-1y+y')-0.5] | Functional = Σ[y(1-1y+0.5y')-1(1-1y+0.5y')²-1(1-1y+y')-0.5] dt |
|---|---|---|---|---|---|
| 0.0000 | 1.0000 | | | | |
| 0.0500 | 1.0144 | 0.0144 | 0.0500 | 0.6588 | 0.0329 |
| 0.1000 | 1.0291 | 0.0147 | 0.0500 | 0.6578 | 0.0329 |
| 0.1500 | 1.0445 | 0.0154 | 0.0500 | 0.6613 | 0.0331 |
| 0.2000 | 1.0610 | 0.0165 | 0.0500 | 0.6690 | 0.0335 |
| 0.2500 | 1.0789 | 0.0179 | 0.0500 | 0.6811 | 0.0341 |
| 0.3000 | 1.0986 | 0.0198 | 0.0500 | 0.6975 | 0.0349 |
| 0.3500 | 1.1207 | 0.0221 | 0.0500 | 0.7186 | 0.0359 |
| 0.4000 | 1.1456 | 0.0249 | 0.0500 | 0.7447 | 0.0372 |
| 0.4500 | 1.1739 | 0.0283 | 0.0500 | 0.7763 | 0.0388 |
| 0.5000 | 1.2064 | 0.0324 | 0.0500 | 0.8139 | 0.0407 |
| 0.5500 | 1.2437 | 0.0373 | 0.0500 | 0.8581 | 0.0429 |
| 0.6000 | 1.2867 | 0.0430 | 0.0500 | 0.9097 | 0.0455 |
| 0.6500 | 1.3364 | 0.0498 | 0.0500 | 0.9694 | 0.0485 |
| 0.7000 | 1.3941 | 0.0577 | 0.0500 | 1.0382 | 0.0519 |
| 0.7500 | 1.4611 | 0.0670 | 0.0500 | 1.1169 | 0.0558 |
| 0.8000 | 1.5389 | 0.0778 | 0.0500 | 1.2064 | 0.0603 |
| 0.8500 | 1.6294 | 0.0905 | 0.0500 | 1.3074 | 0.0654 |
| 0.9000 | 1.7347 | 0.1053 | 0.0500 | 1.4204 | 0.0710 |
| 0.9500 | 1.8572 | 0.1226 | 0.0500 | 1.5456 | 0.0773 |
| 1.0000 | 2.0000 | 0.1428 | 0.0500 | 1.6828 | 0.0841 |
| | | | | α=1 | |
| | | 1.00 | | β=1 | 0.9567 |
| | | Set equal to: | | λ=0.5 | |
| y(0) | 1.00 | | | a=b=1 | |
| y(1) | 2.00 | 1.00 | | h=0.5 | |

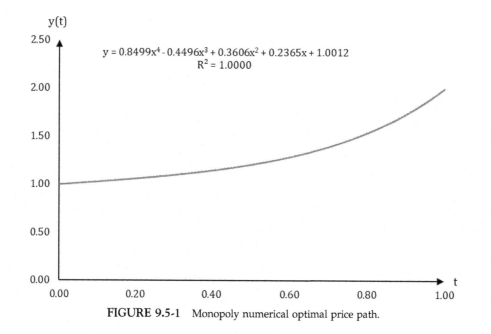

y(t)

y = 0.8499x⁴ - 0.4496x³ + 0.3606x² + 0.2365x + 1.0012
R² = 1.0000

**FIGURE 9.5-1**   Monopoly numerical optimal price path.

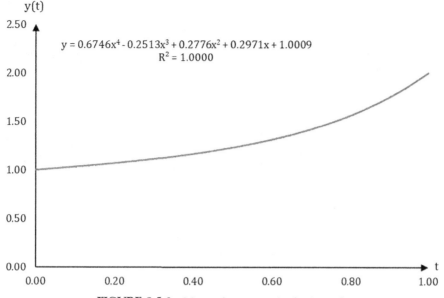

**FIGURE 9.5-2** Monopoly exact optimal price path.

Before starting with our CoV problem, let us derive the *functional* introducing the concept of *social loss function*, which in mathematical terms can be expressed as:

$$\lambda = (Y_n - Y)^2 + \alpha(p - 0)^2 \qquad (\alpha > 0) \tag{9.6-1}$$

where $Y_n$ is the desired natural income level, coupled with the ideal inflation rate $P = 0$; then, the quantity $\lambda$ indicates the undesirable deviation (squared) from ideal the income, plus the undesirable deviation (squared) from the ideal $p$, this weighted by a factor $\alpha$.

From the Lucas aggregate supply, one can derive the following expectation-based Phillips trade-off between $(Y_n - Y)$ and $p$:

$$p = -\beta(Y_n - Y) + \pi \qquad (\beta > 0) \tag{9.6-2}$$

where $\pi$ is the *expected* rate of inflation.

The formation of inflation expectations is assumed to be adaptive, according to the following:

$$\pi' = j(p - \pi) \qquad (0 < j \leq 1) \tag{9.6-3}$$

If $p > \pi$ then $\pi' > 0$ and $\pi$ will be revised upward; if $p < \pi$ then $\pi' < 0$ and $\pi$ will be revised downward.

From Eqs. (9.6-1) and (9.6-2) together we have:

$$\pi' = -\beta j(Y_n - Y) \tag{9.6-4}$$

which is:

$$(Y_n - Y) = \frac{-\pi'}{\beta j} \tag{9.6-5}$$

that leads to a new form, Eq. (9.6-1):

$$p = \frac{\pi'}{j} + \pi \tag{9.6-6}$$

Now, from Eqs. (9.6-4) and (9.6-5), we derive the following new form of the *social loss function* 9.6-1, in terms of $\pi$ and $\pi'$.

$$\lambda(\pi, \pi') = \left(\frac{\pi'}{\beta j}\right)^2 + \alpha \left(\frac{\pi'}{j} + \pi\right)^2 \tag{9.6-7}$$

which will be our integrand function in the following CoV problem

$$\min J(\pi) = \int_0^T \lambda(\pi, \pi') e^{-\rho t} dt \tag{9.6-8}$$

s.t. $\pi(0) = \pi_0 > 0$ and $\pi(T) = 0$ (T given).

The goal is to find an optimal path of $\pi$, to minimize the total present value of the *social loss* $J(\pi)$ over the time interval $[0, T]$, with a target inflation rate $= 0$ at $T$.

The exact general solution via the Euler–Lagrange is found solving the following second-order differential equation:

$$\pi'' + \pi - \Omega \pi = 0$$

where $\Omega \equiv \dfrac{\alpha \beta^2 j(\rho + j)}{1 + \alpha \beta^2}$

and the general solution is:

$$\pi^*(t) = A_1 e^{r_1 t} + A_2 e^{r_2 t} \qquad \text{(particular solution} = 0\text{)}$$

with $A_1 = \frac{-\pi_0 e^{r_2 T}}{e^{r_1 T} - e^{r_2 T}}$, $A_2 = \frac{\pi_0 e^{r_1 T}}{e^{r_1 T} - e^{r_2 T}}$ and $r_1, r_2 = \frac{1}{2}\left(p \pm \sqrt{p^2 + 4\Omega}\right)$.

Now, as usual our goal is not going to much into the details of the exact solution, but rather solving the problem numerically.

Let us assign the following parameters:

$$j = 0.5, \quad \alpha = 1, \quad \beta = 1, \quad \rho = 0.05, \quad \pi_0 = 0.05, \quad \pi_T = 0$$

**TABLE 9.6-1**   Inflation numerical solution.

| t | y = expected rate of inflation π | dy | dt | F = $[(y')/0.5]^2+[(y')/0.5+y]^2$ exp(-0.05t) | Functional = $\Sigma[(y')/0.5]^2+[(y')/0.5+y]^2$exp(-0.05t)dt |
|---|---|---|---|---|---|
| 0.0000 | 5.0000% | | | | |
| 0.0500 | 4.7426% | -0.0026 | 0.0500 | 0.0137 | 0.0007 |
| 0.1000 | 4.4866% | -0.0026 | 0.0500 | 0.0138 | 0.0007 |
| 0.1500 | 4.2317% | -0.0025 | 0.0500 | 0.0139 | 0.0007 |
| 0.2000 | 3.9779% | -0.0025 | 0.0500 | 0.0141 | 0.0007 |
| 0.2500 | 3.7252% | -0.0025 | 0.0500 | 0.0142 | 0.0007 |
| 0.3000 | 3.4734% | -0.0025 | 0.0500 | 0.0144 | 0.0007 |
| 0.3500 | 3.2225% | -0.0025 | 0.0500 | 0.0146 | 0.0007 |
| 0.4000 | 2.9723% | -0.0025 | 0.0500 | 0.0149 | 0.0007 |
| 0.4500 | 2.7228% | -0.0025 | 0.0500 | 0.0151 | 0.0008 |
| 0.5000 | 2.4739% | -0.0025 | 0.0500 | 0.0154 | 0.0008 |
| 0.5500 | 2.2256% | -0.0025 | 0.0500 | 0.0157 | 0.0008 |
| 0.6000 | 1.9776% | -0.0025 | 0.0500 | 0.0160 | 0.0008 |
| 0.6500 | 1.7301% | -0.0025 | 0.0500 | 0.0163 | 0.0008 |
| 0.7000 | 1.4828% | -0.0025 | 0.0500 | 0.0166 | 0.0008 |
| 0.7500 | 1.2356% | -0.0025 | 0.0500 | 0.0170 | 0.0008 |
| 0.8000 | 0.9886% | -0.0025 | 0.0500 | 0.0174 | 0.0009 |
| 0.8500 | 0.7416% | -0.0025 | 0.0500 | 0.0178 | 0.0009 |
| 0.9000 | 0.4946% | -0.0025 | 0.0500 | 0.0182 | 0.0009 |
| 0.9500 | 0.2474% | -0.0025 | 0.0500 | 0.0186 | 0.0009 |
| 1.0000 | 0.0000% | -0.0025 | 0.0500 | 0.0191 | 0.0010 |
| | | -0.05 | | | 0.0158 |
| | | Set equal to: | | j = 0.5 | |
| π(0) | 5.00% | -0.05 | | α = 1 | |
| π(1) | 0.00% | | | β = 1 | |

and our Excel output of the numerical optimization, after launching the Solver, is in Table 9.6-1:

The exact solution corresponds to the numerical solution, as we can see comparing Table 9.6-2 with Table 9.6-1. In Fig. 9.6-1, we plot the optimal path of π with the associated the best fitting curve equation.

## 9.7 The Eisner–Strotz model

The Eisner–Strotz model focuses on finding an optimal capital path $K^*(t)$ that maximizes the total present value firm net profit in the following CoV problem:

$$\max \Pi(K) = \int_0^\infty [\pi(K) - C(K')]e^{-\rho t}dt \tag{9.7-1}$$

$$s.t. \quad K(0) = K_0$$

**TABLE 9.6-2**  Unemployment and inflation model
exact Solution and error vs. numerical
solution.

| t | y Exact | Error |
|---|---|---|
| 0.000 | 0.050 | 0.000 |
| 0.050 | 0.047 | 0.000 |
| 0.100 | 0.045 | 0.000 |
| 0.150 | 0.042 | 0.000 |
| 0.200 | 0.040 | 0.000 |
| 0.250 | 0.037 | 0.000 |
| 0.300 | 0.035 | 0.000 |
| 0.350 | 0.032 | 0.000 |
| 0.400 | 0.030 | 0.000 |
| 0.450 | 0.027 | 0.000 |
| 0.500 | 0.025 | 0.000 |
| 0.550 | 0.022 | 0.000 |
| 0.600 | 0.020 | 0.000 |
| 0.650 | 0.017 | 0.000 |
| 0.700 | 0.015 | 0.000 |
| 0.750 | 0.012 | 0.000 |
| 0.800 | 0.010 | 0.000 |
| 0.850 | 0.007 | 0.000 |
| 0.900 | 0.005 | 0.000 |
| 0.950 | 0.003 | 0.000 |
| 1.000 | 0.000 | 0.000 |

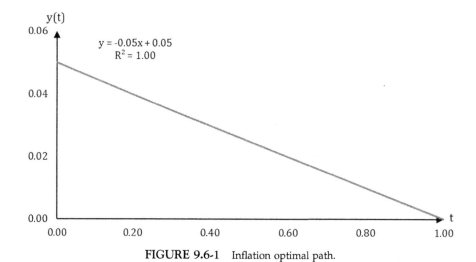

$y = -0.05x + 0.05$
$R^2 = 1.00$

**FIGURE 9.6-1**  Inflation optimal path.

where $\pi(K)$ is a profit quadratic function associated to the capital path defined as follows:

$$\pi = \alpha K - \beta K^2 \qquad (\alpha, \ \beta > 0)$$

and $C(K')$ is the adjustment cost, in which the firm incurs according to the speed of expansion $K'(t)$ defined as:

$$C = aK'^2 + bK' \qquad (a, b > 0)$$

$K'(t)$ can be interpreted economically as the net investment path.

So, our integrand function becomes:

$$F = \pi(K) - C(K') = \left( \alpha K - \beta K^2 - aK'^2 - bK' \right) e^{-\rho t}$$

which leads to the following Euler–Lagrange second-order differential equation:

$$K'' - \rho K' - \frac{\beta}{a} K = \frac{b\rho - \alpha}{2a}$$

whose general exact solution is given by:

$$K^*(t) = A_1 e^{r_1 t} + A_2 e^{r_2 t} + \overline{K}$$

where the characteristic roots are $r_1, r_2 = \frac{1}{2} \left( \rho \pm \sqrt{\rho^2 + \frac{4\beta}{a}} \right)$ and $\overline{K} = \frac{\alpha - bp}{2\beta}$, which is the particular solution and from which we have:

$$K_0 = A_1 + A_2 + \overline{K}$$

Now, referring to the general solution $K^*(t)$ we see that while the second exponential term (where $r_2 < 0$) tends to zero as $t \to \infty$, the first exponential term (where $r_1 > 0$) tends to $\lessgtr \pm \infty$ if $A_1 \lessgtr 0$. Since neither $+\infty$ nor $\infty$ is acceptable for the terminal value of K on economic grounds, the only way out is to set $A_1 = 0$, having $A_2 = K_0 - \overline{K}$ and a new form of the general solution is:

$$K^*(t) = \left( K_0 - \overline{K} \right) e^{r_2 t} + \overline{K}$$

Now, as usual let us solve numerically the problem with the following parameters:

$$\alpha = \beta = a = b = 1, \quad \rho = 0.05, \quad K(0) = 0.20$$

We can adapt our worksheet to the fact that the original problem is expressed in terms infinite planning horizon where $T = \infty$ by expanding as much as possible the time horizon, to find the asymptotic level of $\overline{K} = \frac{1 - 0.05}{2} = 0.475$ resulting from the parameters we have set. We decide to set then $T = 10$, and the numerical output solution is as follows in Table 9.7-1 and Fig. 9.7-1.

As we can see the Solver finds that $K^*$ converges to the particular solution $\overline{K}$ at $T = 10$, as the characteristic root is negative ($r_2 < 0$), with the factor $K_0 - \overline{K}$ that gets close to zero as we move close to $T = 10$.

Fig. 9.7-1 explains the convergence of the optimal capital path to the level of $\overline{K}$ over the time interval in case of $T = 1$ and $T = 10$.

9. Calculus of variations

**TABLE 9.7-1**  Capital numerical solution.

| t | y = K capital | dy | dt | F = $(\alpha y - \beta y^2 - ay'^2 - by')\exp(-0.05t)$ | Functional = $\Sigma[(\alpha y - \beta y^2 - ay'^2 - by')\exp(-0.05t)]dt$ |
|---|---|---|---|---|---|
| 0.0000 | 0.2000 | | | | |
| 0.5000 | 0.3059 | 0.1059 | 0.5000 | -0.0433 | -0.0216 |
| 1.0000 | 0.3710 | 0.0651 | 0.5000 | 0.0819 | 0.0410 |
| 1.5000 | 0.4112 | 0.0402 | 0.5000 | 0.1441 | 0.0721 |
| 2.0000 | 0.4359 | 0.0247 | 0.5000 | 0.1756 | 0.0878 |
| 2.5000 | 0.4511 | 0.0152 | 0.5000 | 0.1909 | 0.0955 |
| 3.0000 | 0.4604 | 0.0093 | 0.5000 | 0.1975 | 0.0988 |
| 3.5000 | 0.4661 | 0.0057 | 0.5000 | 0.1992 | 0.0996 |
| 4.0000 | 0.4696 | 0.0035 | 0.5000 | 0.1981 | 0.0991 |
| 4.5000 | 0.4718 | 0.0022 | 0.5000 | 0.1955 | 0.0977 |
| 5.0000 | 0.4731 | 0.0014 | 0.5000 | 0.1920 | 0.0960 |
| 5.5000 | 0.4740 | 0.0009 | 0.5000 | 0.1880 | 0.0940 |
| 6.0000 | 0.4746 | 0.0006 | 0.5000 | 0.1839 | 0.0920 |
| 6.5000 | 0.4749 | 0.0003 | 0.5000 | 0.1797 | 0.0898 |
| 7.0000 | 0.4751 | 0.0002 | 0.5000 | 0.1755 | 0.0877 |
| 7.5000 | 0.4752 | 0.0001 | 0.5000 | 0.1713 | 0.0857 |
| 8.0000 | 0.4751 | 0.0000 | 0.5000 | 0.1672 | 0.0836 |
| 8.5000 | 0.4751 | -0.0001 | 0.5000 | 0.1631 | 0.0816 |
| 9.0000 | 0.4750 | -0.0001 | 0.5000 | 0.1591 | 0.0796 |
| 9.5000 | 0.4749 | 0.0000 | 0.5000 | 0.1551 | 0.0776 |
| 10.0000 | 0.4750 | 0.0000 | 0.5000 | 0.1512 | 0.0756 |
| | | 0.2750 | $\alpha$ | 1.00 | 1.6129 |
| | | Set equal to: | $\beta$ | 1.00 | |
| k0 | 0.2000 | | a | 1.00 | |
| k10 | 0.4750 | 0.2750 | b | 1.00 | |

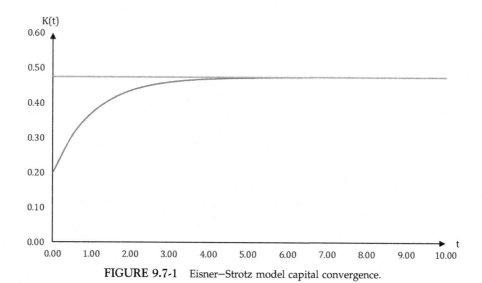

FIGURE 9.7-1  Eisner–Strotz model capital convergence.

## 9.8 The optimal consumption Ramsey model

One of the models often mentioned in the literature of CoV is the Ramsey model, which attempts to model the optimal consumption (and so the optimal savings) path to maximize the present value of a nation utility function over time interval $[0, T]$.

The CoV problem can be stated as follows:

$$\max U(K) = \int_0^T [U(C(t))]e^{-\rho t}dt = \int_0^T [U(f(K(t)) - K'(t))]e^{-\rho t}dt \qquad (9.8\text{-}1)$$

$$s.t.\ K(0) = K_0 \text{ and } K(T) = K_T$$

where $f(k(t)) = C(t) + K'(t)$ is the macroeconomic total output function equal to the economy aggregate demand, made of total consumption plus the total investments (not considering in this context the Government consumption G and the difference between Exports and Imports).

So, let us consider now a Constant Relative Risk Aversion Utility function and an income output function depending on the capital over time, defined as:

$$U(C) = \frac{C^{(1-\gamma)} - 1}{1 - \gamma}; f(k) = bK \qquad (\gamma > 0,\ b > 0)$$

plugging it into the *functional* 9.8-1, the problem becomes:

$$\max U(K) = \int_0^T \left[ \frac{(bK - K')^{1-\gamma}}{1 - \gamma} \right] e^{-\rho t}dt \qquad (9.8\text{-}2)$$

$$s.t.\ K(0) = K_0 \text{ and } K(T) = K_T$$

where we have to find the optimal $K^*(t)$ and indirectly also $C^*(t)$ and $K'^*(t)$.

Again, the general solution found via the Euler–Lagrange equation has a similar form to the one seen before:

$$K^*(t) = A_1 e^{bt} + A_2 e^{(b-\rho)t/\gamma}$$

it must also follow that $A_1 + A_2 = K_0$ and $K(T) = A_1 e^{bT} + A_2 e^{(b-\rho)T/\gamma}$ from which we derive $A_2 = \frac{K_0 e^b - K(T)}{e^b - e^{(b-\rho)T/\gamma}}$.

As usual, with the following parameters:

$$b = 1 \text{ and } \rho = 0.10,\ K_0 = 5,\ K_T = 0 \text{ (no capital left after T) and } K_T = 7$$

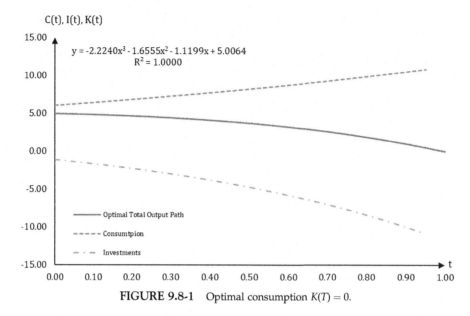

**FIGURE 9.8-1**   Optimal consumption $K(T) = 0$.

We derive our output numerical solution in Fig. 9.8-1, where the different patterns in Consumption, Investments, and Total Output are graphed, together with the equation trendline fitting the optimal path $K^*(t)$, in both scenarios of terminal capital $K_T$ (Fig. 9.8-2).

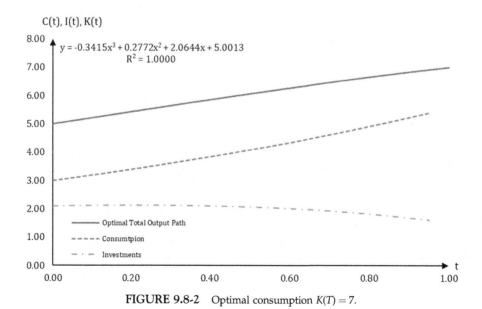

**FIGURE 9.8-2**   Optimal consumption $K(T) = 7$.

## 9.9 Inventory dynamic optimization

The example presented in this section is the case of inventory optimization and a consequent optimal production schedule. The problem is that of a firm receiving an order for $B$ units of product to be delivered by time $T$, seeking an optimal production schedule for filling the order at the specified delivery date at minimum cost.

The unit production cost rises linearly with the production rate, while the unit cost of holding the inventory per unit time is constant.

Let $y(t)$ denote the inventory accumulated by time $t$. Then we have $y(0) = 0$ and we must achieve $y(T) = B$.

The inventory level, at any time, is the cumulated past production, while the rate of change of inventory is the production rate $y'(t) = \frac{dy}{dt}$.

Thus, the firm's total cost at any moment $t$ is expressed as follows:

$$[c_1 y'(t)]y'(t) + c_2 y(t) = c_1 y'(t)^2 + c_2 y(t)$$

where the first term is the total production cost (the product of the unit cost of production and the level of production) and the second term is the total cost of holding the inventory; $c_1$ and $c_2$ are positive constants.

The firm's objective is to determine a production rate $y'(t)$ and an optimal inventory accumulation path $y(t)$ to minimize the total cost over the time interval $[0, T]$. The CoV problem is then formulated as follows:

$$\min J(y) = \int_0^T \left[ c_1 y'(t)^2 + c_2 y(t) \right] dt$$

$$s.t.\ y(0) = 0 \ \text{and}\ y(T) = B \ \text{with}\ y'(t) \geq 0$$

The general exact solution found via the Euler–Lagrange equation is:

$$y^*(t) = \frac{c_2}{c_1} \frac{1}{4} t^2 + k_1 t + k_2$$

With the given boundary conditions it must follow that:

$$k_1 = \frac{B}{T} - \frac{c_2}{c_1} \frac{T}{4} \ \text{and}\ k_2 = 0$$

which complete the general solution $y^*(t)$.

Now, as usual our goal is to give a numerical optimal path of $y^*(t)$, found it computer based via the Excel Solver resolution. We assume then the following parameters:

$c_1 = 10,\ c_2 = 5,\ y(T) = B = 2$

(the quantity of products we are required to deliver) and $T = 1$

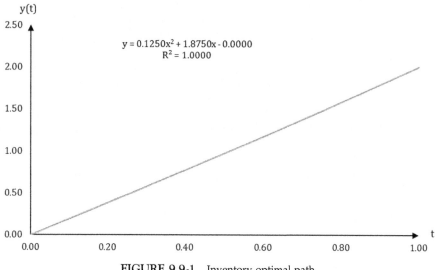

**FIGURE 9.9-1**   Inventory optimal path.

Notice that the fitting equation coefficients in Fig. 9.9-1 are the same as the exact solution (Table 9.9-1).

We have therefore the following coefficients in the equation of $y^*(t)$:

$$\frac{c_2}{c_1}\frac{1}{4} = \frac{5}{10}\frac{1}{4} = 0.125$$

and

$$k_1 = \frac{2}{1} - \frac{5}{10}\frac{1}{4} = 1.875$$

## 9.10 Optimal capital structure and the firm cost of capital

In this example, we will look at a typical issue of Corporate Finance, which is the one of finding the optimal firm capital structure, maximizing the firm value and, at the same time, minimizing the cost of capital (e.g., the *Weighted Average Cost of Capital: WACC*).

Let us assume we have an underlevered publicly traded firm with a capital structure not considered *optimal* by its Chief Financial Officer (CFO), according to the Modigliani–Miller theory[4] and other Capital Structure theories. This is because the firm does not carry

---

[4]See F. Modigliani and M. Miller, "The Cost of Capital, Corporation Finance and the Theory of Investments", *The American Economic Review*, Vol. 48, No. 3, June 1958 and F. Modigliani and M. Miller, "Income Taxes and the Cost of Capital: A Correction", *The American Economic Review*, Vol. 53, No. 3, June 1963.

**TABLE 9.9-1**  Inventory numerical solution.

| t | y Inventory path | dy | dt | $F = [10(dy/dt)^2 + 5y]$ | Functional $= \Sigma[10(dy/dt)^2 + 5y]dt$ |
|---|---|---|---|---|---|
| 0.0000 | 0.0000 | 0.0941 | 0.0500 | 35.8575 | 1.7929 |
| 0.0500 | 0.0941 | 0.0947 | 0.0500 | 36.8013 | 1.8401 |
| 0.1000 | 0.1887 | 0.0953 | 0.0500 | 37.7531 | 1.8877 |
| 0.1500 | 0.2840 | 0.0959 | 0.0500 | 38.7127 | 1.9356 |
| 0.2000 | 0.3800 | 0.0966 | 0.0500 | 39.6797 | 1.9840 |
| 0.2500 | 0.4765 | 0.0972 | 0.0500 | 40.6533 | 2.0327 |
| 0.3000 | 0.5737 | 0.0978 | 0.0500 | 41.6329 | 2.0816 |
| 0.3500 | 0.6716 | 0.0984 | 0.0500 | 42.6177 | 2.1309 |
| 0.4000 | 0.7700 | 0.0991 | 0.0500 | 43.6070 | 2.1803 |
| 0.4500 | 0.8691 | 0.0997 | 0.0500 | 44.6006 | 2.2300 |
| 0.5000 | 0.9688 | 0.1003 | 0.0500 | 45.5988 | 2.2799 |
| 0.5500 | 1.0691 | 0.1009 | 0.0500 | 46.6022 | 2.3301 |
| 0.6000 | 1.1700 | 0.1016 | 0.0500 | 47.6123 | 2.3806 |
| 0.6500 | 1.2716 | 0.1022 | 0.0500 | 48.6306 | 2.4315 |
| 0.7000 | 1.3738 | 0.1028 | 0.0500 | 49.6589 | 2.4829 |
| 0.7500 | 1.4766 | 0.1034 | 0.0500 | 50.6977 | 2.5349 |
| 0.8000 | 1.5800 | 0.1041 | 0.0500 | 51.7450 | 2.5872 |
| 0.8500 | 1.6841 | 0.1047 | 0.0500 | 52.7936 | 2.6397 |
| 0.9000 | 1.7888 | 0.1053 | 0.0500 | 53.8276 | 2.6914 |
| 0.9500 | 1.8941 | 0.1059 | 0.0500 | 54.8784 | 2.7439 |
| 1.0000 | 2.0000 | | | | |
| | | | | | 45.1980 |

|  |  | Set equal to: |  | c1 = cost of production | 10.00 |
|---|---|---|---|---|---|
| y(0) | 0.00 | 2.00 |  | c2 = cost of storage | 5.00 |
| y(1) | 2.00 | 2.00 |  | B=2 | 2.00 |

any debt and the current *Debt-to-Equity* (D/E) ratio is zero. The CFO knows that all the other competitors use at least either some bank debt or corporate bonds, and the objective now is to know how the firm could theoretically reach over the time interval [0, T] the optimal capital structure, to minimize the firm *cost of capital* and maximize the *enterprise value*, which is in this context simply the present value of the unlevered cash flows from $t=0$ to T.

Let us define the *Weighted Average Cost of Capital* as follows:

$$WACC \ = \ K_e[E \ / \ (E+D)] \ + \ [K_d(1-tax)D \ / \ (E+D)]$$

where $E$ = *market value of Equity*; $D$ = *market value of Debt*; $K_e$ = cost of equity, $K_d$ = cost of debt and *tax* = *marginal tax rate*, and where the *cost of equity* is defined according to the *Capital Asset Pricing Model*:

$$K_e \ = \ Rfr \ + \ \beta_L ERP$$

where $\beta_L$ is the *beta levered (systematic risk factor)*, ERP is the *Equity Risk Premium* and Rfr the *Risk-free rate*.

If we go into more details of the *cost of equity*, we notice something of key importance, that is $K_e$ also depends on the D/E ratio of the company, implicitly incorporated in the *betalevered* $\beta_L$. This means that the more the company borrows money from banks, the higher the financial leverage and the higher the risk perceived by the shareholders, who will require a higher remuneration of equity capital.

So, the level of firm D/E is incorporated into $K_e$, via $\beta_L$, as follows[5]:

$$\beta_L \ = \ \beta_U[1+(1-tax)(D \ / \ E)]$$

where $\beta_U$ and the *cost of equity* becomes:

$$K_e \ = \ Rfr \ + \ ERP[\beta_U[1+(1-tax)(D \ / \ E)]$$

Also, the *cost of debt*, $K_d$, usually depends on the D/E ratio of the company, according to the fact that the financial system normally will charge the company a higher default spread if the company has a higher degree of financial leverage because of the increased cost of financial distress.

Now, for the *cost of debt* of our firm, we assume the following linear relation:

$$K_d \ = \ K_d(0) + \ 100bps(D \ / \ E) + 10bps(D \ / \ E)'$$

which means that we make the *cost of debt* $K_d$ increase as a function of both the *D/E ratio* and its slope as well, adding 100 bps (= 1.00%) per unit of D/E and other additional 10 bps for $(D/E)'$ (namely, the higher the slope in D/E path the more the basis points charged).

---

[5]See Aswath Damodaran, *Investment Valuation*, 2012, Wiley, third Edition, chapter 8.

In summary, the WACC is rearranged algebraically as follows:

$$WACC = \left\{ Rfr + ERP\left[\beta_U[1 + (1-t)(\tfrac{D}{E})]\right]\right\} \underbrace{\left[1 - (\frac{\frac{D}{E}}{\frac{D}{E}+1})\right]}_{} + \underbrace{\left[K_d(0) + 100bps\left(\frac{D}{E}\right) + 10bps\left(\frac{D}{E}\right)'\right]}_{}(1-t)\underbrace{\frac{\frac{D}{E}}{\frac{D}{E}+1}}_{}$$

| Cost of Equity | Equity weight | Cost of Debt | Tax saving and debt weight |

which depends both on $D/E(t)$ and $D/E'(t)$, and it will appear in our integrand function under the following CoV problem:

$$\max J(y(t) = D/E(t)) = \int_0^T \frac{1}{(1 + WACC)^t} dt$$

$$s.t. \ (D/E)_0 = 0 \ \text{and} \ (D/E)_T = Free$$

Essentially, we want to maximize the present value of the cash flow stream in the interval $[0, T]$, finding the optimal $D/E$ ratio path (the optimal $y^*(t)$ in the usual notations), which is incorporated into the WACC as explained before. Also, the problem is a *vertical-terminal-line* problem with $y(T) = \left(\frac{D}{E}\right)_T = Free$. So, we let the system find the optimal solution at $T$. As usual, we want to find the numerical solution of the problem, Excel Solver based, and we assume the following data for $K_e$ and $K_d$ (Table 9.10-1).

As the company at $t = 0$ does not carry any debt burden, we assume it can enjoy the best credit rating available (AAA) and a correspondent *cost of debt* of 1.00%. Our linear function in $K_d$ will ensure that a spread is added to this initial *cost of debt* as the $D/E$ moves away from zero.

From Table 9.10-2 and Fig. 9.10-1, the numerical solution of the problem would be to reach a target $\frac{D}{E} = 0.8536$ which implies an optimal capital structure of *Debt Capital* $\cong 46\%$ and *Equity Capital* $\cong 54\%$ being the minimum $WACC = 5.99\%$, with *Enterprise Value* $= 0.9699$, assuming for simplicity a constant unlevered cash flow stream equal to 1 and no terminal value at $T$. The company should obviously check the sustainability of the suggested degree of financial leverage according to its operating margins. Notice that if we pushed the $D/E$ ratio beyond the optimal point, we would have an increasing WACC beyond the optimal point of 5.99%, because of the activation of the distress costs in the formula of $K_d$, obtaining the usual convex WACC curve (Fig. 9.10-2).

**TABLE 9.10-1** Cost of capital inputs.

| COST OF EQUITY INPUTS | | COST OF DEBT | |
|---|---|---|---|
| Risk Free Rate | 0.41% | 1.00% | |
| Equity Risk Premium (ERP) | 5.00% | AAA Rating | |
| Unlevered beta | 1.2000 | | |
| Tax rate | 30.00% | | |

**TABLE 9.10-2**   Numerical Optimal Capital Structure and WACC solutions.

| t | y Optimal Capital Structure Path D/E | dy | dt | F = 1/(1+WACC)$^t$ | Functional = Σ[1/(1+WACC)$^t$]dt | WACC | k$_e$ = rfr + β$_L$(ERP) | k$_d$ = K$_d$(0)+ 100bps(D/E)+10bps(D/E)$^2$ | Natural Boundary Cond. at T |
|---|---|---|---|---|---|---|---|---|---|
| 0.0000 | 0.0000 |  |  |  |  | 6.41% | 6.41% | 1.00% |  |
| 0.0500 | 0.0644 | 0.0644 | 0.0500 | 0.9969 | 0.0498 | 6.33% | 6.68% | 1.19% | 0.00 |
| 0.1000 | 0.1283 | 0.0640 | 0.0500 | 0.9939 | 0.0497 | 6.26% | 6.95% | 1.26% | 0.00 |
| 0.1500 | 0.1915 | 0.0632 | 0.0500 | 0.9910 | 0.0496 | 6.20% | 7.21% | 1.32% | 0.00 |
| 0.2000 | 0.2535 | 0.0620 | 0.0500 | 0.9881 | 0.0494 | 6.16% | 7.47% | 1.38% | 0.00 |
| 0.2500 | 0.3141 | 0.0606 | 0.0500 | 0.9853 | 0.0493 | 6.12% | 7.73% | 1.44% | 0.00 |
| 0.3000 | 0.3729 | 0.0588 | 0.0500 | 0.9824 | 0.0491 | 6.09% | 7.98% | 1.49% | 0.00 |
| 0.3500 | 0.4297 | 0.0568 | 0.0500 | 0.9796 | 0.0490 | 6.07% | 8.21% | 1.54% | 0.00 |
| 0.4000 | 0.4841 | 0.0544 | 0.0500 | 0.9768 | 0.0488 | 6.05% | 8.44% | 1.59% | 0.00 |
| 0.4500 | 0.5359 | 0.0518 | 0.0500 | 0.9740 | 0.0487 | 6.04% | 8.66% | 1.64% | 0.00 |
| 0.5000 | 0.5847 | 0.0488 | 0.0500 | 0.9712 | 0.0486 | 6.03% | 8.87% | 1.68% | 0.00 |
| 0.5500 | 0.6304 | 0.0457 | 0.0500 | 0.9684 | 0.0484 | 6.02% | 9.06% | 1.72% | 0.00 |
| 0.6000 | 0.6726 | 0.0422 | 0.0500 | 0.9656 | 0.0483 | 6.02% | 9.23% | 1.76% | 0.00 |
| 0.6500 | 0.7110 | 0.0385 | 0.0500 | 0.9628 | 0.0481 | 6.01% | 9.40% | 1.79% | 0.00 |
| 0.7000 | 0.7455 | 0.0345 | 0.0500 | 0.9600 | 0.0480 | 6.01% | 9.54% | 1.81% | 0.00 |
| 0.7500 | 0.7757 | 0.0302 | 0.0500 | 0.9572 | 0.0479 | 6.01% | 9.67% | 1.84% | 0.00 |
| 0.8000 | 0.8014 | 0.0257 | 0.0500 | 0.9544 | 0.0477 | 6.00% | 9.78% | 1.85% | 0.00 |
| 0.8500 | 0.8223 | 0.0209 | 0.0500 | 0.9517 | 0.0476 | 6.00% | 9.86% | 1.86% | 0.00 |
| 0.9000 | 0.8381 | 0.0158 | 0.0500 | 0.9489 | 0.0474 | 6.00% | 9.93% | 1.87% | 0.00 |
| 0.9500 | 0.8486 | 0.0105 | 0.0500 | 0.9462 | 0.0473 | 6.00% | 9.97% | 1.87% | 0.00 |
| 1.0000 | 0.8536 | 0.0049 | 0.0500 | 0.9435 | 0.0472 | 5.99% | 10.00% | 1.86% | 0.00 |

0.9699

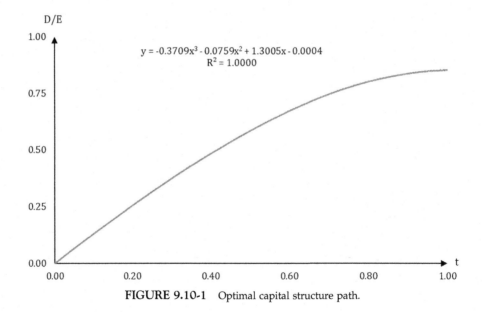

$$y = -0.3709x^3 - 0.0759x^2 + 1.3005x - 0.0004$$
$$R^2 = 1.0000$$

**FIGURE 9.10-1**   Optimal capital structure path.

We can easily inspect that the natural boundary condition for *vertical-line-problems* $\left[\frac{\partial(T,y(T),y'(T))}{\partial y'}\right] = 0$ is also numerically satisfied at $T = 1$.

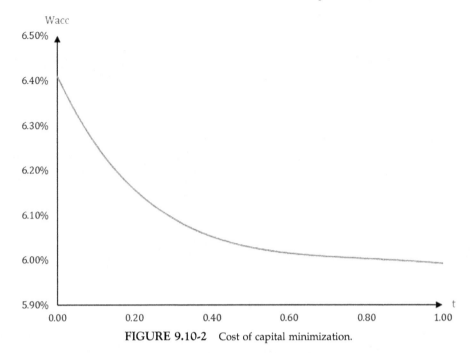

FIGURE 9.10-2    Cost of capital minimization.

## 9.11 Contour lines solution for Calculus of Variations using the VBA code

Let us see now how the second approximate numerical approach (see end of Section 9.2) can be implemented easily in Excel using a simple VBA code.

### EXAMPLE 1

Continuing the **Examples 3.a and 3.b** of Section 9.2, the original problem was to find the extremal of the *functional* in the following problem, with exact optimal path $y^*(t) = \frac{1}{24}t^3 + \frac{23}{24}t + 1$:

$$\min J = \int_0^1 (ty + 2y'^2)dt$$

$$s.t.\ y(0) = 1 \text{ and } y(1) = 2$$

After discretization, according to the form in 9.2-1, we have:

$$\min J = \left[ t_1(1 + \Delta_1 y) + 2\frac{(\Delta_1 y)^2}{(\Delta_1 t)^2} \right] \Delta_1 t + \left[ t_2(1 + \Delta_1 y + \Delta_2 y) + 2\frac{(\Delta_2 y)^2}{(\Delta_2 t)^2} \right] \Delta_2 t$$

III. Dynamic optimization

$$s.t.\ \Delta_1 y + \Delta_2 y = 1$$

With $t_1 = 0.5$, $t_2 = 1$ and $\Delta_1 t = \Delta_2 t = 0.5$ we have:

$$J = \left[ 0.5(1 + \Delta_1 y) + 2\frac{(\Delta_1 y)^2}{(0.5)^2} \right] 0.5 + \left[ 1(2) + 2\frac{(\Delta_2 y)^2}{(0.5)^2} \right] 0.5$$

where $J$ is a function of two independent variables $\Delta_1 y$ and $\Delta_2 y$, problem that we can transform into a one-independent variable problem just setting $J = c$ and taking $\Delta_1 y$ as the only independent variable and $\Delta_2 y$ as the dependent variable. We can then map all the curves as a function of $J = c$ to see when the given constraint $\Delta_1 y + \Delta_2 y = 1$ is met, and at the same time, $J = c$ is chosen at its optimal level.

The *contour map*, as a function of the constant $J = c$, is:

$$\Delta_2 y = \left[ \frac{c - 1.25 - \Delta_1 y(0.25 + 4\Delta_1 y)}{4} \right]^{\frac{1}{2}} \tag{9.11-1}$$

The goal, like in the CoV discretized Lagrange approach, is to find the optimal values of $\Delta_1 y$ and $\Delta_2 y$.

Let us go in Excel now, open a worksheet, and set up the first two *Columns* as in Fig. 9.11-1, where under *Column B* we have inserted Eq. (9.11-1) and *Column A* the independent variable $\Delta_1 y$ divided by intervals of length 0.05, starting from zero.

Going further to the right of our worksheet, under *Column C* we store the constraint of the problem $\Delta_1 y + \Delta_2 y$, while under *Column D* we have an *if statement* that must return **True**, when the *Column C* returns the closest value to what is required by the constraint ($\Delta_1 y + \Delta_2 y = 1$).

| | A | B | C | D | | E | F | G |
|---|---|---|---|---|---|---|---|---|
| 1 | Δ1y | Δ2y | Constraint | s.t. Δ1y+Δ2y=1 | Test | | Δ1y | Δ2y |
| 2 | 0 | =SQRT(($I$2-1.25-0.25*A2-4*A2^2)/4) | =A2+B2 | =IF(ABS(C2-1)<0.001;"True";"False" | =IF(D2="False";0;1) | | 0 | =1-F2 |
| 3 | 0.05 | =SQRT(($I$2-1.25-0.25*A3-4*A3^2)/4) | =A3+B3 | =IF(ABS(C3-1)<0.001;"True";"False" | =IF(D3="False";0;1) | | =A3 | =1-F3 |
| 4 | 0.1 | =SQRT(($I$2-1.25-0.25*A4-4*A4^2)/4) | =A4+B4 | =IF(ABS(C4-1)<0.001;"True";"False" | =IF(D4="False";0;1) | | =F3+0.05 | =1-F4 |
| 5 | 0.15 | =SQRT(($I$2-1.25-0.25*A5-4*A5^2)/4) | =A5+B5 | =IF(ABS(C5-1)<0.001;"True";"False" | =IF(D5="False";0;1) | | =F4+0.05 | =1-F5 |
| 6 | 0.2 | =SQRT(($I$2-1.25-0.25*A6-4*A6^2)/4) | =A6+B6 | =IF(ABS(C6-1)<0.001;"True";"False" | =IF(D6="False";0;1) | | =F5+0.05 | =1-F6 |
| 7 | 0.25 | =SQRT(($I$2-1.25-0.25*A7-4*A7^2)/4) | =A7+B7 | =IF(ABS(C7-1)<0.001;"True";"False" | =IF(D7="False";0;1) | | =F6+0.05 | =1-F7 |
| 8 | 0.3 | =SQRT(($I$2-1.25-0.25*A8-4*A8^2)/4) | =A8+B8 | =IF(ABS(C8-1)<0.001;"True";"False" | =IF(D8="False";0;1) | | =F7+0.05 | =1-F8 |
| 9 | 0.35 | =SQRT(($I$2-1.25-0.25*A9-4*A9^2)/4) | =A9+B9 | =IF(ABS(C9-1)<0.001;"True";"False" | =IF(D9="False";0;1) | | =F8+0.05 | =1-F9 |
| 10 | 0.4 | =SQRT(($I$2-1.25-0.25*A10-4*A10^2)/4) | =A10+B10 | =IF(ABS(C10-1)<0.001;"True";"False | =IF(D10="False";0;1) | | =F9+0.05 | =1-F10 |
| 11 | 0.45 | =SQRT(($I$2-1.25-0.25*A11-4*A11^2)/4) | =A11+B11 | =IF(ABS(C11-1)<0.001;"True";"False | =IF(D11="False";0;1) | | =F10+0.05 | =1-F11 |
| 12 | 0.484375 | =SQRT(($I$2-1.25-0.25*A12-4*A12^2)/4) | =A12+B12 | =IF(ABS(C12-1)<0.001;"True";"F. | =IF(D12="False";0;1) | | =F11+0.05 | =1-F12 |
| 13 | 0.55 | =SQRT(($I$2-1.25-0.25*A13-4*A13^2)/4) | =A13+B13 | =IF(ABS(C13-1)<0.001;"True";"False | =IF(D13="False";0;1) | | =F12+0.05 | =1-F13 |
| 14 | 0.6 | =SQRT(($I$2-1.25-0.25*A14-4*A14^2)/4) | =A14+B14 | =IF(ABS(C14-1)<0.001;"True";"False | =IF(D14="False";0;1) | | =F13+0.05 | =1-F14 |
| 15 | 0.65 | =SQRT(($I$2-1.25-0.25*A15-4*A15^2)/4) | =A15+B15 | =IF(ABS(C15-1)<0.001;"True";"False | =IF(D15="False";0;1) | | =F14+0.05 | =1-F15 |
| 16 | 0.675 | =SQRT(($I$2-1.25-0.25*A16-4*A16^2)/4) | =A16+B16 | =IF(ABS(C16-1)<0.001;"True";"False | =IF(D16="False";0;1) | | =F15+0.05 | =1-F16 |
| 17 | 0.69 | =SQRT(($I$2-1.25-0.25*A17-4*A17^2)/4) | =A17+B17 | =IF(ABS(C17-1)<0.001;"True";"False | =IF(D17="False";0;1) | | =F16+0.05 | =1-F17 |
| 18 | 0.695 | =SQRT(($I$2-1.25-0.25*A18-4*A18^2)/4) | =A18+B18 | =IF(ABS(C18-1)<0.001;"True";"False | =IF(D18="False";0;1) | | =F17+0.05 | =1-F18 |
| 19 | 0.6955 | =SQRT(($I$2-1.25-0.25*A19-4*A19^2)/4) | =A19+B19 | =IF(ABS(C19-1)<0.001;"True";"False | =IF(D19="False";0;1) | | =F18+0.05 | =1-F19 |
| 20 | 0.696 | =SQRT(($I$2-1.25-0.25*A20-4*A20^2)/4) | =A20+B20 | =IF(ABS(C20-1)<0.001;"True";"False | =IF(D20="False";0;1) | | =F19+0.05 | =1-F20 |
| 21 | 0.6965 | =SQRT(($I$2-1.25-0.25*A21-4*A21^2)/4) | =A21+B21 | =IF(ABS(C21-1)<0.001;"True";"False | =IF(D21="False";0;1) | | =F20+0.05 | =1-F21 |
| 22 | 0.697 | =SQRT(($I$2-1.25-0.25*A22-4*A22^2)/4) | =A22+B22 | =IF(ABS(C22-1)<0.001;"True";"False | | | =F21+0.05 | =1-F22 |
| 23 | | | | | | | | |
| 24 | | | | | | | | |
| 25 | | | | Test Macro | =IFERROR(SUM(E2:E21);0) | | | |

**FIGURE 9.11-1**   Example 1 excel set-up.

The *if statement* is:

*If (absolute difference*$(C_i - 1) < \varepsilon)$ *then return True  otherwise return* **False**

with $\varepsilon = 0.001$.

*Column F* just stores the value 1 *if* cell of *Column D* is **True** and the value **0** *if Column D* is **False.** *Cell E25* calculates the sum within the specified Excel range that must be always equal to 1 (namely just one solution is optimal).

*Column F* and *Column G* store the linear equation constraint:

$$\Delta_2 y = 1 - \Delta_1 y$$

Further to the right of our Excel worksheet (see Figure 9.11-3) we decided to store the entire *contour map* with the help of the Excel Data Table tool, like we did in the two-variable calculus of Chapter 2. The Data Table will allow us to graph the set of contour lines, of which just one is the optimal to choose.

**TABLE 9.11-1**   Example 1 excel output.

| $\Delta_1 y$ | $\Delta_2 y$ | Constraint | s.t. $\Delta_1 y + \Delta_2 y = 1$ | Test | $\Delta_1 y$ | $\Delta_2 y$ |
|---|---|---|---|---|---|---|
| 0.0000 | 0.7280 | 0.7280 | False | 0.0000 | 0.0000 | 1.0000 |
| 0.0500 | 0.7241 | 0.7741 | False | 0.0000 | 0.0500 | 0.9500 |
| 0.1000 | 0.7168 | 0.8168 | False | 0.0000 | 0.1000 | 0.9000 |
| 0.1500 | 0.7058 | 0.8558 | False | 0.0000 | 0.1500 | 0.8500 |
| 0.2000 | 0.6910 | 0.8910 | False | 0.0000 | 0.2000 | 0.8000 |
| 0.2500 | 0.6722 | 0.9222 | False | 0.0000 | 0.2500 | 0.7500 |
| 0.3000 | 0.6490 | 0.9490 | False | 0.0000 | 0.3000 | 0.7000 |
| 0.3500 | 0.6210 | 0.9710 | False | 0.0000 | 0.3500 | 0.6500 |
| 0.4000 | 0.5874 | 0.9874 | False | 0.0000 | 0.4000 | 0.6000 |
| 0.4500 | 0.5472 | 0.9972 | False | 0.0000 | 0.4500 | 0.5500 |
| **0.4844** | **0.5149** | **0.9993** | **True** | **1.0000** | 0.5000 | 0.5000 |
| 0.5500 | 0.4395 | 0.9895 | False | 0.0000 | 0.5500 | 0.4500 |
| 0.6000 | 0.3640 | 0.9640 | False | 0.0000 | 0.6000 | 0.4000 |
| 0.6500 | 0.2586 | 0.9086 | False | 0.0000 | 0.6500 | 0.3500 |
| 0.6750 | 0.1794 | 0.8544 | False | 0.0000 | 0.7000 | 0.3000 |
| 0.6900 | 0.1038 | 0.7938 | False | 0.0000 | 0.7500 | 0.2500 |
| 0.6950 | 0.0595 | 0.7545 | False | 0.0000 | 0.8000 | 0.2000 |
| 0.6955 | 0.0530 | 0.7485 | False | 0.0000 | 0.8500 | 0.1500 |
| 0.6960 | 0.0457 | 0.7417 | False | 0.0000 | 0.9000 | 0.1000 |
| 0.6965 | 0.0368 | 0.7333 | False | 0.0000 | 0.9500 | 0.0500 |
| 0.6970 | 0.0251 | 0.7221 | False | 0.0000 | 1.0000 | 0.0000 |

| | | | **Test Macro** | **1.0000** | | |
|---|---|---|---|---|---|---|

Now, it is time to run the VBA Macro to find the optimal solution for *Subroutine* and *Cell L1*.

We just insert the *Subroutine* of Fig. 9.11-2 into the Excel VBA module, which increments by 0.01 the *initial value* of *Cell* L1, where we decided to store our original input of $J = c$ and then via *Cell I2* we make $\Delta_1 y$ and $\Delta_2 y$ under *Column A* and *Column B*, move to find the optimal point. This is the point that returns the optimal solution of the two subintervals in $y(t)$ and where the *contour line* is tangent to the equation of the constraint (which is then satisfied). The *Cell I2* = *Cell L1* stores our optimal $J(y) = c$.

In Table 9.11-1, we have the final Excel output with the optimal $\Delta_1 y$ and $\Delta_2 y$ highlighted in bold (Fig. 9.11-3).

Finally, we just have to build Table 9.11-2 with the optimal numerical path, which returns the same results as the Lagrange approach of Section 9.2, satisfying the exact optimal path $y^*(t) = \frac{1}{24}t^3 + \frac{23}{24}t + 1$. Fig. 9.11-4 graphs the contour map and the point of tangency with the optimal $\Delta_1 y$ and $\Delta_2 y$.

```
Sub Find_CoV_Optimal_Path()


' As the macro increments the value of the functional J = c
' it moves the contour line from left to the right until it meets
' tangent point with constraint line where
' the optimal solution is found

Do Until Range("E25") = 1

    Range("L1").Value = Range("L1").Value + 0.01

Loop

End Sub
```

**FIGURE 9.11-2**    VBA code for the contour line CoV solution.

| I | J | K | L | M | N | O | P | Q | R | S |
|---|---|---|---|---|---|---|---|---|---|---|
| c | =B2 | 3.37 | =L1+0.5 | =M1+0.5 | =N1+0.5 | =O1+0.5 | =P1+0.5 | =Q1+0.5 | =R1+0.5 |
| =L1 | =A2 | =TABLE(I2:A2) | =TABLE(I2:A2) | =TABLE(I2:A2) | =TABLE(I2:A2) | =TABLE(I2:A2) | =TABLE(I2:A2) | =TABLE(I2:A2) | =TABLE(I2:A2) |
| | =A3 | =TABLE(I2:A2) | =TABLE(I2:A2) | =TABLE(I2:A2) | =TABLE(I2:A2) | =TABLE(I2:A2) | =TABLE(I2:A2) | =TABLE(I2:A2) | =TABLE(I2:A2) |
| | =A4 | =TABLE(I2:A2) | =TABLE(I2:A2) | =TABLE(I2:A2) | =TABLE(I2:A2) | =TABLE(I2:A2) | =TABLE(I2:A2) | =TABLE(I2:A2) | =TABLE(I2:A2) |
| | =A5 | =TABLE(I2:A2) | =TABLE(I2:A2) | =TABLE(I2:A2) | =TABLE(I2:A2) | =TABLE(I2:A2) | =TABLE(I2:A2) | =TABLE(I2:A2) | =TABLE(I2:A2) |
| | =A6 | =TABLE(I2:A2) | =TABLE(I2:A2) | =TABLE(I2:A2) | =TABLE(I2:A2) | =TABLE(I2:A2) | =TABLE(I2:A2) | =TABLE(I2:A2) | =TABLE(I2:A2) |
| | =A7 | =TABLE(I2:A2) | =TABLE(I2:A2) | =TABLE(I2:A2) | =TABLE(I2:A2) | =TABLE(I2:A2) | =TABLE(I2:A2) | =TABLE(I2:A2) | =TABLE(I2:A2) |
| | =A8 | =TABLE(I2:A2) | =TABLE(I2:A2) | =TABLE(I2:A2) | =TABLE(I2:A2) | =TABLE(I2:A2) | =TABLE(I2:A2) | =TABLE(I2:A2) | =TABLE(I2:A2) |
| | =A9 | =TABLE(I2:A2) | =TABLE(I2:A2) | =TABLE(I2:A2) | =TABLE(I2:A2) | =TABLE(I2:A2) | =TABLE(I2:A2) | =TABLE(I2:A2) | =TABLE(I2:A2) |
| | =A10 | =TABLE(I2:A2) | =TABLE(I2:A2) | =TABLE(I2:A2) | =TABLE(I2:A2) | =TABLE(I2:A2) | =TABLE(I2:A2) | =TABLE(I2:A2) | =TABLE(I2:A2) |
| | =A11 | =TABLE(I2:A2) | =TABLE(I2:A2) | =TABLE(I2:A2) | =TABLE(I2:A2) | =TABLE(I2:A2) | =TABLE(I2:A2) | =TABLE(I2:A2) | =TABLE(I2:A2) |
| | =A12 | =TABLE(I2:A2) | =TABLE(I2:A2) | =TABLE(I2:A2) | =TABLE(I2:A2) | =TABLE(I2:A2) | =TABLE(I2:A2) | =TABLE(I2:A2) | =TABLE(I2:A2) |
| | =A13 | =TABLE(I2:A2) | =TABLE(I2:A2) | =TABLE(I2:A2) | =TABLE(I2:A2) | =TABLE(I2:A2) | =TABLE(I2:A2) | =TABLE(I2:A2) | =TABLE(I2:A2) |
| | =A14 | =TABLE(I2:A2) | =TABLE(I2:A2) | =TABLE(I2:A2) | =TABLE(I2:A2) | =TABLE(I2:A2) | =TABLE(I2:A2) | =TABLE(I2:A2) | =TABLE(I2:A2) |
| | =A15 | =TABLE(I2:A2) | =TABLE(I2:A2) | =TABLE(I2:A2) | =TABLE(I2:A2) | =TABLE(I2:A2) | =TABLE(I2:A2) | =TABLE(I2:A2) | =TABLE(I2:A2) |
| | =A16 | =TABLE(I2:A2) | =TABLE(I2:A2) | =TABLE(I2:A2) | =TABLE(I2:A2) | =TABLE(I2:A2) | =TABLE(I2:A2) | =TABLE(I2:A2) | =TABLE(I2:A2) |
| | =A17 | =TABLE(I2:A2) | =TABLE(I2:A2) | =TABLE(I2:A2) | =TABLE(I2:A2) | =TABLE(I2:A2) | =TABLE(I2:A2) | =TABLE(I2:A2) | =TABLE(I2:A2) |
| | =A18 | =TABLE(I2:A2) | =TABLE(I2:A2) | =TABLE(I2:A2) | =TABLE(I2:A2) | =TABLE(I2:A2) | =TABLE(I2:A2) | =TABLE(I2:A2) | =TABLE(I2:A2) |
| | =A19 | =TABLE(I2:A2) | =TABLE(I2:A2) | =TABLE(I2:A2) | =TABLE(I2:A2) | =TABLE(I2:A2) | =TABLE(I2:A2) | =TABLE(I2:A2) | =TABLE(I2:A2) |
| | =A20 | =TABLE(I2:A2) | =TABLE(I2:A2) | =TABLE(I2:A2) | =TABLE(I2:A2) | =TABLE(I2:A2) | =TABLE(I2:A2) | =TABLE(I2:A2) | =TABLE(I2:A2) |
| | =A21 | =TABLE(I2:A2) | =TABLE(I2:A2) | =TABLE(I2:A2) | =TABLE(I2:A2) | =TABLE(I2:A2) | =TABLE(I2:A2) | =TABLE(I2:A2) | =TABLE(I2:A2) |
| | =A22 | =TABLE(I2:A2) | =TABLE(I2:A2) | =TABLE(I2:A2) | =TABLE(I2:A2) | =TABLE(I2:A2) | =TABLE(I2:A2) | =TABLE(I2:A2) | =TABLE(I2:A2) |

**FIGURE 9.11-3**    Example 1 excel set-up (Continued).

**TABLE 9.11-2** Example 1 optimal path.

| t | y(t) |
|---|------|
| 0.00 | 1.0000 |
| 0.50 | $= 1+\Delta_1 y = 1.4844$ |
| 1.00 | $= 1.4844+\Delta_2 y = 1.4844+0.5149 \cong 2.0000$ |

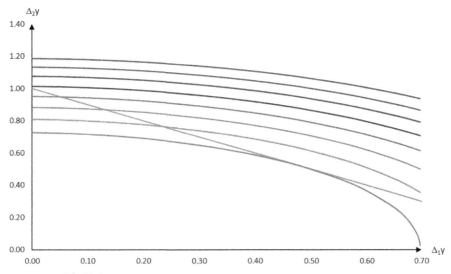

**FIGURE 9.11-4** Example1 (optimal $\Delta_1 y = 0.4844$ and $\Delta_2 y = 0.5149$).

## EXAMPLE 2

The numerical *contour lines* approach, working with just two subintervals, works best if we know somehow that the exact solution $y^*(t)$ is linear in $t$, like in the following CoV problem:

$$\min J = \int_0^2 (y^2 + t^2 y')dt$$

$$s.t.\ y(0) = 0 \text{ and } y(2) = 2$$

After the *functional* discretization, according to the form in 9.2-1, we have:

$$J = \left[ (0 + \Delta_1 y)^2 + t_1^2 \frac{\Delta_1 y}{\Delta_1 t} \right] \Delta_1 t + \left[ (0 + \Delta_1 y + \Delta_2 y)^2 + t_2^2 \frac{\Delta_2 y}{\Delta_2 t} \right] \Delta_2 t$$

$$s.t.\ \Delta_1 y + \Delta_2 y = 2$$

With $t_1 = 1$, $t_2 = 2$ and $\Delta_1 t = \Delta_2 t = 1$ we have:

$$J = \left[ (0 + \Delta_1 y)^2 + (1)^2 \frac{\Delta_1 y}{\Delta_1 t} \right] 1 + \left[ (2)^2 + (2)^2 \frac{\Delta_2 y}{\Delta_2 t} \right] 1$$

Setting $J = c$ we have:

$$c = (\Delta_1 y)^2 + \Delta_1 y + 4 + 4\Delta_2 y$$

The contour lines equations as a function of $c$ is obtained as follows:

$$\Delta_2 y = \frac{\left[ c - (\Delta_1 y)^2 - \Delta_1 y - 4 \right]}{4}$$

The solution is found for $J = c = 10$ with $\Delta_1 y = \Delta_2 y = 1$ as we can see in the following table (Table 9.11-3).

TABLE 9.11-3   Example 2 excel output.

| Δ1y | Δ2y | Constraint | s.t. Δ1y+Δ2y=1 | Test | Δ1y | Δ2y |
|---|---|---|---|---|---|---|
| 0.0000 | 1.5000 | 1.5000 | False | 0.0000 | 0.0000 | 2.0000 |
| 0.0500 | 1.4869 | 1.5369 | False | 0.0000 | 0.0500 | 1.9500 |
| 0.1000 | 1.4725 | 1.5725 | False | 0.0000 | 0.1000 | 1.9000 |
| 0.1500 | 1.4569 | 1.6069 | False | 0.0000 | 0.1500 | 1.8500 |
| 0.2000 | 1.4400 | 1.6400 | False | 0.0000 | 0.2000 | 1.8000 |
| 0.2500 | 1.4219 | 1.6719 | False | 0.0000 | 0.2500 | 1.7500 |
| 0.3000 | 1.4025 | 1.7025 | False | 0.0000 | 0.3000 | 1.7000 |
| 0.3500 | 1.3819 | 1.7319 | False | 0.0000 | 0.3500 | 1.6500 |
| 0.4000 | 1.3600 | 1.7600 | False | 0.0000 | 0.4000 | 1.6000 |
| 0.4500 | 1.3369 | 1.7869 | False | 0.0000 | 0.4500 | 1.5500 |
| 0.5000 | 1.3125 | 1.8125 | False | 0.0000 | 0.5000 | 1.5000 |
| 0.5500 | 1.2869 | 1.8369 | False | 0.0000 | 0.5500 | 1.4500 |
| 0.6000 | 1.2600 | 1.8600 | False | 0.0000 | 0.6000 | 1.4000 |
| 0.6500 | 1.2319 | 1.8819 | False | 0.0000 | 0.6500 | 1.3500 |
| 0.7000 | 1.2025 | 1.9025 | False | 0.0000 | 0.7000 | 1.3000 |
| 0.7500 | 1.1719 | 1.9219 | False | 0.0000 | 0.7500 | 1.2500 |
| 0.8000 | 1.1400 | 1.9400 | False | 0.0000 | 0.8000 | 1.2000 |
| 0.8500 | 1.1069 | 1.9569 | False | 0.0000 | 0.8500 | 1.1500 |
| 0.9000 | 1.0725 | 1.9725 | False | 0.0000 | 0.9000 | 1.1000 |
| 0.9500 | 1.0369 | 1.9869 | False | 0.0000 | 0.9500 | 1.0500 |
| 1.0000 | 1.0000 | 2.0000 | True | 1.0000 | 1.0000 | 1.0000 |

The numerical values of the optimal path $y^*(t)$ over two data intervals are described in the following table (Table 9.11-4):

TABLE 9.11-4   Example 2 optimal
path.

| $t$ | $y(t)$ |
|---|---|
| 0.00 | 0,0000 |
| 1,00 | $= 0 + \Delta_1 y = 1.0000$ |
| 2,00 | $= 1.0000 + \Delta_2 y = 1.0000 + 1.0000 = 2.0000$ |

As $y^*(t)$ turns out to be linear in $t$ two data intervals are enough to derive the exact function. See Fig. 9.11-5 where we find, at the point of tangency, the optimal $\Delta_1 y = \Delta_2 y = 1$. The resulting optimal equation path is in Fig. 9.11-6.

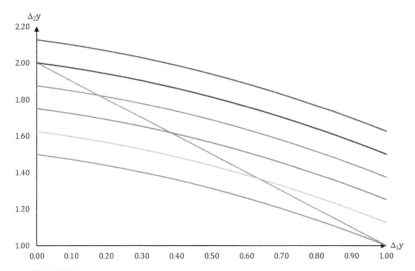

FIGURE 9.11-5   Example 2: contour lines and optimal. $\Delta_1 y = \Delta_2 y = 1$.

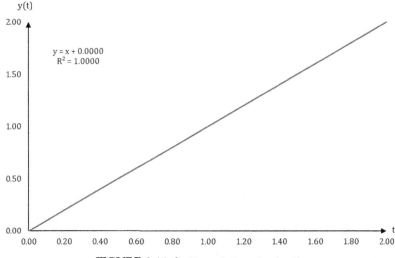

FIGURE 9.11-6   Example 2: optimal path.

III. Dynamic optimization

# 9.12 Calculus of Variations with functionals involving two independent functions

So far, the *functionals* considered have contained only a single function and its first derivative. In this section, we will see how to approach a problem where the *functional* involves two independent functions.

In general, if we had $n$ independent functions we would express our *functional* with matrix notations as follows:

$$J = \int_{t_0}^{T} (F(t, y(t), y'(t)) dt \tag{9.12-1}$$

$$s.t. \ y(t_0) = y_0 \text{ and } y(T) = y_T$$

where:

$$y(t) \triangleq \begin{bmatrix} y_1(t) \\ \cdot \\ \cdot \\ \cdot \\ y_n(t) \end{bmatrix} \text{ and } y'(t) \triangleq \begin{bmatrix} y_1'(t) \\ \cdot \\ \cdot \\ \cdot \\ y_n'(t) \end{bmatrix}$$

The matrix representation of the Euler–Lagrange necessary condition equation is:

$$\frac{\partial F}{\partial y}(y(t), y'(t), t) - \frac{d}{dt}\left[\frac{\partial F}{\partial y'}(y(t), y'(t), t)\right] = 0 \tag{9.12-2}$$

which exactly corresponds to the scalar version. The scalar version is in fact a special case of Eq. (9.12-2), when $y(t)$ is a scalar.

Let us see now how we can modify our Excel worksheet to solve such a problem when $n = 2$.

## EXAMPLE 1

Find the extremal for the following CoV problem:

$$J = \int_{0}^{\frac{\pi}{4}} (y_1^2 + 4y_2^2 + y_1'y_2') dt$$

s.t.

$$y_1(0) = 0, y_2(0) = 1$$

and

$$y_1\left(\frac{\pi}{4}\right) = 1, y_2\left(\frac{\pi}{4}\right) = 0$$

The two Euler equations found from Eq. (9.12-2) are:

$$2y_1 - y_2'' = 0$$

$$8y_2 - y_1'' = 0$$

Contrary to what we have seen in the case $n = 1$, with $n = 2$ we will explicitly use these two differential equations from the matrix version of the Euler−Lagrange equation as new constraints in the Solver parameters, together with the boundary condition constraints.

The way we change the worksheet is also in the number of variables we want to store. With $n = 2$ we need to store two variables, and we do it as follows in Fig. 9.12-1:

What we have done is to insert under *Column B* and *Column D* the two unknown paths to seek, as a function of the optimal $\Delta y_1$ and $\Delta y_2$ will be found launching the computer optimizer.

| | A | B | C | D | E | F | G | H |
|---|---|---|---|---|---|---|---|---|
| 1 | t | y₁ Path | dy₁ | y₂ Path | dy₂ | dt | F = y₁²+4y₂²+y'₁y'₂ | Functional = Σ[y₁²+4y₂²+y'₁y'₂]dt |
| 2 | 0 | 0 | | 1 | | | | |
| 3 | =A2+$A$22/20 | =B2+C3 | -0.022519! | =D2+E3 | -0.05! | =A3-A2 | =B3^2+4*D3^2+(C3/F3)*(E3/F3) | =G3*F3 |
| 4 | =A3+$A$22/20 | =B3+C4 | -0.010862! | =D3+E4 | -0.05! | =A4-A3 | =B4^2+4*D4^2+(C4/F4)*(E4/F4) | =G4*F4 |
| 5 | =A4+$A$22/20 | =B4+C5 | 0.0001129 | =D4+E5 | -0.05! | =A5-A4 | =B5^2+4*D5^2+(C5/F5)*(E5/F5) | =G5*F5 |
| 6 | =A5+$A$22/20 | =B5+C6 | 0.0104062 | =D5+E6 | -0.05! | =A6-A5 | =B6^2+4*D6^2+(C6/F6)*(E6/F6) | =G6*F6 |
| 7 | =A6+$A$22/20 | =B6+C7 | 0.0200161 | =D6+E7 | -0.05! | =A7-A6 | =B7^2+4*D7^2+(C7/F7)*(E7/F7) | =G7*F7 |
| 8 | =A7+$A$22/20 | =B7+C8 | 0.0289425 | =D7+E8 | -0.05! | =A8-A7 | =B8^2+4*D8^2+(C8/F8)*(E8/F8) | =G8*F8 |
| 9 | =A8+$A$22/20 | =B8+C9 | 0.0371864 | =D8+E9 | -0.05! | =A9-A8 | =B9^2+4*D9^2+(C9/F9)*(E9/F9) | =G9*F9 |
| 10 | =A9+$A$22/20 | =B9+C10 | 0.0447502 | =D9+E10 | -0.054 | =A10-A9 | =B10^2+4*D10^2+(C10/F10)*(E10/F10) | =G10*F10 |
| 11 | =A10+$A$22/20 | =B10+C11 | 0.0516381 | =D10+E11 | -0.054 | =A11-A10 | =B11^2+4*D11^2+(C11/F11)*(E11/F11) | =G11*F11 |
| 12 | =A11+$A$22/20 | =B11+C12 | 0.0578561 | =D11+E12 | -0.05! | =A12-A11 | =B12^2+4*D12^2+(C12/F12)*(E12/F12) | =G12*F12 |
| 13 | =A12+$A$22/20 | =B12+C13 | 0.0634124 | =D12+E13 | -0.05! | =A13-A12 | =B13^2+4*D13^2+(C13/F13)*(E13/F13) | =G13*F13 |
| 14 | =A13+$A$22/20 | =B13+C14 | 0.0683178 | =D13+E14 | -0.05! | =A14-A13 | =B14^2+4*D14^2+(C14/F14)*(E14/F14) | =G14*F14 |
| 15 | =A14+$A$22/20 | =B14+C15 | 0.0725856 | =D14+E15 | -0.05! | =A15-A14 | =B15^2+4*D15^2+(C15/F15)*(E15/F15) | =G15*F15 |
| 16 | =A15+$A$22/20 | =B15+C16 | 0.0762317 | =D15+E16 | -0.04! | =A16-A15 | =B16^2+4*D16^2+(C16/F16)*(E16/F16) | =G16*F16 |
| 17 | =A16+$A$22/20 | =B16+C17 | 0.0792753 | =D16+E17 | -0.047 | =A17-A16 | =B17^2+4*D17^2+(C17/F17)*(E17/F17) | =G17*F17 |
| 18 | =A17+$A$22/20 | =B17+C18 | 0.0817381 | =D17+E18 | -0.04! | =A18-A17 | =B18^2+4*D18^2+(C18/F18)*(E18/F18) | =G18*F18 |
| 19 | =A18+$A$22/20 | =B18+C19 | 0.0836454 | =D18+E19 | -0.04! | =A19-A18 | =B19^2+4*D19^2+(C19/F19)*(E19/F19) | =G19*F19 |
| 20 | =A19+$A$22/20 | =B19+C20 | 0.0850253 | =D19+E20 | -0.04( | =A20-A19 | =B20^2+4*D20^2+(C20/F20)*(E20/F20) | =G20*F20 |
| 21 | =A20+$A$22/20 | =B20+C21 | 0.0859094 | =D20+E21 | -0.037 | =A21-A20 | =B21^2+4*D21^2+(C21/F21)*(E21/F21) | =G21*F21 |
| 22 | =PI()/4 | =B21+C22 | 0.0863324 | =D21+E22 | -0.034 | =A22-A21 | =B22^2+4*D22^2+(C22/F22)*(E22/F22) | =G22*F22 |
| 23 | | | | | | | | |
| 24 | | | | | | | | =SUM(H3:H23) |
| 25 | | | | | | | | |
| 26 | | y₁(0) 0 | | y₂(0) 1 | | | | |
| 27 | | y₁(π/4) 1 | | y₂(π/4) 0 | | | | |

FIGURE 9.12-1    Example 1 excel set-up.

Further to the right of our worksheet (from *Column J* to *Column M*) it is the area where we have decided to store the two Euler–Lagrange differential equations conditions. See Fig. 9.12-2.

Now we are ready to compute our optimal solution with the assistance of the Excel Solver that will have to be organized like the one in Fig. 9.12-3.

The optimal computer-based solutions are represented in Table 9.12-1 with the associated graphs in Fig. 9.12-4, while in Fig. 9.12-5 we have graphed the Euler–Lagrange exact solutions for comparison.

To derive the exact solutions from the differential equations of the Euler–Lagrange is a quite complicated steps process that implies solving the second-order differential equations, which is out of the scope of this book.

We give the final solutions for $y_1^*(t)$ and $y_2^*(t)$ as follows:

$$y_1^*(t) = c_1 e^{2t} + c_2 e^{-2t} + c_3 \cos 2t + c_4 \sin 2t$$

$$y_2^*(t) = \frac{1}{2}c_1 e^{2t} + \frac{1}{2}c_2 e^{-2t} - \frac{1}{2}c_3 \cos 2t - \frac{1}{2}c_4 \sin 2t$$

Putting $t = 0$ and $t = \pi/4$ in the two above equations, we have four equations and four unknowns:

$$y_1^*(0) = 0; \qquad y_2^*(0) = 1; \qquad y_1^*\left(\frac{\pi}{4}\right) = 1; \qquad y_2^*\left(\frac{\pi}{4}\right) = 0$$

| J | K | L | M |
|---|---|---|---|
| | **s.t. Conditions from Euler-Lagrange** | | |
| y'₁ | 8y₂-y"₁ = 0 | y'₂ | 2y₁-y"₂ = 0 |
| =(B3-B2)/F3 | | =(D3-D2)/F3 | |
| =(B4-B3)/F4 | =8*D3-(J4-J3)/F3 | =(D4-D3)/F4 | =2*B4-(L4-L3)/F4 |
| =(B5-B4)/F5 | =8*D4-(J5-J4)/F4 | =(D5-D4)/F5 | =2*B5-(L5-L4)/F5 |
| =(B6-B5)/F6 | =8*D5-(J6-J5)/F5 | =(D6-D5)/F6 | =2*B6-(L6-L5)/F6 |
| =(B7-B6)/F7 | =8*D6-(J7-J6)/F6 | =(D7-D6)/F7 | =2*B7-(L7-L6)/F7 |
| =(B8-B7)/F8 | =8*D7-(J8-J7)/F7 | =(D8-D7)/F8 | =2*B8-(L8-L7)/F8 |
| =(B9-B8)/F9 | =8*D8-(J9-J8)/F8 | =(D9-D8)/F9 | =2*B9-(L9-L8)/F9 |
| =(B10-B9)/F10 | =8*D9-(J10-J9)/F9 | =(D10-D9)/F10 | =2*B10-(L10-L9)/F10 |
| =(B11-B10)/F11 | =8*D10-(J11-J10)/F10 | =(D11-D10)/F11 | =2*B11-(L11-L10)/F11 |
| =(B12-B11)/F12 | =8*D11-(J12-J11)/F11 | =(D12-D11)/F12 | =2*B12-(L12-L11)/F12 |
| =(B13-B12)/F13 | =8*D12-(J13-J12)/F12 | =(D13-D12)/F13 | =2*B13-(L13-L12)/F13 |
| =(B14-B13)/F14 | =8*D13-(J14-J13)/F13 | =(D14-D13)/F14 | =2*B14-(L14-L13)/F14 |
| =(B15-B14)/F15 | =8*D14-(J15-J14)/F14 | =(D15-D14)/F15 | =2*B15-(L15-L14)/F15 |
| =(B16-B15)/F16 | =8*D15-(J16-J15)/F15 | =(D16-D15)/F16 | =2*B16-(L16-L15)/F16 |
| =(B17-B16)/F17 | =8*D16-(J17-J16)/F16 | =(D17-D16)/F17 | =2*B17-(L17-L16)/F17 |
| =(B18-B17)/F18 | =8*D17-(J18-J17)/F17 | =(D18-D17)/F18 | =2*B18-(L18-L17)/F18 |
| =(B19-B18)/F19 | =8*D18-(J19-J18)/F18 | =(D19-D18)/F19 | =2*B19-(L19-L18)/F19 |
| =(B20-B19)/F20 | =8*D19-(J20-J19)/F19 | =(D20-D19)/F20 | =2*B20-(L20-L19)/F20 |
| =(B21-B20)/F21 | =8*D20-(J21-J20)/F20 | =(D21-D20)/F21 | =2*B21-(L21-L20)/F21 |
| =(B22-B21)/F22 | =8*D21-(J22-J21)/F21 | =(D22-D21)/F22 | =2*B22-(L22-L21)/F22 |

FIGURE 9.12-2   Example 1 Excel set-up of the euler-lagrange equations.

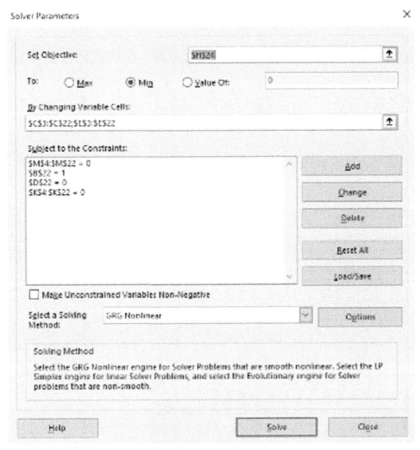

FIGURE 9.12-3    Example 1 excel solver.

to determine the four constants of integrations as:

$$c_1 = \frac{-\frac{1}{2} + e^{-\pi/2}}{e^{-\pi/2} - e^{\pi/2}}; \qquad c_2 = \frac{-\frac{1}{2} - e^{\pi/2}}{e^{-\pi/2} - e^{\pi/2}}; \qquad c_3 = -1; \qquad c_4 = \frac{1}{2}$$

## 9.13 Calculus of Variations constrained problems

So far, we have always dealt with problems with no constraints specified, apart from the boundary conditions.

In this section, we will see two basic examples on the numerical resolution of the following constrained problems in Cov: *Differential Equations* and *isoperimetric constraint* problems

III. Dynamic optimization

**TABLE 9.12-1**    Example 1 values of optimal numerical solution $y_1^*(t)$ and $y_2^*(t)$.

| t | $y_1$ Path | $dy_1$ | $y_2$ Path | $dy_2$ | dt | $F = y_1^2+4y_2^2+y'_1y'_2$ | Functional $= \Sigma[y_1^2+4y_2^2+y'_1y'_2]dt$ |
|---|---|---|---|---|---|---|---|
| - | 0.00 | | 1.00 | | | | |
| 0.0393 | -0.0225 | -0.0225 | 0.9449 | -0.0551 | 0.0393 | 4.3766 | 0.1719 |
| 0.0785 | -0.0334 | -0.0109 | 0.8897 | -0.0552 | 0.0393 | 3.5561 | 0.1396 |
| 0.1178 | -0.0333 | 0.0001 | 0.8343 | -0.0553 | 0.0393 | 2.7816 | 0.1092 |
| 0.1571 | -0.0229 | 0.0104 | 0.7789 | -0.0554 | 0.0393 | 2.0538 | 0.0807 |
| 0.1963 | -0.0028 | 0.0200 | 0.7235 | -0.0554 | 0.0393 | 1.3750 | 0.0540 |
| 0.2356 | 0.0261 | 0.0289 | 0.6682 | -0.0553 | 0.0393 | 0.7485 | 0.0294 |
| 0.2749 | 0.0633 | 0.0372 | 0.6131 | -0.0551 | 0.0393 | 0.1783 | 0.0070 |
| 0.3142 | 0.1080 | 0.0448 | 0.5583 | -0.0548 | 0.0393 | -0.3315 | -0.0130 |
| 0.3534 | 0.1597 | 0.0516 | 0.5040 | -0.0543 | 0.0393 | -0.7766 | -0.0305 |
| 0.3927 | 0.2175 | 0.0579 | 0.4504 | -0.0536 | 0.0393 | -1.1533 | -0.0453 |
| 0.4320 | 0.2809 | 0.0634 | 0.3976 | -0.0528 | 0.0393 | -1.4583 | -0.0573 |
| 0.4712 | 0.3493 | 0.0683 | 0.3459 | -0.0517 | 0.0393 | -1.6891 | -0.0663 |
| 0.5105 | 0.4218 | 0.0726 | 0.2955 | -0.0504 | 0.0393 | -1.8442 | -0.0724 |
| 0.5498 | 0.4981 | 0.0762 | 0.2467 | -0.0488 | 0.0393 | -1.9232 | -0.0755 |
| 0.5890 | 0.5773 | 0.0793 | 0.1996 | -0.0471 | 0.0393 | -1.9268 | -0.0757 |
| 0.6283 | 0.6591 | 0.0817 | 0.1546 | -0.0450 | 0.0393 | -1.8570 | -0.0729 |
| 0.6676 | 0.7427 | 0.0836 | 0.1119 | -0.0427 | 0.0393 | -1.7168 | -0.0674 |
| 0.7069 | 0.8278 | 0.0850 | 0.0717 | -0.0402 | 0.0393 | -1.5102 | -0.0593 |
| 0.7461 | 0.9137 | 0.0859 | 0.0343 | -0.0374 | 0.0393 | -1.2425 | -0.0488 |
| 0.7854 | 1.0000 | 0.0863 | 0.0000 | -0.0343 | 0.0393 | -0.9196 | -0.0361 |
| | | | | | | | -0.1288 |

| | | | | |
|---|---|---|---|---|
| $y_1(0)$ | 0.00 | $y_2(0)$ | 1.00 | |
| $y_1(\pi/4)$ | 1.00 | $y_2(\pi/4)$ | 0.00 | |

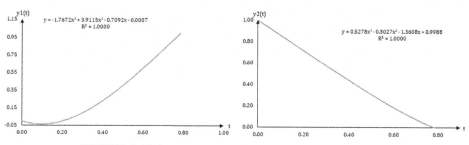

**FIGURE 9.12-4** Example 1: optimal numerical $y_1^*(t)$ and $y_2^*(t)$.

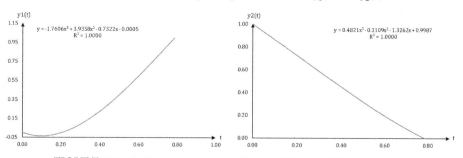

**FIGURE 9.12-5** Example 1: exact $y_1^*(t)$ and $y_2^*(t)$ from Euler–Lagrange.

**1.** Differential Equations Constraint

The CoV problem is specified as follows:

$$J = \int_{t_0}^{T} (F(t, y(t), y'(t))) dt$$

with the following $n$ differential equations that must be satisfied:

$$f_i(y(t), y'(t), t) = 0 \qquad \text{for } i = 1, 2, \ldots, n$$

To solve such a problem, we use the Lagrange multipliers $\lambda(t)$, forming a new version of the *functional J*, called *augmented functional*, which is given by:

$$J_a = \int_{t_0}^{T} \{(F(t, y(t), y'(t)) + \cdots + \lambda_1(t)[f_1(y(t), y'(t), t)] + \lambda_2(t)[f_2(y(t), y'(t), t)$$

$$\times] + \cdots + \lambda_n(t)[f_n(y(t), y'(t), t)]\} dt$$

which, in matrix notation, becomes:

$$J_a = \int_{t_0}^{T} \{F(y(t), y'(t), t) + \boldsymbol{\lambda}^T(t)[\mathbf{f}(y(t), y'(t), t)]\} dt \qquad (9.13\text{-}1)$$

III. Dynamic optimization

where $\lambda^T(t)$ is the transposed $(n \times 1)$ column vector of Lagrange multipliers and $\mathbf{f}(y(t), y'(t), t)$ is the $(n \times 1)$ column vector of the differential equations constraints and where the *augmented integrand function* $F_a$ is defined as:

$$F_a(y(t), y'(t), \lambda(t), t) = F(y(t), y'(t), t) + \lambda^T(t)[\mathbf{f}(y(t), y'(t), t)]$$

The necessary Euler–Lagrange conditions are found instead through the following equations:

$$\frac{\partial F_a}{\partial y}(y(t), y'(t), \lambda(t), t) - \frac{d}{dt}\left[\frac{\partial F_a}{\partial y'}(y(t), y'(t), \lambda(t), t)\right] = 0 \qquad (9.13\text{-}2)$$

$$\frac{\partial F_a}{\partial \lambda}(y(t), y'(t), \lambda(t), t) - \frac{d}{dt}\left[\frac{\partial F_a}{\partial \lambda'}(y(t), y'(t), \lambda(t), t)\right] = 0 \qquad (9.13\text{-}3)$$

## EXAMPLE 1

Find the extremal in the following problem:

$$\min J = \int_{t_0}^{T} \frac{1}{2}[y_1^2 + y_2^2]\, dt$$

$$s.t.\ y_1' = y_2\ (\textit{differential equation constraint})$$

$$\text{and } y_1(0) = 0; y_2(0) = 1; t_0 = 0; T = 1; y_1(T) = y_2(T) = Free$$

Our *augmented functional* is:

$$J_a = \int_{t_0}^{T}\left[\frac{1}{2}(y_1^2 + y_2^2) + \lambda(y_2 - y_1')\right] dt$$

now, from Eq. (9.13-2) we have the following necessary conditions:

$$\frac{\partial F_a}{\partial y_1} - \frac{d}{dt}\left[\frac{\partial F_a}{\partial y_1'}\right] = 0$$

$$y_1(t) + \lambda'(t) = 0$$

and

$$\frac{\partial F_a}{\partial y_2} - \frac{d}{dt}\left[\frac{\partial F_a}{\partial y_2'}\right] = 0$$

$$y_2(t) + \lambda(t) = 0$$

and finally:

$$\frac{\partial F_a}{\partial \lambda} - \frac{d}{dt}\left[\frac{\partial F_a}{\partial \lambda'}\right] = 0$$

$$y_2 = y_1'$$

To solve numerically this problem we have now all the elements to develop our Excel worksheet, similarly to what we have done with the Example 1 of Section 9.12.

After launching the optimizer, this returns Table 9.13-1, while the graph solutions for $y_1^*(t)$ and $y_2^*(t)$ are in Fig. 9.13-1.

2. Isoperimetric constraint

The *isoperimetric constraint* is in the form of:

$$\int_{t_0}^{T} e_i(y(t), y'(t), t) = c_i \qquad \text{for } i = 1, 2, \dots, r$$

TABLE 9.13-1 Example 1 excel output for the optimal numerical paths.

| t | $y_1$ | $dy_1$ | $y_2$ | $dy_2$ | dt | $\lambda(t)$ | Augmented Integrand F $= [0.5(y_1^2+y_2^2)+\lambda(y_2-y_1')]$ | Augmented Functional $= \Sigma[0.5(y_1^2+y_2^2)+\lambda(y_2-y_1')]dt$ | s.t Constraints $y_1+\lambda_1'(t)=0$ | $y_2+\lambda(t)=0$ | $y_1'-y_2=0$ |
|---|---|---|---|---|---|---|---|---|---|---|---|
| 0.0000 | 0.0000 | | 1.0000 | | | -1.0000 | | | | | |
| 0.0500 | 0.0501 | 0.0501 | 1.0025 | 0.0025 | 0.0500 | -1.0025 | 0.5038 | 0.0252 | 0.0000 | 0.0000 | 0.0000 |
| 0.1000 | 0.1005 | 0.0504 | 1.0075 | 0.0050 | 0.0500 | -1.0075 | 0.5126 | 0.0256 | 0.0000 | 0.0000 | 0.0000 |
| 0.1500 | 0.1513 | 0.0508 | 1.0151 | 0.0076 | 0.0500 | -1.0151 | 0.5266 | 0.0263 | 0.0000 | 0.0000 | 0.0000 |
| 0.2000 | 0.2025 | 0.0513 | 1.0252 | 0.0101 | 0.0500 | -1.0252 | 0.5460 | 0.0273 | 0.0000 | 0.0000 | 0.0000 |
| 0.2500 | 0.2544 | 0.0519 | 1.0379 | 0.0127 | 0.0500 | -1.0379 | 0.5710 | 0.0286 | 0.0000 | 0.0000 | 0.0000 |
| 0.3000 | 0.3071 | 0.0527 | 1.0533 | 0.0154 | 0.0500 | -1.0533 | 0.6019 | 0.0301 | 0.0000 | 0.0000 | 0.0000 |
| 0.3500 | 0.3606 | 0.0536 | 1.0713 | 0.0180 | 0.0500 | -1.0713 | 0.6389 | 0.0319 | 0.0000 | 0.0000 | 0.0000 |
| 0.4000 | 0.4153 | 0.0546 | 1.0921 | 0.0208 | 0.0500 | -1.0921 | 0.6825 | 0.0341 | 0.0000 | 0.0000 | 0.0000 |
| 0.4500 | 0.4710 | 0.0558 | 1.1156 | 0.0236 | 0.0500 | -1.1156 | 0.7333 | 0.0367 | 0.0000 | 0.0000 | 0.0000 |
| 0.5000 | 0.5281 | 0.0571 | 1.1420 | 0.0264 | 0.0500 | -1.1420 | 0.7916 | 0.0396 | 0.0000 | 0.0000 | 0.0000 |
| 0.5500 | 0.5867 | 0.0586 | 1.1714 | 0.0293 | 0.0500 | -1.1714 | 0.8582 | 0.0429 | 0.0000 | 0.0000 | 0.0000 |
| 0.6000 | 0.6469 | 0.0602 | 1.2037 | 0.0323 | 0.0500 | -1.2037 | 0.9337 | 0.0467 | 0.0000 | 0.0000 | 0.0000 |
| 0.6500 | 0.7088 | 0.0620 | 1.2392 | 0.0354 | 0.0500 | -1.2392 | 1.0190 | 0.0510 | 0.0000 | 0.0000 | 0.0000 |
| 0.7000 | 0.7727 | 0.0639 | 1.2778 | 0.0386 | 0.0500 | -1.2778 | 1.1150 | 0.0557 | 0.0000 | 0.0000 | 0.0000 |
| 0.7500 | 0.8387 | 0.0660 | 1.3197 | 0.0419 | 0.0500 | -1.3197 | 1.2236 | 0.0611 | 0.0000 | 0.0000 | 0.0000 |
| 0.8000 | 0.9070 | 0.0683 | 1.3651 | 0.0453 | 0.0500 | -1.3651 | 1.3430 | 0.0672 | 0.0000 | 0.0000 | 0.0000 |
| 0.8500 | 0.9777 | 0.0707 | 1.4140 | 0.0489 | 0.0500 | -1.4140 | 1.4776 | 0.0739 | 0.0000 | 0.0000 | 0.0000 |
| 0.9000 | 1.0510 | 0.0733 | 1.4665 | 0.0526 | 0.0500 | -1.4665 | 1.6277 | 0.0814 | 0.0000 | 0.0000 | 0.0000 |
| 0.9500 | 1.1272 | 0.0761 | 1.5229 | 0.0564 | 0.0500 | -1.5229 | 1.7948 | 0.0897 | 0.0000 | 0.0000 | 0.0000 |
| 1.0000 | 1.2063 | 0.0792 | 1.5832 | 0.0603 | 0.0500 | -1.5832 | 1.9809 | 0.0990 | 0.0000 | 0.0000 | 0.0000 |

0.9740

| y1(0) | 0.00 | y2(0) | 1.00 |
|---|---|---|---|
| y1(1) | Free | y2(1) | Free |

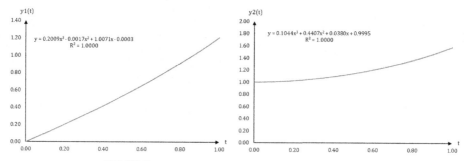

**FIGURE 9.13-1**  Example 1 numerical optimal paths.

that can be put into the form of differential equation seen before just defining the new variable:

$$z_i(t) \triangleq \int_{t_0}^{t} e_i(y(t), y'(t), t) \qquad \text{for } i = 1, 2, \ldots, r$$

where the required boundary conditions are $Z_i(t_0) = 0$ and $Z_i(T) = c_i$.

Now, differentiating $z_i(t)$ with respect to $t$ we obtain:

$$z_i'(t) \triangleq e_i(y(t), y'(t), t) \qquad \text{for } i = 1, 2, \ldots, r$$

or in vector notation:

$$z'(t) = e(y(t), y'(t), t)$$

that we will treat by forming the following *augmented function*.

$$F_a(y(t), y'(t), \lambda(t), z'(t), t) = F(y(t), y'(t), t) + \lambda^T(t)[e(y(t), y'(t), t) - z'(t)] \qquad (9.13\text{-}4)$$

from which we have to derive the following the $n$ usual equations:

$$\frac{\partial F_a}{\partial y}(y(t), y'(t), \lambda(t), z'(t), t) - \frac{d}{dt}\left[\frac{\partial F_a}{\partial y'}(y(t), y'(t), \lambda(t), z'(t), t)\right] = 0 \qquad (9.13\text{-}5)$$

and the additional $r$ equations as well to solve the problem:

$$\frac{\partial F_a}{\partial z}(y(t), y'(t), \lambda(t), z'(t), t) - \frac{d}{dt}\left[\frac{\partial F_a}{\partial z'}(y(t), y'(t), \lambda(t), z'(t), t)\right] = 0 \qquad (9.13\text{-}6)$$

$F_a$ does not contain $z(t)$ so $\frac{\partial F_a}{\partial z} = 0$, while $\frac{\partial F_a}{\partial z'} = -\lambda(t)$; namely:

$$0 - \frac{d}{dt}\left[\frac{\partial F_a}{\partial z'}\right] = \lambda'(t) = 0$$

which implies that the Lagrange multipliers are constants.

## EXAMPLE 2

Find the extremal in the following problem:

$$\min J = \int_{t_0}^{T} \frac{1}{2}\left(y_1^2 + y_2^2 + 2y_1'y_2'\right)dt$$

$$s.t. \int_{t_0}^{T} y_2^2 dt = 8 \ (Isoperimetric\ constraint)$$

with $t_0 = 0$ and $T = 1$.

Let us start defining $z' \triangleq y_2^2$ differentiating the *isoperimetric constraint* with respect to time. According to Eq. (9.13-3) we obtain then the *augmented integrand function*:

$$F_a = \frac{1}{2}y_1^2 + \frac{1}{2}y_2^2 + y_1'y_2' + \lambda\left(y_2^2 - z'\right).$$

From Eq. (9.13-4) we have the usual necessary conditions:

$$y_1 - y_2'' = 0$$

$$y_2 + 2y_2\lambda - y_1'' = 0$$

while from Eq. (9.13-5) we have:

$$\lambda'(t) = 0.$$

Also, the following, from the *isoperimetric constraint*, must be satisfied in the problem:

$$z' = y_2^2$$

$$z(t_0) = 0 \text{ and } z(t_f) = 8$$

In such a problem, with an increased complexity and new constraints to add, we are forced to change the organization of our worksheet. This is mainly due to the isoperimetric constraint. The main part of the worksheet is in Fig. 9.13-2, where we notice the first key difference compared to the previous worksheets seen so far, which is the introduction of the

**FIGURE 9.13-2** (columns A–K)

Header row:

- **A** t
- **B** y1
- **C** dy1
- **D** y2
- **E** dy2
- **F** dt
- **G** z(t)
- **H** z'(t)
- **I** λ(t)
- **J** Augmented Integrand $F = 0.5(y_1'^2 + y_2^2 + y_1' y_2') + \lambda(y_1^2 - z'(t))$
- **K** Augmented Functional $= \Sigma\,[0.5(y_1'^2 + y_2^2 + y_1' y_2') + \lambda(y_1^2 - z'(t))]dt$

| # | A | B | C | D | E | F | G | H | I | J | K |
|---|---|---|---|---|---|---|---|---|---|---|---|
| 2 | 0 | 0 | | 1 | | 0 | | 0 | | 0 | |
| 3 | =A2+0.05 | =B2+C3 | -0.55( | =D2+E3 | 0.189( | =A3-A2 | =G2+H3*F3 | =D3^2 | 6.656 | =0.5*(B3^2+D3^2)+((B3-B2)/F3)*((D3-D2)/F3))+I3*(D3^2-H3) | =J3*F3 |
| 4 | =A3+0.05 | =B3+C4 | -0.50( | =D3+E4 | 0.187( | =A4-A3 | =G3+H4*F4 | =D4^2 | 6.656 | =0.5*(B4^2+D4^2)+((B4-B3)/F4)*((D4-D3)/F4))+I4*(D4^2-H4) | =J4*F4 |
| 5 | =A4+0.05 | =B4+C5 | -0.44( | =D4+E5 | 0.185( | =A5-A4 | =G4+H5*F5 | =D5^2 | 6.656 | =0.5*(B5^2+D5^2)+((B5-B4)/F5)*((D5-D4)/F5))+I5*(D5^2-H5) | =J5*F5 |
| 6 | =A5+0.05 | =B5+C6 | -0.38( | =D5+E6 | 0.181( | =A6-A5 | =G5+H6*F6 | =D6^2 | 6.656 | =0.5*(B6^2+D6^2)+((B6-B5)/F6)*((D6-D5)/F6))+I6*(D6^2-H6) | =J6*F6 |
| 7 | =A6+0.05 | =B6+C7 | -0.31( | =D6+E7 | 0.176( | =A7-A6 | =G6+H7*F7 | =D7^2 | 6.656 | =0.5*(B7^2+D7^2)+((B7-B6)/F7)*((D7-D6)/F7))+I7*(D7^2-H7) | =J7*F7 |
| 8 | =A7+0.05 | =B7+C8 | -0.23( | =D7+E8 | 0.171( | =A8-A7 | =G7+H8*F8 | =D8^2 | 6.656 | =0.5*(B8^2+D8^2)+((B8-B7)/F8)*((D8-D7)/F8))+I8*(D8^2-H8) | =J8*F8 |
| 9 | =A8+0.05 | =B8+C9 | -0.15( | =D8+E9 | 0.165( | =A9-A8 | =G8+H9*F9 | =D9^2 | 6.656 | =0.5*(B9^2+D9^2)+((B9-B8)/F9)*((D9-D8)/F9))+I9*(D9^2-H9) | =J9*F9 |
| 10 | =A9+0.05 | =B9+C10 | -0.07( | =D9+E10 | 0.158( | =A10-A9 | =G9+H10*F10 | =D10^2 | 6.656 | =0.5*(B10^2+D10^2)+((B10-B9)/F10)*((D10-D9)/F10))+I10*(D10^2-H10) | =J10*F10 |
| 11 | =A10+0.05 | =B10+C11 | 0.019( | =D10+E11 | 0.151( | =A11-A10 | =G10+H11*F11 | =D11^2 | 6.656 | =0.5*(B11^2+D11^2)+((B11-B10)/F11)*((D11-D10)/F11))+I11*(D11^2-H11) | =J11*F11 |
| 12 | =A11+0.05 | =B11+C12 | 0.116( | =D11+E12 | 0.145( | =A12-A11 | =G11+H12*F12 | =D12^2 | 6.656 | =0.5*(B12^2+D12^2)+((B12-B11)/F12)*((D12-D11)/F12))+I12*(D12^2-H12) | =J12*F12 |
| 13 | =A12+0.05 | =B12+C13 | 0.218( | =D12+E13 | 0.138( | =A13-A12 | =G12+H13*F13 | =D13^2 | 6.656 | =0.5*(B13^2+D13^2)+((B13-B12)/F13)*((D13-D12)/F13))+I13*(D13^2-H13) | =J13*F13 |
| 14 | =A13+0.05 | =B13+C14 | 0.325( | =D13+E14 | 0.133( | =A14-A13 | =G13+H14*F14 | =D14^2 | 6.656 | =0.5*(B14^2+D14^2)+((B14-B13)/F14)*((D14-D13)/F14))+I14*(D14^2-H14) | =J14*F14 |
| 15 | =A14+0.05 | =B14+C15 | 0.436( | =D14+E15 | 0.128( | =A15-A14 | =G14+H15*F15 | =D15^2 | 6.656 | =0.5*(B15^2+D15^2)+((B15-B14)/F15)*((D15-D14)/F15))+I15*(D15^2-H15) | =J15*F15 |
| 16 | =A15+0.05 | =B15+C16 | 0.552( | =D15+E16 | 0.124( | =A16-A15 | =G15+H16*F16 | =D16^2 | 6.656 | =0.5*(B16^2+D16^2)+((B16-B15)/F16)*((D16-D15)/F16))+I16*(D16^2-H16) | =J16*F16 |
| 17 | =A16+0.05 | =B16+C17 | 0.672( | =D16+E17 | 0.121( | =A17-A16 | =G16+H17*F17 | =D17^2 | 6.656 | =0.5*(B17^2+D17^2)+((B17-B16)/F17)*((D17-D16)/F17))+I17*(D17^2-H17) | =J17*F17 |
| 18 | =A17+0.05 | =B17+C18 | 0.797( | =D17+E18 | 0.121( | =A18-A17 | =G17+H18*F18 | =D18^2 | 6.656 | =0.5*(B18^2+D18^2)+((B18-B17)/F18)*((D18-D17)/F18))+I18*(D18^2-H18) | =J18*F18 |
| 19 | =A18+0.05 | =B18+C19 | 0.926( | =D18+E19 | 0.122( | =A19-A18 | =G18+H19*F19 | =D19^2 | 6.656 | =0.5*(B19^2+D19^2)+((B19-B18)/F19)*((D19-D18)/F19))+I19*(D19^2-H19) | =J19*F19 |
| 20 | =A19+0.05 | =B19+C20 | 1.059( | =D19+E20 | 0.125( | =A20-A19 | =G19+H20*F20 | =D20^2 | 6.656 | =0.5*(B20^2+D20^2)+((B20-B19)/F20)*((D20-D19)/F20))+I20*(D20^2-H20) | =J20*F20 |
| 21 | =A20+0.05 | =B20+C21 | 1.197( | =D20+E21 | 0.131( | =A21-A20 | =G20+H21*F21 | =D21^2 | 6.656 | =0.5*(B21^2+D21^2)+((B21-B20)/F21)*((D21-D20)/F21))+I21*(D21^2-H21) | =J21*F21 |
| 22 | =A21+0.05 | =B21+C22 | 1.340( | =D21+E22 | 0.141( | =A22-A21 | =G21+H22*F22 | =D22^2 | 6.656 | =0.5*(B22^2+D22^2)+((B22-B21)/F22)*((D22-D21)/F22))+I22*(D22^2-H22) | =J22*F22 |
| 24 | | | | | | | Boundary cond. z(tf)=c | | | | =SUM(K3:K22) |

**FIGURE 9.13-2** Example 2 isoperimetric constrained problem excel worksheet set-up.

**FIGURE 9.13-3** (columns L–Q)

| # | L — Isoperimetric constraint | M — s.t. Constraints $y_1'$ | N — $y_2 + 2y_2\lambda(t) - y_1'' = 0$ | O — $y_2'$ | P — $y_1 y_2'' = 0$ | Q — $\lambda'(t) = 0$ |
|---|---|---|---|---|---|---|
| 3 | =D3^2*F3 | =(B3-B2)/F3 | | =(D3-D2)/F3 | | |
| 4 | =D4^2*F4 | =(B4-B3)/F4 | =-(M4-M3)/F4+2*D4*I4+D4 | =(D4-D3)/F4 | =B3-(O4-O3)/F4 | =(I4-I3)/F3 |
| 5 | =D5^2*F5 | =(B5-B4)/F5 | =-(M5-M4)/F5+2*D5*I5+D5 | =(D5-D4)/F5 | =B4-(O5-O4)/F5 | =(I5-I4)/F4 |
| 6 | =D6^2*F6 | =(B6-B5)/F6 | =-(M6-M5)/F6+2*D6*I6+D6 | =(D6-D5)/F6 | =B5-(O6-O5)/F6 | =(I6-I5)/F5 |
| 7 | =D7^2*F7 | =(B7-B6)/F7 | =-(M7-M6)/F7+2*D7*I7+D7 | =(D7-D6)/F7 | =B6-(O7-O6)/F7 | =(I7-I6)/F6 |
| 8 | =D8^2*F8 | =(B8-B7)/F8 | =-(M8-M7)/F8+2*D8*I8+D8 | =(D8-D7)/F8 | =B7-(O8-O7)/F8 | =(I8-I7)/F7 |
| 9 | =D9^2*F9 | =(B9-B8)/F9 | =-(M9-M8)/F9+2*D9*I9+D9 | =(D9-D8)/F9 | =B8-(O9-O8)/F9 | =(I9-I8)/F8 |
| 10 | =D10^2*F10 | =(B10-B9)/F10 | =-(M10-M9)/F10+2*D10*I10+D10 | =(D10-D9)/F10 | =B9-(O10-O9)/F10 | =(I10-I9)/F9 |
| 11 | =D11^2*F11 | =(B11-B10)/F11 | =-(M11-M10)/F11+2*D11*I11+D11 | =(D11-D10)/F11 | =B10-(O11-O10)/F1 | =(I11-I10)/F10 |
| 12 | =D12^2*F12 | =(B12-B11)/F12 | =-(M12-M11)/F12+2*D12*I12+D12 | =(D12-D11)/F12 | =B11-(O12-O11)/F1 | =(I12-I11)/F11 |
| 13 | =D13^2*F13 | =(B13-B12)/F13 | =-(M13-M12)/F13+2*D13*I13+D13 | =(D13-D12)/F13 | =B12-(O13-O12)/F1 | =(I13-I12)/F12 |
| 14 | =D14^2*F14 | =(B14-B13)/F14 | =-(M14-M13)/F14+2*D14*I14+D14 | =(D14-D13)/F14 | =B13-(O14-O13)/F1 | =(I14-I13)/F13 |
| 15 | =D15^2*F15 | =(B15-B14)/F15 | =-(M15-M14)/F15+2*D15*I15+D15 | =(D15-D14)/F15 | =B14-(O15-O14)/F1 | =(I15-I14)/F14 |
| 16 | =D16^2*F16 | =(B16-B15)/F16 | =-(M16-M15)/F16+2*D16*I16+D16 | =(D16-D15)/F16 | =B15-(O16-O15)/F1 | =(I16-I15)/F15 |
| 17 | =D17^2*F17 | =(B17-B16)/F17 | =-(M17-M16)/F17+2*D17*I17+D17 | =(D17-D16)/F17 | =B16-(O17-O16)/F1 | =(I17-I16)/F16 |
| 18 | =D18^2*F18 | =(B18-B17)/F18 | =-(M18-M17)/F18+2*D18*I18+D18 | =(D18-D17)/F18 | =B17-(O18-O17)/F1 | =(I18-I17)/F17 |
| 19 | =D19^2*F19 | =(B19-B18)/F19 | =-(M19-M18)/F19+2*D19*I19+D19 | =(D19-D18)/F19 | =B18-(O19-O18)/F1 | =(I19-I18)/F18 |
| 20 | =D20^2*F20 | =(B20-B19)/F20 | =-(M20-M19)/F20+2*D20*I20+D20 | =(D20-D19)/F20 | =B19-(O20-O19)/F2 | =(I20-I19)/F19 |
| 21 | =D21^2*F21 | =(B21-B20)/F21 | =-(M21-M20)/F21+2*D21*I21+D21 | =(D21-D20)/F21 | =B20-(O21-O20)/F2 | =(I21-I20)/F20 |
| 22 | =D22^2*F22 | =(B22-B21)/F22 | =-(M22-M21)/F22+2*D22*I22+D22 | =(D22-D21)/F22 | =B21-(O22-O21)/F2 | =(I22-I21)/F21 |
| 24 | =SUM(L3:L22) | | | | | |

**FIGURE 9.13-3** Example 2 isoperimetric constrained problem excel worksheet set-up (continued).

differential equation on $z(t)$ under *Column G*. Having $z'(t)$ under *Column H*, $z(t)$ is derived via the Euler method in *Column G* (Fig. 9.13-3).

In Fig. 9.13-2, we have instead the section of the worksheet where we store the *isoperimetric constraint*, together with the necessary Euler—Lagrange conditions.

Launching the Excel Solver parameters (Fig. 9.13-4), where all the constraints of the problem are set, by changing the cells under *Column C, E* and *I* (the lagrange multiplier), the final numerical output results are in Tables 9.13-2 and 9.13-3, while in Fig. 9.13-5 we have the optimal $y_1^*(t)$ and $y_2^*(t)$.

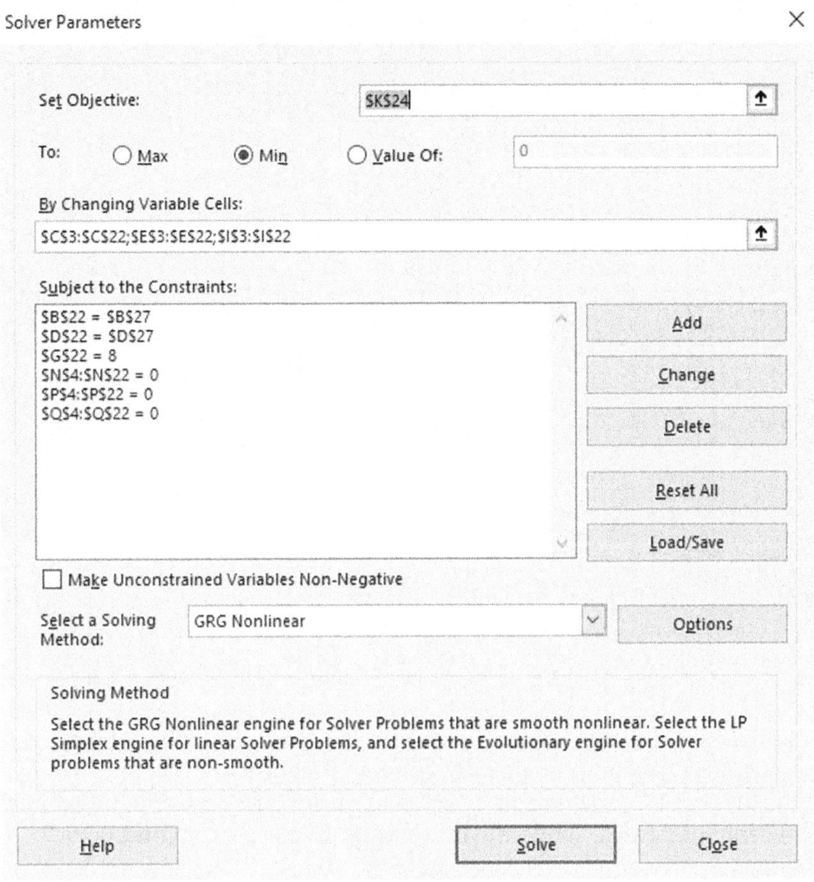

**FIGURE 9.13-4** Example 2 isoperimetric problem (solver set-up).

## 9.14 Checking the Second-Order Conditions in Excel

We conclude this chapter briefly mentioning an important issue in CoV, that is the one of checking the *Second-Order Conditions*, to see whether the extremal found do actually maximizes or minimizes the *functional J(y)*.

Computing our solution numerically we always let the Excel optimizer finding the correct solution. However, one may also check the Second-Order Conditions examining whether the integrand function $F(t, y, y')$ is globally *convex* or *concave* in Excel using the *What-if Analysis Data Table*.

**TABLE 9.13-2**   Example 2 isoperimetric problem excel output results.

| t | y1 | dy1 | y2 | dy2 | dt | z(t) | z'(t) | λ(t) | Augmented Integrand F = $0.5(y_1^2+y_2^2+y_1'y_2')+\lambda(y_2^2-z'(t))$ | Augmented Functional = $\Sigma$ $[0.5(y_1^2+y_2^2+y_1'y_2')+\lambda(y_2^2-z'(t))]dt$ |
|---|---|---|---|---|---|---|---|---|---|---|
| · | 0.00 | | 1.0000 | | | 0.0000 | | 0.0000 | | |
| 0.05 | -0.5502 | -0.5502 | 1.1890 | 0.1890 | 0.0500 | 0.0707 | 1.4138 | 6.6562 | 207.8648 | 10.3932 |
| 0.10 | -1.0512 | -0.5010 | 1.3767 | 0.1876 | 0.0500 | 0.1654 | 1.8952 | 6.6562 | 225.9711 | 11.2986 |
| 0.15 | -1.4963 | -0.4451 | 1.5617 | 0.1850 | 0.0500 | 0.2874 | 2.4388 | 6.6562 | 233.5321 | 11.6766 |
| 0.20 | -1.8790 | -0.3827 | 1.7429 | 0.1813 | 0.0500 | 0.4393 | 3.0378 | 6.6562 | 229.0199 | 11.4510 |
| 0.25 | -2.1931 | -0.3140 | 1.9195 | 0.1766 | 0.0500 | 0.6235 | 3.6845 | 6.6562 | 211.1351 | 10.5568 |
| 0.30 | -2.4323 | -0.2392 | 2.0906 | 0.1711 | 0.0500 | 0.8420 | 4.3706 | 6.6562 | 178.8305 | 8.9415 |
| 0.35 | -2.5908 | -0.1585 | 2.2556 | 0.1650 | 0.0500 | 1.0964 | 5.0878 | 6.6562 | 131.3198 | 6.5660 |
| 0.40 | -2.6630 | -0.0722 | 2.4141 | 0.1585 | 0.0500 | 1.3878 | 5.8281 | 6.6562 | 68.0746 | 3.4037 |
| 0.45 | -2.6433 | 0.0197 | 2.5660 | 0.1519 | 0.0500 | 1.7171 | 6.5845 | 6.6562 | -11.1932 | -0.5597 |
| 0.50 | -2.5266 | 0.1167 | 2.7113 | 0.1453 | 0.0500 | 2.0846 | 7.3511 | 6.6562 | -106.5632 | -5.3282 |
| 0.55 | -2.3080 | 0.2187 | 2.8502 | 0.1390 | 0.0500 | 2.4908 | 8.1239 | 6.6562 | -217.9513 | -10.8976 |
| 0.60 | -1.9826 | 0.3254 | 2.9834 | 0.1332 | 0.0500 | 2.9358 | 8.9008 | 6.6562 | -345.1675 | -17.2584 |
| 0.65 | -1.5458 | 0.4367 | 3.1116 | 0.1282 | 0.0500 | 3.4200 | 9.6823 | 6.6562 | -487.9866 | -24.3993 |
| 0.70 | -0.9933 | 0.5525 | 3.2360 | 0.1244 | 0.0500 | 3.9435 | 10.4717 | 6.6562 | -646.2303 | -32.3115 |
| 0.75 | -0.3206 | 0.6727 | 3.3579 | 0.1219 | 0.0500 | 4.5073 | 11.2754 | 6.6562 | -819.8607 | -40.9930 |
| 0.80 | 0.4766 | 0.7972 | 3.4790 | 0.1211 | 0.0500 | 5.1125 | 12.1031 | 6.6562 | -1,009.0852 | -50.4543 |
| 0.85 | 1.4026 | 0.9260 | 3.6012 | 0.1223 | 0.0500 | 5.7609 | 12.9688 | 6.6562 | -1,214.4723 | -60.7236 |
| 0.90 | 2.4620 | 1.0594 | 3.7270 | 0.1258 | 0.0500 | 6.4554 | 13.8905 | 6.6562 | -1,437.0813 | -71.8541 |
| 0.95 | 3.6594 | 1.1975 | 3.8589 | 0.1319 | 0.0500 | 7.2000 | 14.8913 | 6.6562 | -1,678.6048 | -83.9302 |
| 1.00 | 5.0000 | 1.3406 | 4.0000 | 0.1411 | 0.0500 | 8.0000 | 16.0000 | 6.6562 | -1,941.5311 | -97.0766 |

Boundary cond. z(tf)=c           -421.4990

| | | | | |
|---|---|---|---|---|
| y1(0) | 0.00 | y2(0) | 1.00 | |
| y1(1) | 5.00 | y2(1) | 4.00 | |

This is what the *Second-Order Conditions* also do in theory: checking whether a function (in this case the integrand function) is globally convex or concave.

In fact, in the theory of CoV, there are two theorems for Second-Order Conditions: one provides the sufficient conditions, while the other only the necessary conditions.[6]

1. Sufficiency Theorem

    *In the problem of CoV 9.1-2 if the integrand function $F(t, y, y')$ is concave in the variables $(y, y')$ jointly, then the Euler–Lagrange equation is sufficient for an absolute maximum of $J(y)$. Similarly, if $F(t, y, y')$ is convex in $(y, y')$ jointly, then the Euler–Lagrange equation is sufficient for an absolute minimum of $J(y)$ .*

2. Legendre Necessary Conditions

$$\text{maximization of } J(y) \quad \Rightarrow F_{y'y'} \leq 0 \quad \forall\ t \in [t_0, T]$$

$$\text{minimization of } J(y) \quad \Rightarrow F_{y'y'} \geq 0 \quad \forall\ t \in [t_0, T]$$

$F_{y'y'}$ need to be evaluated along the extremal.

---

[6]See for more details Alpha Chiang, *op. cit.*, chapter 4. See also Akira Takayama, *Mathematical Economics*, 2d ed., Cambridge University Press, 1985, pp. 429–430.

**TABLE 9.13-3** Example 2 isoperimetric problem excel output results (continued).

| Isoperimetric constraint | s.t. Constraints | | | | | |
|---|---|---|---|---|---|---|
| | $y'_1$ | $y_2 + 2y_2\lambda(t) - y_1'' = 0$ | | $y'_2$ | $y_1 \cdot y_2'' = 0$ | $\lambda'(t) = 0$ |
| 0.0707 | -11.0046 | | | 3.7803 | | |
| 0.0948 | -10.0194 | 0.0000 | | 3.7528 | 0.0000 | 0.0000 |
| 0.1219 | -8.9018 | 0.0000 | | 3.7002 | 0.0000 | 0.0000 |
| 0.1519 | -7.6545 | 0.0000 | | 3.6254 | 0.0000 | 0.0000 |
| 0.1842 | -6.2809 | 0.0000 | | 3.5315 | 0.0000 | 0.0000 |
| 0.2185 | -4.7848 | 0.0000 | | 3.4218 | 0.0000 | 0.0000 |
| 0.2544 | -3.1707 | 0.0000 | | 3.3002 | 0.0000 | 0.0000 |
| 0.2914 | -1.4430 | 0.0000 | | 3.1707 | 0.0000 | 0.0000 |
| 0.3292 | 0.3933 | 0.0000 | | 3.0375 | 0.0000 | 0.0000 |
| 0.3676 | 2.3335 | 0.0000 | | 2.9053 | 0.0000 | 0.0000 |
| 0.4062 | 4.3732 | 0.0000 | | 2.7790 | 0.0000 | 0.0000 |
| 0.4450 | 6.5082 | 0.0000 | | 2.6636 | 0.0000 | 0.0000 |
| 0.4841 | 8.7350 | 0.0000 | | 2.5645 | 0.0000 | 0.0000 |
| 0.5236 | 11.0507 | 0.0000 | | 2.4872 | 0.0000 | 0.0000 |
| 0.5638 | 13.4537 | 0.0000 | | 2.4375 | 0.0000 | 0.0000 |
| 0.6052 | 15.9433 | 0.0000 | | 2.4215 | 0.0000 | 0.0000 |
| 0.6484 | 18.5204 | 0.0000 | | 2.4453 | 0.0000 | 0.0000 |
| 0.6945 | 21.1876 | 0.0000 | | 2.5155 | 0.0000 | 0.0000 |
| 0.7446 | 23.9491 | 0.0000 | | 2.6386 | 0.0000 | 0.0000 |
| 0.8000 | 26.8116 | 0.0000 | | 2.8215 | 0.0000 | 0.0000 |
| **8.0000** | | | | | | |

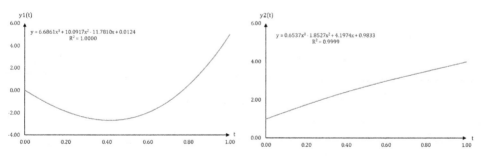

**FIGURE 9.13-5** Example 2 isoperimetric costrained problem numerical optimal paths.

III. Dynamic optimization

## EXAMPLE 1

Let us start with the monopolist optimization case of Section 9.5. Before implementing the *sufficiency theorem* with ($y$, $y'$) jointly one may simply start analyzing in Excel the pattern of the *functional* $F(t, y, y')$ as a function of $dy$ with the Data Table. If one discovers that the *functional* is strictly convex a *minimum* is reached, if strictly concave a *maximum* is reached.

Let us go to our Monopoly case worksheet and just insert a Data Table as follows (Fig. 9.14-1):

The *What if Analysis Data Table* is nothing more than a simulation: here we simulate the behavior of the integrand function F.

Notice that the formula of the Data Table says = **TABLE(;C22)** which means that we take the *Cell C22* as a column input, which is in fact the one-dimensional simulation we want, namely analyze the pattern of $F(t, y, y')$ as a function of $dy$.

We want to discover whether the integrand function is strictly convex when we change $dy$. Notice also that the same results would be reached if we simulated the pattern of the scalar $J(y)$ instead of $F(t, y, y')$.

In this specific example, the pattern discovered is represented in the following Fig. 9.14-2, where we have obtained the strict desired convexity of the *functional*, which means there is just one optimal path that minimizes the given problem.

Now, applying the Data Table to study the behavior of the Functional $F(t, y, y')$ as a function of $F(t, y, y')$ jointly we have to modify our Data Table like in Fig. 9.14-3, simulating along the rows and the columns with a sufficiently large range (here from -100 to +100). The three-dimensional chart obtained is in Fig. 9.14-4, where, again, we confirm the global convexity as a function of ($y$, $y'$) as required by the Sufficiency Theorem.

| | A | B | C | D | E | F | G | H | I | J |
|---|---|---|---|---|---|---|---|---|---|---|
| | $t$ | y = Optimal Price Path P | dy | dt | F = [y{1-1y+0.5y')-1{1- 1y+0.5y')²-1(1-1y+y')-0.5] | Functional = Σ[y{1- 1y+0.5y')-1(1-1y+0.5y')². 1(1-1y+y')-0.5]dt | | | | |
| 1 | | | | | | | | | | |
| 2 | 0 | 1 | | | | | | | | =E22 |
| 3 | =A2+0.05 | =B2+C3 | 0.014388 | =A3-A2 | =-(B3*(1-B3+0.5*C3/D3)-(1-B: | =E3*D3 | | | -1 | =TABLE(;C22) |
| 4 | =A3+0.05 | =B3+C4 | 0.014728 | =A4-A3 | =-(B4*(1-B4+0.5*C4/D4)-(1-B· | =E4*D4 | | | -0.9 | =TABLE(;C22) |
| 5 | =A4+0.05 | =B4+C5 | 0.015417 | =A5-A4 | =-(B5*(1-B5+0.5*C5/D5)-(1-B! | =E5*D5 | | | -0.8 | =TABLE(;C22) |
| 6 | =A5+0.05 | =B5+C6 | 0.016459 | =A6-A5 | =-(B6*(1-B6+0.5*C6/D6)-(1-B( | =E6*D6 | | | -0.7 | =TABLE(;C22) |
| 7 | =A6+0.05 | =B6+C7 | 0.017897 | =A7-A6 | =-(B7*(1-B7+0.5*C7/D7)-(1-B' | =E7*D7 | | | -0.6 | =TABLE(;C22) |
| 8 | =A7+0.05 | =B7+C8 | 0.019757 | =A8-A7 | =-(B8*(1-B8+0.5*C8/D8)-(1-B! | =E8*D8 | | | -0.5 | =TABLE(;C22) |
| 9 | =A8+0.05 | =B8+C9 | 0.022071 | =A9-A8 | =-(B9*(1-B9+0.5*C9/D9)-(1-B' | =E9*D9 | | | -0.4 | =TABLE(;C22) |
| 10 | =A9+0.05 | =B9+C10 | 0.024908 | =A10-A9 | =-(B10*(1-B10+0.5*C10/D10)- | =E10*D10 | | | -0.3 | =TABLE(;C22) |
| 11 | =A10+0.05 | =B10+C11 | 0.028338 | =A11-A10 | =-(B11*(1-B11+0.5*C11/D11)- | =E11*D11 | | | -0.2 | =TABLE(;C22) |
| 12 | =A11+0.05 | =B11+C12 | 0.032428 | =A12-A11 | =-(B12*(1-B12+0.5*C12/D12)- | =E12*D12 | | | -0.1 | =TABLE(;C22) |
| 13 | =A12+0.05 | =B12+C13 | 0.037286 | =A13-A12 | =-(B13*(1-B13+0.5*C13/D13)- | =E13*D13 | | | 0 | =TABLE(;C22) |
| 14 | =A13+0.05 | =B13+C14 | 0.043027 | =A14-A13 | =-(B14*(1-B14+0.5*C14/D14)- | =E14*D14 | | | 0.1 | =TABLE(;C22) |
| 15 | =A14+0.05 | =B14+C15 | 0.049767 | =A15-A14 | =-(B15*(1-B15+0.5*C15/D15)- | =E15*D15 | | | 0.2 | =TABLE(;C22) |
| 16 | =A15+0.05 | =B15+C16 | 0.057688 | =A16-A15 | =-(B16*(1-B16+0.5*C16/D16)- | =E16*D16 | | | 0.3 | =TABLE(;C22) |
| 17 | =A16+0.05 | =B16+C17 | 0.066695 | =A17-A16 | =-(B17*(1-B17+0.5*C17/D17)- | =E17*D17 | | | 0.4 | =TABLE(;C22) |
| 18 | =A17+0.05 | =B17+C18 | 0.077800 | =A18-A17 | =-(B18*(1-B18+0.5*C18/D18)- | =E18*D18 | | | 0.5 | =TABLE(;C22) |
| 19 | =A18+0.05 | =B18+C19 | 0.090481 | =A19-A18 | =-(B19*(1-B19+0.5*C19/D19)- | =E19*D19 | | | 0.6 | =TABLE(;C22) |
| 20 | =A19+0.05 | =B19+C20 | 0.10529: | =A20-A19 | =-(B20*(1-B20+0.5*C20/D20)- | =E20*D20 | | | 0.7 | =TABLE(;C22) |
| 21 | =A20+0.05 | =B20+C21 | 0.12257: | =A21-A20 | =-(B21*(1-B21+0.5*C21/D21)- | =E21*D21 | | | 0.8 | =TABLE(;C22) |
| 22 | =A21+0.05 | =B21+C22 | 0.14275: | =A22-A21 | =-(B22*(1-B22+0.5*C22/D22)- | =E22*D22 | | | 0.9 | =TABLE(;C22) |
| 23 | | | | | | | | | 1 | =TABLE(;C22) |
| 24 | | | | | | =SUM(F3:F22) | | | | |

FIGURE 9.14-1    Example1: one-dimensional Data Table.

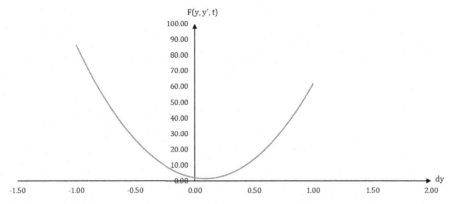

**FIGURE 9.14-2** Example 1: monopoly convex integrand function as a function of *dy*.

| =E22 | -100 | -90 | -80 | -70 | -60 |
|---|---|---|---|---|---|
| -100 | =TABLE(B22;C22) | =TABLE(B22;C22) | =TABLE(B22;C22) | =TABLE(B22;C22) | =TABLE(B22;C22) |
| -90 | =TABLE(B22;C22) | =TABLE(B22;C22) | =TABLE(B22;C22) | =TABLE(B22;C22) | =TABLE(B22;C22) |
| -80 | =TABLE(B22;C22) | =TABLE(B22;C22) | =TABLE(B22;C22) | =TABLE(B22;C22) | =TABLE(B22;C22) |
| -70 | =TABLE(B22;C22) | =TABLE(B22;C22) | =TABLE(B22;C22) | =TABLE(B22;C22) | =TABLE(B22;C22) |
| -60 | =TABLE(B22;C22) | =TABLE(B22;C22) | =TABLE(B22;C22) | =TABLE(B22;C22) | =TABLE(B22;C22) |
| -50 | =TABLE(B22;C22) | =TABLE(B22;C22) | =TABLE(B22;C22) | =TABLE(B22;C22) | =TABLE(B22;C22) |
| -40 | =TABLE(B22;C22) | =TABLE(B22;C22) | =TABLE(B22;C22) | =TABLE(B22;C22) | =TABLE(B22;C22) |
| -30 | =TABLE(B22;C22) | =TABLE(B22;C22) | =TABLE(B22;C22) | =TABLE(B22;C22) | =TABLE(B22;C22) |
| -20 | =TABLE(B22;C22) | =TABLE(B22;C22) | =TABLE(B22;C22) | =TABLE(B22;C22) | =TABLE(B22;C22) |
| -10 | =TABLE(B22;C22) | =TABLE(B22;C22) | =TABLE(B22;C22) | =TABLE(B22;C22) | =TABLE(B22;C22) |
| 0 | =TABLE(B22;C22) | =TABLE(B22;C22) | =TABLE(B22;C22) | =TABLE(B22;C22) | =TABLE(B22;C22) |
| 10 | =TABLE(B22;C22) | =TABLE(B22;C22) | =TABLE(B22;C22) | =TABLE(B22;C22) | =TABLE(B22;C22) |
| 20 | =TABLE(B22;C22) | =TABLE(B22;C22) | =TABLE(B22;C22) | =TABLE(B22;C22) | =TABLE(B22;C22) |
| 30 | =TABLE(B22;C22) | =TABLE(B22;C22) | =TABLE(B22;C22) | =TABLE(B22;C22) | =TABLE(B22;C22) |
| 40 | =TABLE(B22;C22) | =TABLE(B22;C22) | =TABLE(B22;C22) | =TABLE(B22;C22) | =TABLE(B22;C22) |
| 50 | =TABLE(B22;C22) | =TABLE(B22;C22) | =TABLE(B22;C22) | =TABLE(B22;C22) | =TABLE(B22;C22) |
| 60 | =TABLE(B22;C22) | =TABLE(B22;C22) | =TABLE(B22;C22) | =TABLE(B22;C22) | =TABLE(B22;C22) |
| 70 | =TABLE(B22;C22) | =TABLE(B22;C22) | =TABLE(B22;C22) | =TABLE(B22;C22) | =TABLE(B22;C22) |
| 80 | =TABLE(B22;C22) | =TABLE(B22;C22) | =TABLE(B22;C22) | =TABLE(B22;C22) | =TABLE(B22;C22) |
| 90 | =TABLE(B22;C22) | =TABLE(B22;C22) | =TABLE(B22;C22) | =TABLE(B22;C22) | =TABLE(B22;C22) |
| 100 | =TABLE(B22;C22) | =TABLE(B22;C22) | =TABLE(B22;C22) | =TABLE(B22;C22) | =TABLE(B22;C22) |

**FIGURE 9.14-3** Example 1: two-dimensional Data Table $F(y, y', t)$ as a function of $(y, y')$.

## EXAMPLE 2

In Fig. 9.14-5 we have studied the globally concave *functional* for the maximization economic problem seen in Section 9.7 (The Eisner–Strotz model).

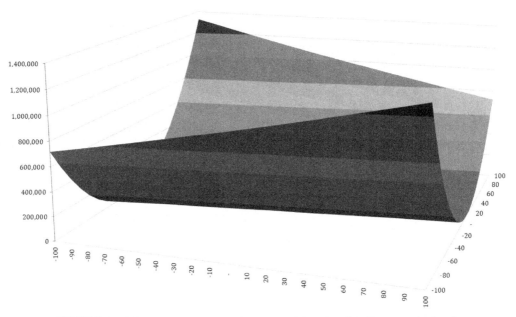

**FIGURE 9.14-4**   Example 1: monopoly integrand function globally convex in $(y, y')$.

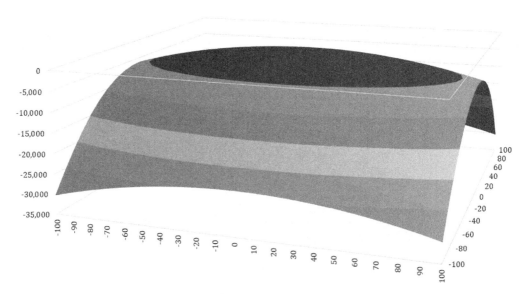

**FIGURE 9.14-5**   Example 2: Eisner–Strotz model integrand function globally concave in $(y, y')$.

## Exercises

1. Solve using the contour lines in Excel the following CoV discrete form of the *shortest distance problem*:

$$J = \sum_{i=1}^{2} \left[1 + \frac{(\Delta_i y)^2}{(\Delta_i t)^2}\right]^{1/2} \Delta_i t = \left[1 + \frac{(\Delta_1 y)^2}{(\Delta_1 t)^2}\right]^{1/2} \Delta_1 t + \left[1 + \frac{(\Delta_2 y)^2}{(\Delta_2 t)^2}\right]^{1/2} \Delta_2 t$$

s.t.

$$y(1) = 7$$

$$y(3) = 17$$

$$\Delta_1 y + \Delta_2 y = 10$$

Plot the solution in a chart.

2. Solve by hand, using the Lagrange multipliers technique, on a discrete basis and over three stages only, the following CoV problem:

$$\min J = \int_0^2 \left[12ty + (y')^2\right] dt$$

s.t.

$$y(0) = 0 \text{ and } y(2) = 8$$

Replicate the exercise in Excel and check the solution.

3. Solve the following CoV problem in Excel using the Solver, and compare the numerical solution to the exact solution:

$$\min J = \int_1^5 \left[3t + (y')^{1/2}\right] dt$$

s.t.

$$y(1) = 3 \text{ and } y(5) = 7$$

III. Dynamic optimization

**4.** Solve the following CoV problem in Excel using the Solver, and compare the numerical solution to the exact solution:

$$\min J = \int_0^1 \left[10ty + (y')^2\right] dt$$

s.t.

$$y(0) = 1 \text{ and } y(1) = 2$$

**5.** Find the extremal for the following CoV problem, involving two independent functions:

$$J = \int_0^{\frac{\pi}{4}} (y_1^2 + y_1' y_2' + y_2^2) dt$$

s.t.

$$y_1(0) = 1, y_2(0) = 3/2$$

and

$$y_1\left(\frac{\pi}{4}\right) = 2, y_2\left(\frac{\pi}{4}\right) = free$$

Set up, to solve the problem, the problem the necessary transversality condition.

**6.** Find the extremal of the following functional in Excel using the Solver, and compare the numerical solution to the exact solution:

$$J = \int_0^T \left[ty + (y')^2\right] dt$$

s.t.

$$y(0) = 1, \ y(T) = 10 \text{ and } T \text{ free}$$

Set up in the problem the necessary transversality conditions.

7. Find the extremal of the following functional in Excel using the Solver, and compare the numerical solution to the exact solution:

$$J = \int_0^2 (y^2 + t^2 y') \, dt$$

s.t.

$$y(0) = 0 \text{ and } y(2) = 2$$

8. Find the extremal of the following functional in Excel using the Solver, and compare the numerical solution to the exact solution:

$$J = \int_0^1 \left[ y + yy' + y' + \frac{1}{2}(y')^2 \right] dt$$

s.t.

$$y(0) = 0 \text{ and } y(1) = 5$$

9. **Unemployment and inflation.** Repeat the problem of finding the optimal path of inflation rate in Section 9.6, transformed now in the following problem with free terminal value:

$$\min J(\pi) = \int_0^1 \lambda(\pi, \pi') e^{-\rho t} dt$$

s.t.

$$\pi(0) = 5\% \text{ and } \pi(1) = Free$$

where:

$$\lambda(\pi, \pi') = \left( \frac{\pi'}{\beta j} \right)^2 + \alpha \left( \frac{\pi'}{j} + \pi \right)^2$$

Utilize the required boundary condition at $T = 1$ and use the following parameters:

$$j = 0.5, \quad \alpha = 1, \quad \beta = 1, \quad \rho = 0.05, \quad \pi_0 = 0.05$$

III. Dynamic optimization

10. **Optimal consumption Ramsey model.** Solve the Ramsey problem, finding the optimal capital path K*(t) such that the following functional is maximized:

$$U(K) = \int_0^1 [U(C(t))]dt = \int_0^1 [U(f(K(t)) - K'(t))]dt$$

s.t.

$$K(0) = 5 \text{ and } K(T) = 3$$

where the production function is:

$$f(K(t)) = rK(t) \qquad (r > 0)$$

with $r = 5\%$ and the utility function is in the following form:

$$U(C(t)) = \widehat{U} - \frac{1}{b}C^{-b} \qquad (b > 0)$$

with $\widehat{U} = 10$, $b = 0.5$.

    Also, find the optimal numerical consumption path $C^*(t) = rK^*(t) - K^{*'}$

11. **Optimal consumption Ramsey model.** Solve the Ramsey problem, finding the optimal capital path K*(t), such that the following functional is maximized:

$$U(K) = \int_0^1 [U(C(t))]e^{-t/4}dt = \int_0^1 [\ln(2K - K')]e^{-t/4}dt$$

s.t.

$$K(0) = 5 \text{ and } K(T) = 7$$

12. **Optimal rate of advertising expenditures.** Let us consider the case of a company that produces a good having a seasonal demand pattern. Rate of sales depends not only on the time of year $t$ but also on the rate of advertising expenditure $s(t)$. The sales response to advertising can be assumed instantaneous so that $q = q(s,t)$. Since the good is assumed to be highly perishable, the rate of production will be maintained at a value equal to the known sales rate. There is the requirement that all the demands must be met. If $q$ is the production rate, production costs are incurred at a rate of $c(q, \dot{q})$, namely, the production costs depend on the production rate and the rate of change of the production rate. Now, since $q = q(s, t)$ we can express the rate of incurring production costs in terms of $s, s' = \frac{ds}{dt}$ and $t$, that is $c(s, s', t)$. The problem is to determine the rate of advertising expenditures $s(t)$ which maximizes the profit from the sale of the good, with a specified unit price $p$ and total revenues $pq$, total cost $C + s$ and therefore profit

equal to $\pi = \bar{p}q - \bar{c}q - s$. The problem is to find the optimal path $s^*(t)$ so that we maximize the following total profit functional:

$$P(s) = \int_0^T [\bar{p}q(s, t) - C(s, \dot{s}, t) - s(t)].$$

Now, let us assume that the quantity produced and sold moves with respect to $s$ according to the following function:

$$q = s - 0.05s^2$$

and total costs are assumed to be instead:

$$C(s, \dot{s}, t) = \bar{c}\left[(s - 0.05s^2) + (ds/dt)^2\right];$$

we can reexpress $P$, with $s(t)$ the state variable, as:

$$P = \int_0^T \left[\bar{p}(s - 0.05s^2) - \bar{c}(s - 0.05s^2) - \bar{c}(ds/dt)^2 - s\right]$$

**a.** Maximize the above functional with: $T = 1$, $\bar{p} = 50$ and $\bar{c} = 5$, $s(0) = 1$ and $s(1) = 5$.

**b.** Assume now a vertical-line-problem with $s(1) = $ *free* and find the optimal rate of advertisement, using the required *natural boundary condition* at $T = 1$ (i.e., $\frac{\partial F(T, s(T), s'(T))}{\partial s'(T)} = 0$).

13. **Optimal adjustment of labor demand.**[7] Consider a firm that has decided to raise the labor input from $L_0$ to an undetermined optimal level $L_T^*$ after encountering a wage shock reduction at $t = 0$. The adjustment of labor input will imply a cost that varies with $L'(t)$, the rate of change of $L(t)$. The problem is to determine the best speed of adjustment toward $L_T^*$ as well as the level of $L_T^*$ itself.

Let the profit function be a function of $L$ only:

$$\pi(L) \qquad (\text{with } \pi''(L) < 0).$$

The cost of adjusting $L$ is assumed to be:

$$C(L') = bL'^2 + k \qquad (b > 0, \, k > 0 \text{ and } L' \neq 0)$$

[7]See Daniel S. Hamermesh "Labor Demand and the Structure of Adjustment Costs". *American Economic Review*, September 1989.

The net profit will be:

$$\Pi(L) = \pi(L) - C(L')$$

The problem of the firm is to maximize the total net profit over time during the process of changing the labor input. The firm has to choose not only the optimal $L_T^*$ but also the optimal $T^*$. This is *a terminal curve problem*, where neither the time nor the state variable is preset.

Moreover, the profit will also include the capitalized value of the profit in the post $T^*$ period, which is affected by the choice of $L_T^*$ and $T$. The profit rate at time $T$ is $\pi(L_T)$ and its present value at $T$, will be $\frac{\pi(L_T)}{\rho}$ and the present value as of $t_0$ will be $\frac{\pi(L_T)}{\rho}e^{-\rho t}$.

The problem is therefore formalized as maximizing the following discounted stream of profits:

$$\text{maximize } \Pi(L) = \int_0^T \left[\pi(L) - bL'^2 - k\right]e^{-\rho t} + \frac{\pi(L_T)}{\rho}e^{-\rho T} \tag{1}$$

s.t.

$$L(0) = L_0$$

and

$$L(T) = L_T \qquad (\text{with } L_T > L_0 \text{ free, } T \text{ free})$$

Problem **(1)** is defined as *Problem of Bolza*, because of the presence outside the integral of the quantity $\frac{\pi(L_T)}{\rho}e^{-\rho T}$, which still varies with $L_T$ and $T$. We can convert Problem **(1)** (see also Alpha Chiang, *op. cit.* Section 3.4) into the following standard version:

$$\text{maximize } \Pi(L) = \int_0^T \left[-bL'^2 - k + \frac{1}{\rho}\pi'(L)L'\right]e^{-\rho t} + \frac{1}{\rho}\pi(L_0) \tag{2}$$

The functional now contains an extra term outside the integral, but it is a constant and therefore it does not affect neither the optimal path $L(t)$ nor the optimal value $L_T$ and $T$.

   **a.** Find the numerical optimal path $L^*(t)$, the optimal value $L_T^*$ and the optimal time $T^*$ with the following profit function, setting the required boundary conditions:

$$\pi(L) = L^{0.5}$$

**b.** Find the numerical optimal path $L^*(t)$ the optimal value $L_T^*$ and the optimal time $T^*$ with the following profit function, setting the required boundary conditions:

$$\pi(L) = 2mL - nL^2$$

where $m = 1$ and $n = 0.05$.

Enumerate and plot the results. In both cases, set $L(0) = 10$, $p=0.05$, $k = 0.9$ and $b = 1$.

**14.** Find the extremal for the following constrained CoV problem, involving two state variables and a constraint represented by a differential equation:

$$J = \int_0^1 (y_1 - y_2^2)dt$$

s.t.

$$\frac{dy_1}{dt} = y_2$$

and boundary conditions as follows:

$$y_1(0) = 0, \quad y_2(0) = 0, \quad y_1(1) = free, \quad y_2(1) = free$$

**a.** Set up the augmented functional.
**b.** Identify via the Euler–Lagrange equations the conditions for the solution of the problem.
**c.** Plot the numerical solutions for the two state variables.

**15.** Find the extremal in the following isoperimetric constrained problem:

$$\min J = \int_0^1 \frac{1}{2}(y_1^2 + y_2^2 + 2y_1'y_2')dt$$

s.t.

$$\int_0^1 y_2^2 dt = 8 \text{ (Isoperimetric constraint)}$$

and

$$y_1(0) = 0, \quad y_2(0) = 0, \quad y_1(1) = \text{free}, \quad y_2(1) = \text{free}$$

**16.** Find the extremal in the following constrained problem, with two differential equation constraints:

$$\min J = \int_0^1 \frac{1}{2}(y_1^2 + y_2^2 + y_3^2)dt$$

s.t.

$$y_1' = y_2 - y_1$$

$$y_2' = -2y_1 - 3y_2 + y_3$$

$$y_1(0) = 5, y_2(0) = 5, \; y_1(1) = \text{free}, y_2(1) = \text{free}$$

**a.** Find the necessary conditions to solve the problem setting up the augmented integrand function and the Euler–Lagrange conditions.

**b.** Once you have identified the system of the five differential equations, set them up in Excel and using the shooting method, changing the two Lagrange multipliers at $t_0 = 0$ (Solver), find the numerical solutions that optimizes the functional.

**c.** Plot the solutions in a chart.

Hint: the augmented integrand function will be given by:

$$F_a(y(t), y'(t), \lambda(t), t) = \frac{1}{2}(y_1^2 + y_2^2 + y_3^2) + \lambda_1[y_2 - y_1 - y_1'] + \lambda_2[-2y_1 - 3y_2 + y_3 - y_2']$$

Now, we just need to find the differential equations of the system via the following five Euler–Lagrange conditions:

$$\frac{\partial F_a}{\partial y_1} - \frac{d}{dt}\left[\frac{\partial F_a}{\partial y_1'}\right] = 0 \Rightarrow \lambda_1' = -y_1 + \lambda_1 + 2\lambda_2$$

$$\frac{\partial F_a}{\partial y_2} - \frac{d}{dt}\left[\frac{\partial F_a}{\partial y_2'}\right] = 0 \Rightarrow \lambda_2' = -y_2 - \lambda_1 + 3\lambda_2$$

$$\frac{\partial F_a}{\partial y_3} - \frac{d}{dt}\left[\frac{\partial F_a}{\partial y_3'}\right] = 0 \Rightarrow y_3 = -\lambda_2$$

$$\frac{\partial F_a}{\partial \lambda_1} - \frac{d}{dt}\left[\frac{\partial F_a}{\partial \lambda_1'}\right] = 0 \Rightarrow y_2 - y_1 - y_1' = 0$$

$$\frac{\partial F_a}{\partial \lambda_2} - \frac{d}{dt}\left[\frac{\partial F_a}{\partial \lambda_2'}\right] = 0 \Rightarrow -2y_1 - 3y_2 + y_3 - y_2' = 0$$

CHAPTER

# 10

# Theory of optimal control

OUTLINE

Elements of Numerical Mathematical Economics with Excel
https://doi.org/10.1016/B978-0-12-817648-1.00010-4

## 10.1 The optimal control problem and the Pontryagin's maximum principle

Differently from the *simplest problem* form 9.1-2 given in the Control of Variables (CoV) section, the *simplest problem* in the *Theory of Optimal Control* is stated as follows:

$$\max_{\{u\}} J(u) = \int_{t_0}^{T} F(t, y, u) dt$$

$$s.t. \quad \dot{y} = f(t, y, u) \quad (equation\ of\ motion) \tag{10.1-1}$$

$$y(t_0) = y_0 \quad y(T) \quad \text{free} \quad (y_0,\ T\ \text{given})$$

$$\text{and } u(t) \in \mathcal{U} \quad \forall t \in [t_0, T].$$

The objective then is to find an admissible $u^*(t)$, which causes the system $\dot{y}(t)$ to follow an admissible path $y^*(t)$ that maximizes the performance measure $J(u)$.

Normally, in the Theory of Optimal Control (OC), the *simplest problem* is always stated in terms of *maximization* and reformulated in terms of *minimization* by simply attaching a minus to the objective *functional*.

Notice the following key differences from the *simplest problem* provided in CoV.

The objective *functional* $J$ contains the variable $u(t)$, called *control variable*, as argument, and this is because $u(t)$ is now the ultimate variable of dynamic optimization. Therefore, Eq. (10.1-1) is still a definite integral, but the integrand function $F$ does not contain anymore the $y'(t)$ argument as in CoV. Now we have a new argument $u(t)$, which represents the control variable.

The control variable $u(t)$ affects the state variable $y(t)$ through the *equation of motion* $\dot{y} = f(t, y, u)$, where we have now denoted with $\dot{y}(t)$ the time derivative $dy/dt$, differently from CoV.[1] What this equation does is providing a mechanism through which the choice of control variable $u(t)$ can be transferred to the state variable $y(t)$.

Normally, the equation of motion takes the form[2] of a first-order differential equation $\dot{y} = f(t, y, u)$, but also a second-order differential equation may appear.

---

[1] See also the approach used by Alpha Chiang in *op. cit.*, Chapter 7.

[2] We will normally deal with *time invariant* (or *autonomous*) first-order ODE in the form of $\dot{y} = f(y(t), u(t))$.

To solve the OC problem given in Eq. (10.1-1), we need to introduce an auxiliary variable called *costate variable*, that works as a Lagrange multiplier and therefore it is denoted by $\lambda(t)$.

The OC Problem 10.1-1 includes an equality constraint $\dot{y} = f(t, y, u)$, and within its resolution process an important mathematical entity is introduced, which is called *Hamiltonian* (denoted by $\mathcal{H}$) defined as:

$$\mathcal{H}(t, y, u, \lambda) \overset{\text{def}}{=} F(t, y, u) + \lambda(t) f(t, y, u) \tag{10.1-2}$$

To solve Problem 10.1-1, we introduce now the most important finding in the OC theory, which is the *maximum principle*, a set of first-order necessary conditions, that originated from the work of the Russian mathematician L. S. Pontryagin and his associates.[3]

The *maximum principle* conditions to solve the OC Problem 10.1-1 are as follows:

$$\max_{\{u\}} \mathcal{H}(t, y, u, \lambda) \quad \forall\, t \in [t_0,\ T]$$

$$\dot{y}(t) = \frac{\partial \mathcal{H}}{\partial \lambda} \quad \text{(equation of motion for } y) \tag{10.1-3}$$

$$\dot{\lambda}(t) = -\frac{\partial \mathcal{H}}{\partial y} \quad \text{(equation of motion for } \lambda)$$

$$\lambda(T) = 0 \quad \text{(transversality condition)}$$

$\max_{u} \mathcal{H}(t, y, u, \lambda)$ means that the Hamiltonian is to be maximized with respect to the control variable $u(t)$ alone.

Eq. (10.1-3) can also be expressed as follows:

$$\mathcal{H}(t, y, u^*, \lambda) \geq \mathcal{H}(t, y, u, \lambda) \quad \forall\, t \in [t_0,\ T] \tag{10.1-4}$$

where $u^*(t)$ is the optimal control and $u(t)$ is any other suboptimal control.

The maximum principle conditions are, in general, not sufficient. The conditions are, however, necessary and sufficient if certain concavity conditions are satisfied. These sufficient conditions are contained in the *Mangasarian* and *Arrow Sufficiency Theorems* that we will see in Section 10.12.

## 10.2 Nonlinear Hamiltonian and linear Hamiltonian (bang-bang control)

It is clear from the *maximum principle* conditions that the resolution of Eq. (10.1-1) must pass through the maximization of the Hamiltonian function $\mathcal{H}$ with respect to the control variable $u(t)$.

[3]L. S. Pontryagin, V. G. Boltyanskii, R. V. Gamkrelidze, and E. F. Mishchenko, *The Mathematical Theory of Optimal Processes*, translated from the Russian by K. N. Trirogoff, Interscience Publishers, New York, 1962.

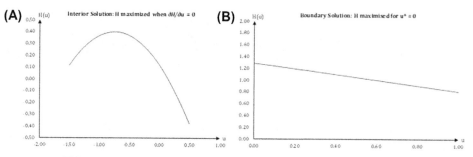

FIGURE 10.2-1   (A) Nonlinear Hamiltonian and (B) linear Hamiltonian.

Now, essentially the following two cases arise in the OC theory for maximizing $\mathcal{H}$:

1. Hamiltonian function is nonlinear in $u(t)$, and usually the control variable $u(t)$ is unconstrained.
2. Hamiltonian function is linear in $u(t)$, and the control variable $u$ is usually constrained (*bang-bang* control problem).

In the first case assuming $\mathcal{H}$ is continuous and differentiable with respect to $u(t)$ we can always apply the first-order condition $\partial\mathcal{H}/\partial u = 0$ to get the solution (see Fig. 10.2-1.A). When a closed set $\mathcal{U}$ is provided, and the control variable is constrained, depending on the shape of $\mathcal{H}$ within the control region $\mathcal{U}$, we may not use the first-order condition because the optimal solution is on the boundary of $\mathcal{U}$.

We will see that the first-order condition $\partial\mathcal{H}/\partial u = 0$ will lead to obtaining a time path control variable $u(t)$ as a function of $\lambda(t)$, therefore having the two variables intimately connected in the OC problems.

In the second case instead, as $\mathcal{H}$ is linear with respect to $u(t)$, the first-order condition does not apply at all, to find the maximum point of $\mathcal{H}$ (see Fig. 10.2-1.B).

Normally in these cases, a restriction on $u(t)$ is specified, such as $u \in [0, 1]$. Therefore, what we need to do is simply studying the shape of the linearity of $\mathcal{H}$ over $\mathcal{U} = [0, 1]$ to identify the optimal $u^*(t)$.

In the linear case essentially $\mathcal{H}$ can be a negative or a positive straight line, with respect to $u(t)$, and the control variable is normally to be chosen on the boundary points of the specified set $\mathcal{U}$, *banging* against one boundary point solution and then *banging* against a second boundary point solution, to maximize the value of $\mathcal{H}$.

In Fig. 10.2-2 instead, different paths in the nonlinear Hamiltonian function have been simulated changing the control variable $u(t)$, of which just one path satisfies the relation 10.1-4 (the dotted line curve), leading to the resolution of Problem 10.1-1 according to the *maximum principle*.

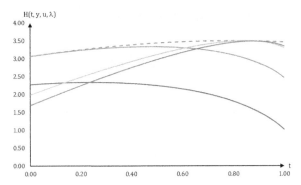

FIGURE 10.2-2   Examples of different $\mathcal{H}$ paths versus the optimal $\mathcal{H}^*$ (dotted line curve).

## 10.3 Setup of the Excel worksheet for optimal control problems

It is time to see how we can implement the OC problems numerically in Excel.

The first two examples are taken purposely from the literature,[4] to let the reader realize that different computational approaches may be implemented to solve these problems.

### EXAMPLE 1 (OPTIMAL CONTROL INVESTMENT PROBLEM)

Let us solve with respect to $u$ the following investment problem, which has the standard form 10.1-1:

$$\max_{\{u\}} J(u) = \int_0^1 \left( y - \frac{1}{2} u^2 \right) dt$$

$$s.t. \ \ \dot{y} = u - \delta y \ \text{and} \ y(0) \ = \ 1, \ y(1) \ = \ free$$

In the model proposed the state variable $y$ represents the available capital (i.e., fixed long-term capital), while its differential $\dot{y}$ represents the variation in the capital stock, namely the net capital expenditures, which are equal to the gross capital expenditures (gross capex), the control variable $u$, minus the total depreciation (with $\delta$ rate of depreciation).

Then, if we pose for simplicity $\Delta t = 1$ we can also write the constraint on $\dot{y}$ as follows:

$$y_{t+1} = y_t + gross\ capex - depreciation = y_t + u - \delta y \ \ \ 0 < \delta \leq 1$$

[4]See Eric Naevdal, Solving Continuous-Time Optimal-Control Problems with a Spreadsheet, *The Journal of Economic Education*, Vol. 34, No. 2 (Spring 2003), pp. 99–122. He solves the cases using the Runge-Kutta method, while the method proposed here to obtain the *costate variable* is the Euler Method, which is less cumbersome than Runge-Kutta and, at the same time, the worksheet is in general organized differently, without resorting to defined-user functions.

The integrand function $\left(y - \frac{1}{2}u^2\right)$ represents instead the profit *performance measure* that we want to maximize, where revenues ($y$) depend on the fixed capital employed and costs depend on the investments made. In the integrand function $y$ can be then interpreted as the Sales-to-Capital ratio (in this specific example Sales-to-Capital $= 1$).

Now, a key step to solve the problem is identifying the Hamiltonian function and in general the complete set of equations under Eq. (10.1-3).

Setting the rate of depreciation $\delta = 1$ we have a nonlinear Hamiltonian function with respect to $u(t)$:

$$\mathcal{H} = y - \frac{1}{2}u^2 + \lambda(u - y)$$

from which we can derive the first-order condition $\frac{\partial \mathcal{H}}{\partial u} = 0$ to get the maximum in $\mathcal{H}$:

$$\frac{\partial \mathcal{H}}{\partial u} = -u + \lambda = 0 \Rightarrow u(t) = \lambda.$$

Notice that the second derivative in $\mathcal{H}$ with respect to $u(t)$ is negative.

Then, from the Hamiltonian, we can derive the given equation of motion for $y(t)$:

$$\frac{dy}{dt} = \frac{\partial \mathcal{H}}{\partial \lambda} = u - y = \lambda - y$$

together with the equation of motion for $\lambda(t)$:

$$\frac{d\lambda}{dt} = -\frac{\partial \mathcal{H}}{\partial y} = -(1 - \lambda) = \lambda - 1.$$

We have now all the differential equations to set up the Excel spreadsheet and solve the problem.

With the help of the usual screenshot the way the worksheet is organized is depicted in Fig. 10.3-1, where we have set up 20 steps of length 0.05 over the time interval [0, *T*].

The above problem essentially consists of solving the differential equation (using the Euler method) for $\lambda(t)$, setting the *Cell H22* $= 0$ (i.e., the transversality condition) by changing *Cell H2*, as in the Excel Solver of Fig. 10.3-2. **This is the Shooting method**.

The optimal Capital Path is then derived through $u(t)$, while the Optimal Investment (the control variable *u*) is derived under *Column E*. It is apparent how all the variables involved are intimately connected for the resolution of the problem.

The final numerical solution is in Table 10.3-1.

The exact continuous solution for $y(t)$ is as follows:

$$y^*(t) = 1 - \frac{1}{2}e^{t-1} + \left(\frac{1}{2}e^{-1} - 1\right)e^{-t}$$

while for $\lambda(t)$ is:

$$\lambda^*(t) = 1 - e^{t-1}.$$

| | A | B | C | D | E | F | G | H | I | J | K |
|---|---|---|---|---|---|---|---|---|---|---|---|
| 1 | t | y Capital Path | dy = (u-y)dt | dt | Investment u = ẏ+y | dy/dt =λ-y | Hamiltonian = (y-1/2u²)+λ(u-y) | λ(t) | dλ/dt | F = y-1/2u² | Functional = Σ [y-1/2u²]dt |
| 2 | 0 | 0 | =(E2-B2)*D2 | | =F2+B2 | =H2-B2 | 0 | 0.6415140823379¦ | =-1+H2 | =B2-1/2*E2^2 | =J2*D2 |
| 3 | =A2+0.05 | =B2+C3 | =(E3-B3)*D3 | =A3-A2 | =F3+B3 | =H3-B3 | =J3+H3*F3 | =H2+I3*D3 | =-1+H3 | =B3-1/2*E3^2 | =J3*D3 |
| 4 | =A3+0.05 | =B3+C4 | =(E4-B4)*D4 | =A4-A3 | =F4+B4 | =H4-B4 | =J4+H4*F4 | =H3+I4*D4 | =-1+H4 | =B4-1/2*E4^2 | =J4*D4 |
| 5 | =A4+0.05 | =B4+C5 | =(E5-B5)*D5 | =A5-A4 | =F5+B5 | =H5-B5 | =J5+H5*F5 | =H4+I5*D5 | =-1+H5 | =B5-1/2*E5^2 | =J5*D5 |
| 6 | =A5+0.05 | =B5+C6 | =(E6-B6)*D6 | =A6-A5 | =F6+B6 | =H6-B6 | =J6+H6*F6 | =H5+I6*D6 | =-1+H6 | =B6-1/2*E6^2 | =J6*D6 |
| 7 | =A6+0.05 | =B6+C7 | =(E7-B7)*D7 | =A7-A6 | =F7+B7 | =H7-B7 | =J7+H7*F7 | =H6+I7*D7 | =-1+H7 | =B7-1/2*E7^2 | =J7*D7 |
| 8 | =A7+0.05 | =B7+C8 | =(E8-B8)*D8 | =A8-A7 | =F8+B8 | =H8-B8 | =J8+H8*F8 | =H7+I8*D8 | =-1+H8 | =B8-1/2*E8^2 | =J8*D8 |
| 9 | =A8+0.05 | =B8+C9 | =(E9-B9)*D9 | =A9-A8 | =F9+B9 | =H9-B9 | =J9+H9*F9 | =H8+I9*D9 | =-1+H9 | =B9-1/2*E9^2 | =J9*D9 |
| 10 | =A9+0.05 | =B9+C10 | =(E10-B10)*D10 | =A10-A9 | =F10+B10 | =H10-B10 | =J10+H10*F10 | =H9+I10*D10 | =-1+H10 | =B10-1/2*E10^2 | =J10*D10 |
| 11 | =A10+0.05 | =B10+C11 | =(E11-B11)*D11 | =A11-A10 | =F11+B11 | =H11-B11 | =J11+H11*F11 | =H10+I11*D11 | =-1+H11 | =B11-1/2*E11^2 | =J11*D11 |
| 12 | =A11+0.05 | =B11+C12 | =(E12-B12)*D12 | =A12-A11 | =F12+B12 | =H12-B12 | =J12+H12*F12 | =H11+I12*D12 | =-1+H12 | =B12-1/2*E12^2 | =J12*D12 |
| 13 | =A12+0.05 | =B12+C13 | =(E13-B13)*D13 | =A13-A12 | =F13+B13 | =H13-B13 | =J13+H13*F13 | =H12+I13*D13 | =-1+H13 | =B13-1/2*E13^2 | =J13*D13 |
| 14 | =A13+0.05 | =B13+C14 | =(E14-B14)*D14 | =A14-A13 | =F14+B14 | =H14-B14 | =J14+H14*F14 | =H13+I14*D14 | =-1+H14 | =B14-1/2*E14^2 | =J14*D14 |
| 15 | =A14+0.05 | =B14+C15 | =(E15-B15)*D15 | =A15-A14 | =F15+B15 | =H15-B15 | =J15+H15*F15 | =H14+I15*D15 | =-1+H15 | =B15-1/2*E15^2 | =J15*D15 |
| 16 | =A15+0.05 | =B15+C16 | =(E16-B16)*D16 | =A16-A15 | =F16+B16 | =H16-B16 | =J16+H16*F16 | =H15+I16*D16 | =-1+H16 | =B16-1/2*E16^2 | =J16*D16 |
| 17 | =A16+0.05 | =B16+C17 | =(E17-B17)*D17 | =A17-A16 | =F17+B17 | =H17-B17 | =J17+H17*F17 | =H16+I17*D17 | =-1+H17 | =B17-1/2*E17^2 | =J17*D17 |
| 18 | =A17+0.05 | =B17+C18 | =(E18-B18)*D18 | =A18-A17 | =F18+B18 | =H18-B18 | =J18+H18*F18 | =H17+I18*D18 | =-1+H18 | =B18-1/2*E18^2 | =J18*D18 |
| 19 | =A18+0.05 | =B18+C19 | =(E19-B19)*D19 | =A19-A18 | =F19+B19 | =H19-B19 | =J19+H19*F19 | =H18+I19*D19 | =-1+H19 | =B19-1/2*E19^2 | =J19*D19 |
| 20 | =A19+0.05 | =B19+C20 | =(E20-B20)*D20 | =A20-A19 | =F20+B20 | =H20-B20 | =J20+H20*F20 | =H19+I20*D20 | =-1+H20 | =B20-1/2*E20^2 | =J20*D20 |
| 21 | =A20+0.05 | =B20+C21 | =(E21-B21)*D21 | =A21-A20 | =F21+B21 | =H21-B21 | =J21+H21*F21 | =H20+I21*D21 | =-1+H21 | =B21-1/2*E21^2 | =J21*D21 |
| 22 | =A21+0.05 | =B21+C22 | =(E22-B22)*D22 | =A22-A21 | =F22+B22 | =H22-B22 | =J22+H22*F22 | =H21+I22*D22 | =-1+H22 | =B22-1/2*E22^2 | =J22*D22 |
| 23 | | | | | | | | | | | |
| 24 | y(0) | 0 | | | | | | Transversality Condition λ(T) = 0 | | | |
| 25 | y(1) | Free | | | | | | | | | =SUM(K3:K22) |

FIGURE 10.3-1  Example 1: worksheet setup.

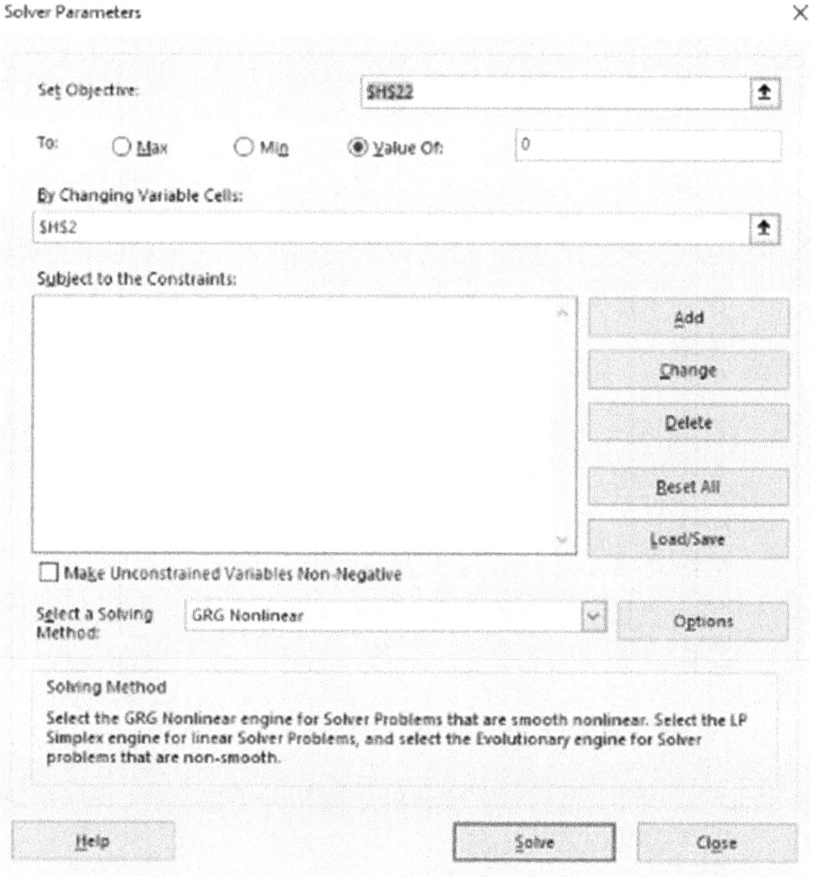

FIGURE 10.3-2  Example 1: setting $\lambda(T) = 0$ in the Excel Solver.

**TABLE 10.3-1**  Example 1: numerical solution.

| t | y Capital Path | dy = (u-y)dt | dt | Investment u = y+y | dy/dt = u-y | Hamiltonian = (y-1/2u²)+λ(u-y) | λ(t) | dλ/dt | F = y-1/2u² | Functional = Σ [y-1/2u²] dt |
|---|---|---|---|---|---|---|---|---|---|---|
| 0.0000 | 0.0000 | 0.0000 |  | 0.6415 | 0.6415 | 0.0000 | 0.6415 | -0.3585 | -0.2058 | 0.0000 |
| 0.0500 | 0.0296 | 0.0296 | 0.0500 | 0.6226 | 0.5930 | 0.2050 | 0.6226 | -0.3774 | -0.1642 | -0.0082 |
| 0.1000 | 0.0569 | 0.0273 | 0.0500 | 0.6028 | 0.5458 | 0.2043 | 0.6028 | -0.3972 | -0.1247 | -0.0062 |
| 0.1500 | 0.0819 | 0.0250 | 0.0500 | 0.5819 | 0.4999 | 0.2036 | 0.5819 | -0.4181 | -0.0874 | -0.0044 |
| 0.2000 | 0.1047 | 0.0228 | 0.0500 | 0.5599 | 0.4552 | 0.2028 | 0.5599 | -0.4401 | -0.0520 | -0.0026 |
| 0.2500 | 0.1253 | 0.0206 | 0.0500 | 0.5367 | 0.4114 | 0.2021 | 0.5367 | -0.4633 | -0.0188 | -0.0009 |
| 0.3000 | 0.1437 | 0.0184 | 0.0500 | 0.5123 | 0.3686 | 0.2013 | 0.5123 | -0.4877 | 0.0125 | 0.0006 |
| 0.3500 | 0.1600 | 0.0163 | 0.0500 | 0.4867 | 0.3266 | 0.2006 | 0.4867 | -0.5133 | 0.0416 | 0.0021 |
| 0.4000 | 0.1743 | 0.0143 | 0.0500 | 0.4596 | 0.2853 | 0.1998 | 0.4596 | -0.5404 | 0.0687 | 0.0034 |
| 0.4500 | 0.1865 | 0.0122 | 0.0500 | 0.4312 | 0.2447 | 0.1991 | 0.4312 | -0.5688 | 0.0936 | 0.0047 |
| 0.5000 | 0.1968 | 0.0102 | 0.0500 | 0.4013 | 0.2045 | 0.1983 | 0.4013 | -0.5987 | 0.1163 | 0.0058 |
| 0.5500 | 0.2050 | 0.0082 | 0.0500 | 0.3698 | 0.1648 | 0.1976 | 0.3698 | -0.6302 | 0.1366 | 0.0068 |
| 0.6000 | 0.2113 | 0.0063 | 0.0500 | 0.3366 | 0.1253 | 0.1968 | 0.3366 | -0.6634 | 0.1546 | 0.0077 |
| 0.6500 | 0.2156 | 0.0043 | 0.0500 | 0.3017 | 0.0861 | 0.1960 | 0.3017 | -0.6983 | 0.1701 | 0.0085 |
| 0.7000 | 0.2179 | 0.0023 | 0.0500 | 0.2649 | 0.0470 | 0.1953 | 0.2649 | -0.7351 | 0.1828 | 0.0091 |
| 0.7500 | 0.2183 | 0.0004 | 0.0500 | 0.2262 | 0.0079 | 0.1945 | 0.2262 | -0.7738 | 0.1927 | 0.0096 |
| 0.8000 | 0.2167 | -0.0016 | 0.0500 | 0.1855 | -0.0313 | 0.1937 | 0.1855 | -0.8145 | 0.1995 | 0.0100 |
| 0.8500 | 0.2132 | -0.0035 | 0.0500 | 0.1426 | -0.0706 | 0.1930 | 0.1426 | -0.8574 | 0.2030 | 0.0102 |
| 0.9000 | 0.2077 | -0.0055 | 0.0500 | 0.0975 | -0.1102 | 0.1922 | 0.0975 | -0.9025 | 0.2030 | 0.0101 |
| 0.9500 | 0.2002 | -0.0075 | 0.0500 | 0.0500 | -0.1502 | 0.1914 | 0.0500 | -0.9500 | 0.1969 | 0.0099 |
| 1.0000 | 0.1907 | -0.0095 | 0.0500 | 0.0000 | -0.1907 | 0.1907 | 0.0000 | -1.0000 | 0.1907 | 0.0095 |

|   |   |   |   |   |   |   |   |   |   |   |
|---|---|---|---|---|---|---|---|---|---|---|
| y(0) | 0 |   |   |   |   |   | Transversality |   |   | 0.0859 |
| y(1) | Free |   |   |   |   |   | Condition λ(T) = 0 |   |   |   |

Table 10.3-2 shows the error of the numerical solutions versus the exact continuous solutions while Figs. 10.3-3 and 10.3-4 depict the numerical paths for $y(t)$ and $u(t)$ versus the exact continuous paths.

TABLE 10.3-2  Error versus exact solutions.

| t | y(t) True | Error on y(t) | $\lambda(t)$ True | Error on $\lambda(t)$ |
|---|---|---|---|---|
| 0.0000 | 0.0000 | | 0.6321 | 0.01 |
| 0.0500 | 0.0304 | 0.00 | 0.6133 | 0.01 |
| 0.1000 | 0.0583 | 0.00 | 0.5934 | 0.01 |
| 0.1500 | 0.0839 | 0.00 | 0.5726 | 0.01 |
| 0.2000 | 0.1072 | 0.00 | 0.5507 | 0.01 |
| 0.2500 | 0.1283 | 0.00 | 0.5276 | 0.01 |
| 0.3000 | 0.1472 | 0.00 | 0.5034 | 0.01 |
| 0.3500 | 0.1639 | 0.00 | 0.4780 | 0.01 |
| 0.4000 | 0.1786 | 0.00 | 0.4512 | 0.01 |
| 0.4500 | 0.1912 | 0.00 | 0.4231 | 0.01 |
| 0.5000 | 0.2018 | 0.01 | 0.3935 | 0.01 |
| 0.5500 | 0.2104 | 0.01 | 0.3624 | 0.01 |
| 0.6000 | 0.2170 | 0.01 | 0.3297 | 0.01 |
| 0.6500 | 0.2216 | 0.01 | 0.2953 | 0.01 |
| 0.7000 | 0.2243 | 0.01 | 0.2592 | 0.01 |
| 0.7500 | 0.2251 | 0.01 | 0.2212 | 0.01 |
| 0.8000 | 0.2240 | 0.01 | 0.1813 | 0.00 |
| 0.8500 | 0.2208 | 0.01 | 0.1393 | 0.00 |
| 0.9000 | 0.2158 | 0.01 | 0.0952 | 0.00 |
| 0.9500 | 0.2088 | 0.01 | 0.0488 | 0.00 |
| 1.0000 | 0.1998 | 0.01 | 0.0000 | 0.00 |

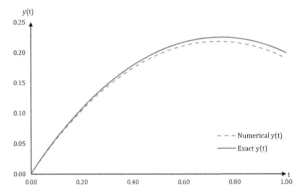

**FIGURE 10.3-3**    Example 1: numerical versus exact optimal capital path $y(t)$.

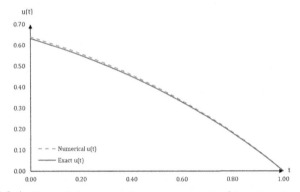

**FIGURE 10.3-4**    Example 1: numerical versus exact optimal investment control path $u(t)$.

## EXAMPLE 2 (OPTIMAL CONTROL BOUNDED INVESTMENT PROBLEM)

Let us solve with respect to $u$ the following modified investment problem in Example 1:

$$\max_{\{u\}} J(u) = \int_0^1 \left( 2y - \frac{1}{2}u^2 \right) dt$$

$$s.t. \quad \dot{y} = u - \delta y \text{ and } y(0) = 0, \, y(1) = 0$$

Here we require the Capital Path be zero at $T = 1$, and this will require changing slightly our spreadsheet, as well as the transversality condition.

In such a case the transversality condition is just reduced to:

$$y(T) = y_T$$

and no restriction is required on $\lambda(T)$.

|   | A | B | C | D | E | F | G | H | I | J | K |
|---|---|---|---|---|---|---|---|---|---|---|---|
|   | t | y Capital Path | dy = (u-y)dt | dt | Investment u = ẏ+y | dy/dt =λ-y | Hamiltonian = (2y- 1/2u²)+λ(u-y) | λ(t) | dλ/dt | F = 2y-1/2u² | Functional = Σ [2y-1/2u²]dt |
| 1 |   |   |   |   |   |   |   |   |   |   |   |
| 2 | 0 | 0 | =(E2-B2)*D2 |   | =F2+B2 | =H2-B2 | 0 | 0.966914921208875 |   |   |   |
| 3 | =A2+0.05 | =B2+C3 | =(E3-B3)*D3 | =A3-A2 | =F3+B3 | =H3-B3 | =J3+H3*(E3-B3) | =H2+I3*D3 | =-2+H3 | =2*B3-1/2*E3^2 | =J3*D3 |
| 4 | =A3+0.05 | =B3+C4 | =(E4-B4)*D4 | =A4-A3 | =F4+B4 | =H4-B4 | =J4+H4*(E4-B4) | =H3+I4*D4 | =-2+H4 | =2*B4-1/2*E4^2 | =J4*D4 |
| 5 | =A4+0.05 | =B4+C5 | =(E5-B5)*D5 | =A5-A4 | =F5+B5 | =H5-B5 | =J5+H5*(E5-B5) | =H4+I5*D5 | =-2+H5 | =2*B5-1/2*E5^2 | =J5*D5 |
| 6 | =A5+0.05 | =B5+C6 | =(E6-B6)*D6 | =A6-A5 | =F6+B6 | =H6-B6 | =J6+H6*(E6-B6) | =H5+I6*D6 | =-2+H6 | =2*B6-1/2*E6^2 | =J6*D6 |
| 7 | =A6+0.05 | =B6+C7 | =(E7-B7)*D7 | =A7-A6 | =F7+B7 | =H7-B7 | =J7+H7*(E7-B7) | =H6+I7*D7 | =-2+H7 | =2*B7-1/2*E7^2 | =J7*D7 |
| 8 | =A7+0.05 | =B7+C8 | =(E8-B8)*D8 | =A8-A7 | =F8+B8 | =H8-B8 | =J8+H8*(E8-B8) | =H7+I8*D8 | =-2+H8 | =2*B8-1/2*E8^2 | =J8*D8 |
| 9 | =A8+0.05 | =B8+C9 | =(E9-B9)*D9 | =A9-A8 | =F9+B9 | =H9-B9 | =J9+H9*(E9-B9) | =H8+I9*D9 | =-2+H9 | =2*B9-1/2*E9^2 | =J9*D9 |
| 10 | =A9+0.05 | =B9+C10 | =(E10-B10)*D10 | =A10-A9 | =F10+B10 | =H10-B10 | =J10+H10*(E10-B10) | =H9+I10*D10 | =-2+H10 | =2*B10-1/2*E10^2 | =J10*D10 |
| 11 | =A10+0.05 | =B10+C11 | =(E11-B11)*D11 | =A11-A10 | =F11+B11 | =H11-B11 | =J11+H11*(E11-B11) | =H10+I11*D11 | =-2+H11 | =2*B11-1/2*E11^2 | =J11*D11 |
| 12 | =A11+0.05 | =B11+C12 | =(E12-B12)*D12 | =A12-A11 | =F12+B12 | =H12-B12 | =J12+H12*(E12-B12) | =H11+I12*D12 | =-2+H12 | =2*B12-1/2*E12^2 | =J12*D12 |
| 13 | =A12+0.05 | =B12+C13 | =(E13-B13)*D13 | =A13-A12 | =F13+B13 | =H13-B13 | =J13+H13*(E13-B13) | =H12+I13*D13 | =-2+H13 | =2*B13-1/2*E13^2 | =J13*D13 |
| 14 | =A13+0.05 | =B13+C14 | =(E14-B14)*D14 | =A14-A13 | =F14+B14 | =H14-B14 | =J14+H14*(E14-B14) | =H13+I14*D14 | =-2+H14 | =2*B14-1/2*E14^2 | =J14*D14 |
| 15 | =A14+0.05 | =B14+C15 | =(E15-B15)*D15 | =A15-A14 | =F15+B15 | =H15-B15 | =J15+H15*(E15-B15) | =H14+I15*D15 | =-2+H15 | =2*B15-1/2*E15^2 | =J15*D15 |
| 16 | =A15+0.05 | =B15+C16 | =(E16-B16)*D16 | =A16-A15 | =F16+B16 | =H16-B16 | =J16+H16*(E16-B16) | =H15+I16*D16 | =-2+H16 | =2*B16-1/2*E16^2 | =J16*D16 |
| 17 | =A16+0.05 | =B16+C17 | =(E17-B17)*D17 | =A17-A16 | =F17+B17 | =H17-B17 | =J17+H17*(E17-B17) | =H16+I17*D17 | =-2+H17 | =2*B17-1/2*E17^2 | =J17*D17 |
| 18 | =A17+0.05 | =B17+C18 | =(E18-B18)*D18 | =A18-A17 | =F18+B18 | =H18-B18 | =J18+H18*(E18-B18) | =H17+I18*D18 | =-2+H18 | =2*B18-1/2*E18^2 | =J18*D18 |
| 19 | =A18+0.05 | =B18+C19 | =(E19-B19)*D19 | =A19-A18 | =F19+B19 | =H19-B19 | =J19+H19*(E19-B19) | =H18+I19*D19 | =-2+H19 | =2*B19-1/2*E19^2 | =J19*D19 |
| 20 | =A19+0.05 | =B19+C20 | =(E20-B20)*D20 | =A20-A19 | =F20+B20 | =H20-B20 | =J20+H20*(E20-B20) | =H19+I20*D20 | =-2+H20 | =2*B20-1/2*E20^2 | =J20*D20 |
| 21 | =A20+0.05 | =B20+C21 | =(E21-B21)*D21 | =A21-A20 | =F21+B21 | =H21-B21 | =J21+H21*(E21-B21) | =H20+I21*D21 | =-2+H21 | =2*B21-1/2*E21^2 | =J21*D21 |
| 22 | =A21+0.05 | =B21+C22 | =(E22-B22)*D22 | =A22-A21 | =F22+B22 | =H22-B22 | =J22+H22*(E22-B22) | =H21+I22*D22 | =-2+H22 | =2*B22-1/2*E22^2 | =J22*D22 |
| 23 |   |   |   |   |   |   |   |   |   |   |   |
| 24 | y(0) | 0 |   |   |   |   | With fixed end point No |   |   |   | =SUM(K3:K22) |
| 25 | y(1) | 0 |   |   |   |   | transversality condition |   |   |   |   |

FIGURE 10.3-5    Example 2: worksheet setup.

In Example 2, different from Example 1, we have in the integrand function a Sales-to-Capital ratio of 2. Setting $\delta = 1$ the Hamiltonian is:

$$\mathcal{H} = 2y - \frac{1}{2}u^2 + \lambda(u-y)$$

and we obtain a slightly different equation of motion for $\lambda(t)$ as:

$$\frac{d\lambda}{dt} = -\frac{\partial \mathcal{H}}{\partial y} = -(2-\lambda) = \lambda - 2.$$

The spreadsheet setup is in Fig. 10.3-5 and the output in Table 10.3-3, which is graphed in Fig. 10.3-7.

We optimize the problem setting the boundary condition $y(T) = 0$ as described in Fig. 10.3-6:

## EXAMPLE 3.A (OPTIMAL CONTROL MINIMUM CONTROL EFFORT INVESTMENT PROBLEM)

The investment problem presented in this example is in the following form, which is different in the integrand function from the previous two examples:

$$\max_{\{u\}} J(u) = \int_0^1 -u^2 dt$$

$$\text{s.t. } \dot{y} = u - \delta y \text{ and } y(0) = 0, \ y(1) = 1.$$

**TABLE 10.3-3**   Example 2: numerical solution.

| t | y Capital Path | dy = (u-y)dt | dt | Investment u = y+y' | dy/dt = u-y | Hamiltonian = (2y - 1/2u²) + λ(u-y) | λ(t) | dλ/dt | F = 2y - 1/2u² | Functional = Σ[2y-1/2u²]dt |
|---|---|---|---|---|---|---|---|---|---|---|
| 0.0000 | 0.0000 | 0.0000 | | 0.9669 | 0.9669 | 0.0000 | 0.9669 | | | |
| 0.0500 | 0.0435 | 0.0435 | 0.0500 | 0.9125 | 0.8691 | 0.4636 | 0.9125 | -1.0875 | -0.3295 | -0.0165 |
| 0.1000 | 0.0821 | 0.0387 | 0.0500 | 0.8553 | 0.7732 | 0.4598 | 0.8553 | -1.1447 | -0.2015 | -0.0101 |
| 0.1500 | 0.1161 | 0.0339 | 0.0500 | 0.7951 | 0.6790 | 0.4559 | 0.7951 | -1.2049 | -0.0839 | -0.0042 |
| 0.2000 | 0.1454 | 0.0293 | 0.0500 | 0.7316 | 0.5863 | 0.4520 | 0.7316 | -1.2684 | 0.0231 | 0.0012 |
| 0.2500 | 0.1701 | 0.0247 | 0.0500 | 0.6649 | 0.4948 | 0.4482 | 0.6649 | -1.3351 | 0.1192 | 0.0060 |
| 0.3000 | 0.1903 | 0.0202 | 0.0500 | 0.5946 | 0.4043 | 0.4443 | 0.5946 | -1.4054 | 0.2039 | 0.0102 |
| 0.3500 | 0.2061 | 0.0157 | 0.0500 | 0.5207 | 0.3146 | 0.4404 | 0.5207 | -1.4793 | 0.2766 | 0.0138 |
| 0.4000 | 0.2173 | 0.0113 | 0.0500 | 0.4428 | 0.2255 | 0.4365 | 0.4428 | -1.5572 | 0.3366 | 0.0168 |
| 0.4500 | 0.2242 | 0.0068 | 0.0500 | 0.3608 | 0.1367 | 0.4325 | 0.3608 | -1.6392 | 0.3832 | 0.0192 |
| 0.5000 | 0.2266 | 0.0024 | 0.0500 | 0.2746 | 0.0480 | 0.4286 | 0.2746 | -1.7254 | 0.4154 | 0.0208 |
| 0.5500 | 0.2246 | -0.0020 | 0.0500 | 0.1837 | -0.0408 | 0.4247 | 0.1837 | -1.8163 | 0.4322 | 0.0216 |
| 0.6000 | 0.2180 | -0.0065 | 0.0500 | 0.0882 | -0.1299 | 0.4207 | 0.0882 | -1.9118 | 0.4322 | 0.0216 |
| 0.6500 | 0.2071 | -0.0110 | 0.0500 | -0.0125 | -0.2195 | 0.4168 | -0.0125 | -2.0125 | 0.4140 | 0.0207 |
| 0.7000 | 0.1916 | -0.0155 | 0.0500 | -0.1184 | -0.3099 | 0.4128 | -0.1184 | -2.1184 | 0.3761 | 0.0188 |
| 0.7500 | 0.1715 | -0.0201 | 0.0500 | -0.2299 | -0.4014 | 0.4088 | -0.2299 | -2.2299 | 0.3166 | 0.0158 |
| 0.8000 | 0.1468 | -0.0247 | 0.0500 | -0.3472 | -0.4940 | 0.4048 | -0.3472 | -2.3472 | 0.2333 | 0.0117 |
| 0.8500 | 0.1174 | -0.0294 | 0.0500 | -0.4708 | -0.5882 | 0.4008 | -0.4708 | -2.4708 | 0.1239 | 0.0062 |
| 0.9000 | 0.0832 | -0.0342 | 0.0500 | -0.6008 | -0.6840 | 0.3968 | -0.6008 | -2.6008 | -0.0141 | -0.0007 |
| 0.9500 | 0.0441 | -0.0391 | 0.0500 | -0.7377 | -0.7818 | 0.3928 | -0.7377 | -2.7377 | -0.1839 | -0.0092 |
| 1.0000 | 0.0000 | -0.0441 | 0.0500 | -0.8818 | -0.8818 | 0.3888 | -0.8818 | -2.8818 | -0.3888 | -0.0194 |

y(0)   0.00
y(1)   0.00

With fixed end point No
transversality condition

Functional total: 0.1442

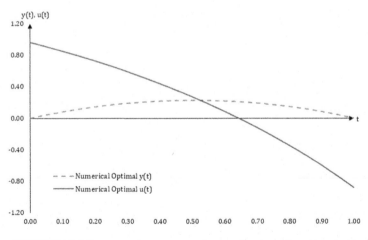

FIGURE 10.3-6    Setting $y(T) = 0$ in the Excel Solver.

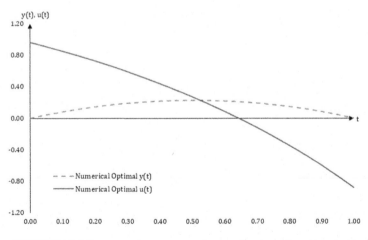

FIGURE 10.3-7    Example 2: numerical optimal policies for $y(t)$ and $u(t)$.

III. Dynamic optimization

When the *performance measure* is in the form $\min \int_{t_0}^{T} u^2 dt$, the OC problem is generally referred as *Minimum Control Effort Problem*.

Assuming we start running the business with zero capital at $t_0 = 0$ in this OC economic application the goal is to accumulate, over the time interval $[0, T = 1]$, a unit of capital, through an Optimal Investment policy $u^*(t)$, minimizing the total costs in the *functional*, which are directly proportional to the investments made $u(t)$.

Notice that a minimum problem has been converted into a maximum problem attaching the negative sign to the integrand function. As usual the quantity $\dot{y} = u - \delta y$ represents the net variation in the available capital, considering a rate of depreciation $\delta$, that we set equal to 1 for simplicity.

For this example, we will go through all the steps of the theoretical solution and then we will present the Excel numerical solution.

**i.** As a first step, let us derive the Hamiltonian function as:

$$\mathcal{H} = -u^2 + \lambda(u - y),$$

from which we can derive the first-order condition $\frac{\partial \mathcal{H}}{\partial u} = 0$ to get the maximum in $\mathcal{H}$:

$$\frac{\partial \mathcal{H}}{\partial u} = -2u + \lambda = 0 \Rightarrow u(t) = \frac{1}{2}\lambda.$$

**ii.** From the equation of motion for $\lambda(t)$ we obtain:

$$\frac{d\lambda}{dt} = -\frac{\partial \mathcal{H}}{\partial y} = -(-\lambda) = \lambda,$$

which is a differential equation with general solution:

$$\lambda^*(t) = ke^t \Rightarrow u^*(t) = \frac{1}{2}ke^t.$$

**iii.** Now, from the equation of motion $\dot{y} = u - y$ we have the following ordinary linear differential equation to solve:

$$\frac{dy}{dt} + y = \frac{1}{2}ke^t$$

which has general solution:

$$y = e^{-\int dt}\left[c + \int \left(e^{\int dt}\frac{1}{2}ke^t\right)dt\right]$$

namely,

$$y = e^{-t}\left[c + \int\left(e^t\frac{1}{2}ke^t\right)dt\right] = e^{-t}\left[c + \int\left(\frac{1}{2}ke^{2t}\right)dt\right]$$

$$y^*(t) = e^{-t}\left[c + \frac{1}{4}ke^{2t}\right] = ce^{-t} + \frac{1}{4}ke^t$$

which is our definite solution.

**iv.** Finally, the boundary conditions $y(0) = 0$, $y(1) = 1$ have to be applied to derive $c$ and $k$.

We have the constant $c$ as

$$y(0) = 0 \Rightarrow c + \frac{1}{4}k = 0 \Rightarrow c = -\frac{1}{4}k,$$

while $k$ is calculated as follows:

$$y(1) = 1 \Rightarrow -\frac{1}{4}ke^{-1} + \frac{1}{4}ke^1 = 1$$

which is:

$$k\left(\frac{1}{4}e - \frac{1}{4e}\right) = 1 \Rightarrow k = \frac{4}{e - \dfrac{1}{e}} = \frac{4e}{e^2 - 1}.$$

The graphed numerical discrete optimal policies compared to the above exact continuous solutions are presented in Fig. 10.3-8.

The numerical solutions have been found setting in the Excel Solver the boundary condition $y(1) = 1$, by changing $\lambda(0)$, as we did in Example 2. The complete numerical solution worksheet is in Table 10.3-4.

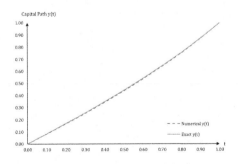 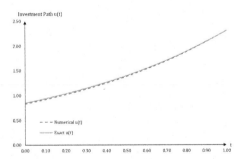

**FIGURE 10.3-8** Example 3.a optimal policies for $y(t)$ and $u(t)$.

**TABLE 10.3-4**  Example 3.a numerical solution.

| t | y Capital Path | dy = (u-y)²dt | dt | Investment u = ẏ+y | dy/dt = λ/2-y | Hamiltonian = -u²+λ(u-y) | λ(t) | dδᵧ/dt | F = -u² | Functional = Σ∫-u²]dt |
|---|---|---|---|---|---|---|---|---|---|---|
| 0.0000 | 0.0000 | | | 0.8290 | 0.8290 | 0.0000 | 1.65779 | | | |
| 0.0500 | 0.0416 | 0.0416 | 0.0500 | 0.8726 | 0.8311 | 0.6889 | 1.7452 | 1.7452 | 0.7614 | 0.0381 |
| 0.1000 | 0.0833 | 0.0418 | 0.0500 | 0.9185 | 0.8352 | 0.6906 | 1.8371 | 1.8371 | 0.8437 | 0.0422 |
| 0.1500 | 0.1254 | 0.0421 | 0.0500 | 0.9669 | 0.8415 | 0.6924 | 1.9337 | 1.9337 | 0.9348 | 0.0467 |
| 0.2000 | 0.1679 | 0.0425 | 0.0500 | 1.0178 | 0.8499 | 0.6941 | 2.0355 | 2.0355 | 1.0358 | 0.0518 |
| 0.2500 | 0.2109 | 0.0430 | 0.0500 | 1.0713 | 0.8604 | 0.6959 | 2.1427 | 2.1427 | 1.1477 | 0.0574 |
| 0.3000 | 0.2546 | 0.0437 | 0.0500 | 1.1277 | 0.8732 | 0.6976 | 2.2554 | 2.2554 | 1.2717 | 0.0636 |
| 0.3500 | 0.2990 | 0.0444 | 0.0500 | 1.1871 | 0.8881 | 0.6993 | 2.3741 | 2.3741 | 1.4091 | 0.0705 |
| 0.4000 | 0.3442 | 0.0453 | 0.0500 | 1.2495 | 0.9053 | 0.7011 | 2.4991 | 2.4991 | 1.5614 | 0.0781 |
| 0.4500 | 0.3905 | 0.0462 | 0.0500 | 1.3153 | 0.9248 | 0.7029 | 2.6306 | 2.6306 | 1.7300 | 0.0865 |
| 0.5000 | 0.4378 | 0.0473 | 0.0500 | 1.3845 | 0.9467 | 0.7046 | 2.7691 | 2.7691 | 1.9169 | 0.0958 |
| 0.5500 | 0.4864 | 0.0486 | 0.0500 | 1.4574 | 0.9710 | 0.7064 | 2.9148 | 2.9148 | 2.1240 | 0.1062 |
| 0.6000 | 0.5363 | 0.0499 | 0.0500 | 1.5341 | 0.9979 | 0.7082 | 3.0682 | 3.0682 | 2.3535 | 0.1177 |
| 0.6500 | 0.5876 | 0.0514 | 0.0500 | 1.6149 | 1.0272 | 0.7099 | 3.2297 | 3.2297 | 2.6078 | 0.1304 |
| 0.7000 | 0.6406 | 0.0530 | 0.0500 | 1.6998 | 1.0593 | 0.7117 | 3.3997 | 3.3997 | 2.8895 | 0.1445 |
| 0.7500 | 0.6953 | 0.0547 | 0.0500 | 1.7893 | 1.0940 | 0.7135 | 3.5786 | 3.5786 | 3.2017 | 0.1601 |
| 0.8000 | 0.7519 | 0.0566 | 0.0500 | 1.8835 | 1.1316 | 0.7153 | 3.7670 | 3.7670 | 3.5475 | 0.1774 |
| 0.8500 | 0.8105 | 0.0586 | 0.0500 | 1.9826 | 1.1721 | 0.7171 | 3.9652 | 3.9652 | 3.9308 | 0.1965 |
| 0.9000 | 0.8713 | 0.0608 | 0.0500 | 2.0870 | 1.2157 | 0.7189 | 4.1739 | 4.1739 | 4.3554 | 0.2178 |
| 0.9500 | 0.9344 | 0.0631 | 0.0500 | 2.1968 | 1.2624 | 0.7207 | 4.3936 | 4.3936 | 4.8260 | 0.2413 |
| 1.0000 | 1.0000 | 0.0656 | 0.0500 | 2.3124 | 1.3124 | 0.7225 | 4.6249 | 4.6249 | 5.3473 | 0.2674 |

y(0)   0.00

y(1)   1.00

With fixed end point No transversality condition                                            2.3898

## EXAMPLE 3.B (SIMILARITY WITH CONSTRAINED CALCULUS OF VARIATIONS)

The same investment problem could have been also tackled with a constrained CoV approach setting the Capital Path variable $y(t) = y_1(y)$ and the gross capex control variable $u(t) = y_2(t)$, obtaining the following CoV problem in two variables:

$$\max_{\{y\}} J(y) = \int_0^1 -y_2^2 dt$$

s.t. $\dot{y}_1 = y_2 - \delta y_1$ and $y(0) = 0, y(1) = 1.$

As usual a minimum problem has been converted into a maximum problem attaching the negative sign to the integrand function.

Setting $\delta = 1$ and resorting to the *augmented functional*, the above OC problem is then transformed in the following CoV problem:

$$\max_{\{y\}} J_a = \int_0^1 -y_2^2 + \lambda(y_2 - y_1 - y_1')dt$$

Let us extract now the *Euler–Lagrange* first-order conditions:

$$\frac{\partial F_a}{\partial y_1} - \frac{d}{dt}\left[\frac{\partial F_a}{\partial y_1'}\right] = 0$$

$$-\lambda(t) + \lambda'(t) = 0 \Rightarrow \lambda = \lambda'$$

and

$$\frac{\partial F_a}{\partial y_2} - \frac{d}{dt}\left[\frac{\partial F_a}{\partial y_2'}\right] = 0$$

$$-2y_2(t) + \lambda(t) = 0 \Rightarrow u = y_2 = \frac{1}{2}\lambda$$

and finally:

$$\frac{\partial F_a}{\partial \lambda} - \frac{d}{dt}\left[\frac{\partial F_a}{\partial \lambda'}\right] = 0$$

$$y_2 - y_1 - y_1' = 0.$$

The worksheet setup will be as in Fig. 10.3-9, where we have included the constraints from the *Euler–Lagrange* first-order conditions, which will be part of the Excel Solver constraints.

| | A | B | C | D | E | F | G | H | I | J | K | L | M |
|---|---|---|---|---|---|---|---|---|---|---|---|---|---|
| 1 | t | Capital Path $y_1$ | $dy_1$ | Investment $u = y_2$ | $dy_2$ | dt | $\lambda(t)$ | Augmented Integrand F = $[-y_2^2 + \lambda\{y_2\cdot y_1\cdot y_1'\}]$ | Augmented Functional = $\Sigma[-y_2^2 + \lambda\{y_2\cdot y_1\cdot y_1'\}]dt$ | | s.t. Constraints | | |
| 2 | 0 | 0 | | | | | 1.65795 | | | | $-\lambda(t)+\lambda'(t) = 0$ | $-2y_2+\lambda(t) = 0$ | $y_2-y_1\cdot y_1'$ |
| 3 | =A2+0.05 | =B2+C3 | 0.0415 | =D2+E3 | 0.8726 | =A3-A2 | =2*D3 | =-D3^2+G3*(D3-B3-(B3-B2)/F3) | =H3*F3 | | =-.03+(.03-G2)/F3 | =-2*D3+G3 | =D3-B3-(B3-B2)/F3 |
| 4 | =A3+0.05 | =B3+C4 | 0.0417 | =D3+E4 | 0.0459 | =A4-A3 | =2*D4 | =-D4^2+G4*(D4-B4-(B4-B3)/F4) | =H4*F4 | | =-G4+(G4-G8)/F4 | =-2*D4+G4 | =D4-B4-(B4-B3)/F4 |
| 5 | =A4+0.05 | =B4+C5 | 0.0420 | =D4+E5 | 0.0483 | =A5-A4 | =2*D5 | =-D5^2+G5*(D5-B5-(B5-B4)/F5) | =H5*F5 | | =-G5+(G5-G4)/F5 | =-2*D5+G5 | =D5-B5-(B5-B4)/F5 |
| 6 | =A5+0.05 | =B5+C6 | 0.0424 | =D5+E6 | 0.0508 | =A6-A5 | =2*D6 | =-D6^2+G6*(D6-B6-(B6-B5)/F6) | =H6*F6 | | =-.06+(.06-G5)/F6 | =-2*D6+G6 | =D6-B6-(B6-B5)/F6 |
| 7 | =A6+0.05 | =B6+C7 | 0.0430 | =D6+E7 | 0.0535 | =A7-A6 | =2*D7 | =-D7^2+G7*(D7-B7-(B7-B6)/F7) | =H7*F7 | | =-G7+(G7-G6)/F7 | =-2*D7+G7 | =D7-B7-(B7-B6)/F7 |
| 8 | =A7+0.05 | =B7+C8 | 0.0436 | =D7+E8 | 0.0563 | =A8-A7 | =2*D8 | =-D8^2+G8*(D8-B8-(B8-B7)/F8) | =H8*F8 | | =-G8+(G8-G7)/F8 | =-2*D8+G8 | =D8-B8-(B8-B7)/F8 |
| 9 | =A8+0.05 | =B8+C9 | 0.0444 | =D8+E9 | 0.0593 | =A9-A8 | =2*D9 | =-D9^2+G9*(D9-B9-(B9-B8)/F9) | =H9*F9 | | =-.09+(.09-G8)/F9 | =-2*D9+G9 | =D9-B9-(B9-B8)/F9 |
| 10 | =A9+0.05 | =B9+C10 | 0.0452 | =D9+E10 | 0.0624 | =A10-A9 | =2*D10 | =-D10^2+G10*(D10-B10-(B10-B9)/F10) | =H10*F10 | | =-G10+(G10-G9)/F10 | =-2*D10+G10 | =D10-B10-(B10-B9)/F10 |
| 11 | =A10+0.05 | =B10+C11 | 0.0462 | =D10+E11 | 0.0657 | =A11-A10 | =2*D11 | =-D11^2+G11*(D11-B11-(B11-B10)/F11) | =H11*F11 | | =-G11+(G11-G10)/F11 | =-2*D11+G11 | =D11-B11-(B11-B10)/F11 |
| 12 | =A11+0.05 | =B11+C12 | 0.0473 | =D11+E12 | 0.0692 | =A12-A11 | =2*D12 | =-D12^2+G12*(D12-B12-(B12-B11)/F12) | =H12*F12 | | =-G12+(G12-G11)/F12 | =-2*D12+G12 | =D12-B12-(B12-B11)/F12 |
| 13 | =A12+0.05 | =B12+C13 | 0.0485 | =D12+E13 | 0.0728 | =A13-A12 | =2*D13 | =-D13^2+G13*(D13-B13-(B13-B12)/F13) | =H13*F13 | | =-G13+(G13-G12)/F13 | =-2*D13+G13 | =D13-B13-(B13-B12)/F13 |
| 14 | =A13+0.05 | =B13+C14 | 0.0498 | =D13+E14 | 0.0767 | =A14-A13 | =2*D14 | =-D14^2+G14*(D14-B14-(B14-B13)/F14) | =H14*F14 | | =-G14+(G14-G13)/F14 | =-2*D14+G14 | =D14-B14-(B14-B13)/F14 |
| 15 | =A14+0.05 | =B14+C15 | 0.0513 | =D14+E15 | 0.0807 | =A15-A14 | =2*D15 | =-D15^2+G15*(D15-B15-(B15-B14)/F15) | =H15*F15 | | =-G15+(G15-G14)/F15 | =-2*D15+G15 | =D15-B15-(B15-B14)/F15 |
| 16 | =A15+0.05 | =B15+C16 | 0.0529 | =D15+E16 | 0.0849 | =A16-A15 | =2*D16 | =-D16^2+G16*(D16-B16-(B16-B15)/F16) | =H16*F16 | | =-G16+(G16-G15)/F16 | =-2*D16+G16 | =D16-B16-(B16-B15)/F16 |
| 17 | =A16+0.05 | =B16+C17 | 0.0547 | =D16+E17 | 0.0894 | =A17-A16 | =2*D17 | =-D17^2+G17*(D17-B17-(B17-B16)/F17) | =H17*F17 | | =-G17+(G17-G16)/F17 | =-2*D17+G17 | =D17-B17-(B17-B16)/F17 |
| 18 | =A17+0.05 | =B17+C18 | 0.0565 | =D17+E18 | 0.0941 | =A18-A17 | =2*D18 | =-D18^2+G18*(D18-B18-(B18-B17)/F18) | =H18*F18 | | =-G18+(G18-G17)/F18 | =-2*D18+G18 | =D18-B18-(B18-B17)/F18 |
| 19 | =A18+0.05 | =B18+C19 | 0.0586 | =D18+E19 | 0.0991 | =A19-A18 | =2*D19 | =-D19^2+G19*(D19-B19-(B19-B18)/F19) | =H19*F19 | | =-G19+(G19-G18)/F19 | =-2*D19+G19 | =D19-B19-(B19-B18)/F19 |
| 20 | =A19+0.05 | =B19+C20 | 0.0607 | =D19+E20 | 0.1043 | =A20-A19 | =2*D20 | =-D20^2+G20*(D20-B20-(B20-B19)/F20) | =H20*F20 | | =-G20+(G20-G19)/F20 | =-2*D20+G20 | =D20-B20-(B20-B19)/F20 |
| 21 | =A20+0.05 | =B20+C21 | 0.0631 | =D20+E21 | 0.1098 | =A21-A20 | =2*D21 | =-D21^2+G21*(D21-B21-(B21-B20)/F21) | =H21*F21 | | =-G21+(G21-G20)/F21 | =-2*D21+G21 | =D21-B21-(B21-B20)/F21 |
| 22 | =A21+0.05 | =B21+C22 | 0.0656 | =D21+E22 | 0.1156 | =A22-A21 | =2*D22 | =-D22^2+G22*(D22-B22-(B22-B21)/F22) | =H22*F22 | | =-G22+(G22-G21)/F22 | =-2*D22+G22 | =D22-B22-(B22-B21)/F22 |
| 24 | | | | | | | | | =SUM(I3:I22) | | | | |
| 26 | y1(0) | 0 | y2(0) 0 | | | | | | | | | | |
| 27 | y1(1) | 1 | y2(1) Free | | | | | | | | | | |

FIGURE 10.3-9   Example 3.b worksheet setup in a constrained Calculus of Variations framework.

From the Excel Solver of Fig. 10.3-10 we maximize the *augmented functional,* by changing directly $dy_1$, $dy_2$ (*Column C* and *Column E*) and $\lambda(0)$.

The results obtained in the numerical solution of Table 10.3-5 are the same as the ones provided in Table 10.3-4. The only Excel limitation of the two-variable CoV approach is that the

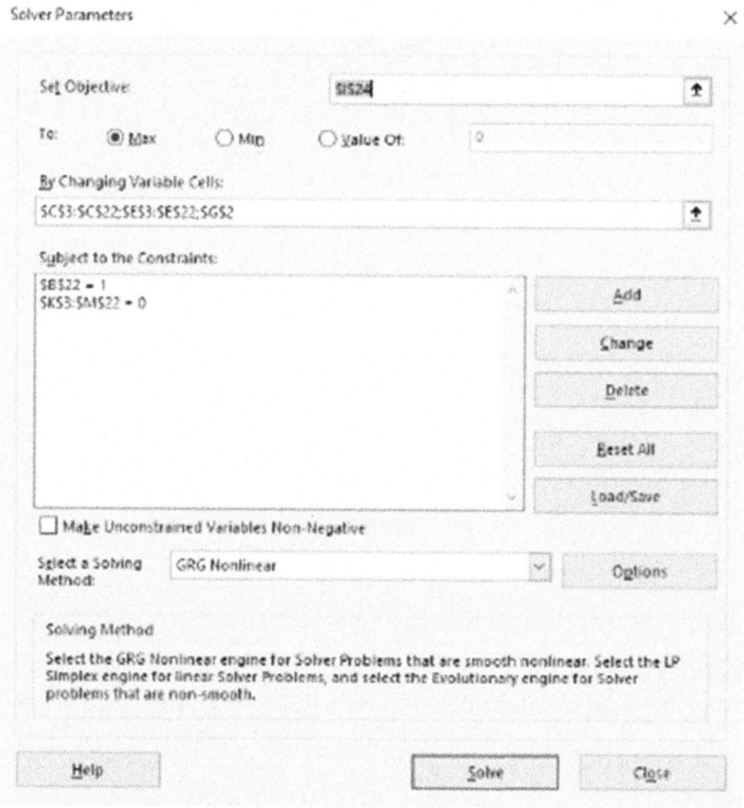

**Solver Parameters**                                                      ✕

Set Objective:                        $I$24                                    ↑

To:   ● Max     ○ Min     ○ Value Of:    0

By Changing Variable Cells:

$C$3:$C$22,$E$3:$E$22,$G$2                                                      ↑

Subject to the Constraints:

$B$22 = 1
$K$3:$M$22 = 0                                                    [ Add ]
                                                                 [ Change ]
                                                                 [ Delete ]
                                                                 [ Reset All ]
                                                                 [ Load/Save ]

☐ Make Unconstrained Variables Non-Negative

Select a Solving Method:    GRG Nonlinear                        [ Options ]

Solving Method

Select the GRG Nonlinear engine for Solver Problems that are smooth nonlinear. Select the LP Simplex engine for linear Solver Problems, and select the Evolutionary engine for Solver problems that are non-smooth.

[ Help ]                              [ Solve ]              [ Close ]

FIGURE 10.3-10   Example 3.a Solver setup.

**TABLE 10.3-5** Example 3.b numerical solution in the Calculus of Variations framework.

| t | Capital Path $y_1$ | $dy_1$ | Investment $u = y_2$ | $dy_2$ | dt | $\lambda(t)$ | Augmented Integrand F = $[-y_2^2 + \lambda(y_2 - y_1 \cdot y_1')]$ | Augmented Functional = $\Sigma[-y_2^2 + \lambda(y_2 - y_1 \cdot y_1')]dt$ |
|---|---|---|---|---|---|---|---|---|
| 0.0000 | 0.0000 | | | | | **1.6580** | | |
| 0.0500 | 0.0416 | 0.0416 | 0.8726 | 0.8726 | 0.0500 | 1.7452 | 0.7614 | 0.0381 |
| 0.1000 | 0.0833 | 0.0418 | 0.9185 | 0.0459 | 0.0500 | 1.8371 | 0.8437 | 0.0422 |
| 0.1500 | 0.1254 | 0.0421 | 0.9669 | 0.0483 | 0.0500 | 1.9338 | 0.9348 | 0.0467 |
| 0.2000 | 0.1679 | 0.0425 | 1.0178 | 0.0509 | 0.0500 | 2.0355 | 1.0358 | 0.0518 |
| 0.2500 | 0.2109 | 0.0430 | 1.0713 | 0.0536 | 0.0500 | 2.1427 | 1.1477 | 0.0574 |
| 0.3000 | 0.2546 | 0.0437 | 1.1277 | 0.0564 | 0.0500 | 2.2554 | 1.2717 | 0.0636 |
| 0.3500 | 0.2990 | 0.0444 | 1.1871 | 0.0594 | 0.0500 | 2.3741 | 1.4091 | 0.0705 |
| 0.4000 | 0.3442 | 0.0453 | 1.2495 | 0.0625 | 0.0500 | 2.4991 | 1.5614 | 0.0781 |
| 0.4500 | 0.3905 | 0.0462 | 1.3153 | 0.0658 | 0.0500 | 2.6306 | 1.7300 | 0.0865 |
| 0.5000 | 0.4378 | 0.0473 | 1.3845 | 0.0692 | 0.0500 | 2.7691 | 1.9170 | 0.0958 |
| 0.5500 | 0.4864 | 0.0486 | 1.4574 | 0.0729 | 0.0500 | 2.9148 | 2.1240 | 0.1062 |
| 0.6000 | 0.5363 | 0.0499 | 1.5341 | 0.0767 | 0.0500 | 3.0682 | 2.3535 | 0.1177 |
| 0.6500 | 0.5876 | 0.0514 | 1.6149 | 0.0807 | 0.0500 | 3.2297 | 2.6078 | 0.1304 |
| 0.7000 | 0.6406 | 0.0530 | 1.6999 | 0.0850 | 0.0500 | 3.3997 | 2.8895 | 0.1445 |
| 0.7500 | 0.6953 | 0.0547 | 1.7893 | 0.0895 | 0.0500 | 3.5786 | 3.2017 | 0.1601 |
| 0.8000 | 0.7519 | 0.0566 | 1.8835 | 0.0942 | 0.0500 | 3.7670 | 3.5475 | 0.1774 |
| 0.8500 | 0.8105 | 0.0586 | 1.9826 | 0.0991 | 0.0500 | 3.9652 | 3.9308 | 0.1965 |
| 0.9000 | 0.8713 | 0.0608 | 2.0870 | 0.1043 | 0.0500 | 4.1739 | 4.3555 | 0.2178 |
| 0.9500 | 0.9344 | 0.0631 | 2.1968 | 0.1098 | 0.0500 | 4.3936 | 4.8260 | 0.2413 |
| 1.0000 | 1.0000 | 0.0656 | 2.3124 | 0.1156 | 0.0500 | 4.6249 | 5.3474 | 0.2674 |
| | | | | | | | | **2.3898** |
| y1(0) | 0.00 | y2(0) | 0.00 | | | | | |
| y1(1) | 1.00 | y2(1) | Free | | | | | |

Solver, when the worksheet is set up the first time, it takes much more time, compared to an OC problem, to compute the optimal solution. This is because more variables and constraints are involved in the problem.

### EXAMPLE 4 (SHORTEST DISTANCE PROBLEM)

The last introductory example is devoted to the classical simplest problem of finding the shortest distance optimal path between two points.

Within the OC theory, the CoV problem to be solved with respect to $y$:

$$\min_{\{y\}} J(y) = \int_{t_0}^{T} \left[ 1 + \frac{(dy)^2}{(dt)^2} \right]^{1/2} dt$$

$$s.t. \ y(t_0) = A, \ y(T) = Z$$

is reformulated as a maximum problem as follows:

$$\max_{\{u\}} J(u) = \int_{t_0}^{T} -(1 + u^2)^{1/2} dt$$

$$s.t. \ \dot{y} = u$$

$$\text{and } y(t_0) = A, \ y(T) = free.$$

Remember that in such a problem with $y(T) = free$ the transversality condition $\lambda(T) = 0$ must be satisfied.

As usual we proceed with the following steps.

**i.** Find the Hamiltonian:

$$\mathcal{H} = -\left(1 + u^2\right)^{\frac{1}{2}} + \lambda u$$

and apply the first-order condition $\frac{d\mathcal{H}}{dt} = 0$ to find the maximum to get:

$$\frac{\partial \mathcal{H}}{\partial u} = -\frac{1}{2}(1 + u^2)^{-\frac{1}{2}} 2u + \lambda = 0 \Rightarrow u(t) = \lambda(1 - \lambda^2)^{-\frac{1}{2}},$$

with negative second derivative:

$$\frac{\partial^2 \mathcal{H}}{\partial u^2} = -\left(1 + u^2\right)^{-\frac{3}{2}} < 0.$$

ii. From the equation of motion for $\lambda(t)$ we obtain the *costate variable*:

$$\frac{d\lambda}{dt} = -\frac{\partial \mathcal{H}}{\partial y} = 0 \Rightarrow \lambda(t) = constant.$$

As the transversality condition $\lambda(T) = 0$ must also be satisfied, then it must follow that:

$$\lambda(t) = constant = 0$$

so that $u(t)$ becomes:

$$u(t) = \lambda\left(1 - \lambda^2\right)^{-\frac{1}{2}} = 0.$$

iii. Now, from the equation of motion $\dot{y} = u$ we have:

$$\dot{y} = 0 \Rightarrow y(t) = constant.$$

Since the initial condition is $y(0) = A$, it must turn out that the optimal path for $y(t)$ is:

$$y^*(t) = A.$$

Let us see now how to implement the shortest distance problem in Excel within the OC framework, setting $y(t_0 = 1) = 7$ and $y(T = 2) = free$. The worksheet will have to be organized as in Fig. 10.3-11.

| | A | B | C | D | E | F | G | H | I | J | K |
|---|---|---|---|---|---|---|---|---|---|---|---|
| | t | y Path | dy = (u)dt | dt | u = ẏ | Hamiltonian = -(1+u²)^(1/2) + λu | dy/dt =dH/dλ = λ(t) u = 0 | λ(t) | dλ/dt =dH/dy = 0 | F = -(1+u²)^(1/2) =dH/dy = 0 | Functional =Σ[-(1+u²)^(1/2)]dt |
| 1 | | | | | | | | | | | |
| 2 | 1 | 7 | | | | | 0 | | | | |
| 3 | =A2+0.05 | =B2+C3 | =(E3)*D3 | =A3-A2 | =C3/D3 | =-((1+E3^2)^0.5)+H3*E3 | 0 | =H2+I3*D3 | 0 | =-((1+E3^2)^0.5) | =J3*D3 |
| 4 | =A3+0.05 | =B3+C4 | =(E4)*D4 | =A4-A3 | =C4/D4 | =-((1+E4^2)^0.5)+H4*E4 | 0 | =H3+I4*D4 | 0 | =-((1+E4^2)^0.5) | =J4*D4 |
| 5 | =A4+0.05 | =B4+C5 | =(E5)*D5 | =A5-A4 | =C5/D5 | =-((1+E5^2)^0.5)+H5*E5 | 0 | =H4+I5*D5 | 0 | =-((1+E5^2)^0.5) | =J5*D5 |
| 6 | =A5+0.05 | =B5+C6 | =(E6)*D6 | =A6-A5 | =C6/D6 | =-((1+E6^2)^0.5)+H6*E6 | 0 | =H5+I6*D6 | 0 | =-((1+E6^2)^0.5) | =J6*D6 |
| 7 | =A6+0.05 | =B6+C7 | =(E7)*D7 | =A7-A6 | =C7/D7 | =-((1+E7^2)^0.5)+H7*E7 | 0 | =H6+I7*D7 | 0 | =-((1+E7^2)^0.5) | =J7*D7 |
| 8 | =A7+0.05 | =B7+C8 | =(E8)*D8 | =A8-A7 | =C8/D8 | =-((1+E8^2)^0.5)+H8*E8 | 0 | =H7+I8*D8 | 0 | =-((1+E8^2)^0.5) | =J8*D8 |
| 9 | =A8+0.05 | =B8+C9 | =(E9)*D9 | =A9-A8 | =C9/D9 | =-((1+E9^2)^0.5)+H9*E9 | 0 | =H8+I9*D9 | 0 | =-((1+E9^2)^0.5) | =J9*D9 |
| 10 | =A9+0.05 | =B9+C10 | =(E10)*D10 | =A10-A9 | =C10/D10 | =-((1+E10^2)^0.5)+H10*E10 | 0 | =H9+I10*D10 | 0 | =-((1+E10^2)^0.5) | =J10*D10 |
| 11 | =A10+0.05 | =B10+C11 | =(E11)*D11 | =A11-A10 | =C11/D11 | =-((1+E11^2)^0.5)+H11*E11 | 0 | =H10+I11*D11 | 0 | =-((1+E11^2)^0.5) | =J11*D11 |
| 12 | =A11+0.05 | =B11+C12 | =(E12)*D12 | =A12-A11 | =C12/D12 | =-((1+E12^2)^0.5)+H12*E12 | 0 | =H11+I12*D12 | 0 | =-((1+E12^2)^0.5) | =J12*D12 |
| 13 | =A12+0.05 | =B12+C13 | =(E13)*D13 | =A13-A12 | =C13/D13 | =-((1+E13^2)^0.5)+H13*E13 | 0 | =H12+I13*D13 | 0 | =-((1+E13^2)^0.5) | =J13*D13 |
| 14 | =A13+0.05 | =B13+C14 | =(E14)*D14 | =A14-A13 | =C14/D14 | =-((1+E14^2)^0.5)+H14*E14 | 0 | =H13+I14*D14 | 0 | =-((1+E14^2)^0.5) | =J14*D14 |
| 15 | =A14+0.05 | =B14+C15 | =(E15)*D15 | =A15-A14 | =C15/D15 | =-((1+E15^2)^0.5)+H15*E15 | 0 | =H14+I15*D15 | 0 | =-((1+E15^2)^0.5) | =J15*D15 |
| 16 | =A15+0.05 | =B15+C16 | =(E16)*D16 | =A16-A15 | =C16/D16 | =-((1+E16^2)^0.5)+H16*E16 | 0 | =H15+I16*D16 | 0 | =-((1+E16^2)^0.5) | =J16*D16 |
| 17 | =A16+0.05 | =B16+C17 | =(E17)*D17 | =A17-A16 | =C17/D17 | =-((1+E17^2)^0.5)+H17*E17 | 0 | =H16+I17*D17 | 0 | =-((1+E17^2)^0.5) | =J17*D17 |
| 18 | =A17+0.05 | =B17+C18 | =(E18)*D18 | =A18-A17 | =C18/D18 | =-((1+E18^2)^0.5)+H18*E18 | 0 | =H17+I18*D18 | 0 | =-((1+E18^2)^0.5) | =J18*D18 |
| 19 | =A18+0.05 | =B18+C19 | =(E19)*D19 | =A19-A18 | =C19/D19 | =-((1+E19^2)^0.5)+H19*E19 | 0 | =H18+I19*D19 | 0 | =-((1+E19^2)^0.5) | =J19*D19 |
| 20 | =A19+0.05 | =B19+C20 | =(E20)*D20 | =A20-A19 | =C20/D20 | =-((1+E20^2)^0.5)+H20*E20 | 0 | =H19+I20*D20 | 0 | =-((1+E20^2)^0.5) | =J20*D20 |
| 21 | =A20+0.05 | =B20+C21 | =(E21)*D21 | =A21-A20 | =C21/D21 | =-((1+E21^2)^0.5)+H21*E21 | 0 | =H20+I21*D21 | 0 | =-((1+E21^2)^0.5) | =J21*D21 |
| 22 | =A21+0.05 | =B21+C22 | =(E22)*D22 | =A22-A21 | =C22/D22 | =-((1+E22^2)^0.5)+H22*E22 | 0 | =H21+I22*D22 | 0 | =-((1+E22^2)^0.5) | =J22*D22 |
| 23 | | | | | | | | | | | |
| 24 | | | | | | | | | | | =SUM(K3:K23) |
| 25 | | | | | | | | | | | |

**FIGURE 10.3-11** Example 4: shortest distance problem worksheet setup within the optimal control framework.

III. Dynamic optimization

As usual, under *Column H* we have the solution of the differential equation on $\lambda(t)$ through the equation of motion $\dot{\lambda}(t)$.

To solve the problem what we need to do is to optimize with the Excel Solver setting the transversality condition $\lambda(T) = 0$, by changing $\lambda(0)$, which is initially set to zero.

The Excel Solver parameters will have to be set up like in Fig. 10.3-12, while the entire numerical solution for the variables involved in the problem is depicted in Table 10.3-6.

The numerical solution $y^*(t) = 7$ is also graphed in Fig. 10.3-13. The solution that optimizes the problem is a horizontal straight line.

## 10.4 Bang-bang control problems

In the previous Section 10.3 we have examined examples where the Hamiltonian function is nonlinear in the control variable $u(t)$. However, as we have seen in Section 10.2, a second important class of OC problems is encountered when the Hamiltonian function is linear in

FIGURE 10.3-12    Example 4: Solver parameters setting $\lambda(T) = 0$.

TABLE 10.3-6 Example 4: Excel numerical solution for the shortest distance problem within the optimal control framework.

| t | y Path | dy = (u)dt | dt | u = ẏ | Hamiltonian = $-(1+u^2)^{1/2} + \lambda u$ | dy/dt=dH/dλ = u = 0 | λ(t) | dλ/dt=dH/dy = 0 | F = $-(1+u^2)^{1/2}$ | Functional = $\Sigma[-(1+u^2)^{1/2}]dt$ |
|---|---|---|---|---|---|---|---|---|---|---|
| **1.0000** | **7.0000** | | | | | | **0.0000** | | | |
| 1.0500 | 7.0000 | 0.0000 | 0.0500 | 0.0000 | -1.0000 | 0.0000 | 0.0000 | 0.0000 | -1.0000 | -0.0500 |
| 1.1000 | 7.0000 | 0.0000 | 0.0500 | 0.0000 | -1.0000 | 0.0000 | 0.0000 | 0.0000 | -1.0000 | -0.0500 |
| 1.1500 | 7.0000 | 0.0000 | 0.0500 | 0.0000 | -1.0000 | 0.0000 | 0.0000 | 0.0000 | -1.0000 | -0.0500 |
| 1.2000 | 7.0000 | 0.0000 | 0.0500 | 0.0000 | -1.0000 | 0.0000 | 0.0000 | 0.0000 | -1.0000 | -0.0500 |
| 1.2500 | 7.0000 | 0.0000 | 0.0500 | 0.0000 | -1.0000 | 0.0000 | 0.0000 | 0.0000 | -1.0000 | -0.0500 |
| 1.3000 | 7.0000 | 0.0000 | 0.0500 | 0.0000 | -1.0000 | 0.0000 | 0.0000 | 0.0000 | -1.0000 | -0.0500 |
| 1.3500 | 7.0000 | 0.0000 | 0.0500 | 0.0000 | -1.0000 | 0.0000 | 0.0000 | 0.0000 | -1.0000 | -0.0500 |
| 1.4000 | 7.0000 | 0.0000 | 0.0500 | 0.0000 | -1.0000 | 0.0000 | 0.0000 | 0.0000 | -1.0000 | -0.0500 |
| 1.4500 | 7.0000 | 0.0000 | 0.0500 | 0.0000 | -1.0000 | 0.0000 | 0.0000 | 0.0000 | -1.0000 | -0.0500 |
| 1.5000 | 7.0000 | 0.0000 | 0.0500 | 0.0000 | -1.0000 | 0.0000 | 0.0000 | 0.0000 | -1.0000 | -0.0500 |
| 1.5500 | 7.0000 | 0.0000 | 0.0500 | 0.0000 | -1.0000 | 0.0000 | 0.0000 | 0.0000 | -1.0000 | -0.0500 |
| 1.6000 | 7.0000 | 0.0000 | 0.0500 | 0.0000 | -1.0000 | 0.0000 | 0.0000 | 0.0000 | -1.0000 | -0.0500 |
| 1.6500 | 7.0000 | 0.0000 | 0.0500 | 0.0000 | -1.0000 | 0.0000 | 0.0000 | 0.0000 | -1.0000 | -0.0500 |
| 1.7000 | 7.0000 | 0.0000 | 0.0500 | 0.0000 | -1.0000 | 0.0000 | 0.0000 | 0.0000 | -1.0000 | -0.0500 |
| 1.7500 | 7.0000 | 0.0000 | 0.0500 | 0.0000 | -1.0000 | 0.0000 | 0.0000 | 0.0000 | -1.0000 | -0.0500 |
| 1.8000 | 7.0000 | 0.0000 | 0.0500 | 0.0000 | -1.0000 | 0.0000 | 0.0000 | 0.0000 | -1.0000 | -0.0500 |
| 1.8500 | 7.0000 | 0.0000 | 0.0500 | 0.0000 | -1.0000 | 0.0000 | 0.0000 | 0.0000 | -1.0000 | -0.0500 |
| 1.9000 | 7.0000 | 0.0000 | 0.0500 | 0.0000 | -1.0000 | 0.0000 | 0.0000 | 0.0000 | -1.0000 | -0.0500 |
| 1.9500 | 7.0000 | 0.0000 | 0.0500 | 0.0000 | -1.0000 | 0.0000 | 0.0000 | 0.0000 | -1.0000 | -0.0500 |
| 2.0000 | 7.0000 | 0.0000 | 0.0500 | 0.0000 | -1.0000 | 0.0000 | **0.0000** | 0.0000 | -1.0000 | -0.0500 |
| | | | | | | | | | | **-1.0000** |

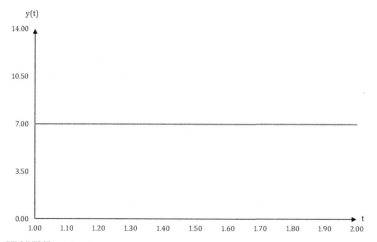

**FIGURE 10.3-13**   Example 4: horizontal straight line optimal path $y^*(t) = 7$.

the control variable $u(t)$, which is usually subject to a constraint, such as to belong to the set $\mathcal{U} = [0,1]$.

As we have seen, in these cases the first-order condition $d\mathcal{H}/dt = 0$ does not hold and what we need to do is to investigate the shape of the linear $\mathcal{H}$ to find the optimal solution, either at one or at the other boundary point of the Hamiltonian function.

The following example is taken from Alpha Chiang,[5] so that the reader can also check some other necessary theoretical details.

## EXAMPLE 1

The problem to be solved is:

$$\max_{\{u\}} J(u) = \int_0^2 (2y - 3u)dt$$

$$s.t. \quad \dot{y} = y + u$$

$$y(0) = 4, \ y(2) = \textit{free}$$

and $u \in \mathcal{U} = [0,2]$.

**i.** The first step is looking for conditions that maximize the Hamiltonian function:

$$\mathcal{H} = 2y - 3u + \lambda(y + u) = (2 + \lambda)y + (\lambda - 3)u$$

which is evidently linear in the control variable $u(t)$.

[5]See Alpha Chiang, *op. cit*, ch. 7, example 2.

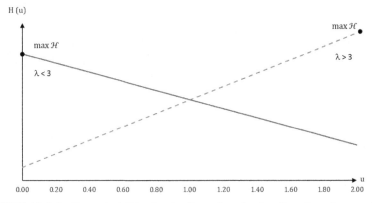

FIGURE 10.4-1  Example 1: Hamiltonian linear function in $u(t)$ and maximum points.

The slope of the line $\mathcal{H}$ is $\frac{d\mathcal{H}}{du} = (\lambda - 3)$ which can be positive or negative, depending on the values taken by $\lambda(t)$.

If $\lambda > 3$ the slope will be positive and the maximum point of $\mathcal{H}$ will be found at the boundary point $u = 2$.

However, if $\lambda < 3$ the slope will be negative and the maximum point will be found at the boundary point $u = 0$.

In formal terms the following will hold for the maximization of $\mathcal{H}$ (Fig. 10.4-1):

$$u^*(t) = \left\{ \begin{matrix} 0 \\ 2 \end{matrix} \right\} \text{if} \lambda(t) \left\{ \begin{matrix} > \\ < \end{matrix} \right\} 3.$$

**ii.** Next step is to determine from the equation of motion the solution for $\lambda(t)$:

$$\frac{d\lambda}{dt} = -\frac{\partial \mathcal{H}}{\partial y} = -2 - \lambda$$

which corresponds to:

$$\frac{d\lambda}{dt} + \lambda = -2$$

which is an ordinary linear differential equation with general solution:

$$\lambda(t) = e^{-\int dt} \left[ k + \int \left( -2e^{\int dt} \right) dt \right] = ke^{-t} - 2$$

Since $\lambda(T) = 0$ for the transversality condition then we have:

$$\lambda(2) = ke^{-2} - 2 = 0 \Rightarrow k = 2e^2$$

and the equation for $\lambda(t)$ becomes:

$$\lambda(t) = 2e^{2-t} - 2.$$

Now, what we need to do is to find the time $t^*$ when the control switches from $u = 2$ to $u = 0$; as we have seen before this will occur when $\lambda = 3$.

So, we have:

$$3 = 2e^{2-t} - 2$$

which is:

$$\frac{5}{2}\frac{1}{e^2} = e^{-t} \Rightarrow e^t = \frac{2}{5}e^2.$$

We calculate then the control switch time $t^*$ as:

$$t^* = \log\frac{2}{5}e^2 \approx 1.0837.$$

The optimal control policy is formulated in two phases:

$$Phase\ I \Rightarrow u_I = u^*[0, t^*) = 2$$

$$Phase\ II \Rightarrow u_{II} = u^*[t^*, 2] = 0$$

iii. Finally, from the equations of motion $\dot{y} = y + 2$ in *Phase I* and $\dot{y} = y + 0$ in *Phase II* and from the initial value $y(0) = 4$, the state variable $y(t)$ is determined for the two phases as:

$$Phase\ I \Rightarrow y_I^* = 2(3e^t - 1)$$

which evaluated in $t^*$ is equal to:

$$y_I^*(t^*) = 2(3e^{t^*} - 1) = 15.7336$$

In $t^*$ the state variable $y_{II}^*$ will assume the same value as $y_I^*$, namely:

$$Phase\ II \Rightarrow y_{II}^* = ce^{1.0837} = 15.7336 \Rightarrow c = 5.3233$$

from which we derive the optimal $y_{II}^*$ as:

$$Phase\ II \Rightarrow y_{II}^* = 5.3233e^t$$

Let us see now in Excel how to implement a numerical approach of a *bang-bang* control problem, comparing the computed solution with the exact solutions explained so far.

The setup of the worksheet is as follows in Fig. 10.4-2.

| | A | B | C | D | E | F | G | H | I | J | K |
|---|---|---|---|---|---|---|---|---|---|---|---|
| | t | y Path | dy = (y+u)dt | dt | Control u =y-y | dy/dt = y+2 up to ≅1 dy/dt=y after | Hamiltonian = 2y-3u+λ(y+u) | λ(t) | dλ/dt | F = 2y-3u | Functional = Σ (2y-3u)dt |
| 1 | | | | | | | | | | | |
| 2 | 0 | 4 | | | =F2-B2 | =B2+2 | =2*B2-3*E2+H2*(B2+E2) | 12.07997742421 | =-2-H2 | | |
| 3 | =A2+0.05 | =B2+C3 | =(E3+B3)*D3 | =A3-A2 | =F3-B3 | =B3+2 | =2*B3-3*E3+H3*(B3+E3) | =H2+I3*D3 | =-2-H3 | =2*B3-3*E3 | =J3*D3 |
| 4 | =A3+0.05 | =B3+C4 | =(E4+B4)*D4 | =A4-A3 | =F4-B4 | =B4+2 | =2*B4-3*E4+H4*(B4+E4) | =H3+I4*D4 | =-2-H4 | =2*B4-3*E4 | =J4*D4 |
| 5 | =A4+0.05 | =B4+C5 | =(E5+B5)*D5 | =A5-A4 | =F5-B5 | =B5+2 | =2*B5-3*E5+H5*(B5+E5) | =H4+I5*D5 | =-2-H5 | =2*B5-3*E5 | =J5*D5 |
| 16 | =A15+0.05 | =B15+C16 | =(E16+B16)*D16 | =A16-A15 | =F16-B16 | =B16+2 | =2*B16-3*E16+H16*(B16+E16) | =H15+I16*D16 | =-2-H16 | =2*B16-3*E16 | =J16*D16 |
| 17 | =A16+0.05 | =B16+C17 | =(E17+B17)*D17 | =A17-A16 | =F17-B17 | =B17+2 | =2*B17-3*E17+H17*(B17+E17) | =H16+I17*D17 | =-2-H17 | =2*B17-3*E17 | =J17*D17 |
| 18 | =A17+0.05 | =B17+C18 | =(E18+B18)*D18 | =A18-A17 | =F18-B18 | =B18+2 | =2*B18-3*E18+H18*(B18+E18) | =H17+I18*D18 | =-2-H18 | =2*B18-3*E18 | =J18*D18 |
| 19 | =A18+0.05 | =B18+C19 | =(E19+B19)*D19 | =A19-A18 | =F19-B19 | =B19+2 | =2*B19-3*E19+H19*(B19+E19) | =H18+I19*D19 | =-2-H19 | =2*B19-3*E19 | =J19*D19 |
| 20 | =A19+0.05 | =B19+C20 | =(E20+B20)*D20 | =A20-A19 | =F20-B20 | =B20+2 | =2*B20-3*E20+H20*(B20+E20) | =H19+I20*D20 | =-2-H20 | =2*B20-3*E20 | =J20*D20 |
| 21 | =A20+0.05 | =B20+C21 | =(E21+B21)*D21 | =A21-A20 | =F21-B21 | =B21+2 | =2*B21-3*E21+H21*(B21+E21) | =H20+I21*D21 | =-2-H21 | =2*B21-3*E21 | =J21*D21 |
| 22 | =A21+0.05 | =B21+C22 | =(E22+B22)*D22 | =A22-A21 | =F22-B22 | =B22+2 | =2*B22-3*E22+H22*(B22+E22) | =H21+I22*D22 | =-2-H22 | =2*B22-3*E22 | =J22*D22 |
| 23 | =A22+0.05 | =B22+C23 | =(E23+B23)*D23 | =A23-A22 | =F23-B23 | =B23+2 | =2*B23-3*E23+H23*(B23+E23) | =H22+I23*D23 | =-2-H23 | =2*B23-3*E23 | =J23*D23 |
| 24 | =A23+0.05 | =B23+C24 | =(E24+B24)*D24 | =A24-A23 | =F24-B24 | =B24 | =2*B24-3*E24+H24*(B24+E24) | =H23+I24*D24 | =-2-H24 | =2*B24-3*E24 | =J24*D24 |
| 25 | =A24+0.05 | =B24+C25 | =(E25+B25)*D25 | =A25-A24 | =F25-B25 | =B25 | =2*B25-3*E25+H25*(B25+E25) | =H24+I25*D25 | =-2-H25 | =2*B25-3*E25 | =J25*D25 |
| 26 | =A25+0.05 | =B25+C26 | =(E26+B26)*D26 | =A26-A25 | =F26-B26 | =B26 | =2*B26-3*E26+H26*(B26+E26) | =H25+I26*D26 | =-2-H26 | =2*B26-3*E26 | =J26*D26 |
| 27 | =A26+0.05 | =B26+C27 | =(E27+B27)*D27 | =A27-A26 | =F27-B27 | =B27 | =2*B27-3*E27+H27*(B27+E27) | =H26+I27*D27 | =-2-H27 | =2*B27-3*E27 | =J27*D27 |
| 38 | =A37+0.05 | =B37+C38 | =(E38+B38)*D38 | =A38-A37 | =F38-B38 | =B38 | =2*B38-3*E38+H38*(B38+E38) | =H37+I38*D38 | =-2-H38 | =2*B38-3*E38 | =J38*D38 |
| 39 | =A38+0.05 | =B38+C39 | =(E39+B39)*D39 | =A39-A38 | =F39-B39 | =B39 | =2*B39-3*E39+H39*(B39+E39) | =H38+I39*D39 | =-2-H39 | =2*B39-3*E39 | =J39*D39 |
| 40 | =A39+0.05 | =B39+C40 | =(E40+B40)*D40 | =A40-A39 | =F40-B40 | =B40 | =2*B40-3*E40+H40*(B40+E40) | =H39+I40*D40 | =-2-H40 | =2*B40-3*E40 | =J40*D40 |
| 41 | =A40+0.05 | =B40+C41 | =(E41+B41)*D41 | =A41-A40 | =F41-B41 | =B41 | =2*B41-3*E41+H41*(B41+E41) | =H40+I41*D41 | =-2-H41 | =2*B41-3*E41 | =J41*D41 |
| 42 | =A41+0.05 | =B41+C42 | =(E42+B42)*D42 | =A42-A41 | =F42-B42 | =B42 | =2*B42-3*E42+H42*(B42+E42) | =H41+I42*D42 | =-2-H42 | =2*B42-3*E42 | =J42*D42 |
| | | | | | | | | Transversality condition λ(T) = 0 | | | |
| 44 | y(0) | 4 | | | | | | | | | =SUM(K3:K43) |
| 45 | y(2) | Free | | | | | | | | | |

FIGURE 10.4-2  Example 1: worksheet setup for the bang-bang optimal control problem.

Notice that from the study of the linear Hamiltonian function, we know that the optimal control policy has to be $u(t) = \begin{Bmatrix} 0 \\ 2 \end{Bmatrix}$ if $\lambda(t) \begin{Bmatrix} > \\ < \end{Bmatrix} 3$ and the equation of motion under *Column F* has been changed accordingly. Then, as usual, under *Column H*, we have the Euler method to derive $\lambda(t)$ from its equation of motion $\frac{d\lambda}{dt} = -2 - \lambda$.

The way to solve the problem is to set initially an arbitrary value in the *Cell H2* and therefore optimizing as depicted in Fig. 10.4-3.

The worksheet solution obtained is in Table 10.4-1, which represents, however, a **suboptimal solution**. What we need to do to compute the **final optimal solution** is to implement in the worksheet the optimal policy $u^*(t) = \begin{Bmatrix} 0 \\ 2 \end{Bmatrix}$ if $\lambda(t) \begin{Bmatrix} > \\ < \end{Bmatrix} 3$ by changing *Column F*, just adding manually the value 2 up to *Cell F23* (this is when $\lambda \cong 3$) as represented in Fig. 10.4-2.

Notice that by doing this the value of the *Functional* under *Cell K44* will increase from the value 54.2509, given by the suboptimal solution in Table 10.4-1, to the value 64.2762, given by the **final optimal solution** in Table 10.4-2.

Notice also that the whole worksheet has been developed over 40 steps, to be more accurate in finding the time $t^*$ at which the control switches from 2 to 0. We can see from the worksheet that $1.05 < t^* < 1.10$ (Figs. 10.4-4 and 10.4-5).

## 10.5 Consumption model

Let us see now some economic models applied with the OC theory starting with a simple consumption model.[6]

[6]Taken from Prof. Richard T. Woodward, *Lecture in Dynamic Optimization*, Department of Agricultural Economics, Texas A&M University.

**FIGURE 10.4-3**   Solver parameters setting $\lambda(T) = 0$ by changing $\lambda(0)$.

The consumption model is expressed as follows:

$$\max_{\{u\}} J(u) = \int_0^1 \log(u4y)dt$$

$$s.t. \ \dot{y} = 4y(1-u) \text{ and } y(0) = 1, \ y(1) = e^2$$

where $u(t)$ is the consumption and $y(t)$ is the total output of the economy over the time interval $[0, 1]$, while $\dot{y} = \frac{dy}{dt}$ is the variation in the total output (i.e., the aggregate investment expenditures).

The objective is to maximize the economy utility function.

**i.** The Hamiltonian is given by:

$$\mathcal{H} = \log(u4y) + \lambda[4y(1-u)].$$

**TABLE 10.4-1** Example 1: suboptimal numerical solution before the optimal control policy is implemented.

| t | y Path | dy = (y+u)dt | dt | Control u = ẏ-y | dy/dt = y+2 up to ≅1 dy/dt = y after | Hamiltonian = 2y-3u+λ(y+u) | λ(t) | dλ/dt | F = 2y-3u | Functional = Σ(2y-3u)dt |
|---|---|---|---|---|---|---|---|---|---|---|
| **0.0000** | **4.0000** | | | 0.0000 | 4.0000 | 56.3199 | **12.0800** | -14.0800 | | |
| 0.0500 | 4.2105 | 0.2105 | 0.0500 | 0.0000 | 4.2105 | 56.4611 | 11.4095 | -13.4095 | 8.4211 | 0.4211 |
| 0.1000 | 4.4321 | 0.2216 | 0.0500 | 0.0000 | 4.4321 | 56.6026 | 10.7710 | -12.7710 | 8.8643 | 0.4432 |
| 0.1500 | 4.6654 | 0.2333 | 0.0500 | 0.0000 | 4.6654 | 56.7444 | 10.1628 | -12.1628 | 9.3308 | 0.4665 |
| 0.2000 | 4.9110 | 0.2455 | 0.0500 | 0.0000 | 4.9110 | 56.8866 | 9.5836 | -11.5836 | 9.8219 | 0.4911 |
| 0.2500 | 5.1694 | 0.2585 | 0.0500 | 0.0000 | 5.1694 | 57.0292 | 9.0320 | -11.0320 | 10.3388 | 0.5169 |
| 0.8000 | 9.0883 | 0.4544 | 0.0500 | 0.0000 | 9.0883 | 58.6213 | 4.4502 | -6.4502 | 18.1766 | 0.9088 |
| 0.8500 | 9.5666 | 0.4783 | 0.0500 | 0.0000 | 9.5666 | 58.7682 | 4.1430 | -6.1430 | 19.1332 | 0.9567 |
| 0.9000 | 10.0701 | 0.5035 | 0.0500 | 0.0000 | 10.0701 | 58.9155 | 3.8505 | -5.8505 | 20.1403 | 1.0070 |
| 0.9500 | 10.6001 | 0.5300 | 0.0500 | 0.0000 | 10.6001 | 59.0632 | 3.5719 | -5.5719 | 21.2003 | 1.0600 |
| 1.0000 | 11.1580 | 0.5579 | 0.0500 | 0.0000 | 11.1580 | 59.2112 | 3.3066 | -5.3066 | 22.3161 | 1.1158 |
| 1.0500 | 11.7453 | 0.5873 | 0.0500 | 0.0000 | 11.7453 | 59.3596 | 3.0539 | -5.0539 | 23.4906 | 1.1745 |
| 1.1000 | 12.3635 | 0.6182 | 0.0500 | 0.0000 | 12.3635 | 59.5084 | 2.8132 | -4.8132 | 24.7270 | 1.2363 |
| 1.1500 | 13.0142 | 0.6507 | 0.0500 | 0.0000 | 13.0142 | 59.6575 | 2.5840 | -4.5840 | 26.0284 | 1.3014 |
| 1.2000 | 13.6991 | 0.6850 | 0.0500 | 0.0000 | 13.6991 | 59.8070 | 2.3657 | -4.3657 | 27.3983 | 1.3699 |
| 1.7500 | 24.0843 | 1.2042 | 0.0500 | 0.0000 | 24.0843 | 61.4767 | 0.5526 | -2.5526 | 48.1686 | 2.4084 |
| 1.8000 | 25.3519 | 1.2676 | 0.0500 | 0.0000 | 25.3519 | 61.6307 | 0.4310 | -2.4310 | 50.7038 | 2.5352 |
| 1.8500 | 26.6862 | 1.3343 | 0.0500 | 0.0000 | 26.6862 | 61.7852 | 0.3152 | -2.3152 | 53.3724 | 2.6686 |
| 1.9000 | 28.0907 | 1.4045 | 0.0500 | 0.0000 | 28.0907 | 61.9401 | 0.2050 | -2.2050 | 56.1815 | 2.8091 |
| 1.9500 | 29.5692 | 1.4785 | 0.0500 | 0.0000 | 29.5692 | 62.0953 | 0.1000 | -2.1000 | 59.1384 | 2.9569 |
| 2.0000 | 31.1255 | 1.5563 | 0.0500 | 0.0000 | 31.1255 | 62.2509 | 0.0000 | -2.0000 | 62.2509 | 3.1125 |

y(0)   4.0000
y(2)   Free

Transversality condition λ(T) = 0

54.2509

**TABLE 10.4-2**  Example 1: optimal numerical solution after the optimal control policy is implemented.

| t | y Path | dy = (y+u)dt | dt | Control u = dy/dt = ẏ-y | dy/dt = y+2 up to ≅1 dy/dt = y after | Hamiltonian = 2y- 3u+λ(y+u) | λ(t) | dλ/dt | F = 2y-3u | Functional = Σ(2y-3u)dt |
|---|---|---|---|---|---|---|---|---|---|---|
| 0.0000 | 4.0000 |  |  | 2.0000 | 6.0000 | 74.4799 | 12.0800 | -14.0800 |  |  |
| 0.0500 | 4.3158 | 0.3158 | 0.0500 | 2.0000 | 6.3158 | 74.6916 | 11.4095 | -13.4095 | 2.6316 | 0.1316 |
| 0.1000 | 4.6482 | 0.3324 | 0.0500 | 2.0000 | 6.6482 | 74.9039 | 10.7710 | -12.7710 | 3.2964 | 0.1648 |
| 0.1500 | 4.9981 | 0.3499 | 0.0500 | 2.0000 | 6.9981 | 75.1166 | 10.1628 | -12.1628 | 3.9962 | 0.1998 |
| 0.7000 | 10.3033 | 0.6152 | 0.0500 | 2.0000 | 12.3033 | 77.4928 | 5.1113 | -7.1113 | 14.6066 | 0.7303 |
| 0.7500 | 10.9508 | 0.6475 | 0.0500 | 2.0000 | 12.9508 | 77.7121 | 4.7727 | -6.7727 | 15.4016 | 0.7951 |
| 0.8000 | 11.6324 | 0.6816 | 0.0500 | 2.0000 | 13.6324 | 77.9320 | 4.4502 | -6.4502 | 17.2649 | 0.8632 |
| 0.8500 | 12.3499 | 0.7175 | 0.0500 | 2.0000 | 14.3499 | 78.1523 | 4.1430 | -6.1430 | 18.6999 | 0.9350 |
| 0.9000 | 13.1052 | 0.7553 | 0.0500 | 2.0000 | 15.1052 | 78.3733 | 3.8505 | -5.8505 | 20.2104 | 1.0105 |
| 0.9500 | 13.9002 | 0.7950 | 0.0500 | 2.0000 | 15.9002 | 78.5948 | 3.5719 | -5.5719 | 21.8004 | 1.0900 |
| 1.0000 | 14.7371 | 0.8369 | 0.0500 | 2.0000 | 16.7371 | 78.8168 | 3.3066 | -5.3066 | 23.4741 | 1.1737 |
| 1.0500 | 15.6180 | 0.8809 | 0.0500 | 2.0000 | 17.6180 | 79.0394 | 3.0539 | -5.0539 | 25.2359 | 1.2618 |
| 1.1000 | 16.4400 | 0.8220 | 0.0500 | 0.0000 | 16.4400 | 79.1294 | 2.8132 | -4.8132 | 32.8799 | 1.6440 |
| 1.1500 | 17.3052 | 0.8653 | 0.0500 | 0.0000 | 17.3052 | 79.3277 | 2.5840 | -4.5840 | 34.6104 | 1.7305 |
| 1.2000 | 18.2160 | 0.9108 | 0.0500 | 0.0000 | 18.2160 | 79.5266 | 2.3657 | -4.3657 | 36.4320 | 1.8216 |
| 1.2500 | 19.1748 | 0.9587 | 0.0500 | 0.0000 | 19.1748 | 79.7259 | 2.1579 | -4.1579 | 38.3495 | 1.9175 |
| 1.8000 | 33.7109 | 1.6855 | 0.0500 | 0.0000 | 33.7109 | 81.9516 | 0.4310 | -2.4310 | 67.4218 | 3.3711 |
| 1.8500 | 35.4851 | 1.7743 | 0.0500 | 0.0000 | 35.4851 | 82.1570 | 0.3152 | -2.3152 | 70.9703 | 3.5485 |
| 1.9000 | 37.3528 | 1.8676 | 0.0500 | 0.0000 | 37.3528 | 82.3629 | 0.2050 | -2.2050 | 74.7056 | 3.7353 |
| 1.9500 | 39.3187 | 1.9659 | 0.0500 | 0.0000 | 39.3187 | 82.5693 | 0.1000 | -2.1000 | 78.6374 | 3.9319 |
| 2.0000 | 41.3881 | 2.0694 | 0.0500 | 0.0000 | 41.3881 | 82.7762 | 0.0000 | -2.0000 | 82.7762 | 4.1388 |

y(0)  4.0000
y(2)  Free

Transversality condition λ(T) = 0                    64.2762

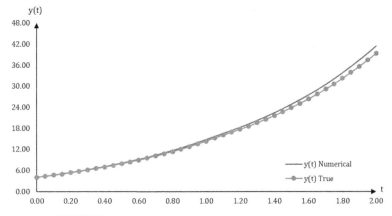

**FIGURE 10.4-4**  Example 1: numerical versus exact $y^*(t)$.

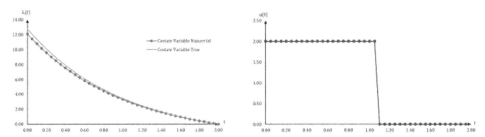

**FIGURE 10.4-5**  Example 1: numerical versus exact $\lambda^*(t)$ and the optimal control policy $u^*(t)$.

Let us check as usual the first-order condition to find the maximum for $\mathcal{H}$:

$$\frac{\partial \mathcal{H}}{\partial u} = \frac{4y}{4yu} - \lambda 4y = \frac{1}{u} - \lambda 4y = 0 \Rightarrow u^*(t) = \frac{1}{\lambda 4y}.$$

The second derivative is:

$$\frac{\partial^2 \mathcal{H}}{\partial u^2} = -\frac{1}{u^2} < 0.$$

In this problem, we find that current consumption is inversely related to the total aggregate output and the costate variable.

**ii.** From the equation of motion for $\lambda(t)$ we obtain:

$$\frac{d\lambda}{dt} = -\frac{\partial \mathcal{H}}{\partial y} = -\left[\frac{1}{y} + 4\lambda(1 - u)\right].$$

III. Dynamic optimization

As $u(t) = \frac{1}{\lambda 4y}$ the above equation of motion becomes:

$$\frac{d\lambda}{dt} = -\frac{\partial \mathcal{H}}{\partial y} = -\left[\frac{1}{y} + 4\lambda\left(1 - \frac{1}{\lambda 4y}\right)\right] = -4\lambda$$

which has general solution:

$$\lambda^*(t) = ke^{-4t}$$

iii. Now, from the equation of motion $\dot{y} = 4y - 4yu$ we have the following ordinary linear differential equation to solve:

$$\frac{dy}{dt} = 4y - 4y\frac{1}{\lambda 4y}$$

which becomes:

$$\frac{dy}{dt} - 4y = -\frac{1}{\lambda}.$$

As $\lambda^*(t) = ke^{-4t}$ we have:

$$\frac{dy}{dt} - 4y = -\frac{1}{k}e^{4t}$$

which is a first-order differential equation with general solution:

$$y(t) = e^{4\int dt}\left[c - \frac{1}{k}\int \left(e^{-4\int dt}e^{4t}\right)dt\right]$$

$$y(t) = e^{4t}\left[c - \frac{1}{k}\int dt\right] = e^{4t}\left[c - \frac{t}{k}\right] = ce^{4t} - t\frac{e^{4t}}{k}.$$

iv. From the boundary conditions $y(0) = 1$, $y(1) = e^2$ we can now determine the two constants of integration as:

$$y(0) = 1 \Rightarrow c = 1$$

$$y(1) = e^2 \Rightarrow e^4 - \frac{e^4}{k} = e^2 \Rightarrow k = \frac{e^4}{e^4 - e^2} \cong 1.1565.$$

The optimal $y^*(t)$ is determined then as follows:

$$y^*(t) = e^{4t} - t\frac{e^{4t}}{1.1565}$$

while the costate variable is:

$$\lambda^*(t) = 1.1565e^{-4t}.$$

We finally obtain $u^*(t)$ as:

$$\mathrm{u}^*(\mathrm{t}) = \frac{1}{\lambda 4y} = \frac{e^{4t}}{4k\left(e^{4t} - \frac{t}{k}e^{4t}\right)} = \frac{1}{(4\cdot 1.1565 - 4t)} = \frac{1}{(4.626 - 4t)}.$$

The Excel worksheet for this model is built as follows (Fig. 10.5-1):

The Solver Parameters window is set up as in Fig. 10.5-2. We maximize *Cell K24* by changing *Cell H2* $= \lambda(0)$ subject to the boundary condition $y(1) = e^2$. Table 10.5-1 is the final computed numerical solution for the variables involved in the problem.

It is worthwhile to notice that for completing the Excel numerical solution is enough for us to identify the theoretical Hamiltonian function and its maximum point $\mathrm{u}^*(\mathrm{t}) = \frac{1}{\lambda 4y}$ which has been inserted in *Column E*. The Excel Solver will compute then the solutions for the state and control variable, passing through the costate variable (Figs. 10.5-3 and 10.5-4).

| | A | B | C | D | E | F | G | H | I | J | K |
|---|---|---|---|---|---|---|---|---|---|---|---|
| 1 | t | Output Path y(t) | dy = 4y(1-u)dt | dt | Consumption u = 1/(λ4y) | dy/dt = 4y(1-u) | Hamiltonian = log(u4y)+ λ[4y(1-u)] | λ(t) | dλ/dt = -4λ | F = 4log(u4y) | Functional = Σ 4log(u4y)dt |
| 2 | 0 | 1 | | | =1/(H2*4*B2) | =4*B2*(1-E2) | =LN(E2*4*B2)+H2*(4*B2*(1-E2)) | 0.9149865140 | =-(H2*4) | | |
| 3 | =A2+0.05 | =B2+C3 | =(4*B3-1/H3)*D3 | =A3-A2 | =1/(H3*4*B3) | =4*B3*(1-E3) | =LN(E3*4*B3)+H3*(4*B3*(1-E3)) | =H2+I3*D3 | =-(H3*4) | =LN(E3*4*B3) | =J3*D3 |
| 4 | =A3+0.05 | =B3+C4 | =(4*B4-1/H4)*D4 | =A4-A3 | =1/(H4*4*B4) | =4*B4*(1-E4) | =LN(E4*4*B4)+H4*(4*B4*(1-E4)) | =H3+I4*D4 | =-(H4*4) | =LN(E4*4*B4) | =J4*D4 |
| 5 | =A4+0.05 | =B4+C5 | =(4*B5-1/H5)*D5 | =A5-A4 | =1/(H5*4*B5) | =4*B5*(1-E5) | =LN(E5*4*B5)+H5*(4*B5*(1-E5)) | =H4+I5*D5 | =-(H5*4) | =LN(E5*4*B5) | =J5*D5 |
| 6 | =A5+0.05 | =B5+C6 | =(4*B6-1/H6)*D6 | =A6-A5 | =1/(H6*4*B6) | =4*B6*(1-E6) | =LN(E6*4*B6)+H6*(4*B6*(1-E6)) | =H5+I6*D6 | =-(H6*4) | =LN(E6*4*B6) | =J6*D6 |
| 7 | =A6+0.05 | =B6+C7 | =(4*B7-1/H7)*D7 | =A7-A6 | =1/(H7*4*B7) | =4*B7*(1-E7) | =LN(E7*4*B7)+H7*(4*B7*(1-E7)) | =H6+I7*D7 | =-(H7*4) | =LN(E7*4*B7) | =J7*D7 |
| 8 | =A7+0.05 | =B7+C8 | =(4*B8-1/H8)*D8 | =A8-A7 | =1/(H8*4*B8) | =4*B8*(1-E8) | =LN(E8*4*B8)+H8*(4*B8*(1-E8)) | =H7+I8*D8 | =-(H8*4) | =LN(E8*4*B8) | =J8*D8 |
| 9 | =A8+0.05 | =B8+C9 | =(4*B9-1/H9)*D9 | =A9-A8 | =1/(H9*4*B9) | =4*B9*(1-E9) | =LN(E9*4*B9)+H9*(4*B9*(1-E9)) | =H8+I9*D9 | =-(H9*4) | =LN(E9*4*B9) | =J9*D9 |
| 10 | =A9+0.05 | =B9+C10 | =(4*B10-1/H10)*D10 | =A10-A9 | =1/(H10*4*B10) | =4*B10*(1-E10) | =LN(E10*4*B10)+H10*(4*B10*(1-E10)) | =H9+I10*D10 | =-(H10*4) | =LN(E10*4*B10) | =J10*D10 |
| 11 | =A10+0.05 | =B10+C11 | =(4*B11-1/H11)*D11 | =A11-A10 | =1/(H11*4*B11) | =4*B11*(1-E11) | =LN(E11*4*B11)+H11*(4*B11*(1-E11)) | =H10+I11*D11 | =-(H11*4) | =LN(E11*4*B11) | =J11*D11 |
| 12 | =A11+0.05 | =B11+C12 | =(4*B12-1/H12)*D12 | =A12-A11 | =1/(H12*4*B12) | =4*B12*(1-E12) | =LN(E12*4*B12)+H12*(4*B12*(1-E12)) | =H11+I12*D12 | =-(H12*4) | =LN(E12*4*B12) | =J12*D12 |
| 13 | =A12+0.05 | =B12+C13 | =(4*B13-1/H13)*D13 | =A13-A12 | =1/(H13*4*B13) | =4*B13*(1-E13) | =LN(E13*4*B13)+H13*(4*B13*(1-E13)) | =H12+I13*D13 | =-(H13*4) | =LN(E13*4*B13) | =J13*D13 |
| 14 | =A13+0.05 | =B13+C14 | =(4*B14-1/H14)*D14 | =A14-A13 | =1/(H14*4*B14) | =4*B14*(1-E14) | =LN(E14*4*B14)+H14*(4*B14*(1-E14)) | =H13+I14*D14 | =-(H14*4) | =LN(E14*4*B14) | =J14*D14 |
| 15 | =A14+0.05 | =B14+C15 | =(4*B15-1/H15)*D15 | =A15-A14 | =1/(H15*4*B15) | =4*B15*(1-E15) | =LN(E15*4*B15)+H15*(4*B15*(1-E15)) | =H14+I15*D15 | =-(H15*4) | =LN(E15*4*B15) | =J15*D15 |
| 16 | =A15+0.05 | =B15+C16 | =(4*B16-1/H16)*D16 | =A16-A15 | =1/(H16*4*B16) | =4*B16*(1-E16) | =LN(E16*4*B16)+H16*(4*B16*(1-E16)) | =H15+I16*D16 | =-(H16*4) | =LN(E16*4*B16) | =J16*D16 |
| 17 | =A16+0.05 | =B16+C17 | =(4*B17-1/H17)*D17 | =A17-A16 | =1/(H17*4*B17) | =4*B17*(1-E17) | =LN(E17*4*B17)+H17*(4*B17*(1-E17)) | =H16+I17*D17 | =-(H17*4) | =LN(E17*4*B17) | =J17*D17 |
| 18 | =A17+0.05 | =B17+C18 | =(4*B18-1/H18)*D18 | =A18-A17 | =1/(H18*4*B18) | =4*B18*(1-E18) | =LN(E18*4*B18)+H18*(4*B18*(1-E18)) | =H17+I18*D18 | =-(H18*4) | =LN(E18*4*B18) | =J18*D18 |
| 19 | =A18+0.05 | =B18+C19 | =(4*B19-1/H19)*D19 | =A19-A18 | =1/(H19*4*B19) | =4*B19*(1-E19) | =LN(E19*4*B19)+H19*(4*B19*(1-E19)) | =H18+I19*D19 | =-(H19*4) | =LN(E19*4*B19) | =J19*D19 |
| 20 | =A19+0.05 | =B19+C20 | =(4*B20-1/H20)*D20 | =A20-A19 | =1/(H20*4*B20) | =4*B20*(1-E20) | =LN(E20*4*B20)+H20*(4*B20*(1-E20)) | =H19+I20*D20 | =-(H20*4) | =LN(E20*4*B20) | =J20*D20 |
| 21 | =A20+0.05 | =B20+C21 | =(4*B21-1/H21)*D21 | =A21-A20 | =1/(H21*4*B21) | =4*B21*(1-E21) | =LN(E21*4*B21)+H21*(4*B21*(1-E21)) | =H20+I21*D21 | =-(H21*4) | =LN(E21*4*B21) | =J21*D21 |
| 22 | =A21+0.05 | =B21+C22 | =(4*B22-1/H22)*D22 | =A22-A21 | =1/(H22*4*B22) | =4*B22*(1-E22) | =LN(E22*4*B22)+H22*(4*B22*(1-E22)) | =H21+I22*D22 | =-(H22*4) | =LN(E22*4*B22) | =J22*D22 |
| 23 | | | | | | | | | | | |
| 24 | | | | | | | | | | | =SUM(K3:K23) |
| 25 | y(0) | 1 | | | | | | | | | |
| 26 | y(1) | $e^2$ = | =EXP(2) | | | | | | | | |

FIGURE 10.5-1 Consumption model Excel worksheet setup.

FIGURE 10.5-2　Consumption model Solver parameters.

## 10.6 Investment model

We will solve now a more complex investment model[7] given by the following:

$$\max_{\{I\}} J(I) = \int_{t_0}^{T} \left( K - aK^2 - I^2 \right) dt$$

s.t. $\dot{K} = I - \delta K$ and $K(t_0) = $ given, $K(T) = $ free, $0 < \delta \leq 1$ and $a > 0$

where $\delta$ is the rate of depreciation, $K$ is the capital stock (state variable), $I$ is the investment made, namely the control variable (gross variation in the capital stock), while $\dot{K}$ represents the net capital expenditures.

[7]See also Michael Hoy *et al.*, *Mathematics for Economics*, The MIT Press, chapter 25.

**TABLE 10.5-1** Consumption model complete numerical solution.

| t | Output Path y(t) | dy = 4y(1-u)dt | dt | Consumption u = 1/(λ4y) | dy/dt = 4y(1-u) | Hamiltonian = log[u4y]+λ4y(1-u) | λ(t) | dλ/dt = -λ | F = 4log(u4y) | Functional = I = 4log(u4y)dt |
|---|---|---|---|---|---|---|---|---|---|---|
| **0.0000** | **1.0000** | | | 0.2732 | 2.9071 | 2.7488 | **0.9150** | -3.6599 | 0.2712 | 0.0136 |
| 0.0500 | 1.1680 | 0.1680 | 0.0500 | 0.2907 | 3.3606 | 2.8336 | 0.7625 | -3.0500 | 0.4535 | 0.0227 |
| 0.1000 | 1.3617 | 0.1936 | 0.0500 | 0.2889 | 3.8729 | 2.9144 | 0.6354 | -2.5416 | 0.6358 | 0.0318 |
| 0.1500 | 1.5841 | 0.2224 | 0.0500 | 0.2981 | 4.4477 | 2.9909 | 0.5295 | -2.1180 | 0.8181 | 0.0409 |
| 0.2000 | 1.8384 | 0.2544 | 0.0500 | 0.3082 | 5.0875 | 3.0630 | 0.4413 | -1.7650 | 1.0005 | 0.0500 |
| 0.2500 | 2.1281 | 0.2896 | 0.0500 | 0.3195 | 5.7928 | 3.1305 | 0.3677 | -1.4709 | 1.1828 | 0.0591 |
| 0.3000 | 2.4561 | 0.3281 | 0.0500 | 0.3322 | 6.5611 | 3.1933 | 0.3064 | -1.2257 | 1.3651 | 0.0683 |
| 0.3500 | 2.8254 | 0.3693 | 0.0500 | 0.3465 | 7.3855 | 3.2510 | 0.2554 | -1.0214 | 1.5474 | 0.0774 |
| 0.4000 | 3.2381 | 0.4126 | 0.0500 | 0.3628 | 8.2529 | 3.3036 | 0.2128 | -0.8512 | 1.7297 | 0.0865 |
| 0.4500 | 3.6951 | 0.4571 | 0.0500 | 0.3815 | 9.1413 | 3.3508 | 0.1773 | -0.7093 | 1.9121 | 0.0956 |
| 0.5000 | 4.1960 | 0.5008 | 0.0500 | 0.4032 | 10.01168 | 3.3923 | 0.1478 | -0.5911 | 2.0944 | 0.1047 |
| 0.5500 | 4.7374 | 0.5415 | 0.0500 | 0.4285 | 10.8292 | 3.4280 | 0.1231 | -0.4926 | 2.2767 | 0.1138 |
| 0.6000 | 5.3127 | 0.5753 | 0.0500 | 0.4585 | 11.5064 | 3.4575 | 0.1026 | -0.4105 | 2.4590 | 0.1230 |
| 0.6500 | 5.9101 | 0.5973 | 0.0500 | 0.4946 | 11.9469 | 3.4807 | 0.0855 | -0.3421 | 2.6413 | 0.1321 |
| 0.7000 | 6.5106 | 0.6005 | 0.0500 | 0.5388 | 12.0103 | 3.4973 | 0.0713 | -0.2851 | 2.8237 | 0.1412 |
| 0.7500 | 7.0858 | 0.5752 | 0.0500 | 0.5941 | 11.5048 | 3.5069 | 0.0594 | -0.2376 | 3.0060 | 0.1503 |
| 0.8000 | 7.5944 | 0.5086 | 0.0500 | 0.6652 | 10.1714 | 3.5094 | 0.0495 | -0.1980 | 3.1883 | 0.1594 |
| 0.8500 | 7.9775 | 0.3831 | 0.0500 | 0.7599 | 7.6627 | 3.5043 | 0.0412 | -0.1650 | 3.3706 | 0.1685 |
| 0.9000 | 8.1534 | 0.1758 | 0.0500 | 0.8922 | 3.5165 | 3.4915 | 0.0344 | -0.1375 | 3.5530 | 0.1776 |
| 0.9500 | 8.0094 | -0.1439 | 0.0500 | 1.0898 | -2.8786 | 3.4705 | 0.0286 | -0.1146 | 3.7353 | 0.1868 |
| 1.0000 | 7.3931 | -0.6164 | 0.0500 | 1.4169 | -12.3273 | 3.4411 | 0.0239 | -0.0955 | | |
| | | | | | | | | | | 2.0032 |

y(0) = **1.0000**

y(1) = **7.3931**      e² = **7.3891**

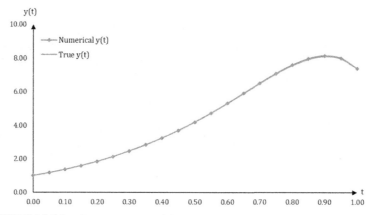

**FIGURE 10.5-3**   Consumption model exact versus numerical aggregate output $y^*(t)$.

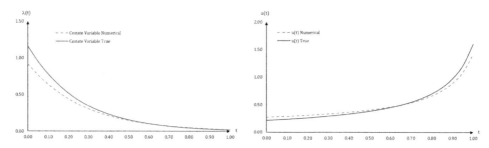

**FIGURE 10.5-4**   Consumption model approximate numerical versus exact solutions for $u^*(t)$ and $\lambda^*(t)$.

The quantity:

$$Q = K - aK^2$$

is the total output of the firm, while:

$$\pi = \left(K - aK^2\right) - I^2$$

is the profit function that we want to maximize, where the costs are directly proportional to the investments made (we assume the price of the output equal to 1\$ and the cost equal to $I^2$dollars).

**i.** As usual we find the Hamiltonian as:

$$\mathcal{H} = K - aK^2 - I^2 + \lambda(I - \delta K).$$

The first-order condition $\frac{d\mathcal{H}}{dI} = 0$ gives:

$$\frac{d\mathcal{H}}{dI} = -2I + \lambda = 0 \Rightarrow I(t) = \frac{\lambda}{2}$$

with negative second derivative:

$$\frac{\partial^2 \mathcal{H}}{\partial I^2} = -2.$$

**ii.** The equation of motion $\dot{\lambda}(t)$ is:

$$\frac{d\lambda}{dt} = -\frac{\partial \mathcal{H}}{\partial K} = -[1 - 2aK - \lambda\delta] = -1 + 2aK + \lambda\delta.$$

We have now all we need to compute the Excel numerical solution without going through the rest of the theoretical continuous solution.

The following parameters data have been assumed in the Excel worksheet: $t_0 = 0$, $T = 1$, $a = 1$, depreciation rate $\delta = 15\%$ and initial capital $K(0) = 5$.

In this case, as $K(T)$ is free, the Excel Solver is optimized considering the transversality condition $\lambda(T) = 0$, by changing $\lambda(0)$, as in Example 1 of Section 10.3 and Example 1 of Section 10.4.

The optimal numerical solution is given by Table 10.6-1.

The case would be then solved under the numerical point of view.

We present next the theoretical solution steps, comparing the exact continuous solution with the above numerical computed solution.

For the theoretical solution, this investment model involves solving a linear system of differential equations.

From steps **i**, **ii**, and from the equation of motion $\dot{K} = I - \delta K$ we have the following linear system:

$$\dot{\lambda} = -1 + 2aK + \lambda\delta$$

$$\dot{K} = \frac{\lambda}{2} - \delta K$$

which, in matrix form, is transformed in the following homogenous linear system:

$$\begin{bmatrix} \dot{\lambda} \\ \dot{K} \end{bmatrix} = \begin{bmatrix} \delta & 2a \\ 1/2 & -\delta \end{bmatrix} \begin{bmatrix} \lambda \\ K \end{bmatrix}$$

whose solutions are given by the following:

$$\lambda(t) = c_1 e^{r_1 t} + c_2 e^{r_2 t} + \overline{\lambda}$$

$$K(t) = \frac{r_1 - \delta}{2a} c_1 e^{r_1 t} + \frac{r_2 - \delta}{2a} c_2 e^{r_2 t} + \overline{K}$$

**TABLE 10.6-1**  Investment model optimal numerical solution.

| t | K Capital Path | $dy=(1-0.15K)dt$ | dt | Gross Capex $=I=\lambda/2$ | Net Capex $y=I-0.15K$ | Hamiltonian $=K-K^2\bar I^2+\lambda(I-0.15K)$ | $\lambda(t)$ | $d\lambda/dt=-1+2\delta K+\lambda\delta$ | $F=K-K^2\bar I^2$ | Functional $=\Sigma[K-K^2\bar I^2]dt$ |
|---|---|---|---|---|---|---|---|---|---|---|
| **0.0000** | **5.0000** | | | **-3.0386** | | **0.0000** | **-6.0772** | 7.7901 | -26.5140 | -1.3257 |
| 0.0500 | 4.8216 | -0.1784 | 0.0500 | -2.8438 | -3.5671 | -6.2257 | -5.6877 | 7.5111 | -24.0598 | -1.2030 |
| 0.1000 | 4.6539 | -0.1677 | 0.0500 | -2.6561 | -3.3541 | -6.2422 | -5.3121 | 7.2505 | -21.8464 | -1.0923 |
| 0.1500 | 4.4965 | -0.1575 | 0.0500 | -2.4748 | -3.1493 | -6.2389 | -4.9496 | 7.2505 | -19.8520 | -0.9926 |
| 0.2000 | 4.3489 | -0.1476 | 0.0500 | -2.2996 | -2.9519 | -6.2755 | -4.5992 | 7.0079 | -18.0570 | -0.9029 |
| 0.2500 | 4.2108 | -0.1381 | 0.0500 | -2.1300 | -2.7617 | -6.2922 | -4.2601 | 6.7826 | -16.4439 | -0.8222 |
| 0.3000 | 4.0819 | -0.1289 | 0.0500 | -1.9657 | -2.5790 | -6.3090 | -3.9314 | 6.5741 | -14.9967 | -0.7498 |
| 0.3500 | 3.9619 | -0.1200 | 0.0500 | -1.8061 | -2.4004 | -6.3258 | -3.6123 | 6.3819 | -13.7013 | -0.6851 |
| 0.4000 | 3.8504 | -0.1114 | 0.0500 | -1.6510 | -2.2286 | -6.3426 | -3.3020 | 6.2056 | -12.5449 | -0.6272 |
| 0.4500 | 3.7474 | -0.1031 | 0.0500 | -1.4999 | -2.0620 | -6.3595 | -2.9997 | 6.0447 | -11.5162 | -0.5758 |
| 0.5000 | 3.6523 | -0.0950 | 0.0500 | -1.3524 | -1.9003 | -6.3764 | -2.7048 | 5.8990 | -10.6051 | -0.5303 |
| 0.5500 | 3.5652 | -0.0871 | 0.0500 | -1.2082 | -1.7430 | -6.3934 | -2.4164 | 5.7679 | -9.8027 | -0.4901 |
| 0.6000 | 3.4857 | -0.0795 | 0.0500 | -1.0669 | -1.5898 | -6.4104 | -2.1338 | 5.6513 | -9.1011 | -0.4551 |
| 0.6500 | 3.4137 | -0.0720 | 0.0500 | -0.9282 | -1.4402 | -6.4275 | -1.8564 | 5.5489 | -8.4935 | -0.4267 |
| 0.7000 | 3.3490 | -0.0647 | 0.0500 | -0.7917 | -1.2940 | -6.4446 | -1.5834 | 5.4605 | -7.9739 | -0.3987 |
| 0.7500 | 3.2914 | -0.0575 | 0.0500 | -0.6570 | -1.1508 | -6.4617 | -1.3141 | 5.3858 | -7.5373 | -0.3769 |
| 0.8000 | 3.2409 | -0.0505 | 0.0500 | -0.5239 | -1.0101 | -6.4789 | -1.0478 | 5.3247 | -7.1794 | -0.3590 |
| 0.8500 | 3.1974 | -0.0436 | 0.0500 | -0.3920 | -0.8716 | -6.4961 | -0.7840 | 5.2771 | -6.8970 | -0.3448 |
| 0.9000 | 3.1606 | -0.0368 | 0.0500 | -0.2609 | -0.7350 | -6.5134 | -0.5218 | 5.2430 | -6.6871 | -0.3344 |
| 0.9500 | 3.1306 | -0.0300 | 0.0500 | -0.1304 | -0.6000 | -6.5307 | -0.2607 | 5.2221 | -6.5481 | -0.3274 |
| 1.0000 | 3.1073 | -0.0233 | 0.0500 | 0.0000 | -0.4661 | -6.5481 | 0.0000 | 5.2146 | | |

| | | | | | | | | | | |
|---|---|---|---|---|---|---|---|---|---|---|
| y(0) | 5 | | | a = 1 | | | Transversality | | | -13.0179 |
| y(1) | Free | | | $\delta = 0.15$ | | | condition $\lambda(T)=0$ | | | |

where $r_1, r_2$ are the eigenvalues associated to the matrix $A = \begin{bmatrix} \delta & 2a \\ 1/2 & -\delta \end{bmatrix}$ that can be found as:

$$r_1, r_2 = \frac{tr(A)}{2} \pm \frac{1}{2}\sqrt{tr(A)^2 - 4\det(A)}$$

namely:

$$r_1, r_2 = \pm\sqrt{\delta^2 + a} = \pm\sqrt{0.15^2 + 1} \cong \pm 1.0112.$$

Setting the two equations of motions $\dot{K} = 0$ and $\dot{\lambda} = 0$

$$\frac{\lambda}{2} - \delta K = 0 \Rightarrow \lambda = 2\delta K$$

$$-1 + 2aK + \lambda\delta = 0 \Rightarrow -1 + 2aK + 2K\delta^2 = 0$$

from which we need to derive the steady state solutions (particular solutions) of the system:

$$\overline{K} = \frac{1}{2(a + \delta^2)} = \frac{1}{2(1 + 0.15^2)} \cong 0.4890$$

and

$$\overline{\lambda} = \frac{\delta}{(a + \delta^2)} = \frac{0.15}{1 + 0.15^2} \cong 0.1467.$$

Now, as usual with the transversality conditions $K(t_0) = K_0$ and $\lambda(T) = 0$ we determine the final complete solutions $K^*(t)$ and $I^*(t)$.

We have:

$$K_0 = \frac{r_1 - \delta}{2a}c_1 + \frac{r_2 - \delta}{2a}c_2 + \overline{K}$$

from which we derive:

$$c_1 = \frac{\left(K_0 - \dfrac{r_2 - \delta}{2a}c_2 - \overline{K}\right)}{\dfrac{r_1 - \delta}{2a}} = \frac{\left[2a(K_0 - \overline{K}) - (r_2 - \delta)c_2\right]}{r_1 - \delta}.$$

Then from $\lambda(T) = 0$ we derive:

$$c_1 e^{r_1 T} + c_2 e^{r_2 T} + \overline{\lambda} = 0.$$

Solving simultaneously the two above equations we have:

$$c_1 = \frac{2a\left(K_0 - \overline{K}\right) + (r_2 - \delta)\overline{\lambda}e^{-r_2 T}}{(r_1 - \delta) - (r_2 - \delta)e^{(r_1 - r_2)T}}$$

$$c_2 = \frac{-2a\left(K_0 - \overline{K}\right)e^{(r_1 - r_2)T} - (r_1 - \delta)\overline{\lambda}e^{-r_2 T}}{(r_1 - \delta) - (r_2 - \delta)e^{(r_1 - r_2)T}}.$$

Therefore, for $K_0 = 5$ and $a = 1$ we have $c_1 \cong 0.8877$ and $c_2 \cong -7.1112$.
The numerical versus continuous exact optimal solutions are given in Figs. 10.6-1 and 10.6-2.

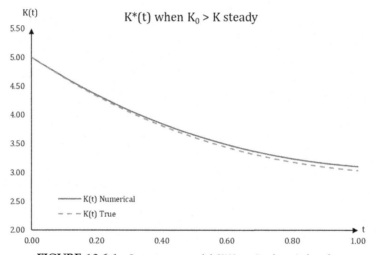

FIGURE 10.6-1    Investment model $K^*(t)$ optimal capital path.

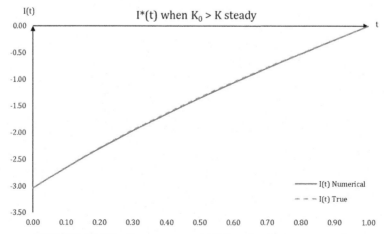

FIGURE 10.6-2    Investment model $I^*(t)$ optimal investment path.

## 10.7 Inventory optimization

Let us go back to the inventory problem presented in Section 9.9.

The problem was that of a firm receiving an order for $B$ units of product to be delivered by time $T$, seeking an optimal production schedule for filling the order at the specified delivery date at minimum cost.

The CoV problems was formalized as follows:

$$\min J(y) = \int_0^T \left[ c_1 y'(t)^2 + c_2 y(t) \right] dt$$

$$s.t. \ y(0) = 0 \text{ and } y(T) = B \text{ with } y'(t) \geq 0$$

The firm's objective is to determine a production rate $y'(t)$ and an optimal inventory accumulation path $y(t)$ to minimize the total cost over the time interval $[0, T]$.

The above CoV problem is transformed in the following OC problem (we leave the min operator):

$$\min J(u) = \int_0^T \left[ c_1 u^2 + c_2 y(t) \right] dt$$

$$s.t. \dot{y} = u \text{ and } y(0) = 0, y(T) = B \text{ with } u(t) \geq 0$$

where $c_1$ (cost of production) and $c_2$ (cost of storage) are positive constants.

The general exact solution found was:

$$y^*(t) = \left[ \frac{c_2}{c_1} \frac{1}{4} \right] t^2 + \left[ \frac{B}{T} - \frac{c_2}{c_1} \frac{T}{4} \right] t$$

Let us see how we can approach numerically the same problem in the OC Excel environment.

**i.** First as usual we identify the following Hamiltonian:

$$\mathcal{H} = c_1 u^2 + c_2 y(t) + \lambda u$$

Let us check as usual the first-order condition to find the maximum for $\mathcal{H}$ (with positive second derivative):

$$\frac{\partial \mathcal{H}}{\partial u} = 2c_1 u + \lambda = 0 \Rightarrow u = -\frac{\lambda}{2c_1}$$

**TABLE 10.7-1** Inventory Optimization Excel Solution in the Optimal Control Framework.

| t | y Inventory Path | $dy = \{u\}dt$ | dt | $\dot{y} = u$ | $u = \dot{z}/2c_1$ | Hamiltonian = $c_1 u^2 + c_2 y + z u$ | $z(t)$ | $dz(q)/dt = -c_2$ | $F = c_1 u^2 + c_2 y$ | Functional = $\int[c_1 u^2 + c_2 y]dt$ |
|---|---|---|---|---|---|---|---|---|---|---|
| 0.0000 | 0.0000 | | | 1.8688 | 1.8688 | -34.9223 | -37.3750 | | 34.9223 | 0.0000 |
| 0.0500 | 0.0941 | 0.0941 | 0.0500 | 1.8813 | 1.8813 | -34.9207 | -37.6250 | -5.0000 | 35.8613 | 1.7931 |
| 0.1000 | 0.1888 | 0.0947 | 0.0500 | 1.8938 | 1.8938 | -34.9191 | -37.8750 | -5.0000 | 36.8066 | 1.8403 |
| 0.1500 | 0.2841 | 0.0953 | 0.0500 | 1.9063 | 1.9063 | -34.9176 | -38.1250 | -5.0000 | 37.7582 | 1.8879 |
| 0.2000 | 0.3800 | 0.0959 | 0.0500 | 1.9188 | 1.9188 | -34.9160 | -38.3750 | -5.0000 | 38.7160 | 1.9358 |
| 0.2500 | 0.4766 | 0.0966 | 0.0500 | 1.9313 | 1.9313 | -34.9145 | -38.6250 | -5.0000 | 39.6801 | 1.9840 |
| 0.3000 | 0.5738 | 0.0972 | 0.0500 | 1.9438 | 1.9438 | -34.9129 | -38.8750 | -5.0000 | 40.6504 | 2.0325 |
| 0.3500 | 0.6716 | 0.0978 | 0.0500 | 1.9563 | 1.9563 | -34.9113 | -39.1250 | -5.0000 | 41.6270 | 2.0813 |
| 0.4000 | 0.7700 | 0.0984 | 0.0500 | 1.9688 | 1.9688 | -34.9098 | -39.3750 | -5.0000 | 42.6098 | 2.1305 |
| 0.4500 | 0.8691 | 0.0991 | 0.0500 | 1.9813 | 1.9813 | -34.9082 | -39.6250 | -5.0000 | 43.5988 | 2.1799 |
| 0.5000 | 0.9688 | 0.0997 | 0.0500 | 1.9938 | 1.9938 | -34.9066 | -39.8750 | -5.0000 | 44.5941 | 2.2297 |
| 0.5500 | 1.0691 | 0.1003 | 0.0500 | 2.0063 | 2.0063 | -34.9051 | -40.1250 | -5.0000 | 45.5957 | 2.2798 |
| 0.6000 | 1.1700 | 0.1009 | 0.0500 | 2.0188 | 2.0188 | -34.9035 | -40.3750 | -5.0000 | 46.6035 | 2.3302 |
| 0.6500 | 1.2716 | 0.1016 | 0.0500 | 2.0313 | 2.0313 | -34.9020 | -40.6250 | -5.0000 | 47.6176 | 2.3809 |
| 0.7000 | 1.3738 | 0.1022 | 0.0500 | 2.0438 | 2.0438 | -34.9004 | -40.8750 | -5.0000 | 48.6379 | 2.4319 |
| 0.7500 | 1.4766 | 0.1028 | 0.0500 | 2.0563 | 2.0563 | -34.8988 | -41.1250 | -5.0000 | 49.6645 | 2.4832 |
| 0.8000 | 1.5800 | 0.1034 | 0.0500 | 2.0688 | 2.0688 | -34.8973 | -41.3750 | -5.0000 | 50.6973 | 2.5349 |
| 0.8500 | 1.6841 | 0.1041 | 0.0500 | 2.0813 | 2.0813 | -34.8957 | -41.6250 | -5.0000 | 51.7363 | 2.5868 |
| 0.9000 | 1.7888 | 0.1047 | 0.0500 | 2.0938 | 2.0938 | -34.8941 | -41.8750 | -5.0000 | 52.7816 | 2.6391 |
| 0.9500 | 1.8941 | 0.1053 | 0.0500 | 2.1063 | 2.1063 | -34.8926 | -42.1250 | -5.0000 | 53.8332 | 2.6917 |
| 1.0000 | 2.0000 | 0.1059 | 0.0500 | 2.1188 | 2.1188 | -34.8910 | -42.3750 | -5.0000 | 54.8910 | 2.7446 |

|  |  |
|---|---|
| y(0) | 0.00 |
| y(1) | 2.00 |

c1 = cost of production　10.0000
c2 = cost of storage　5.0000
B=2　2.0000

Functional = 45.1981

**ii.** Then, from the Hamiltonian, we can rederive the given equation of motion for $y(t)$:

$$\frac{dy}{dt} = \frac{\partial \mathcal{H}}{\partial \lambda} = u$$

together with deriving the equation of motion for $\lambda(t)$:

$$\frac{d\lambda}{dt} = -\frac{\partial \mathcal{H}}{\partial y} = -c_2 \Rightarrow \lambda = -c_2 t - k_1$$

from which we derive $y(t)$ as presented in the CoV:

$$\frac{dy}{dt} = -\frac{(-c_2 t - k_1)}{2c_1} \Rightarrow y(t) = \frac{c_2}{c_1}\frac{1}{4}t^2 + \frac{k_1}{2c_1}t + k_2.$$

**iii.** From the boundary conditions $y(0) = 0$, $y(T) = 2$ we have:

$$k_2 = 0$$

$$y(T) = \frac{c_2}{c_1}\frac{1}{4}T^2 + \frac{k_1}{2c_1}T + k_2 = 2 \qquad \text{with } T = 1$$

$$\frac{c_2}{c_1}\frac{1}{4} + \frac{k_1}{2c_1} = 2 \Rightarrow k_1 = 4c_1 - \frac{c_2}{2} = 40 - \frac{5}{2} = 37.5.$$

with $k_1 = 37.5$ we obtain $\frac{k_1}{2c_1} = 1.875$ from which we have the optimal equation $y^*(t) = 0.125t^2 + 1.875t$ that we indicated in Section 9.9 (Fig. 10.7-1).

We have solved the problem setting the Solver parameters as depicted in Figs. 10.7-2 and 10.7-3.

## 10.8 Two state variables control problems

As we have seen in the CoV, also in the OC theory an important class of problems is represented by the problems where more state variables are involved.

We will present in the following example how the Excel worksheets can be easily used to solve these types of problems as well.

EXAMPLE 1 (MINIMUM CONTROL EFFORT PROBLEM IN TWO VARIABLES)

$$\min_{\{u\}} J = \int_0^2 \frac{1}{2}u^2 dt$$

| | A | B | C | D | E | F | G | H | I | J | K |
|---|---|---|---|---|---|---|---|---|---|---|---|
| 1 | t | y Inventory Path | dy = (u)dt | dt | ẏ = u | u = -λ/2c₂ | Hamiltonian = c₁u²+c₂y+λu | λ(t) | dλ(t)/dt = -c₂ | F = c₁u²+c₂y | Functional = Σ [c₁u²+c₂y]dt |
| 2 | 0 | 0 | | | =F2 | =-H2/(2*10) | =(SHS24*E2^2+SHS25*B2+H2*E2) | -37.37500262! | | =(SHS24*E2^2+SHS25*B2) | =J2*D2 |
| 3 | =A2+0.05 | =B2+C3 | =(E3)*D3 | =A3-A2 | =F3 | =-H3/(2*10) | =(SHS24*E3^2+SHS25*B3+H3*E3) | =H2+I3*D3 | -5 | =(SHS24*E3^2+SHS25*B3) | =J3*D3 |
| 4 | =A3+0.05 | =B3+C4 | =(E4)*D4 | =A4-A3 | =F4 | =-H4/(2*10) | =(SHS24*E4^2+SHS25*B4+H4*E4) | =H3+I4*D4 | -5 | =(SHS24*E4^2+SHS25*B4) | =J4*D4 |
| 5 | =A4+0.05 | =B4+C5 | =(E5)*D5 | =A5-A4 | =F5 | =-H5/(2*10) | =(SHS24*E5^2+SHS25*B5+H5*E5) | =H4+I5*D5 | -5 | =(SHS24*E5^2+SHS25*B5) | =J5*D5 |
| 6 | =A5+0.05 | =B5+C6 | =(E6)*D6 | =A6-A5 | =F6 | =-H6/(2*10) | =(SHS24*E6^2+SHS25*B6+H6*E6) | =H5+I6*D6 | -5 | =(SHS24*E6^2+SHS25*B6) | =J6*D6 |
| 7 | =A6+0.05 | =B6+C7 | =(E7)*D7 | =A7-A6 | =F7 | =-H7/(2*10) | =(SHS24*E7^2+SHS25*B7+H7*E7) | =H6+I7*D7 | -5 | =(SHS24*E7^2+SHS25*B7) | =J7*D7 |
| 8 | =A7+0.05 | =B7+C8 | =(E8)*D8 | =A8-A7 | =F8 | =-H8/(2*10) | =(SHS24*E8^2+SHS25*B8+H8*E8) | =H7+I8*D8 | -5 | =(SHS24*E8^2+SHS25*B8) | =J8*D8 |
| 9 | =A8+0.05 | =B8+C9 | =(E9)*D9 | =A9-A8 | =F9 | =-H9/(2*10) | =(SHS24*E9^2+SHS25*B9+H9*E9) | =H8+I9*D9 | -5 | =(SHS24*E9^2+SHS25*B9) | =J9*D9 |
| 10 | =A9+0.05 | =B9+C10 | =(E10)*D10 | =A10-A9 | =F10 | =-H10/(2*10) | =(SHS24*E10^2+SHS25*B10+H10*E10) | =H9+I10*D10 | -5 | =(SHS24*E10^2+SHS25*B10) | =J10*D10 |
| 11 | =A10+0.05 | =B10+C11 | =(E11)*D11 | =A11-A10 | =F11 | =-H11/(2*10) | =(SHS24*E11^2+SHS25*B11+H11*E11) | =H10+I11*D11 | -5 | =(SHS24*E11^2+SHS25*B11) | =J11*D11 |
| 12 | =A11+0.05 | =B11+C12 | =(E12)*D12 | =A12-A11 | =F12 | =-H12/(2*10) | =(SHS24*E12^2+SHS25*B12+H12*E12) | =H11+I12*D12 | -5 | =(SHS24*E12^2+SHS25*B12) | =J12*D12 |
| 13 | =A12+0.05 | =B12+C13 | =(E13)*D13 | =A13-A12 | =F13 | =-H13/(2*10) | =(SHS24*E13^2+SHS25*B13+H13*E13) | =H12+I13*D13 | -5 | =(SHS24*E13^2+SHS25*B13) | =J13*D13 |
| 14 | =A13+0.05 | =B13+C14 | =(E14)*D14 | =A14-A13 | =F14 | =-H14/(2*10) | =(SHS24*E14^2+SHS25*B14+H14*E14) | =H13+I14*D14 | -5 | =(SHS24*E14^2+SHS25*B14) | =J14*D14 |
| 15 | =A14+0.05 | =B14+C15 | =(E15)*D15 | =A15-A14 | =F15 | =-H15/(2*10) | =(SHS24*E15^2+SHS25*B15+H15*E15) | =H14+I15*D15 | -5 | =(SHS24*E15^2+SHS25*B15) | =J15*D15 |
| 16 | =A15+0.05 | =B15+C16 | =(E16)*D16 | =A16-A15 | =F16 | =-H16/(2*10) | =(SHS24*E16^2+SHS25*B16+H16*E16) | =H15+I16*D16 | -5 | =(SHS24*E16^2+SHS25*B16) | =J16*D16 |
| 17 | =A16+0.05 | =B16+C17 | =(E17)*D17 | =A17-A16 | =F17 | =-H17/(2*10) | =(SHS24*E17^2+SHS25*B17+H17*E17) | =H16+I17*D17 | -5 | =(SHS24*E17^2+SHS25*B17) | =J17*D17 |
| 18 | =A17+0.05 | =B17+C18 | =(E18)*D18 | =A18-A17 | =F18 | =-H18/(2*10) | =(SHS24*E18^2+SHS25*B18+H18*E18) | =H17+I18*D18 | -5 | =(SHS24*E18^2+SHS25*B18) | =J18*D18 |
| 19 | =A18+0.05 | =B18+C19 | =(E19)*D19 | =A19-A18 | =F19 | =-H19/(2*10) | =(SHS24*E19^2+SHS25*B19+H19*E19) | =H18+I19*D19 | -5 | =(SHS24*E19^2+SHS25*B19) | =J19*D19 |
| 20 | =A19+0.05 | =B19+C20 | =(E20)*D20 | =A20-A19 | =F20 | =-H20/(2*10) | =(SHS24*E20^2+SHS25*B20+H20*E20) | =H19+I20*D20 | -5 | =(SHS24*E20^2+SHS25*B20) | =J20*D20 |
| 21 | =A20+0.05 | =B20+C21 | =(E21)*D21 | =A21-A20 | =F21 | =-H21/(2*10) | =(SHS24*E21^2+SHS25*B21+H21*E21) | =H20+I21*D21 | -5 | =(SHS24*E21^2+SHS25*B21) | =J21*D21 |
| 22 | =A21+0.05 | =B21+C22 | =(E22)*D22 | =A22-A21 | =F22 | =-H22/(2*10) | =(SHS24*E22^2+SHS25*B22+H22*E22) | =H21+I22*D22 | -5 | =(SHS24*E22^2+SHS25*B22) | =J22*D22 |
| 24 | | | | | | | c1 = cost of production | 10 | | | |
| 25 | y(0) | 0 | | | | | c2 = cost of storage | 5 | | | =SUM(K2:K22) |
| 26 | y(1) | 2 | | | | | B=2 | 2 | | | |

**FIGURE 10.7-1** Inventory optimization Excel setup in the optimal control framework with $c_1 = 10$, $c_2 = 5$, $B = 2$ (Table 10.7-1).

**FIGURE 10.7-2** Inventory Solver parameters.

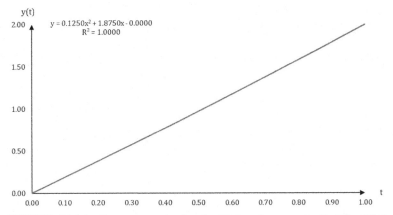

**FIGURE 10.7-3** Inventory optimal path $y^*(t)$ (see the same result of Fig. 9.9-1).

s.t. the following equations of motions conditions:

$$\dot{y}_1(t) = y_2(t)$$

$$\dot{y}_2(t) = -y_2(t) + u(t)$$

and boundary conditions:

$$y_1(2) = 5, y_2(2) = 2$$

**i.** As usual we start working on the Hamiltonian function, to find the necessary conditions that must be satisfied for the optimal control. We have then the following:

$$\mathcal{H} = \frac{1}{2}u^2 + \lambda_1 y_2 + \lambda_2(-y_2 + u)$$

from which we can derive the first-order condition $\frac{\partial \mathcal{H}}{\partial u} = 0$ to get the maximum in $\mathcal{H}$:

$$\frac{\partial \mathcal{H}}{\partial u} = u + \lambda_2 = 0 \Rightarrow u(t) = -\lambda_2.$$

**ii.** Next step is to determine from the equations of motion the solution for $\lambda_1(t)$ and $\lambda_2(t)$:

$$\dot{\lambda}_1(t) = -\frac{\partial \mathcal{H}}{\partial y_1} = 0$$

$$\dot{\lambda}_2(t) = -\frac{\partial \mathcal{H}}{\partial y_2} = -\lambda_1 + \lambda_2$$

III. Dynamic optimization

**iii.** The equations of motion of the two state variables then become:

$$\dot{y}_1(t) = y_2$$

$$\dot{y}_2(t) = -y_2 - \lambda_2$$

Steps **ii** and **iii** taken together form a system of four linear differential equations that will lead to the optimal solutions for the state and costate variables.
The general solutions of the system are:

$$y_1^*(t) = c_1 + c_2(1 - e^{-t}) + c_3\left(-t - \frac{1}{2}e^{-t} + \frac{1}{2}e^t\right) + c_4\left(1 - \frac{1}{2}e^{-t} - \frac{1}{2}e^t\right)$$

$$y_2^*(t) = c_2 e^{-t} + c_3\left(-1 - \frac{1}{2}e^{-t} + \frac{1}{2}e^t\right) + c_4\left(\frac{1}{2}e^{-t} - \frac{1}{2}e^t\right)$$

$$\lambda_1^*(t) = c_3$$

$$\lambda_2^*(t) = c_3(1 - e^t) + c_4 e^t.$$

From the initial conditions $y_1(0) = 0$, $y_2(0) = 0$ we obtain:

$$c_1 = c_2 = 0$$

from which we can derive the two equations that satisfy the endpoint boundary conditions $y_1(2) = 5$, $y_2(2) = 2$:

$$5 = c_3\left(-2 - \frac{1}{2}e^{-2} + \frac{1}{2}e^t\right) + c_4\left(1 - \frac{1}{2}e^{-2} - \frac{1}{2}e^2\right)$$

$$2 = c_3\left(-1 - \frac{1}{2}e^{-2} + \frac{1}{2}e^2\right) + c_4\left(\frac{1}{2}e^{-2} - \frac{1}{2}e^2\right)$$

and the two solution $c_3 = -7.289$, $c_4 = -6.103$, which lead to the optimal solutions for the state variables:

$$y_1^*(t) = 7.289t - 6.103 + 6.696e^{-t} - 0.593e^t$$

$$y_2^*(t) = 7.289 - 6.696e^{-t} - 0.593e^t.$$

From the conditions under steps **i, ii,** and **iii,** we can immediately set up the Excel worksheet, bypassing the cumbersome steps for the exact theoretical optimal solutions of a system in four differential equations.

The way the necessary condition and the equations of motion are implemented in Excel is in Fig. 10.8-1:

The objective now is to get, via the Solver, the boundary conditions satisfied, changing the *Cell K2* and *Cell M2*, where the two values $\lambda_1(0)$ and $\lambda_2(0)$ are stored. This is the Shooting phase of the optimization process (Fig. 10.8-2).

The final solution is given by the following Table 10.8-1, while the exact and numerical solutions are compared in Figs. 10.8-3, 10.8-4.

## Example 1 (continued)

A second (probably better) alternative way to approach this dynamical system problem is to solve simultaneously in Excel the following system in the four linear differential equations, derived from the maximum principle condition (Figs. 10.8-5 and 10.8-6 show the optimal numerical solutions):

$$\dot{y}_1 = y_2$$

$$\dot{y}_2 = -y_2 - \lambda_2$$

$$\dot{\lambda}_1 = 0$$

$$\dot{\lambda}_2 = -\lambda_1 + \lambda_2$$

| | A | B | C | D | E | F | G | H | I | J | K | L | M | N | O | P |
|---|---|---|---|---|---|---|---|---|---|---|---|---|---|---|---|---|
| 1 | t | $y_1$ | $y_2$ | $dy_1 = y_2 dt$ | $dy_2 = (-y_2 - \lambda_2)dt$ | dt | $u = -\lambda_2$ | $dy_1/dt = y_2$ | $dy_2/dt = -y_2 - \lambda_2$ | Hamiltonian = $1/2u^2 + \lambda_1 y_2 + \lambda_2(-y_2 + u)$ | $\lambda_1$ | $d\lambda_1/dt$ | $\lambda_2$ | $d\lambda_2/dt = \lambda_2 - \lambda_1$ | $F = 1/2u^2$ | Functional = $\Sigma\ 1/2u^2 dt$ |
| 2 | 0 | 0 | 0 | | | | =-M2 | =C2 | =-C2-M2 | =1/2*G2^2+L2*C2+N2*(-C2+G2) | -7.17490849( | 0 | -6.15778862 1: | | | |
| 3 | =A2+0.1 | =B2+D3 | =C2+E3 | =C3*F3 | =I3*F3 | =A3-A2 | =-M3 | =C3 | =-C3-M3 | =1/2*G3^2+L3*C3+N3*(-C3+G3) | =K2+L3*F3 | 0 | =M2+N3*F3 | =M3-K3 | =1/2*G3^2 | =O3*F3 |
| 4 | =A3+0.1 | =B3+D4 | =C3+E4 | =C4*F4 | =I4*F4 | =A4-A3 | =-M4 | =C4 | =-C4-M4 | =1/2*G4^2+L4*C4+N4*(-C4+G4) | =K3+L4*F4 | 0 | =M3+N4*F4 | =M4-K4 | =1/2*G4^2 | =O4*F4 |
| 5 | =A4+0.1 | =B4+D5 | =C4+E5 | =C5*F5 | =I5*F5 | =A5-A4 | =-M5 | =C5 | =-C5-M5 | =1/2*G5^2+L5*C5+N5*(-C5+G5) | =K4+L5*F5 | 0 | =M4+N5*F5 | =M5-K5 | =1/2*G5^2 | =O5*F5 |
| 6 | =A5+0.1 | =B5+D6 | =C5+E6 | =C6*F6 | =I6*F6 | =A6-A5 | =-M6 | =C6 | =-C6-M6 | =1/2*G6^2+L6*C6+N6*(-C6+G6) | =K5+L6*F6 | 0 | =M5+N6*F6 | =M6-K6 | =1/2*G6^2 | =O6*F6 |
| 7 | =A6+0.1 | =B6+D7 | =C6+E7 | =C7*F7 | =I7*F7 | =A7-A6 | =-M7 | =C7 | =-C7-M7 | =1/2*G7^2+L7*C7+N7*(-C7+G7) | =K6+L7*F7 | 0 | =M6+N7*F7 | =M7-K7 | =1/2*G7^2 | =O7*F7 |
| 8 | =A7+0.1 | =B7+D8 | =C7+E8 | =C8*F8 | =I8*F8 | =A8-A7 | =-M8 | =C8 | =-C8-M8 | =1/2*G8^2+L8*C8+N8*(-C8+G8) | =K7+L8*F8 | 0 | =M7+N8*F8 | =M8-K8 | =1/2*G8^2 | =O8*F8 |
| 9 | =A8+0.1 | =B8+D9 | =C8+E9 | =C9*F9 | =I9*F9 | =A9-A8 | =-M9 | =C9 | =-C9-M9 | =1/2*G9^2+L9*C9+N9*(-C9+G9) | =K8+L9*F9 | 0 | =M8+N9*F9 | =M9-K9 | =1/2*G9^2 | =O9*F9 |
| 10 | =A9+0.1 | =B9+D10 | =C9+E10 | =C10*F10 | =I10*F10 | =A10-A9 | =-M10 | =C10 | =-C10-M10 | =1/2*G10^2+L10*C10+N10*(-C10+G10) | =K9+L10*F10 | 0 | =M9+N10*F10 | =M10-K10 | =1/2*G10^2 | =O10*F10 |
| 11 | =A10+0.1 | =B10+D11 | =C10+E11 | =C11*F11 | =I11*F11 | =A11-A10 | =-M11 | =C11 | =-C11-M11 | =1/2*G11^2+L11*C11+N11*(-C11+G11) | =K10+L11*F11 | 0 | =M10+N11*F11 | =M11-K11 | =1/2*G11^2 | =O11*F11 |
| 12 | =A11+0.1 | =B11+D12 | =C11+E12 | =C12*F12 | =I12*F12 | =A12-A11 | =-M12 | =C12 | =-C12-M12 | =1/2*G12^2+L12*C12+N12*(-C12+G12) | =K11+L12*F12 | 0 | =M11+N12*F12 | =M12-K12 | =1/2*G12^2 | =O12*F12 |
| 13 | =A12+0.1 | =B12+D13 | =C12+E13 | =C13*F13 | =I13*F13 | =A13-A12 | =-M13 | =C13 | =-C13-M13 | =1/2*G13^2+L13*C13+N13*(-C13+G13) | =K12+L13*F13 | 0 | =M12+N13*F13 | =M13-K13 | =1/2*G13^2 | =O13*F13 |
| 14 | =A13+0.1 | =B13+D14 | =C13+E14 | =C14*F14 | =I14*F14 | =A14-A13 | =-M14 | =C14 | =-C14-M14 | =1/2*G14^2+L14*C14+N14*(-C14+G14) | =K13+L14*F14 | 0 | =M13+N14*F14 | =M14-K14 | =1/2*G14^2 | =O14*F14 |
| 15 | =A14+0.1 | =B14+D15 | =C14+E15 | =C15*F15 | =I15*F15 | =A15-A14 | =-M15 | =C15 | =-C15-M15 | =1/2*G15^2+L15*C15+N15*(-C15+G15) | =K14+L15*F15 | 0 | =M14+N15*F15 | =M15-K15 | =1/2*G15^2 | =O15*F15 |
| 16 | =A15+0.1 | =B15+D16 | =C15+E16 | =C16*F16 | =I16*F16 | =A16-A15 | =-M16 | =C16 | =-C16-M16 | =1/2*G16^2+L16*C16+N16*(-C16+G16) | =K15+L16*F16 | 0 | =M15+N16*F16 | =M16-K16 | =1/2*G16^2 | =O16*F16 |
| 17 | =A16+0.1 | =B16+D17 | =C16+E17 | =C17*F17 | =I17*F17 | =A17-A16 | =-M17 | =C17 | =-C17-M17 | =1/2*G17^2+L17*C17+N17*(-C17+G17) | =K16+L17*F17 | 0 | =M16+N17*F17 | =M17-K17 | =1/2*G17^2 | =O17*F17 |
| 18 | =A17+0.1 | =B17+D18 | =C17+E18 | =C18*F18 | =I18*F18 | =A18-A17 | =-M18 | =C18 | =-C18-M18 | =1/2*G18^2+L18*C18+N18*(-C18+G18) | =K17+L18*F18 | 0 | =M17+N18*F18 | =M18-K18 | =1/2*G18^2 | =O18*F18 |
| 19 | =A18+0.1 | =B18+D19 | =C18+E19 | =C19*F19 | =I19*F19 | =A19-A18 | =-M19 | =C19 | =-C19-M19 | =1/2*G19^2+L19*C19+N19*(-C19+G19) | =K18+L19*F19 | 0 | =M18+N19*F19 | =M19-K19 | =1/2*G19^2 | =O19*F19 |
| 20 | =A19+0.1 | =B19+D20 | =C19+E20 | =C20*F20 | =I20*F20 | =A20-A19 | =-M20 | =C20 | =-C20-M20 | =1/2*G20^2+L20*C20+N20*(-C20+G20) | =K19+L20*F20 | 0 | =M19+N20*F20 | =M20-K20 | =1/2*G20^2 | =O20*F20 |
| 21 | =A20+0.1 | =B20+D21 | =C20+E21 | =C21*F21 | =I21*F21 | =A21-A20 | =-M21 | =C21 | =-C21-M21 | =1/2*G21^2+L21*C21+N21*(-C21+G21) | =K20+L21*F21 | 0 | =M20+N21*F21 | =M21-K21 | =1/2*G21^2 | =O21*F21 |
| 22 | =A21+0.1 | =B21+D22 | =C21+E22 | =C22*F22 | =I22*F22 | =A22-A21 | =-M22 | =C22 | =-C22-M22 | =1/2*G22^2+L22*C22+N22*(-C22+G22) | =K21+L22*F22 | 0 | =M21+N22*F22 | =M22-K22 | =1/2*G22^2 | =O22*F22 |
| 23 | | | | | | | | | | | | | | | | |
| 24 | | $y_1(2)$ | $y_2(2)$ | | | | | | | | | | | | | =SUM(P3:P23) |
| 25 | | 5 | 2 | | | | | | | | | | | | | |

FIGURE 10.8-1 Example 1: two variables optimal control problem Excel setup.

**FIGURE 10.8-2**  Example 1: Solver parameters setting $y_1(2) = 5$ and $y_2(2) = 2$ by changing $\lambda_1(0)$ and $\lambda_2(0)$.

This is done using the numerical Euler method, resorting to the algorithm we have seen in Section 4.5. The Solver will be then used to set the initial conditions on $\lambda_1(0)$ and $\lambda_2(0)$ such that the endpoint boundary conditions are satisfied for the two state variables: $y_1(2) = 5$ and $y_2(2) = 2$. This is the Shooting method. The above system in matrix form becomes instead:

$$
\begin{bmatrix} \dot{y}_1 \\ \dot{y}_2 \\ \dot{\lambda}_1 \\ \dot{\lambda}_2 \end{bmatrix} = \begin{bmatrix} 0 & 1 & 0 & 0 \\ 0 & -1 & 0 & -1 \\ 0 & 0 & 0 & 0 \\ 0 & 0 & -1 & 1 \end{bmatrix} \begin{bmatrix} y_1 \\ y_2 \\ \lambda_1 \\ \lambda_2 \end{bmatrix}
$$

From the results obtained, we see that this method to proceed gives a better approximation of the exact solution, compared to what has been calculated in Table 10.8-1. This can be noticed from the values obtained in the constants $c_3$ and $c_4$.

**TABLE 10.8-1** Example 1: Two variables optimal control problem approximate optimal numerical solution.

| $t$ | $y_1$ | $y_2$ | $\delta y_1=y_2 dt$ | $\delta y_2=(y_2-\lambda_2)dt$ | $dt$ | $u=-\lambda_2$ | $dy_1/dt=y_2$ | $dy_2/dt=y_2-\lambda_2$ | Hamiltonian $=\tfrac12 u^2+\lambda_1 y+\lambda_2(-y_1+u)$ | $\lambda_1$ | $d\lambda_1/dt$ | $\lambda_2$ | $d\lambda_2/dt=-\lambda_1$ | $F=\tfrac12 u^2$ | Functional $=\Sigma\tfrac12 u^2 dt$ |
|---|---|---|---|---|---|---|---|---|---|---|---|---|---|---|---|
| 0.0000 | 0.0000 | 0.0000 | | | | 6.1578 | 0.0000 | 6.1578 | 18.9592 | -7.1749 | 0.0000 | 6.1578 | | | |
| 0.1000 | 0.0550 | 0.5495 | 0.0550 | 0.5495 | 0.1000 | 6.0448 | 0.5495 | 5.4953 | 24.4800 | -7.1749 | 0.0000 | 6.0448 | 1.1301 | 18.2697 | 1.8270 |
| 0.2000 | 0.1587 | 1.0377 | 0.1038 | 0.4882 | 0.1000 | 5.9192 | 1.0377 | 4.8815 | 23.6482 | -7.1749 | 0.0000 | 5.9192 | 1.2557 | 17.5185 | 1.7518 |
| 0.3000 | 0.3056 | 1.4688 | 0.1469 | 0.4311 | 0.1000 | 5.7797 | 1.4688 | 4.3109 | 22.7171 | -7.1749 | 0.0000 | 5.7797 | 1.3952 | 16.7024 | 1.6702 |
| 0.4000 | 0.4903 | 1.8466 | 0.1847 | 0.3778 | 0.1000 | 5.6247 | 1.8466 | 3.7781 | 21.6754 | -7.1749 | 0.0000 | 5.6247 | 1.5503 | 15.8164 | 1.5818 |
| 0.5000 | 0.7077 | 2.1744 | 0.2174 | 0.3278 | 0.1000 | 5.4524 | 2.1744 | 3.2780 | 20.5108 | -7.1749 | 0.0000 | 5.4524 | 1.7225 | 14.8644 | 1.4864 |
| 0.6000 | 0.9532 | 2.4550 | 0.2455 | 0.2806 | 0.1000 | 5.2610 | 2.4550 | 2.8060 | 19.2096 | -7.1749 | 0.0000 | 5.2610 | 1.9139 | 13.8892 | 1.3889 |
| 0.7000 | 1.2223 | 2.6907 | 0.2691 | 0.2358 | 0.1000 | 5.0484 | 2.6907 | 2.3576 | 17.7566 | -7.1749 | 0.0000 | 5.0484 | 2.1265 | 12.7430 | 1.2743 |
| 0.8000 | 1.5106 | 2.8836 | 0.2884 | 0.1908 | 0.1000 | 4.8121 | 2.8836 | 1.9285 | 16.1347 | -7.1749 | 0.0000 | 4.8121 | 2.3628 | 11.5781 | 1.1578 |
| 0.9000 | 1.8141 | 3.0350 | 0.3035 | 0.1515 | 0.1000 | 4.5495 | 3.0350 | 1.5145 | 14.3253 | -7.1749 | 0.0000 | 4.5495 | 2.6254 | 10.3492 | 1.0349 |
| 1.0000 | 2.1288 | 3.1462 | 0.3146 | 0.1112 | 0.1000 | 4.2578 | 3.1462 | 1.1116 | 12.3073 | -7.1749 | 0.0000 | 4.2578 | 2.9171 | 9.0646 | 0.9065 |
| 1.1000 | 2.4505 | 3.2178 | 0.3218 | 0.0716 | 0.1000 | 3.9337 | 3.2178 | 0.7159 | 10.0575 | -7.1749 | 0.0000 | 3.9337 | 3.2412 | 7.7371 | 0.7737 |
| 1.2000 | 2.7755 | 3.2501 | 0.3250 | 0.0323 | 0.1000 | 3.5736 | 3.2501 | 0.3234 | 7.5501 | -7.1749 | 0.0000 | 3.5736 | 3.6013 | 6.3853 | 0.6385 |
| 1.3000 | 3.0999 | 3.2432 | 0.3243 | -0.0070 | 0.1000 | 3.1734 | 3.2432 | -0.0697 | 4.7563 | -7.1749 | 0.0000 | 3.1734 | 4.0015 | 5.0354 | 0.5035 |
| 1.4000 | 3.4195 | 3.1964 | 0.3196 | -0.0468 | 0.1000 | 2.7288 | 3.1964 | -0.4676 | 1.6444 | -7.1749 | 0.0000 | 2.7288 | 4.4461 | 3.7233 | 0.3723 |
| 1.5000 | 3.7304 | 3.1090 | 0.3109 | -0.0874 | 0.1000 | 2.2348 | 3.1090 | -0.8742 | -1.8213 | -7.1749 | 0.0000 | 2.2348 | 4.9401 | 2.4972 | 0.2497 |
| 1.6000 | 4.0284 | 2.9796 | 0.2980 | -0.1294 | 0.1000 | 1.6859 | 2.9796 | -1.2937 | -5.6799 | -7.1749 | 0.0000 | 1.6859 | 5.4990 | 1.412 | 0.1421 |
| 1.7000 | 4.3090 | 2.8066 | 0.2807 | -0.1731 | 0.1000 | 1.0760 | 2.8066 | -1.7305 | -9.9754 | -7.1749 | 0.0000 | 1.0760 | 6.0989 | 0.5789 | 0.0579 |
| 1.8000 | 4.5678 | 2.5876 | 0.2588 | -0.2189 | 0.1000 | 0.3984 | 2.5876 | -2.1893 | -14.7562 | -7.1749 | 0.0000 | 0.3984 | 6.7765 | 0.0794 | 0.0079 |
| 1.9000 | 4.7998 | 2.3202 | 0.2320 | -0.2675 | 0.1000 | -0.3546 | 2.3202 | -2.6747 | -20.0765 | -7.1749 | 0.0000 | -0.3546 | 7.5295 | 0.0629 | 0.0063 |
| 2.0000 | 4.9999 | 2.0010 | 0.2001 | -0.3192 | 0.1000 | -1.1912 | 2.0010 | -3.1921 | -25.9962 | -7.1749 | 0.0000 | -1.1912 | 8.3661 | 0.7094 | 0.0709 |
| | $y_1(2)$ 5.00 | $y_2(2)$ 2.00 | | | | | | | | | | | | | 16.8977 |

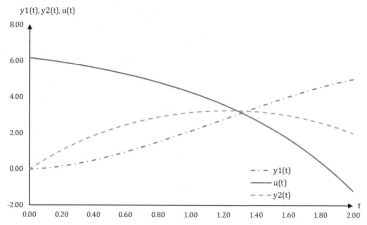

**FIGURE 10.8-3**    Example 1: approximate numerical optimal solution $y_1^*(t)$, $y_2^*(t)$, and $u^*(t)$.

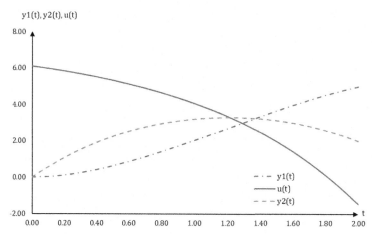

**FIGURE 10.8-4**    Example 1: exact optimal solutions $y_1^*(t)$, $y_2^*(t)$, and $u^*(t)$.

| | A | B | C | D | E | F | G | H | I | J | K | L | M | N |
|---|---|---|---|---|---|---|---|---|---|---|---|---|---|---|
| 1 | t | dt | dy1/dt = y2 | dy1 = [y2]dt | y1 = Σ f(t,y)dt | dy2/dt = -y2-λ2 | dy = [-y2-λ2]dt | y2 = Σ f(t,y)dt | dλ1/dt = 0 | dλ1 = [0]dt | λ1 = Σ f(t,y)dt | dλ2/dt = -λ1+λ2 | dλ2 = [-λ1+λ2]dt | λ2 = Σ f(t,y)dt |
| 2 | 0.0000 | | Given Initial conditions--> | | 0.0000 | Given Initial conditions--> | | 0.0000 | Shooting--> | | -7.2802 | Shooting--> | | -6.1106 |
| 3 | 0.0100 | 0.0100 | 0.0604 | 0.0006 | 0.0006 | 6.0184 | 0.0604 | 0.0604 | 0.0000 | 0.0000 | -7.2802 | 1.1815 | 0.0118 | -6.0988 |
| 4 | 0.0200 | 0.0100 | 0.1201 | 0.0012 | 0.0018 | 5.9668 | 0.0597 | 0.1201 | 0.0000 | 0.0000 | -7.2802 | 1.1934 | 0.0119 | -6.0868 |
| 199 | 1.9700 | 0.0100 | 2.1019 | 0.0210 | 4.9390 | -3.2925 | -0.0329 | 2.1019 | 0.0000 | 0.0000 | -7.2802 | 8.4708 | 0.0847 | 1.1906 |
| 200 | 1.9800 | 0.0100 | 2.0685 | 0.0207 | 4.9597 | -3.3446 | -0.0334 | 2.0685 | 0.0000 | 0.0000 | -7.2802 | 8.5564 | 0.0856 | 1.2762 |
| 201 | 1.9900 | 0.0100 | 2.0345 | 0.0203 | 4.9800 | -3.3971 | -0.0340 | 2.0345 | 0.0000 | 0.0000 | -7.2802 | 8.6428 | 0.0864 | 1.3626 |
| 202 | 2.0000 | 0.0100 | 2.0000 | 0.0200 | 5.0000 | -3.4499 | -0.0345 | 2.0000 | 0.0000 | 0.0000 | -7.2802 | 8.7301 | 0.0873 | 1.4499 |
| 203 | | | | | Boundary Condition | | | Boundary Condition | | | | | | |

**FIGURE 10.8-5**    Euler method to solve the system in four differential equations.

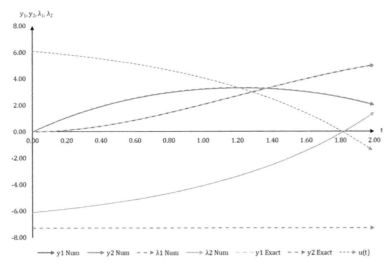

FIGURE 10.8-6   Optimal solution trajectories.

## 10.9 Current-value Hamiltonian

Another important class of problems in the OC theory is when, especially in the economic theory, we have to deal with discounted values, resorting to the factor $e^{-\rho t}$ in the integrand function as follows:

$$F(t, y, u) = G(t, y, u)e^{-\rho t}$$

so that the OC problem becomes:

$$\max J(u) = \int_{t_0}^{T} G(t, y, u)e^{-\rho t}dt$$

$$s.t. \ \dot{y} = f(t, y, u) \quad (equation \ of \ motion)$$

together with the boundary conditions.
   The Hamiltonian becomes then:

$$\mathcal{H} = G(t, y, u)e^{-\rho t} + \lambda f(t, y, u)$$

where the presence of the discount factor $e^{-\rho t}$ increases the complexity of the OC problems and one way to get around is to derive a new Hamiltonian function, free of this discount factor.
   This new form of Hamiltonian function is called *current-value Hamiltonian*, and it is derived as follows.
   Define a new *current-value* Lagrange-multiplier $\lambda$ from:

$$m = \lambda e^{\rho t}$$

as:

$$\lambda = me^{-\rho t}$$

then define the current-value Hamiltonian $\mathcal{H}_c$ as:

$$\mathcal{H}_c \overset{\text{def}}{=} \mathcal{H}e^{\rho t} = [G(t,y,u)e^{-\rho t} + \lambda f(t,y,u)]e^{\rho t}$$

$$\mathcal{H}_c = G(t,y,u) + mf(t,y,u)$$

which is now free of the continuous discount factor.

Now, what we need to do is to derive the new necessary conditions for the *maximum principle* with $\mathcal{H}_c \overset{\text{def}}{=} \mathcal{H}e^{\rho t}$.

The *maximum principle* conditions stated under 10.1-3, are then revised as[8]:

$$\max_{\{u\}} \mathcal{H}_c(t,y,u,\lambda) \quad \forall\, t \in [t_0,\ T]$$

$$\dot{y}(t) = \frac{\partial \mathcal{H}_c}{\partial m} \quad \text{(equation of motion for } y\text{)} \tag{10.9 $-$1}$$

$$\dot{m}(t) = -\frac{\partial \mathcal{H}_c}{\partial y} + \rho m \quad \text{(equation of motion for } m\text{)}$$

$$m(T)e^{-\rho t} = 0 \quad \text{(transversality condition)}$$

## EXAMPLE 1

Let us solve the following problem, first finding the exact continuous solution and then numerically in Excel:

$$\max J(u) = \int_0^1 e^{-\rho t}(y - y^2 - u^2)dt$$

$$s.t.\dot{y} = u - y \text{ and } y(0) = 0,\ y(1) = \text{free.}$$

i. As a first step let us derive the *current-value* Hamiltonian function as:

[8]For the complete proof see Alpha Chiang, *op.cit.*, ch. 8.

$$H_c = (y - y^2 - u^2) + m(u - y),$$

from which we can derive the first-order condition $\frac{\partial H}{\partial u} = 0$ to get the maximum in $\mathcal{H}_c$:

$$\frac{\partial \mathcal{H}_c}{\partial u} = -2u + m = 0 \Rightarrow u(t) = \frac{m}{2}.$$

**ii.** From the equation of motion for $m(t)$ we obtain:

$$\dot{m}(t) = -\frac{\partial \mathcal{H}_c}{\partial y} + \rho m = -[(1 - 2y) - m] + \rho m = 2y - 1 + m + \rho m,$$

which combined with the following equation of motion:

$$\dot{y} = \frac{m}{2} - y$$

forms the following complete system of differential equations:

$$\begin{bmatrix} \dot{m} \\ \dot{y} \end{bmatrix} = \begin{bmatrix} \rho + 1 & 2 \\ 1/2 & -1 \end{bmatrix} \begin{bmatrix} m \\ y \end{bmatrix} + \begin{bmatrix} -1 \\ 0 \end{bmatrix}$$

with general complete solutions:

$$m(t) = c_1 e^{r_1 t} + c_2 e^{r_2 t} + \overline{m}$$

$$y(t) = \frac{r_1 - \rho - 1}{2} c_1 e^{r_1 t} + \frac{r_2 - \rho - 1}{2} c_2 e^{r_2 t} + \overline{y},$$

where $r_1, r_2$ are the eigenvalues associated to the matrix $A = \begin{bmatrix} \rho + 1 & 2 \\ 1/2 & -1 \end{bmatrix}$ that can be found as:

$$r_1, r_2 = \frac{tr(A)}{2} \pm \frac{1}{2}\sqrt{tr(A)^2 - 4\det(A)}.$$

Setting $\rho = 0.05$ we have:

$$r_1, r_2 = \frac{0.05}{2} \pm \frac{1}{2}\sqrt{0.05^2 - 4\cdot(-2.05)} = \frac{0.05}{2} \pm 1.4320$$

from which the eigenvalues are obtained as:

$$r_1 = -1.4070, r_2 = 1.4570.$$

We derive then the coefficients for $y(t)$:

$$\frac{r_1 - \rho - 1}{2} = -1.2285$$

and

$$\frac{r_2 - \rho - 1}{2} = 0.2035.$$

As usual, the steady-state solutions are found setting the two equations of motion equal to zero ($\dot{m} = 0$ and $\dot{y} = 0$), so that we have:

$$\dot{y} = 0 \Rightarrow \bar{y} = \frac{m}{2}$$

$$\dot{m} = 0 \Rightarrow 2y - 1 + m + \rho m = 0$$

with $\bar{y} = \frac{m}{2}$ the last equation becomes:

$$m - 1 + m + \rho m = 0 \Rightarrow \bar{m} = \frac{1}{2 + \rho} = \frac{1}{2.05} \cong 0.4878$$

so that

$$\bar{y} \cong 0.2439.$$

**iii.** Now, the final step is to derive $c_1$ and $c_2$ from the boundary condition $y(0) = 0$ and the transversality condition $m(1) = 0$.

From the two equations:

$$m^*(t) = c_1 e^{-1.4070t} + c_2 e^{1.4570t} + 0.4878$$

$$y^*(t) = -1.2285 c_1 e^{-1.4070t} + 0.2035 c_2 e^{1.4570t} + 0.2439$$

We have $y(0) = 0$:

$$0 = -1.2285 c_1 + 0.2035 c_2 + 0.2439$$

from which we derive:

$$c_1 = \frac{(0.2035 c_2 + 0.2439)}{1.2285}$$

which plugged into $m(1) = 0$ leads to:

$$\frac{(0.2035c_2 + 0.2439)}{1.2285}e^{-1.4070} + c_2 e^{1.4570} + 0.4878 = 0.$$

Solving the above system the two constants are finally obtained as:

$$c_1 = 0.1780 \text{ and } c_2 = -0.1238$$

and the final optimal solutions for $y(t)$ and $m(t)$ are:

$$m^*(t) = 0.1780e^{-1.4070t} - 0.1238e^{1.4570t} + 0.4878$$

$$y^*(t) = -0.2187e^{-1.4070t} - 0.0252e^{1.4570t} + 0.2439.$$

As we have seen in the other cases, to compute the numerical Excel solution, one can just consider the necessary maximum principle conditions, skipping all the above cumbersome steps for the theoretical solutions.

The Excel worksheet setup with all the maximum principle necessary conditions involved in the problems is represented in Fig. 10.9-1.

As usual is key to solve the problem over the Lagrange multiplier $m$ via the Euler method under *Column H*, from the equation of motion $\dot{m}(t)$ stored under *Column I*.

The Solver will find the solution setting the transversality condition $m(T) = 0$ (*Cell H22*) by changing $m(0)$ (*Cell H2*), returning the following result (Figs. 10.9-2 and 10.9-3) (Table 10.9-1).

| | A | B | C | D | E | F | G | H | I | J | K |
|---|---|---|---|---|---|---|---|---|---|---|---|
| | t | y(t) | dy=(u-y)dt | dt | u=ẏ+y | ẏ=m/2-y | H.=(y·1/2u²)+m(u-y) | m(t) | m=2y-1+m+ρm | G=(y·y²-u²) | Functional G=Σ (y·y²-u²)dt |
| 1 | | | | | | | | | | | |
| 2 | 0 | 0 | | | =F2+B2 | =H2/2-B2 | 0 | 0.549276723035914 | =2*B2-1+H2+0.05*H2 | | |
| 3 | =A2+0.05 | =B2+C3 | =(E3-B3)*D3 | =A3-A2 | =F3+B3 | =H3/2-B3 | =J3+H3*F3 | =H2+I3*D3 | =2*B3-1+H3+0.05*H3 | =(B2-B2^2-E2^2) | =J3*D3 |
| 4 | =A3+0.05 | =B3+C4 | =(E4-B4)*D4 | =A4-A3 | =F4+B4 | =H4/2-B4 | =J4+H4*F4 | =H3+I4*D4 | =2*E4-1+H4+0.05*H4 | =(B3-B3^2-E3^2) | =J4*D4 |
| 5 | =A4+0.05 | =B4+C5 | =(E5-B5)*D5 | =A5-A4 | =F5+B5 | =H5/2-B5 | =J5+H5*F5 | =H4+I5*D5 | =2*B5-1+H5+0.05*H5 | =(B4-B4^2-E4^2) | =J5*D5 |
| 6 | =A5+0.05 | =B5+C6 | =(E6-B6)*D6 | =A6-A5 | =F6+B6 | =H6/2-B6 | =J6+H6*F6 | =H5+I6*D6 | =2*B6-1+H6+0.05*H6 | =(B5-B5^2-E5^2) | =J6*D6 |
| 7 | =A6+0.05 | =B6+C7 | =(E7-B7)*D7 | =A7-A6 | =F7+B7 | =H7/2-B7 | =J7+H7*F7 | =H6+I7*D7 | =2*B7-1+H7+0.05*H7 | =(B6-B6^2-E6^2) | =J7*D7 |
| 8 | =A7+0.05 | =B7+C8 | =(E8-B8)*D8 | =A8-A7 | =F8+B8 | =H8/2-B8 | =J8+H8*F8 | =H7+I8*D8 | =2*B8-1+H8+0.05*H8 | =(B7-B7^2-E7^2) | =J8*D8 |
| 9 | =A8+0.05 | =B8+C9 | =(E9-B9)*D9 | =A9-A8 | =F9+B9 | =H9/2-B9 | =J9+H9*F9 | =H8+I9*D9 | =2*B9-1+H9+0.05*H9 | =(B8-B8^2-E8^2) | =J9*D9 |
| 10 | =A9+0.05 | =B9+C10 | =(E10-B10)*D10 | =A10-A9 | =F10+B10 | =H10/2-B10 | =J10+H10*F10 | =H9+I10*D10 | =2*B10-1+H10+0.05*H10 | =(B9-B9^2-E9^2) | =J10*D10 |
| 11 | =A10+0.05 | =B10+C11 | =(E11-B11)*D11 | =A11-A10 | =F11+B11 | =H11/2-B11 | =J11+H11*F11 | =H10+I11*D11 | =2*B11-1+H11+0.05*H11 | =(B10-B10^2-E10^2) | =J11*D11 |
| 12 | =A11+0.05 | =B11+C12 | =(E12-B12)*D12 | =A12-A11 | =F12+B12 | =H12/2-B12 | =J12+H12*F12 | =H11+I12*D12 | =2*B12-1+H12+0.05*H12 | =(B11-B11^2-E11^2) | =J12*D12 |
| 13 | =A12+0.05 | =B12+C13 | =(E13-B13)*D13 | =A13-A12 | =F13+B13 | =H13/2-B13 | =J13+H13*F13 | =H12+I13*D13 | =2*B13-1+H13+0.05*H13 | =(B12-B12^2-E12^2) | =J13*D13 |
| 14 | =A13+0.05 | =B13+C14 | =(E14-B14)*D14 | =A14-A13 | =F14+B14 | =H14/2-B14 | =J14+H14*F14 | =H13+I14*D14 | =2*B14-1+H14+0.05*H14 | =(B13-B13^2-E13^2) | =J14*D14 |
| 15 | =A14+0.05 | =B14+C15 | =(E15-B15)*D15 | =A15-A14 | =F15+B15 | =H15/2-B15 | =J15+H15*F15 | =H14+I15*D15 | =2*B15-1+H15+0.05*H15 | =(B14-B14^2-E14^2) | =J15*D15 |
| 16 | =A15+0.05 | =B15+C16 | =(E16-B16)*D16 | =A16-A15 | =F16+B16 | =H16/2-B16 | =J16+H16*F16 | =H15+I16*D16 | =2*B16-1+H16+0.05*H16 | =(B15-B15^2-E15^2) | =J16*D16 |
| 17 | =A16+0.05 | =B16+C17 | =(E17-B17)*D17 | =A17-A16 | =F17+B17 | =H17/2-B17 | =J17+H17*F17 | =H16+I17*D17 | =2*B17-1+H17+0.05*H17 | =(B16-B16^2-E16^2) | =J17*D17 |
| 18 | =A17+0.05 | =B17+C18 | =(E18-B18)*D18 | =A18-A17 | =F18+B18 | =H18/2-B18 | =J18+H18*F18 | =H17+I18*D18 | =2*B18-1+H18+0.05*H18 | =(B17-B17^2-E17^2) | =J18*D18 |
| 19 | =A18+0.05 | =B18+C19 | =(E19-B19)*D19 | =A19-A18 | =F19+B19 | =H19/2-B19 | =J19+H19*F19 | =H18+I19*D19 | =2*B19-1+H19+0.05*H19 | =(B18-B18^2-E18^2) | =J19*D19 |
| 20 | =A19+0.05 | =B19+C20 | =(E20-B20)*D20 | =A20-A19 | =F20+B20 | =H20/2-B20 | =J20+H20*F20 | =H19+I20*D20 | =2*B20-1+H20+0.05*H20 | =(B19-B19^2-E19^2) | =J20*D20 |
| 21 | =A20+0.05 | =B20+C21 | =(E21-B21)*D21 | =A21-A20 | =F21+B21 | =H21/2-B21 | =J21+H21*F21 | =H20+I21*D21 | =2*B21-1+H21+0.05*H21 | =(B20-B20^2-E20^2) | =J21*D21 |
| 22 | =A21+0.05 | =B21+C22 | =(E22-B22)*D22 | =A22-A21 | =F22+B22 | =H22/2-B22 | =J22+H22*F22 | =H21+I22*D22 | =2*B22-1+H22+0.05*H22 | =(B21-B21^2-E21^2) | =J22*D22 |
| 23 | | | | | | | | | | | |
| 24 | y(0) | 0 | | | | | ρ=5% | Transversality | | | |
| 25 | y(1) | Free | | | | | | condition m(T)=0 | | | =SUM(K3:K22) |

**FIGURE 10.9-1** Example 1: current-value Hamiltonian Excel worksheet setup.

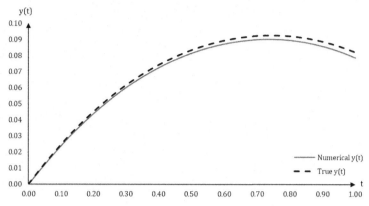

**FIGURE 10.9-2**    Example 1: current-value Hamiltonian optimal $y^*(t)$.

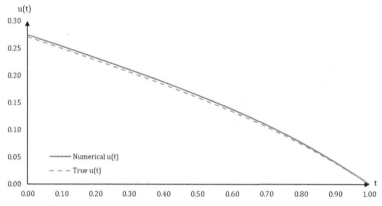

**FIGURE 10.9-3**    Example 1: current-value Hamiltonian optimal $u^*(t)$.

## 10.10 Constraints on the state variable: a linear case with an inventory application with VBA

As in CoV also the OC problems may be constrained. In this section we will see a state-space constrained problem, where both the integrand function and the constraints are linear. Next, we will show how VBA can be used in a *bang-bang* inventory problem.

In the OC theory a state space constrained problem is expressed as follows[9]:

$$\max_{\{u\}} \int_{t_0}^{T} F(t, y, u)dt$$

[9]See for the complete theoretical details (also for Examples one and 2) Alpha Chiang, *op.cit.*, ch. 10. The Excel numerical approach proposed in the Examples does not resort to the theoretical conditions described by Alpha Chiang.

**TABLE 10.9-1** Example 1: current-value Hamiltonian Excel computed solution.

| t | y(t) | dy = (u-y)dt | dt | u = ẏ+y | ẏ = m/2-y | Hc = (y-1/2u²)+m(u-y) | m(t) | ṁ = 2y-1+m+ρm | G = (y-y²-u²) | Functional G = Σ(y-y²-u²)dt |
|---|---|---|---|---|---|---|---|---|---|---|
| 0.0000 | 0.0000 | | | 0.2746 | 0.2746 | 0.0000 | 0.5493 | -0.4233 | -0.0754 | -0.00038 |
| 0.0500 | 0.0126 | 0.0126 | 0.0500 | 0.2641 | 0.2516 | 0.0575 | 0.5283 | -0.4202 | -0.0573 | -0.00029 |
| 0.1000 | 0.0241 | 0.0115 | 0.0500 | 0.2537 | 0.2296 | 0.0591 | 0.5073 | -0.4192 | -0.0409 | -0.00020 |
| 0.1500 | 0.0345 | 0.0104 | 0.0500 | 0.2431 | 0.2087 | 0.0606 | 0.4863 | -0.4204 | -0.0258 | -0.00013 |
| 0.2000 | 0.0439 | 0.0094 | 0.0500 | 0.2325 | 0.1886 | 0.0619 | 0.4651 | -0.4238 | -0.0121 | -0.00006 |
| 0.2500 | 0.0524 | 0.0085 | 0.0500 | 0.2218 | 0.1694 | 0.0631 | 0.4436 | -0.4294 | 0.0004 | 0.00000 |
| 0.3000 | 0.0599 | 0.0075 | 0.0500 | 0.2109 | 0.1509 | 0.0641 | 0.4218 | -0.4373 | 0.0119 | 0.0006 |
| 0.3500 | 0.0666 | 0.0067 | 0.0500 | 0.1997 | 0.1331 | 0.0650 | 0.3994 | -0.4475 | 0.0223 | 0.0011 |
| 0.4000 | 0.0724 | 0.0058 | 0.0500 | 0.1882 | 0.1158 | 0.0659 | 0.3764 | -0.4600 | 0.0317 | 0.0016 |
| 0.4500 | 0.0773 | 0.0049 | 0.0500 | 0.1763 | 0.0990 | 0.0666 | 0.3526 | -0.4751 | 0.0403 | 0.0020 |
| 0.5000 | 0.0815 | 0.0041 | 0.0500 | 0.1640 | 0.0825 | 0.0673 | 0.3280 | -0.4927 | 0.0479 | 0.0024 |
| 0.5500 | 0.0848 | 0.0033 | 0.0500 | 0.1512 | 0.0664 | 0.0680 | 0.3024 | -0.5130 | 0.0547 | 0.0027 |
| 0.6000 | 0.0873 | 0.0025 | 0.0500 | 0.1378 | 0.0505 | 0.0686 | 0.2756 | -0.5361 | 0.0607 | 0.0030 |
| 0.6500 | 0.0890 | 0.0017 | 0.0500 | 0.1237 | 0.0347 | 0.0693 | 0.2474 | -0.5621 | 0.0658 | 0.0033 |
| 0.7000 | 0.0900 | 0.0009 | 0.0500 | 0.1089 | 0.0190 | 0.0699 | 0.2179 | -0.5912 | 0.0700 | 0.0035 |
| 0.7500 | 0.0901 | 0.0002 | 0.0500 | 0.0934 | 0.0032 | 0.0706 | 0.1867 | -0.6237 | 0.0733 | 0.0037 |
| 0.8000 | 0.0895 | -0.0006 | 0.0500 | 0.0769 | -0.0127 | 0.0714 | 0.1537 | -0.6596 | 0.0756 | 0.0038 |
| 0.8500 | 0.0881 | -0.0014 | 0.0500 | 0.0594 | -0.0287 | 0.0722 | 0.1188 | -0.6991 | 0.0768 | 0.0038 |
| 0.9000 | 0.0858 | -0.0023 | 0.0500 | 0.0408 | -0.0450 | 0.0731 | 0.0816 | -0.7426 | 0.0768 | 0.0038 |
| 0.9500 | 0.0827 | -0.0031 | 0.0500 | 0.0211 | -0.0617 | 0.0742 | 0.0421 | -0.7903 | 0.0755 | 0.0038 |
| 1.0000 | 0.0788 | -0.0039 | 0.0500 | 0.0000 | -0.0788 | 0.0755 | 0.0000 | -0.8424 | | |
| y(0) | 0.0000 | | | | | ρ = 5% | | | | 0.0286 |
| y(1) | Free | | | | | Transversality condition m(T) = 0 | | | | |

$$s.t. \ \dot{y} = f(t, y, u)$$

$$h(t, y) \leq c$$

$$y(t_0) = A \quad y(T) = Z.$$

We will propose to solve such a problem (in a *bang-bang* form) within a spreadsheet through the following basic steps.

i. Solve the *bang-bang* problem over the time interval $[0, T]$ as if it were not constrained. Choose as optimal path the computed $y^*(t)$ till the constraint $h(t, y) \leq c$ is satisfied, and this will occur in $t = t_{ou}$, where $t_{ou}$ stands for *time optimal unconstrained*.

ii. Implement the constraint in Excel, moving the state variable $y(t)$ on the constraint equation, and this will occur in $t = t_{oc}$, where $t_{oc}$ stands for *time optimal constrained*.

iii. Once $y(T) = Z$ is satisfied, move the state variable $y(t)$ on the value given by the boundary condition, and this will occur in $t = t_{bc}$, where $t_{bc}$ stands for *time boundary conditions*. This is because $y^*(t)$ anyway is not allowed to go beyond what is stated in the boundary conditions.

## EXAMPLE 1 (OPTIMAL CONTROL BANG-BANG PROBLEM)

Let us consider the following case:

$$\max_{\{u\}} \int_0^3 (4 - t) u \, dt$$

$$s.t. \ \dot{y} = u$$

$$y - t \leq 1$$

$$y(0) = 0 \quad y(3) = 3$$

$$u \in [0, 2]$$

i. The Hamiltonian is as follows:

$$\mathcal{H} = (4 - t)u + \lambda u$$

which is linear in $u$ with slope:

$$\frac{d\mathcal{H}}{du} = (4 - t) + \lambda.$$

In the time interval [0, 3] the quantity (4−t) will be always positive. So, the optimal control policy $u^*(t)$ will be:

$$u^*(t) = \left\{ \begin{matrix} 0 \\ 2 \end{matrix} \right\} \text{ if } \lambda(t) \left\{ \begin{matrix} > \\ < \end{matrix} \right\} 0.$$

Next step is to determine from the equation of motion the solution for $\lambda(t)$:

$$\frac{d\lambda}{dt} = -\frac{\partial \mathcal{H}}{\partial y} = 0 \Rightarrow \lambda(t) = constant.$$

As $\lambda(t)$ turns out to be a positive constant, to reach the optimal solution, the optimal policy is chosen such that $u^*(t) = 2$ and the equation of motion on the state variable becomes $\dot{y} = 2$ from which the optimal unconstrained solution is (setting the constant of integration zero, because of the initial condition $y(0) = 0$):

$$y^*(t) = 2t.$$

Notice that in the unconstrained optimal solution of Table 10.10-1 $y^*(t)$ in the second column has been divided in three areas: the first unmarked area is when the optimal solution satisfies the state space constraint $y \leq t + 1$, the second area in light gray is when the constraint equation is activated, and finally the third dark gray area is when the boundary condition value $y(3) = 3$ is activated.

This process is depicted in Table 10.10-2, which is the optimal constrained solution of the problem.

From the above solutions, we derive the three subperiods where the different optimal solutions are identified, and the consequent optimal control policy $u^*(t)$ is implemented (see Fig. 10.10-1) (Figs. 10.10-2 and 10.10-3).

## EXAMPLE 2 (AN INVENTORY APPLICATION USING VBA)

The second example is about an economic application in inventory and production.

Let $D(t)$ be the demand for the firm's product. To meet this demand, the firm can either draw dawn the inventory available, $X(t)$, or produce the demanded quantity $Q(t)$, or use a combination of the two.

We indicate with $c$ the cost of production and with $s$ the storage cost per unit of goods. These costs are assumed to be constant over time.

The output and the inventory are related, such that:

$$\dot{X}(t) = Q(t) - D(t)$$

which means that the inventory $X(t)$ available accumulates (decumulates) whenever the quantity $Q(t)$ exceeds (or falls short of) the demanded quantity $D(t)$.

The objective is to minimize the total cost $\int_{t_0}^{T} [cQ(t) + sX(t)]dt$ over the period of time $[t_0, T]$ where $Q(t)$ is the control variable (production) and $X(t)$ the state variable (inventory). The level of demanded goods $D(t) > 0$ is given.

**TABLE 10.10-1**   Example 1: *Bang-bang* optimal control problem unconstrained optimal solution.

| t | y | $dy = (u)dt$ | $dt$ | $u = \dot{y}$ | $\dot{y} = u$ | Hamiltonian $= (4+t)u + \lambda u$ | $\lambda(t)$ | $d\lambda/dt = 0$ | $F = (4+t)u$ | $\Sigma = (4+t)u\,dt$ |
|---|---|---|---|---|---|---|---|---|---|---|
| 0.0000 | 0.0000 |  |  | 2.0000 | 2.0000 | 8.0000 | 0.0000 | 0.0000 |  |  |
| 0.0750 | 0.1500 | 0.1500 | 0.0750 | 2.0000 | 2.0000 | 7.8500 | 0.0000 | 0.0000 | 7.8500 | 1.1775 |
| 0.1500 | 0.3000 | 0.1500 | 0.0750 | 2.0000 | 2.0000 | 7.7000 | 0.0000 | 0.0000 | 7.7000 | 0.5775 |
| 0.2250 | 0.4500 | 0.1500 | 0.0750 | 2.0000 | 2.0000 | 7.5500 | 0.0000 | 0.0000 | 7.5500 | 0.5663 |
| 0.3000 | 0.6000 | 0.1500 | 0.0750 | 2.0000 | 2.0000 | 7.4000 | 0.0000 | 0.0000 | 7.4000 | 0.5550 |
| 0.3750 | 0.7500 | 0.1500 | 0.0750 | 2.0000 | 2.0000 | 7.2500 | 0.0000 | 0.0000 | 7.2500 | 0.5438 |
| 0.4500 | 0.9000 | 0.1500 | 0.0750 | 2.0000 | 2.0000 | 7.1000 | 0.0000 | 0.0000 | 7.1000 | 0.5325 |
| 0.5250 | 1.0500 | 0.1500 | 0.0750 | 2.0000 | 2.0000 | 6.9500 | 0.0000 | 0.0000 | 6.9500 | 0.5213 |
| 0.6000 | 1.2000 | 0.1500 | 0.0750 | 2.0000 | 2.0000 | 6.8000 | 0.0000 | 0.0000 | 6.8000 | 0.5100 |
| 0.6750 | 1.3500 | 0.1500 | 0.0750 | 2.0000 | 2.0000 | 6.6500 | 0.0000 | 0.0000 | 6.6500 | 0.4988 |
| 0.7500 | 1.5000 | 0.1500 | 0.0750 | 2.0000 | 2.0000 | 6.5000 | 0.0000 | 0.0000 | 6.5000 | 0.4875 |
| 0.8250 | 1.6500 | 0.1500 | 0.0750 | 2.0000 | 2.0000 | 6.3500 | 0.0000 | 0.0000 | 6.3500 | 0.4763 |
| 0.9000 | 1.8000 | 0.1500 | 0.0750 | 2.0000 | 2.0000 | 6.2000 | 0.0000 | 0.0000 | 6.2000 | 0.4650 |
| 0.9750 | 1.9500 | 0.1500 | 0.0750 | 2.0000 | 2.0000 | 6.0500 | 0.0000 | 0.0000 | 6.0500 | 0.4538 |
| 1.0500 | 2.1000 | 0.1500 | 0.0750 | 2.0000 | 2.0000 | 5.9000 | 0.0000 | 0.0000 | 5.9000 | 0.4425 |
| 1.1250 | 2.2500 | 0.1500 | 0.0750 | 2.0000 | 2.0000 | 5.7500 | 0.0000 | 0.0000 | 5.7500 | 0.4313 |
| 1.2000 | 2.4000 | 0.1500 | 0.0750 | 2.0000 | 2.0000 | 5.6000 | 0.0000 | 0.0000 | 5.6000 | 0.4200 |
| 1.2750 | 2.5500 | 0.1500 | 0.0750 | 2.0000 | 2.0000 | 5.4500 | 0.0000 | 0.0000 | 5.4500 | 0.4088 |
| 1.3500 | 2.7000 | 0.1500 | 0.0750 | 2.0000 | 2.0000 | 5.3000 | 0.0000 | 0.0000 | 5.3000 | 0.3975 |
| 1.4250 | 2.8500 | 0.1500 | 0.0750 | 2.0000 | 2.0000 | 5.1500 | 0.0000 | 0.0000 | 5.1500 | 0.3863 |
| 1.5000 | 3.0000 | 0.1500 | 0.0750 | 2.0000 | 2.0000 | 5.0000 | 0.0000 | 0.0000 | 5.0000 | 0.3750 |
| 1.5750 | 3.1500 | 0.1500 | 0.0750 | 2.0000 | 2.0000 | 4.8500 | 0.0000 | 0.0000 | 4.8500 | 0.3638 |
| 1.6500 | 3.3000 | 0.1500 | 0.0750 | 2.0000 | 2.0000 | 4.7000 | 0.0000 | 0.0000 | 4.7000 | 0.3525 |
| 1.7250 | 3.4500 | 0.1500 | 0.0750 | 2.0000 | 2.0000 | 4.5500 | 0.0000 | 0.0000 | 4.5500 | 0.3413 |
| 1.8000 | 3.6000 | 0.1500 | 0.0750 | 2.0000 | 2.0000 | 4.4000 | 0.0000 | 0.0000 | 4.4000 | 0.3300 |
| 1.8750 | 3.7500 | 0.1500 | 0.0750 | 2.0000 | 2.0000 | 4.2500 | 0.0000 | 0.0000 | 4.2500 | 0.3188 |
| 1.9500 | 3.9000 | 0.1500 | 0.0750 | 2.0000 | 2.0000 | 4.1000 | 0.0000 | 0.0000 | 4.1000 | 0.3075 |
| 2.0250 | 4.0500 | 0.1500 | 0.0750 | 2.0000 | 2.0000 | 3.9500 | 0.0000 | 0.0000 | 3.9500 | 0.2963 |
| 2.1000 | 4.2000 | 0.1500 | 0.0750 | 2.0000 | 2.0000 | 3.8000 | 0.0000 | 0.0000 | 3.8000 | 0.2850 |
| 2.1750 | 4.3500 | 0.1500 | 0.0750 | 2.0000 | 2.0000 | 3.6500 | 0.0000 | 0.0000 | 3.6500 | 0.2738 |
| 2.2500 | 4.5000 | 0.1500 | 0.0750 | 2.0000 | 2.0000 | 3.5000 | 0.0000 | 0.0000 | 3.5000 | 0.2625 |
| 2.3250 | 4.6500 | 0.1500 | 0.0750 | 2.0000 | 2.0000 | 3.3500 | 0.0000 | 0.0000 | 3.3500 | 0.2513 |
| 2.4000 | 4.8000 | 0.1500 | 0.0750 | 2.0000 | 2.0000 | 3.2000 | 0.0000 | 0.0000 | 3.2000 | 0.2400 |
| 2.4750 | 4.9500 | 0.1500 | 0.0750 | 2.0000 | 2.0000 | 3.0500 | 0.0000 | 0.0000 | 3.0500 | 0.2288 |
| 2.5500 | 5.1000 | 0.1500 | 0.0750 | 2.0000 | 2.0000 | 2.9000 | 0.0000 | 0.0000 | 2.9000 | 0.2175 |
| 2.6250 | 5.2500 | 0.1500 | 0.0750 | 2.0000 | 2.0000 | 2.7500 | 0.0000 | 0.0000 | 2.7500 | 0.2063 |
| 2.7000 | 5.4000 | 0.1500 | 0.0750 | 2.0000 | 2.0000 | 2.6000 | 0.0000 | 0.0000 | 2.6000 | 0.1950 |
| 2.7750 | 5.5500 | 0.1500 | 0.0750 | 2.0000 | 2.0000 | 2.4500 | 0.0000 | 0.0000 | 2.4500 | 0.1838 |
| 2.8500 | 5.7000 | 0.1500 | 0.0750 | 2.0000 | 2.0000 | 2.3000 | 0.0000 | 0.0000 | 2.3000 | 0.1725 |
| 2.9250 | 5.8500 | 0.1500 | 0.0750 | 2.0000 | 2.0000 | 2.1500 | 0.0000 | 0.0000 | 2.1500 | 0.1613 |
| 3.0000 | 6.0000 | 0.1500 | 0.0750 | 2.0000 | 2.0000 | 2.0000 | 0.0000 | 0.0000 | 2.0000 | 0.1500 |

y(0)   0.00

y(2)   3.00

15.3638

**TABLE 10.10-2**    Example 1: *Bang-bang* optimal control problem constrained optimal solution.

| t | Linear constraint y = 1+t | Boundary condition y = 3 | y Optimal constrained solution | u= ẏ |
|---|---|---|---|---|
| 0.0000 | 1.0000 | 3.0000 | 0.0000 | |
| 0.0750 | 1.0750 | 3.0000 | 0.1500 | 2.0000 |
| 0.1500 | 1.1500 | 3.0000 | 0.3000 | 2.0000 |
| 0.2250 | 1.2250 | 3.0000 | 0.4500 | 2.0000 |
| 0.3000 | 1.3000 | 3.0000 | 0.6000 | 2.0000 |
| 0.3750 | 1.3750 | 3.0000 | 0.7500 | 2.0000 |
| 0.4500 | 1.4500 | 3.0000 | 0.9000 | 2.0000 |
| 0.5250 | 1.5250 | 3.0000 | 1.0500 | 2.0000 |
| 0.6000 | 1.6000 | 3.0000 | 1.2000 | 2.0000 |
| 0.6750 | 1.6750 | 3.0000 | 1.3500 | 2.0000 |
| 0.7500 | 1.7500 | 3.0000 | 1.5000 | 2.0000 |
| 0.8250 | 1.8250 | 3.0000 | 1.6500 | 2.0000 |
| 0.9000 | 1.9000 | 3.0000 | 1.8000 | 2.0000 |
| 0.9750 | 1.9750 | 3.0000 | 1.9500 | 2.0000 |
| 1.0500 | 2.0500 | 3.0000 | 2.0500 | 1.0000 |
| 1.1250 | 2.1250 | 3.0000 | 2.1250 | 1.0000 |
| 1.2000 | 2.2000 | 3.0000 | 2.2000 | 1.0000 |
| 1.2750 | 2.2750 | 3.0000 | 2.2750 | 1.0000 |
| 1.3500 | 2.3500 | 3.0000 | 2.3500 | 1.0000 |
| 1.4250 | 2.4250 | 3.0000 | 2.4250 | 1.0000 |
| 1.5000 | 2.5000 | 3.0000 | 2.5000 | 1.0000 |
| 1.5750 | 2.5750 | 3.0000 | 2.5750 | 1.0000 |
| 1.6500 | 2.6500 | 3.0000 | 2.6500 | 1.0000 |
| 1.7250 | 2.7250 | 3.0000 | 2.7250 | 1.0000 |
| 1.8000 | 2.8000 | 3.0000 | 2.8000 | 1.0000 |
| 1.8750 | 2.8750 | 3.0000 | 2.8750 | 1.0000 |
| 1.9500 | 2.9500 | 3.0000 | 2.9500 | 1.0000 |
| 2.0250 | 3.0250 | 3.0000 | 3.0000 | 0.0000 |
| 2.1000 | 3.1000 | 3.0000 | 3.0000 | 0.0000 |
| 2.1750 | 3.1750 | 3.0000 | 3.0000 | 0.0000 |
| 2.2500 | 3.2500 | 3.0000 | 3.0000 | 0.0000 |
| 2.3250 | 3.3250 | 3.0000 | 3.0000 | 0.0000 |
| 2.4000 | 3.4000 | 3.0000 | 3.0000 | 0.0000 |
| 2.4750 | 3.4750 | 3.0000 | 3.0000 | 0.0000 |
| 2.5500 | 3.5500 | 3.0000 | 3.0000 | 0.0000 |
| 2.6250 | 3.6250 | 3.0000 | 3.0000 | 0.0000 |
| 2.7000 | 3.7000 | 3.0000 | 3.0000 | 0.0000 |
| 2.7750 | 3.7750 | 3.0000 | 3.0000 | 0.0000 |
| 2.8500 | 3.8500 | 3.0000 | 3.0000 | 0.0000 |
| 2.9250 | 3.9250 | 3.0000 | 3.0000 | 0.0000 |
| 3.0000 | 4.0000 | 3.0000 | 3.0000 | 0.0000 |

*Phase I* time interval $t_{ou} \in [0, 0.975] \Rightarrow u^*(t) = 2$ and $y^*(t) = 2t$

*Phase II* time interval $t_{oc} \in [1.05, 1.95] \Rightarrow u^*(t) = 1$ and $y^*(t) = t + 1$

*Phase III* time interval $t_{bc} \in [2.025, 3] \Rightarrow u^*(t) = 0$ and $y^*(t) = 3$

**FIGURE 10.10-1**    Example 1: summary of the *bang-bang* optimal control problem constrained optimal solution.

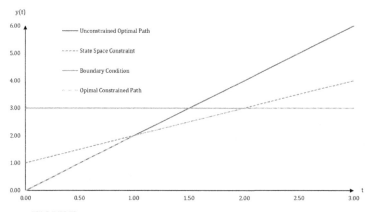

**FIGURE 10.10-2**    Example 1: optimal $y^*(t)$ path in three phases.

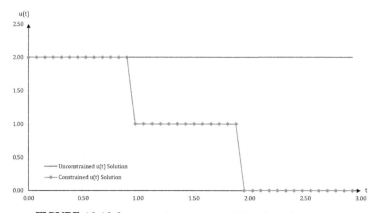

**FIGURE 10.10-3**    Example 1: optimal $u^*(t)$ path in three phases.

Converting the above minimum problem into a maximum problem and assigning the usual notations $y(t)$ and $u(t)$ to the state and control variables, we have the following OC problem:

$$\max_{\{u\}} \int_{t_0}^{T} (-cu - sy)dt$$

$$s.t. \; \dot{y}(t) = u(t) - D(t)$$

$$y(t) \geq 0$$

$$y(0) = y_0 \quad y(T) \geq 0 \; free$$

$$u \in [0, \infty)$$

The unconstrained problem would be solved through the following usual steps.

**i.** The Hamiltonian is as follows:

$$\mathcal{H} = (-cu - sy) + \lambda(u - D)$$

which is linear in $u$ with slope:

$$\frac{d\mathcal{H}}{du} = -c + \lambda$$

and the optimal control policy $u^*(t)$ will be:

$$u^*(t) = \begin{Bmatrix} 0 \\ indeterminate \\ unbounded \end{Bmatrix} \text{if} \; \lambda(t) \begin{Bmatrix} < \\ = \\ > \end{Bmatrix} c.$$

where $c$ is a positive constant.

The first policy is implemented whenever the slope $\frac{d\mathcal{H}}{du} = -c + \lambda$ is negative and $u^*(t) = 0$ is selected. If the slope is positive ($\lambda > c$), being $u \in [0, \infty)$, $u^*(t)$ will be unbounded, and this will not be feasible. The possibility $\lambda = c$ would generate an indeterminate solution.

**ii.** From the equation of motion:

$$\frac{d\lambda}{dt} = -\frac{d\mathcal{H}}{dy} = s \Rightarrow \lambda(t) = st + k_1$$

where $s$ is a positive constant. Since, for the transversality condition, $\lambda(1) = 0$, then $k_1 = -s$ and $\lambda(0) = -s$.

**iii.** From the equation of motion $\dot{y} = u - D$ and optimal control $u^*(t) = 0$ we have

$$y^*(t) = -Dt + k_2.$$

As $y(0) = y_0$ then $k_2 = y_0$.

The variation in the inventory will become $\dot{y} = -D$, namely the inventory will only decumulates due to the demand, until the firms runs into the constraint that the inventory cannot be negative ($y \geq 0$) and the constraint is not satisfied.

It is at this stage that we will need to activate the control production variable solving the problem satisfying the constraints as well.

Let us see first the unconstrained problem implemented in Excel with the following data parameters: production cost $c = 1$, storage cost $s = 1$, constant $D(t) = 5$, inventory at $t_0 = 0$, $y(0) = 1$, and $T = 1$.

The numerical optimal solution with the Solver, setting $\lambda(T) = 0$ by changing $\lambda(0)$, is as follows in Table 10.10-3. It is apparent how the control variable policy $u^*(t) = 0$ suggested by the unconstrained solution would generate a negative inventory at $T = 1$ equal to $y(T) = -4$, because of the initial inventory availability of $y(0) = 1$ and the demand of $D(t) = 5$ in $[0, 1]$.

The constrained problem would also imply, under a theoretical point of view, the definition of the new Lagrangian function as follows:

$$\mathcal{L} = -cu - sy + \Lambda(u - D) + \Theta(u - D)$$

The first-order condition is $\frac{d\mathcal{L}}{d\Theta} = 0$, and the maximum point would be reached when $u(t) = D$. This policy would be activated soon after the given inventory $y(0)$ is exhausted by the unconstrained policy. As the objective is to minimize costs it is not advisable to start producing the quantity $D(t)$ from $t = 0$, rather we satisfy the demand just by the inventory decumulation.

The optimal policy is then identified in two phases as in Fig. 10.10-4.

Notice that in *Phase II*, as it is $\dot{y} = u - D = 0$, it will be $y^*(t) = constant = 0$ because we start with zero inventory at the beginning of *Phase II*, as it has been completely exhausted in *Phase I*.

**TABLE 10.10-3**  Example 2: Inventory problem unconstrained solution.

| t | Demand | y Inventory | dy = (u-D)dt | dt | Control variable = Quantity Produced u = y + D | y** = D | Hamiltonian = (cu + vy)λ(u-D) | λ(t) | dλ/dt = -s | F = cu+vy | Σ = (cu+vy)dt | Σ D dt |
|---|---|---|---|---|---|---|---|---|---|---|---|---|
| 0.0000 | 5.0000 | 1.0000 | -0.1250 | 0.0250 | 0.0000 | 5.0000 | 4.0000 | -1.0000 | 0.0000 | 1.0000 | 0.0219 | 0.1250 |
| 0.0250 | 5.0000 | 0.8750 | -0.1250 | 0.0250 | 0.0000 | 5.0000 | 4.0000 | 0.9750 | 1.0000 | 0.8750 | 0.0188 | 0.1250 |
| 0.0500 | 5.0000 | 0.7500 | -0.1250 | 0.0250 | 0.0000 | 5.0000 | 4.0000 | 0.9500 | 1.0000 | 0.7500 | 0.0156 | 0.1250 |
| 0.0750 | 5.0000 | 0.6250 | -0.1250 | 0.0250 | 0.0000 | 5.0000 | 4.0000 | 0.9250 | 1.0000 | 0.6250 | 0.0125 | 0.1250 |
| 0.1000 | 5.0000 | 0.5000 | -0.1250 | 0.0250 | 0.0000 | 5.0000 | 4.0000 | 0.9000 | 1.0000 | 0.5000 | 0.0094 | 0.1250 |
| 0.1250 | 5.0000 | 0.3750 | -0.1250 | 0.0250 | 0.0000 | 5.0000 | 4.0000 | 0.8750 | 1.0000 | 0.3750 | 0.0063 | 0.1250 |
| 0.1500 | 5.0000 | 0.2500 | -0.1250 | 0.0250 | 0.0000 | 5.0000 | 4.0000 | 0.8500 | 1.0000 | 0.2500 | 0.0031 | 0.1250 |
| 0.1750 | 5.0000 | 0.1250 | -0.1250 | 0.0250 | 0.0000 | 5.0000 | 4.0000 | 0.8250 | 1.0000 | 0.1250 | 0.0000 | 0.1250 |
| 0.2000 | 5.0000 | 0.0000 | -0.1250 | 0.0250 | 0.0000 | 5.0000 | 4.0000 | 0.8000 | 1.0000 | 0.0000 | 0.0031 | 0.1250 |
| 0.2250 | 5.0000 | -0.1250 | -0.1250 | 0.0250 | 0.0000 | 5.0000 | 4.0000 | 0.7750 | 1.0000 | 0.1250 | 0.0063 | 0.1250 |
| 0.2500 | 5.0000 | -0.2500 | -0.1250 | 0.0250 | 0.0000 | 5.0000 | 4.0000 | 0.7500 | 1.0000 | 0.2500 | 0.0094 | 0.1250 |
| 0.2750 | 5.0000 | -0.3750 | -0.1250 | 0.0250 | 0.0000 | 5.0000 | 4.0000 | 0.7250 | 1.0000 | 0.3750 | 0.0125 | 0.1250 |
| 0.3000 | 5.0000 | -0.5000 | -0.1250 | 0.0250 | 0.0000 | 5.0000 | 4.0000 | 0.7000 | 1.0000 | 0.5000 | 0.0156 | 0.1250 |
| 0.3250 | 5.0000 | -0.6250 | -0.1250 | 0.0250 | 0.0000 | 5.0000 | 4.0000 | 0.6750 | 1.0000 | 0.6250 | 0.0188 | 0.1250 |
| 0.3500 | 5.0000 | -0.7500 | -0.1250 | 0.0250 | 0.0000 | 5.0000 | 4.0000 | 0.6500 | 1.0000 | 0.7500 | 0.0219 | 0.1250 |
| 0.3750 | 5.0000 | -0.8750 | -0.1250 | 0.0250 | 0.0000 | 5.0000 | 4.0000 | 0.6250 | 1.0000 | 0.8750 | 0.0250 | 0.1250 |
| 0.4000 | 5.0000 | -1.0000 | -0.1250 | 0.0250 | 0.0000 | 5.0000 | 4.0000 | 0.6000 | 1.0000 | 1.0000 | 0.0219 | 0.1250 |
| 0.4250 | 5.0000 | -1.1250 | -0.1250 | 0.0250 | 0.0000 | 5.0000 | 4.0000 | 0.5750 | 1.0000 | 1.1250 | 0.0281 | 0.1250 |
| 0.4500 | 5.0000 | -1.2500 | -0.1250 | 0.0250 | 0.0000 | 5.0000 | 4.0000 | 0.5500 | 1.0000 | 1.2500 | 0.0313 | 0.1250 |
| 0.4750 | 5.0000 | -1.3750 | -0.1250 | 0.0250 | 0.0000 | 5.0000 | 4.0000 | 0.5250 | 1.0000 | 1.3750 | 0.0344 | 0.1250 |
| 0.5000 | 5.0000 | -1.5000 | -0.1250 | 0.0250 | 0.0000 | 5.0000 | 4.0000 | 0.5000 | 1.0000 | 1.5000 | 0.0375 | 0.1250 |
| 0.5250 | 5.0000 | -1.6250 | -0.1250 | 0.0250 | 0.0000 | 5.0000 | 4.0000 | 0.4750 | 1.0000 | 1.6250 | 0.0406 | 0.1250 |
| 0.5500 | 5.0000 | -1.7500 | -0.1250 | 0.0250 | 0.0000 | 5.0000 | 4.0000 | 0.4500 | 1.0000 | 1.7500 | 0.0438 | 0.1250 |
| 0.5750 | 5.0000 | -1.8750 | -0.1250 | 0.0250 | 0.0000 | 5.0000 | 4.0000 | 0.4250 | 1.0000 | 1.8750 | 0.0469 | 0.1250 |
| 0.6000 | 5.0000 | -2.0000 | -0.1250 | 0.0250 | 0.0000 | 5.0000 | 4.0000 | 0.4000 | 1.0000 | 2.0000 | 0.0500 | 0.1250 |
| 0.6250 | 5.0000 | -2.1250 | -0.1250 | 0.0250 | 0.0000 | 5.0000 | 4.0000 | 0.3750 | 1.0000 | 2.1250 | 0.0531 | 0.1250 |
| 0.6500 | 5.0000 | -2.2500 | -0.1250 | 0.0250 | 0.0000 | 5.0000 | 4.0000 | 0.3500 | 1.0000 | 2.2500 | 0.0563 | 0.1250 |
| 0.6750 | 5.0000 | -2.3750 | -0.1250 | 0.0250 | 0.0000 | 5.0000 | 4.0000 | 0.3250 | 1.0000 | 2.3750 | 0.0594 | 0.1250 |
| 0.7000 | 5.0000 | -2.5000 | -0.1250 | 0.0250 | 0.0000 | 5.0000 | 4.0000 | 0.3000 | 1.0000 | 2.5000 | 0.0625 | 0.1250 |
| 0.7250 | 5.0000 | -2.6250 | -0.1250 | 0.0250 | 0.0000 | 5.0000 | 4.0000 | 0.2750 | 1.0000 | 2.6250 | 0.0656 | 0.1250 |
| 0.7500 | 5.0000 | -2.7500 | -0.1250 | 0.0250 | 0.0000 | 5.0000 | 4.0000 | 0.2500 | 1.0000 | 2.7500 | 0.0688 | 0.1250 |
| 0.7750 | 5.0000 | -2.8750 | -0.1250 | 0.0250 | 0.0000 | 5.0000 | 4.0000 | 0.2250 | 1.0000 | 2.8750 | 0.0719 | 0.1250 |
| 0.8000 | 5.0000 | -3.0000 | -0.1250 | 0.0250 | 0.0000 | 5.0000 | 4.0000 | 0.2000 | 1.0000 | 3.0000 | 0.0750 | 0.1250 |
| 0.8250 | 5.0000 | -3.1250 | -0.1250 | 0.0250 | 0.0000 | 5.0000 | 4.0000 | 0.1750 | 1.0000 | 3.1250 | 0.0781 | 0.1250 |
| 0.8500 | 5.0000 | -3.2500 | -0.1250 | 0.0250 | 0.0000 | 5.0000 | 4.0000 | 0.1500 | 1.0000 | 3.2500 | 0.0813 | 0.1250 |
| 0.8750 | 5.0000 | -3.3750 | -0.1250 | 0.0250 | 0.0000 | 5.0000 | 4.0000 | 0.1250 | 1.0000 | 3.3750 | 0.0844 | 0.1250 |
| 0.9000 | 5.0000 | -3.5000 | -0.1250 | 0.0250 | 0.0000 | 5.0000 | 4.0000 | 0.1000 | 1.0000 | 3.5000 | 0.0875 | 0.1250 |
| 0.9250 | 5.0000 | -3.6250 | -0.1250 | 0.0250 | 0.0000 | 5.0000 | 4.0000 | 0.0750 | 1.0000 | 3.6250 | 0.0906 | 0.1250 |
| 0.9500 | 5.0000 | -3.7500 | -0.1250 | 0.0250 | 0.0000 | 5.0000 | 4.0000 | 0.0500 | 1.0000 | 3.7500 | 0.0938 | 0.1250 |
| 0.9750 | 5.0000 | -3.8750 | -0.1250 | 0.0250 | 0.0000 | 5.0000 | 4.0000 | 0.0250 | 1.0000 | 3.8750 | 0.0969 | 0.1250 |
| 1.0000 | 5.0000 | -4.0000 | -0.1250 | 0.0250 | 0.0000 | 5.0000 | 4.0000 | 0.0000 | 1.0000 | 4.0000 | 0.1000 | 0.1250 |

y(0)  1.00  Free
y(2)  1.00  1.00

Assumptions on costs:
c: Cost of Production
v: Cost of Storage

Transversality condition λ(T) = 0

1.56     5.00

*Phase I* time interval $t_{ou} \in [0, \tau] \Rightarrow u^*(t) = 0$ and $y^*(t) = -5t + 1$

*Phase II* time interval $t_{oc} \in (\tau, 1] \Rightarrow u^*(t) = D = 5$ and $y^*(t) = 0$

FIGURE 10.10-4

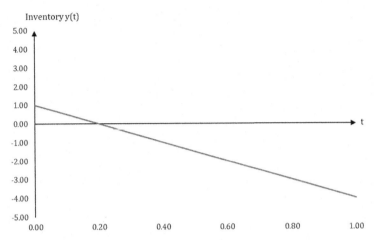

**FIGURE 10.10-5**    Inventory unconstrained optimal path $y^*(t) = -5t + 1$.

The production control in *Phase II* can be activated in Excel through the following simple VBA code:

The macro starts at *Cell* C1 and once it meets the value $\cong 0$, the point at which the initial inventory has been exhausted via the unconstrained policy (i.e., *Cell* $C_k < \varepsilon = 0.00005$), then it activates the control $u(t) = D$, which means that the demand will be satisfied entirely by the current production.

The numerical solution after running the Excel Macro is in Table 10.10-4.

The optimal control policy for the two phases is shown in Fig. 10.10-7, while the optimal path of the inventory $y^*(t)$ is in Fig. 10.10-8.

It is worth to notice how the results obtained are consistent with the modern techniques of the *lean manufacturing* and *just in time* that both aim at the minimization of the stock and the related costs.

Notice also that, in the context of the financial statements accounting, the following equation of motion:

$$\dot{y}(t) = u(t) - D(t)$$

corresponds to the inventory accounting relationship:

$$EI - BI = P - COGS,$$

```
Sub Control_Inventory()

Range("c1").Select

   Do Until ActiveCell < 0.00005

   ActiveCell.Offset(1, 0).Select

Loop


ActiveCell.Offset(0, 0).AddComment.Text Text:= _
   "Inventory exhausted activate control"


' Activate control u = Demand cell column F = cells Column B

   ActiveCell.Offset(1, 3) = ActiveCell.Offset(1, -1)

   ' Start now from first control activated in column F
   ' Activate control u: cells column F = cells Column C

ActiveCell.Offset(1, 3).Select

Do Until ActiveCell = 0


ActiveCell.Offset(1, 0).Select

ActiveCell.Offset(0, 0) = ActiveCell.Offset(0, -4)
Loop
```

FIGURE 10.10-6   VBA code with loops to implement the control policy.

where $EI$ = Ending Inventory, $BI$=Beginning Inventory, $P$=Purchases, and $COGS$=Cost of Goods Sold. The change in inventory is affected by two events: the purchase or manufacture of goods ($P$) and their subsequent sale ($COGS$).

## 10.11 Steepest descent numerical approach for optimal control problems using VBA

The procedure to solve an optimal control problem via the numerical technique of the *steepest descent* method goes through the following basic steps.

1. Simulate an approximate control variable path as initial guess, denoted by $u^{(0)}(t)$, over the time interval $[t_0, T]$ and store it in the Excel worksheet.
2. We will see the following two cases:

**TABLE 10.10-4**  Example 2: inventory problem constrained solution.

| t | Demand | y inventory | dy=(u-D)dt | dt | Control variable = Quantity Produced u = y + D | y = u-D | Hamiltonian = (cu+sy)+λ(u-D) | λ[t] | dλ/dt = -s | F = cu+sy | Z = ∫(cu+sy)dt | Σ dt |
|---|---|---|---|---|---|---|---|---|---|---|---|---|
| 0.0000 | 5.0000 | 1.0000 | 0.1250 | 0.0250 | 0.0000 | 5.0000 | 4.0000 | -1.0000 | 0.0000 | 1.0000 | 0.0210 | 0.1250 |
| 0.0250 | 5.0000 | 0.8750 | 0.1250 | 0.0250 | 0.0000 | 5.0000 | 4.0000 | 0.9750 | 1.0000 | 0.8750 | 0.0188 | 0.1250 |
| 0.0500 | 5.0000 | 0.7500 | 0.1250 | 0.0250 | 0.0000 | 5.0000 | 4.0000 | 0.9500 | 1.0000 | 0.7500 | 0.0166 | 0.1250 |
| 0.0750 | 5.0000 | 0.6250 | 0.1250 | 0.0250 | 0.0000 | 5.0000 | 4.0000 | 0.9250 | 1.0000 | 0.6250 | 0.0125 | 0.1250 |
| 0.1000 | 5.0000 | 0.5000 | 0.1250 | 0.0250 | 0.0000 | 5.0000 | 4.0000 | 0.9000 | 1.0000 | 0.5000 | 0.0094 | 0.1250 |
| 0.1250 | 5.0000 | 0.3750 | 0.1250 | 0.0250 | 0.0000 | 5.0000 | 4.0000 | 0.8750 | 1.0000 | 0.3750 | 0.0063 | 0.1250 |
| 0.1500 | 5.0000 | 0.2500 | 0.1250 | 0.0250 | 0.0000 | 5.0000 | 4.0000 | 0.8500 | 1.0000 | 0.2500 | 0.0031 | 0.1250 |
| 0.1750 | 5.0000 | 0.1250 | 0.1250 | 0.0250 | 0.0000 | 5.0000 | 4.0000 | 0.8250 | 1.0000 | 0.1250 | 0.0000 | 0.1250 |
| 0.2000 | 5.0000 | 0.0000 | -0.1250 | 0.0250 | 0.0000 | 5.0000 | 4.0000 | 0.8000 | 1.0000 | 0.0000 | 0.1250 | 0.1250 |
| 0.2250 | 5.0000 | 0.0000 | 0.0000 | 0.0250 | 5.0000 | 0.0000 | 5.0000 | 0.7750 | 1.0000 | 5.0000 | 0.1250 | 0.1250 |
| 0.2500 | 5.0000 | 0.0000 | 0.0000 | 0.0250 | 5.0000 | 0.0000 | 5.0000 | 0.7500 | 1.0000 | 5.0000 | 0.1250 | 0.1250 |
| 0.2750 | 5.0000 | 0.0000 | 0.0000 | 0.0250 | 5.0000 | 0.0000 | 5.0000 | 0.7250 | 1.0000 | 5.0000 | 0.1250 | 0.1250 |
| 0.3000 | 5.0000 | 0.0000 | 0.0000 | 0.0250 | 5.0000 | 0.0000 | 5.0000 | 0.7000 | 1.0000 | 5.0000 | 0.1250 | 0.1250 |
| 0.3250 | 5.0000 | 0.0000 | 0.0000 | 0.0250 | 5.0000 | 0.0000 | 5.0000 | 0.6750 | 1.0000 | 5.0000 | 0.1250 | 0.1250 |
| 0.3500 | 5.0000 | 0.0000 | 0.0000 | 0.0250 | 5.0000 | 0.0000 | 5.0000 | 0.6500 | 1.0000 | 5.0000 | 0.1250 | 0.1250 |
| 0.3750 | 5.0000 | 0.0000 | 0.0000 | 0.0250 | 5.0000 | 0.0000 | 5.0000 | 0.6250 | 1.0000 | 5.0000 | 0.1250 | 0.1250 |
| 0.4000 | 5.0000 | 0.0000 | 0.0000 | 0.0250 | 5.0000 | 0.0000 | 5.0000 | 0.6000 | 1.0000 | 5.0000 | 0.1250 | 0.1250 |
| 0.4250 | 5.0000 | 0.0000 | 0.0000 | 0.0250 | 5.0000 | 0.0000 | 5.0000 | 0.5750 | 1.0000 | 5.0000 | 0.1250 | 0.1250 |
| 0.4500 | 5.0000 | 0.0000 | 0.0000 | 0.0250 | 5.0000 | 0.0000 | 5.0000 | 0.5500 | 1.0000 | 5.0000 | 0.1250 | 0.1250 |
| 0.4750 | 5.0000 | 0.0000 | 0.0000 | 0.0250 | 5.0000 | 0.0000 | 5.0000 | 0.5250 | 1.0000 | 5.0000 | 0.1250 | 0.1250 |
| 0.5000 | 5.0000 | 0.0000 | 0.0000 | 0.0250 | 5.0000 | 0.0000 | 5.0000 | 0.5000 | 1.0000 | 5.0000 | 0.1250 | 0.1250 |
| 0.5250 | 5.0000 | 0.0000 | 0.0000 | 0.0250 | 5.0000 | 0.0000 | 5.0000 | 0.4750 | 1.0000 | 5.0000 | 0.1250 | 0.1250 |
| 0.5500 | 5.0000 | 0.0000 | 0.0000 | 0.0250 | 5.0000 | 0.0000 | 5.0000 | 0.4500 | 1.0000 | 5.0000 | 0.1250 | 0.1250 |
| 0.5750 | 5.0000 | 0.0000 | 0.0000 | 0.0250 | 5.0000 | 0.0000 | 5.0000 | 0.4250 | 1.0000 | 5.0000 | 0.1250 | 0.1250 |
| 0.6000 | 5.0000 | 0.0000 | 0.0000 | 0.0250 | 5.0000 | 0.0000 | 5.0000 | 0.4000 | 1.0000 | 5.0000 | 0.1250 | 0.1250 |
| 0.6250 | 5.0000 | 0.0000 | 0.0000 | 0.0250 | 5.0000 | 0.0000 | 5.0000 | 0.3750 | 1.0000 | 5.0000 | 0.1250 | 0.1250 |
| 0.6500 | 5.0000 | 0.0000 | 0.0000 | 0.0250 | 5.0000 | 0.0000 | 5.0000 | 0.3500 | 1.0000 | 5.0000 | 0.1250 | 0.1250 |
| 0.6750 | 5.0000 | 0.0000 | 0.0000 | 0.0250 | 5.0000 | 0.0000 | 5.0000 | 0.3250 | 1.0000 | 5.0000 | 0.1250 | 0.1250 |
| 0.7000 | 5.0000 | 0.0000 | 0.0000 | 0.0250 | 5.0000 | 0.0000 | 5.0000 | 0.3000 | 1.0000 | 5.0000 | 0.1250 | 0.1250 |
| 0.7250 | 5.0000 | 0.0000 | 0.0000 | 0.0250 | 5.0000 | 0.0000 | 5.0000 | 0.2750 | 1.0000 | 5.0000 | 0.1250 | 0.1250 |
| 0.7500 | 5.0000 | 0.0000 | 0.0000 | 0.0250 | 5.0000 | 0.0000 | 5.0000 | 0.2500 | 1.0000 | 5.0000 | 0.1250 | 0.1250 |
| 0.7750 | 5.0000 | 0.0000 | 0.0000 | 0.0250 | 5.0000 | 0.0000 | 5.0000 | 0.2250 | 1.0000 | 5.0000 | 0.1250 | 0.1250 |
| 0.8000 | 5.0000 | 0.0000 | 0.0000 | 0.0250 | 5.0000 | 0.0000 | 5.0000 | 0.2000 | 1.0000 | 5.0000 | 0.1250 | 0.1250 |
| 0.8250 | 5.0000 | 0.0000 | 0.0000 | 0.0250 | 5.0000 | 0.0000 | 5.0000 | 0.1750 | 1.0000 | 5.0000 | 0.1250 | 0.1250 |
| 0.8500 | 5.0000 | 0.0000 | 0.0000 | 0.0250 | 5.0000 | 0.0000 | 5.0000 | 0.1500 | 1.0000 | 5.0000 | 0.1250 | 0.1250 |
| 0.8750 | 5.0000 | 0.0000 | 0.0000 | 0.0250 | 5.0000 | 0.0000 | 5.0000 | 0.1250 | 1.0000 | 5.0000 | 0.1250 | 0.1250 |
| 0.9000 | 5.0000 | 0.0000 | 0.0000 | 0.0250 | 5.0000 | 0.0000 | 5.0000 | 0.1000 | 1.0000 | 5.0000 | 0.1250 | 0.1250 |
| 0.9250 | 5.0000 | 0.0000 | 0.0000 | 0.0250 | 5.0000 | 0.0000 | 5.0000 | 0.0750 | 1.0000 | 5.0000 | 0.1250 | 0.1250 |
| 0.9500 | 5.0000 | 0.0000 | 0.0000 | 0.0250 | 5.0000 | 0.0000 | 5.0000 | 0.0500 | 1.0000 | 5.0000 | 0.1250 | 0.1250 |
| 0.9750 | 5.0000 | 0.0000 | 0.0000 | 0.0250 | 5.0000 | 0.0000 | 5.0000 | 0.0250 | 1.0000 | 5.0000 | 0.1250 | 0.1250 |
| 1.0000 | 5.0000 | 0.0000 | 0.0000 | 0.0250 | 5.0000 | 0.0000 | 5.0000 | 0.0000 | 1.0000 | 5.0000 | 0.1250 | 0.1250 |

y(0) = 1.00  Free

x(2) = 5.0000

Assumptions on costs:
c: Cost of Production = 1.00
s: Cost of Storage = 1.00

Transversality condition λ(T) = 0

Z = -4.09    Σ = 5.00

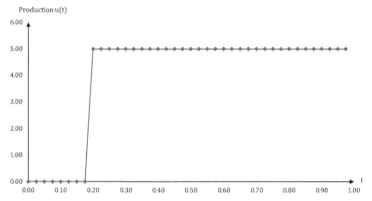

**FIGURE 10.10-7**  Example 2: optimal production policy $u^*(t)$ in Phase I and Phase II.

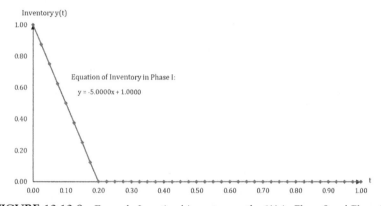

**FIGURE 10.10-8**  Example 2: optimal inventory path $y^*(t)$ in Phase I and Phase II.

**a.** vertical-terminal-line problem where $y(0) = y_0$ and $y(T)$ is free and $\lambda(T) = 0$. Integrate forward over y(t) while integrate backward over $\lambda(t)$.

**b.** *bounded* problem where $y(0) = y_0$ and $y(T) = y_T$ and no restriction is required on $\lambda(T)$. Integrate backward over y(t) while integrate forward over $\lambda(t)$.

**3.** If the following, *stopping criterion* is satisfied:

$$\frac{d\mathcal{H}^{(0)}}{du}(t) = 0 \qquad \forall \; t \in [t_0, T]$$

terminate the iterative procedure otherwise go to the following steps.

**4.** Generate a new policy given by:

$$u^{(1)}(t) = u^{(0)}(t) + \tau \frac{d\mathcal{H}^{(0)}(t)}{du}.$$

III. Dynamic optimization

**5.** If it is still happening that:

$$\frac{d\mathcal{H}^{(1)}}{du}(t) \neq 0,$$

then keep on generating a new control policy iteration as:

$$u^{(i+1)}(t) = u^{(i)}(t) + \tau\frac{d\mathcal{H}^{i}(t)}{du}$$

and stop at the *kth* iteration so that:

$$\frac{d\mathcal{H}^{(k+1)}}{du}(t) = 0 \qquad \forall\ t \in [t_0, T]$$

## EXAMPLE 1 (CASE A. WITH TRANSVERSALITY CONDITION $\lambda(T) = 0$)

Let us go back to Example 1 of Section 10.1:

$$\max_{\{u\}} J(u) = \int_0^1 \left(y - \frac{1}{2}u^2\right)dt$$

$$s.t.\ \dot{y} = u - y \text{ and } y(0) = 1,\ y(1) = \textit{free}$$

According to the transversality condition of the problem, it must be $\lambda(T) = 0$ so that we implement a backward integration over $\lambda(t)$ and a forward integration over $y(t)$.

The worksheet setup of the OC problem becomes (Fig. 10.11-1):

| | A: τ | B: y(t) | C: dy = (u-y)dt | D: dt | E: Investment u = ẏ+y | F: dy/dt = λ-y | G: Hamiltonian = (y-1/2u²)+λ(u-y) | H: λ(t) | I: dλ/dt | J: F = y-1/2u² | K: Functional = Σ[y-1/2u²]dt | Q: dH/du = -u+λ |
|---|---|---|---|---|---|---|---|---|---|---|---|---|
| 2 | 0 | 0 | | | =F2+B2 | =M2-B2 | 0 | =H3-I3*D3 | =-1+H2 | =B2-1/2*E2^2 | =J2*D2 | |
| 3 | =A2+0.05 | =B2+C3 | =(E3-B3)*D3 | =A3-A2 | =U3+0.1*V3 | =M3-B3 | =J3+H3*F3 | =H4-I4*D4 | =-1+H3 | =B3-1/2*E3^2 | =J3*D3 | =-E3+H3 |
| 4 | =A3+0.05 | =B3+C4 | =(E4-B4)*D4 | =A4-A3 | =U4+0.1*V4 | =M4-B4 | =J4+H4*F4 | =H5-I5*D5 | =-1+H4 | =B4-1/2*E4^2 | =J4*D4 | =-E4+H4 |
| 5 | =A4+0.05 | =B4+C5 | =(E5-B5)*D5 | =A5-A4 | =U5+0.1*V5 | =M5-B5 | =J5+H5*F5 | =H6-I6*D6 | =-1+H5 | =B5-1/2*E5^2 | =J5*D5 | =-E5+H5 |
| 6 | =A5+0.05 | =B5+C6 | =(E6-B6)*D6 | =A6-A5 | =U6+0.1*V6 | =M6-B6 | =J6+H6*F6 | =H7-I7*D7 | =-1+H6 | =B6-1/2*E6^2 | =J6*D6 | =-E6+H6 |
| 7 | =A6+0.05 | =B6+C7 | =(E7-B7)*D7 | =A7-A6 | =U7+0.1*V7 | =M7-B7 | =J7+H7*F7 | =H8-I8*D8 | =-1+H7 | =B7-1/2*E7^2 | =J7*D7 | =-E7+H7 |
| 8 | =A7+0.05 | =B7+C8 | =(E8-B8)*D8 | =A8-A7 | =U8+0.1*V8 | =M8-B8 | =J8+H8*F8 | =H9-I9*D9 | =-1+H8 | =B8-1/2*E8^2 | =J8*D8 | =-E8+H8 |
| 9 | =A8+0.05 | =B8+C9 | =(E9-B9)*D9 | =A9-A8 | =U9+0.1*V9 | =M9-B9 | =J9+H9*F9 | =H10-I10*D10 | =-1+H9 | =B9-1/2*E9^2 | =J9*D9 | =-E9+H9 |
| 10 | =A9+0.05 | =B9+C10 | =(E10-B10)*D10 | =A10-A9 | =U10+0.1*V10 | =M10-B10 | =J10+H10*F10 | =H11-I11*D11 | =-1+H10 | =B10-1/2*E10^2 | =J10*D10 | =-E10+H10 |
| 11 | =A10+0.05 | =B10+C11 | =(E11-B11)*D11 | =A11-A10 | =U11+0.1*V11 | =M11-B11 | =J11+H11*F11 | =H12-I12*D12 | =-1+H11 | =B11-1/2*E11^2 | =J11*D11 | =-E11+H11 |
| 12 | =A11+0.05 | =B11+C12 | =(E12-B12)*D12 | =A12-A11 | =U12+0.1*V12 | =M12-B12 | =J12+H12*F12 | =H13-I13*D13 | =-1+H12 | =B12-1/2*E12^2 | =J12*D12 | =-E12+H12 |
| 13 | =A12+0.05 | =B12+C13 | =(E13-B13)*D13 | =A13-A12 | =U13+0.1*V13 | =M13-B13 | =J13+H13*F13 | =H14-I14*D14 | =-1+H13 | =B13-1/2*E13^2 | =J13*D13 | =-E13+H13 |
| 14 | =A13+0.05 | =B13+C14 | =(E14-B14)*D14 | =A14-A13 | =U14+0.1*V14 | =M14-B14 | =J14+H14*F14 | =H15-I15*D15 | =-1+H14 | =B14-1/2*E14^2 | =J14*D14 | =-E14+H14 |
| 15 | =A14+0.05 | =B14+C15 | =(E15-B15)*D15 | =A15-A14 | =U15+0.1*V15 | =M15-B15 | =J15+H15*F15 | =H16-I16*D16 | =-1+H15 | =B15-1/2*E15^2 | =J15*D15 | =-E15+H15 |
| 16 | =A15+0.05 | =B15+C16 | =(E16-B16)*D16 | =A16-A15 | =U16+0.1*V16 | =M16-B16 | =J16+H16*F16 | =H17-I17*D17 | =-1+H16 | =B16-1/2*E16^2 | =J16*D16 | =-E16+H16 |
| 17 | =A16+0.05 | =B16+C17 | =(E17-B17)*D17 | =A17-A16 | =U17+0.1*V17 | =M17-B17 | =J17+H17*F17 | =H18-I18*D18 | =-1+H17 | =B17-1/2*E17^2 | =J17*D17 | =-E17+H17 |
| 18 | =A17+0.05 | =B17+C18 | =(E18-B18)*D18 | =A18-A17 | =U18+0.1*V18 | =M18-B18 | =J18+H18*F18 | =H19-I19*D19 | =-1+H18 | =B18-1/2*E18^2 | =J18*D18 | =-E18+H18 |
| 19 | =A18+0.05 | =B18+C19 | =(E19-B19)*D19 | =A19-A18 | =U19+0.1*V19 | =M19-B19 | =J19+H19*F19 | =H20-I20*D20 | =-1+H19 | =B19-1/2*E19^2 | =J19*D19 | =-E19+H19 |
| 20 | =A19+0.05 | =B19+C20 | =(E20-B20)*D20 | =A20-A19 | =U20+0.1*V20 | =M20-B20 | =J20+H20*F20 | =H21-I21*D21 | =-1+H20 | =B20-1/2*E20^2 | =J20*D20 | =-E20+H20 |
| 21 | =A20+0.05 | =B20+C21 | =(E21-B21)*D21 | =A21-A20 | =U21+0.1*V21 | =M21-B21 | =J21+H21*F21 | =H22-I22*D22 | =-1+H21 | =B21-1/2*E21^2 | =J21*D21 | =-E21+H21 |
| 22 | =A21+0.05 | =B21+C22 | =(E22-B22)*D22 | =A22-A21 | =U22+0.1*V22 | =M22-B22 | =J22+H22*F22 | 0 | =-1+H22 | =B22-1/2*E22^2 | =J22*D22 | =-E22+H22 |
| 24 | y(0) | 0 | y(t) integrated forward | while λ(t) backward | | | Transversality condition λ(T) =0 | | | | =SUM(K3:K22) | =ABS(ROUND(SUM(Q3:Q22)^2;5)) |
| 25 | y(1) | Free | | | | | | | | | | |

**FIGURE 10.11-1**   Example 1: worksheet setup for steepest descent.

The key difference from the standard Solver worksheet setup is how we obtain the control policy *Column E* and costate variable *Column H*.

*Column E* is equal to the following iteration policy where $\tau = 0.1$.

$$u^{(i+1)}(t) = u^{(i)}(t) + \tau \frac{d\mathcal{H}^i(t)}{du}$$

while *Column H* represents the backward in time integration of the costate variable $\lambda(t)$.

This is simply done as follows:

from:

$$(\lambda_{t+1} - \lambda_t) / \Delta_t = \lambda'_t$$

we determine $\lambda_t$ as:

$$\lambda_t = \lambda_{t+1} - (\Delta_t)(\lambda'_t)$$

with final condition to integrate backward in time $\lambda(T) = 0$.

Under *Column U* and *Column V* we store the values of $u^{(i)}(t)$ and $\frac{d\mathcal{H}^i(t)}{du}$ during the iteration process. The stopping criterion is stored in *Cell Q24*.

Starting with $u^0(t) = 0.1$ we obtain a first nonoptimal output as given in Table 10.11-1. Notice that the stopping criterion is not obviously satisfied with the first guess $u^{(0)}(t)$.

The VBA code of the iteration process is developed as follows in Fig. 10.11-2:

Notice how the macro does not perform any calculation, as these are all implemented in the worksheet; the macro just simply moves the calculated values from one area of the worksheet to another area to allow the iteration process *Do Until*, that is to be stopped when the given criterion in *Cell Q24* is satisfied.

The final solution is given in Table 10.11-2 where the stopping criterion equals to zero, while Fig. 10.11-3 compares the steepest descent solution path $y^*(t)$ against the exact solution.

## EXAMPLE 2 (CASE 2.B WITH BOUNDARY CONDITION Y(T) = Y$_T$)

Let us solve now with the steepest descent Example 2 of Section 10.1.

$$\max_{\{u\}} J(u) = \int_0^1 \left(2y - \frac{1}{2}u^2\right) dt$$

$$s.t. \quad \dot{y} = u - y \text{ and } y(0) = 0, \; y(1) = 0$$

In this case, we need to integrate backward over time the state variable $y(t)$ s.t. to the constraint $y(1) = 0$.

Then, we will need to integrate forward $\lambda(t)$ finding the optimal $\lambda(0)$ that leads to the initial value condition $y(0) = 0$. This step will be performed via the Excel Solver, and it represents the necessary prerequisite before running the VBA macro for the steepest descent iteration.

**TABLE 10.11-1**   Example 1: Excel nonoptimal output with first guess $u^{(0)} = 0.1$

| t | y(t) | dy - (u y)dt | dt | Investment u=y+y | dy/dt=z₂y | Hamiltonian = (y 1/2u²)-(u+y) | z(t) | dz/dt | F = y 1/2u² | Functional = Σ (y 1/2u²)dt | dH/du = u-z |
|---|------|--------------|----|------------------|-----------|-------------------------------|------|-------|-------------|----------------------------|-------------|
| 0.0000 | 0.0000 |        |        | 0.6415 | 0.6415 | 0.0000 | 0.6415 | 0.3585 | 0.2058 | 0.0000 | 0.5226 |
| 0.0500 | 0.0048 | 0.0048 | 0.0500 | 0.1000 | 0.6179 | 0.3845 | 0.6226 | 0.3774 | -0.0002 | 0.0000 | 0.5028 |
| 0.1000 | 0.0093 | 0.0045 | 0.0500 | 0.1000 | 0.5935 | 0.3620 | 0.6028 | 0.3972 | 0.0043 | 0.0002 | 0.4819 |
| 0.1500 | 0.0136 | 0.0043 | 0.0500 | 0.1000 | 0.5683 | 0.3293 | 0.5819 | 0.4181 | 0.0086 | 0.0004 | 0.4599 |
| 0.2000 | 0.0177 | 0.0041 | 0.0500 | 0.1000 | 0.5421 | 0.3163 | 0.5599 | 0.4401 | 0.0127 | 0.0006 | 0.4399 |
| 0.2500 | 0.0216 | 0.0039 | 0.0500 | 0.1000 | 0.5151 | 0.2931 | 0.5367 | 0.4633 | 0.0166 | 0.0008 | 0.4367 |
| 0.3000 | 0.0254 | 0.0037 | 0.0500 | 0.1000 | 0.4869 | 0.2699 | 0.5123 | 0.4877 | 0.0204 | 0.0010 | 0.4123 |
| 0.3500 | 0.0289 | 0.0036 | 0.0500 | 0.1000 | 0.4577 | 0.2467 | 0.4867 | 0.5133 | 0.0239 | 0.0012 | 0.3867 |
| 0.4000 | 0.0323 | 0.0034 | 0.0500 | 0.1000 | 0.4273 | 0.2227 | 0.4596 | 0.5404 | 0.0273 | 0.0014 | 0.3596 |
| 0.4500 | 0.0355 | 0.0032 | 0.0500 | 0.1000 | 0.3957 | 0.2011 | 0.4312 | 0.5688 | 0.0305 | 0.0015 | 0.3312 |
| 0.5000 | 0.0386 | 0.0031 | 0.0500 | 0.1000 | 0.3627 | 0.1791 | 0.4013 | 0.5987 | 0.0336 | 0.0017 | 0.3013 |
| 0.5500 | 0.0415 | 0.0029 | 0.0500 | 0.1000 | 0.3282 | 0.1579 | 0.3698 | 0.6302 | 0.0365 | 0.0018 | 0.2698 |
| 0.6000 | 0.0443 | 0.0028 | 0.0500 | 0.1000 | 0.2923 | 0.1377 | 0.3366 | 0.6634 | 0.0393 | 0.0020 | 0.2366 |
| 0.6500 | 0.0470 | 0.0027 | 0.0500 | 0.1000 | 0.2547 | 0.1288 | 0.3017 | 0.6983 | 0.0420 | 0.0021 | 0.2017 |
| 0.7000 | 0.0495 | 0.0025 | 0.0500 | 0.1000 | 0.2154 | 0.1016 | 0.2649 | 0.7251 | 0.0445 | 0.0022 | 0.1649 |
| 0.7500 | 0.0519 | 0.0024 | 0.0500 | 0.1000 | 0.1743 | 0.0863 | 0.2262 | 0.7738 | 0.0469 | 0.0023 | 0.1262 |
| 0.8000 | 0.0542 | 0.0023 | 0.0500 | 0.1000 | 0.1313 | 0.0735 | 0.1855 | 0.8145 | 0.0492 | 0.0025 | 0.0855 |
| 0.8500 | 0.0564 | 0.0022 | 0.0500 | 0.1000 | 0.0963 | 0.0637 | 0.1426 | 0.8574 | 0.0514 | 0.0026 | 0.0426 |
| 0.9000 | 0.0584 | 0.0021 | 0.0500 | 0.1000 | 0.0391 | 0.0573 | 0.0975 | 0.9025 | 0.0534 | 0.0027 | -0.0025 |
| 0.9500 | 0.0604 | 0.0020 | 0.0500 | 0.1000 | -0.0104 | 0.0549 | 0.0500 | 0.9500 | 0.0554 | 0.0028 | -0.0500 |
| 1.0000 | 0.0623 | 0.0019 | 0.0500 | 0.1000 | -0.0623 | 0.0573 | 0.0000 | 1.0000 | 0.0573 | 0.0029 | -0.1000 |

y(0)   0.00      y(t) integrated forward while z(t) backward      0.8327    26.7260

y(1)   Free      Transversality condition z(T)=0

```
Sub Steepest_descent()
Do Until Range("q24") = 0
' Guess first iteration u(0)=0.10
' under Column U and values = 0 under Column V dH/du
' Copy the control policy u(0)=0.1 from Column E to Column X

    Range("E3").Select
    Range(Selection, Selection.End(xlDown)).Select
    Selection.Copy
        ' Store it under column X temporarily
        ActiveWindow.SmallScroll Down:=-27
        Range("X3").Select
    Selection.PasteSpecial Paste:=xlPasteValues, Operation:=xlNone, SkipBlanks _
        :=False, Transpose:=False

    ' Copy dH(0)/du deriving from the first guess iteration
    ' from column Q to V

    Range("Q3").Select
    Range(Selection, Selection.End(xlDown)).Select
    Application.CutCopyMode = False
    Selection.Copy
    ActiveWindow.SmallScroll Down:=-33
        Range("V3").Select
    Selection.PasteSpecial Paste:=xlPasteValues, Operation:=xlNone, SkipBlanks _
        :=False, Transpose:=False

        ' It moves the control policy u(0)from Column X
        ' to Column U then it calculuates u(1) under Column E and Loop continues
    Range("X3").Select
    Range(Selection, Selection.End(xlDown)).Select
    Application.CutCopyMode = False
    Selection.Copy
    ActiveWindow.SmallScroll Down:=-30
        Range("U3").Select
    Selection.PasteSpecial Paste:=xlPasteValues, Operation:=xlNone, SkipBlanks _
        :=False, Transpose:=False
    Application.CutCopyMode = False
    Loop
```

**FIGURE 10.11-2**   Example 1 VBA code for the steepest descent iteration process.

Essentially, we first optimize over $\lambda(t)$ and then over $u(t)$ and $y(t)$ via the steepest descent procedure (Fig. 10.10-4).

Notice the backward integration under *Column B* and the forward integration under *Column H*.

The Solver in Fig. 10.11-5 will find the optimal $\lambda(0)$ to have the initial boundary condition on the state variable satisfied.

The optimal steepest descent solution is in Table 10.11-3 and Fig. 10.11-6.

## 10.12  Checking the sufficient conditions in Excel

As we mentioned at the beginning of this chapter, the maximum principle represents a set of necessary that in general are not sufficient.

When certain concavity conditions are satisfied these necessary conditions become sufficient for the maximization.

**TABLE 10.11-2**  Example 1: steepest descent numerical solution.

| t | y(t) | dy=(u-y)dt | dt | Investment u=y+y' | dy/dt=u-y | Hamiltonian=(y-1/2u²)+λ(u-y) | λ(t) | dλ/dt | F=y-1/2u² | Functional=-∫(y-1/2u²)dt | dH/du=u-uλ |
|---|---|---|---|---|---|---|---|---|---|---|---|
| 0.00000 | 0.0000 |  | 0.0500 | 0.6415 | 0.6415 | 0.0000 | 0.6415 | 0.3585 | 0.2928 | 0.0000 |  |
| 0.0500 | 0.0296 | 0.0296 | 0.0500 | 0.6224 | 0.5985 | 0.2052 | 0.6226 | 0.3774 | 0.1641 | 0.0082 | 0.0002 |
| 0.1000 | 0.0569 | 0.0273 | 0.0500 | 0.6026 | 0.5459 | 0.2044 | 0.6028 | 0.3972 | 0.1246 | 0.0062 | 0.0002 |
| 0.1500 | 0.0819 | 0.0250 | 0.0500 | 0.5817 | 0.5000 | 0.2037 | 0.5819 | 0.4181 | 0.0873 | 0.0044 | 0.0002 |
| 0.2000 | 0.1047 | 0.0229 | 0.0500 | 0.5597 | 0.4552 | 0.2029 | 0.5599 | 0.4401 | 0.0520 | 0.0026 | 0.0002 |
| 0.2500 | 0.1252 | 0.0206 | 0.0500 | 0.5365 | 0.4115 | 0.2021 | 0.5367 | 0.4633 | -0.0187 | -0.0009 | 0.0002 |
| 0.3000 | 0.1437 | 0.0184 | 0.0500 | 0.5122 | 0.3687 | 0.2014 | 0.5123 | 0.4877 | 0.0125 | 0.0006 | 0.0002 |
| 0.3500 | 0.1600 | 0.0163 | 0.0500 | 0.4865 | 0.3267 | 0.2006 | 0.4867 | 0.5133 | 0.0416 | 0.0021 | 0.0002 |
| 0.4000 | 0.1742 | 0.0143 | 0.0500 | 0.4595 | 0.2854 | 0.1999 | 0.4596 | 0.5404 | 0.0687 | 0.0034 | 0.0001 |
| 0.4500 | 0.1865 | 0.0122 | 0.0500 | 0.4311 | 0.2447 | 0.1991 | 0.4312 | 0.5688 | 0.0936 | 0.0047 | 0.0001 |
| 0.5000 | 0.1967 | 0.0102 | 0.0500 | 0.4011 | 0.2046 | 0.1983 | 0.4013 | 0.5987 | 0.1162 | 0.0058 | 0.0001 |
| 0.5500 | 0.2049 | 0.0082 | 0.0500 | 0.3696 | 0.1648 | 0.1976 | 0.3698 | 0.6302 | 0.1366 | 0.0068 | 0.0001 |
| 0.6000 | 0.2112 | 0.0063 | 0.0500 | 0.3365 | 0.1254 | 0.1968 | 0.3366 | 0.6634 | 0.1546 | 0.0077 | 0.0001 |
| 0.6500 | 0.2155 | 0.0043 | 0.0500 | 0.3016 | 0.0862 | 0.1960 | 0.3017 | 0.6983 | 0.1700 | 0.0085 | 0.0001 |
| 0.7000 | 0.2178 | 0.0023 | 0.0500 | 0.2648 | 0.0471 | 0.1952 | 0.2649 | 0.7351 | 0.1828 | 0.0091 | 0.0001 |
| 0.7500 | 0.2182 | 0.0004 | 0.0500 | 0.2262 | 0.0080 | 0.1945 | 0.2262 | 0.7738 | 0.1927 | 0.0096 | 0.0001 |
| 0.8000 | 0.2167 | -0.0016 | 0.0500 | 0.1855 | -0.0312 | 0.1937 | 0.1855 | 0.8145 | 0.1995 | 0.0100 | 0.0000 |
| 0.8500 | 0.2132 | -0.0035 | 0.0500 | 0.1426 | -0.0705 | 0.1929 | 0.1426 | 0.8574 | 0.2030 | 0.0101 | 0.0000 |
| 0.9000 | 0.2076 | -0.0055 | 0.0500 | 0.0975 | -0.1101 | 0.1922 | 0.0975 | 0.9025 | 0.2029 | 0.0101 | 0.0000 |
| 0.9500 | 0.2001 | -0.0075 | 0.0500 | 0.0500 | -0.1501 | 0.1914 | 0.0500 | 0.9500 | 0.1989 | 0.0099 | 0.0000 |
| 1.0000 | 0.1906 | -0.0095 | 0.0500 | 0.0000 | -0.1906 | 0.1906 | 0.0000 | 1.0000 | 0.1906 | 0.0095 | 0.0000 |
| y(0) | 0.00 |  |  |  |  |  |  |  |  | 0.0859 | 0.0000 |
| y(1) | Free |  |  |  |  |  | Transversality condition λ(T)=0 |  |  |  |  |

y(t) integrated forward while λ(t) backward

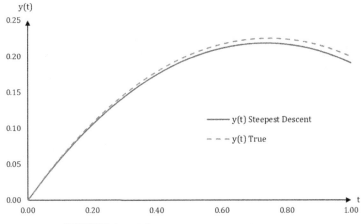

**FIGURE 10.11-3**   Example 1: optimal path $y^*(t)$.

| | A | B | C | D | E | F | G | H | I | J | K | Q |
|---|---|---|---|---|---|---|---|---|---|---|---|---|
| | t | y(t) | dy = (u-y)dt | dt | Investment u = y*y | dy/dt =λ-y | Hamiltonian = (2y- 1/2u²)+λ(u-y) | λ(t) | dλ/dt | F = 2y-1/2u² | Functional = Σ [2y- 1/2u²]dt | dH/du = -u+λ |
| 1 | | | | | | | | | | | | |
| 2 | 0 | =B3-F3*D3 | | | | | 0 | 0.966971273 | | | | |
| 3 | =A2+0.05 | =B4-F4*D4 | =(E3-B3)*D3 | =A3-A2 | =U3+0.1*V3 | =H3-B3 | =J3+H3*(E3-B3) | =H2+I3*D3 | =-2+H3 | =2*B3-1/2*E3^2 | =J3*D3 | =-E3+H3 |
| 4 | =A3+0.05 | =B5-F5*D5 | =(E4-B4)*D4 | =A4-A3 | =U4+0.1*V4 | =H4-B4 | =J4+H4*(E4-B4) | =H3+I4*D4 | =-2+H4 | =2*B4-1/2*E4^2 | =J4*D4 | =-E4+H4 |
| 5 | =A4+0.05 | =B6-F6*D6 | =(E5-B5)*D5 | =A5-A4 | =U5+0.1*V5 | =H5-B5 | =J5+H5*(E5-B5) | =H4+I5*D5 | =-2+H5 | =2*B5-1/2*E5^2 | =J5*D5 | =-E5+H5 |
| 6 | =A5+0.05 | =B7-F7*D7 | =(E6-B6)*D6 | =A6-A5 | =U6+0.1*V6 | =H6-B6 | =J6+H6*(E6-B6) | =H5+I6*D6 | =-2+H6 | =2*B6-1/2*E6^2 | =J6*D6 | =-E6+H6 |
| 7 | =A6+0.05 | =B8-F8*D8 | =(E7-B7)*D7 | =A7-A6 | =U7+0.1*V7 | =H7-B7 | =J7+H7*(E7-B7) | =H6+I7*D7 | =-2+H7 | =2*B7-1/2*E7^2 | =J7*D7 | =-E7+H7 |
| 8 | =A7+0.05 | =B9-F9*D9 | =(E8-B8)*D8 | =A8-A7 | =U8+0.1*V8 | =H8-B8 | =J8+H8*(E8-B8) | =H7+I8*D8 | =-2+H8 | =2*B8-1/2*E8^2 | =J8*D8 | =-E8+H8 |
| 9 | =A8+0.05 | =B10-F10*D10 | =(E9-B9)*D9 | =A9-A8 | =U9+0.1*V9 | =H9-B9 | =J9+H9*(E9-B9) | =H8+I9*D9 | =-2+H9 | =2*B9-1/2*E9^2 | =J9*D9 | =-E9+H9 |
| 10 | =A9+0.05 | =B11-F11*D11 | =(E10-B10)*D10 | =A10-A9 | =U10+0.1*V10 | =H10-B10 | =J10+H10*(E10-B10) | =H9+I10*D10 | =-2+H10 | =2*B10-1/2*E10^2 | =J10*D10 | =-E10+H10 |
| 11 | =A10+0.05 | =B12-F12*D12 | =(E11-B11)*D11 | =A11-A10 | =U11+0.1*V11 | =H11-B11 | =J11+H11*(E11-B11) | =H10+I11*D11 | =-2+H11 | =2*B11-1/2*E11^2 | =J11*D11 | =-E11+H11 |
| 12 | =A11+0.05 | =B13-F13*D13 | =(E12-B12)*D12 | =A12-A11 | =U12+0.1*V12 | =H12-B12 | =J12+H12*(E12-B12) | =H11+I12*D12 | =-2+H12 | =2*B12-1/2*E12^2 | =J12*D12 | =-E12+H12 |
| 13 | =A12+0.05 | =B14-F14*D14 | =(E13-B13)*D13 | =A13-A12 | =U13+0.1*V13 | =H13-B13 | =J13+H13*(E13-B13) | =H12+I13*D13 | =-2+H13 | =2*B13-1/2*E13^2 | =J13*D13 | =-E13+H13 |
| 14 | =A13+0.05 | =B15-F15*D15 | =(E14-B14)*D14 | =A14-A13 | =U14+0.1*V14 | =H14-B14 | =J14+H14*(E14-B14) | =H13+I14*D14 | =-2+H14 | =2*B14-1/2*E14^2 | =J14*D14 | =-E14+H14 |
| 15 | =A14+0.05 | =B16-F16*D16 | =(E15-B15)*D15 | =A15-A14 | =U15+0.1*V15 | =H15-B15 | =J15+H15*(E15-B15) | =H14+I15*D15 | =-2+H15 | =2*B15-1/2*E15^2 | =J15*D15 | =-E15+H15 |
| 16 | =A15+0.05 | =B17-F17*D17 | =(E16-B16)*D16 | =A16-A15 | =U16+0.1*V16 | =H16-B16 | =J16+H16*(E16-B16) | =H15+I16*D16 | =-2+H16 | =2*B16-1/2*E16^2 | =J16*D16 | =-E16+H16 |
| 17 | =A16+0.05 | =B18-F18*D18 | =(E17-B17)*D17 | =A17-A16 | =U17+0.1*V17 | =H17-B17 | =J17+H17*(E17-B17) | =H16+I17*D17 | =-2+H17 | =2*B17-1/2*E17^2 | =J17*D17 | =-E17+H17 |
| 18 | =A17+0.05 | =B19-F19*D19 | =(E18-B18)*D18 | =A18-A17 | =U18+0.1*V18 | =H18-B18 | =J18+H18*(E18-B18) | =H17+I18*D18 | =-2+H18 | =2*B18-1/2*E18^2 | =J18*D18 | =-E18+H18 |
| 19 | =A18+0.05 | =B20-F20*D20 | =(E19-B19)*D19 | =A19-A18 | =U19+0.1*V19 | =H19-B19 | =J19+H19*(E19-B19) | =H18+I19*D19 | =-2+H19 | =2*B19-1/2*E19^2 | =J19*D19 | =-E19+H19 |
| 20 | =A19+0.05 | =B21-F21*D21 | =(E20-B20)*D20 | =A20-A19 | =U20+0.1*V20 | =H20-B20 | =J20+H20*(E20-B20) | =H19+I20*D20 | =-2+H20 | =2*B20-1/2*E20^2 | =J20*D20 | =-E20+H20 |
| 21 | =A20+0.05 | =B22-F22*D22 | =(E21-B21)*D21 | =A21-A20 | =U21+0.1*V21 | =H21-B21 | =J21+H21*(E21-B21) | =H20+I21*D21 | =-2+H21 | =2*B21-1/2*E21^2 | =J21*D21 | =-E21+H21 |
| 22 | =A21+0.05 | 0 | =(E22-B22)*D22 | =A22-A21 | =U22+0.1*V22 | =H22-B22 | =J22+H22*(E22-B22) | =H21+I22*D22 | =-2+H22 | =2*B22-1/2*E22^2 | =J22*D22 | =-E22+H22 |
| 24 | y(0) | 0 | y(t) goes backward because of contraint y(T) = 0 while λ(t) goes forward | | | | | No Restriction on λ(T) | | | =SUM(K3:K22) | =ABS(ROUND(SUM(Q3:Q22)^2;5)) |
| 25 | y(1) | 0 | | | | | | | | | | |

**FIGURE 10.11-4**   Example 2: worksheet setup.

There are two theorems in the OC theory about the sufficient conditions.

**1.** The Mangasarian Sufficiency Theorem

In the problem of OC 10.1-1, the necessary conditions of the maximum principle 10.1-3 are also sufficient for the global maximization of $J(u)$ if (1) both the $F$ and $f$ are concave in the variables $(y, u)$ jointly, and (2) in the optimal solution is true that

$$\lambda(t) \geq 0 \quad \forall t \in [0, T].$$

If $f$ linear jointly in $(y, u)$ then $\lambda(t)$ does not require any sign restriction.

**2.** The Arrow Sufficiency Theorem

III. Dynamic optimization

**FIGURE 10.11-5**   Example 2: setting $y(1) = 0$ by changing $\lambda(0)$.

At any point in time, given the values of $y$ and $\lambda$, let the Hamiltonian function be maximized by a particular $u^*$, obtaining the maximized Hamiltonian as follows:

$$\mathcal{H}^0(t, y, u^*, \lambda) \overset{\text{def}}{=} F(t, y, u^*) + \lambda(t)f(t, y, u^*)$$

where $\mathcal{H}^0(t, y, u^*, \lambda)$ is now a function of the three arguments $(t, y, \lambda)$ that have not been substituted out.

The Arrow theorem states that the necessary conditions of the maximum principle 10.1-3 are also sufficient for the maximization of $J(u)$ if the maximized Hamiltonian $\mathcal{H}^0$ is concave in the variable $y$ for all $t \in [0, T]$ for a given $\lambda$.

Let us apply the Mangasarian sufficient conditions to the economic models proposed in Sections 10.5—10.7.

**TABLE 10.11-3** Example 2: steepest descent numerical solution.

| t | y(t) | dy = (u-y)/dt | dt | Investment u = $\dot{y}$+y | dy/dt = $\dot{y}$ = y | Hamiltonian = $(2y- \frac{1}{2}u^2)+\lambda(u-y)$ | $\lambda(t)$ | $d\lambda/dt$ | F = $2y- \frac{1}{2}u^2$ | Functional = $\Sigma [2y- \frac{1}{2}u^2]dt$ | dH/du = $-u+\lambda$ |
|---|---|---|---|---|---|---|---|---|---|---|---|
| 0.0000 | 0.0000 | | | 0.9669 | 0.9669 | 0.0000 | **0.9669** | | | | |
| 0.0500 | 0.0435 | 0.0434 | 0.0500 | 0.9109 | 0.8691 | 0.4636 | 0.9125 | -1.0875 | -0.3280 | -0.0164 | 0.0016 |
| 0.1000 | 0.0821 | 0.0386 | 0.0500 | 0.8538 | 0.7732 | 0.4598 | 0.8553 | -1.1447 | -0.2002 | -0.0100 | 0.0015 |
| 0.1500 | 0.1161 | 0.0339 | 0.0500 | 0.7937 | 0.6790 | 0.4559 | 0.7951 | -1.2049 | -0.0828 | -0.0041 | 0.0014 |
| 0.2000 | 0.1454 | 0.0292 | 0.0500 | 0.7304 | 0.5863 | 0.4520 | 0.7316 | -1.2684 | 0.0240 | 0.0012 | 0.0013 |
| 0.2500 | 0.1701 | 0.0247 | 0.0500 | 0.6638 | 0.4948 | 0.4482 | 0.6649 | -1.3351 | 0.1200 | 0.0060 | 0.0011 |
| 0.3000 | 0.1903 | 0.0202 | 0.0500 | 0.5936 | 0.4043 | 0.4443 | 0.5946 | -1.4054 | 0.2045 | 0.0102 | 0.0010 |
| 0.3500 | 0.2061 | 0.0157 | 0.0500 | 0.5198 | 0.3146 | 0.4404 | 0.5206 | -1.4794 | 0.2770 | 0.0139 | 0.0008 |
| 0.4000 | 0.2173 | 0.0112 | 0.0500 | 0.4421 | 0.2255 | 0.4365 | 0.4428 | -1.5572 | 0.3369 | 0.0166 | 0.0007 |
| 0.4500 | 0.2242 | 0.0068 | 0.0500 | 0.3603 | 0.1367 | 0.4325 | 0.3608 | -1.6392 | 0.3834 | 0.0192 | 0.0005 |
| 0.5000 | 0.2266 | 0.0024 | 0.0500 | 0.2742 | 0.0480 | 0.4286 | 0.2746 | -1.7254 | 0.4155 | 0.0208 | 0.0003 |
| 0.5500 | 0.2245 | -0.0020 | 0.0500 | 0.1836 | -0.0408 | 0.4247 | 0.1837 | -1.8163 | 0.4322 | 0.0216 | 0.0002 |
| 0.6000 | 0.2190 | -0.0065 | 0.0500 | 0.0882 | -0.1299 | 0.4207 | 0.0882 | -1.9118 | 0.4322 | 0.0216 | 0.0000 |
| 0.6500 | 0.2071 | -0.0110 | 0.0500 | -0.0122 | -0.2195 | 0.4168 | -0.0125 | -2.0125 | 0.4140 | 0.0207 | -0.0002 |
| 0.7000 | 0.1916 | -0.0155 | 0.0500 | -0.1190 | -0.3100 | 0.4128 | -0.1184 | -2.1184 | 0.3762 | 0.0188 | -0.0004 |
| 0.7500 | 0.1715 | -0.0200 | 0.0500 | -0.2292 | -0.4014 | 0.4088 | -0.2299 | -2.2299 | 0.3167 | 0.0158 | -0.0007 |
| 0.8000 | 0.1468 | -0.0247 | 0.0500 | -0.3464 | -0.4940 | 0.4048 | -0.3672 | -2.3472 | 0.2336 | 0.0117 | -0.0009 |
| 0.8500 | 0.1174 | -0.0294 | 0.0500 | -0.4696 | -0.5882 | 0.4008 | -0.4708 | -2.4708 | 0.1245 | 0.0062 | -0.0011 |
| 0.9000 | 0.0832 | -0.0341 | 0.0500 | -0.5994 | -0.6840 | 0.3968 | -0.6008 | -2.6008 | -0.0133 | -0.0007 | -0.0014 |
| 0.9500 | 0.0441 | -0.0390 | 0.0500 | -0.7360 | -0.7818 | 0.3928 | -0.7377 | -2.7377 | -0.1827 | -0.0091 | -0.0017 |
| 1.0000 | 0.0000 | -0.0440 | 0.0500 | -0.8798 | -0.8818 | 0.3868 | **-0.8818** | -2.8818 | -0.3871 | -0.0194 | -0.0020 |
| y(0) | 0.00 | | | y(t) goes backward because of constraint y(T) = 0 while λ(t) goes forward | | | No Restriction on λ(T) | | | **0.1448** | **0.0000** |
| y(1) | 0.00 | | | | | | | | | | |

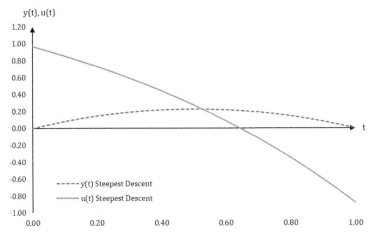

**FIGURE 10.11-6** Example 2: optimal $y^*(t)$ and $u^*(t)$.

| =J22 | -10 | -9.5 | -9 | -8.5 | -8 |
|---|---|---|---|---|---|
| -10 | =TABLE(E22;B22) | =TABLE(E22;B22) | =TABLE(E22;B22) | =TABLE(E22;B22) | =TABLE(E22;B22) |
| -9.5 | =TABLE(E22;B22) | =TABLE(E22;B22) | =TABLE(E22;B22) | =TABLE(E22;B22) | =TABLE(E22;B22) |
| -9 | =TABLE(E22;B22) | =TABLE(E22;B22) | =TABLE(E22;B22) | =TABLE(E22;B22) | =TABLE(E22;B22) |
| -8.5 | =TABLE(E22;B22) | =TABLE(E22;B22) | =TABLE(E22;B22) | =TABLE(E22;B22) | =TABLE(E22;B22) |
| -8 | =TABLE(E22;B22) | =TABLE(E22;B22) | =TABLE(E22;B22) | =TABLE(E22;B22) | =TABLE(E22;B22) |
| -7.5 | =TABLE(E22;B22) | =TABLE(E22;B22) | =TABLE(E22;B22) | =TABLE(E22;B22) | =TABLE(E22;B22) |
| -7 | =TABLE(E22;B22) | =TABLE(E22;B22) | =TABLE(E22;B22) | =TABLE(E22;B22) | =TABLE(E22;B22) |
| -6.5 | =TABLE(E22;B22) | =TABLE(E22;B22) | =TABLE(E22;B22) | =TABLE(E22;B22) | =TABLE(E22;B22) |
| -6 | =TABLE(E22;B22) | =TABLE(E22;B22) | =TABLE(E22;B22) | =TABLE(E22;B22) | =TABLE(E22;B22) |
| -5.5 | =TABLE(E22;B22) | =TABLE(E22;B22) | =TABLE(E22;B22) | =TABLE(E22;B22) | =TABLE(E22;B22) |
| -5 | =TABLE(E22;B22) | =TABLE(E22;B22) | =TABLE(E22;B22) | =TABLE(E22;B22) | =TABLE(E22;B22) |
| -4.5 | =TABLE(E22;B22) | =TABLE(E22;B22) | =TABLE(E22;B22) | =TABLE(E22;B22) | =TABLE(E22;B22) |
| -4 | =TABLE(E22;B22) | =TABLE(E22;B22) | =TABLE(E22;B22) | =TABLE(E22;B22) | =TABLE(E22;B22) |
| -3.5 | =TABLE(E22;B22) | =TABLE(E22;B22) | =TABLE(E22;B22) | =TABLE(E22;B22) | =TABLE(E22;B22) |
| -3 | =TABLE(E22;B22) | =TABLE(E22;B22) | =TABLE(E22;B22) | =TABLE(E22;B22) | =TABLE(E22;B22) |
| -2.5 | =TABLE(E22;B22) | =TABLE(E22;B22) | =TABLE(E22;B22) | =TABLE(E22;B22) | =TABLE(E22;B22) |
| -2 | =TABLE(E22;B22) | =TABLE(E22;B22) | =TABLE(E22;B22) | =TABLE(E22;B22) | =TABLE(E22;B22) |
| -1.5 | =TABLE(E22;B22) | =TABLE(E22;B22) | =TABLE(E22;B22) | =TABLE(E22;B22) | =TABLE(E22;B22) |
| -1 | =TABLE(E22;B22) | =TABLE(E22;B22) | =TABLE(E22;B22) | =TABLE(E22;B22) | =TABLE(E22;B22) |

**FIGURE 10.12-1** Example 1: consumption model data table for Mangasarian conditions.

## EXAMPLE 1 (CONSUMPTION MODEL)

To investigate the joint concavity in $(y, u)$ of the integrand function $F$ we resort to the Excel Data Table as follows (Fig. 10.12-1):

The Excel Data Table will allow us to investigate about the global concavity of the $F = \log(u4y)$ in $(y, u)$ as depicted in Fig. 10.12-2, while the linearity of $f = 4y(1-u)$ in $(y, u)$ also guarantees the concavity of the $f$.

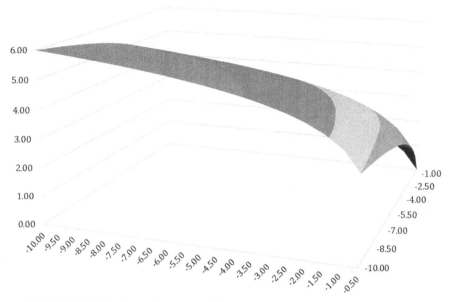

**FIGURE 10.12-2**   Consumption model integrand function global concavity in $(y, u)$.

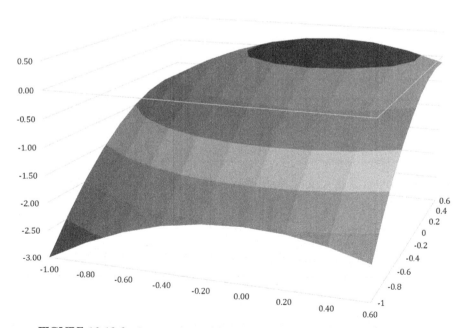

**FIGURE 10.12-3**   Investment model integrand function global concavity in $(y, u)$.

III. Dynamic optimization

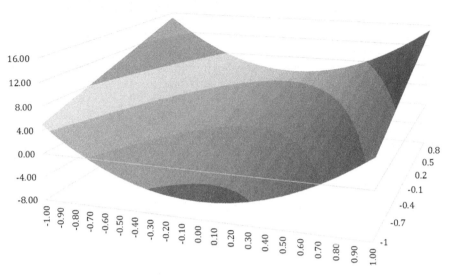

**FIGURE 10.12-4**   Inventory integrand function global convexity in $(y,u)$.

## EXAMPLE 2 (INVESTMENT MODEL)

The second example pertains to the investment model seen in Section 10.6. See Fig. 10.12-3 for the global concavity derived from the equation of integrand function. $f$ is linear in $(y, u)$ and so automatically concave and $\lambda(t)$ does not require any sign restriction.

## EXAMPLE 3 (INVENTORY MODEL)

In this example (see Section 10.7), we have to analyze the convexity conditions as the problem was formulated in terms of minimization. $f = u$ is liner in $u$, and it is also automatically concave, while the joint convexity in $(y, u)$ of the integrand function is shown in Fig. 10.12-4.

## Exercises

1. A first-order system is described by the following equation of motion in the state variable:

$$\dot{y} = -y + u$$

with initial condition $y(0) = 4$ and $y(T)$ free.
Find in Excel the optimal control (unconstrained) that minimizes the following performance measure:

$$J(u) = \int_0^1 \frac{1}{2}u^2 dt + y^2(1)$$

where the function outside the integral can be defined as a salvage value function $h(y(T), T)$.

The costate equation is $\dot{\lambda}(t) = -\lambda(t)$ and the transversality condition to be met is as follows:

$$\frac{\partial h}{\partial y}(y^*(T)) - \lambda^*(T) = 0$$

namely,

$$2y^*(1) = \lambda^*(1)$$

2. Maximize the following performance measure:

$$J(u) = \int_0^1 -u^2 dt$$

s.t.

$$\dot{y}(t) = y + u$$

and $y(0) = 1$, $y(1) = 0$.

3. Solve the following *bang-bang* control problem:

$$\max_{\{u\}} J(u) = \int_0^4 3y dt$$

s.t.

$$\dot{y} = y + u$$

$$y(0) = 5, \ y(4) \ free$$

and $u \in \mathcal{U} = [0, 2]$.

4. Solve the following *bang-bang* control problem:

$$\max_{\{u\}} J(u) = \int_0^4 3y dt$$

s.t.

$$\dot{y} = y + u$$

$$y(0) = 5, \ y(4) \geq 300$$

and. $u \in \mathcal{U} = [0, 2]$.
III. Dynamic optimization

In this problem, terminal time $T$ is fixed, but the terminal state is free to vary, only subject to $y(T) \geq y_{mim}$, and the problem is called to have a *truncated terminal vertical line*. In such a problem the transversality condition to be satisfied will be therefore:

$$(y_T - y_{min})\lambda_T = 0.$$

5. Solve the following *bang-bang* control problem with a *horizontal terminal line*:

$$\max_{\{u\}} J(u) = \int_0^4 -1 dt$$

s.t.

$$\dot{y} = y + u$$

$$y(0) = 5, \ y(T) = 11, T \ free$$

and. $u \in \mathcal{U} = [-1, 1].$

The exact solution is for $T^* = \ln[2] \cong 0.6931$. In such a problem, with a free terminal time but a fixed endpoint, the transversality condition to consider is to be set directly on the Hamiltonian function as follows:

$$H[T] = 0.$$

6. Solve in Excel the following problem, using the numerical technique of the steepest descent, with the VBA program proposed in the chapter:

$$\min_{\{u\}} J(u) = \int_0^1 \frac{1}{2} u^2 dt + y^2(1)$$

$$\dot{y} = -y + u$$

with initial condition $y(0) = 4$ and $y(1)$ *free*.
(Hint: as $y(1)$ is free to vary we need to integrate numerically backward the costate variable, on which we set the boundary condition such that $\frac{\partial h}{\partial y}(y^*(T)) - \lambda^*(T) = 0$, while we integrate forward the state variable).

7. Solve in Excel the following problem, using the numerical technique of the steepest descent, with the VBA code proposed in the chapter:

$$\min_{\{u\}} J(u) = \int_0^1 u^2 dt$$

$$\dot{y} = -y + u$$

with initial condition $y(0) = 4$ and $y(1) = 0$.

(Hint: in this case, as $y(1) = 0$, namely the state variable is bounded, and therefore we need to integrate numerically backward the state variable, while we integrate forward the costate variable. Launch the Solver first to set up the costate variable, such that $y(0) = 4$ and then run the VBA steepest descent VBA program).

8. **Optimal consumption.** Solve the following optimal control consumption model:

$$\max_{\{c(t)\}} J(c(t)) = \int_0^5 b^t \ln(c(t)) dt$$

s.t.

$$\dot{K}(t) = -c(t)$$

$$K(0) = 5, \ K(5) = 0$$

and where $b = \frac{1}{1+0.05}$ is the discount factor and $K(t)$ is the capital available to the consumer. We assume there is no capital appreciation and that only the consumption affects the Capital Path.

9. *Bang-bang* **optimal investment control problem.** Solve the following optimal control investment model:

$$\max_{\{I(t)\}} J(I(t)) = \int_0^1 \left[ K(t) - \frac{1}{2} I(t) \right] dt$$

s.t.

$$\dot{K}(t) = I(t) - \delta K(t)$$

$$K(0) = 1, \ K(1) \, free$$

and $I(t) \in [0, 1]$

where $\delta$ is the capital depreciation rate, set equal to 15% and $K(t)$ is the capital available to the firm.

In Section 10.6 we have assumed the quantities sold at 1\$ move according to the function $Q(K) = K - aK^2$, while here sales are just a linear function of capital $K(t)$. We still assume a unit of quantity sold at 1\$. The total costs are instead estimated 1/2 of the investments made, so that the profit function in the functional becomes:

$$\pi(t) = \left[ K(t) - \frac{1}{2} I(t) \right].$$

**a.** Find the optimal Capital Path $K^*(t)$.

**b.** Find the optimal switch time $t^*$ at which the investment policy needs to be changed.

10. *Bang-bang* **optimal advertising policy control problem.** The model presented here attempts to determine the best advertising expenditure for a firm, which produces a single product and sells it into a market which can absorb no more than $M$ dollars of the product per unit of time, that is, $M$ is the extent of the market. It is assumed that if the firm does no advertising, its rate of sales at any point in time will decrease at a rate proportional to the rate of sales at that time. If a firm advertises, the rate of sales increases at a rate proportional to the rate of advertising, but this increase only affects that share of the market that is not already purchasing the product. We have therefore the following variables in the model:

$$S(t) = \textit{rate of sales at time } t$$

$$\alpha = \textit{constant} > 0$$

$$\gamma = \textit{constant} > 0$$

$$A(t) = \textit{rate of advertising}$$

and the quantity:

$$\left[1 - \frac{S(t)}{M}\right] = \textit{part of the market affected by advertising.}$$

Under these assumptions, the change in rate of sales is given by:

$$\dot{S}(t) = -\alpha S(t) + \gamma A(t)\left[1 - \frac{S(t)}{M}\right].$$

In terms of Maximum Principle, the problem can be formalized as follows:

$$\max_{\{A(t)\}} J(A(t)) = \int_0^T S(t)dt$$

*s.t.*

$$\dot{S}(t) = -\left[\alpha + \frac{\gamma}{M}A(t)\right]S(t) + \gamma A(t)$$

$S(0) = S_0$ and $A(t) \in [0, 10]$.

Use $\alpha = \gamma = 1$, $M = 50$, $T = 1$ as problem data. In case of $S(0) = 70$ and $S(0) = 30$ solve the following points.

**a.** Identify the linear Hamiltonian function $\mathcal{H}$, and find the conditions under which at time $t^*$ the advertisement policy needs to be changed.

**b.** Find the optimal Capital Path $S^*(t)$,

**c.** Find the optimal advertising policy in both initial conditions for $S(0)$.

11. ***Bang-bang* optimal maintenance and replacement model.**[10] Consider a machine whose resale value gradually declines over time, and its output is assumed to be proportional to its resale value. It is possible, somehow, to slow down the rate of decline of the resale value, applying preventive maintenance. The control problem consists of simultaneously determining the optimal rate of preventive maintenance and the optimal sale date $T^*$ of machine. This is a control problem where both the terminal point of the state variable and the terminal time are not fixed, that is, a *terminal curve problem*. The model can be formalized as follows:

$$y(t) = state\ variable;\ resale\ value\ of\ the\ machine.$$

$$u(t) = control\ variable;\ preventive\ maintenance\ at\ time\ t,\ such\ that\ u(t) \in \Omega.$$

$$g(t) = maintenance\ effectiveness\ function,\ i.e.\ money\ added\ to\ the\ resale\ value$$

$$per\ dollar\ spent\ on\ preventive\ maintenance.$$

$$d(t) = obsolescence\ function\ measured\ in\ terms\ of\ dollars\ subracted\ from\ y(t)\ at\ time\ t.$$

$$\rho = discount\ rate\ (if\ applicable).$$

$$\pi = constant\ production\ rate\ in\ dollars\ per\ unit\ time\ and\ per\ unit\ resale\ value.$$

In terms of Maximum Principle, the problem can be then stated as:

$$\max_{\{u(t)\}} J(u(t)) = \int_0^T [\pi y(t) - u(t)] e^{-\rho t} dt + y(T) e^{-\rho T}$$

$$s.t.$$

$$\dot{y}(t) = -d(t) + g(t)u(t) \text{ and } y(0) = y_0$$

---

[10]See Suresh P. Sethi, *Optimal Control Theory: Applications to Management Science and Economics*, Ch. 9, third Edition, Springer, 2018.

and where we denote the function outside the integral as $h(y(T), T) = y(T)e^{-\rho T}$.

This problem turns out to be a *bang-bang* control problem with a linear Hamiltonian function. Build and solve for the optimal control policy $u^*(t)$, optimal path $y^*(t)$, and optimal switch time $t^*$ the following three scenarios of the problem.

a. The first model is without the discount rate and with terminal time of machine resale given, as $T = 36$ *months*, while $y^*(T)$ is instead free.

b. The second model includes the discount rate $\rho$ with terminal time $T = 36$ *months*, while $y^*(T)$ is instead free.

c. The third model includes the discount rate $\rho$ , and it is specified as *terminal curve problem*, so that neither $y^*(T)$ nor the optimal time of resale $T^*$ are preset and therefore are free, and they need to be found by the problem itself, setting up the required transversality conditions for $y^*(T) = free$ as:

$$\frac{\partial h}{\partial y}(y^*(T)) - \lambda^*(T) = 0$$

and $T = free$ as:

$$\mathcal{H}(y^*(T), u^*(T), \lambda^*(T), T) = -\frac{\partial h}{\partial t}(y^*(T), T) = \rho \cdot y(T)e^{-\rho T}.$$

In all the three scenarios, use the following information: $u(t) \in [0, 1]$, $y(0) = 100$, $d(t) = 2$, $\pi = 0.1$, $\rho = 0.05$, and $g(t) = 2/(1 + t)^{1/2}$ and adopt the unit of time of 1 month.

## Linear quadratic regulator problems

The following exercises will consider an important class of optimal control problems, the *linear quadratic regulator (LQR) problems* (or *linear regulator problems*), in that the system to be controlled is linear while the performance measure is quadratic. We have already seen an example of such a problem in Section 10.8 where we have studied the optimal control problem in two state variables. The linear quadratic regulator problems in their general form are formalized as follows. We have a system of $n$ linear state equations described in matrix form as:

$$\dot{y}(t) = A(t)y(t) + B(t)u(t)$$

and the performance measure to be optimized is:

$$J(u) = \frac{1}{2}y^T(T)Hy(T) + \frac{1}{2}\int_{t_0}^{T}[y^T(T)Q(t)y(T) + u^T(t)R(t)u(t)]dt$$

where $T$ is fixed, $H$ and $Q$ are real symmetric positive semidefinite matrices and $R$ is a real symmetric positive definite matrix. It is assumed that state controls are not bounded and the vector $y(T)$ is free.

Solving for the Hamiltonian Maximum Principle conditions, the solution is given by the following $2n$ equations:

$$\begin{bmatrix} \dot{y}(t) \\ -- \\ \dot{p}(t) \end{bmatrix} = \begin{bmatrix} A(t) & | & -B(t)R^{-1}(t)B^T(t) \\ -- -- & | & -- -- -- -- -- -- -- \\ -Q(t) & | & -A^T(t) \end{bmatrix} \begin{bmatrix} y^*(t) \\ -- \\ p^*(t) \end{bmatrix}$$

where this time we have indicated the Lagrange multipliers with $p(t)$.

12. Solve the following LQR problem, which slightly changes Example 1 in Section 10.8.

$$\min_{\{u\}} J(u) = \frac{1}{2}[y_1(T) - 5]^2 + \frac{1}{2}[y_2(T) - 2]^2 + \frac{1}{2}\int_0^2 \frac{1}{2}u^2(t)dt$$

s.t.

$$y(0) = 0 \text{ and } y(2) \text{ free}$$

$$\dot{y}_1(t) = y_2(t)$$

$$\dot{y}_2(t) = -y_2(t) + u(t).$$

Set up in Excel the system of differential equations from the Hamiltonian Maximum Principle conditions, and also define the required transversality conditions at $T$.

13. Consider the system of two linear differential equations:

$$\dot{y}_1(t) = y_2(t)$$

$$\dot{y}_2(t) = 2y_1(t) - y_2(t) + u(t)$$

which needs to be controlled to minimize:

$$J(u) = \frac{1}{2}\int_0^T \left[ y_1^2(t) + \frac{1}{2}y_2^2(t) + \frac{1}{4}u^2(t) \right]dt.$$

Setting up the Hamiltonian Maximum Principle conditions, it turns out to have the following matrices:

$$A = \begin{bmatrix} 0 & 1 \\ 2 & -1 \end{bmatrix}; B = \begin{bmatrix} 0 \\ 1 \end{bmatrix}; Q = \begin{bmatrix} 2 & 0 \\ 0 & 1 \end{bmatrix} \text{ with } R = \frac{1}{2}.$$

Solve the system of differential equations and at the same time minimize the functional, given the following initial conditions on the two state variables:
$y(0) = [-4 \quad 4]$ and $y(T)$ *free*. Set $T = 4$.

**14.** Find the optimal control for the system:

$$\dot{y}_1(t) = ay(t) + u(t)$$

to minimize:

$$J(u) = \frac{1}{2}Hy^2(T) + \int\limits_0^T \frac{1}{4}u^2(t)dt$$

**a.** Solve the problem with $H = 5$, $T = 15$, $a = -0.2$, and $y(0) = 5.0$.

**b.** Solve the problem with $H = 5$, $T = 15$, $a = +0.2$, and $y(0) = 5.0$.

**15.** The following second-order differential system:

$$\dot{y}_1(t) = y_2(t)$$

$$\dot{y}_2(t) = 2y_1(t) - y_2(t) + u(t)$$

needs to be controlled to minimize the performance measure:

$$J(u) = [y_1(T) - 1]^2 + \int\limits_0^T \left\{ [y_1(t) - 1]^2 + 0.0025u^2(t) \right\}dt.$$

Solve the problem with $T = 5$ and $y(0) = [0 \quad 0]$, while $y(T)$ *free*.

**16.** Consider the system of two linear differential equations:

$$\dot{y}_1(t) = y_2(t)$$

$$\dot{y}_2(t) = -y_2(t) + u(t)$$

which needs to be controlled to minimize:

$$J(u) = \frac{1}{2} \int\limits_0^T [y_1^2(t) + y_2^2(t) + u^2(t)]\,dt.$$

Solve the problem setting $y(0) = [4 \quad -2]$, $T = 2$, and $y(T)$ *free*.

17. Consider the system of two linear differential equations:

$$\dot{y}_1(t) = y_2(t)$$

$$\dot{y}_2(t) = -y_2(t) + u(t)$$

which needs to be controlled to minimize:

$$J(u) = \frac{1}{2} \int\limits_0^T [y_1^2(t) + u^2(t)]\,dt.$$

Solve the problem setting $y(0) = [5 \quad 2]$, $T = 2$, and $y(T)$ *free*.

III. Dynamic optimization

## 11.1 Bellman's principle, discrete shortest path problems, and the Excel MINIFS function

The first class of problems that we will develop in the Discrete Dynamic Programming (DDP) is that of finding a *discrete optimal policy* over a sequence of discrete *stages*.

These types of problems are called discrete *shortest path problems,* and they have a large variety of applications in economics.

These problems are typically modeled by a *graph,* as the one depicted in Fig. 11.1-1, which is always specified in terms of a certain number of *vertices* (or *nodes*) and in terms of the corresponding *arcs* connecting the nodes.

To each arc is normally associated a value, which is the cost we have to incur when we decide to pass through that specific arc. The solution of the problem is to find a *minimum-value path* of connected arcs. This optimal sequence is called *optimal (discrete) path.*

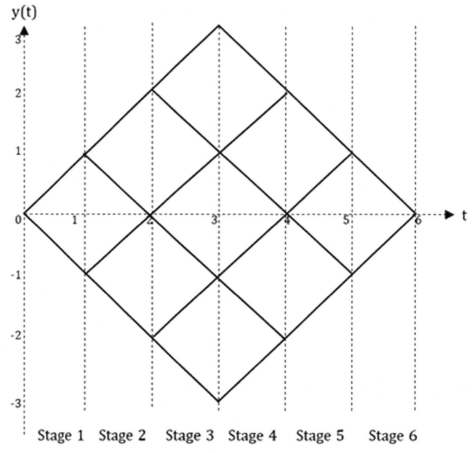

**FIGURE 11.1-1**   Model of a six-stage discrete graph oriented from left to right in a coordinate system.

## EXAMPLE 1 (FIXED ENDPOINT PROBLEM)

Let us solve the graph[1] in Fig. 11.1-2, finding the optimal path, taking the state variable $y(t)$ from *node* 1 to *node* 16. It is an analogue problem to Calculus of Variations (CoV), in that there are several ways of going from first to final node and we need to find the optimal one.

This could be a routing problem, where the traveler has to choose, among various routes, the optimal minimum distance (or cost) route to reach the location of *node* 16 from the location of *node* 1 or it could represent an economic problem, where the goal is to transform, with the minimum cost, the state variable $y(t)$ raw material into a finished good, through a six-stage production process, passing through alternative production subprocesses.

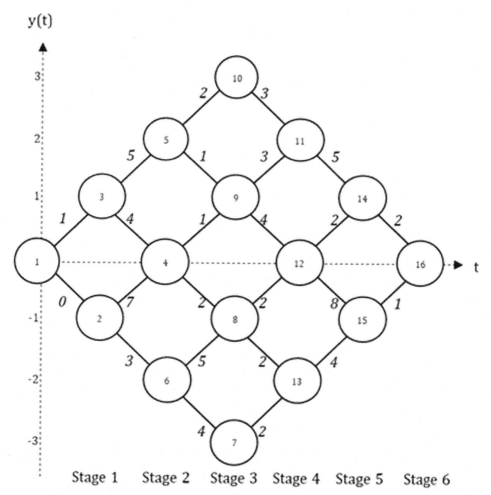

FIGURE 11.1-2     Example 1: Six-stage graph with the numbered nodes (from 1 to 16) and arc values.

---

[1]See Stuart. E. Dreyfus, *Dynamic Programming and the Calculus of Variations*, The Rand Corporation, 1965, chapter I.

For each arc, we have a specific value that can be interpreted as a distance in miles from one location to another in a routing problem, or also, it may represent a cost for a specific stage in a production problem.

Within the DDP theory, the way the problem is solved is resorting to the **Bellman's recurrence relation**, **optimal value function**, or **functional equation of dynamic programming**[2]:

$$J^*_{t_k,T}(t_k, y_k) = \min\left\{ \left[ J^u_{t_k,t_k+1}(t_k, y_k) + J^*_{t_k+1,T}(t_k + 1, y_k + 1) \right], \left[ J^d_{t_k,t_k+1}(t_k, y_k) + J^*_{t_k+1,T}(t_k + 1, y_k - 1) \right] \right\}$$

(11.1-1)

where $t_k = 0, 1, 2\cdots,(T-1)$ and where:

$J^u_{t_k,t_k+1}(t_k, y_k)$ = value of *arc-up* connecting the vertices with coordinates $(t_k,y_k)$ and $(t_k + 1, y_k + 1)$

$J^d_{t_k,t_k+1}(t_k, y_k)$ = value of *arc-down* connecting the vertices with coordinates $(t_k,y_k)$ and $(t_k + 1, y_k - 1)$

$J^*_{t_k,T}(t_k, y_k)$ = value of the **minimum-cost admissible path** connecting the *node* with coordinates $(t_k,y_k)$ to the last *node* with coordinates $(T,y_T)$ (in the above graph the last *node* has coordinates $(6, 0)$).

$$J^*_{T,T}(T, y_T) = 0$$

Specifically, for the Example 1, we calculate the following values of **optimal value function** at each step:

- $J^*_{5,6}(t_5, y_5) = \min[2, 1] = 1$ (to move with the least cost from stage 6 to stage 5, we should move downward from *node* 16 to *node* 15).
- $J^*_{4,6}(t_4, y_4) = \min$

$$\left\{ \begin{array}{c} 2 + 5 = 7 = value\ of\ node\ 11 \\ \min\{[2 + value\ of\ node\ 14], [8 + value\ of\ node\ 15]\} = \min[4,\ 9] = \overline{4} = \overline{val.node\ 12} \\ 4 + value\ of\ node\ 15 = 4 + 1 = 5 = value\ of\ node\ 13 \end{array} \right\} = \overline{4}$$

- $J^*_{3,6}(t_3, y_3) = \min$

$$\left\{ \begin{array}{c} 3 + value\ of\ node\ 11 = 3 + 7 = 10 = value\ of\ node\ 10 \\ \min\left\{\left[4 + J^*_{4,6}\right], [3 + value\ of\ node\ 11]\right\} = \min[8,\ 10] = 8 = value\ of\ node\ 9 \\ \min\left\{\left[2 + J^*_{4,6}\right], [2 + value\ of\ node\ 13]\right\} = \min[6,\ 7] = \overline{6} = \overline{value\ of\ node\ 8} \\ 2 + value\ of\ node\ 13 = 2 + 5 = 7 = value\ of\ node\ 7 \end{array} \right\} = \overline{6}$$

[2]Without loss of generality, we assume here for simplicity that just one *arc-down* and one *arc-up* are connecting each node.

In the above brackets as *node* 8 and *node* 9 pass through *node* 12 and since this has turned out to be the optimal policy $J_{4,6}^*(t_4, y_4)$, to calculate the values of *node* 8 and *node* 9 we have used this optimal policy. For example, for *node* 8 with coordinates $(t_3 = 3, y_3 = -1)$ we have:

- $J_{3,6}^*(t_3, y_3) = J_{t_3}^u(t_3, y_3) + J_{4,6}^*(t_3 + 1, y_3 + 1) = J_{t_3}^u(3, -1) + J_{4,6}^*(4, 0) = 2 + 4 = 6$
- $J_{2,6}^*(t_2, y_2) = \min$

$$\left\{ \begin{array}{l} \min\{[2 + value\, of\, node\, 10], [1 + value\, of\, node\, 9]\} = \min[12, 9] = 9 = value\, of\, node\, 5 \\[4pt] \min\left\{[1 + value\, of\, node\, 9], \left[2 + J_{3,6}^*\right]\right\} = \min[9, 8] = \overline{8 = value\, of\, node\, 4} \\[4pt] \min\left\{\left[5 + J_{3,6}^*\right], [4 + value\, of\, node\, 7]\right\} = \min[11, 11] = 11 = value\, of\, node\, 6 \end{array} \right\} = \overline{8}$$

As *node* 4 and *node* 6 pass through *node* 8, and this constitutes the optimal policy $J_3^*(t_3, y)$ to calculate their values we have used this optimal policy.

- $J_{1,6}^*(t_1, y_1) = \min\left\{ \begin{array}{l} \min\left\{4 + \left[J_{2,6}^*\right], [5 + value\, of\, node\, 5]\right\} = \min[12, 14] = \overline{12 = value\, of\, node\, 3} \\[4pt] \min\left\{7 + \left[J_{2,6}^*\right], [3 + value\, of\, node\, 6]\right\} = \min[15, 14] = 14 = value\, of\, node\, 2 \end{array} \right\} = \overline{12}$

In the above brackets, both *node* 2 and *node* 3 pass through the *node* 4 and since this node constitutes the optimal policy $J_{2,6}^*(t_2, y_2)$ we use this policy to determine the values of *node* 2 and *node* 3.

The last step is determined as follows:

- $J_{0,6}^*(t_0, y_0) = \min\left\{[0 + value\, of\, node\, 2], \left[1 + J_{1,6}^*\right]\right\} = \min[14, 13] = \overline{13}$

where $J_{1,6}^* = value\, of\, node\, 3$.

The optimal path must pass through the nodes indicated with the overline: *node 1* at $t_0$, then *node 3, node 4, node 8, node 12* (which is linked optimally to *node 14*), and finally *node 16*. The total optimal cost is $J^* = 13$. See Fig. 11.1-3.

The implicit principle that has been used to solve the problem above is called the *Bellman principle of optimality* which states:

An optimal policy has the property that whatever the initial state and initial decisions are, the remaining decisions must constitute an optimal policy with regard to the state resulting from the first decision.

The above statement is embedded in Eq. (11.1-1).

It is apparent how this process may become very cumbersome once the number of nodes and vertices increase.

The way Excel can be implemented to solve these types of problems is via the *MINIFS* function.

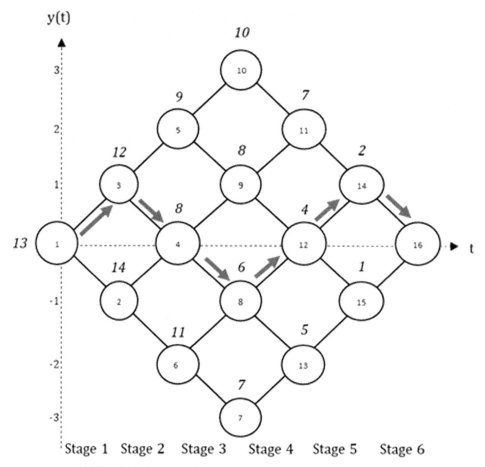

**FIGURE 11.1-3**   Example 1: Values at each node and the optimal path.

The idea is first to rearrange by rows and columns the information contained in the graph of Example 1. This would be done like in Fig. 11.1-4 where *Column A* is the number of the arc, *Column B* is the sink node and *Column C* the source node. *Column D* stores the cost at each arc, while *Column E* returns the optimal policy cost.

Let us implement the optimal policy starting backward from *node* 16.

To find the optimal path from *node* 16 to either *node* 15 or *node* 14 we use the formula in *Column E*, which is equal to the cost to move from stage 6 to stage 5 (either to *node* 15 or to *node* 14) + the minimum cost path to reach the *stage* 16 (zero in this case) with the *MINIFS* formula. As stage 16 is the last stage, there is no previous optimal policy.

Now, let us copy the formula in *Column E* up to the beginning of the worksheet, and see what happens, for example, at *arc* 12 (see Fig. 11.1-5), connecting *node* 8 to *node* 6.

| | A | B | C | D | E |
|---|---|---|---|---|---|
| 1 | Arc | To node | From node | Cost at the arc | Min Cost Optimal Policy to reach current node with Minifs |
| 2 | 1 | 1 | 2 | 0 | |
| 3 | 2 | 1 | 3 | 1 | |
| 4 | 3 | 2 | 4 | 7 | |
| 5 | 4 | 2 | 6 | 3 | |
| 6 | 5 | 3 | 4 | 4 | |
| 7 | 6 | 3 | 5 | 5 | |
| 8 | 7 | 4 | 8 | 2 | |
| 9 | 8 | 4 | 9 | 1 | |
| 10 | 9 | 5 | 9 | 1 | |
| 11 | 10 | 5 | 10 | 2 | |
| 12 | 11 | 6 | 7 | 4 | |
| 13 | 12 | 6 | 8 | 5 | |
| 14 | 13 | 7 | 13 | 2 | |
| 15 | 14 | 8 | 12 | 2 | |
| 16 | 15 | 8 | 13 | 2 | |
| 17 | 16 | 9 | 11 | 3 | |
| 18 | 17 | 9 | 12 | 4 | |
| 19 | 18 | 10 | 11 | 3 | |
| 20 | 19 | 11 | 14 | 5 | |
| 21 | 20 | 12 | 14 | 2 | |
| 22 | 21 | 12 | 15 | 8 | |
| 23 | 22 | 13 | 15 | 4 | |
| 24 | 23 | 14 | 16 | 2 | =D24+MINIFS(E25:E$25:B25:B$25:C24) |
| 25 | 24 | 15 | 16 | 1 | =D25+MINIFS(E$25:E25:B$25:B25:C25) |

FIGURE 11.1-4    Example 1: Worksheet graph setup with backward recursion.

Here the *Column* $E$ calculates the sum of the current *cost* $= 5$, and the *MINIFS* formula returns the minimum cost policy over the previous stages to reach the *node* 8. The *MINIFS* process can be seen in the second screenshot on the right-hand side of Fig. 11.1-5, where we see that we can reach *node* 8 either from *node* 12 *node* 13, and the best policy is to pass through *node* 12 with *cost* 6. Going further backward, to reach *node* 12 we use *node* 14, with cost, instead of using of *node* 15.

To optimally move from *node* 8 to *node* 6 it costs then 11, value stored in *Cell* E13. In *Cell* E13 what the *MINIFS* function does is to look for the *node* 8 in the range B14:B25, returning the minimum value between *Cell* E15 (=6) and *Cell* E16 (=7) (see right-hand side of Fig. 11.1-5) and then, it sums the minimum value to *Cell* D13 (=5). The result is $6 + 5 = 11$.

Table 11.1-1 and Fig. 11.1-6 return the final solution. Table 11.1-1 gives the solution of the graph at *node* 1 with total minimum *cost* $= 13$, through which we can easily move forward identifying the optimal nodes (highlighted in gray) up to *node* 16.

## EXAMPLE 2 (VERTICAL TERMINAL LINE PROBLEM)

Let us solve now in Excel the vertical terminal line problem given in Fig. 11.1-7.

We can easily solve the problem in Excel, as described in Example 1, in the following Table 11.1-2, where the optimal path has been highlighted in gray.

| | A | B | C | D | E |
|---|---|---|---|---|---|
| | Arc | To node | From node | Cost at the arc | Min Cost Optimal Policy to reach current node with Minifs |
| 2 | 1 | 1 | 2 | 0 | =D2+MINIFS(E3:E$25;B3;B$25;C2) |
| 3 | 2 | 1 | 3 | 1 | =D3+MINIFS(E4:E$25;B4;B$25;C3) |
| 4 | 3 | 2 | 4 | 7 | =D4+MINIFS(E5:E$25;B5;B$25;C4) |
| 5 | 4 | 2 | 6 | 3 | =D5+MINIFS(E6:E$25;B6;B$25;C5) |
| 6 | 5 | 3 | 4 | 4 | =D6+MINIFS(E7:E$25;B7;B$25;C6) |
| 7 | 6 | 3 | 5 | 5 | =D7+MINIFS(E8:E$25;B8;B$25;C7) |
| 8 | 7 | 4 | 8 | 2 | =D8+MINIFS(E9:E$25;B9;B$25;C8) |
| 9 | 8 | 4 | 9 | 1 | =D9+MINIFS(E10:E$25;B10;B$25;C9) |
| 10 | 9 | 5 | 9 | 1 | =D10+MINIFS(E11:E$25;B11;B$25;C10) |
| 11 | 10 | 5 | 10 | 2 | =D11+MINIFS(E12:E$25;B12;B$25;C11) |
| 12 | 11 | 6 | 7 | 4 | =D12+MINIFS(E13:E$25;B13;B$25;C12) |
| 13 | 12 | 6 | 8 | 5 | =D13+MINIFS(E14:E$25;B14;B$25;C13) |
| 14 | 13 | 7 | 13 | 2 | =D14+MINIFS(E15:E$25;B15;B$25;C14) |
| 15 | 14 | 8 | 12 | 2 | =D15+MINIFS(E16:E$25;B16;B$25;C15) |
| 16 | 15 | 8 | 13 | 2 | =D16+MINIFS(E17:E$25;B17;B$25;C16) |
| 17 | 16 | 9 | 11 | 3 | =D17+MINIFS(E18:E$25;B18;B$25;C17) |
| 18 | 17 | 9 | 12 | 4 | =D18+MINIFS(E19:E$25;B19;B$25;C18) |
| 19 | 18 | 10 | 11 | 3 | =D19+MINIFS(E20:E$25;B20;B$25;C19) |
| 20 | 19 | 11 | 14 | 5 | =D20+MINIFS(E21:E$25;B21;B$25;C20) |
| 21 | 20 | 12 | 14 | 2 | =D21+MINIFS(E22:E$25;B22;B$25;C21) |
| 22 | 21 | 12 | 15 | 8 | =D22+MINIFS(E23:E$25;B23;B$25;C22) |
| 23 | 22 | 13 | 15 | 4 | =D23+MINIFS(E24:E$25;B24;B$25;C23) |
| 24 | 23 | 14 | 16 | 2 | =D24+MINIFS(E25:E$25;B25;B$25;C24) |
| 25 | 24 | 15 | 16 | 1 | =D25+MINIFS(E$25;E$25;B$25;B$25;C25) |

| | A | B | C | D | E |
|---|---|---|---|---|---|
| | Arc | To node | From node | Cost at the arc | Min Cost |
| 13 | 12 | 6 | 8 | 5 | 11 |
| 14 | 13 | 7 | 13 | 2 | 7 |
| 15 | 14 | 8 | 12 | 2 | 6 |
| 16 | 15 | 8 | 13 | 2 | 7 |
| 17 | 16 | 9 | 11 | 3 | 10 |
| 18 | 17 | 9 | 12 | 4 | 8 |
| 19 | 18 | 10 | 11 | 3 | 10 |
| 20 | 19 | 11 | 14 | 5 | 7 |
| 21 | 20 | 12 | 14 | 2 | 4 |
| 22 | 21 | 12 | 15 | 8 | 9 |
| 23 | 22 | 13 | 15 | 4 | 5 |
| 24 | 23 | 14 | 16 | 2 | 2 |
| 25 | 24 | 15 | 16 | 1 | 1 |

FIGURE 11.1-5    Highlight on node 8 formula with the MINIFS function.

TABLE 11.1-1    Graph worksheet complete solution with MINIFS.

| Arc | To node | From node | Cost at the arc | Min Cost Optimal Policy to reach current node with Minifs |
|---|---|---|---|---|
| 1 | 1 | 2 | 0 | 14 |
| 2 | 1 | 3 | 1 | 13 |
| 3 | 2 | 4 | 7 | 15 |
| 4 | 2 | 6 | 3 | 14 |
| 5 | 3 | 4 | 4 | 12 |
| 6 | 3 | 5 | 5 | 14 |
| 7 | 4 | 8 | 2 | 8 |
| 8 | 4 | 9 | 1 | 9 |
| 9 | 5 | 9 | 1 | 9 |
| 10 | 5 | 10 | 2 | 12 |
| 11 | 6 | 7 | 4 | 11 |
| 12 | 6 | 8 | 5 | 11 |
| 13 | 7 | 13 | 2 | 7 |
| 14 | 8 | 12 | 2 | 6 |
| 15 | 8 | 13 | 2 | 7 |
| 16 | 9 | 11 | 3 | 10 |
| 17 | 9 | 12 | 4 | 8 |
| 18 | 10 | 11 | 3 | 10 |
| 19 | 11 | 14 | 5 | 7 |
| 20 | 12 | 14 | 2 | 4 |
| 21 | 12 | 15 | 8 | 9 |
| 22 | 13 | 15 | 4 | 5 |
| 23 | 14 | 16 | 2 | 2 |
| 24 | 15 | 16 | 1 | 1 |
| | f* | | 13 | |

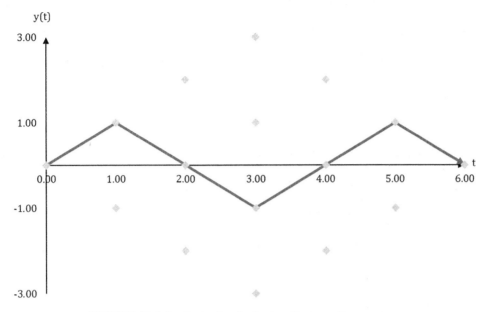

**FIGURE 11.1-6**   Optimal path plot in a $(t, y)$ coordinate system.

Fig. 11.1-8 shows the graph implementation of the Excel optimal trajectory: the total minimum cost of the optimal path is 7, and this optimal path starts from *node* 12 (4,2), passing through *node* 8 (3,1), *node* 4 (2,2), *node* 2 (1, 1), and finally *node* 1 (0, 0) (in brackets are the coordinates of the nodes).

## 11.2 Discrete dynamic systems: tabular method, Excel data table, and Solver

The dynamic programming recurrence algorithm can be also applied to typical OC problems expressed for example by the following:

$$\min_{u\{t\}} J(u) = y^2(2) + 2 \int_{t_0}^{T} u^2(t)dt$$

$$s.t. \ \frac{dy(t)}{dt} = ay(t) + bu(t),$$

$$\text{and } y(t) \in \mathscr{Y}, u(t) \in \mathscr{U} \quad \forall t \in [t_0, T]$$

The goal, as usual, is to find the admissible optimal $u^*(t)$ which causes the system $\dot{y}(t)$ to follow an admissible trajectory $y^*(t)$ that minimizes the given performance measure $J(u)$.

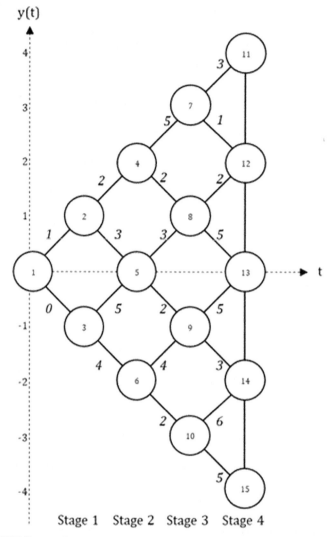

Stage 1    Stage 2    Stage 3    Stage 4

FIGURE 11.1-7    Vertical terminal line graph: Arc values and optimal path.

## EXAMPLE 1.A (TABULAR APPROACH)

Setting in the above problem $\Delta t = 1$ and $T = 2$, we solve the two-stage process described by the discrete equation of motion, with $a = 0$ and $b = 1$:

$$y(k+1) = y(k) + u(k) \quad k = 0, 1.$$

**TABLE 11.1-2**  Example 2: Excel output and optimal path solution with backward recursion.

| Arc | To | From | Cost | Min Cost Optimal Policy |
|-----|----|------|------|-------------------------|
| 1 | 1 | 2 | 1 | 7 |
| 2 | 1 | 3 | 0 | 10 |
| 3 | 2 | 5 | 3 | 8 |
| 4 | 2 | 4 | 2 | 6 |
| 5 | 3 | 5 | 5 | 10 |
| 6 | 3 | 6 | 4 | 11 |
| 7 | 4 | 7 | 5 | 6 |
| 8 | 4 | 8 | 2 | 4 |
| 9 | 5 | 8 | 3 | 5 |
| 10 | 5 | 9 | 2 | 5 |
| 11 | 6 | 9 | 4 | 7 |
| 12 | 6 | 10 | 2 | 7 |
| 13 | 7 | 11 | 3 | 3 |
| 14 | 7 | 12 | 1 | 1 |
| 15 | 8 | 12 | 2 | 2 |
| 16 | 8 | 13 | 5 | 5 |
| 17 | 9 | 13 | 5 | 5 |
| 18 | 9 | 14 | 3 | 3 |
| 19 | 10 | 14 | 6 | 6 |
| 20 | 10 | 15 | 5 | 5 |
| | J* | | 7 | |

$u(0)$ and $u(1)$ have to be selected to minimize the discrete equivalent form of the performance measure $J(u) = y^2(2) + 2 \int_{t_0}^{T} u^2(t)dt$:

$$J(u) = y^2(2) + 2u^2(0) + 2u^2(1)$$

$$s.t.\ 0.0 \leq y(k) \leq 1.5 \quad k = 0, 1, 2$$

and

$$-1.0 \leq u(k) \leq 1.0 \quad k = 0, 1.$$

It will be also assumed that $y(k) \in \mathscr{Y} = [0.0, 0.5, 1.0, 1.5]$ and $u(k) \in \mathscr{U} = [-1.0, -0.5, 0, 0.5, 1.0]$.

The way the computational procedure is implemented is essentially a simulation of the performance measure for all the admissible values that the state and control variables can take over the two steps, as follows.

III. Dynamic optimization

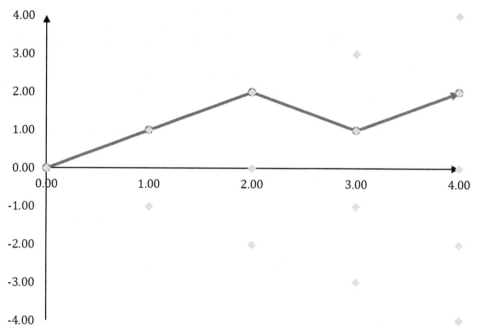

FIGURE 11.1-8 Optimal path plot in a coordinate system.

**i.** Start from last stage: for $k = 1$ and for each of the values that $y(k)$ can assume in $\mathscr{Y} = [0.0, 0.5, 1.0, 1.5]$ calculate the resulting $y(2)$ according to the discrete equation of motion $y(k+1) = y(k)+u(k)$ for each of the value that $u(k)$ can assume in $\mathscr{U} = [-1.0, -0.5, 0, 0.5, 1.0]$ and find the resulting minimum cost path $J_{1,2}^*$ and the associated optimal control (OC) value $u^*(1)$.

**ii.** Go to the first stage: for $k = 0$ and for each of the value that $y(0)$ can assume in $\mathscr{Y} = [0.0, 0.5, 1.0, 1.5]$ calculate the next state value $y(k+1) = y(k)+u(k)$ via each of the value that $u(k)$ can assume in $\mathscr{U} = [-1.0, -0.5, 0, 0.5, 1.0]$ and find the resulting total minimum cost path as $J_{0,2}^* = \min\left[C_{0,2}^*\right]$ and the associated OC value $u^*(0)$, where $C_{0,2}^* = J_{0,1} + J_{1,2}^*$ (the costs simulated for the first stage for different values assumed by state and control variable + the optimal policy cost to arrive at *stage* 1 determined under the step **i.**).

The output solution is given in Table 11.2-1 (the Excel setup) and Fig. 11.2-1 where the optimal path for $y(0) = 1.50$ has been highlighted.

The way the table needs to be read is as follows, assuming the initial condition is $y(0) = 1.50$.

Look for the initial condition $y(0) = 1.50$ under *Current State* $y(0)$ with corresponding minimum cost $J_{0,2}^* = \min[2.25, 1.25, 1.50] = 1.25$ and optimal $u^*(0) = -0.5$ in the second column *Control* $u(0)$. On the same row, we read $y(1) = 1.0$.

**TABLE 11.2-1**   Example 1: Excel output tabular solution.

| Current State y(1) | Control u(1) | Next State y(2) = y(1) + u(1) | Cost y²(2) + 2u²(1) = J(1,2) | Minimum Cost J*(1,2) | Optimal Control Applied at k = 1 |
|---|---|---|---|---|---|
|  | -1.00 | 0.50 | 2.25 |  |  |
|  | -0.50 | 1.00 | 1.50 |  |  |
| 1.50 | 0.00 | 1.50 | 2.25 | 1.50 | -0.50 |
|  | 0.50 | 2.00 | 4.50 |  |  |
|  | 1.00 | 2.50 | 8.25 |  |  |
|  | -1.00 | 0.00 | 2.00 |  |  |
|  | **-0.50** | **0.50** | **0.75** |  |  |
| 1.00 | 0.00 | 1.00 | 1.00 | **0.75** | **-0.50** |
|  | 0.50 | 1.50 | 2.75 |  |  |
|  | 1.00 | 2.00 | 6.00 |  |  |
|  | -1.00 | -0.50 | 2.25 |  |  |
|  | -0.50 | 0.00 | 0.50 |  |  |
| 0.50 | 0.00 | 0.50 | 0.25 | 0.25 | 0.00 |
|  | 0.50 | 1.00 | 1.50 |  |  |
|  | 1.00 | 1.50 | 4.25 |  |  |
|  | -1.00 | -1.00 | 3.00 |  |  |
|  | -0.50 | -0.50 | 0.75 |  |  |
| 0.00 | 0.00 | 0.00 | 0.00 | 0.00 | 0.00 |
|  | 0.50 | 0.50 | 0.75 |  |  |
|  | 1.00 | 1.00 | 3.00 |  |  |

| Current State y(0) | Control u(0) | Next State y(1) = y(0) + u(0) | C*(0,2) = J(0,1) + J*(1,2) | Minimum Cost over last two stages J*(0,2) = min C*(0,2) | Optimal Control Applied at k = 0 |
|---|---|---|---|---|---|
|  | -1.00 | 0.50 | 2.25 |  |  |
|  | **-0.50** | **1.00** | **1.25** |  |  |
| 1.50 | 0.00 | 1.50 | 1.50 | **1.25** | **-0.50** |
|  | 0.50 | 2.00 |  |  |  |
|  | 1.00 | 2.50 |  |  |  |
|  | -1.00 | 0.00 | 2.00 |  |  |
|  | -0.50 | 0.50 | 0.75 |  |  |
| 1.00 | 0.00 | 1.00 | 0.75 | 0.75 | -0.50 |
|  | 0.50 | 1.50 | 2.00 |  |  |
|  | 1.00 | 2.00 |  |  |  |
|  | -1.00 | -0.50 |  |  |  |
|  | -0.50 | 0.00 | 0.50 |  |  |
| 0.50 | 0.00 | 0.50 | 0.25 | 0.25 | 0.00 |
|  | 0.50 | 1.00 | 1.25 |  |  |
|  | 1.00 | 1.50 | 3.50 |  |  |
|  | -1.00 | -1.00 |  |  |  |
|  | -0.50 | -0.50 |  |  |  |
| 0.00 | 0.00 | 0.00 | 0.00 | 0.00 | 0.00 |
|  | 0.50 | 0.50 | 0.75 |  |  |
|  | 1.00 | 1.00 | 2.75 |  |  |

We move now on the *stage 2* table section to read $y(1) = 1.0$, minimum cost $J_{1,2}^* = 0.75$, $y(2) = 0.5$, and OC $u^*(1) = -0.5$.

In summary, the optimal path when $y(0) = 1.5$ is:

$$y(0) = 1.5 \Rightarrow y(1) = 1.0 \text{ via the optimal control } u^*(0) = -0.5$$

then:

$$y(1) = 1.0 \Rightarrow y(2) = 0.50 \text{ via the optimal control } u^*(1) = -0.5$$

with

$$\text{Optimal value function } J_{0,2}^* = 1.25$$

Notice how Table 11.2-1 is originally built backward from *stage 2* to *stage 1* and then retraced forward to identify the optimal path.

| | A | B | C | D | E | F |
|---|---|---|---|---|---|---|
| | Current State y(1) | Control u(1) | Next State y(2) = y(1) + u(1) | Cost y²(2) + 2u²(1) = J(1,2) | Minimum Cost J*(1,2) | Optimal Control Applied at k = 1 |
| 1 | | | | | | |
| 2 | | -1 | =$A$4+B2 | =C2^2+2*B2^2 | | |
| 3 | | -0.5 | =$A$4+B3 | =C3^2+2*B3^2 | | |
| 4 | 1.5 | 0 | =$A$4+B4 | =C4^2+2*B4^2 | =MIN(D2:D6) | =B3 |
| 5 | | 0.5 | =$A$4+B5 | =C5^2+2*B5^2 | | |
| 6 | | 1 | =$A$4+B6 | =C6^2+2*B6^2 | | |
| 7 | | -1 | =$A$9+B7 | =C7^2+2*B7^2 | | |
| 8 | | -0.5 | =$A$9+B8 | =C8^2+2*B8^2 | | |
| 9 | 1 | 0 | =$A$9+B9 | =C9^2+2*B9^2 | =MIN(D7:D11) | =B8 |
| 10 | | 0.5 | =$A$9+B10 | =C10^2+2*B10^2 | | |
| 11 | | 1 | =$A$9+B11 | =C11^2+2*B11^2 | | |
| 12 | | -1 | =$A$14+B12 | =C12^2+2*B12^2 | | |
| 13 | | -0.5 | =$A$14+B13 | =C13^2+2*B13^2 | | |
| 14 | 0.5 | 0 | =$A$14+B14 | =C14^2+2*B14^2 | =MIN(D12:D16) | =B14 |
| 15 | | 0.5 | =$A$14+B15 | =C15^2+2*B15^2 | | |
| 16 | | 1 | =$A$14+B16 | =C16^2+2*B16^2 | | |
| 17 | | -1 | =$A$19+B17 | =C17^2+2*B17^2 | | |
| 18 | | -0.5 | =$A$19+B18 | =C18^2+2*B18^2 | | |
| 19 | 0 | 0 | =$A$19+B19 | =C19^2+2*B19^2 | =MIN(D17:D21) | =B19 |
| 20 | | 0.5 | =$A$19+B20 | =C20^2+2*B20^2 | | |
| 21 | | 1 | =$A$19+B21 | =C21^2+2*B21^2 | | |
| | Current State y(0) | Control u(0) | Next State y(1) = y(0) + u(0) | C*(0,2) = J(0,1) + J*(1,2) | Minimum Cost over last two stages J*(0,2) = min | Optimal Control Applied at k = 0 |
| 22 | | | | | | |
| 23 | | -1 | =$A$25+B23 | =2*B23^2+IFERROR(VLOOKUP(C23,$A$2:$F$21,5,FALSE),"") | | |
| 24 | | -0.5 | =$A$25+D24 | =2*B24^2+IFERROR(VLOOKUP(C24,$A$2:$F$21,5,FAL... | | |
| 25 | 1.5 | 0 | =$A$25+B25 | =2*B25^2+IFERROR(VLOOKUP(C25,$A$2:$F$21,5,FALSE),"") | =MIN(D23:D25) | =B24 |
| 26 | | 0.5 | =$A$25+B26 | | | |
| 27 | | 1 | =$A$25+B27 | | | |
| 28 | | -1 | =$A$30+B28 | =2*B28^2+IFERROR(VLOOKUP(C28,$A$2:$F$21,5,FALSE),"") | | |
| 29 | | -0.5 | =$A$30+B29 | =2*B29^2+IFERROR(VLOOKUP(C29,$A$2:$F$21,5,FALSE),"") | | |
| 30 | 1 | 0 | =$A$30+B30 | =2*B30^2+IFERROR(VLOOKUP(C30,$A$2:$F$21,5,FALSE),"") | =MIN(D28:D31) | =B29 |
| 31 | | 0.5 | =$A$30+B31 | =2*B31^2+IFERROR(VLOOKUP(C31,$A$2:$F$21,5,FALSE),"") | | |
| 32 | | 1 | =$A$30+B32 | | | |
| 33 | | -1 | =$A$35+B33 | | | |
| 34 | | -0.5 | =$A$35+B34 | =2*B34^2+IFERROR(VLOOKUP(C34,$A$2:$F$21,5,FALSE),"") | | |
| 35 | 0.5 | 0 | =$A$35+B35 | =2*B35^2+IFERROR(VLOOKUP(C35,$A$2:$F$21,5,FALSE),"") | =MIN(D34:D37) | =B35 |
| 36 | | 0.5 | =$A$35+B36 | =2*B36^2+IFERROR(VLOOKUP(C36,$A$2:$F$21,5,FALSE),"") | | |
| 37 | | 1 | =$A$35+B37 | =2*B37^2+IFERROR(VLOOKUP(C37,$A$2:$F$21,5,FALSE),"") | | |
| 38 | | -1 | =$A$40+B38 | | | |
| 39 | | -0.5 | =$A$40+B39 | | | |
| 40 | 0 | 0 | =$A$40+B40 | =2*B40^2+IFERROR(VLOOKUP(C40,$A$2:$F$21,5,FALSE),"") | =MIN(D40:D42) | =B40 |
| 41 | | 0.5 | =$A$40+B41 | =2*B41^2+IFERROR(VLOOKUP(C41,$A$2:$F$21,5,FALSE),"") | | |
| 42 | | 1 | =$A$40+B42 | =2*B42^2+IFERROR(VLOOKUP(C42,$A$2:$F$21,5,FALSE),"") | | |

**FIGURE 11.2-1**   Excel setup Discrete Dynamic Programming recurrence relation tabular resolution approach.

It is worth noticing that the *functional relation of dynamic programming*, in the context of these types of problems, will assume the following much broader general form, compared to Eq. (11.1-1):

$$J_{k,T}^{*}(y(k), u(k)) = \min_{\{u(k)\}}\left\{ J_{k,k+1}(y(k), u(k)) + J_{k+1,T}^{*}(y(k+1)) \right\} \qquad (11.2\text{-}1)$$

where:

$$y(k+1) = g(y(k), u(k)).$$

## EXAMPLE 1.B (EXCEL DATA TABLE AND SOLVER)

Another way we can exploit Excel in such a problem is to resort to either the Data Table or the Solver.

Let us analyze the Data Table first, which can be applied easily to a two-stage problem.

First, we set up the problem as follows in Fig. 11.2-2, where under *Column C* we just insert the equation of motion, while on *Column D* the performance measure. For the moment we leave to zero *Column B*, the values of OC, that represent the aim to find.

As a second step now let us go to the Excel ribbon, let us select Data, then What-if Analysis and Data Table, as in Fig. 11.2-3.

Let us build then the following Data Table in Fig. 11.2-4 over the *Cell D4*, which is the objective cell to be simulated and minimized.

As row-input cell we use $u(0) = $ *Cell B2*, while as column-input cell we use $u(1) = $ *Cell B3* because we want the objective cell to be optimized by changing $u(0)$ and $u(1)$. As required by the problem we make $u(k)$ move in the range $\mathcal{U} = [-1.0, -0.5, 0, 0.5, 1.0]$.

In the second table, once the optimal $u(0)$ and $u(1)$ are found, we calculate $y(k+1) = y(k)+u(k)$ as:

- $y(1) = 1.50 + u(0)$, in *Row C16:G16*, for each of the values taken by $u(0)$ in *Row C8:G8*.
- $y(2) = y(1)+u(1)$, in *Range C17:G21*, for each of the values taken by $y(1)$ in *Row C16:G16* and $u(1)$ in *Column B9:B13*, in the step before.

The solution is given in Table 11.2-2 (the minimum cost identified is in *Cell D10* $= J^* = 1.25$.

The alternative way to solve the problem is resorting to the Solver. In this case the solution would be reached setting up the Solver parameters like in Fig. 11.2-5. We want to minimize *Cell D4* of Fig. 11.2-2 by changing the control variables stored in the range B2:B3. The solution is given by Table 11.2-3 and by the graph in Fig. 11.2-6.

|  | A | B | C | D |
|---|---|---|---|---|
| 1 | t | u(k) | y(k+1) = y(k) + u(k) | J = y²(2) + 2u²(0) + 2u²(1) |
| 2 | 0 | 0 | 1.5 | |
| 3 | 1 | 0 | =C2+B2 | |
| 4 | 2 | | =C3+B3 | =2*B2^2+2*B3^2+C4^2 |

FIGURE 11.2-2 Step 1: build the two-stage discrete system with $y(0) = 1.50$.

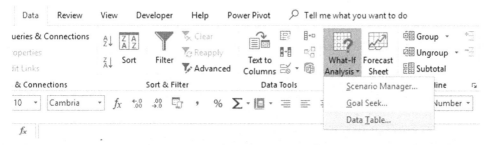

FIGURE 11.2-3 Step 2: go to Data Table.

III. Dynamic optimization

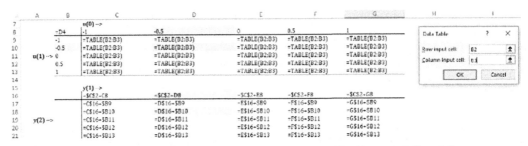

**FIGURE 11.2-4** Step 3: build a Data Table over Cell D4 (the Objective Cell) as follows.

**TABLE 11.2-2** Data Table solution of the two-stage problem with $y(0) = 1.50$.

| t | u(k) | y(k+1) = y(k) + u(k) | $J = y^2(2) + 2u^2(0) + 2u^2(1)$ | $J^*$ |
|---|------|----------------------|-----------------------------------|-------|
| 0.00 | -0.500 | 1.500 | | |
| 1.00 | -0.500 | 1.000 | | |
| 2.00 | | 0.500 | 1.2500 | 1.2500 |

| | | u(0) --> | | | | |
|---|------|-------|-------|------|------|-------|
| | 1.25 | -1.00 | -0.50 | 0.00 | 0.50 | 1.00 |
| | -1.00 | 4.25 | 2.50 | 2.25 | 3.50 | 6.25 |
| | -0.50 | 2.50 | 1.25 | 1.50 | 3.25 | 6.50 |
| u(1) --> | 0.00 | 2.25 | 1.50 | 2.25 | 4.50 | 8.25 |
| | 0.50 | 3.50 | 3.25 | 4.50 | 7.25 | 11.50 |
| | 1.00 | 6.25 | 6.50 | 8.25 | 11.50 | 16.25 |

| | | y(1) --> | | | | |
|---|------|-------|------|------|------|------|
| | 0.50 | | 1.00 | 1.50 | 2.00 | 2.50 |
| | -0.50 | | 0.00 | 0.50 | 1.00 | 1.50 |
| | 0.00 | | 0.50 | 1.00 | 1.50 | 2.00 |
| y(2) --> | 0.50 | | 1.00 | 1.50 | 2.00 | 2.50 |
| | 1.00 | | 1.50 | 2.00 | 2.50 | 3.00 |
| | 1.50 | | 2.00 | 2.50 | 3.00 | 3.50 |

Notice how the Solver finds a better solution than the Data Table solution. This is since the constraint on $u(k)$ is given in the form of a range ($-1 \leq u(k) \leq 1$), rather than through the discrete point values of $\mathscr{U} = [-1.0, -0.5, 0, 0.5, 1.0]$. In the Solver solution $u(0) = u(1) = -0.375$ while $J^* = 1.125$.

### EXAMPLE 1.C (BELLMAN APPROACH WITH STANDARD CALCULUS)

Let us start with the following functional at *step 2* to be optimized with respect to $u(1)$:

$$J_{1,2} = [y(2)]^2 + 2[u(1)]^2.$$

As $y(2) = y(1) + u(1)$ then we have:

$$J_{1,2}(u(1)) = [y(1) + u(1)]^2 + 2[u(1)]^2.$$

**Solver Parameters**                                                    ✕

Se_t Objective:                          $DS4                         ⬆

To:     ○ Ma_x        ◉ Mi_n        ○ _Value Of:       0

B_y Changing Variable Cells:

$B$2:$B$3                                                            ⬆

S_ubject to the Constraints:

| $B$2:$B$3 <= 1 | | _Add |
| $B$2:$B$3 >= -1 | | |
| | | _Change |
| | | _Delete |
| | | _Reset All |
| | | Load/Save |

☐ Ma_ke Unconstrained Variables Non-Negative

S_elect a Solving     GRG Nonlinear                     ⌄     O_ptions
Method:

**Solving Method**

Select the GRG Nonlinear engine for Solver Problems that are smooth nonlinear. Select the LP
Simplex engine for linear Solver Problems, and select the Evolutionary engine for Solver
problems that are non-smooth.

| _Help | | _Solve | | Cl_ose |

FIGURE 11.2-5    Example 1.b: solver parameters.

Let us now differentiate $J_{1,2}(u(1))$ with respect to $u(1)$ to find the optimal $u^*(1)$:

$$\frac{\partial J_{1,2}}{\partial u(1)} = 2[y(1) + u(1)] + 4u(1) = 0 \Rightarrow u^*(1) = -\frac{2}{6}y(1) = -\frac{2}{6}[y(0) + u(0)].$$

We have expressed $u^*(1)$ as a function of $y(0)$ and $u(0)$. Let us cover now *step 1* with the functional over the two steps expressed as follows:

$$J_{0,2} = J_{0,1} + \left\{J_{1,2}^*\right\} = 2[u(0)]^2 + \left\{[y(2)]^2 + 2[u^*(1)]^2\right\}$$
$$= 2[u(0)]^2 + \left\{[y(0) + u(0) + u(1)]^2 + 2[u^*(1)]^2\right\},$$

III. Dynamic optimization

**TABLE 11.2-3**   Example 1.b: solver solution.

| t | u(k) | y(k+1) = y(k) + u(k) | J = y²(2) + 2u²(0) + 2u²(1) |
|---|---|---|---|
| 0.00 | -0.375 | 1.500 | |
| 1.00 | -0.375 | 1.125 | |
| 2.00 | | 0.750 | 1.1250 |

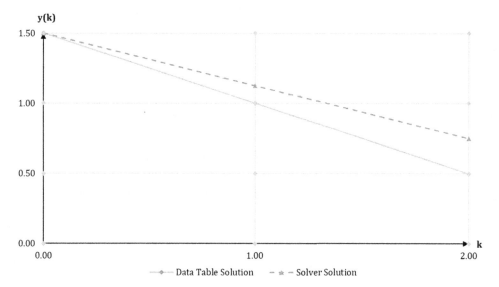

**FIGURE 11.2-6**   Plot of the optimal path $y*(k)$ Solver and Data Table solutions with $y(0) = 1.50$.

which becomes, with $u*(1) = -\frac{2}{6}[y(0) + u(0)]$:

$$J_{0,2} = 2[u(0)]^2 + \left\{ \left[ y(0) + u(0) - \frac{2}{6}[y(0) + u(0)] \right]^2 + 2\left[ -\frac{2}{6}[y(0) + u(0)] \right]^2 \right\}.$$

We can now differentiate with respect to $u(0)$ as follows:

$$\frac{\partial J_{0,2}}{\partial u(0)} = 4u(0) + 2\left[ y(0) + u(0) - \frac{2}{6}[y(0) + u(0)] \right]\left(\frac{4}{6}\right) + 4\left[ -\frac{2}{6}[y(0) + u(0)] \right]\left(-\frac{2}{6}\right) = 0.$$

With the initial condition $y(0) = 1.50$ the above equation leads to the optimal $u*(0)$:

$$\frac{\partial J_{0,2}}{\partial u(0)} = 2 + \frac{16}{3}u(0) = 0 \Rightarrow u*(0) = -0.375.$$

Now that we have obtained $u^*(0) = -0.375$ we can solve the problem going forward to determine $y(1) = 1.50-0.375 = 1.125$, together with $u^*(1) = -\frac{2}{6}y(1) = -0.375$ and $y(2) = 1.125-0.375 = 0.75$, which constitutes the optimal solution leading to $J^*(u) = y^2(2)+2u^2(0)+2u^2(1) = 0.5625 + 2\cdot0.28,125 = 1.125$.

## 11.3 Cargo loading allocation problems: tabular method and the Excel Solver

As described thoroughly by Richard Bellman and Stuart Dreyfus[3] the dynamic programming technique is also useful for the one-dimensional allocation types of process. We will see here the cargo loading problem, that is stated, in its simplest form, in the following terms.

A cargo ship has a maximum capacity $W$, and the cargo is to consist of different quantities $x_i$ of different $N$ items.

Now let:

$$w_i = \text{the weight of the} i_{th} \text{ type of item,}$$

$$v_i = \text{the value of the} i_{th} \text{type of item,}$$

$$x_i = \text{the number of items of type} i \text{loaded.}$$

The problem is to choose the optimal quantities $x_i$, such that the following linear objective function is maximized, subject to the specified constraints:

$$\max_{\{x_i\}} L(x) = \sum_{i=1}^{N} x_i v_i \ (objective\ performance\ measure)$$

$$s.t. \sum_{i=1}^{N} x_i w_i \leq W (total\ weight\ constraint)$$

$$\text{and } x_i, v_i, w_i \geq 0 \ (where\ x_i\ must\ be\ an\ integer)$$

This is a typical linear integer operational research problem that can be solved easily with the Solver. However, we want to show here how the dynamic programming can be an alternative way to approach and solve the problem.

This is done as follows.

Let us define the optimal value function $J_N^*(W)$ as:

$$J_N^*(W) = \max \sum_{i=1}^{N} x_i v_i.$$

[3] *Applied Dynamic Programming*, Princeton University, 1962, chapter I.

In the context of DDP, the problem is essentially restated to find the portion of the available resource $W$ to allocate to each of the $N$ types of items (or $N$ activities).

The functional dynamic recurrence relation that we will use is then expressed as:

$$J_N^*(W) = \max_{\{x_N\}}\{x_N v_N + J_{N-1}^*(W - x_N w_N)\}$$

We have then the following optimal function at each stage:

- $J_1^*(W) = \max\limits_{x_1 w_1 \leq W}\{x_1 v_1\} = \max\limits_{x_1 w_1 \leq W}\left\{\left[\dfrac{W}{w_1}\right] v_1\right\}$

- $J_2^*(W) = \max\limits_{x_1 w_1 + x_2 w_2 \leq W}\{x_2 v_2 + J_1^*(W - x_2 w_2)\} = \max\limits_{x_1 w_1 + x_2 w_2 \leq W}\left\{\left[\dfrac{W}{w_2}\right] v_2 + \max\limits_{x_1 w_1 \leq W}\left[\dfrac{W}{w_1}\right] v_1\right\}$

- $J_3^*(W) = \max\limits_{x_1 w_1 + x_2 w_2 + x_3 w_3 \leq W}\{x_3 v_3 + J_2^*(W - x_3 w_3)\}$

  $= \max\limits_{x_1 w_1 + x_2 w_2 + x_3 w_3 \leq W}\left\{\left[\dfrac{W}{w_3}\right] v_3 + \max\limits_{x_1 w_1 + x_2 w_2 \leq W}\left\{\left[\dfrac{W}{w_2}\right] v_2 + \max\limits_{x_1 w_1 \leq W}\left[\dfrac{W}{w_1}\right] v_1\right\}\right\}$

- Etc....

## Numerical example 1

Let us consider the following data:

$$w_1 = 49, w_2 = 50, w_3 = 51$$

$$v_1 = 20, v_2 = 75, v_3 = 102$$

The optimal solution is to load 2 items of type 2, 0 items of type 1, and 0 items of type 3:

$$x_1 = 0, x_2 = 2, x_3 = 0.$$

Fig. 11.3-1 shows the procedure to obtain the optimal result enumerated in Table 11.3-1. We have divided the maximum capacity $W = 100$ in two ranges, such that:

$$0 \leq W_\alpha < 50$$

$$50 \leq W_\alpha \leq 100$$

| Stage | | Integer Number of items to load $x_n = (W - 100)/w_n$ | $J_n(W_n) = x_n v_n + J_{n-1}(W_n - x_n v_n)$ | Capacity W min | Capacity W max | Remaining Capacity from N-1 | Remaining capacity to be allocated next stage | Total Capacity Utilized | Policy | Optimal Policy such that $J^* = Max J = \Sigma$ $x_n v_n$ |
|---|---|---|---|---|---|---|---|---|---|---|
| 13 | | | | | | | | | | |
| 14 | 1 | =INT(D14/F2) | =B14*F5 | 0 | 50 | | =100-B14*F2 | =100-G14 | 0 Items of type1 | |
| 15 | Item 1 | =INT(E15/F2) | =INT(B15)*F5 | 50 | 100 | | =100-B15*F2 | =100-G15 | 2 Items of type1 | =MAX(C14:C15) |
| 16 | 2 | =INT(D16/50$2) | =B16*G5+C14 | 0 | 50 | =G14 | =F16-B16*5G$2 | =100-016 | 0 items type2 and 0 items type1 | |
| 17 | Item 1 | =INT(D17/5G$2) | =B17*G6+C15 | 0 | 50 | =G15 | =F17-B17*5G$2 | =100-G17 | 0 items type2 and 2 items type1 | |
| 18 | + | =INT(E18/5G$2) | =B18*G6+C14 | 50 | 100 | =G14 | =F18-B18*G2 | =100-G18 | 2 items of type2 0 items type1 | =MAX(C16:C18) |
| 19 | Item 2 | =INT(E19/5G$2) | =B19*G6+C15 | 50 | 100 | =G15 | =F19-B19*G2 | =100-G19 | Not feasible discarded for next stage | |
| 20 | 3 | =INT(D20/5H$2) | =B20*H5+C16 | 0 | 50 | =G16 | =F20-B20*H2 | =100-G20 | 0 items type3 type2 and type1 | |
| 21 | Item 1 | =INT(D21/5H$2) | =B21*H5+C17 | 0 | 50 | =G17 | =F21-B21*H2 | =100-G21 | 0items type3 0 type2 and 2 type1 | |
| 22 | + | =INT(D22/5H$2) | =B22*H5+C18 | 0 | 50 | =G18 | =F22-B22*H2 | =100-G22 | 0 items type3 2 type2 and 0 type1 | =MAX(C20:C23) |
| 23 | Item 2 | =INT(E23/5H$2) | =B23*H5+C16 | 50 | 100 | =F20 | =F23-B23*H2 | =100-G23 | 1 item type1 0 type2 and type1 | |
| 24 | + | =INT(E24/5H$2) | =B24*H6+C17 | 50 | 100 | =F21 | =F24-B24*H2 | =100-G24 | Not feasible | |
| 25 | Item 3 | =INT(E25/5H$2) | =B25*H5+C18 | 50 | 100 | =F22 | =F25-B25*H2 | =100-G25 | Not feasible | |

**FIGURE 11.3-1** Cargo loading setup problem.

**TABLE 11.3-1** Cargo loading problem solution.

| Stage | Integer Number of items to load $x_\alpha$ = (W = 100 )/$w_\alpha$ | $J_i(W_\alpha)$ = $x_\alpha v_\alpha$ + $J_{i-1}(W_\alpha - x_\alpha w_\alpha)$ | Capacity W min | Capacity W max | Remaining Capacity from N-1 | Remaining capacity to be allocated next stage | Total Capacity Utilized | Policy | Optimal Policy such that J* = Max J = $\Sigma$ $x_\alpha v_\alpha$ |
|---|---|---|---|---|---|---|---|---|---|
| 1.00 | 0.00 | 0.00 | 0.00 | 50.00 | | 100.00 | 0.00 | 0 Items of type1 | |
| Item 1 | 2.00 | 40.00 | 50.00 | 100.00 | | 2.00 | 98.00 | 2 Items of type1 | 40.00 |
| 2.00 | 0.00 | 0.00 | 0.00 | 50.00 | 100.00 | 100.00 | 0.00 | 0 items type2 and 0 items type1 | |
| Item 1 | 0.00 | 40.00 | 0.00 | 50.00 | 2.00 | 2.00 | 98.00 | 0 items type2 and 2 items type1 | |
| . | 2.00 | 150.00 | 50.00 | 100.00 | 100.00 | 0.00 | 100.00 | 2 items of type2 0 items type1 | 150.00 |
| Item 2 | 2.00 | 190.00 | 50.00 | 100.00 | 2.00 | 98.00 | 198.00 | Not feasible discarded for next stage | |
| 3.00 | 0.00 | 0.00 | 0.00 | 50.00 | 100.00 | 100.00 | 0.00 | 0 items type3 type2 and type1 | |
| Item 1 | 0.00 | 40.00 | 0.00 | 50.00 | 2.00 | 2.00 | 98.00 | 0items type3 0 type2 and 2 type1 | |
| . | 0.00 | 150.00 | 0.00 | 50.00 | 0.00 | 0.00 | 100.00 | 0 items type3 2 type2 and 0 type1 | 150.00 |
| Item 2 | 1.00 | 102.00 | 50.00 | 100.00 | 100.00 | 49.00 | 51.00 | 1 item type1 0 type2 and type1 | |
| . | 1.00 | 142.00 | 50.00 | 100.00 | 2.00 | -49.00 | 149.00 | Not feasible | |
| Item 3 | 1.00 | 252.00 | 50.00 | 100.00 | 0.00 | 51.00 | 151.00 | Not feasible | |

for each range in the $i_{th}$ activity we assess the maximum integer of quantities loadable of the $i_{th}$ item as integer of $W_\alpha/w_\alpha$.

What we do in Excel is just calculating the value of the functional at each stage for each of the value of the functional at the stage before, as described in Fig. 11.3-1.

In particular, the computational procedure goes through the following steps.

1. Evaluation of $J_i = x_i v_i = \left\lceil \dfrac{W_\alpha}{w_i} \right\rceil v_i$ to choose the quantity $x_i$ (integer) to load.

2. Table look-up for the optimal return $J_{i-1}^*(W_\alpha - x_i w_i)$ obtainable from the item $(i-1)$.

3. Maximization of (1) + (2) subject to $\sum\limits_{i=1}^{N} x_i w_i \leq W$.

## Excel Solver solution

The same solution $x_1 = 0$, $x_2 = 2$, $x_3 = 0$ could have been reached as well via the Excel Solver, within a typical Linear Programming approach, just setting up the Solver parameters to maximize the objective function $L(x) = \sum\limits_{i=1}^{N} x_i v_i$ s.t. to the given constraint $\sum\limits_{i=1}^{N} x_i w_i \leq W$, together with the integer constraint over $x_i$.

The problem would be then set up as follows in Figs. 11.3-2 and 11.3-3:

|  | A | B | C | D | E | F | G | H |
|---|---|---|---|---|---|---|---|---|
| 1 | W Max | =SUMPRODUCT(F5:H5;F8:H8) | | | | w1 | w2 | w3 |
| 2 | | | | | | 49 | 50 | 51 |
| 3 | | | | | | | | |
| 4 | s.t. | =SUMPRODUCT(F2:H2;F8:H8) | <= | 100 | | v1 | v2 | v3 |
| 5 | | | | | | 20 | 75 | 102 |
| 6 | | | | | | | | |
| 7 | | | | | | x1 | x2 | x3 |
| 8 | | | | | | 0 | 2 | 0 |

**FIGURE 11.3-2** Example 1: Cargo loading problem Excel setup for Solver.

Solver Parameters                                                    ✕

Se̱t Objective:                    $B$1|                                    ⬆

To:      ⦿ Ma̱x      ○ Mi̱n      ○ Va̱lue Of:      0

By̱ Changing Variable Cells:

$F$8:$H$8                                                              ⬆

Su̱bject to the Constraints:

| $B$4 = 100 |  | Add |
| $F$8:$H$8 = integer |  |  |
|  |  | Change |
|  |  | Delete |
|  |  | Reset All |
|  |  | Load/Save |

☑ Ma̱ke Unconstrained Variables Non-Negative

Se̱lect a Solving      Simplex LP                          Options
Method:

Solving Method

Select the GRG Nonlinear engine for Solver Problems that are smooth nonlinear. Select the LP
Simplex engine for linear Solver Problems, and select the Evolutionary engine for Solver
problems that are non-smooth.

He̱lp                              So̱lve                    Cḻose

FIGURE 11.3-3    Example 1: Cargo loading problem Solver parameters.

## 11.4 Multistage allocation problems using the Excel Solver

Another important class of problems in DDP is represented by the *multistage allocation processes* (see Richard Bellman, *Dynamic Programming*, chapter I).

Let us assume we have two different production processes and a certain material $\mathscr{X} = x_0$ is to be divided into two nonnegative parts $y_0$ and $(x_0 - y_0)$ to be employed respectively in the two production processes, such that we obtain a return $g(y_0)$ from the first production process and $h(x_0 - y_0)$ from the second production process.

The problem is then to maximize the total return:

$$R_1(x_0, y_0) = g(y_0) + h(x_0 - y_0)$$

Now, as a natural consequence of the production cycle let us assume that after the first production stage, the quantity $y_0$ reduces to $ay_0$ with $0 \leq a \leq 1$ and the quantity $(x_0 - y_0)$ reduces to $b(x_0 - y_0)$ with $0 \leq b \leq 1$.

We are left then with the quantity $x_1 = ay_0 + b(x_0 - y_0)$ to be employed again in the following production stage of the two production processes, so that we divide $x_1$ in the two quantities $y_1$ and $(x_1 - y_1)$ to generate the return at stage 2 as:

$$g(y_1) + h(x_1 - y_1)$$

and the total return at stage 2 as:

$$R_2(x_0, y_0, y_1) = [g(y_0) + h(x_0 - y_0)] + [g(y_1) + h(x_1 - y_1)]$$

as $x_1 = ay_0 + b(x_0 - y_0)$ the above functional equation becomes:

$$R_2(x_0, y_0, y_1) = [g(y_0) + h(x_0 - y_0)] + [g(y_1) + h(ay_0 + b(x_0 - y_0) - y_1)]$$

which is a function in two variables that can be maximized with respect to $y_0$ and $y_1$.

In general, with N stages the problem can be formalized as follows:

$$\max_{\{y_0,\ y_1,y_2,\cdots,y_{N-1}\}} R_N(x_0, y_0, y_1, y_2, \cdots, y_{N-1}) = \max_{\{y_0,\ y_1,y_2,\cdots,y_{N-1}\}} \sum_{k=0}^{N-1} [g(y_k) + h(x_k - y_k)]$$

s.t. $0 \leq y_k \leq x_k$ and $x_{k+1} = ay_k + b(x_k - y_k)$ for $k = 0, 1, 2 \cdots (N - 2)$

Within the DDP, the above problem is solved resorting to the recurrence relation as follows.

Let us define the function:

$f_N$ = maximum return obtained from an N − stage process starting with $x_0$.

We have then:

$$f_N(x) = \max_{\{y_0,\ y_1,y_2,\cdots,y_{N-1}\}} R_N(x_0, y_0, y_1, y_2, \cdots, y_{N-1})$$

while the recurrence equation, separating the objective function at each stage as the sum of the optimal for the current stage and the optimal reached until the stage before is defined as:

$$f_N(x) = \max_{0 \leq y \leq x} \{g(y) + h(x - y) + f_{N-1}[ay + b(x - y)]\}$$

A numerical example will clarify the way the DDP is used in these types of problems.

## Numerical example 1

Let us consider the following data.

$$x_0 = 10, \ N = 4, \ g(y) = 3y, \ h(x - y) = 2(x - y), \ a = 0.75, \ b = 0.80$$

First, the problem can be solved immediately with the Excel Solver setting up the Excel as in Fig. 11.4-1 (the equation of motion is stored under *Column B*), while the Solver parameters setup is in Fig. 11.4-2. The optimal solution is represented in Table 11.4-1.

Secondly, resorting instead to the computations of the Bellman approach, we would separate the solution of the problem into four steps.

**1.** $f_1(x_3) = \max_{0 \le y_3 \le x_3} \{g(y_3) + h(x_3 - y_3)\} = \max_{0 \le y_3 \le x_3} \{3y_3 + 2(x_3 - y_3)\} = \max_{0 \le y_3 \le x_3} \{y_3 + 2x_3\}$

which is maximized for $y_3 = x_3$ obtaining $f_1(x_3) = x_3 + 2x_3 = 3x_3$.

**2.** $f_2(x_2) = \max_{0 \le y_2 \le x_2} \{g(y_2) + h(x_2 - y_2) + f_1\} = \max_{0 \le y_2 \le x_2} \{3y_2 + 2(x_2 - y_2) + 3x_3\}$

From the equation of motion $x_{k+1} = ay_k + b(x_k - y_k)$ we state $x_3$ as a function of $y_2$ and $x_2$ as:

$$x_3 = 0.75y_2 + 0.80(x_2 - y_2),$$

so that $f_2(x_2)$ becomes:

$$f_2(x_2) = \max_{0 \le y_2 \le x_2} \{3y_2 + 2(x_2 - y_2) + 3[0.75y_2 + 0.80(x_2 - y_2)]\} = \max_{0 \le y_2 \le x_2} \{0.85y_2 + 4.4x_2\}$$

whose maximum is reached for $y_2 = x_2$ so that we have $f_2(x_2) = 0.85x_2 + 4.4x_2 = 5.25x_2$

**3.** $f_3(x_1) = \max_{0 \le y_1 \le x_1} \{g(y_1) + h(x_1 - y_1) + f_2(x_2)\} = \max_{0 \le y_1 \le x_1} \{3y_1 + 2(x_1 - y_1) + 5.25x_2\}$

As $x_2 = 0.75y_1 + 0.80(x_1 - y_1)$ we use this relation in $f_3(x_1)$ obtaining the following:

$$f_3(x_1) = \max_{0 \le y_1 \le x_1} \{3y_1 + 2(x_1 - y_1) + 5.25[0.75y_1 + 0.80(x_1 - y_1)]\} = 0.7375y_1 + 6.20x_1,$$

| | A | B | C | D | E | F | G | H | I |
|---|---|---|---|---|---|---|---|---|---|
| 1 | x | | y | g(y) = 3y | h(x-y) = 2(x-y) | Σ g(y) + h(x-y) | | a | b |
| 2 | 0 | 10 | | 10 =3*C2 | =2*(B2-C2) | =D2+E2 | | 0.75 | 0.8 |
| 3 | 1 | =SH$2*C2+$I$2*(B2-C2) | 7.50 =3*C3 | | =2*(B3-C3) | =D3+E3 | | given data | |
| 4 | 2 | =SH$2*C3+$I$2*(B3-C3) | 5.62 =3*C4 | | =2*(B4-C4) | =D4+E4 | | | |
| 5 | 3 | =SH$2*C4+$I$2*(B4-C4) | 4.21 =3*C5 | | =2*(B5-C5) | =D5+E5 | | | |
| 6 | | | | | | | | | |
| 7 | s.t. $0 \le y \le x$ | | | | Σ | =SUM(F2:F5) | | | |

FIGURE 11.4-1   Example 1: multistage allocation problem Excel setup.

Solver Parameters      ✕

Se_t Objective:     SFS7     ⬆

To:   ◉ M_ax    ○ Mi_n    ○ _Value Of:    0

_By Changing Variable Cells:

SCS2:SCS5      ⬆

Su_bject to the Constraints:

SCS2:SCS5 <= SBS2:SBS5      _Add
SCS2:SCS5 >= 0     

C_hange

D_elete

_Reset All

Load/Save

☑ Ma_ke Unconstrained Variables Non-Negative

S_elect a Solving Method:    Simplex LP    ⌄    Options

Solving Method

Select the GRG Nonlinear engine for Solver Problems that are smooth nonlinear. Select the LP Simplex engine for linear Solver Problems, and select the Evolutionary engine for Solver problems that are non-smooth.

Help      _Solve      Cl_ose

**FIGURE 11.4-2**   Example 1: multistage allocation problem solver parameters.

**TABLE 11.4-1**   Example 1: multistage Problem Optimal Solution for $y$.

| | x | y | g(y) = 3y | h(x-y) = 2(x-y) | Σg(y) + h(x-y) | | a | b |
|---|---|---|---|---|---|---|---|---|
| 0.0000 | 10.0000 | 10.0000 | 30.0000 | 0.0000 | 30.0000 | | 0.7500 | 0.8000 |
| 1.0000 | 7.5000 | 7.5000 | 22.5000 | 0.0000 | 22.5000 | | given data | |
| 2.0000 | 5.6250 | 5.6250 | 16.8750 | 0.0000 | 16.8750 | | | |
| 3.0000 | 4.2187 | 4.2188 | 12.6563 | 0.0000 | 12.6562 | | | |
| s.t. | $0 \leq y \leq x$ | | | Σ | 82.0313 | | | |

III. Dynamic optimization

which is maximized for $y_1 = x_1$ obtaining $f_3(x_1) = 6.9375x_1$, where $x_1 = 0.75y_0 + 0.80(x_0 - y_0)$.

**4.**
$$f_4(x_0) = \max_{0 \le y_0 \le x_0} \{g(y_0) + h(x_0 - y_0) + f_3\}$$

$$= \max_{0 \le y_0 \le x_0} \{3y_0 + 2(x_0 - y_0) + 6.9375[0.75y_0 + 0.80(x_0 - y_0)]\}$$

from which we derive $f_4(x_0) = \max_{0 \le y_0 \le x_0} \{0.6531y_0 + 7.55x_0\}$ which is maximized for $y_0 = x_0 = 10$ obtaining the following:

$$f_4(x_0) = (0.6531) \cdot 10 + (7.55) \cdot 10 = 82.031$$

which is the optimal value function solution over the four stages. Notice how the maximum points have always been found at the right admissible extremum of $y_k$, due to the positive linearity of $f_N(x_k)$ over each step.

Once the optimal value of $y_0$ has been found we have then:

$$x_1 = ay_0 + b(x_0 - y_0) = 0.75 \cdot 10 + 0.80 \cdot (10 - 10) = 7.5000$$

$$x_2 = ay_1 + b(x_1 - y_1) = 0.75 \cdot 7.5000 + 0.80 \cdot (7.5000 - 7.5000) = 5.6250$$

$$x_3 = ay_2 + b(x_2 - y_2) = 0.75 \cdot 5.6250 + 0.80 \cdot (5.6250 - 5.6250) = 4.2187$$

## 11.5 Equality constrained optimization problems using the recursive Bellman's approach

DDP can be used as well to solve in stages equality constrained optimization problems. Let us consider the following problem of minimization of the sum of squares, which will turn out to be useful to understand the way the next economic applications have been developed:

$$\max_{\{u_t\}} J = -\sum_{t=0}^{T} u_t^2$$

s.t.

$$\sum_{t=0}^{T} u_t = S \text{ and } u(t) \ge 0.$$

We describe the recursive optimization method in three stages, that is, $T = 3$, with $c = 10$. We proceed beginning from $T = 1$.

$T = 1$

$$J_1^* = \max\left[-u_1^2 - u_0^2\right]$$

Let $S_1$ be the following sum:

$$u_0 + u_1 = S_1$$

from which we have:

$$u_0 = S_1 - u_1,$$

then, the functional becomes:

$$J_1^* = \max\left[-u_1^2 + J_0^*\right] = \max\left[-u_1^2 - (S_1 - u_1)^2\right].$$

Let us maximize with respect to $u_1$ as follows:

$$\frac{\partial J_1}{\partial u_1} = -2u_1 - 2(S_1 - u_1)(-1)$$

$$= -2u_1 + 2S_1 - 2u_1 = -2u_1 + S_1$$

$$\Rightarrow u_1^* = \frac{1}{2}S_1.$$

In case of $u_0 + u_1 = 10$ we have

$$u_1^* = 5, u_0^* = 5$$

$$J_1^* = -\frac{1}{4}S_1^2 - \left(S_1 - \frac{1}{2}S_1\right)^2 = -\frac{1}{2}S_1^2 = -50$$

$T = 2$

In this case the functional becomes:

$$J_2^* = \max\left[-u_2^2 - u_1^2 - u_0^2\right]$$

We know from $T = 1$ that $J_1^* = -\frac{1}{2}S_1^2$ so that we have the functional expressed by:

$$J_2^* = \max\left[-u_2^2 + J_1^*\right] = \max\left[-u_2^2 - \frac{1}{2}S_1^2\right]$$

Let $S_2$ be:

$$S_1 + u_2 = (u_0 + u_1) + u_2 = S_2$$

then, the optimal functional to maximize will be:

$$J_2^* = \max\left[ -u_2^2 + J_1^* \right] = \max\left[ -u_2^2 - \frac{1}{2}(S_2 - u_2)^2 \right].$$

Taking now the derivative with respect to $u_2$ we have:

$$\frac{\partial J_2}{\partial u_2} = -2u_2 - (S_2 - u_2)(-1) = -3u_2 + S_2$$

$$\Rightarrow u_2^* = \frac{1}{3}S_2$$

$$J_2^* = -\left(\frac{1}{3}S_2\right)^2 - \frac{1}{2}\left(S_2 - \frac{1}{3}S_2\right)^2 = -\frac{1}{9}S_2^2 - \frac{1}{2}\left(\frac{4}{9}S_2^2\right) = -\frac{1}{3}S_2^2$$

$T = 3$

The functional is

$$J_3^* = \max\left[ -u_3^2 - u_2^2 - u_1^2 - u_0^2 \right]$$

From $T = 2$ we know that $J_2^* = -\frac{1}{3}S_2^2$ so that now the functional becomes:

$$J_3^* = \max\left[ -u_3^2 + J_2^* \right] = \max\left[ -u_3^2 - \frac{1}{3}S_2^2 \right]$$

Let $S_3$ be:

$$S_2 + u_3 = (u_0 + u_1 + u_2) + u_3 = S_3$$

then, the optimal functional to maximize will be:

$$J_3^* = \max\left[ -u_3^2 + J_2^* \right] = \max\left[ -u_3^2 - \frac{1}{3}(S_3 - u_3)^2 \right].$$

Taking the derivative with respect to $u_3$ we have:

$$\frac{\partial J_3}{\partial u_3} = -2u_3 - \frac{2}{3}(S_3 - u_3)(-1) = -\frac{8}{3}u_3 + \frac{2}{3}S_3$$

$$\Rightarrow u_3^* = \frac{1}{4}S_3$$

**TABLE 11.5-1** Excel Solver solution at each stage ($c = 10$).

| | T=1 | | | T=2 | | | T=3 | |
|---|---|---|---|---|---|---|---|---|
| t | u(t) | J* | t | u(t) | J* | t | u(t) | J* |
| 0 | 5.00 | | 0 | 3.33 | | 0 | 2.50 | |
| 1 | 5.00 | -50.00 | 1 | 3.33 | | 1 | 2.50 | |
| | | | 2 | 3.33 | -33.33 | 2 | 2.50 | |
| | | | | | | 3 | 2.50 | -25.00 |
| s.t. | 10.0000 | 10.0000 | s.t. | 10.0000 | 10.0000 | s.t. | 10.0000 | 10.0000 |

with

$$J_3^* = -\frac{1}{16}S_3^2 - \frac{1}{3}\left(S_3 - \frac{1}{4}S_3\right)^2 = -\frac{1}{16}S_3^2 - \frac{3}{16}S_3^2 = -\frac{1}{4}S_3^2$$

Using Excel, we can easily resort to the Solver and build Table 11.5-1. We see in next paragraph in more detail how the solver is applied.

## 11.6 Dynamic economic problems solved with Discrete Dynamic Programming

Within this section, we will develop some basic discrete dynamic economic problems to show how the techniques seen so far are similarly applied. The first example is a typical optimal consumption and saving model.

### EXAMPLE 1 (OPTIMAL CONSUMPTION AND SAVING)

Let $C_t = u_t$ be the consumption in period $t$, to which a logarithmic utility, namely $U(C_t) = \log(u_t)$, is associated.

Let us assume the consumer generates his own output according to a Cobb–Douglas function as follows:

$$y_t = AK_{t-1}^\alpha \quad \text{with } A \text{ and } \alpha \text{ positive constants.}$$

Also, let $K_t$ be the capital available at the beginning of period $t$ to which the following equation of motion is associated:

$$K_{t+1} = AK_t^\alpha - u_t \geq 0 \quad \text{for } t = 0, 1, 2, \cdots, T \text{ and with a given I condition } K_0.$$

We use $u_t$ to clearly identify the consumption variable in period $t$ as control variable, as we did in the OC theory.

The problem is then to find the optimal consumption for each period $t$ such that the present value of the utility function is maximized.

$$\max_{\{u_t\}} \sum_{t=0}^{T} \beta^t \log(u_t)$$

$$s.t.\ K_{t+1} = AK_t^\alpha - u_t \geq 0 \quad \text{for } t = 0,\ 1,\ 2,\ \cdots, T \text{ and I condition} K_0 \text{ given.}$$

$\beta^t = \left(\frac{1}{1+\rho}\right)^t$ is the discount factor for a given interest rate $\rho$.

The recursive relation associated to this problem can be expressed as follows:

$$J_{t,T}(K, u) = \max\left\{\beta^t [\log(u_t)] + J_{t+1,T}^*(K_{t+1})\right\}$$

$$s.t.\ K_{t+1} = AK_t^\alpha - u_t \geq 0 \text{ and } u_t \geq 0.$$

It is normally assumed that $T = $ entire life cycle and therefore $K_{T+1} = 0$.

Let us solve by hand (and then in Excel) a numerical case with the following data: $t = 0,\ 1,\ 2\ (T = 3)$, for simplicity let's put $A = 1$, $\alpha = 1$, while interest rate is $\rho = 5\%$ and $K_0 = 5$.

The objective function to maximize is the quantity:

$$\sum_{t=0}^{2} \beta^t \log(u_t) = \left\{\beta^0 \log(u_0) + \beta^1 \log(u_1) + \beta^2 \log(u_2)\right\}$$

- We proceed backward and at **stage $T = 2$** we want to maximize the following quantity with respect to $u_2$:

$$J_2 = \beta^2 \log(u_2)$$

$$s.t.\ 0 \leq u_2 \leq K_2$$

As $K_{t+1} = K_t - u_t \geq 0$ we will have $u_t = K_t - K_{t+1}$, that for $t = 2$ becomes $u_2 = K_2 - K_3 = K_2$

So, at $t = 2$ the quantity $\beta^2 \log(u_2)$ is maximized for $u_2 = K_2$, so that we have:

$$J_2^* = \beta^2 \log(K_2) = \beta^2 \log(K_1 - u_1)$$

as $K_2 = K_1 - u_1$ because of the constraint $K_{t+1} = K_t - u_t$.

- At **stage** $T = 1$ we want to maximize the following:

$$J_1 = \max_{\{u_1\}}\{\beta^1 \log(u_1) + J_2^*\} = \max_{\{u_1\}}\{\beta^1 \log(u_1) + \beta^2 \log(K_1 - u_1)\}.$$

Taking the derivative with respect to $u_1$ we obtain:

$$\frac{\partial J_1}{\partial u_1} = \frac{\beta}{u_1} - \frac{\beta^2}{K_1 - u_1} = 0 \Rightarrow u_1 = \frac{\beta K_1}{(\beta^2 + \beta)} = \frac{K_1}{(1+\beta)} = \frac{K_0 - u_0}{(1+\beta)},$$

as $K_1 = K_0 - u_0$.

- At **stage** $T = 0$ we want to maximize the following:

$$J_0 = \max_{\{u_0\}}\{\beta^0 \log(u_0) + J_1^*\} = \max_{\{u_0\}}\left\{\beta^0 \log(u_0) + \beta \log\frac{K_1}{(1+\beta)} + \beta^2 \log\left(K_1 - \frac{K_1}{(1+\beta)}\right)\right\}$$

which becomes, after replacing $K_1 = K_0 - u_0$

$$J_0 = \max_{\{u_0\}}\left\{\beta^0 \log(u_0) + \beta \log\frac{(K_0 - u_0)}{(1+\beta)} + \beta^2 \log\left[(K_0 - u_0) - \frac{(K_0 - u_0)}{(1+\beta)}\right]\right\}$$

$$J_0 = \max_{\{u_0\}}\left\{\beta^0 \log(u_0) + \beta \log\frac{(K_0 - u_0)}{(1+\beta)} + \beta^2 \log\left[\frac{\beta(K_0 - u_0)}{(1+\beta)}\right]\right\}.$$

Once the recursive relation is expressed as a function of $u_0$ we differentiate it now with respect to $u_0$ obtaining:

$$\frac{\partial J_0}{\partial u_0} = \frac{1}{u_0} - \frac{\beta}{(K_0 - u_0)} - \frac{\beta^2}{(K_0 - u_0)} \Rightarrow$$

$$\frac{\partial J_0}{\partial u_0} = \frac{K_0 - u_0 - \beta u_0 - \beta^2 u_0}{u_0(K_0 - u_0)} = 0$$

for $K_0 \neq u_0$ and $u_0 \neq 0$ we have the maximum point $u_0$ as:

$$K_0 - u_0 - \beta u_0 - \beta^2 u_0 = 0 \Rightarrow u_0 = \frac{K_0}{1 + \beta + \beta^2}.$$

For $\rho = 5\%$, $\beta = \frac{1}{(1.05)} \cong 0.9524$ and $K_0 = 5$ we have the numerical values of $u_0$, $u_1$ and $u_2$ as follows:

$$u_0 = \frac{5}{1 + 0.9524 + 0.9524^2} \cong 1.7486$$

and

$$u_1 = \frac{K_0 - u_0}{(1 + \beta)} = \frac{5 - 1.7486}{1.9524} = 1.6653.$$

We can determine then $K_1$ as:

$$K_1 = K_0 - u_0 = 5 - 1.7486 = 3.2514,$$

$K_2$ as:

$$K_2 = K_1 - u_1 = 3.2514 - 1.6653 = 1.5861$$

$K_3 = 0$ as $u_2 = K_2 = 1.5861$

$$K_3 = K_2 - u_2 = 1.5861 - 1.5861 = 0.$$

The scalar associated to the optimal value function for the three stages is then:

$$J_0^* = \{\beta^0 \log(u_0) + \beta^1 \log(u_1) + \beta^2 \log(u_2)\} = \log 1.7486 + 0.9524 \cdot \log 1.6653$$
$$+ 0.9524^2 \cdot \log 1.5861$$

$$J_0^* = 0.5588 + 0.4857 + 0.4184 = 1.4629$$

### Optimal consumption policy

The optimal consumption (and saving) policy consists of consuming a larger portion of wealth as the consumer gets older and finally consuming the remaining wealth during the last period of life.

### Alternative solution (Lagrange multipliers)

The same problem could have been solved via the standard calculus technique of Lagrange multipliers which is the one applied with the Excel Solver.

The problem is expressed as follows:

$$\max_{\{u_0, u_1, u_2\}} \{\beta^0 \log(u_0) + \beta^1 \log(u_1) + \beta^2 \log(u_2)\}$$

$$s.t. \ u_0 + u_1 + u_2 = 5$$

The Lagrange static function in three variables is defined as:

$$\mathscr{L}(u_0, u_1, u_2) = \beta^0 \log(u_0) + \beta^1 \log(u_1) + \beta^2 \log(u_2) + \lambda(u_0 + u_1 + u_2 - 5)$$

Let us derive $\mathscr{L}(u_0, u_1, u_2)$ with respect to $u_0$, $u_1$, $u_2$.

1. $\frac{\partial \mathscr{L}(u_0, u_1, u_2)}{\partial u_2} = \frac{\beta^2}{u_2} + \lambda \Rightarrow u_2 = -\frac{\beta^2}{\lambda}$

2. $\frac{\partial \mathscr{L}(u_0, u_1, u_2)}{\partial u_1} = \frac{\beta}{u_1} + \lambda \Rightarrow u_1 = -\frac{\beta}{\lambda}$

3. $\frac{\partial \mathscr{L}(u_0, u_1, u_2)}{\partial u_0} = \frac{1}{u_0} + \lambda \Rightarrow u_0 = -\frac{1}{\lambda}$

The following must be satisfied:

$$-\frac{\beta^2}{\lambda} - \frac{\beta}{\lambda} - \frac{1}{\lambda} = 5 \Rightarrow \lambda = -0.5719$$

and the optimal values for $u_0, u_1, u_2$ can be determined as:

$$u_0 = -\frac{1}{\lambda} = \frac{1}{0.5719} = 1.7486$$

$$u_1 = -\frac{\beta}{\lambda} = \frac{1/1.05}{0.5719} = 1.6653$$

$$u_2 = -\frac{\beta}{\lambda} = \frac{1/1.05^2}{0.5719} = 1.5860$$

## Excel spreadsheet solution (Solver)

The problem would be set up as in Figs. 11.6-1 and 11.6-2. Then, we show in Tables 11.6-1 and 11.6-2 the sensitivity report with Lagrange multipliers and the final results, respectively. Fig. 11.6-3 shows the graphical discrete dynamic optimal path of consumption.

### EXAMPLE 2 (OPTIMAL MINE ORE EXTRACTION)

A similar economic application to the optimal consumption problem of Example 1 is a natural resource economic problem, which deals with finding the optimal ore extraction from a mine, in a given range of time $[0, \; T]$ and given the initial mine available ore stock.

The problem is formalized as follows:

$$J(u) = \max_{\{u\}} \sum_{t=0}^{T} \beta^t u_t^\alpha$$

s.t. $x_{t+1} = x_t - u_t$        with $x_0$ given.

| | A | B | C | D |
|---|---|---|---|---|
| 1 | α | 1 | | |
| 2 | A Factor | 1 | | |
| 3 | K₀ | 5 | | |
| 4 | Interest rate | 0.05 | | |
| 5 | β = 1/(1+ρ) | =1/(1+B4) | Discount factor | |
| 6 | C(t) = u(t) | | | |
| 7 | | | | |
| 8 | | | | |
| 9 | Time | u(t) Optimal Consumption Path | K(t+1) = AK(t)ᵃ - u(t) | J* = bᵗln[u(t)] |
| 10 | 0 | 1.74860470924491 | 5 | =($B$5^A10)*LN(B10) |
| 11 | 1 | 1.66542308358248 | =C10^$B$1-B10 | =($B$5^A11)*LN(B11) |
| 12 | 2 | 1.58597220564953 | =C11^$B$1-B11 | =($B$5^A12)*LN(B12) |
| 13 | 3 | | =C12^$B$1-B12 | |
| 14 | | | | |
| 15 | | | | =SUM(D10:D12) |

FIGURE 11.6-1    Example 1: optimal consumption model Excel setup.

$\beta^t = \left(\frac{1}{1+\rho}\right)^t$ is the discount factor for a given interest rate $\rho$ and we have denoted with $J(u)$ the discounted cash flow functional related to the ore extraction $u_t$ in period $t$. $u_t^\alpha$ instead is the cash flow function associated to the quantity $u_t$ extracted. $x_{t+1} = x_t - u_t$ gives the equation of motion.

Let us suppose we have the following data: $T = 4$ for $t = 0, 1, 2, 3, \alpha = 0.5$, $x(0) = 1000$ and $\rho = 5\%$.

We can then set up the worksheet of Fig. 11.6-4.

The optimal solution is instead depicted in the following Table 11.6-3 and the optimal path in Fig. 11.6-5.

## EXAMPLE 3 (REFORMULATED INVESTMENT PROBLEM)

Let us go back now to our Example 1 of Section 10.3 where we presented the following stylized investment problem, represented in the standard form of OC theory (see set of Eqs. 10.1-1):

$$\max_{\{u\}} J(u) = \int_0^1 \left[y(t) - \frac{1}{2}u^2(t)\right] dt$$

$$s.t. \quad \dot{y} = u - \delta y \text{ and } y(0) = 1, y(1) = \text{free}$$

What we can do is discretizing the above continuous problem, solving it with DDP Excel approach that we have used so far in this section.

Solver Parameters     ✕

Se_t Objective:     $SD$15     ⬆

To:    ⦿ M_ax    ◯ Mi_n    ◯ V_alue Of:     0

_By Changing Variable Cells:

$B$10:$B$12     ⬆

Su_bject to the Constraints:

| $B$10:$B$12 >= 0 | | _Add |
| $C$11:$C$13 >= 0 | | |
| | | _Change |
| | | _Delete |
| | | _Reset All |
| | | _Load/Save |

☑ Ma_ke Unconstrained Variables Non-Negative

S_elect a Solving Method:    | GRG Nonlinear    ⌄ |    O_ptions

Solving Method

Select the GRG Nonlinear engine for Solver Problems that are smooth nonlinear. Select the LP Simplex engine for linear Solver Problems, and select the Evolutionary engine for Solver problems that are non-smooth.

_Help        S_olve        Cl_ose

**FIGURE 11.6-2**    Example 1: optimal consumption Solver parameters.

The problem can be converted into the typical dynamic programming form:

$$J(u) = \max_{\{u(t)\}} \sum_{t=0}^{T} \left[ y(t) - \frac{1}{2} u^2(t) \right]$$

$$y(t) = y(t-1) + u(t) - \delta y(t) \text{ (equation of motion for capital stock)}$$

where $\delta$ is the depreciation rate and $u(t)$ is the gross investment to be optimized over the range $[0,T]$.

**TABLE 11.6-1**    Excel sensitivity report.

## Variable Cells

| Cell | Name | Final Value | Reduced Gradient |
|------|------|-------------|------------------|
| $B$10 | u(t) Optimal Consumption Path | 1.748604709 | 0 |
| $B$11 | u(t) Optimal Consumption Path | 1.665423084 | 0 |
| $B$12 | u(t) Optimal Consumption Path | 1.585972206 | 0 |

## Constraints

| Cell | Name | Final Value | Lagrange Multiplier |
|------|------|-------------|---------------------|
| $C$11 | K(t+1) = A*K(t)a - u(t) | 3.251395291 | 0 |
| $C$12 | K(t+1) = A*K(t)a - u(t) | 1.585972207 | 0 |
| $C$13 | K(t+1) = A*K(t)a - u(t) | 0 | -0.571883962 |

**TABLE 11.6-2**    Example 1: optimal consumption policy.

| | | |
|---|---|---|
| $\alpha$ | 1.0000 | |
| A Factor | 1.0000 | |
| $K_0$ | 5.0000 | |
| Interest rate | 5.00% | |
| $\beta = 1/(1+\rho)$ | 0.9524 | Discount factor |
| C(t) = u(t) | | |

| Time | u(t) Optimal Consumption | $K(t+1) = AK(t)^a - u(t)$ | $J^* = b^t \ln[u(t)]$ |
|------|--------------------------|---------------------------|------------------------|
| 0.00 | 1.7486 | **5.0000** | 0.5588 |
| 1.00 | 1.6654 | 3.2514 | 0.4858 |
| 2.00 | 1.5860 | 1.5860 | 0.4183 |
| 3.00 | | 0.0000 | |
| | | | **1.4629** |

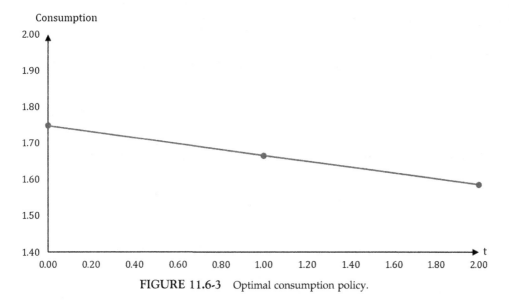

FIGURE 11.6-3    Optimal consumption policy.

|   | A | B | C | D |
|---|---|---|---|---|
| 1 | α | 0.5 | | |
| 2 | ρ | 0.05 | | |
| 3 | β | =1/(1+B2) | Discount factor | |
| 4 | x(0) | 1000 | | |
| 5 | | | | |
| 6 | | | | |
| 7 | **Time** | **u(t) ore extraction optimal path** | **x(t+1) = x(t) - u(t)** | **Cash flow earned from ore extraction in year t DCF(t) = β$^t$u$^α$(t)** |
| 8 | 0 | 287.691722839279 | 1000 | =($B$3^A8)*B8^$B$1 |
| 9 | 1 | 260.944372230367 | =C8-B8 | =($B$3^A9)*B9^$B$1 |
| 10 | 2 | 236.68382967918 | =C9-B9 | =($B$3^A10)*B10^$B$1 |
| 11 | 3 | 214.680075251174 | =C10-B10 | =($B$3^A11)*B11^$B$1 |
| 12 | 4 | | =C11-B11 | |
| 13 | | | | =SUM(D8:D11) |

FIGURE 11.6-4    Example 2: optimal ore extraction Excel setup.

The recursive optimal value function would be defined as follows:

$$J_{t,T}(y, u) = \max_{\{u(t)\}} \left\{ \left[ y(t) - \frac{1}{2}u^2(t) \right] + J^*_{t+1,T}(y(t+1)) \right\}.$$

III. Dynamic optimization

**TABLE 11.6-3**   Example 2: optimal ore extraction solution.

| α    | 0.5000           |
|------|------------------|
| ρ    | 0.0500           |
| β    | 0.9524 Discount factor |
| x(0) | 1,000.0000       |

| Time   | u(t) ore extraction optimal path | x(t+1) = x(t) - u(t) | Cash flow earned from ore extraction in year t DCF(t) = $\beta^t u^\alpha(t)$ |
|--------|--------|--------|--------|
| 0.0000 | 287.6917 | 1,000.0000 | 16.9615 |
| 1.0000 | 260.9444 | 712.3083 | 15.3845 |
| 2.0000 | 236.6838 | 451.3639 | 13.9542 |
| 3.0000 | 214.6801 | 214.6801 | 12.6569 |
| 4.0000 |          | 0.0000   |         |
|        |          |          | 58.9572 |

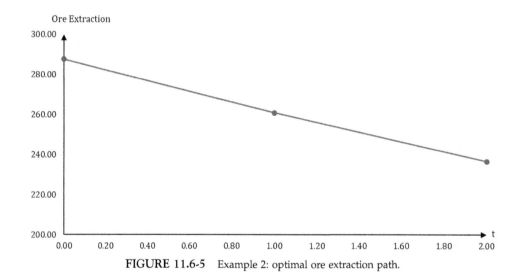

FIGURE 11.6-5   Example 2: optimal ore extraction path.

Supposing $T = 10$ and $\delta = 15\%$ (depreciation period ca. 7 years) the problem can be easily set up in Excel as in Fig. 11.6-6.

The solution is easily found setting the Solver parameters to maximize *Cell F14* of Fig. 11.6-6, by changing the range *B3:B12*, where the control variable $u(t)$ Gross Investment is stored. Table 11.6-4 returns the optimal solution. The optimal solutions for $u(t)$ and $y(t)$ are then graphed in Figs. 11.6-7 and 11.6-8, respectively.

| | A | B | C | D | E | F |
|---|---|---|---|---|---|---|
| 1 | t | u(t) Investment | y(t) = y(t-1) + u(t) | Depreciation = 0.15y(t) | y(t) = y(t-1) + u(t) - Depreciation | J Profit Functional |
| 2 | 0 | 0 | 0 | | 0 | =E2-1/2*B2^2 |
| 3 | 1 | 9.50000000531 | =C2+B3 | =(C3)*0.05 | =C3-D3 | =E3-1/2*B3^2 |
| 4 | 2 | 8.54999999779 | =C3+B4 | =(C4)*0.05 | =C4-D4 | =E4-1/2*B4^2 |
| 5 | 3 | 7.59999996262 | =C4+B5 | =(C5)*0.05 | =C5-D5 | =E5-1/2*B5^2 |
| 6 | 4 | 6.65000005232 | =C5+B6 | =(C6)*0.05 | =C6-D6 | =E6-1/2*B6^2 |
| 7 | 5 | 5.70000004176 | =C6+B7 | =(C7)*0.05 | =C7-D7 | =E7-1/2*B7^2 |
| 8 | 6 | 4.75000002858 | =C7+B8 | =(C8)*0.05 | =C8-D8 | =E8-1/2*B8^2 |
| 9 | 7 | 3.79999998758 | =C8+B9 | =(C9)*0.05 | =C9-D9 | =E9-1/2*B9^2 |
| 10 | 8 | 2.84999998112 | =C9+B10 | =(C10)*0.05 | =C10-D10 | =E10-1/2*B10^ |
| 11 | 9 | 1.89999997466 | =C10+B11 | =(C11)*0.05 | =C11-D11 | =E11-1/2*B11^ |
| 12 | 10 | 0.94999996820 | =C11+B12 | =(C12)*0.05 | =C12-D12 | =E12-1/2*B12^ |
| 13 | | | | | | |
| 14 | | | | | Σ | =SUM(F2:F12) |

FIGURE 11.6-6    Example 3: Discrete Dynamic Programming investment problem Excel setup.

TABLE 11.6-4    Example 3: Discrete Dynamic Programming investment problem Excel solution.

| t | u(t) Investment | y(t) = y(t-1) + u(t) | Depreciation = 0.15y(t) | y(t) = y(t-1) + u(t) - Depreciation | J Profit Functional |
|---|---|---|---|---|---|
| 0 | 0.000000 | 0.000 | | 0.000 | 0.0000 |
| 1 | 9.5000 | 9.5000 | 0.4750 | 9.0250 | -36.1000 |
| 2 | 8.5500 | 18.0500 | 0.9025 | 17.1475 | -19.4037 |
| 3 | 7.6000 | 25.6500 | 1.2825 | 24.3675 | -4.5125 |
| 4 | 6.6500 | 32.3000 | 1.6150 | 30.6850 | 8.5737 |
| 5 | 5.7000 | 38.0000 | 1.9000 | 36.1000 | 19.8550 |
| 6 | 4.7500 | 42.7500 | 2.1375 | 40.6125 | 29.3312 |
| 7 | 3.8000 | 46.5500 | 2.3275 | 44.2225 | 37.0025 |
| 8 | 2.8500 | 49.4000 | 2.4700 | 46.9300 | 42.8688 |
| 9 | 1.9000 | 51.3000 | 2.5650 | 48.7350 | 46.9300 |
| 10 | 0.9500 | 52.2500 | 2.6125 | 49.6375 | 49.1863 |
| | | | | Σ | 173.7313 |

# 11.7 Discrete Dynamic Programming, Optimal Control theory, and Calculus of Variations: a synthesis

This last paragraph of DDP attempts to highlight the similarities and relations among the three dynamic optimization techniques.

First, it is important to stress that the CoV, OC theory, and DDP are essentially alternative ways to solve a dynamic optimization problem. The DDP problem is a discrete-stages approach in its mathematical nature, while the other two are continuous-time-based techniques.

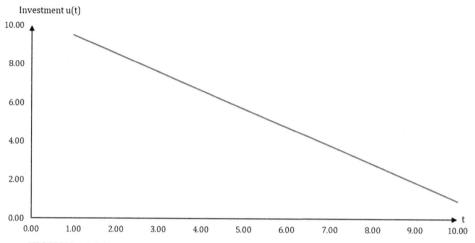

**FIGURE 11.6-7**   Example 3: Discrete Dynamic Programming optimal investment path.

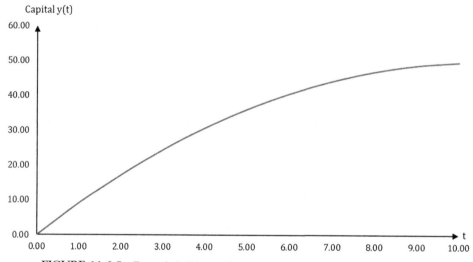

**FIGURE 11.6-8**   Example 3: Discrete Dynamic Programming optimal capital path.

One might have noticed that the shortest path problem in a discrete-stages environment attempts to solve the same CoV minimum distance problem in the continuous-time framework. However, in a discrete-stages environment, we have already a predefined set of arcs (directed from left to right, either with slope upward or downward) together with the arc values and the connected nodes, through which we can define a finite number of admissible paths and from which we build the optimal path. The arc value then is an essential information to find the sought optimal path via the recursive Bellman's relation.

In CoV, instead, we only have the boundary conditions of the state variable, together with the integrand function $F$, which embodies the information about the arc value to find the optimal path via the Euler–Lagrange. Within the CoV the continuous-time counterpart of the relation 11.1-1 can be expressed then as follows:

$$\int_{t_0}^{T} (arc\ value)dt,$$

where the arc value is implicitly derived from the integrand function $F(t,\ y(t),\ y'(t))$, which provides information about a specific path $y^*(t)$, univocally characterized by having at $t_k$ a specific value $y^*(t_k)$ and a specific slope $dy^*(t_k)/dt$. Simply put, the slope might be interpreted as the discrete counterpart of the arcs directed up or down in a graph. The functional $\int_{t_0}^{T} F(t,\ y^*(t), dy^*(t)\ /dt)$ will tell us whether $y^*(t)$ is an optimizing path or not.

Concerning the OC theory in relation to CoV we have already seen that the former is a modern development of the latter and, in many instances, one might model the same problem with the two techniques, as we did with the Inventory Optimization (see Section 10.7 and Section 9.9).

Furthermore, a typical OC problem can be also discretized and solved through the Bellman's recursive approach, as we did for some of the examples seen in this section (see Section 11.2). However, while the OC theory and CoV can be somehow manageable by hand, using the Euler–Lagrange and the Pontryagin's Maximum Principle, the calculations of the Bellman's approach may become practically unfeasible when we deal with a high number of stages (already with $N = 5$ the calculations are complex), and a computer-based computation is needed.

In summary, we describe as follows the main features of the three techniques together with their Excel-based numerical solution alternatives proposed in the book:

1. **CoV:** continuous-time theory solved via the Euler–Lagrange. Numerically, in a discrete-time framework it can be analyzed as a Lagrange multipliers problem (see Eq. (9.2-1) and the fixed endpoints problem in Section 9.2). In Excel, we can use the Solver (i.e., Lagrange multipliers) and for the fixed endpoint problems we have also shown the geometrical method of contour lines, via VBA computer programming.
2. **OC theory:** continuous-time theory solved via the Pontryagin's Maximum Principle. Numerically, in a discrete-time framework, approachable with the Excel Solver and Steepest Descent, via a VBA subroutine.
3. **DDP:** mainly created within the discrete-stages theoretical framework and solved via the Bellman's Recursive Functional. In the continuous-time framework, the Hamilton–Jacobi–Bellman equation applies. In Excel, several techniques have been shown to be useful for the dynamic discrete optimization problems, like the *MINIFS* function, the Solver and the Data Table for two-stage problems.

## Exercises

1. Solve in Excel the directed graphs given in Figs. 1 and 2, finding the shortest path from *node* 1 to *node* 9.
2. You are given a route map as represented in Fig. 3 with costs from node to node of the route. Solve it in Excel for the minimum cost route to choose, to reach destination *h* from current location *a*. You can only travel one way as indicated by the arrows. Plot in a chart the optimal route.
3. Reconsider the problem of Example 1 reformulated in a continuous framework as follows:

$$\dot{y}(t) = u(t)$$

so that the following performance measure is minimized:

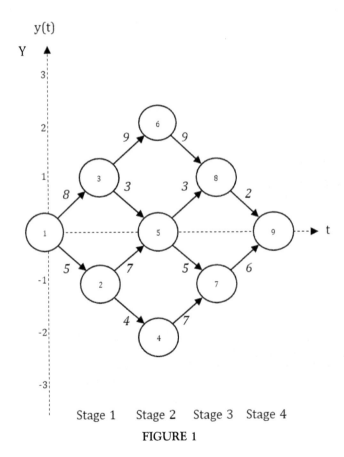

FIGURE 1

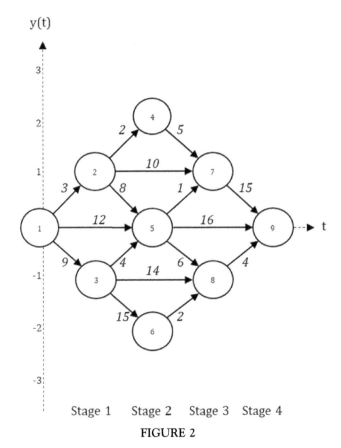

Stage 1    Stage 2    Stage 3    Stage 4

**FIGURE 2**

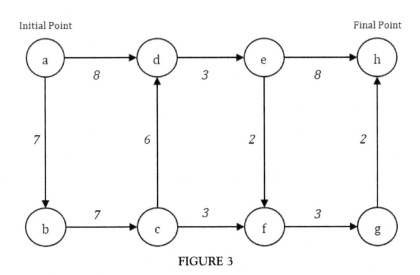

**FIGURE 3**

III. Dynamic optimization

$$J(u) = y(2) + \int_0^2 u^2 dt.$$

With initial condition $y(0) = 1.5$ solve the problem in Excel as if it were a CoV problem for $y(T)$ *free* and $y(T) = 0.5$. Remember to consider the tranversality condition when $y(T)$ is unspecified.

4. Solve in Excel, as well as by hand, setting up the recursive equations, a multistage allocation problem as in Section 11.4, with the following data:

$$x_0 = 10, \quad N = 4, \quad g(y) = 3y, \quad h(x-y) = 2(x-y), \quad a = 0.50, \quad b = 0.70$$

5. Use the Excel Solver to solve the following discrete dynamic problem:

$$\max_{\{u\}} \sum_{t=0}^{3} \left[ 1 + y(t) - u^2(t) \right]$$

s.t.

$$y(t+1) = y(t) + u(t)$$

and $y(0) = 0$.

6. Use the Excel Solver to solve the following discrete dynamic problem:

$$\max_{\{u\}} \sum_{t=0}^{3} \left[ -\frac{2}{3} u(t) y(t) \right] + \ln(y(T))$$

s.t.

$$y(t+1) = y(t)(1 + u(t)y(t))$$

and $y(0) = 1$.

7. Use the Excel Solver to solve the following discrete dynamic problem. Repeat the exercise by hand, using the fundamental recursive equation of dynamic programming 11.2-1.

$$\max_{\{u\}} \sum_{t=0}^{2} \left[ 1 - (y^2(t) + 2u^2(t)) \right]$$

s.t.

$$y(t+1) = y(t) - u(t)$$

and $y(0) = 5$.

(Hint: to solve the problem by hand using the standard calculus begin considering the functional $J_2(u_2) = 1 - y_2^2 - 2u_2^2$ which is maximized for $u_2 = 0$ as it turns out to be $\frac{dJ(u_2)}{du_2} = -4u_2$. As a second step, consider the functional $J_1(u_1) = 1 - y_1^2 - 2u_1^2 + J_2^* = 1 - y_1^2 - 2u_1^2 + \left[1 - (y_1 - u_1)^2 - 0\right]$ which is maximized setting $\frac{dJ(u_1)}{du_1} = 0$, then at the end set up $J_0(u_0) = 1 - y_0^2 - 2u_0^2 + J_1^*$.

The final solution of the optimal path $y^*(t)$ is $y(0) = 5$, $y^*(1) = 2.7273$, $y^*(2) = 1.8182$, while the OC inputs are $u^*(0) = 2.2727$, $u^*(1) = 0.9091$, and $u^*(2) = 0$.

8. Use the Excel Solver and the Data Table to solve the following discrete dynamic problem.

$$\max_{\{u\}} \sum_{t=0}^{2} \left[(y^2(t) + u^2(t))\right] + y^2(3)$$

s.t.

$$y(t+1) = y(t) + u(t)$$

and $y(0) = 1$.

When you use the Data Table, assume $u(t)$ can only take the discrete values $-1.0$, $-0.6$, $-0.20$, $0.4$, $1.0$.

9. **Optimal consumption.** Let $C(t) = u(t)$ be the consumption in period $t$. Solve the following consumption model for $T = 2$ and $T = 4$, with $K(0) = 5{,}000$, discounting rate 5%, $\alpha = 1$, $A = 1$:

$$\max_{\{u\}} \sum_{t=0}^{T} \beta^t \ln[u(t)]$$

s.t.

$$K(t+1) = AK^\alpha(t) - u(t) \geq 0$$

for $t = 0, 1, 2, \cdots, (T-1)$ and initial condition $K(0)$ given above.

10. **Mine ore extraction.** Suppose we are granted operating a mine for 10 years, with initial available ore equal to 1000. We want to choose the optimal ore extraction $u(t)$ such that we maximize the present value of cash flows from the mine over the 10 years. The model can be therefore formalized as follows, where the cash flows are modeled as a power function of the extraction ($0 < \alpha < 1$):

$$\max_{\{u\}} \sum_{t=0}^{T} \beta^t [u(t)]^\alpha$$

s.t.

$y(t+1) = y(t) - u(t) \geq 0$ for $t = 0, 1, 2, \cdots, 9$ and initial condition $y(0) = 1,000$

$$\beta = \frac{1}{(1+0.08)}$$ is the discount factor and parameter $\alpha = 1/2$.

Solve for the optimal ore extraction $u^*(t)$.

**11. Optimal advertising policy.** Let us consider a company that wishes to set an optimal plan for its advertising expenditure over a period of 3 years, assuming the profit available for this expenditure is 50,000 £ at the beginning of the period.

The company knows that reinvesting in advertising will cause the profit increasing, but not directly proportionally with the expenditures made and that it will benefit from these expenditures even after the marketing campaign has been ceased. The problem is to determine the optimal advertising policy over the 3 years horizon, once the company has estimated the quantitative relations between its marketing expenses and the profit generated over the years.

Let us assume the following:

$t = 0, 1, 2$

$I(t) =$ *income availabe at time t.*

$u(t) =$ *portion of the income used for advertising expenses.*

$I(t+1) = I(t) + 200\sqrt{u(t)} =$ *equation ofmotion for the income, i.e.: the relation which*

*shows the increase of the income induced by the advertsing expenses* $u(t)$.

The problem can be therefore formalized in its complete form over the 3 years as follows:

$$\max_{\{u(0),\ u(1),u(2)\}} \{[I(1) - u(1)] + [I(2) - u(2)] + [I(3) - u(3)]\}$$

s.t.

$$I(t+1) = I(t) + 200\sqrt{u(t)} \qquad t = 0, 1$$

$$I(0) = 50,000$$

$$0 \leq u(t) \leq I(t) \quad t = 0, 1, 2$$

It turns out that this problem is suitable to be solved sequentially with the recursive Bellman's approach.

Like all Bellman's problems, if this problem is manually approached using the standard calculus, it will be particularly complicated to be solved; however, in Excel using the GRG Solver, it can be approached quite easily. We just have to identify the equation of motion and the objective functional to optimize.

a. Set up the Excel to find the optimal advertising policy over the 3 years horizon.
b. Solve the same problem for $T = 5$.
c. With $T = 5$ assume now the advertising expenses generate over the immediate following year an increase in income equal to $200u(t)$ while during the second following year an increase equal to $100u(t)$ and then afterward the increases in income generated will be zero, that is, the expenses made in at $t = 0$ will affect the income until $t = 2$, during the first year according to $200u(t)$, while the second year according to $100u(t)$. Find the optimal advertising policy in Excel under this new scenario.

# Special topics

Part IV of this book will cover some special and important topics that have been chosen not only because of their specific importance, but also because they can be considered perfectly complementary to the mathematical economics.

These topics are the dynamic production scheduling and inventory theory, the data and regression analysis, and finally, the Monte Carlo analysis. The inventory theory, the dynamic production scheduling and the Monte Carlo analysis are typically key topics of the *operations research*, while the data analysis belongs to the theory of statistics and data science.

Chapter 12 will cover some production scheduling and the inventory modeling, which represents somehow the continuation and complements of the linear programming and the dynamic programming. The linear programming can be in fact adapted to solve some dynamic programming scheduling problems, while the Wagner–Whitin dynamic inventory and production algorithm leverages on the use the Bellman's principle of optimality.

Chapter 13 will cover the data analysis together with the regression analysis. We will cover some advanced Excel tools to organize and analyze the business data, like the pivot tables, pivot charts, and the slicers; then, the basic descriptive statistics will give the essential tools to analyze statistically the data in Excel. Finally, some inferential statistics is also covered within the basic univariate and multivariate linear regression analysis, which represent the core concepts of the econometric modeling.

The last chapter of this book (Chapter 14) is devoted to the essential Monte Carlo analysis with simulations applied to the games of chances as an introduction to the subject and then applied to some business and financial decision problems, like the NPV. We will also show how to run the basic Bernoulli processes with the Excel random number generator and how to perform the numerical integration using the Monte Carlo simulation.

## 12.1 Multiperiod production models with linear programming

A multiperiod model of production with only production and inventory costs.

These classes of models can be adapted to several production situations and they are suitable when there are from one to several production sources for a single product in each time period over the horizon planning $T$. The product may be stored from one period to the next at a known inventory unit cost. No shortages are planned. Only the direct variable costs of production are considered in the model. The objective is to find the optimal quantities to produce in each time period, to minimize the total costs objective function, as well as meeting the given demand for each period.

*Elements of Numerical Mathematical Economics with Excel*
https://doi.org/10.1016/B978-0-12-817648-1.00012-8

We can formulate the problem as follows:

$$D_t = \text{demand of the product in period } t = 1, 2, \cdots, T$$

$$m = \text{number of sources of product in any period}$$

$$C_{it} = \text{constraint capacity, in units of products, of source } i = 1, 2, \cdots, m \text{ in period } t$$

$$P_{it} = \text{planned quantity to be obtined from source } i \text{ in period } t$$

$$c_{it} = \text{variable unit cost of production from source } i \text{ in period } t$$

$$h_t = \text{variable unit cost of storing a unit of good from period } t \text{ to } t + 1$$

$$I_t = I_{t-1} + P_t - D_t$$

represents the conservation of flow on the inventory (clearing account equation) that must be valid in each period. It is somehow the discrete version of the equation of motion that we have seen in Example 2 of Section 10.10.

The conservation of flow corresponds to the inventory accounting relationship:

$$EI - BI = P - COGS,$$

where **EI** = ending inventory, **BI** = beginning inventory, **P** = purchases and **COGS** = cost of goods sold. The change in inventory is affected by two events: the purchase or manufacture of goods (*P*) and their subsequent sale (*COGS*).

The linear programming problem is to minimize the following:

$$Z = \sum_{t=1}^{T} \sum_{i=1}^{m} c_{it} P_{it} + h_t I_t$$

s.t.

$$P_{it} \leq C_{it}$$

$$I_t = I_{t-1} + \sum_{i=1}^{m} P_{it} - D_t \quad t = 1, 2, \cdots, T$$

$$P_{it} \geq 0 \quad (\text{for all } i \text{ and all } t)$$

$$I_t \geq 0 \quad (\text{for all } t)$$

The objective function $Z$ is the sum over all time periods of the production costs and inventory costs, these being based on the ending inventory. This formulation links subsequent time periods using as a key constraint the fundamental accounting equation of inventory. It is a model that can be used in various real production situations.

These types of models can be also implemented resorting to the *Network Flow Programming*, which is a related (to linear programming) technique utilized often in operations research.

## EXAMPLE 1

Let us consider the demand schedule forecast of the following Table 12.1-1.
We have three sources of production, namely $m = 3$.
The unit cost of regular time production is constant for all periods and equal to:

$$C_{1t} = 100 \quad (for\ all\ t).$$

For overtime production the unit variable cost is:

$$C_{2t} = 107 \quad (for\ all\ t)$$

There is also some production subcontracted, which has cost equal to:

$$C_{3t} = 113 \quad (for\ all\ t)$$

The inventory holding costs are as well constant and equal to:

$$h_t = 2$$

TABLE 12.1-1   Demand schedule.

| Expected Demand | |
| --- | --- |
| D1 | 100 |
| D2 | 150 |
| D3 | 250 |
| D4 | 120 |
| D5 | 110 |
| D6 | 210 |
| D7 | 240 |
| D8 | 290 |
| D9 | 280 |
| D10 | 240 |
| D11 | 240 |
| D12 | 220 |
| D13 | 130 |

Then, there is no initial inventory:

$$I_0 = 0.$$

The model in Excel is specified as in Fig. 12.1-1, where some time periods have been hidden on purpose. The Solver parameters with the constraints are in Fig. 12.1-2. The complete program solution is in Table 12.1-2 with:

$$Z^*_{min} = £\,261,950$$

Notice from Table 12.1-2 how the demand can be satisfied both with the current production and the inventory decumulation.

This happens, for example, in period $t = 3$ where the demand requirement is $D_3 = 250$, satisfied with $P_3 = 180$ (regular production) and the inventory carried forward from previous period $I_2 = 70$. See also what happens in Example 2 in Section 10.10.

A multiperiod model of production with shipment to branches.

| | B | C | D | E |
|---|---|---|---|---|
| 1 | Min Z | =SUMPRODUCT(C16:C68;D16:D68) | | |
| 2 | s.t. | | | |
| 3 | D1 | 100 | | |
| 4 | D2 | 150 | | |
| 13 | D11 | 240 | | |
| 14 | D12 | 220 | | |
| 15 | D13 | 130 | Unit costs | Constraints |
| 16 | P1 | 140 | 100 | 180 |
| 25 | P10 | 180 | 100 | 180 |
| 26 | P11 | 180 | 100 | 180 |
| 27 | P12 | 180 | 100 | 180 |
| 28 | P13 | 130 | 100 | 180 |
| 29 | P1 | 0 | 107 | 36 |
| 32 | P4 | 0 | 107 | 36 |
| 40 | P12 | 36 | 107 | 36 |
| 41 | P13 | 0 | 107 | 36 |
| 42 | P1 | 0 | 113 | 50 |
| 43 | P2 | 0 | 113 | 50 |
| 53 | P12 | 4 | 113 | 50 |
| 54 | P13 | 0 | 113 | 50 |
| 55 | I0 | 0 | 2 | 0 |
| 56 | I1 | 40 | 2 | =C55+C16+C29+C42-C3 |
| 59 | I4 | 60 | 2 | =C58+C19+C32+C45-C6 |
| 65 | I10 | 0 | 2 | =C64+C25+C38+C51-C12 |
| 66 | I11 | 0 | 2 | =C65+C26+C39+C52-C13 |
| 67 | I12 | 0 | 2 | =C66+C27+C40+C53-C14 |
| 68 | I13 | 0 | 2 | =C67+C28+C41+C54-C15 |

FIGURE 12.1-1 Multiperiod production linear program.

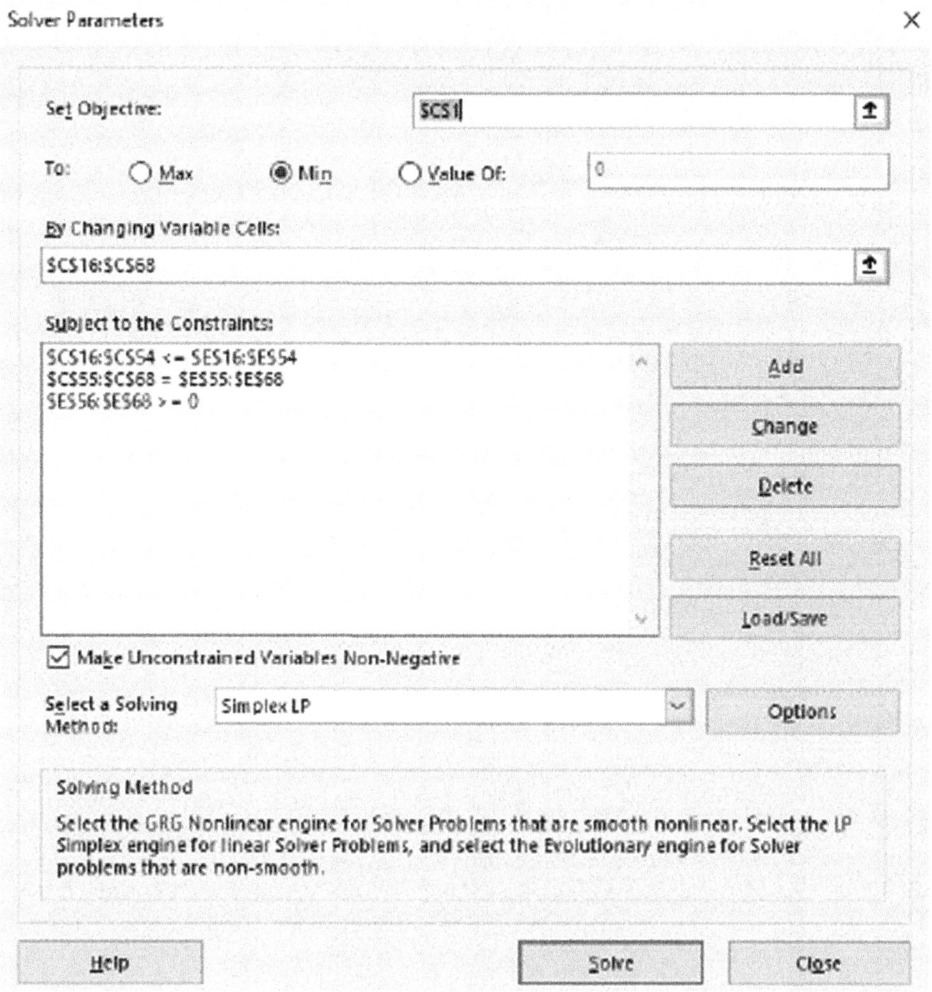

Solver Parameters                                                                    ✕

Se_t Objective:                          $CS1|                                    ⬆

To:      ○ _Max      ◉ Mi_n      ○ _Value Of:      0

_By Changing Variable Cells:

$CS16:$CS68                                                                        ⬆

Su_bject to the Constraints:

| $CS16:$CS54 <= $ES16:$ES54 | | Add |
| $CS55:$CS68 = $ES55:$ES68 | | Change |
| $ES56:$ES68 >= 0 | | Delete |
| | | Reset All |
| | | Load/Save |

☑ Ma_ke Unconstrained Variables Non-Negative

Se_lect a Solving      Simplex LP                          ⌄        Options
Method:

Solving Method

Select the GRG Nonlinear engine for Solver Problems that are smooth nonlinear. Select the LP Simplex engine for linear Solver Problems, and select the Evolutionary engine for Solver problems that are non-smooth.

He_lp                              So_lve                              Cl_ose

FIGURE 12.1-2    Solver parameters.

Many manufacturing groups have one or more production centers with controlled distribution branches.

The production plants ship then the required quantities of finished or semifinished goods to the controlled distribution branches, for finishing and selling (distribution branches with some manufacturing activities) or just selling (pure distribution branches). Together with the controlled distribution branches there are also the third-party distributors.

The model we have discussed so far can be therefore expanded to include the shipment costs from a production center to the distribution branches. We assume one production source plant and pure distribution branches. The inventory is a group consolidated quantity.

**TABLE 12.1-2**   Linear program production planning solution.

| | | Min Z | 261,950 | | |
|---|---|---|---|---|---|
| | | s.t. | | | |
| Demand | D1 | | 100 | | |
| | D2 | | 150 | | |
| | D3 | | 250 | | |
| | D4 | | 120 | | |
| | D5 | | 110 | | |
| | D6 | | 210 | | |
| | D7 | | 240 | | |
| | D8 | | 290 | | |
| | D9 | | 280 | | |
| | D10 | | 240 | | |
| | D11 | | 240 | | |
| | D12 | | 220 | | |
| | D13 | | 130 | Unit costs | Constraints |
| Production regular time | P1 | | 140 | 100 | 180 |
| | P2 | | 180 | 100 | 180 |
| | P3 | | 180 | 100 | 180 |
| | P4 | | 180 | 100 | 180 |
| | P5 | | 180 | 100 | 180 |
| | P6 | | 180 | 100 | 180 |
| | P7 | | 180 | 100 | 180 |
| | P8 | | 180 | 100 | 180 |
| | P9 | | 180 | 100 | 180 |
| | P10 | | 180 | 100 | 180 |
| | P11 | | 180 | 100 | 180 |
| | P12 | | 180 | 100 | 180 |
| | P13 | | 130 | 100 | 180 |
| Production over time | P1 | | 0 | 107 | 36 |
| | P2 | | 0 | 107 | 36 |
| | P3 | | 0 | 107 | 36 |
| | P4 | | 0 | 107 | 36 |
| | P5 | | 0 | 107 | 36 |
| | P6 | | 36 | 107 | 36 |
| | P7 | | 36 | 107 | 36 |
| | P8 | | 36 | 107 | 36 |
| | P9 | | 36 | 107 | 36 |
| | P10 | | 36 | 107 | 36 |
| | P11 | | 36 | 107 | 36 |
| | P12 | | 36 | 107 | 36 |
| | P13 | | 0 | 107 | 36 |
| Production sub contracted | P1 | | 0 | 113 | 50 |
| | P2 | | 0 | 113 | 50 |
| | P3 | | 0 | 113 | 50 |
| | P4 | | 0 | 113 | 50 |
| | P5 | | 0 | 113 | 50 |
| | P6 | | 0 | 113 | 50 |
| | P7 | | 0 | 113 | 50 |
| | P8 | | 0 | 113 | 50 |
| | P9 | | 26 | 113 | 50 |
| | P10 | | 24 | 113 | 50 |
| | P11 | | 24 | 113 | 50 |
| | P12 | | 4 | 113 | 50 |
| | P13 | | 0 | 113 | 50 |
| Inventory | I0 | | 0 | 2 | 0 |
| | I1 | | 40 | 2 | 40 |
| | I2 | | 70 | 2 | 70 |
| | I3 | | 0 | 2 | 0 |
| | I4 | | 60 | 2 | 60 |
| | I5 | | 130 | 2 | 130 |
| | I6 | | 136 | 2 | 136 |
| | I7 | | 112 | 2 | 112 |
| | I8 | | 38 | 2 | 38 |
| | I9 | | 0 | 2 | 0 |
| | I10 | | 0 | 2 | 0 |
| | I11 | | 0 | 2 | 0 |
| | I12 | | 0 | 2 | 0 |
| | I13 | | 0 | 2 | 0 |

We can formulate the problem as follows:

$S_{ti}$ = *sales of the product in period t* = 1, 2, $\cdots$, *T of branch i* = 1, 2, $\cdots$, *m*

$C_t$ = *constraint capacity, in units ofproducts, in period t*

$P_t$ = *planned quantity to be obtined in period t*

$Q_{ti}$ = *sales of the product in period t* = 1, 2, $\cdots$, *T of branch i* = 1, 2, $\cdots$, *m*

$\overline{Q}_{ti}$ = *maximum sales of the product in period t* = 1, 2, $\cdots$, *T of branch i* = 1, 2, $\cdots$, *m*

$p_{ti}$ = *unit price of the product in period t* = 1, 2, $\cdots$, *T applied by branch i* = 1, 2, $\cdots$, *m*

$D_{ti}$ = *shipment (or delivery) of the product in period t* = 1, 2, $\cdots$, *T to branch i* = 1, 2, $\cdots$, *m*

$c_t$ = *variable unit cost of production in period t*

$d_{ti}$ = *variable unit transportation cost of delivering from production plant to branhces in period t*

$h_t$ = *variable unit cost of storing a unit ofgood from period t to t + 1*

$$I_t = I_{t-1} + P_t - \sum_{i=1}^{m} Q_{ti} \ \left(\text{subject to maximum storage } \bar{I}_t\right)$$

the ending consolidated inventory (expressed in quantities) at time t is equal to the beginning inventory, plus the production of the period, minus the quantities sold from all the branches.

The linear programming problem is to find the optimal $Q^*$, $P^*$, $D^*$, and $I^*$ to maximize the following contribution margin:

$$Z = \sum_{t=1}^{T} \sum_{i=1}^{m} p_{ti}Q_{ti} - (c_tP_t + d_{ti}D_{ti} + h_tI_t)$$

s.t.

$$P_t \leq C_t \quad t = 1, 2, \cdots, T$$

$$Q_{ti} \leq \overline{Q}_{ti} \ t = 1, 2, \cdots, T \text{ and } i = 1, 2, \cdots, m$$

$$I_t = I_{t-1} + P_t - \sum_{i=1}^{m} Q_{ti} \quad t = 1, 2, \cdots, T$$

$$P_t \geq 0 \quad t = 1, 2, \cdots, T$$

$$I_t \geq 0 \quad t = 1, 2, \cdots, T$$

$$I_t \leq \bar{I}_t \quad t = 1, 2, \cdots, T$$

## EXAMPLE 2

Let us consider three branches, $m = 3$, and a multiperiod planning of 3 months for 1 year, $T = 3$, so that, for example, for $t = 1$ the objective function becomes:

$$Z_1 = \sum_{i=1}^{3} p_{1i}Q_{1i} - (c_1 P_1 + d_{1i}D_{1i} + h_1 I_1) = (p_{11}Q_{11} + p_{12}Q_{12} + p_{13}Q_{13}) - c_1 P_1$$
$$- (d_{11}D_{11} + d_{12}D_{12} + d_{13}D_{13}) - h_1 I_1.$$

Then, we have for $t = 2$

$$Z_2 = \sum_{i=1}^{3} p_{2i}Q_{2i} - (c_2 P_2 + d_{2i}D_{2i} + h_2 I_2) = (p_{21}Q_{21} + p_{22}Q_{22} + p_{23}Q_{23}) - c_2 P_2$$
$$- (d_{21}D_{21} + d_{22}D_{22} + d_{23}D_{23}) - h_2 I_2.$$

Finally, for $t = 3$ it is:

$$Z_3 = \sum_{i=1}^{3} p_{3i}Q_{3i} - (c_3 P_3 + d_{3i}D_{3i} + h_3 I_3) = (p_{31}Q_{31} + p_{32}Q_{32} + p_{33}Q_{33}) - c_3 P_3$$
$$- (d_{31}D_{31} + d_{32}D_{32} + d_{33}D_{33}) - h_3 I_3.$$

The linear programming can be also solved with the Bellman's approach and the above formulation is nothing but a separation of the objective function that we have seen in the DDP.

Table 12.1-3 presents the data of the problem, while Fig. 12.1-3 is the problem setup in Excel. Using the LP Simplex Solver as in Fig. 12.1-4, we represent the multiperiod optimal production program as in Table 12.1-4.

The optimal solution will of course depend on the time structure (increasing vs. decreasing or stable) of costs and revenues considered together (Table 12.1-4).

**TABLE 12.1-3**  Example 2: production and maximum sales data.

| Production | | | Selling Prices | | | Maximum Sales | | |
|---|---|---|---|---|---|---|---|---|
| Period | Unit Cost | Capacity | Branch A | Branch B | Branch C | Branch A | Branch B | Branch C |
| 1 | 10 | 180 | 20 | 25 | 20 | 60 | 110 | 80 |
| 2 | 11 | 200 | 22 | 27 | 20 | 80 | 170 | 80 |
| 3 | 12 | 160 | 24 | 30 | 22 | 30 | 90 | 60 |

| | A | B | C | D | E | F |
|---|---|---|---|---|---|---|
| 1 | | Max | =SUM(E1:E4) | Revenues | =SUMPRODUCT(C21:C29;E21:E29) | |
| 2 | | | | Production costs | =-SUMPRODUCT(C7:C9;E7:E9) | |
| 3 | | | | Storage costs | =-SUMPRODUCT(C31:C33;E31:E33) | |
| 4 | | | | Shipment costs | =-SUMPRODUCT(C11:C19;E11:E19) | |
| 5 | | | | | | |
| 6 | t | | Production (P) | s.t. Capacity | Unit Cost (c) | |
| 7 | 1 | P1 | 180 | 180 | 10 | |
| 8 | 2 | P2 | 200 | 200 | 11 | |
| 9 | 3 | P3 | 160 | 160 | 12 | |
| 10 | | | Shipment to Branch (D) | | Unit cost (d) | |
| 11 | 1 | P1_A1 | 20 | | 5 | |
| 12 | 1 | P1_B1 | 110 | | 7 | |
| 13 | 1 | P1_C1 | 0 | | 9 | |
| 20 | | | Sales of Branch (Q) | s.t. Max sales | Unit Price (p) | |
| 21 | 1 | A1 | 20 | 60 | 20 | |
| 22 | 1 | B1 | 110 | 110 | 25 | |
| 23 | 1 | C1 | 0 | 80 | 20 | |
| 24 | 2 | A2 | 80 | 80 | 22 | |
| 25 | 2 | B2 | 170 | 170 | 27 | |
| 26 | 2 | C2 | 0 | 80 | 20 | |
| 27 | 3 | A3 | 30 | 30 | 24 | |
| 28 | 3 | B3 | 90 | 90 | 30 | |
| 29 | 3 | C3 | 40 | 60 | 22 | |
| 30 | | | Inventory end period (I) | s.t. Max storage | Unit cost (h) | Inventory end period |
| 31 | 1 | I1 | 50 | 100 | 1 | =C7-SUM(C21:C23) |
| 32 | 2 | I2 | 0 | 100 | 1 | =C31+C8-SUM(C24:C26) |
| 33 | 3 | I3 | 0 | 100 | 1 | =C32+C9-SUM(C27:C29) |

**FIGURE 12.1-3**  Multiperiod production model excel setup.

## 12.2 Wagner–Whitin algorithm for inventory dynamic modeling

When we want to plan the production dynamically over a time horizon, we can also resort to the Wagner–Whitin algorithm, which essentially works like the DDP, in that it seeks to define the optimal production and inventory policy according to the Bellman's principle.

Let us consider a planning horizon which we divide into $N$ periods, with given demand $D_1, D_2, \cdots, D_N$ for each subperiod in $[0, N]$.

Let $Q_t$ be instead the lot size that we need to procure in period $t$. We have a procurement fixed cost of $A_t$ if the lot is ordered in period $t$, as well as a variable cost $C_t$, which varies from period to period.

There is also an inventory cost $h_t$ to carry forward from period $t$ to $t + 1$. The initial inventory is zero and no shortages are to be planned.

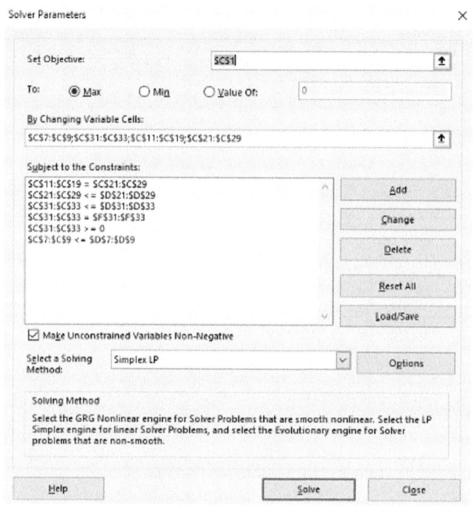

**FIGURE 12.1-4**   Example 2 solver set-up.

The problem is to find the optimal lot sizes $Q_1, Q_2, \cdots, Q_N$ to minimize the total procurement and inventory costs.

The requirement of the period will be satisfied either with the procurement of the current period or with the procurement already done in prior periods. That is, according to the time production cost structure we can essentially decide, either to produce for future demanded quantities at current costs, generating the inventory costs, or to produce at future costs the future required quantities. The algorithm will guide us in selecting the best choice.

**TABLE 12.1-4** Multiperiod production model solution.

| Max | | 4,230 | | Revenues | 13,800 |
|---|---|---|---|---|---|
| | | | | Production costs | -5,920 |
| | | | | Storage costs | -50 |
| | | | | Shipment costs | -3,600 |

| t | | Production (P) | s.t. Capacity | Unit Cost (c) | |
|---|---|---|---|---|---|
| 1 | P1 | 180.0 | 180 | 10.0 | |
| 2 | P2 | 200.0 | 200 | 11.0 | |
| 3 | P3 | 160.0 | 160 | 12.0 | |
| | | Shipment to Branch (D) | | Unit cost (d) | |
| 1 | P1_A1 | 20.0 | | 5.0 | |
| 1 | P1_B1 | 110.0 | | 7.0 | |
| 1 | P1_C1 | 0.0 | | 9.0 | |
| 2 | P2_A2 | 80.0 | | 5.0 | |
| 2 | P2_B2 | 170.0 | | 7.0 | |
| 2 | P2_C2 | 0.0 | | 9.0 | |
| 3 | P3_A3 | 30.0 | | 5.0 | |
| 3 | P3_B3 | 90.0 | | 7.0 | |
| 3 | P3_C3 | 40.0 | | 9.0 | |
| | | Sales of Branch (Q) | s.t. Max sales | Unit Price (p) | |
| 1 | A1 | 20.0 | 60 | 20.0 | |
| 1 | B1 | 110.0 | 110 | 25.0 | |
| 1 | C1 | 0.0 | 80 | 20.0 | |
| 2 | A2 | 80.0 | 80 | 22.0 | |
| 2 | B2 | 170.0 | 170 | 27.0 | |
| 2 | C2 | 0.0 | 80 | 20.0 | |
| 3 | A3 | 30.0 | 30 | 24.0 | |
| 3 | B3 | 90.0 | 90 | 30.0 | |
| 3 | C3 | 40.0 | 60 | 22.0 | |

| | | Inventory end period (I) | s.t. Max storage | Unit cost (h) | Inventory end period |
|---|---|---|---|---|---|
| 1 | I1 | 50.0 | 100.0 | 1.0 | 50.0 |
| 2 | I2 | 0.0 | 100.0 | 1.0 | 0.0 |
| 3 | I3 | 0.0 | 100.0 | 1.0 | 0.0 |

We define the following quantities.

$M_{jk}$ = costs incurred in period $j + 1$ through $k$ as:

$$M_{jk} = A_{j+1} + C_{j+1}Q_{j+1} + \sum_{t=j+1}^{k-1} h_t I_t.$$

$M_{jk}$ denotes then the cost of producing in period $j + 1$ to satisfy the demands from period $j + 1$ through $k$.

As:

$$I_t = Q_{j+1} - \sum_{r=j+1}^{t} D_r = \sum_{r=t+1}^{k} D_r \quad (\text{for } j < t < k)$$

we have

$$M_{jk} = A_{j+1} + C_{j+1}Q_{j+1} + \sum_{t=j+1}^{k-1} h_t \sum_{r=t+1}^{k} D_r.$$

This second version of $M_{jk}$ highlights the fact that if we are in $t$ and we decide to produce for future periods demanded quantities, up to $k$, at current costs, then we will have to sustain the total cost of the inventory carrying forward.

We can write the following recursive equation to optimize:

$$F_k = \min_{0 \leq j < k} [F_j + M_{jk}] \quad (k = 1, 2, \cdots, N)$$

where $F_j$ is the optimal policy up to stage $j$. By enumerating all $j < k$ we can find the value of $j_k^*$ which minimizes $F_j + M_{jk}$.

The procedure is to find the sequence of $F_k$ selecting then the optimal policy proceeding backward.

At this point, to grasp the algorithm, we need to proceed with a numerical example that will be also implemented in Excel.

## EXAMPLE 1

The following data are provided for a planning horizon period of 6 months.
Let us consider one period horizon (we use the forward algorithm):

$$D_1 = 60$$

$$F_1 = F_o + M_{01} = F_o + A_1 + C_1Q_1 = 0 + 150 + 7 \cdot 60 = 570$$

For two periods we have:

$$F_2 = \min \begin{cases} F_o + M_{02} = F_0 + A_1 + C_1(D_1 + D_2) + h_1 D_2 \\ \qquad\qquad = 0 + 150 + 7 \cdot (60 + 100) + 1 \cdot 100 = 1,370 \qquad\qquad = 1,370 \\ F_1 + M_{12} = F_1 + A_2 + C_2 D_2 = 570 + 140 + 7 \cdot 100 = 1,410 \end{cases}$$

The first equation says that we produce for all the two periods at current costs, and since this alternative is less costly than the second, this implies that it is better to produce in the first period for satisfying the demands occurring in $t = 1$ and $t = 2$, generating some inventory costs, rather than producing separately in each period.

In this case the inventory cost generated is equal to:

$$h_1 D_2 = 1 \cdot 100$$

Let us move forward to $t = 3$.

$$F_3 = \min \begin{cases} F_o + M_{03} = F_0 + A_1 + C_1(D_1 + D_2 + D_3) + h_1(D_2 + D_3) + h_2 D_3 \\ \quad = 0 + 150 + 7 \cdot (60 + 100 + 140) + 1 \cdot (100 + 140) + 1 \cdot 140 = 2,630 \\ F_1 + M_{13} = F_1 + A_2 + C_2(D_2 + D_3) + h_2 D_3 = 570 + 1,960 = 2,530 \\ F_2 + M_{23} = F_1 + A_3 + C_3 D_3 = 1,370 + 1,280 = 2,650 \end{cases} = 2,530$$

From the first equation, notice how the quantity $D_3$ is carried forward the first time from $t = 1$ to $t = 2$ at cost $h_1$ then a second time to $t = 3$ at cost $h_2$.

For $t = 4$, we have the following:

$$F_4 = \min \begin{cases} F_o + M_{04} = F_0 + A_1 + C_1(D_1 + D_2 + D_3 + D_4) + h_1(D_2 + D_3 + D_4) + h_2(D_3 + D_4) + h_3 D_4 = 4,830 \\ F_1 + M_{14} = F_1 + A_2 + C_2(D_2 + D_3 + D_4) + h_2(D_3 + D_4) + h_3 D_4 = 4,530 \\ F_2 + M_{24} = F_1 + A_3 + C_3(D_3 + D_4) + h_3 D_4 = 4,650 \\ F_3 + M_{34} = F_3 + A_4 + C_4 D_4 = 4,090 \end{cases} = 4,090$$

For a four-period horizon, $j_k^* = 3$. Looking backward we notice that:

$$F_3 = F_1 + M_{13} = (F_o + M_{01}) + M_{13} + 2,530$$

which implies producing for the first period $D_1$, then at $t = 2$ producing for $D_2$ itself, as well as for $D_3$, then waiting and producing separately for the quantity $D_4$ of the fourth period.

This problem is equivalent to that of finding the shortest path through a graph or network (see Section 11.1).

Using Table 12.2-1, we proceed first by building the cost transportation table from each origin node to the terminal nodes 1, 2, 3, 4, 5, and 6 as in Table 12.2-2.

Based on Table 12.2-2 we select the best policy for each $k = 1, 2, 3, 4, 5, 6$:

$$F_k = \min_{0 \le j < k} [F_j + M_{jk}] \quad (k = 1, 2, \cdots, N)$$

obtaining Table 12.2-3. The ways Tables 12.2-2 and 12.2-3 have been built are shown in Figs. 12.2-2 and 12.2-3, respectively.

**TABLE 12.2-1**   Example 1 data.

| Month | 1 | 2 | 3 | 4 | 5 | 6 |
|---|---|---|---|---|---|---|
| $D_t$ Demand | 60 | 100 | 140 | 200 | 120 | 80 |
| $A_t$ Fixed Cost | 150 | 140 | 160 | 160 | 170 | 190 |
| $C_t$ Variable Prod. Cost | 7 | 7 | 8 | 7 | 6 | 10 |
| $h_t$ Inventory Holding Cost | 1 | 1 | 2 | 2 | 2 | 2 |

**Source:** Lynwood A. Johnson, Douglas C. Montgomery, *Operations Research in Production Planning, Scheduling and Inventory Control*, Table 2.3, p. 76, Copyright © 1974 by John Wiley and Sons, Inc.

**TABLE 12.2-2**   Enumeration of cost $M_{jk}$.

| Arc Index | Origin Node | Terminal Node | Cost $M_{jk}$ |
|---|---|---|---|
| 0_1 | 0 | 1 | 570 |
| 0_2 | 0 | 2 | 1,370 |
| 0_3 | 0 | 3 | 2,630 |
| 0_4 | 0 | 4 | 4,830 |
| 0_5 | 0 | 5 | 6,390 |
| 0_6 | 0 | 6 | 7,590 |
| 1_2 | 1 | 2 | 840 |
| 1_3 | 1 | 3 | 1,960 |
| 1_4 | 1 | 4 | 3,960 |
| 1_5 | 1 | 5 | 5,400 |
| 1_6 | 1 | 6 | 6,520 |
| 2_3 | 2 | 3 | 1,280 |
| 2_4 | 2 | 4 | 3,280 |
| 2_5 | 2 | 5 | 4,720 |
| 2_6 | 2 | 6 | 5,840 |
| 3_4 | 3 | 4 | 1,560 |
| 3_5 | 3 | 5 | 2,640 |
| 3_6 | 3 | 6 | 3,520 |
| 4_5 | 4 | 5 | 890 |
| 4_6 | 4 | 6 | 1,530 |
| 5_6 | 5 | 6 | 990 |

**TABLE 12.2-3** Optimal policies for each k.

| j | k | | | | | |
|---|---|---|---|---|---|---|
| | 1 | 2 | 3 | 4 | 5 | 6 |
| 0 | 570 | 1,370 | 2,630 | 4,830 | 6,390 | 7,590 |
| 1 | | 1,410 | 2,530 | 4,530 | 5,970 | 7,090 |
| 2 | | | 2,650 | 4,650 | 6,090 | 7,210 |
| 3 | | | | 4,090 | 5,170 | 6,050 |
| 4 | | | | | 4,980 | 5,620 |
| 5 | | | | | | 5,970 |
| **Optimal policy** $F_k$ | **570** | **1,370** | **2,530** | **4,090** | **4,980** | **5,620** |

The optimal policy for all the 6-periods planning horizon is given instead in Table 12.2-4, namely the optimal plan is to order (or produce) lots of 60, 240, 0, 200, 200. How do we know that?

We discover this from Table 12.2-3 where the minimum $F_6 = 5,620$ designs a policy such that the last period of production (or procurement) is period five in which we produce also for $k = 6$ the total quantity $200 = 120 + 80$. Moving then backward to $k = 4$ where the minimum cost is $F_4 = 4,090$ whose optimal policy has been already explained before.

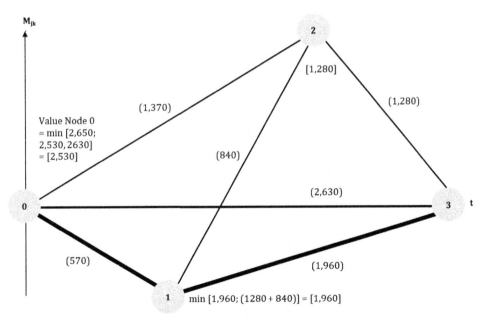

**FIGURE 12.2-1** Network of costs for $t = 3$ (data from Table 12.2-2) and shortest path.

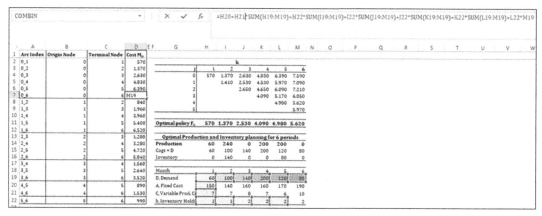

**FIGURE 12.2-2**    Computation of $M_{06}$ of Table 12.2-2.

As we already mentioned, this algorithm is characterized by the implicit application of the Bellman's principle and therefore it can be also approached via the shortest path of a graph (or network).

Let us build then the graph for $t = 3$ as in Fig. 12.2-1 and as we have done in Section 11.1 to solve it. Each arc value represents the cost $M_{jk}$ in round brackets, while in square brackets we have the value of the node.

The thicker line arc connecting nodes 0, 1, and 3 in the graph is our backward solution. Using instead the Excel *MINIFS* function we can also solve the problem, backward, as in Table 12.2-5.

COMBIN    ▾ : × ✓ fx    =VLOOKUP($G9&"_"&M$3:$A:$D:4:FALSE)+MIN(L4:L9)

| Arc Index | Origin Node | Terminal Node | Cost $M_{jk}$ | | | | | | |
|---|---|---|---|---|---|---|---|---|---|
| 0_1 | 0 | 1 | 570 | | | | | | |
| 0_2 | 0 | 2 | 1.370 | | | k | | | |
| 0_3 | 0 | 3 | 2.630 | | | 1 | 2 | 3 | 4 | 5 | 6 |
| 0_4 | 0 | 4 | 4.830 | 0 | 570 | 1.370 | 2.630 | 4.830 | 6.390 | 7.590 |
| 0_5 | 0 | 5 | 6.390 | 1 | | 1.410 | 2.530 | 4.530 | 5.970 | 7.090 |
| 0_6 | 0 | 6 | 7.590 | 2 | | | 2.650 | 4.650 | 6.090 | 7.210 |
| 1_2 | 1 | 2 | 840 | 3 | | | | 4.090 | 5.170 | 6.050 |
| 1_3 | 1 | 3 | 1.960 | 4 | | | | | 4.980 | 5.620 |
| 1_4 | 1 | 4 | 3.960 | 5 | | | | | | L4:L9 |
| 1_5 | 1 | 5 | 5.400 | | | | | | | |
| 1_6 | 1 | 6 | 6.520 | Optimal policy $F_k$ | 570 | 1.370 | 2.530 | 4.090 | 4.980 | 5.620 |
| 2_3 | 2 | 3 | 1.280 | Optimal Production and Inventory planning for 6 periods | | | | | | |
| 2_4 | 2 | 4 | 3.280 | Production | 60 | 240 | 0 | 200 | 200 | 0 |
| 2_5 | 2 | 5 | 4.720 | Cogs = D | 60 | 100 | 140 | 200 | 120 | 80 |
| 2_6 | 2 | 6 | 5.840 | Inventory | 0 | 140 | 0 | 0 | 80 | 0 |
| 3_4 | 3 | 4 | 1.560 | | | | | | | |
| 3_5 | 3 | 5 | 2.640 | Month | 1 | 2 | 3 | 4 | 5 | 6 |
| 3_6 | 3 | 6 | 3.520 | D, Demand | 60 | 100 | 140 | 200 | 120 | 80 |
| 4_5 | 4 | 5 | 890 | A, Fixed Cost | 150 | 140 | 160 | 160 | 170 | 190 |
| 4_6 | 4 | 6 | 1.530 | C, Variable Prod. Cc | 7 | 7 | 8 | 7 | 6 | 10 |
| 5_6 | 5 | 6 | 990 | h, Inventory Holdi | 1 | 1 | 2 | 2 | 2 | 2 |

**FIGURE 12.2-3**    Computation of $F_6 = F_5 + M_{56}$.

**TABLE 12.2-4** Optimal production planning for $k = 6$

| Optimal Production and Inventory planning for 6 periods | | | | | | |
|---|---|---|---|---|---|---|
| Production | 60 | 240 | 0 | 200 | 200 | 0 |
| Cogs = D | 60 | 100 | 140 | 200 | 120 | 80 |
| Inventory | 0 | 140 | 0 | 0 | 80 | 0 |

**TABLE 12.2-5** Tabular backward solution ($t = 3$).

| Arc | To node | From node | Cost at the arc | Min Cost Optimal Policy to reach current node with Minifs |
|---|---|---|---|---|
| 1 | 0 | 1 | 570 | 2,530 |
| 2 | 0 | 2 | 1,370 | 2,650 |
| 3 | 0 | 3 | 2,630 | 2,630 |
| 4 | 1 | 2 | 840 | 2,120 |
| 5 | 1 | 3 | 1,960 | 1,960 |
| 6 | 2 | 3 | 1,280 | 1,280 |
| | | | F* | 2,530 |

For $t = 3$ as already seen before the minimum cost of production would be $F_3 = 2,530$ which implies producing nothing at $t = 3$, then producing $240 = D_2 + D_3 = 100 + 140$ at $t = 2$ and then $D_1 = 60$ at $t = 1$, this process being read of course forward.

## Linear programming versus Wagner–Whitin algorithm

The problem, only with variable costs and in absence of fixed costs, could have also been approached using the linear programming, with one of the models shown in the previous paragraph.

The fact that we also have in this case the fixed costs, these being dynamically determined as a function of the optimal policy undertaken at each step, lead to a particular dynamic cost structure and this prevents us from directly using one of the linear models presented in the previous section. Therefore, the dynamic Wagner–Whitin algorithm is in this case a much more powerful algorithm.

## 12.3 Eliezer Naddor stochastic single-period inventory models

This class of models attempts to answer an important question. Say we are at the beginning of a period; the problem is at what stock level we should have the inventory in order to satisfy an uncertain (stochastic) demand, so that the total expected cost is also minimized?

These models are particularly useful when goods are demanded for a relatively short period of time, after which goods become obsolete (e.g., newspapers, apparel, Christmas items, etc.) or not demanded until the next season (e.g., swimwear). The key characteristic of these situations is that there is only one opportunity of producing (or procuring) the items, i.e., at the beginning of the period.

If the level of inventory is too high a *surplus* in inventory will arise and the costs associated with this are the costs of carrying the inventory, while if the inventory is too low *shortages* will arise and this will lead to even higher costs (e.g., loss of customers, loss of profit, etc.).

Whether producing seasonal items or not, the companies should always find the optimal inventory level, such that demand is always smoothly satisfied, and the costs associated to keeping the inventory are minimized. This is an important aspect that impacts the company financial management area and the whole working capital management (inventory, accounts receivables, and accounts payables).

## Model 1

Assume that the period starts with an inventory level $S$ and as we have said before two situations may arise. In the case of a surplus the cost will be:

$$c_1(S - r)$$

where

$$c_1 = cost\ of surplus$$

$$S = stock\ available$$

$$r = quantity\ required$$

In the case of a shortage we have a shortage cost equal to:

$$c_2(r - S)$$

where

$$c_2 = cost\ of\ shortage$$

We also assume the demand follows a probability density distribution $f(r)$ so that the total expected cost in one period is:

$$C(S) = \int_0^S c_1(S - r)f(r)dr + \int_S^\infty c_2(r - S)f(r)dr.$$

The minimum point of $C(S)$ is found differentiating $C(S)$ with respect to $S$ and setting then the first-order condition. Therefore, we have:

$$\frac{dC}{dS} = c_1 \int_0^S f(r)dr - c_2 \int_S^\infty f(r)dr$$

namely,

$$\frac{dC}{dS} = c_1 F(S) - c_2[1 - F(S)]$$

where $F(S)$ is the cumulative distribution associated to $f(r)$:

$$F(S) = \int_0^S f(r)dr.$$

The first-order condition for an optimum $S^*$ becomes:

$$(c_1 + c_2)F(S^*) - c_2 = 0$$

$$\Rightarrow F(S^*) = \frac{c_2}{c_1 + c_2}$$

and since the second derivative is:

$$\frac{d^2C}{dS^2} = c_1 f(S^*) + c_2 f(S^*) \geq 0$$

the critical point $S^*$ is a minimum.

In summary, $S^*$ satisfying:

$$F(S^*) = \frac{c_2}{c_1 + c_2}$$

returns the minimum point for the expected cost $C(S)$.

## EXAMPLE 1

Let us consider the following demand density distribution:

$$f(r) = 0.02 - 0.0002r$$

with $r$ varying from 0 to 100.

The costs of surplus and shortages are, respectively:

$$c_1 = 1 \ cent$$

$$c_2 = 15 \ cents$$

The optimal solution is equal to $S^* = 75$, and the excel worksheet will have to be set up as in Table 12.3-1.

At *Row* 4 the integrand function is, for example, equal to:

$$= IF(\$H\$2 > A4; \$K\$2 * (\$H\$2 - A4) * B4; \$K\$3 * (A4 - \$H\$2) * B4)$$

where

$$\$H\$2 = cell \ where \ the \ optimal \ stock \ is \ stored$$

$$\$K\$2 = c_1$$

$$\$K\$3 = c_3$$

$$(\$H\$2 - A4) = (S - r)$$

$$(A4 - \$H\$2) = (r - S)$$

TABLE 12.3-1   Excel table for the optimal inventory problem.

|  | A | B | C | D | E |
|---|---|---|---|---|---|
| 1 | 0<r<100 | f(r) = 0.02-0.0002r | Δr | Integrand Function | Integral |
| 2 | 0.0000 | 0.0200 |  | 1.5000 | 0.0000 |
| 3 | 1.0000 | 0.0198 | 1.0000 | 1.4652 | 1.4652 |
| 4 | 2.0000 | 0.0196 | 1.0000 | 1.4308 | 1.4308 |
| 5 | 3.0000 | 0.0194 | 1.0000 | 1.3968 | 1.3968 |
| 6 | 4.0000 | 0.0192 | 1.0000 | 1.3632 | 1.3632 |
| 7 | 5.0000 | 0.0190 | 1.0000 | 1.3300 | 1.3300 |
| 8 | 6.0000 | 0.0188 | 1.0000 | 1.2972 | 1.2972 |
| 9 | 7.0000 | 0.0186 | 1.0000 | 1.2648 | 1.2648 |
| 10 | 8.0000 | 0.0184 | 1.0000 | 1.2328 | 1.2328 |
| 96 | 94.0000 | 0.0012 | 1.0000 | 0.3420 | 0.3420 |
| 97 | 95.0000 | 0.0010 | 1.0000 | 0.3000 | 0.3000 |
| 98 | 96.0000 | 0.0008 | 1.0000 | 0.2520 | 0.2520 |
| 99 | 97.0000 | 0.0006 | 1.0000 | 0.1980 | 0.1980 |
| 100 | 98.0000 | 0.0004 | 1.0000 | 0.1380 | 0.1380 |
| 101 | 99.0000 | 0.0002 | 1.0000 | 0.0720 | 0.0720 |
| 102 | 100.0000 | 0.0000 | 1.0000 | 0.0000 | 0.0000 |
| 103 |  |  |  | Σ | 49.2400 |

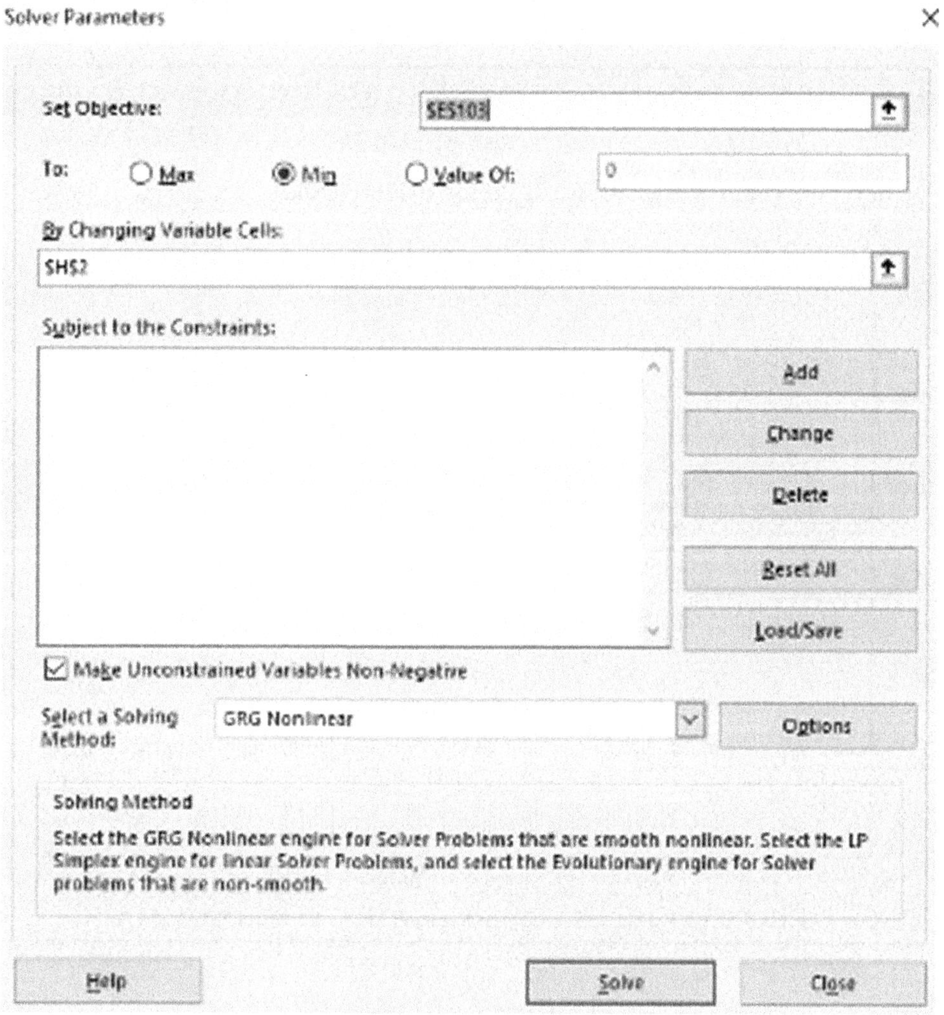

FIGURE 12.3-1   Solver parameters.

$$B4 = f(r)$$

We will resort instead to the Solver in order to minimize the integral in *Cell E103* to find the optimal solution $S^* = 75$ by changing *Cell H2*, which is where we store our stock variable. See Figs. 12.3-1–12.3-3.

The exact solution is to satisfy the following

$$F(S^*) = \frac{c_2}{c_1 + c_2}$$

| G | H | I | J | K | L |
|---|---|---|---|---|---|
| Optimal Stock $S^*$ | 75.00 | | c1 Surplus cost | 1.00 | 1 cent |
| | | | c2 Shortage cost | 15.00 | 15 cents |

**FIGURE 12.3-2**   $S^* = 75$ optimal solution.

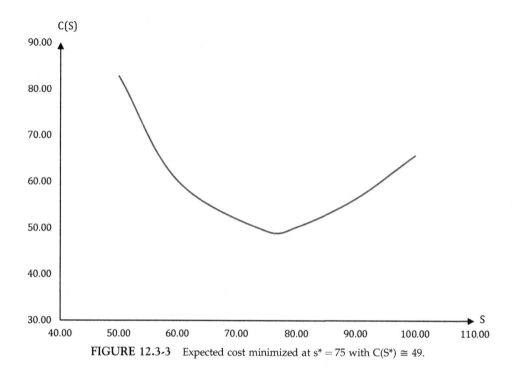

**FIGURE 12.3-3**   Expected cost minimized at $s^* = 75$ with $C(S^*) \cong 49$.

which is:

$$\int_0^S f(r)dr = \frac{c_2}{c_1 + c_2}$$

$$\Rightarrow 0.02S - 0.0001S^2 = \frac{15}{16}.$$

The above equation is equal to zero for the two roots $S_1 = 75$ and $S_2 = 125$, and we choose $S^* = 75$.

The Model I has been essentially transformed in the following discrete formulation:

$$C(S) = \sum_{r=0}^{S} c_1(S-r)f(r)\Delta r + \sum_{r=S+1}^{\infty} c_2(r-S)f(r)\Delta r$$

## Model II

In this case, $r$ will be assumed to occur continuously in the scheduling period and two situations may arise.

When $r \leq S$ the cost will be:

$$c_1\left(S - \frac{r}{2}\right).$$

When $r > S$ the cost will be:

$$c_1 \frac{S}{2}\frac{S}{r} + c_2 \frac{(r-S)}{2}\frac{(r-S)}{r}.$$

The two situations are represented in Figs. 12.3-4 and 12.3-5, respectively.

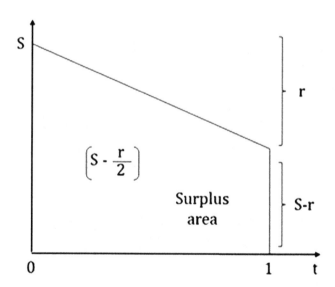

FIGURE 12.3-4   Surplus.

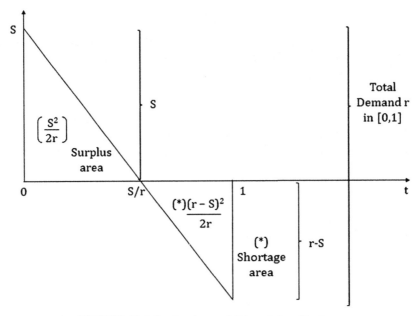

FIGURE 12.3-5   Surplus until S/r and then Shortage.

## Remark

From the theory of inventory, if $I(t)$ is the function representing the inventory over time, the following will be the average inventory over a period $[0, T]$:

$$\bar{I} = \frac{1}{T} \int_0^T I(t)dt$$

being the integral (i.e., the area) the whole inventory generated within the period $[0, T]$.
The cost $C(s)$ will be for Model II the following:

$$C(S) = \int_0^S c_1\left(S - \frac{r}{2}\right)f(r)dr + \int_S^\infty c_1\frac{S^2}{2r}f(r)dr + \int_S^\infty c_2\frac{(r-S)^2}{2r}f(r)dr$$

Now, we want to find the minimum and differentiating $C(S)$ we have:

$$\frac{dC}{dS} = c_1\int_0^S f(r)dr + c_1\int_0^S \frac{S}{r}f(r)dr - c_2\int_s^\infty \frac{(r-S)}{r}f(r)dr$$

$$= c_1F(S) + c_1G(S) - c_2[1 - F(S)] + c_2G(S)$$

$$= (c_1 + c_2)[F(S) + G(S)] - c_2 = (c_1 + c_2)L(S) - c_2$$

where $L(S)=F(S) + G(S)$ and:

$$F(S) = \int_0^S f(r)dr$$

$$G(S) = S \int_S^\infty \frac{1}{r}f(r)dr.$$

Setting now:

$$\frac{dC}{dS} = (c_1 + c_2)L(S) - c_2 = 0$$

we obtain the extreme value of $S^*$ such that the following must result:

$$L(S^*) = \frac{c_2}{c_1 + c_2}.$$

Since the second derivative is positive the critical point $S^*$ is a minimum. The Model II will be discretized as follows:

$$C(S) = \sum_{r=0}^S c_1 \left(S - \frac{r}{2}\right)f(r)\Delta r + \sum_{r=S+1}^\infty c_1 \frac{S^2}{2r}f(r)\Delta r + \sum_{r=S+1}^\infty c_2 \frac{(r-S)^2}{2r}f(r)f(r)\Delta r$$

## EXAMPLE 2

The demand probability density is:

$$f(r) = re^{-r}.$$

The cost of shortage is $c_2 = 19$ *cents* while the cost of surplus is $c_1 = 1$ *cent*. $L(S)$ is:

$$L(S) = \int_0^S re^{-r}dr + S \int_S^\infty \frac{1}{r}re^{-r}$$

$$= |(-r-1)e^{-r}|_0^S + S|-e^{-r}|_S^\infty$$

$$= (-S-1)e^{-S} + 1 + S(-e^{-\infty} + e^{-S})$$

$$= -Se^{-S} - e^{-S} + 1 + Se^{-S} = 1 - e^{-S}$$

which must satisfy the following at $S^*$:

$$1 - e^{-S^*} = \frac{19}{20}$$

from which we have $S^* = 3$.

The numerical Excel solution is in Table 12.3-2, which is set up like in Fig. 12.3-6.

Fig. 12.3-7 represents instead the cost as a function of the stock $S$, with its minimum point for the optimal quantity stock $S^* = 3$.

**TABLE 12.3-2**   Enumeration of Example 2 with optimal $S^* = 3$

| $0 < r < 100$ | $f(r) = r*exp(-r)$ | $\Delta r$ | Integrand Function | Integral |
|---|---|---|---|---|
| 0.0000 | 0.0793 | | 0.2378 | 0.0000 |
| 1.0000 | 0.3679 | 1.0000 | 0.9188 | 0.9188 |
| 2.0000 | 0.2707 | 1.0000 | 0.5407 | 0.5407 |
| 3.0000 | 0.1494 | 1.0000 | 0.2237 | 0.2237 |
| 4.0000 | 0.0733 | 1.0000 | 0.2571 | 0.2571 |
| 5.0000 | 0.0337 | 1.0000 | 0.2870 | 0.2870 |
| 6.0000 | 0.0149 | 1.0000 | 0.2234 | 0.2234 |
| 7.0000 | 0.0064 | 1.0000 | 0.1429 | 0.1429 |
| 8.0000 | 0.0027 | 1.0000 | 0.0813 | 0.0813 |
| 9.0000 | 0.0011 | 1.0000 | 0.0428 | 0.0428 |
| 10.0000 | 0.0005 | 1.0000 | 0.0214 | 0.0214 |
| 11.0000 | 0.0002 | 1.0000 | 0.0102 | 0.0102 |
| 12.0000 | 0.0001 | 1.0000 | 0.0048 | 0.0048 |
| 13.0000 | 0.0000 | 1.0000 | 0.0022 | 0.0022 |
| 14.0000 | 0.0000 | 1.0000 | 0.0010 | 0.0010 |
| 15.0000 | 0.0000 | 1.0000 | 0.0004 | 0.0004 |
| 97.0000 | 0.0000 | 1.0000 | 0.0000 | 0.0000 |
| 98.0000 | 0.0000 | 1.0000 | 0.0000 | 0.0000 |
| 99.0000 | 0.0000 | 1.0000 | 0.0000 | 0.0000 |
| 100.0000 | 0.0000 | 1.0000 | 0.0000 | 0.0000 |
| | | | $\Sigma$ | 2.7578 |

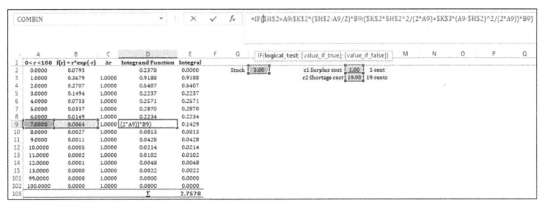

**FIGURE 12.3-6** Excel setup for Example 2 with discrete integrand highlighted.

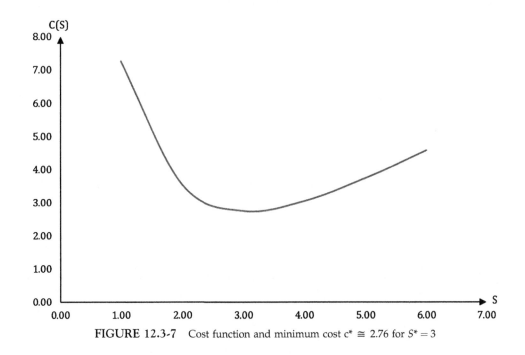

**FIGURE 12.3-7** Cost function and minimum cost $c^* \cong 2.76$ for $S^* = 3$

# Exercises

1. Build a dynamic monthly production schedule $P_t$ over 6 months via a linear program using the data in Table 1 for demands, unit production costs, and costs for holding a unit of inventory. Shortages are not allowed.

TABLE 1

| Month | Demand | Unit Production Costs (£) | Unit Inventory Costs (£) |
|-------|--------|---------------------------|--------------------------|
| 1 | 1,300 | 98 | 5.0 |
| 2 | 1,600 | 104 | 5.0 |
| 3 | 900 | 108 | 5.0 |
| 4 | 700 | 120 | 5.0 |
| 5 | 1,800 | 105 | 5.0 |
| 6 | 2,000 | 105 | 5.0 |

The constraints of the problem are given below:

$$I_t \leq 250 \ (\textit{no more than 250 units can be stored})$$

$$I_t = I_{t-1} + P_t - D_t \quad (\textit{Inventory clearing account equation})$$

$$I_0 = 200$$

$$I_6 = 150$$

$$I_t \geq 0, \ P_t \geq 0 \quad \textit{for } t = 1, \cdots, 6$$

The objective function to minimize is given instead by the following cost function:

$$Z = \sum_{t=1}^{6}(c_t P_t + 4I_t)$$

2. A company has two manufacturing plants (PA and PB) and three sales stores (I, II, and III). The shipping costs from production centers to the store centers, the manufacturing data with capacity constraints, and unit costs of production, as well as the demands data for the store with sales price and maximum sales constraints, are given below in Tables 2-4. Cost of holding a unit of inventory is £ 1, while the maximum storage in the company (either at plant level or store) allowed is 75 units.

TABLE 2

| | SHIPPING COSTS | | |
|-------|---|---|---|
| | | Store | |
| Plant | I | II | III |
| PA | 3 | 8 | 7 |
| PB | 6 | 3 | 4 |

### TABLE 3

| | MANUFACTURING DATA | | | |
| | Plant A (PA) | | Plant B (PB) | |
| Period | Unit Cost (£) | Capacity | Unit Cost (£) | Capacity |
|--------|---------------|----------|---------------|----------|
| 1 | 7 | 180 | 6 | 190 |
| 2 | 9 | 170 | 10 | 195 |

### TABLE 4

| | DEMAND DATA | | | | | |
| | Selling Price | | | Maximum Sales | | |
| Period | I | II | III | I | II | III |
|--------|----|----|-----|-----|-----|-----|
| 1 | 20 | 18 | 17 | 110 | 190 | 145 |
| 2 | 17 | 20 | 22 | 145 | 295 | 155 |

**a.** Identify the objective function to maximize, i.e., $Z = Total\ Revenues - Total\ Costs$.

**b.** Identify and formalize in Excel the various constraints.

**c.** Build in Excel, using the Simplex LP Solver the optimal production schedule over the two periods.

**3.** A company has to organize its aggregate production schedule for the next 3 months. Units may be produced on regular time or overtime. The relevant costs and capacities are shown in Table 5 below.

### TABLE 5

| | MANUFACTURING DATA | | | | |
| | Capacity | | Production Costs | | Demand |
| Period | Regular Time | Over Time | Regular Time | Over Time | |
|--------|--------------|-----------|--------------|-----------|--------|
| 1 | 120 | 25 | 16 | 20 | 70 |
| 2 | 90 | 12 | 18 | 21 | 90 |
| 3 | 80 | 18 | 18 | 24 | 150 |

There is 1 £ cost per unit of inventory held, and the inventory at the beginning of the 2 months is equal to 15 units. Also, sales can be backordered at a cost of 2 £ per unit a month. Backorders occur when demand is temporarily out of stock, and it will be satisfied with future production at an additional cost.

**a.** Identify the objective function with total costs to minimize.

**b.** Identify and formalize in Excel the various constraints.

**c.** Build in Excel, using the Simplex LP Solver the optimal production schedule.

**4.** A company has to plan a production schedule over a four-period horizon, where the requirements by period are 20, 10, 40, and 30 units, respectively. Costs for holding a unit of inventory are $h_1 = 3$, $h_2 = 2$, and $h_3 = h_4 = 1$. No shortages are allowed. The production costs are given in Table 6. These costs are assumed to be constant for the given range of $P$. Maximum production for each period is 35 units. The initial inventory is zero and the final inventory is to be zero as well. Maximum storage capacity is 5 units for period 2 and period 3.

TABLE 6

MARGINAL PRODUCTION COSTS

| Range of Production | Period of Production | | | |
|---|---|---|---|---|
| | 1 | 2 | 3 | 4 |
| $1 \le P_t \le 8$ | 4 | 6 | 6 | 3 |
| $9 \le P_t \le 17$ | 5 | 10 | 8 | 5 |
| $18 \le P_t \le 25$ | 6 | 12 | 10 | 7 |
| $36 \le P_t \le 35$ | 8 | 14 | 12 | 10 |

**Source**: Lynwood A. Johnson, Douglas C. Montgomery, *Operations Research in Production Planning, Scheduling and Inventory Control*, Table 4.5, p. 208, Copyright © 1974 by John Wiley and Sons, Inc.

Develop the Excel model that will generate the optimal production schedule over the four periods.

**5. Wagner–Whitin dynamic programming approach.** Use the demand and manufacturing data gathered in Table 7 to set up the optimal production and inventory schedule over four periods. No shortages are permitted (i.e., when the demand cannot be met, being temporarily out of stock).

TABLE 7

| Month | 1 | 2 | 3 | 4 |
|---|---|---|---|---|
| $D_t$ Demand | 20 | 30 | 40 | 30 |
| $A_t$ Fixed Cost | 30 | 40 | 30 | 50 |
| $C_t$ Variable Prod. Cost | 3 | 3 | 4 | 4 |
| $h_t$ Inventory Holding Cost | 2 | 2 | 1 | 1 |

**Source**: Lynwood A. Johnson, Douglas C. Montgomery, *Operations Research in Production Planning, Scheduling and Inventory Control*, Table 4.8, p. 215, Copyright © 1974 by John Wiley and Sons, Inc.

The following exercises refer to the single-period stochastic Naddor inventory modeling

**6.** Consider the following continuous probability density function for a certain type of goods required in a month:

$$f(r) = \begin{cases} 0 & r < 80 \\ f_2(r) = -\dfrac{1}{5} + \dfrac{r}{400} & 80 \le r < 100 \\ f_3(r) = 1.5 - \dfrac{r}{400} & 100 \le r \le 120 \\ 0 & r > 120 \end{cases}$$

Costs of inventory are as follows:

$$c_1 = cost\ of\ surplus = 200$$

$$c_2 = cost\ of\ shortage = 9,000$$

Like in Model II (slightly modified) of the chapter determine the optimal stock $S^*$, so that the total inventory expected cost, described by the following integral, is minimized:

$$C(S) = \int_{80}^{100} c_1\left(S - \frac{r}{2}\right)f_2(r)dr + \int_{100}^{S} c_1\left(S - \frac{r}{2}\right)f_3(r)dr + \int_{S}^{120} c_1\frac{S^2}{2r}f_3(r)dr + \int_{S}^{120} c_2\frac{(r-S)^2}{2r}f_3(r)dr.$$

**7.** Consider the following case.[1] There are certain rather expensive items (some costing over $ 100,000 each) known as insurance spares which are generally procured at the time a new class of ship is under construction. These spares are bought even though it is known that it is very unlikely that any of them will ever be needed and that they cannot be used on any ship except of that particular class. They are procured in order to provide insurance against the rather serious loss which would be suffered if one of these spares were not available when needed. Also, the initial procurement of these spares is intended to be the only procurement during the lifetime of the ships of that class because it is extremely difficult and costly to procure these spares at a later time.

Suppose that spares cost $ 100,000 each and that a loss of $ 10,000,000 is suffered for each spare that is needed when there is none available in stock. Further, suppose the following probabilities that spares will be needed as replacements during the life term of the class of ship discussed

---

[1]For Exercises 7 and 8 see Eliezer Naddor, *Some models of Inventory and an application*, Management Science, Vol. 2, No. 4, pp. 299–312.

$$f(r) = \begin{cases} 0 & 1 & 2 & 3 & 4 & \text{5 or more} \\ 0.9488 & 0.0400 & 0.0100 & 0.0010 & 0.00020 & 0.0000 \end{cases}$$

How many parts should be procured? In this exercise apply Model I.

8. There are two items with cost of surplus $c_1$, cost of shortage $c_2$, and discrete probability distribution for each item request as follows:

**Item 1**

$$c_1 = \$2,\ c_2 = \$130$$

$$f_1(r) = \begin{cases} 0 & 1 & 2 & 3 \\ 0.4 & 0.3 & 0.2 & 0.1 \end{cases}$$

**Item 2**

$$c_1 = \$5,\ c_2 = \$60$$

$$f_2(r) = \begin{cases} 0 & 1 & 2 \\ 0.2 & 0.5 & 0.3 \end{cases}$$

What is the optimal inventory level for the two items?

9. **Inventory and optimal procurement policy (deterministic single item inventory model).** This is the classical application of finding the optimal *economic order quantity (aka: EOQ)*. See also exercise 17 in Ch. 5.

We have the following data:

$$C = 15\ unit\ variable\ cost\ of\ purchase$$

$$p = 35\ unit\ price\ of\ sales$$

$$D = 30,000\ known\ demand\ rate\ in\ units\ per\ year$$

$$h = 6\ inventory\ carying\ cost\ per\ unit\ and\ per\ year$$

$$K = 400\ fixed\ cost\ of\ a\ replenishement\ order$$

$$Q = order\ quantity$$

The objective function describing the gross margin of the goods sold that we want to optimize, with respect to $Q$, is as follows:

$F(Q) = Total\ Revenues - [Total\ Purhase\ Costs + Total\ Cost\ of\ Orders + Total\ Inventory\ Costs]$

$$F(Q) = pD - \left[ CD + K\frac{D}{Q} + h\frac{Q}{2} \right]$$

**a.** Find in Excel the optimal *economic order quantity* $Q^*$ and the maximum value of the gross profit $F(Q^*)$.

**b.** Plot the function $F(Q)$.

**c.** Calculate the optimal number of orders in a year (assuming 300 working days in a year).

**d.** Calculate the cycle length $T$, namely the length of time between placements of replenishment orders.

*Elements of Numerical Mathematical Economics with Excel*
https://doi.org/10.1016/B978-0-12-817648-1.00013-X

## 13.1  A simple way to organize a spreadsheet using the VBA code and bookmarks

Working on a spreadsheet implies that we are well organized, not only in the worksheet itself, where we are working on, but also in the spreadsheet as a whole, especially when this is made of several worksheets.

An important and simple tip is to recall each worksheet of the spreadsheet using an elementary VBA sub, which will help us to move from a main summary worksheet page (a sort of table of contents) to each detailed worksheet.

The following first method with VBA is the method that one should prefer to organize the spreadsheets.

Let us assume we have a spreadsheet made of $n$ worksheets. We can create the following elementary VBA sub to move from the first page to each worksheet $j$ and vice versa:

*Sub Worksheet_j()*

*Sheets("Worksheet j").Select*

*End Sub*

Let us assign to the first worksheet page the name "Menu," then from each worksheet page we can go back to our Menu page using the following sub:

*Sub Menu()*

*Sheets("Menu").Select*

*End Sub*

Look at Fig. 13.1-1. This is the first Menu page of a spreadsheet (made of four worksheets in total) that we will use in this and next paragraph to show how to implement a dashboard reporting on the sales data of a company. Each button (*form control*) in Fig. 13.1-1 is associated to one VBA sub routine, to recall a specific worksheet. The subs are in Fig. 13.1-2.

A second technique to recall the worksheets in a spreadsheet is using the **Bookmarks**.

FIGURE 13.1-1    Menu page for a sales dashboard.

This is done following the three steps from Fig. 13.1-3 through Fig. 13.1-5, to go to the worksheet "Dashboard" from the Menu worksheet page.Fig. 13.1-4

We can repeat the creation of a Bookmark for the other worksheet names as well.

By default, you will be redirected to *Cell A*1 of the worksheet "Dashboard." If you want the Bookmark to redirect you somewhere else in this worksheet you should specify it in the Bookmark dialogue box.

## 13.2 Pivot tables, Pivot charts, and dynamic dashboards for managerial data analysis

The goal of this paragraph is to go through a business case of an Excel dashboard creation for a standard company sales reporting.

If we click on the Button Sales Data of Fig. 13.1-1, we are redirected to the raw sales data of Table 13.2-1, that we want to analyze in more details.

```
Sub Dashboard()

Sheets("Dashboard").Select

End Sub
Sub Sales()

Sheets("Sales Data").Select

End Sub
Sub Pivot()

Sheets("Pivot").Select

End Sub
Sub Menu()

Sheets("Menu").Select

End Sub
```

FIGURE 13.1-2    Sub to recall each worksheet in a spreadsheet.

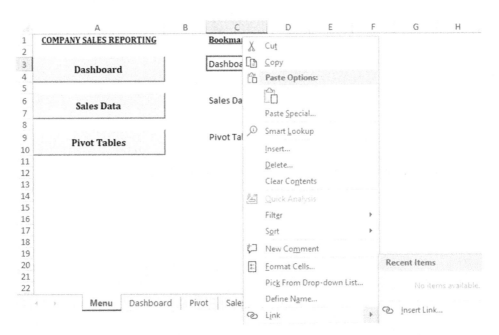

FIGURE 13.1-3    Bookmark Step 1: Right click on cell and then go to link.

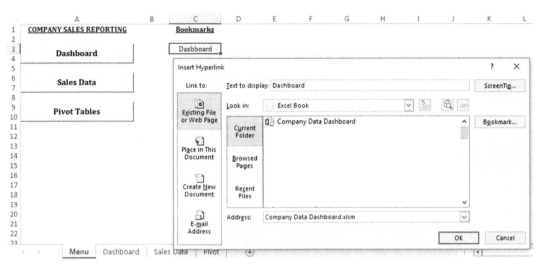

FIGURE 13.1-4   Step 2: Select the spreadsheet name and click on Bookmark.

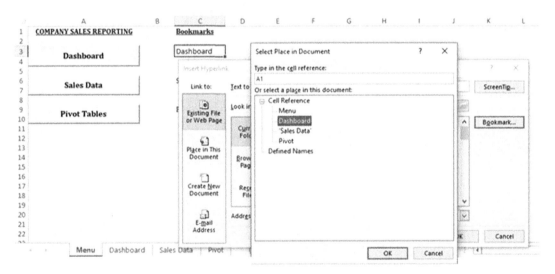

FIGURE 13.1-5   Step 3: Select the worksheet name "Dashboard," then click OK as requested.

The data we want to analyze represent the *ex-post* comparison of the annual budgeted sales (i.e., the objective or goal sales the company wants to reach over a specific period) compared to the actual sales, by each customer for a given period (year, quarter, semester, etc.).

We assume the company is selling its manufactured industrial products to 100 customers, which can be divided into three relevant dimensions:

**i.** Geographic area.

**TABLE 13.2-1**  Budget versus actual sales data by customer in the worksheet "sales data."

| | A | B | C | D | E | F |
|---|---|---|---|---|---|---|
| | CUSTOMER | BUDGET | ACTUAL | SECTOR | MACRO AREA | TYPE OF CUSTOMER |
| 1 | | | | | | |
| 2 | Customer 1 | 10.886.361 | 10.588.500 | TEXTILE | REST OF THE WORLD | END USER |
| 3 | Customer 2 | 3.904.615 | 4.121.000 | RUBBER | EUROPE | END USER |
| 4 | Customer 3 | 3.256.000 | 3.125.623 | TEXTILE | REST OF THE WORLD | END USER |
| 5 | Customer 4 | 2.820.313 | 2.920.313 | RUBBER | EUROPE | RESELLER |
| 6 | Customer 5 | 2.521.000 | 2.775.200 | TEXTILE | EUROPE | END USER |
| 7 | Customer 6 | 2.500.000 | 2.627.234 | RUBBER | AMERICA | RESELLER |
| 8 | Customer 7 | 2.158.000 | 2.580.123 | TEXTILE | EUROPE | RESELLER |
| 95 | Customer 94 | 2.050 | 2.075 | TEXTILE | REST OF THE WORLD | END USER |
| 96 | Customer 95 | 5.089 | 1.718 | RUBBER | EUROPE | END USER |
| 97 | Customer 96 | 3.393 | 1.145 | PACKAGING | EUROPE | RESELLER |
| 98 | Customer 97 | 8.134 | 1.128 | TEXTILE | EUROPE | END USER |
| 99 | Customer 98 | 821 | 1.052 | PACKAGING | EUROPE | RESELLER |
| 100 | Customer 99 | 3.510 | 452 | TEXTILE | EUROPE | END USER |
| 101 | Customer 100 | 11.545 | 0 | TEXTILE | REST OF THE WORLD | END USER |

**ii.** Type of customer.

**iii.** Type of industrial sector in which the customer is categorized.

We want to build now a dynamic sales dashboard, so that each dimension of analysis is interconnected each other and the budget versus the actual sales data are returned in an automatic fashion according to a specific query or filter.

The dashboard will be implemented as follows step-by-step.

## Building the dynamic Pivot tables

To get started, we first need to build the Pivot Tables on our sales data. This can be easily done opening a second worksheet called Pivot, where, from the Ribbon Menu, we will insert three Pivot Tables, respectively, for each of the three customer dimensions (see Fig. 13.2-1). The Source Data of Table 13.2-1, used to build the Pivot Tables, are located in the worksheet called "Sales Data."

The Pivot Tables are then placed in the worksheet named "Pivot" as represented in the following Fig. 13.2-2.

The problem of these Pivot Tables is that they are static, in that the source data *'Sales Data'* !$A$1:$F$101 we have used to create them are themselves static.

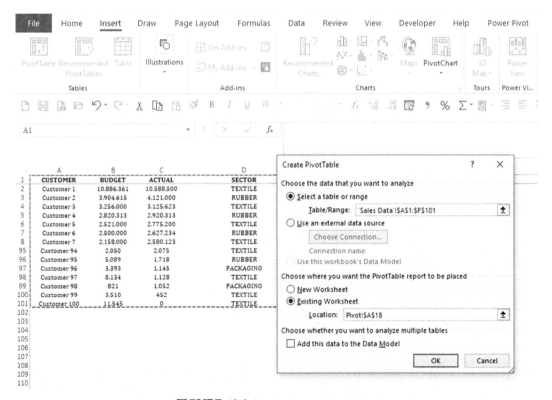

**FIGURE 13.2-1** Inserting a Pivot table.

| | A | B | C | D | E | F | G | H |
|---|---|---|---|---|---|---|---|---|
| 1 | Row Labels | Sum of BUDGET | Sum of ACTUAL | | | Row Labels | Sum of BUDGET | Sum of ACTUAL |
| 2 | PAPER MANUFACTURING | 50,587 | 60,852 | | | END USER | 28,278,661 | 28,532,706 |
| 3 | FOOD INDUSTRY | 117,797 | 124,250 | | | RESELLER | 34,873,774 | 36,853,433 |
| 4 | TIMBER INDUSTRIES | 311,837 | 317,374 | | | Grand Total | 63,152,435 | 65,386,140 |
| 5 | METAL PRODUCTS MANUFACTURING | 420,379 | 461,603 | | | | | |
| 6 | AUTOMOBILES INDUSTRY | 3,879,607 | 4,128,994 | | | | | |
| 7 | PACKAGING | 8,040,605 | 8,365,695 | | | Row Labels | Sum of BUDGET | Sum of ACTUAL |
| 8 | RUBBER | 24,774,184 | 26,120,344 | | | REST OF THE WORLD | 33,954,570 | 34,288,766 |
| 9 | TEXTILE | 25,557,439 | 25,807,028 | | | EUROPE | 23,992,212 | 25,501,565 |
| 10 | Grand Total | 63,152,435 | 65,386,140 | | | AMERICA | 5,205,653 | 5,595,809 |
| 11 | | | | | | Grand Total | 63,152,435 | 65,386,140 |
| 12 | | | | | | | | |

FIGURE 13.2-2    Pivot tables in the worksheet "ssPivot."

Suppose that in Table 13.2-1 we only have a quarter of a year and we want the Pivot Tables to update the new data, as we add the new quarter's data. This is done replacing in the Data Range of each Pivot Table the original source 'Sales Data'!$A$1:$F$101 with the following OFFSET formula (the number 6 at the end is the number of columns of the sales data in Table 13.2-1):

$$= OFFSET('Sales\ Data'!\$A\$1; 0; 0; COUNTA('Sales\ Data'!\$A: \$A); 6)$$

to which a name will be assigned, as in Fig. 13.2-3, from the Name Manager Dialogue Box (which we find under the Tab Formulas in the Ribbon).

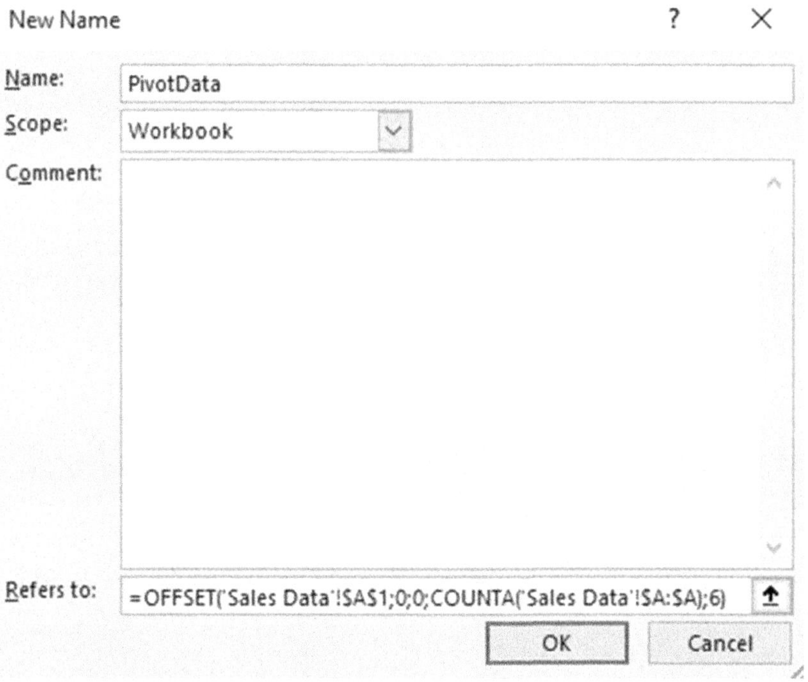

FIGURE 13.2-3    Creating a name with the OFFSET formula from name manager.

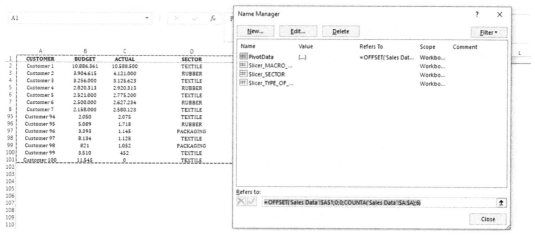

**FIGURE 13.2-4**    Name PivotData created under name manager.

The result of the modified Name Manager dialogue box is in Fig. 13.2-4. The *OFFSET* will guarantee the dynamic updating of the Database, so that the new company customers in the next period of analysis can be captured by the Dashboard without any manual intervention. Very often companies have continuously new customers entering from 1 month to another.

As we said, what we need to do then is to replace in the Pivot Tables the original source *'Sales Data'*!$A$1:$F$101 with this new name "PivotData," as shown in Figs. 13.2-5 and 13.2-6.

| Row Labels | Sum of BUDGET | Sum of ACTUAL | | Row Labels | Sum of BUDGET | Sum of ACTUAL |
|---|---|---|---|---|---|---|
| PAPER MANUFACTURING | 50,587 | 60,852 | | END USER | 28,278,661 | 28,532,706 |
| FOOD INDUSTRY | 117,797 | 124,250 | | RESELLER | 34,873,774 | 36,853,433 |
| TIMBER INDUSTRIES | 311,837 | 317,374 | | **Grand Total** | **63,152,435** | **65,386,140** |
| METAL PRODUCTS MANUFACTURING | 420,379 | 461,603 | | | | |
| AUTOMOBILES INDUSTRY | 3,879,607 | 4,128,994 | | | | |
| PACKAGING | 8,040,605 | 8,365,695 | | Row Labels | Sum of BUDGET | Sum of ACTUAL |
| RUBBER | 24,774,184 | 26,120,344 | | REST OF THE WORLD | 33,954,570 | 34,288,766 |
| TEXTILE | 25,557,439 | 25,807,028 | | EUROPE | 23,992,212 | 25,501,565 |
| **Grand Total** | **63,152,435** | **65,386,140** | | AMERICA | 5,205,653 | 5,595,809 |
| | | | | **Grand Total** | **63,152,435** | **65,386,140** |

**FIGURE 13.2-5**    Click on the Pivot table, then go to the analyze tab on the ribbon, then change data source.

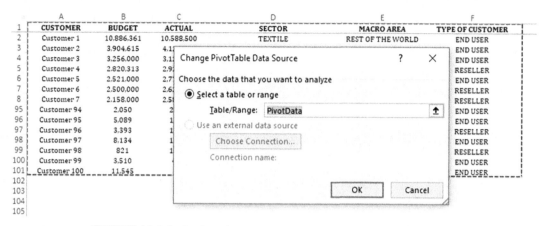

FIGURE 13.2-6   Replace the original data source with the name PivotData.

The whole process of replacing the old data source will allow us to have a dynamic pivot table, so that each time we add a new row to the data source, the Pivot Tables will get updated to reflect the new information as well.

For example, let us add a 101th customer in Packaging, End User, Europe, as highlighted in Fig. 13.2-7, with £ 1.2 mln of Actual Sales. Compare now Fig. 13.2-8 with Fig. 13.2-2 and see how the values of each business dimension has increased by £ 1 mln for Budget and £ 1.2 for Actual.

## Dynamic Pivot charts

Now that the Pivot Tables have been created and made dynamic, we can create for each Pivot Table a Pivot Chart, and this will be dynamic as well, as it is linked automatically to the Pivot Table by Excel.

Clicking anywhere on the Pivot Table we select Pivot Charts from the Excel Ribbon, as in Fig. 13.2-9.

After repeating this for the three Pivot Tables and getting the charts formatted as desired, we start obtaining our Dashboard as in Fig. 13.2-10.

| | A | B | C | D | E | F |
|---|---|---|---|---|---|---|
| 1 | CUSTOMER | BUDGET | ACTUAL | SECTOR | MACRO AREA | TYPE OF CUSTOMER |
| 95 | Customer 94 | 2.050 | 2.075 | TEXTILE | REST OF THE WORLD | END USER |
| 96 | Customer 95 | 5.089 | 1.718 | RUBBER | EUROPE | END USER |
| 97 | Customer 96 | 3.393 | 1.145 | PACKAGING | EUROPE | RESELLER |
| 98 | Customer 97 | 8.134 | 1.128 | TEXTILE | EUROPE | END USER |
| 99 | Customer 98 | 821 | 1.052 | PACKAGING | EUROPE | RESELLER |
| 100 | Customer 99 | 3.510 | 452 | TEXTILE | EUROPE | END USER |
| 101 | Customer 100 | 11.545 | 0 | TEXTILE | REST OF THE WORLD | END USER |
| 102 | **Customer 101** | **1,000,000** | **1,200,000** | **PACKAGING** | **EUROPE** | **END USER** |

FIGURE 13.2-7   New customer inserted.

| Row Labels | Sum of BUDGET | Sum of ACTUAL | | | Row Labels | Sum of BUDGET | Sum of ACTUAL |
|---|---|---|---|---|---|---|---|
| PAPER MANUFACTURING | 50.587 | 60.852 | | | END USER | 29,278,661 | 29,732,706 |
| FOOD INDUSTRY | 117,797 | 124,250 | | | RESELLER | 34,873,774 | 36,853,433 |
| TIMBER INDUSTRIES | 311,837 | 317,374 | | | Grand Total | 64,152,435 | 66,586,140 |
| METAL PRODUCTS MANUFACTURING | 420,379 | 461,603 | | | | | |
| AUTOMOBILES INDUSTRY | 3,879,607 | 4,128,994 | | | | | |
| PACKAGING | 9,040,605 | 9,565,695 | | | Row Labels | Sum of BUDGET | Sum of ACTUAL |
| RUBBER | 24,774,184 | 26,120,344 | | | REST OF THE WORLD | 33,954,570 | 34,288,766 |
| TEXTILE | 25,557,439 | 25,807,028 | | | EUROPE | 24,992,212 | 26,701,565 |
| Grand Total | 64,152,435 | 66,586,140 | | | AMERICA | 5,205,653 | 5,595,809 |
| | | | | | Grand Total | 64,152,435 | 66,586,140 |

FIGURE 13.2-8   Reflecting the new customer in the Pivot tables.

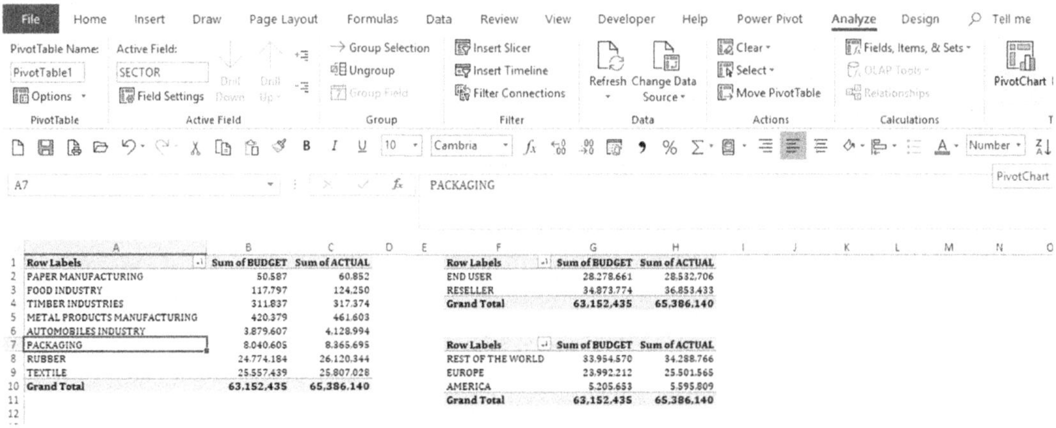

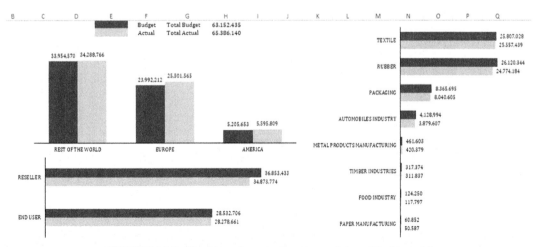

FIGURE 13.2-9   Inserting a Pivot chart from a Pivot table.

FIGURE 13.2-10   Pivot charts in the new worksheet "Dashboard."

IV. Special topics

## Creating the slicers

The Dashboard we have created is still not completely ready to be used, as the objective is somehow to query the charts in order to have from them a dynamic answer filtering on the underlying data.

For example, say we just want to display the sales data versus budget for America, how could we do that? The same, for example, if we want to display the data just for the Resellers and then look at how each sector performs in this subsegment of customers only. Then, we also want to be able to unfilter the data.

In order to do this, Excel offers a very powerful tool which is the **Slicer**.

To do this, we just need to click anywhere inside the Pivot Chart or the Pivot Table, and then we click in the Ribbon **Analyze Tab** the option **Insert Slicer** as shown in Fig. 13.2-11.

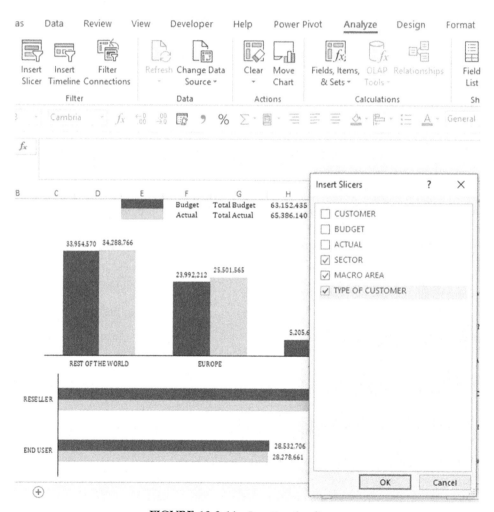

FIGURE 13.2-11    Inserting the slicers.

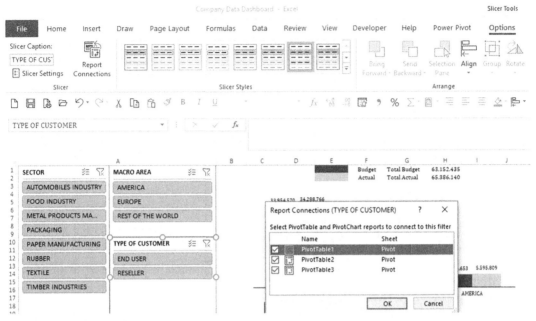

FIGURE 13.2-12   Getting the report connected for each slicer and getting the slicer formatted.

The following step is then to connect for each of the Slicers the Pivot Charts and Pivot Tables each other. This is done simply clicking on each slicer, then clicking on the **Report Connection** tool (the option is also on the Slicers Tool) and flagging all the Pivot Tables we want to connect (see Fig. 13.2-12). This will make the Dashboard dynamic. The Dashboard should look like Fig. 13.2-13.

The Slicers are activated just clicking on the dimension we want to analyze (e.g., Reseller). We can clear the filters clicking on the small funnel with the little red cross located on the up right-hand corner of the slicer, and we can also click on the multiselect option if we want to show multiple fields together.

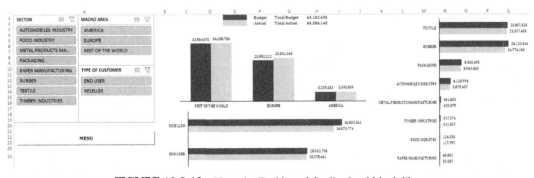

FIGURE 13.2-13   How the Dashboard finally should look like.

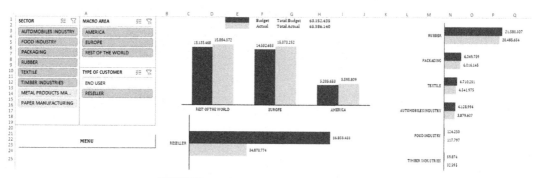

**FIGURE 13.2-14**    Filtering by resellers only.

Say, for example, we only want to show the data for the Type of Customer Reseller; in this case the report would be as Fig. 13.2-14.

Although we can consider the Dashboard complete and ready for our business report, we can undertake a step beyond.

The little problem we have in the dashboard as designed so far is that each time we want to analyze for a specific sales dimension (say from Reseller to End User) we manually need to clear the filter and then run the new filter.

We do not want this. We just want that when we click on a specific Sales dimension the system unfilters the old selections and then creates the new one automatically.

We then need to associate a VBA macro to the Slicers and then creating the buttons (form control) in the worksheet, hiding somewhere the original Excel Slicers. The Dashboard now looks like Fig. 13.2-15.

We show in Fig. 13.2-16 the VBA subs for the dimension Type of Customer, which allows us to clear all the filters previously applied (see first three lines of the code) in any other dimension of sales and then activate the new filter for each type of customer (see the rest of the code with True and False).

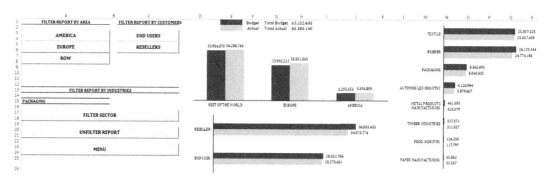

**FIGURE 13.2-15**    Dashboard with VBA buttons.

```
Sub Customers_EndUsers()

    ActiveWorkbook.SlicerCaches("Slicer_MACRO_AREA").ClearManualFilter
    ActiveWorkbook.SlicerCaches("Slicer_SECTOR").ClearManualFilter
    ActiveWorkbook.SlicerCaches("Slicer_TYPE_OF_CUSTOMER").ClearManualFilter

    With ActiveWorkbook.SlicerCaches("Slicer_TYPE_OF_CUSTOMER")
        .SlicerItems("END USER").Selected = True
        .SlicerItems("RESELLER").Selected = False
    End With

End Sub

Sub Customers_Resellers()

    ActiveWorkbook.SlicerCaches("Slicer_MACRO_AREA").ClearManualFilter
    ActiveWorkbook.SlicerCaches("Slicer_SECTOR").ClearManualFilter
    ActiveWorkbook.SlicerCaches("Slicer_TYPE_OF_CUSTOMER").ClearManualFilter

    With ActiveWorkbook.SlicerCaches("Slicer_TYPE_OF_CUSTOMER")
        .SlicerItems("END USER").Selected = False
        .SlicerItems("RESELLER").Selected = True
    End With

End Sub
```

FIGURE 13.2-16    VBA subs on type of customers.

How do we know this specific VBA code? The code simply derives from the recording of the macro while we manually apply the filters and we clear the filters.

If each of these operations is recorded separately (see Fig. 13.2-17), organizing then together all the recorded macros under more VBA modules as desired, we obtain an entire code as in Fig. 13.2-16 (this is just for the dimension Type of Customers). Repeating the same for all the other dimensions of sales, our report will be ready with all the necessary modules.

In our case we have created five modules, as in Fig. 13.2-18, where the first *Module0* is the module that includes the code to move from one sheet to another, while the other four modules are those for the Dashboard analysis.

Notice how in Fig. 13.2-15 the worksheet also includes a way to filter the sector in *Cell A*15 from a drop-down list, using the Data Validation. This is done simply as in Figs. 13.2-19 and 13.2-20: keeping the *Cell A*15 selected, we give to Excel the range of cells from which we want to pick up our sector. In our case the list is in the *Range* = $A$30:$A$38.

Finally, the worksheet panes can be conveniently frozen, hiding the slicers and the sector list to show only the Charts Dashboard and the buttons. If we need to, we can protect the worksheet as well, paying attention to leave the unlocked *Cell A*15 of the drop-down list, otherwise this will not work. This is done from **Format Cell**, **Protection**, leaving unflagged the option **Locked**.

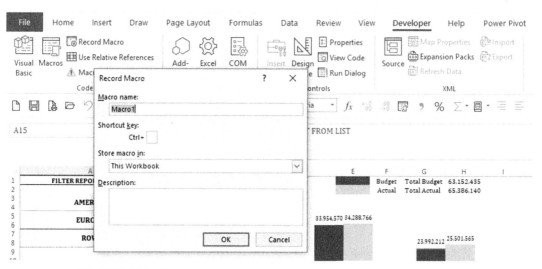

FIGURE 13.2-17    Recording a macro while filtering and unfiltering the slicers.

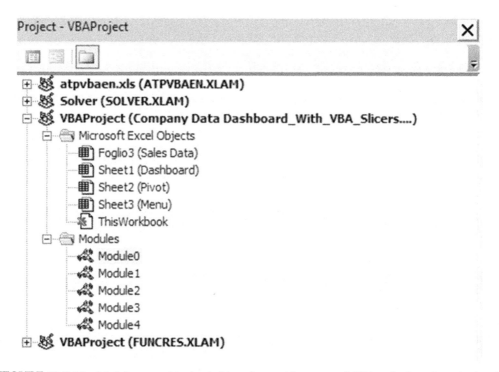

FIGURE 13.2-18    Modules created in the dashboard spreadsheet once all VBA codes have been finalized.

FIGURE 13.2-19   How to insert a drop-down list.

FIGURE 13.2-20   Data validation for Sectors.

## 13.3  Basic descriptive statistics

The study of statistics is usually divided in two macro categories:

**i.** Descriptive Statistics (and its basic concepts will be explained in this paragraph)
**ii.** Inferential Statistics (see **§ 13.5**)

**Descriptive Statistics** is represented by all those methods that organize, summarize, and present data in an informative way. The construction of *frequency tables, histograms, cumulative frequency charts*, and other graphical ways to represent both the quantitative and qualitative data all belong to this part of statistics.

The objective of Descriptive Statistics is also to extrapolate summary statistical indices like the mean (or average) and the standard deviation, called **measures of central tendency** and **measures of dispersion**, respectively.

The purpose of a measure of central tendency is to pinpoint the center of a distribution of data. The measures of dispersion (or spread) indicate how much the data are clustered around the average, indicating then the variability around the central tendency. A small value for a measure of dispersion indicates that the data are clustered closely around the arithmetic mean. The mean is therefore considered representative of the data. Conversely, a large measure of dispersion indicates that the mean is not reliable and that the observations of the distribution are somehow more "cluttered."

Other descriptive indices relevant to the economic analysis are represented by the concentration indices, like the *Gini's Coefficient*, which measures the inequality of income or wealth.

Several times analyzing the entire population, i.e., the entire set of individuals or objects of interest is not possible because it could be too costly, and the researchers resort to the so-called *sample*. A sample is just a portion, or part, of the population of interest.

Here it is where the statistician resorts to a second field of statistics, namely the **Inferential Statistics**, which is represented by all those statistical techniques used to estimate a property of a population, on the basis of a population sample. Techniques like *point intervals, confidence intervals, hypothesis testing, correlation,* and *regression* all belong to this part of statistics.

We will deal here with quantitative variables (which are normally contrasted to the qualitative variables) that can be either discrete, when they can only assume certain values, or continuous, when they can assume any value within a specific range.

Within the quantitative variables there are two measure scales: **interval scale** and the **ratio scale** (being this measure scale our focus of analysis).

The **interval scale** provides the ranking and guarantees that the differences between scale values are equal. However, the zero does not reflect the absence of what is being measured (e.g., for the Celsius and the Fahrenheit scales) and therefore we cannot form ratios in the interval scales (50 degrees does not represent five times as much as 10 degrees temperature and $0°$ degrees does not mean the absence of temperature).

**Ratio scales** represent the strongest level of measurement as they have all the characteristics of interval measurement scales, as well as a true zero point as the origin, which is the absence of what is being measured (for instance, income earned within a month). With ratio scales, we can compute meaningful ratios, add, and subtract.

## EXAMPLE 1 (FREQUENCY DISTRIBUTION CHARTS IN EXCEL FOR A FINANCIAL INDEX MONTHLY RETURNS)

Let us consider again the data of Table 8.1.1 which showed the returns of two financial indices. Consider the Euro Bond Index Return as shown in Table 13.3-1.

In Table 13.3-1, we also have built the intervals in which we have divided the monthly returns, while in *Column D* we have the frequency of occurrences, namely how many times a monthly return appears in a specific interval. This is done using the excel function *FREQUENCY*, entered as an array CSE formula.

$$= FREQUENCY(B2: B37; C2: C37)$$

The frequency chart we can then obtain is in Fig. 13.3-1. The intervals have been built beginning from the most negative return ($-1.68\%$) with constant class width of $0.25\%$. There are some rules to set the interval width, and also a subjective professional judgment is suggested to establish the interval width.

**TABLE 13.3-1** Monthly observations, interval, and absolute frequencies over 3 years.

| | A | B | C | D |
|---|---|---|---|---|
| 1 | **Dates** | **Euro Bond Index Return** | **Interval** | **Frequency** |
| 2 | 31/03/2003 | -0.4919% | -1.6800% | 1 |
| 3 | 30/04/2003 | -0.0418% | -1.4300% | 0 |
| 4 | 30/05/2003 | 1.9091% | -1.1800% | 1 |
| 5 | 30/06/2003 | 0.2069% | -0.9300% | 1 |
| 6 | 31/07/2003 | -1.6806% | -0.6800% | 2 |
| 7 | 29/08/2003 | 0.3118% | -0.4300% | 3 |
| 8 | 30/09/2003 | 1.4298% | -0.1800% | 1 |
| 9 | 31/10/2003 | -1.2182% | 0.0700% | 4 |
| 10 | 28/11/2003 | -0.5030% | 0.3200% | 4 |
| 11 | 31/12/2003 | 1.3562% | 0.5700% | 2 |
| 12 | 30/01/2004 | 0.8333% | 0.8200% | 2 |
| 13 | 27/02/2004 | 1.5521% | 1.0700% | 4 |
| 14 | 31/03/2004 | 0.9682% | 1.3200% | 5 |
| 15 | 30/04/2004 | -1.1664% | 1.5700% | 4 |
| 16 | 31/05/2004 | -0.1268% | 1.8200% | 1 |
| 17 | 30/06/2004 | 0.3185% | 2.0700% | 1 |
| 18 | 30/07/2004 | 0.9714% | 2.3200% | 0 |
| 19 | 31/08/2004 | 1.1774% | 2.5700% | 0 |
| 20 | 30/09/2004 | 0.3475% | 2.5700% | 0 |
| 33 | 31/10/2005 | -0.9149% | 2.5700% | 0 |
| 34 | 30/11/2005 | 0.0472% | 2.5700% | 0 |
| 35 | 30/12/2005 | 0.8179% | 2.5700% | 0 |
| 36 | 31/01/2006 | -0.2961% | 2.5700% | 0 |
| 37 | 28/02/2006 | 0.1683% | 2.5700% | 0 |

For example, based on a predetermined number of classes the formula would be as follows:

$$Interval\ Width = \frac{Max - Min}{\#\ of\ Classes}$$

The Cumulative Absolute Frequency Chart is instead given by Fig. 13.3-2. This is to assess the following:

$$F(x) = Freq(X \leq x)$$

which is the frequency of value occurrences less than a reference value $x$.

Excel offers an automatic tool for descriptive and inferential statistics called **Data Analysis ToolPak** (Fig. 13.3-3), from which, if we select **Descriptive Statistics**, we can find selected measures of central tendency, measures of dispersion, and measures of symmetry and kurtosis.

If we use this tool for our 36 monthly return observations, we obtain the summary descriptive stats in Table 13.3-2.

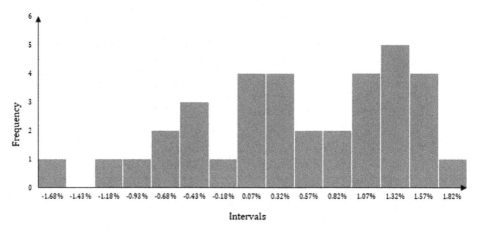

**FIGURE 13.3-1**   Frequency chart of the 36 return observations.

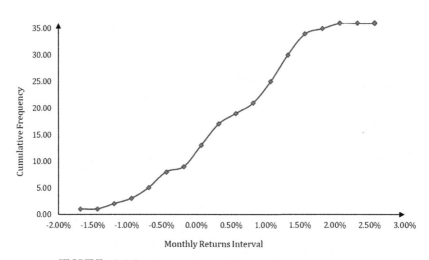

**FIGURE 13.3-2**   Empirical cumulative absolute frequency chart.

## Measures of central tendency

The main indicator is the population **mean**, which is defined as:

$$\mu = \frac{\sum_{i=1}^{N} x_i}{N}$$

where $N$ = population observations.

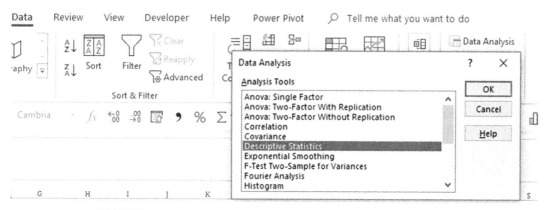

**FIGURE 13.3-3**  Data analysis ToolPak (descriptive and inferential stats).

**TABLE 13.3-2**  Excel data analysis output.

| Descriptive Statistics | |
| --- | --- |
| Mean | 0.3995% |
| Standard Error | 0.1520% |
| Median | 0.4154% |
| Mode | #N/A |
| Standard Deviation | 0.9120% |
| Sample Variance | 0.0083% |
| Kurtosis | -0.61163 |
| Skewness | -0.42565 |
| Range | 3.5897% |
| Minimum | -1.6806% |
| Maximum | 1.9091% |
| Sum | 14.3806% |
| Count | 36 |

The sample mean (in case we cannot observe the entire population) is instead usually denoted by $\overline{X}$ defined as:

$$\overline{X} = \frac{\sum_{i=1}^{n} x_i}{n}$$

where $n = sample\ observations$.

In our case the numerical value of the mean is 14.3806%/36 = 0.3995%, as returned by Table 13.3-2.

A second indicator of central tendency is the **median**, which is equal to 0.4154%.

The median is the middle item observed in a data set (sorted from smallest to largest). The median has the advantage compared to the mean that is not affected by extremely large or small values in the observations, while the mean can be affected by these extreme values.

A third measure of central tendency is the **mode**, which is the most frequently occurring value in the distribution. A distribution can have more than one mode or even no mode, like in our example.

## Measures of dispersion

The **Standard Deviation** is the main indicator of dispersion, being the square root of the **Variance** defined as follows:

$$\sigma^2 = \frac{\sum_{i=1}^{N}(x_i - \mu)^2}{N}$$

The sample variance is instead given by:

$$s^2 = \frac{\sum_{i=1}^{n}(x_i - \mu)^2}{n - 1}$$

and this is what Excel is returning by default in Table 13.3-2, as the sample variance is $s^2 = 0.0083\%$ and $s = 0.9120\%$.

The Standard Error (of the mean) is instead:

$$se(\overline{X}) = \frac{s}{\sqrt{n}}$$

and it represents a measure of dispersion of sample means around the population mean. This is because in theory several samples would be extracted from the population, and then the mean obtained from each sample would be recorded. $se(\overline{X}) = \frac{s}{\sqrt{n}}$ says that the *spread* of the values of $\overline{X}$ about $\mu$ is small for a large sample size as compared to a small sample size.

Another measure of dispersion is the range, which is defined as:

$$\textit{Maximum Value} - \textit{Minimum Value} = 1.9091\% - (-1.6806\%) = 3.5897\%$$

## Measures of symmetry and Kurtosis

The **skewness** represents an index of asymmetry of distributions being analyzed. Perfectly symmetrical distribution will have a skewness equal to zero. The fact that here we have a negative skewness in our example implies that the distribution is *skewed to the left*. This means that the distribution of the Euro Bond index in the observed 3 years is characterized by many small gains and a few extreme losses.

The **coefficient of kurtosis** (or also *excess kurtosis* or just *excess*) is used to assess whether a density is more or less peaked around its center, than the density of a normal curve and negative values are sometimes used to indicate that a density is flattered around its center than the density of a normal curve. The normal curve has zero value of kurtosis.

Excel has a great potential in terms of statistical (and also probabilistic) calculations, and several statistic functions (from basic to advanced) are already available in the system (see Fig. 13.3-4). One should always check with a manual of statistics, the underlying formula used by Excel.

## Geometric average versus arithmetic average in economics and finance

In economics and finance, the geometric average should be used instead of the arithmetic average, and this is simply due to the effect of the compounding.

FIGURE 13.3-4    Excel built-in statistic functions.

Consider again Table 13.3-1. At the beginning of first month we invest a unit of capital and at the end of first period our investment will be:

$$1 - 0.4919\% = 0.9951$$

while at the end of second period we obtain:

$$0.9951 \cdot (1 - 0.0418\%) = 0.9947$$

and so on up to the 36th month.

The monthly average of our investment return should not be calculated then on an arithmetic basis, but on a geometric basis, as follows:

$$R_G = \left[ \prod_{t=1}^{T} (1 + R_t) \right]^{\frac{1}{T}} - 1$$

which is the periodical growth rate, to obtain precisely the capital at the end of the investment horizon.

The above formula comes out from the fact that the monthly average $R_G$ should satisfy the following equation:

$$(1 + R_G)^{T} = 1 \cdot (1 + R_1) \cdot (1 + R_2) \cdot \cdots \cdot (1 + R_j) \cdot \cdots \cdot (1 + R_T).$$

In Excel, we have calculated then the monthly geometric average in Fig. 13.3-5 and Table 13.3-3.

### EXAMPLE 2 (CONSTRUCTION OF A STATISTICAL HISTOGRAM SHOWING THE DENSITY OF FREQUENCY)

A pure statistical histogram (which is slightly different from what is returned by default in Excel) requires the calculation of the so-called **density of frequency** $f(x) = c_i$ which is obtained dividing the relative frequency $p_i$ within an interval (the area of each histogram bar), by the interval width $\delta_i$. Then, the standard statistical histogram can be drawn, with the vertical axis representing the frequency density function $f(x) = c_i$ of the statistical variable that is being measured.

The histogram obtained like that is then the counterpart of a continuous curve for a continuous probabilistic density function, in which the area under the curve returns the cumulative probability.

Let us reconsider the actual sales data of Table 13.2-1 (see Table 13.3-4), and let us construct Table 13.3-5, where for each given interval the frequency (that will represent the area of the bar in the histogram) and the density function (which will represent the height of the bar) are calculated. The statistical histogram is built as in Fig. 13.3-6.

| | A | B | C | D | E | F | G |
|---|---|---|---|---|---|---|---|
| 1 | Dates | Euro Bond Index Return | Interval | Frequency | Cumulative Frequency | Monthly Compounding Factor | Capital Accumulated |
| 2 | 37711 | -0.0049188052676683 | -0.0168 | =FREQUENCY(B2:B37;C2:C37) | =D2 | =1+B2 | =PRODUCT($F$2:F2) |
| 3 | 37741 | -0.000418157448741074 | =C2+0.0025 | =FREQUENCY(B2:B37;C2:C37) | =D3+E2 | =1+B3 | =PRODUCT($F$2:F3) |
| 4 | 37771 | 0.0190909166465811 | =C3+0.0025 | =FREQUENCY(B2:B37;C2:C37) | =D4+E3 | =1+B4 | =PRODUCT($F$2:F4) |
| 5 | 37802 | 0.00206878928252974 | =C4+0.0025 | =FREQUENCY(B2:B37;C2:C37) | =D5+E4 | =1+B5 | =PRODUCT($F$2:F5) |
| 6 | 37833 | -0.0168064263216579 | =C5+0.0025 | =FREQUENCY(B2:B37;C2:C37) | =D6+E5 | =1+B6 | =PRODUCT($F$2:F6) |
| 7 | 37862 | 0.00311798109344563 | =C6+0.0025 | =FREQUENCY(B2:B37;C2:C37) | =D7+E6 | =1+B7 | =PRODUCT($F$2:F7) |
| 8 | 37894 | 0.0142981317254585 | =C7+0.0025 | =FREQUENCY(B2:B37;C2:C37) | =D8+E7 | =1+B8 | =PRODUCT($F$2:F8) |
| 9 | 37925 | -0.0121819592018269 | =C8+0.0025 | =FREQUENCY(B2:B37;C2:C37) | =D9+E8 | =1+B9 | =PRODUCT($F$2:F9) |
| 10 | 37953 | -0.00502951269732321 | =C9+0.0025 | =FREQUENCY(B2:B37;C2:C37) | =D10+E9 | =1+B10 | =PRODUCT($F$2:F10) |
| 11 | 37986 | 0.0135616884371086 | =C10+0.0025 | =FREQUENCY(B2:B37;C2:C37) | =D11+E10 | =1+B11 | =PRODUCT($F$2:F11) |
| 12 | 38016 | 0.00833303841473532 | =C11+0.0025 | =FREQUENCY(B2:B37;C2:C37) | =D12+E11 | =1+B12 | =PRODUCT($F$2:F12) |
| 13 | 38044 | 0.0155213097404385 | =C12+0.0025 | =FREQUENCY(B2:B37;C2:C37) | =D13+E12 | =1+B13 | =PRODUCT($F$2:F13) |
| 14 | 38077 | 0.0096824877777255 | =C13+0.0025 | =FREQUENCY(B2:B37;C2:C37) | =D14+E13 | =1+B14 | =PRODUCT($F$2:F14) |
| 15 | 38107 | -0.011664494384981 | =C14+0.0025 | =FREQUENCY(B2:B37;C2:C37) | =D15+E14 | =1+B15 | =PRODUCT($F$2:F15) |
| 16 | 38138 | -0.0012681328342502 | =C15+0.0025 | =FREQUENCY(B2:B37;C2:C37) | =D16+E15 | =1+B16 | =PRODUCT($F$2:F16) |
| 36 | 38748 | -0.0029606354860815 | =C35 | =FREQUENCY(B2:B37;C2:C37) | =D36+E35 | =1+B36 | =PRODUCT($F$2:F36) |
| 37 | 38776 | 0.0016834734631419 | =C36 | =FREQUENCY(B2:B37;C2:C37) | =D37+E36 | =1+B37 | =PRODUCT($F$2:F37) |
| 38 | | | | | | | |
| 39 | Arithmetic Average =AVERAGE(B2:B37) | | | | | Geometric Average | =G37^(1/36)-1 |
| 40 | | | | | | | |
| 41 | | | | | | With Excel Rate Formula | =RATE(36;;-1;G37) |

**FIGURE 13.3-5** Excel calculation of the monthly geometric avearage.

The mean can be calculated as well from Table 13.3-5, based on the interval classes according to the following formula:

$$\mu = \sum_{i=1}^{n-1} \frac{(x_{i+1} + x_i)}{2} \cdot p_i$$

where $\frac{(x_{i+1}+x_i)}{2}$ is the central point of the $i$th interval and $p_i = \delta_i \cdot c_i$.

The exact average would be the one in Table 13.3-4, calculated as if, somehow, we had the intervals "collapsing" on the observation values.

## Multivariate descriptive stats: covariance and correlation matrix for several variables

The descriptive statistics of Table 13.3-2 can be obtained as well when we are analyzing jointly more quantitative variables.

Let us consider again the six-assets returns of Example 2 in § 8.1. The objective is to build the descriptive stats for all the six assets, as well as the matrix of variances and covariances in one shot, in order to proceed to build the efficient frontier. We have 69 return observations on the six asset indices, arranged in columns as in Table 13.3-6. First, we can run the Data Analysis descriptive statistics tool on the six column returns in one shot, like Fig. 13.3-7. The output will appear in another worksheet simply called "Descriptive Stats" (Table 13.3-7).

As a second step, we want to obtain the matrix of variances and covariances (also of correlations is possible).

Choosing the option Covariance of the Data Analysis dialogue box we have the following window appearing, where we just have to indicate the input range and the output worksheet name (e.g., "Matrix of Var and Covar"). See Fig. 13.3-8 and Table 13.3-8. We can also do the same for the matrix of correlations. See Fig. 13.3-9 and Table 13.3-9.

**TABLE 13.3-3**  Monthly geometric average versus arithmetic average.

| Dates | Euro Bond Index Return | Interval | Frequency | Cumulative Frequency | Monthly Compounding Factor | Capital Accumulated |
|---|---|---|---|---|---|---|
| 31/03/2003 | -0.4919% | -1.6800% | 1 | 1 | 0.9951 | 0.9951 |
| 30/04/2003 | -0.0418% | -1.4300% | 0 | 1 | 0.9996 | 0.9947 |
| 30/05/2003 | 1.9091% | -1.1800% | 1 | 2 | 1.0191 | 1.0137 |
| 30/06/2003 | 0.2069% | -0.9300% | 1 | 3 | 1.0021 | 1.0158 |
| 31/07/2003 | -1.6806% | -0.6800% | 2 | 5 | 0.9832 | 0.9987 |
| 29/08/2003 | 0.3118% | -0.4300% | 3 | 8 | 1.0031 | 1.0018 |
| 30/09/2003 | 1.4298% | -0.1800% | 1 | 9 | 1.0143 | 1.0161 |
| 31/10/2003 | -1.2182% | 0.0700% | 4 | 13 | 0.9878 | 1.0037 |
| 28/11/2003 | -0.5030% | 0.3200% | 4 | 17 | 0.9950 | 0.9987 |
| 31/12/2003 | 1.3562% | 0.5700% | 2 | 19 | 1.0136 | 1.0122 |
| 30/01/2004 | 0.8333% | 0.8200% | 2 | 21 | 1.0083 | 1.0207 |
| 27/02/2004 | 1.5521% | 1.0700% | 4 | 25 | 1.0155 | 1.0365 |
| 31/03/2004 | 0.9682% | 1.3200% | 5 | 30 | 1.0097 | 1.0465 |
| 30/04/2004 | -1.1664% | 1.5700% | 4 | 34 | 0.9883 | 1.0343 |
| 31/05/2004 | -0.1268% | 1.8200% | 1 | 35 | 0.9987 | 1.0330 |
| 31/01/2006 | -0.2961% | 2.5700% | 0 | 36 | 0.9970 | 1.1507 |
| 28/02/2006 | 0.1683% | 2.5700% | 0 | 36 | 1.0017 | 1.1527 |

| Arithmetic Average | 0.3995% |
|---|---|

| Geometric Average | 0.39542% |
|---|---|
| With Excel Rate Formula | 0.39542% |

**TABLE 13.3-4**  Actual sales from Table 13.2-1.

| Customer | Actual sales | Exact Average |
|---|---|---|
| Customer 1 | 10,588,500 | 105,885 |
| Customer 2 | 4,121,000 | 41,210 |
| Customer 3 | 3,125,623 | 31,256 |
| Customer 4 | 2,920,313 | 29,203 |
| Customer 5 | 2,775,200 | 27,752 |
| Customer 6 | 2,627,234 | 26,272 |
| Customer 7 | 2,580,123 | 25,801 |
| Customer 8 | 2,458,236 | 24,582 |
| Customer 9 | 2,252,813 | 22,528 |
| Customer 10 | 1,921,256 | 19,213 |
| Customer 11 | 1,856,000 | 18,560 |
| Customer 12 | 1,849,977 | 18,500 |
| Customer 17 | 1,408,440 | 14,084 |
| Customer 18 | 1,172,574 | 11,726 |
| Customer 93 | 2,264 | 23 |
| Customer 94 | 2,075 | 21 |
| Customer 95 | 1,718 | 17 |
| Customer 96 | 1,145 | 11 |
| Customer 97 | 1,128 | 11 |
| Customer 98 | 1,052 | 11 |
| Customer 99 | 452 | 5 |
| Customer 100 | 0 | 0 |
| **Exact Average** | | **653,861** |

An alternative way to obtain the matrix of variances and covariances from a data set of more than two variables is to use the **OFFSET** function. This function returns a reference to a range that is a specified number of rows and columns from a cell or range of cells. The reference that is returned can be a single cell or a range of cells (in this case an entire column within the covariance function). See Fig. 13.3-10.

## 13.4  Some numerical calculus applied to continuous densities

The numerical techniques of calculus we have seen within the book can also fit the theory of statistics (and probability).

Consider, for example, the concept of mean. In the theory of statistics for a discrete variable, it is given by:

**TABLE 13.3-5** Reclassification of actual sales in intervals for the statistical histogram.

| From | Up to | Delta class | Abs. Frequency | Rel. Freq. $p_i$ | Density $c_i = p_i/\delta_i$ | Cumul. Frequency F(x) | Mean |
|---|---|---|---|---|---|---|---|
| 0 | 5,000 | 5,000 | 14 | 14.00% | 0.0028000% | 14.00% | 350 |
| 5,000 | 25,000 | 20,000 | 10 | 10.00% | 0.0005000% | 24.00% | 1,500 |
| 25,000 | 50,000 | 25,000 | 12 | 12.00% | 0.0004800% | 36.00% | 4,500 |
| 50,000 | 75,000 | 25,000 | 8 | 8.00% | 0.0003200% | 44.00% | 5,000 |
| 75,000 | 100,000 | 25,000 | 6 | 6.00% | 0.0002400% | 50.00% | 5,250 |
| 100,000 | 150,000 | 50,000 | 5 | 5.00% | 0.0001000% | 55.00% | 6,250 |
| 150,000 | 200,000 | 50,000 | 4 | 4.00% | 0.0000800% | 59.00% | 7,000 |
| 200,000 | 300,000 | 100,000 | 4 | 4.00% | 0.0000400% | 63.00% | 10,000 |
| 300,000 | 400,000 | 100,000 | 2 | 2.00% | 0.0000200% | 65.00% | 7,000 |
| 400,000 | 500,000 | 100,000 | 3 | 3.00% | 0.0000300% | 68.00% | 13,500 |
| 500,000 | 600,000 | 100,000 | 3 | 3.00% | 0.0000300% | 71.00% | 16,500 |
| 600,000 | 700,000 | 100,000 | 3 | 3.00% | 0.0000300% | 74.00% | 19,500 |
| 700,000 | 800,000 | 100,000 | 1 | 1.00% | 0.0000100% | 75.00% | 7,500 |
| 800,000 | 900,000 | 100,000 | 1 | 1.00% | 0.0000100% | 76.00% | 8,500 |
| 900,000 | 1,000,000 | 100,000 | 5 | 5.00% | 0.0000500% | 81.00% | 47,500 |
| 1,000,000 | 1,500,000 | 500,000 | 3 | 3.00% | 0.0000060% | 84.00% | 37,500 |
| 1,500,000 | 2,000,000 | 500,000 | 7 | 7.00% | 0.0000140% | 91.00% | 122,500 |
| 2,000,000 | 4,000,000 | 2,000,000 | 7 | 7.00% | 0.0000040% | 98.00% | 210,000 |
| 4,000,000 | 5,000,000 | 1,000,000 | 1 | 1.00% | 0.0000010% | 99.00% | 45,000 |
| 5,000,000 | 6,000,000 | 1,000,000 | 0 | 0.00% | 0.0000000% | 99.00% | 0 |
| 6,000,000 | 7,000,000 | 1,000,000 | 0 | 0.00% | 0.0000000% | 99.00% | 0 |
| 7,000,000 | 8,000,000 | 1,000,000 | 0 | 0.00% | 0.0000000% | 99.00% | 0 |
| 8,000,000 | 9,000,000 | 1,000,000 | 0 | 0.00% | 0.0000000% | 99.00% | 0 |
| 9,000,000 | 10,000,000 | 1,000,000 | 0 | 0.00% | 0.0000000% | 99.00% | 0 |
| 10,000,000 | 11,000,000 | 1,000,000 | 1 | 1.00% | 0.0000001% | 100.00% | 105,000 |

| Average Based on Class Intervals | | | | | | | 679,850 |

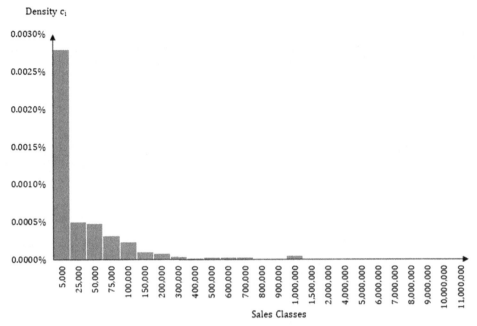

FIGURE 13.3-6   Statistical histogram on actual sales data.

$$\mu = \sum_{i=1}^{N} x_i \cdot p_i$$

while for a theoretical density function $f(x)$ it is given by the following integral:

$$\mu = \int_{-\infty}^{+\infty} x \cdot f(x) dx.$$

We can try then to use the Euler method to calculate the integral (see § 2.2).

## EXAMPLE 1 (NUMERICAL INTEGRATION AS THE AVERAGE OF A DENSITY)

Let us use the following theoretical density function for a statistical variable we are researching on:

$$f(x) = \begin{cases} 1 - \dfrac{1}{2}x & 0 < x < 2 \\ 0 & elsewhere \end{cases}$$

**TABLE 13.3-6**   Monthly returns for six financial indices.

| | A | B | C | D | E | F | G |
|---|---|---|---|---|---|---|---|
| 1 | Dates | MSCI Europe Net | EONIA Capit. 90j Micropal (TR) | S&P 500 (Composite) | Japan TSE 1st Section (Topix) (TR) | S&P/IFCI EMEA (TR) | Lehman Euro-Aggregate (TR) |
| 2 | 29/01/1999 | 2.73% | 0.25% | 7.70% | 3.84% | 9.03% | 1.36% |
| 3 | 26/02/1999 | 0.83% | 0.24% | 0.21% | 0.94% | 5.94% | -1.13% |
| 4 | 31/03/1999 | 2.80% | 0.27% | 5.73% | 15.79% | 5.53% | 0.64% |
| 5 | 30/04/1999 | 5.08% | 0.23% | 5.98% | 6.83% | 11.72% | 1.08% |
| 6 | 31/05/1999 | -3.42% | 0.22% | -0.97% | -3.54% | -1.04% | -0.56% |
| 7 | 30/06/1999 | 2.83% | 0.21% | 6.71% | 11.09% | 7.19% | -1.73% |
| 8 | 30/07/1999 | -2.75% | 0.21% | -6.66% | 6.13% | 0.62% | -0.91% |
| 9 | 31/08/1999 | 2.35% | 0.22% | 0.80% | 4.50% | 2.07% | -0.10% |
| 10 | 30/09/1999 | -1.58% | 0.20% | -3.56% | 5.91% | 1.69% | -0.31% |
| 63 | 27/02/2004 | 2.91% | 0.16% | 1.34% | 0.12% | 6.25% | 1.35% |
| 64 | 31/03/2004 | -2.04% | 0.18% | -0.44% | 16.25% | 8.20% | 0.95% |
| 65 | 30/04/2004 | 1.66% | 0.17% | 0.88% | -2.77% | -8.41% | -0.98% |
| 66 | 31/05/2004 | -0.24% | 0.17% | -0.52% | -5.81% | -0.43% | -0.25% |
| 67 | 30/06/2004 | 1.71% | 0.17% | 2.29% | 6.17% | 3.66% | 0.27% |
| 68 | 30/07/2004 | -1.73% | 0.17% | -2.31% | -5.25% | -1.32% | 0.90% |
| 69 | 31/08/2004 | -0.87% | 0.18% | -0.57% | -0.23% | 1.93% | 1.32% |
| 70 | 30/09/2004 | 1.77% | 0.17% | -1.12% | -4.58% | 5.32% | 0.41% |

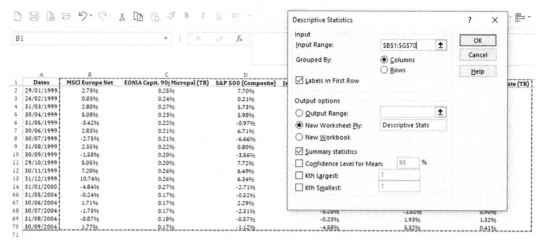

FIGURE 13.3-7   Descriptive stats for the set of six financial indices.

The exact average is simply given by the following definite integral:

$$\mu = \int_{0}^{2} x \cdot \left(1 - \frac{1}{2}x\right) dx = \frac{2}{3}.$$

Using the numerical integration, we have the following Table 13.4-1, while the average as a function of $x$, in the interval from 0 to 2, can be represented in Fig. 13.4-1.

## EXAMPLE 2 (THE MODE AS THE MAXIMUM POINT OF A DENSITY)

We have seen that the mode is the most frequently occurring value in a distribution. Then, if the continuous density function is provided, we can calculate the maximum point as in standard calculus and then use the techniques shown in Chapter 5.

Let us assume our density function is:

$$f(x) = \begin{cases} \dfrac{a^3 x^2}{2} e^{-ax} & x > 0 \\ 0 & elsewhere \end{cases}$$

The exact mode is given by the value $2/a$.

If we assume the parameter estimated is $a = 2$, the following function will have to be considered:

$$f(x) = \begin{cases} 4x^2 e^{-2x} & x > 0 \\ 0 & elsewhere \end{cases}$$

**TABLE 13.3-7** Descriptive stats for the six indices monthly returns.

| MSCI Europe Net | | EONIA Capt. 90j Mercapil (TR) | | S&P 500 (Composite) | | Japan TSE 1st Section (Topix) (TR) | | S&P/IFCI EMEA (TR) | | Lehman Euro-Aggregate (TR) | |
|---|---|---|---|---|---|---|---|---|---|---|---|
| Mean | 0.000989 | Mean | 0.002697 | Mean | 0.000323 | Mean | 0.0026468 | Mean | 0.013336 | Mean | 0.004208 |
| Standard Error | 0.006049 | Standard Error | 0.000097 | Standard Error | 0.006762 | Standard Error | 0.0080106 | Standard Error | 0.0078368 | Standard Error | 0.001101 |
| Median | 0.008268 | Median | 0.002624 | Median | -0.000220 | Median | 0.0012211 | Median | 0.016672 | Median | 0.004917 |
| Mode | #N/A | Mode | #N/A | Mode | #N/A | Mode | #N/A | Mode | #N/A | Mode | #N/A |
| Standard Deviation | 0.050246 | Standard Deviation | 0.000809 | Standard Deviation | 0.056168 | Standard Deviation | 0.0466505 | Standard Deviation | 0.065354 | Standard Deviation | 0.009188 |
| Sample Variance | 0.002525 | Sample Variance | 0.000001 | Sample Variance | 0.003155 | Sample Variance | 0.0044123 | Sample Variance | 0.004271 | Sample Variance | 0.000084 |
| Kurtosis | 0.185660 | Kurtosis | 0.865819 | Kurtosis | 0.564781 | Kurtosis | -0.216242 | Kurtosis | 0.294164 | Kurtosis | -0.452846 |
| Skewness | -0.366065 | Skewness | 0.471331 | Skewness | -0.289935 | Skewness | 0.282249 | Skewness | 0.360945 | Skewness | -0.266886 |
| Range | 0.247881 | Range | 0.002984 | Range | 0.281161 | Range | 0.315030 | Range | 0.325271 | Range | 0.049582 |
| Minimum | -0.138229 | Minimum | 0.001510 | Minimum | -0.121573 | Minimum | -0.152506 | Minimum | -0.151217 | Minimum | -0.017212 |
| Maximum | 0.109653 | Maximum | 0.004895 | Maximum | 0.106588 | Maximum | 0.162524 | Maximum | 0.174054 | Maximum | 0.023269 |
| Sum | 0.063712 | Sum | 0.186064 | Sum | 0.022268 | Sum | 0.184123 | Sum | 0.920207 | Sum | 0.290351 |
| Count | 69 | Count | 69 | Count | 69 | Count | 69 | Count | 69 | Count | 69 |

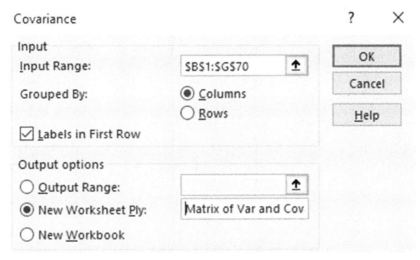

**FIGURE 13.3-8**    Inserting a matrix of variances and covariances.

The maximum point (mode) would be in $x = 1$.

We show in Fig. 13.4-2 the mode using the tangent line technique that we have implemented in **§ 5.1**. The Solver can be used as well, with the nonnegative option flagged.

## 13.5 Univariate, multivariate regression analysis and the ANOVA tables

The regression analysis represents the core concept of econometrics, and it is vastly used within the business and the economic analysis. Before looking at some practical examples, we give a quick review of the classical regression model.

Using the matrix notation, the regression model in general can be formalized as follows:

$$Y = X \cdot \beta + \varepsilon$$

where

$$
\underset{(T \cdot 1)}{Y} = \begin{bmatrix} Y_1 \\ \vdots \\ Y_t \\ \vdots \\ Y_T \end{bmatrix} ; \quad
\underset{(T \cdot K)}{X} = \begin{bmatrix} 1 & X_{11} & X_{12} & \cdots & X_{1K} \\ \vdots & \vdots & \vdots & \vdots & \vdots \\ 1 & X_{t1} & X_{t2} & \vdots & X_{tK} \\ \vdots & \vdots & \vdots & \vdots & \vdots \\ 1 & X_{T1} & X_{T2} & \cdots & X_{TK} \end{bmatrix} ; \quad
\underset{(K \cdot 1)}{\beta} = \begin{bmatrix} \beta_0 \\ \vdots \\ \beta_j \\ \vdots \\ \beta_K \end{bmatrix} ; \quad
\underset{(T \cdot 1)}{\varepsilon} = \begin{bmatrix} \varepsilon_1 \\ \vdots \\ \varepsilon_t \\ \vdots \\ \varepsilon_T \end{bmatrix} ;
$$

so that, for a single $t$th observation the model is:

$$Y_t = \beta_0 + \beta_1 X_{t1} + \beta_2 X_{t2} + \beta_3 X_{t3} + \cdots + \beta_K X_{tK} + \varepsilon_t$$

**TABLE 13.3-8** Matrix of variances and covariances.

| | MSCI Europe Net | EONIA Capit. 90) Micropal (TR) | S&P 500 (Composite) | Japan TSE 1st Section(Topix) (TR) | S&P/IFCI EMEA (TR) | Lehman Euro-Aggregate (TR) |
|---|---|---|---|---|---|---|
| MSCI Europe Net | 0.002488 | | | | | |
| EONIA Capit. 90) Micropal (TR) | -0.000008 | 0.000001 | | | | |
| S&P 500 (Composite) | 0.002373 | -0.000005 | 0.003109 | | | |
| Japan TSE 1st Section(Topix) (TR) | 0.001462 | -0.000015 | 0.002086 | 0.004359 | | |
| S&P/IFCI EMEA (TR) | 0.002334 | -0.000012 | 0.002510 | 0.002435 | 0.004209 | |
| Lehman Euro-Aggregate (TR) | -0.000184 | 0.000001 | -0.000195 | -0.000146 | -0.000146 | 0.000082 |

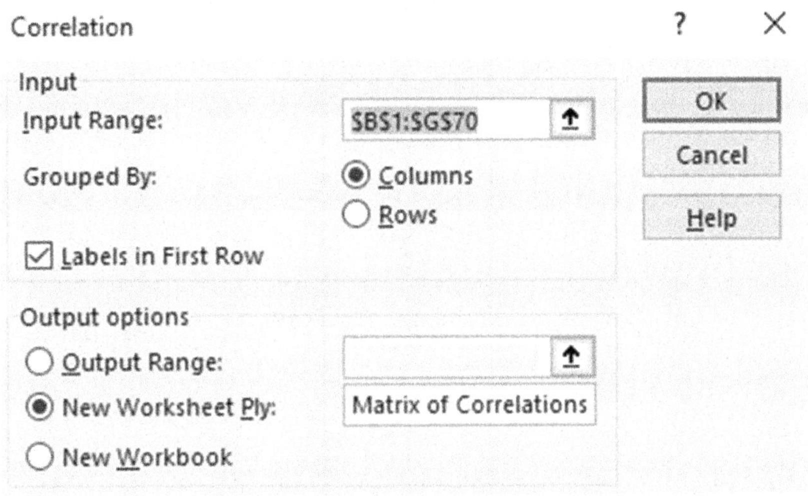

FIGURE 13.3-9   Inserting a matrix of correlations.

where

$Y_t = $ *dependent variable,*
$X_{t1,t2,\cdots,tK} = $ *independent, or explanatory variables, or regressors,*
$\beta_0 \quad = $ *intercept parameter,*
$\beta_{1,2,\cdots,K} \quad = $ *slope parameters,*
$\varepsilon_t \quad = $ *error term, or disturbance.*

The **Classical Normal Linear Regression Model** makes the following essential assumptions:

**(1)** Linear relation existing between the dependent and the independent variable, via the regression parameters, that is, the regression is linear in the parameters.
**(2)** The independent variable is nonstochastic.
**(3)** The expected value of the error term is zero, that is $E(\varepsilon_t) = 0$.
**(4)** *Homoscedasticity,* that is, the variance of the error terms is the same for all observations: $E(\varepsilon_t^2) = \sigma_\varepsilon^2 \ \forall \ t$.
**(5)** No autocorrelation between the disturbances: $E(\varepsilon_i \varepsilon_j) = 0$.
**(6)** Normal distribution of the error term $\varepsilon_t$, that is $\varepsilon_t \sim N(0, \sigma^2)$.

Under these assumptions, usually the estimation method of *Ordinary Least Squares* (**OLS**) is used for the parameters of the Classical Normal Linear Regression Model. An alternative to the least squares method is the method of *maximum likelihood* (**ML**) and under the normality assumption (6), the ML and OLS estimators of the intercept and slope parameters of the regression model are identical.

Using the OLS approach the parameters are estimated minimizing the following quadratic function

**TABLE 13.3-9** Matrix of correlations.

| | MSCI Europe Net | EONIA Capit. 90j Micropal (TR) | S&P 500 (Composite) | Japan TSE 1st Section(Topix) (TR) | S&P/IFCI EMEA (TR) | Lehman Euro-Aggregate (TR) |
|---|---|---|---|---|---|---|
| MSCI Europe Net | 1.000000 | | | | | |
| EONIA Capit. 90j Micropal (TR) | -0.205565 | 1.000000 | | | | |
| S&P 500 (Composite) | 0.853122 | -0.114076 | 1.000000 | | | |
| Japan TSE 1st Section(Topix) (TR) | 0.443925 | -0.276940 | 0.566621 | 1.000000 | | |
| S&P/IFCI EMEA (TR) | 0.721342 | -0.237848 | 0.693794 | 0.568537 | 1.000000 | |
| Lehman Euro-Aggregate (TR) | -0.405876 | 0.197901 | -0.385581 | -0.242985 | -0.247501 | 1.000000 |

| | A | B | C | D |
|---|---|---|---|---|
| 1 | Dates | MSCI Europe Net | EONIA Capit. 90j Micropal (TR) | S&P 500 (Composite) |
| 3 | 36217 | 0.00826785913214079 | 0.00241683754227995 | 0.00212638150104194 |
| 4 | 36250 | 0.0279545840660675 | 0.00268402101194609 | 0.0572858186569032 |
| 5 | 36280 | 0.0508208536572985 | 0.00228347728362199 | 0.0597717151425956 |
| 6 | 36311 | -0.034244616811397 | 0.00218768216760146 | -0.00972500043991364 |
| 7 | 36341 | 0.0283164580178377 | 0.00212518588077382 | 0.0671195089620649 |
| 8 | 36371 | -0.0274889264509865 | 0.00208133034298985 | -0.0666477081476059 |
| 14 | 36556 | -0.0484406889371302 | 0.0026764783063038 | -0.0270756182094266 |
| 66 | 38138 | -0.00240010602861829 | 0.00172797065465424 | -0.00521642160555458 |
| 67 | 38168 | 0.0171237088871212 | 0.00169073897874905 | 0.0229116596146164 |
| 68 | 38198 | -0.0172615453908074 | 0.00171536659983951 | -0.0231327544890496 |
| 69 | 38230 | -0.00870030935109523 | 0.00180674093098787 | -0.00566113602271681 |
| 70 | 38260 | 0.0177451767628038 | 0.00170265265930669 | -0.0111922680368415 |
| 71 | | | | |
| 72 | | Matrix of Var Cov Ret using OFFSET | | |
| 73 | | 0 | 1 | 2 |
| 74 | 0 | =COVAR(OFFSET($B$2:$B$70;0;B$73);OFFSET($B$2:$B$70;0;$A74)) | =COVAR(OFFSET($B$2:$B$70;0;C$73);OFFSET($B$2:$B$70;0;$A74)) | =COVAR(OFFSET($B$2:$B$70;0;D$73);OFFSET($B$2:$B$70;0;$A74)) |
| 75 | 1 | =COVAR(OFFSET($B$2:$B$70;0;B$73);OFFSET($B$2:$B$70;0;$A75)) | =COVAR(OFFSET($B$2:$B$70;0;C$73);OFFSET($B$2:$B$70;0;$A75)) | =COVAR(OFFSET($B$2:$B$70;0;D$73);OFFSET($B$2:$B$70;0;$A75)) |
| 76 | 2 | =COVAR(OFFSET($B$2:$B$70;0;B$73);OFFSET($B$2:$B$70;0;$A76)) | =COVAR(OFFSET($B$2:$B$70;0;C$73);OFFSET($B$2:$B$70;0;$A76)) | =COVAR(OFFSET($B$2:$B$70;0;D$73);OFFSET($B$2:$B$70;0;$A76)) |
| 77 | 3 | =COVAR(OFFSET($B$2:$B$70;0;B$73);OFFSET($B$2:$B$70;0;$A77)) | =COVAR(OFFSET($B$2:$B$70;0;C$73);OFFSET($B$2:$B$70;0;$A77)) | =COVAR(OFFSET($B$2:$B$70;0;D$73);OFFSET($B$2:$B$70;0;$A77)) |
| 78 | 4 | =COVAR(OFFSET($B$2:$B$70;0;B$73);OFFSET($B$2:$B$70;0;$A78)) | =COVAR(OFFSET($B$2:$B$70;0;C$73);OFFSET($B$2:$B$70;0;$A78)) | =COVAR(OFFSET($B$2:$B$70;0;D$73);OFFSET($B$2:$B$70;0;$A78)) |
| 79 | 5 | =COVAR(OFFSET($B$2:$B$70;0;B$73);OFFSET($B$2:$B$70;0;$A79)) | =COVAR(OFFSET($B$2:$B$70;0;C$73);OFFSET($B$2:$B$70;0;$A79)) | =COVAR(OFFSET($B$2:$B$70;0;D$73);OFFSET($B$2:$B$70;0;$A79)) |

FIGURE 13.3-10 Offset function to create a matrix of variances and covariances.

**TABLE 13.4.1**   Numerical integral for the average $\mu = 2/3$.

| x | y'(x) | $x_k - x_{k-1} = h$ | y'(x)*h | $y_k = y_{k-1} + y'*h$ | Average ($y_k$ ; $y_{k-1}$) | y Exact | Step |
|---|---|---|---|---|---|---|---|
| 0.0000 | | | | 0.0000 | 0.0000 | 0.0000 | 0.02 |
| 0.0200 | 0.0198 | 0.0200 | 0.0004 | 0.0004 | 0.0002 | 0.0002 | |
| 0.0400 | 0.0392 | 0.0200 | 0.0008 | 0.0012 | 0.0008 | 0.0008 | |
| 0.0600 | 0.0582 | 0.0200 | 0.0012 | 0.0023 | 0.0018 | 0.0018 | |
| 0.0800 | 0.0768 | 0.0200 | 0.0015 | 0.0039 | 0.0031 | 0.0031 | |
| 0.1000 | 0.0950 | 0.0200 | 0.0019 | 0.0058 | 0.0048 | 0.0048 | |
| 0.1200 | 0.1128 | 0.0200 | 0.0023 | 0.0080 | 0.0069 | 0.0069 | |
| 0.1400 | 0.1302 | 0.0200 | 0.0026 | 0.0106 | 0.0093 | 0.0093 | |
| 0.1600 | 0.1472 | 0.0200 | 0.0029 | 0.0136 | 0.0121 | 0.0121 | |
| 0.1800 | 0.1638 | 0.0200 | 0.0033 | 0.0169 | 0.0152 | 0.0152 | |
| 0.2000 | 0.1800 | 0.0200 | 0.0036 | 0.0205 | 0.0187 | 0.0187 | |
| 0.2200 | 0.1958 | 0.0200 | 0.0039 | 0.0244 | 0.0224 | 0.0224 | |
| 0.2400 | 0.2112 | 0.0200 | 0.0042 | 0.0286 | 0.0265 | 0.0265 | |
| 0.2600 | 0.2262 | 0.0200 | 0.0045 | 0.0331 | 0.0309 | 0.0309 | |
| 1.9400 | 0.0582 | 0.0200 | 0.0012 | 0.6654 | 0.6648 | 0.6649 | |
| 1.9600 | 0.0392 | 0.0200 | 0.0008 | 0.6662 | 0.6658 | 0.6659 | |
| 1.9800 | 0.0198 | 0.0200 | 0.0004 | 0.6666 | 0.6664 | 0.6665 | |
| 2.0000 | 0.0000 | 0.0200 | 0.0000 | 0.6666 | 0.6666 | 0.6667 | |

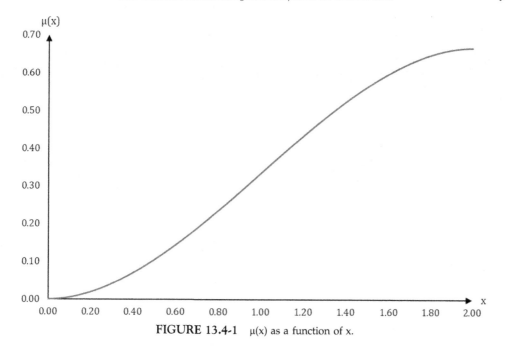

**FIGURE 13.4-1**    μ(x) as a function of x.

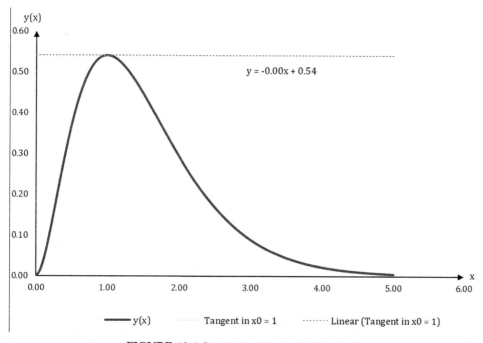

$y = -0.00x + 0.54$

**FIGURE 13.4-2**    Mode of the density function.

$$\min_{\{\beta\}} \sum_{t=1}^{T} \left[ Y_t - \left( \widehat{\beta}_0 + \widehat{\beta}_1 X_{t1} + \widehat{\beta}_2 X_{t2} + \widehat{\beta}_3 X_{t3} + \cdots + \widehat{\beta}_K X_{tK} \right) \right]^2$$

where the symbol $(\widehat{\ })$ has been placed to represent the calculated values of the true parameters.

It is worth highlighting (from the theory of econometrics) the general formulation of the OLS estimator in a matrix notation, which is as follows:

$$\widehat{\beta} = (X^T X)^{-1} X^T Y.$$

The univariate regression is instead expressed in the following simplified form:

$$Y_t = \beta_0 + \beta_1 X_{t1} + \varepsilon_t$$

and the OLS parameters are found minimizing the following quadratic expression (essentially a Nonlinear Optimization Problem):

$$\min_{\{\beta\}} \sum_{t=1}^{T} \left( Y_t - \widehat{\beta}_0 - \widehat{\beta}_1 X_{t1} \right)^2 = \min_{\{\beta\}} \sum_{t=1}^{T} (\varepsilon_t)^2$$

where the term $\left( \widehat{\beta}_0 + \widehat{\beta}_1 X_t \right)$ is the predicted value of $Y$ which can be also denoted by $\widehat{Y}$.

Using the OLS method to estimate $\beta_0$ and $\beta_1$ we can therefore fit a line through the observation on $X$ and $Y$ that best explains the value that $Y$ takes for any value of $X$.

For a univariate regression the formula of the OLS-estimate of the systematic risk $\beta_1$ is indicated as follows:

$$\widehat{\beta}_1 = \frac{Cov(X, Y)}{\sigma_X^2}.$$

The intercept $\beta_0$ is the value of the dependent variable $Y$ when the independent variable $X$ is equal to zero. The OLS-estimate of $\beta_0$ is indicated as follows:

$$\widehat{\beta}_0 = \overline{Y} - \widehat{\beta}_1 \overline{X}$$

where

$$\overline{Y} = \textit{Arithmetic average of } Y$$

$$\overline{X} = \textit{Arithmetic average of } X$$

To perform the regression analyses, Excel offers several alternatives.

i. Built in function =**LINEST** (also working for a Multivariate Regression). See Fig. 13.5-1. Statistics of the regression can be also obtained.

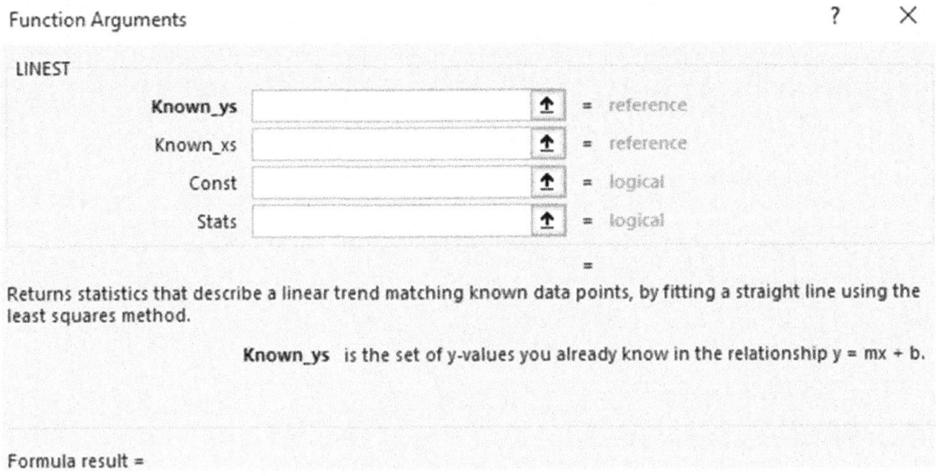

Function Arguments      ?    X

LINEST

| | | | |
|---|---|---|---|
| Known_ys | | ↑ | = reference |
| Known_xs | | ↑ | = reference |
| Const | | ↑ | = logical |
| Stats | | ↑ | = logical |

=

Returns statistics that describe a linear trend matching known data points, by fitting a straight line using the least squares method.

    **Known_ys** is the set of y-values you already know in the relationship y = mx + b.

Formula result =

**FIGURE 13.5-1**   LINEST function.

ii **Data Analysis ToolPak** (also for a Multivariate Regression). See Fig. 13.5-2, where the confidence level can be changed from the level of 95% (given by default) and other options on the residuals may be flagged. The output will return automatically the complete **ANOVA (Analysis of Variance).**

iii. Built-in functions $=SLOPE$ and $=INTERCEPT$ for univariate regressions. No statistics is provided.

iv. **Scatter Chart** with trendlines. This is not a statistical regression tool but just an option called trendline embedded in the scatter chart, working also for the nonlinear curves fitting. It just shows the equation on the scatter chart, with the $R^2$ stat if we want it to be included. It is useful for a quick analysis.

v. As the regression parameters are found minimizing an objective nonlinear function, we can also apply the **Solver** to find the parameters.

vi. We can analytically calculate the parameters resorting to the general matrix formulation $\hat{\beta} = (X^T X)^{-1} X^T Y$.

## EXAMPLE 1 (UNIVARIATE REGRESSION ANALYSIS: INVESTMENT FUND VS. BENCHMARK'S RETURNS)

Within the asset management field, the Regression Analysis is used a lot as a tool to examine the fund's returns together with the benchmark's returns.

The goal of the regression analysis is to estimate the parameter $\beta_1$, which represents in the theory of finance the *standardized* measure of systematic risk (risk that cannot be eliminated

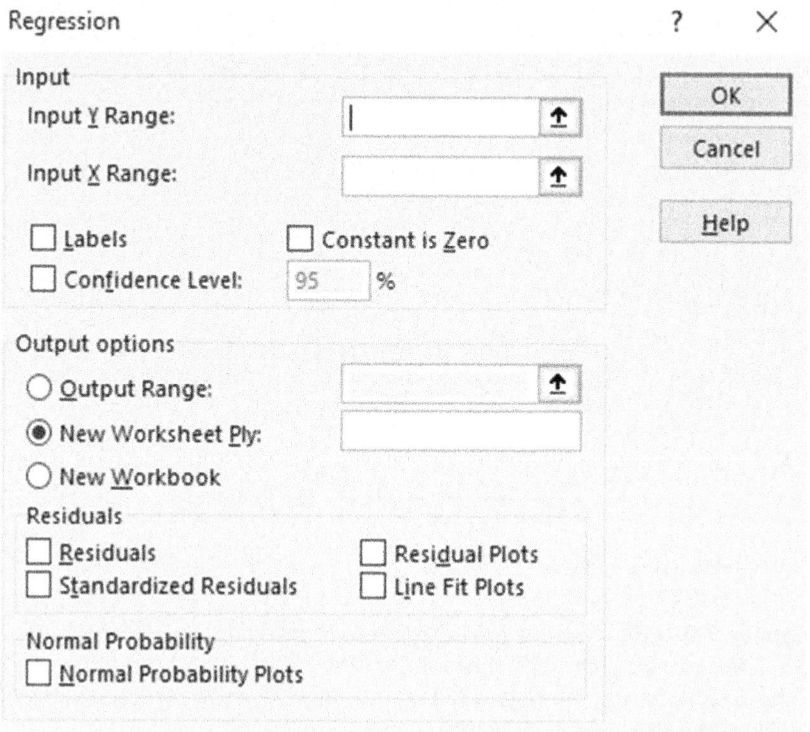

**FIGURE 13.5-2** Regression analysis in the data analysis ToolPak.

by the diversification of the fund), as well as the intercept parameter $\beta_0$, which is instead an indicator of over/under performance of the stock (or fund) we are analyzing versus the benchmark returns (i.e., the market return).

We will show here the regression analysis concerning 104 monthly observations of a fund versus its benchmark.

The regression is in the form:

$$Y_t = \beta_0 + \beta_1 X_{t1} + \varepsilon_t$$

where

$$Y_t = monthly\ returns\ of\ the\ fund.$$

$$X_{t1} = monthly\ returns\ of\ the\ benchmark.$$

First, before using the Data Analysis ToolPak, we can solve the problem using the Solver, as the regression parameters are found solving a minimization problem. This is done using

| | A | B | C | D $(\beta_0 + \beta_1 X_t)$ | E $(Y - \beta_0 - \beta_1 X_t)^2$ | F (Y Estimated-Y Average)^2 | G Total Variation (Y-Y Average) |
|---|---|---|---|---|---|---|---|
| 1 | Objective Function | Fund | Benchmark | | | | |
| 2 | =SUM(E2:E105) | -0.0209 | -0.0086415831 | =$A$4+$A$6*C2 | =(B2-D2)^2 | =(D2-$A$8)^2 | =(B2-$A$8)^2 |
| 3 | $\beta_0$ | 0.0183 | 0.0203364094 | =$A$4+$A$6*C3 | =(B3-D3)^2 | =(D3-$A$8)^2 | =(B3-$A$8)^2 |
| 4 | 0 | 0.0540 | 0.0455983181 | =$A$4+$A$6*C4 | =(B4-D4)^2 | =(D4-$A$8)^2 | =(B4-$A$8)^2 |
| 5 | $\beta_1$ | 0.0014 | -0.0181945729 | =$A$4+$A$6*C5 | =(B5-D5)^2 | =(D5-$A$8)^2 | =(B5-$A$8)^2 |
| 6 | 0.916557921148466 | 0.0170 | 0.0273205564 | =$A$4+$A$6*C6 | =(B6-D6)^2 | =(D6-$A$8)^2 | =(B6-$A$8)^2 |
| 7 | Y Average | -0.046 | -0.0568071725 | =$A$4+$A$6*C7 | =(B7-D7)^2 | =(D7-$A$8)^2 | =(B7-$A$8)^2 |
| 8 | =AVERAGE($B$2:$B$105) | 0.0527 | 0.0486887663 | =$A$4+$A$6*C8 | =(B8-D8)^2 | =(D8-$A$8)^2 | =(B8-$A$8)^2 |
| 9 | | 0.0529 | 0.0657258759 | =$A$4+$A$6*C9 | =(B9-D9)^2 | =(D9-$A$8)^2 | =(B9-$A$8)^2 |
| 10 | SSE (Sum of Squared Errors) | -0.0020 | -0.0131652812 | =$A$4+$A$6*C10 | =(B10-D10)^2 | =(D10-$A$8)^2 | =(B10-$A$8)^2 |
| 11 | =SUM(E2:E105) | -0.0268 | -0.0433385326 | =$A$4+$A$6*C11 | =(B11-D11)^2 | =(D11-$A$8)^2 | =(B11-$A$8)^2 |
| 12 | RSS (Regression Sum of Squares) | 0.0299 | 0.0306832042 | =$A$4+$A$6*C12 | =(B12-D12)^2 | =(D12-$A$8)^2 | =(B12-$A$8)^2 |
| 13 | =SUM(F2:F105) | 0.0039 | 0.0023435419 | =$A$4+$A$6*C13 | =(B13-D13)^2 | =(D13-$A$8)^2 | =(B13-$A$8)^2 |
| 14 | TSS (Total Sum of Squares) | -0.0109 | -0.0030073541 | =$A$4+$A$6*C14 | =(B14-D14)^2 | =(D14-$A$8)^2 | =(B14-$A$8)^2 |
| 15 | =SUM(G2:G105) | 0.0133 | 0.0187874235 | =$A$4+$A$6*C15 | =(B15-D15)^2 | =(D15-$A$8)^2 | =(B15-$A$8)^2 |
| 16 | $R^2$ | 0.0275 | 0.0298822042 | =$A$4+$A$6*C16 | =(B16-D16)^2 | =(D16-$A$8)^2 | =(B16-$A$8)^2 |
| 17 | =(A15-A11)/A15 | -0.0268 | -0.0264891897 | =$A$4+$A$6*C17 | =(B17-D17)^2 | =(D17-$A$8)^2 | =(B17-$A$8)^2 |
| 18 | | 0.0275 | 0.0282086058 | =$A$4+$A$6*C18 | =(B18-D18)^2 | =(D18-$A$8)^2 | =(B18-$A$8)^2 |
| 19 | Slope | -0.0499 | -0.0435883451 | =$A$4+$A$6*C19 | =(B19-D19)^2 | =(D19-$A$8)^2 | =(B19-$A$8)^2 |
| 20 | =SLOPE(B2:B105;C2:C105) | 0.0044 | 0.0094517428 | =$A$4+$A$6*C20 | =(B20-D20)^2 | =(D20-$A$8)^2 | =(B20-$A$8)^2 |
| 21 | Intercept | -0.0340 | -0.0152529638 | =$A$4+$A$6*C21 | =(B21-D21)^2 | =(D21-$A$8)^2 | =(B21-$A$8)^2 |
| 22 | =INTERCEPT(B2:B105;C2:C105) | 0.0085 | 0.0143366437 | =$A$4+$A$6*C22 | =(B22-D22)^2 | =(D22-$A$8)^2 | =(B22-$A$8)^2 |
| 23 | | 0.0335 | 0.0479538980 | =$A$4+$A$6*C23 | =(B23-D23)^2 | =(D23-$A$8)^2 | =(B23-$A$8)^2 |
| 24 | SEE (Standard Error of Estimate) | 0.0354 | 0.0346215669 | =$A$4+$A$6*C24 | =(B24-D24)^2 | =(D24-$A$8)^2 | =(B24-$A$8)^2 |
| 25 | =(A11/102)^(1/2) | 0.0085 | 0.0083280328 | =$A$4+$A$6*C25 | =(B25-D25)^2 | =(D25-$A$8)^2 | =(B25-$A$8)^2 |
| 26 | | -0.0071 | -0.0005353416 | =$A$4+$A$6*C26 | =(B26-D26)^2 | =(D26-$A$8)^2 | =(B26-$A$8)^2 |
| 105 | | -0.0370 | -0.0303973555 | =$A$4+$A$6*C105 | =(B105-D105)^2 | =(D105-$A$8)^2 | =(B105-$A$8)^2 |

**FIGURE 13.5-3**    Setup of the worksheet for the solver regression.

the example of worksheet in Fig. 13.5-3. The optimization is done minimizing the objective function as shown in Fig. 13.5-4.

In Table 13.5-1, we have calculated analytically the following:

$$SSE(Sum\ of\ Squared\ Errors) = \sum_{t=1}^{T=104} \left(Y_t - \widehat{Y}_t\right)^2 (Unexplained\ Variation)$$

$$RSS(Regression\ Sum\ of\ Squares) = \sum_{t=1}^{T=104} \left(\widehat{Y}_t - \overline{Y}\right)^2 (Explained\ Variation)$$

$$TSS(Total\ Sum\ of\ Squares) = \sum_{t=1}^{T=104} \left(Y_t - \overline{Y}\right)^2 (Total\ Variation)$$

It is straightforward to inspect that:

$$\left(Y_t - \overline{Y}\right) = \left(Y_t - \widehat{Y}_t\right) + \left(\widehat{Y}_t - \overline{Y}\right)$$

which means that we divide the total variation of $Y_t$ (from its average) into two components: the first is the distance from $Y_t$ to $\widehat{Y}_t$ (from the true value to the predicted value), the second component is the distance from the predicted value to the average $\overline{Y}$.

FIGURE 13.5-4    Solver for the regression minimizing parameters.

The **Standard Error of Estimate** is given instead by:

$$SEE = \left[ \frac{\sum_{t=1}^{T=104} \left( Y_t - \widehat{\beta}_0 + \widehat{\beta}_1 X_t \right)^2}{T-2} \right]^{1/2} = \left[ \frac{\sum_{t=1}^{T=104} (\varepsilon_t)^2}{T-2} \right]^{1/2} = \left[ \frac{SSE}{T-2} \right]^{1/2} = [1.6083\%/102]^{1/2}$$

$$= 0.012557$$

**TABLE 13.5-1** Solver regression results for 104 monthly returns for a fund versus its benchmark.

| | A | B Fund | C Benchmark | D $(\hat{\beta}_0 + \hat{\beta}_1 X_i)(Y - \hat{\beta}_0 - \hat{\beta}_1 X_i)^2$ | E $(Y - \hat{\beta}_0 - \hat{\beta}_1 X_i)^2$ | F (Y Estimated - Y Average)^2 | G Total Variation (Y-Y Average) |
|---|---|---|---|---|---|---|---|
| 1 | Objective Function | | | | | | |
| 2 | 1.6083% | -2.10% | -0.86% | -0.79% | 0.02% | 0.02% | 0.07% |
| 3 | β₀ | 1.83% | 2.03% | 1.86% | 0.00% | 0.02% | 0.02% |
| 4 | 0.00 | 5.41% | 4.56% | 4.18% | 0.02% | 0.13% | 0.24% |
| 5 | β₁ | 0.14% | -1.87% | -1.72% | 0.03% | 0.05% | 0.00% |
| 6 | 0.91656 | 1.71% | 2.73% | 2.50% | 0.01% | 0.04% | 0.01% |
| 7 | Y Average | -4.62% | -5.68% | -5.21% | 0.00% | 0.33% | 0.27% |
| 8 | 0.5552% | 5.28% | 4.87% | 4.46% | 0.01% | 0.15% | 0.22% |
| 9 | | 5.29% | 6.57% | 6.02% | 0.01% | 0.30% | 0.22% |
| 10 | SSE (Sum of Squared Errors) | -0.26% | -1.32% | -1.21% | 0.01% | 0.03% | 0.01% |
| 11 | 1.6083% | -2.65% | -4.33% | -3.97% | 0.02% | 0.20% | 0.10% |
| 12 | RSS (Regression Sum of Squares) | 3.00% | 3.07% | 2.81% | 0.00% | 0.05% | 0.06% |
| 13 | 14.0207% | 0.40% | 0.23% | 0.21% | 0.00% | 0.00% | 0.00% |
| 14 | TSS (Total Sum of Squares) | -1.05% | -0.30% | -0.28% | 0.01% | 0.01% | 0.03% |
| 15 | 15.7352% | 1.33% | 1.88% | 1.72% | 0.00% | 0.01% | 0.01% |
| 16 | R² | 2.76% | 2.99% | 2.74% | 0.00% | 0.05% | 0.05% |
| 17 | 89.7788% | -2.69% | -2.65% | -2.43% | 0.00% | 0.09% | 0.11% |
| 18 | | 2.76% | 2.82% | 2.59% | 0.00% | 0.04% | 0.05% |
| 19 | Slope | -4.94% | -4.36% | -4.00% | 0.01% | 0.21% | 0.30% |
| 20 | 0.920605 | 0.45% | 0.95% | 0.87% | 0.00% | 0.00% | 0.00% |
| 21 | Intercept | -3.40% | -1.53% | -1.40% | 0.04% | 0.04% | 0.16% |
| 22 | -0.0009479 | 0.86% | 1.43% | 1.31% | 0.00% | 0.01% | 0.00% |
| 23 | | 3.36% | 4.80% | 4.40% | 0.01% | 0.15% | 0.08% |
| 24 | SEE (Standard Error of Estimate) | 3.55% | 3.46% | 3.17% | 0.00% | 0.07% | 0.09% |
| 25 | 0.0125570 | 0.86% | 0.83% | 0.76% | 0.00% | 0.00% | 0.00% |
| 26 | | -0.73% | -0.05% | -0.05% | 0.00% | 0.00% | 0.02% |
| 105 | | -3.71% | -3.04% | -2.79% | 0.01% | 0.11% | 0.18% |

## Coefficient of determination: a measure of goodness of fit

The coefficient of determination is considered a summary measure that indicates how well in the regression the independent variable explains the variation in the dependent variable. Namely, how well the regression line fits the data.

Therefore, the coefficient of determination measures the fraction of the total variance in the dependent variable explained by the independent variable.

We have:

$$Total\ Variation(TSS) = Explained\ Variation(RSS) + Unexplained\ Variation(SSE)$$

and the coefficient of determination $R^2$ is the ratio:

$$R^2 = \frac{Explained\ Variation}{Total\ Variation} = \frac{RSS}{TSS}$$

(sometimes for univariate regressions this ratio is indicated with $r^2$, while for multivariate regressions with $R^2$)
where

$$0 \leq R^2 \leq 1.$$

An $R^2$ of 1 means a perfect fit, that is, $\widehat{Y}_t = Y_t$ for each $t$. On the other hand, an $R^2$ of zero means that there is no relationship between the dependent and the independent variable and the regression line will be horizontal to the $X$ axis.

In Table 13.5-1, we have computed $R^2 = 0.8977$, so that we can conclude that the regression is doing a good job in fitting the pairs of data.

Using the scatter chart and the trendline option, the graphical output of the regression is given in Fig. 13.5-5.

The $R^2$ and the estimated value parameters are slightly different from the ones calculated via the Solver.

Using the functions *SLOPE* and *INTERCEPT*, we obtain the same values as the regression chart trendline equation:

$$= SLOPE(B2: B105; C2: C105) = 0.92006$$

$$= INTERCEPT(B2: B105; C2: C105) = -0.00095$$

## LINEST function

Another way to obtain the regression parameters with some stats associated is the *LINEST* function. The *LINEST* function needs to be input as an array formula, using *Control + Shift + Enter* as represented in Fig. 13.5-6 and Table 13.5-2.

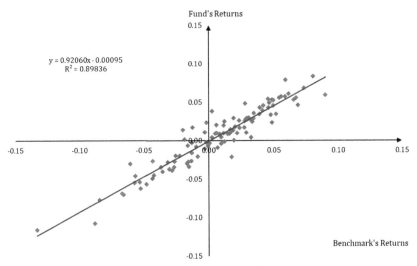

**FIGURE 13.5-5**  Linear regression: Fund's returns versus Benchmark's returns.

The limitation of *LINEST* is the fact that the output returned is not labeled while we should label them in order to avoid confusion when we look at the statistics. Another limitation is that the data arrays of *Y* and *X* must be contiguous.

The strong advantage of *LINEST* is that it is a function and therefore, together with the *OFFSET* function, the data can be treated dynamically.

In general (for univariate and multivariate regressions), the order of stats returned by the *LINEST* function is as follows (Fig. 13.5-7). This is the original Excel Help explanation, where the parameters are denoted by the letter *m*, while the intercept is denoted by *b*, under *Row* 1. Then, under *Row* 2 we have for each parameter the standard error. In *Row* 3, we have the Coefficient of Determination indicated as *r2* and the Standard Error of Estimate **SEE** (indicated here as **se$_y$**) of the dependent variable. In *Row* 4 the multiple regression **F-test** statistic is provided, together with the degrees of freedom *d$_f$*. In *Row* 5, we have the **RSS** (SSreg) and **SSE** (SSresid).

In our Example 1, we have the following values for the **F-test** statistic and *d$_f$*:

$$F_{K,\ [T-(K+1)]} = \frac{\dfrac{RSS}{K}}{\dfrac{SSE}{[T-(K+1)]}} = \frac{Mean\ Regression\ Sum\ of\ Squares}{Mean\ Squared\ Error}$$

where *K* is the number of slope parameters and *T* is the number of observations.

The subscript *K*, [*T*−(*K* + 1)] means that the test *F-test* is run for *K* degrees of freedom, equal to the number of slope parameters at the numerator and [*T*−(*K* + 1)] **degrees of freedom** at the denominator, as a divisor of *RSS* and *SSE*, respectively.

| Linest Output | | |
|---|---|---|
| | $\beta_1$ | $\beta_0$ |
| Coefficients | =LINEST(A2:A105;B2:B105;;TRUE) | =LINEST(A2:A105;B2:B105;;TRUE) |
| Standard Error | =LINEST(A2:A105;B2:B105;;TRUE) | =LINEST(A2:A105;B2:B105;;TRUE) |
| R Sq ; St Er | =LINEST(A2:A105;B2:B105;;TRUE) | =LINEST(A2:A105;B2:B105;;TRUE) |
| F | =LINEST(A2:A105;B2:B105;;TRUE) | =LINEST(A2:A105;B2:B105;;TRUE) |
| RSS ; SSE | =LINEST(A2:A105;B2:B105;;TRUE) | =LINEST(A2:A105;B2:B105;;TRUE) |

FIGURE 13.5-6   Linear regression output using *LINEST*.

TABLE 13.5-2   Example 1: Linear regression output using **LINEST**.

| | $\beta_1$ | $\beta_0$ |
|---|---|---|
| Coefficients | 0.920604926 | -0.000947912 |
| Standard Error | 0.030659873 | 0.001246775 |
| R Sq ; St Er | 0.898364194 | 0.012521571 |
| F | 901.5833266 | 102 |
| RSS ; SSE | 0.141359014 | 0.015992553 |

| | A | B | C | D | E | F |
|---|---|---|---|---|---|---|
| 1 | $m_n$ | $m_{n-1}$ | . . . | $m_2$ | $m_1$ | $b$ |
| 2 | $se_n$ | $se_{n-1}$ | . . . | $se_2$ | $se_1$ | $se_b$ |
| 3 | $r_2$ | $se_y$ | | | | |
| 4 | $F$ | $d_f$ | | | | |
| 5 | $ss_{reg}$ | $ss_{resid}$ | | | | |

FIGURE 13.5-7   Explanation of the linear regression output using *LINEST*.

For the univariate regression in general, and specifically for Example 1 of the returns of the fund versus the returns of the benchmark, we have $K = 1$ and $[T-(K+1)] = 104-2 = 102$, so that the *F statistic* is:

$$F_{2,102} = \frac{0.141359014}{\dfrac{0.015992553}{102}} = 901.58$$

The *F-test* statistic is an indicator of reliability of the regression parameters as a whole. If the regression does a good job of explaining variation in the dependent variable, then the *F statistic* value should be high (like in this case).

As in the univariate regression the *F-significance* duplicates the *P-value* of the slope parameter, we do not normally use this test, while the same relation does not hold in the multivariate regression.

## Data analysis and inferential statistics on the regression parameters

The choice Regression under the Data Analysis ToolPak represented in Fig. 13.5-8 is the most informative tool for the Excel regression analysis. However, it is not a formula and it is just a stand-alone output that we have to repeat for each data set.

The output of Table 13.5-3 returns all the information we already knew from *LINEST* plus other information.

First, we find in it the **adjusted R-squared** which is particularly useful for the multiple regression, as simply taking in this context the R-squared as an indicator of goodness of fit is not enough. In fact, what happens in the multiple regression is that each time we add a variable, somehow, we decrease the unexplained variation, even though the new regressor is slightly correlated with the dependent variable.

Then, an alternative measure of goodness of fit in the multiple regression is:

$$\overline{R}^2 = 1 - \left[\frac{T-1}{T-(K+1)}\right](1-R^2)$$

In the specific case of Table 13.5-3 for a univariate regression, the two values of R-squared almost correspond:

$$\overline{R}^2 = 1 - \left(\frac{103}{102}\right)(1-0.89836) = 0.89737$$

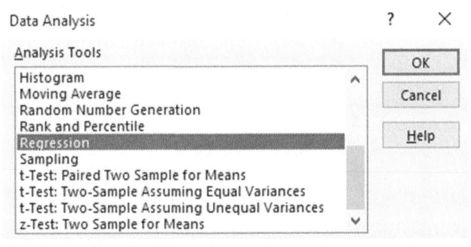

FIGURE 13.5-8   The regression option under data analysis.

**TABLE 13.5-3** The regression data analysis ANOVA output.

**REGRESSION AND ANOVA SUMMARY OUTPUT**

| Regression Statistics | |
|---|---|
| Multiple R | 0.947820761 |
| R Square | 0.898364194 |
| Adjusted R Square | 0.897367765 |
| Standard Error | 0.012521571 |
| Observations | 104 |

ANOVA

| | df | SS | MS | F | Significance F |
|---|---|---|---|---|---|
| Regression | 1 | 0.141359014 | 0.141359014 | 901.5833266 | 1.90003E-52 |
| Residual | 102 | 0.015992553 | 0.000015679 | | |
| Total | 103 | 0.157351568 | | | |

| | Coefficients | Standard Error | t Stat | P-value | Lower 95% | Upper 95% | Lower 95.0% | Upper 95.0% |
|---|---|---|---|---|---|---|---|---|
| Intercept | -0.000094791 | 0.001246775 | -0.760291133 | 0.448834318 | -0.003420884 | 0.00152506 | -0.003420884 | 0.00152506 |
| X Variable 1 | 0.920060493 | 0.030659873 | 30.02637718 | 1.90003E-52 | 0.859791212 | 0.98141864 | 0.859791212 | 0.98141864 |

Table 13.5-3 also returns the usual Standard Error (of Estimate):

$$\text{Standard Error of Estimate}(SEE) = \sqrt{\frac{SSE}{T-K}} = 0.01252.$$

Using the output of Table 13.5-3, we can then perform the inferential statistic analysis on each parameter in terms of **hypotheses test.**

This is done simply looking at the *tStat* and *P-value* for each parameter.

Let us assume we want to test the following **null hypothesis** versus **alternative hypothesis** over $\beta_1$, the slope parameter of the regression:

$$H_0: \ \beta_1 = 0 \ \textit{versus} \ H_0: \ \beta_1 \neq 0$$

This is a **two-sided hypothesis test** (or **two-tailed hypothesis test**).

Using the information in Table 13.5-3, we can reject or accept the null hypothesis $H_0: \ \beta_1 = 0$ using a 95% confidence level.

*Confidence interval*

We can first construct a confidence interval at 95% probability to reject or accept the null hypothesis.

This is built as (we are assuming the variance is not known):

$$\left[\widehat{\beta}_1 - t_c s_{\widehat{\beta}_1}; \ \widehat{\beta}_1 + t_c s_{\widehat{\beta}_1}\right]$$

where $t_c = t_{\alpha/2}$ (with $\alpha = 5\%$ *level of sginificance*) is the critical value to be read in a table of the $t$-distribution probability (also called $t$-student distribution) with $(T-2)$ degrees of freedom, which is approximately 1.9835 with $P = .025$ because this is a two-tailed test.

Alternatively, we can use in Excel the inverse $t$-distribution to find the exact critical value as follows:

$$= T.INV(0.025; 102) = 1.9835$$

The confidence interval at 95% probability is therefore:

$$[0.92060 - 1.9835 \cdot 0.3066; \ 0.92060 + 1.9835 \cdot 0.3066] = [0.8597; 0.9814]$$

which is what is returned in Table 13.5-3 (*lower 95%* and *upper 95%*).

Because we are testing $\beta_1 = 0$ (this is the test proposed by default in Excel) and the value zero is not included in the interval, we can reject $H_0: \ \beta_1 = 0$.

The *tStat* values for $\beta_0$ and $\beta_1$ are calculated, respectively, as follows.

$$\frac{\left(\widehat{\beta}_0 - 0\right)}{s_{\widehat{\beta}_0}} = -0.76029$$

$$\frac{\left(\widehat{\beta}_1 - 0\right)}{s_{\widehat{\beta}_1}} = 30.02637$$

which, again, follow a $t$-distribution with $(T-2) = 102$ degrees of freedom because two parameters have been estimated.

### Calculated tStat versus $t_c$

Another way to reject (or to accept) the null hypothesis is to compare these $t$-statistic values with the critical value $t_c = 1.9835$ from the $t$-distribution and reject the null hypotheses if they are greater than $t_c$.

In conclusion, we reject:

$$H_0: \ \beta_1 = 0$$

which means that the slope coefficient $\widehat{\beta}_1 = 0.92060$ is statistically significant and for each 1% increase in the benchmark's returns the fund's expected return would be 0.92%, while we do not reject:

$$H_0: \ \beta_0 = 0$$

which implies that the fund did not statistically generate a persistent over performance, beyond the returns associated with the market risk of the fund.

### P-value

The test of hypotheses can be also performed looking immediately at the $P$-values.

If the $P$-value is less than the specified **level of significance** we reject the null hypothesis. Otherwise, we do not reject the null hypothesis. In this case, the $P$-value is small enough to reject the null hypothesis $H_0: \ \beta_1 = 0$, and we can conclude that $\beta_1$ is statistically (significantly) different from zero, while we do not reject $H_0: \ \beta_0 = 0$.

The P-values of Table 13.5-3 can be also obtained manually in Excel using:

$$P - value \ = T.DIST(t_c; 102; TRUE) * 2 = 0.4488$$

when $t_c < 0$ (as here for the intercept parameter). Otherwise:

$$P - value \ = T.DIST.RT(t_c; 102; TRUE) * 2 = 1.9003E - 52$$

when $t_c > 0$ and where $RT$ stands for $Right \ Tailed$, as here for the slope parameter.

Analogously the $F$-significance, which is $P$-value for the test $F$, is found as:

$$= F.DIST.RT(901.58; 1; 102) = 1.9003E - 52.$$

As we have mentioned before, notice how in the univariate regression the calculated $F$-significance is the same as the $P$-value of the slope parameter, and this is why for the univariate regressions we do not normally use the $F$-test. The same does not happen in the multivariate case where instead the $F$-test is of paramount importance.

## Obtaining the OLS parameters from the matrix-based notation $\widehat{\beta} = (X^TX)^{-1}X^TY$ in one shot

This is done simply inputting the following array formula, referred to Table 13.5-4, where we have inserted the unit vector parameter.

$$= \{MINVERSE(MMULT(TRANSPOSE(C2:D105); C2:D105))$$
$$* MMULT(TRANSPOSE(C2:D105); B2:B105)\}$$

The above formula will return then for each parameter two output values that have to be summed to obtain the final estimates of the two parameters. See Table 13.5-5.

Notice how the results are identical to what has been returned by the ANOVA Table 13.5-3. The advantage of this formula is that it can be treated dynamically, over the Excel data ranges.

## Prediction interval

Let us continue Example 1, and what we want to do now is to build a prediction estimate of $Y$,

$$\widehat{Y} = \widehat{\beta}_0 + \widehat{\beta}_1 X_{t1}$$

given a predicted value of $X$, together with the prediction interval.

**TABLE 13.5-4** Inserting a unit vector as independent variable.

| | A | B | C | D | E | F | G | H |
|---|---|---|---|---|---|---|---|---|
| 1 | Objective Function | Fund | Unit Vector | Benchmark | $(\widehat{\beta}_0 + \widehat{\beta}_1 X_t)(Y - \beta_0 - \beta_1 X_t)^2$ | | (Y Estimated-Y Average)^2 | Total Variation (Y-Y Average) |
| 2 | 1.5993% | -2.10% | 1.00 | -0.86% | -0.89% | 0.01% | 0.02% | 0.07% |
| 3 | $\beta_0$ | 1.83% | 1.00 | 2.03% | 1.78% | 0.00% | 0.01% | 0.02% |
| 4 | -0.00094791 | 5.41% | 1.00 | 4.56% | 4.10% | 0.02% | 0.13% | 0.24% |
| 5 | $\beta_1$ | 0.14% | 1.00 | -1.87% | -1.82% | 0.04% | 0.06% | 0.00% |
| 6 | 0.92060493 | 1.71% | 1.00 | 2.73% | 2.42% | 0.01% | 0.03% | 0.01% |
| 7 | Y Average | -4.62% | 1.00 | -5.68% | -5.32% | 0.01% | 0.35% | 0.27% |
| 8 | 0.5552% | 5.28% | 1.00 | 4.87% | 4.39% | 0.01% | 0.15% | 0.22% |
| 9 | | 5.29% | 1.00 | 6.57% | 5.96% | 0.00% | 0.29% | 0.22% |
| 10 | SSE (Sum of Squared Errors) | -0.26% | 1.00 | -1.32% | -1.31% | 0.01% | 0.03% | 0.01% |
| 11 | 1.5993% | -2.65% | 1.00 | -4.33% | -4.08% | 0.02% | 0.22% | 0.10% |
| 12 | RSS (Regression Sum of Squares) | 3.00% | 1.00 | 3.07% | 2.73% | 0.00% | 0.05% | 0.06% |
| 13 | 14.1359% | 0.40% | 1.00 | 0.23% | 0.12% | 0.00% | 0.00% | 0.00% |
| 14 | TSS (Total Sum of Squares) | -1.05% | 1.00 | -0.30% | -0.37% | 0.00% | 0.01% | 0.03% |
| 15 | 15.7352% | 1.33% | 1.00 | 1.88% | 1.63% | 0.00% | 0.01% | 0.01% |
| 16 | $R^2$ | 2.76% | 1.00 | 2.99% | 2.66% | 0.00% | 0.04% | 0.05% |
| 17 | 89.8364% | -2.69% | 1.00 | -2.65% | -2.53% | 0.00% | 0.10% | 0.11% |
| 18 | | 2.76% | 1.00 | 2.82% | 2.50% | 0.00% | 0.04% | 0.05% |
| 19 | Slope | -4.94% | 1.00 | -4.36% | -4.11% | 0.01% | 0.22% | 0.30% |
| 20 | 0.920605 | 0.45% | 1.00 | 0.95% | 0.78% | 0.00% | 0.00% | 0.00% |
| 21 | Intercept | -3.40% | 1.00 | -1.53% | -1.50% | 0.04% | 0.04% | 0.16% |
| 22 | -0.0009479 | 0.86% | 1.00 | 1.43% | 1.23% | 0.00% | 0.00% | 0.00% |
| 23 | | 3.36% | 1.00 | 4.80% | 4.32% | 0.01% | 0.14% | 0.08% |
| 24 | SEE (Standard Error of Estimate) | 3.55% | 1.00 | 3.46% | 3.09% | 0.00% | 0.06% | 0.09% |
| 25 | 0.0125216 | 0.86% | 1.00 | 0.83% | 0.67% | 0.00% | 0.00% | 0.00% |
| 105 | | -3.71% | 1.00 | -3.04% | -2.89% | 0.01% | 0.12% | 0.18% |

**TABLE 13.5-5**  Matrix-based solution of the regression parameters.

| $\beta$ Estimated $= (X^TX)^{-1}X^TY$ | |
| --- | --- |
| $\beta_0$ | $\beta_1$ |
| -0.0009479 | 0.9206049 |
| 0.0057240 | -0.0244381 |
| -0.0066719 | 0.9450430 |

The 104th observation of the benchmark from Table 13.5-1 was $-3.04\%$; suppose we expect another even worse negative month of about $-4\%$ in the benchmark because of the shrinking global economy and other specific economic factors. Then, according to the regression line estimated the expected (or forecasted) return of the portfolio would be:

$$\widehat{Y}_{105} = -0.00094791 + 0.92060492 \cdot (-0.04) = -0.03777211 \cong -0.038$$

The estimated variance of the prediction error of $Y$ given $X$ is denoted by $s_f^2$, and it is as follows:

$$s_f^2 = s^2 \left[1 + \frac{1}{T} + \frac{(X - \overline{X})^2}{(T-1)s_X^2}\right]$$

where $s_X^2$ = variance of the indepedent variable = 0.00161935 and $f$ stands for forecast.
Then

$$s_f^2 = 0.01252157^2 \left[1 + \frac{1}{104} + \frac{(-0.04 - 0.00705994)^2}{(103) \cdot 0.00161935}\right] = 0.000160379.$$

We can build now a prediction interval at 95% with 102 degrees of freedom with:

$$t_c = T.INV(0.025; 102) = 1.9835$$

as follows:

$$\widehat{Y}_{105} \pm t_c s_f$$

namely:

$$-0.0377 \pm 1.9835 \cdot \sqrt{0.000160379}$$

$$[-0.06289 ; \; -0.01265].$$

Thus, we would expect a 95% chance that the actual return will fall between $-6.29\%$ and $-1.26\%$.

## EXAMPLE 2 (MARGINAL PROPENSITY TO CONSUME FOR THE US ECONOMY)

Econometrics helps us to investigate about the economic theory formulation. A classical example is the Keynesian concept of *Marginal Propensity to Consume*, which was stated by Keynes in *The General Theory of Employment, Interest and Money*:

> The fundamental psychological law…is that men [women] are disposed, as a rule and on average, to increase their consumption as their income increases, but not as much as the increase in their income.

At the time of Keynes, Econometrics was only at the beginning and Keynes here postulated that the marginal propensity to consume is:

$$MPC = \frac{\Delta C}{\Delta Y},$$

namely the rate of change of consumption for a unit change in income is greater than zero but less than one.

Econometrics can help to assess the marginal propensity to consume using a linear regression model.

Let us try then to use the following univariate linear model to estimate the marginal propensity to consume (MPC) in the US economy over 3 years with quarterly GDP and private Consumption Expenditures data:

$$C_t = \beta_0 + \beta_1 GDP_t + \varepsilon_t$$

where

$$C_t = \text{Level of Prvate Consumption at each period observed in \$ Bln.}$$

$$GDP_t = \text{Level of GDP at each period observed in \$ Bln.}$$

The data we will use for the estimate of the regression are in Table 13.5-6.

The ANOVA analysis is shown in Table 13.5-7. We estimate the MPC from the slope parameter $\widehat{\beta_1} = 0.7225$.

From the *F-test* we see immediately that the regression as a whole is doing a good job in explaining the variation in consumption.

At 5% level of significance we reject the null hypothesis:

$$H_0: \beta_1 = 0$$

**TABLE 13.5-6**  Quarterly data for US consumption and GDP.

| Year | Quarter | Gross Domestic Product ($ Bln) | Personal consumption expenditures ($ Bln) |
|------|---------|-------------------------------|-------------------------------------------|
|      | Q2      | 4,402                         | 3,053                                     |
| 2016 | Q3      | 4,448                         | 3,060                                     |
|      | Q4      | 4,527                         | 3,185                                     |
|      | Q1      | 4,339                         | 3,014                                     |
| 2017 | Q2      | 4,501                         | 3,136                                     |
|      | Q3      | 4,562                         | 3,136                                     |
|      | Q4      | 4,649                         | 3,272                                     |
|      | Q1      | 4,483                         | 3,098                                     |
| 2018 | Q2      | 4,638                         | 3,221                                     |
|      | Q3      | 4,686                         | 3,228                                     |

*Source: U.S. Bureau of Economic Analysis*

**TABLE 13.5-7**  ANOVA analysis for the univariate regression consumption versus GDP.

REGRESSION AND ANOVA SUMMARY OUTPUT

| Regression Statistics |  |
|-----------------------|--------------|
| Multiple R            | 0.949378743  |
| R Square              | 0.901319998  |
| Adjusted R Square     | 0.888984997  |
| Standard Error        | 28.46862607  |
| Observations          | 10           |

ANOVA

|            | df | SS     | MS     | F      | Significance F |
|------------|----|--------|--------|--------|----------------|
| Regression | 1  | 59,221 | 59,221 | 73.070 | 2.70197E-05    |
| Residual   | 8  | 6,484  | 810    |        |                |
| Total      | 9  | 65,704 |        |        |                |

|             | Coefficients  | Standard Error | t Stat     | P-value  | Lower 95%    | Upper 95%   | Lower 95.0%  | Upper 95.0% |
|-------------|---------------|----------------|------------|----------|--------------|-------------|--------------|-------------|
| Intercept   | -128.3400448  | 382.4888972    | -0.3355393 | 0.745848 | -1010.361023 | 753.6809337 | -1010.361023 | 753.6809337 |
| X Variable 1| 0.72259633    | 0.084532912    | 8.5481064  | 2.7E-05  | 0.527663085  | 0.917529574 | 0.527663085  | 0.917529574 |

while we do not reject:

$$H_0: \beta_0 = 0$$

As we are doing the test of hypotheses at 95% probability (i.e., 5% of significance), with 8 degrees of freedom our critical value from the $t$-student distribution is:

$$= T.INV(0.025; 8) = -2.3060$$

TABLE 13.5-8  Confidence interval at 95% probability (5% of significance).

|  | $t_c$ | Confidence Interval | |
|---|---|---|---|
| Intercept | -2.30600 | -1,010.36 | 753.68 |
| X Variable 1 | -2.30600 | 0.52766 | 0.91753 |

and the intervals for the two parameters are reproposed in the following Table 13.5-8:

As we can reject the null hypothesis at 5% level of significance, we have strong evidence that the null hypothesis is false, and the result found of $MPC = \hat{\beta}_1 = 0.7225$ is statistically significant (for the time period considered Fig. 13.5-9).

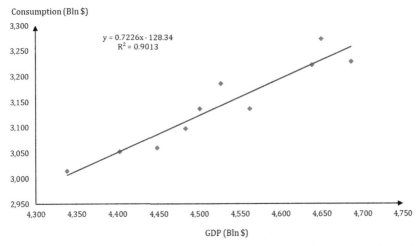

FIGURE 13.5-9  Scatter chart and linear regression of consumption versus GDP (Quarterly data from Table 13.5-6).

## EXAMPLE 3 (MULTIVARIATE REGRESSION AND THE COBB—DOUGLAS PRODUCTION FUNCTION)

As we have remarked at the end of **§ 6.7** the Cobb—Douglas mathematical economic production function can be estimated through a preliminary transformation of the nonlinear mathematical form:

$$Y = A\left(L^\alpha K^\beta\right)$$

where

$Y$ = total production.

$L$ = labor input (e.g., person-hours of the workforce).
$K$ = capital input (e.g., machine-hours referred to the fixed capital employed or real value of equipment).

The following linear logarithmic form is a linear multiple regression in two independent variables:

$$\log(Y) = \log(A) + \alpha \cdot \log(L) + \beta \cdot \log(K).$$

Using available data, we will take therefore the *natural log level* of each data series and then regress $Y$ on both $L$ and $K$. The correct econometric model would also include the disturbance term; therefore, we would transform the following:

$$Y_t = A\left(L_t^\alpha K_t^\beta\right)e_t^\varepsilon$$

into the following:

$$\log(Y_t) = \log(A) + \alpha \cdot \log(L_t) + \beta \cdot \log(K_t) + \varepsilon_t.$$

The model is linear in the parameters and is therefore a linear regression model. Notice, though, it is nonlinear in the variables $Y$ and $L$, $K$ but linear in the logs of these variables. The above formulation is also called a *regression log-linear model*.

From § **6.6** we know that:

**i.** $A$ = factor of productivity.
**ii.** $\alpha$ and $\beta$ are the output elasticities of capital and labor, respectively. Output elasticity measures the responsiveness of output to a change in levels of either labor or capital used in production. For example, if $\alpha = 0.8$, it means that a 1% increase in labor will determine a 0.80% increase in production, other things remaining equal.

## The returns to scale

$\alpha$ and $\beta$ also determine the *returns to scale*, which describe what happens in the long run to the output production $Y$ when both inputs production $L$ and $K$ change equi-proportionally.
We can have the following three cases:

**i.** $\alpha + \beta = 1$ (constant returns to scale).
**ii.** $\alpha + \beta < 1$ (decreasing returns to scale).
**iii.** $\alpha + \beta > 1$ (increasing returns to scale).

Let us consider the following data set (Table 13.5-9) taken from the original article by Charles W. Cobb and Paul H. Douglas, *A Theory of Production* (The American Economic Review, mar. 1928).
The regression parameters OLS-estimators are obtained as follows in Table 13.5-10, where $A = e^{-0.1773}$.

**TABLE 13.5-9** Indices of manufacturing, number of workers, and capital stock and natural logs.

| Year | Index of Manufactures | Relative Number of Workers, 1899 = 100 | Relative Capital Stock, 1899 = 100 | ln Y | Unit Vector | ln L | ln K |
|------|------|------|------|------|------|------|------|
| 1899 | 100 | 100 | 100 | 4.6052 | 1.0000 | 4.6052 | 4.6052 |
| 1900 | 101 | 105 | 107 | 4.6151 | 1.0000 | 4.6540 | 4.6728 |
| 1901 | 112 | 110 | 114 | 4.7185 | 1.0000 | 4.7005 | 4.7362 |
| 1902 | 122 | 118 | 122 | 4.8040 | 1.0000 | 4.7707 | 4.8040 |
| 1903 | 124 | 123 | 131 | 4.8203 | 1.0000 | 4.8122 | 4.8752 |
| 1904 | 122 | 116 | 138 | 4.8040 | 1.0000 | 4.7536 | 4.9273 |
| 1905 | 143 | 125 | 149 | 4.9628 | 1.0000 | 4.8283 | 5.0039 |
| 1906 | 152 | 133 | 163 | 5.0239 | 1.0000 | 4.8903 | 5.0938 |
| 1907 | 151 | 138 | 176 | 5.0173 | 1.0000 | 4.9273 | 5.1705 |
| 1908 | 126 | 121 | 185 | 4.8363 | 1.0000 | 4.7958 | 5.2204 |
| 1909 | 155 | 140 | 198 | 5.0434 | 1.0000 | 4.9416 | 5.2883 |
| 1910 | 159 | 144 | 208 | 5.0689 | 1.0000 | 4.9698 | 5.3375 |
| 1911 | 153 | 145 | 216 | 5.0304 | 1.0000 | 4.9767 | 5.3753 |
| 1912 | 177 | 152 | 226 | 5.1761 | 1.0000 | 5.0239 | 5.4205 |
| 1913 | 184 | 154 | 236 | 5.2149 | 1.0000 | 5.0370 | 5.4638 |
| 1914 | 169 | 149 | 244 | 5.1299 | 1.0000 | 5.0039 | 5.4972 |
| 1915 | 189 | 154 | 266 | 5.2417 | 1.0000 | 5.0370 | 5.5835 |
| 1916 | 225 | 182 | 298 | 5.4161 | 1.0000 | 5.2040 | 5.6971 |
| 1917 | 227 | 196 | 335 | 5.4250 | 1.0000 | 5.2781 | 5.8141 |
| 1918 | 223 | 200 | 366 | 5.4072 | 1.0000 | 5.2983 | 5.9026 |
| 1919 | 218 | 193 | 387 | 5.3845 | 1.0000 | 5.2627 | 5.9584 |
| 1920 | 231 | 193 | 407 | 5.4424 | 1.0000 | 5.2627 | 6.0088 |
| 1921 | 179 | 147 | 417 | 5.1874 | 1.0000 | 4.9904 | 6.0331 |
| 1922 | 240 | 161 | 431 | 5.4806 | 1.0000 | 5.0814 | 6.0661 |

**Source** (up to the 4th column): Cobb, Charles W. and Douglas, Paul H. "*A Theory of Production*", The American Economic Review: Papers and Proceedings of the Fortieth Annual Meeting of the American Economic Association, Vol. 18, No. 1, (Mar. 1928), pp.139-165. Reproduced with permission of the American Economic Review.

**TABLE 13.5-10** OLS parameter estimators.

| $\beta_{\text{Estimated}} = (X^T X)^{-1} X^T Y$ | | |
|------|------|------|
| $\beta_0 = \ln(A)$ | $\beta_1$ | $\beta_2$ |
| -0.1773 | 0.8073 | 0.2331 |
| 6,800 | -2,147 | 720 |
| -10,675 | 3,773 | -1,503 |
| 3,875 | -1,626 | 783 |

| COBB-DOUGLAS PRODUCTION FUNCTION PARAMETERS | | |
|------|------|------|
| A | $\alpha$ | $\beta$ |
| 0.837520 | 0.807278 | 0.233053 |

The log-linear estimated regression would be then as follows:

$$\widehat{\log}(Y_t) = -0.1773 + 0.8073 \cdot \log(L_t) + 0.2330 \cdot \log(K_t)$$

and consequently, the mathematical original nonlinear form would be:

$$Y = 0.8375\left(L^{0.8073}\,K^{0.2330}\right)$$

According to the regression, ANOVA output at 5% level of significance we reject both:

$$H_0:\ \beta_1 = 0$$

and

$$H_0:\ \beta_2 = 0$$

while we do not reject

$$H_0:\ \beta_0 = 0.$$

The confidence intervals for each parameter in Table 13.5-11 (*upper 95%* and *lower 95%*) are found using the following critical values of *t*-student distribution (for a two-tailed test at 0.05 significance: see Table 13.5-12):

$$t_c = T.INV(0.025; 21) = 2.0796$$

TABLE 13.5-11   Regression stats and ANOVA summary output.

| REGRESSION SUMMARY OUTPUT |
| --- |

| Regression Statistics | |
| --- | --- |
| Multiple R | 0.978480817 |
| R Square | 0.957424709 |
| Adjusted R Square | 0.953369919 |
| Standard Error | 0.058138438 |
| Observations | 24 |

ANOVA

| | df | SS | MS | F | Significance F |
| --- | --- | --- | --- | --- | --- |
| Regression | 2 | 1.596221004 | 0.798110502 | 236.121919 | 4.0379E-15 |
| Residual | 21 | 0.070981638 | 0.003380078 | | |
| Total | 23 | 1.667202641 | | | |

| | Coefficients | Standard Error | t Stat | P-value | Lower 95% | Upper 95% | Lower 95.0% | Upper 95.0% |
| --- | --- | --- | --- | --- | --- | --- | --- | --- |
| Intercept | -0.177309685 | 0.434293047 | -0.408271986 | 0.687206963 | -1.080471517 | 0.725852148 | -1.080471517 | 0.725852148 |
| ln L | 0.807278222 | 0.145076163 | 5.564513189 | 1.60135E-05 | 0.505575825 | 1.108980618 | 0.505575825 | 1.108980618 |
| ln K | 0.233053476 | 0.063529743 | 3.668415217 | 0.001431523 | 0.100936143 | 0.365170809 | 0.100936143 | 0.365170809 |

**TABLE 13.5-12** Confidence Interval at 95% Probability (5% of significance).

|  | $t_c$ | Confidence Interval | |
|---|---|---|---|
| Intercept | -2.079614 | -1.080471517 | 0.725852148 |
| ln L | -2.079614 | 0.505575825 | 1.108980618 |
| ln K | -2.079614 | 0.100936143 | 0.365170809 |

In the multiple regression, using the $F$-test, we can instead test simultaneously the hypothesis that all the slope coefficients are jointly equal to zero:

$$H_0: \beta_1 = \beta_2 = 0.$$

The $F$ statistic is calculated as:

$$F_{K, \, [T-(K+1)]} = \frac{\dfrac{RSS}{K}}{\dfrac{SSE}{[T-(K+1)]}}$$

with $K$ = number of slope parameters and $T$ = number of observations.
    In this case, the calculated $F$ is

$$F_{2, \, [24-(3)]} = \frac{\dfrac{1.5962}{2}}{\dfrac{0.07098}{21}} = 236.12$$

and the critical value $F_c$ is to be found using the following right-tailed inverse distribution of the $F$-probability (in this case a **one-tailed test** is used):

$$= F.INV.RT(0.05; 2; 21) = 3.4668.$$

Since $F_{2, \, [24-(3)]} = 236.12 > F_c = 3.47$, we reject at the 0.05 significance the null hypothesis that both slope coefficients are equal to zero. This can be also seen immediately used the *Significance F* in Table 13.5-11, which is less than our specified level of significance (0.05).
    The *Significance F* in Table 13.5-11 reports a *P-value* of $4.0379E-15 = 4.0379 \times 10^{-15}$ which represents the smallest level of significance at which the null hypothesis can be rejected, which is less than the level of significance 0.05 and therefore the null hypothesis is rejected. The *P-value* can be found manually in Excel using the following $F$ distribution probability:

$$= F.DIST.RT(236.12; 2; 21) = 4.0379E - 15$$

## Exercises

1. Table 1 gives data on GNP and four definitions of the money stock for the United States for 1970–83.

TABLE 1

| Year | GNP ($ billion) | M1 | M2 | M3 | L |
|------|-----------------|-------|---------|----------|----------|
| 1970 | 992.7 | 216.6 | 628.2 | 677.5 | 816.3 |
| 1971 | 1,077.60 | 230.8 | 712.8 | 776.2 | 903.1 |
| 1972 | 1,185.90 | 252 | 805.2 | 886 | 1,023.00 |
| 1973 | 1,326.40 | 265.9 | 861 | 985 | 1,141.70 |
| 1974 | 1,434.20 | 277.6 | 908.5 | 1,070.50 | 1,249.30 |
| 1975 | 1,549.20 | 291.2 | 1,023.30 | 1,174.20 | 1,367.90 |
| 1976 | 1,718.00 | 310.4 | 1,163.60 | 1,311.90 | 1,516.60 |
| 1977 | 1,918.30 | 335.4 | 1,286.70 | 1,472.90 | 1,704.70 |
| 1978 | 2,163.90 | 363.1 | 1,389.10 | 1,647.10 | 1,910.60 |
| 1979 | 2,417.80 | 389.1 | 1,498.50 | 1,804.80 | 2,117.10 |
| 1980 | 2,631.70 | 414.9 | 1,632.60 | 1,990.00 | 2,326.20 |
| 1981 | 2,957.80 | 441.9 | 1,796.60 | 2,238.20 | 2,599.80 |
| 1982 | 3,069.30 | 480.5 | 1,965.40 | 2,462.50 | 2,870.80 |
| 1983 | 3,304.80 | 525.4 | 2,196.30 | 2,710.40 | 3,183.10 |

**Source**: FRASER, Economic Report of the President, 1985, GNP data from Table B-1, p. 232; money stock data from Table B-61, p. 303.

 

 

a. Regress GNP versus each definition of money. Which definition of money seems to be closely related to nominal GNP?

b. Run now a multiple regression of GNP versus all the money data supplies.

c. Calculate in Excel the estimator $\hat{\beta} = (X^T X)^{-1} X^T Y$ for the multiple regression you have run under point b.

d. Obtain the ANOVA tables for each regression you have run.

**2.** Table 2 gathers the data for $Y = demand\ of\ roses$ in a town and the following independent variables.

$X_2 = quantity\ of\ roses\ sold$

$X_3 = average\ wholesale\ price\ of\ carnations$

$X_4 = average\ weekly\ family\ disposable\ income\ in\ town$

$X_5 = the\ trend\ variable\ taking\ values\ of\ 1,\ 2,\ and\ so\ on,\ for\ the\ period\ 1971{-}III\ to\ 1975{-}II$

    **a.** Run multiple linear regression and calculate the $\widehat{\beta} = (X^TX)^{-1}X^TY$.
    **b.** Run multiple log-linear regression and calculate the $\widehat{\beta} = (X^TX)^{-1}X^TY$.
    **c.** Obtain the ANOVA tables and compare the $F$ test for the two regressions and draw conclusions about the two regressions.

## TABLE 2

| Year and Quarter | Y | X2 | X3 | X4 | X5 |
|---|---|---|---|---|---|
| 1971 III | 11,484 | 2.26 | 3.49 | 158.11 | 1 |
| IV | 9,348 | 2.54 | 2.85 | 173.36 | 2 |
| 1972 I | 8,429 | 3.07 | 4.06 | 165.26 | 3 |
| II | 10,079 | 2.91 | 3.64 | 172.92 | 4 |
| III | 9,240 | 2.73 | 3.21 | 178.46 | 5 |
| IV | 8,862 | 2.77 | 3.66 | 198.62 | 6 |
| 1973 I | 6,216 | 3.59 | 3.76 | 186.28 | 7 |
| II | 8,253 | 3.23 | 3.49 | 188.98 | 8 |
| III | 8,038 | 2.6 | 3.13 | 180.49 | 9 |
| IV | 7,476 | 2.89 | 3.2 | 183.33 | 10 |
| 1974 I | 5,911 | 3.77 | 3.65 | 181.87 | 11 |
| II | 7,950 | 3.64 | 3.6 | 185.00 | 12 |
| III | 6,134 | 2.82 | 2.94 | 184.00 | 13 |
| IV | 5,868 | 2.96 | 3.12 | 188.20 | 14 |
| 1975 I | 3,160 | 4.24 | 3.58 | 175.67 | 15 |
| II | 5,872 | 3.69 | 3.53 | 188.00 | 16 |

*Source*: Damodar N. Guajarati, *Basic Econometrics*, Ch. 7 (Table 7.6, p. 236), 4th Edition, Mc-Graw Hill, 2004.

**3.** Table 3 puts together the excess (over a risk-free rate) monthly returns of a mutual fund versus its benchmark.

**TABLE 3**

| Number of Observations | Excess Return of the Fund (EF) | Excess Returns of the Benchmark (EB) | $EB^2$ |
|:---:|:---:|:---:|:---:|
| 1 | 0.0095 | -0.0357 | 0.0013 |
| 2 | 0.0419 | 0.0654 | 0.0043 |
| 3 | 0.1207 | 0.0819 | 0.0067 |
| 4 | 0.0169 | 0.0419 | 0.0018 |
| 5 | 0.0750 | 0.0247 | 0.0006 |
| 6 | -0.0125 | -0.0177 | 0.0003 |
| 7 | 0.0331 | 0.0170 | 0.0003 |
| 8 | 0.0609 | 0.0461 | 0.0021 |
| 9 | -0.0222 | -0.0333 | 0.0011 |
| 10 | 0.0475 | 0.0366 | 0.0013 |
| 11 | -0.0231 | -0.0417 | 0.0017 |
| 12 | 0.0210 | 0.0329 | 0.0011 |
| 13 | -0.0346 | -0.0156 | 0.0002 |
| 14 | 0.0406 | 0.0527 | 0.0028 |
| 15 | 0.1217 | 0.0790 | 0.0062 |
| 16 | 0.1691 | 0.1386 | 0.0192 |
| 69 | -0.0132 | -0.0068 | 0.0000 |

According to the model of Treynor–Mazuy,[1] we want to run the following regression:

$$EF = \alpha + \beta EB + \gamma EB^2$$

to assess whether the fund shows a market timing *ability* or not.

Remark: this regression is called *second-degree polynomial regression* as the only explanatory variable on the right-hand side appears with various powers (here up to 2), thus making the regression a multiple regression model. Since the second-degree polynomial (or the k*th* degree polynomial) is linear in the parameters, these can be estimated by the usual OLS methodology.

Essentially, there will be market timing ability when the fund is able to anticipate major turns in the stock market (i.e., the benchmark). This is so when the characteristic line of the fund versus its benchmark is not perfectly straight but shows a *curvature* upward. Therefore, the $\gamma$ factor in our regression is the coefficient that we want to study statistically (whether this is statistically significant or not).

---

[1]See Jack. K. Treynor and Kay K. Mazuy, "*Can Mutual Funds Outguess the Market?*," Harvard Business Review, July–August 1966.

**a.** Run the multiple regression (polynomial in two independent variables) and draw conclusions about the market timing of the mutual fund. Run also a standard univariate regression.

**b.** Obtain the ANOVA tables.

**c.** Build a frequency chart and a density chart for the returns of the fund.

4. A company shows the following historical sales data (Table 4):

   **a.** Run the linear regression model and obtain the ANOVA table.

   **b.** Make a prediction of the quantity sold for year 2019 and build the prediction interval at 95%.

   **c.** Use the built-in Excel Forecast Sheet to make a sale prediction for 2019.

   **d.** Plot the results.

TABLE 4

| Year | n | Quantities Sold |
|------|----|----------------|
| 2010 | -4 | 99,600 |
| 2011 | -3 | 99,300 |
| 2012 | -2 | 95,500 |
| 2013 | -1 | 91,500 |
| 2014 | 0 | 88,600 |
| 2015 | 1 | 86,400 |
| 2016 | 2 | 83,600 |
| 2017 | 3 | 78,200 |
| 2018 | 4 | 75,800 |

5. The parent company revenues and the branch revenues of a company, over 3 years and by quarter, are compared in Table 5.

   **a.** Run a linear regression of the branch revenues versus the parent company revenues (the independent variable) and make an estimate for the budget for Q1 and Q2 of Year 4.

   **b.** Obtain the ANOVA table and plot the regression.

6. Table 6 shows for a group of companies the relation between their profits and some explanatory variables.

TABLE 5

| Year | Quarters | Parent Revenues | Branch Revenues |
|------|----------|-----------------|-----------------|
| Y1 | 1 | 132 | 62 |
| | 2 | 150 | 63 |
| | 3 | 135 | 60 |
| | 4 | 156 | 66 |
| Y2 | 5 | 155 | 70 |
| | 6 | 145 | 67 |
| | 7 | 139 | 65 |
| | 8 | 152 | 68 |
| Y3 | 9 | 178 | 74 |
| | 10 | 160 | 65 |
| | 11 | 168 | 70 |
| | 12 | 180 | 72 |

TABLE 6

| Profit (Thousands) | Employees | Number of consecutive dividend | Inventory (Thousands) |
|--------------------|-----------|--------------------------------|-----------------------|
| 2,800 | 140 | 12 | 1,800 |
| 1,300 | 65 | 21 | 320 |
| 1,230 | 130 | 42 | 820 |
| 1,600 | 115 | 80 | 76 |
| 4,500 | 390 | 120 | 3,600 |
| 5,700 | 670 | 64 | 8,400 |
| 3,150 | 205 | 43 | 508 |
| 640 | 40 | 14 | 870 |
| 3,400 | 480 | 88 | 5,500 |
| 6,700 | 810 | 98 | 9,875 |
| 3,700 | 120 | 44 | 6,500 |
| 6,440 | 590 | 110 | 9,130 |
| 1,280 | 440 | 38 | 1,200 |
| 4,160 | 280 | 24 | 890 |
| 3,870 | 650 | 60 | 1,200 |
| 980 | 150 | 24 | 1,300 |

Mason, Lind, Marchal, *Statistical Techniques in Businsess and Economics* (Ch. 13, Exercise 19, p. 498), Irwin Mc-Graw Hill, 10th Ed. 1999.

**a.** Run a multiple regression with ANOVA table in all three independent variables, and using the global $F$-test, test simultaneously the hypothesis that all the slope coefficients are jointly equal to zero:

$$H_0: \beta_1 = \beta_2 = \beta_3 = 0.$$

**b.** Conduct a test of hypothesis for the individual regression coefficients and then, of these, drop the one which is not appearing statistically significant using the ANOVA table.

**c.** Run now a new regression and compare the ANOVA table versus the one of point a.

**d.** As we have seen the assumptions for regression also require that the residuals remain constant for all predicted values $\hat{Y}$ of the dependent variable. This condition is called homoscedasticity. A way to check for this is to plot and evaluate the behavior of residuals versus the predicted values. Do this for the second regression in two independent variables and draw conclusion about the homoscedasticity.

CHAPTER

# 14

# Essential Monte Carlo analysis

The Monte Carlo method is a simulation technique pioneered in the field of physics, within the Manhattan Project, during World War II, by Stanislaw Ulam, John Von Neuman, and Nicholas Metropolis.

The name Monte Carlo was coined by N. Metropolis because of the similarity of the statistical simulation to games of chances, whose outcomes are strongly determined by a randomizing device (roulette wheels, dice, cards, etc.) and because in the town of Monte Carlo (also called Monaco) the famous Casino gambling is located.

We will see in this chapter the essentials of the Monte Carlo simulation, beginning with some games of chance simulation as a short introduction to the generation of random numbers in Excel, together with the basics of the Bernoulli processes; then, we will see some Monte Carlo business and financial modeling; finally, we will see how the Monte Carlo method can be used in the numerical integration.

## 14.1 The Monte Carlo method and the generation of random numbers

In essence, the algorithm of Monte Carlo (MC) is based on randomly drawing the hypothetical observations assuming for them a specific probability distribution function, via the **inverse transformation method** (ITM).

From the theory of probability we know that for a given **probability space** $(\Omega, A, P[\cdot])$, where $\Omega$ is a sample space, A is a collection of events (each a subset of $\Omega$), and $P[\cdot]$ is a probability function with domain A, a random variable, denoted by $X$ or $X(\cdot)$, is a function with domain $\Omega$ and counter-domain the real line $\Re$.

Thinking in terms of a random experiment, $\Omega$ is the totality of outcomes of that random experiment, and the function, or random variable $X(\cdot)$, with domain $\Omega$, makes some real number correspond to each outcome of the experiment.

For example, consider the experiment of tossing a single coin. Let the random variable $X$ denote the number of heads. $\Omega = \{head, tail\}$, and $X(\omega) = 1$ if $\omega = head$, and $X(\omega) = 0$ if $\omega = tail$; so, the random variable $X$ associates a real number with each outcome of the experiment.

In the MC method, the objective is to implement a procedure through which we search the random variable $X \in \Re$ several times.

All this works as follows.

First the cumulative distribution function of a random variable $X$, denoted by $F_X(x)$ is defined to be that function with domain the real line $\Re$ and counter-domain the interval $[0, 1]$ which satisfies $F_X(x) = p[X \leq x]$ for every real number $x$.

Usually, you start from the observations to infer the probability (or frequency) distribution, while in the MC method the objective is revered: we assume a probability distribution function and starting from the counter-domain $[0, 1]$ we search then for the several hypothetical observations (the random variable numbers).

Essentially, we are interested in the random observations $x$ for the random variable $X$ with cumulative distribution function $F(x)$. As the cumulative distribution is defined as $F(x) = p[X \leq x]$, with $p$ between 0 and 1, we can obtain our random observation as follows:

$$x = F^{-1}(p).$$

We define an inverse of $F$ and we substitute the probability value in $F^{-1}$, which then returns the random observation $x$.

In general, the steps to randomly drawing the observations from $F(x)$ can be then summarized as follows.

i. Generate a uniform random number between 0 and 1, that is, the probability $p$ to be input in the inverse $F^{-1}$.

ii. Evaluate $F^{-1}(p)$ to obtain the random observation $x$.

iii. Run step (i) and (ii) several times (this is the actual experiment of simulation of observations and it is usually run up to 10,000 times). This will guarantee to approximate the true average $\mu(x)$ and standard deviation $\sigma(x)$ of the population.

The MC method is somehow based on the "a posteriori" or *frequency* definition of probability. What the MC method does is tossing a coin (the experiment) 100 and even 1000 of times, so that the relative frequency of $\omega = head$ will approximate the true probability $^{1}/_{2}$, noting here that although the relative frequencies of the different outcomes are predictable, the actual outcome of an individual throw is unpredictable.

We mention the fact that the ITM can be used for obtaining analytically $F^{-1}$ for many common probability distributions, while for the normal distribution the inverse cumulative distribution $F^{-1}$ cannot be computed analytically and in this case the *central limit theorem* is used. Luckily in Excel, we do not need to go into the details of such a calculation as the following function in Fig. 14.1-1 is available for the normal distribution.

For a discrete empirical random variable distribution, in the form of:

$$X = \begin{cases} x_1 & x_2 & \cdots & x_j & \cdots & x_n \\ p_1 & p_2 & \cdots & p_j & \cdots & p_n \end{cases}$$

the MC technique slightly changes, and this will be shown in Example 3 of the next paragraph Section 14.2, in the context of a warehouse optimal choice, with stochastic demand for a good.

The tool Data Analysis can also be used to generate the random numbers from specified probabilistic distributions available, as shown in Fig. 14.1-2. We will see this further on within the Bernoulli processes.

## EXAMPLE 1 (EXCEL RANDOM NUMBER GENERATION AND THE DIGITAL TOSSING OF A COIN)

Let us apply the MC method to the example we have mentioned before regarding the tossing of a coin.

We use the Excel function *Rand()* to generate the random number between 0 and 1. It is a digital **Bernoulli experiment** of tossing the coin several times, seeing what happens in terms of frequency between heads and tails.

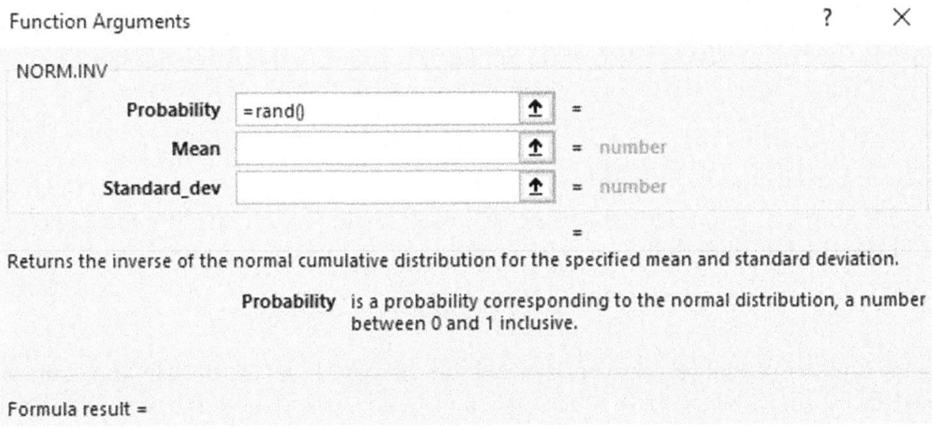

FIGURE 14.1-1  Excel normal cumulative inverse NORM.INV.

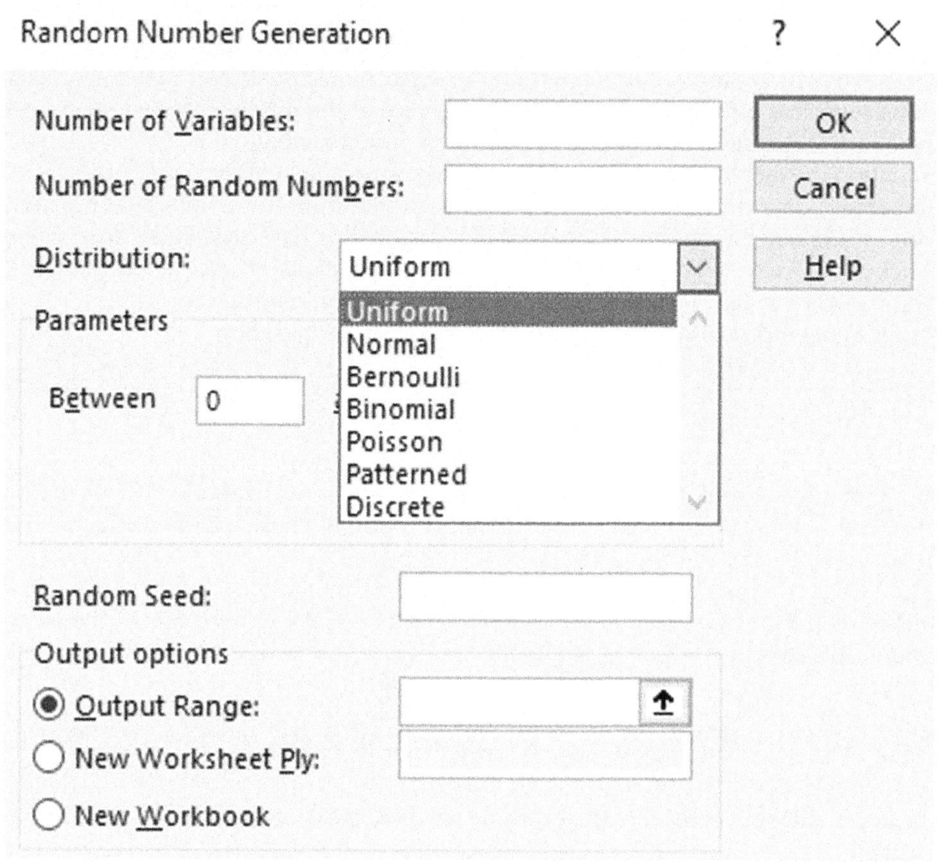

FIGURE 14.1-2   The random number generation from Data Analysis.

As we have said $\Omega = \{head,\ tail\}$, and $X(\omega) = 1$ if $\omega = head$, and $X(\omega) = 0$ if $\omega = tail$.

The following in Excel would need to be implemented. We generate a sequence of random observations from a uniform distribution between 0 and 1, as implemented in Fig. 14.1-3.

The result is in Table 14.1-1 from which it is apparent that $\text{Prob}(X = 1) \cong 0.50$.

## EXAMPLE 2 (TOSSING TWO DICE)

Consider now the experiment of tossing two dice. $\Omega$ can be described by the 36 points displayed in Fig. 14.1-4, such that:

$$\Omega = \{(i,\ j):\ i = 1, \cdots, 6\ and\ j = 1, \cdots, 6\}$$

Several random variables can be defined; for instance, let $X$ denote the sum of the upturned faces; so, $X(\omega) = (i + j)$ if $\omega = (i,\ j)$. Also, let $Y$ denote the absolute difference

| | A | B | C |
|---|---|---|---|
| 1 | Tossing Coin | | Prob(Head) |
| 2 | Experiment | | =COUNTIF(C5:C1422;"1")/COUNT(C5:C1422) |
| 3 | | | |
| 4 | Digital Toss (Simulation Runs) | Rand # | 1 Head; 0 Tail |
| 5 | 1 | =+RAND() | =IF(B5<0.5;0;1) |
| 6 | =A5+1 | =+RAND() | =IF(B6<0.5;0;1) |
| 7 | 2 | =+RAND() | =IF(B7<0.5;0;1) |
| 8 | =A7+1 | =+RAND() | =IF(B8<0.5;0;1) |
| 9 | =A8+1 | =+RAND() | =IF(B9<0.5;0;1) |
| 10 | =A9+1 | =+RAND() | =IF(B10<0.5;0;1) |
| 11 | =A10+1 | =+RAND() | =IF(B11<0.5;0;1) |
| 12 | =A11+1 | =+RAND() | =IF(B12<0.5;0;1) |
| 13 | =A12+1 | =+RAND() | =IF(B13<0.5;0;1) |
| 1416 | =A1415+1 | =+RAND() | =IF(B1416<0.5;0;1) |
| 1417 | =A1416+1 | =+RAND() | =IF(B1417<0.5;0;1) |
| 1418 | =A1417+1 | =+RAND() | =IF(B1418<0.5;0;1) |
| 1419 | =A1418+1 | =+RAND() | =IF(B1419<0.5;0;1) |
| 1420 | =A1419+1 | =+RAND() | =IF(B1420<0.5;0;1) |
| 1421 | =A1420+1 | =+RAND() | =IF(B1421<0.5;0;1) |
| 1422 | =A1421+1 | =+RAND() | =IF(B1422<0.5;0;1) |

**FIGURE 14.1-3**   Tossing a coin more than 1000 times.

**TABLE 14.1-1**   Coin toss experiment and Monte Carlo results.

| Tossing Coin | | Prob(Head) |
|---|---|---|
| Experiment | | 0.4803 |
| **Digital Toss (Simulation Runs)** | **Rand #** | **1 Head; 0 Tail** |
| 1 | 0.070 | 0 |
| 2 | 0.803 | 1 |
| 2 | 0.235 | 0 |
| 3 | 0.368 | 0 |
| 4 | 0.858 | 1 |
| 5 | 0.764 | 1 |
| 6 | 0.262 | 0 |
| 7 | 0.165 | 0 |
| 8 | 0.025 | 0 |
| 1411 | 0.996 | 1 |
| 1412 | 0.159 | 0 |
| 1413 | 0.084 | 0 |
| 1414 | 0.579 | 1 |
| 1415 | 0.013 | 0 |
| 1416 | 0.447 | 0 |
| 1417 | 0.594 | 1 |

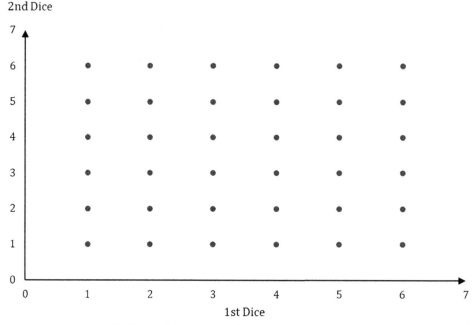

**FIGURE 14.1-4** The sample space $\Omega$ of tossing two dice.

between the upturned faces; then $Y(\omega) = |i - j|$ *if* $\omega = (i, j)$. We see that $X$ can take on the values 2, 3, ... , 12 and $Y$ can take on the values 0, 1, ... , 5.

We want to use now the MC method to estimate the following probabilities:

$$Prob(X = 7) \text{ and } Prob(Y = 2)$$

The first true probability is equal to $P(X = 7) = \frac{6}{36}$ that can be represented as in Fig. 14.1-5, while $P(Y = 2) = \frac{8}{36}$ is represented in Fig. 14.1-6.

In Fig. 14.1-7, we represent how the random numbers using the *RANDBETWEEN* formula have been generated and the two probabilities calculated in Excel.

Notice how a single experiment is made here of more than 2,000 dice tosses with the associated result in *Cell D2* and *Cell E2* with the *Countif* function. Then, two Data Table, have been built in *Column G* and *Column I*, to repeat the experiment over more than 2,000 times. The way this is done is just using, as a Column Input Cell of the Data Table formula, any empty cell in the worksheet.

Table 14.1-2 shows instead the numerical results.

## EXAMPLE 3 (FRENCH ROULETTE)

The French Roulette is a casino game where the wheel (i.e., the roulette) is numbered from single zero to 36 and therefore we have 37 colored numbers, where the zero is normally colored in green and the others either in red or black. In the game, players can choose to wager on either a single number, various groupings of numbers, the colors red or black,

2nd Dice

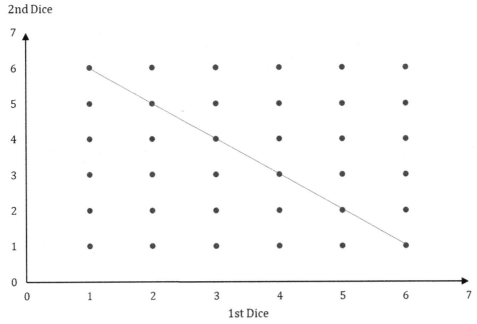

**FIGURE 14.1-5**   On the diagonal $N(X = 7) = 6$ and $\text{Prob}(X = 7) = 6/36$.

2nd Dice

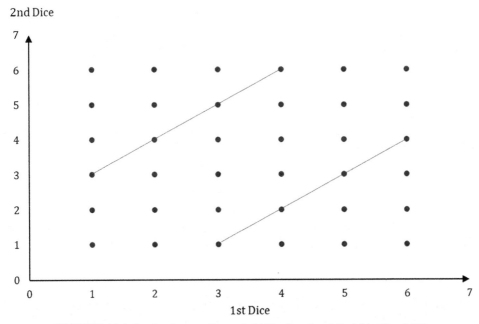

**FIGURE 14.1-6**   On the two diagonals $N(Y = 2) = 8$ and $\text{Prob}(Y = 2) = 8/36$.

IV. Special topics

| | A | B | C | D | E | F | G | H | I |
|---|---|---|---|---|---|---|---|---|---|
| 1 | Dice Dots | | | p[(i+j) = 7] | p[Abs(i-j) = 2] | | | | |
| 2 | From | to | One Experiment with over 2,000 tosses | =COUNTIF(D7:D2069;"7")/COUNT(D7:D2069) | =COUNTIF(E7:E2069;"2")/COUNT(E7:E2069) | | | | |
| 3 | 1 | 6 | True Probability | =6/36 | =8/36 | | | | |
| 4 | | | Monte Carlo Probability over 2,000 Experiments | =AVERAGE(G7:G2069) | =AVERAGE(I7:I2069) | | | | |
| 5 | | | | | | | | | |
| 6 | Digital Toss (Simulation Runs) | 1st dice | 2nd dice | X = i+j = 7 | Y = Abs(i-j) = 2 | Data Table | =D2 | Data Table | =E2 |
| 7 | 1 | =RANDBETWEEN(1;6) | =RANDBETWEEN(1;6) | =B7+C7 | =ABS(B7-C7) | 1 | =TABLE(;G4) | 1 | =TABLE(;L5) |
| 8 | =A7+1 | =RANDBETWEEN(1;6) | =RANDBETWEEN(1;6) | =B8+C8 | =ABS(B8-C8) | =F7+1 | =TABLE(;G4) | =H7+1 | =TABLE(;L5) |
| 9 | =A8+1 | =RANDBETWEEN(1;6) | =RANDBETWEEN(1;6) | =B9+C9 | =ABS(B9-C9) | =F8+1 | =TABLE(;G4) | =H8+1 | =TABLE(;L5) |
| 10 | =A9+1 | =RANDBETWEEN(1;6) | =RANDBETWEEN(1;6) | =B10+C10 | =ABS(B10-C10) | =F9+1 | =TABLE(;G4) | =H9+1 | =TABLE(;L5) |
| 11 | =A10+1 | =RANDBETWEEN(1;6) | =RANDBETWEEN(1;6) | =B11+C11 | =ABS(B11-C11) | =F10+1 | =TABLE(;G4) | =H10+1 | =TABLE(;L5) |
| 12 | =A11+1 | =RANDBETWEEN(1;6) | =RANDBETWEEN(1;6) | =B12+C12 | =ABS(B12-C12) | =F11+1 | =TABLE(;G4) | =H11+1 | =TABLE(;L5) |
| 13 | =A12+1 | =RANDBETWEEN(1;6) | =RANDBETWEEN(1;6) | =B13+C13 | =ABS(B13-C13) | =F12+1 | =TABLE(;G4) | =H12+1 | =TABLE(;L5) |
| 14 | =A13+1 | =RANDBETWEEN(1;6) | =RANDBETWEEN(1;6) | =B14+C14 | =ABS(B14-C14) | =F13+1 | =TABLE(;G4) | =H13+1 | =TABLE(;L5) |
| 15 | =A14+1 | =RANDBETWEEN(1;6) | =RANDBETWEEN(1;6) | =B15+C15 | =ABS(B15-C15) | =F14+1 | =TABLE(;G4) | =H14+1 | =TABLE(;L5) |
| 16 | =A15+1 | =RANDBETWEEN(1;6) | =RANDBETWEEN(1;6) | =B16+C16 | =ABS(B16-C16) | =F15+1 | =TABLE(;G4) | =H15+1 | =TABLE(;L5) |
| 17 | =A16+1 | =RANDBETWEEN(1;6) | =RANDBETWEEN(1;6) | =B17+C17 | =ABS(B17-C17) | =F16+1 | =TABLE(;G4) | =H16+1 | =TABLE(;L5) |
| 18 | =A17+1 | =RANDBETWEEN(1;6) | =RANDBETWEEN(1;6) | =B18+C18 | =ABS(B18-C18) | =F17+1 | =TABLE(;G4) | =H17+1 | =TABLE(;L5) |
| 19 | =A18+1 | =RANDBETWEEN(1;6) | =RANDBETWEEN(1;6) | =B19+C19 | =ABS(B19-C19) | =F18+1 | =TABLE(;G4) | =H18+1 | =TABLE(;L5) |
| 2069 | =A2068+1 | =RANDBETWEEN(1;6) | =RANDBETWEEN(1;6) | =B2069+C2069 | =ABS(B2069-C2069) | =F2068+1 | =TABLE(;G4) | =H2068+1 | =TABLE(;L5) |

**FIGURE 14.1-7**   Tossing two dice more than 2000 times with Monte Carlo.

**TABLE 14.1-2**   Dice toss experiment and Monte Carlo results.

| Dice Dots | | | p[(i+j) = 7] | p[Abs(i-j) = 2] |
|---|---|---|---|---|
| From | to | | | |
| 1 | 6 | One Experiment with over 2,000 tosses | 16.19% | 23.41% |
| | | True Probability | 16.67% | 22.22% |
| | | Monte Carlo Probability over 2,000 Experiments | 16.68% | 22.23% |

| Digital Toss (Simulation Runs) | 1st dice | 2nd dice | X = i+j = 7 | Y = Abs(i-j) = 2 | Data Table 0.1619 | | Data Table 0.2341 | |
|---|---|---|---|---|---|---|---|---|
| 1 | 1 | 4 | 6 | 3 | 1 | 0.1561 | 1 | 0.214 |
| 2 | 2 | 1 | 4 | 1 | 2 | 0.1643 | 2 | 0.237 |
| 3 | 4 | 1 | 8 | 3 | 3 | 0.1566 | 3 | 0.224 |
| 4 | 1 | 5 | 6 | 1 | 4 | 0.1653 | 4 | 0.230 |
| 5 | 6 | 5 | 8 | 4 | 5 | 0.1634 | 5 | 0.230 |
| 6 | 3 | 6 | 8 | 4 | 6 | 0.1701 | 6 | 0.222 |
| 7 | 5 | 5 | 5 | 0 | 7 | 0.1609 | 7 | 0.202 |
| 8 | 4 | 6 | 4 | 2 | 8 | 0.1546 | 8 | 0.234 |
| 9 | 4 | 1 | 9 | 1 | 9 | 0.1794 | 9 | 0.219 |
| 10 | 4 | 4 | 8 | 4 | 10 | 0.1701 | 10 | 0.229 |
| 11 | 1 | 2 | 3 | 0 | 11 | 0.1658 | 11 | 0.228 |
| 12 | 1 | 3 | 7 | 1 | 12 | 0.1653 | 12 | 0.215 |
| 13 | 6 | 2 | 7 | 5 | 13 | 0.1609 | 13 | 0.222 |
| 2,063 | 5 | 3 | 2 | 0 | 2,063 | 0.1571 | 2,063 | 0.233 |

whether the number is odd or even, or if the numbers are high (19-36) or low (1-18). The game starts when the *croupier* spins the Roulette in one direction, then spins a ball in the opposite direction.

Let us suppose we wager on a single number. We mathematically have a 1 out of 37 chance at winning a straight bet on a single number, which is 2.70%.

Using the same MC technique as in Example 2, we show the result of *p(single number = 20)* (Table 14.1-3).

## Bernoulli processes

As we have mentioned, the random numbers (from a specified distribution) can be generated via the **Excel Data Analysis ToolPak**.

**TABLE 14.1-3** French Roulette and Monte Carlo results.

| French Roulette | | | | p(# = 20) |
|---|---|---|---|---|
| From | to | One Experiment with over 2,000 tosses | | 2.76% |
| 0 | 36 | True Probability | | 2.70% |
| | | Monte Carlo Probability over 2,000 Experiments | | 2.70% |
| Digital Roulette Spinning (Simulation Runs) | Roulette # | Data Table | | 0.028 |
| 1 | 28 | 1 | | 0.026 |
| 2 | 29 | 2 | | 0.024 |
| 3 | 0 | 3 | | 0.035 |
| 4 | 1 | 4 | | 0.031 |
| 5 | 8 | 5 | | 0.023 |
| 6 | 26 | 6 | | 0.025 |
| 7 | 36 | 7 | | 0.028 |
| 8 | 33 | 8 | | 0.030 |
| 9 | 5 | 9 | | 0.024 |
| 10 | 15 | 10 | | 0.027 |
| 11 | 28 | 11 | | 0.026 |
| 12 | 35 | 12 | | 0.028 |
| 13 | 4 | 13 | | 0.026 |
| 2,063 | 16 | 2,063 | | 0.026 |

We will show here how we can use that in the interesting case of the Bernoulli random (or Stochastic) processes, with number of successes distributed according to a binomial distribution.

A Bernoulli process is a sequence of **independent Bernoulli trials**.

Consider a random experiment consisting of these $n$ repeated independent Bernoulli trials when $p$ is the probability of success $s$ at each individual trial. The term repeated is used to indicate that the probability of $s$ remains the same from trial to trial, which means that the process has the property of *memorylessness*. In other words, the trials are *independent* and *identically distributed* (a.k.a. as *iid*) and the probability of any specified outcome, say $\{(f, f, s, f, s, s,..., f, f)\}$ is given by the multiplication $qqpqpp...qq$.

We want to get the probability of obtaining exactly $x$ successes in the $n$ trials, and this probability is given by a binomial distribution (as a function of $x$):

$$P = [X = x] = P[Exactly\ x\ successes\ and\ (n - x)\ failures\ in\ n\ trials]$$

$$= \binom{n}{x} p^x q^{n-x} \quad for\ x = 0, 1, \cdots, n$$

since each outcome of the experiment that has exactly $x$ successes has probability $p^x q^{n-x}$ and there are $\binom{n}{x}$ possible outcomes.

Using the Excel Data Analysis ToolPak, we can obtain this binomial density distribution, within an experiment of independent Bernoulli trials.

In Figs. 14.1-8 and 14.1-9, we have replicated two densities with $P = .50$ and $P = .25$ with $n = 10$ Bernoulli trials.

| | A | B | C | D | E | F | G |
|---|---|---|---|---|---|---|---|
| 1 | x (p = 0.50) | x | Density Binomial p = 0.50 | | x (p = 0.25) | x | Density Binomial p = 0.25 |
| 2 | 3 | 0 | 0.0009 | | 3 | 0 | 0.0592 |
| 3 | 7 | 1 | 0.0108 | | 4 | 1 | 0.1816 |
| 4 | 8 | 2 | 0.0445 | | 0 | 2 | 0.2820 |
| 5 | 6 | 3 | 0.1203 | | 2 | 3 | 0.2516 |
| 6 | 7 | 4 | 0.2113 | | 3 | 4 | 0.1482 |
| 7 | 7 | 5 | 0.2368 | | 2 | 5 | 0.0582 |
| 8 | 6 | 6 | 0.1998 | | 4 | 6 | 0.0159 |
| 9 | 5 | 7 | 0.1201 | | 2 | 7 | 0.0029 |
| 10 | 4 | 8 | 0.0443 | | 1 | 8 | 0.0004 |
| 11 | 3 | 9 | 0.0105 | | 1 | 9 | 0.0000 |
| 12 | 2 | 10 | 0.0007 | | 3 | 10 | 0.0000 |
| 13 | 4 | | | | 1 | | |
| 14 | 5 | Tot Prob | 1.0000 | | 4 | Tot Prob | 1.0000 |
| 15 | 4 | | | | 0 | | |
| 16 | 2 | | | | 5 | | |
| 17 | 8 | | | | 3 | | |
| 9998 | 5 | | | | 4 | | |
| 9999 | 5 | | | | 4 | | |
| 10000 | 6 | | | | 3 | | |
| 10001 | 3 | | | | 2 | | |

FIGURE 14.1-8    Two binomial densities with 10 Bernoulli trials for each density.

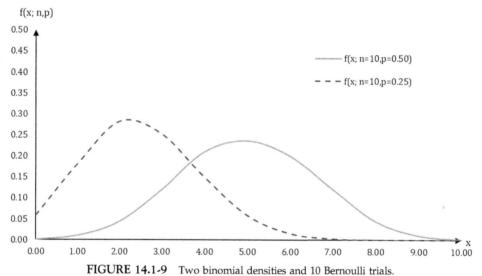

FIGURE 14.1-9    Two binomial densities and 10 Bernoulli trials.

This is done using the number generator tool in Data Analysis as shown in Figs. 14.10 and 14.1-11 where the probability parameter has been changed. 10,000 random occurrences of success are generated in *Column A* and then the density binomial is obtained with the *Countif* for each *x* out of 10,000.

The densities return the probability of having exactly *x* successes over the *n* trials.

The Bernoulli processes are suitable for several applications and some examples can be made.

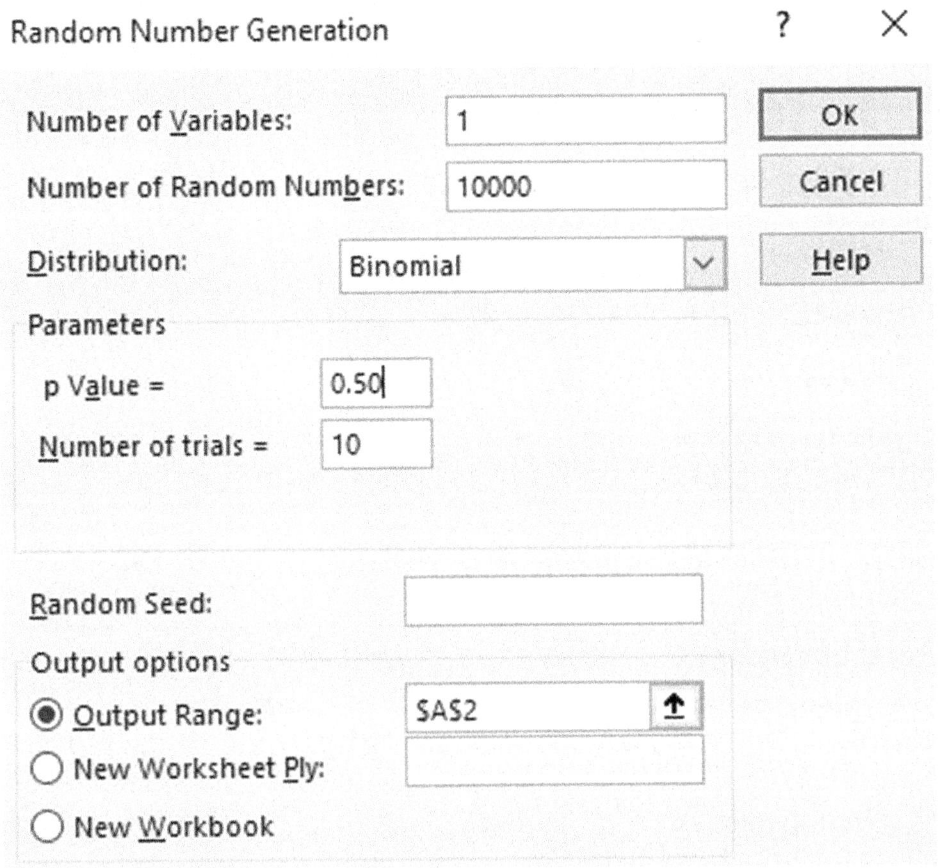

FIGURE 14.1-10  Bernoulli trials and binomial distribution $P = .50$.

For instance, Fig. 14.1-12 is the case of $n = 12$ Bernoulli trials of tossing a coin to get the probability of obtaining exactly $x = 8$ heads, considering $P = 1/2$.

Fig. 14.1-13 represents instead the case of modeling arrivals, with $n = 15$ Bernoulli trials, where we measure the probability of seeing, in an $n = 15$ min period, exactly $x = 2$ cars passing in a place in 2 separate minutes, respectively, considering that the probability of success is $P = 2/15$. Each minute we can have a success or a failure of seeing a car passing. These models lead to the Poisson processes, if we relax the assumption that the cars should pass in separate minutes.

## 14.2 The Monte Carlo method for business decisions

The MC applications for business and finance decisions are extremely wide. Practically in all the areas where we face uncertainty, we can apply the MC method.

Random Number Generation                    ?      ✕

| Number of Variables: | 1 | OK |
|---|---|---|
| Number of Random Numbers: | 10000 | Cancel |
| Distribution: | Binomial ⌄ | Help |

Parameters

p Value =        0.25|

Number of trials =    10

Random Seed:        [          ]

Output options

⦿ Output Range:      SES2      ⬆

◯ New Worksheet Ply:    [          ]

◯ New Workbook

FIGURE 14.1-11    Bernoulli trials and binomial distribution $P = .25$.

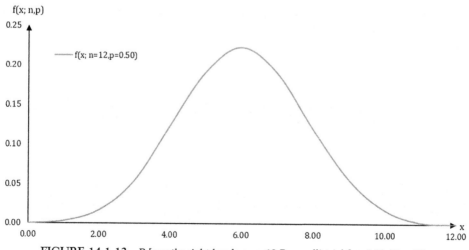

FIGURE 14.1-12    P [exactly eight heads over 12 Bernoulli trials] $\cong 0.12$ $(P = .50)$.

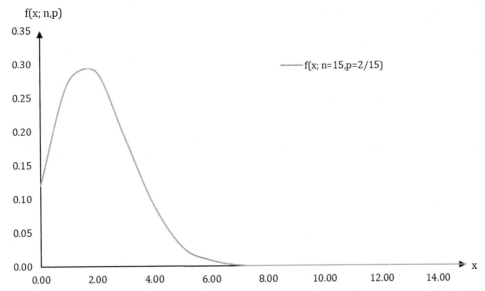

FIGURE 14.1-13   P [exactly two cars passing at the $i$th and $j$th minute within 15 min] $\cong 0.29$ ($P = 2/15$).

We will show three cases.

First, we will look at two cases in the field of corporate finance. The first corporate finance example will concern the risk assessment of a company ability to pay its interests. The second example is a typical case of capital budgeting valuation project, using the NPV (Net Present Value) and the IRR (Internal Rate of Return). In both the above cases we assume the continuous normal distribution.

The third case is where we have instead a discrete empirical distribution, and the MC method is needed for deciding which warehouse among three alternatives a wholesaler should decide to rent, considering a stochastic demand of a new type of timber that he will need to stock and sale. We have mentioned before that in this case we do not use the ITM to obtain the random observations, but an alternative approach.

## EXAMPLE 1 (RISK ASSESSMENT WITH A NORMAL DISTRIBUTION)

Let us consider the information gathered in Table 14.2-1 regarding the key data of the income statement of a company (this example and the input data in Table 14.2-1 come from the article "Expect the Unexpected: Risk Assessment Using Monte Carlo Simulations" by Douglas Ayres, James Schmutte, Jason Stanfield, The Journal of Accountancy, Nov. 2017, pp. 43–48, AICPA).

The first step is to identify the **stochastic variables** on which we want to apply the MC method. In this case, we decide to simulate the expected Sales and the expected Variable Costs. Then, on that basis we obtain the expected Ebit and the expected **Interest Coverage Ratio** (ICR), which are defined as the **output variables** of the model.

The problem the CFO faces is that of assessing the probability of having an ICR lower than a specific threshold, determined within the bank loan contract. In this case as a condition of

**TABLE 14.2-1**   Income statement key data.

|  | Stochastic Variable | Expected Value | Standard Deviation |
|---|---|---|---|
| Sales | 1 | 10,000,000 | 500,000 |
| Variable Costs % | 2 | 35.00% | 2.00% |
| Operating fixed costs |  | 5,000,000 |  |
| Interest Expenses |  | 500,000 |  |
| Expected EBIT |  | 1,500,000 |  |
| Expected Interest Coverage |  | 3.00 |  |

the loan, it is assumed the lender requires that the company always maintain an interest coverage ratio, defined as earnings before interest and taxes (Ebit) divided by the interest expenses, of at least 1.5. In general, when a company's ICR is lower than this level its ability to meet the interest expenses may be questionable. While the company is financially sound and expects to be profitable, its profits face two major sources of uncertainty. First, revenues fluctuate due to variations in product mix and sales volume. Second, the firm's costs present an element of uncertainty due to factors such as variations in the sales mix, efficiencies in operations, changes to input prices, etc.

What we do now is to simulate on the two stochastic variables, randomly drawing their observations from each probability distribution (in this case a normal distribution is assumed). To perform the random draw (as if we tossed a coin several times) we use the Excel function:

$$= NORM.INV(RAND(); Mean\ Value; Standard\ Deviation)$$

which returns the inverse of the normal cumulative distribution for the specified mean and standard deviation.

The *NORM.INV* function syntax has the following arguments (see also Fig. 14.1-1):

i. First argument. Probability required. A probability corresponding to the normal distribution. In this case, we will randomly generate from the codomain [0, 1] of the cumulative distribution.

ii. Second argument. Mean required. The arithmetic mean of the distribution will be taken from Table 14.2-1.

iii. Third argument. Standard deviation required. The standard deviation of the distribution will be taken from Table 14.2-1.

We generate now several Sales and Variable Costs observations from the inverse distribution, as in Fig. 14.2-1.

Notice how we have simulated once in *Cell* C19 for the Sales and in *Cell* D19 for the Variable Costs, via the *NORM.INV* and then repeated 1,000 times those simulations using the Data Table from *Cell* C23 for the Sales and D23 for the Variable Costs.

| | B | C | D | E | F | G |
|---|---|---|---|---|---|---|
| | | Stochastic Variable | Expected Value | Standard Deviation | | |
| 4 | | | | | | |
| 5 | Sales | 1 | 10000000 | 500000 | | |
| 6 | Variable Costs % | 2 | 0.35 | 0.02 | | |
| 7 | Operating fixed costs | | 5000000 | | | |
| 8 | Interest Expenses | | 500000 | | | |
| 9 | | | | | | |
| 10 | Expected EBIT | | =D5*(1-D6)-D7 | | | |
| 11 | Expected Interest Coverage | | =(D5*(1-D6)-D7)/D8 | | | |
| 12 | | | | | | |
| 18 | | | | | | |
| 19 | Simulation | =NORM.INV(RAND();$D$5;$E$5) | =NORM.INV(RAND();$D$6;$E$6)*C19 | 5000000 | =C19-D19-E19 | =F19/$D$8 |
| 20 | | | | | | |
| 21 | Simulations | Sales | Variable Costs | Fixed Costs | Ebit | ICR |
| 22 | 1 | =C19 | =D19 | 5000000 | =C22-D22-E22 | =F22/$D$8 |
| 23 | 2 | =TABLE(;C15) | =TABLE(;C15) | 5000000 | =C23-D23-E23 | =F23/$D$8 |
| 24 | 3 | =TABLE(;C15) | =TABLE(;C15) | 5000000 | =C24-D24-E24 | =F24/$D$8 |
| 27 | 6 | =TABLE(;C15) | =TABLE(;C15) | 5000000 | =C27-D27-E27 | =F27/$D$8 |
| 28 | 7 | =TABLE(;C15) | =TABLE(;C15) | 5000000 | =C28-D28-E28 | =F28/$D$8 |
| 29 | 8 | =TABLE(;C15) | =TABLE(;C15) | 5000000 | =C29-D29-E29 | =F29/$D$8 |
| 30 | 9 | =TABLE(;C15) | =TABLE(;C15) | 5000000 | =C30-D30-E30 | =F30/$D$8 |
| 1016 | 995 | =TABLE(;C15) | =TABLE(;C15) | 5000000 | =C1016-D1016-E1( | =F1016/$D$8 |
| 1017 | 996 | =TABLE(;C15) | =TABLE(;C15) | 5000000 | =C1017-D1017-E1( | =F1017/$D$8 |
| 1018 | 997 | =TABLE(;C15) | =TABLE(;C15) | 5000000 | =C1018-D1018-E1( | =F1018/$D$8 |
| 1019 | 998 | =TABLE(;C15) | =TABLE(;C15) | 5000000 | =C1019-D1019-E1( | =F1019/$D$8 |
| 1020 | 999 | =TABLE(;C15) | =TABLE(;C15) | 5000000 | =C1020-D1020-E1( | =F1020/$D$8 |
| 1021 | 1000 | =TABLE(;C15) | =TABLE(;C15) | 5000000 | =C1021-D1021-E1( | =F1021/$D$8 |

**FIGURE 14.2-1** Simulation runs on the stochastic variables Sales and Variable Costs.

The way this is done is to use an empty cell (in this case *Cell C*15) of the worksheet as Column Input Cell of the Data Table simulation. Once the Sales and Variable Costs have been randomly "tossed" or drawn, we estimate the **output variables**, i.e., the Ebit (the operating fixed costs include the depreciation costs as well) and the ICR, which is the ratio Ebit/Interest Expenses.

As we are interested in analyzing the ICR values and the probability of having the ICR lower than 1.5, in the results of the following Table 14.2-2, we have calculated the normal distribution of the ICR, using the Excel function *NORM.DIST* (density and cumulative), as well as the underlying data for the discrete frequency chart. This is done using the excel function *FREQUENCY*, entered as an array CSE formula, pressing *Ctrl + Shift + Enter*.

The discrete frequency chart, the normal density probability distribution, and the cumulative distribution are shown, respectively, from Figs. 14.2-2 to 14.2-4.

In the light of the MC simulation, assuming a normal distribution in Sales and Variable Costs with the specified means and standard deviation, the conclusion of the CFO is that the probability of having the ICR lower than 1.50, i.e., what the loan contract says, is approximately 2.20%, and this is a reassuring result for him.

This probability has been calculated considering the results of ICR on *Column G* using the *COUNTIF* function in Excel to count all interest coverage values of *Column G* that fall below the threshold of 1.5, comparing this total to the total number of observations (1000):

$$= \frac{COUNTIF(G22:G1021;" < 1.5")}{COUNT(G22:G1021)}.$$

As it is assumed that the stochastic variables move according to normal distributions, the charts are virtually identical to the underlying distribution.

**TABLE 14.2-2**   Example 1: Monte Carlo result together with the frequency data.

| | Stochastic Variable | Expected Value | Standard Deviation | | | | |
|---|---|---|---|---|---|---|---|
| Sales | 1 | 10,000,000 | 500,000 | | | | |
| Variable Costs % | 2 | 35.00% | 2.00% | | | | |
| Operating fixed costs | | 5,000,000 | | | | | |
| Interest Expenses | | 500,000 | | | | | |
| | | | | | | | |
| Expected EBIT | | 1,500,000 | | | | | |
| Expected Interest Coverage | | 3.00 | | | | | |
| | | | | | | | |
| **Results of Simulation** | | **Average** | **Standard Deviation** | **Min** | **Max** | **Range for Frequency Chart** | |
| Interest Coverage Ratio (ICR) | | 2.9743 | 0.73 | 0.6981 | 5.467 | 0.20 | |
| EBIT | | 1,487,172 | 362,676 | | | | |
| | | | | | | | |
| % Covenant Failure ICR < 1.50 | | 1.70% | | | | | |

| Simulation | 9,462,254 | 3,441,248 | 5,000,000 | 1,021,005 | 2.0420 | | | | |
|---|---|---|---|---|---|---|---|---|---|

| Simulations | Sales | Variable Costs | Fixed Costs | Ebit | ICR | ICR Norm Dist | ICR Range | Frequency | ICR Cumul. Dist |
|---|---|---|---|---|---|---|---|---|---|
| 1 | 9,462,254 | 3,441,248 | 5,000,000 | 1,021,005 | 2.0420 | 24.08% | 1.0000 | 3 | 0.32% |
| 2 | 10,174,662 | 4,273,594 | 5,000,000 | 901,068 | 1.8021 | 14.90% | 1.2000 | 4 | 0.72% |
| 3 | 10,943,290 | 3,907,774 | 5,000,000 | 2,035,516 | 4.0710 | 17.54% | 1.4000 | 3 | 1.50% |
| 4 | 10,018,837 | 3,395,539 | 5,000,000 | 1,623,298 | 3.2466 | 51.26% | 1.6000 | 15 | 2.91% |
| 5 | 10,764,083 | 3,424,020 | 5,000,000 | 2,340,063 | 4.6801 | 3.46% | 1.8000 | 23 | 5.27% |
| 995 | 10,155,987 | 3,689,369 | 5,000,000 | 1,466,618 | 2.9332 | 54.91% | 199.8000 | 0 | 100.00% |
| 996 | 10,458,430 | 4,044,352 | 5,000,000 | 1,414,079 | 2.8282 | 53.89% | 200.0000 | 0 | 100.00% |
| 997 | 9,966,705 | 3,654,660 | 5,000,000 | 1,312,045 | 2.6241 | 48.95% | 200.2000 | 0 | 100.00% |
| 998 | 10,010,189 | 3,543,933 | 5,000,000 | 1,466,256 | 2.9325 | 54.91% | 200.4000 | 0 | 100.00% |
| 999 | 10,211,405 | 3,516,925 | 5,000,000 | 1,694,480 | 3.3890 | 46.71% | 200.6000 | 0 | 100.00% |
| 1,000 | 9,851,133 | 3,403,526 | 5,000,000 | 1,447,607 | 2.8952 | 54.67% | 200.8000 | 0 | 100.00% |

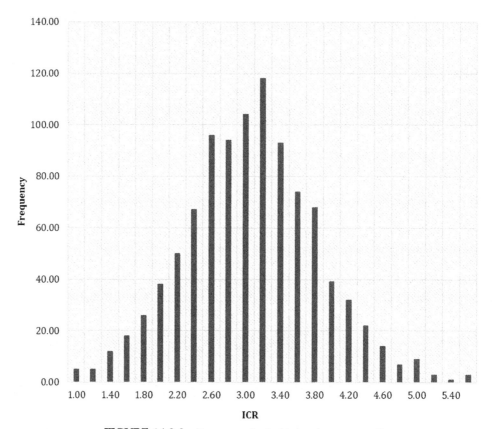

**FIGURE 14.2-2**   Frequency chart of interest coverage ratio.

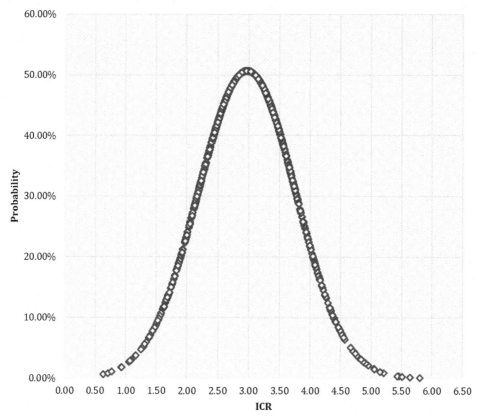

**FIGURE 14.2-3** Normal distribution of interest coverage ratio.

## EXAMPLE 2 (CAPITAL BUDGETING)

The Capital Budgeting is the process through which the companies optimally select their investment opportunities, based on some financial performance measures, such as the Net Present Value (NPV) or the Internal Rate of Return (IRR).

The NPV is mathematically formalized as follows (for simplicity, just one cash outlay is assumed):

$$NPV = \sum_{t=1}^{n} \frac{CF_t}{(1+r)^t} - CF_0$$

where

$$CF_t = Cash\ flow\ in\ period\ t$$

$$r = required\ rate\ of\ return;\ the\ Weighted\ Average\ Cost\ of\ Capital\ (Wacc)\ is\ considered$$

$$CF_0 = Cash\ Outlay\ at\ the\ beginning\ of\ the\ project.$$

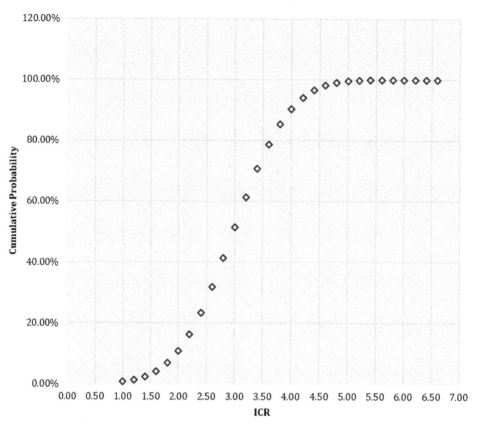

FIGURE 14.2-4  Cumulative distribution of interest coverage ratio.

*Ceteris paribus* the project with the highest (and positive) NPV should be normally selected among the other competing projects. Negative *NPV* projects should be discarded.

The *IRR* is instead the actual return (ex post, or expected based on the cash flows projection), of the project, which is found to satisfy the following equation:

$$\sum_{t=1}^{n} \frac{CF_t}{(1+IRR)^t} - CF_0 = 0$$

The IRR should be at least equal to the Weighted Average Cost of Capital (Wacc) required by the suppliers of capital of the project, and among various projects we select the one with the highest IRR (higher than the cost of capital). A potential supplier of capital will not invest in the project, unless its actual return (i.e., the *IRR*) meets or exceeds what the supplier could earn (the *Wacc*) elsewhere in a comparable risk investment. The *Wacc* is the required return that the investor demands for a comparable risk investment.

In case of mutually exclusive projects, with the same initial cash outlay, there may be instances in which the two criteria lead to a ranking conflict, due to the different cash flow patterns (i.e., for two projects A and B, based on NPV Project A is better, while based on IRR Project B is better). In this case, selecting the project using the NPV would be more appropriate, as it makes the more realistic assumption of the reinvestment of cash flows at the required Cost of Capital.

To begin with the capital budgeting process for each investment project, we have to model its cash flow pattern, which normally starts with a cash outlay, right at the beginning of the project. In this example, we use as the main criterion the NPV and we will just evaluate whether to undertake or not a single project.

Let us begin with the summary data in Table 14.2-3, where we have already identified the so-called stochastic variables, on which the expected cash flow pattern will depend. We have identified the following four stochastic variables:

**i.** Sales as of the end of period 1
**ii.** Sales growth over the investment horizon of 5 years
**iii.** Variable Costs as of the end of period 1
**iv.** Variable Costs growth over the investment horizon of 5 years

For each of the above stochastic variables we have specified its mean value and the standard deviation, calculated on a historical data set. We assume these variables follow a normal distribution.

Table 14.2-4 shows the free cash flows of the investment (i.e., Cash flows available to Equity and Bond Holders) and the **first step** is to calculate the NPV and IRR of the project assuming the Wacc of the project is 10% indicated in Table 14.2-3.

The NPV and IRR results are in Table 14.2-5.

The Excel formulas for *NPV* and *IRR* are, respectively, shown in Figs. 14.2-5 and 14.2-6. The *IRR* formula in Fig. 14.2-6 is for cash flows distributed evenly within the investment horizon, otherwise the *XIRR* should be used, for scheduled cash flows in specific dates, over the investment horizon. The Guess option is to suggest Excel the closest value to the true *IRR*, otherwise a rate of 10% is used by default.

**TABLE 14.2-3**　Summary data for the investment project (Worksheet 1).

|  | A | B | C | D | E | F | G |
|---|---|---|---|---|---|---|---|
| 1 |  | Stochastic Variable | Input | Mean | Standard Deviation | Distribution |  |
| 2 | Initial Outlay |  | -60,000 |  |  |  |  |
| 3 | Revenue t$_i$ | 1 | 60,000 | 59,500 | 700 | Normal |  |
| 4 | g | 2 | 3.00% | 2.700% | 0.800% | Normal |  |
| 5 | Var. Costs in t$_i$ | 3 | 32,500 | 32,000 | 800 | Normal |  |
| 6 | Variable Costs growth rate | 4 | 2.50% | 2.40% | 0.250% | Normal |  |
| 7 | Wacc |  | 10.00% |  |  |  |  |
| 8 | Fixed Costs |  | 4,000 |  |  |  |  |

**TABLE 14.2-4**   After tax cash flow projection (Worksheet 1).

| | A | B | C | D | E | F | G |
|---|---|---|---|---|---|---|---|
| | | | | | | | |
| 10 | | Years | | | | | |
| 11 | Item | 0 | 1 | 2 | 3 | 4 | 5 |
| 12 | Revenues | | 60,000 | 61,800 | 63,654 | 65,564 | 67,531 |
| 13 | Variable costs | | -32,500 | -33,313 | -34,145 | -34,999 | -35,874 |
| 14 | Fixed Costs | | -4,000 | -4,000 | -4,000 | -4,000 | -4,000 |
| 15 | EBITDA | | 23,500 | 24,488 | 25,509 | 26,565 | 27,657 |
| 16 | - Depreciation | | -9,000 | -9,000 | -9,000 | -9,000 | -9,000 |
| 17 | EBIT | | 14,500 | 15,488 | 16,509 | 17,565 | 18,657 |
| 18 | - Taxes (t = 40%) | | -5,800 | -6,195 | -6,603 | -7,026 | -7,463 |
| 19 | NOPAT | | 8,700 | 9,293 | 9,905 | 10,539 | 11,194 |
| 20 | + Depreciation | | 9,000 | 9,000 | 9,000 | 9,000 | 9,000 |
| 21 | - Change in Working Capital | | -3,000 | -1,500 | 0 | 1,700 | 2,800 |
| 22 | Operating Cash Flow | | 14,700 | 16,793 | 18,905 | 21,239 | 22,994 |
| 23 | - Capex | -60,000 | | | | | |
| 24 | Free Cash Flow | -60,000 | 14,700 | 16,793 | 18,905 | 21,239 | 22,994 |

**TABLE 14.2-5**   Net present value and internal rate of return (Worksheet 2).

| Year | 0 | 1 | 2 | 3 | 4 | 5 |
|---|---|---|---|---|---|---|
| Cash Flow | -60,000 | 14,700 | 16,793 | 18,905 | 21,239 | 22,994 |
| NPV | 10,229 | | | | | |
| Wacc | 10.00% | | | | | |
| IRR | 15.96% | | | | | |

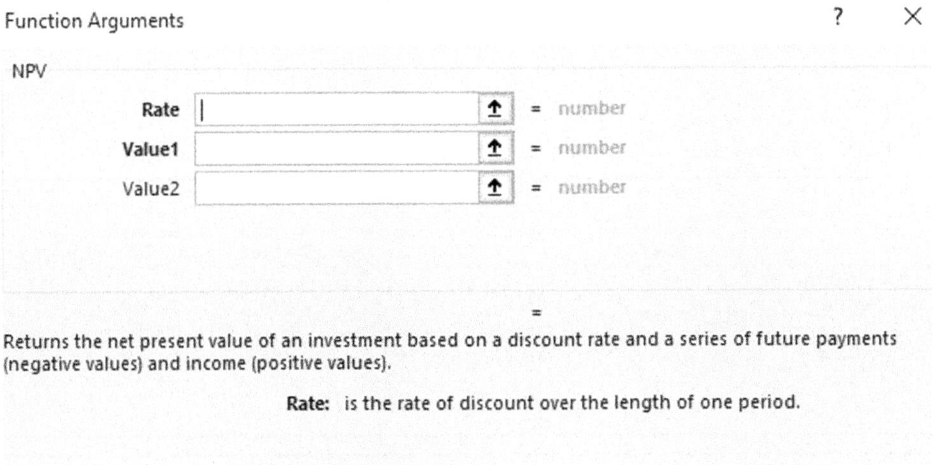

Function Arguments                                    ?    ✕

NPV

Rate    [                    ] ↑    =  number

**Value1**  [                    ] ↑    =  number

Value2   [                    ] ↑    =  number

=

Returns the net present value of an investment based on a discount rate and a series of future payments (negative values) and income (positive values).

Rate:  is the rate of discount over the length of one period.

**FIGURE 14.2-5**   Excel net present value formula.

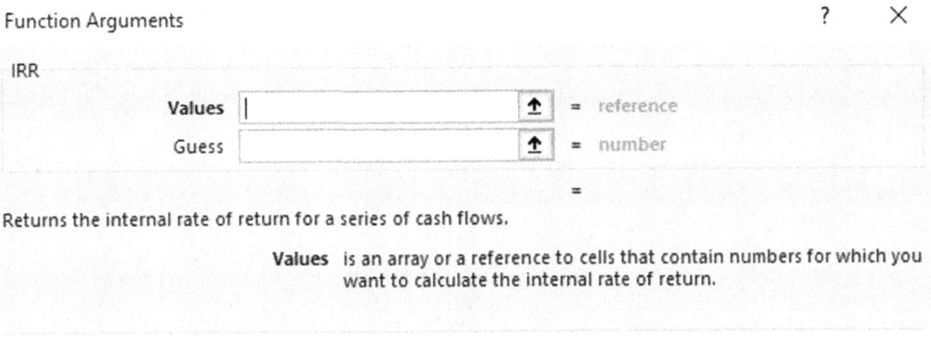

Function Arguments                                              ?    X

IRR

| | | |
|---|---|---|
| **Values** | \| | ↑ = reference |
| **Guess** | | ↑ = number |
| | | = |

Returns the internal rate of return for a series of cash flows.

**Values** is an array or a reference to cells that contain numbers for which you want to calculate the internal rate of return.

**FIGURE 14.2-6**   Excel internal rate of return formula.

## Remark on NPV in Excel

We need to pay attention to the fact that the terminology we have used in the textbook for the NPV criterion is slightly different from the Excel NPV terminology. The Excel NPV is just the Present Value of all the values we input in the formula, which means that in Excel we have to omit the first cash outlay at $t = 0$ only inserting then the cash flows from the first period we want to discount, as shown in Fig. 14.2-7. The cash outlay (this is not discounted) is negatively added separately.

As a **second step** we want to analyze the profile of the NPV by changing the discount rate, and this is the same as discovering the IRR of the project. This is done using the Data Table as in Fig. 14.2-8, where we simulate various NPVs by changing the discount rate. We see that the NPV function crosses the horizontal axis at the IRR value (see Fig. 14.2-9).

| | A | B | C | D | E | F | G |
|---|---|---|---|---|---|---|---|
| 1 | Year | 0 | 1 | 2 | 3 | 4 | 5 |
| 2 | Cash Flow | -60000 | 14700 | 16792.5 | 18905.2125 | 21238.8048125 | 22993.9657928125 |
| 3 | NPV | =B2+NPV(B4:C2:G2) | | | | | |
| 4 | Wacc | 0.1 | | | | | |
| 5 | IRR | =IRR(B2:G2) | | | | | |

**FIGURE 14.2-7**   Excel internal rate of return and net present value formulas for Example 2 (Worksheet 2).

| | Data Table | |
|---|---|---|
| | **Discount Rate** | **=B3** |
| | 0.05 | =TABLE(;B4) |
| | =D9+0.05 | =TABLE(;B4) |
| | 0.12 | =TABLE(;B4) |
| IRR | 0.159613744000726 | =TABLE(;B4) |
| | 0.18 | =TABLE(;B4) |
| | =D13+0.05 | =TABLE(;B4) |
| | =D14+0.05 | =TABLE(;B4) |
| | =D15+0.05 | =TABLE(;B4) |
| | =D16+0.05 | =TABLE(;B4) |
| | =D17+0.05 | =TABLE(;B4) |
| | =D18+0.05 | =TABLE(;B4) |

**FIGURE 14.2-8**   Excel Data Table simulation for the net present value profile (Worksheet 2).

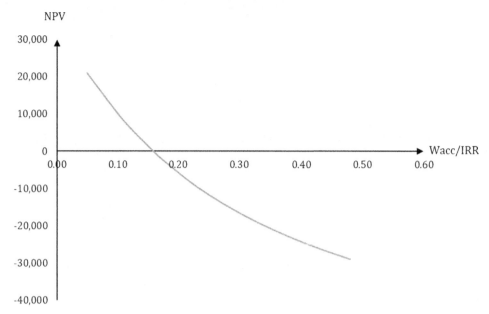

**FIGURE 14.2-9**    Excel Data Table simulation for the net present value profile and internal rate of return.

In general, the nonsimulated results lead us to the conclusion that the project should be accepted, as the *NPV* is positive (£ 10,229) and the *IRR* (15.96%) is higher than the *Wacc* (10%).

The **third step** is now to perform the MC simulation, to investigate in more details how the *NPV* values behave, as if one could actually see the cash flow pattern several times, assuming the stochastic variables follow a normal density distribution.

The way this is done is in Fig. 14.2-10 where we have randomly drawn, via the *NORM.INV*, the observations for each of the stochastic variable (one at a time from *Column B* to *Column M*) with the resulting associated *NPV* and *IRR*. The last column is instead the general simulation of *NPV* considering the change in the four stochastic variables taken together. See Table 14.2-6 for the results.

**FIGURE 14.2-10**    Monte Carlo simulation of net present value and internal rate of return for each stochastic variable and then taken together (Worksheet 1).

**TABLE 14.2-6**   Results (Worksheet 1).

| | A | B | C | D | E | F | G | H | I | J | K | L | M | N |
|---|---|---|---|---|---|---|---|---|---|---|---|---|---|---|
| 24 | Free Cash Flow | -60.000 | 14.700 | 16.793 | 18.905 | 21.239 | 22.994 | | | | | | | |
| 26 | | Non- | Changing | Changing | Changing Var. | Changing Var. | All. Stoc. Var. | | | | | | | |
| 27 | | Simulated | Sales @ t1 | Sales g | Costs | Costs g | Together | | | | | | | |
| 28 | IRR | 15.96% | 15.54% | 15.54% | 16.65% | 16.03% | n/a | | | | | | | |
| 29 | NPV | 10.229 | 9.071 | 9.476 | 11.456 | 10.365 | 9.434 | | | | | | | |
| 31 | | Sales | NPV | IRR | g | NPV | IRR | Var. Costs | NPV | IRR | Var.Costs g | NPV | IRR | NPV |
| 32 | Average | 59.492 | 9.071 | 15.30% | 2.67% | 9.476 | 15.54% | 32.025 | 11.456 | 16.65% | 2.40% | 10.365 | 16.03% | 9.434 |
| 33 | Standard Deviation | 691 | 1.707 | 0.98% | 0.76% | 2.101 | 1.14% | 811 | 1.905 | 1.08% | 0.26% | 354 | 0.19% | 3.218 |
| 34 | Simulation Runs | Data Tab. | 10.229 | 15.96% | Data Tab. | 10.229 | 15.96% | Data Tab. | 10.229 | 15.96% | Data Tab. | 10.229 | 15.96% | |
| 35 | 1 | 60.000 | 10.229 | 15.96% | 3.00% | 10.229 | 15.96% | 32.500 | 10.229 | 15.96% | 2.50% | 10.229 | 15.96% | 10.229 |
| 36 | 2 | 59.348 | 9.639 | 15.63% | 4.19% | 8.436 | 14.99% | 33.352 | 9.860 | 15.75% | 2.57% | 10.597 | 16.16% | 9.930 |
| 37 | 3 | 59.441 | 7.924 | 14.64% | 1.87% | 11.549 | 16.66% | 32.334 | 9.725 | 15.67% | 2.25% | 9.930 | 15.80% | 6.734 |
| 38 | 4 | 59.685 | 8.989 | 15.25% | 1.60% | 4.858 | 12.96% | 31.016 | 10.386 | 16.05% | 2.41% | 10.149 | 15.92% | 9.519 |
| 39 | 5 | 59.321 | 7.811 | 14.58% | 2.05% | 12.957 | 17.40% | 31.606 | 10.677 | 16.22% | 2.78% | 10.112 | 15.90% | 7.915 |
| 40 | 6 | 59.295 | 9.743 | 15.68% | 3.61% | 7.324 | 14.37% | 32.051 | 11.677 | 16.78% | 2.67% | 9.929 | 15.80% | 10.958 |
| 1030 | 996 | 58.985 | 8.929 | 15.22% | 3.44% | 11.157 | 16.46% | 31.728 | 11.580 | 16.73% | 2.17% | 10.853 | 16.29% | 11.215 |
| 1031 | 997 | 60.112 | 6.384 | 13.76% | 4.26% | 5.884 | 13.55% | 32.453 | 13.947 | 18.06% | 2.39% | 10.524 | 16.12% | 14.094 |
| 1032 | 998 | 59.546 | 10.691 | 16.22% | 3.61% | 10.974 | 16.36% | 31.672 | 10.499 | 16.11% | 2.34% | 9.804 | 15.73% | 12.923 |
| 1033 | 999 | 59.140 | 12.094 | 17.02% | 2.96% | 7.374 | 14.40% | 32.552 | 10.441 | 16.08% | 2.42% | 10.263 | 15.98% | 8.055 |
| 1034 | 1.000 | 59.580 | 8.116 | 14.75% | 2.22% | 3.838 | 12.36% | 33.145 | 9.885 | 15.77% | 1.98% | 10.222 | 15.96% | 6.410 |

Consider again Fig. 14.2-10 from *Column B* and *Column D*. Here we have randomly drawn the observations of the Sales, under *Column B* for 1000 times; then, for each of this observation we have a specific value of *NPV* via the Data Table simulation, using the *NPV* formula in *Cell B29* and as a column input the *Cell C12* (Sales) of Table 14.2-4. The same has been done for the IRR. This process is repeated for each of the four stochastic variables separately, one at a time until *Column M*. This is because we would like to analyze first the effect of simulating each stochastic variable on the NPV.

At the end of Fig. 14.2-10, under *Column N*, we have instead the *NPV* calculated taking into account the changes in the stochastic variables considered together.

These results are shown in Table 14.2-6 (*Row 28* and *Row 29*) where, together the nonsimulated results of $NPV = £10,229$ and $IRR = 15.96\%$, we can read the values of average *NPV* for each stochastic variable simulation taken separately. Then, we have the NPV value as a result of simulating all the variables together. The conclusion is still that we accept the project, but the *NPV* turns out to range from a minimum average of £ 9,071 to a maximum of £ 11,456. We can consider the average $NPV = £ 9,434$ as the one to expect (see *Column N* in Table 14.2-6). The IRR is instead on average 16%. Each time the worksheet is opened, we may see slightly different figures, as the simulations will be activated.

If we analyze instead the standard deviations (*Row 33* in Table 14.2-6) of the *NPV*, we may reasonably conclude that the growth rate in sales has the major impact on the *NPV*, while the least impact would be given by the growth rate in the variable costs. We see this, drawing the normal distribution densities as in Fig. 14.2-11.

## EXAMPLE 3 (STOCHASTIC DEMAND AND THE OPTIMAL CHOICE OF A WAREHOUSE)

In this example, we will see how to use the MC method when a discrete empirical distribution in the following form is used:

$$X = \begin{cases} x_1 & x_2 & \cdots & x_j & \cdots & x_n \\ p_1 & p_2 & \cdots & p_j & \cdots & p_n \end{cases}$$

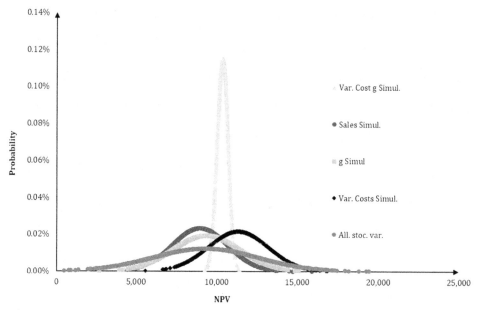

FIGURE 14.2-11   Normal density distributions associated to each net present value simulation.

In such cases what we need to do is to simply allocate the possible values of a random number to the various observations in the above discrete probability distribution, directly proportional to the respective probabilities of those observations.

Let us suppose we have a timber wholesaler that is about to decide to stock and sale a new type of timber, and he/she knows the following stochastic weekly timber demand (expressed in cubic meters):

$$X = \begin{cases} 0 & 5 & 10 & 15 & 20 & 25 \\ 0.10 & 0.10 & 0.20 & 0.30 & 0.20 & 0.10 \end{cases}$$

where $\mu(X) = 13.50$.

Here below we show how 100 random numbers can be allocated to each occurrence of the random variable $X$:

$$X = \begin{cases} 0 & 5 & 10 & 15 & 20 & 25 \\ 0.10 & 0.10 & 0.20 & 0.30 & 0.20 & 0.10 \\ \textit{from 00} & \textit{from 10} & \textit{from 20} & \textit{from 40} & \textit{from 70} & \textit{from 90} \\ \textit{to 09} & \textit{to 19} & \textit{to 39} & \textit{to 69} & \textit{to 89} & \textit{to 99} \end{cases}$$

We essentially use the occurrences in the 100 random numbers to reconstruct the occurrences in the random variable, weekly demand, $X$. If 15 is the random number drawn, then it will be allocated to the range (10–19), which is associated to the 10% probability

TABLE 14.2-7 Warehouse data and revenue per cubic meter.

| | Capacity | 10 weeks rent | Rev./cubic meter |
|---|---|---|---|
| Warehouse A | 100 | 2,000 | |
| Warehouse B | 135 | 2,500 | 100 |
| Warehouse C | 170 | 2,800 | |

and a weekly demand of 5 cubic meters. For the 30% probability, we use an interval of 30 random numbers and so on.

To trade the new type of timber the wholesaler needs to rent a new warehouse and the following three alternatives are presented, where the cost of the rent also includes all other ancillary costs. Table 14.2-7 includes the capacity of each warehouse, the rent, and the revenue per cubic meter, which does not change (the price is taken as given by the market).

The timber procurement is to be done only once every 10 weeks, and the rent is expressed accordingly.

Now, the problem the wholesaler faces is which warehouse to select, considering that the demand is stochastic.

If the wholesaler selects a too small warehouse compared to demand then the entire demand will not be satisfied, risking renting an additional warehouse, otherwise if the wholesaler selects a too large warehouse, compared to the actual demand, the extra costs will have to be paid.

If we used the criterion of the weekly expected demand value $\mu(X) = 13.50$, we would select the Warehouse B, which exactly fits the demand of timber for the 10 weeks period (135). However, using the more detailed MC simulation analysis Warehouse B does not turn out to be the best choice.

Let us consider a simulation sample of 50 weeks which is almost a year. The following Table 14.2-8 show how each random number is associated to the random variable $X = weekly\ demand$ observations.

We show in Fig. 14.2-12 the details of these calculations for the first set of 10 weeks (Column B and C).

TABLE 14.2-8 Random Numbers and Random Drawn of Demand Observations over the 50 weeks.

| Week | Rand | Demand | Week | Rand | Demand | Week | Rand | Demand | Week | Rand | Demand | Week | Rand | Demand |
|---|---|---|---|---|---|---|---|---|---|---|---|---|---|---|
| 1 | 77 | 20 | 11 | 13 | 5 | 21 | 83 | 20 | 31 | 75 | 20 | 41 | 85 | 20 |
| 2 | 17 | 5 | 12 | 5 | 0 | 22 | 54 | 15 | 32 | 65 | 15 | 42 | 64 | 15 |
| 3 | 7 | 0 | 13 | 5 | 0 | 23 | 8 | 0 | 33 | 59 | 15 | 43 | 12 | 5 |
| 4 | 35 | 10 | 14 | 26 | 10 | 24 | 12 | 5 | 34 | 36 | 10 | 44 | 8 | 0 |
| 5 | 19 | 5 | 15 | 11 | 5 | 25 | 11 | 5 | 35 | 83 | 20 | 45 | 76 | 20 |
| 6 | 89 | 20 | 16 | 80 | 20 | 26 | 21 | 10 | 36 | 94 | 25 | 46 | 45 | 15 |
| 7 | 88 | 20 | 17 | 79 | 20 | 27 | 22 | 10 | 37 | 0 | 0 | 47 | 31 | 10 |
| 8 | 36 | 10 | 18 | 49 | 15 | 28 | 25 | 10 | 38 | 62 | 15 | 48 | 44 | 15 |
| 9 | 14 | 5 | 19 | 36 | 10 | 29 | 99 | 25 | 39 | 73 | 20 | 49 | 12 | 5 |
| 10 | 0 | 0 | 20 | 60 | 15 | 30 | 15 | 5 | 40 | 52 | 15 | 50 | 38 | 10 |
| Total Demand | | 95 | | | 100 | | | 105 | | | 155 | | | 115 |

| | A | B | C | D | E | F | G |
|---|---|---|---|---|---|---|---|
| 1 | Weekly demand random | | | | | | |
| 2 | | 0 | 5 | | 10 | 15 | 20 | 25 |
| 3 | X | | | | | | |
| 4 | | 0.1 | 0.1 | | 0.2 | 0.3 | 0.2 | 0.1 |
| 5 | | | | | | | |
| 6 | RN from | 0 | 10 | | 20 | 40 | 70 | 90 |
| 7 | to | 9 | 19 | | 39 | 69 | 89 | 99 |
| 8 | | | | | | | |
| 9 | Week | Rand | Demand | | Week | Rand | Demand | Week |
| 10 | 1 | =RANDBETWEEN(0;99) | =IF(B10<10;$B$2;IF(B10<20;$C$2;IF(B10<40;$D$2;IF(B10<70;$E$2;IF(B10<90;$F$2;IF(B10<100;$G$2)))))) | | =A19+1 | =RANDBE =IF(E10< =D19+1 |
| 11 | =A10+1 | =RANDBETWEEN(0;99) | =IF(B11<10;$B$2;IF(B11<20;$C$2;IF(B11<40;$D$2;IF(B11<70;$E$2;IF(B11<90;$F$2;IF(B11<100;$G$2)))))) | | =D10+1 | =RANDBE =IF(E11< =G10+1 |
| 12 | =A11+1 | =RANDBETWEEN(0;99) | =IF(B12<10;$B$2;IF(B12<20;$C$2;IF(B12<40;$D$2;IF(B12<70;$E$2;IF(B12<90;$F$2;IF(B12<100;$G$2)))))) | | =D11+1 | =RANDBE =IF(E12< =G11+1 |
| 13 | =A12+1 | =RANDBETWEEN(0;99) | =IF(B13<10;$B$2;IF(B13<20;$C$2;IF(B13<40;$D$2;IF(B13<70;$E$2;IF(B13<90;$F$2;IF(B13<100;$G$2)))))) | | =D12+1 | =RANDBE =IF(E13< =G12+1 |
| 14 | =A13+1 | =RANDBETWEEN(0;99) | =IF(B14<10;$B$2;IF(B14<20;$C$2;IF(B14<40;$D$2;IF(B14<70;$E$2;IF(B14<90;$F$2;IF(B14<100;$G$2)))))) | | =D13+1 | =RANDBE =IF(E14< =G13+1 |
| 15 | =A14+1 | =RANDBETWEEN(0;99) | =IF(B15<10;$B$2;IF(B15<20;$C$2;IF(B15<40;$D$2;IF(B15<70;$E$2;IF(B15<90;$F$2;IF(B15<100;$G$2)))))) | | =D14+1 | =RANDBE =IF(E15< =G14+1 |
| 16 | =A15+1 | =RANDBETWEEN(0;99) | =IF(B16<10;$B$2;IF(B16<20;$C$2;IF(B16<40;$D$2;IF(B16<70;$E$2;IF(B16<90;$F$2;IF(B16<100;$G$2)))))) | | =D15+1 | =RANDBE =IF(E16< =G15+1 |
| 17 | =A16+1 | =RANDBETWEEN(0;99) | =IF(B17<10;$B$2;IF(B17<20;$C$2;IF(B17<40;$D$2;IF(B17<70;$E$2;IF(B17<90;$F$2;IF(B17<100;$G$2)))))) | | =D16+1 | =RANDBE =IF(E17< =G16+1 |
| 18 | =A17+1 | =RANDBETWEEN(0;99) | =IF(B18<10;$B$2;IF(B18<20;$C$2;IF(B18<40;$D$2;IF(B18<70;$E$2;IF(B18<90;$F$2;IF(B18<100;$G$2)))))) | | =D17+1 | =RANDBE =IF(E18< =G17+1 |
| 19 | =A18+1 | =RANDBETWEEN(0;99) | =IF(B19<10;$B$2;IF(B19<20;$C$2;IF(B19<40;$D$2;IF(B19<70;$E$2;IF(B19<90;$F$2;IF(B19<100;$G$2)))))) | | =D18+1 | =RANDBE =IF(E19< =G18+1 |
| 20 | Total Demand | | =SUM(C10:C19) | | | | =SUM(F1 |

**FIGURE 14.2-12**   Excel worksheet for simulation of the weekly demand.

**TABLE 14.2-9**   Profit for each of the Warehouses.

| | Profit 1st 10 weeks | Profit 2nd 10 weeks | Profit 3rd 10 weeks | Profit 4rd 10 weeks | Profit 5th 10 weeks | Total Profit | Choice | Prob |
|---|---|---|---|---|---|---|---|---|
| Warehouse A | 7,500 | 8,000 | 8,000 | 8,000 | 8,000 | **39,500** | | 0.00% |
| Warehouse B | 7,000 | 7,500 | 8,000 | 11,000 | 9,000 | **42,500** | | 16.90% |
| Warehouse C | 6,700 | 7,200 | 7,700 | 12,700 | 8,700 | **43,000** | x | 83.10% |

For each of the warehouse we calculate then the profit considering the demands simulated in Table 14.2-8 for the sample of 50 weeks, as in Table 14.2-9, considering the fact that each warehouse is constrained by the capacity in Table 14.2-7.

The total profit of the Warehouse A ($P\ WA$) has been calculated, for example, as:

$$P\ WA = (95 \cdot 100 + 100 \cdot 100 \cdot 4 - 2,000 \cdot 5) = 39,500$$

because of the constraint of 100 cubic meters capacity in four 10 weeks periods.

We will generate now 1000 artificial profits for each warehouse obtaining Table 14.2-10 from which we can conclude that the best choice is the Warehouse C, as the probability of having the largest profit from this warehouse appears in 83.10% out of 1000 simulated trials.

## 14.3 Numerical integration

An interesting application of the MC method is also concerning the possibility of extrapolating the area under the curve, i.e., the integral.

The idea behind can be represented as in Fig. 14.3-1.

We fill with a certain number of dots the square and the circle inscribed in it as in Fig. 14.3-1, then we count the dots of each figure and we derive the area of the circle as the ratio between the total number of dots of the circle and the total number of dots in the square, times 1

TABLE 14.2-10   Profit generation with Monte Carlo.

| Data Table | P WA | P WB | P WC | Choice |
|---|---|---|---|---|
| 1 | 39,500 | 42,500 | 43,000 | Warehouse C |
| 2 | 40,000 | 49,500 | 50,000 | Warehouse C |
| 3 | 40,000 | 48,500 | 47,000 | Warehouse B |
| 4 | 40,000 | 49,000 | 51,000 | Warehouse C |
| 5 | 40,000 | 53,500 | 56,500 | Warehouse C |
| 6 | 40,000 | 54,000 | 55,500 | Warehouse C |
| 7 | 40,000 | 53,000 | 57,500 | Warehouse C |
| 8 | 39,500 | 47,000 | 47,500 | Warehouse C |
| 9 | 40,000 | 50,500 | 53,500 | Warehouse C |
| 10 | 40,000 | 55,000 | 62,500 | Warehouse C |
| 990 | 40,000 | 54,000 | 55,000 | Warehouse C |
| 991 | 40,000 | 48,500 | 47,500 | Warehouse B |
| 992 | 40,000 | 54,500 | 59,500 | Warehouse C |
| 993 | 40,000 | 51,500 | 54,000 | Warehouse C |
| 994 | 40,000 | 49,500 | 50,000 | Warehouse C |
| 995 | 40,000 | 51,500 | 52,500 | Warehouse C |
| 996 | 40,000 | 54,000 | 58,500 | Warehouse C |
| 997 | 40,000 | 54,000 | 57,500 | Warehouse C |
| 998 | 40,000 | 49,000 | 48,500 | Warehouse B |
| 999 | 40,000 | 55,000 | 63,000 | Warehouse C |
| 1,000 | 40,000 | 52,500 | 58,500 | Warehouse C |

(the true area of the square). As the number of dots $\rightarrow \infty$, the ratio will eventually approximate $\pi \cdot r^2 \cong 3.1416 \cdot 0.5^2 = 0.785$, namely the area of a circle with a *radius* equal to 0.50.

The same reasoning will be applied to calculus for the numerical integration of a function. Consider, for example, the following exponential function:

$$y = e^x.$$

We will perform now the MC integration using Excel as in Fig. 14.3-2, whose results are in Table 14.3-1.

In *Column B* and *Column C* of Fig. 14.3-2, we generate the random numbers in the interval from 1 to 2. These points will generate the following square scatter plot made with all the 2000 random points generated.

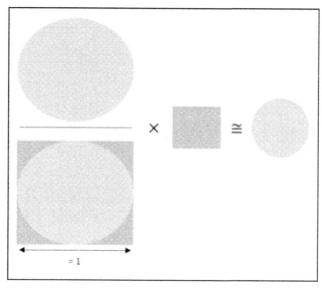

**FIGURE 14.3-1**    Representation of the Monte Carlo integration.

| | A | B | C | D | E | F | G | H |
|---|---|---|---|---|---|---|---|---|
| 1 | | Range of integration | | Iterations | True Area | =EXP(C2)-EXP(B2) | Monte Carlo Area | |
| 2 | x | 1 | 2 | =MAX(A6:A2005) | Numerical Area 2,000 trials | =(C2-B2)*(C3-B3)*COUNTIF(F6:F2005,"1")/D2 | =AVERAGE(H5:H2005) | |
| 3 | y | 0 | =EXP(C2) | | | | | |
| 4 | | | | | | | | |
| 5 | Rand | x Rand | y Rand | x | Exp(x) | Binary Test | Data Table | =F2 |
| 6 | 1 | =$B$2+($C$2-$B$2)*RAND() | =$B$3+($C$3-$B$3)*RAND() | =IF(C6<EXP(B6);B6;0) | =IF(C6<EXP(B6);C6;0) | =IF(E6=0;0;1) | 1 | =TABLE(;H2) |
| 7 | 2 | =$B$2+($C$2-$B$2)*RAND() | =$B$3+($C$3-$B$3)*RAND() | =IF(C7<EXP(B7);B7;0) | =IF(C7<EXP(B7);C7;0) | =IF(E7=0;0;1) | 2 | =TABLE(;H2) |
| 8 | 3 | =$B$2+($C$2-$B$2)*RAND() | =$B$3+($C$3-$B$3)*RAND() | =IF(C8<EXP(B8);B8;0) | =IF(C8<EXP(B8);C8;0) | =IF(E8=0;0;1) | 3 | =TABLE(;H2) |
| 9 | 4 | =$B$2+($C$2-$B$2)*RAND() | =$B$3+($C$3-$B$3)*RAND() | =IF(C9<EXP(B9);B9;0) | =IF(C9<EXP(B9);C9;0) | =IF(E9=0;0;1) | 4 | =TABLE(;H2) |
| 10 | 5 | =$B$2+($C$2-$B$2)*RAND() | =$B$3+($C$3-$B$3)*RAND() | =IF(C10<EXP(B10);B10;0) | =IF(C10<EXP(B10);C10;0) | =IF(E10=0;0;1) | 5 | =TABLE(;H2) |
| 11 | 6 | =$B$2+($C$2-$B$2)*RAND() | =$B$3+($C$3-$B$3)*RAND() | =IF(C11<EXP(B11);B11;0) | =IF(C11<EXP(B11);C11;0) | =IF(E11=0;0;1) | 6 | =TABLE(;H2) |
| 12 | 7 | =$B$2+($C$2-$B$2)*RAND() | =$B$3+($C$3-$B$3)*RAND() | =IF(C12<EXP(B12);B12;0) | =IF(C12<EXP(B12);C12;0) | =IF(E12=0;0;1) | 7 | =TABLE(;H2) |
| 13 | 8 | =$B$2+($C$2-$B$2)*RAND() | =$B$3+($C$3-$B$3)*RAND() | =IF(C13<EXP(B13);B13;0) | =IF(C13<EXP(B13);C13;0) | =IF(E13=0;0;1) | 8 | =TABLE(;H2) |
| 1999 | 1994 | =$B$2+($C$2-$B$2)*RAND() | =$B$3+($C$3-$B$3)*RAND() | =IF(C1999<EXP(B1999);B1999;0) | =IF(C1999<EXP(B1999);C1999;0) | =IF(E1999=0;0;1) | 1994 | =TABLE(;H2) |
| 2000 | 1995 | =$B$2+($C$2-$B$2)*RAND() | =$B$3+($C$3-$B$3)*RAND() | =IF(C2000<EXP(B2000);B2000;0) | =IF(C2000<EXP(B2000);C2000;0) | =IF(E2000=0;0;1) | 1995 | =TABLE(;H2) |
| 2001 | 1996 | =$B$2+($C$2-$B$2)*RAND() | =$B$3+($C$3-$B$3)*RAND() | =IF(C2001<EXP(B2001);B2001;0) | =IF(C2001<EXP(B2001);C2001;0) | =IF(E2001=0;0;1) | 1996 | =TABLE(;H2) |
| 2002 | 1997 | =$B$2+($C$2-$B$2)*RAND() | =$B$3+($C$3-$B$3)*RAND() | =IF(C2002<EXP(B2002);B2002;0) | =IF(C2002<EXP(B2002);C2002;0) | =IF(E2002=0;0;1) | 1997 | =TABLE(;H2) |
| 2003 | 1998 | =$B$2+($C$2-$B$2)*RAND() | =$B$3+($C$3-$B$3)*RAND() | =IF(C2003<EXP(B2003);B2003;0) | =IF(C2003<EXP(B2003);C2003;0) | =IF(E2003=0;0;1) | 1998 | =TABLE(;H2) |
| 2004 | 1999 | =$B$2+($C$2-$B$2)*RAND() | =$B$3+($C$3-$B$3)*RAND() | =IF(C2004<EXP(B2004);B2004;0) | =IF(C2004<EXP(B2004);C2004;0) | =IF(E2004=0;0;1) | 1999 | =TABLE(;H2) |
| 2005 | 2000 | =$B$2+($C$2-$B$2)*RAND() | =$B$3+($C$3-$B$3)*RAND() | =IF(C2005<EXP(B2005);B2005;0) | =IF(C2005<EXP(B2005);C2005;0) | =IF(E2005=0;0;1) | 2000 | =TABLE(;H2) |

**FIGURE 14.3-2**    Monte Carlo integration of $y = e^x$ between 1 and 2.

**TABLE 14.3-1**    Monte Carlo integration result.

| | Range of integration | | Iterations | True Area | 4.6708 | Monte Carlo Area |
|---|---|---|---|---|---|---|
| x | 1.0000 | 2.0000 | 2,000 | Numerical Area 2,0 | 4.6994 | 4.6709 |
| y | 0.0000 | 7.3891 | | | | |

| Rand | x Rand | y Rand | x | Exp(x) | Binary Test | Data Table | 4.6994 |
|---|---|---|---|---|---|---|---|
| 1 | 1.1291 | 2.4547 | 1.1291 | 2.4547 | 1.0000 | 1 | 4.6810 |
| 2 | 1.0909 | 4.9611 | 0.0000 | 0.0000 | 0.0000 | 2 | 4.7327 |
| 3 | 1.4554 | 2.0698 | 1.4554 | 2.0698 | 1.0000 | 3 | 4.6847 |
| 4 | 1.6779 | 2.1807 | 1.6779 | 2.1807 | 1.0000 | 4 | 4.7844 |
| 5 | 1.9360 | 4.3041 | 1.9360 | 4.3041 | 1.0000 | 5 | 4.5960 |
| 6 | 1.3402 | 5.3429 | 0.0000 | 0.0000 | 0.0000 | 6 | 4.7438 |
| 7 | 1.3391 | 2.1982 | 1.3391 | 2.1982 | 1.0000 | 7 | 4.5295 |
| 8 | 1.0588 | 5.8671 | 0.0000 | 0.0000 | 0.0000 | 8 | 4.6403 |
| 1,994 | 1.4880 | 0.6180 | 1.4880 | 0.6180 | 1.0000 | 1,994 | 4.5110 |
| 1,995 | 1.2770 | 4.6931 | 0.0000 | 0.0000 | 0.0000 | 1,995 | 4.6219 |
| 1,996 | 1.2087 | 6.2174 | 0.0000 | 0.0000 | 0.0000 | 1,996 | 4.7142 |
| 1,997 | 1.9507 | 4.9832 | 1.9507 | 4.9832 | 1.0000 | 1,997 | 4.7290 |
| 1,998 | 1.1221 | 3.7684 | 0.0000 | 0.0000 | 0.0000 | 1,998 | 4.6588 |
| 1,999 | 1.7584 | 6.8374 | 0.0000 | 0.0000 | 0.0000 | 1,999 | 4.6662 |
| 2,000 | 1.6712 | 1.8652 | 1.6712 | 1.8652 | 1.0000 | 2,000 | 4.6921 |

In *Column D* and *Column E* of Fig. 14.3-2, for both variables $y$ and $x$ we impose an *if* statement to generate the area of random points under the curve $y = e^x$. This will generate Figs. 14.3-4.

*Column F* in Fig. 14.3-2 is just a binary test that will return the times the *if* statement is actually *true*, which is the number of points under the curve we are looking for, if we sum them all.

The approximate numerical area is therefore calculated in *Cell F*2 with the *Countif* formula which is divided by the number of MC trials (2,000) and then multiplied by the true area of

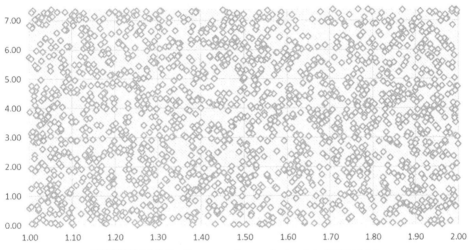

**FIGURE 14.3-3**    Square scatter random points (2000 trials).

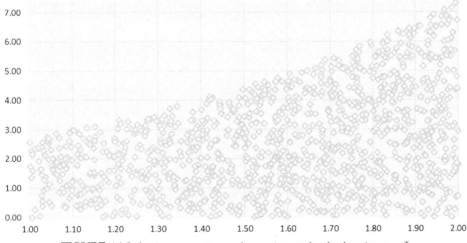

**FIGURE 14.3-4**    Square scatter random points under the function $y = e^x$.

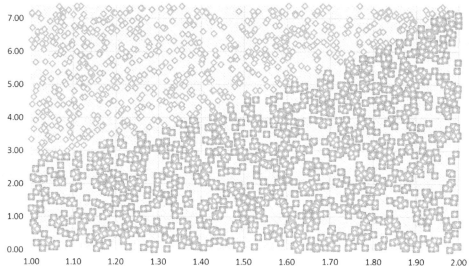

**FIGURE 14.3-5**   Darker area is the Monte Carlo numerical area.

the square in Fig. 14.3-3 delimited by the pairs (1, 0) and (2, 7.3891), with width equal to (2 − 1) and height equal to (7.3891 − 0) being then the true *Square Area* = 7.3891.

We can then fine-tune the numerical area simulating as well on this *Cell F2* via the Data Table under *Column H*, with any empty cell in the worksheet as a column input cell. The result is the grand average in *Cell G2* which approximates the following exact integral:

$$\int_1^2 e^x dx = 7.3890 - 2.7182 = 4.6708.$$

Putting together then Fig. 14.3-3 with Fig. 14.3-4, we obtain the following Fig. 14.3-5, from which it is apparent how we have extrapolated the area under the curve of the function $y = e^x$ using the MC method.

## Exercises

1. Run a three-coin digital flip Monte Carlo experiment and calculate the probability of having two heads, in case you throw the three fair coins eight times. See Table 1 below which represents the sample space $\Omega$ of this experiment.
2. Consider a fair coin and run $n = 5$ Bernoulli independent trials of coin flip.
   **a.** What is the probability of obtaining exactly $x = 2$ heads, considering $p = \frac{1}{2}$ ?
   **b.** Plot the binomial distribution for $x = \#$ *of Heads* from 0 to 5.
   Do this using the random number generator tool in Excel.

TABLE 1

| Flip | Coin A | Coin B | Coin C |
|------|--------|--------|--------|
| 1 | H | H | H |
| 2 | H | H | T |
| 3 | H | T | T |
| 4 | T | T | T |
| 5 | T | T | H |
| 6 | T | H | H |
| 7 | T | H | T |
| 8 | H | T | H |

3. We are required to conduct a poll in a town where on average we know that 40% of the population agrees and 60% disagrees with a new town decree. If we interview 10 people (randomly chosen) solve for the following.
   a. What is the probability that exactly 3 people out of the 10 interviewed will agree?

   b. What is the probability that the first three people interviewed will agree, and the other seven disagree?

**Poisson processes and some applications.** In this chapter, we have seen that if we relax the assumption that an event occurs exactly in a separate period of time, like in the Bernoulli independent experiments and binomial distribution, we can use the Poisson distribution, given by:

$$P[X = x] = \frac{e^{-\lambda}\lambda^x}{x!} \quad \text{with } E(X) = \lambda.$$

We can model therefore the number of occurrences of a happening in a period of time of length $t$ with a Poisson distribution with parameter $\lambda = vt$. If the random variable $Z(t)$ denotes the number of occurrences of the happening in a time interval of length $t$, then:

$$P[Z(t) = z] = \frac{e^{-vt}(vt)^z}{z!} \quad \text{for } z = 0, 1, 2, \ldots$$

Solve the following exercises using the Excel random number generator tool.

4. Plot three Poisson distributions with:
   a. $\lambda = 4.0$
   b. $\lambda = 1.0$
   c. $\lambda = 0.5$
5. Suppose that the average number of calls arriving at the switchboard of a corporation is 30 calls per hour. Assume that the number of calls arriving during any time period has a Poisson distribution and assume the time is measured in minutes. Therefore, 30

calls per hour is 0.5 calls per minute, so that the mean rate of occurrence is 0.5 calls per minute. Solve the following points.

    **a.** What is the probability that no calls will arrive in 3-minute period? (Hint: in this case $\lambda = 0.5 \cdot 3$ and $P[\textit{No calls in } 3 \textit{ min period}] = e^{-vt} \cong 0.223$).

    **b.** What is the probability that more than five calls will arrive in a 5-minute interval?

    **c.** Plot the Poisson distribution for each case.

6. Some cars arrive at a queue with an average rate of occurrence of four per minute. Assume the cars arrive at the queue with a Poisson distribution, and determine the probability that at least two cars will add to the queue in a 30-second interval. Plot the Poisson distribution.

7. **Inventory.** A merchant knows that the number of a certain kind of item that he can sell in a given period of time is Poisson distributed. How many of these items should the merchant stock, so that the probability will be 0.95 that he will have enough items to meet the customer demand for a time period of length T? Let $v$ denotes the *mean rate of occurrence* per unit time and K the unknown quantity he should stock. Solve now the following point.

    **a.** If the merchant sells an average of two items per day, how many should he stock so that he will have a probability at least 0.95 of having enough stock to meet the demand in 1-month period? (Hint: we denote X as the demand and K as the stock of the items and the solution requires finding K so that $P[X \leq K] \geq$

$$0.95 \text{ or } \sum_{k=0}^{K} \frac{e^{-(2 \cdot 30)}(60)^k}{k!} \geq 0.95.)$$

8. **Inventory.** A merchant knows that the number of items he sells in a month is distributed according to a Poisson distribution. On average, he sells 48 items per year. If at the beginning of a month he has in stock only two items, what is the probability that he will not be able to meet the customer demand? (Hint: 48 items sold per year means 4 per month, so that $v = 4$ and $\lambda = 4$; as in the previous case, denote with X the customer demand and with K the stock, so that we need to find $P[\textit{Demand } X > \textit{Stock } K = 2]$.)

**Solve the following Monte Carlo applications for business decisions.**

9. A company shows average sales data for £ 5 M, with standard deviation for £ 1.5 M, variable costs for £ 3 M and standard deviation for £ 0.5M., and operating fixed costs (including depreciations) for £ 1 M. Assuming a normal distribution in the two stochastic variables sales and variable costs, construct a Monte Carlo simulation for the $Ebit = s - vc - fc$ and build an empirical histogram.

10. A company is planning the launch of a new product, and they project for this new product the following data for unit price and quantities. The company has employed various marketing techniques to determine the unit price (Table 2).

    **a.** Run a Monte Carlo simulation for the possible total sales outcomes assuming a normal distribution. Run therefore the iterations for unit sales, price, and quantity.

    **b.** Build an empirical histogram and construct a 95% empirical probability interval in which total sales may fall.

TABLE 2

| NEW PRODUCT DATA | | |
| --- | --- | --- |
| | **Unit sales Price** | **Quantity Sold** |
| Mean | 1,000 | 2,000 |
| St. Dev | 100 | 200 |

**11.** A company shows for a given month the following customer order data (Table 3):

TABLE 3

| CUSTOMER ORDER DATA | |
| --- | --- |
| Mean of Customer Orders in £ | 623,538 |
| St. Dev | 211,714 |

**a.** Assume a normal distribution construct an empirical histogram and an interval at 95% probability in which the possible customer orders may likely fall in the future. To do this, run a Monte Carlo simulation of 1000 customer orders.

**Monte Carlo numerical integration**

**12.** Calculate numerically the following definite integrals and compare the results versus the exact solutions:

$$\int_1^2 x^2 dx;$$

$$\int_1^2 \frac{1}{x} dx;$$

$$\int_1^2 \ln x dx.$$

# Index

'Note: Page numbers followed by "f" indicate figures, "t" indicate tables and "b" indicate boxes.'